HANDBOOK OF PSYCHOTHERAPY SUPERVISION

HANDBOOK OF PSYCHOTHERAPY SUPERVISION

edited by

C. Edward Watkins, Jr.

John Wiley & Sons, Inc.
New York • Chichester • Weinheim • Brisbane • Singapore • Toronto

Copyright © 1997 by John Wiley & Sons, Inc.
Published by John Wiley & Sons, Inc.

Library of Congress Cataloging-in-Publication Data:
Handbook of psychotherapy supervision / C. Edward Watkins, Jr.
        p.   cm.
    Includes bibliographical references.
    ISBN 0-471-11219-4 (cloth)
    1. Psychotherapists—Supervision of. 2. Psychotherapy—Study and
teaching—Supervision.   I. Watkins, C. Edward.
    RC459.H36   1997
    616.89'14—dc20   96-35571
                                                      CIP

Printed in the United States of America

10   9   8   7

To a Valued Contributor
Now Past

Norman I. Kagan

Series Preface

This series of books is intended to provide scientists and practitioners in the mental health disciplines with up-to-date summaries and critiques of clinical theory, diagnosis, assessment, intervention, and prevention. The major common thread binding the series is its focus on the scientific basis underlying effective clinical work.

It is extremely difficult for scientific investigators to keep up with the burgeoning empirical work, even with regard to specific disorders; it is impossible for the practicing clinician, especially those who treat a range of disorders, to do so. Each book in this series attempts to distill the most pertinent information covered by that book's topic and presents it in a scientifically valid and practitioner-friendly manner. Great strides have been made in recent years in all aspects of clinical practice and especially in developing valid diagnostic criteria, scientifically acceptable assessment processes, and effective disorder-specific treatments; less progress has been made with prevention efforts, but exciting large-scale longitudinal studies are underway. Our biggest problem is getting the current scientific information available in a utilizable form; that is the major purpose of this series.

W. EDWARD CRAIGHEAD
University of Colorado
Boulder, Colorado

Preface

Allen Hess's book *Psychotherapy Supervision: Theory, Research, and Practice* was published in 1980. Since then, the field of psychotherapy supervision has continued to evolve, with the growth of new models, research, and practice (e.g., Watkins, 1996, in press). Even with such evolution and growth, we have lacked a relatively comprehensive source book, such as Hess's book, to bring us up to date on the current state of the field of psychotherapy supervision. This is the primary reason for this *Handbook*—to provide an informed and informative treatment of many of the key areas that have been and continue to be so central to the enterprise of psychotherapy supervision.

In conceiving this book, I drew not only on Hess's (1980) previous effort but also on Bergin and Garfield's (1994) latest edition of their *Handbook of Psychotherapy and Behavior Change.* I attempted to structure this book along the lines that had seemed so successful for them. For example, you will find that the major section headings used here are quite similar to theirs. With this book, I specifically wished to put together a resource that would (a) get at many of the supervision topics addressed earlier (e.g., theories and models; see Hess, 1980, Chapters 10 to 15), (b) bring information on those topics up to date, and (c) give more emphasis to supervision research and the conduct of it. What resulted was this seven-part *Handbook.*

In Part I, psychotherapy supervision is defined; some of the factors that influence supervisor functioning are considered; and the methodology and design of psychotherapy supervision research are reviewed. Part II focuses on the variety of models of psychotherapy supervision. For this part of the book, I asked all authors to address three basic questions: (a) What is your approach to supervision? (b) How do you put it into practice? and (c) Is there any research support for it?

Part III addresses some of the teaching formats, tools, and models that are used in psychotherapy education. In Part IV, the focus shifts to some specialized forms and modes of psychotherapy supervision, for example, group therapy supervision and family therapy supervision.

With Part V, we shift yet again, this time to research. Authors of these chapters were asked to do the following: (a) review and critique the research that has been done thus far, (b) identify what needs to be done, and (c) provide some direction or an agenda as to how we can go about doing what needs to be done.

Part VI gives attention to several important issues in psychotherapy supervision, for example, gender, ethnicity, and training. And, finally, Part VII serves as a wrap-up or conclusion, bringing the book to a close.

This *Handbook,* as I see it, is most suitable for two audiences: (a) graduate students who are enrolled in supervision courses or seminars and who, thereby, want to learn about the many facets of the psychotherapy supervision endeavor; and (2) mental health professionals who want to get a relatively comprehensive, current reading about psychotherapy supervision. Furthermore, what you will find in this *Handbook* is, I believe, relevant for and applicable to graduate students and mental health professionals of varied specialities (e.g., clinical, counseling, or school psychology; psychiatry; social work; counselor education; or psychiatric nursing).

In putting together their chapters, I asked contributors to provide a current treatment—introduction, overview, critique—of their topic area. The various authors were chosen because of their recognized expertise and the many substantive contributions they have made to the field.

Whereas this book provides a rather broad picture of much that is taking place within psychotherapy supervision, it still has limits in coverage. There are, after all, some important areas not dealt with here (e.g., sex therapy supervision). Such limits seem worth keeping in mind.

There are many people who helped make this book a reality. First, I would like to thank the many chapter contributors; their fine work made all of this possible, and I am much indebted to them. Second, thanks to Kelly Franklin of John Wiley for helping me navigate through the book editing and publishing waters. Third, thanks to Lee Ward, typist extraordinaire, for her ever-expert, ever-efficient, ever-ready assistance. Finally, thanks to the Psychology Department at the University of North Texas, and especially Ernie Harrell, department head, for supporting my efforts in putting this book together.

ED WATKINS

REFERENCES

Bergin, A. E., & Garfield, S. L. (Eds.). (1994). *Handbook of psychotherapy and behavior change* (4th ed.). New York: Wiley.

Hess, A. K. (Ed.). (1980). *Psychotherapy supervision: Theory, research, and practice.* New York: Wiley.

Watkins, C. E., Jr. (Chair). (1996, August). *The future of psychotherapy training—some selected theory-driven perspectives.* Symposium presented at the annual meeting of the American Psychological Association, Toronto.

Watkins, C. E., Jr. (Ed.). (in press). Special section: Supervising psychotherapy—new developments, advances, and possibilities. *The Clinical Supervisor.*

Contents

PART III: TRAINING MODELS FOR PSYCHOTHERAPY SUPERVISION

PART IV: SPECIALIZED FORMS AND MODES

PART V: RESEARCHING PSYCHOTHERAPY SUPERVISION

PART VI: PROFESSIONAL, ETHICAL, AND LEGAL ISSUES

Contributing Authors

David A. Altfeld, Ph.D.
National Institute of Psychotherapies

Robert Banchero, Ph.D.
Counseling/Clinical/School Psychology
University of California–Santa Barbara

Judith S. Beck, Ph.D.
Beck Institute for Cognitive Therapy and Research

Dana Becker, Ph.D.
Early Adolescence Transitions Project
Temple University

Harold S. Bernard, Ph.D.
Department of Psychiatry
New York University Medical Center

Janine M. Bernard, Ph.D.
Department of Counselor Education
Fairfield University

Larry E. Beutler, Ph.D.
Counseling/Clinical/School Psychology
University of California–Santa Barbara

Jeffrey L. Binder, Ph.D.
Core Faculty
Georgia School of Professional Psychology

Donald B. Boulet, Ph.D.
Department of Psychology
University of Ottawa

Thomas G. Daniels, Ph.D.
Department of Psychology
Sir Wilfred Grenfell College

Paul A. Dewald, M.D.
Professor Emeritus, Psychiatry
St. Louis University School of Medicine

Gary M. Diamond, M.Ed.
Philadelphia Child Guidance Center

Michael Duffy, Ph.D.
Department of Educational Psychology
Texas A & M University

Albert Ellis, Ph.D.
Institute for Rational Emotive Therapy

Michael V. Ellis, Ph.D.
Department of Counseling Psychology
University at Albany, State University of New York

Alan E. Fruzzetti, Ph.D.
Department of Psychology
University of Nevada

Rodney K. Goodyear, Ph.D.
Division of Counseling Psychology
University of Southern California

Richard P. Halgin, Ph.D.
Department of Psychology
University of Massachusetts–Amherst

Allen K. Hess, Ph.D.
Department of Psychology
Auburn University

Elizabeth L. Holloway, Ph.D.
Department of Counseling Psychology
University of Wisconsin

Allen E. Ivey, Ed.D.
Division/Human Servies and Applied Behavioral Science
University of Massachusetts–Amherst

Henya Kagan (Klein), Ph.D.
Mason Media, Inc.

Norman I. Kagan, Ph.D. (deceased)
Department of Educational Psychology
University of Houston

Samuel Knapp, Ph.D.
Professional Affairs Officer
Pennsylvania Psychological Association

Thomas R. Kratochwill, Ph.D.
Department of Educational Psychology
University of Wisconsin

Nicholas Ladany, Ph.D.
Department of Counseling Psychology
Lehigh University

Michael J. Lambert, Ph.D.
Department of Psychology
Brigham Young University

Kathleen M. Lepage, B.S.
School Psychology Program
University of Wisconsin

Howard A. Liddle, Ed.D.
Center for Family Studies
University of Miami School of Medicine

Bruce S. Liese, Ph.D.
Department of Family Medicine and Psychiatry
University of Kansas Medical Center

Marsha M. Linehan, Ph.D.
Department of Psychology
University of Washington

Steven R. López, Ph.D.
Department of Psychology
University of California–Los Angeles

Alvin R. Mahrer, Ph.D.
Department of Psychology
University of Ottawa

Julia McGivern, Ph.D.
Department of Educational Psychology
University of Wisconsin

Brian W. McNeill, Ph.D.
Department of Counseling Psychology
Washington State University

Pamilla Morales, Ph.D.
Department of Educational Psychology
Texas A & M University

Carlton E. Munson, D.S.W.
School of Social Work
University of Maryland

Mary Lee Nelson, Ph.D.
Department of Educational Psychology
University of Washington

Susan Allstetter Neufeldt, Ph.D.
Counseling/Clinical/School Psychology
University of California–Santa Barbara

John C. Norcross, Ph.D.
Department of Psychology
University of Scranton

Benjamin M. Ogles, Ph.D.
Department of Psychology
Ohio University

C. H. Patterson, Ph.D.
Professor Emeritus, Educational Psychology
University of Illinois

Sandra A. Rigazio-DiGilio, Ph.D.
School of Family Studies
University of Connecticut

Paul Rodenhauser, M.D.
Department of Psychiatry
Tulane University School of Medicine

Cal D. Stoltenberg, Ph.D.
Department of Educational Psychology
University of Oklahoma

Hans H. Strupp, Ph.D.
Department of Psychology
Vanderbilt University

Leon VandeCreek, Ph.D.
School of Professional Psychology
Wright State University

Jennifer A. Waltz, Ph.D.
Department of Psychology
University of Montana

Bruce E. Wampold, Ph.D.
Department of Educational Psychology
University of Wisconsin

C. Edward Watkins Jr., Ph.D.
Department of Psychology
University of North Texas

Paul J. Woods, Ph.D.
Institute for Rational Therapy and Behavioral Medicine

Gary Yontef, Ph.D.
Gestalt Therapy Institute of Los Angeles

PART I

Conceptual and Methodological Foundations

CHAPTER 1

Defining Psychotherapy Supervision and Understanding Supervisor Functioning

C. EDWARD WATKINS JR.
University of North Texas

All mental health preparation programs, be they in psychology, psychiatry, social work, counselor education, or psychiatric nursing, provide some form of clinical supervision to those who perform therapeutic services (e.g., Rodenhauser, 1992). A number of surveys have also shown that many practicing professionals, whatever their work setting, provide supervision to therapists in training and devote a fair portion of their time to doing so (Watkins, 1995). By all accounts, psychotherapy supervision is considered to be important in learning to function effectively as a psychotherapist and is a role that many view as highly relevant to both their professional practice and professional identity.

Psychotherapy supervision is important because, among other possibilities, it provides supervisees with feedback about their performance; offers them guidance about what to do in times of confusion and need; allows them the opportunity to get alternate views and perspectives about patient dynamics, interventions, and course of treatment; stimulates or enhances curiosity about patients and the treatment experience; contributes to the process of forming a therapist "identity"; and serves as a "secure base" for supervisees, letting them know that they are not alone in their learning about and performing of psychotherapy (Cooper & Witenberg, 1983; Greben, 1991; Hart, 1982; Hoffman, 1994). Furthermore, psychotherapy supervision serves a critical quality-control function, ensuring that (a) patients are provided with acceptable care, (b) therapists do no harm, (c) therapists possess sufficient skills to function as "therapists," and (d) those who lack such skills are not allowed to continue without some form of remediation (Harrar, VandeCreek, & Knapp, 1990; Knapp & VandeCreek, Chapter 30, this volume; Stoltenberg & Delworth, 1987; Watkins, 1994). Therefore, it is easier to see why psychotherapy supervision plays such an important and key role in psychotherapy training.

This chapter sets the stage for the subsequent ones. It provides a working definition of psychotherapy supervision and considers some of the factors that make up and influence supervisory functioning (e.g., theories/models and roles).

Note: I would like to thank Janine Bernard, Ph.D., and Paul Rodenhauser, M.D., for the comments they offered on an earlier version of this chapter.

WHAT IS PSYCHOTHERAPY SUPERVISION?

A Working Definition

If you examine various clinical supervision books, you find various (though similar) definitions of the term *psychotherapy supervision.* But which one is best? How might we best define "supervision" for our purposes here?

Consider the following definition offered by Bernard and Goodyear (1992):

> An intervention that is provided by a senior member of a profession to a junior member or members of that same profession. This relationship is evaluative, extends over time, and has the simultaneous purposes of enhancing the professional functioning of the junior member(s), monitoring the quality of professional services offered to the clients she, he, or they see(s), and serving as a gatekeeper for those who are to enter the particular profession. (p. 4)

This definition can serve as a good point of orientation for the succeeding chapters. But to employ the definition, it might be useful to briefly consider some of its component parts.

Relationship.   Supervision takes place in a relational context; it is first and foremost a relationship between senior and junior professional members. All supervisory approaches (e.g., see Part II, Chapters 3 to 14) recognize the relational component of psychotherapy supervision, but the emphasis they accord it varies (cf. Goodyear & Bradley, 1983). Some speak of the supervisory relationship as a learning alliance (Fleming & Benedek, 1983); others see it as being the "essence" of the supervision experience (Patterson, 1983); and still others appear to consider it a "medium" (a means to an end) for the teaching of needed skills and techniques (Linehan, 1980). Whatever the view taken, however, the supervisor-supervisee relationship appears to be a necessary ingredient to the making, doing, and being of the supervision process itself and seemingly facilitates or potentiates whatever takes place within that process.

Evaluation.   If supervisees are to receive feedback about their performance; are to be told about their therapeutic strengths and weaknesses; are to be informed about their skills or areas of functioning that need to be developed, further enhanced, or improved; and if patient care is to be monitored and protected, then supervision must be evaluative. There is no way that cannot be so even though evaluation can come in different forms. In psychotherapy training programs, for example, students not only receive critical feedback about their performance and progress, they can be graded as well. Grading is typically either pass-fail or satisfactory-unsatisfactory, or a letter grade is assigned for work completed. In other cases, in which an already graduated professional voluntarily chooses to be supervised by a more experienced professional, the evaluation can exclusively involve the provision of feedback about performance, skills, and effectiveness. Whatever the nature of the supervisory relationship, some form of evaluation is involved, and that is how it must always be.

Extends Over Time.   Supervision is a process wherein learning and growth occur. For that to happen, however, time is required. Supervisees must have opportunities to work with varied patients; to experience the therapeutic process as it unfolds; to track and scrutinize their treatment efforts over time (what and with whom do they do well, not well, and why); and to try out different interventions, strategies, and techniques along the way (to see what fits and what does not fit for them). All of this is part of the "learning and growth" referred to previously. But none of it can be rushed or hurried. Again, time is requisite.

How much time, then, is needed for supervision to take place? How much time is needed for a supervisee to be in a relationship with a particular supervisor? From this author's observations of university training programs, supervisor and supervisee often work together for a full academic year (about 9 months). It is rather common, too, for these supervisees to work with more than one supervisor during that time period (Greenberg, 1980). Furthermore, more than one (academic) year of psychotherapy practice and supervision may be required.

In many practice sites that train psychotherapists (e.g., mental health centers or counseling centers), supervisor and supervisee can work together for anywhere from about 4 to 12 months, depending on the nature of the setting and its primary training goals and needs. Again, these supervisees commonly work with more than one supervisor during that time period. In still other training situations, for example, psychoanalytic training institutes, the supervisor-supervisee relationship may well last longer than 12 months. And further still, the supervision relationship between already practicing professionals and their supervisors can last longer yet—even several years in duration for some (see McCarthy, Kulakowski, & Kenfield, 1994).

Enhancing Professional Functioning.   Supervision is all about helping the therapist become better and more effective with regard to conceptual ability, intervention, assessment, and implementation, among other areas. By means of supervision, it is the supervisor's hope and intention that therapist functioning will thereby be enhanced. That hope and intention apply for all theories and models of supervision and training (see Parts II and III), whatever their conceptual thrust may be.

Monitoring Quality of Professional Service.   What type of care is the patient receiving? Supervisors are ultimately responsible for the treatment that their supervisees' patients receive; they must then be ever attentive to the quality of that treatment and how it serves the patient in the process. If supervisees are providing sufficient to high-quality treatment, how can they be helped to make it even better? If treatment quality is less than sufficient, what can supervisors do to bring it up to at least an acceptable level? If supervisees are unable to bring their treatment efforts up to such a level, or if they are actually harming patients, what steps must the supervisor take to help both supervisee and patient move ahead? Those questions are integral to the supervision endeavor and must be dealt with if patient care is to be improved upon and protected. Without good monitoring of service quality, patient welfare can be sorely compromised or even jeopardized (Knapp & VandeCreek, Chapter 30, this volume); that cannot be allowed to happen.

Serving as Gatekeeper.   Consistent with their monitoring function, supervisors are gatekeepers as well. If they deem that a supervisee (e.g., a master's or doctoral student) still lacks the needed therapy skills after supervised training, they can require that he or she engage in remediation. In some cases that can mean additional training and supervision; in other cases, it may become clear that the supervisee is in need of personal therapy as well as additional training and supervision. Whatever the form of remediation, supervisees are judged not ready to enter the profession and are not allowed to do so; the supervisor is responsible for making such a judgment and in that way serves as a keeper of the gate.

Summary

This working definition, then, seems to capture the essentials of psychotherapy supervision: who is involved (a senior and junior member of a profession), how they are involved (by means of relationship), the purposes of their interaction (to enhance functioning, monitor quality, and provide gatekeeping), and some key characteristics of that interaction (it is evaluative and extends over time).

FACTORS THAT COMPOSE AND INFLUENCE
SUPERVISORY FUNCTIONING

Let us now look at some of the elements that make up "supervisory functioning." What factors influence what supervisors do, why they do it, and how they do it? These questions relate to the supervisor's goal of facilitating both supervisee and patient growth. To answer the questions, we need to focus on the supervisor's (a) assumptive world, (b) theory or model, (c) supervisory style, (d) roles and strategies, (e) foci, (f) format of supervision, and (g) techniques (see Friedlander & Ward, 1984; Rodenhauser, Painter, & Rudisill, 1985; Shanfield & Gil, 1985). Those factors can all be seen as "interrelated sources of variability among supervisors" (Friedlander & Ward, 1984, p. 542).

Assumptive World.   *Assumptive world* refers to the supervisor's "past professional and life experience, training, values, and general outlook on life" (Bernard & Goodyear, 1992, p. 35). The assumptive world is a product, then, of the professional and the personal (e.g., working with patients and supervisees and interacting with other individuals in various roles and capacities). It reflects our values, assumptions, and overall perspective on life and living, the world at large, and our place in it. The assumptive world logically affects the next factor or level of functioning—choice of a theory or model.

Theory or Model.   A *theory* can be defined as "an attempt to organize and integrate knowledge and to answer the question 'Why?'" (Patterson & Watkins, 1996, p. 1). Or as Lazarus (1993) has put it, "a theory endeavors to answer the question of *why* and *how* certain processes arise, are maintained, can be modified, or are extinguished, and to make predictions therefrom" (p. 675, emphasis in original). According to Patterson and Watkins (1996), a good theory ideally possesses the following characteristics: importance (i.e., it addresses something that matters), precision and clarity, parsimony and simplicity, comprehensiveness, operationality, empirical validity, fruitfulness, and practicality. A theory, then, represents an effort to understand, organize, and predict relative to some phenomenon or phenomena (e.g., human functioning). It is a valuable road map that enables us to better navigate the territory we need to cross (Krumboltz, 1991).

In psychotherapy, for example, one's theory can offer understanding about patient problems (how they came to be, how they are maintained, what can be done about them, and why). One's theory of psychotherapy supervision may offer understanding about variables such as the supervisor-supervisee relationship, supervisee dynamics, supervisee resistance and transference, supervisory interventions, and the process of supervisee growth and development. Thus, whatever the nature of the therapy or supervision theory, each allows one to systematize, organize, understand, and predict relative to the therapeutic and supervision situations, respectively; each reflects one's values, assumptions, and perspective about the treatment and supervision endeavors.

In considering the role of theory, one important question arises: Are the practitioner's theory of therapy and theory of supervision the same or different? Chapters 3 through 14 (Part II) illustrate that for some their views of therapy and supervision are much the same—leading to what has been termed *psychotherapy-based supervision* approaches in the clinical literature (e.g., Bradley, 1989). For others, their supervision approach seems to be more integrative in nature, yet they recognize that key concepts from their therapy theory (e.g., irrational beliefs) still have relevance for their view of supervision as well (e.g., helping supervisees recognize and combat their own irrational beliefs about being the "perfect" therapist). As you read the chapters in Part II, you will see those two perspectives in evidence.

What might now be said about the other term, *model?* Is it the same as a theory? A few decades back, Simon and Newell (1963) stated that "in contemporary usage the term 'model' is . . . simply a synonym for 'theory'" (p. 89). From this author's observations, those terms are still often used synonymously today. So when you hear the words "one's theory of supervision" or "one's model of supervision," those phrases are usually somewhat interchangeable.

Yet models have been differentiated from theories. For example, Chapanis (1961) refers to models as analogies—looser constructions than theories that, nevertheless, can contribute to our ability to describe, understand, and predict certain phenomena. Models tend to be less precise than theories, but they can provide us with a road map of sorts by which to navigate.

It may be that the term *model* fits best for most of the chapters in Part II (and Part III as well). *Supervision theory* may be too strong a term for what is described there, whereas *supervision model* is not. That is a consideration the reader may wish to keep in mind as he or she reads that section.

Supervisory Style.   *Supervisory style* refers to supervisors' rather consistent, characteristic manner of relating to their supervisees. For instance, is the supervisor primarily facilitative in manner? dictatorial? passive? Shanfield's (see Shanfield & Gil, 1985) research identified four basic supervisor styles—task-oriented, expert, confrontative and directive, and facilitative—that vary across eight dimensions (e.g., control of supervisory session, activity level). Later research has further confirmed the consistent, enduring nature of supervisor style in psychotherapy supervision (Shanfield, Mohl, Matthews, & Hetherly, 1992). In essence, style is the characteristic fashion in which the supervisor relates to supervisees and implements his or her assumptive world and theory or model in supervision.

Roles/Strategies.   *Role* refers to "a function . . . assumed by someone [an advisory *role*]" (Guralnick, 1972, p. 1233). *Strategy* (though often used to refer to a technique or specific intervention) can also be defined in the same way (e.g., Rodenhauser et al., 1985). Some of the different roles/strategies that supervisors can assume include teacher, lecturer, instructor (Hess, 1980; Holloway, 1984; Holloway & Aposhyan, 1994; Rodenhauser et al., 1985); counselor, therapist (Hess, 1980; Holloway, 1984); consultant (Holloway, 1984; Rodenhauser et al., 1985); colleague, collegial-peer (Hess, 1980; Holloway, 1984); monitor (Hess, 1980; Holloway, 1984); case reviewer (Hess, 1980); model and mentor (Holloway & Aposhyan, 1994); and administrator and interactor (Rodenhauser et al., 1985). Supervision requires us to perform different roles at different times. Because of the nature of our assumptive world, theory-model, and style, we may understandably give more emphasis to and feel more comfortable engaging in certain supervisory roles as opposed to others.

Foci.   The term *foci* refers to the factors or processes that receive primary attention during the supervision session. To draw again on Rodenhauser et al. (1985), four such focal points are professional/organizational factors, assessment/planning processes, implementation/ intervention/evaluation processes, and personal factors. Professional/organizational factors relate to matters of record keeping, billing procedures, and ethical and legal concerns.

Assessment/planning processes involve issues of treatment planning, decision making, and modality determination. Implementation/intervention/evaluation processes involve teaching supervisees about relevant treatment concepts (e.g., transference), parallel process, and patient regression. Personal factors include concerns about culture, gender, and ethnicity (e.g., therapist-patient differences), discussions of referrals when needed, and consideration of the impact of countertransference on the therapist's treatment efforts.

Each of these four foci requires specific attention in supervision at various times. Furthermore, each can be addressed by means of various supervisor roles or strategies. For example, the professional/organizational, assessment/planning, implementation/intervention/evaluation, and personal may all be dealt with—depending on the specific nature of the problem—via the administrative, teacher-instructional, consultative, and interactive roles, among others (see Rodenhauser et al., 1985, pp. 221–222, for some good examples).

Format of Supervision.   *Format* refers to the form or forms by which supervision is delivered. For example, is supervision done individually or in a group? Is it performed face to face? Format would logically be affected by and flow from the previously identified factors of supervisory functioning (e.g., foci, theory/model).

Techniques.   *Techniques* refer to the supervisor's actual interventions used in supervision. According to Loganbill, Hardy, and Delworth (1982), supervisory interventions can take varied forms. Some might be facilitative (e.g., offering support and encouragement) or confrontive (e.g., identifying a conflict or discrepancy between the supervisee's verbal and nonverbal behavior). Others might be conceptual (e.g., helping the supervisee think about patient dynamics). Still others might be prescriptive (e.g., telling the supervisee what seems needed in a particular therapeutic situation) or catalytic (e.g., encouraging the supervisee to experiment with different techniques in therapy). Techniques involve doing; they are active and are engaged in for a particular reason to bring about some desired or expected result. Of all the factors discussed thus far, technique would be the most specific level of operation in supervisor functioning.

A Multilayered Conceptualization

All the foregoing factors lead to a *multilayered conceptualization* of supervisor functioning. Such a conceptualization is graphically depicted in Table 1.1. The top layer is the broadest and most influential, ultimately affecting all layers that lie below it. Each succeeding layer would be more specific in nature and each would, in turn, affect all layers that lie below it. Although other layers could perhaps be added to this conceptualization, those shown identify most if not *the* most important factors that affect supervisor functioning.

(It is vital to say that this conceptualization is not something this author has devised. It borrows much from Friedlander and Ward's, 1984, earlier work; what is different here, however, is that the training, conceptual, and research efforts of Rodenhauser and Shanfield have been incorporated into this conceptualization. As a result, some of the levels are now slightly different in name and meaning.)

Summary

Many factors influence supervisory functioning. This multilayered view considers several of those factors—assumptive world, theory/model, style, roles/strategies, foci, format, and techniques—that seem most important in understanding how and why supervisors do what they do.

**Table 1.1   Factors That Compose and Influence Supervisor Functioning:
A Multilayered Conceptualization**

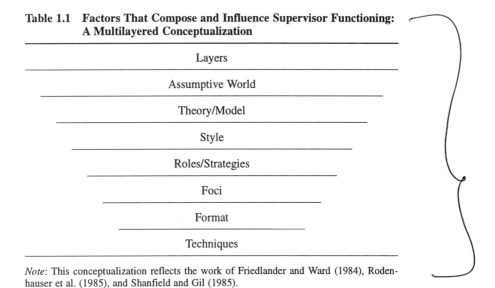

Layers
Assumptive World
Theory/Model
Style
Roles/Strategies
Foci
Format
Techniques

Note: This conceptualization reflects the work of Friedlander and Ward (1984), Rodenhauser et al. (1985), and Shanfield and Gil (1985).

Admittedly, the supervisor is but one member of a group that includes the supervisee
and patient. What about the factors that influence supervisee and patient functioning, as
well as the supervisory mix as a whole? That question or portions of it will be substantively addressed in some of the chapters that follow.

CONCLUSION

Psychotherapy supervision is a critical if not *the* most critical facet of the psychotherapy
training endeavor. Such supervision is offered across all mental health preparation programs and is offered by many practicing professionals as well. This chapter has considered a definition of psychotherapy supervision and some of the primary variables that
seemingly influence supervisory functioning. It is hoped that this definition and multilayered conceptualization will, to some extent, set the stage for what follows.

REFERENCES

Bernard, J. M., & Goodyear, R. K. (1992). *Fundamentals of clinical supervision*. Boston: Allyn &
Bacon.

Bradley, L. J. (1989). *Counselor supervision: Principles, process, and practice* (2nd ed.). Muncie,
IN: Accelerated Development.

Chapanis, A. (1961). Men, machines, and models. *American Psychologist, 16*, 116–131.

Cooper, A., & Witenberg, E. G. (1983). Stimulation of curiosity in the supervisory process of psychoanalysis. *Contemporary Psychoanalysis, 19*, 248–264.

Fleming, J., & Benedek, T. (1983). *Psychoanalytic supervision: A method of clinical teaching*. New
York: International Universities Press.

Friedlander, M. L., & Ward, L. G. (1984). Development and validation of the Supervisory Styles
Inventory. *Journal of Counseling Psychology, 31*, 541–557.

Goodyear, R. K., & Bradley, F. O. (1983). Theories of counselor supervision: Points of convergence
and divergence. *The Counseling Psychologist, 11*(1), 59–67.

Greben, S. E. (1991). Interpersonal aspects of the supervision of individual psychotherapy. *American Journal of Psychotherapy*, *45*, 306–316.

Greenberg, L. (1980). Supervision from the perspective of the supervisee. In A. K. Hess (Ed.), *Psychotherapy supervision: Theory, research and practice* (pp. 85–91). New York: Wiley.

Guralnick, D. B. (Ed.). (1972). *Webster's new world dictionary*. New York: World Publishing.

Harrar, W. R., VandeCreek, L., & Knapp, S. (1990). Ethical and legal aspects of clinical supervision. *Professional Psychology: Research and Practice*, *21*, 37–41.

Hart, G. (1982). *The process of clinical supervision*. Baltimore: University Park Press.

Hess, A. K. (1980). Training models and the nature of psychotherapy supervision. In A. K. Hess (Ed.), *Psychotherapy supervision: Theory, research and practice* (pp. 15–25). New York: Wiley.

Hoffman, L. W. (1994). The training of psychotherapy supervisors: A barren scape. *Psychotherapy in Private Practice*, *13*, 23–42.

Holloway, E. L. (1984). Outcome evaluation in supervision research. *The Counseling Psychologist*, *12*(4), 167–174.

Holloway, E. L., & Aposhyan, H. M. (1994). The supervisor as teacher, model, and mentor for careers and psychotherapy. *Journal of Career Assessment*, *2*, 191–197.

Krumboltz, J. D. (1991). The 1990 Leona Tyler Award Address: Brilliant insights—platitudes that bear repeating. *The Counseling Psychologist*, *19*, 298–315.

Lazarus, A. A. (1993). Theory, subjectivity and bias: Can there be a future? *Psychotherapy*, *30*, 674–677.

Linehan, M. M. (1980). Supervision of behavior therapy. In A. K. Hess (Ed.), *Psychotherapy supervision: Theory, research and practice* (pp. 148–180). New York: Wiley.

Loganbill, C., Hardy, E., & Delworth, U. (1982). Supervision: A conceptual model. *The Counseling Psychologist*, *10*(1), 3–42.

McCarthy, P., Kulakowski, D., & Kenfield, J. A. (1994). Clinical supervision practices of licensed psychologists. *Professional Psychology: Research and Practice*, *25*, 177–181.

Patterson, C. H. (1983). A client–centered approach to supervision. *The Counseling Psychologist*, *11*(1), 21–25.

Patterson, C. H., & Watkins, C. E., Jr. (1996). *Theories of psychotherapy* (5th ed.). New York: HarperCollins.

Rodenhauser, P. (1992). Psychiatry residency programs: Trends in psychotherapy supervision. *American Journal of Psychotherapy*, *46*, 240–249.

Rodenhauser, P., Painter, A. F., & Rudisill, J. R. (1985). Supervising supervisors: A series of workshops. *Journal of Psychiatric Education*, *9*, 217–224.

Shanfield, S. B., & Gil, D. (1985). Styles of psychotherapy supervision. *Journal of Psychiatric Education*, *9*, 225–232.

Shanfield, S. B., Mohl, P. C., Matthews, K. L., & Hetherly, V. (1992). Quantitative assessment of the behavior of psychotherapy supervisors. *American Journal of Psychiatry*, *149*, 352–357.

Simon, H. A., & Newell, A. (1963). The uses and limitations of models. In M. Marx (Ed.), *Theories in contemporary psychology* (pp. 89–104). New York: Macmillan.

Stoltenberg, C. D., & Delworth, U. (1987). *Supervising counselors and therapists: A developmental approach*. San Francisco: Jossey-Bass.

Watkins, C. E., Jr. (1994). The supervision of psychotherapy supervisor trainees. *American Journal of Psychotherapy*, *48*, 417–431.

Watkins, C. E., Jr. (1995). Psychotherapy supervision in the 1990s: Some observations and reflections. *American Journal of Psychotherapy*, *49*, 568–581.

CHAPTER 2

Methodology, Design, and Evaluation in Psychotherapy Supervision Research

BRUCE E. WAMPOLD
University of Wisconsin—Madison
ELIZABETH L. HOLLOWAY
University of Wisconsin—Madison

CAUSAL MODEL OF SUPERVISION

Supervision is not a simple, easily conceptualized, and straightforward phenomenon because of its connection with other aspects of therapist training and psychotherapy practice. Although supervision as an instructional method has not yet been defined with specificity, in this chapter we outline a general causal model for research in supervision that recognizes the pragmatic and methodological linkages among supervision, therapist training, and psychotherapy. As is typical with generic modeling, certain instances will not be accommodated by the causal model presented here. The purpose of the model, however, is to depict the simplest framework that generates a sufficiently rich contextual backdrop for clinically relevant research. Nevertheless, it becomes apparent that even this parsimonious model will spawn complexities for which existing research methods are inadequate. Methodologically, there is nothing unique about supervision; rather, it is the complexity of the phenomenon itself that adds unique methodological considerations. Consequently, complex research strategies are needed to capture the complexity of supervision.

Figure 2.1 presents our causal model of supervision. Before discussing elements of the model and how research might be applied to understand the elements and their interrelationship, several aspects of this model need elaboration. Four aspects of this model have implications for how research in supervision is conceptualized. First, all the arrows are bidirectional, indicating that reciprocal causal relations exist. In some instances, it is difficult to conceive of the reciprocal causality; for example, the ethnicity of either the supervisor or the therapist is unlikely to be affected by the supervisory process. Any supervision research that assumes that therapist and supervisor characteristics affect the supervisory process but not vice versa is, however, obviously unrealistic. The purpose of supervision is to affect the ability of the therapist to deliver efficacious psychotherapy by changing therapist characteristics including, but certainly not limited to, skill level, role expectations, therapeutic orientation, values, attitudes, beliefs, and, in some cases, emotional well-being and cultural attitudes (Holloway, 1992, 1995). Specifying the directionality of causal relations is critical to understanding where a given research study fits in the causal model.

The second perspicuous aspect of Figure 2.1 is that the outcome of supervision is not

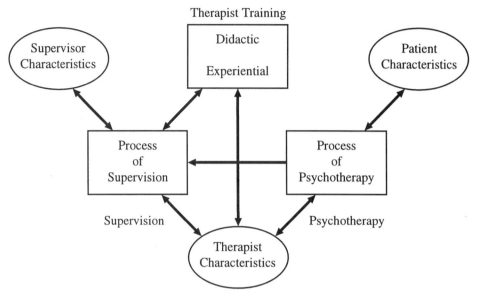

Figure 2.1   Causal Model of Supervision Research

depicted distinctly from other elements. In our conceptualization, the outcome of super-vision is manifest in the causal relations from the process of supervision to therapist char-acteristics. Therefore, whether it be changes in skill level, attitudes, self-understanding, or some other characteristic, the effect of supervision results most proximally in some mod-ification of therapists' characteristics. These changes in the therapist will then, it is hoped, result in the delivery of more efficacious treatment.

A third aspect of the model, related to the previous two, is that *all* effects of supervi-sion are transmitted through therapist characteristics. Certainly, an important, although the most distal, outcome of supervision is that the patient improves. In our model, this distal outcome of supervision is mediated entirely by changes in therapist characteristics. We make this argument logically rather than empirically. In traditional supervision, the ther-apist meets with the supervisor individually or in groups, but typically contact with the patient is limited to the therapist, suggesting the impossibility of supervision affecting the patient in any way other than through the therapist. One notable exception to this situa-tion occurs in those instances in which the supervisor takes the additional role of being a cotherapist with the trainee, as is occasionally the case in modalities other than individ-ual therapy (e.g., group or family therapy; Everett, 1980).

A fourth aspect is that causal forces other than supervision are working on the thera-pist. Of course, there are the usual threats to internal validity, such as maturation, history, and so forth. If the therapist is also a trainee, however, then an important influence on him or her is the concurrent therapist training, including didactic and experiential course work, interaction with other trainees, workshops attended, and so on. As discussed later, unless these experiences are controlled experimentally, they will always provide alternative expla-nations for any change in therapist characteristics or more distal outcomes, such as patient improvement. The heuristic model developed by Holloway (1995; Chapter 15, this volume) provides one example of a model that identifies influential contextual factors that have been identified in the empirical literature.

In following sections, we discuss the elements of the general causal model (see Figure

2.1), choice of operations that reflect the elements, and research designs that examine the relationships among the elements. We have avoided critiquing supervision research by examining inadequacies of extant research because previous reviews of supervision research have ably exposed the methodological limitations of this research (e.g., Ellis, Ladany, Krengel, & Schult, 1996). Our goal is to provide a schema for understanding how supervision research can contribute to a connected and coherent understanding of the phenomenon of supervision.

SUPERVISION ELEMENTS

Therapist Characteristics

A plethora of therapist characteristics potentially could affect the process and outcome of supervision, and many ways to categorize these characteristics exist. Because those therapist characteristics that have been identified as important in the study of psychotherapy should also be important in the study of supervision, we have, for heuristic purposes, adapted the taxonomy of therapist characteristics in the context of psychotherapy proposed by Beutler, Machado, and Neufeldt (1994).

Essentially, Beutler et al. (1994) classified characteristics into four taxons constructed by crossing two dichotomous dimensions, as shown in Figure 2.2. One dimension, objective/subjective, refers to whether the characteristics are inferred from therapist's self-report (subjective) or can be determined from sources other than self-report (objective). The other

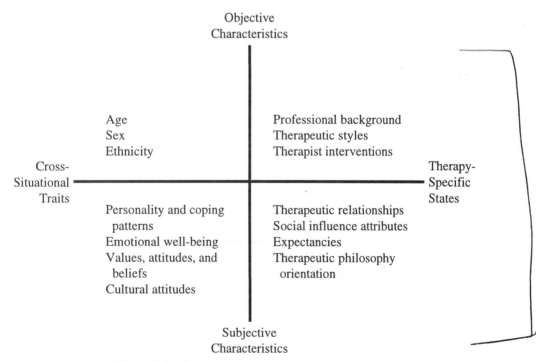

Figure 2.2   Classification of Therapist Characteristics

dimension, cross-situational traits/therapy-specific states, alludes to whether characteristics are stable, enduring, and exist independently of the supervision or psychotherapy (cross-situational traits) or are specific to the supervision and/or therapy context.

Although the purpose of this chapter is not to review the supervision research literature, examination of the therapist characteristics taxonomy presented in Figure 2.2 raises some prickly research design issues, many of which fit under the rubric of construct validity. Although the issue of the construct validity of research designs has been well explicated generally (Cook & Campbell, 1979) and in relation to counseling and psychotherapy specifically (Heppner, Kivlighan, & Wampold, 1992; Wampold & Poulin, 1992), the consequences of inadequate construct validity are profound.

First, it should be realized that the names of the characteristics in each of the four taxons are ambiguous with regard to their level of abstraction. Clearly, some characteristics, such as the personality of the therapist (subjective/cross-situational trait), refer to psychological constructs, whereas others, such as age (objective/cross-situational trait), refer to observed variables. Suppose one is interested in the relation of the psychological construct of extroversion to some supervision process phenomenon; one then infers the level of this characteristic (i.e., extroversion) with some valid operation or operations (e.g., a paper-and-pencil self-report measure of extroversion). Age, however, although easily obtainable, theoretically would be useless unless it were conceptualized as an indicator of some psychological process, construct, or phenomenon. One might hypothesize that the nature of the supervision offered may be dependent on the roles the supervisor and supervisee take (Ellis & Dell, 1986; Ellis, Dell, & Good, 1988; Friedlander, Keller, Peca-Baker, & Olk, 1986). Accordingly, one might speculate that the roles assumed by the participants when there is a large difference in age between the supervisor and the supervisee would be different from those assumed when the ages of the participants are nearly the same (Doehrman, 1976).

Another issue related to the construct validity of supervision research is related to confusion between levels of a construct and the construct itself. This confusion occurs when two or three levels of a continuous variable are chosen such that the levels are in a narrow range (i.e., do not span the continuum). As an example, consider the apparently straightforward construct related to therapist experience, which would be classified as an objective, supervision-specific state (Beutler et al., 1994). This is an important construct because it has been hypothesized that supervision process is a function of therapist experience. Typically, however, experience is operationalized by comparing practicum students with interns (Worthington, 1987), which, considering the continuum from novice therapist to expert, represents a restricted portion of the experience variable.

Another complication when studying therapist characteristics is that many of the characteristics are confounded or interact with one another to (presumably) affect supervision process and outcome. It would be surprising to find that therapists' ethnicity and cultural attitudes are not related in some fashion. Indeed, many studies have shown that American ethnic minority subjects' preferences for and judgments of therapists are moderated by their cultural affiliation (Coleman, Wampold, & Casali, 1995). Given a supervisor who is an American ethnic minority and a therapist who is a European American, any relationship built between the two is likely to be a function of both participants' expectations, cultural attitudes, and ethnicity, as well as the interaction among these characteristics (Martinez & Holloway, in press; Peterson, 1991). Attributing effects to the ethnicity of the therapist surely would be misleading because the meaning of ethnicity is derived primarily from the social context in which it exists, in this case the social context of supervision.

Moreover, issues of culture and diversity are very much intertwined with the dynamics of interpersonal relationships, particularly power and involvement (Holloway, 1995; Martinez & Holloway, in press). For example, it has been found that female trainees are less likely to be encouraged to use responses that signify higher levels of power in the supervisory relationship vis-à-vis male trainees (Nelson & Holloway, 1990).

Appropriate operationalization of therapist characteristics is crucial in our conceptualization of supervision because the superordinate goal of supervision is to make the supervisee a more effective therapist. The characteristics in Figure 2.2 were included in Beutler et al.'s (1994) taxonomy because they have been thought to be, at one time or another, related to treatment outcomes. If a therapist characteristic is related to treatment outcomes and if the characteristic is modifiable, then supervision could be appropriately focused on changing this characteristic of the therapist. Of course, the most obvious therapist characteristic that would be the focus of supervision would be therapeutic skill level.

Supervisor Characteristics

Supervisor characteristics are classified according to the Beutler model as well (refer to Figure 2.2). All the characteristics displayed in Figure 2.2 are relevant to supervisors. Of course, there are characteristics specific to supervision, such as supervisory style, supervisor interventions, and supervisory theoretical orientation, that could be added to the taxonomy. Moreover, the issues discussed earlier with regard to therapist characteristics also are applicable to supervisor characteristics.

One of the issues in studying supervisor characteristics is the importance of characteristics of the supervisor as therapist. For example, in the area of experience, the supervisor has experience as a therapist and experience as a supervisor. Similarly, the supervisor has a level of competence in both therapeutic as well as supervisory contexts. To assume that characteristics of the supervisor in the therapeutic context are synonymous with characteristics in the supervisory context is to equate the therapeutic and supervisory processes, a position that is unsupported by research in supervision (Holloway, Freund, Gardner, Nelson, & Walker, 1989; Lambert, 1974; Pierce & Schauble, 1970, 1971; Wedeking & Scott, 1976).

The situation is further complicated when the matching of supervisor and therapist characteristics is considered because the characteristics can either influence each other (e.g., Beutler & NcNabb, 1981; Guest & Beutler, 1988) or potentially lead to conflict (e.g., Kennard, Stewart, & Gluck, 1987). For example, it has been found that therapists tend to adopt the theoretical orientation of the supervisor and maintain that orientation for several years (Guest & Beutler, 1988). In those instances in which theoretical orientation of the therapist is initially discordant with that of the supervisor, however, conflict may affect the supervision process. For example, a behavioral supervisor may question the therapist about the behavioral antecedents of the patient's problematic behavior. The therapist may not be able to respond in the desired way because he or she does not know the answer; a behavioral analysis was not conducted because of therapist orientation. The supervisor may then make attributions about the therapist based on the therapist's inability to provide the desired information, and these attributions may or may not be consistent with the therapist's therapeutic competence in his or her area. Kennard et al. (1987) found that similar theoretical orientation and interpretive style contributed to trainees' reported positive supervisory experiences.

Supervision Process (as Distinct From Outcome)

In therapy, classification of certain phenomena either as process or as outcome is dependent on the definition of process and outcome adopted (see Orlinsky, Grawe, & Parks, 1994); consequently, we do not think it important that a definition be given that makes a distinct boundary between process and outcome in supervision. Nevertheless, as a heuristic tool we define process to include those activities that occur in the supervision session as well as the participants' (viz., supervisor and therapist) perceptions of those events and observers' rating of those events. Outcome is then any phenomena representing a change or state that persists beyond the confines of the actual supervision session.

One of the earliest and most persistent lines of research in supervision has simply been to describe the interactions in supervision. In the most basic incarnation of this method, coding systems were developed or adapted from other areas of research; supervisor and/or therapist behaviors were classified according to the coding system; and then the frequencies of the codes were obtained. A comprehensive review of the observational systems used in supervision research appears elsewhere (Holloway & Poulin, 1994). One of the pervasive findings of this line of research was that the supervisor spends more time giving information, opinions, and suggestions than providing emotional support or attending to the therapist's emotional needs, demonstrating that supervision differs from the prototypic conception of psychotherapy and is more in line with educative processes (Carroll, 1996; Holloway, 1984; Holloway & Wampold, 1983; Holloway & Wolleat, 1980; Lambert, 1974; Rickards, 1984; Wedeking & Scott, 1976).

When coding behavior within the supervision process, issues of construct validity as well as epistemology need to be considered. It should be recognized that any coding system used attends to some aspect of the supervision process and ignores others. For example, the Penman system (1980), used by Holloway and her colleagues (Holloway et al., 1989; Nelson & Holloway, 1990), operationalizes power and involvement, two constructs hypothesized to underlie interpersonal interactions (e.g., Leary, 1957). Carroll (1996) devised a coding system that focused on task (e.g., teaching, consultation, evaluation) rather than on relationship.

In many areas of psychology and related disciplines that have examined social interactions, frequencies of codes (i.e., base rates) are an inadequate method to describe social phenomena because the essence of social interchange is exhibited in the pattern of behavior and not in the frequency of behavior. That is, the examination of the contingent nature of the codes reveals important aspects of the interaction above and beyond information provided by frequencies. The simplest question in such analyses is whether the emission of a specified behavior by one of the participants increases (or decreases) the probability that the other participant will respond with a specified behavior. A class of data-analytic procedures to answer this question and more sophisticated questions of behavioral contingency has come to be known as *sequential analysis* (e.g., Gottman & Roy, 1990; Wampold, 1992). Several supervision studies have used sequential analysis (Holloway & Poulin, 1994). It should be noted that the sequential patterns found in streams of behavior between supervisor and therapist are constructs in and of themselves. For example, Nelson and Holloway (1990) attached the descriptor *ascending patterns* to interchanges in which low power responses were followed by high power responses to reflect a construct related to the power dynamics between supervisor and therapist.

Studies that use coding schemes to assess frequency of events or sequential patterns rely on the central epistemological assumption that there exists a real phenomenon and that this phenomenon can be reliably observed. Although some coding systems were developed pan-theoretically, the names of the categories and their descriptions represent a system that is atomistic in that the supervision phenomenon is classified into a finite number of categories and assumes that analysis of the results of this classification (either by examining rates or sequential connections) are informative. The construals of the participants (i.e., the meanings given to the events by the participants) are thought to be either nonexistent or not important.

Research designs that recognize that participants' description of their experience provide critical information about a phenomenon are beginning to be recognized as legitimate research strategies for understanding psychotherapy and related activities (Heppner, Kivlighan, & Wampold, 1992; Qualitative Research, 1994). Recently, interpretive methods have been applied to supervision (Carroll, 1996; Neufeldt, Karno, & Nelson, 1996; Poulin, 1992; Skovholt & Ronnestad, 1992; Worthen & McNeill, 1996). It should be noted that interpretive methods used to describe the meanings of events are philosophically different from positivist and postpositivist methods that examine events in supervision; moreover, the degree to which meaning is described and extracted from the data varies according to the interpretive method used. Interpretive methods have their own strategies to assess rigor and relevance. Integrity of an interpretive study rests on its congruence to the philosophical perspective that informs the method (Holloway & Carroll, 1996). As an example of interpretive research, Worthen and McNeill (1996) used a phenomenological approach to describe trainees' perspectives of "good supervision." This study used the participants' willingness and skill in articulating their reflections on the supervision process and in attributing meaning to events in supervision. When ,interviewed, the trainees described the characteristics of the supervision interview that freed them to reveal their vulnerabilities and difficulties in supervision.

LINKING ELEMENTS OF SUPERVISION

Simply describing the characteristics of the participants in supervision or the supervisory process limits understanding of the ways that these elements may relate to one another as well as the role of contextual factors outside the supervisory relationship. Researchers have sought to examine the relationship of these factors in order to make causal connections among the characteristics of the participants, the process of supervision, and most important, the outcome of the endeavor. The most researched link is between supervisor and/or therapist characteristics and process with the presumed causal direction being from the characteristics to the process. Some studies have examined the effect of the process on the supervisor and supervisee; although these studies could be classified as supervision-outcome studies, as we will see, the scope of outcome research is severely limited (Holloway & Neufeldt, 1995).

Supervisor/Therapist Characteristics → Supervision Process

In terms of research design, studies that examine the influence of supervisor and therapist characteristics on the supervision process are restricted to passive designs in which the relationship between the characteristics and aspects of the supervisory process is determined. Logically, experimental designs are precluded because subjects in studies cannot be randomly assigned to various characteristics. As passive designs, the usual inferential problems are present.

The first issue is whether the true causal direction is consistent with research claims. That is, is the hypothesized causal direction from the participant characteristic to the supervision process, as claimed in the research? One of the competing hypotheses in passive designs is that the true causal direction is opposite to that hypothesized (Cook & Campbell, 1979). In many supervision studies, however, the opposite causal path is precluded. For instance, supervision studies have examined the relationship between participant gender and supervision process (e.g., Goodyear, 1990; Robyak, Goodyear, Prange, & Donham, 1986); it is not logical to assume that the supervision process affects the participants' gender. So, threats resulting from ambiguous causal direction in such cases are minimal.

Nevertheless, the causal direction can be ambiguous and often bidirectional. Limiting the causal direction from supervisor characteristics to supervision process (or outcome) may constrain realistic conceptualizations of supervision. Certainly, supervisor expectations of supervisory roles and the learning tasks (subjective/supervision-specific state) prior to the commencement of therapy can be classified as a supervisor characteristic (e.g., Wiley & Ray, 1986). Even so, these expectations may be influenced by the supervision interaction during the course of supervision. For example, the supervisor may have the expectation that the therapist is in need of considerable personal growth and is willing to enter into such a process; but when the therapist resists entreaties toward this goal, the supervisor likely will modify his or her expectations. Such expressed expectations are built on experience with supervising therapists but also are modified in particular instances of supervision. That is, expectations are a result of past experience but are affected considerably by the ongoing supervision process. It has been found that the therapist's personality characteristics and client situations modify the manner in which the supervisor responds to the therapist's learning needs (e.g., Tracey, Ellickson, & Sherry, 1989).

Although threats resulting from ambiguous causal direction may not be problematic, interpretation of these passive designs becomes extremely equivocal when one considers both the participants' characteristics and their perspectives vis-à-vis the supervision process within the session. To understand the inferential problems, this chapter considers, in some detail, supervision studies that have examined developmental models of supervision (e.g., Stoltenberg & Delworth, 1987). Developmental models hypothesize that the supervision process will be a function of the developmental level of the trainee. Although developmental level has been defined in various ways (e.g., on the basis of skill level or cognitive styles), most studies have operationalized developmental level by assessing the level of training (e.g., beginning practicum, advanced practicum, and internship), although there are notable exceptions (e.g., Hill, Charles, & Reed, 1981; Miars et al., 1983). The assumptions of such an operationalization are (a) that the key feature of the developmental model (e.g., skill level) is reflected in the training level (i.e., that more advanced students have higher levels of skill), and (b) that the supervision process is a function of this developmental construct. Now consider an instance in which supervisors rate some aspect of the supervision process (e.g., environmental structure) and suppose that these ratings vary as a function of the training level of the supervisee. Given the assumptions postulated earlier, it is assumed that these results provide evidence for a developmental model of supervision because the supervision process varies as a function of the experience level of the supervisee. Nevertheless, there are many inferential ambiguities inherent in such designs.

To understand the developmental result fully, one must take into account the characteristics of the supervisor, particularly the supervisor's expectations for training. The supervisor may have the expectation that supervision should be structured differently for beginning practicum, advanced practicum, and intern students and thus will respond that he or she provides three forms of supervision, regardless of the variation in supervision actually provided. That is, supervisor reports of the supervision process may reflect their belief that their instructional strategies are governed by therapist experience, when in fact they are not. Krause and Allen (1988), corroborating the results of Wiley and Ray (1986), reported that although supervisors thought they expected they would be more collegial and unstructured with advanced trainees, the trainees did not report such differences. Of course, to complicate matters, it might be that there were differences, but the trainees did not perceive or report them, raising the exacerbating factor of perspective differences, which is discussed later.

Supervision Process → Therapist Characteristics: The Outcome of Supervision

In the general causal model, outcomes of supervision are found in changes in therapist characteristics or are mediated by changes in therapist characteristics. The goal of supervision is to change some characteristic of the therapist (e.g., skill level), which in turn will result in the competent delivery of psychotherapy, which in turn will result in positive changes in the patient. Clearly, the outcome of supervision can be assessed by examining the therapist, the psychotherapy process, and the psychotherapy outcome. Moreover, each of these outcomes can be accessed through various perspectives (i.e., the person making the ratings of the outcome). Before discussing research strategies that are appropriate for identifying the causal link between supervision process and outcome, we first examine the outcome of supervision in some detail.

Although we have limited outcome to refer to changes in behavior, moods, states, or other phenomena that persist beyond the individual session in supervision, many classes of outcome need to be differentiated. As illustrated in Figure 2.3, these outcomes have been

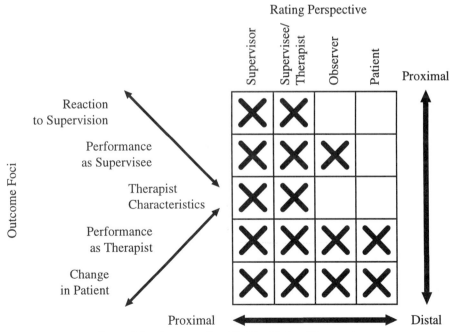

Figure 2.3   Outcome Classified by Foci and Perspective

classified along two dimensions, each of which is scaled according to distance from the supervision interaction. Clearly, several combinations of foci and perspective are not possible. For example, the patient cannot rate the performance of the therapist in supervision nor can the patient indicate the therapist's reaction to supervision. The two dimensions are now discussed.

Rating Perspective.   The horizontal dimension, which is designated as the *rating perspective*, refers to the person who is making the ratings (used generically) of the outcome. Because the supervisor and the therapist are the actual participants in the process (viz., supervision), their perspective is most proximal to the supervision phenomenon. Observers are usually trained in psychotherapy and/or supervision and thus are closer to these phenomena than would be patients, who may not even be cognizant of the fact that their therapist is receiving supervision (in spite of ethical obligations that require the client's knowledge of supervision). It should be noted that Holloway and Poulin (1994) systematically examined rating perspectives and the inherent issues of the meaning that raters ascribe to their ratings by using Poole, Folger, and Hewe's (1987) taxonomy of structured meaning.

It is consequential for supervision research to note that concordance among perspectives relative to a single outcome focus may be low. That is, the perspectives of the participants of the supervision/therapy processes rating the same aspect of the process (e.g., therapist performance in therapy) may not be consistent. In therapy, differences among therapists, patients, and observers have been well documented in the areas of therapy process (e.g., Cooley & Lajoy, 1980; Dill-Standiford, Stiles, & Rorer, 1988; Fuller & Hill, 1985), therapy outcome (e.g., Bachelor, 1991; Stiles & Snow, 1984), and the relationship between process and outcome (e.g., Bloch & Reibstein, 1980; Elliot, 1983; Eugster & Wampold, in press; Wampold & Kim, 1989).

Clearly, perspective is influenced by level of knowledge and the meaning attributed to events (Holloway & Poulin, 1994). The implication for supervision research is that any of the outcome foci cannot be considered an objective phenomenon such that ratings of it from various perspectives are interchangeable. Participants, because of their roles, look for and emphasize different aspects. The fact that Eugster and Wampold (in press) found that patients value the real relationship whereas therapists value therapeutic skill instead raises the issue about which of these two therapeutic perspectives is the legitimate outcome measure for supervision research. Of course, supervision research could be focused profitably on the systematic differences among perspectives and the processes underlying those differences. Clearly, however, the complexity of measuring the outcome of supervision is increased when one considers the perspective issue.

Outcome Foci.   The vertical dimension is denoted as *outcome foci*, to indicate on which aspect of the supervision/therapy enterprise the assessment is focused. The most immediate outcome of supervision is centered on the participants' reaction to a single session of supervision. In research studies, participants have been asked to make judgments about supervisory relationship, supervisory style, and satisfaction with the supervision (see Holloway, 1984, and Holloway & Neufeldt, 1995, for summaries of such research).

The next level of outcome foci is related to the performance of the supervisee in supervision. Surprisingly, little research has used any evaluative measure of therapist behavior in *supervision* (Holloway, 1984, 1992). It seems reasonable that the therapist's behavior in supervision would affect the supervisor's evaluation of the therapist. Indeed, Ward, Friedlander, Schoen, and Klein (1985) found, in an analogue setting, that the manner in which the therapist presented him- or herself affected supervisor evaluations of the therapist, but that information about client progress was more salient to the supervisors than was self-presentational style. However, Ward et al.'s study was designed to assess whether assessments of the therapist were affected by their behavior in the supervision session rather than considering therapist behavior in the supervision session as an outcome per se. This raises the question of whether therapist behavior in the supervision session is a valid outcome measure. Skovholt and Ronnestad (1992) have argued that supervision as a productive learning experience is dependent on the therapist being reflective; that is, the therapist must be able to reflect on the therapeutic process. Moreover, this reflective stance is a skill separate from those skills that are strictly necessary for the therapeutic endeavor. That is, reflection is the skill necessary to use supervision effectively to hone one's clinical skills. According to this view, one of the goals of supervision would be to assist the therapist to reflect in supervision on the therapeutic situation and therapist role, and consequently reflection in supervision would be an appropriate outcome measure. Indeed, Poulin (1992), in a grounded theory dimensional analysis of supervision, found that supervisors choose teaching strategies based in part on the capability of therapists to engage in a reflective process in supervision.

Therapist characteristics represent the next most distal foci in supervision. This level involves judgments of change in therapist characteristics resulting from the supervision process. Therapeutic skill falls into this category and is clearly a primary goal of supervision, but many other therapist characteristics are subsumed here as well, including attitude, expectations, emotional well-being, and so forth. Our perspective is that changes in therapist characteristics represent the primary goal of supervision. Although this claim is debatable; it could be argued that the ultimate goal of supervision is to effect positive change in the patient. Our position is that in most supervision contexts, and particularly in the context of therapists-in-training, the supervisor may intervene in supervision in such a way that the therapist subsequently affects the patient positively and that the effect on the patient was an explicit goal of the supervision intervention. However, almost certainly a superordinate goal was to increase the skill of the therapist so that the therapist would recognize similar therapeutic situations in the future and be able to intervene successfully in such situations; that is, the supervisor hopes that therapist learning generalizes to the therapist's treatment of other patients. Although patient change is the ultimate goal of the supervision/therapeutic process, change in all patients of the therapist/supervisee, present and future, is paramount rather than the patient of the case that is the focus of an instance of supervision. In those cases in which the patient is in crisis and/or there is imminent danger (e.g., suicide), however, the goals of supervision change and supervision becomes much more focused on the patient. In these conditions, as would be expected, the supervisor becomes increasingly more directive with the therapist to ensure patient outcome (Tracey et al., 1989).

The next most distal level is performance of the therapist in therapy. This level involves the actual behavior of the therapist in the therapy endeavor. The final, and most distal, level involves changes in the patient. The outcome foci are presented as a wedge to indicate the primacy, as an outcome, of therapist characteristics. The relation among the foci and the primacy of therapist characteristics is discussed next.

Relation Among Outcomes in Supervision.   Given the argument of the primacy of therapist characteristics as an outcome of supervision and the chronology of the outcome foci, the relation among the outcome foci can be conceptualized as being mediated by therapist characteristics, as presented in Figure 2.4. If reactions to supervision and performance as supervisee are legitimate outcomes of supervision, then they should be predictive causally of change in therapist characteristics. For example, favorable ratings of the performance of the supervisee in supervision need to lead to change in therapist characteristics, such as skill level, in order for performance in supervision to be a legitimate supervision outcome foci. Research linking degree of reflectivity in supervision (Skovholt & Ronnestad, 1992) to development of therapeutic skill is needed to establish reflectivity in supervision as a valid outcome measure. Unfortunately, no research has established the connection between ratings of supervisors in supervision with changes in characteristics of the therapist (Holloway, 1992). Because supervision research and practice have focused on therapist reactions to supervision, it is important to establish the connection between these variables and therapist characteristics (i.e., the left portion of Figure 2.4 involving reaction to supervision, performance as supervisee, and therapist characteristics). It should be noted that reaction to supervision and performance of the therapist in supervision are often used in training contexts to evaluate trainees.

The connection between therapist characteristics and performance as therapist and change in patients also is problematic. These connections have been the subject of much research in therapy (e.g., Beutler et al., 1994). Nevertheless, the causal connections among these constructs have not been established (Wampold, in press). For example, competence in administering treatments has been found to be weakly correlated (e.g., O'Malley et al., 1988) or even negatively correlated (Svartberg & Stiles, 1992) with patient change. Moreover, decades of research have failed to find robust connections between therapist characteristics and patient outcomes (Beutler et al., 1994). We know that much of the variance in therapeutic outcome is due to therapists (Crits-Christoph et al., 1991; Crits-Christoph & Mintz, 1991; Luborsky et al., 1986), but delineation of these therapist characteristics has lagged behind. Again, the lack of empirical results to establish the mediating effects of therapist characteristics confuses the establishment of outcome measures in supervision. Even though supervision researchers are interested in patient outcome data, the connections between therapist characteristics, performance as therapist, and patient change (i.e., the right side of Figure 2.4) are the primary foci of psychotherapy researchers.

Another aspect of Figure 2.4 is related to arraying outcomes according to their distance from the supervision phenomenon. Generally, magnitude of the relation between constructs is proportional to the distance between them. For example, correlations of Grade 1 intelligence with Grade 2 achievement are greater than correlations of Grade 1 intelligence and Grade 6 achievement. Similarly, it would be expected that the further the outcome measure from the process of supervision, the smaller will be the magnitude of the relation between supervision process and outcome. Not surprisingly, relatively strong correlations have been found between supervision process and participants' reaction to supervision (e.g., Holloway & Wampold, 1983). Detection of a relation between supervision process

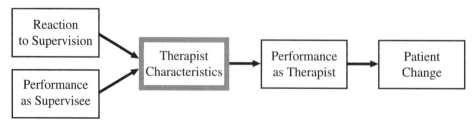

Figure 2.4   Causal Relations of Outcomes in Supervision

and the patient's rating of patient change (the most distal outcome) would be expected to be extremely small. It may well be that the connection between supervision process and distal outcomes will need to be established by studies focusing on various pieces of the mediated causal process displayed in Figure 2.4 rather than by trying to establish relations among distal elements. For example, Carey, Williams, and Wells (1988) found a correlation between supervisor characteristics (viz., supervisor trustworthiness as rated by therapist) and therapist performance in therapy, two relatively distal elements. Dodenhoff (1981) found that trainees who were interpersonally attracted to their supervisors demonstrated greater skill and had increased patient change when rated by their supervisors, but not when rated by the patient or by themselves.

Process of Psychotherapy → Process of Supervision

The process of supervision is both implicitly and explicitly influenced by the process of psychotherapy. The explicitly stated connection is the "what" of supervision. The topics of supervision typically are related to aspects of the client (including client characteristics, diagnosis, and severity), the trainee's conceptualization of the case, treatment plans, and the therapeutic interaction. These aspects of therapy enter supervision via the trainee's report, video- or audiotapes of the therapeutic session, or case notes.

There is an additional hypothesized influence of therapy on supervision through an implicit process related to supervision/therapy dynamics. The therapist may reenact the therapy process in supervision, creating a dynamic labeled *parallel process* (Doehrman, 1976; Ekstein & Wallerstein, 1958). For example, the therapist who is feeling helpless and powerless in the face of the patient's helplessness and hopelessness of depression may reenact this sense of defeat within the supervision dyad by resisting any suggestions to intervene. Friedlander, Siegel, and Brenock (1989) used rating systems to code both the therapy session and the supervision session and found that characteristics of the communication patterns of supervision mirrored the patterns of therapy.

Therapist Training → Process of Supervision and Therapist Characteristics

Clearly, one of the primary goals of therapist training is to develop and improve the clinical skills of the therapist. It is also reasonable to expect, however, that therapist training will affect the supervision process and characteristics of the therapist that are related to supervision as well as to therapy (Holloway, 1995). For example, the therapist, as a student in a training program, may have experiences directly related to supervision, such as taking a formal didactic or practica in supervision, reading about supervision, talking to other students who are being supervised, and so forth. The therapists are also learning about clinical skills and therapy research, which gives them an increasing knowledge base that most likely changes their expectations about the supervisor and the supervision process. In spite of the likelihood that therapist training affects supervision, no studies have been conducted in this area.

CONCLUSIONS

The purpose of this chapter was to conceptualize the major components of supervision in a causal model that explains how the components are related and to discuss the manner in which research might profitably be applied to understand the components and their relationships. Understanding research via this model has shown the complexity of supervision and the consequent difficulty in studying these intricacies. Any criticism of supervision research should be considered in light of this complexity. Individual researchers are left with the task of simplifying the phenomenon so that research can be realistically conducted.

REFERENCES

Bachelor, A. (1991). Comparison and relationship to outcome of diverse dimensions of the helping alliance as seen by client and therapist. *Psychotherapy: Theory, Research, and Practice, 28,* 534–549.

Beutler, L. E., Machado, P. P. P., & Neufeldt, S. A. (1994). Therapist variables. In A. E. Bergin & S. L. Garfield (Eds.), *Handbook of psychotherapy and behavior change* (4th ed., pp. 229–269). New York: Wiley.

Beutler, L. E., & McNabb, C. E. (1981). Self-evaluation for the psychotherapist. In C. E. Walker (Ed.), *Clinical practice of psychology* (pp. 397–439). Elmsford, NY: Pergamon.

Bloch, S., & Reibstein, J. (1980). Perceptions by patients and therapists of therapeutic factors in group psychotherapy. *British Journal of Psychiatry, 137,* 274–278.

Carey, J. C., Williams, K. S., & Wells, M. (1988). Relationships between dimensions of supervisors' influence and counselor trainees performance. *Counselor Education and Supervision, 28,* 130–139.

Carroll, M. (1996). *Couseling supervision: Theory, skills and practice.* London: Cassell.

Coleman, H. K. L., Wampold, B. E., & Casali, S. (1995). Ethnic minorities' ratings of ethnically similar and European American counselors: A meta-analysis. *Journal of Counseling Psychology, 42,* 55–64.

Cook, T. D. A., & Campbell, D. T. (1979). *Quasi-experimentation: Design and analysis issues for field settings.* Boston: Houghton Mifflin.

Cooley, E. J., & Lajoy, R. (1980). Therapeutic relationship and improvement as perceived by clients and therapists. *Journal of Clinical Psychology, 36,* 562–570.

Crits-Christoph, P., Baranackie, K., Jurcias, J. S., Carroll, K., Luborsky, L., McLellan, T., Woody, G., Thompson, L., Gallagier, D., & Zitrin, C. (1991). Meta-analysis of therapist effects in psychotherapy outcome studies. *Psychotherapy Research, 1,* 81–91.

Crits-Christoph, P., & Mintz, J. (1991). Implications of therapist effects for the design and analysis of comparative studies of psychotherapies. *Journal of Consulting and Clinical Psychology, 59,* 20–26.

Dill-Standiford, T. J., Stiles, W. B., & Rorer, L. G. (1988). Counselor-client agreement on session impact. *Journal of Counseling Psychology, 35,* 47–55.

Dodenhoff, J. T. (1981). Interpersonal attraction and direct-indirect supervisor influence as predictors of counselor trainee effectiveness. *Journal of Counseling Psychology, 28,* 47–52.

Doehrman, M. J. (1976). Parallel processes in supervision and psychotherapy. *Bulletin of the Menninger Clinic, 40* (I), 1–104.

Ekstein, R., & Wallerstein, R. S. (1958). *The teaching and learning of psychotherapy.* New York: Basic Books.

Elliot, R. (1983). "That in your hands": A comprehensive process analysis of a significant event in psychotherapy. *Psychiatry, 46,* 113–129.

Ellis, M. V., & Dell, D. M. (1986). Dimensionality of supervisor roles: Supervisors' perceptions of supervision. *Journal of Counseling Psychology, 33,* 282–291.

Ellis, M. V., Dell, D. M., & Good, G. E. (1988). Counselor trainees' perceptions of supervisor roles: Two studies testing the dimensionality of supervision. *Journal of Counseling Psychology, 35,* 315–324.

Ellis, M. V., Ladany, N., Krengel, M., & Schult, D. (1996). Clinical supervision research from 1981 to 1993: A methodological critique. *Journal of Counseling Psychology, 43,* 35–50.

Eugster, S. L., & Wampold, B. E. (in press). Systematic effects of participant role on evaluation of the psychotherapy session. *Journal of Consulting and Clinical Psychology.*

Everett, C. A. (1980). Supervision of marriage and family therapy. In A. Hess (Ed.), *Psychotherapy supervision* (pp. 367–380). New York: Wiley.

Friedlander, M. L., Keller, K. E., Peca-Baker, T. A., & Olk, M. E. (1986). Effects of role conflict on counselor trainees' self-statements, anxiety level, and performance. *Journal of Counseling Psychology, 33,* 1–5.

Friedlander, M. L., Siegel, S. M., & Brenock, K. (1989). Parallel processes in counseling and supervision: A case study. *Journal of Counseling Psychology, 36,* 149–157.

Fuller, F., & Hill, C. E. (1985). Counselor and helpee perceptions of counselor intentions in relation to outcome in a single counseling session. *Journal of Counseling Psychology, 32,* 329–338.

Goodyear, R. K. (1990). Gender configurations in supervisory dyads: Their relation to supervisee influence and strategies and to skill evaluation of the supervisee. *The Clinical Supervisor, 8(3),* 67–79.

Goodyear, R. K., & Robyak, J. E. (1982). Supervisors' theory and experience in supervisory focus. *Psychological Reports, 51,* 978.

Gottman, J. M., & Roy, A. (1990). *Sequential analysis: A guide for behavioral researchers.* Cambridge: Cambridge University Press.

Guest, P. D., & Beutler, L. E. (1988). Impact of psychotherapy supervision on therapist orientation and values. *Journal of Consulting and Clinical Psychology, 56,* 653–658.

Heppner, P., Kivlighan, D., & Wampold, B. (1992). *Research design in counseling.* Pacific Grove, CA: Brooks/Cole.

Hill, C. E., Charles, D., & Reed, K. G. (1981). A longitudinal analysis of changes in counseling skills during doctoral training in counseling psychology. *Journal of Counseling Psychology, 28,* 428–436.

Holloway, E. L. (1984). Outcome evaluation in supervision research. *The Counseling Psychologist, 12*(4), 167–174.

Holloway, E. L. (1992). Supervision: A way of teaching and learning. In S. D. Brown & R. W. Lent (Eds.), *Handbook of counseling psychology* (pp. 177–214). New York: Wiley.

Holloway, E. L. (1995). *Clinical supervision: A systems approach.* Thousand Oaks, CA: Sage.

Holloway, E. L., & Carroll, M. (1996). Reaction to special section on Supervision research: Comment on Ellis et al. (1996), Ladany et al. (1996), Neufeldt et al. (1996), and Worthen and McNeill (1996). *Journal of Counseling Psychology, 43,* 51–55.

Holloway, E. L., Freund, R. D., Gardner, S. L., Nelson, M. L., & Walker, B. E. (1989). Relation of power and involvement to theoretical orientation in supervision: An analysis of discourse. *Journal of Counseling Psychology, 36,* 88–102.

Holloway, E. L., & Neufeldt, S. A. (1995). Supervision: Its contributions to treatment efficacy. *Journal of Consulting and Clinical Psychology, 63,* 207–213.

Holloway, E. L., & Poulin, K. (1994). Discourse in supervision. In J. Siegfried (Ed.), *Therapeutic and everyday discourse as behavior change: Towards a micro-analysis in psychotherapy process research.* Norwood, NJ: Ablex.

Holloway, E. L., & Wampold, B. E. (1983). Patterns of verbal behavior and judgments of satisfaction in the supervision interview. *Journal of Counseling Psychology, 30,* 227–234.

Holloway, E. L., & Wolleat, P. L. (1980). Relationship of counselor conceptual level to clinical hypothesis formation. *Journal of Counseling Psychology, 27,* 539–545.

Kennard, B. D., Stewart, S. M., & Gluck, M. R. (1987). The supervision relationship: Variables contributing to positive versus negative experiences. *Professional Psychology: Research and Practice, 18,* 172–175.

Krause, A. A., & Allen, G. J. (1988). Perceptions of counselor supervision: An examination of Stoltenberg's model from the perspectives of the supervisor and supervisee. *Journal of Counseling Psychology, 35,* 77–80.

Lambert, M. J. (1974). Supervisory and counseling process: A comparative study. *Counselor Education and Supervision, 14,* 54–60.

Leary, T. (1957). *Interpersonal diagnosis of personality: A theory and a methodology for personality evaluation.* New York: Ronald.

Luborsky, L., Crits-Christoph, P., McLellan, T., Woody, G., Piper, W., Liberman, B., Imber, S., & Pilkonis, P. (1986). Do therapists vary much in their success? Findings from four outcome studies. *American Journal of Orthopsychiatry, 46*, 501–512.

Martinez, R. P., & Holloway, E. L. (in press). The supervision relationship in multicultural training. In D. Pope-Davis & Coleman, H. K. L. (Eds.), *Handbook of multicultural competence.* Thousand Oaks, CA: Sage.

Miars, R. D., Tracey, T. J., Ray, P. B., Cornfeld, J. L., O'Farrell, M., & Gelson, C. J. (1983). Variation in supervision process across trainee experience levels. *Journal of Counseling Psychology, 30*, 403–412.

Nelson, M. L., & Holloway, E. L. (1990). Relation of gender to power and involvement in supervision. *Journal of Counseling Psychology, 37*, 473–481.

Neufeldt, S. A., Karno, M. P., & Nelson, M. L. (1996). A qualitative study of experts' conceptualization of supervisee reflectivity. *Journal of Counseling Psychology, 43*, 3–9.

O'Malley, S. S., Foley, S. H., Rounsaville, B. J., Watkins, J. T., Sotsky, S. M., Imber, S. D., & Elkin, I. (1988). Therapist competence and patient outcome in interpersonal psychotherapy of depression. *Journal of Consulting and Clinical Psychology, 56*, 496–501.

Orlinsky, D. E., Grawe, K., & Parks, B. K. (1994). Process and outcome in psychotherapy—NOCH EINMAL. In A. E. Bergin & S. L. Garfield (Eds.), *Handbook of psychotherapy and behavior change* (4th ed., pp. 270–376). New York: Wiley.

Penman, R. (1980). *Communication processes and relationships.* London: Academic.

Peterson, R. K. (1991). Issues of race and ethnicity in supervision: Emphasizing who you are, not what you know. *The Clinical Supervisor, 9*, 15–31.

Pierce, R. M., & Schauble, P. G. (1970). Graduate training of facilitative counselors: The effects of individual supervision. *Journal of Counseling Psychology, 17*, 210–217.

Pierce, R. M., & Schauble, P. G. (1971). Study on the effects of individual supervision in graduate school training. *Journal of Counseling Psychology, 18*, 186–187.

Poole, M. S., Folger, J. P., & Hewes, D. E. (1987). Analyzing interpersonal interaction. In M. E. Roloff & G. R. Miller (Eds.), *Interpersonal processes: New directions in communication research* (pp. 221–256). Newbury Park, CA: Sage.

Poulin, K. (1992). *Toward a grounded pedagogy of practice: A dimensional analysis of counseling supervision.* Dissertation Abstracts 9505214 UMI Dissertation Services, Bell & Howell Co., 3200 N. Zeb Rd., Ann Arbor, MI 48106 (1-800-521-0600).

Qualitative Research in Counseling Process and Outcome [Special Section]. (1994). *Journal of Counseling Psychology, 41* (4).

Rickards, L. D. (1984). Verbal interaction and supervisor perception in counselor supervision. *Journal of Counseling Psychology, 31*, 262–265.

Robyak, J. E., Goodyear, R. K., Prange, M. E., & Donham, G. (1986). Effects of gender, supervision, and presenting problems on practicum students' preference for interpersonal power bases. *Journal of Counseling Psychology, 33,* 159–163.

Skovholt, T. M., & Ronnestad, M. H. (1992). *The evolving professional self: Stages and themes in therapist and counselor development.* New York: Wiley.

Stiles, W. B., & Snow, J. S. (1984). Counseling session impact as viewed by novice counselors and their clients. *Journal of Counseling Psychology, 32*, 3–12.

Stoltenberg, C. D., & Delworth, U. (1987). *Supervising counselors and therapists.* San Francisco: Jossey-Bass.

Svartberg, M., & Stiles, T. C. (1992). Predicting patient change from therapist competence and patient-therapist complementarity in short-term anxiety-provoking psychotherapy: A pilot study. *Journal of Consulting and Clinical Psychology, 60*, 304–307.

Tracey, T. J., Ellickson, J. L., & Sherry, P. (1989). Reactance in relation to different supervisory environments and counselor development. *Journal of Counseling Psychology, 36*, 336–344.

Wampold, B. E. (1992). The intensive examination of social interactions. In T. R. Kratochwill & J. R. Levin (Eds.), *Single-case research design and analysis: New directions for psychology and education* (pp. 93–131). Hillsdale, NJ: Lawrence Erlbaum.

Wampold, B. E. (in press). Methodological problems with identifying efficacious psychotherapies. *Psychotherapy Research.*

Wampold, B. E., & Kim, K. H. (1989). Sequential analysis applied to counseling process and outcome: A case study revisited. *Journal of Counseling Psychology, 36,* 357–364.

Wampold, B. E., & Poulin, K. L. (1992). Counseling research methods: Art and artifact. In S. D. Brown & R. W. Lent (Eds.), *Handbook of counseling psychology* (2nd ed., pp. 71–109). New York: Wiley.

Ward, L. G., Friedlander, M. L., Schoen, L. G., & Klein, J. C. (1985). Strategic self-presentation in supervision. *Journal of Counseling Psychology, 32,* 111–118.

Wedeking, D. F., & Scott, T. B. (1976). A study of the relationship between supervisor and trainee behaviors in counseling practicum. *Counselor Education and Supervision, 15,* 259–266.

Wiley, M. O., & Ray, P. B. (1986). Counseling supervision by developmental level. *Journal of Counseling Psychology, 33,* 439–445.

Worthen, V., & McNeill, B. W. (1996). A phenomenological investigation of "good" supervision events. *Journal of Counseling Psychology, 43,* 25–34.

Worthington, E. L. (1987). Changes in supervision as counselors and supervisors gain experience: A review. *Professional Psychology: Research and Practice, 18,* 189–208.

PART II

Approaches to Psychotherapy Supervision

CHAPTER 3

The Process of Supervision in Psychoanalysis

PAUL A. DEWALD
St. Louis University School of Medicine
and
St. Louis Psychoanalytic Institute

In most psychoanalytic training programs, the education and training of a psychoanalyst are based on a tripartite model involving the candidate's personal psychoanalysis, the completion of a didactic curriculum, and the analysis of several patients under the supervision of a senior analytic teacher.

The personal analysis allows the candidate to acquire firsthand experience of being a patient and increasing awareness of his or her own internal conscious and unconscious mental processing and functions. It is hoped that modification of the neurotic conflicts, symptoms, or inhibitions within the candidate will also occur, resulting in partial reorganization of the candidate's personality in an advance toward psychic maturation. There is no expectation of complete elimination of neurotic processes within the candidate, but the goal of a training analysis is to allow the candidate access to his or her own unconscious mental processes and an awareness of how the mind functions.

The didactic curriculum involves a series of seminars (with appropriate reading assignments) that include the understanding of normal as well as psychopathological development, the general theory of motivation and the understanding of behavior, the various pathological syndromes conceptualized on the basis of psychodynamic and psychoanalytic thinking, and a series of technical seminars dealing with the generally accepted procedures and techniques of therapeutic analysis. This material covers the indications for or against psychoanalysis, the recognition and understanding of the various phases of the treatment, and the modifications of technique that are applicable to a given psychoanalytic situation. These technical courses can, however, offer or describe only a general and nonspecific presentation of psychoanalytic technique and practice. They are usually augmented in the curriculum by a series of case presentations or continuous case conferences in which candidates are exposed in detail to cases other than their own, from which to observe a spectrum of psychodynamic and psychoanalytic interactions.

The third leg of the tripartite system is the experience of supervision in which the candidate conducts the analysis of patients with the help of a supervising analyst. The supervisor is someone designated by the institute to fulfill this function, based upon the evaluation of this individual and his or her teaching, conceptual, and technical skills. In most institutes, the candidate is expected to have a different supervisor for each required case. This process of supervision usually begins on a weekly basis and continues for the duration of that psychoanalytic treatment, although the frequency of supervisory sessions varies with the candidate's progress and with the nature of the treatment experience. In some institutes supervisors are assigned, and in some they are selected by the student.

GOALS OF SUPERVISION

Although the specific goals of a particular supervisory experience may vary, the general orientation is that in supervision the candidate's access to his or her own internal psychological experience and function, as well as the theoretical and technical learning that has occurred during the curriculum, will be synthesized and applied to the analysis of the particular case at hand. In that way, the three components of psychoanalytic education become progressively integrated and contribute to the development of the candidate's "psychoanalytic instrument." This concept involves the candidate learning to use him- or herself and his or her own access to unconscious processes in the interactions with the patient and to become comfortable in the role of analyst in a therapeutic relationship.

Simultaneously, the candidate learns to observe the analytic process as it unfolds and receives feedback about his or her progress and understanding. The candidate also receives specific instruction in applying psychoanalytic techniques to the case under observation.

Inasmuch as the candidate will have several supervisory experiences during the course of his or her education, another aim is to have the student exposed to different analysts with their inevitable differences in theoretical understanding, style, technique, and personal qualities. Thus, the candidate experiences a variety of different models of psychoanalytic understanding and technique. The student ultimately, then, does not identify with any one particular individual but can integrate the various experiences in keeping with his or her own personality and style of interaction. This process optimally will allow development of a uniquely personal psychoanalytic identity that can become the basis for future development of more sophisticated analytic skills and understanding.

Another goal of psychoanalytic supervision is to give the candidate an opportunity to observe the natural evolution of a psychoanalytic process, as illustrated by the case at hand and the experience in the student's interactions with that particular patient. This experience includes the evaluation of such factors as the indications for and against analysis, the nature of analytic capacities in different patients, the "fit" between analyst and analysand, and how they influence the overview and ultimate outcome of the psychoanalytic process. Additionally, the aim is to provide the candidate with an experience in evaluation of analytic progress, as well as the ultimate indications and process involved in the natural planned termination of an analytic procedure.

Another significant function of supervision is the supervisor's need to evaluate the candidate's educational progress and developing skill and to report to the institute on the candidate's level of function. At times such reporting may lead to a "syncretistic dilemma," as the supervisory reports have a significant impact on the candidate's academic progression through the institute structure. The supervisor may at times experience conflict between the wish to be liked by the candidate (and avoid the reputation of being "tough" or "mean") and the obligation to be candidly objective in the evaluation process.

STYLES OF SUPERVISION

Supervisors vary considerably in their own understanding and perceptions of the analytic process, as well as their skills as teachers and their abilities to conceptualize what they do in their own clinical practice situations. They also vary greatly in their skills in communicating their knowledge and experience to others. Candidates also vary enormously in terms of innate skills, as well as in the rate and style of learning and the acquisition of skills in the technical process of conducting an analysis. The nature of the patient and his or her aptitude and capacities to use the analytic procedure effectively also have a major impact on the entire supervisory situation. A "naturally good" patient can make a poor student look competent, and a difficult or unanalyzable case can make a good student seem to have major difficulties.

There is also a significant variation in the supervisory process whether the case is an early or later one in the candidate's experience. The comparison of prior experience with other supervisors, as contrasted with the current one, and whatever differences may exist with the technical interventions by the candidate's personal training analyst also contribute to a highly idiosyncratic and variable situation in regard to the supervisory experience. The reputation of the supervisor and the scuttlebutt among candidates regarding his or her style are other factors influencing the total supervisory situation.

It is therefore likely that no two supervisions, either with different candidates or with different supervisors, or even with the same supervisor or the same candidate with a different supervisor, will be precisely similar. Enormous variability exists in the impact and evolution of the supervisory experiences during the education and training of psychoanalytic candidates.

THE PSYCHOANALYTIC THEORY OF SUPERVISION

Most psychoanalytic supervisors consider supervision to be a process in some ways similar and in other ways quite different from therapeutic psychoanalysis. Similar to the establishment of a therapeutic (working) alliance in therapeutic analysis, a learning alliance must evolve between the supervisor and the candidate. One of the important functions of the supervisor is to establish a situation of comfort and safety that will allow the candidate openly and honestly to report the experience and interactions between him- or herself and the patient in a way that allows the supervisor a reasonable view and understanding of the analyst/analysand interactions. This requires that the supervisor be sensitive to the learning needs of the candidate and place the candidate's educational needs and experience ahead of the supervisor's own particular clinical or theoretical interests.

The development of a successful learning alliance also involves the candidate experientially discovering that the supervisor can empathically recognize and accept some of the issues and conflicts in the candidate's experience. It also involves learning that feedback from the supervisor will be predominantly constructively helpful and aimed at improving the candidate's skill, even if at times it may involve pointing out difficult or painful limitations or errors.

If a solid learning alliance does not evolve between supervisor and candidate, the result may be a conflict-dominated situation in which the supervisor's evaluative function becomes intensified in the minds of both candidate and supervisor. If that occurs, the candidate may become more intensely motivated to please and impress the supervisor or to hide errors and uncertainties rather than openly and honestly report his or her experience in the effort to learn and benefit from the supervisor's responses.

The supervisor must be aware of the multiple potential transferences and countertransferences that may be mobilized in the psychoanalytic supervisory situation. As in any psychoanalytic experience, the analysand will have a variety of transference responses to the candidate analyst, who will also have a variety of countertransference responses to the analysand. These must be recognized by the supervisor, who then needs to exercise the educational judgments involved in whether (and if so when) to call them to the candidate analyst's attention. Additionally, the candidate analyst will have a variety of conscious and unconscious transference reactions and responses to the supervisor and the supervisory situation. Some of these may be specific to the supervisor-candidate pair; some may parallel his or her experience with the patient in the analysis (parallel process); and some may be displaced from the candidate's own analyst, as well as from the candidate's relationship to the institute and to the supervisor as the representative of the institute. The supervisor and the candidate's training analyst may have their own personal relationship, which can vary from positive and collegial to competitive or negative, and a variety of unspoken transferences between these two faculty members may exist with the candidate as the vehicle for transmitting them from one to the other. When the supervisor makes a suggestion that is alien to or merely different from the candidate's experience in his or her personal analysis, the candidate may be in a situation of conflicting loyalties that adds an additional complexity to the supervisory situation.

The supervisor will usually respond to different candidates primarily based on reality perceptions, but at other times transference-countertransference responses may significantly color or impact the learning process and the supervisory relationship.

Another conflict for the candidate may arise out of the differences in personality, analytic style, and theoretical conceptualization, as well as possibly the teaching ability of the various supervisors with whom he or she is working simultaneously. Each supervisor may prefer or expect that the candidate will use and accept his or her theoretical and conceptual model and supervisory style as the most effective one for the future development of the student. For the candidate, this may create a situation of competing loyalties and identifications; and there may be problems in regard to learning from one or more of the supervisors in question. Another source of transference conflict is that early in a candidate's psychoanalytic experience, the patient may become aware (either explicitly or through manifest technical shifts made by the candidate) that a supervisor is involved. Such knowledge can activate a variety of questions in the patient's mind, as well as defensive processes in the candidate analyst for whom this situation may become competitive or threatening. The analysand's fantasies about the presence and nature of the supervision becomes an important component of the analysis that the beginning candidate frequently finds difficult to expose and address.

One of the significant components of learning in any discipline involves identification by the student with the instructor. This is particularly important in professional education as the teacher not only imparts cognitive knowledge but also serves as a role model for the student's future career. Such factors as enthusiasm, attitudes toward the profession, values, ways of thinking and problem solving, skills, capacity for interpersonal relationships, and general demeanor are components of identification that lead to the development of a positive or a negative ego ideal. Identification can arise out of positive feeling and admiration, but it can also reflect concerns such as negative feelings, fear and identification with the aggressor, passivity and the wish to be taken care of, or inhibition and fear of independent development.

In psychoanalytic education, the supervisor's sophistication in regard to the multiple forms and meanings of identification makes it possible to recognize this tendency in the candidate and to try to avoid encouraging pure imitation in the candidate's identification. Most candidate analysands identify with their training analyst, which may be a source of tension or comfort. It is hoped that both the supervisor and the training analyst can recognize the conflict and help the candidate understand it. As mentioned earlier, there are also identifications with other supervisors, as well as classroom teachers. The final synthesis of a psychoanalytic ego ideal should reflect these multiple partial identifications and not be based on pure imitation of any one person.

In psychoanalytic education, if the candidate is still in his or her training analysis, the possibility exists for the supervisor to suggest to the candidate that a particular issue or problem be taken up in the personal analysis. This is particularly the case when interfering countertransference or other forms of learning impairment seem to be active. It is important, however, for the supervisor to observe whether there appears to be a change in the attitude or behavior in question and whether the candidate seems to have processed the issue in the training analysis.

When the candidate supervisee has completed the training analysis, however, it becomes necessary for the supervisor to rely on the candidate's efforts at self-observation or self-analysis when dealing with some of the transferential or neurotic inhibitions in the teaching/learning or therapeutic process. Dealing with countertransference interference can become difficult because if the candidate is unable to observe or identify the interference in question, the supervisor has no one else to help with the issue.

He or she then must be the one to discuss some of the candidate's countertransference or transference responses that are interfering with the learning process. This brings the teaching/learning situation closer to the boundary line of a therapeutic process for the supervisee, which may become inappropriate given the fact that the supervisor can have only limited access to the candidate's inner psychic life on which to base interpretation or understandings of the candidate's neurotic or residual difficulties.

Although there is general reluctance to recommend a return for further personal analysis in a particular supervisee, it may at times become necessary in order to preserve the supervisory relationship and avoid having it become a therapeutic one. Such decisions are usually not made unilaterally by the supervisor alone, however, but should be part of an overall institute educational evaluation and assessment of the candidate's progress rather than be based exclusively on a single supervisory relationship.

For most candidates, assuming the role of analyst, particularly in their first or second cases, is a major developmental experience. It involves identification with the "grown-ups" and with the training analyst; as well as with the additional components of success, of progression, of rivalry, of feeling alone, or of achieving a new level of performance and function. The supervisor may need to assist the candidate in assuming this new role, which adds to the complexity of the total emotional situation of the student. The student is the analyst to his or her analysand but, simultaneously, is the analysand of the training analyst. The student is a junior colleague of the supervisor and is also expected to be critically and intellectually challenging in his or her role in the seminar or classwork situation. Simultaneously, the student (particularly the older analytic student) is the spouse, parent, or head of his or her family and is also a professional who has additional responsibilities and relationships beyond the analytic institute. In essence, the supervisor has to recognize the enormously complex and multifaceted position of the student's function and identity and the potential conflicts among these various roles.

Another source of potential conflict is the supervisor's role in evaluating the progress, skill, and competence, as well as the integration and conceptual adequacy of the student analyst. In most psychoanalytic institutes, the training analyst is no longer expected or even allowed to have impact on or to provide information for evaluations of the progress in the institute of his or her candidate analysand. This is now done to preserve the typical setting and integrity of the training analysis and the candidate's confidentiality and privacy in the institute environment. The candidate's participation in seminars and classrooms provides one type of evaluative function, predominantly of cognitive skill or understanding. The evaluation by the classroom or seminar teacher is based on a more limited exposure by virtue of the varying level and style of participation by students in the classroom setting.

These limitations mean that the supervisor becomes the major evaluator of how well the student is integrating his or her tripartite experience and of how he or she is progressing in the therapeutic capacity to function as an analyst. For both student and supervisor, this may promote a more conflicted learning situation, and the student may become significantly motivated to please and gain approval of the supervisor in order to facilitate progress through the institute. In the student's mind, this may at times conflict with the process of learning, and the supervisor must be careful to assess the difference between limitations or errors based on lack of experience and conceptual ignorance and those based on the student's aptitude, personal or transferential issues, or significant learning inhibitions or blocks. The student also needs to feel reassured that whatever evaluation occurs will be fair and objective and will assess the student's progress and success as well as his or her errors, limitations, or failures.

DIFFERENCES IN PEDAGOGIC THEORY

Psychoanalytic supervising analysts differ considerably in their philosophy of supervision and conceptual understanding of the role of the supervisor in psychoanalytic education. These differences are impacted by the supervisor's idiosyncratic characterological predisposition, as well as the nature of his or her training and supervisory experiences during candidacy. Many psychoanalytic institutes do not make an organized effort to develop the roles of the supervisor and to discuss or consider the supervisory situation and technique and their part in the educational process. Frequently, it is assumed that because someone can analyze effectively he or she is able to supervise effectively as well. Thus, many times analysts are appointed training analyst and supervising analyst simultaneously, without significant evaluation of their understanding of supervision and their teaching skills or capacity to interact in a one-to-one supervisory situation. Research on the process of supervision in psychoanalysis has been meager, and there is no generally accepted model of supervision or of the theory of pedagogy that is involved.

For some supervisors the major thrust of their supervisory work is on the didactic and conceptual as well as on the technical learning situation as applied to the case at hand. It is assumed that the student has the most active interest in learning the practical technique of psychoanalysis and that, particularly during the early cases, the student needs instruction and understanding of the rationale for technical interventions and the nature of the analytic process. The student at this stage in training will frequently be technically identified with the training analyst and will also be concerned lest he or she make serious errors. The student may, therefore, tend somewhat rigidly to adhere to the type of technical program introduced in technique courses in the curriculum.

Other supervisors adopt the conceptual position that the student will need the most help in recognizing and dealing with some of his or her own emotional and countertransference responses to the role of analyst and to the specific patient in question. These supervisors emphasize the importance of the student bringing into the supervisory situation his or her own feelings, reactions, personal associations, and other subjective experiences that accompany the analyst's role. This type of supervisor will tend to emphasize empathic resonance, emotional interplay, and the interpersonal elements and will point out manifestations of countertransference responses as they occur in the student's presentation of the clinical material.

Those who focus on the conceptual understanding and cognitive processes as primary in the supervisory situation point out that given the limited access of the supervisor to the mental processes of the student, emphasis on countertransference conflict or emotional factors is based on inference and guesswork and cannot accurately portray or elucidate the student's psychological state. Indeed, they frequently see such supervisory style as intrusive and akin to "wild analysis."

On the other hand, those who emphasize the importance of the supervisor's dealing with the student's responsive connections to the patient point out that the cognitive element is only one part of the total analytic undertaking and does not include an extremely important component of the analytic process, namely, the affective and emotional tie between patient and candidate analyst.

Some supervisors take an active interventional approach, presenting ongoing comments and pointing out various components of material as the student presents it. In so doing, the supervisor actively shapes the nature of the interaction with the candidate and to some extent directly influences the therapeutic process. Those who follow this approach argue that particularly in early cases the student has little idea of what is of significance and what is relatively less important and that the student needs guidance in developing the kind of psychoanalytic process that makes for an appropriate and optimal learning experience. Other supervisors tend to remain more quiet, less interventional, and more manifestly accepting of the candidate's own work without active comment. This form of supervision focuses on the candidate's needs to have his or her own experience and to make his or her own mistakes, thereby emphasizing experiential and active, rather than passive, learning processes.

Some supervisors prefer to work from the candidate's process notes, emphasizing the unfolding chronological material of the various analytic sessions, as well as the time and sequence from session to session. Their reasoning is that this approach tends to be closer to the primary data and at the beginning of an analytic career the student is not sufficiently able to recognize the associative flow and linkages in the patient's verbal and nonverbal productions. The experienced supervisor (who is also affectively less involved while listening) is in a position to recognize meanings and patterns to the material that are beyond the capacity of the student to appreciate at this point in his or her analytic development. The data to allow this recognition may show up only in the presentation of detailed process notes.

Other supervisors prefer to have the student not work from notes (except in particular situations or in reporting the details of a particular fantasy or dream) and instead encourage the student to associate and to report in a spontaneous and unfocused way. They emphasize the construct that the student will have listened to the material and will have organized it (consciously and unconsciously) in keeping with the interactions between the patient and the candidate and that it will, therefore, reflect the essence of the psychoanalytic process. These supervisors also contend that the student may use notes for defensive purposes, which may interfere with the student's ability to allow free-floating personal associations and affective or empathic responses to the analysand.

Much of what transpires in the mind of an analyst during the therapeutic sessions remains silent and inaccessible to the analysand and may result only in brief interventions or comments to the patient. Therefore, the student does not observe the mind of an analyst at work during his or her training analysis, nor does it occur in a sustained way during various clinical conferences. To make up for this, some supervisors tend actively to verbalize to the student their method of listening and the associative patterns, conceptual and technical options, and possible dynamic meanings they observe as the material unfolds. This is done so that the student has a model for how an analyst thinks and listens to material during the analytic experience, thereby filling a gap for which there is no other access in depth or consistency. Other supervisors tend to believe that such a teaching technique unduly influences and pressures the candidate to identify with them, and these supervisors tend to keep their associations to themselves and not to think out loud as openly or consistently.

A similar difference of opinion exists in connection with the framing of interventions and interpretations. Some supervisors demonstrate actively what technical interventions they would have made and why, reasoning that the candidate needs a model other than that of the training analyst. Those who do this generally emphasize the multiple options and alternatives available at any point in the analytic interaction. Other supervisors believe such teaching techniques encourage blind imitation and that they can lead to the supervisor subtly taking over the treatment of the case. As a result, they tend to avoid this type of modeling.

Another variable in supervisory style is the degree of feedback that is offered to the student as the process of the supervisory session proceeds. Some see active encouragement and support as part of the supervisor's role and function, with praise and reassurance offered when appropriate as well as direct constructive criticism or suggestion of alternatives when required. Even if the student is having significant difficulty with the analytic process, this reinforcement is used to try to highlight and emphasize any of the positive things that the student is accomplishing, thereby encouraging further efforts and rewarding the student for appropriate attempts at learning progress. Other supervisors, however, tend to remain more neutral and to adopt a stance more akin to the therapeutic one in which judgments about what is good or bad are essentially reserved for quiet, silent reflection in the mind of the analyst or supervisor. In this supervisory model, the rationale is to help the student become capable of self-directed motivation and to achieve reinforcement by the success of the process and the pleasure in being effective as an analyst.

There are also significant differences in regard to supervision when it occurs early in the candidate's career as compared with later or postgraduate supervisory experiences. The assumption is that as the candidate gains more experience and is more comfortable and familiar with the analytic posture and with the role of analyst, and as the candidate is becoming more proficient technically, other aspects of the psychoanalytic process and experience can be brought into play in the supervisory situation. In other words, the situation shifts from the student-teacher relationship in early cases and becomes more a junior-senior colleague peer relationship. The types of conceptual, technical, or countertransferential issues that are being discussed can become more sophisticated and more challenging and can more appropriately go beyond the format or the material of the case in question and become a more generalized consultation and opportunity for discussion of more advanced topics.

Experience in progression committee evaluations when multiple supervisors share observations of the same student suggests, however, that many of the same difficulties emerge in later cases as occurred in early ones. But these difficulties are resolved more rapidly and completely in the later cases.

HOW I DO IT

My own style of supervision is based on the assumption that my role is to be a teacher and a model, so that the student can conceptualize the position and functions of an analyst. To this extent, I tend to use an active and didactic style, with considerable explication of my own thought processes as I discuss the issues that come up with the candidate. I attempt to maintain a focus on the needs of the student analyst, making my own professional interests secondary to the learning of the candidate at whatever point in his or her career development the student is at the moment. I therefore attempt to assess the candidate's primary motivations, which most of the time in early cases involve the wish to learn practical technique, to learn to frame interpretations, and to understand the dynamic patterns. The beginner also needs help to recognize and become comfortable with transference and countertransference interactions.

Particularly in beginning cases, the processes of setting up the psychoanalytic situation and of developing a therapeutic alliance are of primary interest for my work with the candidate, in order that a subsequent progressive analytic process in which the candidate can participate and observe will unfold.

My usual frequency of supervision is once a week for beginning candidates, and this continues for a prolonged time, usually one year and possibly longer, depending on how the candidate is progressing. For most candidates, it is helpful to continue regular supervision until the middle phase of the analytic process has evolved and the transference relationship is significantly activated. With more advanced candidates or in postgraduate work, I tend to see the person at weekly intervals initially, but once I am satisfied with the individual's capacities and progress, this may be reduced to less frequent interactions. The importance of the termination phase and the role of natural planned termination usually require that the candidate be supervised at a more frequent rate during the actual termination phase in the treatment. In cases in which the frequency of the supervision had been reduced from once a week, I may resume weekly supervision during the termination phase, particularly in early cases, so that the candidate can have the full benefit of a developed and affectively significant termination experience with the case.

Although I use myself as an active model of psychoanalytic thinking, I make it a point to attempt to provide the candidate with multiple alternatives to any particular intervention I might suggest. I try to point out how the dynamic processes and experiences of the individual patient interact with the dynamic processes of the candidate analyst; and this context will determine the nature of the interaction between them. I hope this helps to avoid various types of cookbook formulations and blind imitation.

The emphasis on the patient's perceptions of the analytic situation and of the analyst's interventions in it represents, however, a persistent learning need, one for which the candidate benefits from the experience of the supervisor. I therefore prefer in the beginning of a case to work from reasonably detailed process notes, inasmuch as I feel a need to observe the sequence of associations and the details of what the patient or the analyst has said or done in order to gain a fair assessment of that context. I recognize that process notes can express only some of the highlights of the analytic interaction, and I am aware that shortly after the particular analytic session, a great deal of the material and sequence has been forgotten by the candidate. I am also aware that the candidate's emphasis on accessing the primary data may interfere with his or her use of him- or herself as an associative instrument. But I still find it more useful in explicating the details of the analytic process to have at least a semblance of the primary data available. Candidates frequently are not aware of the nuances indicated by some of the data they report (at times inadvertently), and this gives access to some of the interactional processes that may have escaped their notice during the time of the analytic sessions.

I encourage candidates not to take detailed notes during the analytic sessions and instead to try to write an outline that can be fleshed out after the session is over. I am aware, however, that for many candidates the desire to get the data recorded and the pressures of time may encourage the taking of notes during the session. If this becomes a significant distraction, I then begin to challenge the note taking procedure more firmly. Subsequently, when the candidate is more comfortable and when I am more familiar with the candidate's style and the availability of the candidate's associative processes, I encourage the candidate to depart from routine use of process notes and, at least in part, to summarize in a more free-flowing and associational way the unfolding of the analytic sessions.

I also believe that the integration of the tripartite model of analytic education requires that the candidate develop a capacity to objectify his or her personal experience from his or her own analysis. I therefore do not hesitate to frequently call the candidate's attention to a particular countertransference enactment, not to interpret it, but to encourage the candidate to reflect openly on it, or to take it back to his or her own personal analysis. Not infrequently I may demonstrate or allude to certain technical errors or countertransference responses of my own, or certain common and characteristic countertransference responses that occur in candidates at the level of their training. The reason for this is to allow the candidate more comfort and freedom to express his or her own misgivings, shortcomings, and self-doubts, all of which are expected during the educational process. The need is to avoid the image of the all-knowing or all-correct and always omniscient supervisor and the struggling candidate whose mistakes are so glaringly apparent.

In this connection, I also tend to be active in my interactions in regard to assessment of the candidate's activity and functioning. I believe it is particularly important to encourage, through appropriate praise, positive performance or improvement in an area that the candidate had found difficult previously. I point out how much better it was this time than last, and in those ways seek to reinforce the candidate's confidence and self-esteem and capacity to enjoy the analytic work and have it be less like an examination by the supervisor. Too often, supervisors transpose analytic abstinence to the teaching/learning process of supervision, to the detriment of the pedagogy involved.

With similar reasoning, I always show the candidate my written evaluative report to the institute prior to the time that I submit it to the Progression Committee. In this way, the candidate has complete access to what I am reporting about him or her, and I also offer the candidate an opportunity to assess whether he or she believes that it is an accurate, objective, and fair kind of evaluative statement. Candidates appreciate this even if their difficulties are described, and in my mind it contributes to the development of a better learning alliance. For me, the evidence of a solid learning alliance includes the candidate's greater willingness candidly to describe what he or she actually said, as well as to reveal the errors that he or she has made and the countertransference feelings or responses that he or she has been experiencing. The candidate actively questioning or disagreeing with something I have said, or asking for more extensive explanations, or actively attempting a formulation without passively waiting for me to ask or initiate it are further signs of a solid learning alliance.

I also openly indicate that the techniques or conceptual models I espouse may be very different from those of other supervisors or those of their own training analyst and in this way emphasize the candidates' needs ultimately to integrate the different components of their experiences into ones that match their own personal styles and character structures. When differences of opinion among different theoretical models occur, I tend to illustrate them as alternate ways of observing the same primary clinical data and point to the various places at which the candidate has multiple ways of responding or interpreting the material that is presented by the patient. I repeatedly point out how analysts are constantly making choices of how to respond (or not respond) to the patient's material, which offers feedback and suggestive influence to the patient as to where the analyst's interests, opinions, and judgments lie in regard to what is important. This also means checking to see how much the patient is telling us what we want to hear.

Another important teaching principle is the need not to overload the candidate with too much material in any one particular interaction or session of the supervisory process. In other words, although there may be many things that could be commented on in a particular supervisory session, I select only those that are the most important at that time, recognizing that the others are not going to be addressed then. If an issue is significant, it will come up again at some other time or in some other context, at which time it can be addressed without overloading the student beyond his or her ability to usefully absorb my comments.

As students become more comfortable in the role of analyst and as their technical capacity and skill improve, I begin to use the clinical material of the specific case in more generalized ways, with attempts to compare how this particular case may differ or be similar to others, as well as to get beyond the immediate clinical situation and into more conceptual and possibly theoretical perspectives. This process tends to enrich the supervisory interaction and focus of discussion for both participants. The aim is to make the case an illustration of general principles and concepts, rather than to stay narrowly focused on the specific psychoanalytic experience of this particular patient.

In today's educational world, candidates or postgraduates not infrequently live at a geographical distance from the institute or from the location of the supervisor. As a result, supervision by telephone has become a fairly common undertaking. This involves significant limitations in the supervisory situation and requires getting used to, by both the student and the supervisor. In the usual analytic supervisory situation, smiles, nodding, and facial or hand gestures help to provide the kind of feedback and reinforcement that was described earlier. More of such overt feedback has to become verbal in the telephone contacts. There is also a more impersonal and somewhat "disembodied" quality to the interaction that may feel awkward at first. It is possible that future technical developments of speaker or video telephone hookups will make telephone supervision easier, but at present, significant supervision can still occur over geographic distances and may be the only option available.

RESEARCH ON PSYCHOANALYTIC SUPERVISION

For many years, it was assumed that if one were a skilled analyst one would be able to do skilled supervision. It has become increasingly apparent that this is not the case. Some individuals may be effective as the intuitive and empathic treating analyst but may have difficulty in presenting their constructs and concepts in an articulate and understandable form. In the role of teacher, emphasis is more on clarity of conceptualization of constructs and ideas.

A variety of studies on the supervisory process have been undertaken within the discipline of psychoanalysis, and some of these studies have also applied psychoanalytic and psychodynamic thinking to various forms of psychotherapy supervision.

Eckstein and Wallerstein (1958) were among the first to study and report systematically about the supervisory process. Fleming and Benedek (1966) were pioneers in the study of the supervisory situation through the use of audiotape recordings of their supervisory sessions, developing extrapolations from these carefully studied supervisory interactions. These led to the development of a conceptual model of supervision in the psychoanalytic situation.

The COPE Study Group on Supervision of the American Psychoanalytic Association, chaired by Robert Wallerstein, consisted of a group of senior supervising analysts who met to discuss in depth the process notes of a supervisory situation provided by a candidate's supervisor who was himself *not* part of the study group. The group extensively studied and critiqued a number of early sessions of a psychoanalytic supervision. The individual members of the group presented their own interpretations and understandings of the supervision as well as of the analytic process itself. This eventuated in the monograph *Becoming a Psychoanalyst* (Wallerstein, 1981).

More recently another COPE group has begun to collect a library of audiotaped recordings of supervisory sessions made in different psychoanalytic institutes. These are made available anonymously to analytic study groups from institutes other than the one where the recording was done. In this way, the aim is to provide primary data for discussion and study of the supervisory process, but to do so while maintaining the privacy and anonymity of the patient, the candidate analyst, and the supervisor in question. There has been a general reluctance to provide this kind of recording, but progressively more are being collected and thus becoming available in a lending library arrangement for institutes to study and thus enhance the development of supervision skills and process.

The American Psychoanalytic Association Committee on Institutes regularly conducts site visits at different institutes of the association. As part of these site visits, there is observation of the supervision taking place, with visitors from the committee observing firsthand the interaction between students and supervisors. The data from these observations and the identity of the individuals and institute involved have remained confidential and sealed. Some general awareness of the kinds of supervisory processes occurring in different institutes has been gleaned, however, at least by the members of the committee.

Dewald (1987) recorded at random 18 psychoanalytic supervisory sessions from different phases of one particular student analysis. After the conclusion of the supervisory relationship and of the case, he studied the recordings in detail to demonstrate and illlustrate the process. Each of the recordings was critiqued by him, and the candidate in question also had access to the recorded sessions and was then able to write an evaluative critique of the supervisory experience from her point of view. This study was published as *Learning Process in Psychoanalytic Supervision: Complexities and Challenges* and has been used in various locations to study the details of a supervisory process.

The International Psychoanalytic Association has organized a series of biannual precongress meetings on the subject of supervision in psychoanalysis, with various supervising analysts throughout the world meeting to discuss issues and problems in that area of psychoanalytic training.

Many psychoanalytic institutes conduct ongoing supervisory seminars in which material from supervision is presented for general discussion and elucidation of the supervisory process. Although this does not qualify as formal research nor are the various individual seminar sessions necessarily transcribed or published, they nevertheless can provide a stimulus for further understanding of the supervisory process.

There are also small groups of supervisors who informally organize themselves into a peer study group on supervision and who discuss the supervisory process in considerable depth and detail based on the presentations of supervision material by group members. This has eventuated in a number of publications on the process of supervision (e.g., Jacobs, David, & Meyer, 1995) but does not qualify as genuine and publicly accessible research.

SUMMARY

It is generally acknowledged that supervision is one of the major pillars of psychoanalytic education and that the psychoanalytic supervisory situation is an extremely intense, long-term, and significant component in the development of the professional skill and understanding of a psychoanalyst. There are significant variations in the way by which various individuals understand the supervisory experience, from the standpoint of both the candidate and the supervisor. Although there are major differences in philosophy, conceptualization, and technique of supervision, there are also some similarities that seem to be generally acknowledged in the candidate/supervisor experience.

REFERENCES

Dewald, P. A. (1987). *Learning process in psychoanalytic supervision: Complexities and challenges.* Madison, CT: International Universities Press.

Ekstein, R., & Wallerstein, R. S. (1958). *The teaching and learning of psychotherapy.* New York: Basic Books.

Fleming, J., & Benedek, T. (1966). *Psychoanalytic supervision.* New York: Grune and Stratton.

Jacobs, D., David, P., & Meyer, D. J. (1995). *The supervisory encounter.* New Haven and London: Yale University Press.

Wallerstein, R. S. (Ed.). (1981). *Becoming a psychoanalyst.* New York: International Universities Press.

CHAPTER 4

Supervision of Psychodynamic Psychotherapies

JEFFREY L. BINDER
Georgia School of Professional Psychology
HANS H. STRUPP
Vanderbilt University

> In general, it may be said that knowledge is acquired by concentrated study and schooling
> . . . and skills by something at least vaguely resembing apprenticeship. . . . Psychoanalytic edu-
> cation must include both of these avenues since we don't know of any better ones. (Burke,
> 1991, p. 30)

A BRIEF HISTORY

As soon as Freud acquired a following for his approach to the treatment of mental disorders, methods for teaching psychoanalysis had to be developed. The first pedagogic model
was based on a "master-apprentice" relationship. Informal groups met regularly to be
taught, supervised, and analyzed by Freud. The roles of teacher and analyst were interchangeable, as were the roles of student and analysand. Personal psychoanalysis was considered to be the cornerstone of training to be a psychoanalyst by reducing the interferences emanating from neurotic conflicts. In the 1920s, the establishment of formal
psychoanalytic institutes and societies led to the development of formal training procedures
and standards. The "tripartite" model of analytic training consisted of didactic course work,
supervised treatment of several patients, and personal analysis (Doehrman, 1976;
Moldawsky, 1980). This model remains the predominant format for psychodynamic therapy training on the basis of established tradition and faith as opposed to empirical evidence
for its effectiveness (Binder, 1993a).

Once formal training procedures were developed, the blurred roles of teacher and analyst, which had been accepted as part of the original informal training experience, became
controversial. The underlying issue concerned how supervision of treatments could be
most effectively accomplished. A more fundamental pedagogic question concerned the
processes by which therapeutic skills are acquired. Two opposing positions crystallized.
The Hungarian position, represented by the Budapest Institute, advocated combining the
roles of supervisor and analyst, based on the assumption that therapeutic skills are acquired
secondary to the resolution of neurotic conflicts. The Vienna position, represented by that
institute, advocated separation of educational experiences from pursuit of resolution of
personal conflicts, based on the assumption that therapeutic skills had to be formally
taught, although their effective implementation required minimal interference from the
analyst's neurotic conflicts (Caligor, 1984; Thorbeck, 1992).

These two positions concerning the role of the supervisor have varied in relative influence over the decades, with the prevalent philosophy of supervision partly determined by the zeitgeist of the current analytic theory in vogue. Before the 1960s, the dominant supervision philosophy reflected the Vienna position, which was associated with drive-structural personality theory and the orthodox model of psychoanalytic treatment. The supervisor was viewed as an educator whose role was didactic and who transmitted knowledge about principles and procedures. The supervision was patient-centered, with the student bringing clinical problems and being given technical advice. From the 1960s to the late 1970s, the Hungarian position was at least implicitly in evidence, as object relations theories of personality gained prominence along with a more interactive view of the therapeutic process (e.g., the role of the analyst changing from a "blank screen" to that of "participant observer"). The supervisor was viewed as a therapeutic facilitator who pointed out blind spots in the trainee's experiences in treatment. The supervision was therapist-centered, with the student receiving essentially focused therapy that consisted of confrontation and clarification of countertransferences around personal conflicts that interfered with treatment of the patient under consideration. From the early 1980s to the present time, the Vienna and Hungarian positions appear to have become integrated, reflecting the hegemony of the concept of *parallel process* as a framework guiding the supervisor's efforts. The supervision is treatment-centered, with the student simultaneously discussing the treatment and unwittingly enacting with the supervisor important dynamics occurring in his or her relationship with the patient. The supervisor's role, then, is both to provide relevant theoretical and technical observations and to intervene in a therapeutic manner to interpret the parallel process (Davidson, 1987; Teitelbaum, 1990; Thorbeck, 1992; Wolstein, 1994).

Currently, there is no widespread consensus on the best philosophy and methods for conducting psychodynamic supervision. The most prevalent model, however, is characterized by a particular form of integration of didactic and therapeutic roles. The enterprise is viewed as an educational activity, but the typical supervisor applies psychodynamic clinical theories and methods usually associated with therapy to achieve the educational goals of supervision. This situation is not surprising—clinical supervisors are rarely trained in pedagogic theories, principles, and methods specifically tailored to the supervision process. Therefore, they use the knowledge and skills with which they are most familiar and comfortable. On the other hand, the position has a certain logic because psychodynamic therapy supervision and psychodynamic therapies have many features in common. In both situations, there are complementary roles: One role involves learning new interpersonal skills, whereas the other involves fostering the acquisition of those skills. These roles taken together can be characterized as a collaborative working arrangement, with the shared aim of changing one of the parties in an agreed-upon direction. Also, in both situations the working arrangement involves a process in which both technical and relationship factors contribute to the eventual outcome.

Whether this integration—or confounding—of educational and therapeutic roles is the most effective approach to therapy supervision is discussed later. First, to anticipate this discussion we review what we believe to be a representative sample of the abundant literature on psychodynamic therapy supervision. We occasionally review literature that is not specifically concerned with psychodynamic therapy but which nevertheless appears to be relevant to our topic. This situation occurs most often with regard to empirical studies. For the most part, we restrict the review to literature published over the past 20 years, which we believe is a practical compromise between the dual goals of presenting a historical overview and focusing on contemporary thinking.

Although the pertinent literature is sizable, the vast majority is theoretical/clinical, with empirical data practically nonexistent. The calls for research on psychotherapy training (and clinical training in general) have become so frequent and fervent that they resemble incantations (Alpher, 1991; Beutler & Kendall, 1995; Binder, 1993a; Binder et al., 1993; Buckley, Conte, Plutchik, Karasu, & Wild, 1982; Davidson, 1987; Dewald, 1987; Glass, 1986; Henry, Strupp, Butler, Schacht, & Binder, 1993; Holloway & Neufeldt, 1995; Langs, 1994; Rodenhauser, 1994; Stein & Lambert, 1995; Strupp, Butler, & Rosser, 1988; Watkins, 1995). The magic is not working, however, as evidenced by the absence for the first time of a chapter on training in the encyclopedic fourth edition of the *Handbook of Psychotherapy and Behavioral Change* (Bergin & Garfield, 1994). In the preface to this most recent edition of the *Handbook*, the authors explain omitted chapter topics as reflecting "current trends." Thus, the outlook appears bleak for increased research on therapy training. Unfortunately, research on psychodynamic therapy training has always lagged behind training for more behaviorally oriented models.

Although research on therapy training is meager, empirical studies of therapy process and outcome, including psychodynamic therapies, continue to flourish. Since the psychodynamic supervision process has much in common with the psychodynamic therapy process, it seems reasonable to examine the former using conceptual categories comparable to those that have proven useful in examining the latter. Individual adult psychotherapy process-and-outcome research typically addresses characteristics of both parties in the dyadic relationship, technical and relationship factors, and the interaction of these factors as constituents of the therapeutic process. Finally, all these factors are examined with respect to outcome. Accordingly, our review will be organized as follows: (a) characteristics of the trainee; (b) characteristics of the supervisor; (c) the conception of the supervision process, including how change is assumed to occur; (d) technical and relationship factors; (e) goals of supervision; and (f) evidence for the efficacy of supervision with respect to therapeutic skill acquisition and improved treatment outcomes. For each topic, we first examine the theoretical/clinical literature and then discuss relevant findings from empirical studies.

CHARACTERISTICS OF THE TRAINEE

There do not appear to be any noteworthy differences between trainee characteristics that are discussed by psychodynamic clinicians and clinicians representing other orientations. Consequently, their observations are combined. The personal characteristics that are assumed to be required to learn psychotherapy seem to aid the trainee in assuming the roles of student, therapist, and patient. The capacity to assume alternately all three roles is generally considered to be a necessary requirement for psychodynamic supervision. The specific characteristics that trainees must possess can be roughly grouped into three categories: (a) generic to all learning—openness to learning, curiosity, thoughtfulness, initiative; (b) probably generic to all learning but with special application to learning psychotherapy—self-reflection, emotional and interpersonal self-monitoring, recognition of interpersonal patterns, flexibility (personal, theoretical, and clinical), motivation to change, ability to apply theory to clinical data, accepting the expertise of the supervisor; and (c) relatively specific to doing psychotherapy—psychological-mindedness, capacity to relate, willingness to deal with uncomfortable feelings and insights, empathy, openness to discussion of personal issues (Berger & Bucholz, 1993; Chrzanowski, 1984; Davidson, 1987; Dewald, 1987; Doehrman, 1976; Ekstein & Wallerstein, 1972; Gediman & Wolkenfeld,

1980; Glickauf-Hughes, 1994; Haesler, 1993; Halgin & Murphy, 1995; Issacharoff, 1984; Josephs, 1990; Langs, 1979; Lesser, 1984; Levenson, 1984; Mollon, 1987; Rodenhauser, 1994; Sarnat, 1992; Schimel, 1984; Shechter, 1990; Teitelbaum, 1990; Thorbeck, 1992).

Several issues regarding personal characteristics of the therapist trainee have been recurrently discussed in the psychodynamic supervision literature.The first issue concerns the importance of the supervisor's sensitivity to the individual learning needs and experiences of each trainee. Supervision strategies must be tailored to these individual features (Davidson, 1987; Thorbeck, 1992). An extension of this perspective are the "developmental" models of supervision, which posit changing teaching strategies over time in response to the trainee's progressive acquisition of knowledge and skills (Holloway, 1987). The second issue concerns the vulnerable "professional self-esteem" of the novice therapist (Josephs, 1990; Teitelbaum, 1990). Some evidence exists that talented novice therapists are more particularly susceptible than less talented novices to feeling incompetent in their work (Buckley et al., 1982). Another issue is the interference in supervision contributed by trainee psychopathology (Glickauf-Hughes, 1994; Langs, 1979). If it is assumed that trainee psychopathology can seriously interfere with learning through clinical supervision, then it follows that personal therapy can be a crucial factor in maximizing the learning experiences. In a survey of trainees representing various theoretical orientations, Allen, Szollos, and Williams (1986) estimated that at least 25% of the trainees entered personal therapy while they were being supervised. Furthermore, practitioners routinely consider their personal therapy experiences to have had a major positive impact on their clinical performance (Norcross & Prochaska, 1982). There is no convincing empirical evidence that personal therapy enhances a trainee's performance in supervision, however (Glass, 1986; Halgin & Murphy, 1995; Strupp et al., 1988).

The lack of evidence for the contribution of personal therapy in enhancing clinical learning by no means implies that interpersonal skills are unimportant for the therapy trainee. Indeed, no idea has as much consensus among psychodynamic therapy teachers as the critical importance of interpersonal skills for conducting effective treatment (Strupp et al., 1988). There is, however, disagreement about the extent to which interpersonal skills can be learned—or at least improved—as opposed to their being innate and impervious to learning (Binder et al., 1993; Rodenhauser, 1994). Accumulating empirical evidence indicates that both novices and experienced therapists have most difficulty in dealing with the interpersonal consequences of hostile attitudes, sentiments, and behaviors from their patients (Binder et al., 1993; Henry, Strupp et al., 1993; Josephs, 1990; Strupp et al., 1988). The extent to which interpersonal skills can be taught, or at least enhanced, through supervision remains an empirical question.

CHARACTERISTICS OF THE SUPERVISOR

A common, if often tacit, assumption particularly characteristic of psychodynamically oriented supervisors is that the primary skills required to teach psychotherapy are also those required to conduct therapy (Ekstein & Wallerstein, 1972). Accordingly, characteristics of an effective supervisor include self-reflection and self-monitoring of the emotional/interpersonal processes associated with supervisor-trainee interactions, along with the ability to oscillate between identifying with and observing the experiences of the trainee and the trainee's patient (Caligor, 1984; Doehrman, 1976; Gediman & Wolkenfeld, 1980; Martin, Mayerson, Olsen, & Wiberg, 1977; Schimel, 1984). Specific characteristics and skills are emphasized according to the theoretical model favored by the supervisor: Ego psychological supervisors emphasize detecting and conveying awareness of the trainee's maladaptive ego coping functions (Ekstein & Wallerstein, 1972); interpersonally oriented supervisors emphasize detecting and conveying awareness of countertransferences and fostering "participant observation" (Issacharoff, 1984; Lesser, 1984).

Some characteristics identified by therapy teachers are as applicable to any good teacher as they are to a good supervisor of psychotherapy. These characteristics include flexibility about theory, technical principles, and the trainee's learning and therapy styles as well as his or her nervousness and mistakes; a respectful attitude; the ability to be supportive and nonjudgmental; humility toward knowledge; curiosity; a relaxed and patient manner; thoughtfulness; and the ability to convey principles and concepts with clarity (Chrzanowski, 1984; Cooper & Witenberg, 1984; Davidson, 1987; Feiner, 1994; Haesler, 1993; Halgin & Murphy, 1995; Lesser, 1984; Levenson, 1984; Mollon, 1987; Rodenhauser, 1994; Schimel, 1984; Shechter, 1990). Other characteristics that have been mentioned include the ability to think out loud in order to model clinical inference processes and technical strategy formation, a willingness to allow students to view the supervisor's own therapy performance (e.g., through video recordings), and the ability to collaborate with trainees in deciding upon working arrangements and goals (Berger & Bucholz, 1993; Corradi, Wasman, & Gold, 1980; Dewald, 1987).

Therapy trainees (clinical and counseling psychology graduate students, psychiatry residents) have been extensively surveyed to obtain their views of the characteristics that determine an effective therapy supervisor. These characteristics include expertise, trustworthiness, interpersonal attractiveness, tolerance of trainee mistakes, provision of clear and direct feedback, confrontation of student mistakes in an atmosphere of safety, openness to feedback about their own style of relating, significant investment of time in the endeavor, and a keen interest in a student's learning as evidenced by viewing tape recordings of his or her work. Trainees have also provided a picture of the characteristics associated with a poor supervisor: disinterest and ineptness; vague communications that are sometimes authoritarian; exploitative treatment; tendency to avoid interpersonal issues in the supervisory relationship; focus on personal shortcomings of the trainee or being absorbed in him- or herself; and occasional sexist attitudes (Allen et al., 1986; Shanfield, Matthews, & Hetherely, 1993).

The characteristics associated with poor supervisors have been explained as evidence of significant psychopathology (Langs, 1979) or as evidence of more subtle "narcissistic needs and vulnerabilities" that are associated with an excessive need to be liked and admired or to be in control (Teitelbaum, 1990). A more temporary and benign form of supervisory ineffectiveness is associated with the novice supervisor, who in his or her zeal to teach does not attend to the individual learning needs of each trainee (Davidson, 1987).

MODELS OF THE SUPERVISORY PROCESS

Teaching strategies must be designed around a conception of the interpersonal processes that form the context for teaching and learning. The most influential conception in the area of psychodynamic supervision is the model of parallel process (Doehrman, 1976; Ekstein & Wallerstein, 1972). The core of this model is the notion that similar interpersonal dynamics are concurrently enacted in the therapy dyad and in the supervisory dyad. Variations of this process model represent alternative views concerning the origin of the interpersonal dynamics, the interrelationships of therapy and supervisory dynamics, and the prevalence and utility of parallel process for teaching and learning. There can be little doubt that the popularity among psychodynamic supervisors of parallel process as a pedagogic model stems from its foundation in psychoanalytic clinical observations and theory. The supervisor can use familiar clinical skills to deal with teaching and learning issues in a context viewed as a "quasi-therapeutic encounter" (Sarnat, 1992). Perhaps the first discussion of parallel process was by Searles (1965), who referred to a "reflection process" occurring among patient, trainee, and supervisor. When the trainee was struggling with an inchoate conflict in the patient that could not be verbalized to the supervisor, he or she was seen as having identified with the patient and as enacting that conflict with the supervisor. The incentive for this process was to receive help with the therapeutic problem, which could occur if the supervisor deciphered the meanings of the trainee's enactments. The process was one-directional, originating in the therapy dyad and directed toward the supervisory dyad.

The conception of parallel process was intensively studied by Ekstein and Wallerstein (1972) and introduced to the field in their classic treatise on the teaching of psychoanalytic therapy. These authors conceptualized the process from an ego psychological perspective. For the novice therapist, the emotional stresses of commencing to do psychotherapy and of being supervised produce ego regression to familiar forms of adaptation that may be maladaptive in the current circumstances. When these ego adaptive functions and their interpersonal manifestations interfere with empathic attunement to patients, they become "learning problems." When they interfere with optimal receptiveness to supervisory teaching, they become "problems about learning." The regressive ego adaptations in the form of maladaptive attitudes, sentiments, and behavior patterns can be strikingly similar in their appearance in therapy and supervision; hence, they are viewed as components of parallel processes. When occurring in supervision, they can evoke countertransference reactions from the supervisor. Ekstein and Wallerstein believe that when these "problems" are identified and worked through with the aid of circumscribed therapeutic interventions by the supervisor, the transmission of didactic knowledge occurs with relative ease. Their conception of the supervisor's role implicitly combines the functions of teacher and therapist, with the latter role being narrowly focused on removing emotional interferences to learning. Whereas these interferences and their maladaptive interpersonal manifestations are generally assumed to originate in either the supervisory dyad or the therapeutic dyad, Ekstein and Wallerstein emphasize the flow of parallel process from the latter to the former.

Doehrman (1976) provided empirical support for the influence of parallel process in her intensive naturalistic study of several patient-trainee-supervisor triads. She elaborated on, and somewhat modified, Ekstein and Wallerstein's explanation of the origin of parallel process. Doehrman viewed the supervisor's role as composed of the conflicting functions of teacher and evaluator. This situation contributes to an emotionally charged atmosphere, which promotes regressive transference in both parties. The trainee is prone to act out in his or her therapies conflicts that originated in the supervisory relationship, either by identifying with the supervisor and acting toward the patient as he or she experienced the supervisor acting toward him or her or, by counteridentification, acting toward the patient in the opposite fashion. The impact on the therapy continues until the supervisory impasse is resolved. Doehrman conceived of the influence of parallel process as multidirectional. Based on her systematic observations, however, she concluded that the most prevalent direction of influence originates in the supervisory dyad and moves toward the therapy dyad. It is worth noting that most subsequent writings on the subject emphasize the direction of influence from the therapy dyad to the supervisory dyad. Perhaps this reflects the reluctance of supervisors to face interpersonal problems originating within the supervisory dyad.

Parallel process has also been conceptualized from a Neo-Sullivanian (interpersonal) viewpoint. By his or her participant observation in the therapy relationship, the trainee is receptive to reactions evoked by the patient. In the supervisory relationship, the trainee shifts from receiver of an evoking message to transmitter of the message, evoking similar reactions in the supervisor. The incentives activating this process involve the contagious influence of interpersonal processes and the desire for help from the supervisor (Caligor, 1984).

One view of parallel process is that it is comparable to transference and countertransference processes. It is viewed as unavoidable and, if recognized and worked with, can be an invaluable aid to teaching psychodynamic therapy (Berger & Bucholz, 1993; Caligor, 1984; Haesler, 1993; Sachs & Shapiro, 1976; Teitelbaum, 1990). An opposing position conceives of parallel process as infrequent, of limited educational value, and symptomatic of impasses either in therapy or in supervision, or both. It might also be symptomatic of deficiencies in the supervisor's teaching skills (Bromberg, 1984; Chrzanowski, 1984; Dewald, 1987; Haesler, 1993; Issacharoff, 1984; Lesser, 1984; Schimel, 1984; Wolstein, 1994). From an interpersonal perspective, Feiner (1994) takes the position that parallel process is more apparent than real, because the model refers to similarities in broad classes of behavior and ignores critical differences in the therapy and supervisory dyads associated with their respective unique contexts. Finally, in a systematic empirical study of one patient-student-supervisor triad, Alpher (1991) adduced evidence of a limited role for parallel process at critical points in therapy. Rodenhauser (1994) proposed a model of the supervisor's development in this role, in which the recognition of parallel process is a developmental achievement. The novice supervisor progresses from emulating his or her own prior supervisors to developing a conceptualization of supervision as a set of procedures, culminating in a proficiency at monitoring parallel process.

An alternative version of the parallel process model emphasizes the comparability of interpersonal roles and functions in therapy and supervision rather than of the content similarity of interpersonal themes. In this Neo-Sullivanian version of the model, the trainee is a "participant observer" in both therapy and supervision, and both relationships involve the "collaborative exploration" of issues within an immediate interpersonal context (Cooper & Witenberg, 1984; Lesser, 1984). The assumption is that self-monitoring and self-reflecting skills that are learned in supervision are generalized to therapy. An idiosyncratic view of the supervision process was proposed by Langs (1979). Transferences and countertransferences of the trainee and supervisor are introjected by the trainee's patient. The patient in turn may initiate "unconscious curative efforts" that are manifested as implicit communications to the trainee. If the supervisor and trainee can decipher the meanings of these communications, they can implement reparative efforts. This model probably has limited appeal because of the emphasis on trainee and supervisor pathology and because of the implied expectation that the supervisor be somewhat omniscient.

The concept of parallel process as well as competing conceptions are used to describe the *context* in which teaching and learning take place. In order to explain *how* learning occurs, psychoanalytic supervisors commonly employ the developmental concept of *internalization*. A prototypic developmental progression of internalization processes occurs as follows: The beginning phase of supervision is characterized by the development of a "learning alliance" and the learning of basic technical strategies and tactics (Feiner, 1994; Gediman & Wolkenfeld, 1980; Haesler, 1993; Holloway & Neufeldt, 1995; Shechter, 1990). The first mental processes associated with these activities are compliance with and imitation of the supervisor. The first internalizations are in the form of introjections of the supervisor. These introjections are "unmetabolized" experiences of the actual internal image of the supervisor that guide global, concrete emulations of the supervisor's way of working. In this stage, the trainee is reliant on explicit and specific guidance from the supervisor. In the intermediate stage of supervision, the trainee learns to apply theory to practice and acquires a deeper comprehension of therapeutic processes as well as proficiency with therapeutic skills. The mental processes associated with these developments are identifications with selected aspects of the supervisor's functioning. Thus, a trainee gradually acquires the capacity for spontaneous reflection on his or her functioning within the supervisory dyad and begins to generalize this capacity to the therapy dyad. The supervisor relies on the strategy of relatively more nondirective coaching. In the advanced phase of supervision, the trainee works with increasing spontaneity and autonomy. The underlying mental processes involve progressive consolidation of a professional identity in which internalizations are fully "metabolized" and experienced as smooth unself-conscious parts of the professional identity. The supervisor's role is that of a consultant who is available when needed. The supervisory function has been internalized by the trainee, who is now able to self-reflect spontaneously within the therapy sessions (Casement, 1991; Dewald, 1987; Haesler, 1993; Halgin & Murphy, 1995; Shechter, 1990).

Empirical investigations of the role of internalization processes in the acquisition of therapeutic skills are essentially nonexistent. One notable exception is a study of the effects of manual-guided training in a form of time-limited dynamic therapy that was conducted by Strupp and his colleagues (Strupp, 1993). One of the findings from this study was that therapists whose established introjects were characterized by self-directed hostility were more receptive to adhering to prescribed therapy techniques but also had more difficulty in maintaining a positive interpersonal atmosphere with their patients (Henry, Schacht, Strupp, Butler, & Binder, 1993). Although this finding is not directly applicable to internalizations of the supervisor during supervision, it does point to more complex interactions between internalizations and therapeutic skills than is reflected in current conceptions of mental processes associated with learning in therapy supervision.

STRATEGIES AND TECHNIQUES FOR CONDUCTING SUPERVISION

Before turning to strategies and tactics, it would be informative to review briefly the data sources and formats that have been proposed for psychodynamic supervision. The traditional source of data for supervision has been the trainee's recollections of therapy sessions, in the form of chronologically ordered written notes or more free-associative musings. The rationale for this type of data is that the supervisor views the patient through the trainee's eyes, thereby allowing the supervisor to work with the trainee's apperceptions. Those who favor the trainee's recollections without the aid of notes assume that, as with free association in therapy, important themes will spontaneously emerge (Ekstein & Wallerstein, 1972; Langs, 1979; Mollon, 1987). A more contemporary approach to data relies on tape recordings (audio or video). The rationale for tape recordings is that they are more accurate and complete (Bromberg, 1984; Corradi et al., 1980; Gill & Hoffman, 1982; Luborsky & Auerbach, 1969). On the other hand, some supervisors maintain that recordings are an unjustifiable intrusion on the sanctity of the therapy relationship (Tennen, 1988). The traditional format for psychodynamic supervision, a dyad composed of trainee and supervisor, remains the most prevalent. A surprising number of supervisors, however, recommend the advantages of a small-group format. These advantages include providing for a range of viewpoints on clinical issues and avoiding the regressive transferences and countertransferences that tend to arise in the emotionally charged atmosphere of a supervisory dyad (Caligor, 1984; Corradi et al., 1980; Issacharoff, 1984; Sachs & Shapiro, 1976; Wolstein, 1994).

As mentioned earlier, in the 1970s and 1980s, the hegemony of the parallel process concept encouraged a reliance on a therapeutic role for the psychodynamic supervisor. This role reflected a learning strategy of addressing "resistances" to learning on the part of the trainee. The more or less tacit assumption was that once the trainee was freed from resistances to learning through therapeutic interventions by the supervisor, the transmission of knowledge would flow spontaneously (Chrzanowski, 1984; Ekstein & Wallerstein, 1972; Issacharoff, 1984, Searles, 1965). Sarnat (1992) observed that the therapeutic role for the supervisor had advantages, because it could not be assumed that personal issues of the trainee that impede his or her performance could be effectively addressed in personal therapy. On the other hand, he also pointed out the dangers of exploitation and inappropriate intrusions on the student that could result from the supervisor's therapeutic role.

The modern role for the psychodynamic supervisor is characterized by attentiveness to didactic issues and appreciation of the supervisor's contribution to learning problems, in addition to dealing with trainee countertransferences. The pedagogic philosophy of the supervisor determines the instructional focus, which may be on teaching specific theory and techniques, on recognizing participation in conflictual interpersonal processes, or on encouraging trainee learning by experience (Dewald, 1987). It is becoming more common for supervisors to take the position that the salient learning strategy at any point in the trainee-supervisor dyad is primarily determined by contextual needs (Berger & Bucholz, 1993; Davidson, 1987; Haesler, 1993; Josephs, 1990; Newman, 1986; Thorbeck, 1992) or the phase of the trainee's development (Hanlon, 1990). Regardless of which learning strategy is favored, it is widely recommended to scrupulously avoid attitudes of hostility and disrespect toward the trainee (Davidson, 1987; Langs, 1979). Following this advice is crucial to establishing and maintaining a good learning alliance, which is considered to be an important part of the foundation for a productive learning experience (Haesler, 1993; Holloway & Neufeldt, 1995).

As we have seen, among psychodynamic therapy teachers the most prevalent view of how therapeutic skills are acquired is the process of internalization of learning experiences. The clinical lineage of this view is evident by the focus on interpersonal activities between the participants. Accordingly, the most widely discussed specific teaching strategy is "modeling" therapeutic mental activities and behaviors for the trainee. Whatever other teaching aims are associated with a supervisor's interventions, a cardinal aim is to model specific technical strategies and tactics as well as more general attitudes such as curiosity and patience (Caligor, 1984; Halgin & Murphy, 1995; Sachs & Shapiro, 1976; Shechter, 1990).

Another form of modeling may be highly effective but particularly difficult for supervisors to perform: "Thinking out loud" takes the trainee through the supervisor's stages in thinking about clinical data during the effort to achieve clinical understanding and case formulation, as well as to develop therapeutic strategies (Dewald, 1987). Another form of modeling through "thinking out loud" involves sharing with trainees examples of the supervisor's videotaped therapy sessions. The supervisor can simultaneously illustrate and discuss clinical concepts, principles, strategies, and techniques. Although the teaching advantages are evident, many supervisors are reluctant to expose their performances (Corradi et al., 1980).

Modeling therapeutic activities probably has instructional value, although how much is a question yet to be investigated. Levenson (1984) has asserted that therapy knowledge and skills cannot be taught exclusively through being told about them. Simply teaching strategies and techniques "by the numbers" will not guarantee therapeutic competence, nor will interpreting trainee countertransferences straightforwardly result in acquisition of therapeutic skills. Levenson does not stray far from a technical emphasis, however; he recommends an "algorithmic" approach in which the trainee is taught a series of practical strategies and procedures that are not wedded to theory. Other teachers place even more emphasis on encouraging the trainee's active involvement in the learning process, in order to achieve a thorough comprehension of the rationales behind technical strategies (Binder, 1993a; Bromberg, 1984; Cooper & Witenberg, 1984; Haesler, 1993; Lesser, 1984).

A specific strategy for actively involving the trainee in the learning process involves fostering an interest in "asking good questions" and promoting the skills to do this. This strategy aims to teach skills in forms of inquiry, both how to frame good questions and how to pursue their answers (Feiner, 1994). Teaching forms of inquiry is a more generic instructional strategy (by this we mean relevant to many domains of knowledge and skill) than is characteristic of many supervisory activities that, as we have seen, are heavily influenced by clinical theory and experience. A related generic instructional strategy involves "coaching" trainees to discover for themselves the therapeutic strategies and styles that work for them. Coaching is conducted through demonstrating, advising, questioning, and providing critical feedback, with the aim of learning forms of inquiry for framing problems and gaining understanding in unique contexts (Schon, 1987). We will make a case later for the importance of this strategy.

THE GOALS AND THE OUTCOMES OF SUPERVISION

The blending of therapeutic and educational roles has been characteristic of psychodynamic supervision; therefore, the distinction between therapy and supervision often has been defined with regard to the goals of these respective endeavors. Ekstein and Wallerstein (1972) conceptualized the primary goal of therapy as the resolution of inner conflicts whatever their external manifestations. In contrast, they conceptualized the primary goal of supervision as the acquisition of therapeutic skills, regardless of what inner conflicts might encumber the trainee. Therapeutic interventions in the service of educational goals, for example, are supposed to enhance the trainee's empathic capacities (Chrzanowski, 1984; Issacharoff, 1984; Langs, 1979) and to reduce narcissistic vulnerabilities associated with the novice role (Teitelbaum, 1990).

The goals of instructional interventions include learning clinical theory and techniques, applying theory to clinical data, and applying techniques to particular patients (Dewald, 1987; Gediman & Wolkenfeld, 1980). Supervision also aims to encourage component attitudes and skills that contribute to therapeutic techniques; these include curiosity, patience, and learning to observe and explore "significant patterns" in the data (Cooper & Witenberg, 1984; Lesser, 1984; Schimel, 1984). Developing and practicing therapeutic skills with the aid of supervision should lead to increasingly autonomous functioning, the development of a personal therapeutic style, and the ability to improvise when the need arises (Dewald,

1987; Gediman & Wolkenfeld, 1980; Haesler, 1993; Schon, 1987). The fundamental generic skills of self-monitoring and self-regulating must also be acquired and increasingly perfected, because they underlie so many other performance skills (Berger & Bucholz, 1993; Bromberg, 1984; Casement, 1991; Haesler, 1993; Mollon, 1987; Schon, 1987).

Whereas a plethora of opinions about methods for psychodynamic therapy supervision have been disseminated in the literature, empirical evaluation of the impact of supervision methods on skill acquisition or treatment outcome is rare. This state of affairs is true for supervision of all therapy orientations (Beutler & Kendall, 1995; Binder, 1993a; Holloway & Neufeldt, 1995; Stein & Lambert, 1995) but perhaps especially true for psychodynamic therapy supervision (Strupp et al., 1988). Doehrman (1976) concluded from her study of psychodynamic supervision that the "resolution of transference binds" in trainee-supervisor dyads was associated with the resolution of transference binds in the trainee-patient dyads. Hence, effective supervisory techniques appeared to include (a) circumscribed therapeutic interventions directed at emotionally based teaching and learning problems and (b) modeling of interpretive interventions. These findings have never been replicated with more stringent research methods, but this has not diminished their appeal to countless psychodynamic supervisors.

The most common type of empirical study of supervision involves surveys of student satisfaction. Surveys of psychology doctoral students and psychiatry residents have yielded a set of characteristics associated with the "good" supervisor: spends a substantial amount of time with trainees; emphasizes trainee concerns, both intellectual and emotional, in working with patients; presents a theory-based framework for understanding therapeutic processes; teaches practical skills; models a disciplined focus on specific clinical material; respects the development of individual therapeutic styles; and, most important, communicates clearly and specifically about concepts, principles, and evaluative feedback. In contrast, the "poor" supervisor is characterized as disinterested in trainees, conveying rigid attitudes about what is right and wrong, being critical, manifesting superficial understanding of clinical material, and communicating vaguely and ambiguously (Allen et al., 1986; Shanfield et al., 1993). Although these satisfaction surveys offer useful guidelines for supervisors, they do not produce hard evidence for what actually contributes to therapy skill acquisition.

There are several trends evident from empirical investigations of therapy training, of which supervision of cases is the centerpiece (these studies include psychodynamic, interpersonal, and cognitive-behavioral therapy models). There is strong evidence that technical skills can be taught. There is, however, a consistently weak relationship between adherence to prescribed therapy techniques and global ratings of therapeutic competence. The same holds true for the association between technical adherence and treatment outcome (Beckham, 1990; Binder, 1993a; Butler & Strupp, 1993). It appears that therapy instruction is more successful in inculcating the form rather than the substance of therapy. We teach best what we understand, and we understand more about the nature of techniques than about other therapeutic skills.

The strongest contributor to successful therapy outcome is a solid therapeutic alliance (Alexander & Luborsky, 1986; Horvath & Greenberg, 1986). Interpersonal skills in establishing and maintaining an alliance with the patient are essential, particularly in the face of inevitable and often serious stresses on the therapeutic relationship (Safran, Crocker, McMain, & Murray, 1990). Evidence from a variety of sources indicates, however, that interpersonal skills are enormously difficult to teach, and success on this front, particularly when measured by how effectively therapists are able to cope with various forms of patient hostility, has been less than satisfactory (Binder, 1993b; Buckley et al., 1982; Butler & Strupp, 1993; Henry, Strupp et al., 1993). Even after specialized training, therapists' interpersonal competence appears to be eroded by difficult patients (Foley, O'Malley, Rounsaville, Prusoff, & Weissman, 1987). Because such complications associated with teaching therapeutic skills exist, it is not surprising that the scanty empirical evidence available points to only "modest" improvements in treatment outcome as a consequence of training (Beutler & Kendall, 1995; Stein & Lambert, 1995). A much stronger recurrent finding is the variability in treatment outcomes across therapists and across patients for a given therapist (Binder, 1993a; Butler & Strupp, 1993). This finding suggests both variability in training effectiveness across therapists, as well as the vulnerability of therapists to potential difficulties in any given therapeutic relationship.

Reviews of the scanty empirical data about teaching methods that contribute to therapy skill acquisition and/or enhanced treatment outcome reveal a suggestive trend: Structured learning experiences designed to teach specific procedures and skills in a progression from simple to more complex performances may be particularly effective (Binder, 1993a; Lambert & Arnold, 1987). As mentioned earlier, Strupp and his colleagues have conducted an empirically rigorous investigation of the impact of systematic training in a form of time-limited dynamic therapy on skill acquisition and therapy process and outcome (Strupp, 1993). Although the "trainees" were experienced clinical psychologists and psychiatrists who were learning to incorporate new therapeutic strategies into their existing therapeutic styles, the results may be generalized with caution to novices. It was found that technical skills were most enhanced through a structured approach to supervision when (a) each supervisory session was structured around specific learning tasks (e.g., identifying implicit references to transference issues); (b) discussion was focused on the trainee's thought processes associated with how clinical understanding was achieved and therapeutic strategies were devised; (c) emphasis was on self-reflection and self-monitoring while the therapeutic process was ongoing; (d) positive and negative evaluative feedback was spelled out precisely in terms of the trainee's behavior (Henry, Schacht, Strupp, Butler, & Binder, 1993).

The value of structured learning experiences and precise communication of ideas has also been emphasized by the representatives of other research-based therapy training programs (including psychodynamic, cognitive, and behavioral models). These recommendations include: (a) teach case conceptualizations that are precise and anchored in the patient's interpersonal experience in order to guide therapeutic interventions; (b) a positive therapeutic alliance is crucial to treatment outcome, therefore basic relationship skills (which are necessary for establishing and maintaining an alliance) should be taught before more specialized technical procedures; (c) the educational impact of supervision is enhanced by structuring tasks and by precise communications about concepts, principles, and evaluative feedback; (d) the use of clearly and precisely written treatment manuals facilitates the teaching of concepts, principles, technical strategies, and tactics; (e) the use of tape recordings aids the comprehension of ideas and the development of skills in detecting important patterns of interpersonal process in the therapeutic dyad; (f) the supervision of trainees in a small group increases the diversity of observations and ideas and is a cost-effective teaching format; (g) the integration of didactic experiences and supervised practice experiences should occur more frequently and should be more carefully planned (Binder et al., 1993).

REFLECTIONS ON TEACHING PSYCHOTHERAPY
AND A PROPOSAL

Improvements in teaching psychodynamic therapy have involved technical innovations such as the use of videotape recordings and the more precise specification of therapeutic principles and procedures that are offered in treatment manuals. These improvements have not been grounded in advances in pedagogic concepts that serve to guide instruction in therapy knowledge and skills. Guiding concepts and principles for the teaching of psychodynamic therapy consist primarily of an amalgam of clinical concepts stretched to serve as pedagogic principles that are loosely organized around the instructional model of "master and apprentice." Although clinical theories and their associated intervention strategies undoubtedly are useful for comprehending and managing emotional and interpersonal obstacles to learning, they should not be expected to guide efforts to teach complex cognitive skills. Pedagogic theories, principles, and procedures that are designed to understand and guide the development of competencies would be more appropriate. They also could be useful in comprehending and rectifying certain recurrently identified deficiencies in psychotherapy training (Binder, 1993a).

These deficiencies have emerged regularly in the course of "manual-guided" psychotherapy training and research projects in which the consequences of therapy training are subjected to rigorous empirical analyses. A stable finding is that prescribed technical strategies and tactics can be effectively taught. It has been observed, however, that the learning of new techniques by novice and experienced therapists is often an exceedingly inefficient process, characterized by much floundering, repetition of errors, and, in the case of experienced therapists, temporary deterioration of previous levels of performance (Dewald, 1987; Henry, Strupp et al., 1993; Rodenhauser, 1994). One common explanation for these phenomena assumes a clinical perspective; these problems result from stress-induced temporary ego regressions and/or problems of internalization resulting from insufficient exposure to supervisor modeling or competing models presented by different supervisors (Dewald, 1987). An alternative view suggests that a major pedagogic problem is posed by the "gap" between didactic experiences associated with course work about therapy and the experience of actually doing therapy (Corradi et al., 1980). Other identified training deficiencies include noticeable variation across therapists in the consistency of technical adherence that is maintained (Henry, Strupp et al., 1993) and the absence of a strong association between technical adherence and ratings of overall therapeutic competence. A strong association between technical adherence and positive treatment outcome is also lacking (Beckham, 1990; Butler & Strupp, 1993; Binder, 1993a).

We propose that concepts and principles that have been developed by cognitive-instructional psychologists in the course of investigating the progress from novice to expert irrespective of knowledge domain could be applied to understanding and improving the teaching of therapeutic skills (Binder, 1993a). The abstract knowledge acquired in course work, and to some extent in supervision, is referred to as "declarative" knowledge. This knowledge consists of theories, concepts, principles, and facts, along with certain rules on how to apply them (Bransford & Vye, 1988). With regard to therapy training, treatment manuals have improved the content specificity of declarative knowledge. The latter, however, may be mentally retained in an "inert" form, that is, knowledge that is not spontaneously accessible to the user at appropriate times (Bransford, Franks, Vye, & Sherwood, 1989). In order to proficiently apply therapeutic concepts, principles, and procedures, "procedural" knowledge is required. This type of knowledge refers to cognitive strategies for *when* and *how* to act in the immediate context. Procedural knowledge is composed of cognitive strategies that are grounded in abstract principles and concepts. These forms of knowledge serve as guidelines for action in the immediate context, because they are associated with past experiences of action-consequence sequences in the same or similar situations (Bransford & Vye, 1988). This form of knowledge is usually tacit and automatic. Schon (1987) refers to it as "knowing-in-action," by which is meant spontaneous, skillful execution of performances, without the person necessarily being able verbally to explicate the algorithms for his or her performance. The difficulty an expert faces in explicating the essentials of his or her performance is perhaps why no one has become a proficient golfer merely by reading an instructional book by Jack Nicklaus and why listening to an expert therapy supervisor think out loud about a case does not appear to be an efficient method for learning to do therapy.

The lack of bridging instructional experiences between didactic course work and therapy supervision, which is a typical situation in the teaching of psychodynamic therapy, is conducive to the acquisition of inert knowledge about the conduct of therapy. Evidence for this belief was produced in a study of performance differences between novice psychodynamic therapists in supervision and very experienced psychodynamic therapists who were judged by their peers as "outstanding" (Church, 1993). The specific performances studied were the recognition and interpretive management of implicit references to transference. The novices demonstrated theoretical understanding of transference but were unable to translate this understanding into effective practice. In other words, they manifested declarative knowledge but lacked commensurate procedural knowledge.

Although procedural knowledge can be acquired during supervision, the acquisition process is probably inefficient. Procedural knowledge is most efficiently acquired in learning situations that provide active involvement of the learner, who is exposed to a pre-arranged sequence of progressively more complex clinical problems, knowledge, and methods (Binder, 1993a; Bransford et al., 1989). These systematic conditions are unlikely to occur spontaneously in therapy supervision, in which the vicissitudes of patients' lives and the characteristically unsystematic nature of moment-to-moment supervisory activities create a relatively context-determined, free-form learning experience. Indirect evidence for this assertion comes from the Vanderbilt training study that was previously cited. In that study, it was observed that experienced psychodynamic therapists were much less adept at recognizing and managing implicit references to transference than was reflected by their self-ratings (Henry, Strupp et al., 1993). The concert stage is probably not the best place to first practice basic piano technique, and the therapy session may not be the best place to first practice basic therapy technique. The placement of major responsibility on therapy supervision for the initial and continuing acquisition of procedural knowledge may contribute to the deficiencies in learning and application of therapy strategies and tactics, a problem cited earlier. We propose that therapy supervision is a method best suited for refining therapeutic skills and elaborating procedural knowledge *after* an initial foundation of declarative and procedural knowledge has been constructed with the aid of structured learning experiences that bridge course work and supervision of real cases (Binder, 1993a).

Another more serious deficiency in psychotherapy supervision can be inferred from the enormous difficulties that therapists manifest in attempting to detect and then effectively manage the reciprocal hostile interaction patterns that inevitably arise to disrupt therapeutic alliances (Henry, Schacht, & Strupp, 1986; Safran et al., 1990; Strupp, 1980). The skills required to manage interpersonal processes within a therapy dyad constitute perhaps the most important facet of therapeutic competence. These skills involve much more than adherence to prescribed techniques, however. It appears that with difficult interpersonal situations, relatively strict technical adherence tends to produce poor therapeutic process (Foley et al., 1987; Henry, Strupp et al., 1993).

This situation is not so surprising when one realizes that technical expertise refers to rules or algorithms for dealing with problems that have clear and familiar parameters. Psychotherapy is an interpersonal process, however, and interpersonal relationships exemplify what have been referred to as "indeterminate zones" (Schon, 1987). These are problem domains that are characterized by uncertainty, uniqueness, and conflict. As an indeterminate zone, the interpersonal context of psychotherapy is characterized by problem situations that are often ambiguous, contextually unique, and continuously shifting. The prescribed use of even manual-guided techniques as a problem-solving strategy will often be insufficient. What is needed is a particular sort of procedural knowledge that allows for on-the-spot appraisals and reappraisals of the problem situation while one is acting within it. Moreover, based on the unique problem context encountered at the moment, capacities are required for deriving new understandings and new ways of framing the immediately encountered problems, as well as innovative strategies to guide action (Schon, 1987).

The particular sort of procedural knowledge required for this type of activity Schon (1987) has called "reflection-in-action." It is the basis for the ability to *improvise* in problem situations in which standard principles and rules may not apply. We suggest that true therapeutic competence and effectiveness involve becoming proficient in the capacities for reflection-in-action and improvisation. These capacities are essential for comprehending and managing the interpersonal difficulties (i.e., transference and countertransference enactments) that inevitably arise within therapeutic relationships. We further suggest that the concepts, principles, and procedures that are provided by treatment manuals and that are emphasized in manual-guided training (including supervision) can serve as broad parameters for the comprehension and conduct of psychotherapy. It should be recognized, however, that these parameters offer only a sketchy map of the therapeutic terrain on which moment-to-moment movements often must be improvised.

We propose filling the gap between the classroom teaching of declarative knowledge about what therapy is and the generally unsystematic teaching of procedural knowledge through supervision. The purpose of filling this gap between teaching environments would be to foster the integration of declarative and procedural forms of therapeutic knowledge, as well as the initial capacity for improvisation. The gap would be filled with structured sequences of therapeutic problem-detection and problem-solving exercises under conditions that simulate actual clinical experiences. These conditions could be developed through application of interactive computer technology. Video-recorded and computer-digitized segments of real or simulated therapy situations, along with accompanying narratives that offer relevant concepts and principles, could be used as the learning environment for therapy trainees to be coached and to practice identifying and managing various sorts of interpersonal processes associated with therapeutic work and therapeutic dilemmas. For example, a critical skill in conducting psychodynamic therapy is recognition in patient communications of implicit references to transference. The trainee could be exposed to video illustrations accompanied by relevant theoretical narrative, and he or she could be guided through interactive computer programs that offer practice in detecting such communication patterns, along with immediate feedback about the performance of that particular skill. A particular emphasis could be on practicing to identify and cope with "negative process," that is, with various sorts of interpersonal problems created by provocative patient actions. We believe that structured educational activities of this sort are especially needed to improve the basic relationship skills that novice therapists possess when they begin to encounter real patients.

Supervision of actual patients is a teaching format best suited for refining therapeutic skills with an ever broader diversity of persons, problems, and therapeutic situations *after* an initial foundation of declarative and procedural knowledges has been constructed with the aid of structured learning experiences that bridge course work and supervision. The heart of supervision involves the coached practicing of skills under the pressure of responsibility for actual persons. We propose that the trainee would have more self-confidence and use more efficiently what the supervisor has to offer if the trainee brings to it a previously established foundation of therapeutic declarative and procedural knowledges.

CONCLUSION

We have reviewed a representative sample of the literature on psychodynamic psychotherapy supervision, identified what we consider to be several noteworthy deficiencies in the endeavor, and proposed an outline for improving the format of psychodynamic psychotherapy training. We also believe that any new techniques and procedures should be systematically evaluated. We realize that this would entail an investment of substantial resources in training research, a recommendation that thus far has been largely ignored. We remain hopeful, however, and plan to implement our proposals with the resources at our disposal.

REFERENCES

Alexander, L. B., & Luborsky, L. (1986). The Penn helping alliance scales. In L. S. Greenberg & W. M. Pinsof (Eds.), *The psychotherapeutic process: A research handbook* (pp. 325–366). New York: Guilford.

Allen, G. J., Szollos, S. J., & Williams, B. E. (1986). Doctoral students' comparative evaluations of best and worst psychotherapy supervision. *Professional Psychology: Research and Practice, 17,* 91–99.

Alpher, V. S. (1991). Interdependence and parallel process: A case study of structural analysis of social behavior in supervision and short-term dynamic psychotherapy. *Psychotherapy, 28,* 218–231.

Beckham, E. E. (1990). Psychotherapy of depression research at a crossroads: Directions for the 1990s. *Clinical Psychology Review, 10,* 207–228.

Berger, S. S., & Bucholz, E. S. (1993). On becoming a supervisee: Preparation for learning in a supervisory relationship. *Psychotherapy, 30,* 86–92.

Bergin, A. E., & Garfield, S. A. (Eds.). (1994). *Handbook of psychotherapy and behavioral change* (4th ed.). New York: Wiley.

Beutler, L. E., & Kendall, P. C. (1995). Introduction to the special section: The case for training in the provision of psychological therapy. *Journal of Consulting and Clinical Psychology, 63,* 179–181.

Binder, J. L. (1993a). Is it time to improve psychotherapy training? *Clinical Psychology Review, 13,* 301–318.

Binder, J. L. (1993b). Observations on the training of therapists in time-limited dynamic psychotherapy. *Psychotherapy, 30,* 592–598.

Binder, J. L., & Strupp, H. H. (1993). Recommendations for improving psychotherapy training based on experiences with manual-guided training and research: An introduction. *Psychotherapy, 30,* 571–572.

Binder, J. L., Strupp, H. H., Bongar, B., Lee, S. S., Messer, S., & Peake, T. H. (1993). Recommendations for improving psychotherapy training based on experiences with manual-guided training and research: Epilogue. *Psychotherapy, 30,* 599–600.

Bransford, J. D., Franks, J. J., Vye, N. J., & Sherwood, R. D. (1989). New approaches to instruction: Because wisdom can't be told. In S. Vosniadou & A. Ortony (Eds.), *Similarity and analogical reasoning* (pp. 470–497). New York: Cambridge University Press.

Bransford, J. D., & Vye, N. J. (1988). *Research on cognition and its implications for instruction: An overview.* Unpublished manuscript. Vanderbilt University, Nashville, TN.

Bromberg, P. M. (1984). The third ear. In L. Caligor, P. M. Bromberg, & J. D. Meltzer (Eds.), *Clinical perspectives on the supervision of psychoanalysis and psychotherapy* (pp. 29–44). New York: Plenum.

Buckley, P., Conte, H. R., Plutchik, R., Karasu, T. B., & Wild, K. V. (1982). Learning dynamic psychotherapy: A longitudinal study. *American Journal of Psychiatry, 139,* 607–1610.

Burke, M. O. (1991). A philosophy of psychoanalytic training. *Psychoanalytic Psychologist, 11,* 28–31.

Butler, S. F., & Strupp, H. H. (1993). Effects of training experienced dynamic therapists to use a psychotherapy manual. In N. E. Miller, L. Luborsky, J. P. Barber, & J. P. Docherty (Eds.), *Psychodynamic treatment research* (pp. 191–210). New York: Basic Books.

Caligor, L. (1984). Parallel and reciprocal processes in psychoanalytic supervision. In L. Caligor, P. M. Bromberg, & J. D. Meltzer (Eds.), *Clinical perspectives on the supervision of psychoanalysis and psychotherapy* (pp. 1–28). New York: Plenum.

Casement, P. J. (1991). *Learning from the patient.* New York: Guilford.

Chrzanowski, G. (1984). Can psychoanalysis be taught? In L. Caligor, P. M. Bromberg, & J. D. Meltzer (Eds.), *Clinical perspectives on the supervision of psychoanalysis and psychotherapy* (pp. 45–58). New York: Plenum.

Church, E. (1993). Reading the transference in adolescent psychotherapy: A comparison of novice and experienced therapists. *Psychoanalytic Psychology, 10,* 187–205.

Cooper, A., & Witenberg, E. G. (1984). Stimulation of curiosity in the supervisory process. In L. Caligor, P. M. Bromberg, & J. D. Meltzer (Eds.), *Clinical perspectives on the supervision of psychoanalysis and psychotherapy* (pp. 59–74). New York: Plenum.

Corradi, M., Wasman, M., & Gold, F. S. (1980). Teaching about transference: A videotape introduction. *American Journal of Psychotherapy, 34,* 564–571.

Davidson, L. (1987). Integration and learning in the supervisory process. *The American Journal of Psychoanalysis, 47,* 331–341.

Dewald, P. A. (1987). *Learning process in psychoanalytic supervision: Complexities and challenges.* Madison, WI: International Universities Press.

Doehrman, M. J. (1976). Parallel process in supervision and psychotherapy. *Bulletin of the Menninger Clinic, 40,* 1–104.

Ekstein, R., & Wallerstein, R. S. (1972). *The teaching and learning of psychotherapy* (2nd ed.). Madison, WI: International Universities Press.

Feiner, A. H. (1994). Comments on contradictions in the supervisory process. *Contemporary Psychoanalysis, 30,* 57–75.

Foley, S. H., O'Malley, S. S., Rounsaville, B. J., Prusoff, B. A., & Weissman, M. M. (1987). The relationship of patient difficulty to therapist performance in interpersonal psychotherapy of depression. *Journal of Affective Disorders, 12,* 207–217.

Gediman, H. K., & Wolkenfeld, J. (1980). The parallelism phenomenon in psychoanalysis and supervision: Its reconsideration as a triadic system. *Psychoanalytic Quarterly, 49,* 234–255.

Gill, M. M., & Hoffman, I. (1982). *Analysis of transference* (Vol. 2). New York: International Universities Press.

Glass, J. (1986). Personal therapy and the student therapist. *Canadian Journal of Psychiatry, 31,* 304–311.

Glickauf-Hughes, C. (1994). Characterological resistances in psychotherapy supervision. *Psychotherapy, 31,* 58–66.

Haesler, L. (1993). Adequate distance in the relationship between supervisor and supervisee. *International Journal of Psycho-Analysis, 74,* 547–555.

Halgin, R. P., & Murphy, R. A. (1995). Issues in the training of psychotherapists. In B. Bongar & L. E. Beutler (Eds.), *Comprehensive textbook of psychotherapy. Theory and practice* (pp. 434–455). New York: Oxford University Press.

Hanlon, J. (1990). Modes of internalizing the supervisor. *Psychoanalysis and Psychotherapy, 8,* 5–10.

Henry, H. P., Schacht, T. E., & Strupp, H. H. (1986). Structured analysis of racial behavior: Application to a study of interpersonal process in differential psychotherapeutic outcomes. *Journal of Consulting and Clinical Psychology, 54,* 27–31.

Henry, W. P., Schacht, T. E., Strupp, H. H., Butler, S. F., & Binder, J. L. (1993). Effects of training in time-limited dynamic psychotherapy: Mediators of therapists' responses to training. *Journal of Consulting and Clinical Psychology, 61,* 441–447.

Henry, W. P., Strupp, H. H., Butler, S. F., Schacht, T. E., & Binder, J. L. (1993). Effects of training in time-limited dynamic psychotherapy: Changes in therapist behavior. *Journal of Consulting and Clinical Psychology, 61,* 434–440.

Holloway, E. L. (1987). Developmental models of supervision: Is it development? *Professional Psychology: Research and Practice, 18,* 209–216.

Holloway, E. L., & Neufeldt, S. A. (1995). Supervision: Its contributions to treatment efficacy. *Journal of Consulting and Clinical Psychology, 63,* 207–213.

Horvath, A., & Greenberg, L. S. (1986). The development of the working alliance inventory. In L. S. Greenberg & W. M. Pinsoff (Eds.), *The psychotherapeutic process: A research handbook* (pp. 529–556). New York: Guilford.

Issacharoff, A. (1984). Countertransference in supervision. Therapeutic consequences for the supervisee. In L. Caligor, P. M. Bromberg, & J. D. Meltzer (Eds.), *Clinical perspectives on the supervision of psychoanalysis and psychotherapy* (pp. 89–105). New York: Plenum.

Josephs, L. (1990). The concrete attitude and the supervision of beginning psychotherapists. *Psychoanalysis and Psychotherapy, 8,* 11–22.

Lambert, M. J., & Arnold, R. C. (1987). Research and the supervisory process. *Professional Psychology: Research and Practice, 18,* 217–224.

Langs, R. (1979). *The supervisory experience.* New York: Jason Aronson.

Langs, R. (1994). Supervision in training institutes. *Contemporary Psychoanalysis, 30,* 75–82.

Lesser, R. M. (1984). Illusions, anxieties, and questions. In L. Caligor, P. M. Bromberg, & J. D. Meltzer (Eds.), *Clinical perspectives on the supervision of psychoanalysis and psychotherapy* (pp. 143–152). New York: Plenum.

Levenson, E. A. (1984). Follow the fox. In L. Caligor, P. M. Bromberg, & J. D. Meltzer (Eds.), *Clinical perspectives on the supervision of psychoanalysis and psychotherapy* (pp. 153–168). New York: Plenum.

Martin, G. C., Mayerson, P., Olsen, H. E., & Wiberg, J. L. (1977). Candidates' evaluation of psychoanalytic supervision. *Bulletin of the American Psychoanalytic Association, 34,* 407–424.

Moldawsky, S. (1980). Psychoanalytic psychotherapy supervision. In A. K. Hess (Ed.), *Psychotherapy supervision. Theory, research and practice* (pp. 126–135). New York: Wiley.

Mollon, P. (1987). Anxiety, supervision and a space for thinking: Some narcissistic perils for clinical psychologists in learning psychotherapy. *British Journal of Medical Psychology, 62,* 113–122.

Newman, C. (1986). Psychoanalytic supervision and the larger truth. *The American Journal of Psychoanalysis, 46,* 263–269.

Norcross, J. C., & Prochaska, J. O. (1982). A national survey of clinical psychologists: Views on training, career choice, and APA. *Clinical Psychologist, 35,* 3–6.

Rodenhauser, P. (1994). Toward a multidimensional model for psychotherapy supervision based on developmental stages. *Journal of Psychotherapy Practice and Research, 3*, 1–15.

Sachs, D., & Shapiro, S. (1976). On parallel process in therapy and teaching. *Psychoanalytic Quarterly, 45*, 394–415.

Safran, J. D., Crocker, P., McMain, S., & Murray, P. (1990). Therapeutic alliance rupture as a therapy event for empirical investigation. *Psychotherapy, 27*, 154–165.

Sarnat, J. E. (1992). Supervision in relationship: Resolving the teach-treat controversy in psychoanalytic supervision. *Psychoanalytic Psychology, 9*, 387–403.

Schimel, J. L. (1984). In pursuit of the truth. An essay on an epistemological approach to psychoanalytic supervision. In L. Caligor, P. M. Bromberg, & J. D. Meltzer (Eds.), *Clinical perspectives on the supervision of psychoanalysis and psychotherapy* (pp. 231–242). New York: Plenum.

Schon, D. A. (1987). *Educating the reflective practitioner* San Francisco: Jossey-Bass.

Searles, H. F. (1965). The information value of the supervisor's emotional experiences. In *Collected papers on schizophrenia and related subjects* (pp. 157–176). New York: International Universities Press.

Shanfield, S. B., Matthews, K. L., & Hetherely, V. (1993). What do excellent psychotherapy supervisors do? *American Journal of Psychiatry, 150*, 1081–1084.

Shechter, R. A. (1990). Becoming a supervisor: A phase in professional development. *Psychoanalysis and Psychotherapy, 8*, 23–28.

Stein, D. M., & Lambert, M. J. (1995). Graduate training in psychotherapy: Are therapy outcomes enhanced? *Journal of Consulting and Clinical Psychology, 63*, 182–196.

Strupp, H. H. (1980). Success and failure in time-limited psychotherapy. Further evidence (Comparison 4). *Archives of General Psychiatry, 37*, 947–954.

Strupp, H. H., (1993) The Vanderbilt psychotherapy studies: Synopsis. *Journal of Consulting and Clinical Psychology, 61*, 431–433.

Strupp, H. H., & Binder, J. L. (1984). *Psychotherapy in a new key: A guide to time-limited dynamic psychotherapy*. New York: Basic Books.

Strupp, H. H., Butler, S. F., & Rosser, C. L. (1988). Training in psychodynamic therapy. *Journal of Consulting and Clinical Psychology, 56*, 689–695.

Teitelbaum, S. H. (1990). Supertransference: The role of the supervisor's blind spots. *Psychoanalytic Psychology, 7*, 243–258.

Tennen, H. (1988). Supervision of integrated psychotherapy. A critique. *Journal of Integrative and Eclectic Psychotherapy, 7*, 167–175.

Thorbeck, J. (1992). The development of the psychodynamic psychotherapist in supervision. *Academic Psychiatry, 16*, 72–82.

Watkins, C. E., Jr. (1995). Psychotherapy supervisor development. On musings, models, and metaphor. *Journal of Psychotherapy Practice and Research, 4*, 150–158.

Wolstein, B. (1994). Notes on psychoanalytic supervision (brief commentary). *Contemporary Psychoanalysis, 30*, 182–191.

CHAPTER 5

The Interpersonal Approach to the Supervision of Psychotherapy

ALLEN K. HESS
Auburn University at Montgomery

If this were a chapter concerning psychotherapy supervision from a "traditional" theoretical viewpoint, we could proceed with little preamble to the issues concerning the teaching and learning of psychotherapy and counseling.[1] The interpersonal perspective, however, poses certain dilemmas. No single, clear theoretical statement, no single theorist who articulated the complete interpersonal viewpoint, and no institute or set of journals serve as a signature for the interpersonal viewpoint. Yet the central propositions of the interpersonal perspective are self-evident to the point that stating the propositions may lead the reader to say "So what? We knew that already." The reader may respond as did the shocked first-year student who reported to his parents after the first day in English class at college, "Do you know that we have been speaking prose for years?"

This self-evidence leads to another paradox. A theory can lack a "cultural presence" in which "no one has to know about it or take it into account to appear less than ignorant; no one will be held accountable for ignoring it" (Dworkin as cited in Paris, 1994, p. xvii). A handbook such as this one that lacked a psychodynamic or behavioral perspective would need to explain that absence. The lack of an interpersonal chapter would regrettably not be challenged. It is with pleasure, then, that we can embark here in creating for this approach a "cultural presence."

This chapter first provides the flavor of the interpersonal approach by presenting its basic precepts. This presentation is necessarily nonexhaustive because interpersonal theory has developed a rich and diverse literature, but the précis helps the reader understand the second section. The second section applies the interpersonal approach to the supervisory situation. What becomes apparent is the seamless way the interpersonal approach encompasses everyday interactions, the individual and group psychotherapy situation, and the supervision of psychotherapy. In effect, the interpersonal approach is a theory of psychotherapy supervision and perhaps the only wholly articulated one. The basis for this assertion follows.

[1]The terms *psychotherapy* and *counseling* are used interchangeably here as the operations of psychotherapists and counselors are indistinguishable.

The author extends gratitude to Kathryn D. Hess, Sigrid A. Hess, Sheila Mehta, and Peter Zachar for suggesting changes that have improved the chapter, although they should not be held accountable for the suggestions the author was too obdurate to adapt.

63

THE INTERPERSONAL APPROACH

Psychology is the study of experience; psychotherapy is the involvement by one in the stability and change of another's experience; and supervision is the development of psychotherapy skills in the student. The interpersonal approach speaks to the core of psychology, psychotherapy, and the supervision of psychotherapy because its focus is the human experience in relationship. For Kelly (1955) the root metaphor of a theory was the "focus" of that theory and the area to which it could be maximally applied. The "scope" of a theory is the phenomena to which it is or could be extended. Interpersonal theory does not concern itself with rats, cats, and pigeons, although it contains a learning theory with five processes ranging from simple association (Sullivan's, 1953, parataxic mode) through the eduction of relations (higher order judgments; Carson, 1969). Interpersonal theory does not live or die by the couch or the dream although mental processes are integral to its approach.

The focus of interpersonal theory is the relationship people have with others. That relationship is the essence of their psychological development or ontogeny. Whereas psychoanalytic approaches provide the "text" and interiorization of personal experience (making sure the individual owns experiences that may have external sources) and behaviorism provides a "context" trying to show the exterior determinants of human experience (pseudo-objectifying what are nonquantifiable experiences), *the interpersonal approach provides the relationship between text and context.*[2] Strupp (1958) recognized "that psychotherapy is characterized not only by its techniques, but also the personal relationship between the patient and his therapist" (p. 34; cf. Strupp, 1962). Perhaps the best way to understand interpersonal psychotherapy supervision is to consider some basic precepts of the interpersonal approach.

Precepts

1. *There is a psychological reality.* One can convincingly argue that the psychological reality is more palpable than physical reality in human affairs. For example, consumers will rush to a store that offers $10 off a $20 item but not travel to a shop that offers 10% off a $200 item. Logically, one would more likely travel to save $20 than $10, but consumers will be more attracted to the 50% savings than the 10% savings. Clearly, more than logic determines our psychological reality.

2. *These realities are based on a "psychologic" rather than a "rational" logic.* Consider two students who claim to be absent for a final exam because of a flat tire. The professor gives a makeup exam consisting of a 5-point question on a sheet of paper and a 95-point item on the back side of the sheet. The latter question is, "Which tire was flat?" One's immediate response to the chances that both students answered the same, given no collusion or factuality to the story, would be 1 in 16. However, logically the answer is 1 in 4. Or, finally, consider that you have a $10 or a $20 bill in your pocket. You add a $10 bill. Later, without looking, you remove a $10 bill. What are the chances that the remaining bill is a $10 bill? It may seem that the odds are 1 in 2 that a $10 bill remains, but the odds are 2 in 3 that the remaining bill is a $10 bill. Emotions, too, determine or value our cognitions. For example, our graduate admissions committee circulates folios to three gradu-

---

[2]The principles of the interpersonal approach are italicized, in no order of relative importance, for the reader's ease in recounting them.

ate faculty for their decision as to admit or deny admission to our program. One faculty member, Bob, was upset that another, Ginny, always gave the folios to Bill. Bob complained to me and attributed various prejudices to Ginny about why she never gave him any folios. I asked Ginny why she gave the folios to Bill and not to Bob. She said she knew Bill did not like to perform this departmental service so she was pestering him with the task (Ginny and Bill have a relationship based on nettling each other). She said she had no problem giving Bob the folios but will miss pestering Bill. Bob had a reality different from Ginny's. I went back to my office with a good example for this chapter. We decide and act based on the realities as we know them.

3. *Two modes of communication are central to the interpersonal experience.* The *analogic* mode uses similarity as its basis, has no negative cases ("I do not mean to hurt you" obviously means the speaker has infliction of pain on his or her mind), has a "thingness" quality, is psychological, has scope, operates with a "primary process" quality, and is imbued with emotion. It dwells in the semantics of relationship but has no syntax for the unambiguous definition of relationship. That is, the experience of the relationship is all-encompassing whereas inconsistencies and their resolutions are irrelevant. On the other hand, the *digital* mode operates by convention, based on social consensus, is precise, and has negative cases. For example, "I did not buy flowers for my wife because she suspects me of infidelity" is logical, operates with "secondary process" characteristics, has a powerful syntax but no semantics, and is cognitive. The analogic is the experience whereas the digital is the account of the experience. Paradox begins here as the account of the experience is putatively digital but is experiential for both the sender and the receiver of the communication (see the earlier sentences about the flowers.)

4. *The essence of human experience involves cognitive and emotional processes.* Cognition, working through the digital mode, tends to be enduring and obeys rules of syntax. Emotions are quick to erupt in a seemingly unpredictable fashion, to co-opt or short-circuit cognitions, and to focus around a particular interpersonal event. When anxiety and *security operations*, Sullivan's term for defensive maneuvers, can be assuaged so the person can examine his or her emotions, patterns can be detected. These can lead to "corrective emotional experiences."

For example, a student, Tam, who was like a daughter to me and my family, died tragically at the age of 22 from lupus. I thought the minister delivered a bad sermon. I became increasingly angry over the next few days. I reflected on how I handled my parents' deaths and realized that I had taken care of all the chores at work that needed attention during my absence for mourning, arranged for my family's travel to my parents' funerals, and after practical affairs were in place, became rageful at the medical (mal)treatment I felt my parents had received. Similarly, I took care of notifying the student's adviser and other faculty and fellow students of Tam's death before I allowed myself to feel Tam's death. Several days after her death, the minister delivered that horrible sermon. I was furious at him for not learning enough about her to deliver a decent eulogy. I found someone in authority who botched his responsibilities in a time when he was needed and found a target for my anger. What does this affective-emotive-behavioral pattern mean about my personality, patterns, identity formation, and the possibility for personal growth?

5. The interpersonal approach sees *people as more or less aware of their mental life*, with the notion of an unconscious-preconscious-conscious dimension as less useful and a potential philosophical snare. The paradigmatic shift from the behaviorism of the 1950 to 1970 era and the cognitivism of the 1970 to 1990 era to an emergence of emotions (Hess, 1996) makes the interpersonal even more relevant today. Mental life and levels of awareness are back in fashion, newly conceptualized and thriving. The need to explore one's mental life fits the interpersonal approach well, as seen by research such as Cacioppo, Petty, Feinstein, and Jarvis (1996) on the need for cognition, Haviland and Reise (1996) on the absence of emotional sense, and Goldberg (1990) on the openness to experience factor of the Big Five.

6. *The search for cause and effect is often chimerical, or a wild goose chase in the functionalistic interpersonal approach.* When we probe for unconscious motivation, the implicit question we are asking is the "why?" of an action. The "what for" of a behavior or a feeling or a cognition is there when the "why" remains obscure, unknowable, and often misleading. Is it important to know why a dependent woman and a narcissistic man (my construals of their personality constellations) became the way they are or is it more important to know how they are functioning today in a marriage that seems fully satisfying to both? Why a person was born with certain genetic endowments or into a particularly beneficial or malignant home can be important, but more important is what the individual does with the hand he or she is dealt. Abraham Lincoln is supposed to have said that a person, after the age of 40, is responsible for his or her face. One may be endowed with beauty or not. Yet in the decades since birth, a person etches character lines on his or her persona. Those lines are the person's responsibility. The way a person answers the "what for" question leaves a residue both physically and mentally. Interpersonal theory is functionalistic in the tradition of William James and John Dewey.

7. Having placed cause and effect in a secondary role, it is easy to see that the *past, present, and future melt away in importance in the face of the contemporaneous.* Field theory (Lewin, 1951) places primacy on the field-as-currently-perceived. The past, the present, and the future are construed in the here and now. One patient searched the past for 2 years in therapy trying to find out why he sexually failed his wife. Only when he was continually brought to his present relationship with her and the functional payoff of his playing the role of an impotent husband did dream fragments emerge that allowed him flashes of an image of his mother. He recalled his mother, when he was 11 years old, giving him rubdowns while he was naked and of his lying in bed with her. Sex had come to mean incest for him. As his anxiety waxed and waned, he experienced less or more of the fragment until he knew he had to change or face the responsibility of not changing.

8. *The interpersonal approach uses units of analysis that function on multiple levels.* These include the molecular or even microscopic concept of the "gaze" (Buber, 1965a, 1965b, 1970) through behavioral and communicative sequences (Benjamin, 1974, 1994; Lakoff, 1982) to the molar or even macro existential essence of one's identity. Buber might examine the "Thank-you-for-shopping-Kmart" mantra that the clerks are taught and see the paradox of seemingly trying to welcome the customer but in such an automatic way as to put off the customer instead. As the recipient of this gratuitous gratitude, I responded in a personal way to the cashier one day, saying, "Gosh, it seems you have had a long day." Her masklike face broke into a grin and she said, "It sure has been. A few of the cashiers are down with the flu and we are picking up the slack. Gee, thank you for noticing." Buber recognized personalizing the impersonal on the level of what he terms the "gaze" or smallest unit of interpersonal interaction. He sees this molecular approach as the pathway to the macroscopic concept of the person's identity.

McAdams (1995) describes a useful three-level approach by which we can know personality. Level I consists of traits. Thus, an MMPI, or a content analysis of a TAT, or a sociometric rating or a behavioral count of out-of-seat-time of an unruly student provides the basis for decontextualized, nonconditional constructs. That is, we can say a person is a "2–7 anxious depressive code type," or high in nApp (need for approval), or undisciplined, which provides dispositional, trait statements. Level II, "personal concerns," involves one's strivings, defenses, motives, and goals. Information on this level can be found in the ecology of people's lives, their salient settings and the scripts or patterns they follow in that ecology. Level III concerns the problem of the overall unity and purpose of one's life, one's identity. Identity is an evolving internalized life story or personal myth.

For the interpersonal theorist, all three levels are valid ways of understanding. Communication occurs on multiple levels, each having both characteristic and interrelated units. For example, a pressured use of a word may be a subtle emanation that is behaviorally recognizable (Level I), may express a particular response to an anxiety-laden recurrent pattern, and may characterize part of the identity of the person. One cannot ignore or reduce Level II motives or defenses as typical of an extrovert or anxious person. Nor can one reduce a Level I description to some component of identity. The three levels are irreducible. This multilevel approach places more responsibility on the interpersonal theorist and clinician to master micro and macro explanations and provides two important advantages to the interpersonal supervisor. First, there are so many more tools at his or her disposal. Second, relating with supervisees of different theoretical stripes should be easy for the interpersonal supervisor.

9. *The interpersonal includes the subjective within a wholly empirical base.* The interpersonal approach is based on the person's experience, yet this experience is empirical and subject to assessment. One can research molecular behaviors such as posture, eye contact, and facial expression (Mahl, 1968), self and other rating scales (Leary, 1957), larger sequences of behavior such as complementary relationships (Benjamin, 1974, 1994; Duke & Nowicki, 1982), and molar narrative accounts (Bennis, Schein, Steele, & Berlew, 1968) in developing empirically grounded bases for inferences and interventions in the interpersonal approach.

10. *The interpersonal recognizes the repetitive patterns of communications (behaviors, feelings, and cognitions).* Benjamin (1974, 1994) applied sophisticated statistical models to reveal communications patterns. Mahl (1968) showed a frame-by-frame analysis of a family therapy session to reveal certain ritualistic ways the therapist and family employ to gain one another's attention. And Berne (1964) became immortalized in showing the public the *Games People Play*, a best-seller that is still one of the clearer expositions of the interpersonal approach.

11. *Interpersonal interaction is the basis for the human experience and is theater for diagnosis, psychotherapy, and supervision.* If personality is "the relatively enduring pattern of recurrent interpersonal situations that characterize a human life" (Sullivan, 1953, pp. 110-111), if people interact by way of a "reciprocal process in which (1) complementary needs are resolved, or aggravated, (2) reciprocal patterns of activity are developed, or disintegrated, and (3) foresight of satisfaction, or rebuff, or similar needs is facilitated" (Sullivan, 1953, p. 198), and if each step in an interactive process narrows the following behavioral and communicative options, then interacting with someone allows me to experience the way he or she evokes responses in me.

Similarly, I can observe my typical responses, or countertransference strain, in similar and different situations and explore the way I respond to others. Sullivan knew hysterics irritated him; he believed they wasted time he could be spending treating schizophrenics who needed him. I notice that when I behave like a cheerleader, I am usually dealing with a depressed person. Clarity and support characterize my voice, message, and feelings when I work with schizophrenics. Diagnostic cues abound in the interaction; psychotherapy is possible only through interaction.

12. *Emotions are contagious and fundamental to the human experience.* Sullivan (1953, p. 80) uses the metaphor of the "good and satisfactory nipple-in-the-lips," the "good but unsatisfactory nipple-in-the-lips," the "wrong nipple-in-the-lips," and the "evil nipple" to express the idea that what is conveyed to the infants in relationship with their caregiver is an emotional exchange. Caregiving does not mean merely physical nourishment but refers to the anxieties, tensions, avoidances, and rejections versus the secure and satisfying place-in-the-world that infants and all other human beings crave. The emotional exchange is known to us all when we reflect on our reactions to different people. I recall several friends whose mere presence brightens a room for everyone there. Some people evoke suspicion and distrust, and others can have a group doubled over in laughter in a few moments.

One person needs only to be in interaction with another, no matter the role he or she occupies, to effect change. Kaiser's play *Emergency* (Fierman, 1965) describes a psychotherapist who is hired to treat a psychiatrist by the psychiatrist's wife after the psychiatrist lost a patient to suicide and suffered withdrawal. The wrinkle is the psychotherapist is to enter the relationship with the psychiatrist as a patient of the psychiatrist, all fees being paid by the wife, unknown to the psychiatrist. The psychotherapist is supposed to effect change from his position as a patient. Kaiser's idea is that one universal disorder, the "illusion of fusion," results in duplicitous communication, the cure for which is authentic communication. Given that communication is a complex affair with affective tones and latent meanings comprising most of a communication, Kaiser questions whether it matters that the participants are called patient or doctor as long as communication is nonduplicitous. When with another person, the feelings you experience and he or she experiences will be communicated.

13. *One cannot not behave.* Since the analogic mode can have only the positive instance, even silence is a communication. One beautiful irony of classical psychoanalysis is that the analysand's utterances are interpretable, and when the analysand is silent, that, too, can be interpreted as resistance (Haley, 1963). As stated earlier (precept 3), if someone tells you, "I really am not thinking of breaking up with my spouse," the positive instance must be considered. The implications for teaching students to assume an attentive, open posture but not needing to act since the patient has to behave can often boost the student through a most difficult stage of learning how to conduct psychotherapy: that of being asocial.

14. *Psychotherapy involves being asocial.* Two rules distinguish ordinary discourse from psychotherapy conversation. In contrast with the ordinary conversant, the psychotherapist can be asocial (Young & Beier, 1982). I can choose not to respond to a patient's request for a tissue or to respond with silence when asked to tell him or her the time. If the psychotherapist senses a ploy or part of a pattern of interaction that needs confrontation, he or she can behave in a way that would be considered rude or out of sorts in a social situation. Of course, the effective psychotherapist does not just confront without sufficient time to process the interaction. Learning must occur. The proper use of confrontation is not for the therapist's need gratification but as a tool useful in examining some problematic pattern of conduct.

15. *Cure occurs through authentic communication.* I have wondered why psychotherapists of various theoretical persuasions put patients on couches or have them snap rubber bands on their wrists to eliminate bad habits or encourage patients to beat pillows on the pathway toward self-actualization, yet, when seeking a psychotherapist for him- or herself, the psychotherapist looks for someone who will listen caringly and communicate authentically (Hess, 1987). Surely all the various theories have points that are useful and practitioners who are skilled. Yet, the interpersonal position maintains that the medium and the message of psychotherapy is the relationship, a view that is confirmed when psychotherapists seek their own psychotherapist. For example, Stampfl (Stampfl & Levis, 1967), the creator of implosive therapy, exposes phobic patients in a most unrelenting fashion to the object they find most repugnant and terror provoking. When asked afterward why they allowed themselves to be subjected to this terror, they said that Dr. Stampfl's warmth, care, and concern were their source of strength. Interestingly, such prominent theorists and practitioners as Lazarus (1995) and Davidson (1995) are finding their allegiance to behavioral models waning in favor of a more interpersonal stance. The trend to use "integrative," "transtheoretical," or "eclectic" notions has gathered momentum. However, do not construe my position as supporting eclecticism.

16. *Purposive eclecticism is a muddling of metaphors.* Pepper (1942) describes accidental and purposive eclecticism. The former is natural when someone explores ideas from various viewpoints and is an outgrowth of intellectual curiosity. On our pathway toward developing theoretical sophistication, accidental eclecticism is where we happen to be at a particular moment. Purposive eclecticism is the attempt to meld different theories into one. The latter becomes a problem when the metatheoretical assumptions and the root metaphors of the theories differ. Such exercises end with mixed metaphors or a "model muddle."

For example, provoking frustration, for the closed energy system metaphor, usually results in mobilization of some form of a defense mechanism. For the growth or the ego psychoanalytic model, it may invoke introspection and subsequent creativity. Learning theories might predict that frustration provokes displays of primitive behavior. If a psychotherapist mixes models, then predictions, and perhaps more important, the ability to see where one erred, can be lost in the model muddle. Interpersonal theory incorporates the key aspects of human behavior, which most theories must address although they will do it partially, leaving the interpersonal therapist able to use knowledge from other approaches while remaining faithful to its root metaphor, the human relationship.

THE SUPERVISION OF PSYCHOTHERAPY

Psychotherapy supervision "is a relationship in which one person's skills in conducting psychotherapy and his or her identity as a therapist are intentionally and potentially enhanced by the interaction with another person" (Hess, 1987, pp. 255-256). How does this interaction begin in successful psychotherapy supervision? Something occurs in the life of the supervisee[3] that brings him or her to supervision. The supervisee has usually completed some prerequisite courses that lead to a practicum or has completed an academic program and is embarking on an internship. Or a new job or the licensing process may have brought the person to the supervisor. Sometimes a practitioner feels the need for continuing development or is stuck with a case and needs to see the case through the eyes of a professional he or she respects and trusts.

In each of these possibilities there is either an implicit or an explicit expression of trust. A student in a training or internship program is assigned a teacher or supervisor, and trust is implied in the role of the latter. The institution or agency by way of the assignment has implied that the supervisor is competent, interested, and trustworthy. Dysfunctional supervision can occur when these qualities (Carifio & Hess, 1987) are lacking in the supervi-

[3]The terms *student* and *supervisee* are used interchangeably as are the terms *teacher* and *supervisor.*

sor. In the case in which supervision has more of an elective quality, the supervisee may say to the supervisor when contracting for his or her services: "I am interested in going over a case with you since you have helped me with such cases before (or you have helped my colleague with similar cases, or you might be someone I can learn from, or you seem as if you will do me no harm)." The parenthesized comments are succeedingly more "unconscious" or unstated, the last of which may remain unstated even to the supervisee. Now the last statement may raise an eyebrow or two. What sort of harm do we mean?

Learning Tasks.   The supervision has several learning tasks. Sometimes the supervision may occur with the simple goal of demystification of psychotherapy (Hess, 1986; Yogev, 1982). That is, the new therapists have primitive and idealized notions of psychotherapy learned from the media or from their own therapy experience or from our cultural folklore.

Supervision may have the teaching of technique as a goal. The group psychotherapist, hypnotist, behavior analyst, or interpersonal theorist suggests readings and helps the student implement the strategies and tactics of the orientation. Much of traditional supervision is focused on this task.

The third task may be the development of the therapist's personality as the fulcrum for personality change. Indeed, all three of the tasks have in common the therapist's emerging identity as a psychotherapist who can realize certain ideals as a healer or comforter without the impediment of accompanying idealizations, who can use techniques competently both to help the patient and to bring personal satisfaction of the competence motive, and who can congeal an identity or, better yet, who can develop an internalized learning process that can provide a fulfilling identity as a master of psychotherapy.

Thus, the supervisees entrust their future identity to the supervisor. Students risk exposing their work, their self-as-a-psychotherapist, and the possibility of condemnation and shame (Talbot, 1995). The supervisee's presence, in all but the psychopathic supervisee, suggests the opportunity to work on the identity development of the supervisee as a therapist. Simultaneously, the supervisor has the opportunity to develop his or her identity as a "psychotherapist's psychotherapist," or a supervisor, more of which will be discussed later.

The Inception

The two[4] participants meet within one of the contexts noted earlier, that is, in the student-teacher, intern-supervisor, or junior colleague–expert role (Hess, 1980a) and proceed by defining their roles and expectations. Naturally, such issues as whether the supervision is graded and how the grades are transmitted to whatever authority, such as a faculty or a licensing board, should be discussed at this point.

Evaluation.   Humans are constantly evaluating and self-evaluating (Jarvis & Petty, 1996), which raises anxiety that inhibits learning. I find the typical supervisee highly motivated, eager to do well, and fraught with evaluation anxiety, having been well conditioned in the art of grade seeking from kindergarten through graduate school. Anxiety-laden grade seeking can interfere with the type of learning involved in supervision. In fact, it appears that "It is not possible to view a social object or a social act without at the same time making an assessment on dimensions closely corresponding to good/bad, pleasant/unpleasant, etc." (Markus & Zajonc, 1985, p. 210), and "*evaluation* . . . is assumed to be among the most

---

[4]The dyadic model will be used here but the same principles hold for multiple supervisions that include more than one supervisee or more than one supervisor.

pervasive and dominant human responses" (Jarvis & Petty, 1996, p. 172). I defuse evaluation by agreeing with the student that what occurs in supervision stays in supervision except (a) actions involving imminent harm and (b) obligations to provide training committees with a grade or performance evaluation. The latter I further defuse by saying that progress will be noted as a 5 or 6 on a 1–7 point scale or 8 or 9 on a 1–10 scale used by some agencies.

Intrinsic motivation can be used best by reducing the role of formal reward and coercive power (an "A" grade or a setback on the practicum or internship, respectively), and instead, using informal expert and referent power (French & Raven, 1959). The fundamental goal of interpersonal supervision is to inculcate internalized learning processes. Simply put, the learning that stays with people 1 and 5 and 20 years later is not mediated by the search for an "A" but is the residue of nourishing supervisory experiences. These take the form of internalized sets of images and processes. We learn better from endogenous motivations, and when what we learn is used successfully, our sense of competence works to help form our identity—in this case, that of a competent psychotherapist. Barnat (1974) describes the "affirmation hunger" of the budding psychotherapist as a powerful drive in supervision.

Some Ethical Concerns.   Newman (1981) outlines most of the overt ethical issues that need discussion. These include the superordinate-subordinate relationship of the supervisor and student, the qualifications to supervise, the responsibilities of the supervisor, the trainees' interests, the goals, the methods, and the confidentiality of supervision.

Are Psychotherapy and Supervision Indistinguishable?   The goal of supervision is to develop the psychotherapist's use of his or her cognitions, affect, and conduct in helping other people (Hess, 1980b, 1987). The goal is not psychotherapy of the supervisee. To conduct supervision as psychotherapy of the student is to violate the basic learning contract. Students should go to a psychotherapist, not to a supervisor, for psychotherapy (Burns & Holloway, 1989). In a psychotherapy setting, the psychotherapist should be free of conflicting interests such as grading the student or having any gatekeeping function. The goals of supervision are to educate students, to coach their performance (sometimes even taking the role of cheerleader to encourage their attempts at a new therapeutic technique), and to help the trainees develop their "therapeutic personality." If the supervision has as its goal the psychotherapy of the student, then malpractice may be occurring. Too often the supervisor who is untrained in supervision and has no real commitment to read the literature and to student development may fall back on his or her own extant skills, that is, to do psychotherapy. On the other hand, the process of growing a therapeutic personality in supervision appears indistinguishable from psychotherapy.

In supervision, the issues to which the supervisee attends, the way he or she intervenes, what the student chooses to bring to the supervision are all a function of his or her values and are open to inquiry. The problems students have in conducting psychotherapy depend on their personality. Naturally, the material of supervision will involve personal issues. Nevertheless, the focus should always be on the issues as they relate to the student as psychotherapist, not to the student as patient. To avoid the former is to do partial supervision; to focus on the latter may be malpractice. How does the supervisor know the difference?

Several key issues help the supervisor define appropriate supervision. First, students may invite the supervisor to enter their affective anamnestic world to help with a case. For example, a student of mine was furious with a university counseling center client, a coed who wore puffy bedroom slippers, a robe with a nightie under it, and hair curlers to the session. Her concern was whether to date the fellow with the Ferrari or the Corvette. The novice psychotherapist was a devout Roman Catholic who was contemplating marriage. He realized his emotional reaction was out of proportion to the coed's actions. He brought up his fears that his fiancee would not be as serious as he was about the marriage and about his intellectualism. The coed signified the "shadow" or was a screen on which he could play out his fears of a frivolous wife. That became relevant for supervision as to that case in particular and as to learning to abstain from gratifying or acting out one's emotions in psychotherapy.

It is a poor supervisor who uses supervision to do psychotherapy on each student rather than focusing on how the student may be more effective with his or her case. Although emotions should be subject to supervision, the personal history becomes part of a territory that may better be reserved for psychotherapy. Rubin (1989) opines,

> I speak and hear often about how supervision is not therapy. This is not in dispute. Yet it may not always be either helpful or necessary to dichotomize our listening and intervention skills in the therapeutic and supervisory situations. . . . The use of the supervisor's skills as psychotherapist—identifying difficulties; considering the appropriate timing and focus of an intervention; having the ability to tolerate and contain the anxieties encountered on both sides; and finding the means to communicate to the other—are of particular significance in the critical supervisory process. (p. 395)

A second key issue in distinguishing psychotherapy from supervision is whether the student's case remains the content of the supervision. The process of interpersonal supervision is certainly the supervisory interaction between the supervisor and the student, but the content should remain centered on the student's case. For example, a rigid, rule-bound, humorless student brought a case of child psychotherapy to supervision. She was puzzled about why the child sat mute in the play therapy room. I asked her what had happened from the beginning of the session including how she greeted the child. She said she explained to the child that in play he could do whatever he wanted. Then he hurled a drum against the wall. She told him he could not do that. Then he started banging two trucks together loudly. She told him he could not do that. He tossed items around. She told him he could not do that. Supervision became a matter of asking her to take his role, to examine what she told him about the rules, and then to recall what she told him in the room. Could she see any contradictions? Was his response understandable given the conflict? Focusing on her rigidity in supervision would have made her more rigid. Focusing on the child, for whom she had empathy, allowed her to ask for guidance. I told her that concerns for the room, for noise in the clinic, for her safety should the child throw toys were reasonable. Perhaps modifying her opening comments to the child may be in order. She mentioned the problem of unclear communication in the first session and then told the child what was and was not allowed in the play therapy room. The next session went better. She happily reported that the child interacted with her instead of disliking her.

The Emotional Tone of Supervision. The supervision is being defined at this stage in several other ways. To what extent will the supervisor be open to the student's opinions or prefer a more didactic teaching role? Who will speak, for how long, and in what order? There are both symmetries and complementarities to relationships. In this case, the asymmetry of a gatekeeper and a novice wishing into a profession may stimulate powerful authoritarian conflicts. Relationships operate simultaneously on multiple levels, resulting in potential dilemmas. For example, when a teacher holds a seminar in the classroom or in his or her home, most of the role structure might remain the same, but in the home the student is faced with a new level of intimacy or openness to a side of the teacher not usually available to the student. In cotherapy, the senior clinician or teacher may invite critical analysis of an intervention, making the role relationship more horizontal and even reversing the roles briefly. Of course, at a deeper level the relationship is being defined in terms of the "residual rules" (Scheff, 1963) or "things that go without saying" such as what are the rules of interaction that will be acceptable to both parties. If the experience is graded in some fashion, can the student avoid the role strain or double bind of critiquing the person who is grading the student? Are some rules that are spoken (supervisor as cotherapist: "you can criticize me") actually followed? Does the teacher react in a pique when the student's adulation is not forthcoming regarding an intervention the two people regard differently?

Some issues at this phase of supervision are captured in Peterson and Siddle (1995) who outline (a) privacy rights, (b) loyalty in relationships, (c) obligations connected with promising silence, and (d) professional ethical codes. These issues may or may not be explicitly discussed but are always issues that help supervision succeed or fail.

Ellis and Douce (1994) see three sets of ethical concerns in group supervision of novice therapists. Supervisor issues include supervisor anxiety and choice of intervention; group process issues include competition versus collaboration, and supervisor-supervisee issues include balancing of responsibilities for student and patient growth, parallel process, power struggles, sexual attraction, and individual differences. These concerns can become the preoccupation of the "detailed inquiry" phase of supervision discussed later.

Manifest goals are usually stated, but Lehman, Gorsuch, and Mintz (1985) indicate that the goals of psychotherapy are moving targets, with emerging problems occurring in more than half (56%) of the cases. So, too, the goals of psychotherapy supervision may shift. The seemingly consensual goal statements agreed upon by the supervisor and the supervisee may become replaced or redefined during the supervision since the nature of interpersonal communication involves learning how each party attributes semantic value to statements.

Communication and Signification: Defining the Interpersonal Supervision. In fact, communication rules are negotiated from the outset in the interactions of supervision. Much like the child who was told to do anything in the play therapy room but learned that was not what the psychotherapist meant, what actually happens in supervision redefines the manifest rules. The interpersonal supervisor listens to the student's language to assess the student's construal of both theory and the patient. This allows the student to learn to understand the client's subjective world and to have a way of entering that world in the same way the supervisor is engaging in learning about the student. The following discussion concerns material that occurs in the "detailed inquiry" stage but has its seeds in the first supervisory interactions.

Consider Lakoff's (1982) description of the Level 1 statement that is "meaningful at face value" and seems self-evident (p. 141), the Level 2 statement that is "not fully intelligible on its surface" (p. 141), needing assumptions in order to make sense of the utterance, and the Level 3 statement that "does not make sense and no amount of interpretation, using conventional, agreed upon (implicit) rules will help" (p. 141). Thus, a statement such as "Visiting relatives can be a nuisance" or "They don't know how good meat tastes" (Lakoff, 1982, p. 134) illustrates both the ambiguity of language and the fact that we usually have little difficulty understanding the meaning since the statements are embedded in context that provides clarity by way of naturally occurring redundancies. We know, for example, that if the speaker had just described an impending automobile trip, the "relatives" statement referred to the nuisance of travel as opposed to the bothersomeness of an imminent visit to the speaker's house. Some statements that we might play with include (a) a sign I saw on the road declaring "Slow Men Working" (which might be urging caution or expressing criticism at state highway workers), (b) a faculty member's response to an invitation to a colleague's retirement party: "I would like nothing more than attending Joe's retirement party" (does the faculty rejoice with Joe or at Joe's departure?), and (c) my response to the nurse who approached me with a large tetanus-serum-filled needle and asked, "Which arm would you like it in?" I replied, "Yours" to the mirth of her colleagues and then her, as the needle disappeared in my left arm. She was gentle with me, actually, since I provided plenty of contextual cues to help her understand my meaning. Grinning, tilting my head, and laughing (with her, not at her) provided more of a wholeness to the message than can be conveyed in my comment to her.

In ordinary discourse, we remain largely on the manifest Level I. Close friends and relatives believe they have the privilege or even obligation to metacommunicate or communicate about our Level I statements. Thus can someone close say "You interrupt me too darned often" and expect no reprisal; you are "hooked" or enmeshed in the relationship. Ordinary discourse allows you to see the other as rude. Psychotherapy and supervision discourse involves more Level II statements (e.g., "Do you realize that you grimace when . . .") and even forays into Level III statements (e.g., "When you grimace and turn away, I feel that you may be experiencing me as . . ."). This license to engage in Level II statements in psychotherapy makes psychotherapeutic discourse different and is one element of the teaching-learning process of the interpersonal approach.

Level III communication seems uncanny (Sullivan, 1953, 1954). When my wife walks and I jog, we often begin together and for a few minutes discuss some issue or another. Then we proceed at different speeds. When we rejoin each other, we do not pick up where we left off as we had earlier in our marriage. Each of us has processed information over the half hour and we resume the conversation as if we both had been in conversation during the time away from each other. It seems that the intersubjective experience or the ability for a patient and therapist to know each other's meaning may have this quality of Level III communication. The supervisor who can approach this level of experiencing with a patient is gifted. The supervisor who can help the student be aware of this level and use it in supervision may be rare. Intersubjectivity has received some attention in clinical literature (Buechler, 1993; Cushman, 1994; Ricci, 1995). The area begs for empirical research.

Current wisdom sees ambiguous language as accruing meaning via recontextualization. That is, as we construct the context in which the communication occurs we can understand the intent of the message or, in communications-theory terms, redundancy limits the many ambiguous interpretations to that which is consistent with the other messages and levels of discourse. Meaning between the supervisor and the supervisee will become defined as they establish the way supervision will be conducted. These particulars include how often to meet, what types of cases to discuss, with what kinds of divisions of authority between a clinic-based supervisor and the university-based faculty supervisor (or between the university supervisor and the field administrator), for how many sessions (of both therapy service delivered and supervision received), for how long a session, using what kind of modality (e.g., videotape, audiotape, process notes, cotherapy), and with which learning goals in mind. Language will become the obvious medium of exchange, not transference, not reward structures, not a hierarchy of needs (although we will observe phenomena that each of these ideas helps us capture in words), but a particular kind of exchange between two human beings, the essence of both psychotherapy and especially its supervision.

Theoretical Orientation.   One clear strength of the interpersonal approach involves the theoretical orientation of the student. In supervision, theoretical disparities between the supervisor and supervisee may arise at this time. The supervisor has a certain way of understanding clinical cases that will be imparted. The interpersonal supervisor is in a peculiar position, as alluded to earlier. He or she is usually schooled in several of the more prosaic theories. For example, I learned psychoanalytic, rational emotive, social learning, operant, gestalt-humanistic, and, finally, interpersonal approaches. So we can offer supervision to and communicate with many other professors' students. What I have to offer, however, is an approach that subsumes the other approaches while avoiding that already mentioned plague of epistemology, eclecticism. The interpersonal approach involves several important concepts and several ways of understanding other theories' crucial constructs, so I enjoy finding out what the student knows about various schools of psychotherapy. An assessment of what the student understands is important and actually leads us to the next stage or phase of supervision.

The Reconnaissance

At this point, I must let you know that these stages are a matter of emphasis and transition rather than sharply demarcated stages or divisions. In fact, stage theorists regarding psychotherapy supervision tend to take themselves so seriously that they may have reified or made concrete a theory that is a convenient abstraction. To be sure, supervisees may go through stages in discarding naivete, but for a stage theory to be useful, the stages should be occurring in a way that the first stage always occurs first. There should be an invariance to students' progress from one to another stage, and the stages need to be isomorphic or appear similarly across students. There is no evidence that this is the case. The worrisome part of the stage theorists' beliefs is whether they will respect the students who do not fit into their Procrustean supervision. The supervisor at this phase may want to restate what he or she understands to be the goal and process of supervision, and the supervisee may agree or take this opportunity to modify the supervisor's understanding. The supervisor should and must allow the student to help structure the goals and processes or the seeds of discord and missed learning opportunities may be sown. This stage may last from minutes to hours. In the latter case, supervision may be stillborn. In concluding this stage, the supervisor should be able to make a summary statement of the relationship, its goals, and the methodology of supervision so the next stage can begin. This summary may please and even startle the supervisee who may see how powerful a tool acute listening and summarizing can be in the hands of a skilled practitioner. The supervisee should have been heard and now may confront the task on which they have agreed.

The Detailed Inquiry

Modes of Learning.   The supervisor and supervisee should have an idea about the learning task and methods used to work on the task. For the new student, the task may be how to begin psychotherapy; this may include the fears and expectations of the student, how to strike a balance between information gathering and listening for the client's concerns on an emotional level, setting times and fees, and establishing the limits of confidentiality and privilege in psychotherapy (Zaro, Barach, Nedelman, & Dreiblatt, 1977). Perhaps a role play of how to begin and end a first session may be appropriate. With more advanced students, goals may include questions such as timing of interventions and other "wisdom" questions (Hanna & Ottens, 1995) or issues that involve higher order issues or work with specialized client populations or techniques.

1. Sullivan (Carson, 1969, pp. 35-36) incorporates five types of learning that serve as heuristics. The beginning student might be likened to someone who is "learning by anxiety," which is to say that the student will try what reduces his or her anxiety or terror. Ironically, the typical patient for new psychotherapists-in-training is the close-to-hopeless case, or so it seems to the student. I trained with drug addicts, prostitutes, and career schizophrenics. These clients were less desirable, so the staff passed them on to the trainees, I suppose the overt logic being I could do little harm to these people. Often the client had "broken in" a number of other students. In fact, I recall wondering whether the neurotic, who exhibited guilt, anxiety, and a working through of their problems, was not a myth. Only later in my career did I see the more classical "Yavis" patient who could afford experienced clinicians. Sometimes the supervisor must provide support for the student working with recalcitrant cases.

2. The second learning mode is the "learning by trial and success" or whatever seemed to work we shall try again. Perhaps a student had exposure to crisis intervention techniques as an undergraduate suicide hotline volunteer. That will serve as a dominant response or schema on which to rely in times of stress. Sometimes a student will be wedded to a theory in this stage and can be weaned through support and encouragement to enlarge his or her therapeutic armamentarium. The fragile, rigid student may exhibit "theoretical resistance" or a stuckness on the technique that fuels conflict (or the supervisor may be stuck on insisting that his or her theory is the Holy Grail the student must master). Letting the student try his or her technique and waiting for the results may give the supervisor the best sort of leverage in teaching the student. Gentle feedback at this time, especially if the supervisor can hear the student ask for help in whatever way the student can admit the need for guidance, is the best route for supervision. An alternative student position is to claim incompetence. This reminds me of the janitor observing the two rabbis praying. They bewailed their sins, the first begging for forgiveness while the second asked for atonement. The janitor dropped his broom and beseeched the Lord to forgive him for his sins and grant him atonement and the wisdom to prevent future sins that a frail person such as he might commit. The first rabbi glanced at the second rabbi and said, "Look who thinks he is a big sinner!" The helpless posture may serve as a form of resistance, too.

3. The third type or level of learning involves "learning by rewards and punishments," differing from the prior type of learning in that someone intervenes to reward or punish performance. This involves correction by the supervisor, but the supervisor must remain mindful of the student's sensitivities (Barnat, 1980; Cohen, 1980; Greenburg, 1980; Marshall & Confer, 1980). Remember the wise physician who feels the healthy arm before touching the potentially broken arm. First the clinician establishes a base rate for how the healthy arm feels, then allows the patient to get used to the clinician's touch, and finally when some desensitization has occurred, the clinician gently feels the injured limb. This model serves the supervisor well in correcting the student: Be sure to reward first before correcting. John Masefield said, "Once in a century a person may be ruined or made insufferable by praise. But surely once in a minute something generous dies for want of it."

4. The fourth type of learning is "trial-and-error learning by human example," which involves both observation and language mediation. The student who trusts the supervision may try out techniques he or she reads about and receives feedback from the responses of the patient and from reviewing the results in supervision. Notice the reduced anxiety levels or greater tolerance for risk on the supervisee's part that is necessary for this activity to succeed. The student, with prior planning in supervision, tries a technique and can cope with failure as well as success.

5. The fifth type of learning is termed "learning by eduction of relations." This entails a deeper understanding of the client and the therapist's stimulus impact, and a level of self-assured skill attainment or a consolidation of one's therapeutic personality. The therapist gains knowledge of his or her blind spots and weaknesses and the development of mechanisms either to avoid their harmful effects or to turn them to strengths. For example, many a psychotherapist's need to help may intrude in listening to the efforts of prior therapists to rescue a client. One such supervisee with a great need to impress the supervisor with his efforts came to supervision exhausted, having tried to rescue the patient from her many travails. I laughed and said he was working too hard. Psychotherapy should not be that much work. He was advised to sit back and listen for a session, to abjure from any helping, and to practice a wan smile and occasionally supportive but noncommittal response. I told him that if the session was a failure, the responsibility was entirely mine. He was surprised at the patient's ability to solve some of her own problems. Learning the asocial response often occurs here. He had to learn a mechanism (he mimicked my wan smile, head tilt, and supportive grunt) by which he could break his need to rescue.

Psychotherapeutic wisdom (Hanna & Ottens, 1995) resides in the realm of the eduction of relations. Students learn therapist abstinence or refraining from their natural response in favor of a response, perhaps an asocial one, that promotes a deepening of relationship and understanding. Going against one's personal impulse allows the psychotherapist to know him- or herself better and also to risk that the client can learn by this confrontation. What happens when I do not play the cheerleader for a depressed person? Perhaps he or she can enter with me into a different type of relationship than the patient has had with or elicited from others.

In a parallel fashion, the ability to use one's personality in a psychotherapeutic manner is part of clinical wisdom. The student's use of timing, humor, and self-disclosure toward furthering the psychotherapeutic gain for a patient are important aspects that are learned in this phase of supervision.

Conducting Supervision. The supervisor cannot do all and be all to each supervisee. The student may come to supervision anxious about his or her first case. The goal may be reducing the student's anxiety by role playing how to start the first session. Another student may enter supervision to learn about hypnotherapy, and a third may enter supervision to find out why his or her patients seem not to get beyond a certain point of intimacy in psychotherapy. The interpersonal supervisor keeps the task in mind while helping the student learn to understand the meaning of the relationship between the psychotherapist and the patient. For example, role playing with the anxious student gives the student a way to help understand anxious patients. Teaching hypnosis successfully means understanding a powerful relationship imbued with many nuances. Certainly the third example is centered on meaning and relationship. Essentially, the supervisor's task is helping the student to understand, participate, and consequently, by participation, to intervene in the patient's life. This involves helping the patient to understand his or her own life and to construct meaning to the way the patient thinks, feels, and behaves.

Confrontation. The interpersonal approach to supervision (and psychotherapy) requires the supervisor to confront the student. Confrontation may be one of the most misunderstood concepts in clinical psychology. It does not necessarily mean anything harsh or mean spirited. I have seen "provocative" supervisors tell students such brutal statements as "You seem to have no compassion for your patients" or "Your patients do not relate to you." Teaching by trauma is contrary to everything we know about learning. Moreover, it seems impossible to sort out any truth value regarding the supervisor's statements from the obvious hatred the supervisor is expressing. Neither psychotherapy nor supervision gives license to the practitioner to act out his or her own problems. Rather, a responsibility is imposed to abstain from such acting out. Appropriate confrontation takes more beneficial forms.

Imposition Versus Unfolding.   Buber (1965a) sees as demonic the imposition of wills that occurs in our contemporary society and in psychotherapy. Supervisors who force their will on a student are not allowing the student to realize his or her potential toward becoming a fully functioning psychotherapist. Buber sees unfolding as the path to actualizing. In supervision, beneficial confrontation takes the form of unfolding. The student who says his or her patients seem not to get beyond a certain point of intimacy with the student may be asked by the supervisor to describe what he or she means. Perhaps a tape recording may be played. The supervisor may ask about the student's ideas about what type of intimacy and revelations he or she expects, where those expectations arose, and what would happen if the patient fulfilled these expectations. The supervisor wants to know what Level II referents the student is meaning. The supervisor who is using supervision for his or her own growth may recognize his or her own anticipations of the student's answers as a way of understanding the supervisor's own Level III referents. When the supervisor "misses" the student's interpretation of a term, the supervisor can know what the student means and what "autistic" (or the supervisor's own) processes can interfere in the supervisor's understanding of the student. If the supervisor engages in these processes, he or she cannot help but model open listening and respectful inquiry. These will help the student explore issues. For example, the student may have to understand what intimacy means to him or her. Are the student's expectations reasonable or constructed on a misunderstanding of psychotherapy? Is the student attending to his or her needs to find intimacy in psychotherapy rather than to its appropriateness for the patient? What sort of signals might he or she be sending to patients that prevent them from engaging in more intensive psychotherapy? Rather than imposing an interpretation or "provoking" a student, unfolding leads to learning how to understand and effectively intervene in lives without violating those lives.

The Parallel Process.   Since the student psychotherapist is involved in both the psychotherapy and the supervision, it is not surprising that dynamics between the supervisor and student psychotherapist and the student psychotherapist and client pairs may be similar or parallel (Doehrman, 1976). Although this parallel process is interesting to observe and is even expected, the effective and caring supervisor will not tell the student of this insight. It is just as harmful as telling an adolescent that he or she is experiencing homosexual panic. The mentioning of the term in the latter case may preemptively congeal an identity that is confused and needs to be sorted out. In the former case, mentioning parallel process will force the student into the patient role. This preempts the possibility of the student's discovering his or her own power to produce a dynamic in psychotherapy, albeit a dynamic the student may want to change. For example, one supervisee had trouble with a patient who brought her newborn into the sessions, popped open her blouse and brassiere, and proceeded to breastfeed during the session. I observed that the student's own blouse was open several buttons farther down than was appropriate, she wore an elegant brassiere, and she found it necessary to lean forward during the supervision as if listening to my every word. The easy, self-gratifying position would be to point out the parallel process, but effective supervision would have been stopped, with the probable attribution about the supervisor's mentation. Instead, I made sure I focused on her face or other appropriate and neutral place and asked about what she thought were the patient's motivations, about what feelings were aroused in her, about what that meant about the psychotherapy. She said that she felt cheapened, as if the baby came first and psychotherapy were diminished. The baby could be a foil to avoid problems (Anderson, 1995; Imber, 1995). I asked in what ways the psychotherapy was the same and how it differed with other patients and how it compared with supervision. Further, we discussed what sort of intervention might be appropriate for the psychotherapy. She was relieved and conducted effective psychotherapy with the patient.

Later in supervision when she felt helpless with a patient, she mentioned how similar it was to when she would come home and her mother would hoist her skirt or dress to check her underwear. The mother's controlling intrusiveness persisted into the psychotherapist's adulthood. She would feel exposed, pinioned, helpless, and outraged. We discussed how this feeling may have been the same or may have differed from how she felt when certain ill-considered administrative changes were made at her place of work. She was able to confront the administration affirmatively and felt enough worth to move to a better position at another agency. The trapped feelings had been allayed. Although she was gifted with sensitive intuition, her psychotherapy now had an additional sense of confidence and skill. Making her open blouse the subject of discussion would have debased the supervision and put her in the child role in which her undergarments were the subject of inspection. Only resistance, contempt, and the feeling of violation of the supervision contract would have resulted. Instead, we both had a lesson in constructively using time with another human being.

The Map and the Field.   Interpersonal supervision is concerned with helping the student apply the theories learned in classrooms and books to the cases in the consulting room. Similarly, interpersonal supervision is involved in helping the student identify an issue in psychotherapy and finding resources in reflection, supervision, and reading. For example, in a group psychotherapy session with sex offenders, a prisoner was angry with the female student therapist. He chastised her about wearing an inappropriately short and provocative skirt. After the session, the supervisor-cotherapist asked what the student thought was going on. Although she knew the problem was the patient's (the student's skirt was entirely appropriate), she was stumped at the dynamics. The supervisor suggested that she consider certain defense mechanisms that might be operating. The student began to think about wish fulfillment and projection, then recalled the patient's denying any responsibility for the child molestation, claiming that the child victim was dressed provocatively. Supervision helps articulate the map and the field.

Since the maps are linguistic, the communications and semeiotic approaches of Anchin and Kiesler (1982), Hayakawa (1958, 1962, 1964), Mitroff and Johnson (1981), Ruesch (1957, 1961), Scheflin (1974), and Watzlawick, Beavin, and Jackson (1967) are the codebooks by which the student can understand how to relate clinical literature to clinical experience. Any student or supervisor wanting to master the core works of the interpersonal approach should follow his or her reading of Buber and Sullivan with the preceding set of books.

The Termination

Perhaps the end of the internship, practicum, or other set term for supervision has arrived or a "substantial amount of work" has been accomplished. (I will omit termination due to student problems that merits more serious treatment than we can give here.) Termination in the natural course of the relationship can either undo or cement much of the work of supervision.

First, some summary statement of where the student is with his or her cases is in order, and a similar statement by the supervisor about student strengths should be made. Indeed, the student should have successfully mastered some aspects of psychotherapy and have constructed a self-as-a-psychotherapist. The supervisor might recognize the student's gains. Depending on the relationship and the supervisor's style, such recognition may range from an acknowledgment to an enthusiastic celebration. For example, the office-centered formal supervision might include a shift in postures in the chairs, whereas cotherapists may celebrate over dinner at a restaurant. The affirmation might include discussion of the student's next assignment or career transition, and the exchange of phone, fax, or e-mail numbers. Some confidence-building measures are called for that signify a shift in relationship and are congruent with the existing relationship.

There should be no surprises or unfinished business arising at this time. Efforts to get in a few more supervisory moments are counterproductive. I recall a supervisee who, having done well during the academic term, revealed to me in the last session that she was a practicing witch. I suggested that this seemed important to her and she needed to express this to someone with whom she felt she could work on this during her next assignment. Nonetheless, she had related well to the rehabilitation clients she had seen and motivated them to deal with their physical and emotional disabilities constructively. Her accomplishments should not be lost in her obviously troubling religious commitment.

Eudaimonia.   Waterman (1990, 1993) has explored two concepts of happiness. He philosophically and empirically defined *hedonic enjoyment* and *eudaimonia*. The former refers to the positive affect that accompanies the satisfaction of needs. It tends toward the consummatory. The latter refers to the daimon or true self. Eudaimonia calls for each person to know and actualize his or her innate, diverse, distinctive potential for excellence. Personal expression of the daimon is consistent with feeling challenged, competent, and assertive, having a high level of concentration and high goals, investing a great degree of effort, and knowing how well one is doing. More eudaimonia leads to more actualizing needs and satisfactions. It is cumulative.

So it is with supervision. Both the supervisor and supervisee in successful supervision should be experiencing eudaimonia. Telfer (as cited in Waterman, 1990, p. 54) defined eudaimonia as "what is *worth* desiring and worth having in life" (italics in the original). Life must be the individual's work of art.

As Rabbi Zusya lay dying, his students anxiously gathered about him. They were puzzled by his serenity as he was about to meet his Maker. Zusya reassured them that the Almighty would not ask him why he was not the measure of Moses, but rather how well did he measure up to Zusya.

REFERENCES

Anchin, J. C., & Kiesler, D. J. (Eds.). (1982). *The handbook of interpersonal psychotherapy.* Elmsford, NY: Pergamon.

Anderson, M. K. (1995). "May I bring my newborn baby to my analytic hour?": One analyst's experience with this request. *Psychoanalytic Inquiry, 53,* 358–368.

Barnat, M. (1974). Some characteristics of supervisory identification in psychotherapy. *Psychotherapy: Theory, Research and Practice, 11,* 189–192.

Barnat, M. (1980). Psychotherapy supervision and the duality of experience. In A. K. Hess (Ed.), *Psychotherapy supervision: Theory, research and practice* (pp. 51–67). New York: Wiley.

Benjamin, L. S. (1974). Structural analysis of social behavior. *Psychological Review, 81,* 392–425.

Benjamin, L. S. (1994). SASB: A bridge between personality theory and clinical psychology. *Psychological Inquiry, 5,* 273–316.

Bennis, W. G., Schein, E. H., Steele, F. I., & Berlew, D. E. (1968). *Interpersonal dynamics: Essays and readings on human interaction* (rev. ed.). Homewood, IL: Dorsey.

Berne, E. (1964). *Games people play: The psychology of human relationships.* New York: Grove.

Buber, M. (1965a). *The knowledge of man: Selected essays.* New York: Harper & Row.

Buber, M. (1965b). *Between man and man.* New York: Macmillan.

Buber, M. (1970). *I and thou.* New York: Scribner's.

Buechler, S. (1993). Clinical applications of an interpersonal view of the emotions. *Contemporary Psychoanalysis, 29,* 219–236.

Burns, C. I., & Holloway, E. L. (1989). Therapy in supervision: An unresolved issue. *The Clinical Supervisor, 7,* 47–60.

Cacioppo, J. T., Petty, R. E., Feinstein, J. A., & Jarvis, W. B. G. (1996). Dispositional differences in cognitive motivation: The life and times of individuals varying in need for cognition. *Psychological Bulletin, 119,* 197–253.

Carifio, M., & Hess, A. K. (1987). Who is the ideal supervisor? *Professional Psychology, 18,* 244–250 .

Carson, R. C. (1969). *Interaction concepts in personality.* Chicago: Aldine.

Cohen, L. (1980). The new supervisee views supervision. In A. K. Hess (Ed.), *Psychotherapy supervision: Theory, research and practice* (pp. 78–84). New York: Wiley.

Cushman, P. (1994). Confronting Sullivan's spider: Hermeneutics and the politics of therapy. *Contemporary Psychoanalysis, 30,* 800–844.

Davison, G. C. (1995). A failure of early behavior therapy (circa 1966), or, why I learned to stop worrying and to embrace psychotherapy integration. *Journal of Psychotherapy Integration, 5,* 107–112.

Doehrman, M. J. G. (1976). Parallel processes in supervision and psychotherapy. *Bulletin of the Menninger Clinic, 40,* part 1.

Duke, M. P., & Nowicki, S., Jr. (1982). A social learning theory analysis of interactional theory concepts and a multidimensional model of human interaction constellations. In J. C. Anchin & D. J. Kiesler (Eds.), *The handbook of interpersonal psychotherapy* (pp. 78–94). Elmsford, NY: Pergamon.

Ellis, M. V., & Douce, L. A. (1994). Group supervision of novice clinical supervisors: Eight recurring issues. *Journal of Counseling and Development, 72,* 520–525.

Fierman, L. B. (Ed.). (1965). *Effective psychotherapy: The contribution of Hellmuth Kaiser.* New York: Free Press.

French, J. R. P., & Raven, B. H. (1959). The bases of social power. In D. Cartwright (Ed.), *Studies in social power* (pp. 150–167). Ann Arbor: University of Michigan Press.

Goldberg, L. (1990). An alternative "description of personality": The Big Five structure. *Journal of Personality and Social Psychology, 59,* 1216–1229.

Greenburg, L. (1980). Supervision from the perspective of the supervisee. In A. K. Hess (Ed.), *Psychotherapy supervision: Theory, research and practice* (pp. 85–91). New York: Wiley.

Haley, J. (1963). *Strategies of psychotherapy.* New York: Grune and Stratton.

Hanna, F. J., & Ottens, A. J. (1995). The role of wisdom in psychotherapy. *Journal of Psychotherapy Integration, 5,* 195–219.

Haviland, M. B., & Reise, S. P. (1996). Structure of the Twenty-Item Toronto alexithymia scale. *Journal of Personality Assessment, 66,* 116–125.

Hayakawa, S. I. (1958). *Symbol, status, and personality.* New York: Harcourt, Brace & World.

Hayakawa, S. I. (Ed.). (1962). *The use and misuse of language.* Greenwich CT: Fawcett.

Hayakawa, S. I. (1964). *Language in thought and action* (2nd ed.). New York: Harcourt, Brace & World.

Hess, A. K. (1980a). Training models and the nature of psychotherapy supervision. In A. K. Hess (Ed.), *Psychotherapy supervision: Theory, research and practice* (pp. 15–25). New York: Wiley.

Hess, A. K. (Ed.). (1980b). *Psychotherapy supervision: Theory, research and practice.* New York: Wiley.

Hess, A. K. (1986). Growth in supervision: Stages of supervisee and supervisor development. *The Clinical Supervisor, 4,* 51–67.

Hess, A. K. (1987). Psychotherapy supervision: Stages, Buber and a theory of relationship. *Professional Psychology, 18,* 251–259.

Hess, A. K. (1996). Celebrating the twentieth anniversary of *Criminal Justice and Behavior:* The past, present and future of forensic psychology. *Criminal Justice and Behavior, 23,* 236–250.

Imber, R. R. (1995). The role of the supervisor and the pregnant analyst. *Psychoanalytic Psychology, 12,* 281–296.

Jarvis, W. B. G., & Petty, R. E. (1996). The need to evaluate. *Journal of Personality and Social Psychology, 70,* 172–194.

Kelly G. A. (1955). *The psychology of personal constructs.* New York: Norton.

Lakoff, R. T. (1982). The rationale of psychotherapeutic discourse. In J. C. Anchin & D. J. Kiesler (Eds.), *Handbook of interpersonal psychotherapy* (pp. 132–146). Elsmford, NY: Pergamon.

Lazarus, A. A. (1995). Different types of eclecticism and integration: Let's be aware of the dangers. *Journal of Psychotherapy Integration, 5,* 27–39.

Leary, T. (1957). *Interpersonal diagnosis of personality.* New York: Ronald Press.

Lehman, R. S., Gorsuch, R. L., & Mintz, J. (1985). Moving targets: Patients' changing complaints during psychotherapy. *Journal of Consulting and Clinical Psychology, 53,* 49–54.

Lewin, K. (1951). *Field theory in social science: Selected theoretical papers.* New York: Harper & Row.

Mahl, G. F. (1968). Gestures and body movements in interviews. In J. M. Schein (Vol. Ed.), H. F. Hunt, J. D. Matarzzo, & C. Savage (Assoc. Eds.), *Research in psychotherapy: Vol. III* (pp. 295–346). Washington DC: American Psychological Association.

Markus, H., & Zajonc, R. B. (1985). The cognitive perspective in social psychology. In G. Lindzey & E. Aronson (Eds.), *Handbook of social psychology* (Vol. 1, pp. 137–230). Hillsdale, NJ: Lawrence Erlbaum.

Marshall, W. R., & Confer, W. N. (1980). Psychotherapy supervision: Supervisees' perspective. In A. K. Hess (Ed.), *Psychotherapy supervision: Theory, research and practice* (pp. 92–100). New York: Wiley.

McAdams, D. P. (1995). What do we know when we know a person? *Journal of Personality, 63,* 365–396.

Mitroff, G., & Johnson, M. (1981). *Metaphors we live by.* Chicago: University of Chicago Press.

Newman, A. S. (1981). Ethical issues in the supervison of psychotherapy. *Professional Psychology, 12,* 609–695.

Paris, B. J. (1994). *Karen Horney: A psychoanalyst's search for self-understanding.* New Haven: Yale University Press.

Pepper, S. C. (1942). *World hypotheses.* Berkeley: University of California Press.

Peterson, C. C., & Siddle, D. A. T. (1995). Confidentiality issues in psychological research. *Australian Psychologist, 30,* 187–190.

Ricci, W. F. (1995). Self and intersubjectivity in the supervisory process. *Bulletin of the Menninger Clinic, 59,* 53–68.

Rubin, S. S. (1989). At the border of supervision: Critical moments in psychotherapists' development. *American Journal of Psychotherapy, 43,* 387–397.

Ruesch, J. (1957). *Disturbed communication.* New York: Norton.

Ruesch, J. (1961). *Therapeutic communication.* New York: Norton.

Scheff, T. J. (1963). The role of the mentally ill and the dynamics of mental disorder: A research framework. *Sociometry, 26,* 436–453.

Scheflin, A. E. (1974). *How behavior means.* Garden City NY: Anchor.

Stampfl, T. G., & Levis, D. J. (1967). Essentials of implosive therapy: A learning-based psychodynamic behavioral therapy. *Journal of Abnormal Psychology, 72,* 496–503.

Strupp, H. H. (1958). The psychotherapist's contribution to the treatment process. *Behavioral Science, 3,* 34–67,

Strupp, H. H. (1962). The therapist's contribution to the treatment process: Beginnings and vagaries of a research program. In H. H. Strupp & L. Luborsky (Vol. Eds.), *Research in psychotherapy: Vol. II* (pp. 25–40). Washington DC: American Psychological Association.

Sullivan, H. S. (1953). *The interpersonal theory of psychiatry.* New York: Norton.

Sullivan, H. S. (1954). *The psychiatric interview.* New York: Norton.

Talbot, N. L. (1995). Unearthing shame in the supervisory experience. *American Journal of Psychotherapy, 49,* 338–348.

Waterman, A. S. (1990). Personal expressiveness: Philosophical and psychological foundations. *Journal of Mind and Behavior, 11,* 47–74.

Waterman, A. S. (1993). Two conceptions of happiness: Contrasts of personal expressiveness (eudaimonia) and hedonic enjoyment. *Journal of Personality and Social Psychology, 64,* 678–691.

Watzlawick, P., Beavin, J. H., & Jackson, D. D. (1967). *Pragmatics of human communication.* New York: Norton.

Yogev, S. (1982). An eclectic model of supervision: A developmental sequence for beginning psychotherapy students. *Professional Psychology, 13,* 236–243.

Young, D. M., & Beier, E. G. (1982). Being asocial in social places: Giving the client a new experience. In J. C. Anchin & D. J. Kiesler (Eds.), *The handbook of interpersonal psychotherapy* (pp. 262–273). Elmsford, NY: Pergamon.

Zaro, J. S., Barach, R., Nedelman, D. J., & Dreiblatt, I. S. (1977). *A guide for beginning psychotherapists.* Cambridge, England: Cambridge University Press.

CHAPTER 6

Supervision in Dialectical Behavior Therapy

ALAN E. FRUZZETTI
University of Nevada
JENNIFER A. WALTZ
University of Montana
MARSHA M. LINEHAN
University of Washington

OVERVIEW OF DIALECTICAL BEHAVIOR THERAPY

Dialectical behavior therapy (DBT), developed by Marsha Linehan, is a comprehensive intervention package (Linehan, 1993a, 1993b) designed specifically for treating parasuicidal individuals typically diagnosed with borderline personality disorder. In controlled outcome trials, DBT has been shown to be effective in reducing parasuicidal behavior and inpatient psychiatric hospitalization days (Linehan, Armstrong, Suarez, Allmon, & Heard, 1991) and effective in reducing anger and improving social adjustment (Linehan, Tutek, Heard, & Armstrong, 1994). Over the course of a 1-year, posttreatment, follow-up, these improvements are generally maintained (Linehan, Heard, & Armstrong, 1993). Although it is far beyond the scope and nature of this chapter to explicate DBT, a general overview of its theory and structure will inform the discussion of supervision from a DBT perspective.

The treatment is called *dialectical behavior therapy* because it utilizes a dialectical theory of the process of change that balances an orientation toward change with a concomitant emphasis on acceptance and validation. Thus, DBT integrates traditional, change-oriented behavioral analysis and therapy (skill training, problem solving, contingency management, exposure, etc.) with more acceptance- and validation-based treatment strategies (Linehan, in press). The dialectical worldview employed in DBT maintains that finding the truth or utility in alternative, even seemingly contradictory, positions is sometimes essential for change. Thus, with difficult clients who have enormous, life-threatening problems and few resources, the goal is to find a synthesis that includes an acceptance of clients (as worthwhile, valued, human beings), an understanding or appreciation of their dysfunctional behaviors and pain, *and* a focus on helping (even pushing) them to make significant, seemingly impossible changes in order to survive. Therapy is a constant balance and integration of acceptance/validation and change/problem-solving strategies.

The treatment specifies a hierarchy of treatment stages and targets and focuses therapy time accordingly. The pretreatment target is commitment, which includes orienting the client to the treatment and getting an informed commitment, or agreement, to the therapy. Then, in Stage 1 of the therapy, targets involve client stability, safety, and connection to the therapist. Specific Stage 1 targets are (a) reducing life-threatening suicidal and para-suicidal behaviors and aggression and violence toward others; (b) decreasing any "ther-apy-interfering" behavior (i.e., behaviors of the client or therapist that interfere with or compromise effective treatment); (c) reducing client behaviors that significantly interfere with achieving or maintaining a basically safe and dignified quality of life (e.g., signifi-cant psychological difficulties, substance abuse, homelessness); and (d) increasing client skills. After Stage 1 goals are largely met, Stage 2 focuses on reducing post-traumatic stress. Finally, in Stage 3, increasing client self-respect and focusing on other life goals are targeted.

In its empirically validated form, DBT integrates several components or modes of treat-ment, each with unique functions: (a) skills training, most often done in groups, to enhance client capabilities by teaching new skills in emotion regulation, self-regulation (mindful-ness), interpersonal effectiveness, and distress tolerance; (b) individual therapy, to help clients apply new skills and to help maintain and enhance client motivation; (c) phone con-sultation with the client (or milieu therapy), to provide support and technical advice in applying skills in vivo and to facilitate generalization to the natural environment; and (d) a supervision group, to enhance therapist capabilities, maintain therapist motivation, bal-ance the therapy overall, and deal with administrative issues.

DBT as Treatment of the Therapist

In part because DBT was developed to treat extremely distressed, often emotionally demanding and difficult clients, DBT supervision and consultation is considered an inte-gral and ongoing part of the treatment. Working with borderline, parasuicidal clients can be extremely difficult for the therapist because clients' suicidal ideation and suicidal and parasuicidal behaviors are so prevalent and because clients often engage in behaviors that threaten or unbalance the therapy. Maintaining effective treatment in the context of clients' terrible emotional pain, frequent suicide attempts and other parasuicidal behavior, verbal attacks on the therapist, slow progress, and frequent client discouragement is very diffi-cult. In DBT, the therapist treats the client while the therapist is "treated" by the supervi-sor and/or the supervision/consultation team. Thus, in DBT we seek to enhance client out-comes by anticipating and minimizing (or even preventing) therapist burnout. Therefore, we also seek to enhance therapist training, effectiveness, and competence, and also satis-faction and enjoyment with our work.

Most other therapies view supervision as a necessary step in training in that particular treatment modality, but one that ends when the therapist has developed competence in the delivery of the therapy. Then, supervision or consultation is sought only occasionally, when the therapy is problematic, ineffective, or troubling to the therapist. In DBT, how-ever, ongoing supervision and consultation are viewed as essential parts of the therapy. The treatment or supervision team manages, shapes, supports, balances, or "treats" the thera-pist in order to facilitate effective management, shaping, support, balancing, or "treat-ment" of the client. Although comprehensive supervision may be required in other approaches (e.g., psychoanalysis), in most other therapies the supervision process does end eventually.

The one exception to this may be found among the family systems therapies. For exam-ple, in Milan systemic family therapy (Boscolo, Cecchin, Hoffman, & Penn, 1987), as in other family systems therapies, the therapist "joins" the family, albeit in a particular role, and is thereafter viewed as part of the family system. Therefore, the consultation team observes the interactions between the therapist and the family members, providing balance that allows a new systemic equilibrium to be achieved, and helps to prevent misalignments (lack of balance) between the therapist and individual family members, negative collusion, and so on.

DBT, in this same sense, is a systemic therapy. The therapy is not arbitrarily differentiated from supervision. The transactions among the therapist, other members of the supervision team, and the client *are* the therapy. Thus, ongoing supervision and consultation are part of the therapy for all DBT clients at all stages of treatment and for all DBT therapists at all stages of therapist development.

The DBT Supervision Model Parallels the DBT Psychotherapy Model

Many forms of psychotherapy employ a supervision model that parallels or resembles the therapy structure or process itself. This is also true in DBT. In fact, the structure and process of DBT supervision are nearly identical to the structure and process of the therapy; only the targets differ substantively.

In DBT, the treatment can loosely be described in stages, including pretreatment (in which clients become oriented and agree to treatment guidelines) and then according to the treatment hierarchy, as mentioned earlier. In DBT supervision, there is also a natural progression of stages, from presupervision, in which the prospective therapist becomes oriented to the treatment and agrees or commits to training, to a therapy skills acquisition phase (which starts prior to seeing clients using DBT), to teaching skills in skill-training groups, and to skill application with individual clients. Just as DBT includes group skills training to enhance capabilities, DBT training usually begins with skill acquisition through course work, study groups, or intensive workshop training. And in DBT training, those skills are further developed and applied in the context of individual or group supervision.

Many other parallels are obvious. In DBT, clients participate in ongoing assessment to monitor progress; in DBT supervision, therapists are videotaped for evaluation of strengths and problems in delivering the therapy, and regular assessments are made of therapist adherence to the therapy and competence in its delivery, using the DBT Expert Rating Scale (Linehan, Lockard, Wagner, & Tutek, 1996). In DBT, problem-solving and other change-oriented strategies are continually balanced with acceptance and validation strategies. This is true in training and supervision as well. Similarly, a balance of communication styles is sought in DBT and in DBT supervision. In DBT, therapists seek to empower clients by consulting with them on how to succeed and how to manage their environment, trying not to do for clients what they can do for themselves. In DBT supervision, the team consults with therapists also, similarly encouraging them to develop and apply skills as needs arise. And, just as skills in emotion regulation, mindfulness (self-regulation), distress tolerance, and interpersonal effectiveness are seen as the building blocks to effective action on the part of the client, these same skills are learned, practiced, and applied by DBT therapists in the development and delivery of the therapy.

Overall, the structure of DBT also suggests a general structure of supervision, with different modes serving different functions. Similarly, particular therapy assumptions and processes guide the supervision process. But before going into these in detail, it is important to consider first any prerequisites for becoming a DBT therapist, and how a commitment to DBT training is established.

GETTING STARTED: CHOOSING TO LEARN DBT

Who Can or Should Learn DBT

In many ways, DBT is an equal opportunity therapy. That is, people with diverse degrees and therapy experiences can learn DBT. Individuals with quite different educational and work backgrounds have become competent DBT therapists. Nevertheless, as a comprehensive approach to intervention, many skills are required to learn and perform DBT effectively: (a) As a functional contextual therapy (Linehan, 1994), therapists must be proficient with functional or behavioral analysis, be familiar with basic research in human learning, and have experience in traditional behavioral and cognitive therapies; (b) from a dialectical perspective, DBT therapists must be cognitively and interpersonally flexible and must be willing and able to synthesize multiple, often contradictory, points of view about a problem; (c) therapists must be able to tolerate the risks and difficulties inherent in working with suicidal clients; and finally, (d) it is essential for DBT therapists to like (at least most of the time) the difficult clients for whom DBT has been developed. In some settings, the term *borderline* is used quite pejoratively. In DBT, while acknowledging the often demanding nature of the work and the frequent dysfunctional behavior of clients, we seek to engage clients collaboratively as human beings, in a genuine relationship, without arbitrary "therapeutic distance" that can sometimes be experienced as patronizing. Of course, not all of these proficiencies are necessary to begin training in DBT. Prospective DBT therapists should, however, have these skills as goals and values.

Presupervision: Orienting and Getting a Commitment From Therapists

Before clients begin treatment in DBT, considerable energy and attention are applied to helping them get oriented to DBT and make a fully informed agreement, or commitment, regarding participation in DBT. In general, this involves exposing them to the dialectical process by highlighting both the reasons why DBT may be necessary to help them move their lives out of their present misery, and simultaneously, how difficult DBT really is and why they should consider other options. In the process, it is hoped that clients become collaborative participants in their therapy, understand and agree to the treatment hierarchy (including working on reducing parasuicide as the primary target and participation in both group skills training and individual therapy), and agree to whatever assessments are necessary (including daily diary monitoring cards) and whatever other requirements might be present in a particular setting (such as minimal length of participation in therapy, fees; see Linehan, 1993a, for more details).

A similar process is desirable regarding DBT training and supervision. In the presupervision phase, prospective therapists need to be oriented to what DBT involves, the theory on which it is predicated, and what is expected of them, prior to making a commitment to training. Although it may be understandable for enthusiastic DBT therapists and supervisors to try to "sell" DBT to prospective DBT therapists, a more dialectical approach employs the orienting and commitment DBT strategies to explore genuinely both the advantages (e.g., learning an effective, empirically validated treatment, enhancing capabilities) and potential disadvantages (e.g., DBT is demanding, clients often make only slow progress) of embarking on DBT training. It is also essential for the supervisor or supervision team to be clear at this stage about precisely what is expected from the therapist (e.g., expectations regarding attendance and participation, respect for patient, ethical behavior, length of commitment to the clinic or team, and other agreements).

There are a number of avenues through which prospective therapists can make informed decisions about learning DBT. First, they can read overviews of the treatment (e.g., Linehan & Kehrer, 1993) and published articles about its efficacy (Linehan et al., 1991; Linehan et al., 1993; Linehan et al., 1994). In most settings (assuming neither confidentiality nor liability are issues), prospective DBT therapists can sit in on supervision/consultation meetings and possibly even observe a tape of a DBT session to enhance their understanding of what learning and doing DBT might be like. Most important, prospective DBT therapists should engage in an honest discussion of the pros and cons of DBT training with the supervisor or supervision team.

It is essential that the issues involved in a fully-informed commitment to learning the therapy not be underestimated. DBT clients can be very difficult (parasuicidal behaviors, suicidal threats, hostility, depression and withdrawal, etc.) and often have interpersonal histories that include abandonment (even by therapists). Consequently, fears of abandonment are common, and clients have few skills to regulate their emotions (at least initially). They therefore often behave in ways that make it difficult to stay committed to them and the therapy. So committing to DBT means committing to trying very hard to make the therapy work even when the client may be extraordinarily difficult to work with. Of course, the rewards inherent in working with DBT clients can be enormous as well, so full attention to both sides of this issue is essential at this presupervision stage. Most important is that prospective DBT therapists make a well-informed, carefully considered commitment to their training that includes a full appreciation of the responsibilities, and potential rewards, of doing DBT.

THERAPIST SKILL ACQUISITION

DBT therapists must become adept in a number of domains prior to (or simultaneous with) DBT training. Mastery of many skill domains (e.g., listening, supporting—therapy "nonspecifics") may be necessary to become proficient in any approach to psychotherapy. There may be some skills, or combinations of skills, however, that are more specific to DBT. In addition, some skills are best learned in structured settings, whereas others necessarily must be shaped in context. DBT is no exception.

Didactic Training

Some knowledge and skills can be learned in formal course work. For example, in didactic settings, DBT trainees can learn the basic skills of behavioral analysis, problem solving, contingency management, and other forms of behavior therapy and can achieve a basic knowledge of experimental and applied psychology, particularly regarding learning theories, emotion regulation, and cognitive processing. Some trainees are already quite proficient in these areas; others have some skills but need others. It is possible for the DBT supervision and consultation team to include readings and didactics, or even to bring in experts as teachers and consultants, in order to compensate for members' limited training in these areas or to enhance abilities and knowledge to even more expert levels. General knowledge of DBT, its theory, structure, and so on can similarly be acquired through course work, intensive DBT workshops, or an ongoing DBT study group.

Practica and Experiential Training

Other skills necessary in the effective delivery of DBT are, however, not as easily taught in formal settings. This section identifies several important areas in which DBT therapists should attempt to become skillful in order to be most effective. Sometimes these skills may be enhanced through practice, supervision, or focused outside experiences. Sometimes it is useful for a therapist to enter therapy him- or herself in order to become skillful in all these domains. Regardless of method, these are important skills for DBT therapists to possess.

Therapeutic Genuineness.   The highest level of validation in DBT is that of "radical genuineness," in which the therapist "believes in the individual and his or her capacity to change and move towards ultimate life goals." The client "is responded to as a person of equal status, due equal respect" (Linehan, in press). Being genuine in this way means seeing clients as more than their role as patients. Many therapies, particularly with difficult and dysfunctional clients, encourage or condone maintaining distance from clients, staying only in the therapist role. In DBT, being in a genuine relationship with the client is viewed as essential to successful therapy and to clients achieving their goals. This requires fairly high adjustment, and proficiency in dialectics, on the part of the therapist. That is, therapists are vulnerable in DBT and must be able simultaneously to engage in a "real" relationship with the client *and* recognize, and respond according to, therapeutic responsibility.

Genuineness also includes having and using social reinforcement skills. It is important that genuine warmth and caring are not withheld from the client. Rather, it may be important to articulate these feelings and not rely on clients to perceive them accurately. It is, of course, important also to identify and label clients' dysfunctional or maladaptive behaviors (in a nonpejorative way, of course). Being honest about these behaviors, neither pretending that abnormal behavior is normal nor treating the client as overly fragile, is also a sign of genuineness. These skills are life skills, the same ones essential in any meaningful relationship, and can be enhanced simply by taking risks with friends and family members or by talking openly and honestly in the DBT supervision team. Similarly, modeling in the supervision group or in therapy sessions conducted by supervisors or peers can enhance the development of these repertoires.

Tolerating Distress.   DBT therapists therefore also need to be able to tolerate client distress and regulate their own emotions without distancing from (or punishing) clients. This involves therapists' themselves becoming sophisticated in the use of the DBT skills of mindfulness, emotion regulation, and distress tolerance. Many clients live in severe emotional distress and are chronically suicidal. It is imperative that therapists develop the abilities to tolerate clients' distress and their ever-present risk of suicide and still engage in effective, therapeutic behavior. DBT often involves pushing clients to try new skills in difficult situations and can elicit intense responses from clients. Being mindful of as many factors as possible, including one's own distress, is essential in knowing when to push clients for change versus when to stop pushing and instead support and validate.

Because a history of being in invalidating environments is a core component of the theory of borderline personality disorder on which DBT is based (Linehan, 1993a), invalidation by the therapist is a particularly acute problem. When clients' communication of their experiences puts demands on the therapist that are above a preferred level (difficult to tolerate) or for which the therapist has no readily available response, the risk of invalidation is heightened. Developing and utilizing good distress tolerance skills, however, can balance these risks and facilitate more validating therapeutic behavior.

Appreciation of Diversity.   Cultural sensitivity, or appreciation of diversity across a variety of dimensions (e.g., cultural practices, affective experiencing, social issues such as poverty) may in part be taught in the classroom. But having a variety of experiences may also be necessary to fully appreciate these phenomena. In order to validate clients, we must first truly come to understand their experiences from their perspectives, while simultaneously doing so from our own perspective (Linehan, in press). Consequently, narrow life experiences, including limited therapy experiences, may result in therapists' having difficulty understanding clients' experiences and then inadvertently invalidating clients and their perspectives, with likely devastating effects.

There are many ways that therapists can augment their own previous experiences to include more diverse life experiences. For example, therapists from one particular ethnic or racial group can read about or see films about people from other groups. Therapists can also attend churches, synagogues, mosques, and so forth, that are unfamiliar, go to ethnic festivals, read alternative newspapers, and so on. We can also spend time in less frequented parts of town to gain an appreciation of the lives of people from other social and demographic groups. Therapists, by definition, have high levels of education and in general come from more affluent families. Coming into contact with real poverty can be enlightening and can enhance appreciation of our clients' sometimes desperate behaviors regarding their quality of life. Talking within the supervision group about emotional experiences can sometimes highlight enormous diversity in emotional regulation and emotional processing and can foster a deeper appreciation for other team members. These efforts may both minimize therapists' potential for invalidating clients and enrich their own lives in other ways.

Interpersonal Sensitivity.   Because invalidating environments are such an integral part of the theory underlying DBT, it is important for DBT therapists to possess skills to discriminate accurately the private experiences (especially affect) that clients may have and to identify and label them correctly, thereby validating clients' private experiences. Invalidation of clients is particularly a risk when client behaviors are not public (either they occur only when alone or are private feelings or thoughts). Therapists can mitigate against this risk by developing specific interpersonal sensitivity skills. Such repertoires may be learned in other types of therapy training (e.g., functional analytic psychotherapy; Kohlenberg & Tsai, 1991), or therapists may already be quite skilled at this. Practicing DBT emotion regulation and interpersonal effectiveness skills may help. Either way, these are essential skills in doing DBT.

Receive Feedback and Supervision Nondefensively.   Because DBT is a complicated treatment intervention package developed for difficult clients who have not succeeded in other treatments, progress is often slow. Consequently, the supervision team is called upon to evaluate regularly what the therapist could be doing differently. It is thus essential when receiving supervision to recognize that this work is difficult and that even expert DBT therapists require ongoing supervision. Part of the dialectic philosophy of change maintains that there may be utility, or truth, from multiple perspectives. Thus, even effective interventions may be second-guessed in DBT, so embracing the spirit of moving toward more and more competent treatment delivery is preferable to defensiveness and stubbornness. Needing to be "right" is anathema to the spirit of DBT.

In general, most novice DBT therapists already have at least some of these skills. Improvement of some skill can result from practice or from exposure or participation in particular kinds of experiences, as noted. However, the supervision team is ultimately where therapists apply these skills. Thus, it is essential to establish a safe and collaborative supervision team in which members can be genuine with one another in identifying one anothers' skills and skill limitations, in a supportive, nonpejorative way.

THERAPIST SKILL APPLICATION:
THE DBT SUPERVISION/CONSULTATION TEAM

As mentioned earlier, the DBT supervision/consultation team is an integral and ongoing part of the treatment and provides the primary vehicle for becoming proficient at DBT. As such, the main tasks of ongoing DBT supervision occur here. This section explores the main tasks and possible methods of structuring a DBT consultation group.

Consultation Agreements

DBT consultation team members make a number of agreements that, although standard in DBT, must be discussed within the team so that a genuine agreement can be achieved. The purpose of these agreements is both to orient team members and to provide reminders of some important tenets of DBT in their interactions with one another.

Dialectical Agreement.   Members of the supervision group agree to accept and try to employ a dialectical philosophy. In practice, this means searching for the legitimacy, or utility, in anyone's perspective, rather than expending resources on ascertaining The Truth. In a dialectical philosophy, there is no absolute truth, so efforts are directed instead toward validation, synthesis, and effective action. It is important not to confuse synthesis with compromise. Although compromise is certainly possible, it can sometimes imply a "giving up" of a strong opinion. In a dialectical synthesis, it is possible to find a way to balance and simultaneously validate even opposing strong opinions or feelings.

Consultant to the Patient Agreement.   Team members agree to consult with the client on how to interact effectively with other professionals (including other members of the team) and not to act as intermediaries, telling other professionals how to interact with the client.

Consistency Agreement.   Consultation group members agree that members of the team are not necessarily expected to be consistent in their analyses nor in the ways they deal with clients (including the same client). Not only would it be a violation of the dialectic agreement to expect consistency, but the world is full of inconsistency and in the therapeutic context such inconsistency may have value for the client in learning to use skills in such an unpredictable, yet relatively benevolent, environment. In some ways, this may just as well be called the "inconsistency" agreement, because members are agreeing that there is no inherent value in consistency over inconsistency.

There is some basic consistency within a DBT framework, however. Although therapists may understand or interact with clients quite differently, therapists do agree to be attentive, or "awake," to clients; to look for and reinforce progress; and not to reinforce dysfunctional behaviors or a lack of improvement. Thus, the consistency agreement allows DBT therapists to utilize different styles and to consider different behaviors, but consistently in the service of DBT treatment targets.

Phenomenological Empathy Agreement.   Consultation team members agree to search for nonpejorative, phenomenologically empathic interpretations of client behavior. The idea here is to view behavior contextually, avoid judgment, and avoid "blaming the victim" whenever possible. It is important to understand and validate clients' behavior empathically from their perspective while simultaneously staying in the perspective of the therapist. Similarly, team members agree to search for nonpejorative, phenomenologically empathic interpretations of therapist behavior, and to avoid being judgmental of therapists.

Fallibility Agreement.   There is an explicit understanding that all therapists are fallible. Although the goal is always doing the best DBT possible, the understanding is that even the best efforts will have shortcomings. It is hoped that this agreement results in a reduction in defensiveness in the supervision and consultation process. It is important to note that because therapists are fallible, they will likely violate all of the other agreements mentioned here at various times. The job of the team is simply to try to synthesize opposing perspectives and move on toward effective action.

Observing Limits Agreement.   Members of the consultation group agree that therapists are to observe their own personal and professional limits in their delivery of DBT. Therapists *observe* limits in DBT rather than set them, recognizing that limits may change according to context or circumstances in the lives of clients and therapists and that therapists are different. Thus, therapists continually observe, or watch, their limits and use their observations to guide the therapy. Because of the difficult nature of working with chronically suicidal and parasuicidal clients, this agreement has particular importance as a supervision goal as well and is discussed in depth later on.

General Structure and Functions of a DBT Consultation Group

Organization.   There is no particular structure necessary in a DBT consultation group. Some employ shared leadership responsibilities and others designate a permanent or rotating leader. Most groups meet weekly for 1 or 2 hours, but the length of time groups meet should be predicated on how long it takes for members to get what they want from the consultation team. In some rural settings or in regions with few other DBT therapists nearby, phone consultation meetings supplemented by mailing audiotapes (certified mail, no identifying information included) may be utilized. Similarly, the number of participants can vary according to the practical constraints of number of cases, time needed for supervision, and so forth.

At least two members are needed for a group, although a more useful minimum might be three, so that at least one person can attempt to synthesize opposing views. When there are only two people, and one of them is the "expert," clearly functioning as a supervisor, then DBT supervision resembles more traditional psychotherapy supervision. It is also possible to combine traditional, one-on-one supervision with an ongoing DBT consultation group. This may be particularly desirable when resources allow and DBT trainees are just starting out. What is most important in DBT supervision is learning and applying the therapy effectively and competently, and this always includes some form of supervision or consultation.

Agenda.   Although group members can negotiate the agenda, it should be set at the beginning of every meeting so that sufficient time is allocated to more important topics. Some topics that are particularly important and useful include (a) updates of cases by every therapist, including any difficulties a therapist is having; (b) observation and discussion of at least a segment of videotape from one or more sessions; (c) an update on group skill training (what skills are being taught currently, difficulties and strengths among skill group members) and an exchange of information among individual therapists and skill trainers; (d) problems in learning or applying DBT that team members are experiencing; (e) discussion of institutional issues as they arise (clinic, research, funding, policies, or other issues); and (f) a review or enhancement of DBT principles and strategies.

Treatment Development and Implementation.   Clearly, the primary function of the team is to assess the client and the therapy in order to develop, modify, and implement DBT effectively and competently. Thus, the majority of time is spent on reviewing cases, watching videotapes of sessions, and consulting about the treatment. In general, when discussing an individual case, the team should follow the treatment hierarchy, first discussing commitment to therapy issues, then parasuicidal behaviors, and so on. It is important as well for team members to pause and evaluate the overall treatment development and implementation for a particular client on a regular basis. Is the conceptualization consistent with the data? Is the hierarchy being followed? Are gains being made? Is there a balance of acceptance/validation and problem-solving/change strategies? Is the therapist observing his or her limits? What does the therapist need to do to move up the adherence and competence scale (DBT Expert Rating Scale)? All other aspects of the group are in the service of these goals.

Cheerleading.   Because progress can often be slow with borderline and chronically suicidal clients, it is common for therapists to become demoralized. One important function of the treatment team is to cheer on the therapist by highlighting even small improvements in the therapy process or that the clients make in their lives, supporting and encouraging the therapist in general, and finding other ways to "remoralize" discouraged therapists. Being an effective "cheerleader" requires vigilance to identify incipient discouragement as well as a willingness to validate, support, and encourage others. In DBT supervision, it may be important to cheerlead by articulating a "belief" in the client, the therapist, or the supervision process itself and in each person's capacity for change and improvement, even when little has been demonstrated.

Developing and Maintaining DBT Skills and the Skillful Use of DBT Strategies.   It is essential to find time to develop and enhance DBT skills and strategies on a regular basis. Although it may be possible to schedule special times for advanced learning, this is frequently impractical. Therefore, often the only time skill development and enhancement can be accomplished is during the regular supervision meeting. In order to ensure group members' continuing advancement, it may be useful to rotate responsibility for presenting specific skills or strategies on a monthly basis, although, of course, all members attempt to employ all the DBT components. For example, depending on how large the group is, it may be possible to rotate responsibility for a brief mindfulness exercise at every consultation meeting. Similarly, members can alternate responsibility for reviewing one of the skill-training modules. Members can also alternate paying particular attention to (a) DBT communication strategies; (b) DBT case management strategies; (c) dialectical strategies; (d) consultation group agreements; (e) the DBT Expert Rating Scale, which rates adherence and competence in the delivery of DBT; and (f) other aspects of DBT as they become relevant to group members.

Handling Disagreements.   Most disagreements that occur in the consultation team meetings can be handled effectively by referring to the consultation team agreements. The potential for "staff splitting" is high, however, and it is common for trainees and experts alike to stray from these agreements in many situations. In DBT, we take the position that it is staff members who "split" the staff, not clients. Thus, we try to find ways to accept our own responsibility for dissension and try to repair rifts when they occur. We also attempt to prevent difficulties by regularly "checking in" with one another, trying to maintain a willingness to discuss even difficult topics and refocusing attention on enjoying and appreciating one another whenever possible.

Of course, the ability to implement or adhere to the consultation team agreements is predicated on mutual respect among the members of the team. When a member has personal difficulties that intrude into the group, demonstrates unethical behavior, or consistently engages in anti-DBT strategies, the working alliance of the group is compromised. In these situations, it is essential to deal directly with the issues as soon as they become apparent. This may be done in the group and sometimes requires outside consultation. Recalling that the supervision process is part of the therapy can help block avoidance of difficult issues because the ethical and/or effective delivery of the treatment is at stake.

Maintaining a Dialectical Balance

The general "process" goal in DBT supervision is to try to achieve and maintain a dialectical balance. A dialectical approach is essential both in balancing therapists in their interactions with clients and in balancing team members' interactions with one another. This may be accomplished in part by following the structures and agreements already delineated. In addition, supervisors and other team members can search for "what is being left out," or overlooked, in the therapist's conceptualization of client behavior or use of DBT strategies or in the team's deliberations.

The fundamental dialectic in DBT is between an orientation toward acceptance and validation (of the client, therapist, consultation team members, the therapy itself, etc.) and an orientation toward change (in the conceptualization, treatment methods employed, client, team, therapist behaviors, etc.). The delicate balance of acceptance and change is just as important in supervision as it is in the therapy. It is important to consider both sides of this balance in depth and then attempt to synthesize them.

Validation and Acceptance.   Just as the therapist uses validation to foster a safe therapeutic environment of acceptance of the client, members of the supervision team employ validation strategies to foster an accepting and safe supervision environment in which the therapist's experiences are understood and the therapist is valued. In both environments, successful validation leads to different types of acceptance, which in turn foster change. Of course, acceptance that replaces prior invalidation or avoidance *is* a change.

In DBT, there are multiple types and levels of validation, all of which are relevant in DBT supervision (see Linehan, in press, for a comprehensive description of validation in DBT). For supervision purposes, perhaps the most salient level of validation is "radical genuineness," discussed earlier in the context of the therapy relationship. It is just as essential to the supervision and consultation process that team members consistently strive to be radically genuine with one another. This means synthesizing two positions: (a) Therapists are not fragile and therefore should be treated respectfully and with candor; and (b) therapists are not invulnerable and therefore need support and validation.

During the supervision process, it is important to identify and communicate the wisdom, or validity, in the work of the therapist. This does not mean that everything that DBT therapists do has validity. On the contrary, most supervision time is dedicated to how therapists can do better, try harder, and be more competent DBT therapists. Allowing the balance to include validation can be achieved first by observing therapists directly (or on video or audiotape), noticing in particular their emotional responses, assumptions, and thought processes about their clients, as well as their performance of DBT skills and strategies. It is then useful to give feedback overall and elicit reactions from therapists whose work is being evaluated. Finally, it is important to try to synthesize both supervisor and therapist experiences into a balance of understanding of reactions and effective action vis-à-vis the client.

Problem-Solving and Other Change Strategies. In DBT supervision, as in DBT itself, there are many change strategies and modes of problem solving. At the heart of any effective change strategy is a clear and workable (defined in behavioral terms) definition of the problem. When problem-solving difficulties the therapist has in delivering effective DBT, identifying or defining the type of problem naturally suggests avenues for correction and improvement. In addition to observation and discussion, the use of role plays is particularly effective in both assessing and altering problematic therapist behaviors.

Most problematic therapist behaviors are a result of a skill deficit or counterproductive reinforcement contingencies governing the use of skillful therapy behaviors. We consider both of these possibilities. First, sometimes problems in therapy arise because the therapist does not possess the requisite skills (e.g., the therapist does not know how to implement a particular intervention). Although sometimes difficult to identify, the solution is straightforward: When skill deficits become apparent, therapists need to return to the skill acquisition modes (discussed earlier).

Often, however, the therapist has the necessary skills or repertoires but does not use them in a particular situation. When therapists demonstrate skillful therapy behavior in some situations and not in others, any "unskillful" behavior is likely a result of (a) insufficient reinforcement of these behaviors by the client and/or the consultation team (e.g., good DBT might be ignored by the supervision team or client progress might be slow or difficult to identify); (b) the application of punishing consequences for the skillful therapy behavior (e.g., the client escalates in hostility and attacks the therapist); or (c) a pattern of avoidance on the part of the therapist (e.g., fear or other emotions are avoided by *not* engaging in the skillful behavior, thereby negatively reinforcing unskilled behavior). Careful behavioral analyses comparing the situations of skillful versus unskillful behavior should identify the controlling variables. Then, a number of strategies can be employed to allow for an effective change in contingencies resulting in more effective and competent DBT. Typically, behavior therapy strategies such as shaping and strengthening procedures, response disinhibition, response inhibition, and so on are quite effective (Linehan & McGhee, 1994).

Use DBT Skills to Solve DBT Problems

Although it may be obvious, difficulties that arise in DBT supervision should be approached by using the same skills and strategies employed by DBT itself. In addition to the ones already discussed, several others deserve mention.

DBT Communication Strategies. The DBT communication styles of irreverent and reciprocal communication should both be utilized in DBT supervision. Reciprocal communication is responsive, warm, and genuine, often affectively intense, and can involve self-disclosure. Irreverent communication is offbeat and unorthodox and is used to get others' attention, help "unstick" therapists, present an alternative view (even an "off-the-wall" one), or help elicit an alternative affective response. Typically, neither clients nor therapists expect irreverence in the context of serious conversations. It is important to be clear that this is a communication *style* and never is intended to demean or invalidate. When supervision discussions become repetitive, tiresome, and unproductive, it may be quite useful to search for an irreverent way of reframing the difficulty or a reciprocal way of more fully engaging the participants.

Consultation Strategy.   The supervision corollary to the DBT consultant-to-the-therapist strategy (regarding dealing with the client) is that members of the supervision team consult with one another on *how to deal with one another* and other professionals and do not intervene on behalf of others on the team except when absolutely necessary. This does not mean that team members do not support and validate one another. Rather, this strategy emphasizes the importance of collaborative attempts to resolve problems in a respectful manner.

In addition, this strategy can be used to facilitate enhancing therapist skills. For example, treating specific psychological problems in DBT often involves "importing" other protocols into DBT (e.g., treatment protocols for insomnia or panic disorder). If a particular set of skills is required for effective treatment, the consultation group can act as consultant to the therapists in finding ways to get them trained in these additional skills.

In Vivo Supervision and Consultation.   Just as phone consultation is used in DBT to enhance generalization of skills into the natural environment, phone supervision may be used during client emergencies. Similarly, live observation of sessions can be utilized to give immediate feedback to therapists. Other strategies, such as cotherapy or "bug in the ear" supervision, could be employed to allow for in vivo assessment of treatment difficulties and to maximize the generalization of skills learned in the supervision/consultation team.

SUPERVISION AND CONSULTATION TARGETS

Adherence to and Competence in DBT

The Importance of Adherence to DBT Protocols.   The primary target of training, supervision, and consultation in DBT is the competent delivery of DBT. Providing DBT that closely adheres to the manuals (Linehan, 1993a, 1993b) and is performed at a high level of competence has been demonstrated to be effective in treating borderline and chronically suicidal clients. Thus, the goal is to make decisions in the treatment that conform to DBT principles and strategies whenever possible, because this is the form of the treatment that has empirical support.

It is common for therapists trained in other approaches, when under stress, to consider "mixing" treatments, or temporarily abandoning DBT in favor of more familiar intervention strategies. Under situations of high arousal, new learning is more difficult, and high stress and arousal are common with very distressed and suicidal clients. So, this tendency can be understandable. The target here is delivering excellent DBT, however, not excellent therapy of some other variety.

Clinical Science and DBT.   The DBT values of assessing and demonstrating efficacy suggest that the effectiveness of the therapy be monitored continuously with all clients using whatever assessment devices are practical (e.g., daily diary cards, assessment batteries at fixed intervals, periodic interviews). It is similarly important to monitor therapist adherence and competence in order to evaluate therapists, to evaluate training and supervision, and to test the integrity of a treatment condition in research (Waltz, Addis, Koerner, & Jacobson, 1993). Regardless of setting, rating therapist adherence and competence facilitates identifying both improvements (which can be reinforced) and problems (which can become a focus in the supervision and consultation meetings).

Rating Adherence and Competence.   Traditionally, adherence and competence are rated subjectively by supervisors (or members of the consultation group). A new scale (DBT Expert Rating Scale) has been developed, however, to quantify therapist adherence and competence (Linehan et al., 1996). Again, regardless of method, systematic monitoring of the extent to which therapists are doing DBT (as opposed to utilizing other treatments), and doing so in a competent and effective manner, is essential in therapist development.

One of the advantages of tracking therapist adherence is that it helps in the assessment of the therapist and therefore helps to organize training and supervision time. For example, therapists who receive low adherence marks are likely engaging in therapy-interfering behavior of one kind or another (they have insufficient skills, are not using DBT strategies, etc.). These problems can be readily identified for supervision. In contrast, high adherence and competence ratings include mostly good choices in the use of DBT strategies, which are in turn delivered effectively. Getting higher ratings can be goals, and it is easy for therapists to identify one or more specific DBT skills or strategies for practice and mastery to help move up the adherence scale.

Shaping Therapist Adherence and Competence

A few additional processes are involved in enhancing DBT performance by therapists (i.e., maximizing their adherence to DBT).

Observing Limits.   As previously mentioned, in DBT therapists try not to set limits, but rather to observe them. This includes two parts: (a) monitoring honestly personal and professional limits regarding what therapists are willing (and not willing) to do in the service of their clients and what client behaviors they are (and are not) willing to tolerate; and (b) moving quickly to apply change strategies to client behaviors when they threaten or intrude across therapist limits. Thus, in DBT it is the job of therapists and the supervision team, not of the clients, to take care of therapist limits. This in turn helps to prevent therapist burnout, which allows the most effective treatment to continue to be provided.

Using the term *observing* limits (as opposed to setting them) reflects the DBT flexibility regarding limits and the focus on observing natural, as opposed to arbitrary limits. The only a priori limits for therapist behavior are ethical ones. For client behavior, the only a priori limit usually is that therapy is suspended when clients drop out of either part of the treatment package (skills training or individual therapy). Consultation team members regularly include observing natural limits in discussions of therapy cases.

From a DBT perspective, natural limits vary among therapists and over time within the same therapist. Both events in therapists' lives and in client and supervision interactions influence limits. For example, being overworked or sick often results in a narrowing of limits, whereas an optimal workload, satisfying personal life, and effective supervision team likely foster broader limits.

What is perhaps most important in DBT supervision, in terms of observing limits, is helping therapists monitor exactly where their limits are at all times. Limits that are arbitrarily narrow and "protective" of the therapist result in unnecessary withholding from the client. On the other hand, pretending that limits are broader than they really are leads to burnout and ineffective treatment. It is essential in DBT supervision to push therapists to observe their limits, to be more or less flexible, depending on their genuine limits at any time. It is especially useful to anticipate therapist behaviors that allow clients to cross limits and to address these potential threats to the therapy early in the therapy process.

Monitor Enthusiasm.   It is helpful if all members of the supervision team monitor their own and others' enthusiasm for their work versus discouragement and demoralization. Breaches in observing limits can be the source of discouragement. However, periods of discouragement are common in work with DBT clients. It is important to analyze the factors contributing to discouragement. Whatever the factors, team members can use cheerleading, highlighting successes, higher levels of positive reinforcers for therapists' effective work, validation, effective problem solving, or other strategies to reignite therapist enthusiasm and satisfaction.

In addition, the team may proactively work on "team building" in preventing discouragement of team members. There are many team activities that could function this way. For example, scheduling social time outside the work setting can help put working relationships in a new, often invigorated context. Or, consultation team members could go to a conference, workshop, or other training opportunity as a group, combining social and professional activities. Regardless of the method employed, working together effectively as a team is enhanced with good communication, time to get to know one another, and shared activities.

Stay Behavioral and Dialectical.   By this time, the importance of both these goals should be clear. Nevertheless, low adherence usually occurs in times of elevated client distress and often heightened team distress. Thus, returning to DBT's behavioral roots reminds us that it is important not to reinforce therapy-interfering behaviors by the client, therapist, or supervision/consultation team. Rather, we should always reinforce therapists and team members for doing good, adhering, competent DBT. Staying dialectical means searching for alternative explanations, conceptualizations, and ways of understanding client and therapist behaviors. This then allows effective validation and change strategies to be employed.

Specific Targets Early in Training.   There are a number of common reasons that novice DBT therapists receive lower adherence ratings. It may be useful to identify many of these initial skill deficits early so that therapists and supervisors can work efficiently toward competent delivery of DBT. Novice DBT therapists frequently (and expert ones sometimes) (a) forget to follow the core structures of DBT (e.g., analyzing diary cards); (b) do not observe the treatment hierarchy within sessions; (c) underestimate the sophistication required, and allocate insufficient time and effort to thorough behavioral analysis of client (or therapist, or supervisor) target behaviors; (d) have difficulty integrating problem solving into the behavioral analysis (weaving solutions into chains); (e) do not perform sufficiently thorough or effective problem solving (including good targeting, a collaborative problem-solving process; commitment/agreement to solution; troubleshooting the solution, and reviewing the success of the solution later on, making modifications as required); and (f) engage in "passive" supervision-interfering behavior (e.g., nonparticipation in the supervision group process, not videotaping sessions).

As the training and supervision process progresses, therapists move from paying attention primarily to their own behavior as therapists to a more complete focus on client behavior. As DBT is learned fully and becomes "natural," therapists are better able to integrate and synthesize their own behaviors with those of their clients, identifying and analyzing interactions between them. Because supervision is part of the treatment, it is essential also to integrate interactions that occur in the supervision/consultation group into a coherent examination of the entire therapy process.

Enjoy DBT, DBT Clients, DBT Supervision.   We have already established the difficult nature of working with borderline and chronically suicidal clients in general. It should also be apparent that learning DBT and practicing it competently involves considerable dedication and skill. It is important not to forget, however, that practicing DBT competently can be extremely rewarding professionally and personally and can be quite enjoyable. Not paying attention to the satisfying parts of doing DBT not only would be "therapy-interfering," it would be a darn shame.

FUTURE DIRECTIONS

As described earlier, ongoing supervision and consultation are essential components of the underlying theory of dialectical behavior therapy, and DBT as a whole has been shown to be an effective treatment. In reality, however, the role of supervision and consultation per se in DBT remains a hypothesis. From a research perspective, we know very little about what kinds of supervision are most effective in fostering adherence and competence. The supervision and consultation processes presented in this chapter represent an attempt to describe the structures and processes of DBT in its empirically validated form. Further research is needed on supervision models in general, the specific functions of supervision in DBT, and the relative efficacy of various supervision approaches. These efforts will likely result in more effective services for our clients and, therefore, increasingly satisfying professional experiences for DBT therapists.

REFERENCES

Boscolo, L., Cecchin, G., Hoffman, L., & Penn, P. (1987). *Milan systemic family therapy: Conversations in theory and practice.* New York: Basic Books.

Kohlenberg, R. J., & Tsai, M. (1991). *Functional analytic psychotherapy: Creating intense and curative therapeutic relationships.* New York: Plenum.

Linehan, M. M. (1993a). *Cognitive-behavioral treatment of borderline personality disorder.* New York: Guilford.

Linehan, M. M. (1993b). *Skills training manual for treating borderline personality disorder.* New York: Guilford.

Linehan, M. M. (1994). Acceptance and change: The central dialectic in psychotherapy. In S. C. Hayes, N. S. Jacobson, V. M. Follette, & M. J. Dougher (Eds.), *Acceptance and change: Content and context in psychotherapy* (pp. 73–86). Reno, NV: Context Press.

Linehan, M. M. (in press). Validation and psychotherapy. In A. Bohart & L. S. Greenberg (Eds.), *Empathy and psychotherapy: New directions to theory, research, and practice.* Washington, DC: American Psychological Association.

Linehan, M. M., Armstrong, H. E., Suarez, A., Allmon, D., & Heard, H. L. (1991). Cognitive-behavioral treatment of chronically parasuicidal borderline patients. *Archives of General Psychiatry, 48,* 1060–1064.

Linehan, M. M., Heard, H. L., & Armstrong, H. E. (1993). Naturalistic follow-up of a behavioral treatment for chronically parasuicidal borderline patients. *Archives of General Psychiatry, 50,* 971–974.

Linehan, M. M., & Kehrer, C. A. (1993). Borderline personality disorder. In D. H. Barlow (Ed.), *Clinical handbook of psychological disorders* (2nd ed., pp. 396–441). New York: Guilford.

Linehan, M. M., Lockard, J., Wagner, A., & Tutek, D. A. (1996). *DBT Expert Rating Scale.* Unpublished scale. Seattle: University of Washington.

Linehan, M. M., & McGhee, D. E. (1994). A cognitive-behavioral model of supervision with individual and group components. In S. Greben & R. Ruskin (Eds.), *Clinical perspectives on psychotherapy supervision* (pp. 165–188). Washington, D. C.: American Psychiatric Press.

Linehan, M. M., Tutek, D. A., Heard, H. L., & Armstrong, H. E. (1994). Interpersonal outcome of cognitive behavioral treatment for chronically suicidal borderline patients. *American Journal of Psychiatry, 151,* 1771–1776.

Waltz, J. A., Addis, M. E., Koerner, K., & Jacobson, N. S. (1993). Assessment of adherence and competence. *Journal of Consulting and Clinical Psychology, 61,* 620–630.

CHAPTER 7

Supervision in Rational Emotive Behavior Therapy

PAUL J. WOODS
Institute for Rational Therapy and Behavioral Medicine
ALBERT ELLIS
Institute for Rational-Emotive Therapy

Rational-emotive therapy has been known for years and has been referred to, both formally and informally, as RET. This term for the type of therapy that we actually use, however, is misleading. So in order to better communicate the fact that it is not only cognitive but also behavioral, we have recently changed the name to *rational emotive behavior therapy* (REBT). This is a little more awkward, but we opt for reality rather than ease of expression.

In REBT, we view the endeavor of supervision as one of education, training, and practice with critical and constructive feedback. In using the term *supervision* in this chapter, we do not refer to taking responsibility for the work of another therapist. This point, along with some of the others discussed later, has been made in an earlier chapter on supervision in REBT (Wessler & Ellis, 1980). Other thoughts and comments in that chapter are still timely and relevant, and the reader is referred to it as a companion to the present chapter. Our discussion in this chapter focuses on the teaching of REBT skills and various supervisory practices aimed at facilitating the mastery of REBT approaches in psychotherapy and counseling.

EDUCATIONAL ASPECTS OF SUPERVISION

Supervision has a strong educational component; our experience has shown that people beginning their training in REBT, whether they are young professionals or have extensive experience in other forms of psychotherapy, often fail to grasp the fundamental principles of REBT. So the first objective is to familiarize professionals with various writings discussing the principles and practice of REBT (e.g., Bernard, 1991; Dryden & DiGiuseppe, 1990; Ellis, 1962, 1991; Ellis & Dryden, 1987; Ellis & Grieger, 1977, 1986; Walen, DiGiuseppe, & Dryden, 1992). Background materials such as these are a proper, and likely necessary, beginning for training. At this stage, it is important for those in training to appreciate that REBT concentrates on detecting and changing self-disturbing philosophies. Teaching supervisees to identify self-disturbing attitudes and beliefs, persuading clients that they are, indeed, a main cause of their emotional disturbances, and then showing them how they can be challenged and changed are the principal areas of attention and those in which close and careful supervision is highly desirable. We do not expect one to learn REBT skills simply by reading theory or even by reading or listening to actual therapy transcripts or recordings anymore than we would expect someone to learn to play a musical instrument by reading books on musicology and listening to a musician play the instrument.

At the Institute for Rational-Emotive Therapy in New York and at affiliated training institutes and programs around the world, we introduce people to REBT through workshops conducted by professionals highly experienced in the theory and its application. These workshops include lectures on the fundamentals of REBT, as well as live demonstrations employing volunteers from the workshop participants. We also recommend books, articles, and recordings and prefer that attendees have done some of this background work before the workshops.

Fundamentals of REBT and the Complexity of the ABC Model

One way of conceptualizing the focus of training is shown in Figure 7.1. At the top of this figure is the well-known ABC theory of emotional and behavioral disturbance. The remaining part of the figure represents the psychotherapeutic treatment. In the ABC theory, A stands for *activating event,* B stands for the *beliefs* one holds about such activating events and includes evaluations of them, and C stands for *consequences,* which involve both emotions and behavior. It would be quite erroneous to assume that the use of ABC indicates or implies simplicity. In actuality, A can be *anything that the individual is capable of contemplating.* This includes focusing one's attention on imagining and thinking about events from the past (which are, of course, pulled from one's memory bank), events that are ongoing, and events that are fantasized or predicted to occur in the future. As can also be *internal,* such as one's feelings of anxiousness, which can be viewed and evaluated so as to produce higher states of arousal, more anxiety, and ultimately panic. An A can also be an *inference* that one draws from a particular experience—for example, inferring that the ice one is skating on is dangerously thin when it really isn't. (Since inferences are cognitive processes, beginners often make the mistake of classifying them as Bs.) As can also be about Cs, as when one contemplates one's own anger and creates feelings of guilt over having been angry. As can be about Bs, which is a main part of REBT therapy. That is, people are taught to contemplate their own beliefs and evaluations and focus critical and skeptical attention on them. But complexity can increase manyfold more.

See, for example, Woods and Grieger (1993): This case study of a bulimic young woman involved six ABC sequences with a wide variety of complexities. A1 (body image) was simple, but then A2 consisted of A1 (body image) plus C1 (emotional upset about her body image). A3 consisted of C2 (increased emotional upset and a high dose of laxatives). A4 consisted of C3 (bingeing). A5 consisted of C2 (increased emotional upset and a high dose of laxatives), C3 (bingeing), and C4 (additional dose of laxatives). A6 consisted of the total components of all five of the preceding ABC sequences. So the A in the ABC theory of REBT is not at all simple, and the ABC conceptualization is applicable to very complex circumstances. It is important for supervisees to be aware of such complexity, but not to be overwhelmed by it. It is desirable for them to feel *empowered* by the potential of REBT to be applied to complex human emotional and behavioral problems and to be optimistically confident that they can learn such applications.

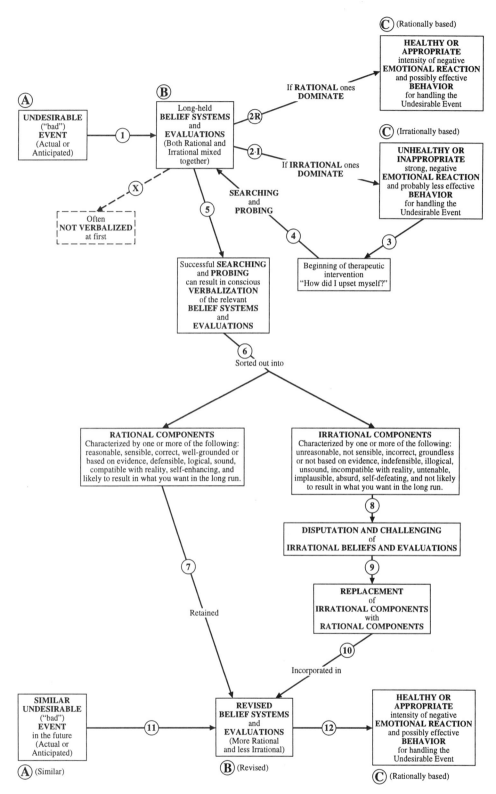

Figure 7.1 Rational Emotive Behavior Therapy and Theory Flowchart

103

Basic Issues of Understanding for the Supervisee

To explain Figure 7.1 more thoroughly, we start at the upper left-hand corner with A. That is, something one is focusing attention on, even if only briefly. Path 1 leads from A to B, where this focus of attention is contemplated and existing attitudes, beliefs, and evaluations are aroused or "triggered off." B exists in the cerebral cortex or thinking part of the brain and can be activated *without actually being verbalized.* That is, the "software program" can run and cause its effects without involving the vocal mechanism. If the contemplation of the activating event is dominated by rational (self-helping) components, then path 2-R will lead to a C with healthy or appropriate emotional reactions and more likely effective behavior for dealing with the problem at A. If the activating event is undesirable, then the emotional reactions at the end of path 2-R *will be negative.* The intensity will be *lower,* but not necessarily low. That is, rational thinking about very bad events may still result in strong negative feelings. Our position is not to be confused with the "power of positive thinking" or "every cloud has a silver lining" approach. Also, there is no guarantee that effective behavior will follow rational thinking, for the individual might not have the necessary skills, such as for assertive behavior or for fixing something that is broken.

If the contemplation of the problem at A is dominated by irrational components, then path 2-I will lead to a C with unhealthy or inappropriately stronger negative emotional reactions and probably less effective behavior for dealing with the problem at A. Here one is more likely to "kick the flat tires of life" and to scream at them, rather than to arrange for them to be better dealt with. Clients are motivated to seek out REBT because they are spending too much time in this box of irrationally based Cs.

Therapeutic intervention begins by following path 3 to raise the question, "How did I upset myself?" And path 4 directs a searching and probing of B, which will be recalled was often not verbalized at all, or at best was incompletely verbalized at the time it was first activated. Clients and some beginning therapists are tempted to go back to A and describe at length all the details of what happened. This is to be resisted so that attention can be directed at the main cause of the emotional upset, B. This probing and searching function requires sophisticated skills to be developed by therapists in training. First, it is important to be familiar with the theory and clinical and research data on the contents of the irrational thinking that causes each of the types of emotional distress humans experience. This knowledge guides the appropriate questions, put forth to the client as hypotheses, that will help obtain a clear and reasonably complete "printout" of the beliefs and evaluations triggered off by the activating event. Skills are also required for completing the client's statements, filling in the *implied* aspects. A client, for example, might make a statement such as, "He knew he was going to be late for the meeting, and he never called to let us know." This will be recognized as merely a description of A, even though the client believes it to be the cause of his anger. The therapist, however, recognizes the presence of the *implied* B—"*as he should have!*" and "teases" it out of the client.

Another important skill to be worked on in supervision is that of discriminating between inferences and actual beliefs. An *inference* is a conclusion drawn from the experience of an activating event that may or may not be correct. But even though it is a cognitive process, it is still considered to be part of A. In order to uncover the Bs, we assume the inference is correct rather than argue against it, and then probe for what evaluative beliefs exist about this "correct" observation.

Suppose, for example, that a wife experiences some neglect and coldness from her partner, infers from this that he no longer loves her, and feels depressed. If the therapist argues against the inference and convinces the wife that her husband does still really love her but is preoccupied with business problems, then she is likely to feel less depressed, and it would seem as if this were an effective strategy for therapy. The trouble is that the beliefs (Bs) related to the possibility of her husband not loving her have not been uncovered, challenged, or changed. Hence, REBT would argue that efficient therapy has hardly been conducted at all. The therapist has merely helped the client to change the A, and if the A is no longer present it will not trigger off the Bs leading to depression. But the client's irrational beliefs are still there—"If my husband doesn't love me, as he *must,* I'm an unlovable worthless person!" These Bs will be able to create depression again in the future if activated. So the temptation on the part of some therapists to argue against the inference is to be resisted for the time being. *After* the depression-producing irrational beliefs have been uncovered, disputed, and replaced, *then* it may be desirable to go back and check the client's assessment of reality. If, indeed, her husband does still love her, it is preferable for her to realize this fact and correct her inference when the therapeutic "cleansing" of her depression-producing thoughts and beliefs has been completed.

Success in the searching and probing of B will lead by path 5 to a fairly complete or representative sampling of the Bs so that each component can be critically and skeptically examined individually. Following path 6, each one is to be labeled and sorted into "rational" (self-helping) or "irrational" (self-defeating) categories. For this task, the therapist needs to be aware of basic aspects of logic and scientific thinking. For example, we live in a cause-and-effect world, and therefore when something *has happened,* no matter how bad or undesirable it is, it is not rational or useful to believe that it shouldn't have happened. Things happen when causal conditions are present, and when the necessary and sufficient conditions are present the event *will occur* exactly as it *should.* Before a therapist can convince a client of this, it is necessary for the therapist to realize and accept it first.

Preceding this process of classifying components of the B, it is useful to have discussed or have the client read about the basic irrational beliefs and to understand why they are irrational. These basic irrational beliefs are (a) demandingness, (b) catastrophizing or "awfulizing," that is, exaggerating the badness of events, (c) low frustration tolerance or "can't-stand-it-itis," and (d) self or other global rating: believing that people as a whole deserve to be damned, blamed, or condemned for their wrongdoing. With this background, and with the unstated, implicit beliefs brought out during the probing and searching, the process of classifying each component of the B can proceed with relatively little disagreement between therapist and client.

All components agreed to be rational by both therapist and client are left alone and, on path 7, are intended to be retained in the revised B. The irrational components, however, are to be given a great deal of attention. Path 8 leads to what can be considered to be the most important part of REBT, the disputation of irrational beliefs. Effective skills by the therapist are required here for successful REBT, and comprehensive disputation strategies are discussed in many REBT publications (e.g., DiGiuseppe, 1991; Ellis, 1994; Kopec, Beal, & DiGiuseppe, 1994; Walen, DiGiuseppe, & Dryden, 1992, Part IV). Skipping this step, and merely learning to think in a rational way, will not be as effective; the new rational alternatives can be conceived of as being stored in another part of the thinking brain while the old irrational "programs" will continue to be stored, untouched, and be retrievable again in the future. But disputations and challenges can be conceived of as additional branches in the neural network where the irrational component was stored, so that when it is activated again in the future, the individual will immediately be reminded of these disputations and challenges before self-defeating philosophies can do the emotional damage they used to do.

Following the successful completion of such disputational challenges, the individual is then at a loss, so to speak, about how to think about the problem of unfortunate events that are almost sure to keep occurring at A. Supervisees are instructed, following path 9, how to tease out or suggest alternatives to the client. Sometimes creating rational alternatives presents a greater challenge than one might expect. Many people have become so used to the destructive ways they have been thinking for years, or even decades, that they cannot readily come up with alternatives, even after they have convinced themselves that their old ways of thinking were irrational.

It is best, therefore, for supervisees to become aware of a great many alternative ways of contemplating problems, and if their clients can't come up with any on their own, to be able to suggest several alternatives on the spot. It is finally intended that these new rational alternatives be reviewed and practiced so that they can be readily incorporated, by path 10, into a revised set of belief systems and evaluations. Then when similar problems arise in the future, path 11 will lead to the more rational beliefs and evaluations that then produce, by path 12, healthy or appropriate levels of negative feelings and possibly more effective behavior for handling the A.

Unfortunate activating events or adversities (A) will always keep occurring in one's life. If, however, one constructs fewer irrational beliefs (iBs) about them, one can improve them, live with them, create fewer of them oneself, and acquire consistent rational self-helping effective new philosophies (Es) that help one at different times successfully carry out these new ways of living. Being, then, both less disturbed and less disturb*able*, one can go on— by oneself or with the help of an REBT practitioner—to actualize or enjoy oneself more.

Working within this formulation shown in Figure 7.1 in a consistent and disciplined manner is likely to lead to increased skills at "self-therapy" so that clients can function better throughout the rest of their lives. For instructions with this formulation using prepared homework forms, see Woods (1991). Repeated, systematic practice can produce a level of proficiency so that nothing has to be written down; the skilled client can run rapidly through the entire chart in his or her head. For example, the client is taught to react to emotional distress at C as if it were an alarm signal. Then, path 3, "Wait a minute! How am I getting myself so upset?" Paths 4 and 5 lead to "This is what I've been telling myself." Path 6, "Part of that is so irrational, and [path 8] this is why." Path 9, "I certainly can think this way instead." Then through path 10 a revision of the original Bs is activated and the emotional distress is lowered.

For a complete guide to the process and practice of REBT that has been designed as a client workbook to accompany therapy, but is also useful for educational aspects of supervision, see Grieger and Woods (1993).

TRAINING ASPECTS OF SUPERVISION

General Goals and Skills

In REBT, the therapist-client relationship is important, for clients are not likely to remain in therapy without a good relationship. But the relationship *itself* is not seen as "curative." Being empathic, understanding, knowledgeable, patient, tolerant, and so on, will help to keep clients returning, doing their homework, and working on their therapeutic goals. But an *intense* therapist-client relationship is to be avoided for it can be iatrogenic in several ways: (a) It can foster a dependency on the therapist, which can thereby increase disturbance producing, irrational needs for love, support, respect, and approval; (b) it may encourage intense feelings to develop toward the therapist so that these become the focus of attention rather than *outside* relationships; and (c) it can interfere with therapy if the therapist becomes fearful to challenge, confront, debate, and dispute the client because such actions might "harm the relationship."

So it is important to recognize that the main focus of attention is the irrational beliefs at B that are causing the emotional distress and inappropriate, self-defeating behavior at C. If progress can then be made at reducing emotional distress and inappropriate behaviors, the client will likely react toward the therapist with such relief and appreciation that relationship issues take care of themselves.

Professionals with sound basic clinical and counseling skills who have experience in interviewing and discussing problems with clients are able, in our experience, to most quickly and effectively learn REBT. They are to be cautioned, however, against adopting an "eclectic" approach when such an approach would be in opposition to the theory and practice of REBT. An approach, for example, that would place great emphasis on uncovering unconscious memories of early childhood experiences would not find a happy "marriage" with REBT. The communication and interpersonal skills developed from prior experience as a therapist are useful and helpful, but incorporating conflicting theoretical positions into REBT training and practice would be counterproductive. Thus it is better for therapists to put their professional biases in storage for a time while they are learning the theory and practice of REBT. Then when their cognitive-behavioral skills are developed, they can compare and contrast them with their prior skills, and it is hoped, test the effectiveness of each in actual practice.

It is important to be clear about this. We are not opposed to therapists using previously learned skills. As long as a basic REBT framework is used, a number of effective therapeutic techniques may be used *within that framework.* That is, we caution against using other strategies *instead of,* rather than *in addition to,* the major focus of identifying, disputing, and replacing irrational beliefs (iBs).

In supervising therapists in REBT, it is important, therefore, to watch for the temptation of supervisees to use the well-learned skills they acquired prior to using REBT skills. Therapists trained in nondirective listening may find it easier to continue than to change to a more active-directive approach. Professionals with a strict behavioristic approach may want to manipulate environmental circumstances and set up contingent consequences to follow behavioral changes rather than to work on their clients' mediating cognitions. Others may strive to provide symptomatic relief, such as with relaxation training or distracting procedures, rather than strive for fundamental philosophic change. And those who use social skill training and assertiveness training, which are useful and valuable, may still focus on teaching these to clients, but they still do not change irrational belief systems. The REBT supervisor, therefore, guards against the temptation of experienced professionals to *mainly* or *only* use their already well-learned skills so as to avoid trying out the unfamiliar domain of REBT.

Specific REBT Skills and a Model for Supervision

Following are a number of specific skills and goals for REBT therapy. The supervisor wants to be aware of them and look for their presence or absence in therapy sessions under review. Obviously, only a few will appear in any one segment being supervised, but notes can be made when reviewing a number of sessions from a given therapist in training so that the supervisor can make suggestions regarding skills that have not been observed.

1. Fundamental insights for clients to achieve (Grieger & Boyd, 1980, pp. 83–85):

   a. The world we occupy involves cause-and-effect relationships, and insight number 1 recognizes that this applies to behavior as well as all other conditions. Simply stated, behavior has antecedent factors that cause it to occur. It does not occur by itself; there are preceding external and internal events operating in a causal relationship to all behavior.

   b. Insight number 2 is that emotional and behavioral reactions are caused to a large extent by ideas, beliefs, evaluations, and philosophies held by the person. In the ABCs of REBT, this insight recognizes that Cs are primarily caused by Bs and not by As. Or, in the words of Epictetus, "People are disturbed not by things, but by the views they take of them." This insight is particularly important, for not much progress will be made in REBT (nor quite likely, we would opine, in any other form of therapy either) unless it is accepted.

   c. Insight number 3 consists of becoming aware of and acknowledging the causes of one's own emotional distress. This involves becoming aware of one's own irrational beliefs and appreciating the role they play in causing one's emotional distress and self-defeating behaviors. This is very important and *empowering,* for it shows clients that they are not helpless victims of earlier life experiences or other outside forces. This insight sets the stage for the final two.

   d. That any thoughts, particularly the irrational ones just identified, may be questioned and challenged is insight number 4. Clients at the beginning of therapy often tend to accept their thinking and beliefs uncritically, and this insight shows them that they can be skeptical and questioning.

   e. The final basic insight, number 5, is that the thoughts, beliefs, and evaluations found to be invalid or self-defeating (irrational) can be reduced and replaced with better ones.

In supervising, it is important to detect whether or not the client has achieved these insights.

2. Identifying and specifying the ABCs:

   In discussing emotional or behavioral problems with the client, it is desirable for the supervisee to ask for specific ones rather than to talk in generalities. Then it is best to identify the As and Cs first to "tie each end down." Following a minimum of discussion of As and Cs, which clients often want to go on and on about, it is good to then focus a lot of attention on the Bs—not only the actual overt and covert (self-talk) statements and thoughts that took place at the time of the emotional episode in question, but also the implied but unstated beliefs and evaluations as well as general beliefs and philosophies. Therapists in supervision are encouraged to be specific at this point and encouraged to write down the ABCs along with the client, so that both can have the entire emotional episode in "black and white" out in the open to critically examine. Clients will often remark that they didn't realize what they were really thinking and how irrational some of it was until they saw it in writing in front of them.

3. Systematic progress through the therapeutic process

   Within reason, some degree of discipline and consistency is desirable through the therapeutic change process. We are uncomfortable with therapy sessions that begin with questions such as, "Well, what do you want to talk about today?" In REBT, homework plays an important role. One type of homework involves working through the sequences shown in Figure 7.1. This process can be broken down in any way that seems reasonable, but one way of demarcating steps along the way is shown in Figure 7.2. First, specifying the ABCs just discussed under number 2 is seen in the section of Figure 7.2 called "Preliminary Practice." Therapists in training may assume too much understanding on the part of clients, and it is good not to rush too quickly over this basic beginning. In supervision, we want to be fairly sure that not only does the therapist understand the basic ABCs of any emotional/behavioral episode under consideration, but that the client in the session being supervised also is comfortable with this separation of events in what seems to be a smooth, unseparated sequence. That is, the input/processing/output components of an emotional/behavioral episode flow together and can occur in a short period of time. Training clients to make these separations is a basic step and because it is a new experience for most not as easy as it may seem. Clients are easily confused at this point, as are many therapists in training as well. So it is good to listen for clarifying questions being asked by the therapist to assure that the client understands what the As, the Bs, and the Cs are.

Preliminary practice can be conducted in the office and then phase I assigned as written homework. Phase I adds to the preliminary practice by next including the searching and probing of the B so as to obtain a reasonably complete survey of all the thoughts, beliefs, and evaluations held by the client about events such as the one under consideration. The client returns to the next session having done the best he or she could, and the work is reviewed by the therapist. This process was discussed earlier in the section "Educational Aspects of Supervision," and in supervision we listen for the effectiveness of the therapist in obtaining a reasonably complete "printout" of the "software program."

Following completion of Phase I, the Bs are sorted into rational and irrational components, Phase II. If feasible, this is done during the same session that Phase I was reviewed, and then Phase III is assigned for written homework. This is just one box in the schematic diagram, but it constitutes, perhaps, the most important phase of REBT work. This was also discussed earlier in the section "Educational Aspects of Supervision." Written homework is brought to the next session and reviewed by the therapist. In supervision, we listen for effective help given by the therapist to the client so that the client does indeed accept the disputation and becomes convinced that each belief in question was irrational—that is, unreasonable, foolish, in conflict with reality, self-defeating, and so forth.

Then the final Phase IV involves replacing each irrational belief with a rational alternative. Again, this is assigned as written homework to be returned for discussion, help, and correction in the next session.

It is unlikely that supervision will cover enough sessions to follow all of these steps. But, in any session being supervised, we would expect to be able to identify where the therapist is in this scheme with the client. In fact, at any point in REBT therapy, we would expect to be able to specify precisely where in this scheme the therapy session is. In "live" supervision, when the supervisee appears confused, suggestions can be made on the basis of Figures 7.1 and 7.2, as to where to go next.

So, much of what is covered in the educational aspects of supervision gets directly transferred and applied to the training aspects of supervision.

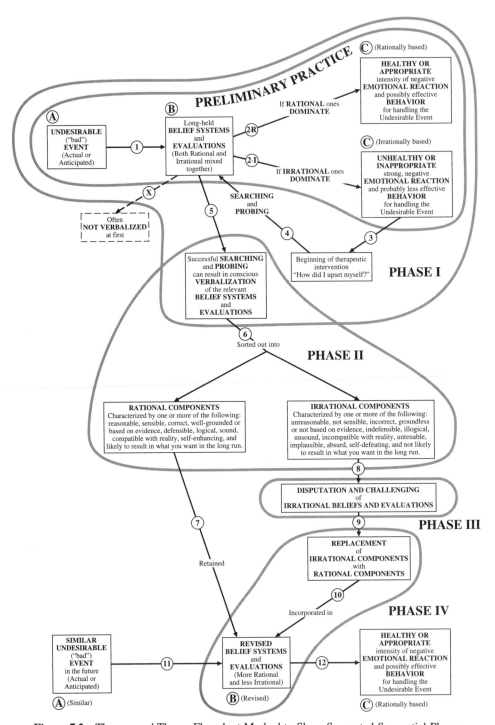

Figure 7.2 Therapy and Theory Flowchart Marked to Show Suggested Sequential Phases

110

EVALUATION OF SUPERVISEES' PERFORMANCE

Some of the problems with supervisees described in the supervision literature apparently stem, we believe, from irrational beliefs held by the supervisee. For example, problems such as self-deprecation and helplessness (Bauman, 1972), evaluation anxiety and performance anxiety (Liddle, 1986), resistance caused by a perceived threat to autonomy (Glickauf-Hughes, 1994), anxiety about facing the unknown (Mollon, 1989), shame and low self-esteem (Eckler-Hart, 1987; Glickauf-Hughes, 1994), evaluation of one's self (Cohen, 1980; Muller, 1985), and perfectionism (Arkowitz, 1990) in the supervisee are largely caused, in our view, by irrational beliefs that would be most desirable to dispute and change. Such deterrents to good professional performance would best be reduced by a thorough understanding and application of REBT principles by the supervisee personally during the process of training and practice. To a limited extent, some of these issues can be dealt with when supervising small groups of supervisees, but a more satisfactory result might require individual work with an REBT therapist.

At the least, evaluation of performance is best conducted in an atmosphere of acceptance and tolerance for mistakes by the supervisor for the supervisee, by the supervisee for him- or herself, and by the supervisee for the supervisor. We would like to see everyone apply REBT to him- or herself, so that the supervisor doesn't become angry with supervisees or vice versa, and so that supervisees don't make themselves anxious about their own inadequacies or make themselves feel threatened by or resentful of criticism.

Evaluation can focus on the same model described earlier in the sections covering educational and training aspects. In any particular therapy session, work will be somewhere in Figure 7.2 if REBT is being applied. Thus, a verbal, taped, or written evaluation would be directed at how well that segment of REBT was being conducted. Was it thorough and effective? Was the client led to the next step? Was homework assigned? And so on. If the segment was lacking in some way, then specific, constructive suggestions would be made to the supervisee.

The evaluation process can also be helped by the use of lists of specific REBT skills that can be found in a number of sources (e.g., Bard, 1980; Ellis, 1985; Ellis & Dryden, 1987; Grieger & Boyd, 1980; Wessler & Wessler, 1980; Yapp & Dryden, 1994).

PREFERABLE CHARACTERISTICS AND TRAITS
FOR REBT PRACTITIONERS

Does an REBT practitioner have to have personal therapy and special personal characteristics in order to be effective? No, not exactly. Many different kinds of individuals have been found to practice REBT effectively, and their own personal experience as a client may be preferable but hardly necessary.

Most of the traits that have been recommended for practically all therapists and that supervisors can look for and abet in REBTers are fairly obvious. They include a vital interest in helping people; strong empathy; ability to cope with and ameliorate their own disturbances; patience, persistence, and willingness to do hard work; consistent ethical, responsible, and professional behavior; optimism and encouragement; knowledge of and acceptance of wide cultural, ethnic, and religious diversity of their clients; and acceptance of their own limitations (Ellis, 1985).

In addition, because REBT is a special kind of active-directive, disputational, and homework-arranging therapy, it is highly preferable that supervisors investigate and encourage their supervisees to acquire and enhance the following traits and propensities:

1. To be adept at giving their clients unconditional acceptance, or what Rogers (1961) calls unconditional positive regard. Clients are to be fully accepted as persons *whether or not* they are competent and *whether or not* they are "nice" and lovable.

2. To be active-directive, persuasive *teachers* of REBT theory and practice, including especially to persistently demonstrate to clients how they can always give themselves unconditional self-acceptance (USA) as well as be ethical, cooperative members of their social group.

3. To fully accept how difficult it is for most clients to change and to stay changed and how, therefore, both they and their therapists had better work *forcefully* and *persistently* at changing their thoughts, feelings, and behaviors, and often to keep working to improve them for the rest of their lives.

4. To often monitor and to dispute their own irrationalities that are likely to interfere with their personal and therapeutic effectiveness and thereby to serve as reasonably good models for their clients' self-improvement efforts. To check, and especially work to modify their own irrational beliefs (iBs) that they *absolutely must* succeed with all their clients; that they *have to be* respected and loved by clients; that their clients *unquestionably should* be responsible, receptive, and hard working; and that the therapy they do *must* be thoroughly easy, enjoyable, and rewarding.

5. To fully accept the point that people largely upset themselves with their dysfunctional, irrational beliefs (iBs) and that they can therefore significantly change these beliefs and make themselves less disturbed and less disturbable. But to also see that every person has many cognitive, emotional, and behavioral aspects of disturbance, all of which complexly interact, and that therefore many thinking, feeling, and action methods are often required for personality change. Although most people have some similar tendencies to disturb themselves, all of them have widespread individual differences. All clients, consequently, are to be viewed as individuals in their own right and not to be rigidly assessed or treated in a few "right" REBT ways.

6. Science has many fairly strict and "proper" outlooks and procedures. But it also is uniquely open-minded, flexible, undogmatic, and ready to make major changes. REBT practitioners, if well trained and supervised, will be "scientific" in their theory and practice. But, as the postmodern thinkers have pointed out, science is created and practiced by fallible, and definitely subjective, humans. It has no absolute under-all-conditions-and-at-all-times "truths." Neither does psychotherapy! So, while trying to efficiently practice REBT, supervisees had better remain "scientifically" open minded, flexible, undogmatic, and ready to make major changes. Supervisors of REBT try to be "scientific" in their own life and their own therapeutic practice and to keep working to help their supervisees think, feel, and act similarly. They don't *have to* be great supervisors. But they can *preferably* try to be.

REFERENCES

Arkowitz, S. W. (1990). Perfectionism in the supervisee. *Psychoanalysis and Psychotherapy*, 8(1), 51–68.

Bard, J. A. (1980). *Rational emotive therapy in practice*. Champaign, IL: Research Press.

Bauman, W. F. (1972). Games counselor trainees play: Dealing with trainee resistance. *Counselor Education & Supervision*, 11, 251–256.

Bernard, M. E. (Ed.). (1991). *Using rational-emotive therapy effectively: A practitioner's guide.* New York: Plenum.

Cohen, L. (1980). The new supervisee views supervision. In A. K. Hess (Ed.), *Psychotherapy supervision: Theory, research and practice.* New York: Wiley.

DiGiuseppe, R. (1991). Comprehensive cognitive disputing in RET. In M. E. Bernard (Ed.), *Using rational-emotive therapy effectively* (pp. 173–195). New York: Plenum.

Dryden, W., & DiGiuseppe, R. (1990). *A primer on rational-emotive therapy.* Champaign, IL: Research Press.

Eckler-Hart, A. (1987). True and false self in the development of the psychotherapist. *Psychotherapy, 24*(4), 683–692.

Ellis, A. (1962). *Reason and emotion in psychotherapy.* New York: Lyle Stuart. Paperback ed.: New York: Citadel Press.

Ellis, A. (1985). *Overcoming resistance.* New York: Springer.

Ellis, A. (1991). The revised ABC's of rational-emotive therapy (RET). *Journal of Rational-Emotive & Cognitive-Behavior Therapy, 9,* 139–172.

Ellis, A. (1994). *Reason and emotion in psychotherapy* (rev. and updated). New York: Birch Lane Press.

Ellis, A., & Dryden, W. (1987). *The practice of rational-emotive therapy (RET).* New York: Springer.

Ellis, A., & Grieger, R. (1977). *Handbook of rational-emotive therapy.* New York: Springer.

Ellis, A., & Grieger, R. (1986). *Handbook of rational-emotive therapy: Vol. 2.* New York: Springer.

Glickauf-Hughes, C. (1994). Characterological resistances in psychotherapy supervision. *Psychotherapy, 31,* 58–66.

Grieger, R., & Boyd, J. B. (1980). *Rational-emotive therapy: A skills-based approach.* New York: Van Nostrand Reinhold.

Grieger, R., & Woods, P. J. (1993). *The rational-emotive therapy companion: A clear, concise, and complete guide to being an RET client.* Roanoke, VA: The Scholars' Press.

Kopec, A. M., Beal, D., & DiGiuseppe, R. (1994). Training in RET: Disputational strategies. *Journal of Rational-Emotive & Cognitive-Behavior Therapy, 12,* 47–60.

Liddle, B. (1986). Resistance in supervision: A response to perceived threat. *Counselor Education and Supervision, 26,* 117–127.

Mollon, P. (1989). Anxiety, supervision and a space for thinking: Some narcissistic perils for clinical psychologists in learning psychotherapy. *British Journal of Medical Psychology, 62,* 113–122.

Muller, R. (1985). *The therapist-in-training and the transfer case: Beyond the transfer triangle.* Amherst: University of Massachusetts Press.

Rogers, C. R. (1961). *On becoming a person.* Boston: Houghton Mifflin.

Walen, S., DiGiuseppe, R., & Dryden, W. (1992). *A practitioner's guide to rational-emotive therapy* (2nd ed.). New York: Oxford University Press.

Wessler, R. L., & Ellis, A. (1980). Supervision in rational-emotive therapy. In A. K. Hess (Ed.), *Psychotherapy supervision* (pp. 181–191). New York: Wiley.

Wessler, R. A., & Wessler, R. L. (1980). *The principles and practice of rational-emotive therapy.* San Francisco: Jossey-Bass.

Woods, P. J. (1991). Orthodox RET taught effectively with graphics, feedback on irrational beliefs, a structured homework series, and models of disputation. In M. E. Bernard (Ed.), *Using rational-emotive therapy effectively* (pp. 69–109). New York: Plenum.

Woods, P. J., & Grieger, R. M. (1993). Bulimia: A case study with mediating cognitions and notes on a cognitive-behavioral analysis of eating disorders. *Journal of Rational-Emotive & Cognitive-Behavior Therapy, 11,* 159–172.

Yapp, R., & Dryden, W. (1994). Supervision of REBT therapists: The thirteen-step self-supervision inventory. *The Rational Emotive Behavior Therapist, 2,* 16–24.

CHAPTER 8

Cognitive Therapy Supervision

BRUCE S. LIESE
University of Kansas Medical Center
JUDITH S. BECK
Beck Institute for Cognitive Therapy and Research

> Dr. Allen views himself as a cognitive therapist. In his first session with Bill and Kathy, he learns that the couple recently suffered the loss of their only child, who was killed by a drunk driver. Dr. Allen spends most of the session eliciting the couple's thoughts about their son's death. The couple vividly describe the traumatic incident, and they explain that they feel guilty because they believe, "Certainly we could have done *something* to save his life." Upon hearing this guilty thought, Dr. Allen vigorously disputes it. By the end of the session, however, Bill is agitated and Kathy is withdrawn and despondent. Obviously, Dr. Allen's interventions have made the couple feel worse. They never return to therapy.

This vignette illustrates that the effective provision of cognitive therapy can be an extremely complex, challenging process. When done properly, it is likely to facilitate symptom reduction and enhance psychological and interpersonal functioning. When done poorly, however, it may actually be harmful to patients who are already psychologically vulnerable.

Initially, the purpose of supervision is to help therapists gain knowledge and skills that will enable them to provide effective cognitive therapy. Over time, however, therapists who do not receive continued supervision are likely to "drift." Dr. Allen has drifted away from standard cognitive therapy; he no longer follows the cognitive model taught to him several years earlier. He fails to explore the couple's goals for therapy. He does not fully conceptualize Bill or Kathy prior to conducting his interventions. He uses logical disputation rather than guided discovery to change the couple's maladaptive thoughts. And he neglects to ask them for feedback at critical times during the session.

Ongoing supervision is essential for minimizing the likelihood that cognitive therapists will drift away from standard cognitive therapy. Perhaps if Dr. Allen had been receiving ongoing supervision, he would have effectively set an agenda, conceptualized this couple, used guided discovery, and asked for feedback during the session.

Cognitive therapy supervision can be as complex and challenging as cognitive therapy itself. Thus, it is surprising that so little has been written about cognitive therapy supervision (Perris, 1994). The existing literature generally focuses on training issues in the context of outcome studies (e.g., Shaw, 1984; Shaw & Wilson-Smith, 1988) and the manualized nature of cognitive therapy (e.g., Dobson & Shaw, 1988, 1993), rather than on the supervision process.

This chapter begins with an overview of cognitive therapy and the misconceptions that interfere with the effective provision of cognitive therapy. The structure, content, and process of cognitive therapy supervision are then presented and problems that may arise in the process of supervision are discussed.

OVERVIEW OF COGNITIVE THERAPY

The Evolution of Cognitive Therapy

Cognitive therapy was developed by Dr. Aaron T. Beck more than 30 years ago as a treatment for depression (Beck, 1964; Beck, Rush, Shaw, & Emery, 1979). Since that time, Beck and his colleagues have applied cognitive therapy to a wide variety of problems, and outcome studies have demonstrated its efficacy for panic disorder (Barlow, Craske, Cerney, & Klosko, 1989; Beck, Sokol, Clark, Berchick, & Wright, 1992; Clark, Salkovskis, Hackmann, Middleton, & Gelder, 1992), generalized anxiety (Butler, Fennell, Robson, & Gelder, 1991), social phobia (Gelernter et al., 1991; Heimberg et al., 1990), major depressive disorder (see Dobson, 1989, for meta-analysis), inpatient treatment of depression (Bowers, 1990; Miller, Norman, Keitner, Bishop, & Dow, 1989; Thase, Bowler, & Harden, 1991), substance abuse (Woody et al., 1983), eating disorders (Agras et al., 1992; Fairburn, Jones, Peveler, Hope, & Doll, 1991; Garner et al., 1993) and couples problems (Baucom, Sayers, & Scher, 1990). Additional outcome studies are currently under way investigating the effectiveness of cognitive therapy for other disorders, including chronic pain, personality disorders, sexual dysfunction, and as adjunctive treatment for schizophrenia and bipolar illness.

Cognitive therapy places primary emphasis on cognitive processes, including the identification and modification of core beliefs, conditional assumptions, and automatic thoughts. A basic assumption is that the manner in which individuals process information influences their emotions, behavior, and physiology in reliable, predictable ways. The model in Figure 8.1 (Liese & Larson, 1995, p. 24) reflects the "basic" model of cognitive therapy, including the influence of early life experiences. Cognitive formulations have been described for most major psychiatric disorders. These refinements to the basic cognitive model are outlined in the following sections for depression, anxiety, marital problems, personality disorders, and substance abuse.

Applications of Cognitive Therapy

Depression.   Individuals who are depressed hold pervasive, negative, maladaptive beliefs about themselves, their personal worlds, other people, and the future (Beck et al., 1979). These beliefs mediate their interpretations of experiences and subsequent thoughts, emotions, and actions. For example, the core belief "I am unlovable" may lead an individual in certain situations to think "I'll always be abandoned," which is likely to lead to feelings of sadness, despair, and (behaviorally) to interpersonal withdrawal.

Anxiety.   Anxious individuals hold beliefs that involve vulnerability to harm and danger (Beck & Emery with Greenberg, 1985). Individuals with anxiety disorders make dire predictions about what will happen to them or others, including failure, humiliation, and physical harm. For example, a common cognition among patients with panic disorder is "My racing heart means I'm having (or am about to have) a heart attack." Social phobics frequently believe, "If I take interpersonal risks I'm likely to be terribly embarrassed." Gen-

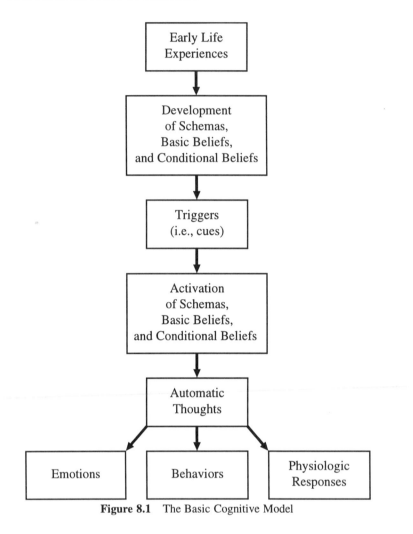

Figure 8.1   The Basic Cognitive Model

eralized anxiety disorder patients have a preponderance of "What if . . . ?" thoughts about a variety of situations.

Marital Problems.   Beck (1988) explains that couples develop relationship problems as a result of unrealistic expectations and negative thoughts and beliefs they develop over time about each other (e.g., "My partner should know exactly what I need" or "My partner does things just to hurt me"). Distressed couples tend to misperceive and miscommunicate with each other. According to Beck, "The essence of marital cognitive therapy consists of exploring with troubled partners their unrealistic expectations, self-defeating attitudes, unjustified negative explanations, and illogical conclusions" (p. 14).

Personality Disorders.   Individuals with personality disorders have numerous rigid, global, negative beliefs about themselves, their personal worlds, and other people (Beck, Freeman, & Associates, 1990; Layden, Newman, Freeman, & Morse, 1993; Young, 1994). These beliefs, which develop as a result of certain early life experiences, may influence personality disorder patients in profoundly negative ways (emotionally, behaviorally, and interpersonally). Each personality disorder has a distinctive set of associated beliefs. For example, dependent persons believe that they are "basically incapable" and can get along in life only by relying on others. Histrionic persons believe that they are "nothing" unless they entertain others. Antisocial persons believe that they are inherently weak and must attack or exploit others to avoid being harmed themselves (J. Beck, 1996, in press).

Substance Abuse.   Individuals with substance use problems can be distinguished from those who do not have substance use problems by their idiosyncratic drug-related thought processes (Beck, Wright, Newman, & Liese, 1993; Liese, 1994; Liese & Franz, 1996; Liese & Beck, 1996). For example, many cigarette smokers believe that "smoking is a good way to relieve boredom." In contrast, individuals who have never smoked are highly unlikely to hold this belief. Liese and Franz (1996) present a cognitive developmental model of substance abuse that emphasizes the importance of early life experiences in the development of addictive behaviors (see Fig. 8.2). Similar to cognitive models of personality disorders, this model emphasizes the relevance of early developmental processes to present emotion and behavior patterns.

Although the formulation and nature of interventions vary according to diagnosis, the basic conceptualization of patients according to the cognitive model (Fig. 8.1) remains constant. Individuals with psychiatric disorders consistently demonstrate distortions in their perceptions and thinking that influence how they react emotionally, behaviorally, and physiologically. When they learn to evaluate their cognitions and perceive themselves, others, and their worlds more accurately, their moods and coping strategies (i.e., behaviors) improve.

MISCONCEPTIONS OF COGNITIVE THERAPY

Interestingly, numerous misconceptions of cognitive therapy have arisen over the past 30 years. An important task of the cognitive therapy supervisor is to assess the therapist's ideas about cognitive therapy and determine the presence of such misconceptions. For example, many therapists misperceive cognitive therapy as dismissing the importance of emotions, interpersonal factors, and the therapeutic alliance and overemphasizing conscious, controlled processing (Clark, 1995). Therapists with these misconceptions apply cognitive techniques in a narrow fashion. Without an appreciation for the broad context of the patient's experience in therapy, such therapists are likely to be relatively ineffective.

Gluhoski (1994) describes seven specific misconceptions of cognitive therapy:

1. Cognitive therapy focuses on techniques for immediate symptom reduction while ignoring personality reorganization.
2. Cognitive therapy is superficial and mechanistic.
3. Cognitive therapy ignores the role of childhood experiences in determining adult psychopathology.
4. Cognitive therapy neglects interpersonal factors that contribute to and maintain psychopathology.
5. The therapeutic relationship is irrelevant in cognitive therapy.
6. The cognitive model does not address the motivation for maintaining problematic symptoms.
7. Cognitive therapists are only concerned with distorted thinking and view emotions as minimally important.

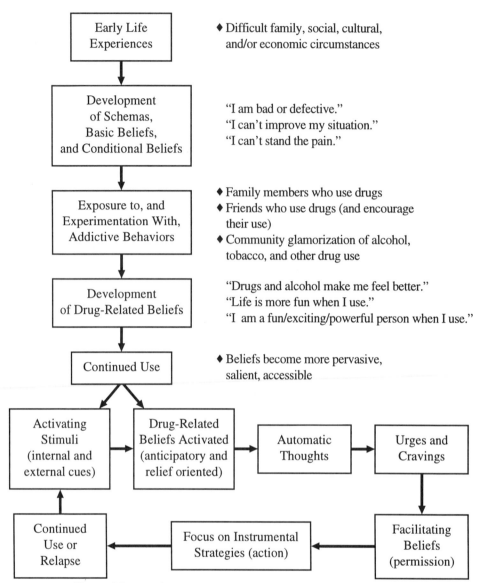

Figure 8.2   The Cognitive Developmental Model of Substance Abuse

Cognitive therapy supervision directly addresses and challenges these misconceptions. For example, in her second supervision session, Dr. Smith proudly reveals that she taught a patient about *all* of the cognitive distortions *in their first therapy session*. In response, Dr. Smith's supervisor carefully explores her views of the cognitive therapy process and learns that Dr. Smith has a relatively mechanistic and simplistic view of cognitive therapy. Her supervisor begins to teach Dr. Smith about the importance of collaboration, generation of a problem list, development of the therapeutic relationship, and the need to choose cognitive interventions based on an accurate, thorough case conceptualization.

Challenging the Misconceptions

The following list presents challenges to therapists' misconceptions of cognitive therapy. Supervisors teach therapists these basic tenets of cognitive therapy when therapists manifest evidence of having the misconceptions described earlier.

1. Cognitive therapy *does* provide techniques for immediate symptom reduction, but it also provides strategies for complex personality reorganization when needed.

2. Cognitive therapy is *not* superficial or mechanistic. Effective cognitive therapists seek to understand *both* the patients' current experiences and the contribution of their early histories to their perceptions and reactions to the world. They carefully plan treatment within and across sessions based on their case conceptualizations. They select interventions with a specific rationale in mind, considering factors such as the strength of the therapeutic relationship, the priority of skills to be learned, and so forth.

3. Cognitive therapists *do* assume that most adult psychopathology has roots in early life experiences. When appropriate, they help patients understand the influence of subtle and blatant early-life traumas on their current functioning. For example, supervisors encourage cognitive therapists to use the cognitive developmental model (Fig. 8.2) to understand their patients' substance use problems.

4. Effective cognitive therapy *does* recognize and acknowledge that most psychological problems have interpersonal components. Cognitive therapists help patients identify and evaluate their negative views of other people that adversely influence their relationships with them (e.g., "People will hurt me.").

5. The therapeutic relationship is *highly* important in cognitive therapy. With the most straightforward, uncomplicated depressed or anxious patients, the therapist needs to display good counseling skills, inspire hope, be collaborative, help solve problems, teach skills, facilitate quick symptom relief, and elicit and respond appropriately to patients' feedback. For more complicated patients, especially those with personality disorders, the therapeutic relationship becomes a central focus in therapy as therapists help patients identify and modify distorted thoughts and beliefs about the therapist (and they are helped to generalize this learning to other relationships). Supervisors encourage therapists to pay careful attention to the interpersonal processes that occur during treatment (i.e., transference and countertransference) and to resolve any therapeutic difficulties as directly as possible (Safran & Segal, 1990).

6. Cognitive therapy *does* address individuals' motives for maintaining problematic symptoms. For example, an important and salient concept in cognitive therapy is "compensatory strategies." *Compensatory strategies* are coping responses designed to compensate for skill deficits. Compensatory strategies, typically overlearned and overused, are likely to become problematic symptoms. For example, some individuals with social anxiety are vulnerable to heavy alcohol consumption because this symptom may be maintained to numb (i.e., circumvent) the discomfort associated with social interaction. Cognitive therapists may use the advantages-disadvantages analysis to examine the maintenance of depressive, anxious, avoidant, addictive, and other maladaptive behaviors. They may also use guided discovery to challenge beliefs that maintain such compensatory strategies.

7. Cognitive therapists *are* attentive and empathetic to patients' emotional states. In fact, a major goal of cognitive therapy is to reduce emotional distress. This is usually accomplished, not through emotional expression alone (i.e., catharsis), but through the exploration, conceptualization, and modification of the thoughts and beliefs that underlie emotional distress.

[handwritten margin note: Supervisory role to teach CBT / reorient to basic tenents]

Hence, cognitive therapy supervisors must elicit and address therapists' conceptions of cognitive therapy. When *mis*conceptions exist, supervisors educate therapists through instruction, discussion, role play, assigned readings, and direct observation of cognitive therapy.

THE STRUCTURE OF COGNITIVE THERAPY SUPERVISION

Cognitive therapy supervision, like psychotherapy, is most likely to be helpful if it is well structured, focused, and educational. Both supervisor and therapist are responsible for session structure and content. In the following sections, we describe a structure that facilitates productive cognitive therapy supervision.

Frequency of Supervision Sessions

Supervisors typically arrange for individual supervision sessions on a weekly basis. This schedule enables therapists to reflect on weekly psychotherapy sessions and apply concepts and techniques learned in the previous week. In weekly supervision, supervisors encourage therapists to discuss at least one patient in depth and generalize what they learn to other patients.

If possible, therapists also participate in group supervision to complement individual supervision sessions. Group cognitive therapy supervision is typically at least 90 minutes in length, scheduled at least biweekly. Group supervision sessions tend to be more didactic than individual sessions and focus on common problems or themes, rather than on individual therapists' difficulties. At times, group supervision may shift to individual therapists' difficulties wherein the group and supervisor together conceptualize a patient and generate a treatment plan. Liese, Shepherd, Cameron, and Ojeleye (1995) advocate a group supervision process wherein trainees directly observe an "expert" conducting cognitive therapy, followed by discussion of the therapy process. (For the remainder of this chapter, we focus primarily on the individual supervision process.)

Structure of Each Supervision Session

The length of typical weekly cognitive therapy supervision sessions is 60 minutes. The structure of supervision is similar to that of cognitive therapy sessions (J. Beck, 1995b), including check-in, agenda setting, bridge from the previous supervision session, inquiry about previously supervised cases, review of homework, prioritization and discussion of agenda items, assignment of new homework, capsule summaries, and therapists' feedback about the session. (See Table 8.1 for a comparison of the structure of therapy and supervision sessions.) Though sessions are structured, supervisors do not allow structure to compromise the supervisory relationship. That is, supervisors do not follow the structure in such a rigid manner that the interpersonal process becomes cold and impersonal. Elements of the supervision session are briefly described in Table 8.1.

Check-In. Cognitive therapy supervision sessions begin with a check-in, initiated by a simple question such as, "How are you today?" The primary purpose of the check-in is to "break the ice," though when supervisors detect significant problematic feelings (e.g., anxiety, depression) they collaboratively decide how to address these. In addressing therapists' personal issues, supervisors proceed carefully and deliberately in an effort to provide appropriate help (and serve as positive role models) to therapists.

**Table 8.1   Comparative Structures of Cognitive Therapy Sessions
and Supervision Sessions**

Step	Cognitive Therapy Session	Supervision Session
1	Agenda setting	Check-in
2	Mood check	Agenda setting
3	Bridge from previous therapy session	Bridge from previous supervision session
4	Inquiry about primary problem(s)	Inquiry about previously supervised therapy case(s)
5	Review of homework since previous therapy session	Review of homework since previous supervision session
6	Prioritization and discussion of agenda items	Prioritization and discussion of agenda items
7	Assignment of new homework	Assignment of new homework
8	Therapist's capsule summaries (throughout session and at end)	Supervisor's capsule summaries (throughout session and at end)
9	Elicit feedback from patient (throughout session and at end)	Elicit feedback from therapist (throughout session and at end)

Agenda Setting.   In setting the agenda, the supervisor asks, "What would you like to work on today?" or "What difficulties are you having?" The supervisor teaches the therapist to carefully prepare for supervision sessions by generating and prioritizing agenda items prior to each session. Initially, some therapists may find it difficult to generate agenda items. Nonetheless, they are encouraged to do so in order to use the time most productively. Typical therapist agenda items might include conceptualization of a particular case, appropriate techniques for treating specific clinical disorders, and interpersonal strategies for dealing with difficult patients. Supervisors usually contribute items to the agenda, based on their review of therapy tapes.

Bridge From Previous Supervision Session.   In order to bridge from the previous session, the supervisor asks questions such as, "What did you learn last time?" or "What did we discuss that was most important or useful to you?" The supervisor encourages therapists to review concepts or skills discussed in the last session and relate how they made use of these during the week.

Inquiry About Previously Supervised Therapy Cases.   In order to facilitate continuity in case management, supervisors inquire about previously supervised therapy cases (as needed) in each session. Though the primary focus of cognitive therapy supervision is typically on one (tape-recorded) patient session, it is occasionally useful to review progress or difficulties with previously supervised cases. Such discussions are likely to be brief, unless a patient is in crisis or the therapist or supervisor assesses the need for more extended discussion.

Review of Homework.   Assigning and reviewing homework (e.g., reading, conceptualizing patients in writing, experimenting with new techniques) is an essential part of cognitive therapy supervision. As in therapy, supervisors and therapists collaboratively set homework assignments, discuss their potential value, and review completed assignments at each session. By reviewing homework, supervisors convey the message that it is important. When therapists fail to complete assignments, supervisors discuss any obstacles that have interfered with homework completion.

Prioritization and Discussion of Agenda Items. The majority of cognitive therapy supervision revolves around the discussion of agenda items. Direct instruction is the predominant style of supervision in cognitive therapy, though guided discovery is also employed. Prior to the session, the supervisor prepares by reviewing therapists' needs (based on previous supervision sessions and therapists' recorded therapy sessions). For example, if a therapist is unfocused in a therapy session, the supervisor might decide to review the structure of cognitive therapy sessions or discuss the therapist's case conceptualization and the direction therapy should take.

Therapists' questions, opinions, doubts, and concerns are also elicited, encouraged, and discussed, especially when the supervisor is teaching complex skills, the therapist shows discomfort in a session, or the therapist appears to have difficulty with a particular patient or clinical issue. For example, if a supervisor observes that a therapist is condescending toward a patient, the supervisor encourages the therapist to talk about his or her thoughts and feelings about the patient. The supervisor addresses these thoughts and feelings and helps the therapist to modify maladaptive thought processes that contribute to the negative interaction.

Whenever appropriate, role playing is used by supervisors to demonstrate techniques. Role playing is particularly helpful for teaching new, complex, or difficult techniques, wherein the supervisor demonstrates the technique (i.e., plays the role of the therapist) and the therapist plays the role of the patient. Dr. Allen's difficult session with the couple (presented at the beginning of this chapter) would have provided an excellent opportunity for a supervisor to demonstrate advanced empathy and case conceptualization skills.

Assignment of New Homework. As agenda items are discussed, the supervisor makes an effort to identify homework likely to facilitate the acquisition and maintenance of knowledge and skills. Certain textbooks and manuals are required: the fourth edition of the *Diagnostic and Statistical Manual of Mental Disorders* (DSM-IV; American Psychiatric Association, 1994) and fundamental cognitive therapy texts (Beck et al., 1979, 1985, 1990, 1993; J. Beck, 1995a). Other readings are suggested as needed. For example, a supervisor may assign Burns's (1989) *The Feeling Good Handbook* as a patient self-help resource for depression. Safran and Segal's (1990) text on *Interpersonal Process in Cognitive Therapy* may be useful when therapists need to learn more about the therapeutic relationship. Therapists are encouraged, between supervision sessions, to listen to instructional audio- and videotapes of "experts" conducting cognitive therapy.

Supervisors might suggest that therapists use certain cognitive therapy techniques themselves, such as the Daily Thought Record or Weekly Activity Scheduling. Doing so helps therapists better explain these activities to patients. It also helps them to appreciate the difficulty of motivating oneself to do homework.

Supervisor's Capsule Summaries. Capsule summaries involve supervisors' reflections on, and synthesis of, material discussed thus far in the current supervision session. The supervisor uses capsule summaries to keep the session focused and to emphasize important points. Optimally, supervisors provide brief summaries (or they ask therapists to summarize) prior to changing topics and at the end of the supervision session.

Elicit Feedback From Therapist.   Supervisors elicit feedback throughout the supervision session and at the end of each session. Since much of the supervision process in cognitive therapy involves teaching therapists important concepts and skills, it is essential for the supervisor to ask about the acquisition of these concepts and skills. After teaching new material or providing substantive conceptual material about a patient, the supervisor asks questions such as, "What do you think of this theoretical model (or technique)?" or "How do you think you will use this technique?" At the end of each session the supervisor asks: "What have you gotten out of this session?" or "What have you learned today?"

Tape Recording of Therapy Sessions

An essential part of the supervision process in cognitive therapy is the audio or video tape recording of therapy sessions. Tape recording provides an accurate and reliable record of the events that have occurred during a session. Without such a record, supervisors would have to rely exclusively on therapists' biased views of their own sessions. Though initially anxiety provoking to some therapists, the tape recording of sessions is among the most valuable features of cognitive therapy supervision. When therapists are reluctant to record sessions, supervisors facilitate their doing so by exploring and addressing their automatic thoughts (e.g., "Recording will cramp my style" or "Taping will make the patient really uncomfortable").

Review of Tape-Recorded Sessions

Supervisors (and sometimes therapists) review entire tape-recorded therapy sessions prior to conducting supervision. This essential practice enables supervisors to assess therapists' strengths and weaknesses, as well as to prioritize issues and topics to be discussed in supervision. During the supervision session, supervisors may either describe a particular therapist-patient interaction or they may actually play important taped segments of the session and discuss these. Generally, therapists learn substantially from listening to and rating their own tape-recorded therapy sessions. Standardized supervision instruments, described in the following section, greatly facilitate review of sessions.

Use of Standardized Supervision Instruments

Cognitive therapy supervisors use standardized supervision instruments such as *The Cognitive Therapy Adherence and Competence Scale* (CTACS; Liese, Barber, & Beck, 1995) when evaluating therapists' tape-recorded sessions. Positive items of the CTACS (i.e., those that reflect optimum therapist functioning) are listed in Table 8.2.

As supervisors review tape-recorded sessions, they note therapists' performance on each of the items of the CTACS. For example, they list (preferably verbatim) the therapists' strategies for agenda setting, mood check, bridge from the previous session, and so forth. On items that are more subtle, such as empathy and warmth, they list examples of empathetic responses or expressions of warmth. After listening to the entire recorded session, the supervisor rates each of the 25 items on a scale from 0 (low) to 6 (high) based on their written notes and reflections on the entire session. These ratings and corresponding supervisory notes provide the material and structure for discussing therapy cases and sessions.

Table 8.2   Positive Items of the Cognitive Therapy Adherence and Competence Scale (CTACS)

Cognitive Therapy Structure

1. *Agenda*—Set an excellent, comprehensive, agenda; identified important target problems; prioritized and followed agenda.

2. *Mood check*—Did an excellent job of asking about mood; followed up with clarification; put important mood-related concerns on agenda; addressed concerns.

3. *Bridge from previous visit*—Discussed previous session with patient; emphasized important issues; related previous session to present agenda items; added unresolved issues to present agenda.

4. *Status of current problems*—Asked excellent questions about primary problem and then followed up with appropriate responses and interventions.

5. *Reviewing previous homework*—Thoroughly reviewed previous homework or discussed incomplete homework.

6. *Assigning new homework*—Collaboratively assigned excellent, detailed homework; discussed fully with patient and began to plan and practice homework in the session.

7. *Capsule summaries*—Reliably and accurately provided excellent capsule summaries that were meaningful to patient; therapist checked capsule summaries for accuracy and revised when appropriate.

8. *Patient summary and feedback*—Asked for summary and feedback throughout the session; responded in a positive, supportive manner; appropriately adjusted behaviors based on patient's feedback.

9. *Focus-structure*—Used time extremely effectively by directing the flow of conversation and redirecting when necessary; session seemed well paced, focused, and structured.

Development of a Collaborative Therapeutic Relationship

10. *Socialization to cognitive therapy model*—Did an outstanding job of describing relevant model, concepts, process, structure; applied these to patient in a timely manner; checked patient's understanding and elicited feedback.

11. *Warmth/genuineness/congruence*—Appeared optimally warm, genuine, caring, and congruent.

12. *Acceptance/respect*—Appeared fully accepting, respectful, nonjudgmental.

13. *Attentiveness*—Was extremely attentive to important obvious and subtle cues.

14. *Accurate empathy*—Demonstrated excellent empathy skills and insight; shared insights with patient.

15. *Collaboration*—Extremely collaborative; shared responsibility for defining patient's problems and potential solutions; functioned as a team.

Development and Application of the Case Conceptualization

16. *Eliciting automatic thoughts*—Excellent job of eliciting ATs; effectively related these to patient's problems.

17. *Eliciting core beliefs and schemas*—Excellent job of eliciting core beliefs/schemas; effectively related these to patient's problems.

18. *Eliciting meaning/understanding/attributions*—Excellent job of asking for meaning of salient events and beliefs; followed up appropriately and substantially.

19. *Addressing key issues*—Raised extremely important and salient key issues (e.g., adaptability, autonomy, commitment, integrity, intimacy, responsibility, spirituality, spontaneity); related key issues to schemas, core beliefs, conditional beliefs, automatic thoughts, emotions, and behaviors.

20. *Case conceptualization: linking past to present*—Inquired about developmental processes when appropriate; linked accurately to current beliefs, thoughts, emotions, behaviors; elicited feedback from the patient regarding accuracy and usefulness.

Table 8.2   (Continued)

21. *Sharing the conceptualization with patient*—Provided patient with an excellent, thorough conceptualization of his or her problems; elicited feedback from patient regarding accuracy and usefulness.

Cognitive and Behavioral Techniques

22. *Guided discovery*—Skillfully used a balance of open-ended questions, reflective, confrontive, and interpretive responses to guide patient's understanding of important issues.
23. *Asking for evidence/alternative views*—Asked in a timely and effective manner for patient's evidence for maladaptive beliefs; where appropriate asked for alternative views; appropriately followed up.
24. *Use of alternative cognitive and behavioral techniques*—Did an outstanding job of selecting and applying standardized methods.
25. *Overall performance as a cognitive therapist*—Performance in this session is excellent; cognitive therapy is practiced at a level equal to or superior to supervisor's own level of proficiency; therapist apparently knows the relevant treatment manual extremely well; applies the cognitive case formulation with ease and flexibility; this represents "state of the art" cognitive therapy.

Source: Liese, Barber, and Beck, 1995.

THE CONTENT OF COGNITIVE THERAPY SUPERVISION

Cognitive therapists must acquire substantial knowledge and skills in the following areas in order to be effective: diagnosis of psychological problems and associated cognitive models; case conceptualization; development and maintenance of the therapeutic relationship; and basic counseling skills, structure, and techniques. These areas are described here.

Diagnosis of Problems and Associated Cognitive Models

An essential skill for cognitive therapists is advanced diagnosis. Therapists should be intimately familiar with the fourth edition of the *Diagnostic and Statistical Manual of Mental Disorders* (APA, 1994). Most experienced therapists recognize depression and anxiety. To effectively plan and carry out therapy, however, a cognitive therapist must be able to distinguish among subtle variations of anxiety (e.g., obsessive-compulsive disorder, generalized anxiety disorder, and agoraphobia), mood disorders (e.g., dysthymia, major depressive episode, bipolar illness), and other psychiatric problems. Cognitive therapists must also recognize and distinguish among the personality disorders, because these may be more subtle and yet have profound effects on the therapeutic relationship, the treatment planning, and the course of therapy (J. Beck, 1996, in press).

Cognitive Case Conceptualization

The cognitive case conceptualization is defined as the "collection, synthesis, and integration of data about the patient" (Liese, 1994, p. 20). According to J. Beck (1995a), the "cognitive conceptualization provides the framework for the therapist's understanding of a patient" (p. 13), and greatly facilitates the cognitive therapy process. A diagram to aid in the process of conceptualization is presented in Figure 8.3 (J. Beck, 1995a, p. 139).

Supervisors encourage the use of cognitive case conceptualization diagrams from the

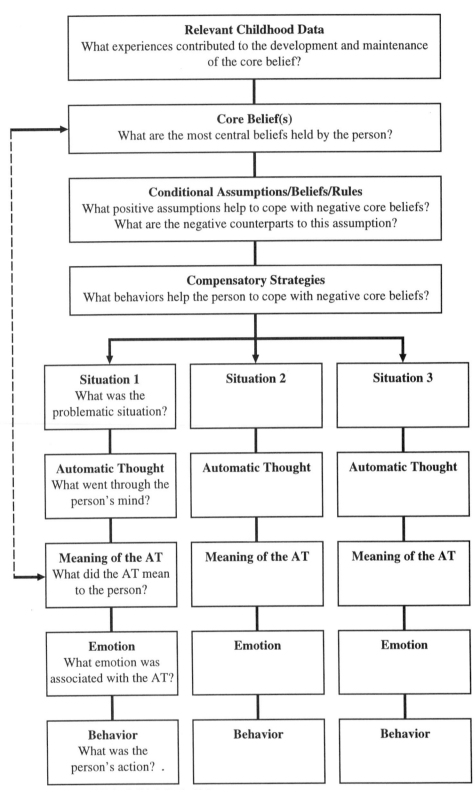

Relevant Childhood Data
What experiences contributed to the development and maintenance
of the core belief?

Core Belief(s)
What are the most central beliefs held by the person?

Conditional Assumptions/Beliefs/Rules
What positive assumptions help to cope with negative core beliefs?
What are the negative counterparts to this assumption?

Compensatory Strategies
What behaviors help the person to cope with negative core beliefs?

Situation 1 What was the problematic situation?	**Situation 2**	**Situation 3**
Automatic Thought What went through the person's mind?	**Automatic Thought**	**Automatic Thought**
Meaning of the AT What did the AT mean to the person?	**Meaning of the AT**	**Meaning of the AT**
Emotion What emotion was associated with the AT?	**Emotion**	**Emotion**
Behavior What was the person's action? .	**Behavior**	**Behavior**

Source: Copyright 1993 by Judith S. Beck, Ph.D.

Figure 8.3   Cognitive Conceptualization Diagram

beginning of supervision. Therapists are instructed to complete these diagrams for each patient as soon as they have collected enough data to detect significant patterns of thinking, feeling, and behaving in response to situations. Supervisors continually urge therapists to modify their conceptualizations as they collect new data to refine or refute their hypotheses. Therapists are also taught to share their conceptualization diagrams with patients. To facilitate this process, supervisors may demonstrate, by means of role playing, the completion of a blank case conceptualization diagram.

Basic Counseling Skills

It is essential for cognitive therapists to have solid basic counseling skills. Specifically, they should be warm, genuine, accurately empathetic, and focused. Unfortunately, many practicing psychotherapists do not possess these most basic skills. Therapists' deficits may range from being distant and unresponsive to being excessively emotional or attached to patients. Some therapists possess basic counseling skills, but they fail to vary their styles according to the patient's needs.

Teaching therapists to attend to patients' verbal and nonverbal cues can help them appropriately vary their levels of warmth, overt empathy, and support. For example, with a dependent patient in crisis, high levels of warmth and overt support may be desirable (especially early in therapy). In contrast, a highly autonomous, obsessive-compulsive personality disorder patient might require more distance early in the therapy relationship.

Structuring Therapy Sessions

Structure and focus are important cognitive therapy skills. Supervisors encourage therapists to follow the basic structure of cognitive therapy (see Table 8.1) and focus on the problems, beliefs, automatic thoughts, and maladaptive behaviors that are most troublesome to the patient. Some patients are uncomfortable with the standard structure, and therapists need to know how to assess such discomfort and negotiate variable levels of structure to keep patients engaged in therapy.

Cognitive and Behavioral Techniques

Cognitive therapists need to be familiar with a wide range of cognitive and behavioral techniques (including experiential techniques for their patients with personality disorders). Supervisors describe and role-play techniques in the supervision session and suggest readings (e.g., McMullin, 1986) to supplement these discussions. Supervisors emphasize that techniques are secondary in importance to collaboration. Techniques are selected according to therapists' conceptualizations of their patients, their shared goals, the problems being discussed, stage of therapy, and strength of the therapeutic relationship.

Most texts on cognitive therapy (e.g., Beck et al., 1979, 1985, 1990, 1993; J. Beck, 1995a; McMullin, 1986) provide detailed descriptions of cognitive therapy techniques. Common techniques include Daily Thought Records, Weekly Activity Schedules, identifying cognitive distortions, the downward arrow technique, assertiveness training, relaxation exercises, positive self-statement logs, and many more.

Implementing techniques effectively takes time, patience, and practice. Supervisors stress that inexperienced cognitive therapists are unlikely to know (especially in advance) precisely which techniques will be most useful at specific points in therapy. With experience and careful attention to the case conceptualization, however, therapists do learn to select techniques more effectively. To facilitate the learning process, therapists are urged to use cognitive therapy techniques (e.g., the Daily Thought Record) themselves to deal with personal problems and issues.

INTERPERSONAL PROCESS IN COGNITIVE THERAPY SUPERVISION

Supervision, like psychotherapy, is an interpersonal process wherein some therapists and supervisors experience significant emotional reactions. Effective supervisors help therapists recognize the thoughts and beliefs that contribute to their emotional reactions both in therapy and in supervision. For example, Dr. Carter tells his supervisor that he wants to "fire" his avoidant patient because "she never does anything I ask her to do!" He further exclaims, "I feel as if therapy with her is a real waste of my time!" In response, Dr. Carter's supervisor inquires about what the patient's avoidant behaviors mean to Dr. Carter. Through this process, Dr. Carter is helped to understand that his patient's behaviors are not a direct reflection of his competence. Dr. Carter and his supervisor then discuss his responsibility to conceptualize and empathize with his patient's difficulties and modify his approach in therapy to facilitate the patient's progress.

Addressing Therapists' Personal Issues

Cognitive therapy supervisors are expected to be attentive to therapists' personal issues (i.e., problems) when these interfere with the effective delivery of therapy. Supervisors need to conceptualize these difficulties, just as therapists conceptualize their patients. The following list of questions may be helpful when evaluating therapists' personal issues:

1. What are the therapist's strengths?
2. What are the therapist's weaknesses?
3. What are the therapist's past educational and professional experiences?
4. What theoretical constructs are used by the therapist to conceptualize patients (i.e., how does the therapist view psychological problems and change processes)?
5. What were the therapist's prior supervision experiences, and how can the current supervisor guide the process most effectively?
6. What is the therapist's communication style, and how does this style relate to the process of psychotherapy and supervision?
7. How does the therapist handle delicate ethical matters?
8. How well does the therapist attend to administrative matters (e.g., being on time, keeping appointments, completing paperwork)?
9. Does the therapist have any significant psychological difficulties?

Problems inevitably emerge in the process of cognitive therapy supervision. Problems may relate directly to the supervisor, the therapist or, more commonly, to an interaction of the two individuals. Supervisors need to conceptualize how and why difficulties arise and collaboratively problem-solve with therapists, just as therapists need to identify and address difficulties in the psychotherapeutic relationship.

Problems Related to the Supervisor

Following are three types of supervisory styles that may lead to problems in the supervision process: The Mister Rogers Supervisor; Attila the Supervisor; and The "How do *you* feel?" Supervisor. Each of these styles is briefly described, and some beliefs associated with each are listed.

The Mister Rogers Supervisor.   Many therapists have had supervisors like Mister Rogers: warm, pleasant, kind, and good-natured, but failing to provide substantial critical feedback or education. Therapists supervised by "Mister Rogers" may develop exaggerated positive views of their competencies and not progress as they should. Some likely thoughts and beliefs associated with Mister Rogers supervisors are

"It is bad when someone's feelings get hurt."

"If I am nice and kind, no one will ever dislike me."

"Therapists are fragile and will be destroyed by any criticism."

Attila the Supervisor.   These supervisors believe that there is only one correct way to do things: *their* way. They may become upset or angry when therapists do not follow their commands. Some specific beliefs of these supervisors are

"I need to be right all the time."

"It's awful if someone in my command doesn't do what I say."

"Not listening to me is a sign of disrespect."

"Disrespect is intolerable."

The "How Do You *Feel?" Supervisor.*   This supervisor believes that everything learned in supervision results from therapists' reflections on personal feelings about the patient (i.e., countertransference). The patient comes in, for example, wishing to quit smoking and the supervisor asks the therapist: "How do *you* feel when your patient wants to quit smoking?" rather than asking, "What is your conceptualization of this patient?" or "What interventions are most appropriate for smoking cessation?" or "What will you do next?"

Problems Related to the Therapist

In this section, three types of therapist styles are described that may lead to problems in the supervision process: unfocused therapists, passive or avoidant therapists, and defensive or aggressive therapists. Consistent with the supervisor section described earlier, each of these styles is briefly described and some beliefs associated with each are listed.

Unfocused Therapists.   Some psychotherapists have difficulties focusing in therapy sessions and in supervision. Such difficulties may be due to stylistic preferences, prior training, or conscious choice. Beliefs associated with therapists' lack of focus may include

"I need to know everything, and I should jump around to get it all."

"If we talk enough, the important stuff will eventually emerge."

"Focusing is too difficult or uncomfortable."

"If we do focus too much, we might focus on the wrong issue."

Passive or Avoidant Therapists.   Some therapists do not actively participate in the supervision process. These therapists seem aloof, distant, or uninterested. Beliefs associated with such passivity or avoidance in supervision may be

"If I reveal my thoughts, I'll reveal my weaknesses."

"If my supervisor sees me as imperfect, I'm a failure."

"I shouldn't have to make a strong effort; my supervisor should always tell me what to do."

"I need to show my supervisor my best side."

Defensive or Aggressive Therapists.   Some therapists respond to supervision with defensive explanations for their behaviors or with aggressiveness when supervisors question them. Beliefs associated with defensiveness and aggressiveness might include

"I need to be perfect" or "My supervisor needs to believe I'm perfect."

"I know better than my supervisor."

"If I don't defend my position, I'm weak or inadequate."

"It's catastrophic when I'm wrong."

"If I'm aggressive, my therapist won't criticize me."

Solutions for Problems in Supervision

Problems in supervision are addressed first by carefully conceptualizing the therapist, supervisor, and supervisory relationship, focusing on how and why problems may have occurred. Some problems arise because of the therapist's lack of experience with cognitive therapy or supervision. Supervisors of passive therapists, for example, may need to socialize (i.e., teach) therapists the skills associated with preparing for sessions: preparation of an agenda, thoughtful case conceptualization, and so forth.

Some therapists have difficulties in supervision because they have misconceptions or maladaptive beliefs such as those described earlier (e.g., "I need to be perfect!"). When this is the case, supervisors elicit therapists' misconceptions about cognitive therapy and they help therapists test and modify these beliefs. This process serves a dual purpose: It removes roadblocks to effective supervision (i.e., it improves the supervisory relationship), and it provides a model for how therapists can elicit and help change patients' maladaptive beliefs.

Since supervision problems may result from a supervisor's style or approach, it is essential for supervisors to routinely elicit feedback from therapists about the effectiveness of their supervision. When therapists express difficulties with supervisors, it is important for supervisors to listen carefully and objectively to their concerns. By taking appropriate responsibility for problems, supervisors are likely to contribute substantially to the supervision process, sharpen their supervisory skills, and modify their own maladaptive beliefs about therapy or supervision.

CONCLUSIONS

Cognitive therapy has evolved substantially over the years. Unfortunately, many cognitive therapists are unaware of the important changes that have taken place (i.e., they have misconceptions about cognitive therapy). Cognitive therapy supervision has at least three important purposes: (a) to teach cognitive theory and techniques, (b) to correct misconceptions of cognitive therapy, and (c) to reduce the likelihood of therapist drift. Most of the supervisor's actual time in cognitive therapy supervision is spent teaching theory and skills to therapists. An extremely valuable component of supervision, however, involves teaching therapists about their own personal (cognitive) processes as they manifest these in therapy.

REFERENCES

Agras, W. S., Rossiter, E. M., Arnow, B., Schneider, J. A., Telch, C. F., Raeburn, S. D., Bruce, B., Perl, M., & Koran, L. M. (1992). Pharmacologic and cognitive-behavioral treatment for bulimia nervosa: A controlled comparison. *American Journal of Psychiatry, 149,* 82–87.

American Psychiatric Association. (1994). *Diagnostic and statistical manual of mental disorders* (4th ed.). Washington, DC: Author.

Barlow, D., Craske, M., Cerney, J. A., & Klosko, J. S. (1989). Behavioral treatment of panic disorder. *Behavioral Therapy, 20,* 261–268.

Baucom, D., Sayers, S., & Scher, T. (1990). Supplementary behavioral marital therapy with cognitive restructuring and emotional expressiveness training: An outcome investigation. *Journal of Consulting and Clinical Psychology, 58,* 636–645.

Beck, A. T. (1964). Thinking and depression: II. Theory and therapy. *Archives of General Psychiatry, 10,* 561–571.

Beck, A. T. (1988). *Love is never enough.* New York: Harper & Row.

Beck, A. T., & Emery, G. (with Greenberg, R. L.). (1985). *Anxiety disorders and phobias: A cognitive perspective.* New York: Basic Books.

Beck, A. T., Freeman, A., & Associates (1990). *Cognitive therapy of personality disorders.* New York: Guilford.

Beck, A. T., Rush, A. J., Shaw, B. F., & Emery, G. (1979). *Cognitive therapy of depression.* New York: Guilford.

Beck, A. T., Sokol, L., Clark, D. A., Berckick, R. J., & Wright, F. D. (1992). A crossover study of focused cognitive therapy for panic disorder. *American Journal of Psychiatry, 149,* 776–783.

Beck, A. T., Wright, F. W., Newman, C. F., & Liese, B. (1993) *Cognitive therapy of substance abuse.* New York: Guilford.

Beck, J. S. (1995a). *Cognitive therapy: Basics and beyond.* New York: Guilford.

Beck, J. S. (1995b, August). New developments in the supervision of cognitive therapists. In E. Watkins (Chair), *Supervising psychotherapy: New developments, advances, and possibilities.* Symposium conducted at the annual meeting of the American Psychological Association, New York.

Beck, J. S. (1996). Cognitive therapy of personality disorders. In P. Salkovskis (Ed.), *Frontiers of cognitive therapy* (pp. 165–181). New York: Guilford.

Beck, J. S. (in press). Cognitive approaches to personality disorders. In L. J. Dickstein, M. B. Riba, & J. M. Oldham (Eds.), *American Psychiatric Association review of psychiatry.* Washington, DC: American Psychiatric Press.

Bowers, W. A. (1990). Treatment of depressed inpatients: Cognitive therapy plus medication, relaxation plus medication, and medication alone. *British Journal of Psychiatry, 156,* 73–78.

Burns, D. D. (1989). *The feeling good handbook: Using the new mood therapy in everyday life.* New York: Morrow.

Butler, G., Fennell, M., Robson, D., & Gelder, M. (1991). Comparison of behavior therapy and cognitive-behavior therapy in the treatment of generalized anxiety disorder. *Journal of Consulting and Clinical Psychology, 59,* 167–175.

Clark, D. A. (1995). Perceived limitations of standard cognitive therapy: A consideration of efforts to revise Beck's theory and therapy. *Journal of Cognitive Psychotherapy: An International Quarterly, 9,* 153–172.

Clark, D. M., Salkovskis, P. M., Hackmann, A., Middleton, H., & Gelder, M. (1992). A comparison of cognitive therapy, applied relaxation, and imipramine in the treatment of panic disorder. *British Journal of Psychiatry, 164,* 759–769.

Dobson, K. S. (1989). A meta-analysis of the efficacy of cognitive therapy for depression. *Journal of Consulting and Clinical Psychology, 57,* 414–419.

Dobson, K. S., & Shaw, B. F. (1988). The use of treatment manuals in cognitive therapy: Experience and issues. *Journal of Consulting and Clinical Psychology, 56,* 673–680.

Dobson, K. S., & Shaw, B. F. (1993). The training of cognitive therapists: What have we learned from treatment manuals? *Psychotherapy, 30,* 573–577.

Fairburn, C. G., Jones, R., Peveler, R. C., Hope, R. A., & Doll, H. A. (1991). Three psychological treatments for bulimia nervosa: A comparative trial. *Archives of General Psychiatry, 48,* 463–469.

Garner, D. M., Rockert, W., Davis, R., Garner, M. V., Olmstead, M. P., & Eagle, M. (1993). Comparison of cognitive-behavioral and supportive-expressive therapy for bulimia nervosa. *American Journal of Psychiatry, 130,* 37–46.

Gelernter, C. S., Uhde, T. W., Cimbolic, P., Arnkoff, D. B., Vittone, B. J., Tancer, M. E., & Bartko, J. J. (1991). Cognitive-behavioral and pharmacological treatments of social phobia: A controlled study. *Archives of General Psychiatry, 48,* 938–945.

Gluhoski, V. L. (1994). Misconceptions of cognitive therapy. *Psychotherapy, 31,* 594–600.

Heimberg, R. G., Dodge, C. S., Hope, D. A., Kennedy, C. R., Zollo, L. J., & Becker, R. E. (1990). Cognitive behavioral group treatment for social phobia: Comparison with credible placebo control. *Cognitive Therapy and Research, 14,* 1–23.

Layden, M. A., Newman, C. F., Freeman, A., & Morse, S. B. (1993). *Cognitive therapy of borderline personality disorder.* Needham Heights, MA: Allyn & Bacon.

Liese, B. S. (1994). Brief therapy, crisis intervention and the cognitive therapy of substance abuse. *Crisis Intervention and Time-Limited Treatment, 1,* 11–29.

Liese, B. S., Barber, J., & Beck, A. T. (1995). *The Cognitive Therapy Adherence and Competence Scale.* Unpublished instrument, University of Kansas Medical Center, Kansas City.

Liese, B. S., & Beck, A. T. (1996). Back to basics: Fundamental cognitive therapy skills for keeping drug-dependent individuals in treatment. In J. J. Boren, L. S. Onken, & J. D. Blaine (Eds.), *Beyond the therapeutic alliance: Keeping drug dependent individuals in treatment* (pp. 210–235). National Institute on Drug Abuse Monograph. Washington, DC: Government Printing Office.

Liese, B. S., & Franz, R. A. (1996). Treating substance use disorders: Lessons learned and implications for the future. In P. Salkovskis (Ed.), *Frontiers of cognitive therapy* (pp. 470–508). New York: Guilford.

Liese, B. S., & Larson, M. W. (1995). Coping with life-threatening illness: A cognitive therapy perspective. *Journal of Cognitive Psychotherapy: An International Quarterly, 9,* 19–34.

Liese, B. S., Shepherd, D. D., Cameron, C. L., & Ojeleye, A. E. (1995). Teaching psychological knowledge and skills to family physicians. *Journal of Clinical Psychology in Medical Settings, 2,* 21–38.

McMullin, R. E. (1986). *Handbook of cognitive therapy techniques.* New York: Norton.

Miller, I. W., Norman, W. H., Keitner, G. I., Bishop, S. B., & Dow, M. G. (1989). Cognitive-behavioral treatment of depressed inpatients. *Behavior Therapy, 20,* 25–47.

Perris, C. (1994). Supervising cognitive psychotherapy and training supervisors. *Journal of Cognitive Psychotherapy: An International Quarterly, 8,* 83–101.

Safran, J. D., & Segal, Z. V. (1990). *Interpersonal process in cognitive therapy.* New York: Basic Books.

Shaw, B. F. (1984). Specification of the training and evaluation of cognitive therapists for outcome studies. In J. B. W. Williams & R. L. Spitzer (Eds.), *Psychotherapy research: Where we are and where we should go* (pp. 92–128). New York: Guilford.

Shaw, B. F., & Wilson-Smith, D. (1988). Training therapists in cognitive-behavior therapy. In C. Perris, I. M. Blackburn, & H. Perris (Eds.), *Cognitive psychotherapy: Theory and practice* (pp. 140–148). Heidelberg: Springer-Verlag.

Thase, M. E., Bowler, K., & Harden, T. (1991). Cognitive behavior therapy of endogenous depression: Part 2. Preliminary findings in 10 unmedicated inpatients. *Behavior Therapy, 22,* 469–477.

Woody, G. E., Luborsky, L., McClellan, A. T., O'Brien, C. P., Beck, A. T., Blaine, J., Herman, I., & Hole, A. (1983). Psychotherapy for opiate addicts: Does it help? *Archives of General Psychiatry, 40,* 1081–1086.

Young, J. E. (1994). *Cognitive therapy for personality disorders: A schema-focused approach* (rev. ed.). Sarasota, FL: Professional Resource Press.

CHAPTER 9

Client-Centered Supervision

C. H. PATTERSON
Asheville, North Carolina

Bernard and Goodyear (1992) group methods of supervision into two classes. The first includes those methods that derive from or are grounded in a theory or system of psychotherapy. The earliest, and still the major, such approach is that of psychoanalysis and its offshoots: "The psychotherapy-based supervisor is one whose supervision is based totally and consistently on the supervisor's theory of psychotherapy or counseling" (Bernard & Goodyear, 1992, p. 12). These authors include client-centered supervision in this category. They note that "there are fewer purely psychotherapy-based supervisors than one might think" (p. 13). Although these authors' eclectic supervision is theory-based, they say that "it must be noted, however, that the theoretical underpinning of these two theories [humanistic and behavior theories] are contradictory" (p. 19). It appears that eclectic supervision was included here because it does not fit into their second category.

The second major category of supervision includes the so-called developmental approaches. The recent and current literature consists almost entirely of discussions of these approaches. It is curious that the developmental approaches ignore the fact that both therapy and supervision are interpersonal relationships.

The developmental approaches to supervision also ignore the theoretical orientations of both the supervisee and the supervisor. Yet each has an approach, or some idea about how therapy should be done, whether or not it is a conscious or recognized theory. The developmental approaches thus fail to consider how the supervisor and supervisee are to reconcile differences or reach agreement on what is expected of the supervisee—what the criteria for the supervisee's practice and performance are.

The client-centered approach to supervision, first described by Patterson (1964), is the focus of this chapter. It is a theory-based approach deriving from client-centered therapy.

THE CURRENT STATE OF SUPERVISION

In actual practice, most supervision does not appear to follow either a theory-based or developmental approach, being atheoretical or eclectic. The reason is that most supervisors do not subscribe to or follow a particular theory of psychotherapy or of supervision and consider themselves to be eclectic. This situation creates problems for supervisees.

There is little, if any, agreement on the preparation of the student for supervised practice. Courses on theory and practice may be taken from different instructors with differing theoretical orientations or with no theoretical orientation. Instructors may or may not have a commitment to a particular theory. They may have been discouraged from making a commitment to any particular theory, or they may have been encouraged to develop their own theory. Supervisors also may or may not be committed to a consistent philosophy or theory. If both student and supervisor claim to be eclectic, there may be little agreement on what this means in actual practice.

The current situation has led this author (Patterson, 1992) to suggest a change in the programs for the education of psychotherapists. Each program would commit itself to two or three theoretical orientations depending on the competence and expertise of its faculty. Each student would enroll in a theories course that covers the major theories in some depth, using a text such as Patterson and Watkins (1996) or Ford and Urban (1963). Students would then select the theory they prefer and enroll in an advanced course covering that theory, with an instructor who is an expert in it. Students would then continue in supervision with that instructor. If a student desires training in a theory that is not a specialty of a faculty member in that institution, he or she would be facilitated in transferring to an institution offering such training. This approach is considered an interim one, pending the time when there would be agreement on one system of psychotherapy—a universal system (Patterson, 1995; Patterson & Hidore, 1996).

This writer has attempted a similar approach to the education of psychotherapists. Early on (at the University of Illinois, 1956–1977) students in the supervised practicum had an introductory course with exposure to the major theories. In the supervised practicum, a seminar (4 hours per week) was conducted in which the students were exposed to a client-centered approach, reading Porter (1950), then later Patterson (1959, 1974).

More recently (at the University of North Carolina at Greensboro, 1984–1994), I accepted for supervision only those students who had had my course on client-centered therapy, requiring that they had read *The Therapeutic Relationship* (Patterson, 1985), among others.

In most programs preparing students for the practice of psychotherapy, students are assigned to supervisors without regard to the theoretical orientation of the student or the supervisor. The student may or may not have had a basic theory course with the supervisor. As a result, mismatches are common. This means that the early stages of supervision are taken up with (a) the supervisee trying to learn where his or her supervisor is coming from and (b) the supervisor engaging in teaching or informing the student about his or her approach. The process of supervision is thus slowed considerably.

MY APPROACH TO SUPERVISION

The desirability and advantages of the supervisor and supervisee sharing the same theoretical basis for psychotherapy have not been adequately recognized. Matarazzo and Patterson (1986) are the only ones to address this issue. They write: "It appears important for supervisor and supervisee to have a similar theoretical orientation" (p. 838).

My position on this is clear. It is not simply desirable or important, but necessary that the supervisor and supervisee be committed to a theory—and the same theory:

> The supervisor has a commitment to a theory, and the supervisee must have at least a tentative commitment to a theory; it should be obvious that if learning is to occur, they must be committed to the same theory. (Patterson, 1983, p. 22)

The Supervisory Process

Orientation of the Supervisee.   Supervisees meet in a group prior to the first individual supervision session. Most recently (1990–1994), a videotape of a published interview (Freeman, 1992) with me on client-centered supervision was shown. This interview provides an orientation to the supervisory process and is followed by discussion with the supervisees. The points made in the interview and the following discussion include the following:

1.   As a result of the course, supervisees are familiar with the client-centered therapist conditions of empathic understanding, respect, therapeutic genuineness, and concreteness (Patterson, 1985). Students recognize and accept that these conditions are necessary for therapeutic personality change (Rogers, 1957). The emphasis is that therapy is not a matter of skills, but of basic attitudes; nevertheless, it is necessary that therapists be able to implement these attitudes with clients. Three simple rules for the beginning therapist are emphasized:

   a. The therapist listens, the client talks. Therefore, keep your mouth shut. You can't listen to the client while you are talking.

   b. Never ask a question—unless you don't understand what the client is saying.

   c. Remain in the responsive mode. The client initiates, the therapist follows.

2.   It is not expected that supervisees should accept that the therapist conditions are sufficient as well as necessary for therapeutic personality change. It is emphasized that supervisees are expected to *test the assumption that they are sufficient*. This means that the supervisees are not to depart from these conditions, thus abandoning the assumption, and try other techniques. Although theoretically it may be that the assumption is not correct, supervisees are not prepared to go beyond them. Engaging in other practices would involve the supervisee's being irresponsible. As a corollary to this requirement, it is emphasized that the supervisor is responsible for the supervisee's clients, and *supervisees are not permitted* to experiment on their clients.

Parenthetically, in my experience during some 35 years of supervision, supervisees have been universally successful in working with clients without going beyond these conditions, often to their surprise when they realize this at the end of the semester.

3.   Supervisees are told the criteria by which they will be evaluated. These consist of effectiveness in providing the therapeutic conditions. Knowing these criteria, supervisees are able to evaluate themselves. Earlier at the University of Illinois, I gave supervisees the option of being evaluated on the basis of an audiotape of a therapy session they submitted at the end of the semester. The tape would be rated by trained raters. No supervisee chose this option to my evaluation.

4.   Supervisees were expected to audiotape their sessions, provided their clients agreed to be taped. Clients seldom refused to be taped.

5.   In preparation for supervision, supervisees are expected to review their tapes and make notes during the review, including questions they wish to bring into supervision. It is impossible for the supervisor to listen to all of the tape recordings; therefore, supervisees are expected to select tapes and sections of tapes that they wish to work on during supervision. Although it might be expected that supervisees would present their best tapes, this is not the case. They select those tapes and sections of tapes in which they realize they did poorly or were confused about their performance and on which they want help.

These practices allow for the development of a supervisory atmosphere that minimizes threat and anxiety for the supervisee. They provide a structure that facilitates supervisee learning (Freeman, 1993). Because the supervisee knows where the supervisor is coming from—they share the same theoretical system—and has the criteria by which he or she is being evaluated, evaluative comments or statements by the supervisor are practically nonexistent. Supervisees make their own evaluative comments. Similarly, the need for and the amount of feedback from the supervisor are minimized: The supervisee gives him- or herself feedback. The stage is set for a relationship that is immediately productive. So-called stages in the process are not present. There is a smooth progression, or supervisee progress.

The Actual Process.   The supervisor provides a client-centered—or supervisee-centered—relationship. He or she is genuine in the process, respects the supervisee, and empathizes with the supervisee's relationship with the client, putting her- or himself in the place of the supervisee in the relationship. The supervisee has the responsibility for the supervision process—selecting the taped material to be considered and raising questions, problems or issues.

   1.   Because the supervisor bears the responsibility for the supervisee's clients and not every tape, or a tape for each client, can be included in the supervisory session, each session begins with the supervisee reviewing each of his or her clients. This may be more, or less, detailed, depending on the client. Also, it is considered important that at least one continuing client is followed in some detail by the supervisor.

   2.   There is little concern with diagnosing or labeling clients and little if any discussion of personality dynamics. Such an approach views the client as an object to be analyzed and evaluated rather than as a person to be accepted and understood. Supervisees are, however, helped to be sensitive to evidence of severe disturbances or organic problems, as well as indications of conditions that would warrant referral. Such conditions become apparent in the course of a therapy that focuses on the client's frame of reference and perceptions.

   3.   The supervisor does not engage in didactic instruction to any great extent because the supervisee has had a course in the theory being practiced. When a question or problem involving an element of the theory or its application arises and it is considered by the supervisor to be an issue of interest or concern to other supervisees, it is brought up for discussion in a group meeting.

   4.   Supervision is not therapy. Nevertheless, both are interpersonal relationships, and they have some commonalities, as already noted: empathic understanding, respect, and genuineness. But these conditions are implemented somewhat differently. The focus is not on the supervisee's personality or problems, but upon his or her relationship with his or her clients. The supervisee's personality becomes of concern only if it detrimentally affects the therapy. Then it is dealt with only in terms of this situation, that is, the supervisor responds to the difficulty in the supervisee's relationships with his or her clients. Yet because of the overlap in supervision and therapy, "one should not be surprised to find at times the line between supervision and therapy becomes difficult to determine" (Bonney, 1994, p. 35).

   If it becomes apparent that the supervisee's personal adjustment is pervasive and interferes with his or her ability to function as a therapist, psychotherapy should be recommended. In extreme cases, when clients could be hurt, the supervisee should be discontinued from the practicum or internship.

Group Meetings.   Supervisees meet regularly in a group with the supervisor. Problems, questions, and issues arising in individual sessions are discussed. With the supervisee's permission, sections of tapes may be played. Professional and ethical issues are considered,

[handwritten margin note: ✳ not training vs. training (inst).]

including record keeping, privileged communication, confidentiality, duty to warn, referrals (e.g., because of suspicion of physiological or neurological conditions or indications
of the desirability of medication), and other topics.

Example

The following excerpts are from a supervisory session with a supervisee who was intern-
ing at a family service agency. This session took place near the end of the third month of
his internship. At the beginning of the semester, he reported that he was to see his first
family group (one of those discussed later) that evening and that he was concerned about
how to approach it, because he had not had a course in family therapy. I recalled for him
what I had said in a brief discussion of family therapy in one of the class sessions in the
course he had had with me: The function of the therapist in family therapy (and in group
therapy also) is (a) as in individual therapy to listen and respond with empathic understanding and (b) to facilitate each person's understanding of the others in the family or
group. If there is evidence that one participant fails to understand, or misunderstands, what
another participant has said, respond with "It seems to me that what he or she was saying
was . . ." or "I heard her or him saying . . ." or a similar response, to help participants to
more accurately hear and understand one another. In the group session the next day, he
reported with satisfaction that the meeting had gone very well.

In the following excerpt, the supervisee begins immediately without the supervisor (this
author) saying anything. He proceeds as usual by reviewing his clients, here in more detail
than is often the case, as they are clients that we have followed closely in previous sessions. SEE is the supervisee; SOR is the supervisor. The family consists of mother, father,
son, and daughter.

SEE: Well, I had a hard time—as I sat in group yesterday—I was having a hard time sort
        of recapturing all that's happened in the last week. Let me go through the clients
        and maybe that will spark fresh memories. [SOR: uhuh]. Ahh—I can't remember—
        did I tell you that the family with the boy who had been running off and making
        all those disruptive phone calls to his mother at work and at school—he—I guess
        two weeks ago tomorrow—that would have been after I last saw you—they took
        him down to the Baptist Adventure Camp.

SOR: Yeah—they were going to do that.

SEE: And that was hard. I talked to the mother that morning. The supervisor of the nurs-
        ing program she is in had wanted some confirmation that the family was in coun-
        seling—she wanted some reassurance before the mother reenrolled for the spring
        quarter [SOR: uhuh] and—ah—so I called the mother, as I wasn't going to talk to
        this woman—she had left a message on the machine—until I had permission from
        the mother, and in the course of talking to her about that it became apparent that
        she was pretty emotional about—understandably—about having to take her son
        off and leaving him somewhere. This was a significant milestone for the family in
        terms of the family development. . . . And I talked to her again on Monday, I guess
        and they had taken him down again [to the camp] on Friday, and I'm not sure
        whether it was Saturday or Sunday that he had run away and—oh—but they had
        found him and taken him back—and she was going to call that day to find out how
        he was doing—you know—he had no access to the telephone there. I haven't heard
        anything more from them. Again I invited her to be in touch if there was a need.

So—let me get it all straight—the nine-year-old boy I have been seeing where the sexual abuse by his cousin came to light recently. I had a good session with him a week ago . . . [continues reviewing this case, including a meeting with the parents]. You know, it seems to me that ongoing couple's work, or some individual work for the father would be helpful for the boy. I guess I'm not real sure where my role is in broaching all of that. I guess it's still very much a gray area for me as to what my role is, as to sharing my perception—my thoughts about what might be useful. At this point I suspect the father—it seemed early to me to talk with the father about individual work. . . .

SOR: Now you're going to continue seeing him twice [a week], then once.
SEE: I think so.

[SEE continues talking about the idea that the boy has an attention deficit disorder. There have been no apparent results of treatment with Ritalin™.]

SEE: But the mother did report that there had been some significant changes at home in his behavior, especially with homework.
SOR: But you're thinking that at some point you feel that he [the father] could benefit from individual therapy.
SEE: I think so. He described his own depression. Do you have any thought on that, on—
SOR: Well, uh, I'm thinking probably that at some point he may focus on himself when they are both there and you might just suggest that he might want to talk about these things without his wife present—then the problem would be whether you could do it. [SEE: uhuh]. It's been a kind of a pattern of parent education and it might not be easy to shift for both of you.
SEE: [Goes on to suggest the possibility of the father joining a parent group for male survivors of child abuse, at the agency—the father is such a survivor.] So I think if it came to that I would certainly refer him, rather than trying to do that myself— O.K., that feels better. So it appears that things are moving in a positive direction.

[The SEE goes on to review other cases for a considerable period of time. Several families were involved. Then]:

SEE: The 38-year-old woman who is on the tape called me and wanted to know if I could see her that morning. She went to work and was unable to stay, and—ah— said she was feeling like she was going to hurt herself. I was supposed to go to a workshop, but I hesitantly agreed to see her, and did. I think it was the right thing to do—hindsight, the powerful tool that it is, tells me that she probably could have made it without it [the appointment]. But—I didn't know that at the time. [SOR: Yeah.] What I've learned since told me that. She brought her 200 Valiums™ with her, poured them all out on the table during our session. We met for about an hour and a half during which she—ahh—well, it's amazing—I listened to the tape—I listened to part of the tape right after that session. She talked in the session about how up and down she felt. She—the night before—she takes Elavil™ daily and was prescribed Tranxene™ to help her sleep. [A psychiatrist monitors her drug treatment.] She had taken four instead of two the night before—said she had taken the four hoping she wouldn't wake up, but had. When she talked about the rapid cycling up and down I wondered if that was a product of the medication [SOR: uhuh] and suggested that we try to get in touch with her psychiatrist to find out whether that might be the case or not. So we did track him down and I talked to him a bit and told him what was going on and then he talked to her briefly, and she told him as she told me that she didn't want to be hospitalized. She had been hospitalized twice—once involuntarily—and she said, she had told me on the phone and she told me before and she told me in the session that she had a gun and that if either of us tried to have the police come and commit her involuntarily that she would have the gun out and she would force the police to kill her—that she wouldn't hurt them, that she would lead them to think that she might and force them to blow her away—to use her term. So she was pretty distraught, certainly. [SOR: uhuh] And by the end of the hour and a half I felt fairly certain that she wouldn't do anything to hurt herself. She called me later in the day—she called me several times during the day. I guess in the session I had talked to her about hospitalization in terms of it being a way for people who—ahh, felt like they might hurt themselves but still had some desire to live, to get help. Well, when she talked to me on the phone in the afternoon, I had an interesting, or what for me was a very illuminating misunderstanding. She almost always speaks in the third person and she said: "You don't do anything but sit there." (I had broached the topic of hospitalization again.) And I took that to be a criticism of me—that I didn't do anything in sessions but just sit there—so I responded—as clearly as I can remember—I wrote it down last night when I was listening to the tape, something like "so you're trying to provoke a different response from me." And then— I don't think she really understood that—she said: "No up there at the hospital you just sit there and watch TV." So that was very interesting to me. What she was saying was that in the hospital all you do is just sit there—how is that going to help me? But because of where I was coming from I read that [SOR: Yeah, right] as "you just sit there."

SOR: She was picturing the hospital and herself.

SEE: So that was very interesting and instructive. And I think my response was a very appropriate one and it did in fact clarify what it was she was talking about. But it was telling me that I was somehow feeling at least mildly attacked or questioned or criticized [SOR: Yeah] and that's the way I read her comment. So she made it through the day.

[The SEE then talks for a time about the client calling him frequently on the telephone, sometimes at his home, and discusses the possibility of seeing her twice a week to reduce the phone contacts. Then]:

SOR: Let me express a feeling I have: What about the possibility you're doing something to create a dependency relationship with her?

SEE: Well, I think that has happened.

SOR: Yeah, but whether it is something you have contributed to . . .

SEE: [Pause] Well, I don't know. I mean, I wouldn't rule it out. I don't—I mean she's obviously a very needy woman who has very little [SOR: Yeah] support coming from anywhere else. I guess I would ask you, did you hear specific things [SOR: Well] that made you wonder about that or worry about that?

SOR: I listened to the tape from where you set it on to the end. You're presenting her with two different roles. Part of the time you're responding to her but then part of the time because of your concern about suicide you're taking over and questioning and probing. And these are inconsistent. You're showing this concern about possible suicide—getting a contract. [The SEE had picked this up from another course or his reading.] At one point she said she wouldn't do it—at one point you say: "Have you been feeling that way lately, that you might use them?" And when she said "No," you said "Good"—showing your own feeling. And I think you may be communicating to her that you're really worried about her—what she might do, what might happen. And I don't say she's manipulating you. But this is a possible reason why people—they talk about a suicide gesture—that she's using these things, talking about—a kind of gesture to get your concern, to get you involved in some way. So that she's becoming dependent rather than independent. I think she's getting two kinds of messages from you.

SEE: Yeah. Yeah. I see that. Uhuh. Well, it's interesting, because in thinking about that now I have felt that and I've—I think in the phone contacts since I haven't seen her since last Tuesday I've been—I've been more limited in my responses.

SOR: Yeah. Not more reassuring, maybe?

SEE: No. I think consciously—because I think the history of all these phone calls has told me as long as I offer that to her she's going to continue to seek it. And if I throw her back on her own resources that she's got more ability to do it than she would want me to think. An example of that being that her husband, from whom she is separated, was arrested for nonpayment of child support—from a previous marriage and she called me and was all teary about—she couldn't get anyone to cosign the bail bond—she was obviously, I think, wanting me to say I would. But I didn't even think of biting on that one—I guess the thing that you're raising the question makes me think more about is, should I have said I would see her today, you know. [SOR: Yeah] Do I need to, from here on out, say there are our scheduled appointment times [SOR: Yeah] particularly if there is a true emergency, there is a crisis response and assessment team at _____ hospital. I think that's what's going to be necessary. I think—I see what you're saying here. I guess what's still unclear to me in a situation where you have someone who is talking about suicide is—uh—morally, ethically, is it sufficient to respond—is there a responsibility to do more.

SOR: But when you do that you're damaging your relationship.

SEE: Yeah. Then I guess the response is then to know what the potential hazards are if you see a need to do that and make the choice.

SOR: I think people in general—and the current literature and everything overemphasize the danger. Everybody who talks about suicide isn't going to do it. People who are vulnerable—like you—have got to protect yourselves and I think too easily panic and lose confidence in the client and take over.

SEE: Well, it's certainly been a good experience, working with her—very different than anybody I've ever worked with before certainly. And has raised this whole realm of boundary questions in a way I haven't had to deal with before. But I think it's caused me to think about what was the cost of intervening in that way at this point, and—ah—I can see in this session too—of this tape—which was a long session with her last Tuesday, that I skated between different roles at that time too.

[There is a period of listening with the supervisee to a portion of a tape with the client. In addition to the difficulty of listening to a tape recording of a tape recording, the client's voice has a childish pitch as a result of a recent experimental treatment for her stuttering, consisting of injection of a substance into her voice box.]

SEE: This tape is very hard to hear. [Tape not audible for a while. SEE then responds to the client. Ther. is the supervisee: Ther: There may be a part of you that wants to open up in the same way but it's been so tight for so long it's hard to accept that change.

SEE: A little bit of interpretation?

SOR: Yeah. [Client speaks inaudibly.]

SEE: She didn't really respond to it. I couldn't hear what that little bit was. I think she said "I'm just so tired." I was seeing it metaphorically, and she just didn't get it.

SOR: Yeah. Well, it seems to me that you have this hypothesis of a multiple personality and you're trying to find something.

SEE: Well, that was it. I was smuggling it in there as _____ [my teaching assistant] would say—to see whether it would turn anything up.

[We continue to listen to the tape though it wasn't possible for the supervisor to hear clearly what the client was saying, partly because of her voice quality. The supervisee's statements were audible, and some of these were commented on by the supervisor.]

Ther. [to client]: With your voice being different now, do you sound more to yourself like you did when you were little? Younger?
Client: I never thought of that.

SEE: See, hindsight tells me that I could have phrased that—I could have commented on her voice [SOR: Yeah] instead of questioning her about it—towards the same—the same end, or by saying "Your voice has a childlike quality to it."

SOR: Yeah, right.

SEE: Even though I'm getting to be a more experienced counselor, I still feel—I guess I feel a lack of an experience base to help me temper expectations—especially with a very different client like this. [SOR: Yeah] I think that uncertainty—I don't know if it's impatience—I guess it is uncertainty as much as anything. [SOR: Yeah] It's part of what has led to my shifting gears and roles.

SOR: Yeah. It's difficult to get in and stay in her field of reference.

SEE: Yeah. At one point during this session she—she was saying "You can't know what my life has been like." And I simply said: "Yes, you're right. I cannot know." And that's really true. I can be with her, but . . .

SOR: You can try, as far as you can.

SEE: But there's an obvious limit to that.

SOR: There's a limit with everybody, but with some much more than with others.

SEE: I don't have anything else pressing. Do you—any threads that you . . .

SOR: I think this is an interesting case and I see a—I think I have some concern that—uh—the best way to help her is to give her all the responsibility—and yet—you feel you have some responsibility about the pills and the gun and those kind of things. And yet when you show your concern about it—it bothers you—it just communicates to her that this must be serious, and it can lead her without manipulating you, bringing up things like this when she wants your attention, and something from you. And yet in the long run that's not going to help her independence. She's got to take responsibility for everything all the time.

SEE: Yeah.

SOR: I think of _____'s [a former student] case where for 30 years therapists took responsibility for her—she was hospitalized much of the time—and _____ is giving it all back to her, consistently and completely—with a miraculous change.

SEE: Yeah. Well, I've seen that and what you're noting on this tape really fits with what I've experienced in the past week in dealing with her—and—not seeking to be reassuring.

SOR: Right.

SEE: And I'm seeing more how she can do it for herself.

SOR: Yeah. If you really let her, she can.

SEE: But what's become clear to me in the course of my time here talking about this is that—uh—my seeking to reassure her is probably going to only increase the likelihood that she will lose her job, for example. Now I can't say, as things go on, that she may not lose her ability to—uh—function well enough to hold her job. But neither can I take responsibility for that—but I think what you've pointed out and what I've experienced in the last weeks suggests that—well, to use the codependency lingo, the more I enable her to be irresponsible the more she will be.

SOR: Yeah. As you say, you're setting limits more, and in a real emergency she goes somewhere else. You'll see her twice a week and that's going to be it.

SEE: Because I think what I've seen is the real emergencies—is going to be a crisis that is going to require a response that I am not going to be able to provide anyway.

Well, it's interesting—I don't remember when it was—I remember—saying at some point—and I'd be interested in your response to this—that borderline personalities can eat up a client-centered therapist, and I've been mulling that over. And I guess what I've made of it is that there's an assumption there that—uh—because a client-centered therapist seeks to be responsive you're more apt to be manipulated. And may not set the kind of limits that are necessary—uh—

SOR: Yeah. The concept of borderline personality is very popular now—but it's very vague.

SEE: It's a catchall. [The session closes with a discussion of borderline personalities, or psychopathic personalities as clients.]

Little comment on this excerpt appears to be necessary. It is clear that the supervisee takes responsibility for the session, explores issues and problems, and comes to his own insights and decisions. The supervisor listens, responds, and follows the lead of the supervisee.

The Supervisee's Perceptions

The supervisee was interviewed briefly on videotape by Suzanne Freeman, following his viewing of the videotape of her interview with the supervisor (Freeman, 1992). IOR designates the interviewer and IEE the interviewee.

IOR: Can you give us a little information about what your thinking and expectations were before supervision?

IEE: Well, I'd had Dr. Patterson for his advanced theories course, so I had developed something of a personal relation with him through that. I think I was intrigued by the notion of being supervised by someone of his experience and background so there was a sense of excitement and anticipation—a little bit of anxiety because I wasn't sure whether his approach would be one which was doctrinaire or whether he would have expectations that I didn't feel able to meet. But I thought of it as an opportunity that I didn't want to pass up, certainly.

IOR: Can you speak to how you felt—did he clarify for you the roles and responsibilities of you as a supervisee and him as a supervisor?

IEE: Yeah. That was really the first thing that he did. I think he refers to that as struc-
       turing the relationship. And that was done very clearly and overtly at the start of
       the semester. It was the only time he did anything of that sort, letting me know what
       the minimal expectation—letting me know it would be primarily my role to bring
       things to our supervision and for me to be responsible to determine what these ses-
       sions would consist of.

IOR: And, how did that occur—you taking responsibility for the sessions?

IEE: Well, it took the form of me having listened to audiotapes of my sessions, and
       bringing those, or segments of those, to the actual supervisory sessions. And—
       uh—making choices about what portions I wanted him to hear. How he was intent
       on developing an in-depth understanding of at least one of my clients, so that was
       something that could be built on session to session. But it also included my bring-
       ing questions that I had that came up either in the context of a session [with a
       client] or about some aspect of counseling that then provided the focus for dis-
       cussion that came out of that.

IOR: Uhuh. Comment on this idea: If a student is being evaluated in supervision, and a
       student has the responsibility for what the student brings into the session, then
       likely the student is going to bring in their very best work. How did that work for
       you? How did you experience that kind of freedom?

IEE: Well, certainly there is the temptation to want to put a good face on things, but I
       think it became clear to me very quickly that I wasn't going to learn very much if
       that was all I did. And my motivation to be the best I could for the clients I was
       working with ultimately led me to wanting to use Dr. Patterson for time in super-
       vision to figure things out that were posing difficulties or things that represented
       hard spots for me. So I think I fairly quickly went beyond the urge to present things
       that would make me look or sound good.

IOR: Can you think of a specific time when you were struggling with a case and you
       brought the difficulty into the discussion? How was it handled? Did Dr. Patterson
       give you what you should have said, did he ask questions? How did he help you
       with the specific problem that you brought in?

IEE: Well, I can think of one particular instance where I was—uh—approaching termi-
       nation with one of my clients and was concerned that I should have been more active
       in the session than I was, and I was seeking some clarification from Dr. Patterson
       about my perceptions of that, and as he listened to the tape to know of my question
       around that for the most part he reflected what it was I was raising and in a sense
       guided me as I thought about what I was concerned about and why and—uh—he
       helped me become clearer about what I had done in the session and whether that had
       been an appropriate response to what the client brought to the session or not.

IOR: Were you aware of the core conditions being present in that supervisory relation-
       ship? Empathy, respect—

IEE: Uhuh. Very definitely, and I commented to Dr. Patterson at the end of the semes-
       ter that one of the things I found most impressive about the process—and about him
       as an individual was the fact that I experienced a high level of congruence between
       the things that I had heard about in his course and understand about a relationship-
       based approach to counseling and seeing those things being demonstrated by him
       in his relationship with me.

IOR: O.K. Now, he says that he divides the didactic role—the teaching role—in one ses-
       sion, and the facilitative role in another session. How did that work for you?

IEE: Well, I think there was very definitely a distinction about how he functioned in those two roles. We had a group process at the same time under way with several of us graduate students and that tended to be more of a—well, to be the time in which didactic processes happened. Dr. Patterson would sometimes bring a specific topic to that group or he would respond to one that came out of a question or difficulty that one of us was having. But the time in individual supervision was much more—ahh—responding to what I brought rather than coming with an agenda of his own that he felt I needed to hear about or be part of.

IOR: Uhuh. In those individual sessions would you say that there was therapy going on for you, or would you say that it was therapeutic in some way within the session?

IEE: I think—it was therapeutic for me at different points —ahh—I worked at different things that were issues for me as a becoming counselor. I certainly did not feel that the process was therapy, or conceived as such. That was not my goal or was it his goal—that it be therapy for me. The focus was my clients and me in the process of being helpful to those people.

IOR: Over the semester do you feel that you changed as a counselor because of what went on in supervision?

IEE: Very definitely. I think that really for the first time in the program I felt both an invitation and an expectation to—ahh—submit to a discipline which was represented by the core conditions and the invitation to test the hypothesis whether the conditions were necessary and sufficient in doing psychotherapy with an individual client and—ahh—that discipline was not one that I submitted to easily but I'm grateful to have had the chance to do that, and I see real value in having had that experience, certainly.

IOR: O.K. Are there any other comments that you would like to make about the experience? Anything that . . .

IEE: Only to say that it really was a very productive experience. Qualitatively different than a previous supervisory experience, to the extent that I did feel a different responsibility placed with me for what the nature and the content of the individual sessions would be—ahh—and that was scary sometimes in the sense that it would have been easier to have been lazy and—ahh—let that revert to Dr. Patterson as the supervisor. But I think, especially coming to a point of conclusion in a program, it was important to feel that responsibility and decide what I was going to do with it.

IOR: Thank you very much.

CONCLUSION

The approach to supervision described here has several advantages:

1. The supervisor and supervisee have a common or shared philosophy and theory of psychotherapy, namely, client-centered theory.
2. The supervisor follows the principles of this system in the supervisory process.
3. The result is a climate or atmosphere in which threat and anxiety are minimized, thus providing an optimum learning situation.
4. The supervisor, in respecting the supervisee, allows the supervisee to direct the sessions by selecting and presenting the materials to be considered by the supervisor.
5. The supervisee knows the criteria by which he or she is being evaluated, thus allowing him or her to apply these criteria in evaluating him- or herself.

6. Supervision begins at a high level, precluding a slow process in which the supervisee must attempt to understand and adapt to the system and criteria of the supervisor. There is no long, drawn-out process of so-called stages in supervision.

7. Although this approach has been designated as client-centered, it is a basic, generic approach. The focus is on elements or conditions commonly recognized as client-centered, but that are actually elements common to all the major theories. Client-centered therapy does not have a monopoly on these conditions. Students or supervisees are informed that whether or not they eventually decide to continue as client-centered therapists, these elements are necessary in any system they might choose. Other elements can be added from their preferred theory. However, any additions can be, and usually are, inconsistent with client-centered philosophy, and the result is not client-centered therapy.

REFERENCES

Bernard, J. M., & Goodyear, R. K. (1992). *Fundamentals of clinical supervision*. Boston: Allyn & Bacon.

Bonney, W. (1994). Teaching supervision: Some practical issues for beginning supervisors. *The Psychotherapy Bulletin, 29*(2), 31–36.

Ford, D. H., & Urban, H. B. (1963). *Systems of psychotherapy*. New York: Wiley.

Freeman, S. (1992). C. H. Patterson on client-centered supervision: An interview. *Counselor Education and Supervision, 31*, 219–226.

Freeman, S. C. (1993). Structure in counseling supervision. *The Clinical Supervisor, 11*(1), 245–252.

Matarazzo, R. G., & Patterson, D. R. (1986). Methods of teaching therapeutic skill. In S. L. Garfield & A. E. Bergin (Eds.), *Handbook of psychotherapy and behavior change* (3rd ed., pp. 821–843). New York: Wiley.

Patterson, C. H. (1959). *Counseling and psychotherapy: Theory and practice*. New York: Harper-Collins.

Patterson, C. H. (1964). Supervising students in the counseling practicum. *Journal of Counseling Psychology, 11*, 47–53.

Patterson, C. H. (1974). *Relationship counseling and psychotherapy*. New York: HarperCollins.

Patterson, C. H. (1983). A client-centered approach to supervision. *The Counseling Psychologist, 11*(1), 21–25.

Patterson, C. H. (1985). *The therapeutic relationship*. Pacific Grove, CA: Brooks/Cole.

Patterson, C. H. (1992). The education of counselors and psychotherapists: A proposal. *Asian Journal of Counseling, 2*(1), 81–88.

Patterson, C. H. (1995). A universal system of psychotherapy. *The Person-Centered Journal, 2*(1), 54–62.

Patterson, C. H., & Hidore, S. (1996). *Effective psychotherapy: A caring, loving relationship*. Northvale, NJ: Jason Aronson.

Patterson, C. H., & Watkins, C. E., Jr. (1996). *Theories of psychotherapy* (5th ed.). New York: HarperCollins.

Porter, E. H., Jr. (1950). *An introduction to therapeutic counseling*. Boston: Houghton Mifflin.

Rogers, C. R. (1957). The necessary and sufficient conditions of therapeutic personality change. *Journal of Consulting Psychology, 21*, 95–103.

CHAPTER 10

Supervision From a Gestalt
Therapy Perspective

GARY YONTEF
Gestalt Therapy Institute of Los Angeles

Although the literature on supervision from a Gestalt therapy perspective is quite sparse, there is an oral tradition in which supervision closely follows the principles of Gestalt therapy. This is true of supervision of Gestalt therapy and also supervision of regular psychotherapy by Gestalt therapists.

SUPERVISION AND GESTALT THERAPY THEORY

Gestalt therapy is an existential therapy that emphasizes existence as people experience it and deemphasizes abstract explanatory schema. Gestalt therapy methodology is phenomenological, using and refining immediate experience or felt sense rather than interpreting the unconscious.

Gestalt therapy and Gestalt therapy supervision use phenomenological focusing and experimentation to clarify the exact experience of supervisor, supervisee, and patients. Supervisees are helped to put aside (into "brackets") inferences, assumptions, interpretations, theoretical beliefs, and so forth so they can be impacted by the obvious (the "given"). Special attention is given to the awareness of the awareness process, especially to how awareness is limited or distorted, and to awareness of the here-and-now contact between therapist and patient and between supervisor and supervisee.

Gestalt therapy thinking is based on field theory (Yontef, 1993). A field analysis regards all phenomena through the lens of a "field." Fields are complex wholes composed of multiple forces interacting in the here and now (the principle of contemporaneity) and changing over time ("process"). In field theory, all phenomena are considered as processes changing over time rather than as static structures. Phenomena are not known absolutely but can be known only from some perspective.

Gestalt therapy and Gestalt therapy supervision encompass as much of the whole field and its multiple interrelating aspects as possible (e.g., biological, social, individual, family, cultural). The supervisor helps the supervisee relate to the entire context in which they operate and the various factors that come into play. This includes appreciating the inevitable

The author is indebted to Arnold Beisser for a supervision course at the Gestalt Therapy Institute of Los Angeles in 1982.

existence and phenomenological validity of different perspectives. Using field process thinking, Gestalt therapy emphasizes contemporaneous relations in the field as they are experienced at any one time and as they develop over time (process). In the field process approach, development or action over time is emphasized over static, structural thinking.

In field theory, all existence is relationship, from electrical charges of subatomic particles through the cosmic movement of star systems. Human identity is a matter of relationship between "me" and "not me," between self and other. In Gestalt therapy theory, contact between organism and environment is considered the "simplest and first reality" (Perls, Hefferline, & Goodman, 1951/1994).

Gestalt therapy personality theory is a radical ecological field theory. Most theories assume the separate existence of individuals and environment and then add interaction. Not so in Gestalt therapy, in which the individual and the environment are considered only phenomenological differentiations of the organism/environment field (Perls et al., 1951/1994, p. 3; Yontef, 1993). A Gestalt therapy understanding always relates individuals to a context or field; in Gestalt therapy there is no other meaningful way to understand a person. From birth onward, people form their sense of self through relationship to others.

The basic unit of relationship is contact. Contact is what one is in touch with and is the basic unit underlying both awareness and motoric behavior (Perls et al., 1951/1994). Gestalt therapy aligns around two forms of contact: awareness and relationship. The goal is increased awareness (being in contact with self and other); the medium is contact between therapist and patient and between supervisor and supervisee. True to the existential and phenomenological basis of Gestalt therapy, the Gestalt therapist makes contact on the model of an existential dialogue (discussed later) and does not attempt to maintain an impersonal demeanor or to foster a transference neurosis.

People regulate themselves organismically through the actions or processes called the "contact boundary." The *contact boundary* is a function or organ of the entire organism/environment field. The individual components of boundary processes are awareness (what one is in contact with), motor behavior (what one does), and feeling (affect). The contact boundary differentiates the field and has the dual functions of joining the individual with others and also maintaining separation. Separation creates and preserves autonomy and protects the organism. But it is only by active exchange with the rest of the field that life and growth are possible. People grow by assimilating that which is novel, that is, different from self and varying from the static. This is especially true of meeting and acknowledging other people as people.

People establish their sense of self by the boundary between me and not me, especially between I and thou (another person conceived as a person) or the boundary between I and it (others being treated as a means to an end). Any "aiming" in relationship points to an I-it mode of operation. (Dialogue in Gestalt therapy is discussed later.) Self-identity in Gestalt therapy theory does not occur by an isolated I, by looking inward, but by distinguishing self and not-self, by the operation of the boundary processes of identification/alienation.

Supervision Is Creative Adjustment

Through boundary processes, people engage in *creative adjustment;* that is, they adjust to the environment and also adjust the environment to the self: "All contact is creative adjustment of the organism and environment" (Perls et al., 1951/1994, p. 6). People must adjust to the environment in which they live, or else they are outcasts, dysfunctional, or a hazard to others. But merely adjusting to the environment is conformity without creativity. People also need to adjust the environment to them, that is, shape the environment so that it conforms to human needs and values.

Individuals maintain themselves and grow by awareness of their needs, environmental needs, and conditions and resources and by accepting and assimilating from the environment that which is appropriate and rejecting that which is not. Assimilation means supporting maintenance and growth by taking in novelty, breaking down (destruct), and integrating, making the novelty part of oneself. For example, food that is assimilated is tasted, chewed, and digested. To take in without assimilation is introjection. Beliefs and other environmental inputs that are introjected rather than truly assimilated keep self-functioning from being whole, as aware as needed, integrated, harmonious, and fully responsive to actual conditions in the field.

Of necessity, most exchanges are governed by habit, with full awareness being reserved for transactions requiring it. With awareness, individuals learn from experience and either adjust self or attempt to adjust the environment until satisfaction is achieved. When the awareness does not develop as needed, psychotherapy is indicated.

Gestalt therapy focuses on awareness of the awareness process, that is, what one is aware of, what important information or feelings are not allowed to come into figural awareness, and precisely how people control what is allowed to come to awareness. Immediate experience is a clear sensing or contemporaneous knowing of the obvious, the "given" (i.e., what stands out as figure), and the meaning (i.e., the relationship between the figure and its background). In health, figure formation and action taken are organized by the dominant contemporaneous need. By the phenomenological work of differentiating what is immediately experienced from fixed statements about experience, the process of interrupting awareness and action based on awareness comes into awareness and becomes open to conscious choice.

The Paradoxical Theory of Change (Beisser, 1970)

Growth occurs by recognition of self and other, identifying with self-experience, and accepting the experience of others.

The Gestalt therapy theory of change is called the paradoxical theory of change. The paradox of the paradoxical theory of change is this: Significant change does not occur by trying to be what one is not, but rather growing from identifying with what one is. Trying to change based on disowning how one is sets up internal dichotomies that stymie growth. On the contrary, identifying with the actuality of one's existence enables learning and growth: It gives grounding that can support movement. Therefore the methodology of Gestalt therapy prefers interventions that align with patients' awareness (inclusion or empathy), help patients acquire tools to focus their own awareness, and create phenomenological experimentation that improves awareness. The methodology of Gestalt therapy supervision aligns with the experience of patient and supervisee.

Dialogic Relationship

The heart of Gestalt therapy is its view of the nature of the contact between therapist and patient. The therapeutic relationship in Gestalt therapy is based on a special form of contact called the *existential dialogue* (Hycner, 1985, 1991; Hycner & Jacobs, 1995; Jacobs, 1989, 1992; Yontef, 1993). This relationship has three major characteristics: (a) inclusion:

the therapist empathically experiences the closest possible approximation to the experience of the patient thereby confirming the patient's human existence; (b) the empathic understanding is communicated through the therapist's genuine, congruent, authentic, and caring presence and genuine and unreserved communication, showing warm acceptance and respect and being appropriately transparent, vulnerable, congruent, and authentic; (c) the Gestalt therapist is committed to dialogue, surrendering to the between. This is a form of contact without aiming, with truth and healing emerging from the interaction rather than what is already known by therapist or patient.

Gestalt therapy supervision is a modified form of dialogue, one that helps the supervisee dialogue with patients. In Gestalt therapy, meeting the patient and facilitating the patient's growth is the only goal. The patient is an end in him- or herself and not a means to an end. Although Gestalt therapy has a dialogic attitude toward supervision, supervision also has the goal of the supervisee serving the needs of his or her patients. To some extent, this makes the therapist a means to an end rather than an end in him- or herself and the I-thou interspersed with more I-it than in the psychotherapy dialogue. However, the Gestalt therapy supervisor makes the relationship as dialogic as possible.

COMPONENTS OF SUPERVISION

Supervision has the goals of meeting societal and agency needs, the growth of the therapist, and the protection and growth of patients. The work is done through administrative, educative, and consultative components. The concentration of the three components varies according to context and stage of learning.

Administrative Component

Since Gestalt therapy is a radical ecological field theory, supervision must be oriented to the context in which it occurs. The administrative component is oriented to the needs of the context in which supervisor and supervisee are operating, especially those of sponsoring and regulating agencies. The supervisor is an agent of interchange between the supervisee and the larger field, including the hierarchy of the agency and larger social, political, and social systems. This includes the supervisor's responsibility and authority to steer, oversee, and evaluate the supervisee's performance in regard to adherence to agency policy and goals, professional standards of practice and ethics, and legal standards. The supervisor informs the supervisee about and helps the supervisee deal with the structural organization of the field, including policy and policy making, funding, accreditation issues, training standards, and so forth. The supervisor brings to the supervisee the perspective of the whole field, the perspective of time, and attention to the nuances of the multiple relations in the field.

Administrative supervision from a Gestalt therapy perspective is a process of creative adjustment, that is, helping the supervisee adjust to the system and also giving support and guidance for responsible fighting for social change both within the agency and within society. The supervisor helps supervisees bring their viewpoint to the larger field. Neither blind conformity nor blind rebellion is condoned.

Gestalt therapists conduct administrative supervision with maximal respect for the principles of Gestalt therapy. A clear dialogue is encouraged in which the requirements of the field are made clear by the supervisor, and the experience of the supervisees and patients are invited and respectfully considered. This invitation includes nondefensive receptivity to how supervisees and patients are affected by agency policy, by the supervisor, and by the supervision process, as well as their thoughts and recommendations. Gestalt therapy philosophy demands that all people—be they supervisor, supervisee, or patient—be treated as an end in themselves and not as a mere means to an end. Their welfare as self-defined is considered primary. This attitude horizontalizes responsibility and authority to the maximal extent possible in the situation.

Educative Function

The educative component of supervision is centered on the teacher or supervisor imparting knowledge to the supervisee. In this mode, the supervisor has a plan of what the supervisee needs to know to facilitate professional development. This includes what the supervisee needs to know to treat his or her patients, what the supervisee needs to know for professional development, and any particular knowledge, expertise, or special interest of the supervisor. Although Gestalt therapy is distinctly experiential, didactic teaching is an indispensable part of Gestalt therapy supervision. For example, Gestalt therapy philosophy and methodology is a supervision teaching topic with both Gestalt and non-Gestalt supervisees.

Non-Gestalt therapists have found useful Gestalt therapist supervisors' emphasis on, and expertise with, immediacy, the paradoxical theory of change, empathic attunement to the flow of affect of the patient (and therapist), and working with the interruptions of patients' awareness of the flow of their affect. They have also found useful the dialogic emphasis in Gestalt therapy that has a developed theory for the active engagement of the therapist-as-a-person and an integration of the relationship factors of therapy and the use of technical interventions, that is, phenomenological experimentation to enhance awareness of feeling, motivation, possibilities, and so forth.

The Gestalt therapy supervisor will usually have specialized or advanced knowledge to teach Gestalt therapists in addition to basic Gestalt therapy theory. For example, the supervisor will often have a useful background in understanding character development, the requirements of treatment with particular patients, details of the sequence, progress of therapy, and so forth.

Consultation

The consultation component of supervision is supervisee centered. It is oriented to the supervisee's growth and to assisting the supervisee with specific problems, issues, and concerns. These are usually about patients. This segment is the most experiential and the most focused on the therapist-supervisee as a person. Its three dominant topics of understanding are (a) therapy systems and methodology, (b) patient character structure and therapeutic requirements, and (c) self-understanding (especially countertransference).

Each therapist must have an understanding of psychotherapy process (i.e., methodology), the character and needs of each particular patient, and self-understanding. Each therapist needs to have a good understanding of factors generic to all psychotherapy but also needs a clear and integrated understanding of the particular form of therapy he or she practices. A Gestalt therapist obviously needs to know the clinical and metatheory of Gestalt therapy in addition to generic factors.

Consultation especially focuses on understanding particular patients and particular clinical issues. Although many issues that need to be explored run across patient categories, understanding the patient is of prime importance. The supervisor helps the supervisee gain a full four-dimensional picture of each patient, including character structure, social history, expected course of therapy, cautions, and particularities of treatment. The understanding needs to be in-depth rather than simplistic, and to account for changes over time rather than be static.

The Gestalt therapy literature is particularly strong in describing personality processes of people in general and how to recognize and understand the personality processes of individuals. The Gestalt therapy literature is weaker in recognizing patterns of personality functioning of groups of individuals, that is, diagnosis. Since the ability to diagnose is essential in supervision, Gestalt therapy supervisors have the responsibility to supply what is missing in the Gestalt therapy literature from their own experience and understanding of Gestalt therapy theory and also from knowledge assimilated from the wider field of psychological knowledge. Recently, there has been a beginning recognition of this general need (see Yontef, 1993, on the general issue of diagnosis and on diagnosis and treatment of the borderline and narcissistic personality disorders in Gestalt therapy).

The consultation process must also help the supervisee to understand his or her own process, including his or her preferences, values, needs, the degree and type of dedication to the task of helping patients, his or her perspectives on relations (e.g., dialogue or fostering transference), and his or her stance on the importance of patient self-determination. According to the theory of Gestalt therapy, good therapy cannot be done unless the therapist understands his or her own biases and emotional reactions, including but not limited to countertransference.

In Gestalt therapy, all emotional reactions are not considered either transference or countertransference. Emotional reactions to the patient's work and the interactions with the patient that are in awareness and present centered, albeit influenced by the therapist's background history, need to be differentiated from emotional reactions triggered by the interaction with the patient that are determined by forces from the therapist's past and that are relatively out of awareness. Having an emotional reaction to the patient that is motivated unknowingly by a characteristic of the therapist or someone in the therapist's background is very different from a reaction that is largely reactive to what is actually happening. One of the biggest dangers to patients occurs when the therapist has an emotional reaction, especially a defensive one, and does not know and admit it.

The most obvious examples occur when the therapist has a warm, sad, protective, or affectionate response to the patient. When it is countertransferential, the response might be because of codependence or because the patient resembles someone in the therapist's past. When out of awareness, it might be a part of forming an inaccurate picture of the patient, failure to make timely interventions, or even an indulgent attitude enabling patient irresponsibility and failure to grow. On the other hand, when the therapist accurately sees the patient and knowingly is affected, for example, feeling warm, affectionate, and so forth, a verbal or nonverbal expression of this feeling can be extremely important to the patient.

Clinical Example. A supervisee reported a feeling of cold resentment and withholding toward a patient. Description revealed a very needy patient who repeatedly presented crises, expected solutions from the therapist, did not take responsibility for work in or out of therapy, acted pathetic and helpless, and repeatedly left the therapist with a message of having let her down. The patient was a borderline patient, and many therapists would have a feeling of shame or failure, resentment, guilt, and so forth in response to her. For this young trainee, there were not only the feelings of frustration that came from the poor boundary regulation of the therapeutic relationship, but a strong countertransferential element in that the patient was very much like the therapist's mother.

When the supervisee realized that the patient elicited unfinished business with his mother, he was able to separate the transferred feelings and work on them in his own psychotherapy. But this was not enough. Learning about the dynamics, boundaries, and sequence of treatment with the borderline patient enabled him to be present in a way that was more contactful, making clearer the therapeutic frame and limits, and make interventions (empathic reflections, interpretations, and guided experiments) that were more effective in getting the patient more centered and in a better position to do the necessary therapeutic work.

With awareness and present-centeredness, a therapist can use his or her emotional reaction for diagnostic purposes and as the basis for appropriately chosen and effective interventions. Gestalt therapy is particularly effective in helping therapists learn how to recognize, understand, contain, and appropriately express emotions. With this understanding, there is usually a growth in the therapist's capacity to make loving contact with the patient in a manner that facilitates the therapeutic work.

Another form of self-understanding that consultation clarifies is recognizing the therapist's limitations and strengths so that practice can be limited to what is within the therapist's training and competence, so that patients are properly informed of these limits, and so that when the patient's needs are beyond the therapist's training and ability, self-understanding can guide the therapist to refer such patients to other therapists and/or get special training and/or supervision as needed.

Gestalt therapy consultation helps supervisees broaden their thinking to include different perspectives and alternative interventions. Consultation from a Gestalt therapy perspective brings to figural awareness alternative ways of understanding and/or intervening, either already existing or spontaneously created. A special characteristic of Gestalt therapy practice and supervision is the creating of phenomenological experimentation. Gestalt therapy and Gestalt therapy supervision cannot be manualized without doing violence to its nature (Yontef, 1995).

THE THERAPEUTIC RELATIONSHIP AND THE GOALS OF SUPERVISION

Supervision has the goals of the growth of the therapist and the growth and protection of patients. Continued growth of the therapist is a major supervision objective at all levels of experience and competence. Although administrative supervision might be considered successful if the therapist reaches a fixed or mandated standard, consultation is oriented to open-ended growth. But consultation is also supervision, and the growth work of the therapist is constructed around improvement of patient services, that is, the increased effectiveness, satisfaction, and creativity of the therapy.

Growth in supervision and therapy is through the medium of relationship. In consultation, as in therapy, the Gestalt therapy attitude about relationship is to be as dialogic and horizontal as possible, consistent with the primary goals. It is the responsibility of the supervisor-consultant to set an atmosphere conducive to learning. This includes acceptance of the person of the supervisee, even while working with weaknesses, flaws, and lack of self-support. The conducive atmosphere encourages striving for excellence through experiencing and experimenting, rather than through imitation and/or perfectionistic harshness.

A safe learning environment is one in which the supervisee feels safe and cared for and leaves supervision sessions with a more accurate and accepting sense of self as person and therapist. To the degree that this is not the case, the atmosphere is not safe and learning is diminished. Of course, when the supervisee does not meet minimal standards, the establishment of such a psychologically safe environment is quite difficult.

The growth of the therapist through the supervisory dialogue is a model for the growth of the patient through the therapeutic dialogue. Both the consulting and therapeutic relationships in Gestalt therapy have the same characteristics of dialogue: inclusion-empathy, presence, and commitment to dialogue. The supervisor is attuned to the experience of the supervisee and, through him or her, to the experience of the patient. The supervisor is attuned to what the supervisee experiences in the supervision session and also in the session with the patient.

Of course, supervisee growth, patient growth and protection, and agency requirements can conflict and bring about a tension that affects the supervisory relationship. But the supervisor can continue to be empathic and authentically present and can facilitate dialogue even through this tension.

Since there is usually at least a minimal hierarchical relationship between supervisor and supervisee, and it is hoped that the supervisor does know more than the supervisee, supervision can be a fertile ground for growing shame (Yontef, 1993, 1996). Shame, the globalized sense of not being enough, can be enhanced or decreased in supervision, depending largely on the attitude of the supervisor.

The Gestalt therapy supervisor is present as a person, not just as an authority—present with a warm, authentic, and disclosed presence and genuine and unreserved communication. It is important that the supervisor's flaws be allowed to show and be acknowledged by the supervisor so that a vertical relationship is not established, that is, one in which the supervisor is inordinately elevated into charismatic stature and the supervisee demoted to a lower caste, admiring the supervisor's flawlessness. The vertical relationship is a potent shame trigger. When the supervisor is present as a person and the supervisee's experience is explicated and respected, then a real dialogue is possible.

In a supervisory or therapeutic dialogue, the supervisor or therapist does not aim and control the interaction, but rather is committed to dialogue, to surrendering to what transpires between the participants. The factor of not aiming is modified by administrative supervision and patient protection requirements. The Gestalt therapy supervisor, however, maximizes the dialogue and makes the relationship as nonauthoritarian as possible.

The philosophy of Gestalt therapy takes a strong stand on respect for differences: The phenomenological base of Gestalt therapy requires respect for multiple valid realities. Even though the supervisor may have a distinct point of view and a responsibility for the patient's welfare, the supervisor in the Gestalt therapy model must respect supervisees' felt sense of the situation with the patient, their sense of what support is needed in supervision to increase their therapeutic effectiveness, and the fact that each therapist has a somewhat different set of values, skills, creative supports, weaknesses, and so forth.

Self-examination is indicated when supervisees come to resemble a supervisor too closely. If the therapist is to help the patient identify with him- or herself, then the therapist has to be able to do the same. The job of supervisors is to encourage clear differentiation between themselves and supervisees.

In order to improve supervisees' effectiveness as therapists, personal self-esteem must be enhanced and their confidence as therapists must be increased. An important part of this process is the supervisees' learning to have self-esteem while acknowledging flaws. Shame-prone supervisees will need help with their shame and with understanding the shame process if they are to be able to be honest about weaknesses and still not be lost in shame or shame defenses (Yontef, 1993, 1996). Of course, it is necessary to distinguish between flaws and weaknesses needing remediation and those to be accepted.

Beyond the process of meeting minimal standards and understanding the orientation of the supervisor, the supervisee needs help in developing his or her own unique style of therapy. Gestalt therapists take a strong stance in favor of encouraging creative professionals and not skilled technicians. This means that there is not a right way to do therapy and that not all therapists can or should do therapy with the same style. Moreover, the style of a therapist evolves over time and needs creative adaptation to individual patients and settings. This contrasts with any view of orthodoxy and/or manualization.

Gestalt therapy is an integrative framework for therapists. Some who are supervised by a Gestalt therapist but are not Gestalt therapists may have a different framework. But a framework is needed, preferably one that allows integration of insights, data, techniques, and so forth from a variety of sources.

In Gestalt therapy supervision, this framework is constructed, not introjected; organismic framework construction requires assimilation. As therapists assimilate, as they apply their healthy aggression to destructing the material they are taught and struggle to make sense of their patients' characters, the therapy process, and their own reactions, they will optimally develop their own personal framework for integration—one that recognizes their strengths, weaknesses, interests, and values. For myself, Gestalt therapy was an ideal starting point for the process of building a personal integrating framework (Yontef, 1993). Supervisees who are able to organismically regulate themselves are more likely to facilitate the same in their patients.

I believe that the responsibility and authority for the consultation work of supervision are shared by supervisor and supervisee. Although there are administrative supervisory responsibilities that cannot be delegated, the educative and consulting components can be shared and in Gestalt therapy are shared.

The ultimate organizing idea of supervision is, of course, the welfare of the patient. Supervisees and supervisors have responsibilities in this task that are not shared. Supervisees have the responsibility of bringing into supervision accurate and representative data, especially of difficulties, and of defining their own needs to the supervisor. Supervisors have the responsibility of giving honest and clear feedback, suggestions, and evaluation. Both have the responsibility of recognizing ethical and competence limits.

COMPARISON OF SUPERVISION AND PSYCHOTHERAPY

Although supervision is not psychotherapy, the difference is largely in the structure rather than in the process. Supervision focuses on improving service to the patient, and the growth work of the supervisee is subsumed under that task. Supervision also has authority-administrative aspects that are different from psychotherapy. There are, however, parallels in task, structure, and process between psychotherapy and psychotherapy supervision. This is true also of Gestalt therapy training.

In the service of the growth of the supervisee, supervision in the Gestalt therapy mode deals extensively with the supervisee's experience during both the supervision session and psychotherapy. As in therapy, Gestalt therapy supervision deals with awareness of the awareness process, identification of need, and organismic self-regulation. These all focus on the limitations of the vision of the supervisee, distortions of awareness, and countertransference. In doing therapy, as in most of life, many transactions are not regulated with focal awareness, but by habit and intuition. Supervisees and patients learn to be aware as needed so that action can be regulated by an explicit knowledge of the dominant need. There is not a sharp line to delineate how far this therapy-like aspect of the consultation is legitimate in supervision and when it becomes psychotherapy.

The process and task of therapy and supervision of therapy certainly have parallels. But they also have differences. The personal exploration in psychotherapy follows whatever the patient might need to explore, and the contract is virtually totally on the growth and maintenance of the patient. That is the task. In supervision, the focus is on the functioning of the supervisee as a therapist and on furtherance of the growth of the supervisee's patient(s). The growth work of the supervisee that is necessary to this task is included in effective consultation. When extensive experiential exploration is needed, or when this is the primary focus, then the relationship is more psychotherapeutic than supervisory.

Context and contract influence how experiential the supervision is. When there is extensive administrative supervisory responsibility and authority, deep experiential work lacks clear boundaries and violates the ethical code of the American Psychological Association. Being therapist and also doing evaluation and grading, making decisions that affect the supervisee's career, and enforcing agency rules all make deep experiential work ill advised. There is inherent danger of violation of the therapeutic need for acceptance and empathic attunement when supervising, and there is danger of violation of the task or duties of administrative supervision by becoming empathically attuned to the detriment of administrative supervisory responsibilities.

There is, however, more flexibility when the supervision is primarily consultative and there is no administrative responsibility. When a supervisee wants deeper exploration and is at an advanced competence level as a therapist and has sufficient experience as a patient in psychotherapy, spending time in consultation on psychotherapeutic endeavors can be quite beneficial.

It often happens that the supervision moves from description of the patient to discussion of the interaction to realization of a countertransference block of the supervisee. Working with this in the direct, Gestalt therapy experiential manner can be extremely effective. In certain circumstances, there are advantages to having experiential exploration in the supervision process. Working experientially can dissolve blocks in therapist functioning that would not be resolved by therapy alone or by more didactic or intellectualized approaches to consultation. On the other hand, having the data of the supervisee's functioning as therapist opens certain avenues of exploration of personal functioning that might not be obvious in the usual therapeutic context.

It should be noted, however, that when the consultation sessions become partially psychotherapeutic there is also danger of diluting either the consultation or the therapy, or both. For example, a change to a therapy focus could avoid a difficulty as therapist, and change to an educative focus could avoid an emotional issue.

MODES OF SUPERVISION

Gestalt therapy supervision occurs in individual, group, and peer-group modalities. These groups can be of various sizes, usually three to six members, meeting from frequencies varying from once a week to once a month. The groups use the full variety of methods discussed more fully later. They include talking about patients, role-playing patients with various group members being therapist, working on countertransference, using didactic discussion, and bringing in real patients for a session in front of the group.

In addition, Gestalt therapy supervision occurs in postgraduate Gestalt therapy training groups in a style that emphasizes practice doing therapy in the group and receiving immediate feedback and facilitation from the trainer and other group members.

There is a wide variety of approaches to training groups in Gestalt therapy. In addition to the variation between various training institutes, there is also variation from country to country. In the United States, the basic preparation to be a therapist generally precedes Gestalt therapy training, that is, Gestalt therapy training is usually postgraduate. On the other hand, in some countries Gestalt therapy is a primary route to becoming a psychotherapist. Of course, there are additional responsibilities and requirements for such training programs.

Typically, training starts with either an experiential group for the trainees or at least an initial phase of training that is largely experiential. This is designed to ensure that trainees have the skill to recognize their own awareness process, are able to make dialogic contact in the learning context, and have "hands on" experience at phenomenological focusing and experimentation. This is also a time to focus on emotional and characterological functioning within the group, for example, issues of safety, anxiety, competition, and so forth.

Usually, there is also didactic teaching even during this early phase. This can be a parallel course, a designated time set aside in the experiential training group, or moving the group from experiential phase to a phase with increased didactic discussion. Sometimes the didactic teaching is programmatic (lecture or discussion), and sometimes it is kept spontaneous so that the learning and creating of theory are not dictated by an authoritative code of teaching but rather arise from contemporaneous interaction. Often there are minilectures and theoretical discussions after experiential work.

Following these two phases, a phase follows that is increasingly marked by the trainees working as therapist with one another and the group leader moving from the primary role of group therapist to the primary role as supervisor. The didactic and therapeutic-experiential aspects continue in this phase but are increasingly dedicated to supervising practice in the group.

In the best Gestalt therapy training, this phase is supplemented by teaching about issues that are necessary for clinical or theoretical sophistication but that are not adequately represented in the Gestalt therapy literature or taught in the earlier didactic phases, for example, teaching about psychodynamics or character diagnosis. There are also didactic presentations of additional topics, for example, shame and guilt, group process, working with couples, treatment of certain diagnostic groups, body-oriented treatment, treatment of PTSD, and so forth.

At this point, trainees need direct consultation about their actual clinical work and the patients they work with. Some programs include this, and when they do not, trainees often seek additional supervision from experienced Gestalt therapists.

The better quality programs require that trainees undergo Gestalt psychotherapy.

A few programs have a qualification process in which trainees are tested for their understanding of the theory and for their clinical understanding and are tested actually doing Gestalt therapy. To my knowledge, there has been no research on the objectivity, reliability, or validity of this process.

METHODOLOGY OF GESTALT THERAPY SUPERVISION

Supervision is largely working with supervisees in order to address the needs of patients. It is helping therapists to better help patients. This is done in administrative supervision, educative supervision, and consultation. The major categories of education and consultation are understanding the character of the patient, understanding therapeutic methodology and application to the particular patient, and explicating countertransference.

It is in line with the theory of Gestalt therapy that the boundaries be made clear between supervisor and supervisee. This includes expectations, requirements, goals, methods, time frame, evaluation procedures, consequences, and so forth. Clear structure is necessary to enable the flow of free and creative process, for freedom and creativity require structure and discipline. When the general direction of the supervision is agreed on, then the supervisee is given maximum freedom to direct the supervisory work and apply the principles according to his or her own unique values, personality, and contemporaneous needs.

Experiential Method: Preference for Description

Gestalt therapy supervision favors descriptive methods rather than intellectualized explanatory methods. Supervisees are trained to separate the continuum of immediate experience (awareness) from assumptions and explanations. This is consistent with the phenomenological and field theory base of Gestalt therapy. Immediate experience is descriptive and includes straightforward observations of internal sensations, categorical and vitality affects, and external observations. Phenomenological work involves focusing on and reporting the continuum of awareness. This focusing is the methodological heart of both Gestalt therapy and Gestalt therapy supervision.

Of course, Gestalt therapist supervisors use the usual talk-about procedures that most supervisors use. Our preference, however, is to be experience-near, horizontally dialogic, and experientially experimental.

Supervision in the Gestalt therapy mode will often include direct observation by the supervisor via one-way mirror, video- and audiotaping, or in-the-room observation. These have largely replaced the detailed process reports by memory that also gave similar data, albeit not as objective, not as complete, and much more time consuming for the supervisee.

Role playing is frequently used in individual and group supervision and can be very effective. The supervisee can play the patient, and the supervisor or another group member can be therapist. Various forms of role reversal can be used. This technique can enable the supervisor and supervisee to transmit more holistically detailed information than can summary statements. The supervisor being therapist in the role playing communicates a more complete and subtle picture than is possible with more abstract methods.

In role playing, various group members can take a turn with different approaches to being therapist, while the therapist can play his or her patient and experience an approximation of what it is like. Role playing enables supervisees to experiment with new approaches and experience how they feel and can then work on the technique or their feelings and modify the technique before experimenting directly with the patient.

Sometimes patients volunteer to have a session at a consultation group. All of the superiority of direct observation is present, plus the possible gains for the patient of getting feedback from persons other than the therapist. Naturally, the feedback to the patient is done with discretion, and there is usually a separate feedback session with the therapist after the patient leaves. The chief drawback of this method is the anxiety and potential shame experience of both therapist and patient and the difficulty of making these arrangements. The safety and effectiveness of this method depend on the discernment and sensitivity of the supervisor and the group.

As in therapy, creativity and experimentation in supervision are encouraged with focus on the here and now. For example, a young male therapist talked about a patient he seemed to be frustrated with. He talked about the patient's character, behavior, and history. The patient was a young borderline with a background of being abused and was still in a dysfunctional mode of behavior.

The supervisee's face was tight—like a mask—his voice clipped. The supervisor asked, "What are you experiencing right now?" With some intermediate experiential facilitation, the supervisee realized that he was frustrated and angry at the patient and feeling ashamed of that. His tight musculature and voice were signs of defense against shame affect. Further exploration revealed two introjected assumptions that were previously beneath his threshold of awareness. He believed that he should be caring and not feel frustrated with a patient; he believed that he should be able to quickly move any patient beyond his or her stuck point. In his eyes, he had failed on both counts, hence the feeling of shame.

Both beliefs were contrary to his actual experience with the patient and contrary to the supervisor's belief that therapists have feelings and it is not their job to move patients. The supervisee found it helpful to have the shame expressed and to discover that the supervisor felt much more positive toward the supervisee than the supervisee felt toward himself, and he also found another belief system to consider. Over a period of time, the supervisee's harsh self-demands were discussed as well as what was reasonable to expect in learning to do therapy, how to treat borderline patients, what was reasonable to expect in the course of such therapy, and how to understand his own feelings as a therapist.

Role of Theory in Supervision

Gestalt therapy's reputation for being pejorative about the value of intellectual discussion makes it important to clarify the role of theory in Gestalt therapy supervision. I believe that an adequate level of theoretical understanding is indispensable for a Gestalt psychotherapist, and an even higher level of theoretical understanding is required for a supervisor or trainer of psychotherapists. Gestalt therapy that is effective and safe must be guided by understanding the basic principles. Without knowing the paradoxical theory of change, field theory, phenomenology, dialogic existentialism, the principle of contemporaneity, organism/environment field, contact boundary and boundary disturbances, figure/ground formation and destruction cycle, role of experimentation, the Gestalt therapy theory of anxiety and impasse, and so forth, trainees are likely either to do a hodgepodge "eclectic" therapy, turn Gestalt therapy into a form of encounter group or undisciplined behavior modification, or even into a diluted and undisciplined psychodynamic variant. For the Gestalt therapist supervising non-Gestalt therapists, a firm theoretical understanding is necessary to build a bridge between the Gestalt therapy perspective and that of the non-Gestalt supervisee and to translate among the various systems and systems' languages.

Unfortunately, sometimes therapists who are cool to theory and/or not very proficient at intellectual understanding treat Gestalt therapy as a justification for avoiding the hard work of theoretical understanding. It is even more unfortunate that some Gestalt therapy programs and supervisors do an inadequate job of teaching the theory and dealing with deficits in cognitive understanding or ability.

Theory is not only a guide to the methodology of the therapy system, but also to the needs of persons with particular character structures or the needs of particular contexts. It can also be a guide to the needs of a supervisee or trainee. For example, a trainee who had difficulty getting and providing a clear focus on important issues when working with patients benefited from a phenomenological focus in supervision and therapy on his awareness continuum and his obsessive interruption with small details. Learning about the phenomenological perspective (e.g., bracketing, recognizing the obvious, staying with immediate experience, and allowing explanatory understanding to come later) helped him understand better how to work with patients.

Theory can also clarify the strengths and weaknesses of the supervisor. During my first year as a supervisor, I was on the Psychology Department faculty at the University of California, Los Angeles. I supervised a graduate student in the departmental clinic who specifically asked for Gestalt therapy supervision. He had been working with Ivar Lovaas in treating autistic children with his peculiar brand of aversive conditioning. When I saw the trainee through the one-way mirror doing "Gestalt therapy" with ordinary patients, it was clear that he was harsh, abusive, clearly using Gestalt therapy (then still not recovered from the 1960s encounter attitude) to batter and vanquish the patient. When I confronted him with this, he was quite defensive and confronted me with, "Do you need to change my personality?" Because I was inexperienced and also had not adequately developed my understanding of the dialogic relationship and ways of achieving a phenomenological understanding, it was difficult for me to serve the dual goals of protecting the patient and facilitating the growth of the supervisee. It would also have been helpful if I had been as clear then as I can be now about models of psychotherapy and the needs of patients, how to work with the immediate experience of the supervisee and clarify his or her values, effective alternatives in treatment, and how Gestalt therapy differs from other therapies, for example, that of Lovaas.

Parallel Process

As the work proceeds in supporting the therapist, focusing on and protecting the patient, there often arise parallels between the dynamics of the patient-therapist relationship and that of the supervisor-supervisee relationship. The therapist sometimes does to the supervisor what the patient does to him or her, and conversely, the therapist often does to the patient what the supervisor does to him or her. It is hoped that this latter is a more benevolent parallel process, but not always. For example, a sarcastic supervisor may result in the therapist being sarcastic with the patient. Another example: A supervisee repeatedly brought up difficulties with a particular patient and asked for suggestions. To each suggestion the supervisee's response was "Yes, but . . ." Then I suggested he role-play the patient. Lo and behold, the patient also clearly asked for help and then said, "Yes, but . . ." in response to all attempts to help. In this case, the therapist was too "helpful"; he tried to satisfy the requests instead of exploring what was happening between them. As supervisee and in his role playing the patient, at first he elicited the same behavior from the supervisor. The supervisor needed to change his response in order to explore what was happening in the supervision process to facilitate the therapist's doing the same with his patient.

SEQUENCE OF SUPERVISION

Supervision is a process; it develops over time. It matures with the experience of the supervisee, the assimilation by the supervisee of what the particular supervisor has to offer, and the ripening of the supervisory relationship. The stages are not clearly and definitively delineated in Gestalt therapy theory, but here we can present a preliminary discussion of the process.

Supervision often moves from a predominantly administrative, authority-based supervision to a more education-oriented supervision and then on to pure consultation. The degree of oversight necessary for students obviously differs from that necessary for experienced clinicians. A licensed therapist who comes to a privately engaged consultant has a different supervisory relationship from that of a graduate student with an assigned administrative supervisor in an agency.

The beginning phase goes from the first contact until there is a clear working relationship in which structure is established and there is at least a minimal level of trust. The clearer and better the foundation at the beginning, the more support there will be for education and consultation to succeed.

Structural clarification includes the mundane; for example, time and place for supervision sessions, whether the supervision will be over the entire caseload of the supervisee or will be intensive supervision of a part of the caseload. What will be the source of data?

It is important at the beginning of supervision to clarify requirements, expectations, goals, and the evaluation process. Among the issues of evaluation that need clarification are (a) what will be evaluated and by what criteria, (b) when and how will evaluations be made, (c) who will make them, (d) to whom will they be reported, (e) how will the evaluations be communicated to the supervisee, (f) will the supervisee have a chance to react before it becomes a part of his or her record, and (g) will the supervisee have the opportunity to evaluate the supervisor and/or the evaluating process? Will evaluations be geared to minimal standards, or will excellence also be noted? What are the consequences that flow from the evaluation? In some settings, evaluating criteria have been changing from patient welfare to how few sessions the therapist can get by with. When criteria are not in the welfare of the patient or fair to the supervisee, efforts to change the system are part of the responsibilities of both the supervisor and the supervisee.

Ideally, the early journey of supervision moves toward mutuality and cooperation in working together. The more clearly the structure is established in the beginning of supervision, the more middle and later phases of supervision can focus on education and consultation with a minimal intrusion of authority issues. The Gestalt therapy supervisor in the consultant mode asks the question, "How can I help?" It is best if the supervisee takes the most active lead in setting the focus. The supervisor and supervisee dialogue and focus to find what is useful and what is not useful for that particular supervisee at that particular time in that particular context.

As structure is established in this beginning phase, as the dialogue begins and advances, trust is built and standards set ("How do you know when you do a good job?"). Ideally, expectations become more realistic, a more trusting relationship develops, and the supervisory work becomes more sharply focused on advancing knowledge, addressing weakness, and building on strengths.

The supervisee gains in clarity about his or her responsibility for defining need, asking for the kind of help needed, and for being receptive to the help when offered. Both supervisor and supervisee learn to respect the supervisee's need for autonomy and individuality. The supervisee learns that the process and effort of supervisor, supervisee, and patient need to be respected and that outcome alone is not an adequate standard for judgment. In all phases, both supervisor and supervisee need to monitor what is helpful, what feels bad but is helpful, and what is hurtful and injurious.

As in therapy, various forms of resistance arise in the beginning phase of supervision.

INTERFERENCES

Resistance, impediments, and barriers are a vital part of the life process. Without resistance there is no life. In Gestalt therapy the patient's avoidance of awareness (resistance to awareness) is one of the most important processes that is brought into awareness. By identifying these processes and identifying with them, the choices the patient makes no longer have to be made by habit and without awareness; they can be made with full awareness and discrimination of needs and dangers. This is also true in supervision.

Unrealistic expectations by supervisor, supervisee, or agency impede the learning of the supervisee and diminish the quality of psychotherapy practice. One example is wanting or needing to give simplistic or magic answers to complex issues. If either the supervisor gives or the supervisee accepts easy answers, it obscures and distracts from the hard work of exploring, learning, and experimenting.

One interference with learning is to avoid working on understanding difficult patients, issues, or countertransference by simply getting rid of difficult clients and avoiding supervisory work that might lead to increased self-support of the therapist and improved quality of treatment for the patient. Sometimes supervisees will avoid improving understanding and practice by dismissing the lack of progress of a patient as due to diagnosis, for example, because he or she is a borderline or has a narcissistic personality disorder.

Another interference is the need to be admired and have disciples. Although the supervisee can have this difficulty, for example, with patients, in this context the interference is by the supervisor. Many supervisors who have this narcissistic need to be adulated and looked up to cannot acknowledge the need. Thus, parallel to the countertransference of a therapist taking positive transference from the patient as if literally true because of the therapist's need for confirmation and narcissistic gratification, the supervisor can take the admiration of the supervisee as if literally true out of the need to be a charismatic leader.

An obvious interference with good supervision is the supervisor not wanting to be a supervisor or the supervisee not wanting to be supervised. This is especially likely in agency settings in which the supervision is an extra burden on the supervisor and an imposed requirement for the supervisee, as opposed to the privately engaged consultant.

Of course, the basis of these forms of interference and the many others not discussed here involves the expected full range of personality and situational variables, for example, narcissistic vulnerability, shame and guilt, and so forth.

VERIFICATION AND THE NEED FOR RESEARCH

Verification happens at several levels and in several ways. Of course, each patient, supervisee, and supervisor must phenomenologically observe over time—observe self, other, relationship, and developments—to know the process and outcome in the particular situation.

In training and supervision groups, shared observations and evaluation over time occur regularly. For example, when working with a training group over a period of time, all group members observe the trainer's supervision, take part themselves in the discussion and feedback, and see changes or lack of changes over time. Over the course of each training period, the changes are publicly observable.

Obviously, this is not systematic research. There is a need for more attention in Gestalt therapy to a clearer theory of research and more process and outcome research on therapy and supervision (for summary of research on Gestalt therapy, see Yontef, 1995). This research could be in the naturalistic science model prevalent in psychology or could be in a more phenomenological research manner.

REFERENCES

Beisser, A. (1970). The paradoxical theory of change. In J. Fagan & I. Shepherd (Eds.), *Gestalt therapy now* (pp. 77–80). Palo Alto: Science & Behavior Books.

Hycner, R. (1985). Dialogical Gestalt therapy: An initial proposal. *The Gestalt Journal, 8*(1), 23–49.

Hycner, R. (1991). *Between person and person: Toward a dialogical psychotherapy*. New York: The Gestalt Journal Press.

Hycner, R., & Jacobs, L. (1995). *The healing relationship in Gestalt therapy: A dialogic-self psychology*. New York: The Gestalt Journal Press.

Jacobs, L. (1989). Dialogue in Gestalt theory and therapy. *The Gestalt Journal, 12*(1), 25–67.

Jacobs, L. (1992). Insights from psychoanalytic self-psychology and intersubjectivity theory for Gestalt therapists. *The Gestalt Journal, 15*(2), 25–60.

Perls, F., Hefferline, R., & Goodman, P. (1994). *Gestalt therapy: Excitement and growth in the human personality*. Highland, NY: The Gestalt Journal Press. Originally published in 1951.

Yontef, G. (1993). *Awareness, dialogue and process: Essays on Gestalt therapy*. New York: The Gestalt Journal Press.

Yontef, G. (1995). Gestalt therapy. In A. Gurman & S. Messer (Eds.), *Essential psychotherapies* (pp. 261–303). New York: Guilford.

Yontef, G. (1996). Shame and guilt in Gestalt therapy: Theory and practice. In R. Lee & G. Wheeler (Eds.), *The missing voice: A Gestalt approach to working with shame* (pp. 351–380). Cleveland, OH: GIC Press.

CHAPTER 11

The Experiential Model
of On-the-Job Teaching

ALVIN R. MAHRER
DONALD B. BOULET
University of Ottawa

There are two main purposes of this chapter. The first is to describe the experiential model of on-the-job teaching. Doing this means flagging some experiential training propositions such as the following: (a) The role of the on-the-job experiential teacher may be sculpted out and differentiated from many traditional components of the role of supervisor; (b) in the experiential model of teaching, the heavy emphasis is on the continuous development and improvement of the trainee's competence and skills; (c) it is useful, we believe, to discover and explore the trainee's own personal, inner, natural framework or approach to psychotherapy and to see if there is a goodness-of-fit with that of experiential psychotherapy; (d) experiential teaching includes a pronounced emphasis on periods of skill-developing concentrated practice; and (e) experiential teaching includes presentation and study of the teacher's own tapes. The second purpose is to describe some concrete methods that seem useful in helping the on-the-job teacher to teach how to do experiential psychotherapy.

A MODEL OF ON-THE-JOB TEACHING

Of the various roles and models of supervision, we follow in the tradition of the on-the-job teacher (e.g., Hess, 1980; Ivey, 1971; Langs, 1979; Liddle, 1988; Tarachow, 1963). In our model, the role of supervisor is minimized, the role of teacher is maximized, and the two roles are rather sharply differentiated from each other.

Is There an Experiential Theory of Supervision or Teaching-Training?

Not really. At least there does not seem to be any full-fledged, respectable theory that provides a legitimate conceptual foundation for what the experiential teacher does. Instead, there is a collection of low-level, working principles to help achieve the aims and goals of doing this kind of on-the-job teaching.

It may seem sensible that there ought to be some commonality between the aims and goals of a given psychotherapy and those of supervision or training of that therapy, and even between the actual methods of doing the therapy and doing the supervision or training (e.g.,

Bartlett, 1983; Carifio & Hess, 1987). There is probably some commonality and probably some consistency among the aims, goals, and methods of experiential psychotherapy (Mahrer, 1966a) and those of experiential on-the-job teaching. But commonality and consistency do not mean that the aims, goals, and methods of experiential on-the-job training are derived or deduced from those of experiential psychotherapy. Even further, it would probably be stretching far too much to try and drape a single theoretical framework over both the therapy and the on-the-job training, or even to say that the low-level working principles of experiential on-the-job training could or should be dignified as a theory.

What Are the Main Aims or Goals of Experiential On-the-Job Teaching?

1. *The trainee is gradually and continuously to increase competency in the experiential skills.* A main goal is that the trainee is gradually and continuously increasing the level and the range of experiential skills and also continuously increasing competency in these skills (cf. Ivey, 1971; Langs, 1979; Liddle, 1988; Tarachow, 1963). In other words, the training is successful if the trainee performs better than a month or so ago and performs significantly better than many months ago. Gradually increasing the level of competency is the goal, rather than attaining some predetermined acceptable level of competency. Likewise, gradually increasing the range of skills is the goal, rather than learning a predetermined set of experiential skills. The key is steadily increasing both the level and range of competencies and skills.

What skills is the trainee to learn? Each experiential session should follow a series of four steps or phases (Mahrer, 1996a), and the skills are nested under each of the steps or phases. There is a rather defined set of skills for the trainee to acquire gradually and continuously.

In the first step, the trainee is to enable the person to live and be in a specific moment of strong feeling, and to access, be in touch with, and sense the deeper inner experiencing. Here are the main skills the trainee is gradually to improve: (a) The trainee is to learn how to give opening instructions that can elicit scenes of strong feeling; (b) the trainee is to enable the person to find some scene, time, situation in which the feeling is quite strong; (c) the trainee is to show the person how to enter into, to live and be in, the scene of strong feeling and to search for and discover the precise moment of heightened feeling; and (d) in the moment of strong feeling, the trainee is to be able to access, receive, be open to, be in touch with, and sense the inner deeper potential for experiencing. There are explicit ways of accomplishing these parts of the first step.

In the second step, the person is to welcome, appreciate, accept, and have good integrative relationships with the accessed inner deeper experiencing. The trainee is to become proficient in a package of about a dozen methods, each of which is designed to help attain this second step in the session.

The third step enables the person to undergo a qualitative, radical change into being the inner deeper experiencing in the context of earlier life scenes: (a) The trainee is to have the skills for enabling the person to find earlier life scenes; (b) the trainee enables the person to undergo a radical shift into being the inner deeper potential for experiencing in the context of the alive, real, immediate, earlier life scene; and (c) the trainee learns methods to show the person how to find other life scenes and how to be the inner deeper potential for experiencing in these scenes.

The final step of the session enables the person to be the qualitatively new person and to be free of bad-feelinged scenes, in the context of the present and prospective future:

(a) The trainee shows the person how to find prospective scenes and new behaviors; (b) the trainee enables the person to be the qualitatively new person in these prospective scenes; (c) the trainee uses methods to enable the person to rehearse and refine prospective new ways of being and behaving in the next few days or so; and (d) the trainee enables the new person to engage in a provisional commitment to a selected new way of being and behaving in the present and prospective world.

The goal is steady, gradual, increased competency in the depth and breadth of skills contained in each step and under each of the substeps.

The emphasis on gradually increasing competency in the range of these specific experiential skills may be contrasted with an aim of providing trainees with a set of skills that are regarded as supposedly basic, fundamental, and common across most approaches. Accordingly, experiential skills do not necessarily include most common meanings of empathy, confrontation, simple questioning, problem identification, self-awareness, establishing a therapist-client relationship, and so on (cf. Alonso, 1985; Holloway, 1992; Worthington, 1987).

Furthermore, the goal of steadily increasing competency applies to beginning trainees as well as to trainees who may be further along or who may be seasoned in some other approach (cf. Hill, Charles, & Reed, 1981; Loganbill, Hardy, & Delworth, 1982; Stoltenberg, 1981). Wherever they start, the goal is to keep increasing competency in the level of proficiency and in the range of skills.

2. *The trainee is to achieve and to increase competence in attaining effective and successful sessions.* From the beginning and throughout the training, the trainee is to be able to achieve effective and successful sessions. At first, the sessions may be only mildly effective and successful. From then on, the goal is to increase the proportion and the level of genuinely effective and successful sessions.

What is the meaning of an effective and successful session? What are the indications of an effective and successful session? One is that the trainee is to be able to achieve the four steps of each session. Much as in supervising and training in rational-emotive therapy, the trainee is to be able to achieve the steps that comprise the carrying out of an effective and successful session as laid down by the therapy (Wessler & Ellis, 1980).

Achieving competence in the four steps of each session means that each session thereby enables the kinds of changes that are the hallmark of an effective and successful experiential session. There are two.

a. The person is enabled to become a qualitatively new person. There is a genuine change in who and what the new person is, in the very core and identity of this new person, and in how this new person is and acts and interacts. The change is from the inside out, for it starts with the discovery of what is deeper inside this person, then enables what is deeper to be welcomed and appreciated (integration) and to become a central part of the new person (actualization).

b. The new person is to be free of the bad-feelinged scenes and situations that were front and center for the old person in the session. There is a letting go of and a freedom from the scenes and situations that were so bothersome, painful, and troubling for the person who started the session.

A main goal is for the trainee to learn how to achieve effective and successful experiential sessions. This goal is to be achieved rather early in the training and can occur acceptably with a beginning level of a relatively small number of skills. As the trainee gradually increases the level and range of skills, there should be accompanying increases in the proportion and degree of effective and successful sessions.

What Are Some Secondary Aims or Goals of Experiential On-the-Job Teaching?

There are two, one coming early in and one coming after the training.

1. *See if there is a goodness-of-fit between the experiential approach to psychotherapy and the trainee's own, personal, natural approach to psychotherapy.* In order to learn how to do this therapy, it is almost essential that the experiential way of thinking—the theory of what people are like; the notions of personality structure, of change, of what psychotherapy is and how it works; the directions of change that can be attained; the way that pain and unhappiness are understood—all of this should make sense to the trainee. Even more important, there is to be a solid goodness-of-fit between the experiential approach and what may be called the trainee's own personal, natural approach to psychotherapy. Accordingly, early in training, the teacher aims at trying to discover the trainee's own personal, natural way of thinking, the trainee's inner deeper approach to psychotherapy (Mahrer & Boulet, 1995; Rogers, 1957). If this is cordial and congruent with the experiential approach, it is likely that the trainee can achieve the major goals of this kind of training. If not, the trainee probably cannot.

2. *The trainee is to learn how to be in cotraining throughout his or her entire career.* The cotraining may be with one other colleague or perhaps with a small group. It may occur once every few weeks or months or so, but further training is to continue throughout the therapist's career.

The trainee is to learn enough about how to be a trainee and how to be a trainer or teacher so that the main goals continue throughout the therapist's career. That is, the therapist is gradually to (a) keep increasing competency in experiential skills, to become better and better in more and more skills and (b) become more and more competent in achieving more effective and successful sessions.

Supervision and On-the-Job Teaching: What Are Some Similarities and Differences?

The on-the-job teaching of experiential psychotherapy has some similarities to and some differences from what is ordinarily called supervision.

1. *Continually increasing competency in skills is a main goal in on-the-job teaching, but not necessarily in all kinds of supervision.* The on-the-job teacher is there mainly to enable the trainee to keep on gaining more and more competency in a gradually broadening range of skills. This is perhaps the main function of the on-the-job teacher. Most of what occurs in most training sessions is focused on the heightening of competency in particular skills. Furthermore, once the trainee is able to have reasonably effective sessions, the continuing goal is to keep on gaining more competency in more and more skills.

In the supervision model, such teaching is typically part of the role of most supervisors and may even warrant being called a substantive part (e.g., Alonso, 1985; Holloway & Hosford, 1983). But most of what the supervisor does is not especially aimed at a central goal of gradually increasing the trainee's competency in a gradually broadening breadth of skills.

Many supervisors are responsible for the trainee's becoming sufficiently competent to do what the supervisor is supervising the trainee to do. Often this includes training to an adequate level of competency. There seems to be a significant difference, however, between this goal and the on-the-job teacher's main goal of continuously trying to increase the trainee's competence in both the depth and breadth of experiential skills. Evidence of continuous improvement can be quite different from evidence of attaining a predetermined level of adequacy. They do differ.

2.   *The teaching and learning of experiential psychotherapy largely determine the aims and goals of the training; versus, the setting or program may well determine the aims and goals of the supervision.* Who and what are largely responsible for determining the aims and goals of the training? This is a subtle but powerful issue. The answers to this question play a large hand in determining what the teacher's or supervisor's job is, what the trainee's job is, and the degree to which the trainee is judged as successful in the training.

For the experiential teacher, it is the sheer teaching and learning of experiential psychotherapy that largely determine the aims and goals of the training. This is why the trainee is here, and this is what the trainee is to learn. The trainee is gradually to increase competency in the experiential skills. The trainee is to achieve, and to increase, competency in attaining effective and successful sessions.

But this is only one perspective. Another perspective holds that the aims and goals of training may be largely determined by the needs and requirements of the program, the internship or field training or residency, or by the needs and requirements of the setting, the clinic, the hospital unit, the agency, the setting in which the trainee is working and training.

Since each perspective can be justified in its own aims and goals, it can seem sensible to try and satisfy both sets of aims and goals. Arguments can easily be mounted against the extremes of either set of aims and goals to the exclusion of the other. In actual operation, however, it seems that one set of aims and goals must generally be emphasized over the other, especially when there is, as there often is, some antimony between whether the aims and goals are largely determined by the teaching and learning of experiential psychotherapy or by the setting or program. Our perspective is the former rather than the latter, when there has to be a choice.

3.   *The teacher helps the trainee to evaluate progress and learning; versus, the supervisor is responsible for formal evaluation of the trainee.* In most training programs, someone has to decide if the trainee passes or fails and has or has not completed the training program satisfactorily. It is common that a part of the role of supervisor is serving as a formal judge and evaluator of the satisfactory or unsatisfactory progress of the trainee and whether or not the trainee is judged as having completed the training program (e.g., Bernard & Goodyear, 1992).

In general, the experiential teacher declines the role of serving as a formal judge of the trainee. The preference is for that particular role to be the responsibility of a third person, someone other than the on-the-job teacher, someone who accepts the formal responsibility for deciding if the trainee is or is not progressing adequately and if the trainee has or has not satisfactorily completed the training program.

On the other hand, the experiential teacher accepts responsibility for helping the trainee to engage in almost continuous evaluation of progress, of strengths and weaknesses, of whether training is or is not moving along in a satisfactory way. Virtually every training session touches on this kind of evaluation and assessment. The teacher does this. The trainee does this. They do it together. They may both provide helpful information to the formal judge and evaluator.

In extreme cases, both teacher and trainee typically can discuss that the training is running into serious problems, that perhaps the training ought to be discontinued, and that progress is conspicuously inadequate. Both teacher and trainee can acknowledge that the trainee has missed most of the training sessions or that there has been little or no increase in competencies and skills or that the trainee is apparently unable to have successful sessions. In these extreme instances, both teacher and trainee may well have serious and careful input into decisions to be made by the third person who holds the responsibility for formal and official evaluation. But these extreme cases are generally rare.

Perhaps the main reason for uncoupling the role of formal, official evaluator from the role of on-the-job teacher is that the goals and aims of the on-the-job teacher can probably be more effectively achieved if the on-the-job teacher is not also the formal and official evaluator of the trainee. Both teacher and trainee informally evaluate each other in many or most of the training sessions, but this is different from both claiming the right to be the formal and official evaluator of each other (cf. Bartlett, 1983).

4. *Final, ultimate administrative responsibility for the client does—or does not—lie in the hands of the on-the-job teacher?* In supervision, there is often an understanding that more or less final, ultimate responsibility for the client's treatment lies in the hands of the supervisor (e.g., Bernard & Goodyear, 1992; Blocher, 1983; Loganbill et al., 1982). Professionally, ethically, legally, administratively, the supervisor is responsible for the client's treatment.

The experiential on-the-job teacher accepts that an integral part of teaching involves issues around ensuring that the client's welfare is uppermost, involving the possibility of some harm coming to the client, of what to do in crises, and of involving the client's family or employer or medical or legal authorities. Teaching deals with issues such as (a) ways in which the trainee may be preventing the patient from having successful sessions; (b) ways in which the trainee is helping to make life more painful for the patient; (c) how the trainee's level of competence may be insufficient to deal with this particular patient; and (d) whether the trainee should or should not have further sessions with this patient. Teaching raises lots of relevant professional, ethical, moral, and administrative issues dealing with the welfare of the patient.

For purposes of maximizing what experiential on-the-job teaching tries to achieve, however, the optimal administrative structure is one in which there is another resource who holds ultimate, final, administrative authority and responsibility for the client. When both trainee and on-the-job teacher work in an institution, agency, program, clinic, then it is best if some office in the institution holds ultimate professional responsibility for the welfare of the clients of the institution. Within this administrative structure, it is the responsibility of the experiential on-the-job teacher and trainee to see to it that relevant issues are brought to the attention of the responsible professional and to ensure that this person is consulted on issues involving the welfare of the client.

What are the reasons for this optimal administrative setup? The main reason is that the aims and goals of experiential teaching are best served when the teacher is free from holding ultimate responsibility for the client's treatment. These aims and goals cannot usefully be attained if the teacher is the one who determines that the client should have some sessions with the teacher, if the trainee tells the client that the client can have sessions with the teacher when the client deems it to be helpful, if the teacher is the one who has sessions with the client's family, or if the teacher has the contact with the employer or physician or legal authority.

This administrative arrangement is optimal for experiential on-the-job teaching. On the other hand, for many kinds of supervision, it makes sense that more or less final, ultimate professional and administrative responsibility for the client rests in the hands of the supervisor as supervisor. For example, outside experiential psychotherapy, but inside many approaches to supervision, the supervisor may take final responsibility for the treatment plan, for bringing in other professionals, for the supervisor's having sessions with the client, and for executing professional actions involving the client's protection or welfare in regard to the client's extratherapy world.

5. *The aims and goals of experiential teaching do not emphasize probing into the trainee's personality or into how the trainee relates to the teacher.* In some approaches to supervision, it may be that the supervisor spends some time getting into such matters as the trainee's personality, the trainee's personal qualities and problems, the way the trainee interacts and relates with the supervisor (e.g., Bernard & Goodyear, 1992; Ekstein & Wallerstein, 1972; Hess, 1980; Mueller, 1982; Mueller & Kell, 1972; Orzek, 1984; Russell, Crimmings, & Lent, 1984; Searles, 1955, 1965). There are some reasons why these topics may be sensible and helpful topics in supervision.

One reason is that the supervisor may hold that the way the trainee relates to the supervisor contains many elements of the way the patient and trainee relate to each other. Talking about the relationship can be a salient part of both psychoanalytic-psychodynamic therapy and supervision (Ekstein & Wallerstein, 1972). Second, many supervisors accept that the trainee's own personal issues, problems, conflicts, and personality play a large part in what happens in the therapeutic process, and therefore these issues are to be open to scrutiny by the supervisor. Third, many supervisors accept that one of the aims and goals of supervision is to foster the personal growth of the trainee, and this may well involve delving into rather personal issues. Finally, whether it contributes to the aims and goals of supervision, whether it is simply important for the supervisor, or whether the supervisor is mindful that it is a significant part of the way the supervisee evaluates supervision, many supervisors value the supervisee's being happy, pleased, and satisfied with the supervisor (cf. Carifio & Hess, 1987), and this again can involve getting into topics that are personal to the trainee and to the trainee-supervisor relationship.

The experiential teacher does not dispute the relevance of these considerations in many other approaches. The aims and goals of experiential teaching do not, however, emphasize probing into the trainee's personality or into how the experiential trainee relates to the teacher. The experiential teacher and the group of trainees may have fun together, may well like one another, and may even remember one another fondly, but there are some reasons why there is no special emphasis on probing into the trainee's personality or into how the trainee and teacher relate to each other.

   a. The goal of experiential teaching is for the trainee to become a better experiential psychotherapist, to learn the experiential skills. The goals of an experiential therapy session are to enable the person to become a qualitatively new person and to be free of bad-feelinged scenes. It is doubtful that trying to turn the trainee into a qualitatively new person who is free of bad-feelinged scenes is going to be accompanied with a manifest improvement in particular experiential skills. It is hard to see how the goals of experiential on-the-job teaching would be achieved by spending time showing the trainee, who may or may not be so inclined with this particular teacher, how to become a qualitatively new person who is free of bad-feelinged scenes.

b. In experiential psychotherapy, change is said to occur on the basis of the four steps, and not especially because of a fine patient-therapist relationship. It is therefore not so important to have a fine trainee-teacher relationship on the presumption that the trainee can use that relationship in doing better therapy.

c. In experiential psychotherapy, the trainee learns how to disengage from his or her own personality and to join with or "align" with the patient (Mahrer, Boulet, & Fairweather, 1994). Although this may be hard to imagine, what is perhaps even harder to imagine is that aligning with the patient means that the trainee's personal issues, problems, and difficulties thereby have little effect on the effectiveness of this trainee with this patient. Besides, in experiential psychotherapy, one of the skills to be learned is how to be aligned and then make use of any immediate personal feelings, thoughts, issues, problems, and difficulties. Accordingly, the trainee's personal issues are not things to be worked on or probed into by the supervisor. In actual work, the trainee's own personal issues are either substantially set aside or are in a position to be used constructively in the work.

d. The main aim of the training sessions is for the trainee to gain increasing competency in the various skills. It seems highly unlikely that using the sessions to try and delve into the trainee's personality issues, problems, and difficulties, even if it could be done in the training sessions, would add materially to the trainee's gaining increasing competency in more and more skills.

e. If the experiential teacher wanted to "do something" about the trainee's personality issues and insides, the likelihood of accomplishing anything effective would be almost zero in the training session. It is almost ludicrous to picture the teacher carrying out a full-blown experiential session in a training group. Doing that would almost certainly fail to achieve what an experiential session should help achieve, and also what a training session should achieve. It just won't work.

f. Trainees who are serious about learning experiential psychotherapy are almost certainly to be patients in experiential psychotherapy. Indeed, one of the characteristics of professional experiential psychotherapists is that they are almost always patients in experiential psychotherapy throughout their entire professional lives (Mahrer, 1996a), and this usually starts when they are being serious trainees. They may be the patient with a professional experiential psychotherapist, or they may engage in experiential self-change, or they may alternate therapist and patient roles in working with a colleague-partner.

g. The major role of the teacher is that of teacher. It is not fitting that the teacher carry out any of the other roles that include probing into the trainee's personality. The teacher does not fulfill a role of the professional gatekeeper who screens out the personally unfit, the special supervisor to whom you can entrust precious stories about your childhood, the one who knows more about your twisted insides than you do, the good parent-supervisor who is genuinely interested in you as a person, not just as a trainee, the superior who has a right to dig into your personality while you have no such right over hers, the one who can control and judge your professional worth on the basis of your deep-seated personality makeup, or the special supervisor who knows you so well and still makes you feel positively regarded, loved, understood, inspired, treasured, supported, and respected (e.g., Carifio & Hess, 1987; Fleming & Benedict, 1966; Marshall & Confer, 1980; Mueller & Kell, 1972; Russell et al.,

1984; Searles, 1965). Many supervisory roles call for the supervisor declaring that the trainee's personality is fair game. The role of experiential teacher does not.

All in all, the experiential teacher spends little or no time probing into the trainee's personality or into how the trainee seems to relate to the teacher (cf. Cohen & DeBetz, 1977; Lambert, 1980; Weiner & Kaplan, 1980).

What Are Some Characteristics of Successful Experiential On-the-Job Teachers?

1. *The teacher is a seasoned therapist and teacher.* Typically, the teacher is a seasoned and skilled experiential psychotherapist with many years of practice and a high plateau of competence. The teacher often has also accrued years of being the trainee in experiential teaching-training groups and has become a seasoned teacher in the context of these groups before taking on the formal role of the experiential teacher of his or her own training group. This usually means that experiential teachers tend to start out at the top, with a great deal of seasoning, competence, and experience as a therapist and teacher (cf. Watkins, 1990, 1993; Worthington, 1987).

2. *The teacher does not necessarily have the typical characteristics of the traditional therapist.* The fine experiential teacher tends to love teaching and has an impressive track record of doing a good job with trainees. But there is little if any emphasis on having the characteristics ordinarily associated with a traditional therapist. That is, the experiential teacher is not necessarily characterized as being open, honest, congruent, sharing, trusting, respectful, accepting, prizing, noncritical, caring, supportive, flexible, attentive, empathic, and the like (Albott, 1984; Blocher, 1983; Bruch, 1974; Carifio & Hess, 1987; Coche, 1977; Finch, 1977; Glitterman & Miller, 1977; Hess, 1980, 1987; Holloway & Hosford, 1983; Kutzik, 1977; Melchiode, 1977; Rogers, 1957; Sachs & Shapiro, 1976; Storm & Heath, 1985). These may be characteristics of a fine supervisor and a fine traditional therapist, but they are not necessarily the characteristics of a fine experiential teacher.

These may also be the characteristics a supervisor would want to have in order to be liked by supervisees and to get a good evaluation by supervisees (cf. Dodenhoff, 1981; Worthington & Roehlke, 1979). For the experiential teacher, however, it is probably better not to enter into the games of mutual evaluation, grading, and assessment.

3. *The experiential teacher has minimal private hidden thoughts about the trainee.* It is rare that the teacher has a private stream of thoughts such as, "He needs support from me." "She is becoming defensive toward what I am suggesting, and she has the same kind of problem with her patient." "When he has a better relationship with me, I can get into his tendency to control patients." It is doubtful that the experiential teacher would have private hidden thoughts about the trainee. It is hard to have such thoughts when both teacher and trainee are concentrating on the tape, rather than on what is occurring between the two of them. It is hard to have private thoughts about the trainee's personality and way of relating to the teacher when these topics play little or no role in experiential teaching.

It seems that the model of on-the-job teacher may differ in some ways from the ordinary model of the psychotherapy supervisor. It is suggested that even though there are lots of ways of being a supervisor, a working distinction may be drawn between most meanings of "supervisor" and "on-the-job teacher."

HOW DOES THE ON-THE-JOB TEACHER TEACH
HOW TO DO EXPERIENTIAL PSYCHOTHERAPY?

Few if any of these ways of teaching how to do experiential psychotherapy are limited to on-the-job teachers of experiential psychotherapy. Many of these ways may be and are used by teachers, trainers, and supervisors of other therapeutic approaches.

What Are Some Working Practicalities of an Experiential Training Group?

In order to attain the aims and objectives of experiential training, it seems better to have a training group rather than to have individual sessions with each trainee.

1. *What should the trainee know about experiential psychotherapy before starting training?* The trainee should have some working acquaintance with the experiential model of human beings, and the experiential model of psychotherapy. The trainee should have a picture of this model of the structure of personality, of the origins of personality, of what human beings are like, of what human beings can be, and of what makes human beings feel and act and build the kinds of worlds that they do. The trainee should have a working acquaintance with the experiential model of the goals of this therapy, of what can be accomplished in each session, of the four steps of change in each session, and of the various ways and methods of accomplishing these steps.

The trainee should also accept that this model of human beings and of psychotherapy makes some reasonable sense. It may not be a perfect fit, but at least it can be accepted with or without grinding reservations.

The trainee need not be a scholar of the experiential model of human beings or of psychotherapy. Nor does the trainee need any prerequisite training in personality theories, psychotherapies, or any of the so-called foundational fields of knowledge such as neurology, chemistry, anatomy, physiology, or any other field.

In order to be in the training group, the trainee need not have any skills or competencies in doing experiential psychotherapy. Nor is it helpful if the trainee has so-called basic skills in interviewing, establishing therapist-client relationships, and carrying out methods and techniques often regarded as fundamental or even useful in doing psychotherapy. Indeed, most of the basic knowledge and skills considered requisite for many training programs are either unessential or downright inhibitory to constructive and productive participation in an experiential training group.

2. *What are the size and composition of the training group?* Most training groups include approximately three to six trainees. This enables each trainee to have an adequate number of turns to be the presenter.

The group can be fun, can enable trainees to become better experiential therapists, and can attain the goals of on-the-job training even when the people in the group vary in many characteristics. Groups can be successful when they are mixed in terms of little or no experience versus decades of experience doing therapy; in terms of knowledge and skills in experiential psychotherapy; and in terms of age, sex, and sexual preferences (e.g., Brodsky, 1980; Keefe & Maypole, 1983; Munson, 1987).

It also does not matter whether the trainees have white skin and the teacher has black skin, the trainees are all male and the teacher female, the trainees are all heterosexual and the teacher homosexual (cf. Brody, 1984; Munson, 1987). What is important is that most of their attention is on the tape, rather than on one another, and that they are all dedicated to attaining the goals of experiential training, rather than fulfilling mutual roles of supervisor and supervisees.

3. *What should the office be like to accommodate the trainees?* In order to listen to the tape and to allow for the group's own loud noises and privacy, the office should be sound-proofed. Perhaps the most important equipment is the tape recorder. An office may have the tape recorder on a coffee table with plenty of room for food and drink. The tape recorder is the centerpiece. The office may also include a blackboard and anything else to accommodate the teacher and the trainees.

4. *What is the climate of the training group?* The climate should involve three to six people concentrated on the tape, being puzzled and excited by what is happening on the tape. They are searching, discussing, making suggestions, trying to figure out, arguing, agreeing, disagreeing, and proposing. The group may be quiet, thoughtful, raucous, yelling, laughing, open, puzzled, excited, or all of these. Sometimes it is clear who is the teacher, and sometimes it is not so clear. Sometimes there is careful listening to the tape; sometimes there is mostly talk. This kind of climate seems to characterize most of our sessions, but reviews of group supervision typically say little about the climate (e.g., Bernard & Goodyear, 1992; Holloway & Johnston, 1985).

Try to Help Discover the Trainee's Own Natural Approach to Psychotherapy and See if It Is Reasonably Cordial With the Experiential Approach to Psychotherapy

Experiential teaching starts by trying to discover what may be termed the trainee's own natural approach to psychotherapy (Mahrer & Boulet, 1995). The "natural approach" to psychotherapy consists of what may be described as the trainee's deep-seated, inner framework of what psychotherapy is and how it works, what therapists and patients are like, what kinds of changes can occur, how they can occur, what therapists and patients can do to help change occur, and other parts of the trainee's natural deeper theory of psychotherapy.

Essentially, training starts by trying to see if there is a reasonable goodness-of-fit between the experiential approach to psychotherapy and the trainee's own natural approach to psychotherapy.

Natural approach to psychotherapy means more than merely the affiliation or school the trainee professes. It goes beyond saying that he or she is a Jungian or that he or she likes the experiential model of human beings and of psychotherapy, or that he or she is eclectic. Instead, the natural approach refers to the built-in notions that have a direct effect on what is done in the moment-to-moment process of psychotherapy. The natural approach is made of such working principles as the following: (a) Patients with weak egos will fall apart if you put too much stress on them; (b) patients can make substantial changes in just about every session; (c) psychopaths do not do well in intensive psychotherapy; (d) it takes a fair number of sessions to build a working alliance; (e) therapy is aimed at reducing symptoms of mental disorders; (f) patients with aggressive problems are to learn other ways of expressing their anger; (g) the purpose of the initial session is to assess the problem and mental disorder, and (h) female patients are to be seen by female therapists, and the goal is for the woman to be able to stand up for herself.

How can the teacher help to discover the trainee's own natural approach to psychotherapy? One way is to start with the trainee's own tapes, especially when the trainee is free to do therapy his or her own way, rather than to try to be an experiential therapist or a client-centered therapist or a psychodynamic therapist. In addition, the trainee may study tapes of sessions by other therapists.

The trainee should study the session to find points at which the trainee is excited and satisfied with what is happening and those at which the trainee is bothered and dissatisfied with what is happening. The teacher's job is to help the trainee probe further inside these exciting and bothersome moments in search of the underlying principles, the guiding ideas, the trainee's underlying beliefs about what patients are like, how therapy works, and the aims and goals of therapy. Beyond the rhetoric, beyond the surface sources of what the trainee says, the teacher can discover the trainee's inner, deeper, natural approach.

If these intrinsic, built-in beliefs are cordial with those of experiential psychotherapy, if the trainee's natural approach to psychotherapy has reasonable goodness-of-fit with experiential psychotherapy, then the trainee and teacher can move on to the teaching and learning of this therapy. If, in all honesty, the trainee's natural approach is far from that of experiential psychotherapy, at least for now, and especially if it is at odds with that of experiential psychotherapy, then it seems wisest for the trainee to work with a teacher or supervisor closer to the trainee's own natural approach. This is a friendly screening, but one that has quite practical consequences for both the experiential teacher and the trainee.

When It Is the Trainee's Turn to Present, the Trainee Prepares by Determining What Part of the Tape Should Be Studied, and Why That Part of the Tape Should Be Studied

The trainee tapes each session. Audiotapes are easier to use than videotapes (cf. Goldberg, 1983, 1985). Preparing for the training session consists of selecting one or two excerpts to study in the group. There are some guidelines to help the trainee select helpful excerpts, and it is the teacher's responsibility to ensure that the trainees know the kinds of excerpts to choose and also that there is a reasonable balance of the various kinds of excerpts chosen by each trainee.

In getting ready for the meeting of the training group, the trainee should try to be honest in choosing the reason for bringing that excerpt to the group. The following are some possible reasons:

1. The trainee is genuinely proud of that part of the session. It went rather well, at least as far as the trainee is concerned. The trainee may not be quite sure what seemed to go well or precisely why that part of the session seemed to be the one to play, but the trainee is still proud of that part.

2. There was an impressive change in the patient. Right here, the patient actually became the deeper potential. This is what is supposed to happen, but it is impressive when the change actually occurs.

3. This excerpt shows that the trainee is improving in learning this particular skill. In an earlier training session, the trainee was to practice a defined skill. This excerpt seems to show that the trainee is now able to use this skill fairly well.

4. This excerpt contains something puzzling or inexplicable or novel to the trainee. She actually felt blood dripping from her nose at the moment when the patient was describing an incident in which there was a lot of blood coming from his nose. It was strange because it was so real.

5. This excerpt contains a problem, a place in which the trainee did poorly, ran into difficulty, there was trouble, the trainee knew something went terribly wrong, the trainee was bothered and frustrated and worried by how poorly things were going, or the trainee messed up.

6. In this excerpt, the trainee has the same kind of problem he or she seems to run into a lot. Over and over again, the trainee has trouble achieving step 2. It happened again right here.

7. This excerpt illustrates the same conceptual issue that seems so compelling to the trainee. The training session can open the way to discussing conceptual issues (e.g., Wessler & Ellis, 1980), especially when they are nicely illustrated here in the taped excerpt and the discussion is solidly anchored in what is happening right here in the excerpt.

How Can You Study the Tape to Help Improve Competency and Skill?

Typically, around half of the training session is devoted to studying the tape and the rest is spent in trying to help improve competency and skill. Participants, including the teacher, listen to the tape by closing their eyes and trying to assume the role of the therapist in the taped excerpt (Mahrer, 1996a; Mahrer, Boulet, & Fairweather, 1994).

1. *The whole group participates in leading the training session, including the trainee who is presenting the excerpt.* Generally, it can be clear who is the teacher, but not necessarily. The trainee is usually the one who chairs the session. Even more, anyone in the group is quite free to raise an issue, to ask to hear that part again, to comment on how the trainee seems to be doing. Everyone seems to participate in trying to learn, to figure something out, to probe into this or that, and to get better. The whole group participates in the training, although the teacher is usually the one who knows more.

2. *The main emphasis is usually on the topic or issue that the trainee selected, but the teacher often adds one or two other topics or issues.* The trainee typically introduces the session by emphasizing the topic or issue he or she wants to focus on. He or she might say, "I had real trouble in trying to use this method, in step 2, of helping the patient welcome and appreciate the deeper potential. I need help in how to do it better." Although this focus is honored and respected, the teacher often finds some other topic or issue that seems to call for attention. The other issue or topic may be related to the one the trainee brought up. The teacher says, "Well, there may be another problem here, because you didn't seem to finish getting step 1. Let's get at this issue first." Or the teacher is drawn toward some other topic or issue: "But there is something else. You are really living in this scene. You're very good at this. See how this makes it so much easier for the patient to live and be in this scene."

3. *When there is a problem in the session, listen for the cause and the solution in the trainee, not in the patient.* When something seems to be going wrong, when there seems to be a problem, it is safe, attractive, and easy to blame the patient either directly or indirectly. The trainee says, "As soon as we come to the last step, to change, to really being different, she stops. She won't do it!" "He can't have strong feelings, so we can't even get started!" "She can't put attention on something. As soon as she gets near something threatening, she goes off to something else. She's too threatened!"

If something seems to be wrong, if there is a problem in the session, teachers might assume that a good case could be made that it is the patient's fault, but they should look for what the trainee did that was wrong or done poorly or what the trainee did not do but could and should have done (Mahrer, 1996a; Mahrer, Murphy, Gagnon & Gingras, 1994). One reason is that a teacher can almost always find an answer to the problem in what the trainee did wrong, quite aside from setting out to find what there is about the patient to warrant blame. If the trainee is going to improve, it seems easier to improve something the trainee did or did not do. Blaming the patient mainly helps the trainee get better in blaming patients. Finally, it seems more useful to consider the patient's role as merely a kind of immediate condition so that one can say, "When the patient is being like this or when the patient is doing that . . ."

For the trainee to improve, the more helpful perspective should pull teachers to find the cause of the problem in the trainee, rather than in the patient. Teachers may look for what the trainee might do once the trainee helped bring about the problem. But the best payoff for training is to look for what the trainee did wrong or poorly to help bring about the problem in the first place.

4. *When there is a good change in the patient, find what the trainee did rather well.* This is the job of the teacher, but the job should be spread around to include the trainee and the rest of the group. Be on the alert for good changes in the patient. These include little changes that are nevertheless good ones, such as when the patient seems to come up with other times when he could have been this new inner experiencing in the past. The good changes may refer to some big and impressive ones, such as when the patient declares energetically that she finally talked seriously with her mother and it was wonderful or the patient seems like a whole new person who is free of those pounding headaches. In any case, the trainee is to be comfortable enough to present these as "show-and-tell," and both the teacher and the others in the group are also to be on the lookout for these good changes.

Once the teacher locates the good change, he or she should try to figure out what the trainee did well and how the trainee or trainee and patient conjointly helped to bring about that good change: "I think that what you did was this and that, and here is how the patient helped, and all this helped make for this good change. What do you think?" If it seems warranted, the teacher should show the trainee how it might have been done even better and how doing this or that might have helped even more.

5. *When there is an emphasis on developing a particular method or skill, listen for how well or poorly the trainee is doing it.* Sometimes the trainee opens the training session by wanting to focus on how well or how poorly he or she is doing in regard to a particular skill or method the trainee has been practicing: He or she has been trying to improve the opening instructions or how to go to other earlier life experiences in step 3. In one training session, the group found that the trainee went into the final step without making the context one of playfulness and unreality. The trainee had practiced doing this after the last training session, and now the focus was on how well or poorly the trainee was doing this method in the tape the trainee was playing. Either the trainee or the teacher can pay attention to the methods and skills the trainee is focusing on and can listen for how the trainee is doing with regard to that particular method or skill.

6. *Listen for what and how the trainee could do better.* In listening to the tape, the teacher can be alert to places where the trainee could do something better. It is as if the teacher sees what the trainee is trying to accomplish here, and the teacher can show how to do it more easily, more effectively, and better.

The teacher may suggest some other method that the trainee can also use: "Think about using this other method too. It helps to use several methods. Besides, you don't seem to use this one much, and it is a good method. Try it out."

The teacher can suggest how to do it better. The trainee used a method in step 2; the teacher says, "I can show you how to do it better. Listen, see right here . . ."

The teacher can show the trainee what she might have done to accomplish this more easily, more effectively. She wants to enable the person to be more welcoming and appreciative of the deeper potential in step 2, and the trainee is using some methods fairly well: "It can help if you let the patient know what you both are working on next. Explain what you are trying to accomplish. Doing this first can make this step easier, I think."

7. *Stop the tape; what would you do right now?* As the group listens to the tape, it is helpful to stop the tape and ask the trainees what they would do right here. Almost always, it seems best to stop the tape when the patient has just done something. For example, the patient has just presented the trainee with some kind of challenge. Or in step 4, the patient comes up with a new behavior that scares the therapist. What can the therapist do now? The teacher should stop the tape when the patient is providing a good example of some challenge, some problem.

The teacher should give each trainee a chance to come up with a few things that may be done at that point. The teacher should talk about these options, replay that part of the tape, and invite each trainee to try out and sample what he or she might do right then.

8. *Relisten to the tape, this time from the new perspective.* Studying and learning from the tape enables the trainee to see and hear something more, perhaps something new. This new perspective can allow the trainee to take a fresh look at what is occurring on the tape, on opportunities and possibilities. The trainee may hear something somewhat different, somewhat new: "Yes, I hear it now. He is almost proud of yelling at his uncle! He's feeling satisfied, proud of himself. Yeah!" The trainee can appreciate the presented opportunities: "Right here, this would be the place. I could have joined her and gone even further. Yes." The trainee can now hear what he or she did that seemed so helpful: "That's what I did that worked! I was actually chuckling right along with him. I liked what he was saying. That's what seemed to do it. I can hear it now."

9. *Use the tape as a springboard into conceptual, practical, and professional issues.* There are times when the excerpt will knock on the door of relevant and related conceptual, practical, ethical, and professional issues. This excerpt leads directly into a discussion of how much genuinely deep-seated change can occur in a single session. This other excerpt brings up the issue of how to schedule sessions for a patient who is coming to town for a concentrated weekend of sessions. A third excerpt opens an issue of the therapist's accepting or declining the role of consultant to a government committee that reports to the therapist's patient.

It is the teacher's job to steward these discussions and to make sure that the focus returns to the tape itself. Sometimes the teacher or a trainee may go to the board and outline the experiential model. Sometimes the discussion gets quite excited and lively. Yet the focus remains the tape, and it is the teacher who makes sure that the excerpt is honored, rather than the discussion straying too far away or disappearing into thin air.

The Teacher's Turn: How Can Trainees Benefit From Listening to Tapes of the Teacher's Own Sessions?

An important part of experiential training is that trainees listen to the teacher's tapes. Every so often, it is the teacher's turn to present his or her own tapes.

It is almost embarrassing that studying tapes of exemplars, of seasoned practitioners, is not a mandated part of the training of psychotherapists (Mahrer, 1987, 1996a, 1996b;

Mahrer & Boulet, 1989). There is probably no other profession whose trainees are to learn their craft without seeing, studying, and learning from the actual work of exemplars. Students in other fields usually have rich opportunities to learn from studying the work of fine cellists, surgeons, plumbers, ballerinas, dentists, electricians, architects, or lawyers. Imagine a violinist who never heard a violinist performing; this is the model we proudly follow and aggressively defend. What a pity. Learning how to do psychotherapy could and should include the careful study of the work of fine practitioners. Nor is this a new idea:

> I believe that one excellent method of beginning to experience what is involved in psychotherapy is to listen to recordings—recordings of initial and early interviews, recordings of interviews in which the client is deeply involved in himself and in the relationship. It is certainly most desirable if the recordings can be taken from various orientations of therapy and can include both experienced and inexperienced therapists. (Rogers, 1957, p. 79)

What a refreshing proposal!

During on-the-job training, it is somewhat sad that trainees do not routinely get the chance to listen to and to study 20 hours, or 10 or 5 hours, of tapes of the teacher's and other seasoned practitioners' actual sessions (cf. Baum & Gray, 1992; Gandolfo & Brown, 1987; Goldberg, 1983, 1985; Halgin & Murphy, 1995; Heilveil, 1983). In one little step toward giving trainees this opportunity, the teacher takes his or her turn at presenting a tape to the training group.

There are several reasons for on-the-job teachers to take their turn in presenting tapes. One is that the trainee can learn from studying parts of the session the teacher presents as reasonably good and parts of the session the teacher is satisfied with or even rather proud of. The emphasis is on relatively good sessions rather than on the rare sessions of such wondrous caliber that the trainee is overwhelmed by the magic, overawed by the teacher's virtuosity, and overcome with the depressing unlikelihood of ever becoming such a dazzling practitioner. A second reason is to present something that is somewhat puzzling or inexplicable, maybe a little strange, perhaps perplexing. The trainee is invited to present these kinds of tapes. So does the teacher. The third reason is for the teacher, just like the trainee, to present tapes that illustrate problems. It can be hard for the trainee to present mistakes, honest errors, and problems. It can be hard for the teacher to present tapes on which the teacher goofed, made sophomoric mistakes, was awful, or committed equalizing bloopers. There are occasions when the teacher can welcome a chance to study and to discuss his or her own poor performance, even with the help of the trainees.

Practice, Practice, Practice: Individually Tailored, Competency-Developing Training Sessions

Right here on the tape, the trainee did something wrong, or could have done something better, or went in the wrong direction, or failed to take advantage of something, or should have done this or that. The tape provides a fine opportunity to practice what could or should have been done. By stopping the tape right here, when the patient did this, said that, was being like this, the trainee has a great opportunity to practice doing what he or she could or should have done. So do the other trainees in the group. Give the trainees a chance to practice doing it right, or better. Try it out. Model what the trainee should or could have done. It is practice time, a little bit right here in the group, and in getting ready for practice outside the group.

The teacher assigns a designated skill for the trainee to practice as a simple homework assignment. The trainee is to take the tape and, on his or her own or with a partner, is to spend 15 minutes or so practicing, over and over again, sheer skill learning. Practice doing the opening instructions until they are significantly better. Practice doing this particular method of accessing the deeper potential. Practice this additional skill of enabling the patient to become more welcoming of the deeper potential. Practice this designated skill that the teacher teaches the trainee to use, or to use better, or to use under this specific patient condition on the tape.

Here is a specific way of learning a skill, of developing competence by explicitly targeting and practicing the designated skill (cf. Lambert, 1980; Lambert & Arnold, 1987). Learning how to play the piano or how to serve a tennis ball or how to throw a hook in boxing usually requires hours of practice. Psychotherapy has the rare distinction of being perhaps the only profession in which most practitioners are to achieve competence with little or no actual training-to-criterion, dedicated learning of skills, and actual practice of the competencies. Doing experiential psychotherapy requires the development of skills through sheer hours of practice. Every training session should include some kind of homework to enable the trainee to practice, practice, practice.

One Good Reason for Research Is to Help Discover More Useful Ways of Teaching Trainees the Skills for Attaining Successful and Effective Experiential Sessions

Perhaps the main goal of experiential on-the-job teaching, the payoff, is that the trainee improves the skills of having successful and effective experiential sessions. It is relatively easy to tell if this session enabled the patient to become a qualitatively new person, free of the bad-feelinged scene. It is relatively easy to tell if the trainee was able to attain the four steps. It is relatively easy to tell if the trainee was successful and effective in using particular skills and methods.

Researchers are adept at finding all sorts of reasons to do research on supervision. Of all the reasons, the one that would be most helpful to experiential teaching is to assist in discovering more useful ways of teaching trainees the skills for getting successful and effective sessions. This chapter spelled out some methods that grew out of simple trial and error. More careful research can help to discover better methods (cf. Lambert, 1980; Lambert & Arnold, 1987).

How can this kind of research be done? One way is to study tapes of teaching sessions in which the direct consequences included (a) improvement in the skills that were assigned as homework; (b) improvement in the depth and breadth of skills as shown by the successful and effective achievement of the four steps; and (c) improvement in achieving successful and effective experiential sessions. Studying these tapes should help in discovering new and better teaching methods.

CONCLUSION

There were two main aims of this chapter. One was to feature a role of on-the-job teacher of experiential psychotherapy. To achieve the particular goals of increasing competency in experiential skills and in attaining effective and successful sessions, the role of on-the-job teacher of experiential psychotherapy is probably more useful than is the traditional role of supervisor. A second aim was to describe some concrete ways of doing on-the-job teaching of experiential psychotherapy. Some of these concrete methods are probably also found in other kinds of psychotherapy training programs. Others of these concrete methods may be somewhat distinctive, but they may also be useful in other kinds of psychotherapy training programs.

REFERENCES

Albott, W. (1984). Supervisory characteristics and other sources of supervision variance. *The Clinical Supervisor, 2*, 27–41.

Alonso, A. (1985). *The quiet profession: Supervisors of psychotherapy.* New York: Macmillan.

Bartlett, W. E. (1983). A multidimensional framework for the analysis of supervision of counseling. *Counseling Psychologist, 11*, 9–17.

Baum, B. E., & Gray, J. J. (1992). Expert modeling, self-observation using videotape, and acquisition of basic therapy skills. *Professional Psychology: Research and Practice, 23*, 220–225.

Bernard, J. M., & Goodyear, R. K. (1992). *Fundamentals of clinical supervision.* Boston: Allyn & Bacon.

Blocher, D. H. (1983). Toward a cognitive developmental approach to counselor supervision. *Counseling Psychologist, 11*, 27–34.

Brodsky, A. M. (1980). Sex role issues in the supervision of therapy. In A. K. Hess (Ed.), *Psychotherapy supervision: Theory, research, and practice* (pp. 509–522). New York: Wiley.

Brody, C. M. (Ed.). (1984). *Women therapists working with women: New theory and process of feminist therapy.* New York: Springer.

Bruch, H. (1974). *Learning psychotherapy: Rationale and ground rules.* Cambridge: Harvard University Press.

Carifio, M. S., & Hess, A. K. (1987). Who is the ideal supervisor? *Professional Psychology: Research and Practice, 3*, 244–250.

Coche, E. (1977). Training of group therapists. In F. W. Kaslow (Ed.), *Supervision, consultation, and staff training in the helping professions* (pp. 235–263). San Francisco: Jossey-Bass.

Cohen, R., & DeBetz, B. (1977). Responsive supervision of the psychiatric resident and clinical psychology intern. *American Journal of Psychoanalysis, 37*, 51–64.

Dodenhoff, J. T. (1981). Interpersonal attraction and direct-indirect supervisor influence as predictors of trainee effectiveness. *Journal of Counseling Psychology, 28*, 47–52.

Ekstein, R., & Wallerstein, R. S. (1972). *The teaching and learning of psychotherapy* (2nd ed.). New York: International Universities Press.

Finch, W. A. (1977). The role of the organization. In F. W. Kaslow (Ed.), *Supervision, consultation, and staff training in the helping professions* (pp. 61–80). San Francisco: Jossey-Bass.

Fleming, H., & Benedict, T. (1966). *Psychoanalytic supervision.* New York: Grune and Stratton.

Gandolfo, R. L., & Brown, R. (1987). Psychology interns' ratings of actual and ideal supervision of psychotherapy. *Journal of Training and Practice in Professional Psychology, 1*, 15–28.

Glitterman, A., & Miller, I. (1977). Supervisors as educators. In F. W. Kaslow (Ed.), *Supervision, consultation, and staff training in the helping professions* (pp. 100–114). San Francisco: Jossey-Bass.

Goldberg, D. A. (1983). Resistance to the use of video in individual psychotherapy training. *American Journal of Psychiatry, 140*, 1172–1176.

Goldberg, D. A. (1985). Process notes, audio, and the video tape: Modes of presentation in psychotherapy training. *The Clinical Supervisor, 3*, 3–13.

Halgin, R. P., & Murphy, R. A. (1995). Issues in the training of psychotherapists. In B. Bongar & L. E. Beutler (Eds.), *Comprehensive textbook of psychotherapy: Theory and practice* (pp. 434–455). New York: Oxford University Press.

Heilveil, I. (1983). *Video in mental health practice.* New York: Springer.

Hess, A. K. (1980). Training models and the nature of psychotherapy supervision. In A. K. Hess (Ed.), *Psychotherapy supervision: Theory, research and practice* (pp. 15–25). New York: Wiley.

Hess, A. K. (1987). Psychotherapy supervision: Stages, Buber, and a theory of relationship. *Professional Psychology, Research and Practice, 18,* 251–259.

Hill, C. E., Charles, D., & Reed, K. G. (1981). A longitudinal analysis of changes in counseling skills during doctoral training in counseling psychology. *Journal of Counseling Psychology, 28,* 428–436.

Holloway, E. L. (1992). Supervision: A way of teaching and learning. In S. D. Brown & R. W. Lent (Eds.), *Handbook of counseling psychology* (pp. 177–214). New York: Wiley.

Holloway, E. L., & Hosford, R. E. (1983). Towards developing a prescriptive technology of counselor supervision. *Counseling Psychologist, 11,* 73–77.

Holloway, E. L., & Johnston, R. (1985). Group supervision: Widely practiced, but poorly understood. *Counselor Education and Supervision, 24,* 332–340.

Ivey, A. E. (1971). *Microcounseling: Innovations in interviewing training.* Springfield, IL: Charles C Thomas.

Keefe, T., & Maypole, D. E. (1983). *Relationships in social service practice.* Monterey, CA: Brooks/Cole.

Kutzik, A. J. (1977). The medical field. In F. W. Kaslow (Ed.), *Supervision, consultation, and staff training in the helping professions* (pp. 25–60). San Francisco: Jossey-Bass.

Lambert, M. J. (1980). Research and the supervisory process. In A. K. Hess (Ed.), *Psychotherapy supervision: Theory, research, and practice* (pp. 525–530). New York: Wiley.

Lambert, M. J., & Arnold, R. C. (1987). Research and the supervisory process. *Professional Psychology: Research and Practice, 18,* 217–224.

Langs, R. (1979). *The supervisory experience.* New York: Jason Aronson.

Liddle, H. A. (1988). Systematic supervision: Conceptual overlays and pragmatic guidelines. In H. A. Liddle, D. C. Breunlin, & R. C. Schwartz (Eds.), *Handbook of family therapy training and supervision* (pp. 153–171). New York: Guilford.

Loganbill, C., Hardy, E., & Delworth, U. (1982). Supervision: A conceptual model. *Counseling Psychologist, 10,* 3–42.

Mahrer, A. R. (1987). If there really were a specialty of psychotherapy: Standards for post-doctoral training in psychotherapy. *The Humanistic Psychologist, 15,* 83–94.

Mahrer, A. R. (1996a). *The complete guide to experiential psychotherapy.* New York: Wiley.

Mahrer, A. R. (1996b). Studying distinguished practitioners: A humanistic approach to discovering how to do psychotherapy. *Journal of Humanistic Psychology, 36,* 31–48.

Mahrer, A. R., & Boulet, D. B. (1989). A post-doctoral plan for the education and training of counsellors. *Canadian Journal of Counselling, 23,* 388–389.

Mahrer, A. R., & Boulet, D. B. (1995). *The discovery of the trainee's own deeper approach to psychotherapy.* Symposium address at the annual convention of the American Psychological Association, New York.

Mahrer, A. R., Boulet, D. B., & Fairweather, D. R. (1994). Beyond empathy: Advances in the clinical theory and methods of empathy. *Clinical Psychology Review, 14,* 183–198.

Mahrer, A. R., Murphy, L., Gagnon, R., & Gingras, N. (1994). The counsellor as a cause and cure of client resistance. *Canadian Journal of Counselling, 28,* 125–134.

Marshall, W. R., & Confer, W. N. (1980). Psychotherapy supervision: Supervisees' perspective. In A. E. Hess (Ed.), *Psychotherapy supervision: Theory, research and practice* (pp. 92–100). New York: Wiley.

Melchiode, G. A. (1977). Psychoanalytically oriented individual therapy. In F. W. Kaslow (Ed.), *Supervision, consultation, and staff training in the helping professions* (pp. 155–174). San Francisco: Jossey-Bass.

Mueller, W. J. (1982). Issues in the application of "Supervision: A conceptual model" to dynamically oriented supervision: A reaction paper. *Counseling Psychologist, 10,* 43–46.

Mueller, W. J., & Kell, B. L. (1972). *Coping with conflict: Supervising counselors and psychotherapists*. New York: Appleton-Century-Crofts.

Munson, C. E. (1987). Sex roles and power relationships in supervision. *Professional Psychology: Research and Practice, 18*, 236–243.

Orzek, A. (1984). Mentor-mentee match in training program based on Chickering's vectors of development. *The Clinical Supervisor, 2*, 71–77.

Rogers, C. R. (1957). Training individuals to engage in the therapeutic process. In C. R. Strother (Ed.), *Psychology and mental health* (pp. 76–92). Washington, DC: American Psychological Association.

Russell, R. K., Crimmings, A. M., & Lent, R. W. (1984). Counselor training and supervision: Theory and research. In S. D. Brown & R. W. Lent (Eds.), *Handbook of counseling psychology* (pp. 625–681). New York: Wiley.

Sachs, D. M., & Shapiro, S. H. (1976). On parallel processes in therapy and teaching. *Psychoanalytic Quarterly, 45*, 394–415.

Searles, H. (1955). The informational value of the supervisor's emotional experiences. *Psychiatry, 18*, 135–146.

Searles, H. (1965). *Collected papers on schizophrenia and related subjects*. New York: International Universities Press.

Stoltenberg, C. (1981). Approaching supervision from a developmental perspective: The counselor complexity model. *Journal of Counseling Psychology, 28*, 59–65.

Storm, C., & Heath, A. (1985). Models of supervision: Using therapy theory as a guide. *The Clinical Supervisor, 3*, 87–92.

Tarachow, S. (1963). *An introduction to psychotherapy*. New York: International Universities Press.

Watkins, C. E., Jr. (1990). Development of the psychotherapy supervisor. *Psychotherapy, 27*, 553–560.

Watkins, C. E., Jr. (1993). Development of the psychotherapy supervisor: Concepts, assumptions, and hypotheses of the supervisor complexity model. *American Journal of Psychotherapy, 47*, 58–74.

Weiner, I., & Kaplan, R. (1980). From classroom to clinic: Supervising the first psychotherapy client. In A. K. Hess (Ed.), *Psychotherapy supervision: Theory, research, and practice* (pp. 41–50). New York: Wiley.

Wessler, R. L., & Ellis, A. (1980). Supervision in rational-emotive therapy. In A. K. Hess (Ed.), *Psychotherapy supervision: Theory, research and practice* (pp. 181–191). New York: Wiley.

Worthington, E. L., Jr. (1987). Changes in supervision as counselors and supervisors gain experience: A review. *Professional Psychology: Research and Practice, 18*, 189–208.

Worthington, E. L., Jr., & Roehlke, H. S. (1979). Effective supervision as perceived by beginning counselors-in-training. *Journal of Counseling Psychology, 26*, 64–73.

CHAPTER 12

Clinical Supervision From a Developmental Perspective: Research and Practice

CAL D. STOLTENBERG
University of Oklahoma
BRIAN W. MCNEILL
Washington State University

Developmental models of clinical supervision have been described as the *zeitgeist* of supervision models (Holloway, 1987, p. 209), the most heuristic (Worthington, 1987), as well as the most researched and the most visible themes in recent years (Bernard & Goodyear, 1992). This chapter briefly traces the history of developmental models of supervision and provides an overview of the most recent and comprehensive of these models, the *integrated developmental model* (IDM; Stoltenberg & Delworth, 1987). The chapter summarizes the current state of the supervision research as it relates to this model and ends with an analysis of where the model needs further refinement and more extensive empirical investigation.

A treatise on human development and the utility of this metaphor for the process of clinical supervision is beyond the scope of this chapter and has been adequately addressed elsewhere (see Stoltenberg & Delworth, 1987). We think, however, that it is crucial that the process of supervision should carefully incorporate the concept of change over time (Stoltenberg & Delworth, 1987) in considering the needs and responses of trainees. As discussed later, the research literature appears to support many of the key constructs of developmental models, including differential characteristics and training needs of supervisees, reactions to supervision, and behavior of supervisors across levels of experience (Stoltenberg, McNeill, & Crethar, 1994).

Although some supervision models that articulate a developmental framework do so as an extension of a developmental model of counseling or psychotherapy (e.g., Eckstein & Wallerstein, 1972; Mueller & Kell, 1972), a fundamental assumption of others is articulated by Loganbill, Hardy, and Delworth (1982). They argue that developmental models should be constructed specifically for the supervision process, not as extensions of approaches to counseling or psychotherapy. Unless one assumes that the issues faced by clients in psychotherapy and supervisees in supervision are fundamentally the same, which strikes us as flawed, we are left with the need to construct a model idiosyncratic to the supervision context, an issue echoed by Bernard and Goodyear (1992). This is the intent of the IDM.

EARLY DEVELOPMENTAL MODELS

Extensive discussions of early developmental models of supervision exist elsewhere (e.g., Russell, Crimmings, & Lent, 1984; Stoltenberg & Delworth, 1987; Worthington, 1987), so we limit our discussion here to a brief overview to set the context for discussing the IDM. Similar to individual counselor development, the model of supervision reflected by this perspective has developed into a complex integration of changing characteristics and needs of trainees and how these interact with various domains of counselor/psychotherapist activity and the supervision process.

In their 1987 book, Stoltenberg and Delworth review and critique seven developmental models of clinical supervision using Bartlett's (1983) categorization framework. Hogan's (1964) four-stage model was presented as one of the earliest models (other than Fleming, 1953) relying on developmental constructs. Although the presentation of this model was quite brief and, therefore, lacked detail, it had an important impact on subsequent model building. Indeed, along with the cognitive development work of Harvey, Hunt, and Schroder (1961) and Hunt (1971), Hogan's model formed the basis for Stoltenberg's (1981) developmental model of supervision.

Stoltenberg's (1981) *counselor complexity model* extended Hogan's (1964) work by more formally integrating developmental constructs into a supervision model. Additional guidelines for optimal supervision environments were proposed that more carefully delineated how supervision should be conceptualized across trainee experience levels from dependent novices to independently functioning "master counselors." Worthington (1984) noted in his review that this was the most heuristic model to date and stimulated the most empirical research.

Another important contribution to developmental supervision model building was the work of Littrell, Lee-Borden, and Lorenz (1979). This article integrated four existing models of training counselors: teaching, counseling/therapeutic, consulting, and self-supervision. The model proposed that the appropriate use of these approaches followed an orderly progression beginning with teaching and ending with self-supervision.

Other models addressed by Stoltenberg and Delworth (1987) included Ralph (1980), Yogev (1982), and Blocher (1983). These models, however, have had less impact on the field than the one proposed by Loganbill et al. (1982). Similar to Stoltenberg's (1981) model, Loganbill et al. (1982) relied heavily on existing models of human development to construct their supervision model. Loganbill et al.'s is a three-stage model that suggested that trainees will continue to recycle through the same stages at deepening levels with respect to different content issues. The longest (monograph) of the seven models reviewed by Stoltenberg and Delworth (1987), Loganbill et al. (1982) elaborated on the elements of supervision (supervisor, supervisee, their relationship, and the environment), supervision interventions, and assessment.

In a landmark review of the supervision literature, Worthington (1987) examined 16 models of supervision of varying detail that incorporated the developmental perspective. He describes the models as having subtle differences, but being quite similar, with all of them using rather broad depictions of counselor development although lacking in specific details. In addition, Worthington (1987) notes that the stages of development are the focus of these models, but little attention is given to transitions among stages or how one gets from one to another.

In their chapter in the *Handbook of Counseling Psychology*, Russell et al. (1984) organized their discussion of models into two categories: Ericksonian linear stage theories and step-by-step skill mastery or conflict resolution theories (similar to Stoltenberg and Delworth's, 1987, organismic and mechanistic distinctions, respectively). The former rely heavily on sequential stages to describe psychotherapist development (e.g., Hogan, 1964; Littrell et al., 1979; Stoltenberg, 1981) whereas the latter group of models propose a recycling through phases (usually three) either across certain critical issues in training (e.g., Loganbill et al., 1982) or for each new supervisor (Eckstein & Wallerstein, 1972; Mueller & Kell, 1972). As noted earlier, Russell et al. (1984) suggest that these models are "simplistic and vague" and go on to recommend that future research should focus on "the integration of the developmental approaches to supervision," particularly, incorporating step-by-step methods of task or conflict resolution with stage models.

In a review of the supervision literature in the most recent edition of the *Handbook of Counseling Psychology,* Holloway (1992) failed to examine new developmental models of supervision, incorrectly noting that "no new models of supervision have appeared" (p. 179) since the earlier edition. One important new model of supervision has appeared since 1984. The remainder of this chapter discusses this model, the IDM (Stoltenberg & Delworth, 1987), along with some of its recent extensions (e.g., Stoltenberg, 1993; Stoltenberg et al., 1995).

THE INTEGRATED DEVELOPMENTAL MODEL OF SUPERVISION

Although developmental models of supervision have stimulated considerable research and, as noted earlier, have commanded the most attention in recent years, the perspective has received criticism. Russell et al. (1984) accurately note that at that time current developmental models were too simplistic and inadequately addressed professional development, a position also supported by Worthington (1987). On the other hand, Holloway (1987) criticizes some developmental models as being "exceedingly complex" and more elaborate than what we typically expect of "truth" (p. 211).

Bernard and Goodyear (1992) note some of the disadvantages of developmental models. Their criticism includes an observation that current models do not account for the possibility that, occasionally, advanced trainees may need supervision conditions typically associated with beginning trainees. In addition, they believe that these models do not allow for divergent routes to development for different trainees. Finally, they argue that current models do not account for relapse or failure to progress on the part of the trainee.

The IDM attempts to address some of the shortcomings of earlier developmental models. The IDM presents a more complex model that addresses the criticism of Bernard and Goodyear (1992) in its examination of specific structures across varying professional activities or domains. We agree with Russell et al. (1984) that prior models are incomplete and somewhat simplistic. Given the brevity of the journal article format in which these models were presented, this is to be expected. Also, early reports of these models are intended to lay out a framework from which other issues could be examined. None are intended to be complete. By focusing an entire book on a particular model, Stoltenberg and Delworth (1987) are able to address many of these issues with the IDM. In addition, consistent with Russell et al.'s (1984) recommendations, the IDM uses step-by-step approaches to task and conflict resolution (mechanistic development) within an overall linear stage model (organismic) to more fully articulate the process of growth over time. In addition, recent work (Stoltenberg et al., 1995) more carefully addresses influence strategies for supervision, consistent with Worthington's (1987) recommendations. Finally, Eichenfield and Stoltenberg (1996) recently discussed the problems of relapse and failure to develop for certain trainees.

The argument that developmental models may be too complex (Holloway, 1987) is curious. As argued by Stoltenberg and Delworth (1988), professional development *is* a complicated process and one that requires an awareness of a multitude of factors and how they interact. Our recent work (e.g., Stoltenberg, 1993; Stoltenberg et al., 1995) has focused on further delineating mechanisms of the IDM. Although more simple models are more readily comprehensible, they lack the elegance to capture important aspects of the process. Unfortunately, more complicated models also tend to increase the specificity necessary in empirical investigations that can create problems for the researcher and present the practitioner with a number of issues to consider at any given time.

The space constraints of a single chapter necessarily limit the detail with which we can present the IDM. Interested readers are encouraged to examine other literature to broaden their understanding of the model (e.g., Stoltenberg, 1993; Stoltenberg & Delworth, 1987; Stoltenberg et al., 1995; Stoltenberg, McNeill, & Delworth, 1997). However, key concepts and assumptions related to the model and a brief discussion of applications are presented.

Overarching Structures and Specific Domains

Some early models of counselor/psychotherapist development suggest that growth tends to occur in uniform stages. One was a Level 1, 2, 3, and so on trainee. This global view tends to obscure important differences in levels of development at which the trainee may be functioning across different professional activities or domains. For example, a trainee may function at a relatively high level of autonomy when conducting individual psychotherapy with a depressed client, but he or she may be an appropriately dependent novice when doing marital or family therapy. Similarly, a trainee with significant assessment training and experience but little psychotherapy training and experience may function at a high level in the former domain but may perform at a dramatically lower level in the latter domain. Thus, a single trainee may obviously be functioning at different developmental levels in different domains, requiring different supervision conditions for each.

Other models have suggested that one continues to recycle through stages in an everdeepening (Loganbill et al., 1982) or spiraling manner (Hess, 1986). In the extreme, these models contradict the notion that once development has occurred in a given domain, it should be consolidated by changes in cognitive structures. These models also lack markers that indicate how one monitors development across issues or when certain issues become prominent.

Stoltenberg and Delworth (1987) have proposed using three overriding structures to monitor trainee development through three levels across various domains of clinical training and practice, thus integrating mechanistic and organismic models and providing markers to assess development across domains. These three structures are

Self and Other Awareness
    (Cognitive)
    (Affective)
Motivation
Autonomy

Briefly stated, trainees will begin with a primary focus on the self that includes attempting to keep in mind the skills and interventions they are learning while dealing with performance anxiety and evaluation apprehension. They will be highly motivated, wanting to learn quickly to get past the anxiety and uncertainty of the beginner. Also, they will tend to be dependent on their supervisors or other "experts" for advice and guidance. Toward the end of Level 1, as skills and confidence have increased, trainees can become quite confident (perhaps overly so) in their abilities and the impact of counseling.

Level 2 trainees have acquired sufficient skills, knowledge, and experience to enable them to attend less to their own uncertainties, including what they should do next, and experience reduced anxiety and apprehension. As with late Level 1, at times Level 2 trainees will be quite confident, perhaps overly so, in their abilities and skills. This presents the opportunity to increase their focus on the client (other awareness), which sets into motion both positive and negative influences on their work. Thus, although it is now possible for them to adequately empathize (affective component) and begin to understand the client's perspective (cognitive component), this richer database can create confusion and emotional turmoil in the trainee as simple approaches and interventions no longer appear adequate. Motivation often suffers in this stage as the trainee may exhibit high motivation when things are going well and remarkably decreased motivation for professional work and development when confusion and ambivalence are predominant. Similarly, one notices variations in autonomy, with negative independence (counterdependence) at times and dependence at other times.

Successful resolution of Level 2 issues sets the stage for movement into Level 3. Characteristics of this level of trainee include an ability to be appropriately and insightfully self-aware, but also being able to empathize with and understand the client's perspective. Additionally, motivation tends to stabilize at this level with fewer peaks and valleys. Finally, relatively autonomous functioning characterizes the work of this professional, who has an accurate understanding of relative professional strengths and weaknesses integrated with insightful self-understanding. This level of development is further expanded by Stoltenberg and Delworth (1987) in their discussion of the Level 3i (integrated) professional. This person is capable of functioning with Level 3 structures across a number of domains of activity and can move comfortably across domains utilizing information and perspectives for each to enable more comprehensive professional practice.

Naturally, transitions among levels occur that change the quality of the trainee's characteristics and behavior. Consequently, supervision environments must change to augment development and appropriately challenge each level of trainee. We elaborate upon this, as space allows, in subsequent sections.

The domains of professional activity alluded to here can be conceptualized in varying degrees of specificity. In general, Stoltenberg and Delworth (1987) offer the following categories:

Intervention Skills Competence
Assessment Techniques
Interpersonal Assessment
Client Conceptualization
Individual Differences
Theoretical Orientation
Treatment Goals and Plans
Professional Ethics

Obviously, each of these could be further reduced to more specific domains (e.g., types of intervention skills, assessment techniques), but the general categories serve to highlight the fact that one must attend carefully to the focal activity in which the trainee is engaging to adequately assess the developmental level at which the trainee is functioning at any given time. To highlight the importance of specificity, Stoltenberg (1993) has suggested a slightly different collection of domains for consultant training. Consequently, *global* labeling of developmental levels becomes less useful in supervision (and research), although easier to understand and more simple to apply. Assessment of level for specific domains, however, becomes crucial for providing appropriate supervision environments for trainees across contexts.

LEVELS OF DEVELOPMENT

In the following sections, we briefly discuss important issues for Level 1, 2, and 3 trainees. The narrative is used to augment the outlines of material presented in Table 12.1.

Level 1

Beginning trainees come to us with varying backgrounds in experience related to the domains of activity typically associated with professional psychology. It is important to understand that these experiential differences may place trainees at different points along the developmental continuum for various domains; thus, not all trainees function the same. In addition, other trainees come to us with personal or psychological problems that work to confound the training process (see Eichenfield & Stoltenberg, 1996, for a discussion).

The prototypical beginning trainee, however, has had limited exposure to counseling/psychotherapy, assessment, consultation, and so on. As is typical for most people who enter into a new field of experience, novices tend to be anxious and rely on teachers and supervisors to provide specific guidance as they learn counseling, assessment, conceptualization, and other skills. Their motivation usually is high, largely because it is rather uncomfortable to perceive oneself as inadequate. Thus, a strong desire to learn quickly and reduce the high anxiety can be quite the motivator.

Consistent with the strong motivation to learn is a dependent approach toward supervision and training. It would be inappropriate for someone who has not yet mastered even rudimentary skills to exhibit much autonomous functioning, so this dependency on authority figures is appropriate and desirable. Level 1 trainees must rely on their supervisors and teachers to educate and train them in the theories, techniques, and concepts relevant for professional practice.

The early education and training of beginners usually focuses on an introduction to theories and techniques. Various approaches can be taken, but usually certain skills are taught that enable the trainee to acquire some (initially limited) repertoire of behaviors or strategies to use in sessions with clients (for counseling, psychotherapy, assessment, and so on). Learning these skills and strategies necessarily tends to result in a predominant focus on the self by the trainee. Performance is often positively evaluated by the degree to which he or she can faithfully perform a given technique or follow general guidelines. Little attentional space is left for considering the client's perspective or his or her affective reactions to the counselor.

Table 12.1 Integrated Developmental Model

Developmental Levels

Level	Motivation	Autonomy	Self-Other Awareness
I	High motivation High anxiety Focus on acquisition of skills	Dependent on supervisor Need for structure, positive feedback, minimal direct confrontation	Limited self-awareness Focus on self: anxiety performance Objective self-awareness Learns from outside source Difficulty seeing strengths, weaknesses
Transition Issues	May reduce for learning new approaches or techniques	May desire more autonomy than is warranted	Switches focus more to client and away from own thoughts—performance
II	Fluctuating, at times quite confident More complexity shakes confidence; result often is confusion, despair, vacillation	Dependency-autonomy conflict At times more assertive; develops own ideas Independent functioning; may want specific help Other times dependent, evasive	Can focus more on client; empathize with affect; understand worldview May become enmeshed so not effective Issue is appropriate balance
Transition Issues	Increased desire to personalize orientation	Becomes more conditionally autonomous; better understanding of parameters of competence	Moves focus to include more reactions of self to client
III	Stable Remaining doubts not disabling Concerned with total professional identity and how therapist role fits in	Firm belief in own autonomy, not easily shaken Sense of when it is necessary to seek consultation	Accepting of self, strengths, and weaknesses High empathy, understanding Can focus on client and process information, including own reactions Can use self in sessions

Table 12.1   (Continued)

| | Levels Across Domains | | |
Domain	Level I	Level II	Level III
Transition to 3i	Contrasts domains in which motivation is stable with those in which it is less so	More able to move conceptually and behaviorally from one domain to another Professional identity is solid across most domains	Personalized understanding crosses domains Monitors impact of personal life changes on professional identity/performance
Intervention Skills, Competence	Fundamental counseling skills Structured format for skill implementation Desire for learning and practice Applies skills to client	More developed skills but not well integrated Ability to focus on client leads to confusion about what to do	Well-developed skills More creative and integrative in application of skills Can make changes as deemed necessary based on idiosyncratic client needs
Assessment Techniques	Fits client into diagnostic categories Structured "by the book" Focus on consistency in results rather than discrepancies	Possible loss of interest in "impersonal" assessments as focus is on client Little understanding of implication of label for client	Solid sense of role of assessment Diagnostic classifications influenced by setting and client environment
Interpersonal Assessment	Ignores or attributes too much pathology to normal responses Difficulty in responding to unexpected statements Reliance on supervisor to validate or provide alternate conceptualizations	More aware of client's perspective May overaccommodate Difficulty separating accurate perceptions from countertransference	Avoids stereotypic thinking Focuses on client and personal reactions to client Understanding often more complete than supervisor's

(table continues)

191

Table 12.1 (Continued)

Levels Across Domains

Domain	Level I	Level II	Level III
Client Conceptualization	Focuses on discrete pieces of information, often selected for consistency with theoretical orientation	More accurate More complete understanding of client's perspective Danger of overaccommodation	Sees how client interacts to produce whole person Understands diagnostic label, focus on pattern relevant for client as individual
Individual Differences	Relies too heavily on own experiences, perceptions of world Develops stereotypes Self-focused, empathy difficult to achieve	Awareness increases Still has some stereotypic thinking; sees client as exception Greater openness to varieties of human experience	Views client as individual and person-in-context
Theoretical Orientation	Tends to focus on one approach May rule out alternatives Limited flexibility	More personalized, selective approach Unsure when to pursue which orientation, approach or how to vary Difficulty in justifying choices	Knowledgeable, flexible Not driven by theory Theories' strengths and weaknesses acknowledged Enjoys dialogue about different views
Treatment Goals	Difficult to visualize process from intake to termination Difficult to translate goals into specific interventions or vice versa	Difficult to be specific May have confusion from conflicting conceptualizations, hard to develop tight plan Easily discouraged when initial treatment plans do not work	Great progress here Plans flow from assessment and conceptualizations appropriately altered as a result of interventions Plans more focused, coherent, realistic
Professional Ethics	Depends on supervisor to resolve ethical dilemmas Rote memorization of code without integration	Understands ramifications of ethical decisions Concerned with protection of client	Broadened perspective Can handle complex issues Motivated to look at other codes; personally integrated ethics

Note: Adapted from *Supervising Counselors and Therapists* by C. Stoltenberg and U. Delworth, 1987, San Francisco: Jossey-Bass.

The supervisor's task is to convey the necessary introductory information to the trainee that will allow him or her to begin to conceptualize the counseling, assessment, or other process yet avoid going too deeply into issues that can confuse this level of trainee. Skill development is also important and requires presentation of techniques and so forth via observation (of the supervisor or others), role-playing, practice, and repetitions. Encouraging an early focus of the trainee on self-performance is appropriate so he or she can accurately monitor skill development. Some attention is necessary, however, to the client's response to interventions so that the trainee becomes aware of the importance of this source of feedback. The supervisor should provide most of the structure for training, which should help reduce trainee anxiety and facilitate the most efficient use of supervision and other training experiences. The research literature is supportive of this view of beginners and their supervisory needs (see Stoltenberg & Delworth, 1987; Stoltenberg, McNeill, & Crethar, 1994; Worthington, 1987).

Carefully constructed learning experiences in controlled situations leading to clinical experiences with mildly distressed clients under close supervision should enable the trainee to acquire adequate skills, a rudimentary theoretical model, and understanding of the process. This should result in some degree of confidence and efficacy on the part of the trainee. As this occurs, we are approaching the transition from Level 1 to Level 2. To encourage this transition, the supervisor needs to carefully redirect the trainee's attention from adequate performance of skills, interventions, and so forth, to attending more to the client's conceptual and affective experience. At the same time, encouraging an appropriate increase in autonomy should be a goal as well as providing less structure for supervision. This will set the stage for movement into Level 2.

Appropriate supervisors for Level 1 trainees will have advanced in their own development to at least Level 2 (see following discussion). Often, advanced trainees under the supervision of a professional can do an excellent job of providing a facilitative supervision environment for beginners. Having only recently dealt with these same issues, Level 2 counselors (as supervisors) can empathize with and accurately convey information to Level 1 trainees in supervision.

Level 2

In our experience, what Stoltenberg and Delworth (1987) conceptualize as the Level 2 trainee roughly coincides with advanced practicum status (e.g., third or fourth semester of *supervised* practicum) at least for domains that have been the target of training. Of course, in other domains receiving less (or no) attention, the trainee will remain at Level 1 and should be supervised accordingly. By Level 2, however, the trainee has mastered most of the basic listening and attending skills and has experienced some success in his or her work with clients (intervention skills competence domain). At the same time, however, the supervision process has identified not only the trainee's strengths, but also his or her weaknesses, as the trainee struggles to understand why he or she is unable to be effective with all clients. The trainee now begins to realize the real limitations of the counseling process, and these struggles may have negative effects on his or her level of motivation.

The primary conflict for the trainee at this level is a vacillation between dependency and autonomy. Trainees become more assertive in developing their own ideas in intervening with clients and may even resist discussing certain cases if they suspect that the supervisor will disagree or suggest on an alternative approach. At the same time, however, the trainee remains dependent on the supervisor for advice and direction in cases in which he or she still lacks the experience with certain client issues or types.

This struggle also affects the motivation level of the trainee. Exposure to more difficult client types and problems and subsequent lack of effectiveness with all clients results in the questioning of the trainee's skills and shakes his or her level of confidence. As a result, motivation level fluctuates as the trainee becomes discouraged or distant with clients one week and then may exhibit a high enthusiasm the next week. Some students at this stage also begin to question their career decision to become a therapist and may distance themselves cognitively or affectively from the therapeutic process.

At this stage, the trainee exhibits less of a self-focus and is able to attend more to the client and empathize with the client's emotional experience. This focus, however, can result in frustration for the trainee, as the complexity of the counseling process has become more apparent. The danger for the trainee at this point is overidentification with the client to the extent of being unable to provide effective interventions, along with the potential to engage in countertransference reactions. The trainee may become enmeshed in the client's viewpoint, losing the objectivity necessary to provide effective treatment.

The characteristics of the Level 2 counselor are especially apparent in the domain of *intervention skills competence* as the trainee is increasingly comfortable with a wide array of intervention skills, although these skills are not well integrated within an overriding theoretical orientation or conceptual schema. Trainees will make repeated requests for more experience with diverse client types and problems yet fail to acknowledge or resist supervisor recommendations to expand their repertoire. *Interpersonal assessment* may be severely limited due to the trainee's strong focus on the client's perspective. The trainee may be unable to separate responses to clients based on accurate perceptions from countertransferance reactions and may exhibit a lack of awareness in regard to this process. Whereas *client conceptualizations* are based on a more complete understanding of the client's perspective, they will also be largely based on the client's viewpoint without integration of other sources of information (e.g., objective psychological test data) as discrepancies or inconsistencies in information gathered are ignored or overlooked.

The foregoing characteristics of the Level 2 trainee have led Stoltenberg and Delworth (1987) to characterize this stage as one of "trial and tribulation." The task of the supervisor with Level 2 trainees is to provide a fine balance between structure and support and a degree of autonomy and challenge in fostering the independence and confidence level of the trainee. Highly structured directives and didactic advice are likely to be met by resistance and even anger by the trainee for "always telling me what to do." It is important, however, for the supervisor to remain aware of the overriding concern of client welfare. Thus, the supervisor must be prepared to articulate his or her rationale for providing direction in certain client cases and must respond to trainee resistance and anger in a nondefensive, facilitative manner.

Client assignment should reflect a blend of cases in which the trainee exhibits confidence and independence, with more difficult, challenging cases requiring the application of underdeveloped skills and exposure to diverse client types and problems.

It is also extremely important to monitor the trainee's progress during this stage optimally by viewing session videotapes or by direct observation. In our experience, it is not uncommon for supervisors to back off on these activities as advanced trainees are viewed as "knowing what they are doing." Given the issues characteristic of the Level 2 trainee, supervisees may selectively present client cases with which they feel successful and avoid those with which they have difficulties as manifestations of autonomy or lack of self-awareness. In some cases, trainees may actively avoid discussion of client cases in which they suspect the supervisor will challenge their choice of interventions. Thus, at this stage it is not adequate to simply respond to what trainees may appropriately present as needing direction on and allow complete autonomy in all cases through simple discussion of ongoing clients or monitoring of progress notes.

In order to enhance growth, trainees must be challenged to articulate their rationales for responding to various client concerns, and the cases for which supervisees may resist input, feel uncertain about, or become angry and impatient with may be the most important foci of the supervision session. Process comments by supervisors can increase self-awareness on the part of trainees enmeshed in only the client's viewpoint. These are consistent with Loganbill et al.'s (1982) description of "catalytic interventions," which are intended to "stir things up" and increase trainee's awareness. Conceptual interventions in which trainees are required to articulate alternative intervention plans or varying conceptualizations of the same client case by supervisors help to challenge and expand new information by trainees (see Table 12.2 for descriptions of categories of interventions across levels).

Despite the difficult issues experienced by supervisees at Level 2, research studies suggest that trainees at this level begin to demonstrate an increased readiness and openness to discussion and processing of personal issues of self-awareness, defensiveness, transference-countertransference, and the supervisory relationship (Heppner & Roehlke, 1984; McNeill & Worthen, 1989). A recent phenomenological investigation of "good" supervision events by Worthen and McNeill (1996) found that intermediate supervisees indeed experienced a fragile and fluctuating level of confidence and a generalized state of disillusionment and demoralization with the efficacy of providing therapeutic interventions and were anxious and sensitive to supervisor evaluation. Trainees in this study felt that their anxiety level decreased when supervisors helped to "normalize" their struggles as part of their ongoing development, and this type of intervention was often communicated in the form of a personal self-disclosure. They also characterized the supervisory relationship as one experienced as empathic, nonjudgmental, and validating, with encouragement to explore and experiment. These conditions appeared to set the stage for nondefensive analysis as their confidence was strengthened. In addition, participants reported an increased perception of therapeutic complexity, an expanded ability for therapeutic conceptualizing and intervening, a positive anticipation to reengage in previous difficulties and issues they had struggled with, and a strengthening of the supervisory alliance.

The style or manner in which a supervisor points out or confronts Level 2 issues may vary depending on the degree of sensitivity or defensiveness on the part of the trainee and in this sense requires more advanced skills or experience on the part of the supervisor, perhaps analogous to the development of therapeutic timing and acumen on the part of counselors. As a result, the Level 2 trainee may provide too much of a challenge for inexperienced supervisors or as an initial supervisory assignment for supervisors in training.

Level 3

Stoltenberg and Delworth (1987) have characterized developmental Level 3 as "the calm after the storm" as the trainee is relatively free of the Level 2 fluctuations and is able to focus on further growth and respond to challenge within and across domains. This increased stability most often facilitates rapid development and often coincides with trainees' experience (in some domains) during the latter part of the predoctoral internship. It is further promoted by the engagement in full-time clinical work and increased intensive supervision. Motivation at this stage is again high and stable. Although the trainee may experience doubts in his or her work, these doubts are not disabling, and commitment to

Table 12.2 Supervision Across Levels

Level	Supervision Environment	
I	*General considerations*—Provide structure and keep anxiety at manageable levels. Supervisor perceived as expert and role model. Confidence in trainee develops in response to greater clarity of theory/process and skills. Encourage early development of autonomy (instruction often easier than problem solving). Encourage appropriate risk taking.	
	Client assignment	Mild presenting problems or "maintenance cases."
	Interventions	Facilitative (supportive, encouraging) Prescriptive (suggest approaches, etc.) Conceptual (some, tie theory-DX-TX) Catalytic (late Level 1, see Level 2)
	Mechanisms	Observation (video or live) Skills training Role-playing Interpret dynamics (limited, client or trainee) Readings Group supervision Appropriate balance of ambiguity/conflict Address strengths, then weaknesses Closely monitor clients
II	*General considerations*—Less structure provided, encourage more autonomy particularly during periods of "regression" or stress. Clarify ambivalence, continue modeling, but less of a didactic focus. May see trainee reactance against supervision/supervisor.	
	Client assignment	More difficult clients with more severe presenting problems (e.g., personality disorders), shakes confidence.
	Interventions	Facilitative Prescriptive—used only occasionally Confrontive—now able to handle confrontation Conceptual—introduce more alternative views Catalytic—process comments, highlight countertransference, affective reactions to client or supervisor
	Mechanisms	Observation (video or live) Role-playing—although less important Interpret dynamics—see catalytic above, parallel process Group supervision Broaden clientele
III	*General considerations*—Most structure provided by trainee, more focus on personal/professional integration, career decisions. Don't assume Level 3 for all domains. Focus on bringing up lower-level domains and encourage development toward Level 3i. Assess for "pseudo 3's" and alert trainee to parallel process (if supervising other trainees).	
	Interventions	Facilitative Confrontive—occasionally necessary Conceptual—from personal orientation Catalytic—in response to blocks or stagnation
	Mechanisms	Peer supervision Group supervision Strive for integration

the profession as well as to the further development of a professional identity is strong. At this level, the trainee is open to personal exploration of motivations toward becoming a therapist and the implications of these motivations on therapeutic interactions.

Level 3 trainees exhibit a strong sense of autonomy in their clinical work but appropriately consult with the supervisor when necessary, or when seeking further professional growth. In terms of self- and other awareness, trainees demonstrate a higher level of insight into personal strengths and weaknesses and address areas of weakness with increased confidence and nondefensiveness. Accurate empathy with clients (first emerging in Level 2) remains a focus but is tempered by an ability to pull back in an objective manner and process reactions, feelings, and thoughts. Thus, the Level 3 therapist is now able to fully access and utilize the array of information available from the client, personal responses to the client, and theoretical and empirical information developed in training to date.

Level 3 trainees possess a variety of intervention skills across diverse client types but are still challenged to better integrate interventions with treatment plans and client conceptualizations in order to be flexible within sessions. At this time, trainees may also seek out additional training with new or unfamiliar techniques. It is important to remember, however, that they may function at Level 1 in these new areas if they are significantly different from prior training experiences. Client conceptualizations are reflective of a greater complexity and integration of diverse sources of information. A conceptualization of one client may differ from another with the same diagnostic label, accounting for individual unique client patterns.

The supervisor of the Level 3 trainee avoids an intrusive and overly structured supervisory environment. The primary task in the supervision of these trainees is to carefully assess consistency in performance across domains (particularly those in which the trainee is functional at Levels 1 or 2), identify any deficits, and work toward integration across domains. Thus, careful monitoring of client sessions, progress notes, written conceptualizations, assessment reports, and so forth remains important. As a result of increased levels of insight and self-awareness, supervisees at Level 3 not only display an openness, but also a preference to further acknowledge and confront issues of transference-countertransference, therapy-supervision overlap, and parallel processes in supervisory and client relationships (McNeill & Worthen, 1989; Rabinowitz, Heppner, & Roelke, 1986). It remains important for the supervisor to establish a supportive supervisory environment in which confrontation is not avoided. Joint exploration of personal issues affecting therapy is necessary in order to fully examine the implications of these issues. Gently leading trainees to personal self-discoveries has more impact than simply imparting information. Worthen and McNeill (1996) found that intern-level supervisees exhibited a basic sense of confidence and autonomy and that inadequacies were identified as domain specific. Interestingly, they also reported previous unrewarding supervision experiences, perhaps resulting in an aversion to overt evaluation and a strong desire for more rewarding supervision. In common with lesser experienced trainees, the interns also viewed good supervision as characterized by an empathic, nonjudgmental relationship with encouragement to experiment and explore, and they were pleased when their struggles were normalized. As a result, positive outcomes of good supervision events were similar to those of their less experienced peers. In addition, their confidence was affirmed and they reported an increased impetus for refining a professional identity.

Given the issues apparent in the Level 3 trainee, it is important to match these trainees with a supervisor whose own functioning is at or above the level of the trainee so as to not impede development. Supervisees at this level may also look toward supervisors for advice concerning professional development (e.g., job searches).

Empirical Research

Stoltenberg et al. (1994) exhaustively reviewed the supervision research reported in the literature since Worthington's (1987) article. They examined the methodology used in the 50 or so studies and summarized the results. More specifically, however, they carefully reviewed the 12 studies that included in their methodology the possibility of examination of levels of counselor development or, minimally, levels of counseling experience. Of these 12 studies, only 2 reported finding no effect for experience. One of these two studies (Borders, Fong, & Neimeyer, 1986) had a restricted range of experience levels for the supervisees who participated (functionally masters students). The other study (Ellis, Dell, & Good, 1988) only allowed for an indirect examination of levels of participant experience. The remaining studies reviewed, however, reflected differences in counselors as a function of experience (or measured developmental level) from beginning through intermediate to postdoctoral (e.g., Cummings, Hallberg, Martin, Slemon, & Hiebert, 1990; Hillerbrand & Claiborn, 1990; Martin, Slemon, Hiebert, Hallberg, & Cummings, 1989; McNeill, Stoltenberg, & Pierce, 1985; Robyak, Goodyear, Prange, & Donham, 1986; Winter & Holloway, 1991). Stoltenberg et al. (1994) reported that

In agreement with Worthington's (1987) conclusions, we can say there is support for general developmental models, perceptions of supervisors and supervisees are consistent with developmental theories, the behavior of supervisors changes as counselors gain experience, and the supervision relationship changes as counselors gain experience. (p. 419)

An interesting study by Tracey, Ellickson, and Sherry (1989) highlighted the importance of attending to specific domains when choosing supervision environments. In their study, beginning and advanced practicum students viewed videotapes of supervision environments designed to vary in terms of structure (high or low structure provided by supervisor) and content (suicidal client or relationship issues). Their results indicated that all of the participants preferred highly structured supervision (directive teaching and prescription) in response to the suicidal condition (low experience for all trainees). In reaction to the relationship condition, however, beginners continued to prefer high structure, but more advanced trainees preferred low-structured supervision. This difference highlights the importance of not assuming advanced level of development across topics and domains, but rather reinforces the need to assess specific developmental levels for trainees.

A recent study utilizing single-subject designs by Bear and Kivlighan (1994) provided additional support for the IDM. An experienced supervisor worked with both a beginning and an advanced supervisee. In response to the beginning trainee, who was more dependent, the supervisor was more structured and directive. For the advanced trainee, who responded more autonomously, the supervisor was more collaborative and collegial. The directive and structured supervisor interventions produced more deep-elaborative information processing by the beginner whereas this preferred type of processing was stimulated by the collegial or consultative supervisor interventions for the advanced trainee.

Although issues of gender, multicultural, and gay and lesbian supervision have been discussed in the literature (e.g., Stoltenberg & Delworth, 1987; Stoltenberg, McNeill, & Crethar, 1995), few empirical investigations have been conducted to examine their interaction with developmental models (see Stoltenberg, McNeill, & Crethar, 1994, for a review). Given the importance of these issues, readers are encouraged to examine the general guidelines provided by Stoltenberg and Delworth (1987), and those of Vasquez and McKinley (1982) for ethnic and racial minority trainees. In addition, recommendations regarding the influence of gender issues on training and supervision have been addressed by Brodsky (1980) and Gilbert (1992), and for gay and lesbian clients by Buhrke and Douce (1991), which have relevance for supervision and training.

Future Directions

As Stoltenberg et al. (1994) point out in their review of the literature related to counselor development, research investigating developmental constructs would benefit from the use and development of measures specifically designed for the supervision process, as well as from measures designed to address constructs relevant to individual supervision models. More diverse research paradigms including longitudinal designs, case studies, and qualitative methodologies are also needed in the investigation of counselor development. It is also imperative that any investigations into counselor growth or development control or account for trainee developmental level or differences in experience (although this remains a crude index). Research studies need to clearly explicate how "beginning," "intermediate," and "advanced" trainees are operationally defined.

Developmental theorists must also begin to attend and account for the unique training and supervisory needs of trainees representative of diversity in terms of race, ethnicity, gender, and sexual identity. For example, the influence of a trainee's level of ethnic identity on the development of counseling skills as suggested by Vasquez and McKinley (1982) has yet to be empirically investigated. In addition, a number of authors (e.g., Hunt, 1987; Zuniga, 1987) recommend that the variety of issues that diverse trainees face in training programs, such as racism, backlash as a result of "political correctness," and hostile environments, should be dealt with in the supervisory relationship. Thus, it is incumbent on all supervisors to take responsibility to create a supervisory relationship and environment in which these issues are openly dealt with (McNeill, Hom, & Perez, 1995). To facilitate this task, supervisors must be knowledgeable in regard to issues of diversity in working with trainees and clientele. Finally, Worthen and McNeill's (1996) innovative investigation into the phenomenological experiences of supervisees suggests a greater role for the supervisory relationship in developmental theorizing, as trainees in this study frequently cited the importance of their relationship with their supervisors as crucial to the process of development.

CONCLUSION

Refinement of developmental models of supervision continues as does the empirical investigation of the utility of this perspective. Although the research to date is generally supportive of the tenets of the IDM, considerably more research is necessary to validate specific counselor-trainee characteristics according to level as well as the recommended supervisory environments. Recent expansions of the model for other areas of professional practice (Stoltenberg, 1993; Stoltenberg et al., 1997) also need to be investigated. In addition, work should continue to explore the interpersonal influence mechanisms used for different types of trainees over time (cf. Stoltenberg et al., 1995).

Supervision, like psychotherapy, is a complex undertaking. Rather than "shooting from the hip" or relying on simple formulations of complicated processes, practitioners and researchers of clinical supervision need constantly to attend to the specifics of supervisee developmental level(s) and the concomitant supervision environments. Consistent with Kiesler's (1966) recommendations for psychotherapy research, Stoltenberg et al. (1994) suggested that "Efforts should be directed at determining which level of supervisor using which supervisory interventions is most effective in supervising which level of trainee at a given point in time working with what types of clients in what contexts" (p. 422).

REFERENCES

Bartlett, W. E. (1983). A multidimension framework for the analysis of supervision of counseling. *The Counseling Psychologist, 11,* 9–17.

Bear, T. M., & Kivlighan, D. M., Jr. (1994). Single-subject examination of the process of supervision of beginning and advanced supervisees. *Professional Psychology: Research and Practice, 25,* 450–457.

Bernard, J. M., & Goodyear, R. K. (1992). *Fundamentals of clinical supervision.* Boston: Allyn & Bacon.

Blocher, D. H. (1983). Toward a developmental approach to counseling supervision. *The Counseling Psychologist, 11,* 27–34.

Borders, L. D., Fong, M. L., & Neimeyer, G. J. (1986). Ego development and counseling ability during training. *Counselor Education and Supervision, 29,* 71–83.

Brodsky, A. (1980). Sex role issues in the supervision of therapy. In A. K. Hess (Ed.), *Psychotherapy supervision: Theory research and practice* (pp. 509–524). New York: Wiley.

Buhrke, R. A., & Douce, L. A. (1991). Training issues for counseling psychologists in working with lesbian women and gay men. *The Counseling Psychologist, 19,* 216–234.

Cummings, A. L., Hallberg, E. T., Martin, J., Slemon, A., & Hiebert, B. (1990). Implications of counselor conceptualizations for counselor education. *Counselor Education and Supervision, 30*(2), 120–134.

Eckstein, R., & Wallerstein, R. (1972). *The teaching and learning of psychotherapy* (2nd ed.). New York: International Universities Press.

Eichenfield, G., & Stoltenberg, C. D. (1996). The sublevel 1 trainee: Some developmental difficulties encountered with counselor training. *The Clinical Supervisor, 14,* 25–37.

Ellis, M. V., Dell, D. M., & Good, G. E. (1988). Counselor trainee's perceptions of supervisor roles: Two studies testing the dimensionality of supervision. *Journal of Counseling Psychology, 35,* 315–324.

Fleming, J. (1953). The role of supervision in psychiatric training. *Bulletin of the Menninger Clinic, 17,* 157–159.

Gilbert, L. A. (1992). Gender and counseling psychology: Current knowledge and directions for research and social action. In S. D. Brown & R. W. Lent (Eds.), *Handbook of counseling psychology* (2nd ed., pp. 383–418). New York: Wiley.

Harvey, O. J., Hunt, D. E., & Schroder, H. M. (1961). *Conceptual systems and personality organization.* New York: Wiley.

Heppner, P. P., & Roehlke, H. J. (1984). Differences among supervisees at different levels of training: Implications for a developmental model of supervision. *Journal of Counseling Psychology, 31,* 76–90.

Hess, A. K. (1986). Growth in supervision: Stages of supervisee and supervisor development. *The Clinical Supervisor, 4,* 51–67.

Hillerbrand, E., & Claiborn, C. D. (1990). Examining reasoning skill differences between expert and novice counselors. *Journal of Counseling and Development, 68,* 684–691.

Hogan, R. A. (1964). Issues and approaches in supervision. *Psychotherapy: Theory, Research, and Practice, 1*, 139–141.

Holloway, E. L. (1987). Developmental models of supervision: Is it development? *Professional Psychology: Research and Practice, 18*(3), 209–216.

Holloway, E. L. (1992). Supervision: A way of teaching and learning. In S. D. Brown & R. W. Lent (Eds.), *Handbook of counseling psychology* (2nd ed., pp. 177–214). New York: Wiley.

Hunt, D. E. (1971). *Matching models in education: The coordination of teaching methods with student characteristics.* Toronto: Ontario Institute for Studies in Education.

Hunt, P. (1987). Black clients: Implications for supervision of trainees. *Psychotherapy: Theory, Research and Practice, 24*, 1094–119.

Kiesler, D. J. (1966). Some myths of psychotherapy research and the search for a paradigm. *Psychological Bulletin, 65*, 110–136.

Littrel, J. M., Lee-Boden, N., Lorenz, J. (1979). A developmental framework for counseling supervision. *Counselor Education and Supervision, 19*, 129–136.

Loganbill, C., Hardy, E., & Delworth, U. (1982). Supervision: A conceptual model. *The Counseling Psychologist, 10*(1), 3–42.

Martin, J. S., Slemon, A. G., Hiebert, B., Hallberg, E. T., & Cummings, A. L. (1989). Conceptualizations of novice and experienced counselors. *Journal of Counseling Psychology, 36*, 393–396.

McNeill, B. W., Hom, K. L., & Perez, J. A. (1995). The training and supervisory needs of racial/ethnic minority students. *Journal of Multicultural Counseling and Development, 23*, 246–258.

McNeill, B. W., Stoltenberg, C. D., & Pierce, R. A. (1985). Supervisees' perceptions of their development: A test of the counselor complexity model. *Journal of Counseling Psychology, 32*(4), 630–633.

McNeill, B. W., & Worthen, V. (1989). The parallel process in psychotherapy supervision. *Professional Psychology: Research and Practice, 20*, 329–333.

Mueller, W. J., & Kell, B. L. (1972). *Coping with conflict: Supervising counselors and psychotherapists.* New York: Appleton-Century-Crofts.

Rabinowitz, F. E., Heppner, P. P., & Roehlke, H. J. (1986). Descriptive study of process outcome variables of supervision over time. *Journal of Counseling Psychology, 33*(3), 292–300.

Ralph, N. B., (1980). Learning psychotherapy: A developmental perspective. *Psychiatry, 43*, 243–250.

Robyak, J. E., Goodyear, R. K., Prange, M. E., & Donham, G. (1986). Effects of gender, supervision, and presenting problems on practicum students' preference for interpersonal power bases. *Journal of Counseling Psychology, 33*(2), 159–163.

Russell, R. K., Crimmings, A. M., & Lent, R. W. (1984). Counselor training and supervision: Theory and research. In S. D. Brown & R. W. Lent (Eds.), *Handbook of counseling psychology* (pp. 625–681). New York: Wiley.

Stoltenberg, C. D. (1981). Approaching supervision from a developmental perspective: The counselor complexity model. *Journal of Counseling Psychology, 28*(1), 59–65.

Stoltenberg, C. D. (1993). Supervising consultants in training: An application of a model of supervision. *Journal of Counseling and Development, 72*, 131–138.

Stoltenberg, C. D., & Delworth, U. (1987). *Supervising counselors and therapists.* San Francisco: Jossey-Bass.

Stoltenberg, C. D., & Delworth, U. (1988). Developmental models of supervision: It is development-response to Holloway. *Professional Psychology: Research and Practice, 19*(2), 134–137.

Stoltenberg, C. D., McNeill, B. W., & Crethar, H. C. (1994). Changes in supervision as counseling and therapists gain experience: A review. *Professional Psychology: Research & Practice, 25*, 416–449.

Stoltenberg, C. D., McNeill, B. W., & Crethar, H. C. (1995). Persuasion and development in counselor supervision. *The Counseling Psychologist, 23*, 633–648.

Stoltenberg, C. D., McNeill, B. W., & Delworth, U. (1997). *IDM: The Integrated Development Model of clinical supervision.* San Francisco: Jossey-Bass.

Tracey, T. J., Ellickson, J. L., & Sherry, P. (1989). Reactance in relation to different supervisory environments and counselor development. *Journal of Counseling Psychology, 36*(3), 336–344.

Vasquez, M. J., & McKinley, D. (1982). A conceptual model—reactions and extension. *The Counseling Psychologist, 10*(1), 59–63.

Winter, M., & Holloway, E. L. (1991). Relation of trainee experience, conceptual level, and supervisor approach to selection of audiotaped counseling passages. *The Clinical Supervisor, 9,* 87–103.

Worthen, V., & McNeill, B. W. (1996). A phenomenological investigation of "good" supervision events. *Journal of Counseling Psychology, 43,* 25–34.

Worthington, E. L., Jr. (1984). Empirical investigation of supervision of counselors as they gain experience. *Journal of Counseling Psychology, 31,* 63–75.

Worthington, E. L., Jr. (1987). Changes in supervision as counselors and supervisors gain experience. *Professional Psychology: Research and Practice, 18*(3), 189–208.

Zuniga, M. E. (1987). Mexican-American clinical training: A pilot project. *Journal of Social Work Education, 23,* 11–20.

CHAPTER 13

Integrative Approaches
to Psychotherapy Supervision

JOHN C. NORCROSS
University of Scranton
RICHARD P. HALGIN
University of Massachusetts

> Psychotherapists who will be extant in the year 2000 will have to be . . . enormously more broadly trained than the subspecialized people turned out today.
> —Gardner Murphy, *Psychology in the Year 2000*

Psychotherapy supervision is a complex and demanding activity, and the introduction of integrative perspectives does nothing to relieve the pressure on supervisors and supervisees. On the contrary, the supervision—and practice—of integrative psychotherapy seems to require more from trainees and their mentors than does single-school therapy systems. Not only must the conventional difficulties in producing competent clinicians be resolved, but an integrative approach must also help students to acquire mastery of multiple treatment combinations and to adjust their therapeutic approach to fit the needs of their clients. Nonetheless, if we are to train psychotherapists more broadly than, in Gardner Murphy's words, "the subspecialized people we turn out today," an intensive apprenticeship with integrative supervisors is needed (Norcross, 1988).

Integrative psychotherapy supervision thus constitutes one of our most formidable challenges and, simultaneously, one of our most promising opportunities. In this chapter, we begin by defining psychotherapy integration and delineating various objectives of integrative supervision. Moving from these general considerations to our own form of prescriptive eclectic supervision, we address, in turn, the principles, pragmatics, and potential liabilities of integrative approaches to supervision.

DEFINING PSYCHOTHERAPY INTEGRATION

There are numerous pathways to the integration of the psychotherapies and thus multiple approaches to integrative supervision. The three predominant pathways at present are common factors, technical eclecticism, and theoretical integration. All three are characterized by a desire to look beyond the confines of single theories and the techniques traditionally associated with them, but they do so in rather different ways and at different levels (Norcross & Newman, 1992).

Common Factors

The common factors approach seeks to determine the core ingredients that different therapies share, with the eventual goal of creating more parsimonious and efficacious treatments based on those commonalities. This search is predicated on the belief that commonalities are more important in accounting for therapy outcome than are the unique factors that differentiate among them. The writings of Jerome Frank (1982; Frank & Frank, 1991) and Sol Garfield (1980, 1992) have been among the most influential contributions to this approach.

Judging from experience and the literature, little psychotherapy supervision is conducted from an explicit common factors perspective. What can be gleaned is that supervisors enjoin their trainees to cultivate the consensual therapeutic commonalities, such as development of a therapeutic alliance, opportunity for catharsis, acquisition and practice of new behaviors, and fostering positive expectancies (Grencavage & Norcross, 1990; Weinberger, 1995). As Goldfried (1980, p. 996) argues:

> To the extent that clinicians of varying orientations are able to arrive at a common set of strategies, it is likely that what emerges will consist of robust phenomena, as they have managed to survive the distortions imposed by the therapists' varying theoretical biases.

In specifying what is common across disparate orientations, we may also be selecting what works best among them.

The dilemma is that one cannot function "commonly" or "nonspecifically" in therapy or training (Omer & London, 1988). Hence we must operationalize specific clinical behaviors associated with common factors for purposes of supervision and education. Until such time, integrative supervision from a common factors perspective is largely relegated to the prevalent, but still frequently unheeded, reminder that the so-called common factors in psychotherapy, principally the therapeutic relationship, account for more outcome variance than do technical interventions (Lambert, 1992; Lambert & Ogles, Chapter 24, this volume).

More than commonalities are evident across the therapies; there are unique or specific factors attributable to different therapies as well. One of the important achievements of psychotherapy research, observe Lambert and Bergin (1992), is demonstration of the differential effectiveness of psychotherapies with specific disorders and with specific types of people. Integrative supervision will thus emphasize those factors common across therapies highlighted in research while capitalizing on the contributions of specific techniques. The proper use of common *and* specific factors will probably be most effective for clients and most congenial to practitioners (Garfield, 1992). That is, we will gradually integrate by combining fundamental similarities and useful differences across the schools.

Technical Eclecticism

Eclectics seek to improve their ability to select the best treatments for the person and the problem on the basis of clinical experience and empirical research. The focus is on predicting for whom interventions will work: The foundation is actuarial rather than theoretical (Lazarus, Beutler, & Norcross, 1992). Proponents of technical eclecticism use procedures drawn from different sources without necessarily subscribing to the theories that spawned them, whereas the theoretical integrationist draws from diverse systems that may be epistemologically or ontologically incompatible.

In practice and in supervision, this integrative approach is widely known as technical eclecticism (Lazarus, 1976, 1989, 1992), systematic eclecticism (Beutler, 1983; Beutler & Clarkin, 1990), pragmatic blending (Halgin, 1986, 1989), or prescriptive eclecticism (Diamond, Havens, & Jones, 1978; Norcross, 1994). Our own approach to psychotherapy supervision and the bulk of this chapter emanate from prescriptive eclecticism, which endeavors to customize the technical interventions and the relationship stances to the unique needs of each individual. This customizing or prescriptive matching, it should be emphasized, applies with equal cogency to trainees assisting their clients and to supervisors assisting their trainees. Eclectic supervisors are continually involved in a parallel process of tailoring their supervision to the individual student and of enhancing their student's ability to tailor psychological treatment to individual clients.

Theoretical Integration

In this pathway to psychotherapy integration, two or more therapies are synthesized in the hope that the result will be better than the constituent therapies alone. Theoretical integration aspires to more than a simple combination; it seeks an emergent theory that is more than the sum of its parts, and that leads to new directions for practice and research. As the name implies, there is an emphasis on integrating the underlying *theories* of psychotherapy—what London (1986) has eloquently labeled "theory smushing"— along with the integration of therapy techniques from each—what London has called "technique melding." The various proposals to integrate psychoanalytic and behavioral theories illustrate this direction, as do grander schemes to meld all the major systems of psychotherapy.

Theoretical integration refers to a commitment to a conceptual or theoretical creation beyond eclecticism's pragmatic blending of procedures. Or to take a culinary metaphor (cited in Norcross & Napolitano, 1986, p. 253): "The eclectic selects among several dishes to constitute a meal, the integrationist creates new dishes by combining different ingredients." A corollary to this distinction, rooted in the theoretical integrator's early stage of development, is that current practice is largely eclectic; theory integration represents a promissory note for the future.

In supervision, the distinctions among technical eclecticism and theoretical integration are not always apparent or functional. Few supervisees receiving broad-band supervision would be able to distinguish among them (Norcross & Arkowitz, 1992). Moreover, we hasten to add that these integrative strategies are not mutually exclusive. No technical eclectic can totally disregard theory, and no theoretical integrationist can ignore the technique. Although our own supervision involves the systematic selection from an array of interpersonal and technical interventions spawned by different theoretical traditions, our work also involves transtheoretical melding of the commonalities among these different traditions. In the words of Wachtel (1991, p. 44):

> The habits and boundaries associated with the various schools are hard to eclipse, and for most of us integration remains more a goal than a constant daily reality. Eclecticism in practice and integration in aspiration is an accurate description of what most of us in the integrative movement do much of the time.

Although our clear focus in this chapter is prescriptive eclectic supervision, we employ the term *integrative* throughout. We do so in recognition of (a) the term's more inclusive connotation and representation of the psychotherapy integration movement, (b) its broader acceptance and use in clinical circles, and (c) its emerging preference among eclectics as their self-identification (Norcross & Prochaska, 1988).

DELINEATING THE OBJECTIVES OF INTEGRATIVE SUPERVISION

Before considering the principles and pragmatics of integrative supervision, we and other trainers are confronted with a critical decision with respect to supervision objectives. The major choice is whether the objective of the supervision is to train students to competence in a single psychotherapy system and subsequent referral of some clients to more appropriate treatments, or whether the objective is to train students to accommodate most of these clients themselves by virtue of their competence in multimethod, multimodality psychotherapy (Norcross, Beutler, & Clarkin, 1990). Either integrative alternative would probably constitute an improvement over current training paradigms.

Single-System Competence and Systematic Referral

A modest but still significantly integrative objective in psychotherapy supervision is to ensure students' competence in a single therapy system, say, for example, psychodynamic, cognitive, or experiential, for those clients and problems for whom that therapy system is indicated and then ensure their ability to make systematic referral for clients and problems for which that therapy system is contraindicated. Psychotherapists can function effectively in a single and comfortable theoretical system providing they have the ethics and talent to discriminate which clients can benefit from their preferred system and which cannot. Referral of the latter group of clients can then systematically be made to clinicians competent to offer the indicated service.

The two essential tasks for the supervisor here are to train students to recognize the respective contraindications of their single psychotherapy system and to educate them in making informed referral decisions. Helping single-system advocates to relinquish clients for whom another approach is better suited will entail attention to both the prescriptions of the empirical research and the limitations of their theoretical commitments (Norcross et al., 1990).

Many therapy supervisors routinely adhere to such an integrative approach without recognizing its integrative objectives. Frequently the "treatment of choice" is that associated with a particular brand of therapy, for example, cognitive therapy for panic disorder, or conjoint sessions for marital conflict, or psychodynamic therapy for personality disorders. The primary problem is not from narrow-gauge therapists per se, but from therapists who impose that narrowness on their clients (Stricker, 1988). Furthermore, competence in pure-form or single-theory psychotherapies is a necessary prerequisite to integration. As a movement, psychotherapy integration relies on the constituent elements provided by the respective "brand-name" therapies—the clinical methods, the interpersonal stances, and the research findings. So do students rely on single-system therapies in reaching their integration; after all, one cannot integrate what one does not know.

Integrative Practice

A broader and more ambitious undertaking in supervision is to aim for student competence in integrative psychotherapy wherein the student is able to provide the indicated treatment for most clients. Of critical importance to this decision is the assumption that students can learn to practice several models competently. Although we are uncertain whether most mental health trainees are capable of acquiring such skill, especially those trainees in 2-year graduate programs, plentiful evidence has accumulated to suggest that it is possible for a given therapist to selectively apply in an effective way methods drawn from different perspectives (e.g., Beutler & Consoli, 1992; Hardy & Shapiro, 1985; Lazarus, 1992; Prochaska & DiClemente, 1992). Our own training experiences over the last decade also affirm the possibility of producing competent integrative psychotherapists, although additional time and effort are required in light of the more ambitious training goals.

THE OPTIMAL TIMING FOR INTEGRATIVE TRAINING

The previous section on choosing between single-system competence and systematic referral, on the one hand, and competence in integrative psychotherapy, on the other, was organized around varying objectives of integrative supervision. This choice point can also be organized around the temporal sequence of students' professional development.

The strong consensus is that the sophisticated adoption of an integrative perspective occurs *after* learning specific therapy systems and techniques (see Andrews Norcross, & Halgin, 1992; Beutler et al., 1987; Guest & Beutler, 1988; Halgin, 1988; Norcross, 1986; Robertson, 1986). Thus, at the beginning of graduate work, supervision would focus primarily on competence in a single system of therapy and systematic referral, whereas in the later stages of professional development, supervision may opt for integrative practice.

From the beginning of psychotherapy training and supervision, however, students would be exposed to all therapeutic approaches with minimal judgment being made as to their relative contributions to truth. Theoretical paradigms would be introduced as tentative and explanatory notions, varying in level of experience, goals, and methodology. Multiple systems of psychotherapy would be presented critically, but within a paradigm of comparison and integration (see Prochaska & Norcross, 1994, for example). Integrative frameworks and informed pluralism would thereby be introduced at the beginning of training (Halgin, 1985), but formal supervision in integrative psychotherapy would occur later in the sequence.

"Deep structure" integration will take considerable time and probably come about only after the therapist has had years of clinical experience (Messer, 1992; Norcross & Newman, 1992). Expert psychotherapists represent their domain on a semantically and conceptually deeper level than do novices. Conceptual learning about psychotherapy integration is probably necessary but not sufficient to achieve a deep structure integration. For therapists to integrate at a deeper level requires that they first understand and integrate within each individual therapy and, only then, across therapies. Psychotherapy experience and disciplined reflection on that experience is needed to attain a mature and abiding synthesis.

Psychotherapy integration, in other words, may take two broad forms that are differentially accessible to novice versus expert therapists (Schacht, 1991). The first form, accessible to neophytes, emphasizes conceptual products that enter the educational arena as content additions to the curriculum. The second form of integration, largely limited to more experienced therapists, emphasizes a special mode of thinking. This form enters the educational arena through accumulated and supervised experiences that promote fluent performance and creative metacognitive skills.

In the remainder of this chapter, we address a specific form of integration supervision—prescriptive eclecticism—in the context of assisting advanced psychotherapy students toward the development of competence in integrative practice. As mentioned earlier, this supervision assumes that the trainee has been exposed to the range of theories and techniques that underpin psychotherapy integration, has at least 2 years of clinical experience, and has acquired a rudimentary understanding of differential treatment selection and psychotherapy integration.

CARDINAL PRINCIPLES OF INTEGRATIVE SUPERVISION

Customize Supervision to the Individual Student

In prescriptive eclecticism, we are centrally concerned with tailoring treatment intervention and interpersonal stances to client needs. Just as we ask our students to be prescriptive in their clinical work, we, too, should customize our supervision to their unique needs and clinical strategies. This is the fundamental, overarching principle of our integrative supervision, which is explicated in more detail in what follows.

Conduct a Needs Assessment

Trainees invariably present with multiple agendas—some manifest and some latent—and diverse needs, some of which are quite out of their awareness. Assuming that all students present with identical needs subscribes to a variant of the "uniformity myth" (Kiesler, 1966).

As in clinical work, supervision should ideally begin with a needs assessment: What do they want and/or need from the supervisory experience? Are they here to facilitate personal growth? To ventilate about therapy frustrations? To validate their theoretical allegiances? To evaluate technical weaknesses? To analyze countertransferential reactions? To achieve all of these (e.g., "to become a better therapist") or none of these (e.g., "because I was assigned to you")? Because of such patterns, initial and continual redefinition of supervision objectives is required. Supervisees come with a panoply of preconceptions and needs, many unrecognized, and it is best to examine these at the outset and to modify them as the trainee obtains experience.

There are occasions, of course, when the supervisee's preferences are in conflict with the supervisor's judgment as to legitimate needs. For example, when asked how he best handled negative feedback in supervision, one advanced trainee seriously replied, "By ignoring it [!]." However, as in this case, the disparities sometimes are uncovered early by tactful inquiry and can become a focus of supervision. The supervisee's desires should be elicited, articulated, and considered but will not necessarily commit the supervisor to that tack (Norcross, Beutler, & Clarkin, 1990).

Construct Explicit Contracts

In addition to assessing needs and clarifying expectations, both clinical experience and supervision research highlight the importance of sharing perceptions of the supervision relationship. Hassenfeld and Sarris (1978) attribute mutual failure in a supervisory relationship to discrepant perceptions of each other and their appropriate roles.

Supervision goals and contracts, like psychotherapy itself, should be explicit. Interpersonal roles, attendance expectations, evaluation methods, and provisions for revising the contract should be established at the outset, with both parties entering into the agreement. The acquisition of objectives should be reviewed periodically with the trainee in a two-way dialogue, rather than simply as a critique of the student by the supervisor.

Blend Supervision Methods

Integrative supervision is necessarily eclectic in therapeutic content and pedagogical method. In terms of content, the supervisor's work is determined by both the needs of the clients being discussed and the needs of the trainee. Thus, one supervision might entail more of a directive-educative supervisory approach in which the trainee needs to learn specific techniques for the treatment of a focused clinical problem. Another supervision might involve an approach that is predominantly exploratory, due either to the historical roots of the client's conflicts or to the countertransference struggles of the therapist (Halgin & Murphy, 1995). In an integrative supervision, the supervisor may bring together the techniques of several models. For example, a pragmatically blended supervision might involve the integration of psychodynamic, interpersonal, person-centered, and behavioral techniques (Halgin, 1986). In this kind of supervision, the supervisor makes choices about the extent to which the supervisee will benefit from work that is exploratory, relationship focused, supportive, or directive.

In terms of method, integrative supervision generally entails a wide variety of techniques and stances associated with diverse psychotherapy systems. Structure should follow function. As the situation dictates, supervision might involve didactic presentations, reading assignments, open-ended discussions, personal modeling, experiential activities, video demonstrations, case examples, and minicase conferences. The supervisor may need to adapt interpersonal stances across supervisees and even in their work with each supervisee when their clients are treated with divergent interventions. As Hess (1980) points out, a supervisor can flexibly and fruitfully vary among the roles of lecturer, teacher, case reviewer, collegial peer, monitor, and therapist throughout the course of one supervision or over many supervision contacts.

Address "Relationships of Choice"

Historically, prescriptive eclectic supervision was associated with the systematic selection of clinical techniques, the classical definition of technical eclecticism; however, psychotherapy will never be so technical to overshadow the power of a therapist's ability to form a therapeutic relationship. Nor are the predictors and contributors to these interpersonal stances beyond the scope of psychological science. It is regrettable that the historical emphasis on technique selection has led to a relative neglect of tailoring interpersonal stances to fit particular client needs (Lazarus et al., 1992).

Contemporary supervision from an integrative perspective addresses the effort of psychotherapists to differentially employ or customize their interpersonal stance. One way to conceptualize the issue, paralleling the notion of "treatment of choice" in terms of techniques is how clinicians determine therapeutic "relationships of choice" in terms of relational styles. This broadens the meaning of prescriptive eclecticism to denote selection not only of specific clinical procedures but also of relationship stances.

Operate From a Coherent Framework

Although clinical supervision should be sensitive and tailored to the needs of the student and to the particulars of the case, it must also operate from a coherent conceptual framework. The presence of a systematic schema determines in large part whether prescriptive eclecticism is experienced as intelligible or bewildering.

Allen, Szollos, and Williams (1986) found that integrative supervision within a superordinate framework is associated positively with the quality of the learning experience. Conversely, relatively less valued integrative or eclectic supervisors neglected this need by failing to ground their interventions and decisions within a larger, guiding perspective. "Atheoretical" supervisors may lack the big picture—an encompassing structure that organizes the case formulations and gives priority to clinical intervention.

In the past, supervision from an integrative stance was frequently performed from the supervisor's idiosyncratic and unarticulated perspective. With the publication of formal and systematic accounts of integrative practice, however, integrative supervision can now be directed by systematic and empirically based frameworks for differential treatment. Exemplars include Beutler's systematic eclectic psychotherapy, Lazarus's multimodal therapy, Prochaska and DiClemente's transtheoretical therapy, and Wachtel's integrative psychodynamic and behavioral approach (see Norcross & Goldfried, 1992).

These integrative models specify the basis for treatment selection and guide the supervisor in enabling students to determine the treatments and relationships of choice. Decisional models are provided for selecting the technical procedures and relationship stances from various therapeutic orientations to be applied in given circumstances and with given clients. All told, integrative models offer a coherent framework and the "big picture" by which a multiplicity of theories and methods can be organized into an integrated understanding.

Match Supervision to Trainee Variables

As we have repeatedly said, the determinants of therapist behavior are too numerous and the needs of the supervisee too heterogeneous to provide the identical supervisory experience to each and every student. The prescriptive nature of supervision will obviously blend methods traditionally associated with diverse systems of psychotherapy but will do so systematically as a function of numerous trainee variables. It is impossible to specify in advance which of these variables will become predominant in any supervisory relationship, but our experience and research lead us to consider three: therapy approach, clinical experience, and cognitive style (Norcross et al., 1990).

Therapy Approach.   Within limits, the "how" of supervision (method) should parallel the "what" of supervision (content). In other words, the supervision approach should mirror the therapeutic approach (Frances & Clarkin, 1981). When the supervisee's treatment approach entails verbal, insight-oriented work, supervision profitably explores the student's countertransference reactions to both client and supervisor. Similarly, didactic instruction and role playing in the supervision hour are especially congruent with more behavioral, action-oriented approaches. There may, however, also be some value to conceptualizing supervision as a complement to treatment. Work on countertransference, for example, would not be limited to the supervision of insight-oriented treatment but would also be extended to students who are prone to ignore it in treatment (Stricker, 1988).

Clinical Experience.   The developmental needs of clinical supervisees shift over the course of their training (Worthington, 1987). General experience in supervision (e.g., Blumenfield, 1982; Hart, 1982; Hess, 1980) and developmental models of supervision (e.g., Hogan, 1964; Loganbill, Hardy, & Delworth, 1982; Stoltenberg, 1981; Stoltenberg & McNeil, Chapter 12, this volume) suggest that different supervisory styles are differentially effective for trainees at varying levels of experience. Beginning students are most interested in the acquisition of specific interviewing and therapy techniques; advanced practicum students are more inclined toward the development of alternative formulations; interns tend to be most intrigued by examination of personal dynamics affecting therapy.

Likewise, Heppner and Roehlke (1984) observed that beginning practicum students sought skills and support, moderately advanced trainees sought to expand their conceptual skills and theoretical knowledge, and more advanced students expressed the desire to explore personal issues that might affect their ability to provide treatment (cf. Nelson, 1978; Wiley & Ray, 1986; Worthington, 1984). As with any "stage model," the steps obviously overlap and the emphases are relative rather than absolute.

From such literature, we conclude that the goals of supervision should reflect the developmental stage of the trainee (Guest & Beutler, 1988). Supervisory goals should begin with support and training in technical skill and progress to a consideration of more complex theoretical concepts and should finally endeavor to the work of solidifying and integrating theory and technique with personal response patterns. These later skills include special focus on interpersonal dynamics, particularly transference and countertransference. In oversimplified terms, students move from techniques to knowledge to self. It is not a small coincidence that most psychotherapy clients evidence a similar pattern, particularly those engaged in long-term treatment.

Cognitive Style.   A nascent body of research indicates that the conceptual level of the trainee is an important consideration in fitting the supervision to the student. One aspect refers to students' level of conceptual complexity and includes the degree of self-initiative, ability to generate concepts, and tolerance for ambiguity (Handley, 1982). Students high in conceptual development benefit more from a self-directed instructional approach, whereas those lower in conceptual development perform better with externally oriented and externally controlled training programs (e.g., Hunt & Sullivan, 1974; Rosenthal, 1977).

Another aspect of cognitive style is *interpersonal reactance,* a concept Beutler and Clarkin (1990) have discussed and researched in detail as a client variable. Like the high-reactant client who is resistant to therapist directiveness, the high-reactant student is likely to be resistant to a directive and authoritarian supervisor. This student is likely to do best with a reflective and evocative supervisor who focuses on the student's experience and is less direct in recommending technical procedures. This student is contrasted to the low-reactant (externally focused) student who is likely to respond well to supervisor directives.

Attending to Trainees' Personal Idioms

Even with similar cognitive styles and comparable levels of training, each trainee manifests an idiographic style. It is important for supervisors to recognize each trainee's *personal idiom* (Hogan, 1964), the unique meshing of personality and method. Supervisors who fail to recognize and appreciate each trainee's personalized approach will likely provoke considerable upset if the supervisor's own style is being imposed on the trainee.

One of the most appealing aspects of an integrative approach is that an individualized treatment plan can be formulated for each client's unique needs. A similar principle holds true for the trainee: The student's unique style, interests, and experiences can be used to inform a general approach to treatment and specific treatment plans for each client. For example, some students are naturally more animated and evocative in their interpersonal style; these individuals can use this natural style to conduct therapy in which they take a more active role. In contrast, trainees whose personal style is naturally quieter and less active may work best with a therapeutic approach in which they are placid participants in a relationship that is more serene and less energized. Supervisors who are attentive to these individualized styles of personality can help the trainee use special attributes to benefit the therapy, obviously within appropriate limits. Supervisors who try to coerce a change in personality may find that trainees feel as if they are enacting a script that never seems right.

Assess Therapeutic Skills

The acquisition of technical and relational competencies can be enhanced by incorporating into the supervisory process formal methods of assessing therapeutic skills that have evolved from psychotherapy manuals. Criteria-based rating scales for therapeutic skills have now been developed for cognitive therapy, psychodynamic therapy, experiential and Gestalt therapy, interpersonal therapy, and behavior therapy programs, among others. These scales can be applied to the audio- and videotapes on which supervision is often based, not only defining the procedures that are considered to be of value to the particular manual but also describing the behaviors that comprise their effective utilization. Moreover, by applying different scales to the same psychotherapy session, supervision can explore both differences and similarities among therapeutic approaches (Norcross et al., 1990).

To our knowledge, criteria-based rating skills have not yet been developed for broad-spectrum integrative psychotherapies. This is an obvious lacuna in integrative supervision (and integrative practice) that will need to be rectified for the movement to advance (Goldfried, Castonguay, & Safran, 1992). In the meantime, integrative supervisors can employ treatment manuals and rating scales pertinent to the single-system psychotherapy being offered in some cases. In those cases being treated by integrative therapy, expert ratings and relevant integrative publications can be used to outline criteria for implementing the treatment.

Nurture the Supervisory Relationship

The therapeutic relationship has long been established as a primary curative factor in psychotherapy. It does not involve a great leap of understanding to perceive the supervisory relationship as being comparably important in fostering growth in clinical trainees (Lambert & Arnold, 1987). Carifio and Hess (1987) reviewed the supervision literature and concluded that the ideal supervisor possesses "high levels of empathy, respect, genuineness, flexibility, concern, investment, and openness" (p. 244). Like good therapists, good supervisors are those who use appropriate teaching, goal setting, and feedback; they tend to be seen as supportive, noncritical individuals who respect their supervisees.

Integrative psychotherapists have an interesting opportunity when they conduct supervision; they have the opportunity to apply to the supervisory relationship some of the same methods that are effective in integrative psychotherapy. This does not mean that they should look for ways to convert the supervision into a therapy of sorts; in fact, such an approach is considered objectionable by most trainees (Carifio & Hess, 1987; Rosenblatt

& Mayer, 1975). Yet, the supervisor can blend the methods of several theoretical approaches; for example, supportive, directive, exploratory, and interpersonal techniques can be blended within a supervision in such a way that the supervisee feels supported, understood, and well educated (Halgin, 1985). The supervisory relationship offers an optimal, in vivo context within which to model these crucial training goals.

With experienced supervisees, we strive for mutuality in psychotherapy supervision (Phillips & Kanter, 1984). The ideal relationship can be characterized as a process of mutual exploration and bidirectional exchanges with an "inquiring colleague" (Kagan, 1980). While neither abdicating our professional responsibilities nor denying disparities in knowledge and power between us, we strive for an empathic and collaborative relationship. We hope to create an environment that encourages trainees to express their insecurities, to disagree respectfully, and to suggest alternatives, even if these temporarily increase our discomfort. A critical question that guides us is, "Will trainees be able to present what makes them look bad or only what makes them look good?"

The latter is engendered by a dogmatic and authoritarian style of supervision. An authoritarian style on the part of the supervisor appears to be particularly detrimental (Allen et al., 1986). Supervisors who demand conformity and punish divergence from the "party line" jeopardize their supervisory relationship and subvert central tenets of psychotherapy integration (Cherniss & Equatios, 1977; Moskowitz & Rupert, 1983).

Share Our Work With Supervisees

Although modeling has been shown to be a particularly effective procedure for teaching complex behaviors, it is used surprisingly little in teaching and supervising psychotherapy. Most clinical educators use consultant techniques to pass on knowledge about the methods of psychotherapy. Rather than discuss the mistakes they have committed, they are inclined to report the successes they have achieved. Rather than disclose the anxieties with which they contend in their clinical work, they are likely to boast in ways that communicate an inflated sense of competence and self-assurance.

At the beginning of his supervision of a marital therapy practicum, Prochaska (Beutler et al., 1987) attempts to reduce the anxiety of students and to model collegial openness by playing an audiotape of his first therapy case, which happened to be a conjoint marital session. The students appreciate the honest sharing of a case in which their professor was passive and controlled first by one spouse and then by the other.

Sharing our own clinical work with trainees initiates a rich dialogue in which the supervisor is willing to be vulnerable. By agreeing to such vulnerability, the supervisor can make a strong commitment to a trusting and open relationship. What a wonderful opportunity for the trainee to observe the work of the expert! Open discussion of our actual clinical work will also sensitize us to the complexity of this work. When faced with trainees' asking us to explain—and defend—why a given intervention was chosen, we will assuredly become aware of how difficult practicing within an integrative approach is; and with this awareness, we will be more sensitive to the challenges our trainees confront.

Evaluate the Outcomes

As with psychotherapy itself, it is increasingly difficult to speak of psychotherapy training and supervision without reference to its demonstrated efficacy. The introduction of an integrative perspective does nothing to reduce the subtle and complex effects of supervision and probably only enlarges the task of measuring supervision outcomes.

Whereas descriptions of integrative supervision have appeared in the literature (e.g., Beutler et al., 1987; Halgin, 1986; Norcross, 1986, 1988; Robertson, 1986; Tennen, 1988), empirical evaluations have not. The same can be said for virtually all supervision adhering to a single theoretical tradition (Binder, 1993; Lambert & Ogles, Chapter 24, this volume), but this convergence is hardly redeeming. The competence of our graduates and, indeed, the adequacy of our clinical training are typically assumed rather than verified (Stevenson & Norcross, 1987). Little research has been conducted on evaluating supervision in either pure-form or integrative systems of psychotherapy (cf. Beutler, 1988; Greenberg & Goldman, 1988; Strupp, Butler, & Rosser, 1988), but recent developments in manualization, adherence measurement, and competency judgments show promise.

LOGISTICS OF INTEGRATIVE SUPERVISION

It follows logically that just as integrative psychotherapists are guided by data, so supervisors should be primarily guided by available evidence in their selection of supervision methods (Norcross et al., 1990). Unfortunately, empirical research to date has not rendered many definitive judgments in this regard (Lambert & Arnold, 1987; Matarazzo & Patterson, 1986). Nonetheless, a few sprinkles of evidence and many years of experience in integrative supervision have led us to the following logistical decisions.

Regarding method, our form of integrative supervision is conducted in both individual and group formats. The former is devoted to supervision of individual cases and is based on review of audiotapes and videotapes of therapy sessions. Observation behind a one-way mirror is desirable and arranged whenever mutual schedules permit. Live supervision may or may not be involved, depending again on the trainee's competence and needs. We rarely conduct cotherapy in individual psychotherapy since it can undermine the supervisee's position and complicate the real and transference relationships.

Despite their initial anxiety, supervisees appreciate our reliance on more than their edited verbal reports about what transpired during their psychotherapy contacts. We find that recordings and direct observation offer excellent opportunities for the supervisor to be in touch with the proceedings of the therapy. This closer contact with the therapy helps us to obtain an independent evaluation of client functioning beyond the supervisee's reports; to watch habitual, maladaptive "pulls" of the client unfold in supervision; and to compare the supervisee's "experienced" or "felt" therapeutic relationship to a more objective reality. Supervisees' evaluations (Allen et al., 1986; Nelson, 1978) and empirical research (e.g., Alberts & Edelstein, 1990; Stein, Karasu, Charles, & Buckley, 1975) indicate that direct observation and videotapes are, in fact, the preferred supervisory methods.

This is not to suggest that we totally eschew the use of process notes or critical incidents. In some cases, live observation or videotaping may represent iatrogenic intrusions into the therapy process, and we may thus opt for an alternative approach involving process notes recorded immediately after the session. At other times, process notes offer valuable data about the therapist's own perspective and countertransference and add an important dimension to the supervision.

The group supervision seminar or team combines myriad methods and formats. Representative examples include didactic presentations, reading assignments, discussion periods, personal modeling, group role plays, experiential activities, film demonstrations, case examples, and minicase conferences. The group supervision context provides trainees with an important opportunity to share their work with peers, while at the same time taking advantage of the collected wisdom of their peers and the more advanced trainees who participate.

Three techniques have proven effective in expanding our own theoretical horizons. First, we formulate the same case from disparate theoretical perspectives, leading students to examine points of convergence and contention (Saltzman & Norcross, 1990), therapeutic choices in the treatment, and relative indications and contraindications for particular treatment plans. A more sophisticated technique is to formulate the same case from multiple integrative perspectives to determine points of convergence and contention among their treatment recommendations. Second, at times we engage in a series of "thought experiments" for psychotherapists (e.g., Shapiro, 1986) in order to lift our theoretical blinders and to liberate our restricted range of thinking. And third, we have occasionally conducted cosupervision with an invited colleague (Norcross, 1988). This approach is particularly beneficial when the intervention involves a specialty with which the primary supervisor is less familiar. For example, a specialized behavior therapy technique for treating a specific disorder can be more effectively taught by an expert. Sometimes, a consultant can help a supervision that feels "stuck." In this situation, the ideas and perspective of an uninvolved consultant can bring a refreshing view to a case that has become stagnated, and therefore frustrating, for the supervisor and the trainee. Of course, it takes courage for a supervisor to make such a public admission that he or she is not omniscient.

As with psychotherapy, the pedagogical method assumes a secondary position to the interpersonal relationship in supervision. We invite supervisees to recognize their undue preoccupation with technology at the expense of the relationship, which Mahoney (1986) has labeled the "tyranny of technique." Techniques are most adequately construed as strategies for structuring and communicating the therapeutic message, but they should not be confused with it.

Integrative supervisors provide feedback to students in a variety of ways within a coherent conceptual framework. Addressing the history of psychotherapy training, Matarazzo and Garner (1992) conclude that the refinement of feedback to the learner has been of great importance in imparting skill. We have moved away from trainees' case reporting and reconstructed tales of therapy heroics (Norcross, 1988) to the use of audiotape, observation through one-way mirrors, and videotaped self-confrontation. This progression has substantially increased the accuracy and completeness of information about what has ensued in therapy and thereby has enhanced supervision.

As have legions of other supervisors, we have found it instructive to examine the recurrence of parallels between supervision and psychotherapy. These parallel processes can take many forms. In one manifestation, trainees may behave in supervision in a way that is similar to how their client behaves in psychotherapy. In another manifestation, the dynamics between supervisee and supervisor may mimic those of the therapeutic relationship. Trainees bring similar interpersonal and defensive patterns to all relationships, psychotherapy and supervision included. When these repetitive relationship patterns are addressed in supervision, the trainee's awareness and performance can be enhanced in all interpersonal pursuits, including but not limited to psychotherapy.

In prescriptive eclectic supervision, in addition, we intentionally invoke a relatively unique and constructive form of parallel process. The customizing or prescriptive matching applies both to trainees' conducting their psychotherapy and to supervisors' conducting their supervision. As eclectic supervisors, we are continually involved in a parallel process of tailoring supervision to each of our students as they tailor the psychological treatment to each of their clients. The net result is a synergistic enterprise that fits supervisor, supervisee-therapist, and client.

Finally, there is the matter of the supervisory relationship. As should be evident in much of what has already been said, the relationship is simultaneously a context and a process for change in supervision. We as supervisors have the opportunity of providing our students with wonderful gifts. Ideally, they will finish their work with us knowing more about therapy, more about clients, more about us, and most important, more about themselves. The supervision can be viewed as a laboratory in which creative experiments take place. As supervisors, we have a great deal of responsibility for ensuring that subjects—the clients and the trainees—in the experiment are treated with the greatest of sensitivity and care. When we, the supervisors, make it clear that we are also subjects in this exciting experiment, we enhance the probability of integrative success.

STRENGTHS AND LIABILITIES OF INTEGRATIVE SUPERVISION

Much as we insist on our trainees identifying the relative indications and contraindications of various treatment options for their clients, we are equally adamant about identifying the indications and contraindications of integrative supervision. This is not to say that integrative approaches possess an inordinate number of either strengths or weaknesses, but rather that we endeavor to model an informed pluralism toward our own work as well. In what follows we briefly address several strengths and liabilities of integrative supervision posed by its practitioners (supervisors) and its recipients (supervisees).

Heide and Rosenbaum (1988) surveyed 14 psychotherapists regarding their experiences in using single versus combined theoretical models in psychotherapy. Contrary to predictions, the two conditions did not differ in self-reported anxiety. When using a single orientation, however, psychotherapists reported being significantly more self-controlled, conventional, precise, and reserved. When using a combined or integrative model, they said they were more imaginative, adventuresome, spontaneous, and changeable. Our take on integrative supervision is that it is more imaginative, adventuresome, and challenging—for good and bad.

The ultimate objective of psychotherapy integration is to tailor therapeutic approaches to individual clients in such a way as to enhance outcome. It does so by matching clients' needs, by being more flexible, and by promoting therapist growth in mastering multiple methods and continuing their development. Likewise, the ultimate objective of integrative supervision is to tailor the supervision approach to individual trainees in such a way as to enhance the outcome of both their clients and their training. The integrative enterprise entails exploration, experimentation, and freedom.

But if the clash of theoretical persuasions is the ring of freedom, it is also the sound of occasional disequilibrium. We phrase several of these sources of disequilibrium in the way we often hear them: as anxious, absolutist threats to therapeutic identity and competence (Norcross, 1990).

- *"But which of these many paths shall I take at any one point?"* Should the student promote action or explore mental content; challenge or understand irrational cognitions; work on actual or projected relationships; empathize or redirect during a session (Messer, 1986)? Of course, these choices are not as dualistic, as either/or, as they are phrased. Nevertheless, the change in style implies a change in identity, a transformation of sorts (Rosenbaum, 1988).

Both integrative supervision and integrative practice entail shifts within a single session, across many sessions with the same person, or between sessions with different people. The result can be anxiety and perplexity, occasionally articulated but more frequently not.

• *"It is just too damn hard!"* Psychotherapists adhering to a unitary theoretical model and a single treatment format are likely to employ similar technical interventions and relationship stances across clinical encounters. By contrast, prescriptive eclectics tailoring their practice to individual clients will necessarily employ a wide array of interventions, relationships, and formats. Students and supervisors alike complain of additional work and of increased mental effort. Like switch hitters in baseball and like bilingual children, the participants in integrative supervision pull double duty in the short run for more flexible and comprehensive skills in the long run.

• *"If today is Wednesday and it's 5 P.M., then this must be cognitive-behavioral therapy!"* Akin to those whirlwind European tours, frequent visits to diverse therapeutic communities require considerable physical stamina and mental preparation.

• *"Oh, I don't like doing this type of psychotherapy!"* Therapists are not as personally attached or psychologically comfortable with some therapies as they are with other therapies, even controlling for competence in them. Several psychotherapeutic methods and relationships simply don't "fit." Students thus may be asked to render a treatment indicated for a given client even though they don't particularly enjoy it.

• *"I am becoming a jack of all trades, master of none."* This frequently cited disadvantage of integration (Norcross & Prochaska, 1988) is not an identity we eagerly embrace, but it is one that, like many stereotypes, has a grain of truth to it. This concerns the inherent conflict between depth and breadth (Norcross, 1988). An indisputable disadvantage of aiming to establish multiple competence is that it will necessitate longer and more comprehensive training than will a single competency. When students are delayed in acquiring competence of multiple methods of psychotherapy, they are apt to feel more frustrated. The future promises of increased efficacy and applicability as a result of integrative therapy hold more appeal for supervisors than for supervisees at times.

• *"You can call it scientific, but I'm flying by the seat of my pants."* or *"What gives us the right to practice integratively in the absence of firm data?"* These anxious vacillations reflect the same core conflict: Therapists fear the prospect of unsystematic practice as well as the pretense of science. Prescriptive matching decisions are interactive, cumulative, and crude. Therapists lack compelling research on many clinical disorders and client variables to practice differentially with confidence. Integrative practice does require clinical judgment and "leaps of faith" in the absence of compelling outcome studies on every type of client, problem, and context.

• *"I am opening myself up here to chaos! Who knows what can happen?"* The ambiguity and uncertainty of differential practice can be emotionally taxing (even as it is exciting and spontaneous). Clinical experiences will not be as predictable and controlled as a pure-form therapy practiced uniformly.

• *"I don't know whether I can tolerate the tension created by the shifts between clients."* Wachtel (1991) points out that many students, when first introduced to multitheoretical approaches, are puzzled by the mechanics of technique shifts and are dismayed by a concern that their own attempts might prove to be awkward and disruptive.

In broader strokes, these and other liabilities highlight two central issues regarding integrative supervision. First, such practice and supervision engender a rich variety of countertransferential reactions and can exact a toll on the clinician (Halgin & McEntee, 1993). Integrative practice—"when worlds collide"—offers fertile ground for the generation of emotional responses in both its proponents and detractors (Rosenbaum, 1988). Second, the decision to opt for integrative supervision requires a cost-benefit analysis for each of us—the intellectual challenge versus the internal conflicts, the gratifying openness versus the anxious ambiguity—that is part and parcel of the process of becoming an integrative psychotherapist.

CONCLUDING COMMENTS

In integrative supervision of psychotherapy, the importance of modeling informed pluralism and synthetic thinking cannot be overemphasized. Not unlike our children, our students learn to emulate what we do more closely than what we say (cf. Beutler et al., 1987). But too often, supervisors teach integration in the form of value *statements* instead of value *actions* (Robertson, 1986). Supervisors should reliably model the curiosity and incisiveness central to psychotherapy success as well as to psychotherapy integration.

This is not to say that "anything goes" is accepted or that uncritical acceptance is prized. As a Maharini of Jaipus was once reported to have said: "Keep an open mind; an open mind is a very good thing, but don't keep your mind so open that your brains fall out."

As we have emphasized throughout this chapter, supervision methods and models should be consistent with the pluralistic and empirical nature of psychotherapy integration itself. Our intention is not necessarily to produce card-carrying, flag-waving "eclectic" or "integrative" psychotherapists. This scenario would simply replace enforced commitment to a single system with enforced conversion to an integrative system, a change that may be more pluralistic and liberating in content but certainly not in process. Instead, our goal is to educate therapists to think and, perhaps, to behave integratively—openly, synthetically, but critically—in their clinical pursuits (Norcross et al., 1990).

Put another way: The emphasis of integrative supervision, in its many and varied guises, should be placed squarely on "*how* to think" rather than on "*what* to think." This modified focus engenders informed pluralism and self-evolving clinical styles, in contrast to young disciples or mindless imitators. The training process can then progress from imitative learning to creative learning (Flemming, 1953), a transition from therapy skills to skilled therapists (Grater, 1985). With such an attitude and philosophy, supervisors will find that not only are their students changing but they also are developing and growing over the course of a given supervision and over the duration of their career (Stoltenberg, McNeill, & Crethar, 1994; Watkins, 1993, 1995).

REFERENCES

Alberts, G., & Edelstein, B. (1990). Therapist training: A critical review of skill training studies. *Clinical Psychology Review*, *10*, 497–511.

Allen, G. J., Szollos, S. J., & Williams, B. E. (1986). Doctoral students' comparative evaluations of best and worst psychotherapy supervision. *Professional Psychology: Research and Practice*, *17*, 91–99.

Andrews, J. D. W., Norcross, J. C., & Halgin, R. P. (1992). Training in psychotherapy integration. In J. C. Norcross & M. R. Goldfried (Eds.), *Handbook of psychotherapy integration* (pp. 563–592). New York: Basic Books.

Beutler, L. E. (1983). *Eclectic psychotherapy: A systematic approach*. Elmsford, NY: Pergamon.

Beutler, L. E. (1988). Introduction: Training to competency in psychotherapy. *Journal of Consulting and Clinical Psychology, 56*, 651–652.

Beutler, L. E., & Clarkin, J. (1990). *Systematic treatment selection: Toward targeted therapeutic interventions.* New York: Brunner/Mazel.

Beutler, L. E., & Consoli, A. J. (1992). Systematic eclectic psychotherapy. In J. C. Norcross & M. R. Goldfried (Eds.), *Handbook of psychotherapy integration* (pp. 264–297). New York: Basic Books.

Beutler, L. E., Mahoney, M. J., Norcross, J. C., Prochaska, J. O., Sollod, R. M., & Robertson, M. (1987). Training integrative/eclectic psychotherapists II. *Journal of Integrative and Eclectic Psychotherapy, 6*, 296–332.

Binder, J. L. (1993). Is it time to improve psychotherapy training? *Clinical Psychology Review, 13*, 301–318.

Blumenfield, M. (Ed.). (1982). *Applied supervision in psychotherapy.* New York: Grune and Stratton.

Carifio, M. S., & Hess, A. K. (1987). Who is the ideal supervisor? *Professional Psychology: Research and Practice, 18*, 244–250.

Cherniss, C., & Equatios, E. (1977). Styles of clinical supervision in community mental health programs. *Journal of Consulting and Clinical Psychology, 45*, 1195–1196.

Diamond, R. E., Havens, R. A., & Jones, A. C. (1978). A conceptual framework for the practice of prescriptive eclecticism in psychotherapy. *American Psychologist, 33*, 239–248.

Fleming, J. (1953). The role of supervision in psychiatric training. *Bulletin of the Menninger Clinic, 17*, 157–169.

Frances, A., & Clarkin, J. F. (1981). Parallel techniques in supervision and treatment. *Psychiatric Quarterly, 53*, 242–248.

Frances, A., Clarkin, J. F., & Perry, S. (1984). *Differential therapeutics in psychiatry.* New York: Brunner/Mazel.

Frank, J. D. (1982). Therapeutic components shared by all psychotherapies. In J. H. Harvey & M. M. Parks (Eds.), *Psychotherapy research and behavior change: 1981 Master Lecture Series.* Washington, DC: American Psychological Association.

Frank, J. D., & Frank, J. B. (1991). *Persuasion and healing* (3rd ed.). Baltimore: Johns Hopkins University Press.

Garfield, S. L. (1980). *Psychotherapy: An eclectic approach.* New York: Wiley.

Garfield, S. L. (1992). Eclectic psychotherapy: A common factors approach. In J. C. Norcross & M. R. Goldfried (Eds.), *Handbook of psychotherapy integration.* New York: Basic Books.

Goldfried, M. R. (1980). Toward the delineation of therapeutic change principles. *American Psychologist, 25*, 991–999.

Goldfried, M. R., Castonguay, L. G., & Safran, J. D. (1992). Core issues and future directions in psychotherapy integration. In J. C. Norcross & M. R. Goldfried (Eds.), *Handbook of psychotherapy integration* (pp. 593–616). New York: Basic Books.

Grater, H. A. (1985). Steps in psychotherapy supervision: From therapy skills to skilled therapist. *Professional Psychology: Research and Practice, 16*, 605–610.

Greenberg, L. S., & Goldman, R. L. (1988). Training in experiential therapy. *Journal of Consulting and Clinical Psychology, 56*, 696–702.

Grencavage, L. M., & Norcross, J. C. (1990). Where are the commonalities among the therapeutic common factors? *Professional Psychology: Research and Practice, 21*, 372–378.

Guest, P. D., & Beutler, L. E. (1988). The impact of psychotherapy supervision on therapist orientation and values. *Journal of Consulting and Clinical Psychology, 56*, 653–658.

Halgin, R. P. (1985). Teaching integration of psychotherapy models to beginning therapists. *Psychotherapy, 22*, 555–563.

Halgin, R. P. (1986). Pragmatic blending of clinical models in the supervisory relationship. *The Clinical Supervisor, 3*(4), 23–46.

Halgin, R. P. (Ed.). (1988). Special section: Issues in the supervision of integrative psychotherapy. *Journal of Integrative and Eclectic Psychotherapy, 7*, 152–180.

Halgin, R. P. (1989). Pragmatic blending. *Journal of Integrative and Eclectic Psychotherapy, 8,* 320–328.

Halgin, R. P., & McEntee, D. J. (1993). Countertransference dilemmas in integrative psychotherapy. In G. Stricker & J. Gold (Eds.), *Comprehensive textbook of psychotherapy integration* (pp. 513–522). New York: Plenum.

Halgin, R. P., & Murphy, R. A. (1995). Issues in the training of psychotherapists. In B. Bongar & L. E. Beutler (Eds.), *Comprehensive textbook of psychotherapy: Theory and practice* (pp. 434–455). New York: Oxford University Press.

Handley, P. (1982). Relationship between supervisors' and trainees' cognitive styles and the supervision process. *Journal of Counseling Psychology, 29,* 508–515.

Hardy, G. E., & Shapiro, D. A. (1985). Therapist response modes in prescriptive vs. exploratory psychotherapy. *British Journal of Clinical Psychology, 24,* 235–245.

Hart, G. M. (1982). *The process of clinical supervision.* Baltimore: University Park Press.

Hassenfeld, I., & Sarris, J. (1978). Hazards and horizons of psychotherapy supervision. *American Journal of Psychotherapy, 32,* 393–401.

Heide, F. J., & Rosenbaum, R. (1988). Therapists' experiences of using single versus combined theoretical models in psychotherapy. *Journal of Integrative and Eclectic Psychotherapy, 7,* 41–46.

Heppner, P. P., & Roehlke, J. J. (1984). Differences among supervisees at different levels of training: Implications for a developmental model of supervision. *Journal of Counseling Psychology, 31,* 76–90.

Hess, A. K. (1980). Training models and the nature of psychotherapy supervision. In A. K. Hess (Ed.), *Psychotherapy supervision.* New York: Wiley.

Hess, A. K. (Section Editor). (1987). Advances in psychotherapy supervision. *Professional Psychology: Research and Practice, 18,* 187–259.

Hogan, R. A. (1964). Issues and approaches in supervision. *Psychotherapy: Theory, Research, and Practice, 1,* 139–141.

Hunt, D. E., & Sullivan, E. V. (1974). *Between psychology and education.* Hinsdale, IL: Dryden.

Kagan, N. (1980). Influencing human interaction: Eighteen years with IPR. In A. K. Hess (Ed.), *Psychotherapy supervision.* New York: Wiley.

Kiesler, D. J. (1966). Some myths of psychotherapy research and the search for a paradigm. *Psychological Bulletin, 65,* 110–136.

Lambert, M. J. (1992). Psychotherapy outcome research: Implications for integrative and eclectic therapists. In J. C. Norcross & M. R. Goldfried (Eds.), *Handbook of psychotherapy integration* (pp. 94–129). New York: Basic Books.

Lambert, M. J., & Arnold, R. C. (1987). Research and the supervisory process. *Professional Psychology: Research and Practice, 18,* 217–224.

Lambert, M. J., & Bergin, A. E. (1992). Achievements and limitations of psychotherapy research. In D. K. Freedheim (Ed.), *History of psychotherapy: A century of change* (pp. 360–390). Washington, DC: American Psychological Association.

Lazarus, A. A. (1976). *Multimodal behavior therapy.* New York: Springer.

Lazarus, A. A. (1989). *The practice of multimodal therapy.* Baltimore: Johns Hopkins University Press. (Originally published in 1981 by McGraw-Hill)

Lazarus, A. A. (1992). Multimodal therapy: Technical eclecticism with minimal integration. In J. C. Norcross & M. R. Goldfried (Eds.), *Handbook of psychotherapy integration* (pp. 231–263). New York: Basic Books.

Lazarus, A. A. (1993). Tailoring the therapeutic relationship, or being an authentic chameleon. *Psychotherapy, 30,* 404–407.

Lazarus, A. A., Beutler, L. E., & Norcross, J. C. (1992). The future of technical eclecticism. *Psychotherapy, 29,* 11–20.

Loganbill, C., Hardy, E., & Delworth, U. (1982). Supervision: A conceptual model. *The Counseling Psychologist, 10,* 3–42.

London, P. (1966). Major issues in psychotherapy integration. *International Journal of Eclectic Psychotherapy, 5*(3), 1–12.

London, P. (1986). *The modes and morals of psychotherapy* (2nd ed.). New York: Hemisphere.

Luborsky, L., Crits-Cristoph, P., Alexander, L., Margolis, M., & Cohen, M. (1983). Two helping alliance methods for predicting outcomes of psychotherapy: A counting signs vs. a global rating method. *Journal of Nervous and Mental Disease, 171*, 480–491.

Mahoney, M. J. (1986). The tyranny of technique. *Counseling and Values, 30*, 169–174.

Matarazzo, R. G., & Garner, A. M. (1992). Research on training for psychotherapy. In D. K. Freedheim (Ed.), *History of psychotherapy: A century of change.* Washington, DC: American Psychological Association.

Matarazzo, R. G., & Patterson, D. (1986). Research on the teaching and learning of therapeutic skills. In S. L. Garfield & A. E. Bergin (Eds.), *Handbook of psychotherapy and behavior change* (pp. 821–843). New York: Wiley.

Messer, S. B. (1986). Behavioral and psychoanalytic perspectives at therapeutic choice points. *American Psychologist, 41*, 1261–1272.

Messer, S. B. (1992). A critical examination of belief structures in integrative and eclectic psychotherapy. In J. C. Norcross & M. R. Goldfried (Eds.), *Handbook of psychotherapy integration* (pp. 130–167). New York: Basic Books.

Moskowitz, S., & Rupert, P. (1983). Conflict resolution within the supervisory relationship. *Professional Psychology: Research and Practice, 14*, 632–641.

Nelson, G. (1978). Psychotherapy supervision from the trainee's point of view: A survey of preferences. *Professional Psychology, 9*, 539–550.

Norcross, J. C. (Section Editor). (1986). Training integrative/eclectic psychotherapists. *International Journal of Eclectic Psychotherapy, 5*, 71–94.

Norcross, J. C. (1988). Supervision of integrative psychotherapy. *Journal of Integrative and Eclectic Psychotherapy, 7*, 157–166.

Norcross, J. C. (1990, August). *Countertransference confessions of a prescriptive eclectic.* Paper presented at the annual conference of the Society for the Exploration of Psychotherapy Integration, Philadelphia.

Norcross, J. C. (1994). *Prescriptive eclectic therapy.* Videotape in the APA Psychotherapy Videotape Series. Washington, DC: American Psychological Association.

Norcross, J. C., & Arkowitz, J. (1992). The evolution and current status of psychotherapy integration. In W. Dryden (Ed.), *Integrative and eclectic psychotherapy: A handbook* (pp. 1–40). London: Open University Press.

Norcross, J. C., Beutler, L. E., & Clarkin, J. F. (1990). Training in differential treatment selection. In *Systematic treatment selection: Toward targeted therapeutic intervention* (pp. 289–307). New York: Brunner/Mazel.

Norcross, J. C., & Goldfried, M. R. (Eds.). (1992). *Handbook of psychotherapy integration.* New York: Basic Books.

Norcross, J. C., & Napolitano, G. (1986). Defining our journal and ourselves. *International Journal of Eclectic Psychotherapy, 5*, 249–255.

Norcross, J. C., & Newman, C. F. (1992). Psychotherapy integration: Setting the context. In J. C. Norcross & M. R. Goldfried (Eds.), *Handbook of psychotherapy integration* (pp. 3–45). New York: Basic Books.

Norcross, J. C., & Prochaska, J. O. (1988). A study of eclectic and integrative views revisited. *Professional Psychology: Research and Practice, 19*, 170–174.

Omer, H., & London, P. (1988). Metamorphosis in psychotherapy: End of the systems era. *Psychotherapy, 25*, 171–180.

Phillips, G. L., & Kanter, C. N. (1984). Mutuality in psychotherapy supervision. *Psychotherapy, 21*, 178–183.

Prochaska, J. O., & DiClemente, C. C. (1992). The transtheoretical approach. In J. C. Norcross & M. R. Goldfried (Eds.), *Handbook of psychotherapy integration* (pp. 300–334). New York: Basic Books.

Prochaska, J. O., & Norcross, J. C. (1994). *Systems of psychotherapy: A transtheoretical analysis* (3rd ed.). Pacific Grove, CA: Brooks/Cole.

Robertson, M. (1986). Training eclectic psychotherapists. In J. C. Norcross (Ed.), *Handbook of eclectic psychotherapy* (pp. 416–435). New York: Brunner/Mazel.

Rosenbaum, R. (1988). Feelings toward integration: A matter of style and identity. *Journal of Integrative and Eclectic Psychotherapy, 7*, 52–60.

Rosenblatt, A., & Mayer, J. E. (1975). Objectionable supervisory styles: Students' views. *Social Work, 20*, 184–189.

Rosenthal, N. R. (1977). A prescriptive approach for counselor training. *Journal of Counseling Psychology, 24*, 231–237.

Saltzman, N., & Norcross, J. C. (Eds.). (1990). *Therapy wars: Contention and convergence in differing clinical approaches.* San Francisco: Jossey-Bass.

Schacht, T. E. (1991). Can psychotherapy education advance psychotherapy integration? *Journal of Psychotherapy Integration, 1*, 305–319.

Shapiro, S. J. (1986). Thought experiments for psychotherapists. *International Journal of Eclectic Psychotherapy, 5*(1), 69–70.

Stein, S. P., Karasu, T. B., Charles, E. S., & Buckley, P. J. (1975). Supervision of the initial interview. *Archives of General Psychiatry, 32*, 265–268.

Stevenson, J. F., & Norcross, J. C. (1987). Current status of training evaluation in clinical psychology. In B. Edelstein & E. Berler (Eds.), *Evaluation and accountability in clinical training* (pp. 77–116). New York: Plenum.

Stoltenberg, C. (1981). Approaching supervision from a developmental perspective: The counselor complexity model. *Journal of Counseling Psychology, 28*, 59–65.

Stoltenberg, C. D., McNeill, B. W., & Crethar, H. C. (1994). Changes in supervision as counselors and therapists gain experience: A review. *Professional Psychology: Research and Practice, 25*, 416–449.

Stricker, G. (1988). Supervision of integrative psychotherapy: Discussion. *Journal of Integrative and Eclectic Psychotherapy, 7*, 176–180.

Strupp, H. H., Butler, S. F., & Rosser, C. L. (1988). Training in psychodynamic psychotherapy. *Journal of Consulting and Clinical Psychology, 56*, 689–695.

Tennen, H. (1988). Supervision of integrative psychotherapy: A critique. *Journal of Integrative and Eclectic Psychotherapy, 7*, 167–175.

Wachtel, P. L. (1991). From eclecticism to synthesis: Toward a more seamless psychotherapeutic integration. *Journal of Psychotherapy Integration, 1*, 43–54.

Watkins, C. E., Jr. (1993). Development of the psychotherapy supervisor: Concepts, assumptions, and hypotheses of the Supervisor Complexity Model. *American Journal of Psychotherapy, 47*, 58–74.

Watkins, C. E., Jr. (1995). Considering psychotherapy supervisor development: A status report. *Psychotherapy Bulletin, 29*(4), 32–34.

Weinberger, J. (1995). Common factors aren't so common: The common factors dilemma. *Clinical Psychology: Science and Practice, 2*, 45–69.

Wiley, M. O., & Ray, P. B. (1986). Counseling supervision by developmental level. *Journal of Counseling Psychology, 33*, 439–445.

Williams, S. & Halgin, R. P. (in press). Issues in psychotherapy supervision between the white supervisor and the black supervisee. *Professional Psychology.*

Worthington, E. L. (1984). An empirical investigation of supervision of counselors as they gain experience. *Journal of Counseling Psychology, 31*, 63–75.

Worthington, E. L. (1987). Changes in supervision as counselors and supervisors gain experience: A review. *Professional Psychology, 18*, 189–208.

CHAPTER 14

Systemic Cognitive-Developmental Supervision: A Developmental-Integrative Approach to Psychotherapy Supervision

SANDRA A. RIGAZIO-DIGILIO
University of Connecticut
THOMAS G. DANIELS
*Sir Wilfred Grenfell College of Memorial
University of Newfoundland*
ALLEN E. IVEY
University of Massachusetts

PSYCHOTHERAPY SUPERVISION TRENDS

Over the past 15 years, two shifts have been occurring in the psychotherapy supervision literature. The first, exemplified by Stoltenberg and McNeill (Chapter 12, this volume), represents a move from pathogenic, problem-oriented approaches to salutogenic, developmental perspectives. The second, illustrated by Norcross and Halgin (Chapter 13, this volume) is associated with a move from school-specific approaches to integrative perspectives.

Systemic cognitive-developmental supervision (SCDS) (Rigazio-DiGilio, 1996a, in press; Rigazio-DiGilio & Anderson, 1991, 1994) is an alternative supervision model that synthesizes these primary shifts within a co-constructive framework. This chapter defines the theoretical foundations upon which SCDS is based, directly links these foundations to the immediacy of the supervision process, and illustrates highly specific assessment and intervention strategies that can be used by psychotherapy supervisors across mental health disciplines.

The Status of Developmental Supervisory Perspectives

Psychotherapy supervision literature has been moving from deficit and reparative approaches to developmental and holistic perspectives, focused on supervisee growth and adaptation (cf. Borders,1986; Carey, 1988; Duhl, 1985; Hess, 1986; Liddle, 1988; Stoltenberg & Delworth, 1987). Much of the initial work focused on hierarchical developmental models. The primary sequence of supervision and the corresponding stages of supervisee development were elaborated. This literature has been invaluable in aiding supervisors to identify the critical issues that must be addressed at different phases of supervision and supervisee growth.

The continued advancement of developmental supervision models is being encouraged throughout several mental health disciplines. For example, Liddle (1991), Holloway

(1987), Anderson, Rigazio-DiGilio, and Kunkler (1995), and Borders (1989) suggest that each field work toward linking developmental theories more directly to the immediate work of supervision. Others suggest that we generate developmental conceptualizations that transcend traditional, stage-specific formulations of supervision and supervisee growth (e.g., Anderson et al., 1995; Ivey & Rigazio-DiGilio, 1991).

SCDS offers an alternative developmental perspective that addresses these recommendations. To begin with, SCDS provides a direct bridge between developmental theory and supervisory practice. That is, the model provides one way to access and assess a supervisee's current cognitive-developmental profile in the immediacy of the supervisory encounter and to co-construct learning environments aimed at enhancing and extending these profiles toward increased perceptual, conceptual, and executive competence. Additionally, SCDS primarily draws on holistic assumptions that view supervisee growth as an idiosyncratic journey. The journey toward professional competence is influenced by the dialectic transactions that occur between supervisees, their developmental histories, and their wider contextual fields. In this regard, the model acknowledges the nonlinear changes in cognitive complexity that accompany supervisee growth over the career span.

The Status of Integrative Supervisory Perspectives

Whereas interest in synthesizing individual, systemic, and ecosystemic approaches into integrative models of psychotherapy has been growing (cf. Breunlin, Schwartz, & Mac Kune-Karrer, 1992; Case & Robinson, 1990; Lebow, 1987; Worthington, 1987), admittedly less has been written about the supervision models necessary to facilitate this process (cf. Bagarozzi & Anderson, 1989; Breunlin, Rampage, & Eovaldi, in press; Piercy & Sprenkle, 1986). The models that do exist address several themes. Integrative models introduce supervisees to different theories, therapies, and strategies and provide broad metaframeworks to organize assessment and treatment efforts across psychotherapy schools and modalities. Many models additionally provide an overarching structure that assists supervisors to tailor their work to the unique needs of the supervisee, the client, and the dynamics of the therapeutic and supervisory relationships. By addressing these more sophisticated themes, integrative supervision models tend to represent advanced forms of professional growth for both psychotherapists and supervisors. That is, such models require the intentional use of a wide repertoire of conceptual, perceptual, and executive skills from diverse theories and approaches, and of skills that address the needs of those seeking psychotherapy or supervision.

SCDS represents one such integrative model. For example, SCDS assessment and intervention strategies can be applied to supervision regardless of the supervisor's or supervisee's preferred approach. As such, the model can be used across schools and disciplines. Further, the SCDS classification matrix assists supervisors to draw from a broad range of supervisory perspectives and approaches to tailor their work to the unique issues and concerns of their supervisees. To understand this supervision model, a brief overview of the therapeutic model from which SCDS is derived is necessary.

DEVELOPMENTAL COUNSELING AND THERAPY: THE PSYCHOTHERAPY THEORY UNDERLYING SCDS

Systemic cognitive-developmental supervision represents an isomorphic translation of a co-constructive, developmental, and integrative psychotherapy model called *developmental counseling and therapy* (DCT; cf. Ivey, 1986, 1991; Rigazio-DiGilio, Gonçalves, &

Ivey, 1994). DCT, along with its extension to families (*systemic cognitive-developmental therapy* (SCDT; cf. Rigazio-DiGilio, 1996b; Rigazio-DiGilio & Ivey, 1991, 1993) and networks (DCT/SCDT; cf. Ivey, 1991; Rigazio-DiGilio, 1994a, 1996a), offers conceptually coherent developmental frameworks that are easily learned and directly applicable to the therapeutic process (Borders, 1994). The models provide highly specific, yet flexible assessment and treatment strategies that assist psychotherapists to understand a client's[1] current cognitive-developmental worldview and to help facilitate the developmental processes associated with effective adaptation.

The DCT/SCDT Framework

DCT and its companion, SCDT, represent alternative approaches to treatment that combine the descriptive and analytic potency of human and systemic developmental theories with the client-focused power of therapeutic practice. Additionally, each model imparts an integrative metaframework that can be used to organize familiar therapeutic approaches and strategies within a developmental classification matrix. As such, the DCT/SCDT framework suggests ways to work across seemingly divergent schools and disciplines, using a co-constructive, developmental paradigm (Rigazio-DiGilio, 1994b). The assumptions undergirding DCT and SCDT have useful implications for psychotherapist training (Rigazio-DiGilio, 1994c) and supervision (Anderson et al., 1995; Carey, 1988; Ivey, 1991; Rigazio-DiGilio, 1996a, in press; Rigazio-DiGilio & Anderson, 1991, 1994).

The Theoretical Underpinnings of DCT and SCDT

DCT and SCDT are based on a synthesis of neo-Platonic philosophies (cf. Plotinus, see Merlan, 1967), developmental theories (cf. Carter & McGoldrick, 1989; Gilligan, 1982; Kegan, 1982; Piaget, 1954/1923) and constructivist thought (cf. Kelly, 1955; Vygotsky, 1986/1934; Watzlawick, 1984). This synthesis generates a reinterpretation of human and systemic development and offers a new contextual understanding of how individual and collective worldviews are constructed.

The Developmental Framework. In terms of the developmental framework undergirding DCT and SCDT, traditional, hierarchical perspectives of human and systemic development that imply sequential growth toward increasing levels of cognitive or organizational complexity are recast to encompass spherical and recursive perspectives. To indicate this concept of holism versus hierarchy, DCT and SCDT metaphorically transform the cognitive-developmental levels proposed by Piaget for use within a holistic framework of human and systemic growth and adaptation. This change is highlighted by the use of the term *orientation,* rather than level, to express the various ways individuals and systems make sense of their experience, construct meaning, and operate in their worlds.

The Constructivist Framework. The constructivist framework underlying DCT and SCDT posits that development occurs as a function of a dialectic relationship among individuals, families, and the wider environment. In effect, individuals and families do not develop as pawns of the environment or as independent from their environment. Rather, it is the transaction among individual, family, and environment that creates the dynamic

---

[1]The term *client* refers to individuals, partners, families, and wider systems involved in the therapeutic process.

interplay for development to occur (cf. Harland, 1987; Harre, 1983; Vygotsky, 1986/1934). To highlight this social constructivist perspective, the term *co-construction* is used. Individuals co-construct their worldviews as they participate in the environment. Additionally, individuals co-construct and then share collective worldviews by participating in resonating experiences within committed relationships that evolve within a wider sociocultural context (Rigazio-DiGilio & Ivey, 1991, 1993, 1995). Therapy and supervision are also viewed as a dialectic, co-constructive process of change.

The Interplay Between Developmental and Co-Constructivist Perspectives.   These two constructs—orientations and co-constructivism—lay the groundwork for understanding how individuals and families construct and modify their worldviews, over time and within different contexts. In effect, DCT and SCDT posit that our developmental history, fashioned by the family and the wider sociocultural context that surrounds the family, shapes our worldview. Given these constructs, it becomes difficult to view differences and atypical behavior as deficits. DCT and SCDT therefore reject pathological descriptions of client behavior. Instead, cognitions, behaviors, and emotions are viewed as natural and logical consequences of the transactions that occur among one's developmental and contextual histories and the current environmental, personal, and systemic demands for adaptation and change (Ginter, 1989; Ivey, 1986; Rigazio-DiGilio, 1994a; Rigazio-DiGilio & Ivey, 1995).

DCT and SCDT Cognitive-Developmental Orientations

Four cognitive-developmental orientations are used to classify the various worldviews individuals and collective systems[2] can access to experience, make sense of, and operate in their worlds: sensorimotor/elemental, concrete/situational, formal/reflective, and dialectic/systemic. It is suggested that individuals, families, and wider systems capable of intentionally accessing several of these orientations have a wide repertoire of cognitive, behavioral, and affective options to draw on when facing situational or developmental tasks. These individuals and collective systems have developed a strong foundation within several orientations, and therefore, can draw upon the multiple *competencies* available within each orientation.

Conversely, individuals and collective systems that are unable to access a multitude of orientations or haphazardly move across orientations have a limited repertoire of options from which to draw. In these instances, strong foundations are not constructed within each orientation, and individuals and collective systems are more apt to rely on the *constraints* associated with an orientation. In support of this concept, it has been found that subjects

---

[2]The SCDT construct of *collective worldviews* suggests that families use unique filters to mediate collective understandings of the world and of life tasks. Despite the fact that this construct has been defined in the literature for well over 15 years (cf. Constantine, 1986; Kantor, 1983; Proctor, 1985; Reiss, 1981), this level of systems thinking is often considered quite elusive. For example, many trained within an individualistic paradigm have difficulty conceptualizing how a group of family members could primarily rely on one frame of reference to make sense of their world. In this regard, supervisees need to be exposed to the many factors (e.g., power-differentials, differentiation, individuation, life-cycle issues, cultural issues, legacies) that influence the co-construction of collective worldviews. By being exposed to these phenomena, they will learn to identify how some families construct a true synthesis of all individual members' orientations, how other families rely on a dominant member's (e.g., mother, son, identified patient) or subsystem's (e.g., parental, parent-child) worldview to mediate their collective understanding of the world and their life tasks, and how some families gravitate toward a neutral orientation that provides a common, safe ground for all members to come together.

who can function within multiple orientations report fewer physical and emotional symptoms than subjects with access to only one orientation (Heesacker, Prichard, Rigazio-DiGilio, & Ivey, in work)

The Sensorimotor/Elemental Orientation.   Clients with access to the sensorimotor/elemental orientation use their sensory experiences—what they see, hear, and feel—to construct meaning within their world. Competencies include the ability to engage in direct emotional experiences, to monitor emotional transactions without becoming bewildered, and to identify personal feelings. When constrained within this orientation, however, clients can be easily overwhelmed by affective situations, and tend to restrict effective use of their cognitive and behavioral repertoires.

The Concrete/Situational Orientation.   Clients operating within the concrete/situational orientation can describe actions and events and can think and act in highly predictable ways. Competencies include the ability to accurately apply if/then reasoning and to anticipate consequences. Constrained clients rigidly rely on a narrow range of behaviors and experience difficulty with abstract and affectual perspectives.

The Formal/Reflective Orientation.   Clients operating in the formal/reflective orientation can articulate recurring patterns manifest in their person-environment transactions. Competencies such as multiple perspective taking, synthesizing ideas and concepts, and reflecting on one's own functioning are evident. Clients who overintellectualize, minimize, or neglect affectual and behavioral data and who have difficulty transferring their abstractions into effective actions are considered to be constrained within this orientation.

The Dialectic/Systemic Orientation.   Clients who recognize the recursive influences of intrafamilial and sociocultural contexts on their development operate within the dialectic/systemic orientation. Competencies include the ability to remain aware of contextual influences; to examine, deconstruct, and reconstruct rules and assumptions; and to seek solutions that incorporate resources from the self, the other, and the wider environment. Constraining factors include a proclivity to become overwhelmed by a multiplicity of perspectives and to assume a cynical disposition detached from effective action.

The Predominant Cognitive-Developmental Orientation.   Research indicates that individuals (Rigazio-DiGilio & Ivey, 1990) and families (Rigazio-DiGilio, in work) tend to adhere to a "predominant orientation" when considering the issues promoting treatment. Empirical and clinical data confirm that these predominant orientations can be drawn out and assessed through the natural language of the therapeutic dialogue (Ivey & Ivey, 1990; Lanza, Rigazio-DiGilio, & Kunkler, 1993; Rigazio-DiGilio, 1994a, in work; Rigazio-DiGilio & Ivey, 1990, 1991; Rigazio-DiGilio, Lanza, & Kunkler, 1994).[3] Additionally, when asked questions intended to facilitate explorations in various orientations, clients are able to reframe their presenting issues using multiple perspectives and alternatives for change.

---

[3]Highly specific, open-ended assessment questions, along with linguistically oriented individual and collective profiles for each orientation are available for psychotherapists to use in the assessment phase of treatment. Further, specific questions intended to facilitate client explorations within each orientation are also available for use within both the assessment and treatment phases of psychotherapy (e.g., Ivey, Gonçalves, & Ivey, 1989; Ivey & Rigazio-DiGilio, 1991; Ivey, Rigazio-DiGilio, & Ivey, 1991; Rigazio-DiGilio, 1994a; Rigazio-DiGilio, Gonçalves, & Ivey, 1994; Rigazio-DiGilio & Ivey, 1991).

Co-Constructing Therapeutic Environments to Enhance Client Development

The aim of DCT and SCDT is to enhance client access to a variety of orientations so as to increase emotional, cognitive, and behavioral options. This is facilitated when psychotherapists co-construct, with their clients, different therapeutic environments that invite client explorations within each orientation. Highly specific questioning strategies and treatment interventions, explicated within DCT and SCDT, can be tailored to the contextual issues of each client to initiate access to more than one orientation.

Horizontal Development.   Although treatment protocols are similar for DCT and SCDT, the course of specific therapeutic encounters varies according to the developmental needs of each client. In general, clients are first assisted to construct enhanced emotional, cognitive, and behavioral options within the orientation most familiar to them—their predominant cognitive-developmental orientation. The goal of horizontal development is to reinforce adequate access to and utilization of the possible intrapersonal and interpersonal resources within this orientation. This type of intervention requires that the psychotherapist use *style-matching strategies* to help co-construct an environment that allows clients to exercise the many potentials found within their primary orientation.

Vertical Development.   The second change strategy, vertical development, assists clients to tap resources and perspectives within underutilized or unfamiliar orientations. Here, clients are guided to explore the feelings, thoughts, and behaviors that are generated from different cognitive-developmental orientations. The psychotherapist assumes a *style-shifting* posture that facilitates client exploration and experimentation within these different orientations. Once clients demonstrate comfort and facility accessing a particular orientation, the psychotherapist resumes a style-matching posture to enhance further horizontal development within the new orientation. This cycle is repeated throughout psychotherapy to help clients gain access to as many orientations as possible—and hence, gain multiple perspectives and a wider range of cognitive, behavioral, and affective options to deal with the presenting issues.

The Four Psychotherapy Environments.   DCT and SCDT identify four psychotherapy environments, associated with each of the four cognitive-developmental orientations—*environmental structuring, coaching, consulting, and collaborating.*[4] There are highly specific DCT and SCDT questioning strategies that correspond to each of these environments and that can be used to assist clients to remain focused within a particular orientation long enough for change to be initiated and reinforced. Additionally, DCT and SCDT offer classification matrices that can be used to organize strategies and techniques from across many schools and disciplines. These allow psychotherapists to organize strategies, approaches, theories, and modalities that are familiar to them into the four DCT/SCDT psychotherapy environments.[5] Once developed, each psychotherapist's unique classification matrix can be used to co-construct coherent, developmentally oriented, and culturally sensitive treatment plans.

[4]See Kunkler and Rigazio-DiGilio,1994; Ivey, 1986, 1991; Ivey and Rigazio-DiGilio, 1994; Rigazio-DiGilio, 1994a, 1994c; Rigazio-DiGilio, Gonçalves, and Ivey, 1994; and Rigazio-DiGilio and Ivey, 1991, 1993 for full descriptions of these therapeutic environments.

[5]Examples of classification matrices have been constructed for individual (Ivey, 1986, 1991; Rigazio-DiGilio, Gonçlaves, & Ivey, 1994; Rigazio-DiGilio & Ivey, 1991), family (Rigazio-DiGilio & Ivey, 1991, 1993; Kunkler & Rigazio-DiGilio, 1994), and network (Ivey, 1991; Rigazio-DiGilio, 1994a) psychotherapy.

This form of practice is an advanced integrative process that continues throughout the career span of any psychotherapist. The key variables to be understood include the nature and complexities of each cognitive-developmental orientation and the specific use of language skills and strategies to fashion interventions that promote horizontal or vertical development.[6]

DCT and SCDT suggest that by being fully conscious of the selection and intentionality of specific questions and strategies within the session, the psychotherapist is able to help each client feel accepted and to explore and master cognitive, affectual, and behavioral resources inherent within each orientation. Knowledge of and practice with identifying orientations and co-constructing psychotherapy environments make visible the process of moving clients from one orientation to another.

SYSTEMIC COGNITIVE-DEVELOPMENTAL SUPERVISION

Systemic cognitive-developmental supervision posits that supervisee growth is an individualistic journey that transcends stage-specific, linear-hierarchial conceptualizations. The complex and recursive nature of supervisee growth is considered a natural process toward increased professional competence. SCDS provides specific concepts and tools for supervisors to understand and work with each psychotherapist in a truly personalized fashion. The model clarifies several developmental and structural processes of supervision that can be tapped to propel supervisee maturation.

The SCDS Framework

SCDS as a Supervision Model.   As an alternative model to individual or family supervision, SCDS presents specific assessment and questioning strategies that can be directly applied to the supervisory context. Additionally, because this approach represents an isomorphic translation of DCT and SCDT, psychotherapists supervised within the model are provided the opportunity to learn each therapeutic model in its own right, and to learn the metatheoretical framework used to transcend existing boundaries among diverse individual, systemic, and ecosystemic approaches.

SCDS as a Metatheoretical Framework.   As a metatheoretical framework, SCDS offers a developmental classification schema that integrates various supervisory interventions and strategies that supervisors can draw on in a theoretically coherent fashion. Because the model is not school specific, it can be applied to supervision regardless of the supervisor's or supervisee's preferred approaches or primary disciplines. Further, this schema allows supervisors to incorporate their own unique practices into the overarching framework of the model.

The Theoretical Underpinnings of SCDS

Four theoretical assumptions, derived from DCT and SCDT, undergird this supervision model:

[6]Helpful readings include those who advocate for a developmental paradigm (cf. Combrinck-Graham, 1986; Liddle, 1988), those who advocate for integrative frameworks (cf. Feixas, 1990; Feldman, 1989; Pinsof, 1983), and those who offer strategies for developing one's own personal model of integrative psychotherapy (cf. Ivey, Ivey, & Simek-Morgan, 1994; Lebow, 1987).

1. Supervisee development is holistic, recursive, and nonhierarchical in nature.
2. Supervisee development is co-constructed within the person-environment dialectic of the supervisory relationship, including supervisor, psychotherapist, client, and professional contexts.
3. The developmental processes of supervision are culturally embedded.
4. Supervisee development can be assessed and stimulated via linguistic channels.

Supervisee Development Is Holistic.   "Therapists enter supervision with a unique background of personal and professional experiences that organize the way they conceptualize and approach clinical and supervisory information" (Rigazio-DiGilio & Anderson, 1994, p. 98). Consistent with DCT and SCDT theory, this supervision model identifies four cognitive-developmental orientations that psychotherapists can draw on in their clinical work. Descriptors of these orientations, along with corresponding competencies and constraints, are detailed in Table 14.1.

SCDS posits that psychotherapists who have access to the resources within several cognitive-developmental orientations are able to construct robust clinical conceptualizations and to develop and implement comprehensive treatment plans uniquely suited to the clients they serve. Conversely, psychotherapists with limited access to various orientations have fewer resources to draw on in terms of assessment and treatment. Therefore, the primary goal of supervision is to empower psychotherapists to access the primary resources found within each of the orientations so as to enhance and expand conceptual, perceptual, and executive skills.

Over time, clients may need access to several of the therapeutic environments in order to understand and work through developmental and situational tasks. If psychotherapists learn to move within and among several orientations, they can access the environments best suited to each therapeutic alliance. The client-focused psychotherapist would therefore need to be comfortable working within each orientation to facilitate horizontal and vertical development. This would be in contrast to approaches that—intentionally or inadvertently—expect clients to work through their issues within a limited range of orientations more compatible to specific schools of thought or psychotherapist preferences.

SCDS supervisors help psychotherapists establish clinical skills within all four orientations. Work moves in a systematic fashion based on the needs of the clients, the cognitive-developmental range of the psychotherapist, and the goals of supervision. The course of supervision does not simply flow through the four phases from sensorimotor/elemental, to concrete/situational, to formal/reflective, and then to dialectic/systemic. Instead, SCDS supervisors view and respond to supervisees in a holistic manner. Movement through the orientations is recursive and idiosyncratic, reflecting an oscillating pattern of growth rather than a linear course of development. It is therefore not unusual to re-enter an orientation previously explored as the needs of client and psychotherapist dictate.

Supervision Is a Co-Constructive Process.   SCDS supervisors remain alert to the dialectic relationships among the psychotherapist, the supervisor, the client, and the professional contexts. The power to influence is viewed as a dynamic force that shifts among all participants over time. A linear or static model of the power differentials that emerge during the supervisory process is not consistent with this approach. In classical forms of supervision, the "power" is seen to rest with the supervisor, and in more contemporary models, the power is seen to be re-distributed over time—from the supervisor to the psychotherapist—as the psychotherapist "matures." In a co-constructive view of the super-

Table 14.1   The Four SCDS Cognitive-Developmental Orientations

SCDS posits that supervisees have access to skills within four cognitive-developmental orientations. Each orientation offers different conceptual, perceptual, and executive resources that supervisees can draw on during therapeutic and supervisory encounters. *Competencies* represent the skills available to supervisees who can flexibly access a variety of orientations. *Constraints* reflect the ways supervisees who over-rely on a particular orientation might be limited within the borders of that orientation.

Orientation	Competencies	Constraints
Sensorimotor/Elemental		
Supervisees use direct sensory experiences to understand and work with their clients. They may request help organizing clinical information into workable hypotheses, clarifying intense emotional exchanges, and developing structured plans for each session.	Flexible supervisees can draw on here-and-now skills. They can directly experience and track emotional exchanges without becoming reactive or overwhelmed. They can identify their own personal feelings during therapy and supervision, permitting them to work through issues of transference and countertransference.	Over-reliant supervisees are affected by intense emotional exchanges and are prone to their own hyperstimulation. They are drawn to affective involvements that interfere with their conceptual and executive skills. Interventions are based on what feels right at the time, resulting in random, haphazard treatment planning.
Concrete/Situational		
Supervisees can describe events that take place in therapy and supervision. Their ability to articulate cause and effect transactions permits them to operate with predictability. They may request help regarding how to accomplish interventions and develop treatment plans. They often ask supervisors to validate versus question their observations, interpretations, and actions.	Supervisees with access to several orientations can apply if/then reasoning and can develop linear hypotheses so as to better anticipate client reactions. Their descriptions of basic dynamics that occur during therapy and supervision are usually keenly accurate.	Supervisees constrained within this orientation depend on one set of hypotheses or techniques, even in the face of opposing clinical data. They have difficulty seeing alternative perspectives, viewing situations from affective or reflective vantage points, and applying circular reasoning. Finally, they have difficulty recognizing how specific interventions fit into a wider, comprehensive treatment plan.

(table continues)

231

Table 14.1 (Continued)

Orientation	Competencies	Constraints
Formal/Reflective		
Supervisees can analyze situations from multiple perspectives and can use reflective and circular reasoning. They often request help deciphering typical patterns within or across cases or in relation to themselves, as well as assistance in examining theoretical/ therapeutic themes.	Supervisees with access to several orientations synthesize ideas and strategies across various models and can modify their treatment plans based on clinical or supervisory feedback. They can examine how their own patterns impact therapy and supervision. They can directly link what they are doing with an overall treatment plan.	Rigid supervisees can provide in-depth assessments and treatment plans but have difficulty transferring these to effective executive skills during therapy. They minimize affective and behavioral data, preferring to analyze themes across situations. They have difficulty recognizing or challenging their assumptions.
Dialectic/Systemic		
Supervisees challenge the assumptions undergirding their conceptualizations. They seek out the origins of what and how they learn, and the rules governing their thoughts, feelings, and actions. They request help organizing their thoughts and questions into appropriate treatment plans. They overexamine their cognitions and need assistance with low-inference analysis. They seek assurance of their treatment plans because they recognize the limitations inherent in any one choice.	Supervisees who can access several orientations are aware of wider contextual and historical influences and seek solutions aimed at clients and the broader environment. They can assist clients through the deconstruction and reconstruction of rules, assumptions, and themes.	Supervisees constrained within this orientation can be so overwhelmed by multiple and contextual perspectives that they cannot commit to a plan of action. They easily render any sense of reality meaningless, versus treating ideas as alternate and perhaps viable constructions. Clients are often unable to integrate the complexity of their ideas.

Table 14.1 is reproduced here by permission of Sandra A. Rigazio-DiGilio, copyright 1995.

visory relationship, however, power shifts during the course of supervision depending on the topics and issues being explored, the events occurring, and the relationship developing between the participants. For example, a supervisor who possesses great expertise in one school of psychotherapy will be able to assume a learner role when the psychotherapist examines the clinical utility of interventions from approaches outside the supervisor's field of expertise.

Given the holistic and co-constructive perspective of supervisee development, the SCDS supervisor does not possess a preconceived map regarding what speed or direction supervisee progress should take (Rigazio-DiGilio, in press). Instead, they possess a framework to understand where the psychotherapist is at and a flexible supervisory style that accommodates to the specific supervisory and clinical needs of the moment. In this regard, SCDS does not follow one inevitable path, from the level of novice to the level of mature clinician. Rather, the journey is personal and meandering, has many turns and twists, and often leads back into itself. The SCDS supervisor is responsive to this recycling course and is able to work within the psychotherapist's frame of reference.

The Cultural Experience of Supervision.   Cultural issues and individual differences have a significant impact on the course and outcome of psychotherapy and supervision and need to be explored (cf. Cheatham & Stewart, 1990; Falicov, 1988; Pedersen, 1991; Rigazio-DiGilio & Ivey, 1995; Sue, 1991). The issues that emerge in the supervisory alliance are imbued with cultural and individual influences. Every interaction between client and psychotherapist and between psychotherapist and supervisor can be considered a cultural exchange. This contextual aspect of psychotherapy and supervision is always paramount in the supervisor's mind. Because DCT and SCDT operate within the worldview of the clients, the influence and importance of culture, as interpreted by each individual and collective system, assumes great prominence (Arciniega & Newlon, 1994). Individual and systemic worldviews emerge from the culture in which they were developed and, as such, reflect particular predispositions and proclivities of that culture. These variations in worldviews should be a constant consideration in every therapeutic and supervisory relationship. For example, it is not uncommon for some psychotherapists to paraphrase or reframe the needs of a client from a different culture into words or ideas more compatible with the psychotherapist's culture. In cases such as this, electronic (i.e., audio or video) and live supervision are effective interventions to help the psychotherapist "hear" clients "in-their-own-language" and work on treatment plans based on expressed client need, rather than the interpreted expectations of the psychotherapist.

Issues pertaining to gender, class, ethnic heritage, ability and disability, and age are all appropriate areas to explore during therapeutic and supervisory encounters. Many of these issues are often excluded from supervision and considered secondary to clinical data. If not explored in supervision, however, one can assume these issues will remain in the background of the therapeutic alliance.

Assessing and Stimulating Supervisee Growth via Linguistic Channels

SCDS Questioning Strategies.   At the beginning of supervision, the psychotherapist is asked a series of open-ended questions pertaining to the case being discussed (e.g., "How do you conceptualize this client?") and the supervisory objectives (e.g., "What would you like to focus on in supervision?") (Table 14.2). The supervisor uses only basic attending skills as the psychotherapist responds so that psychotherapist language is not significantly influenced by the dialogue during this assessment phase. The responses provide direct evi-

Table 14.2 Sample SCDS Questioning Strategies for Supervisory Assessment and Intervention

Open-Ended Assessment Questions

Therapy How do you make sense of this case? How do you conceptualize this client?
Supervision What would you like to focus on in supervision? What do you need from supervision?

Intervention Questions to Promote Horizontal and Vertical Development

Client	Self-as-Therapist	Therapeutic Process	Supervisory Process
Sensorimotor/ Elemental			
How does this client express emotions?	How do you feel as you describe them?	How is this client feeling toward you?	How does my reaction affect you?
What direct behaviors seem most relevant to understanding this client?	What direct experiences do you attend to to make sense of this case?	How do your feelings about this client affect how you act toward her in session?	What are you feeling before you come/during/after supervision?
How do you define the emotional climate between this couple?	How do you define your own emotional experience in session?	When they question your competence, what feelings arise for you?	How are your feelings about our supervisory interaction affecting you right now?
Concrete/Situational			
What do they do and say to each other?	Can you tell me exactly what you did?	What did they do to prompt that reaction?	Could you describe what just occurred?
What happens between the couple that leads you to this hypothesis?	How could you better execute that kind of intervention in the next session?	How did they respond to you when you asked that question to the father?	Can you describe what part of our interaction was helpful to you today?
What happens when you ask them to talk together?	How could you present yourself more confidently in session?	What do you think will happen if you ask them to do that next session?	Can you describe exactly what I did that brought you to that conclusion?

Formal/Reflective

What themes are evident that help you understand this case?	Does your reaction to this situation seem familiar to you?	What approach seems to match this family best?	How is our relationship similar to others in your life?
What patterns repeat that help you understand this case?	Have you done or felt similar things in other relationships?	What themes surface when he thinks you are challenging him?	Can we discuss the pattern that is recurring between us?
Does the couple always respond that way during intimate conversations?	Does this reaction you are having match what occurs when you terminate with other cases?	What are the repeating patterns of interaction occurring between you and this couple?	Do you notice any themes in how we interact together at times of high anxiety or challenge?

Dialectic/Systemic

What rules does this client operate from?	What rules are you operating from?	What rules guide the therapy relationship?	What rules guide the work we do here?
What are the origins of the rules guiding the client's way of perceiving this?	What are the origins of the rules that guide your way of thinking and acting?	Who set these rules in this relationship, and how are these rules challenged?	How did these rules come to define our relationship? Can we challenge the rules?
Is this client able to challenge the assumptions underlying his beliefs?	Do you notice flaws or constraints in these assumptions you have about therapy?	Can you and he discuss how the rules governing therapy are constraining growth?	How do our unique backgrounds influence our work together?

Table 14.2 is reproduced here by permission of Sandra A. Rigazio-DiGilio, copyright 1995.

dence of the psychotherapist's primary and ancillary orientations in relation to the particular issues being discussed and also establish the goals of supervision. Coded observations of videotaped supervision sessions indicate that the primary and ancillary cognitive-developmental orientations used by psychotherapists to conceptualize particular clients and supervisory needs can be identified in their natural language (Rigazio-DiGilio, 1996a; Rigazio-DiGilio & Anderson, 1991).

A second set of exploratory questions is used to determine the range of access psychotherapists have in any given orientation (horizontal movement), and the degree to which they can explore issues across orientations (vertical movement). These questions also can be used, throughout the supervisory process, to facilitate movement within and across orientations. Table 14.2 presents a four-by-four matrix of sample questioning strategies that align the cognitive-developmental orientations with significant areas of clinical practice: the client, the self-as-therapist, the therapeutic process, and the supervisory process.

Questions that target the four areas of practice within one orientation are structured to facilitate horizontal movement and are aimed at establishing an adequate foundation within that particular orientation. For example, sustained explorations within the sensorimotor/elemental orientation can be accomplished by asking questions, such as "How do you define the emotional climate between this couple?" (client); "How do you define your own emotional experience in session?" (self-as-therapist); "How do your feelings about this client affect how you act toward her in session?" (therapeutic process); and, "How are your feelings about our supervisory interaction affecting you right now?" (supervisory process).

Questions that range across the four orientations within one area of practice are used to facilitate vertical movement. For example, exploratory questions regarding the therapeutic process might include the following: "When they question your competence, what feelings arise for you?" (sensorimotor/elemental); "What did they do to prompt this reaction from you?" (concrete/situational); "Have these types of interactions occurred between you and other families during this particular phase of treatment?" (formal/reflective); and "What assumptions are you making about these types of interactions?," "How are these assumptions limiting you and your clients?," " What might be some alternative ways of conceptualizing what is occurring?," and "How could these alternative perspectives change the way these interactions occur?" (dialectic/systemic).

SCDS Supervisory Environments.   As suggested within the DCT and SCDT models, there are four supervisory environments that correspond to each of the cognitive-developmental orientations. The *directive environment* provides firm and gentle parameters that permit psychotherapists to explore sensory-based experience that is generated in their clinical work or during the supervisory encounter. A *coaching environment* helps psychotherapists clearly delineate the thoughts, feelings, and behaviors of self, client, and supervisor from a linear, interactive frame in order to act more predictably during the therapeutic or supervisory encounter. A *consultative environment* stresses the facilitation of reflective and integrative skills and is used to assist psychotherapists to identify patterns of behaviors, thoughts, and feelings across clients, self, therapeutic exchanges, and supervisory exchanges. Additionally, this environment assists psychotherapists to incorporate new theories and approaches to treatment within their own overarching treatment paradigm. Finally, a *collaborative environment* focuses on the cognitive and metacognitive processes supporting a psychotherapist's belief system about clients, psychotherapy, and supervision.

These four environments can be co-constructed using the SCDS questioning strategies presented in Table 14.2, and using a wide array of supervisory modalities and techniques to facilitate conceptual, perceptual, and executive skill mastery within (horizontal development) and skill extension across (vertical development) orientations. Samples of these interventions are presented in Table 14.3, along with descriptions of the four environments and the primary objectives associated with each.

Style-Matching/Reinforcing the Psychotherapist's Foundation. The process of co-constructing supervisory environments that correspond with the psychotherapist's predominant orientation is referred to as style-matching. Here, supervisors intentionally apply interventions and strategies that assist psychotherapists to master a wide range of skills within the targeted orientation.

For example, Alexis,[7] a psychotherapist over-relying on the sensorimotor/elemental orientation, became overwhelmed by the intensity of a family's interaction and emotional tone. She had difficulty organizing a coherent conceptualization of the family and employing therapeutic strategies to understand or extend the family's worldview. The supervisor co-constructed a directive supervisory environment that assisted Alexis to develop a capacity to handle intense emotion and to learn to attend to specific aspects of a session so that she could develop comprehensive hypotheses. Additionally, the supervisor assisted Alexis to develop a treatment plan, and to then implement therapeutic strategies associated with this plan. Supervisor and psychotherapist co-therapy teams, along with live supervision with bug-in-the-ear and phone-in technology, were used to help Alexis feel the direct guidance and support of the supervisor. She became more able to sit with the anxiety of emotional exchanges. Video observation assisted Alexis to learn how to attend to salient aspects of the session so as to develop clear client conceptualizations and treatment plans. Finally, role plays were used so that Alexis could practice the implementation of treatment plans and rehearse her ability to handle intense affect in the safety of the supervisory context.

Style-Shifting/Expanding Supervisee Development. Style-shifting is the process of assisting psychotherapists to extend and master clinical skills within new or underutilized orientations. To accomplish this, the supervisor initially assumes a style-mismatching posture toward an underutilized orientation. The orientation chosen is influenced by material offered in supervision that suggests a psychotherapist's willingness to move toward unfamiliar territory. Once the psychotherapist indicates the ability to use perceptual, conceptual, and executive skills associated with the new orientation, the supervisor resumes a style-matching posture. This reinforces new learnings, moving the psychotherapist to skill mastery.

Building on the previous example, Alexis came to understand, over time, that there were particular client personality characteristics and therapeutic phases, related to high emotionality and anxiety, that were particularly challenging to her. As co-therapy, live supervision, and role plays began to allay some of her anxiety and help her move more predictably in session, she became curious about the patterns that reoccurred with specific client types and in relation to specific treatment phases. Building on this formal/reflective curiosity, the supervisor and Alexis co-constructed a consultative environment aimed at understanding and confronting these recurring patterns. This environment emerged through the use of SCDS questioning strategies, such as "What are the patterns that are being repeated across cases?" and "What other types of clients trigger this reaction for you?" These questions led to the analysis of patterns and other similarities across cases through the use of edited videotapes that reflected the major themes introduced in the supervision dialogue (i.e., Alexis's defensive posture when confronted by skeptical male clients, her

---

[7]The supervisee's name has been changed for purposes of confidentiality.

Table 14.3 The Four SCDS Environments Associated With Each Cognitive-Developmental Orientation

The primary objective of SCDS is to assist supervisees to access the broad range of perceptual, conceptual, and executive resources available within each of the four cognitive-developmental orientations. This holistic directive requires supervisors to co-construct—with their supervisees—environments that facilitate both horizontal (skill mastery) and vertical (skill extension) development. Four supervisory environments, corresponding to each of the cognitive-developmental orientations, can be used to tailor supervision to the unique needs of the supervisee.

Supervision Environment	Supervision Objectives	Sample Supervision Modalities/Techniques
Sensorimotor/Elemental: *Structured Environment* To co-construct this environment, the supervisor uses a directive style that permits supervisees to safely explore sensory-based data and integrate salient aspects of these data into a coherent and workable framework.	1. Develop skills in case conceptualization. 2. Clarify and directly experience client and therapist feelings. 3. Reduce anxiety. 4. Identify transference/countertransference issues.	1. Live supervision / bug-in-ear or phone in. 2. Supervisor/supervisee teams doing therapy. 3. Electronic supervision focused on case conceptualization. 4. Team supervision focused on case conceptualization. 5. Instruction, independent readings. 6. Role plays, sculpting, experiential exercises.
Concrete/Situational: *Coaching Environment* To co-construct this environment, the supervisor uses a semidirective, coaching style to assist supervisees to frame thoughts, feelings, and behaviors from an if/then linear perspective and to assist them to act more predictably in the therapeutic encounter.	1. Learn/practice strategies and techniques. 2. Become proficient at if/then reasoning. 3. Enhance tracking skills. 4. Increase predictability. 5. Understand decision-making process across therapy and supervision environments.	1. Live supervision with pre/mid/post session coaching. 2. Electronic supervision focused on conceptual and executive mastery. 3. Practice exercises focused on conceptual and executive skills. 4. Case presentation focused on accurate description.

Formal/Reflective:
Consulting Environment

To co-construct this environment the supervisor takes on a consultation role, working with the supervisee to better understand the constancy of patterns within self, client, therapeutic theories and therapies, and therapeutic and supervisory relationships. This environment stresses work on reflective and abstract, analytical skills.

1. Reflect/analyze self and clinical data.
2. Generalize assessment and intervention skills.
3. Identify themes and patterns in self, client, therapy, and supervision.
4. Co-construct parallel analogs to help clients expand perspectives and actions.

1. Edited electronic segments focused on identifying similar patterns and themes across cases and therapeutic encounters.
2. Assistance in constructing and using integrative metaframeworks.
3. Independent, self-analysis exercises.

Dialectic/Systemic:
Collaborating Environment

To co-construct this environment, supervisor and supervisee engage in a collegial, collaborative venture, focused on core cognitive and meta-cognitive processes such as the person-environment dialectic and personal constructs.

1. Recognize/challenge assumptions and rules.
2. Recognize/challenge developmental and contextual influences on worldview constructions and behaviors.
3. Evaluate parameters of one's beliefs and constructions.

1. Supervision focused on epistemological and ontological issues.
2. Cotherapy.
3. Peer consultation.
4. Co-constructing hypotheses and plans.
5. Analyzation of self and therapeutic framework for generalizability and unrecognized bias.

Table 14.3 is reproduced here by permission of Sandra A. Rigazio-DiGilio, copyright 1995.

defensive posture when creating alliances with adolescent females, and her difficulties in psychotherapy if clients are reticent to explore issues she deems important).

By looking holistically at a number of cases over time, Alexis was able to assume a more reflective posture about the nature and origins of her reactions. This new understanding provided a stronger foundation in the formal/reflective orientation and served as a point of departure toward other orientations. For example, when Alexis became anxious regarding her new understanding, a return to the sensorimotor/elemental orientation was undertaken. When she requested assistance in knowing how to identify precursors to her reaction and to intervene more effectively, a move to a coaching environment was initiated by the supervisor and Alexis. Finally, should Alexis wish to challenge the origins of some of her assumptions regarding challenge and protection, a move to a more collaborative environment will be in order.

The process of style-shifting, including style-matching and style-mismatching, involves the use of language and interventions that enable psychotherapists to develop clinical skills within all four orientations. The supervisory team needs to be able to establish and maintain in-depth analyses of issues at all four orientations and across all four areas of practice depicted in Table 14.2. Supervisory competencies associated with supervision of this nature include linguistic skills, theoretical and pragmatic knowledge across treatment methods, and an understanding of the DCT and SCDT framework to establish environments that integrate the needs of the client, the psychotherapist, and the supervisory relationship. Only by modeling developmental supervision will psychotherapists be enabled to use developmental counseling and therapy methods with individuals, families, and wider systems seeking treatment.

RESEARCH

A research base, suggesting the validity and utility of DCT and SCDT constructs and questioning strategies, is beginning to emerge. Research concerning the supervisory implications of SCDS also has been initiated. Finally, the combined clinical and empirical support for DCT and SCDT has led to new investigations about each model. In this section, the studies pertinent to the fundamental assumptions undergirding SCDS are reported.

Clinical Findings

1. *Can therapists be trained to identify and use cognitive-developmental orientations in clinical practice?*

DCT and SCDT have been used to successfully treat children and families with transitional difficulties (Ivey & Ivey, 1990), agoraphobics (Gonçalves, 1988; Gonçalves & Ivey, 1992), anxiety disorders (Gonçalves & Machado, 1987), victims of physical accidents (Kenny & Law, 1991), Japanese university students (Fukuhara, 1984; Tamase & Rigazio-DiGilio, in press), students preparing to enter the workplace (Mailler, 1991), men who batter (Lanza et al., 1993; Rigazio-DiGilio et al., 1994), and inpatient depressives (Rigazio-DiGilio & Ivey, 1990). These findings demonstrate that the cognitive-developmental orientations represented in client language can be accessed and assessed throughout the course of treatment, and that these data can be used to design and monitor developmentally appropriate and culturally sensitive treatment plans. Fukuhara also demonstrated the differences that occur in cognitive processing before, during, and after treatment.

2. *Have cognitive-developmental concepts been examined in the supervisory context?*

Rigazio-DiGilio (1996a) and Rigazio-DiGilio and Anderson (1991) coded videotapes of marriage and family therapy supervisees to show the viability of using SCDS questioning strategies and the companion linguistic profiles to identify the orientations used by supervisees to conceptualize clients and determine supervisory goals. This research indicated that the predominant cognitive-developmental orientation of supervisees can be identified in the here and now of the supervisory dialogue.

Empirical Findings

1. *How have DCT / SCDT concepts been psychometrically validated?*

Using an inpatient depressive population, Rigazio-DiGilio and Ivey (1990) validated the existence of DCT constructs and the viability of the DCT questioning strategies to facilitate patient explorations within each of the cognitive-developmental orientations.[8] It was found that interviewers could access an individual's predominant orientation in language that could be reliably classified by independent raters (.90). Further, it was found that the DCT questioning strategies designed to promote patient explorations within each of the orientations actually accomplished this objective with a high degree of predictive validity (89% of the responses). All patients involved in the study were able to develop alternative perspectives on their problems, and to commit to try a new behavior that they designed during the interview process. This is, in fact, basic to the dialectic nature of the counseling encounter; that is, if we can expand the contexts that clients operate within, the net result will be enhanced understandings and wider ranges of alternative options from which to choose.

Heesacker, Prichard, Rigazio-DiGilio, and Ivey (in work) have conducted factor analytic studies of DCT constructs with 1,700 subjects in two settings. The factor structure for the four orientations was validated with unusual clarity. A prominent component of the study found that subjects who were able to function within multiple orientations reported fewer psychological and physical problems than those functioning within single orientations.

2. *What research on DCT, SCDT, and SCDS is currently under way?*

Several current projects focus on SCDT constructs. One is being conducted to investigate the construct validity of the four collective orientations as each is manifested in family communication, and to determine the type of relationship that exists between a family's collective predominant orientation and the individual orientations of key family members. A second is being conducted to investigate the predictive validity of the sequential set of SCDT questioning strategies and to determine if family members can collectively explore their issues within each of the cognitive-developmental orientations using language that can be reliably identified by independent raters.

---

[8]This research actually used an extended version of the DCT questioning sequence, with early and late components to each of the four primary cognitive-developmental orientations. The questions were highly predictive in helping patients to view their issues from within each of the resulting eight orientations.

Two ancillary research projects are also under way. The first involves the development of a measure for individuation based on the holistic and developmental conceptualizations of the DCT model. The second involves the measurement of cognitive complexity in marital and family therapy graduate students, again using the holistic, developmental conceptualizations of DCT.

Finally, three studies in Japan should be cited, as each illustrates a cross-cultural promise for DCT. Fukuhara (1984) found that as psychotherapy progressed, a college student moved from sensorimotor cognition to concrete descriptions, and finally to formal and reflective thought. The second study found an increase in affective expression using DCT-type questions (Tamase & Kato, 1990). The third focused on whether Japanese students would change the developmental orientations of their verbalizations as they told stories about their daily lives in response to questions within the concrete and formal orientation (Tamase & Mitsutake, 1993). The results, though small, were in the predicted direction.

In summary, whereas early clinical and research data are promising, much more research and clinical trials will be necessary to both validate and enrich these models of treatment and supervision. The implications of these empirical studies for supervision are indirect, but potentially powerful. Although the research will add important confirming data, the clinical and supervisory applications of DCT and SCDT have already been positively received by practitioners and supervisors seeking more egalitarian models of psychotherapy and supervision. As the field of psychotherapy supervision increasingly moves toward developmental and integrative approaches, the concepts and strategies contained in the DCT model can open up new pathways to understand and explore the multiplicity and complexity inherent in any therapeutic or supervisory encounter.

REFERENCES

Anderson, S., Rigazio-DiGilio, S., & Kunkler, K. (1995). Training and supervision in marriage and family therapy: Current issues and future directions. *Family Relations: Journal of Applied Family and Child Studies, 44,* 489–500.

Arciniega, M., & Newlon, B. (1994). Counseling and psychotherapy: Multicultural considerations. In D. Capuzzi & G. Gross (Eds.), *Counseling and psychotherapy: Theories and interventions* (pp. 557–587). Columbus, OH: Macmillan/Merrill.

Bagarozzi, D., & Anderson, S. (1989). *Personal, marital and family myths: Theoretical formulations and clinical strategies.* New York: Norton.

Borders, L. D. (1986). Facilitating supervisee growth: Implications of developmental models of counseling supervision. *Michigan Journal of Counseling and Development, 17*(2), 7–12.

Borders, L. D. (1989). A pragmatic agenda for developmental supervision research. *Counselor Education and Supervision, 29,* 16–24.

Borders, L. D. (1994). Potential of DCT/SCDT in addressing two elusive themes of mental health counseling. *Journal of Mental Health Counseling, 16,* 75–78.

Breunlin, D., Rampage, C., & Eovaldi, M. (in press). Family therapy supervision: Toward an integrative perspective. In R. Mikesell, D. Lusterman, & S. McDaniel (Eds.), *Family psychology and systems therapy: A handbook.*

Breunlin, D., Schwartz, R., & Mac Kune-Karrer, B. (1992). *Metaframeworks.* San Francisco: Jossey-Bass.

Carey, J. (1988, August). *A cognitive-developmental model of supervision.* A presentation at the annual meeting of the American Psychological Association, Atlanta, GA.

Carter, B., & McGoldrick, M. (1989). *The changing family life cycle.* Boston: Allyn & Bacon.

Case, E., & Robinson, N. (1990). Toward integration: The changing world of family therapy. *The American Journal of Family Therapy, 18,* 153–160.

Cheatham, H., & Stewart, J. (Eds.). (1990). *Black families: Interdisciplinary perspectives.* New Brunswick, NJ: Transaction.

Combrinck-Graham, L. (1986). A developmental model for family systems. *Family Process, 24*(2), 139–150.

Constantine, L. (1986). *Family paradigms.* New York: Guilford.

Duhl, B. (1985). Toward cognitive-behavioral integration in training systems therapists: An interactive approach to training in generic systems thinking. *Journal of Psychotherapy and the Family, 1*(4), 91–108.

Falicov, C. (1988). Learning to think culturally. In H. Liddle, D. Breunlin, & R. Schwartz (Eds.), *Handbook of family therapy training and supervision.* New York: Guilford.

Feixas, G. (1990). Approaching the individual, approaching the system: A constructivist model for integrating psychotherapy. *Journal of Family Psychology, 4,* 4–35.

Feldman, L. (1989). Integrating individual and family therapy. *Journal of Integrative and Eclective Psychotherapy, 8,* 41–52.

Fukuhara, M. (1984, November). *Is love enough?—From the viewpoint of counseling adolescents.* Paper presented at the 42nd annual conference of the International Association of Psychologists, Mexico City.

Gilligan, C. (1982). *In a different voice: Psychological theory and women's development.* Cambridge, MA: Harvard University Press.

Ginter, E. (1989). Slayers of monster-watermelons found in the mental health patch. *Journal of Mental Health Counseling, 11,* 77–85.

Gonçalves, O. (1988, February). *Developmental counseling and therapy: Treatment strategies for agoraphobia.* Presentation at 1988 Conference on Counseling Psychology, University of Southern California, Los Angeles.

Gonçalves, O., & Ivey, A. (1992). Developmental therapy: Clinical applications. In K. Kuehlwein & H. Rosen (Eds.), *Cognitive therapy in action: Evolving innovative practice.* San Francisco: Jossey-Bass.

Gonçalves, O., & Machado, P. (1987). A terapia como co-construçao: Das metáforas do cliente às metáforas do terapeuta [Therapy as co-construction: From client's metaphors to therapist's metaphors]. *Jornal de Psicologia, 6,* 14–20.

Harland, R. (1987). *Superstructuralism.* London: Methuen.

Harre, R. (1983). *Personal being.* Cambridge, MA: Harvard University Press.

Heesacker, M., Prichard, S., Rigazio-DiGilio, S., & Ivey, A. (in work). *Development of paper-and-pencil measures for cognitive-developmental processes and cognitive-developmental orientations.*

Hess, A. K. (1986). Growth in supervision: Stages of supervisee and supervisor development. In F. W. Kaslow (Ed.), *Supervision and training: Models, dilemmas, and challenges.* Binghamton, NY: Haworth.

Holloway, E. L. (1987). Developmental models of supervision: Is it development? *Professional Psychology: Research and Practice, 18*(3), 209–216.

Ivey, A. (1986). *Developmental therapy: Theory into practice.* San Francisco: Jossey-Bass.

Ivey, A. (1991). *Developmental strategies for helpers.* Pacific Grove, CA: Brooks/Cole.

Ivey, A., Gonçalves, O., & Ivey, M. (1989). Developmental therapy: Theory and practice. In O. Gonçalves (Ed.), *Advances in the cognitive therapies: The constructive-developmental approach* (pp. 99–110). Porto, Portugal: APPORT.

Ivey, A., & Ivey M. (1990). Assessing and facilitating children's cognitive development: Developmental counseling and therapy in a case of child abuse. *Journal of Counseling & Development, 68,* 299–305.

Ivey, A., Ivey, M., & Simek-Morgan, L. (1994). *Counseling and psychotherapy from a multicultural perspective* (3rd ed.). Englewood Cliffs, NJ: Prentice Hall.

Ivey, A., & Rigazio-DiGilio, S. (1991). The standard cognitive-developmental interview. In A. E. Ivey, *Developmental strategies for helpers* (pp. 289–290). Pacific Grove, CA: Brooks/Cole.

Ivey, A. E., & Rigazio-DiGilio, S. A. (1994). Developmental counseling and therapy: Can still another theory be useful to you? *The Journal for the Professional Counselor, 9,* 23–48.

Ivey, A., Rigazio-DiGilio, S., & Ivey, M. (1991). The standard cognitive-developmental classification system. In A. E. Ivey, *Developmental strategies for helpers* (pp. 301–306). Pacific Grove, CA: Brooks/Cole.

Kantor, D. (1983). The structural analytic approach to the treatment of family developmental crisis. In J. C. Hansen (Ed.), Family Therapy Collection: Vol. 7. *Clinical implications of the family life cycle* (pp. 12–34). Rockville, MD: Aspen Systems.

Kegan, R. (1982). *The evolving self.* Cambridge, MA: Harvard University Press.

Kelly, G. (1955). *The psychology of personal constructs* (Vols. 1 & 2). New York: Norton.

Kenny, D., & Law, J. (1991). Developmental counseling and therapy with involuntary midlife career changers. *Journal of Young Adulthood and Middle Age, 3,* 25–39.

Kunkler, K., & Rigazio-DiGilio, S. (1994). Systemic cognitive-developmental therapy: Organizing structured activities to facilitate family development. *Simulation and Gaming: An International Journal of Theory, Design, and Research, 25,* 75–87.

Lanza, A., Cramer, D., Kunkler, K., & Rigazio-DiGilio, S. (1995). *Connecticut's family violence education program: A systematic evaluation.* University of Connecticut research manuscript.

Lanza A., & Rigazio-DiGilio, S., & Kunkler, K. (1993, October). *Developmental counseling and therapy: An integrative approach to battering.* Presented at the annual American Association for Marriage and Family Therapy Conference, Anaheim, CA.

Lebow, J. (1987). Developing a personal integration in family therapy: Principles for model construction and practice. *Journal of Marital and Family Therapy, 13,* 1–14.

Liddle, H. (1988). Use of the family life cycle paradigm in training. In C. Falicov (Ed.), *Family transitions* (pp. 132–154). New York: Guilford.

Liddle, H. A. (1991). Training and supervision in family therapy: A comprehensive and critical analysis. In A. S. Gurman & D. P. Kniskern (Eds.), *Handbook of family therapy* (Vol. 2, pp. 638–697). New York: Brunner/Mazel.

Merlan, P. (1967). Plotinus. In P. Edwards (Ed.), *Encyclopedia of philosophy* (Vol. 6, pp. 721–734). New York: Macmillan.

Pedersen, P. (Ed.). (1991). Special Issue: Multiculturalism as a fourth force in counseling. *Journal of Counseling and Development, 70.*

Piaget, J. (1954). *The language and thought of the child.* New York: New American Library. (Original work published, 1923)

Piercy, F. P., & Sprenkle, D. H. (1986). Family therapy theory building: An integrative training approach. In F. Piercy (Ed.), *Family therapy education and supervision* (pp. 23–45). Binghamton, NY: Haworth.

Pinsof, W. (1983). Integrative problem-centered therapy: Toward the synthesis of family and individual psychotherapies. *Journal of Marital and Family Therapy, 9,* 19–35.

Proctor, H. (1985). A construct approach to family therapy and systems intervention. In E. Button (Ed.), *Personal construct theory and mental health* (pp. 47–59). Cambridge, MA: Brookline Books.

Reiss, D. (1981). *The family's construction of reality.* Cambridge, MA: Harvard University Press.

Rigazio-DiGilio, S. (1994a). A co-constructive developmental approach to ecosystemic treatment. *Journal of Mental Health Counseling, 16,* 43–74.

Rigazio-DiGilio, S. (1994b). Beyond paradigms: The multiple implications of a co-constructive-developmental model. *Journal of Mental Health Counseling, 16,* 205–211.

Rigazio-DiGilio, S. (1994c). Systemic cognitive-developmental therapy: Training practitioners to access and assess cognitive-developmental orientations. *Simulation and Gaming: An International Journal of Theory, Design, and Research, 25,* 61–74.

Rigazio-DiGilio, S. A. (1996a, October). *Systemic cognitive-developmental supervision.* A presentation at the 54th annual meeting of the American Association for Marriage and Family Therapy, Toronto, Canada.

Rigazio-DiGilio, S. A. (1996b). Systemic cognitive-developmental therapy: A co-constructive, non-pathological, and integrative approach to treating partners and families. *Directions in Psychology: National Program of Continuing Education and Certification Maintenance* (pre-approved APA, NBCC CEU Lesson Plans). New York: The Hatherleigh Company, Ltd., *6,* 3-1 to 3-18.

Rigazio-DiGilio, S. (in press a). Integrative supervision: Pathways to tailoring the supervisory process. In T. Todd & C. Storm (Eds.), *Marriage and family therapy supervision: The complete supervisor.* Needham Heights, MA: Allyn & Bacon.

Rigazio-DiGilio, S. (in work). Systemic cognitive-developmental therapy: Empirical support.

Rigazio-DiGilio, S., & Anderson, S. (1991, October). *Supervisee-focused supervision: A cognitive-developmental model.* A presentation at the 49th annual American Association for Marriage and Family Therapy Conference, Dallas, TX.

Rigazio-DiGilio, S., & Anderson, S. (1994). A cognitive-developmental model for marital and family therapy supervision. *The Clinical Supervisor, 12,* 93–118.

Rigazio-DiGilio, S., Gonçalves, O., & Ivey, A. (1994). Developmental counseling and therapy: A model for individual and family treatment. In D. Capuzzi & D. Gross (Eds.), *Counseling and psychotherapy: Theories and interventions* (pp. 471–513). Columbus, OH: Macmillan/Merrill.

Rigazio-DiGilio, S., & Ivey, A. (1990). Developmental therapy and depressive disorders: Measuring cognitive levels through patient natural languages. *Professional Psychology, 21,* 470–475.

Rigazio-DiGilio, S., & Ivey, A. (1991). Developmental counseling and therapy: A framework for individual and family treatment. *Counseling and Human Development, 24* (1), 1–20.

Rigazio-DiGilio, S., & Ivey, A. (1993). Systemic cognitive-developmental therapy: An integrative framework. *The Family Journal: Counseling and Therapy for Couples and Families, 1,* 208–219.

Rigazio-DiGilio, S., & Ivey, A. (1995). Individual and family issues in intercultural counseling and therapy: A culturally-centered perspective. *Canadian Journal of Counseling, 29,* 244–261.

Rigazio-DiGilio, S., Lanza, S., & Kunkler, K. (1994). The assessment and treatment of relationship violence: A co-constructive developmental approach. *Family Counseling and Therapy, 2,* 1–24.

Stoltenberg, C. D., & Delworth, U. (1987). *Supervising counselors and therapists: A developmental approach.* San Francisco: Jossey-Bass.

Sue, D. (1991). A model for cultural diversity training. *Journal of Counseling and Development, 70,* 99–105.

Tamase, K., & Kato, M. (1990). Effects of questions about faculty and affective aspects of life events in an introspective interview. *Bulletin of Nara University of Education, 39,* 151–163.

Tamase, K., & Mitsutake, K. (1993). Effect of developmental intervention on cognitive levels of verbal responses in an experimental interview. *Bulletin of Nara University of Education, 42,* 167–181.

Tamase, K., & Rigazio-DiGilio, S. A. (in press). Expanding client worldviews: Investigating developmental counseling and therapy assumptions. *International Journal for the Advancement of Counseling.*

Vygotsky, L. (1986). *Thought and language* (A. Kozulin, Trans.). Cambridge, MA: MIT Press. (Original work published 1934).

Watzlawick, P. (Ed.). (1984). *The invented reality.* New York: W. W. Norton.

Worthington, E. (1987). Treatment of families during life transitions: Matching treatment to family response. *Family Process, 26,* 295–308.

PART III

Training Models for Psychotherapy Supervision

CHAPTER 15

Structures for the Analysis and Teaching of Supervision

ELIZABETH L. HOLLOWAY
University of Wisconsin-Madison

In recent years, interest has developed in understanding how supervisors can be trained to do supervision rather than focusing only on how supervision was being done (Bernard & Goodyear, 1992; Holloway, 1995; Holloway & Neufeldt, 1995). Early models of supervision relied on existing conceptual structures that were analogous to the supervision contexts, that is, counseling, social role, and developmental theories (cf. Bernard & Goodyear, 1992). In 1982 and 1983, *The Counseling Psychologist* published two issues dedicated totally to counseling supervision (Bartlett, Goodyear, & Bradley, 1983; Whitely, 1982). These two volumes emphasized conceptual models of supervision that reflected the influence of counseling (Bordin, 1983; Hosford & Barman, 1983; Patterson, 1983; Wessler & Ellis, 1983) and developmental theories (Blocher, 1983; Loganbill, Hardy, & Delworth, 1982) in understanding supervision. Developmental theories of supervision captured the interest of researchers, and many of the studies undertaken through the 1980s reflect this interest. Begun in the early 1970s as a part of the facilitative conditions movement (Holloway, 1992; Martin, Goodyear, & Newton, 1987, 1995; Russell, Crimmings, & Lent, 1984), the intensive examination of discourse in supervision was the other primary research focus during this period. These 15 years of research and conceptualization have provided an initial basis of knowledge to address the challenge of teaching professionals the structures and skills for effective supervision practice.

The purpose of the *systems approach to supervision* (SAS; Holloway, 1995) is to provide a framework and a language based on the empirical, conceptual, and practice knowledge to guide supervision teaching and practice. Those factors that have consistently been identified as salient to the process and outcome of supervision (Holloway & Neufeldt, 1995; Russell, Crimmings, & Lent, 1984) have been used to build a dynamic model that can assist in systematic assessment of the supervisee's learning needs and the supervisor's teaching interventions. The model can be used as a frame of reference for an individual practitioner to think through a dilemma for case consultation or for training in supervision. It provides a strategy for systematically using a "case method" approach that encompasses the presentation of client histories, accompanied at times with examples of the supervision interaction and followed with a conceptualization of the supervision situation and suggestions for interventions. It is an effort to understand supervision by offering a common language that is relevant to supervisors and educators across different theoretical points of view. The model is meant to raise questions about what each supervisor does rather than to tell a supervisor what to think and what to do. SAS provides four components of support for educators and practitioners to uncover their own thinking, attitudes, decision making, and behaviors: (a) a descriptive base, (b) guidelines stating common goals and imperatives, (c) a way to discover meaning as it relates to participants and the profession, and (d) a systematic mode of inquiry to determine objectives and strategies for interaction during supervision. Although the confines of this chapter prevent the detailed discussion of these knowledge bases, the heuristics of the model are presented. The reader is referred to Holloway (1995) for a complete presentation of the theoretical and empirical underpinnings of the components of SAS.[1]

GOALS OF THE SAS MODEL

The primary goal of supervision is the establishment of an ongoing relationship in which the supervisor designs specific learning tasks and teaching strategies related to the supervisee's development as a professional. In addition, the supervisor empowers the supervisee to enter the profession by understanding the skills, attitudes, and knowledge demanded of the professional and guiding the relationship strategically to facilitate the trainee's achievement of a professional standard. Specifically, the SAS model contends that

1. The goal of supervision is to provide an opportunity for the supervisee to learn a broad spectrum of professional attitudes, knowledge, and skills in an effective and supportive manner.
2. Successful supervision occurs within the context of a complex professional relationship that is ongoing and mutually involving.
3. The supervisory relationship is the primary context for facilitating the involvement of the learner in reaching the goals of supervision. The essential nature of this interpersonal process bestows power to both members as they form the relationship.
4. For the supervisor, both the content and process of supervision become an integral part of the design of instructional approaches within the relationship.
5. As the supervisor teaches, the trainee is further empowered by acquiring the skills and knowledge of the professional work, and gaining knowledge through experiencing and articulating interpersonal situations.

DIMENSIONS OF THE SYSTEMS APPROACH

Seven dimensions have emerged from the empirical, conceptual, and practice knowledge bases of supervision. These dimensions have been integrated conceptually into the SAS model as the seven factors depicted in Figure 15.1 (pp. 252–253). The seven factors are represented as wings connected to the body of supervision, that is, the relationship. Task and function are represented in the foreground of the interaction with the more covert influences of supervisor, trainee, client, and institution in the background. The relationship is the core factor and contains the process of the supervision interaction. This is the foundation of SAS. It is understood that the components of the model are also part of a dynamic process in that they mutually influence one another and are highly interrelated. The graphic model is used to identify anchor points in this complex process and to encour-

[1]From *Clinical Supervision: A Systems Approach* (Chapters 1, 2, 3, and 4) by E. L. Holloway, 1995. Copyright by Sage Publications, Thousand Oaks, CA. Adapted with permission of the author.

age supervisors to discover and name the most salient factors in a particular piece of work as related to (a) the nature of the task, (b) what function the supervisor was carrying out, (c) the character of the relationship, and (d) what contextual factors were relevant to the process.

THE RELATIONSHIP OF SUPERVISION

In the SAS relationship is the container of dynamic process in which the supervisor and the supervisee negotiate a personal way of utilizing a structure of power and involvement that accommodates the trainee's progression of learning. This structure becomes the basis for the process by which the trainee will acquire knowledge and skills—the empowerment of the trainee. Both the supervisor and supervisee are responsible for establishing a relational structure that is flexible enough to accommodate the trainee's particular professional needs in an intense, collaborative learning alliance. The supervisor, however, exercises the guiding function (i.e., how the supervisor is different from the trainee) of evaluation and support within the structure of this professional relationship. The structure and character of the relationship embody all other factors, and in turn all factors are influenced by the relationship.

There has been considerable research on the relationship and process of supervision (cf. Holloway, 1992; Russell et al., 1984). From the empirical base and practice knowledge, this author has identified three essential elements: (a) interpersonal structure of the relationship—the dimensions of power and involvement, (b) phase of the relationship—relational development specific to the participants, and (c) supervisory contract—the establishment of a set of expectations for tasks and functions of supervision (see Figure 15.1).

Interpersonal Structure: Power and Involvement

Power and involvement are helpful constructs in understanding the nature of the supervisory relationship. Supervision is a formal relationship in which the supervisor's task includes imparting expert knowledge, making judgments of trainees' performance, and acting as a gatekeeper to the profession. Formal power, or power attributed to the position, rests with the supervisor, and in this regard the supervisory relationship is a hierarchical one. However, the exercise of power cannot be accomplished independently. The mutually influential process of relationship and the ongoing interaction between individuals allow for a shared influence to emerge. Power may take very different forms dependent on the personal and institutional resources available and the type of involvement of the individuals, a point of view not always given consideration (Hinde, 1979).

Three preferred methods have been used in supervision research to describe the power of the supervisor: French and Raven's (1960) sociological typology; Strong, Hill, and Nelson's (1988) circumplex model; and Penman's (1980) communication matrix. Leary's (1957) circumplex model, however, on which both the Strong et al. (1988) and Penman (1980) classification systems are based, provides a framework to place power in a relational system that includes an *involvement*, or affiliation, dimension that, in his view, every relationship has by definition. This theory of interpersonal relations undergirds the SAS interpersonal structure of the supervision relationship (power through involvement). Although the relationship takes on a unique character that can be defined by power and involvement, the participants bring their own history of interpersonal style. These interpersonal histories influence how the supervisor and the trainee ultimately present themselves in forming their new relationship.

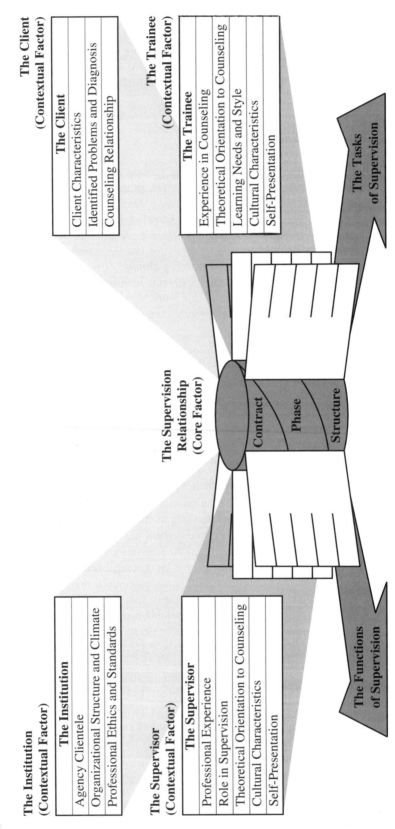

The Institution
(Contextual Factor)

The Institution

Agency Clientele
Organizational Structure and Climate
Professional Ethics and Standards

The Client
(Contextual Factor)

The Client

Client Characteristics
Identified Problems and Diagnosis
Counseling Relationship

The Supervisor
(Contextual Factor)

The Supervisor

Professional Experience
Role in Supervision
Theoretical Orientation to Counseling
Cultural Characteristics
Self-Presentation

The Trainee
(Contextual Factor)

The Trainee

Experience in Counseling
Theoretical Orientation to Counseling
Learning Needs and Style
Cultural Characteristics
Self-Presentation

The Supervision
Relationship
(Core Factor)

Contract

Phase

Structure

The Tasks
of Supervision

The Functions
of Supervision

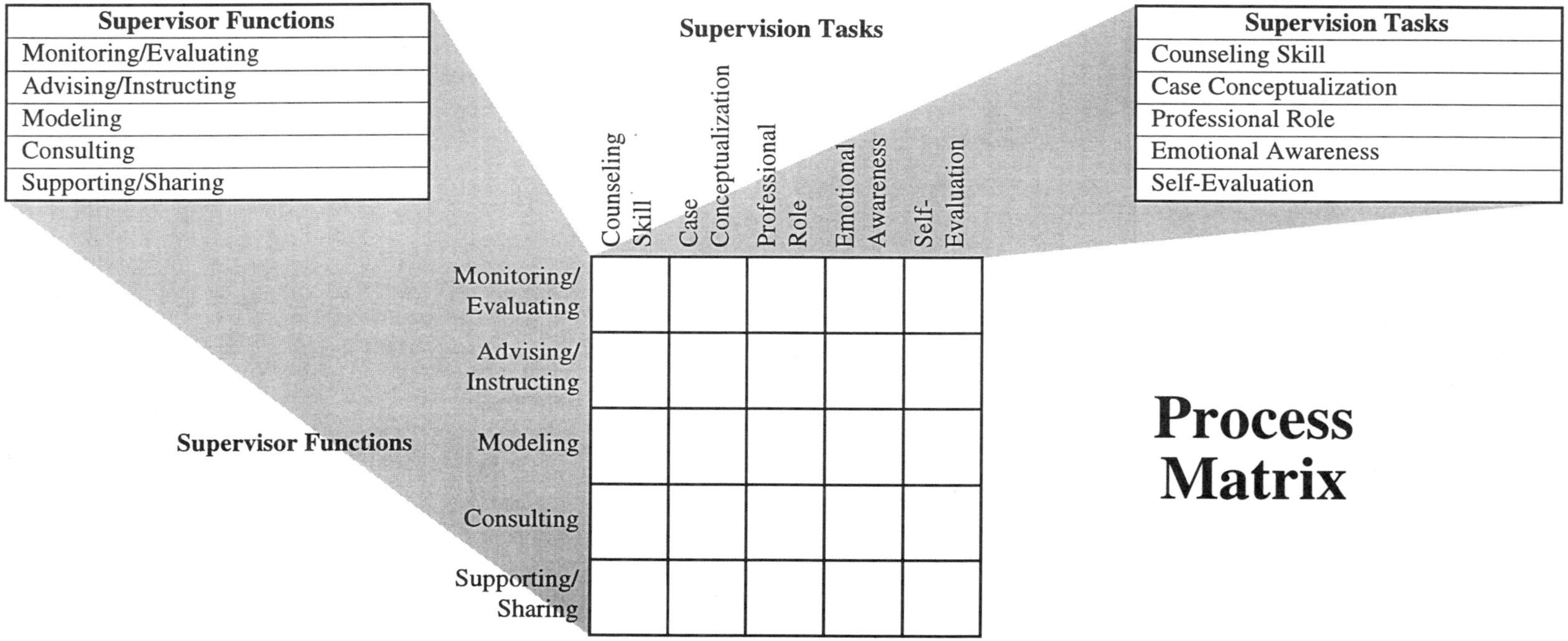

Supervision Tasks

Supervision Tasks
Counseling Skill
Case Conceptualization
Professional Role
Emotional Awareness
Self-Evaluation

Process Matrix

Supervisor Functions

Supervisor Functions
Monitoring/Evaluating
Advising/Instructing
Modeling
Consulting
Supporting/Sharing

Supervision Tasks

	Counseling Skill	Case Conceptualization	Professional Role	Emotional Awareness	Self-Evaluation
Monitoring/Evaluating					
Advising/Instructing					
Modeling					
Consulting					
Supporting/Sharing					

Supervisor Functions

Figure 15.1 The SAS model: Tasks, functions, relationship, and contextual factors.

From *Clinical Supervision: A Systems Approach* by E. L. Holloway, 1995. Copyright by Sage Publications, Thousand Oaks, CA. Reprinted with permission of the author.

Involvement might also be referred to as intimacy that includes "attachments," the degree to which each person uses the other as a source of self-confirmation (Miller & Rogers, 1987). Affiliation influences the exercise and effect of power in the dyadic relationship and is crucial in creating more individualized versus more role-bound relationships. Both participants determine the distribution of power or the degree of attachment to each other (Morton, Alexander, & Altman, 1976). The degree of relational influence potential will determine the degree of social bonding and thus the persuasiveness of the relationship. As the relationship develops, the participants will utilize more personally relevant interpersonal, psychological, and differentiated information to make predictions of each other's behavior and thus reduce interpersonal uncertainty. The basis of mutuality adjusts to these new levels of personal knowledge (Morton et al., 1976).

Phases of the Relationship

In the development of informal relationships, two factors have consistently been observed. First, as a relationship evolves, the participants rely less on general cultural and social information and more on idiosyncratic information of the participant. Predictions regarding the other person's behaviors come from information that differentiates the person from other members of his or her corresponding social group. The other becomes unique in the eyes of the perceiver, and the relationship is said to have moved from being noninterpersonal to being interpersonal (Miller, 1976).

As the relationship evolves to an interpersonal one, there is a process of reduced uncertainty. After initial interactions, participants come to know each other better and are thus more accurate in their predictions about the other person's reactions to their messages. With decreased uncertainty, they are better able to use control strategies and communicative modes that will reduce the level of conflict in the relationship. Participants also become increasingly more vulnerable and more willing to risk self-disclosure, whereas in the initial stages, genuine self-disclosure is seldom observed (Morton et al., 1976).

These findings are interesting in light of Rabinowitz, Heppner, and Roehlke's (1986) supervision study. They found that whether at an advanced or a beginning level, supervisees sought to reduce ambiguity and increase support and assurance from their supervisor at the beginning of the relationship. Advanced trainees, although still seeking initial support, more quickly desired experiences that included personal challenge and confrontation regarding their own interpersonal behaviors in counseling and supervision. Although some of these findings have been interpreted to reflect a developmental shift in the trainee, they might also be viewed as indicating a natural development in a relationship to attempt to reduce uncertainty as interactional patterns become established. Extrapolating from the friendship studies, it could be suggested that the advanced supervisees, having a blueprint for the relationship of supervision from previous experience, were able to truncate the discomfort of uncertainty and resultant need for reassurance by relying on known general expectancies for supervisory roles. Thus, they could move more quickly to establish specific expectancies of an interpersonal (as opposed to a noninterpersonal) relationship by self-disclosing aspects of self-relevancy to their counseling performance. On the other hand, the beginning-level trainee might still be discovering the role expectations of the supervisor and the trainee, since these general cultural, social, and formal rules must be discovered before moving to an interpersonal relationship.

The development of an interpersonal relationship promotes a focus on shared idiosyncratic rules created just for that particular relationship, albeit supervision is a formal, professional relationship defined by certain relational rules and is more role bound than are friend-ship relations. Supervision initially provides a general expectancy base for certain interactive behaviors; however, as the relationship develops, it is individualized around the learning needs of the trainee and the teaching approaches of the supervisor. The participants will need to learn these idiosyncratic reciprocal rules in the interactive process (Miller & Rogers, 1987).

Of itself, phase does not determine the level of involvement in the relationship. Indi-vidual differences also play a part. Altman and Taylor (1973) have named the process of providing more personal information *social penetration,* which is significantly affected by both phase of relationship as well as by personal characteristics. Some individuals, because of their personal or cultural history, have a predisposition to reveal themselves, while others are more reluctant. There is evidence that still other factors may influence the course of supervision. For example, Tracey, Ellickson, and Sherry's (1989) research demonstrated that both the individual presentational style of the trainee (defined as *reac-tance potential*) and the urgency of the client's problem (a possible suicide threat) had a significant effect on the participants' need for a more structured and supportive approach. Research studies ultimately demonstrate the absolute need to consider all of the contex-tual factors that influence supervisory behaviors in devising any strategy in supervision.

SAS has described the relationship phases of supervision in a way that reflects the con-vergence of findings in friendship research (Berger & Calabrese, 1975; Morton et al., 1976) and supervision relationships (Mueller & Kell, 1974; Rabinowitz et al., 1986). Mueller and Kell's (1972) labeling system—beginning, mature, and termination—has been used to describe phases of the supervisory relationship identified in the empirical litera-ture (see Table 15.1; Holloway, 1992; Worthington, 1987).

Supervision Contracts

Each supervisor and supervisee will have idiosyncratic expectations of roles and function in supervision. Some will be the result of experience in engaging in supervision and others will be more directly related to the personal and cultural characteristics of both participants. As in any working relationship, the clarity of these expectations directly affects the rela-tionship and the establishment of specific learning goals. Because the trainee is in a posi-tion of relatively lesser evaluative and expert power, the supervisor has a responsibility to ensure that the trainee is clearly informed of the evaluative structure of the relationship, the expectancies and goals for supervision, the criteria for evaluation, and the limits of con-fidentiality in supervision.

Inskipp and Proctor (1989) have identified the contract as critical to establishing a way of being together in the supervisory relationship. Not only do the participants negotiate spe-cific tasks, but they also define the parameters of the relationship. The negotiation of norms, rules, and commitments at the beginning of any relationship can reduce uncer-tainty and move the involvement to a level of trust that will promote the degree of vul-nerability needed for the task to be done. This clarification sets up both content and rela-tional characteristics to be expected in the relationship and establishes a trajectory for types of interactions in which the supervisor and the supervisee will engage. The super-visor, by initiating the contract, is dealing directly with the inherent uncertainty of the system. By acting openly and purposefully, the supervisor increases the probability that both participants will behave congruently with established expectations (Miller & Rogers, 1987). More important, the supervisee will receive an opportunity to participate in the construction of the relationship.

Table 15.1   Phases of the Supervision Relationship

Developing Phase

- Clarifying relationship with supervisor
- Establishment of supervision contract
- Supporting teaching interventions
- Developing competencies
- Developing treatment plans

Mature Phase

- Increasing individual nature of relationship, becoming less role bound
- Increasing social bonding and influence potential
- Developing skills of case conceptualization
- Increasing self-confidence and self-efficacy in counseling
- Confronting personal issues as they relate to professional performance

Terminating Phase

- Understanding connections between theory and practice in relation to particular clients
- Decreasing need for direction from supervisor

Note: From *Clinical Supervision: A Systems Approach* by E. L. Holloway, 1995, p. 51. Copyright by Sage Publications, Thousand Oaks, CA. Reprinted with permission of the author.

The supervisor must be alerted to the changing character of the relationship and must thereafter initiate discussion on renewed goals and relational expectations. Not only will the trainee's learning needs change as experience increases or clients develop, but also his or her increasing skill and interpersonal confidence will influence issues of relational control. Ongoing negotiation of topics and processes is built on the initial contract for teaching and learning and the quality of relationship that the participants have built. The supervision session often begins with the supervisor asking the trainee what he or she would like to discuss—a negotiation of the topic of conversation (Poulin, 1992). Although there may be shifts in direction throughout the course of the interview, these are often points of subtle negotiation between the participants.

TASKS OF SUPERVISION

In SAS, the teaching tasks and supervisory function are used to describe the action of the supervision process. A task is defined as "a definite piece of work assigned or expected of a person" (*Random House College Dictionary*, 1984). The tasks of supervision are defined by a body of professional knowledge requisite of the counselor role. It is from this larger pool of knowledge that the supervisor and the student will choose those specific learning goals that match the individual needs of the trainee. The numerous characteristics and skills identified in the literature can be grouped into five broad areas (Hess, 1980; Holloway, 1992; Loganbill, Hardy, & Delworth, 1982). Categories of teaching objectives include counseling skills, case conceptualization, professional role, emotional awareness, and self-evaluation. Each of these categories is briefly defined hereafter.

Counseling Skills.   The task of counseling skills focuses on what action to take with the client or on any of the specific skills that the supervisor identifies as both fundamental to counseling knowledge and specifically relevant to a particular trainee. Counseling skills might include communication patterns, empathy, personalization, and techniques of counseling such as symptom prescription, desensitization, and reinforcement.

Case Conceptualization.   Case conceptualization involves the supervisor and the supervisee in understanding the client's psychosocial history and presenting problem and in the development of a conceptual framework that is applicable across many different types of clients and that is simultaneously congruent with the therapist's beliefs of human development and change.

Professional Role.   Professional role relates to how the trainee will use appropriate external resources for the client; apply principles of professional and ethical practice; learn tasks of recordkeeping, procedure, and appropriate interprofessional relationships; and participate in the supervisory relationship.

Emotional Awareness.   Emotional awareness refers to the trainee's self-awareness of feelings, thoughts, and actions that result from working with the client and with the supervisor. Both intra- and interpersonal awareness are relevant to counseling and supervision.

Self-Evaluation.   Self-evaluation is the willingness and skill to recognize one's own limits of competence and effectiveness as they relate to client treatment and participation in supervision.

FUNCTIONS OF SUPERVISION

A function is "the kind of action or activity proper to a person or thing; the purpose for which something is designed or exists; to perform a specialized action or activity" (*Random House College Dictionary,* 1984). Role labels have been useful in providing a common language for describing supervisor functions in educational and mental health supervision (Bernard & Goodyear, 1992; Ellis & Dell, 1986; Ellis, Dell, & Good, 1988; Hess, 1980). The five primary functions that the supervisor engages in while interacting with the supervisee are (a) monitoring/evaluating, (b) instructing/advising, (c) modeling, (d) consulting, and (e) supporting/sharing. Notice that here these roles have been transformed (from a noun to a verb) and simplified in order to emphasize their dynamic nature as well as to suggest a more cohesive approach to the role of supervisor. Each of these functions can be characterized by behaviors typical of their respective social role and the form of relational power governing that function.

Monitoring/Evaluating.   The monitoring and evaluative function is restricted to instances in which the supervisor communicates judgments and evaluation of the trainee's behavior as it relates to his or her professional role. In these instances, because the reward and coercive power of the supervisor is being exercised, the hierarchy of the relationship is accentuated and communication is largely controlled by the supervisor (i.e., unidirectional). The supervisor's *act* of monitoring and evaluating performance is a function of supervision and is distinguished from the *criteria* for evaluation. In training situations, the evaluation may be a formal and standardized procedure, whereas in supervision that takes place between peers or in post-training, it is often less explicit. In any case, the supervisor's opinion and judgment, implicit or explicit, is important.

Instructing/Advising.   The instructing/advising function consists of the supervisor providing information, opinions, and suggestions based on professional knowledge and skill (Holloway & Poulin, 1994). Characterized as a "teacher-student" communication, it is largely controlled by the supervisor (i.e., unidirectional), emphasizes the hierarchy of the relationship, and is marked by considerable interpersonal distance.

Modeling.   The supervisor acts as a model of professional behavior and practice, both implicitly in the supervisory relationship and explicitly by role playing for the supervisee or client. As a mentor, a more implicit process, the supervisor becomes a role model of professional practice and conduct. Communication here is largely bidirectional: Interpersonal distance is reduced because the exercise of referent power is a collaborative process.

Consulting.   The supervisor facilitates problem solving of clinical and professional situations by seeking information and opinions from the supervisee. Again, the use of expert and referent power is most relevant. Communication is bidirectional and interactive as the participants collaborate on fact finding and problem solving.

Supporting/Sharing.   The supervisor supports the supervisee through empathic attention, encouragement, and constructive confrontation. Supervisors often support trainees at a deep interpersonal level by sharing their own perception of trainees' actions, emotions, and attitudes. This direct communication may include confrontation, which can increase the affiliation of the participants if done constructively and appropriately. Communication is bidirectional and interactive, and the participants are highly engaged with little interpersonal distance.

TASK + FUNCTION = PROCESS

Supervisor tasks and functions are the combination of the supervisor and the trainee working together on a particular type of problem with a particular approach; in other words, what are the objectives and what teaching/learning strategies are adopted. This pragmatic, heuristic approach is characterized by the presence of task and function in the ongoing interchange between supervisor and trainee. The interrelatedness of identifying "what" is the teaching task with deciding "how" one will function to accomplish that task is known as the process of supervision. In the transcripts that follow (see Figure 15.1), it is possible to identify the factors of task and function and then use this information to chart them in transcripts as a graphic matrix. Hypothetically, a supervisor may engage in any of the teaching objectives with any of the functions or strategies. Realistically, there are probably some task and function matches that are more likely to occur in supervision, for example, the use of a supporting function when working with interpersonal emotional awareness

or as an advising function when focusing on counseling skills.

Although the deliberate choice of such matches will be influenced by certain factors such as the trainee's experience, the client's situation, and the relationship structure between supervisor and trainee, nonetheless the task and function can be identified in the process of the interview. Using this method of matching task and function, supervisors can analyze the effectiveness of a prior session and plan supervisory focus and strategies for subsequent sessions. The efficacy of matches between task and function in the interview can be examined because the analysis includes the trainee's immediate response to the supervisor's interventions as well as more long-term indices of trainee learning placing the immediate discourse within the context of the ongoing teaching goals.

The supervisor's identification of tendencies for using certain functions or tasks, or for using them in particular combinations, can be informative with respect to the supervisor's style of supervision. Specific knowledge about supervisory actions can encourage the supervisor to question or reflect on past behavior. Are the choices of task and function primarily a reflection of the supervisor's comfort with a particular style of presentation? Are there choices that are most frequent with a particular trainee? Or at a particular phase of the supervisory relationship? Do the choices of task and function facilitate the empowerment of the trainee?

Questions can be generated from the simple identification of task and function and can encourage further exploration of factors influencing the supervisor's actions. There are many factors that might influence the choice of learning objective and the approach to working with a supervisee, and research in supervision has attempted to identify them. Other factors also influence the understanding of the supervisor's effectiveness in choosing a particular task and function. Although sometimes these factors are apparent, just as often they may exist only at a latent, rather than a manifest, level of the interaction. The contextual factors of supervision are defined and uncovered in supervision interviews and, in some cases, in participants' comments on their supervisory behaviors. These "contextual" factors will be discussed next.

CONTEXTUAL FACTORS OF SUPERVISION

Contextual factors of supervision, conditions that are related empirically and practically to the supervisor's and supervisee's choice of task and function and the formation of the relationship, include the supervisor, the trainee, the client, and the institution. The description of these factors completes the SAS model (see Figure 15.1). Whereas task and function are inferred from the process of communication, contextual factors are sometimes not obviously differentiated from the actual interactional process. Participants in an interaction are perceiving, intending, and understanding their own and the other person's messages "inside their heads" as they are engaged in the conversation. Factors that might influence information processing and decision making in supervision must be inferred by the observer. Although such inferential information is useful, it is different from information that might be gained from asking supervisors or trainees to reflect on their own or on the other's actions (Holloway, 1995; Neufeldt, Karno, & Nelson, 1996; Schon, 1983; Skovoldt & Ronnestad, 1992).

Supervisor Factor

The ideal supervisor has been described as a person who exhibits high levels of empathy, understanding, unconditional positive regard, flexibility, concern, attention, investment, curiosity, and openness (Carifio & Hess, 1987). Although such personal qualities are valuable in any relationship, these descriptors focus almost entirely on the intra- and interpersonal characteristics of an individual. They implicitly suggest that supervisors are born and not made. All individuals bring to supervision their own interpersonal characteristics, knowledge, abilities, and cultural values. Even so, supervisors express these characteristics uniquely as the foundation on which the supervisory role is built. Supervisors can enhance their own interpersonal style by the manner in which they use their repertoire of interpersonal skills and clinical knowledge to be deliberate, systematic, and relevant in their professional role.

Early researchers of supervision focused on determining the importance of supervisors' use of facilitative conditions in the supervisory relationship. More recently, gender, theoretical orientation, and experience level have been found to be related to trainee satisfaction with supervision, as well as supervisors' planning behaviors, in-session verbal behaviors, and preferred interpersonal power bases (cf. Holloway, 1992; Russell, Crimmings, & Lent, 1984).

In SAS, five factors have been identified in the empirical or conceptual literature as relevant to the supervisor's performance. These are: (a) professional experience in counseling and supervision; (b) expectations concerning roles for the supervisor and the supervisee; (c) theoretical orientation to counseling; (d) cultural characteristics including race, ethnicity, and gender; and (e) self-presentation. A brief definition and illustrative transcripts are included to clarify their functional meaning in the SAS model.

Professional Experience.   It has been suggested in the supervision literature that the supervisor engages in a developmental process of change that unfolds as the supervisor engages in the unique demands of the supervisory role (Lamb, Roehlke, & Butler, 1986). Whether this is accurate remains to be determined. Empirically, at least, the amount of experience in counseling and supervision appears to be related to the types of judgments made by supervisors regarding self-disclosure, trainee performance, and instructional approach to supervision.

Roles.   Social role theories outline the behavior considered to be a part of the supervisory relationship, specifically the role of the supervisor. The most frequently recognized roles are teacher, counselor, and consultant; however, the roles of evaluator, lecturer, and model of professional practice have been used to describe supervisor behaviors and attitudes (Goodyear & Bradley, 1983; Hess, 1980).

Theoretical Orientation.   The supervisor has the task of teaching trainees the application of theoretical principles of counseling as they are relevant to the individuals and cases trainees will encounter. Thus, supervisors rely explicitly and implicitly on their own knowledge base to determine what to teach as well as how to teach it. Trainees sometimes state a desire to learn a particular approach to counseling; however, supervisors and trainees are often assigned to one another without any consideration for the background of the supervisor or the expectations of the trainee. Or, supervisors of a particular theoretical orientation may choose to take only those who want to learn their approach. Process research has indicated that theoretical orientation to counseling appears to be related to the structure of the supervisory relationship (Beutler, 1988; Carroll, 1995; Goldberg, 1985; Holloway et al., 1989). A supervisor's theoretical orientation is manifestly salient to his or her teaching of personality or counseling theory as it is relevant to client behavior.

Cultural Elements.   The supervisor brings to the relationship his or her way of viewing human behavior, interpersonal relations, and social institutions that is largely influenced by cultural socialization. Because cultural perspective is relevant to the conceptualization of both professionalism and mental health, the SAS model considers cultural values as salient to the supervisor's attitudes and actions. Cultural characteristics include gender, ethnicity, race, sexual orientation, religious beliefs, and personal values that strongly influence an individual's social and moral judgments. In the SAS model, the relationship of supervision is understood from a perspective of power and involvement—inherent qualities in cross-cultural and cross-gender interactions that indicate the complex, sometimes subtle, but always critical aspects of supervisory work. The relation of race and ethnicity to the supervisory process has been researched in the context of the supervisor and trainee relationship. In a survey study of field supervision, McRoy, Freeman, Logan, and Blackmon (1986) concluded that although there were numerous potential difficulties in cross-cultural supervisory relationships, only a few actual instances were reported. African American supervisors reported that language differences; communication styles; the role and authority of the supervisor; personality conflicts; and differences in opinions, backgrounds, and life experiences may be problematic. The interaction between power in role and power in society is evident in that African American supervisors experienced situations in which white students questioned their competency and were actually unwilling to accept supervision. White supervisors reported that lack of trust, poor communication, lack of knowledge of cultural differences, failure to clarify values, language barriers, prejudice or bigotry, differing expectations, and student defensiveness may all cause problems in the relationship. Unfortunately, it is often difficult for students and supervisors to identify such sensitive situations and discuss them openly.

The relation of gender to the perception of interpersonal power and interactional processes has been studied relatively frequently in supervision. Nelson (1993), in a conceptual review, examined the importance of gender in therapeutic and counseling relationships. In general, same-gender dyads have reported closer relationships. Women trainees were perceived to use more dependent styles to seek influence, but there was no difference in males' and females' use of power strategies to influence client change. Interactional analysis of matched and mismatched gender dyads in supervision (Nelson & Holloway, 1990) showed that male and female supervisors used more powerful messages with female trainees, and female trainees were much less likely than males to use high-power messages.

Specific training in didactic and experiential curriculum is necessary to overcome cross-cultural barriers of communication. There are numerous writings on instructional approaches to sensitize students, educators, and supervisors to such issues in theory and practice (cf. Bernard & Goodyear, 1992). Specifically addressing cross-cultural events in practice, Pope-Davis (1992) has developed a multimedia program to facilitate counseling and counselor training. The SAS model is meant to encourage supervisors to recognize the importance of cultural factors in supervision and to pay attention to how these issues interact with each of the other factors of the model.

Self-Presentation.   In SAS, the term *self-presentation* is used to refer to each participant's interpersonal presentation of self. This term originates in the social psychological literature concerned with impression formation. Although initially there was some suggestion that self-presentational behaviors were restricted to those activities that an individual deliberately regulated to communicate a particular image of him- or herself to others (Baumeister, 1982), it has been suggested more recently that this definition is too narrow (DePaulo, 1992). DePaulo argues that verbal and nonverbal behaviors in interpersonal contexts can include more than superficial concerns and are important in developed relationships. Additionally, self-presentation is seen to include behaviors that are produced automatically; these are expressive behaviors that have become habitual and are no longer deliberate, but were originally purposefully regulated (Schlenker, 1984). In the interpersonal psychotherapy literature, such behaviors are referred to as "a person's style of relating," habitual ways of behaving that have been learned early in life and are maintained through adulthood (Teyber, 1988). It might be argued that in supervision, self-presentational style is always a factor; however, it is under particular conditions that style becomes prominent and decidedly the primary factor in the course of the communication.

Friedlander and Schwartz (1985) reviewed the social psychological literature on self-presentation and drew from it those principles that were particularly relevant to the therapeutic context. In supervision, Ward, Friedlander, Schoen, and Klein (1985) used the self-presentation construct to examine supervisors' judgments of trainees in relation to trainees' self-presentational style. Study of the supervisor's style has not used the self-presentational construct as a basis for understanding the supervisor's general interpersonal behavior but, rather, has examined the supervisor's perceived style specific to the role of supervisor (Friedlander & Ward, 1984) and the development of the supervisory relationship (Efstation, Patton, & Kardash, 1990). It has also examined the supervisor's pattern of verbal behavior in the process of supervision (Holloway & Poulin, 1994).

In SAS, self-presentation will be used to refer to the affective, verbal, and nonverbal behaviors that the participants engage in to convey a particular desired impression to the other. These behaviors may be habitual and require no conscious monitoring or may be purposely regulated. They characterize the individual and become the supervisor's individual manner of enacting his or her role.

Trainee Factors

Who is the ideal supervisee? The psychological health and personal character of the therapist have been considered to be of primary importance in the traditional training of the analyst. In-depth personal therapy has been regarded as a critical element in the training process to (a) enhance the therapist's ability as an unbiased clinical observer and to mitigate the effects of countertransference; (b) demonstrate experientially the validity of therapy as a treatment; (c) model firsthand the techniques of psychotherapy; and (d) improve the psychological health of the therapist and ameliorate the stresses of practice (Wampler & Strupp, 1976). In the 1980s, as models of supervision began to attend to the actual process and strategy of supervision (Goodyear & Bradley, 1983; Hess, 1980; Loganbill et al., 1982; Stoltenberg, 1981), researchers became interested in characteristics of the supervisee that may influence the supervisory relationship (cf. Holloway, 1984; Russell et al., 1984; Worthington, 1987). The trainee's cultural experience, gender, cognitive and ego development, professional identity, experience level in counseling, theoretical orientation to counseling, and self-presentation were identified in the empirical and conceptual literature as important factors in supervision. In SAS, these characteristics of the trainee have been grouped into five trainee factors: (a) experience in counseling, (b) theoretical orientation in counseling, (c) learning style and needs, (d) cultural characteristics, and (e) self-presentation.

Experience in Counseling.   Experience level has been a frequently studied factor in supervision research. The trainee's familiarity with the professional role and tasks of counseling appears to be related to the supervisor's expectation of trainee competence and the trainee's needs. The experience of the learner has also been connected to need for support and structure in supervision. Experience in counseling should not be confused with cognitive or ego developmental factors that may influence the trainee's performance or the supervisor's choice of supervisory method. In SAS, developmental cognitive and ego characteristics of the trainee are discussed under learning style and needs and self-presentation, respectively.

Theoretical Orientation.   The theoretical orientation of the trainee has not received much attention in the research literature (Holloway, 1992, 1995); however, most supervisors would concur that the views a trainee holds about human behavior and change will certainly be a part of supervision. Perhaps, because much research in supervision has been about supervisees early in their professional training, there is not a clear theoretical designation expected of these individuals. Instead, the focus is on the development of a personal model of counseling that matches generally expected principles of personality and counseling theory.

Learning Style/Needs.   In the SAS model, learning style and needs refers generally to that identified group of developmental factors relevant to the trainee's approach to and perception of the supervisory experience (Holloway, 1995). Developmental characteristics such as conceptual level (Harvey, Hunt, & Schroder, 1961) and ego development (Loevinger, 1976) have been examined in light of the acquisition of counseling skills such as empathy and clinical hypothesis formation (e.g., Borders, Fong, & Neimeyer, 1986). Stoltenberg and Delworth (1987) prescribed matches between the developmental characteristic of conceptual level and the degree of structure in supervision. For example, the greater the tolerance for ambiguity and the more relativistic the thinking, the greater opportunity for the supervisor to offer a more unstructured approach to supervision. Unfortunately, there are few empirical findings to guide the supervisor in choosing those strategies that would reflect a structured versus an unstructured learning environment. At this point, reflected interviews of supervision may offer the greatest insight into the relevance of such factors to actual decision making and to the practice of the trainee or supervisor. Poulin's (1992) dimensionalization of reflected interviews of expert supervisors found that the supervisor thought of trainee characteristics in three categories: as a person, a counselor, and a student. Within these categories, the supervisors counseled the trainees' learning needs within the context of the style in which they learned and their readiness to assimilate and make use of the knowledge (see Holloway, 1995).

Cultural Characteristics.   This area includes gender, ethnicity, race, sexual orientation, religious beliefs, and personal values that may be central to an individual's group identity, similar to the cultural factors of the supervision. In SAS, cultural values are seen as salient to the trainees' attitudes and actions toward their clients and supervisors, that is, in any interpersonal situation. Research in this supervision area is relatively limited, although there has been significantly more research on the relation of cultural variables to counseling relationship and effectiveness (cf. Atkinson, Morten, & Sue, 1989; Pedersen, 1985; Sue & Sue, 1990; Tyler, Brome, & Williams, 1991). The structure of power and involvement in the supervisory relationship may be particularly complex in a cross-cultural context because of the added complexity of power in the general society between minority and nonminority groups (Martinez & Holloway, 1996; Solomon, 1983). There has been limited research on the relation of gender and role (supervisor/supervisee) to process characteristics of power and involvement (Nelson & Holloway, 1990). Although similar studies examining ethnic or racial minorities in cross-cultural situations do not exist at this time, it is likely that the positional power of the supervisor or trainee might be in contradiction to the usual social arrangements and may thus conceivably be problematic.

Self-Presentation.   Self-presentation is a social-psychological term that refers to the regulation of one's behaviors to create a particular impression on others (Jones & Pittman, 1982). A brief discussion of this construct appears on pages 261–262. The trainee's interpersonal and emotional characteristics in supervisory and counseling relationships have been included in the research on self-presentational behaviors (Ward et al., 1985). Constructs such as interpersonal patterns (Friedlander, Siegel, & Brenock, 1989), reactance potential (Tracey et al., 1989), defensiveness, and counter defensiveness have been studied in relation to the process of supervision and relationship variables.

Client Factors

The client is always present in the supervision. Indeed, the supervisor's raison d'être is to ensure that the trainee can deliver effective service to the client. Yet, ironically, there is little research that examines client change or characteristics as an outcome or in relation to the supervision process (Holloway & Neufeldt, 1995). In SAS, there are three client factors: (a) client characteristics, (b) client identified problem and diagnosis, and (c) counseling relationship.

Client Characteristics.   An important and frequently researched area has been on the variety of client attributes in relation to the process and outcome of psychotherapy. Characteristics and variables that have been studied are social class, personality traits, age, gender, intelligence, race, and ethnicity. Some of these characteristics have some real practical value in determining the appropriateness of brief versus long-term therapy and premature termination (Garfield, 1994). The relevance to these general client characteristics, rather than specific diagnostic attributes, has not been studied within the context of supervision and/or training. Pragmatically, however, the supervisor frequently considers the client's age, ethnicity, gender, and race in determining the appropriateness of the match between counselor and client as well as in problem solving various difficulties that may emerge in the counseling relationship. The literature on matching client gender and/or ethnic minority status with therapists suggests that although there appears to be a preference for ethnically similar counselors, this is not consistently evident in the empirical literature (Coleman, Wampold, & Casali, 1994). It behooves the supervisor to recognize that any or all such variables as social desirability, attitudes, or values may play an important role in the counselor potential effectiveness. The attribution of ineffectiveness may be placed on the lack of similarity between client and therapist on more obvious variables rather than on a more in-depth discussion of other characteristics of the client and/or counselor that may be inhibiting progress.

Identified Problem and Diagnosis.   The identification of the client's problem is often the first topic for discussion in supervision. This might include a formal DSM IV assessment and diagnosis or a more problem-solving description of the client's presenting concern. New clients may be introduced to the trainee's caseload after careful screening by the agency or the supervisor or both. Supervisors in practice often screen clients for begin-ning-level trainees to ensure that they will be assigned only cases appropriate to their level of competence. Supervisors also may choose cases for trainees based on the supervisor's areas of expertise. Occasionally, clients may be dealing with issues that are similar to a life circumstance that the trainee has not yet resolved, and the supervisor then refers the client rather than risk the almost certain countertransference that would emerge in the ther-apeutic relationship. Additionally, other characteristics of the client are relevant to the supervisor's and the trainee's choice of topic of supervision and the manner in which they engage with each other.

The supervisor is responsible for assuring that the client will receive adequate treatment from the supervisee. In part, this assessment of the match between the supervisee's area and level of competence and the client's needs will depend on the severity of the client's problem. Axis IV of the DSM IV is reserved for rating the severity of the psychosocial stressors in an individual's life. The degree of stress is then examined in light of the client's mental condition or the nature of the problem and past adaptability to living in order to determine the course of treatment. If a client is severely depressed or aggressive and is experiencing a very high number of stressors, then the supervisor and counselor may need to do a specific assessment for suicide and/or homicide potential.

Counseling Relationship.   The counseling relationship is an important basis from which to understand the impact of different treatment strategies as well as the effectiveness of the trainee in creating a therapeutic relationship (Holloway & Neufeldt, 1995). The reen-actment of the relationship dynamics in the supervisory situation is a familiar phenome-non to supervisors and has been termed *parallel process* (Doehrman, 1976; Ekstein & Wallenstein, 1958). Parallel process occurs when the central dynamic process of the coun-seling relationship is unconsciously acted out by the trainee in the supervision relation-ship. The trainee may be experiencing difficulty with the client and feels powerless to change the situation therapeutically, so he or she takes on interpersonal strategies similar to the client's form of resistance. If the supervisor does not recognize the dynamic as a part of the counseling situation and the trainee's feelings of powerlessness, then the super-visor may collude with this reenactment by adopting a role similar to the trainee's in the counseling relationship. The obvious result is an impasse in supervision. A supervisor who recognizes the parallel process can intervene directly with the trainee, thus breaking the impasse in supervision while concurrently modeling effective interpersonal strategies for the trainee. Thus, with effective supervisory intervention, the trainee begins to understand, both experientially and conceptually, the meaning of the client's behavior and is able to resume a therapeutic approach to the problem.

Institutional Factors

Supervision, whether as a part of a training program or as continuing professional devel-opment, takes place in the context of institutional organizations, such as in-house depart-mental clinics, university counseling centers, hospitals, or community mental health or other service settings. The role of supervision in respect to the service demands of the orga-nization is an important consideration in establishing goals and functions of supervision. Yet, the influence of organizational variables on supervision has rarely been investigated or discussed in the professional literature (Holloway & Roehlke, 1987). Institutional char-acteristics are defined in SAS as organizational clientele, organizational structure and cli-mate, and professional ethics and standards (see Figure 15.1).

Organizational Clientele.   The clientele served by the agency is relevant to the trainee's type of clinical training and, in some instances, perhaps to supervisory strategies. There has been little research on this topic, but there are a number of supervisory articles that discuss the specialized training needs of trainees working with different types of clinical groups; for example, incest survivors, male perpetrators, substance abusers, medically related syndromes, and many more. Clientele in the program are often required to have specialized knowledge, certain personal experiences, or, in some cases, membership or former membership in the clinical group. There are also more informal ways that the predominant clientele may affect the program. Freundenberger (1977) noted that clinics that offer services exclusively to a particularly disturbed psychiatric population may find that the incidence of job stress and staff burnout is abnormally high among the staff. Agencies that work with specific age groups or developmental stages (for example, adolescents, families, children, and the elderly) may also have specialized requirements for admittance to training or for specifically endorsed supervisory techniques.

Organizational Structure and Climate.   Ekstein and Wallerstein (1958) depicted the many roles necessary for the training program to exist within an institutional setting. Their clinical "rhombus" concept consists of six interactions among the four roles of the supervisor: agency administrator, clinical supervisor, supervisee-therapist, and client. Each of these roles suggests different motivations and goals, yet all four must seek to accommodate the goals of the other three. Dodds (1986) discussed the necessary balance between goals and motivations of the training institution and the service agency. He suggested that the success of the supervisor-supervisee relationship would depend on the degree to which the supervisor could function as a teacher and the supervisee could function as a staff, albeit less experienced, professional. Both participants of the training dyad must understand and be motivated to function in roles prescribed to them by their organizations. Organizational norms and politics often intrude on the supervisory relationship. In a survey that asked interns to indicate their level of readiness for the professional demands of the internship, participants most frequently expressed concern over their lack of preparedness for dealing with organizational politics (Cole, Kolko, & Craddick, 1981).

Cherniss (1980) suggests that the environment within an agency can lead to the transmission of burnout between workers and thereby influence the training program. Because of the close, ongoing relationship between supervisor and supervisee, it is likely that this environmental stress will be carried into the supervisory relationship. Supervisors and supervisees are subject to bringing environmental norms and stressors into their relationship and ultimately to transmit these attitudes to the counseling situation; thus, it seems important for them to understand their roles and behaviors in the context of organizational conditions.

Professional Ethics and Standards.   The supervisory relationship is considered a critical component of professional training. Professional organizations [e.g., Association of Counselor Education and Supervision (ACES) Ethical Standards for Counseling Supervisors, 1989; American Psychological Association (APA) Ethical Guidelines for Practice, 1992] charge supervisors with the responsibility of the treatment of the client by the supervisee, the teaching program for the supervisee, and the protection of the profession from incompetent and/or impaired professionals. Within an agency or organization, the supervisor must also follow specific obligations, standards, and rules regarding client service and training programs. Supervisors often find themselves balancing the standards of the profession with the immediate service needs of the agency. Thus, supervisors must consider all levels of standards and ethics as they relate to their responsibilities. First, as a representative and model of the profession, they must act in compliance with the ethics and standards for delivery of services. Second, they must oversee the trainee's compliance with these ethics. Third, they must act ethically in the role of supervisor. Finally, they must teach ethical standards and guide the trainee in making ethical decisions.

Dual relationships represent one of the most problematic ethical issues facing supervisors. The supervisor must not only ensure that the trainee not engage in a dual relationship with the client, but must also maintain the primacy of the supervisory role over any other role with the trainee. Just as any sexual contact is prohibited between client and counselor, any form of sexual contact between supervisor and trainee is a violation of the ethical code (APA, Principle 1.19, 1992; ACES, Principle 2.15, 1993). In a survey by Pope, Levenson, and Schover (1979) of those students that reported having had a sexual contact with an instructor (10% of sample), the majority indicated that the sexual relationship was with their supervisor. Because of the evaluative power of the supervisor over the trainee, there is the potential for exploitation of the trainee, the resultant risk of inadequate supervision of cases, and a serious breach in the teaching contract with the trainee (Bartell & Rubin, 1990).

A dual relationship between supervisor and trainee may also be a consequence of the supervisor's engaging the trainee in personal therapy concurrent with a supervisory relationship (ACES, Principle 2.16, 1989). The distinction between the process of counseling and that of supervision may sometimes appear similar, especially under circumstances in which the trainee is working through an emotional issue as it relates to the client and/or the counseling relationship. The supervisor first and foremost must uphold the supervisory contract and deal with personal issues of the trainee only as they are relevant to the provision of clinical services and professional function. In addition, any examination of this process should reveal the relevance of all discussion to the supervisory goals.

APPLYING THE SAS MODEL TO TEACHING SUPERVISION

The seven components of the systems approach to supervision (SAS) model used in analyzing the supervision process have been described and include the factors of supervision (task and function), the relationship of supervision, and the contextual factors (supervisor, trainee, institution, and client). Although, for purposes of explication, these factors have been talked about in isolation, they are indeed interrelated, often occurring together in the same supervisory session.

Potentially, there are a multitude of relationships that are directly or indirectly part of any discussion of training in supervision. Each supervisor may have several trainees, and in turn each trainee may have several clients. Further, in the group consultation there is not only the relationship between each supervisor and the trainer, but additionally the relationships among the various supervisor members. Clearly, not all of these relationships will be discussed explicitly in the group, nor will the trainer know all of these relationships in detail. When supervisor members raise issues in the group, however, their perspective will be shaped by their observation and experience of these various relationships and contexts.

Any discussion of the teaching of supervision must involve a discussion of the practice of supervision and the practice of counseling. All three processes—teaching supervision, supervision practice, and counseling practice—are necessarily linked by their concurrence and the supervisors' and supervisees' roles in the group consultation on supervision and the counseling relationship, respectively. Because the distinctions among these three contexts of teaching and practicing are easily confused, for the sake of clarity they are named as follows: the *counseling relationship* refers to each or all of the counselor trainee's counselor-client dyads. The *supervisory relationship* refers to each or all of the supervisor's supervisor-trainee dyads. The *consultative group* refers to the group of supervisors who meet with a trainer to discuss and learn about their practice of supervision. By understanding the linkage among these three relational contexts, the tasks and processes of teaching supervision in a group setting might be further illuminated. The group consultation may deal with any of the roles or issues that emerge in these three interrelated contexts.

Central to the purpose of the supervision consultation group are questions that relate to supervisory performance of each relationship. The supervisors face two enormous tasks: What should I teach? and How should I create a relationship that facilitates the trainee's learning the teaching objectives? With these questions as a point of departure, the trainer can begin by providing a context for the supervisor's experience. Reference to the model may assist the supervisor in identifying the source or sources of the current dilemma, how these factors interrelate, and how the factors influence the three relational contexts. In the teaching of supervision, this author encourages supervisors to consider the following questions while reflecting on their work:

1. What factors are influencing the participants' judgments in guiding the supervision process?
2. What characteristics of the contextual factors have they relied on in their decision making?
3. What characteristics have they not considered but that on reflection seem important in designing a teaching approach in supervision?
4. What kind of roles do they tend to manifest in supervision, and are these the most beneficial for learning to take place?
5. What tasks of supervision do they focus on with particular trainees?

Supervision Consultation Case Analysis[2]

Through my years of teaching supervision, I have collected tales of supervisors' struggles to become more effective in teaching the practice of counseling. Common themes have emerged across the years. I have chosen one common theme to illustrate the application of the SAS model in teaching supervision. The supervisor's original intervention and thinking are depicted in the "Supervisor's Dilemma" section of Figure 15.2. The strategic analysis, including salient factors and critical discoveries that emerged from the discussion, is described in the "SAS Analysis" section. Finally, the "Process Matrix of Supervision" sections, indicating the original task and function of the supervisor and the suggested target for intervention, is depicted. The purpose of the diagrams is to emphasize the evolutionary change in focus throughout the process of the consultation and to demonstrate the way in which the SAS model may be used graphically in case analysis.

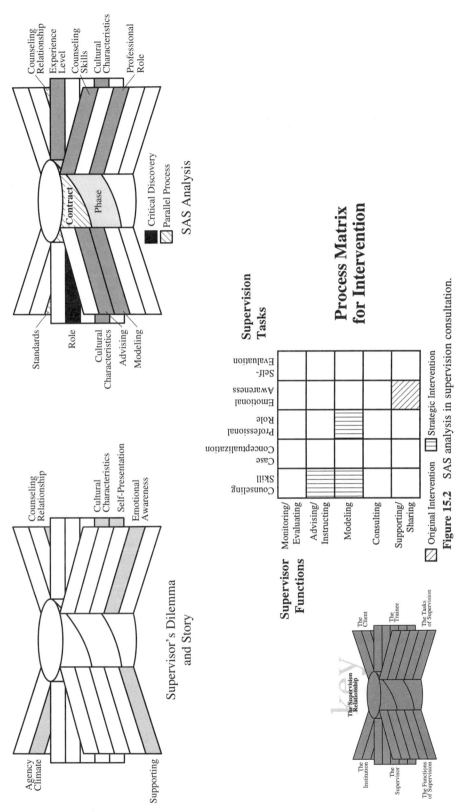

Figure 15.2 SAS analysis in supervision consultation.

From *Clinical Supervision: A Systems Approach* by E. L. Holloway, 1995. Copyright by Sage Publications, Thousand Oaks, CA. Reprinted with permission of the author.

The Supervisors' Dilemma.   Both supervisors came to me in disarray. Their trainees were not accepting supervision. They were unwilling to talk about their own feelings and thoughts about the counseling relationship and about the supervisory relationship. What was the cause of their supervisees' resistance? The supervisors were deeply concerned about the supervisees' futures as counselors because they were unable to engage in the supervisory process. The supervisors were advanced in their clinical skills and experience and were dedicated professionals. They were supervising beginning-level practicum students because of their commitment to training professionals and because of their enjoyment of the supervision process.

The Clinical Service Setting.   This was a small non-profit community agency that offered services to low-income people. All counseling sessions of trainees were audiotaped for supervision purposes.

The Trainees.   The trainees were both mature individuals who had entered the counseling profession from other fields. They were eager to learn how to do counseling and were involved in their placement setting. One trainee was a European American male who had been a teacher for five years. The other trainee was a bicultural, European American and Native American female and had worked extensively in community action organizations prior to returning to the university for counselor training.

The Supervisors' Story

REBECCA: My supervisee is having difficulty establishing boundaries with her client, and it seems at times that the two of them are friends chatting on the street. I have explored with the trainee the difference between friendships and therapy and felt that although she had an intellectual understanding of this, she wasn't able to translate this into the practice of her role. The chatting, although somewhat diminished in the sessions, seems unpredictable, and I don't think she can recognize the boundaries between the two roles. So that is when I decided to begin a process of emotional exploration with her. I've worked really hard at bringing her into her own awareness and felt satisfied with her willingness to self-disclose about her personal feelings in reference to this client. In fact, I followed this up with two more supervisory sessions in which we probed the meaning of friendships in her culture and the need to feel accepted as a person and professional. I really enjoyed the complexity and connection between the professional boundaries and their connection with the cultural background of the counselor. I began to teach her about the importance of separation and the implications of dual relationships and ethics. She really became very tearful and then shut down. I didn't really understand what had happened and then in the next and last session before today she came in very angry with me for intruding into her personal world and my lack of sensitivity to cultural background. She insisted that I stick to supervision and teach her the skills of the profession and not try to be her therapist. I was so shocked at the intensity of her reaction and even more shocked that she felt I was mixing up the boundaries.

GEORGINE: I really know what you are going through. My trainee seems completely incapable of exploring his own emotional response to his client. He's really trying to befriend his client and is actually giving her feedback on how he sees her as a woman. I think that he is trying to assure her that she is a nice person, someone he would find attractive. I am so exasperated with him. He is unable or unwilling to get at what made it so necessary to reach across his professional boundaries like this. I have confronted him several times on this inappropriate behavior with the client. Last time I observed his counseling session with this client I was totally undone. He seemed to be deliberately seductive with her. In the last supervision session, he told me in no uncertain terms to lay off him about exploring his feelings about the client and that what he really needed was to learn the skills of being a counselor. If he wanted therapy, he'd pay a counselor for it.

THE CONSULTATION: Both supervisors sat across from me for their joint consultation hour. Rebecca is a very thoughtful, still type of person. Her quiet intelligence is probably the first view you have of her. There is a persistence and tenacity in the way she takes hold of an idea and runs underground with it. She has a keen set of antennae that pick up the nuances of behaviors and their meaning. She looked pretty discouraged today, and running through it was something of a rage, at least what might be the glimpse of a rage for Rebecca. She started her tale at a higher pitch than usual and I was immediately alerted to the type of intensity she held.

Georgine held a certain serenity about her. She has a great way of being quietly present, delivering searing confrontations with hardly a ripple in her composure and yet with a support and warmth that leaves a lingering feeling that you are cared about in spite of the fact that there are clearly things you need to change. They looked at me expectantly, knowing my predilection for complex interpersonal analysis. I could feel their suggestion that I begin an exploration of their feelings in their respective supervision relationships. I felt tugged by the seduction of their intensity and our history of untangling the webs of emotion and behavior in relationship. I knew just as surely that it must be different this time. They needed to be taught rather directly the boundaries of their roles and the meaning of the contract and development of the supervisory relationship, just as surely as their students needed to understand the boundaries of their roles as counselors. I needed to give to them what their students were asking, that is, to understand experientially the importance of skill acquisition in empowerment. As boring and interpersonally ignorant as it may seem to them in this moment, I must remind them of the purpose of their supervision contract and the level of experience of their trainees. I offered them the possibility that their trainees just did not know how to show warmth and genuineness within the frame of a counseling relationship. This was indeed a parallel process with the counseling and supervisory relationship that needed to be stopped at the consultative level. We needed to engage in a clear and careful analysis of their supervisory method.

And so initially we began a process of examining the skills that the trainees lacked and thought about supervisory approaches to teach these skills. We kept the focus on skills that might help facilitate the trainees in learning the role of counselor. I could tell they were dubious and really quite wanted to divert our attention to their feelings about not being appreciated as supervisors after all their work and attention to these fledgling counselors. I resisted and waited until we had dealt with the skills and teaching methods; and then we ventured into talk of relationship, culture, and gender and how these factors were influencing their involvement with their trainees.

The SAS Analysis.   The supervisors had not misread the difficulty the counselors were having in the development of the counseling relationships, but they had chosen a counseling function to focus almost exclusively on the trainees' emotional awareness to address this issue. The counselors initially found themselves following this lead, but then felt that they were being seduced into a counseling relationship and being denied the skills they needed to act differently. The supervisors needed to return to their understanding of the supervisory contract. Had they maintained the boundaries of the supervisory relationship? They needed to examine the phase of relationship and the level of experience of the trainee. They were in fairly new relationships in which deep self-disclosure might have been seen as premature. Their persistent focus on the trainees' self-disclosure was overly intense. Although initially an appropriate venture, it soon became overly demanding and seemingly unrelated to the client the trainee had to face each week. These were beginning-level counselors, and they needed to learn a level of skill that could help them implement their intellectual understanding of the counselor role. They needed skills other than their friendship skills to create a facilitative and warm relationship. The supervisor's own preference for interpersonal awareness and counseling-type interventions in supervision, that is, their expectation of the role of the supervisor being too narrowly defined, prevented them from acknowledging the need to provide skill training to these trainees. The importance of the gender and cultural differences between the supervisors and their trainees also played a role in their lack of sensitivity to the trainee's anger. The supervisors assumed that the trainee's use of relationship skills was based on some dysfunctional reason for needing to be friends with their clients. Although they were able to engage in a conversation with their trainees about cultural mores and tradition in professional relationships, in action they were defying those norms in their persistence for self-disclosure and more intimate conversation. The trainees felt that their behaviors with their clients were being interpreted in a way that maligned their intentions.

Eventually, the trainees were able to explain their intentions to their supervisors from a cultural and gender perspective. The supervisors were able to specifically identify those behaviors of the trainees that were ineffective in the counseling context, and the trainees were able to suggest ways they would be with the client that would ameliorate the situation but still feel genuine and culturally and gender congruent. Rebecca finally began a discussion of counseling approaches that were most effective with her trainee's own cultural group and the differences in relational structure and role that would be expected in cultures other than European American. For both supervisors, understanding the meaning of their initial supervisory focus on personal awareness from a cultural and gender perspective was important in finding a way to appropriately relate to their supervisees. Note in Figure 15.2 that the consultative process is situated in the institutional factors wing and that the existing and potential parallel processes—among the trainees counseling relationships, the supervisory relationship, and the consultative relationship—are highlighted.

CONCLUSION

The SAS model invites practitioners and educators of supervision to reflect on what they do in supervision, to ask difficult questions about the meaning of their work, to uncover their own intuitive knowledge, and to use a common language to communicate this knowing to others. The model attempts to integrate the research and practice knowledge of supervision and synthesize it in a way that is immediately practical and relevant to the understanding and teaching of supervision. I have tried to be explicit and concrete about a complex instructional method without suggesting that there is a "how to" or "should do" of supervision. The case example is presented to demonstrate how the framework might be applied in the context of teaching supervision. Although the confines of a chapter have prevented me from fully explaining the connection between the empirical literature (for a detailed description of research supporting the model see Holloway, 1995) and the SAS model, I hope that the reader will be able to make use of the application aspect of the model.

REFERENCES

Altman, I., & Taylor, D. A. (1973). *Social penetration: The development of interpersonal relationships*. New York: Holt, Rinehart and Winston.

American Psychological Association. (1992). *American Psychological Association ethical guidelines for practice*. Washington, DC: Author.

Atkinson, D. R., Morten, G., & Sue, D. W. (1989). *Counseling American minorities: A cross-cultural perspective* (3rd ed.). Dubuque, IA: Brown.

Bartell, P. A., & Rubin, L. J. (1990). Dangerous liaisons: Sexual intimacies in supervision. *Professional Psychology: Research and Practice, 21* (6), 442–450.

Bartlett, W. E., Goodyear, R. K., & Bradley, F. O. (Eds.). (1983). Supervision in counseling II. *The Counseling Psychologist, 11*(1).

Baumeister, R. F. (1982). A self-presentational view of social phenomena. *Psychological Bulletin, 91*, 3–26.

Berger, C. E., & Calabrese, A. M. (1975). Some explorations in initial interaction and beyond: Toward a developmental theory of interpersonal communication. *Human Communication Research, 1*, 99–112.

Bernard, J. M., & Goodyear, R. K. (1992). *Fundamentals of clinical supervision*. Boston: Allyn & Bacon.

Beutler, L. E. (Ed.). (1988). Training to competency in psychotherapy [Special Issue]. *Journal of Counseling Psychology, 56*(5).

Blocher, D. (1983). Toward a cognitive developmental approach to counseling supervision. *The Counseling Psychologist, 11*(1), 27–34.

Borders, L. D., Fong, M. L., & Neimeyer, G. J. (1986). Counseling student's level of ego development and perceptions of clients. *Counselor Education and Supervision, 26*, 37–49.

Bordin, E. S. (1983). A working alliance based model of supervision, *The Counseling Psychologist, 11*(1), 35–42.

Carifio, M. S., & Hess, A. K. (1987). Who is the ideal supervisor? *Professional Psychology: Research and Practice, 3*, 244–250.

Carroll, M. (1996). *Counseling supervision: Theory, skills, and practice*. London, UK: Cassell.

Cherniss, C. (1980). *Staff burnout: Job stress in the human services*. New York: Russell Sage.

Cole, M., Kolko, D., & Craddick, R. (1981). The quality and process of the internship experience. *Professional Psychology, 12*, 377–384.

Coleman, H. L. K., Wampold, B. E., & Casali, S. L. (1994). Ethnic minorities' ratings of ethnically similar and European American counselors: A meta-analysis. *Journal of Counseling Psychology, 42*, 247–294.

DePaulo, B. M. (1992). Nonverbal behavior and self-presentation. *Psychological Bulletin, 111*, 203–243.

Dodds, J. B. (1986). Supervision of psychology trainees in field placements. *Professional Psychology: Research and Practice, 17*, 296–300.

Doehrman, M. J. (1976). Parallel processes in supervision and psychotherapy. *Bulletin of the Menninger Clinic, 40*(I), 1–104.

Efstation, J. F., Patton, M. J., & Kardash, C. M. (1990). Measuring the working alliance in counselor supervision. *Journal of Counseling Psychology, 37*, 322–329.

Ekstein, R., & Wallerstein, R. S. (1958). *The teaching and learning of psychotherapy*. New York: Basic Books.

Ellis, M. V., & Dell, D. M. (1986). Dimensionality of supervisor roles: Supervisors' perceptions of supervision. *Journal of Counseling Psychology, 33*, 282–291.

Ellis, M. V., Dell, D. M., & Good, G. E. (1988). Counselor trainees' perceptions of supervisor roles: Two studies testing the dimensionality of supervision. *Journal of Counseling Psychology, 35,* 315–324.

Fredenberger, J. J. (1977). Burn-out: The organizational menace. *Training and Development Journal, 31* (7), 26–27.

French, J. R. P., Jr., & Raven, B. H. (1960). The bases of social power. In D. Cartwright & A. Zander (Eds.), *Group dynamics: Research and theory* (2nd ed., pp. 607–623). New York: Peterson.

Friedlander, M. L., & Schwartz, G. S. (1985). Toward a theory of strategic self-presentation in counseling and psychotherapy. *Journal of Counseling Psychology, 32,* 483–501.

Friedlander, M. L., Siegel, S. M., & Brenock, K. (1989). Parallel processes in counseling and supervision: A case study. *Journal of Counseling Psychology, 36,* 149–157.

Friedlander, M. L., & Ward, L. G. (1984). Development and validation of the supervisory styles inventory. *Journal of Counseling Psychology, 4,* 541–557.

Garfield, S. L. (1994). Research on client variables in psychotherapy. In A. E. Bergin & S. L. Garfield (Eds.), *Handbook of psychotherapy and behavior change* (4th ed., pp. 190–228). New York: Wiley.

Goldberg, D. A. (1985). Process, notes, audio, and videotape: Modes of presentation in psychotherapy. *The Clinical Supervisor, 3*(3), 3–13.

Goodyear, R. K., & Bradley, F. (1983). Theories of counselor supervision: Points of convergence and divergence. *The Counseling Psychologist, 11,* 59–68.

Harvey, O. J., Hunt, D. E., & Schroder, H. M. (1961). *Conceptual systems and personality organization.* New York: Wiley.

Hess, A. K. (Ed.). (1980). *Psychotherapy supervision: Theory, research and practice.* New York: Wiley.

Hess, A. K. (1983). Learning counseling and psychotherapy skills: A challenge in personal and professional identity. In G. Sumprer & S. Walfish (Eds.), *Clinical, counseling and community psychology: A student guide to graduate training and professional practice.* New York: Irvington.

Hinde, R. A. (1979). *Towards understanding relationships.* New York: Academic.

Holloway, E. L. (1984). Outcome evaluation in supervision research. *The Counseling Psychologist, 12*(4), 167–174.

Holloway, E. L. (1992). Supervision: A way of teaching and learning. In S. D. Brown & R. W. Lent (Eds.), *Handbook of counseling psychology* (pp. 177–214). New York: Wiley.

Holloway, E. L. (1995). *Clinical supervision: A systems approach.* Thousand Oaks, CA: Sage.

Holloway, E. L., Freund, R. D., Gardner, S. L., Nelson, M. L., & Walker, B. R. (1989). The relation of power and involvement to theoretical orientation in supervision: An analysis of discourse. *Journal of Counseling Psychology, 36,* 88–102.

Holloway, E. L., & Neufeldt, S. A. (1995). Supervision: Contributors to treatment efficacy. *Journal of Consulting and Clinical Psychology, 65,* 207–213.

Holloway, E. L., & Poulin, K. (1994). Discourse in supervision. In J. Siegfried (Ed.), *Therapeutic and everyday discourse as behavior change: Towards a micro-analysis in psychotherapy process research.* Norwood, NJ: Ablex.

Holloway, E. L., & Roehlke, H. J. (1987). Internship: The applied training of a counseling psychologist. *The Counseling Psychologist, 2,* 205–206.

Hosford, R. E., & Barmann, B. (1983). A social learning approach to counselor supervision. *The Counseling Psychologist, 11*(1), 51–58.

Inskipp, F., & Proctor, B. (1989). *Skills for supervising and being supervised.* Principle of Counseling audiotape series. East Sussex, England: Alexia Publications.

Jones, E. E., & Pittman, T. S. (1982). Toward a general theory of strategic self-presentation. In J. Suls (Ed.), *Psychological perspectives on the self.* Hillsdale, NJ: Lawrence Erlbaum.

Lamb, D., Roehlke, H. & Butler, A. (1986). Passages of psychologists: Career stages of internship directors. *Professional Psychologist: Theory, Research, & Practice, 17,* 158–160.

Leary, T. (1957). *Interpersonal diagnosis of personality: A theory and a methodology for personality evaluation.* New York: Ronald Press.

Loevinger, J. (1976). *Ego development: Conceptions and theories*. San Francisco: Jossey-Bass.

Loganbill, C., Hardy, E., & Delworth, U. (1982). Supervision: A conceptual model. *The Counseling Psychologist, 10*(1), 3–42.

Martin, J. S., Goodyear, R. K., & Newton, F. B. (1987). Clinical supervision: An intensive case study. *Professional Psychology: Research and Practice, 18,* 225–235.

Martinez, R., & Holloway, E. L. (1997). The supervision relationship in multicultural training. In D. Pope-Davis & H. Coleman (Eds.), *Multicultural counseling competencies: Assessment, education, and supervision* (pp. 325–349). Thousand Oaks, CA: Sage.

McRoy, R. G., Freeman, E. M., Logan, S. L., & Blackmon, B. (1986). Cross-cultural field supervision: Implications for social work education. *Journal of Social Work Education, 22,* 50–56.

Miller, F. E., & Rogers, L. E. (1987). Relational dimensions of interpersonal dynamics. In M. E. Roloff & G. R. Miller (Eds.), *Interpersonal processes: New directions in communication research* (pp. 117–139). Beverly Hills: Sage.

Miller, G. R. (1976). *Explorations in interpersonal communication*. Newbury Park, CA: Sage.

Morton, T., Alexander, C., & Altman, I. (1976). Communication and relationship definition. In G. Miller (Ed.), *Explorations in interpersonal communication* (pp. 105–125). Beverly Hills, CA: Sage.

Mueller, W. J., & Kell, B. L. (1972). *Coping with conflict: Supervising counselors and psychotherapists*. Englewood Cliffs, NJ: Prentice Hall.

Nelson, M. L. (1993). A current perspective on gender differences: Implications for research in counseling. *Journal of Counseling Psychology, 40,* 200–209.

Nelson, M. L., & Holloway, E. L. (1990). Relation of gender to power and involvement in supervision. *Journal of Counseling Psychology, 37,* 473–481.

Neufeldt, S. A., Karno, M. P., & Nelson, M. L. (1996). A qualitative study of experts' conceptualization of supervisee reflectivity. *Journal of Counseling Psychology, 43,* 3–9.

Patterson, C. H. (1983). A client-centered approach to supervision. *The Counseling Psychologist, 11*(1), 21–26.

Pedersen, P. (Ed.). (1985). *Handbook of cross-cultural counseling and therapy*. Westport, CT: Greenwood.

Penman, R. (1980). *Communication processes and relationships*. London: Academic Press.

Pope, K. S., Levenson, H., & Schover, L. R. (1979). Sexual intimacy in psychology training: Results and implications of a national survey. *American Psychologist, 34,* 682–689.

Pope-Davis, D. B., Reynolds, A. L., & Vasquez, L. A. (1992). *Multicultural counseling: Issues of ethnic diversity*. Videotape series, Iowa City: AVC Marketing, The University of Iowa.

Poulin, K. (1992). *Towards a grounded pedagogy of practice: A dimensional analysis of counseling supervision*. Dissertation Abstracts, 9505214 UMI Dissertation Services, Bell & Howell Co., 3200 N. Zeb Rd., Ann Arbor, MI 48106 (1-800-521-0600).

Rabinowitz, F. E., Heppner, P. P., & Roehlke, H. J. (1986). Descriptive study of process and outcome variables of supervision over time. *Journal of Counseling Psychology, 33,* 292–300.

Random House College Dictionary, Revised Edition. (1975). New York: Random House.

Russell, R. K., Crimmings, A. M., & Lent, R. W. (1984). Counselor training and supervision: Theory and research. In S. Brown & R. Lent (Eds.), *The handbook of counseling psychology* (pp. 625–681). New York: Wiley.

Schlenker, B. R. (1984). Identities, identifications, and relationships. In V. Dorlega (Ed.), *Communication, intimacy, and close relationships* (pp. 71–104). San Diego, CA: Academic Press.

Schon, D. A. (1983). *Educating the reflective practitioner*. San Francisco: Jossey-Bass.

Skovholdt, T. M., & Ronnestad, M. H. (1992). *The evolving professional self: Stages and themes in therapist and counselor development*. Chichester, England: Wiley.

Solomon, B. (1983). Power: The troublesome factor in cross-cultural supervision. *Smith College Journal School for Social Work, 10,* 27–32.

Stoltenberg, C. (1981). Approaching supervision from a developmental perspective: The counselor complexity model. *Journal of Counseling Psychology, 28,* 59–65.

Stoltenberg, C. D., & Delworth, U. (1987). *Supervising counselors and therapists.* San Francisco: Jossey-Bass.

Strong, S. R., Hills, H. I., & Nelson, B. N. (1988). *Interpersonal communication rating scale (Revision).* Unpublished manuscript, Department of Psychology, Virginia Commonwealth University, Richmond.

Sue, D. W. & Sue, D. (1990). *Counseling the culturally different: Theory and practice* (2nd ed.). New York: Wiley.

Supervision Interest Network, Association for Counselor Education and Supervision. (1993). ACES Ethical Guidelines for Counseling Supervisors. *ACES Spectrum, 53* (4), 5–8.

Teyber, E. (1988). *Interpersonal process in psychotherapy: A guide for clinical training.* Chicago: Dorsey Press.

Tracey, T. J., Ellickson, J. L., & Sherry, P. (1989). Reactance in relation to different supervisory environments and counselor development. *Journal of Counseling Psychology, 36,* 336–344.

Tyler, F. B., Brome, D. R., & Williams, J. E. (1991). *Ethnic validity, ecology, and psychotherapy: A psychosocial competence model.* New York: Plenum.

Wampler, L. D., & Strupp, H. H. (1976). Personal therapy for students in clinical psychology: A matter of faith? *Professional Psychology, 6,* 195–201.

Ward, L. G., Friedlander, M. L., Schoen, L. G., & Klein, J. C. (1985). Strategic self-presentation in supervision. *Journal of Counseling Psychology, 32,* 111–118.

Wessler, R. L., & Ellis, A. (1983). Supervision in counseling: Rational-emotive therapy. *The Counseling Psychologist, 11* (1), 43–50.

Whitely, J. (Ed.). (1982). Supervision in counseling I. *The Counseling Psychologist, 10*(1).

Worthington, E. L. (1987). Changes in supervision as counselors and supervisors gain experience: A review. *Professional Psychology: Research and Practice, 18,* 189–208.

CHAPTER 16

Microcounseling: A Training and Supervision Paradigm for the Helping Professions

THOMAS G. DANIELS
Sir Wilfred Grenfell College of Memorial
University of Newfoundland
SANDRA A. RIGAZIO-DIGILIO
University of Connecticut
ALLEN E. IVEY
University of Massachusetts

Microcounseling was originally conceived as a behavioral training program for teaching beginning counselors specific skills for the interview (Ivey, Normington, Miller, Morrill, & Haase, 1968). But since that time, it has expanded to become a theoretical model in itself, and it also serves to provide a basic vocabulary for discussing verbal and nonverbal behaviors in both the clinical and supervision session. (The terms *microcounseling* and *microtraining* are used interchangeably.)

Microcounseling reveals that we can *name* what actually occurs behaviorally in the session, and this concrete naming provides the possibility of a clear common language between supervisor and supervisee. With this mutual understanding, it becomes feasible to supervise using microskills concepts and/or complement microtraining with virtually any other supervision system ranging from psychodynamic to cognitive-behavioral to humanistic, and with both beginning and advanced trainees. We believe that effective supervision requires basic microskills understandings that can then serve as a foundation for further work and mastery.

The remainder of this chapter presents microcounseling as a training system, research on microcounseling, and supervision within the microcounseling framework and concludes with implications for the future.

MICROCOUNSELING AS A TRAINING SYSTEM

Ivey and Authier (1978) state: "Microcounseling is designed to bridge the gap between theory and practice, between classroom and interview session, between what is said and what is done" (p. 15).

Appreciation is expressed to Dr. Allen Ivey, Jossey-Bass Publishers, and Brooks/Cole Publishers for graciously permitting the use of their respective copyrighted materials.

Material contained in this chapter also appears in Daniels, T. G., & Ivey, A. E. (in press). *Microcounseling* (3rd ed.). Springfield, IL: Charles C Thomas.

Microcounseling is both a teaching/supervisory technology and a conceptual framework. As a teaching technology, microcounseling is a systematic approach for teaching skills of therapeutic communication through a multicomponent training package. The strength of microcounseling is derived from the diverse approaches to learning that are incorporated within the training system and operationalized through the use of videotapes (modeling), instructional manuals, self-observation, practice, and feedback from the supervisor.

THE BASIC MICROCOUNSELING MODEL

The full microcounseling program for teaching a given skill (or skill sequences) consists of the following sequential steps:

1. *The trainee conducts a baseline interview (about 5 minutes in length) with a client that is recorded on videotape or audiotape.* The interview may be about a real or a role-played situation, and there may or may not be agreement between the trainee and client about the topic.

2. *Following this baseline interview, the trainee works through a written manual that describes the skill (or skill sequence) being taught.* Manuals are commercially available or trainers may develop their own manuals for specific purposes.

3. *The trainee views video models of experts demonstrating the effects that the use, misuse, or absence of the skill(s) has on communication.*

4. *The trainee now views her or his own baseline taped interview. The supervisor discusses the trainee's behavior in relation to a predetermined criterion level for that skill. The supervisor emphasizes the positive aspects of the trainee's behavior.*

5. *The supervisor and trainee now review the skill(s) together and plan for the next interview between trainee and client.* Throughout the training, the supervisor maintains a warm, supportive relationship with the trainee and stresses the positive aspects of the trainee's behavior as it is being shaped toward a predetermined criterion.

6. *The trainee now conducts another taped interview in which the trainee emphasizes in the interview the skill(s) being taught. The supervisor reviews and discusses this tape with the trainee.*

Microcounseling is effective in either a one-to-one or a group teaching context (Daniels & Ivey, in press; Forsyth & Ivey, 1980; Ivey, 1994; Ivey & Authier, 1978). For group instruction, the standard microcounseling procedure of lecture, manuals, and the use of video models is used. An additional practice component is used with group applications. Following the demonstration of the skill via lecture, manuals, and models, trainees are divided into groups of three or four. Using a training group of four as an example, two trainees pair off, one acting as the helper and the other the helpee. While they role-play a counseling situation for 3 or 4 minutes, the other two trainees act as observers/cotrainers. Following this role play, the observers give feedback to the trainee who had the role of helper. The roles then shift so that through the practice component, each trainee gets to act in the role of helper, helpee, and cotrainer. The supervisor moves from group to group assisting when necessary. The supervisor requires good group facilitative skills, and each of the trainee roles must be explicitly laid out in advance.

Microcounseling/microtraining is based on the following essential propositions:

1. Only one skill at a time is taught in a given microtraining session. A single skill is learned to a predetermined criterion, and over time the trainees gradually develop and integrate a repertoire of helping behaviors. This proposition appears to be essential for beginners or when there is a special need to focus on key dimensions. Recently, however, it has been indicated that several skills, skill sequences, or complex counseling strategies (e.g., psychodynamic dream analysis) can be effectively taught in microcounseling, particularly to advanced trainees and when a clear cognitive framework is provided (Ivey, Ivey, & Simek-Morgan, 1997).

2. Several diverse approaches to learning employed here underlie the trainee's skill growth. Modeling and social reinforcement are linked to social learning theory (Bandura, 1977). Shaping the trainee's behavior toward a predetermined criterion has operant underpinnings. Baker and Daniels (1989) suggest that the trainee's growth in helping knowledge can be explained in terms of cognitive-behavioral elements inherent in the microcounseling process. More recently Daniels (1992) and Daniels and Ivey (in press) suggested that trainee conceptual growth can be explained in constructivist terms.

3. Self-observation and self-confrontation can be instrumental in behavior change as the trainee is able to compare and contrast her or his behavior with that of expert models.

4. Microcounseling is often perceived as real counseling/interviewing. What often starts off as role playing often becomes real interaction (Daniels & Ivey, in press; Ivey, 1991; Ivey & Authier, 1978; Ivey, 1994).

5. The trainee must have opportunities to extend the skills outside the analogue situation. Studies indicate that skill maintenance is related to opportunities for continued practice and supervision following training (Daniels & Ivey, in press; Kasdorf & Gustafson, 1978). Using behavioral contracts to have the skill used in real helping can be useful here.

MICROCOUNSELING AS A CONCEPTUAL/METAFRAMEWORK

What started as a procedure for teaching identifiable skills of therapeutic communication has evolved through research and theorizing into a metaframework for both counselor training and the counseling process. Central to this metaframework is the construct of the *culturally effective intentional helper* (Ivey, 1994; Ivey & Gluckstern, 1976a, 1976b; Nwachuku & Ivey, 1991). The culturally effective individual (counselor or client) can flexibly communicate with self and others, within cultures, and among diverse groups. This is facilitated by generating maximum verbal and nonverbal behaviors and by planning and reflecting on creative and appropriate helpful courses of action (Forsyth & Ivey, 1980).

Intentionality addresses the most basic issues of counselor competence, flexibility, and client effective living. Ivey and Authier (1978) state that

The person who acts with intentionality has a sense of capability . . . is one who can generate alternative behaviors in a given situation and "come at" a problem from different vantage

points. The intentional individual is not bound to one course of action but can respond in the
moment to changing life situations as he/she looks forward to longer-term goals. (p. 57)

The conceptual framework is represented by the Microskills Hierarchy (Figure 16.1),
which summarizes the successive steps to culturally effective intentional interviewing
(Ivey, 1994). The microtraining process is the vehicle through which this is accomplished,
and both beginning and experienced counselors are trained to increase their response capability.

The organizing principle for the hierarchy is the Five-Stage Interview Process. Different theoretical approaches to helping employ these or similar stages to interviewing but
may emphasize different stages (Brammer, Shostrum, & Abrego, 1989; Ivey, 1983). Ivey
(1994) offers a detailed treatment of the components of the hierarchy; a brief description
of the skills and dimensions of the hierarchy are offered here. It should be noted that both
the technical aspects of the skill and the underlying constructs that give the skill its validity are emphasized in the microtraining.

1. The skills of the hierarchy and interview are founded on individually and culturally
   appropriate attending behavior. Attending behavior involves culturally appropriate
   eye contact, body language, vocal qualities, and verbal tracking.
2. The next level in the hierarchy consists of several skill dimensions referred to as
   the *basic listening sequence* (BLS). The BLS facilitates rapport building, establishing the qualitative therapeutic environment, gathering information, clarification of both content and feelings of client communications, and observing client
   reactions.

- *Questioning* skills facilitate the gathering of information, expressing interest, and
  providing opportunities for exploration. Open questions lead the client toward making
  a more comprehensive and self-revealing response. Typically, open questions begin
  with "what," "how," "why," or "could." Closed questions often begin with "do" or
  "is" and tend to lead the client to more restrictive answers such as "yes" or "no" or
  one-word responses. Both types of questions have a variety of purposes in an interview (e.g., open questions are often a good way to start an interview, and closed
  questions are good for history taking, but an overuse of these latter is believed to
  inhibit communication; Ivey, 1994).
- *Client observation skills* are concerned with on-the-spot clinical judgment of the
  client, including paying attention to both verbal and nonverbal behavior. For instance,
  the therapist might notice that when the client talks about difficult or embarrassing
  issues he or she breaks eye contact or may blush. Over time, the therapist learns to
  understand the meaning of the client's behaviors in the interview setting. Clinical
  judgments and strategies in counseling that involve timing of responses and appropriate delivery of therapeutic strategies are clearly predicated on the therapist's ongoing observations of the client (Holloway & Neufeldt, 1995).
- *Encouraging, paraphrasing,* and *summarization* promote hearing the client accurately
  and communicating this understanding to the client. These are crucial clarifying and
  relationship-building skills. Encouragers tend to be selective minimal verbal responses
  such as "Ummm," "Uh-huh," "Go on . . .," "Tell me more . . .," or the restatement of
  a word or two just mentioned by the client; or nonverbal gestures such as reinforcing

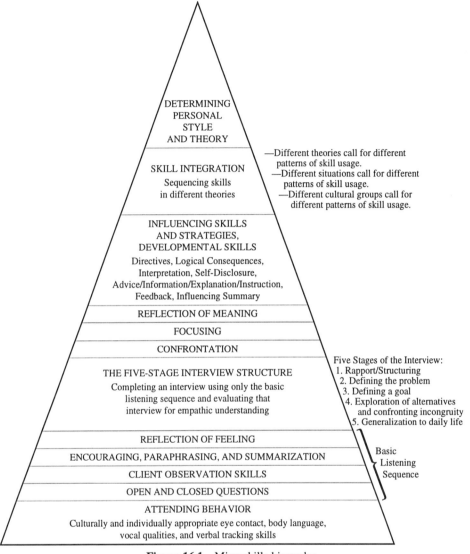

Figure 16.1 Microskills hierarchy.

Source: From *Intentional Interviewing and Counseling, Facilitating Client Development in a Multicultural Society* (3rd ed.), by Allen Ivey, Brooks/Cole Publishing Company, Pacific Grove, CA. Copyright © 1994 by Allen Ivey. Used by permission of Allen Ivey.

hand gestures or head nods. The purpose of encouragers is to communicate to the client "I am with you . . . continue." A paraphrase is a selective restatement of the essence of the client's previous statement or two. The focus is on the *content* of the client's verbalizations. A summarization is similar to a paraphrase in that the essence of the client's verbalizations is restated; however, here the restatement covers several themes of the client's thinking. Summarization can be a useful way to end a session, a series of sessions, or begin a subsequent session.

- Through *reflection of feelings,* selective attention is given to the affective dimensions of the client's experiencing. The importance of the affect construct in counseling is considered axiomatic.

Attending behavior and the BLS help to accomplish four general goals: (a) achieving an overall summary of the client's issues, (b) establishing the key facts of the client's situation, (c) determining the client's central feelings and emotions, and (d) helping determine the basic structure of the client's thinking (Ivey, 1994). Several constructs that both underlie and give validity to attending behavior and the BLS are emphasized in the training. These include a valuing of attention, acknowledgment, reinforcement, contact, recognition, affirmation, focus, information valuing, clarity, continuity, structure, logic, and affect.

3. The *five-stage interview structure* becomes possible when the therapist has the previous skills and dimensions in place. Within microcounseling, the interview is understood as a five-stage process: (a) establishing rapport and structuring, (b) defining the problem, (c) defining outcomes and goals, (d) confronting client incongruity and generating alternatives, and (e) generalizing and transferring learning to daily life. Ivey (1994) has shown how attending behavior and the BLS operate through the five-stage interview process to conduct interviews in the fields of management, medicine, and counseling (including decisional counseling, person-centered counseling, and assertiveness training). This interview structure could serve as a goal-oriented framework for any given session or series of sessions.

4. *Confrontation, focusing,* and *reflection of meaning* reflect increasingly higher levels of therapeutic facilitation. Like other skills and dimensions of the hierarchy, these are not unique to any particular theoretical system or modality. Through therapeutic confrontation, the therapist addresses discrepancies or incongruities among aspects of the client's feelings, cognitions, or behavior. Discovering such discrepancies can help the client deal with incongruities in his or her functioning and can be a stepping-stone to therapeutic movement. Focusing is another dimension through which the helper can direct the therapeutic conversation. Ivey (1994) states that "Focusing adds precision to client observation and to the microskills through selective attention to certain aspects of client talk. People tend to talk about what others will listen to or reinforce" (p. 216). A number of foci are possible in the therapeutic encounter and include the client, a main theme or problem, another person or family, mutual or group issues, the interviewer, and cultural or environmental or contextual issues. In reflection of meaning, the therapist recognizes the uniqueness of the individual's experiences at the level of meaning, values, beliefs, and goals, and hence at deeper levels of the client's experiencing and interpretation of those experiences.

5. The *influencing skills and strategies* and *developmental skills* tend to reflect upper-moderate to high-impact influencing strategies in helping the client take action. *Directives* indicate action(s) the therapist wants the client to take, such as tasks to complete and how to do them. *Logical consequences* help increase the client's awareness of cause-effect relationships in his or her functioning, which better enables the outcome prediction of certain courses of action. *Interpretation* provides the client with an alternative way of looking at a situation and the knowledge that multiple interpretations are possible. This encourages cognitive and behavioral flexibility in the client. Through appropriate *self-disclosure,* the therapist shares something of

herself or himself with the client that, among other things, may serve as important modeling for the client. Through *advice, information, instruction, opinion,* and *suggestion,* clients are given new information and ideas that help broaden their information and experience base, facilitating decision making and goal planning. *Feedback* provides information to the client about how he or she is viewed by others. The *influencing summary* pulls together, at the end of a session or period of counseling, the various influencing strategies employed by the therapist.

Developmental assessment and skills are derived directly from *developmental counseling and therapy* (DCT) (Ivey, 1986, 1991; also see Chapter 14, this volume). In summary, DCT holds that clients operate on, and therefore discuss issues from, four different cognitive-developmental orientations that parallel Piagetian levels of cognitive development. At each level, certain predominant features are present. At the *sensorimotor* level, the client somewhat exclusively focuses on the here and now; thought and emotion are his or her experience. The *concrete* functioning client is more information focused and provides information replete with details and specifics. The *formal-operational* client is able to reflect on self or situations—these are the important foci for that client. And finally, the client functioning at the *dialectic/systemic* level is able to see self-in-context and in relation to family culture and the environment. Developmental questioning skills focus on determining the predominant cognitive-developmental orientation of the client. DCT facilitates the development of client construction within a predominant cognitive-developmental orientation, as well as helping the client experience different cognitive orientations.

6. *Skill integration* requires the therapist to put it all together. When the skills and dimensions of the hierarchy and concepts of intentional interviewing are organized into a smooth and effective treatment plan, helping the client becomes possible. Different therapeutic systems and modalities tend to emphasize different microskills. Figure 16.2 indicates how interviewers of differing theoretical orientations use the microskill leads.

7. The summit of the hierarchy may be considered an opening to future counselor and therapist growth and development—*co-constructing one's own personal style and theory of helping.* This is a new development in microcounseling, for previously Ivey had called this "determining one's own personal style and theory of helping." The reframing of the last level of the hierarchy represents a conscious movement of the microcounseling framework toward constructivism, and social constructivism in particular. Microcounseling recognizes that numerous theoretical orientations have made a contribution to helping and that individual personality and style will help determine which strategies of helping are preferable. Yet, there is a need to involve clients in the choice of how they will be helped. At issue is co-constructing *with* the client what is therapeutically useful. Furthermore, over time, one's own style and theory of helping will evolve as more and more clients are encountered.

Studies showed that when people are trained in the quantitative microskills, they are also rated high in qualitative dimensions of helping, such as empathy, warmth, congruence, and genuineness [see the following section of this chapter]. The qualitative dimensions of the helping relationship that have become fundamental to the microcounseling model include empathy, concreteness, immediacy, respect and warmth, genuineness, and positive regard. Generally speaking, good relationship skills tend to correlate with successful client outcomes, and these qualitative dimensions tend to underlie good relationship skills (Ivey,

MICROSKILL LEAD	Nondirective	Modern Rogerian person-centered	Behavioral	Psychodynamic	Gestalt	Trait and factor	Tavistock group	Decisional vocational	Business problem solving	Medical diagnostic interview	Correctional interrogation	Traditional teaching	Student-centered teaching	Eclectic
ATTENDING SKILLS														
Open question	○	○	◐	◐	●	●	○	◐	◐	◐	●	○	●	◐
Closed question	○	○	●	○	◐	◐	○	◐	◐	●	●	●	◐	◐
Encourage	◐	◐	◐	○	◐	◐	○	◐	◐	◐	◐	○	◐	◐
Paraphrase	●	●	◐	◐	○	◐	○	◐	◐	◐	◐	○	◐	◐
Reflection of feeling	●	●	○	◐	◐	○	◐	○	○	○	○	○	◐	◐
Reflection of meaning	◐	●	○	◐	○	○	◐	○	○	○	○	○	◐	◐
Summarization	◐	◐	◐	◐	○	◐	◐	◐	◐	◐	◐	○	●	◐
INFLUENCING SKILLS														
Feedback	○	●	○	○	◐	○	○	◐	◐	○	○	○	●	◐
Advice/information/instruction/other	○	○	◐	○	○	●	○	●	●	◐	◐	●	●	◐
Self-disclosure	○	●	○	○	○	○	○	○	○	○	◐	○	◐	◐
Interpretation	○	○	○	●	◐	○	●	◐	◐	◐	◐	○	◐	◐
Logical consequences	○	○	◐	○	◐	◐	○	◐	◐	●	●	●	◐	◐
Directive	○	○	●	○	●	◐	○	◐	●	●	●	●	◐	◐
Influencing summary	○	○	◐	◐	○	◐	○	●	●	◐	◐	◐	◐	◐
CONFRONTATION (Combined Skill)	◐	◐	◐	◐	●	◐	●	◐	◐	◐	●	◐	◐	◐
FOCUS														
Client	●	●	●	●	●	●	○	◐	◐	◐	●	◐	●	◐
Counselor, interviewer	○	◐	○	○	○	○	○	○	○	○	○	○	◐	◐
Mutual/group/"we"	○	○	○	○	○	○	●	○	○	○	○	○	◐	◐
Other people	○	○	◐	◐	◐	○	◐	○	○	○	◐	○	◐	◐
Topic or problem	○	○	◐	◐	○	●	○	●	●	●	●	●	●	◐
Cultural/environmental context	○	○	◐	○	○	◐	○	◐	◐	○	○	○	◐	◐
ISSUE OF MEANING (Topics, key words likely to be attended to and reinforced)	Feelings	Relationship	Behavior problem solving	Unconscious motivation	Here and now behavior	Problem solving	Authority, responsibility	Future plans	Problem solving	Diagnosis of illness	Information about crime	Information/facts	Student ideas/info/facts	Varies
AMOUNT OF INTERVIEWER TALK-TIME	Low	Medium	High	Low	High	High	Low	High	High	High	Medium	High	Medium	Varies

Legend

● Frequent use of skill
◐ Common use of skill
○ May use skill occasionally

Figure 16.2 Examples of microskill leads used by interviewers of differing theoretical orientations.

Source: From *Intentional Interviewing and Counseling,* 2nd ed., by Allen Ivey. Copyright © 1988, 1983 by Brooks/Cole Publishing Company, a Division of International Thomson Publishing Inc. Used by permission of Brooks/Cole Publishing Company, Pacific Grove, California 93850.

1994; Luborsky, 1993; Sexton & Whitson, 1994). The qualitative dimensions are further discussed in the section on supervision.

RESEARCH ON MICROSKILLS

More than 300 empirical investigations of microcounseling have been conducted (Daniels & Ivey, in press), and both narrative and meta-analytic reviews of this literature have been published (Baker & Daniels, 1989; Baker, Daniels, & Greeley, 1990; Ford, 1979; Kaplan, 1983; Kasdorf & Gustafson, 1978; Kurtz, Marshall, & Banspach, 1985; Matarazzo & Patterson, 1986; Russell, Crimmings, & Lent, 1984; Van Der Molen, Smit, Hommes, & Lang, 1995). Only selected representative studies will be cited here.[1]

Researchers have investigated the microcounseling paradigm from a variety of angles. In two meta-analyses of microcounseling research, Baker and Daniels (1989) analysed 81 studies and Van Der Molen et al. (1995) analysed 19 microcounseling studies and using Glass's effect size (ES) statistic found mean ES of 0.85 and 1.41 respectively, which, according to Cohen (1979) indicate large experimental effects. These meta-analyses indicate that microcounseling was effective for teaching such higher-order skills/dimensions as discriminating facilitative conditions, generating alternatives, goal development, evaluation and appraisal interviews, assertiveness training, and test interpretation. Baker and Daniels further found that microtraining programs of varying lengths appear to be effective for teaching both low-order or high-order skills. The most significant training results, however, appear to occur when all the components of the microtraining program were employed.

Van Der Molen et al. conducted a meta- and narrative-analysis of 19 studies from The Netherlands covering the period of 1977 to 1994. These studies involved training undergraduate and graduate psychology students, paraprofessionals, individuals with shyness, and mentally deficient individuals. This analysis looked at three major dimensions: (a) knowledge of content and function of the skills being taught (including microskills and higher-order skills such as patient directedness and interview appraisal), (b) acquisition of helping skills, and (c) experience in social situations (such as reduction of shyness and social avoidance, increase in general social well-being, and social cognition). The overall experimental effect of microcounseling on acquisition of knowledge of skills yielded a mean ES = 2.38; on skill acquisition the mean ES = 1.28; and on experience of social situations the mean ES = 0.88; all large effect sizes. This review highlights the importance of including in the training the knowledge of the content and function of the skills being taught. Specifically, the pooled effects of studies where knowledge of the skills was included in the training yielded an ES of 1.41 in comparison to an ES of 1.06 in the group of studies in which this knowledge was excluded.

A number of early microcounseling studies indicated that microtrained helpers have a positively influenced client behavior. Kelley (1971) found that clients of microtrained helpers showed an increase in their talk time in the interview (with a concomitant decrease in trainee talk time). Hearn (1976) found that clients of microtrained helpers showed an increase in self-focus. More recently, when health professionals such as dental students were taught patient-centered communication skills, a number of positive results were found, including patient-directedness (Van den Ende, Schaub, & Lang, 1979). And finally,

---

[1]For a comprehensive review of microtraining research, see Daniels and Ivey (in press) together with Kasdorf and Gustafson (1978).

Bensing (1991) indicated a number of positive patient outcomes when physicians used communication skills such as the microskills.

Extending the paradigm, microtraining as treatment has been successfully used to teach social/communication skills to psychiatric patients (Ivey, 1973), shy individuals (Van Der Molen, 1990), mildly mentally retarded individuals (Bleeker, 1990), and couples with communication problems (Van Der Molen, Gramsbergen-Hoogland, Wolters, & DeMeijer, 1987). Microcounseling has also been effectively used to teach grade-school students generating alternatives (Poitras-Martin & Stone, 1977), sharing behaviors (DeVoe & Sherman, 1978), conflict reduction (Forbes, 1978), and attending (Carr, 1983).[2]

Other studies have found that when trainees are taught the basic microskills, they tend to show an increase in qualitative dimensions such as empathy (Daniels, 1972; Daniels, Denny, & Andrews, 1988; Van Der Molen et al., 1995), genuineness (Gallagher & Hargie, 1989), and warmth and congruence (Spruce & Snyders, 1982) and tend to make fewer errors of therapeutic communication than do the controls (Daniels et al., 1988).

With respect to skill retention, it appears that skills learned in microcounseling have differential rates of retention in follow-up periods as long as one year (Bleeker, 1990; Daniels et al., 1988; Dickson & Mullan, 1990; Scroggins & Ivey, 1978). Generally, the opportunity for skill practice and continued supervision appears to be positively correlated with skill use and retention.

Numerous studies have investigated the various components of modeling, instruction, practice, and feedback both individually and in combination within a microtraining context. Modeling appears to be effective both alone and in combination with other components such as instruction and manuals, the latter adding incremental validity to the training (Peters, Cormier, & Cormier, 1978; Russell et al., 1984). No significant difference was found between media of model (live vs. written vs. video) nor sex of model in a microcounseling context (Musser 1982; Robinson, Froehle, & Kurpuis, 1979). Regarding practice, mental practice/rehearsal appear effective as actual practice in teaching microskills, empathy, and test interpretation skills (Baker, Johnson, Kopala, & Strout, 1985; Munson, Zoerink, & Stadulis, 1986).

The effects of supervisory feedback within microtraining tend to be mixed. Whereas Stone (1981) suggested that supervisory feedback may add incremental validity to the microtraining process, Ford (1979) suggested that microcounseling may be effective with or without supervision. Hayman (1977) found that inexperienced graduate students appeared to benefit from supervision most; for the most experienced subjects supervisory feedback appeared somewhat detrimental. Others have found both high- and low-structured supervision conditions to be more effective than didactic-control conditions but that high-structured supervision with an added cognitive component was particularly effective (Berg & Stone, 1980; Kaplan, 1983). Walker (1978) found that trainee counseling behavior was no different whether feedback was given by instructor or by peer. Finally, Sharf and Lucas (1993) suggested that using computer simulations for assessing correct counselor responses within a microcounseling context were effective. In general, the more components of the microcounseling program used the more effective the outcome (Baker & Daniels, 1989; Stone, 1981; Stone & Vance, 1976; Uhlemann, Lea, & Stone, 1976; Wallace, Horan, Baker, & Hudson, 1975).

Finally, a number of studies compared microcounseling to other training approaches and

---

[2]Daniels and Ivey (in press) discuss the successful extension of microcounseling in nonpsychoeducational settings.

found microcounseling to be as effective as either *human resources development* (HRD) or *interpersonal process recall* (IPR) for teaching a variety of counseling skills (Baker et al., 1990; Crabb, Moracco, & Bender, 1983; Toukmanian, Capelle, & Rennie, 1978). One study showed that students in microcounseling improved in empathy more than did students in an HRD program (Toukmanian & Rennie, 1975). Arbeitman (1984) found that microcounseling was better than IPR for teaching volunteers affective sensitivity and empathic communication. Others found combinations of microcounseling and HRD or microcounseling and IPR to be effective (Pereira, 1978; Welsh, 1976). Several studies found microcounseling to be superior to either didactic instruction, discussion, or film (Bouchard et al., 1980; Lomis & Baker, 1985; Sawyer & Sawyer, 1981; Wallace, Marks, & Martin, 1981).

The effect of microtraining on trainee personality has been difficult to determine from this line of research. Studies that combine microtraining with other learning such as information on personality or information on counseling theories have shown trainee gains on personality measures such as the MMPI and POI (Paradise & Potter, 1977; Scroggins & Ivey, 1978). The effects of microtraining alone, however, could not be determined. Other studies failed to provide convincing evidence that certain personality attributes correlate with success in microcounseling (Berg & Stone, 1980; Simek-Downing, 1981). These and other studies, however, indicated that trainees positively value the microcounseling process.

In summary, microcounseling has proven itself to be a powerful and flexible training paradigm for teaching both lower- and higher-order skills/dimensions to a variety of professional and lay populations both within and outside psychoeducational contexts. The microcounseling program appears to be more effective than no-treatment or control conditions and in some cases appears to be more effective than other approaches for teaching communication skills. There is also a small but growing body of evidence suggesting that microtrained helpers have positive effects on their clients. Although there is no evidence about which sequencing of the steps in microcounseling is most effective, the greatest experimental effects appear to occur when all the components of microcounseling are present.

SUPERVISION IN MICROCOUNSELING

Microcounseling supervision has been employed within a variety of ideological frameworks including the *psychoeducator model* of helping (Ivey & Authier, 1978) and the *medical model* (Daniels & Ivey, in press; Van den Ende et al., 1979). The microcounseling supervisor is committed to the trainee's becoming a maximally flexible and competent helper who is able to facilitate client adaptation and growth within a wide variety of cultural, environmental, and contextual situations. The skills and dimensions of this model are also the tools of supervision through which the supervisor systematically shapes the trainees toward becoming the culturally effective intentional helper.

Supervision and the Qualitative Learning Environment

The supervisor-student relationship in microcounseling operates under the umbrella of a variety of qualitative dimensions. Within the microtraining process, the qualitative dimensions of empathy, concreteness, immediacy, respect, warmth, genuineness, and positive regard are emphasized to the trainee both in terms of being discussed and modeled by the supervisor. The supervisory relationship is one characterized by a warm, supportive, and respectful relationship with the trainee. These dimensions provide a safe learning environment. Individual differences among trainees are respected and valued, and there is an emphasis on the positive aspects of the trainee's behavior. Enhancing statements to the trainee such as "I like the way you responded to the client's feelings" or "Your genuine concern shows through" exemplify these supervisory qualities. The trainee's voice is heard and respected. The trainee is valued for his or her decision to be a helper, and the hard work the trainee puts into learning is demonstrably valued by the supervisor through empathic understanding and supportive, encouraging verbal and nonverbal behavior. Positive regard for the trainee is, therefore, demonstrated.

Just as we as supervisors strive to help our trainees avoid vagueness in their communications with clients, concreteness in supervision is likewise valued (Holloway & Neufeldt, 1995). Feedback, particularly with respect to changes the supervisor might suggest for trainee behavior should be made specific and concrete by saying "Could you give me an example of . . ." Such an approach leaves it clear in the trainee's mind what is required of him or her and even how to go about making change. Questioning and giving directives can be useful supervisory tools for facilitating concreteness.

Dealing with the trainee's behavior in the microcounseling session is a valued focus in the here-and-now of training and thus exemplifies immediacy. When appropriate, the relationship between supervisor and trainee can also be dealt with in the present. When supervising the advanced/experienced trainee for whom supervisory feedback, as the research indicates, can be threatening, the use of immediacy narrows to the present both the field of focus and the range of issues that need to be resolved in supervision.

Finally, through consistent congruence between the supervisor's verbal and nonverbal behaviors, genuineness is demonstrated and encouraged in the trainee.

Supervision and the Microskills

There is a tendency in supervision to be highly abstract. Although there may be a place for this, review of the endless counseling tapes and supervisory process sessions frequently reveals little attention to the concrete specifics of the session. One of the most valuable contributions of microcounseling is that it provides a clear and objective language or vocabulary to describe specifically and concretely what is happening in supervision.

The microcounseling approach is ultimately concrete and can be an important part of supervision that is often overlooked. For example, rather than say to the trainee, "Your client isn't able to express much emotion with you," the supervisor can comment, "You used very few reflections of feeling in the interview, and you tended to focus on the client's wife rather than the client himself. Consider changing your focus to the client. Deliberately emphasize 'how' questions with a feeling emphasis. This will help the client express emotion, and then you can reflect the feeling to encourage him to continue." Such a comment gives the trainee concrete rather than vague feedback and directions for change. Furthermore, the supervisor's strategic use of questioning, paraphrasing, and encouraging can help the trainee clarify what he or she is doing at any point in time and where he or she is going with a particular theme in the practice interviews. Similarly, the supervisor may appropriately use other skills of the hierarchy in interacting with the trainee. As trainees become more adept with the microskills and learn more about themselves in terms of their unique role as helpers, they work toward more self- and cosupervision.

The skills/dimensions of the microskills hierarchy are best learned through the systematic steps of the microtraining process outlined earlier in this chapter. The training process is organized around the five-stage interview structure, which serves as an organizing framework for both the course of the therapeutic relationship and a given therapeutic session. The microskills are discrete skills that are operationally defined and can be objectively observed, evaluated, and practiced. For the beginner, particular emphasis is placed on attending behavior and the BLS as these are seen as foundational to both the five-stage interview structure and the higher-level skills and dimensions of the hierarchy (Ivey, 1994).

Forsyth and Ivey (1980) provide a useful synopsis for supervising microskills training. Beginning helpers are introduced to the complexity of the interviewing process by learning single, discrete skills. The impact of these skills on client communications and the helping relationship is observed firsthand through viewing both the trainee's own behavior as well as that of experts on videotape. Furthermore, in group practice, trainees observe their peers in interviewing interactions and are encouraged to fine-tune their knowledge of the skills by giving feedback to their peers. A further useful exercise in a microcounseling course is to have the trainees use the microskills hierarchy as a taxonomy to rate written interview transcripts or taped interviews. Through this active involved process, the trainee learns the basic communication skills, the constructs underlying these skills, and the interviewing process in a gradual step-by step fashion.

In microcounseling, the trainee gradually learns to analyse the generation of phrases and sentences by both herself and himself and the client. If the microtraining process has been successful, beginning helpers will learn to recognize how their verbal behavior impacts client communication. It is common for clients at the beginning of helping to respond mostly in terms of content issues, and Forsyth and Ivey (1980) state that "they avoid expression of feeling, and tend to be vague rather than concrete, non-immediate, and lack self-respect. If the helping process has been successful, this pattern of responding changes" (p. 245). Similarly, beginning helpers tend to be more advice oriented, ask a lot of closed questions, and tend to be more topic oriented than client oriented. Following microcounseling, the research has shown that trainees tend to be more comprehensive in their verbal repertoire, ask more open questions, make more reflection of feeling statements, and show higher levels of the qualitative dimensions.

With respect to level of skill competence, Ivey (1994) identifies four levels of skill attainment in microcounseling and how these are achieved in supervision:

Level 1, Identification. The most elementary mastery of the skills requires the ability to identify and classify interviewing behavior. Most often this will be done by observing others' behavior in a practice session or through an examination.

Level 2, Basic mastery. This involves being able to perform the skill in an interview, for example, demonstrating that the trainee can use both open and closed questioning even though he or she may not use the skills at a high level.

Level 3, Active mastery. Intentional interviewing demands that the trainee has a variety of skills that he or she can use for specific purposes, for example, attending behavior skills should increase client talk time in the interview, whereas the absence of them usually reduces client talk. Active mastery means that the trainee can produce specific client results from his or her interviewing leads and behavior.

Level 4, Teaching mastery. One way to achieve a deeper mastery of a skill is to teach that skill to someone else. In addition, many clients can gain from being taught skills of interviewing to improve their communication skills.

The attainment of Levels 1 and 2 for the beginning helper appears to be a reasonable goal. The advanced/experienced helper should strive for Levels 3 and 4. The microcounseling supervisor may establish predetermined levels of skill attainment and work with the trainee to attain this level of competency. As a rule, higher levels of the microskills hierarchy are associated with the more advanced skills and thus are the focus of training for the advanced trainee rather than for the beginner.

As the helper becomes more expert in the skills and constructs of therapeutic communication, he or she is able to analyze various therapeutic modalities and systems from the microskills perspective. From this analysis, the helper is able to be more precise about how therapists of varying orientations differ in their communications. The logical extension of this exercise is that the helper will have concrete guidelines for learning alternative therapeutic orientations (Chadbourne, 1975; Ivey, 1988; Sherrard, 1973). Figure 16.2 showed the various patterns of microskill usage in various theoretical systems and can serve as a guide for the advanced trainee as he or she learns theory-specific skills. A more complete treatment of how the microskills adapt to varying theoretical systems can be found in Forsyth and Ivey (1980) and Ivey, Ivey, and Simek-Morgan (1997).

For the advanced trainee who is competent in the use of the microskills, the supervisory focus is on refining skill usage and integrating microskills into broader and more sophisticated helping systems. Furthermore, this trainee learns the uses and roles of the more advanced constructs and dimensions of interaction such as *therapeutic confrontation*. The supervisor as well may use therapeutic confrontation to facilitate trainee self-reflection and analysis. Forsyth and Ivey (1980) provide a most useful example of the value of confrontation in supervision. They state:

> Confrontation appears in a supervisor lead when he or she reflects to the beginning counselor "You say you enjoy and believe in the Rogerian mode of helping, but as I examine your interview, I see only one reflection of feeling in a half hour. How do you put that together?" Confrontation—the pointing out of discrepancies—can be most powerful in bringing espoused theory and theory of practice into harmony. (p. 247)

As the advanced trainee is introduced to influencing skills and strategies and developmental skills, more precise attention is paid to the impact of therapist behavior on client behavior. One way this can be accomplished is to have the trainee and the supervisor rate videotapes independently and later compare notes and observations. Particular attention is paid to nonverbal dimensions of the helper-client relationship, such as breaks in eye contact or unusual changes in body language by either helper or client that may reflect discomfort on the part of either helper or client. Attention should be paid to any lack of verbal and nonverbal synchrony between helper and client and that this lack of congruence should be analyzed as to its meaning. Furthermore, any trouble spots (e.g., therapist deviates from usual style) in the therapeutic situation should be analyzed.

An emphasis on the importance of cultures, environments, and contexts in helping has been part of the microcounseling model for more than 20 years (Ivey, 1994; Ivey & Gluckstern, 1976a, 1976b). The trainee gradually learns how helping skills differentially play out in these various contexts. For example, it has been discovered that direct eye contact (an important component of attending behavior) is appropriate for European Americans and European Canadians but may be inappropriate for certain African Americans, Native Americans, Déné, and Latinas and Latinos for whom direct eye contact can indicate a lack of respect (Ivey, 1994). Cross-cultural training is one way to emphasize how helping plays out in different cultures. The focus here in supervision is on consciousness raising with respect to the impact that forms of oppression such as sexism and racism have on both clients and helpers (Forsyth & Ivey, 1980; Ivey, 1994). The supervisor should strive to confront his or her own cultural (or other) biases and model an appreciation of other cultures, environments, and contexts.

SUMMARY AND IMPLICATIONS FOR THE FUTURE

The paradigm presented in this chapter addresses the basic question, "How does the counseling and psychotherapy supervisor help the trainee bridge the gap between training and practice, between skill-oriented learning and process-oriented practice, between the often decontextualized analogue situation and the highly contextualized environment of the therapeutic setting?" Microcounseling is offered as a comprehensive conceptual framework for training and supervision in interviewing and therapy. Furthermore, microcounseling complements other models and systems such as DCT that, when combined with microcounseling, offer a co-constructive, integrative, and developmentally oriented model of helping, training, and supervision.

Empirical investigations of microcounseling have been extensive and support the effectiveness of this training system. Particularly promising are the findings supporting microcounseling for teaching higher-order skills. Toth and Stockton (1996), for instance, have successfully adapted microcounseling to teach group interventions, which highlights the flexibility of the microcounseling paradigm. As well, there are an increasing number of nonanalogue and prospective designs offering support for the construct validity of the microcounseling paradigm; however, more of this kind of research is needed (Holloway & Neufeldt, 1995). Although there are studies that indicate that microtrained helpers have a positive effect on client behavior, perhaps the greatest challenge to be met is to determine the effectiveness of the microtrained helper in helping clients in the real world. The research on the role of personality in microcounseling has been inconclusive; there are, however, implications in this line of research for streamlining and increasing efficiency of training (i.e., a matching of supervisor and trainee) (Cormier, 1990). And finally, research on the adaptation of microcounseling to train supervisors is warranted.

The implications for training and supervision are clear. This model provides a step-by-step program of learning helping behaviors and constructs from simple behavioral skills such as attending behavior to more complex developmentally oriented strategies of DCT. Microcounseling is also a formal theoretical model of supervision that readily extends to supervision within other theoretical systems and modalities as well as various conceptual systems including behavioral and psychodynamic. Skills, constructs, and strategies of helping are identified and learned, and a common language between the trainee and supervisor follows through which effective supervision becomes possible.

With a number of important trends emerging in the field of counseling psychology that, on the one hand, reflect an increasing emphasis on synthesizing and integrating approaches to helping (Garfield & Bergin, 1986; Goldfried & Padawer, 1982; Ivey, 1991; Lazarus, 1981) and on the other hand, a reexamining of the central importance of culture, race, and gender in the therapeutic process (Ivey, 1991), the implications for using microcounseling are clear. As a powerful and flexible training paradigm and metaframework, microcounseling offers both the supervisor and the trainee a range of opportunities for conceptual and skill growth and a framework for developing learning and therapeutic strategies applicable in various pluralistic contexts.

REFERENCES

Arbeitman, D. A. (1984). The interrelationship, measurement and teaching of affective sensitivity and empathic communication: An experimental study. *Dissertation Abstracts International, 45,* 2677.

Baker, S. B., & Daniels, T. G. (1989). Integrating research on the microcounseling program: A meta-analysis. *Journal of Counseling Psychology, 36,* 213–222.

Baker, S. B., Daniels, T. G., & Greeley, A. (1990). Systematic training of graduate-level counselors: Narrative and meta-analytic reviews of three major programs. *The Counseling Psychologist, 18,* 355–420.

Baker, S. B., Johnson, E., Kopala, M., & Strout, N. (1985). Test interpretation competence: A comparison of microskills and mental practice training. *Counselor Education and Supervision, 25,* 31–43.

Bandura, A. (1977). *Social learning theory.* Englewood Cliffs, NJ: Prentice Hall.

Bensing, J. (1991). *Doctor-patient communication and the quality of care: An observation study into affective and instrumental behavior in general practice.* Amsterdam: NIVEL.

Berg, K., & Stone, G. (1980). Effects of conceptual level and supervision on counselor skill development. *Journal of Counseling Psychology, 27,* 500–509.

Bleeker, J. (1990). *Effects of social skills training program for mildly mentally retarded adolescents.* Unpublished doctoral dissertation, Lisse: Swets & Zeitlinger.

Bouchard, M., Wright, J., Mathieu, M., Lalonde, F., Bergeron, G., & Toupin, J. (1980). Structured learning in teaching therapists social skills training: Acquisition, maintenance, and impact on client outcome. *Journal of Consulting and Clinical Psychology, 48,* 491–502.

Brammer, L., Shostrum, E., & Abrego, P. (1989). *Therapeutic psychology: Fundamentals of counseling and psychotherapy* (5th ed.). Englewood Cliffs, NJ: Prentice Hall.

Carr, J. D. (1983). The microcounseling paradigm in the teaching of senior high school students attending behavior. *Dissertation Abstracts International, 44,* #7.

Chadbourne, J. (1975). *The efficacy of the Ivey Taxonomy of group leader behavior for use with classroom teachers.* Unpublished doctoral dissertation, University of Massachusetts.

Cohen, J. (1979). *Statistical power analysis for the behavioral sciences* (rev. ed.). New York: Academic Press.

Cormier, S. (1990). Systematic training of graduate-level counselors: A reaction. *The Counseling Psychologist, 18,* 446–454.

Crabb, W. T., Moracco, J., & Bender, R. (1983). A comparative study of empathy training with programmed instruction for lay helpers. *Journal of Counseling Psychology, 30,* 221–226.

Daniels, T. G. (1972). *Microcounseling: Training for accurage empathy in lay-personnel.* Unpublished master's thesis, St. Xavier University, Antigonish, Nova Scotia.

Daniels, T. G. (1992, June). *A technology of constructivism.* Paper presented at the Annual Conference of the Canadian Guidance and Counselling Association, Ottawa.

Daniels, T. G., Denny, A., & Andrews, D. (1988). Using microcounseling to teach R.N. nursing students skills of therapeutic communication. *Journal of Nursing Education, 27,* 246–252.

Daniels, T. G., & Ivey, A. E. (in press). *Microcounseling* (3rd ed.). Springfield, IL: Charles C Thomas.

DeVoe, M. W., & Sherman, T. M. (1978). A microtechnology for teaching prosocial behavior to children. *Child Study Journal, 8,* 83–91.

Dickson, D., & Mullan, T. (1990). An empirical investigation of the effects of a microcounselling programme with social work students: The acquisition and transfer of component skills. *Counselling Psychology Quarterly, 3,* 267–284.

Forbes, W. D. (1978). Effects of microcounseling training on junior high school student's knowledge, attitudes and behavior related to interpersonal conflict reduction. *Dissertation Abstracts International,* 2752-A.

Ford, D. (1979). Research on training counselors and clinicians. *Review of Educational Research, 49,* 87–130.

Forsyth, D., & Ivey, A. E. (1980). Microtraining: An approach to differential supervision. In A. Hess (Ed.), *Psychotherapy supervision: Theory, research and practice* (pp. 242–261). New York: Wiley.

Gallagher, M. S., & Hargie, O. D. (1989). Evaluation of a microskills programme with field-based counsellors: Effects on core attitudes and counselling skills. *Counselling Psychology Quarterly, 2*, 405–417.

Garfield, S. L., & Bergin, A. E. (Eds.). (1986). *Handbook of psychotherapy and behavior change* (3rd ed.). New York: Wiley.

Goldfried, M. R., & Padawer, W. (1982). Current status and future directions in psychotherapy. In M. R. Goldfried (Ed.), *Converging trends in psychotherapy.* New York: Springer.

Hayman, M. (1977). The influence of supervisor feedback in the microcounseling format. *Dissertation Abstracts International,* 5950-A.

Hearn, M. (1976). Three models of training counsellors: A comparative study. *Dissertation Abstracts International,* 5353-B.

Holloway, E. L., & Neufeldt, S. (1995). Supervision: Its contributions to treatment efficacy. *Journal of Consulting and Clinical Psychology, 63*, 207–213.

Ivey, A. E. (1971). *Microcounseling: Innovations in interviewing.* Springfield, IL: Charles C Thomas.

Ivey, A. E. (1973). Media therapy: Educational change planning for psychiatric patients. *Journal of Counseling Psychology, 20*, 338–343.

Ivey, A. E. (1983). *Intentional interviewing and counseling.* Monterey, CA: Brooks/Cole.

Ivey, A. E. (1986). *Developmental therapy: Theory into practice.* San Francisco: Jossey-Bass.

Ivey, A. E. (1988). *Intentional interviewing and counseling* (2nd ed.). Pacific Grove, CA: Brooks/Cole.

Ivey, A. E. (1991). *Developmental strategies for helpers.* Pacific Grove, CA: Brooks/Cole.

Ivey, A. E. (1994). *Intentional interviewing and counseling: Facilitating client development in a multicultural society.* Pacific Grove, CA: Brooks/Cole.

Ivey, A. E., & Authier, G. (1978). *Microcounseling: Innovations in interviewing, counseling, psychotherapy, and psychoeducation.* Springfield, IL: Charles C Thomas.

Ivey, A. E., & Gluckstern, N. (1976a). *Basic attending skills.* N. Amherst, MA: Microtraining, Inc.

Ivey, A. E., & Gluckstern, N. (1976b). *Basic influencing skills, leader and participant manuals.* N. Amherst, MA: Microtraining, Inc.

Ivey, A. E., Ivey, M., & Simek-Morgan, L. (1997). *Counseling and psychotherapy from a multicultural perspective* (3rd ed.). Needham Heights, MA: Allyn & Bacon.

Ivey, A. E., Normington, C., Miller, C., Morrill, W., & Haase, R. (1968). Microcounseling and attending behavior: An approach to prepracticum counselor training. *Journal of Counseling Psychology, 15*, 1–12.

Kaplan, D. (1983). Current trends in practicum supervision research. *Counselor Education and Supervision, 23*, 215–226.

Kasdorf, J., & Gustafson, K. (1978). Research related to microcounselling. In A. E. Ivey, & G. Authier (Eds.), *Microcounseling: Innovations in interviewing counseling, psychotherapy and psychoeducation* (pp. 323–376). Springfield, IL: Charles C Thomas.

Kelley, J. (1971). The use of reinforcement in microcounseling. *Journal of Counseling Psychology, 18*, 268–272.

Kurtz, P. D., Marshall, E. K., & Banspach, S. W. (1985). Interpersonal skill-training research: A 12-year review and analysis. *Counselor Education and Supervision, 25*, 249–263.

Lazarus, A. A. (1981). *The practice of multi-modal therapy.* New York: McGraw-Hill.

Lomis, M. J., & Baker, L. L. (1985). Microtraining of forensic psychiatric patients for empathic counseling skills. *Journal of Counseling Psychology, 32*, 84–93.

Luborsky, L. (1993). Recommendations for training therapists based on manuals for psychotherapy research. *Psychotherapy, 30*, 578–580.

Matarazzo, R. G., & Patterson, D. (1986). Research on the teaching and learning of therapeutic skills. In S. Garfield & A. Bergin (Eds.), *Handbook of psychotherapy and behavior change* (pp. 821–843). New York: Wiley.

Meichenbaum, D. (1977). *Cognitive-behavior modification.* New York: Plenum.

Munson, W., Zoerink, D., & Stadulis, R. (1986). Training potential therapeutic recreators for self-efficacy and competence in interpersonal skills. *Therapeutic Recreation Journal, 20,* 53–62.

Musser, B. (1982). Empathy training of seminarians: A comparison of three variations of micro-training. *Dissertation Abstracts International, 43,*(03).

Nwachuku, U., & Ivey, A. E. (1991). Culture-specific counseling: An alternative training model. *Journal of Counseling and Development, 70,* 106–111.

Paradise, L., & Potter, T. (1977). *Changes in personality characteristics in trainees in a counseling method course.* (EDRS Document #142873).

Pereira, G. (1978). *Teaching empathy through skill-building versus interpersonal anxiety-reduction methods: A comparison of microcounseling and interpersonal process recall.* Ann Arbor, MI: University Microfilms International.

Peters, G., Cormier, L., & Cormier, W. (1978). Effects of modeling, rehearsal, feedback, and remediation on acquisition of a counseling strategy. *Journal of Counseling Psychology, 25,* 231–237.

Poitras-Martin, D., & Stone, G. (1977). Psychological education: A skill-oriented approach. *Journal of Counseling Psychology, 24,* 153–157.

Robinson, S., Froehle, T., & Kurpuis, D. (1979). The effects of sex of model and media of model presentation on skill development of counselor trainees. *Journal of Counseling Psychology, 26,* 74–80.

Russell, R., Crimmings, A., & Lent, R. (1984). Counselor training and supervision: Theory and research. In S. Brown & R. Lent (Eds.), *Handbook of counseling psychology* (pp. 625–681). New York: Wiley.

Sawyer, H., & Sawyer, S. (1981). *A teacher-parent communication approach.* (ERDS Document #203566)

Scroggins, W., & Ivey, A. (1978, March). Teaching and maintaining microskills with a residence hall staff. *Journal of College Student Personnel,* 158–161.

Sexton, T., & Whitson, S. (1994). The status of the counseling relationship: An empirical review, theoretical implications, and research directions. *The Counseling Psychologist, 22,* 6–78.

Sharf, R., & Lucas, M. (1993). As assessment of computerized simulation of counseling skills. *Counselor Education and Supervision, 32,* 254–266.

Sherrard, P. (1973). *Predicting group leader/member interaction: The efficacy of the Ivey Taxonomy.* Unpublished doctoral dissertation, University of Massachusetts.

Simek-Downing, L. (1981). *Training university students in counseling and psychotherapy.* Unpublished doctoral dissertation, University of Massachusetts.

Spruce, M. F., & Snyders, F. (1982). An assessment of a microcounseling model for nurse training in facilitative skills. *South African Journal of Psychology, 12,* 81–87.

Stone, G. (1981). Effect of different strategies within a microtraining situation. *Counselor Education and Supervision, 20,* 310–311.

Stone, G., & Vance, A. (1976). Instruction, modeling and rehearsal: Implications for training. *Journal of Counseling Psychology, 23,* 272–279.

Toth, P. & Stockton, R. (1996). A skills-based approach to teaching group counseling interventions. *Journal for Specialists in Group Work, 21,* 101–109.

Toukmanian, S., Capelle, R., & Rennie, D. (1978). Counselor trainees awareness of evaluative criteria: A neglected variable. *Canadian Counsellor, 12,* 177–183.

Toukmanian, S., & Rennie, D. (1975). Microcounseling versus human relations training: Relative effectiveness with undergraduate trainees. *Journal of Counseling Psychology, 22,* 345–352.

Uhlemann, M., Lea, G., & Stone, G. (1976). Effects of modeling and instruction on low-functioning trainees. *Journal of Counseling Psychology, 23,* 509–513.

Van den Ende, E. R., Schaub, R. M. H., & Lang, G. (1979). *Evaluation of a communication skill training for dentists.* Unpublished report. Department of Personality and Educational Psychology, University of Groningen.

Van Der Molen, H. (1990). Being bored with embarrassment: Effects of a course for shy people on experience, behavior and cognition. *De Psycholoog, 11,* 520–526.

Van Der Molen, H., Gramsberger-Hoogland, Y., Wolters, F., & Meijer, M. de. (1987). Effectiveness of a communications skills training for married couples. *Tijdschrift voor Psychotherapy, 13,* 114–127.

Van Der Molen, H., Smit, G. N., Hommes, M. A., & Lang, G. (1995). Two decades of microtraining in The Netherlands: Narrative and meta-analysis. *Educational Research and Evolution, 1,* 347–378.

Walker, M. (1978). The effects of preferred versus assigned associates and peer versus instructor feedback on acquisition of a counseling strategy. *Dissertation Abstracts International,* 6553-A.

Wallace, G., Marks, R., & Martin, J. (1981). Training psychiatric nursing staff in social approval skills. *Canadian Journal of Behavioral Sciences, 13,* 171–180.

Wallace, W. G., Horan, J., Baker, S. B., & Hudson, G. (1975). Incremental effects of modeling and performance feedback in teaching decision-making counseling. *Journal of Counseling Psychology, 22,* 570–572.

Welsh, C. (1976). *Counselor training in interview skills: Interpersonal process recall in microcounseling.* Unpublished doctoral dissertation, McGill University.

CHAPTER 17

Interpersonal Process Recall: Influencing Human Interaction

HENYA KAGAN (KLEIN)
University of Houston
NORMAN I. KAGAN

ORIGIN

In 1962, Norman Kagan and his colleagues (Kagan, 1980; Kagan, Krathwohl, & Miller, 1963) first observed and later described a phenomenon that seemed to have utility for effecting knowledge and improvements in human interaction. They named the basic method IPR (*interpersonal process recall*). It took 5 years of controlled studies (Kagan & Krathwohl, 1967) to discover when and how the phenomenon could be useful; it took several more years of research and development to produce and validate a film series, an Instructor Manual, and a Student Manual (Mason Media, Inc., 1995), so that instructors in education, industry, medicine, and a variety of mental health programs could be trained to offer an IPR course to their participants.

What Norman Kagan and his colleagues observed in 1962 was that if individuals are videorecorded while they are relating to one another and are then shown the recording immediately after the interaction, they are able to recall thoughts and feelings in amazing detail and depth. Usually, there is some self-evaluation as well as a detailed narrative of the impact on the person of the "others" with whom they were relating. If a remote control stop-start switch is given to the individuals so that they can stop and start the playback at will, they generally verbalize a wealth of understanding about their underlying motives, thoughts, and feelings during the interpersonal transaction (Kagan, 1980, p. 262). They also found in these initial experiences that the phenomenon could be more reliable and that more information about underlying feelings could be elicited if the persons viewed the videotape with the help of someone specially trained in encouraging the viewer to verbalize and elaborate on that which is recalled during the viewing.

Kagan et al. (1963) found that "the person who facilitated the recall was most effec-

This chapter is dedicated to the memory of both my beloved daughter Gili Klein and my husband, Norman I. Kagan.

The chapter is a revised summary of research and development in IPR in the last 32 years. The basic processes and description of early developments and research reports on IPR have appeared in journals, books, and monographs. This summary thus includes some material that has been reported elsewhere and is mainly based on the chapter written by Norman I. Kagan that appeared in Hess (1980).

tive when he or she actively encouraged another individual, usually a student, to describe *underlying thoughts and feelings* rather than self-confrontation" (Kagan, 1980, p. 261). The facilitator's role required that he or she ask questions such as, "Can you tell me what you felt at that point?" "Can you recall more of the details of your feelings . . . where did you feel these things . . . what parts of your body responded?" and "What else do you think (the other) thought about you at that point?" The catalyst's role is that of an active inquiring colleague. The word *inquirer* was chosen to describe the facilitative person in an IPR session. The basic discovery then was not just of the value of video playback alone but of this unique combination of human role and technology (Kagan, 1980, p. 263).

IPR proved in time to be a method by which mental health workers and myriad other professional and paraprofessional groups could learn and improve their ability to interview, communicate with, and help other people (Kagan & Kagan, 1990, 1991). It also proved to be a useful vehicle for developing affective sensitivity scales (Campbell, Kagan, & Krathwohl, 1971; Danish & Kagan, 1971), for formulating theory about human interaction (Kagan, 1975), for the study of medical inquiry (Elstein, Kagan, Shulman, Jason, & Loupe, 1972), for the study of teacher-student relationships (Bird, 1977), for the reduction of job-related stress in the workplace [Kagan & Kagan, 1992; Kagan, Kagan (Klein), & Watson, 1995], and for accelerating client growth in therapy (Hartson & Kunce, 1973; Schauble, 1970; Van Noord & Kagan, 1976).

THE IPR MODEL—A METHOD FOR INFLUENCING HUMAN INTERACTION

Rowe (1972) found that if, in addition to the experiential processes of the model, students were also taught theoretical constructs, their skill development was significantly augmented. Based on her findings, theoretical constructs about interpersonal communication were integrated into the IPR model. In 1990, a *Theory and Introduction* film was added to the IPR film series. Accordingly, the entire film series and the Instructor Manual were revised. The revisions were completed in 1995.

An overview of the theory is presented here. Students are cautioned that acceptance or rejection of the theory is not crucial to learning from the IPR model. Instructors are encouraged to modify or substitute their own theoretical constructs (Kagan, 1980, p. 273).

Basic Elements

People need one another. First and foremost, that people need one another is part of our basic nature [Kagan, Holmes, & Kagan (Klein), 1995]. For millions of years, our ability to rely on one another is what permitted us to survive on earth. Alone in nature, an individual is extremely vulnerable and helpless. We survived only because we lived in community [Kagan, Holmes, & Kagan (Klein), 1995]. People are the greatest source of stimulation for one another (Kagan, 1980).

But, *people learn to fear one another.* Just as people can be the most potent source of stimulation for one another, they can also be their own most potent source of pain and horror. Most of these fears are learned in childhood. Because one's earliest, most impressionable imprinted experiences are as a very small being in a large person's world, vague feelings of fear and helplessness may, to a greater or lesser extent, persist throughout one's life (Kagan, 1980, p. 273).

This is why so many of the "gut-level" feelings that we repeatedly hear people eventually admit in the course of IPR sessions appear infantile—living vestiges of early fears. We hear things such as, "I don't know why I feel he's going to hurt me, but it almost feels like any minute I'm going to be picked up, as if I were very small and beaten or thrown away" or "It feels as if, if I'm not careful, he'll get up and walk out; he'll leave me and I just know that I won't be able to survive on my own. I'll die." We develop "interpersonal allergies" to situations and people [Kagan, Holmes, & Kagan (Klein), 1995].

Fear of people usually clusters around four "bottom-line" fears: (a) If I'm not careful, I will be hurt; (b) If I'm not careful, I will hurt others; (c) If I'm not careful, I will be engulfed; (d) If I'm not careful, I will engulf others (Mason Media, Inc., 1994, p. 7). We fear disapproval, punishment, and being hurt physically or emotionally. We fear abandonment, being left or rejected. These fears contribute to a very real sense of vulnerability that can persist or be triggered throughout our lives.

In childhood and adolescence, as we strive for independence, for identity and integrity, we experience the fear of being controlled by another or of being too dependent on another. We also experience the fear of using another for our own needs without concern for them [Kagan, Holmes, & Kagan (Klein), 1995, p. 7]. These fears are usually vague and seem irrational to us because we cannot adequately ascribe them to a reasonable source. They are usually unlabeled and unstated and so are inaccessible to the logic of language. Such feelings are denied or not recognized, and the source is not subject to cognitive scrutiny. The "enemy" remains unknown (Kagan, 1980, p. 273).

Manifestations and Typology

The basically opposed states, that is, the need for people and the fear of people, manifest themselves in a variety of behaviors.

People are unable to give up attempts to achieve interpersonal intimacy, despite their fears of such contact. This approach-avoidance behavior seems to characterize most human interactions. People appear both to approach and retreat from direct, simple intimacy with others. This approach-avoidance syndrome appears to be a cyclical process: Intimacy is followed by relative isolation, which is followed by new bids for intimacy (Kagan, 1980, p. 274).

This movement toward and away from people appears to establish a specific range of psychologically "safe" distances unique for each individual. People "settle in" at a psychological distance where they are more or less intimate with one another and yet able to feel tolerably safe from the potential dangers they sense in the situation. They seek and establish relationships with people who will accept their particular kind of "contract" (Kagan, 1980, p. 274).

The individual's movement toward and away from others may be summarized as an attempt to find a balance between the pain of boredom and loneliness when contact is too distant and the experience of anxiety when the interpersonal contact is too close. Because the need for interpersonal contact, or any contact, is so strong, people continuously seek what they can from an interpersonal relationship, yet they carefully constrain themselves at a distance by the imagined frightening potential of the relationship [Kagan, 1980; Kagan, Holmes, & Kagan (Klein), 1995].

The greater the fear, the further is the distance one establishes. The further the psychological distance one's approach-avoidance syndrome places one from another, the more rigidly the individual maintains that position. Those who gain most easily from psychological "growth" experiences are those who already are able to be close with others. Those who are most resistive are those who are most frightened. The further the distance one establishes, the greater the likelihood that substitutes for human contact will be sought. As people become less frightened of one another, their ability to achieve sustained intimate contact grows, permitting them to become more flexible, more effective, and healthier (Kagan, 1970, p. 274).

The fears people have of one another usually become translated into an interpersonal mythology and expectation, a "slogan" that enables them to avoid the frightening interpersonal nightmares. For example, "People have always perceived me in X ways and ultimately react to me accordingly, and they always will."

These anticipated reactions by others foster a self-fulfilling prophecy in which people make their nightmares happen. They expect others to react to them in certain ways, and so they search for and create evidence that indeed the others do react to them in the ways expected and feared. It is as if one paints a picture and then puts oneself into it. According to Horney (1945), the effect of a neurosis is its purpose. The position one finds oneself in interpersonally is the position one has carefully maneuvered into, sometimes with much difficulty and cunning (Kagan, 1980, p. 275).

One of the manifestations of this approach-avoidance dynamic is in the way in which people send and receive messages. Much of "direct" communication is acknowledged neither by the sender nor by the receiver. As people interact, they sense one another on many levels, but they label or acknowledge only a limited range of what they send or perceive. An example of this process is illustrated in the following old slogan:

A Diplomat

A diplomat is a gentleman who can tell a lie in such a way to another gentleman (who also is a diplomat) that the second gentleman is compelled to indicate that he really believes the first gentleman, although he knows that the first gentleman is a liar, who knows that the second gentleman does not believe him. Both let on that each believes the other, while both know that both are liars.

What Kagan was suggesting (Kagan, 1980, p. 275) is that to a greater or lesser extent people behave diplomatically. People have an almost uncanny ability to hear one another's most subtle messages, although they acknowledge and label only a small part of what they perceive and of what they do actually react to. Kagan (1980) saw this "feigning of clinical naivete" as an almost universal characteristic. Feigning is sometimes justified by participants as a fear that the other may cry or become angry and rejecting. More often, however, the reluctance to label messages honestly is based on an unwillingness to become *that* involved with the other.

Sometimes, however, even obvious messages are not seen or heard despite what looks like attentiveness by the other. This complete tuning-out usually occurs at times when neophyte teachers, counselors, or medical students are deeply immersed in their own thought processes, anxiously belaboring their next moves. Extensive covert analysis, especially when accompanied by anxiety, limits one's ability to attend to the other. Extremely anxious teachers literally do not see many of the behaviors they are actually observing.

Another manifestation of the approach-avoidance dynamic is in lifestyle, the basic interpersonal patterns that people characteristically rely on to survive in a world they need, yet perceive as dangerous. Here a two-stage model helps organize the observations. People have typical response styles in the immediacy of their interactions (first stage), but they also have long-term interpersonal postures (the second stage of the model) (Kagan, 1980, p. 275).

The initial stage's first three "styles" are similar to a typology first proposed by Horney (1945). The basic styles are "attack"—a continuum of aggressive behaviors ranging from assertiveness to attacking; "withdraw"—ranging from mildness to withdrawal; and "conform"—ranging from cooperation to conformity.

The long-term lifestyle may be different from what the immediate response style implies. That is, a person who relies primarily on aggressive behaviors may act in ways that invite others to engage him or her in animated, lively interaction; conversely, the same behavioral style may be adopted to achieve a long-term withdrawal posture.

The second stage of the model consists of six such "interpersonal postures." First, a person's immediate response to others may follow an aggressive continuum with attack at one extreme. He or she may tend to rely on attack as an adaptive technique. This is exemplified by the nasty person, the grouch, and by the person who has a short fuse that is prominently displayed but whose interpersonal posture or long-term lifestyle is one of relative isolation. The surface attacks keep the individual isolated and distant from other people as a basic way of life. Here the response mode is to attack, and the long-term pattern is one of withdrawal. The extreme of this mode achieves the long-term position of distance or withdrawal from human interaction.

Other people attack and achieve a lifestyle not of withdrawal but of a degree of conformity to a particular group or a set of norms. Such people attack to conform. Their theme seems to be, "Don't tread on me, don't disturb the things that I want to believe and the people I want to obey or believe in." Again, this serves as a way of maintaining a degree of safety. It is a behavioral pattern that, however imperfect, is relied on and clung to often tenaciously, because it is perceived as having permitted one to survive in a hostile environment. For example, the gang member who attacks in order to conform to the group's rules thus achieves a sense of safety in a hostile environment.

Another response has an extreme to withdraw under immediate interpersonal threat or encounter, to pull back, or to escape. As a result, one may adopt an interpersonal posture of attack as an overall life pattern. In this category is the traditional passive-aggressive personality (Kagan, 1980, p. 276).

One may also withdraw in order to conform—to remain loyal to a group or to an unchallenged set of standards or beliefs. The surface behavior lies on a continuum of withdrawal, and the long-term posture is one of conformity.

Finally, the person whose immediate interpersonal response is relative *conformity* acts, in the extreme, very chameleonlike. The two overall postures that may accompany a conformity response are *attack* and *withdraw*. Social manipulators fit these categories. Rather than think of the preceding behaviors as discreet entities, each should be considered along a continuum; that is, *attack* refers to a range of behaviors from assertive to aggressive hostility. Thus, the behaviors are not necessarily negative or maladaptive (Kagan, 1980, p. 276).

Less effective people tend to rely on a single interpersonal pattern and posture. A characteristic of more effectively functioning people is their ability to establish and maintain interpersonal intimacy while remaining flexible in their response mode. Depending on the situation and their goals within each situation, they respond somewhere along the continuum of behaviors (Mischel, 1968). Conversely, people who are generally unable to establish and maintain interpersonal intimacy tend to rely on a single response mode and are quite inflexible in their ability to deviate from it. Their behavioral repertoire is constricted, allowing them to experiment in limited ways and with much fear (Kagan, 1980, p. 276).

The concepts described are included in the IPR materials. Again, the theoretical constructs are offered to the student as a set of cognitive road maps. Students and instructors are encouraged to use these concepts as stimuli for their own theory building. As a point of departure for discussion, students/participants may reject all or any part that does not make sense to them and may substitute other constructs that are more compatible with their beliefs or experiences.

Elements of Facilitating Communication

This first unit of training discusses specific response modes of effective interviewer communication. The unit delineates four characteristics of therapeutic responses: exploratory, listening, affective recognition, and metacommunication (previously called "honest labeling"). The first phase of this unit emerged from early attempts to develop a behavioral counseling rating scale. Kagan's conclusion was that, among other undefined characteristics, successful counselors (a) focus much of their attention on client's affect, (b) listen carefully and try to understand fully the client's communication while conveying to the client that they are trying to understand, (c) could be extremely frank and honest (but gentle) rather than manipulative or evasive in responding to the client, and (d) respond so as to encourage the client to explore further and to assume an active role in the counseling process (Kagan, 1980, p. 263). These four behaviors were then used as a basis for rating of the trainee-client interviews. The first stage in the revised training system is to share these four concepts with the neophyte by means of a 52-minute color film in which a narrator presents examples and then simulation exercises for student practice (Kagan, 1980, p. 263).

Counselor Recall

The next phase was designed to help counselors overcome two dynamics that often interfere with the counselor's ability to understand the client or to communicate that understanding (Kagan, 1980, p. 264). It appeared that people "read" one another's most subtle communications fairly well, but as socialized beings they often pretended that they read only the surface phenomena, that is, the "official" message. Beginning counselors acted as if they did not perceive or understand the meaning behind many of their clients' statements, but during recall they indicated that indeed they did understand, yet were unable to act on their perceptions. In IPR sessions in which the counselor was the sole focus of the recall process, the "feigning of clinical naivete" became clear. "I knew she [the client] was very unhappy underneath that put-on smile, but—and I know this is stupid—I was afraid she might cry if I told her I knew she was 'hurting,' and then I would feel that I had made her cry" (Kagan, 1980, p. 264).

The second dynamic is of "tuning out," of actually not seeing or hearing the other person for periods of time during the session. This usually occurred when the students were especially concerned about the impression they hoped to make on the client (Kagan, 1980, p. 264).

After recall sessions, these two dynamics (feigning clinical naivete and tuning out) were exhibited less often by students. Typically, through this counselor-recall procedure, students learned to recognize where and how they failed to hear or to deal with client messages. Students also usually became more sensitive to their own feelings in human interaction.

Inquirer Training

The next phase is learning the inquirer role. The specific questions one asks in the inquirer role and, even more important, the learning-by-discovery philosophy of the recall process are useful skills and attitudes for students to have within their repertoire (Kagan, 1980, p. 264). In studying the inquirer role, most participants also learn that assertive behavior is not necessarily hostile behavior. The inquirer role, though relatively nonjudgmental, is nonetheless confronting and assertive. It requires that one ask questions such as, "How did you want the other person to perceive you?" "Were there any other thoughts going through your mind?" "Were those feelings located physically in some part of your body?" The safety of reviewing a video or audiotape recording of behavior (rather than face-to-face interaction in which the next moment in time is unknown) and the clearly structured cues to be used in the inquirer role generally enable students in the inquirer role to use and become more comfortable with assertive, non-hostile behaviors. As students proceed through a series of structured exercises in which they study and practice the inquirer role, they learn not only to conduct recall sessions for one another without reliance on the instructor but also to develop important new and useful human interaction skills. From the instructor's viewpoint, of course, an extremely time-consuming process can now be assumed by students for one another. From an administrator's point of view, an expensive supervisory process is replaced by one of modest cost (Kagan, 1980, p. 265).

Client Recall

Awareness of and sensitivity to their own feelings and often inappropriate behaviors seemed to help students improve with their next clients or patients; however, awareness of self was not often enough. An IPR tool was fashioned to provide client feedback and to afford the students additional experience using exploratory probes, the primary mode used in recall. In this phase, the students themselves are required to perform the function of inquirer with another student's client. Thus, the counselor has an opportunity to practice new behavior (i.e., the exploratory probes basic to the inquirer role) with the support of the videotape and the realization that he or she is working with a peer's client, not his or her own. When the students later switch roles, the counselor's partner does recall with one of the counselor's clients. Thus, both students learn—the one in the counselor role and the other in the inquirer role. By this phase, students are ready for such feedback and are not overwhelmed by it (especially since it is a peer, not the supervisor, who is the client's inquirer). The instructor or a staff member is available for assistance with any technical problems and to discuss students' reactions to the role of inquirer and to the feedback they received from their clients (Kagan, 1980, p. 265). Students usually learn, often to their amazement, that they can be both confrontive and supportive and that questions or comments raised by the interviewer that might be embarrassing or bold in most social settings are appropriate and productive in a counseling or medical interview when accompanied by communication of concern or interest. Students also learn how clients react to them and which of their behaviors clients found helpful and which they did not. Students are often amazed to learn the extent to which clients are deeply concerned about the counselor's feelings toward them. This awareness creates a readiness in students for the next phase of the system (Kagan, 1980, p. 266).

Mutual Recall

It is one thing for students to learn experientially that an important part of the client's concern involves the counselor's and, especially, the client's anticipations. It is quite another matter, however, for students to *learn to use the relationship itself* as a case in point to help clients understand their interpersonal behavior and feelings and to learn new patterns of relating. Again, with the developmental task defined and awareness of the probable readiness of the student for new learning recognized, an IPR experience was fashioned to help achieve this goal (Kagan, 1980, p. 266).

Counselor and client are videotaped as before. During the recall session, both counselor and client remain in the same room and are joined by an inquirer. Both counselor and client are encouraged to recall their thoughts and feelings, especially how they perceived each other and what meanings they ascribed to each other's behaviors. A situation is thus created in which two people, a client and a student, are helped to talk about each other *to* each other. Such mutual recall sessions typically enable students to improve their communication with clients about the here-and-now of their interaction. Students become more involved, more concerned, more assertive, and more honest with their clients. They use the ongoing counselor-client relationship as a case in point to help clients understand their relationships with others in their lives (Kagan, 1980, p. 266).

EVALUATIONS OF THE MODEL

The early version of the model was used in conjunction with a graduate practicum (Kagan & Krathwohl, 1967). A pre-, post-, and between-treatment design, replicated with three different samples in each of the three academic quarters, was used, permitting an analysis of the effectiveness of IPR-based supervision and of intensive traditional supervision. The design also permitted a comparison between the outcomes of IPR and traditional supervision.

The IPR model did not include the affect simulation films, which had not been adequately tested at the time. Each treatment was limited to a total of only 10 hours during an 8-week period. Eight students participated during the first 8-week period and 14 students during each of the next two academic quarters.

A *t*-test for paired observations was computed across all 18 pairs of counselors to evaluate the relative effectiveness of each of the treatments.

There were statistically significant differences ($p < .05$) in counseling skills as rated on a double-blind basis by independent judges between the groups. Differences were found to be in favor of the IPR treatment on counselor behaviors in the categories of "affective," "understanding," "specific," "exploratory," and "effective" (Kagan, 1980, p. 267).

In fewer than 10 sessions, Kingdon (1975) found that clients of counselors given IPR supervision made greater gains than clients of counselors supervised by other means.

Further evaluation of the model, now expanded to include affect simulation, has been done. Controlled studies indicated that the model reliably enables students to make significantly greater gains than do control students who received more didactic training (Danish & Brodsky, 1970; Kagan & Schauble, 1969; Spivack & Kagan, 1972). The model has been found effective in understanding interpersonal relationships within other cultures (Kagan & Byers, 1973, 1975). It has been in use in Australia, Japan, New Guinea, Malaysia, Hong Kong, Germany, Holland, Denmark, Sweden, Great Britain, Israel, and with native groups in Alaska (Kagan, 1980, p. 271). IPR was translated into several languages and studied in many cultures (Feidel & Bolm, 1981; Kagan & Kagan, 1990). Especially exciting for mental health workers was the finding that the IPR model could be used to help paraprofessionals learn basic counseling skills. Dendy (1971) provided a 50-hour program to undergraduate bachelor-degree candidates. Among his findings were significant improvement in interviewing skills, significant growth on an affective sensitivity scale, and no loss of skills during a 3-month no-training period (Kagan, 1980, p. 271).

Archer and Kagan (1973) then found that these same undergraduates could, in turn, train other undergraduates, so that the peer-instructed students scored significantly higher than did other students who experienced an encounter group of similar duration. They also scored higher than a comparable no-treatment group, not only on measures of affective sensitivity and self-actualization, but also on scales given to roommates and other peers not in the study. When provided with lists of all participants, dormitory residents selected IPR-trained students significantly more often than either the encounter-trained student or the control group member as the ones they "would be willing to talk to about a personal problem." This finding suggests that dormitory residents were able to identify the increased therapeutic skills of those peer-instructed students in the IPR group (Kagan, 1980, p. 272).

Heiserman (1971) applied a 16-hour variation of the model to a population of court caseworkers who did not seem to perceive their role as requiring or including counseling skills. No significant gains were found. The learning potential of IPR has its limitations. Measurable success has not yet been achieved in rehabilitating alcoholics with IPR (Kagan, 1980, p. 272).

The majority of IPR validation studies have been pre-and postevaluations of the impact of all or major segments of the model. There have been relatively few intramodel studies examining the impact of each of the major elements. Some evidence was obtained by making physiological recordings of individuals watching stimulus vignettes (Archer et al., 1972), followed by a recording of their physiological behaviors during video playback as they watched each vignette (Kagan, 1980, p. 272). Katz and Resnikoff (1977) found a systematic, controlled way to test the validity of the basic recall process. They trained persons to provide an ongoing account of the intensity of their feelings on an event recorder as they interacted with another person and again during a videotape recall of the recorded interaction. Significant correlates between ongoing affect and recalled affect were found in all four of their experimental groups. In another intramodel study, Grossman (1975) found evidence to support the basic premise that the affect simulation vignettes do indeed have an impact on people.

Kagan Affective Sensitivity Scale (KASS)

During the early 1960s, Kagan developed the Kagan Affective Sensitivity Scale, or the KASS, to measure sensitivity to emotions in interpersonal interactions, both globally as well as with specific populations of people, settings, and particular emotions (Kagan, 1994).

The KASS is an objective, machine-scored instrument. The scale consists of 18 vignettes of interactions followed by multiple-choice items about the filmed participants' affective states (Kagan, 1994). All scenes are candid; no actors or role playing was used. Currently, Form H of the KASS is administered and requires approximately 80 minutes to complete. Internal consistency, as measured by the Kuder-Richardson correlation coefficient, shows a reliability coefficient of .78 for the total scale (Kagan, 1994). Several studies were undertaken to establish discriminant validity of Form H (Kagan & Kagan, 1992; Kagan, 1994). Form H has the potential to be used as a screening device in areas such as counseling, teaching, medicine, and law. On the basis of early results, a low score appears to be predictive of poor performance in these fields, whereas high scores do not seem to determine future success (Kagan, 1994).

The KASS has also been used in various settings as a pre-, post-, and follow-up measurement of successful IPR training (Bird, 1977; Kagan, Burke, & Lieberman, 1982; Kagan & Schneider, 1987; Lieberman, 1981; Weise, 1992). Spaulding (1993) found significant differences in the scores between two groups on the Empathy subscale of the KASS. The group that used only recall scored significantly higher on Empathy than did the group that used only the IPR manual.

Kagan, Kagan (Klein), and Watson (1995) used KASS Form F as one of several pre-, post-, and follow-up measurements in a study that compared seven types of stress-reduction treatments, including IPR, with Emergency Medical Service personnel of a metropolitan fire department. Results found significant pre- and postdifferences regardless of specific treatment. However, IPR alone was found to be slightly more effective than any other single treatment used.

OTHER APPLICATIONS OF IPR TRAINING

Although originally designed for use with counselors, psychiatrists, and other mental health workers, the IPR model had an immediate appeal in undergraduate medical education. Most students enter medical school with an interest in human health and disease. Because of the extensive knowledge they must acquire before they can be helpful to patients, they are usually not permitted to interview patients for some time. Certainly, it would be beneficial if they were able to gain experience at interviewing earlier in their medical training (Kagan, 1980, p. 269; Kagan, 1984). IPR seemed to offer a solution. Under the direction of Jason (Jason, Kagan, Werner, Elstein, & Thomas, 1971), IPR was adapted for use with medical students.

Evaluations of the program (Resnikoff, 1968; Werner & Schneider, 1974) indicated that medical students made statistically significant gains in interviewing skills and in sensitivity to interpersonal messages. A similar approach was later used in medical inquiry studies to demystify the diagnostic processes employed by highly competent medical specialists (Elstein et al., 1972).

The transfer learning from the classroom or workshop setting where students practice counseling each other or trained clients to the actual work setting with real patients and clients can be a difficult transition for some students. To aid in the transfer of skills to other settings students should be encouraged to apply the various recall formats (i.e., counselor recall, client recall, and mutual recall) to the clinical setting with real clients or patients in which video recording is impractical (e.g., on medical rounds), simple audio cassette recorders have been effectively used. In clinics, internists trained in IPR demonstrated significant gains over non-IPR trained controls (Robbins et al., 1979).

To facilitate transfer-of-learning to the students' own personal "support system," IPR courses have been offered to couples. The student and his or her partner enroll in the course together. Several of the lab sessions are devoted to the couple's individual and mutual recall of their taped interactions. Joe and Fran Kertesz have offered such couples' IPR courses at Michigan State University (Kagan, 1980, p. 270).

Helffenstein and Wechsler (1982) found IPR to be the treatment of choice for the rehabilitation of brain-injured patients. Barrand (1990) found significant improvement in the lives of Lupus sufferers as a result of IPR training. Ross Harris and Norman Kagan have used IPR to study the covert behavior of an Australian airline cockpit crew during simulated crises (Kagan & Kagan, 1990).

WHY DOES IPR WORK?

Why is IPR an effective learning program? There are certainly several terms and more than one learning theory that could be applied to define and describe the importance of the IPR model. Kagan (1980, p. 278) explains the IPR model as follows:

1. Most people have never had opportunities to develop adequate skills that enable and facilitate intimate interpersonal encounters. The program confronts this problem by beginning with nonthreatening exercises in skill definition and skill practice.

2. Skills training is not enough. If people are uncomfortable or even frightened of one another, simply teaching them ways to become closer may have limited utility. People need help in confronting their most feared interpersonal nightmares. By experiencing them from a position of maximum safety and security, it is possible for people to learn to deal with and overcome such fears. Filmed simulations seem to offer this security by encouraging people to discuss, experience, and label the kinds of stress that would ordinarily evoke overwhelming anxiety. Furthermore, simulation enables people to develop an awareness and understanding of their underlying thoughts and feelings without being overwhelmed by them. Videotape feedback of their reactivity to perceived simulated threats offers people the opportunity to experience and examine their most frightening interpersonal nightmares from a secure position. Whenever physiological feedback has been included, the potential for learning has been further increased. As anxiety is reduced, new behaviors can be considered, learned, and applied to real-life interactions (Kagan, 1980, p. 279).

3. Meeting in small groups with others to describe reactions to simulated situations helps participants to expand their repertoire of descriptive words and phrases for covert behaviors. It also provides an atmosphere of intimacy and sharing with others, thereby enabling them to recognize that others share similar fears, and reduces feelings of aloneness and shame (Kagan, 1980, p. 279).

4. In the IPR inquirer recall format, the participant is encouraged to verbalize his or her perceptions, aspirations, thoughts, and feelings about an actual recorded dyadic session. By examining an actual behavioral sample, he or she has the opportunity to recognize the daily expression of interpersonal patterns of interpersonal distancing. The recall process is, in itself, a practice of new behavior, wherein the participant verbalizes previously unexpressed thoughts and feelings during the recall process and recognizes the nonthreatening nature of these statements. If the inquirer is supportive, the participant has little to defend against except his or her own self-perceptions. The participant is encouraged to engage in an exciting learning-by-discovery experience, rather than in an analysis of the extent to which "appropriate" goals were or were not achieved.

Provided with this support and with ample feedback available from the videotape recorder, it is intriguing to hear neophytes describe complex dynamics of which even astute supervisors had not been aware. People are truly the best authority on their own dynamics and the best interpreter of their own experience. Kagan (1980) states that Ronchi's (1973) formulations further clarify why the inquirer role works. In a sense, the inquirer is an active agent in fostering perceptions of personal intention and self-control. Learning and practicing the inquirer role make the model more efficient, while simultaneously providing people with the necessary skills to assist others in the learning-by-discovery process.

5. People ordinarily associate assertive behavior with hostile behavior. Practicing the inquirer role helps them to learn assertive but nonpunitive and nonhostile relationship skills. It is here, as well as elsewhere in the program, that what might be thought of as "interpersonal courage" is nurtured (Kagan, 1980, p. 280).

6. In the client-recall phase of IPR, participants learn directly from the client about interpersonal communication and the nature of helping. The participant's previously unverbalized hunches are confirmed or denied. The participant learns to recognize how the client's lifestyle is enacted in the here-and-now of the client's relationships. Participants learn that as clients talk with counselors, teachers, and others about concerns outside the immediate dyadic relationship, much of their energy is focused on how they feel about the person they are with and how they want the other to feel about them (Kagan, 1980, p. 280).

7. It is one thing for participants to recognize and understand the importance of the here-and-now of an interaction. It is, however, entirely a different matter for them to incorporate this understanding into their behavior, to learn to respond to others in new ways, and, particularly, to risk being more direct with others in the immediacy of the interaction. The mutual-recall format helps people to reduce their fears and to shorten the interpersonal distancing that blocks this kind of interaction. In the presence of a third person seated between them and with the here-and-then experience of the videotape playback, people are usually able to risk describing their mutual perceptions in each other's presence, the aspirations they had for themselves, and what they wanted from each other. This here-and-then situation enables two people to practice relating in a new way (Kagan, 1980, p. 280).

8. Typically, participants act as clients for one another in these training sessions. At the end of the series, whenever possible, participants then engage in interviewer, client, and mutual-recall sessions with people from the actual populations they are to influence. For instance, teachers are videotaped in their classrooms and conduct a teacher-recall session with a colleague as inquirer. Subsequently, the colleague conducts a recall session of the students in the classroom without the original teacher's presence. Finally, a fellow teacher conducts a mutual recall in which both teacher and students are encouraged to describe their reactions and covert behaviors to each other. This facilitates transfer-of-learning beyond the IPR seminar and lab rooms. This process is also cost effective (Kingdon, 1975). Trainees are encouraged to apply the methods to their daily work rather than to think of the experience as a one-shot learning sequence or course. For instance, medical students are encouraged to use the methods during their clinical experiences and to focus on both affect and cognitive inquiry processes during recall.

The ongoing developmental process of IPR continues to invent new ways of assisting people who wish to grow in their interpersonal understanding and skills. However, as Kagan (1980, p. 282) said, "much remains to be done."

REFERENCES

Archer, J., Jr., Feister, T., Kagan, N., Rate, R., Spierling, T., & Van Noord, R. (1972). A new methodology for education, treatment and research in human interaction. *Journal of Counseling Psychology, 19,* 275–281.

Archer, J., Jr., & Kagan, N. (1973). Teaching interpersonal relationship skills on campus: A pyramid approach. *Journal of Counseling Psychology, 20,* 535–541.

Barrand, J. (1990). *The effects on Lupus sufferers of an IPR-based couple course.* Unpublished manuscripts. Department of Family Medicine, University of Sydney, Sydney, Australia.

Bird, D. J. (1977). *The relationship between the training of teachers in the theory and practice of Interpersonal Process Recall and the subsequent effect on the attitudes of the Eaton Rapids Intermediate School students.* Unpublished doctoral dissertation, Michigan State University, East Lansing.

Campbell, R. J., Kagan, N., & Krathwohl, D. R. (1971). The development and validation of a scale to measure affective sensitivity (empathy). *Journal of Counseling Psychology, 18,* 407–412.

Danish, S. J., & Brodsky, S. L. (1970). Training of policemen in emotional control and awareness. *Psychology in Action, 25,* 368–369.

Danish, S. J., & Kagan, N. (1971). Measurement of affective sensitivity: Toward a valid measure of interpersonal perception. *Journal of Counseling Psychology, 18,* 51–54.

Dendy, R. F. (1971). *A model for the training of undergraduate residence hall assistants as paraprofessional counselors using videotape techniques and Interpersonal Process Recall (IPR).* Unpublished doctoral dissertation, Michigan State University, East Lansing.

Elstein, A. S., Kagan, N., Shulman, L., Jason, H., & Loupe, M. J. (1972). Methods and theory in the study of medical inquiry. *Journal of Medical Education, 47,* 85–92.

Feidel, D., & Bolm, G. (1981). Self-confrontation through videoplayback in courses of medical psychology—A summary evaluation of Kagan's Interpersonal Process Recall method in a German adaptation. *Medizinesche Psychologie, 7,* 61–75.

Grossman, R. W. (1975). *Limb tremor responses to antagonistic and informational communication.* Unpublished doctoral dissertation, Michigan State University, East Lansing.

Hartson, D. J., & Kunce, J. T. (1973). Videotape replay and recall in group work. *Journal of Counseling Psychology, 20,* 437–441.

Heiserman, M. S. (1971). *The effect of experiential-videotape training procedures compared to cognitive-classroom teaching methods on the interpersonal communication skills of juvenile court caseworkers.* Unpublished doctoral dissertation, Michigan State University, East Lansing.

Helffenstein, D. A., & Wechsler, F. S. (1982). The use of Interpersonal Process Recall (IPR) in the remediation of interpersonal and communication skill deficits in the newly brain-injured. *Clinical Neuropsychology, 4,* 139–143.

Hess, A. K. (Ed.). (1980). *Psychotherapy supervision: Theory, research and practice.* New York: Wiley.

Horney, K. (1945). *Our inner conflicts: A constructive theory of neurosis.* New York: Norton.

Jason, H., Kagan, N., Werner, A., Elstein, A., & Thomas, J. B. (1971). New approaches to teaching basic interview skills to medical students. *American Journal of Psychiatry, 127,* 1404–1407.

Kagan, N. (1975). Influencing human interaction—Eleven years with IPR. *The Canadian Counselor, 9,* 74–97.

Kagan, N. (1980). Influencing human interaction—Eighteen years with IPR. In A. K. Hess (Ed.), *Psychotherapy supervision: Theory, research and practice* (pp. 262–283). New York: Wiley.

Kagan, N. (1984). The physician as therapeutic agent: Innovations in training. In C. Van Dyke, L. Temoshok, & L. S. Zegans (Eds.), *Emotions in health and illness: Applications to clinical practice.* New York: Grune and Stratton.

Kagan, N. I. (1994). Kagan Affective Sensitivity Scale, Form H. *Examiner's Manual.* Houston, TX: Mason Media, Inc.

Kagan, N., Burke, J. B., & Lieberman, M. (1982). *The use of physiological recall to develop interpersonal effectiveness in medical students.* Final report, Grant # MH15473-03). Washington, DC: National Institutes of Mental Health.

Kagan, N., & Byers, J. (1973). IPR workshops conducted for the United Nations World Health Organization in New Guinea and Australia. World Health Organization, Manila.

Kagan, N., & Byers, J. (1975). IPR workshops conducted for the United Nations World Health Organization in New Guinea and Australia. World Health Organization, Manila.

Kagan, N. I., & Kagan, H. (1990). IPR—A validated model for the 1990s and beyond. *The Counseling Psychologist, 18,* 436–440.

Kagan, N. I., & Kagan, H. (1991). Personal exploration through video. In Peter Dowrick (Ed.), *A practical guide to using video in the behavioral sciences.* New York: Wiley.

Kagan, N. I., & Kagan, H. (1992, May). A controlled study of stress reduction in the Houston Fire Department's E.M.S. personnel. *Fire Chief,* 8–11.

Kagan, N. I., Kagan (Klein), H., & Watson, M. (1995). Stress reduction in the workplace: The effectiveness of psychological training programs. *Journal of Counseling Psychology, 42*(1), 71–78.

Kagan, N., & Krathwohl, D. R. (1967). *Studies in human interaction: Interpersonal Process Recall stimulated by videotape.* East Lansing: Michigan State University.

Kagan, N., Krathwohl, D. R., & Miller, R. (1963). Stimulated recall in therapy using videotape—A case study. *Journal of Counseling Psychology, 10,* 237–243.

Kagan, N., & Schauble, P. G. (1969). Affect simulation in Interpersonal Process Recall. *Journal of Counseling Psychology, 16,* 309–313.

Kagan, N., & Schneider, J. (1987). Toward the measurement of affective sensitivity. *Journal of Counseling and Development, 65,* 459–464.

Kagan, N. I., Holmes, M., & Kagan (Klein), H. (Eds.). (1995). *Interpersonal Process Recall Manual.* Houston: Mason Media, Inc.

Katz, D., & Resnikoff, A. (1977). Televised self-confrontation and recalled affect: A new look at videotape recall. *Journal of Counseling Psychology, 24,* 150–152.

Kingdon, M. A. (1975). A cost/benefit analysis of the Interpersonal Process Recall technique. *Journal of Counseling Psychology, 22,* 353–357.

Lieberman, M. G. (1981). *Psychophysiological correlates of measures of empathy.* Unpublished doctoral dissertation, Michigan State University, East Lansing.

Mischel, W. (1968). *Personality and assessment.* New York: Wiley.

Resnikoff, A. (1968). *The relationship of counselor behavior to client response and an analysis of a medical interview training procedure involving simulated patients.* Unpublished doctoral dissertation, Michigan State University, East Lansing.

Robbins, A. S., Kaus, D. R., Heinrich, R., Abrass, I., Dreyer, J., & Clyman, B. (1979). Interpersonal skills: Evaluation in an internal medicine residency. *Journal of Medical Education, 54,* 885–894.

Ronchi, D. (1973, May). *Attribution theory and video playback: A social psychological view.* Paper presented at the Annual Meeting of the American Educational Research Association, New Orleans.

Rowe, K. K. (1972). *A 50-hour intensified IPR training program for counselors.* Unpublished doctoral dissertation, Michigan State University, East Lansing.

Schauble, P. G. (1970). *The acceleration of client progress in counseling and psychotherapy through Interpersonal Process Recall (IPR).* Unpublished doctoral dissertation, Michigan State University, East Lansing.

Spaulding, J. (1993). *Increasing empathy and interpersonal skills in community college students through the use of Interpersonal Process Recall.* Unpublished candidacy paper, University of Houston.

Spivack, J. S., & Kagan, N. (1972). Laboratory to classroom—The practical application of IPR in a masters level pre-practicum counselor education program. *Counselor Education and Supervision, 23,* 3–15.

Van Noord, R. W., & Kagan, N. (1976). Stimulated recall and affect simulation in counseling: Client growth reexamined. *Journal of Counseling Psychology, 23,* 28–33.

Weise, K. R. (1992). *A contemporary historical study of the Danforth Principal Preparation Program at the University of Houston.* Unpublished doctoral dissertation, University of Houston.

Werner, A., & Schneider, J. M. (1974). Teaching medical students interactional skills. *New England Journal of Medicine, 290,* 1232–1237.

CHAPTER 18

The Discrimination Model

JANINE M. BERNARD
Fairfield University

The *discrimination model* was conceived as a teaching tool. In the mid-1970s, when I joined the Counselor Education faculty at Purdue University, I was asked to assume primary responsibility for the supervision course. Having recently received my doctorate, I was close enough to the experience of assuming the role of supervisor for the first time to understand my students' need for an aid to organize their initial supervision interventions. My intent was to present them with the simplest of maps to direct their activities as supervisors-in-training. As I attempted to reduce supervision to its simplest components, it seemed to me that supervisors must decide what to address with the trainee and find the most functional style to do so. These two axes became the basis for the discrimination model (Bernard, 1979).

THE SUPERVISOR'S FOCUS IN SUPERVISION

In determining what the supervisor should address within supervision, I went in a slightly different direction from others who had been writing in this area at the time. Rather than viewing the internal reality of the supervisee as the central focus of supervision, I chose to address the supervisee in the activity of conducting a counseling session as the focus. This minor adjustment reverberated to change the experience not only for the supervisee, but for the supervisor. By focusing on the supervisee in action, I had to assume that supervision must relate directly to that activity. Therefore, it was necessary to further analyze the activity of counseling in order to determine categories of counselor input. In other words, if I could identify the component factors that described the activity of counseling, I could help direct the supervisor's attention. (Like Kagan, 1980, I believed that much more happened in counseling than one could attend to; this was so for the supervisor as well as for the counselor. Therefore, the supervisor needed an aid to organize all the data being generated by a counseling session.) At the same time, I realized that the number of factors had to be limited in order to make the map functional. The result was the three focus areas of the model: process skills, conceptualization skills, and personalization skills.

The essence of process skills was the observable activity of the trainee. (Because of the different uses of the term *process,* a better description of this category might be *intervention skills.*) Intervention skills range from the simple to the complex and include all trainee

310

behaviors that distinguish counseling as a purposeful therapeutic interpersonal activity. From the greeting of a client to attempts to empathize, confront, or interpret behavior, as well as pacing a session and using silence, the skill of the trainee in delivering an intervention is the focus of this category.

A more subtle activity that is occurring during a counseling session is the trainee's use of *conceptualization skills*. Often, the supervisor can only hypothesize about these while observing a session and must interview the trainee to determine the level of conceptualization. This category includes the trainee's ability to make some sense of the information that the client is presenting, to identify themes, and to discriminate what is essential information from what is not. In addition to the assessment aspect of conceptualization, the trainee must choose an appropriate response to the client. The choice of such a response (e.g., to confront a discrepancy in the client's message) is a conceptualization skill; the delivery of the confrontation is an intervention skill. It is at this point, where the trainee and the supervisor appreciate the overlap of skills, that supervision becomes dynamic.

The contribution of the trainee as an individual, including his or her personality, cultural background, sensitivity toward others, and sense of humor, makes up the third category of skills. In order to avoid other psychological constructs, the awkward term *personalization skills* was chosen to describe this dimension of counseling. As with conceptualization, it can be difficult for the supervisor to appreciate all the personalization skills that are being used by the trainee during direct observation of a counseling session. For example, a supervisor of a race different from the trainee and client may not recognize when the trainee is pulling from his or her cultural background to relate to the client. Because personalization skills are the most unique to each trainee, they are the most likely to be misinterpreted by the supervisor, sometimes even after they have been discussed. The personalization skills of the trainee may be the most important to the client, at least initially. As can be derived from their label, these skills may also be viewed as the most personal to the trainee, making the supervisor's scrutiny regarding personalization skills either highly satisfying or uniquely uncomfortable.

Lanning (1986) added a fourth category of skills to the discrimination model, that of *professional behavior,* referring to issues of ethical behavior, professional development, record keeping, and the like. Although this is an important dimension of supervision, I would contend that this category could be collapsed into the original three skill areas. For example, if a trainee forms a dual relationship with a client, is this a deficit of knowledge or personal integrity? In other words, is the problem one of conceptual understanding or personalization? Being late for a counseling session may also be construed as an intervention issue (a nontherapeutic behavior) or a personalization issue (a disrespect for the client).

As the preceding examples illustrate, for every skill there is a potential skill deficit. Therefore, supervisors are often as much aware of the lack of intervention, conceptualization, or personalization skills as of their presence. Furthermore, when skills are lacking, it may become more difficult to identify (through observation) the source of the deficiency. For example, if the supervisor thinks a trainee didn't *do* much in a session, the supervisor must determine whether this was because the trainee didn't know what to do (conceptualization), didn't know how to do what needed to be done (intervention), or didn't feel comfortable enough to do anything (personalization). Simply being aware that inactivity has several potential sources, however, will make the supervisor more astute in how he or she works with the trainee.

THE SUPERVISOR'S ROLE IN SUPERVISION

The insight of the supervisor to assess or identify the areas of focus and/or difficulty for the trainee is only part of the supervisory role. The supervisor must interact with the trainee in ways that are productive to learning and improving clinical skill. The second half of the discrimination model describes three general roles that the supervisor might adopt for the purposes of enhancing the trainee's development, these being teacher, counselor, and consultant.

When the supervisor assumes the teacher role, he or she takes responsibility for determining what is necessary for the trainee to learn in order to become more competent. Thus, a comment such as "I'd like you to consider doing a role play with this client" would be a teacher response. A teacher also evaluates the level of performance. Therefore, a statement such as "That was an excellent session with Mike" would also fall in the teacher category.

When the supervisor assumes the counselor role, he or she is typically addressing the interpersonal or intrapersonal reality of the trainee. By doing so, the supervisor is asking the trainee to reflect on the meaning of an event for him- or herself in much the same way that counselors ask clients to do. Therefore, the supervisor as counselor is more likely to instigate moments for the trainee when things "come together," when thoughts, behavior, and personal reality merge to enhance professional development. Many of the earlier supervision models that addressed "personal growth" relied heavily on the counselor role in supervision.

Finally, the supervisor may take on the role of consultant, allowing the trainee to share the responsibility for his or her learning. When assuming the consultant role, the supervisor becomes a resource for the trainee but encourages the trainee to trust his or her own thoughts, insights, and feelings about the work with the client. The consultant role can be the most difficult to implement because of the autonomy it requires of the trainee. Just as with other types of instruction, it is far easier to tell someone how to do something than to create a context for learning. The consultant role is more about the latter.

There are two ways to view the supervisor roles: Each supervisor statement can be analyzed using the three role definitions, or the roles can be viewed more globally as metaphors for the entire interaction (Bernard & Goodyear, 1992). Both approaches are of value, but for different reasons. Starting with role as metaphor, let's assume that Supervisor B is working with Trainee A during her first practicum. It is obvious to Supervisor B that Trainee A is floundering in her sessions, not having grasped the pertinent process variables for helping clients state their issues. Thus, Supervisor B assumes that she will need to use the teacher role primarily with this trainee. The following interaction depicts the beginning of their supervision session:

SUPERVISOR B: Well, how do you think that last session went, A?

TRAINEE A: I was really quite pleased with it. I felt less nervous than I felt last week.

SUPERVISOR B: Yes, you seemed relaxed, and that was good. Were you equally pleased with how you and the client were working together?

TRAINEE A: I'm not sure I know what you mean.

SUPERVISOR B: Um, do you think the client got much out of the session?

TRAINEE A: Yes, I do. She told me in the hallway that she felt a lot better than when she got there.

SUPERVISOR B: Well, I'm glad that she felt better, but I had some questions about the actual process of the session. It seemed to me that you lacked a certain focus on the reasons she came to counseling.

TRAINEE A: So you don't think it was a good session.
SUPERVISOR B: I didn't say that . . .

This example illustrates the reason for considering role both as metaphor *and* as individual response. Supervisor B chooses "teacher" as her metaphor, but she quickly finds herself in a less than productive interaction because she relies too heavily on consultant statements as part of her teaching style. Supervisor B has determined that Trainee A is floundering, yet she asks Trainee A to evaluate her session before Supervisor B gives her any feedback. By attempting to appear egalitarian, Supervisor B sets her trainee up to fail in her response to the question. It would have been more fruitful for Supervisor B to structure the session with teacher responses, such as "I saw you struggle some in this last session. I'd like to use a good part of our session today identifying those moments when you seemed at a loss and seeing if we can come up with some ways for you to handle similar moments in the future. Does that sound as if it would be helpful to you?" By "showing her cards" immediately, Supervisor B would have planted herself squarely in the teacher role; at the same time, she would have protected Trainee A from having to evaluate her session when she clearly did not yet have the insight to do so in a way that would lead to a positive response from her supervisor.

A supervisor's accurate insight into the trainee's work can be compromised, if not undone, by an inexpert use of roles. For example, the use of the supervisor as counselor role can make the trainee so uncomfortable as to block learning. It is for this reason that all three roles should be considered for each focus area.

Table 18.1 depicts the 3 × 3 matrix of possible choices for a supervisor working with a trainee who will be named Paul. The supervisor has listened to an audiotape of Paul conducting his second counseling session with a woman we will call Tabitha, a 20-year-old African American woman who has sought counseling because she is in an abusive relationship. Paul is Caucasian and in his mid-twenties. In the session, Tabitha starts discussing her sometimes "embarrassment" at being black in light of the constant local incidents of blacks getting in trouble, dropping out of school, and so forth. Paul, obviously at a loss as to how to respond, makes some comment that a lot of whites break the law and drop out of school, too. Tabitha continues to state that she feels "guilty by association." There is also a lot of nervous laughter on Tabitha's part during this segment of the session. Table 18.1 illustrates the range of responses available to the supervisor.

As the reader considers Table 18.1, some supervisor interventions will be evaluated as more relevant and/or more helpful than are others. This, of course, is the purpose of the discrimination model, to encourage supervisors to consider a variety of responses, and to discriminate among them for the maximum development potential for the trainee.

THE MODEL IN USE

Choosing the Supervisor Role

There is a tendency to pair only one of the possible supervisor roles with each of the three supervision foci. Some supervisors adopt a teacher role whenever the trainee seems to be struggling with interventions, a consultant role when conceptualization is the issue, or a counselor role when personalization is the issue. Although these pairings are logical, they limit the supervisor's repertoire and, therefore, his or her impact. As can be seen by review-

Table 18.1 Discrimination Model Example Using the Case of Paul and Tabitha

Focus of Supervision	Supervisor Role		
	Teacher	*Counselor*	*Consultant*
Intervention	Supervisor models a different reaction to Tabitha's comment, one that reflects some insight into Tabitha's developmental struggle.	Supervisor reflects on Paul's apparent discomfort when he responds to Tabitha's initial statement and the power of this discomfort to block alternate interventions.	Supervisor encourages a conversation with Paul about different intervention possibilities with Tabitha and asks Paul to hypothesize about Tabitha's possible reaction to each.
Conceptualization	Supervisor reviews models of racial identity development with Paul and discusses the implications of Tabitha's statement.	Supervisor comments on Paul's discomfort with Tabitha and suggests that this may have caused Paul to forget information he has learned elsewhere. Supervisor suggests that Paul discuss his discomfort, as well as his thoughts about Tabitha's comment, then and now.	Supervisor asks Paul to write down as many explanations of Tabitha's response as he can produce. The supervisor also suggests that Paul consider Tabitha's response in light of her presenting problem for at least one explanation.
Personalization	Supervisor asks Paul to read Sue and Sue (1990) about the challenges of majority population counselors in assisting minority clients at different racial-identity development stages for the purpose of identifying relevant information for Paul's work with Tabitha.	Supervisor works with Paul to understand the range of his reactions to Tabitha, his feelings about working in context when black-white racial issues are a focus, and in light of Tabitha's presenting problem, his feelings about being both white and male.	Using an interpersonal process recall technique (Kagan, 1976), supervisor helps Paul identify a variety of reactions Paul was having during the targeted segment in his session with Tabitha.

ing Table 18.1, the *focus* of the supervision interaction is the entry point only. For example, consider the intervention/counselor combination given in Table 18.1. One could argue that if the trainee is uncomfortable with a particular client, causing him to falter in his interventions, that the focus should be personalization rather than intervention. Yet, by entering the supervision interaction through a focus on intervention, the supervisor (a) pinpoints the consequence of the trainee's discomfort with this client; (b) directs the trainee toward the ultimate solution (i.e., when the trainee is able to use different types of interventions with this client he may feel more confident and, thus, less uncomfortable); and (c) diminishes the possibility of the trainee becoming overly defensive. If, instead, the supervisor focuses on personalization from the role of counselor, the supervision session will no doubt evolve in a different manner with different results for the trainee.

This example brings us to another important point, the rarity of a supervision issue being planted in one focus area only. Discomfort within the trainee when assuming the responsibility of conducting therapy will limit his or her willingness to attempt new interventions. Unclear conceptualization will frustrate the trainee, thus blending personalization and conceptualization. Inability to think on his or her feet will make it difficult to intervene competently. At the same time, it is important for the supervisor to help the trainee identify the primary focus that seems to be causing difficulty. For example, one trainee I worked with recently was aware only of his panic in his early counseling sessions. As we worked together, however, it became obvious to me that he was entering each counseling session unprepared conceptually. Because each session had been so uncomfortable for him, he had avoided doing his "homework" between sessions. Once supervision helped him to conceptualize better (using both teacher and consultant roles), his panic subsided.

Finally, the supervisor should be sensitive to an overuse of any of the supervisor roles or a particular area of focus. Some supervisors are "natural" teachers and prefer to give their supervisees as much feedback as they can during supervision. Others are frustrated therapists who can cause the reaction I once heard: "Would you please tell my supervisor to stop *counseling* me!" Other supervisors seem to get stuck on one focus, seeing everything as a conceptualization issue or a personalization issue. Supervisors can check their focus easily by reviewing their notes after observing or listening to a counseling session or their supervision notes after meeting with a trainee. If all of a supervisor's notes fall into the same category and this is replicated across trainees, it may say as much about the supervisor as about any individual trainee.

The Importance of Technology

The assumptions of the discrimination model reflect educational practices as much as therapeutic practices. Therefore, early on, it became clear that the model depended on direct samples of the trainee's work (Bernard, 1981). In other words, it is virtually impossible to use self-report as the basis for this supervision model. Just as teachers benefit from watching themselves teach, and dancers learn from seeing themselves dance, counselors can continue to benefit from reviewing accurate samples of their work. For the supervisor, it is imperative to observe directly or, at the very least, listen to audiotapes of the trainee's work, unless the exclusive focus of supervision is the internal reality of the trainee. What is presented in self-report is a metaphor of the session rather than the session itself. A metaphor can be highly significant for supervision, but in the final analysis, it is still a metaphor.

The need for technology is especially acute in regard to the intervention and personalization foci. How many times during a case conference has a supervisor heard a trainee explain a successful implementation of an intervention only to have a videotape or audio-tape show a different reality? Without direct access to the trainee's work, the supervisor is not in a position to correct a faulty intervention or to offer suggestions for making an intervention more fruitful. As for personalization, by definition this focus centers on the trainee's blind spots. Occasionally, these will be evident during self-report, but often a trainee will distance him- or herself from those moments of countertransference or personal discomfort. The time between the counseling session and the supervision session allows for such denial. The supervisor will be much more helpful to the trainee if he or she can, at some level, *experience* the personalization issue with the trainee. A simple audiorecording makes this much more likely to occur.

Another important reason for obtaining direct samples of a trainee's work has to do with what was mentioned earlier regarding the supervisor's hypothesis about the conceptualization or personalization of the trainee. The supervisor accumulates hunches about what the trainee is thinking and feeling during a counseling session. Checking out these assumptions is an important part of supervision. When the supervisor's hunches are different from the trainee's self-report, this is important feedback either for the supervisor or for the trainee. In other words, either the supervisor is misreading the situation or the trainee's internal reality is different from what is observable in the counseling session. Either way, this situation provides important data for supervision, data that would not be available if observation or taping of the session were not done.

Thus far, I have focused on all the precautionary reasons to use technology in supervision, but there are many positive reasons to do so also. It is a delight to see or hear a trainee experience a moment of immediacy with a client or resist being "hooked" by a client's irrational blaming or deliver an intervention with near perfect timing, resulting in a therapeutic experience for the client. Sharing these moments with trainees can add tremendous dimension to the supervisory relationship. In addition, with appropriate releases, these samples of work well done and/or struggles resolved can provide invaluable learning experiences for future trainees.

Expansions of the Discrimination Model

Stenack and Dye (1982) conducted research to determine if a clear distinction existed among the three supervision roles proposed by the discrimination model. They were able to identify five supervisor activities for each of the roles (p. 302):

Supervisor as Teacher

1. Evaluate observed counseling session interactions.
2. Identify appropriate interventions.
3. Teach, demonstrate, or model intervention techniques.
4. Explain the rationale behind specific strategies and/or interventions.
5. Interpret significant events in the counseling sessions.

Supervisor as Counselor

1. Explore trainee feelings during counseling session or supervision session.
2. Explore trainee feelings concerning specific technique and/or interventions.

3. Facilitate trainee self-exploration of confidence and/or worries in the counseling session.
4. Help trainee define personal competencies and areas for growth.
5. Provide opportunities for trainees to process their own affect or defenses.

Supervisor as Consultant

1. Provide alternative interventions and/or conceptualizations for trainee use.
2. Encourage trainee brainstorming of strategies and/or interventions.
3. Encourage trainee discussion of client problems, motivation, etc.
4. Solicit and attempt to satisfy trainee needs during the session.
5. Allow trainee to structure the supervision session.

Neufeldt, Iversen, and Juntunen (1995) have developed a manual for training supervisors using the Stenack and Dye (1982) outline as their initial focus. Each supervision behavior is explained in detail, and a supervision vignette is included to demonstrate the behavior. Neufeldt et al. refer to the Stenack and Dye behaviors as "beginning supervision strategies." They follow these with "advanced supervision strategies" that, they assert, combine two or more of the three supervisor roles. The eleven advanced strategies delineated by Neufeldt et al. (p. 48) are as follows:

1. Encourage trainee's exploration of change theory.
2. Help trainee conceptualize a case (including developing valid information, setting the problem, and developing a change strategy).
3. Explore trainee's feelings to facilitate understanding of the client.
4. Facilitate trainee's identification and use of cues in client's and trainee's behavior.
5. Explore trainee's intentions in a session.
6. Help trainee assess compatibility between in-session behavior and theory of change.
7. Present a developmental challenge.
8. Explore trainee-client boundary issues.
9. Use parallel process to model appropriate strategies for dealing with clients.
10. Reframe trainee ideas and behaviors in a positive manner and build on them.
11. Help trainee process feelings of distress aroused by the client's experience.

As with the beginning supervision strategies, the authors offer an explanation and brief supervision vignette to demonstrate each advanced strategy.

In order to understand how Neufeldt et al. (1995) view each of the advanced strategies as combining supervisor roles, let us look more closely at the first strategy: "Encourage trainee's exploration of change theory." Neufeldt et al. (pp. 57–58) include the following behaviors to complete this strategy:

Supervisor asks trainee how he or she thinks people change (consultant).
Supervisor labels the answer as trainee's espoused theory of human change (teacher).
Supervisor investigates the trainee's experiences of change in his or her life (counselor).

From this analysis, supervisor facilitates the trainee's understanding of his or her practical theory of change and so labels it (teacher).

Supervisor asks trainee to look at ways in which espoused theory and practical theory overlap and ways in which they differ (consultant).

This analysis of advanced strategies that combine roles is helpful to the practicing supervisor, who must learn to weave roles skillfully in order to accomplish more complex learning tasks. The Neufeldt et al. (1995) text is a significant contribution to this end.

Combining the Discrimination Model With Developmental Models of Supervision

The discrimination model provides a matrix of choices for the supervisor. Developmental models (e.g., Johnson & Moses, 1988; Loganbill, Hardy, & Delworth, 1982; Stoltenberg & Delworth, 1987) have addressed the more specific needs of trainees at different points in their development. Referring to developmental models, therefore, can assist the supervisor in using the discrimination model matrix more deliberately.

Loganbill et al. (1982) described the developmental process as moving the trainee from *stagnation* (naively unaware or being "stuck") through *confusion* (erratic cognitive and behavioral fluctuations, disorganization, and dependency on the supervisor) in order to ultimately have the trainee experience *integration* (emotional and cognitive comfort with a significant new learning). The eight critical issues used by Loganbill et al. (1982) to evaluate the trainee (as stuck, in confusion, or integrated) were adapted from Chickering's (1969) developmental tasks of youth and included competence, emotional awareness, self-directedness, conceptual integration, respect for individual differences, purpose and direction, personal motivation, and professional ethics. This path from stagnation to integration is revisited over and over again as new interventions are learned, new frameworks are considered, and new insights are attained.

We have sufficient evidence that novice trainees prefer a relatively high level of structure from their supervisors (Heppner & Roehlke, 1984; Reising & Daniels, 1983; Stoltenberg, McNeill, & Crethar, 1994; Worthington, 1987; Worthington & Roehlke, 1979). Referring back to Loganbill et al. (1982), therefore, it seems that while in the throes of confusion, the trainee may not be able to take advantage of supervision that is highly consultative or may be more agitated by the supervisor as counselor than assisted if this supervisor role exacerbates the trainee's sense of groundlessness. Rather, the structure that is usually associated with the teacher role may be the most efficient to guide the trainee when confusion is at its peak (whereas the consultant or counselor roles may be more helpful when the trainee is in a state of stagnation). Furthermore, because a trainee will be in different states around different issues (e.g., at integration around personal motivation, at confusion around respect for individual differences, and at stagnation regarding competence for advanced techniques), the supervisor will need to be able to comfortably adopt different roles as different trainee states are identified.

Johnson and Moses (1988) took the Loganbill et al. (1982) model and integrated it with discrimination model concepts. For each of the critical issues in supervision as described by Loganbill et al. (e.g., respect for individual differences), Johnson and Moses asserted that there was a behavioral aspect (intervention), a cognitive aspect (conceptualization), and an affective aspect (personalization). For example, a female trainee might intellectually understand the "cycle of violence" and may be skillful in demonstrating counseling approaches used with victims of abuse but may still find herself experiencing annoyance with the client for allowing herself to be victimized, which may block her from communicating the appropriate amount of support for the client. In this case, the supervisor would need to address the trainee's annoyance, perhaps initially moving her from stagnation to confusion, and with additional work, to integration. A balance of support and challenge offered by the supervisor is needed to keep the trainee moving in a positive direction. The many options within the roles of teacher, counselor, and consultant are adequate for this purpose, according to Johnson and Moses (1988).

Less is known about the ongoing supervision needs of more seasoned therapists and the development of supervisors (Worthington, 1987). We know that the consultation role is more useful for counselors once they have more of the basic skills integrated into their style. We do not, however, know about differential applications of the consultation role based on the sophistication of the supervisee. We also have no empirical data regarding the interplay of the counselor and consultant roles in working with seasoned supervisees. Nevertheless, an appreciation of developmental differences, at least throughout training programs and for entry-level practitioners, is an important dimension for using the discrimination model beneficially.

Training Supervisors to Use the Discrimination Model

The discrimination model has been used most regularly to introduce novice supervisors to the process of supervision. Because of its atheoretical nature, the model translates well to different therapeutic modalities. Furthermore, the delineation of supervisor foci and roles is helpful to novice supervisors who desire anchors for their initial attempts to supervise. As was noted by Borders and Fong (1994), supervisor development has some parallels to therapist development, with the novice supervisor responding well to structure. The discrimination model provides some of that structure.

In addition to its utility for novice supervisors, the model has been beneficial for the present cohort of seasoned supervisors. When I first presented the model to experienced supervisors, I was apprehensive about its utility for that group. As is generally known within the mental health professions, however, the more experienced the supervisor, the more likely that the supervisor learned his or her craft through apprenticeship. Therefore, thinking of supervision in other than a therapeutic modality seems to be invigorating and useful to seasoned practitioners. In addition, because many seasoned supervisors still rely on self-report, the exercise of using technology, including the taping of supervision sessions for analysis, proves to be provoking.

Using the model to train supervisors, novice or experienced, is explained in detail elsewhere (Bernard, 1981; Bernard & Goodyear, 1992). Therefore, I will not repeat the entire process here. I would, however, like to emphasize some of the more critical activities for supervisor learning.

Give Ample Time to Focus.   It is easy to view the three focus categories as self-evident and move on to supervisor role. In doing so, however, supervisors-in-training forgo an opportunity to appreciate the richness of the therapeutic process, as well as their limits in perceiving all that is relevant for trainee learning within each counseling session. For all training groups I have conducted, the entire group watches 20 to 30 minutes of a therapy session, and the participants are asked to take notes as if the therapist were their supervisee and they would be responsible for conducting a supervision session after viewing the therapy session. Once everyone has a set of notes, the three focus areas are introduced and are placed on a chalkboard or overhead projector with each category heading a column. Then participants are asked to share their observations about the supervisee's performance. It is important for the trainer to take an almost alter-ego style in labeling each feedback item. The following is an example of a conversation with participants from a recent workshop conducted by the author:

P1:   I thought she [therapist in the tape] was distant, aloof. I wanted her to *do something*.
B: You've stated this as both a lack of skill, not doing anything, and as a personal issue, being distant and aloof. Do you have a hypothesis about which might be the bigger issue?
P1:   I assume it's the personal issue. I didn't see any evidence that she had any warmth for the client.
P2:   I disagree. I thought she started the session with a lot of warmth, but when the client started to "yes, but" her, she seemed to pull back. I think she got overwhelmed and just didn't know what to do.
B: So you agree that there was a personal element, that is, being overwhelmed, but you think the cause was her inability to find her way out of a difficult interaction, which would be more of a conceptual issue.
P2:   Right.

Two things are going on during this activity. First, supervisors are learning that their first comments often dilute the focus area of concern with another focus area. For example, the first participant says that the therapist isn't doing anything (which could be easily corrected), although her real concern is that the therapist is aloof (perhaps more difficult to alter). As the trainer asks the participants questions to help them clarify their comments, everyone is hearing how misleading feedback can be if the foci are blurred (which is different from when the supervisor chooses one focus area as a beginning point, knowing that he or she wants to address another as well). Second, participants start to realize that what they saw, heard, and focused on when observing a given therapy session can be different from what other supervisors saw, heard, and focused on. Experienced supervisors can have "overdeveloped" antennae, meaning that they become quick at making certain hypotheses, even if by doing so they ignore other important data.

Use Multiple Examples.   Because the training activity just described can produce a great deal of discussion and insight into the supervision process, it is tempting to accept a thorough analysis of the focus aspect of the discrimination model relative to one counseling session (and one supervisee) as sufficient. This is usually a mistake. No matter how animated or fruitful the discussion, participants will learn more about themselves if they apply the model to more than one supervisee, especially if the supervisees are distinct on at least one focus category. It is when the activity of using the model is repeated that participants start to appreciate their own personal patterns, sometimes irrespective of the supervisee. Furthermore, it is possible that during an initial activity, a participant found him- or herself to be in agreement with most of what others in the training group had to say; a second round, however, might find his or her perspective quite unique.

Be Literal.   As participants describe what they see or hear or react to in a trainee's counseling session, hold them to what they say, not to what they mean. If a participant says, "I didn't like how he leaned forward during the session," help him or her realize that this is an observation that addresses the intervention used. If the discussion eventually evolves to the realization that the participant thought the trainee was being seductive, allow the group an opportunity to appreciate the potential consequences (positive and negative) of delivering personalization feedback through intervention language.

Allow for Practice of the Roles.   Addressing focus allows participants an opportunity to gain insight with relatively low risk. Asking them to demonstrate supervisor role behavior may be perceived as a bit more threatening. Accepting participants' descriptions of their supervision roles, however, would parallel the limits of self-report supervision. Participants are more likely to know their preferred role as metaphor than they are to have an accurate sense of the roles that are used if their supervisory interventions are analyzed statement by statement. The latter, therefore, offers supervisors an opportunity to move beyond stagnation or confusion to a higher developmental level.

The roles also are far simpler conceptually than they are behaviorally. Activities that ask participants to change role on cue or that ask participants to conduct a simulated supervision session with the use of two of the three roles exclusively can be challenging. Furthermore, if the same supervisee (i.e., two participants simulating the same supervisee who was seen on tape earlier in the training) is supervised by two supervisors using different predominant roles, tapes of these simulations can offer excellent samples of the role's power to influence the direction of learning.

Preparing the Trainee for the Model

"What is it that my supervisor is looking for?" For new trainees or counselors working with a new supervisor, this is a legitimate question. Trainees have typically invested a great deal of psychic energy, as well as significant time and money, in pursuing training in psychotherapy of one sort or another. By the time a clinical supervisor enters the picture, the desire for a successful experience is high.

By describing the categories of intervention skills, conceptualization skills, and personalization skills, the supervisor can move the trainee into the context of the supervisory experience. Not only does this exercise give the supervisor and trainee a common language, it allows the trainee to hear feedback with a more discriminating ear as supervision progresses (Bernard, 1994a). In addition, by framing some social habits as personalization skills, the trainee may more easily grasp their effect on the counseling process.

Whatever the model used by the supervisor, evaluation should be consistent. Therefore, the supervisor also prepares the trainee for working with the discrimination model by describing evaluation criteria based on the focus areas of the model. Table 18.2 illustrates one such evaluation instrument that has been used to evaluate trainees at the culmination of their first practicum. By viewing such a list of skill attainment at the beginning of and throughout supervision, the trainee becomes a full partner in the use of the model.

As important as it is to explain the focus areas to the trainee, it has also proved useful to describe the roles available to the supervisor when conducting supervision. This can encourage dialogue between supervisor and trainee about how counselors learn, as well as providing trainees a vehicle for communication when supervision does not seem to be meeting their needs. For example, it might be beneficial for the trainee to hear something like the following: "There are a few different ways that I can assist you in becoming more expert. When I take a teacher role, I'll be attempting to assist you directly. You'll probably feel pretty comfortable at these times because I'll be doing a good deal of the work. When

Table 18.2   Evaluation Instrument Consistent With Discrimination Model

---

Supervisee's Name:_____   **Date:** _____

1 = needs improvement 2 = adequate 3 = good 4 = excellent

Intervention skills:

Ability to "manipulate" the process toward some desired outcome. For example, if your client has been evasive, ability to intervene to help your client be more concrete.	1	2	3	4
Ability to be in control of the session.	1	2	3	4
Ability to be flexible regarding skills.	1	2	3	4
Ability to be creative regarding skills.	1	2	3	4

Conceptualization skills:

Ability to be able to follow the client's issues as presented during the session.	1	2	3	4
Ability to be able to see the relevance of "sub-themes" to the client's issues.	1	2	3	4
Ability to be able to identify a direction to pursue in the session based on a sound rationale.	1	2	3	4
Ability to have an appreciation for your personal assumptions about the client's issues (espoused theory).	1	2	3	4
Ability to be able to evaluate your interventions for change (practical theory) based on your espoused theory.	1	2	3	4
Ability to identify interventions that complement your conceptualization of the client.	1	2	3	4
Ability to reevaluate your conceptualization of the client on an ongoing and more sophisticated level as you work with the client.	1	2	3	4

Personalization skills:

Ability to recognize your personal assets and liabilities, accenting the former and restraining the latter.	1	2	3	4
Ability to be in touch with your feelings in your sessions and throughout supervision, allowing you to become a better counselor as you mature as a professional.	1	2	3	4
Ability to demonstrate interpersonal and intrapersonal depth and flexibility.	1	2	3	4
Ability to work successfully with persons different from yourself.	1	2	3	4

Professional behavior:

Readiness for supervision and an ability to use feedback constructively.	1	2	3	4
Ability to exhibit professional behavior that reflects the ethical codes of the counseling profession.	1	2	3	4
Ability to exhibit behavior reflective of the responsibility and maturity expected of a professional.	1	2	3	4
Ability to exhibit an appropriate understanding of boundaries.	1	2	3	4

Additional comments:

Supervisor	Supervisee	Date

I believe it's important for you to risk your own strategy, I will probably assume a consultant role. Those times will challenge you more and you'll probably feel on less sure ground."

Conversations about roles can originate from the trainee as well. If trainees are aware of the options, they can communicate a readiness for a role: "I feel as if I've been getting in my own way in my session with Julie. I wonder if you could help me figure out what's going on" (a request for the counselor role). Finally, when the roles have been introduced to the trainee, the supervisor can give process feedback that relates to the roles: "You know, George, I've felt for a couple of weeks now that it's important for you to take more responsibility for planning your counseling sessions. But every time I assume a consultant role, you barrage me with questions, which more or less invites me back into a teacher role. Have you been aware of that pattern?"

In short, working conjointly within the context of the discrimination model communicates a respect for the trainee as a partner in his or her own learning. At the same time, it holds the trainee accountable by making both the process and the goals of supervision less mysterious (Ladany & Friedlander, 1995).

SPECIFIC ISSUES IN USING THE DISCRIMINATION MODEL

Theoretical Issues

The discrimination model was conceived to be atheoretical. Regardless of how trainees envision the helping process, they must deal with the issues of their conceptual grasp of the process, their mastery of intervention skills, and the interpersonal and intrapersonal dynamics that occur during the counseling session. In fact, the model has been used successfully with trainees working within a systemic framework, supervisees within a cognitive behavioral training setting, and trainees with a psychodynamic orientation, to name just a few.

It is its atheoretical nature that distinguishes the discrimination model as a model of supervision from an induction into a particular school of thought regarding the helping process. Bernard and Goodyear (1992) described the latter as *psychotherapy-based supervision*. Psychotherapy-based supervision will rely on the same principles for the supervision process as for the therapy process. The classic example of psychotherapy-based supervision is psychodynamic theory in which part of training includes the process of undergoing psychoanalysis and clinical supervision revolves significantly around transference and countertransference issues. By contrast, the discrimination model operates parallel to the theory of psychotherapy being conducted, not within it. There are advantages and disadvantages to this approach.

By providing a language for supervision that is different from psychotherapy, the two are less likely to be fused and the trainee is less apt to perceive him- or herself as a client. Furthermore, because the discrimination model attempts to be "evenhanded," regarding the contribution of interventions, conceptualization, and personal attributes to the outcome of the therapeutic process, it may serve to balance a theoretical orientation that seems to weigh these areas differentially. This may be important if the trainee is weakest in an area that receives the least scrutiny within a theoretical orientation (which, due to self-selection, is quite likely). As one trainer stated about her theory of choice: "In the normal course of therapy, I'd give the 'person of the therapist' credit for only about 10% of the outcome.

But if that 10% isn't there, the other 90% doesn't have a chance." Such a declaration serves as an argument for a supervision model that is distinct from the therapy model.

Although there is much to be said for a distinction between therapy and supervision, there are also disadvantages to an atheoretical supervision model. There is much in the literature to suggest that trainees are theoretically unsophisticated and require theoretically consistent supervision to attain entry-level competence (e.g., Freeman, 1992). Persons holding this view tend to regard supervision as an ideal opportunity for modeling therapeutic conditions and have an inherent assumption of the isomorphic properties of supervision.

Cultural Issues

Only in recent years have the helping professions given serious attention to multicultural supervision. As a result, the professional literature in this area is limited and empirical studies are only beginning to appear (Leong & Wagner, 1994). When it was initially developed, the discrimination model was no exception to the overall insensitivity to cultural variables within supervision.

Just as the model can be said to be atheoretical, it is also acultural. This does not imply that using the model denies the importance of culture, but that cultural awareness must be infused into its use. Although all three focus areas are affected by cultural factors, a discussion of the personalization skills category can be used as an example of the importance of culture when using the model.

As has been expressed by many authors (e.g., McGoldrick, Pearce, & Giordano, 1982), what is often attributed to personality is, instead, an expression of cultural background. Tone of voice, gregariousness, sense of humor, and nonverbal behavior are all highly culturally determined. Clinical supervisors, therefore, must be cognizant of this as they evaluate personalization skills. Additionally, behaviors cannot be evaluated out of context. The supervisor must take into account the multicultural reality of the counselor-client interaction, as well as the counselor-supervisor interaction. The supervisor must also evaluate the cultural "fit" between him- or herself and the client (i.e., the fit may be better between trainee and client than either of these to the supervisor). Only after such an analysis can the supervisor begin to consider personalization skills. Even then, the wise clinical supervisor will take a posture of respectful inquiry rather than an evaluative posture regarding this category, especially if the trainee and/or trainee and client represent cultural groups far removed from the bulk of the supervisor's experience.

It should be noted that for this discussion, culture does not include only race and ethnic background, but also gender, economic background, and so forth. In fact, training workshops have often found gender to be a highly salient factor when supervisors watch trainee tapes. A male trainee can be seen as "sexist and insensitive" by female supervisors, while being perceived as "vulnerable" by the male supervisors. Although both perspectives have some validity, it is important for supervisors to realize the extent to which their first impressions are moderated by gender.

Recent research has shed some additional light on the role that culture plays within supervision, information that can be applied to the use of the discrimination model. Hilton, Russell, and Salmi (1995) studied the relationship between supervisor and supervisee when these persons represented different races and found that being accepted and feeling psychologically safe are necessary ingredients for productive supervision. Perhaps surprisingly, when the independent variable of race was considered, it did not emerge as a main effect. A pilot study conducted by Fukuyama (1994) revealed that for doctoral internship students, a sensitivity to race and culture was highly significant for a successful supervisory experience.

These two studies are particularly interesting when the developmental supervision literature is reviewed. Several foremost studies in the developmental supervision literature (Heppner & Roehlke, 1984; Rabinowitz, Heppner, & Roehlke, 1986) suggest a developmental progression in supervision. This progression begins with the novice supervisee's need for structure and support and ends with the advanced supervisee's readiness to discuss personal issues and how these relate to the process of counseling. It may be fruitful to consider a similar developmental process operating within multicultural supervision as an explanation for differing results between studies such as Hilton et al. (1995) and Fukuyama (1994). The fact that Hilton et al. found a main effect for level of support but no main effect for race and no interaction effects may be explained by the fact that the supervisees used in the study were novices. The ability of Fukuyama's subjects to address the effect of race and cultural dynamics as operating within their supervisory context may be a function of their advanced developmental stage as doctoral internship students (Bernard, 1994b). Therefore, as the supervisor chooses both focus area and role, he or she is well advised to do so within a developmental context that takes into account development across several variables, including culture. Too much challenge, for example, through a focus on personalization regarding cultural issues, may flood the novice trainee into cultural denial rather than produce the desired effect of increasing cultural awareness.

Research Outcomes

Although models may appear sound intuitively, they are greatly enhanced by empirical evidence of their viability. The discrimination model has received some support, either through explicit study of the model or research efforts that used the model to frame hypotheses (e.g., Ellis & Dell, 1986; Ellis, Dell, & Good, 1988; Glidden & Tracey, 1989; Goodyear, Abadie, & Efros, 1984; Goodyear & Robyak, 1982; Putney, Worthington, & McCullough, 1992; Stenack & Dye, 1982, 1983; Yager, Wilson, Brewer, & Kinnetz, 1989).

Some key findings regarding the utility of the discrimination model are worth noting. Stenack and Dye (1983) found that the supervisor role directly influenced supervisee focus during supervision sessions. Specifically, the teacher role shifted trainees from feelings to actions; the counselor role caused a reduction in thoughts and an increase in the focus on feelings; and the consultant role increased a focus on thoughts and decreased focus on feelings and actions. These findings suggest that the supervisor role may have predominance within a supervision session, regardless of focus. For example, if the supervisor chooses the consultant role, he or she will invite a cognitive evaluation of interventions, conceptualizations, or personalization (depending on focus). As Stenack and Dye (1983) note, therefore, the supervisor should be trained to evaluate the trainee's needs and choose a role that will most effectively address those needs.

Second, the role of consultant has been found to be less distinctive than that of teacher or counselor in several studies (Ellis & Dell, 1986; Glidden & Tracey, 1989; Goodyear et al., 1984; Stenack & Dye, 1982). One hypothesis is that this role does not enjoy the same clarity of definition as both the teacher and counselor roles (Bernard & Goodyear, 1992). A second possibility may have to do with the samples used for several of these studies. Often, the supervisors are doctoral students working with master's level students during their first practicum. Referring again to developmental concepts, it is likely that the supervisees in these studies were not ready to take advantage of the consultant role, thus making these reactions less rewarding and thus appearing "fuzzier." Finally, it must be questioned whether the consultant role was more vulnerable than the other roles to the time constraints involved in these studies.

CONCLUSION

The discrimination model was developed to be technically eclectic and to be used differentially to specific situations. Its strength is the flexibility it allows the supervisor; a potential weakness is that it is not driven by any theoretical approach and, therefore, allows for less modeling as part of supervision. In recent years, the model has been expanded to include professional issues (Lanning, 1986; Lanning & Freeman, 1994; Lanning, Whiston, & Carey, 1994), to address developmental concepts (Johnson & Moses, 1988), and to propose supervisor interventions that blend roles (Neufeldt et al., 1995). Cultural, as well as individual and developmental, variables need to be considered for implementation of the model. Finally, additional research will assist supervisors in refining their use of the model.

REFERENCES

Bernard, J. M. (1979). Supervisor training: A discrimination model. *Counselor Education and Supervision, 19,* 60–68.

Bernard, J. M. (1981). Inservice training for clinical supervisors. *Professional Psychology, 12,* 740–748.

Bernard, J. M. (1994a). Receiving and using supervision. In H. Hackney & L. S. Cormier (Eds.), *Counseling strategies and interventions* (4th ed., pp. 169–189). Boston, MA: Allyn & Bacon.

Bernard, J. M. (1994b). Multicultural supervision: A reaction to Leong and Wagner, Cook, and Fukuyama. *Counselor Education and Supervision, 34,* 159–171.

Bernard, J. M., & Goodyear, R. K. (1992). *Fundamentals of clinical supervision.* Boston, MA: Allyn & Bacon.

Borders, L. D., & Fong, M. L. (1994). Cognitions of supervisors-in-training: An exploratory study. *Counselor Education and Supervision, 33,* 280–294.

Chickering, A. W. (1969). *Education and identity.* San Francisco: Jossey-Bass.

Ellis, M. V., & Dell, D. M. (1986). Dimensionality of supervisor roles: Supervisors' perceptions of supervision. *Journal of Counseling Psychology, 33,* 282–291.

Ellis, M. V., Dell, D. M., & Good, G. E. (1988). Counselor trainees' perceptions of supervisor roles: Two studies testing the dimensionality of supervision. *Journal of Counseling Psychology, 35,* 315–324.

Freeman, S. C. (1992). C. H. Patterson on client-centered supervision: An interview. *Counselor Education and Supervision, 31,* 219–226.

Fukuyama, M. A. (1994) Critical incidents in multicultural counseling supervision: A phenomenological approach to supervision research. *Counselor Education and Supervision, 34,* 142–151.

Glidden, C. E., & Tracey, T. J. (1989, August). *The structure of perceived differences in supervision across developmental levels.* Paper presented at the annual meeting of the American Psychological Association, New Orleans.

Goodyear, R. K., Abadie, P. D., & Efros, F. (1984). Supervisory theory into practice: Differential perception of supervision by Ekstein, Ellis, Polster, and Rogers. *Journal of Counseling Psychology, 31,* 228–237.

Goodyear, R. K., & Robyak, J. E. (1982). Supervisors' theory and experience level in supervisory focus. *Psychological Reports, 51,* 978.

Heppner, P. P., & Roehlke, H. J. (1984). Differences among supervisees at different levels of training: Implications for a developmental model of supervision. *Journal of Counseling Psychology, 31,* 76–90.

Hilton, D. B., Russell, R. K., & Salmi, S. W. (1995). The effects of supervisor's race and level of support on perceptions of supervision. *Journal of Counseling and Development, 73,* 559–563.

Johnson, E., & Moses, N. C. (1988, August). *The dynamic developmental model of supervision.* Paper presented at the annual convention of the American Psychological Association, Atlanta.

Kagan, N. (1976). *Influencing human interaction.* Mason, MI: Mason Media; or Alexandria, VA: American Counseling Association.

Kagan, N. (1980). Influencing human interaction—eighteen years with IPR. In A. K. Hess (Ed.), *Psychotherapy supervision: Theory, research, and practice* (pp. 262–286). New York: Wiley.

Ladany, N., & Friedlander, M. L. (1995). The relationship between the supervisor working alliance and trainees' experience of role conflict and role ambiguity. *Counselor Education and Supervision, 34,* 220–231.

Lanning, W. (1986). Development of the supervisor emphasis rating form. *Counselor Education and Supervision, 25,* 191–196.

Lanning, W., & Freeman, B. (1994). The Supervisor Emphasis Rating Form-Revised. *Counselor Education and Supervision, 33,* 294–304.

Lanning, W., Whiston, S., & Carey, J. C. (1994). Factor structure of the supervisor emphasis rating form. *Counselor Education and Supervision, 34*, 41–51.

Leong, F. T. L., & Wagner, N. M. (1994). Cross-cultural counseling supervision: What do we know? What do we need to know? *Counselor Education and Supervision, 34,* 117–131.

Loganbill, C., Hardy, E., & Delworth, U. (1982). Supervision: A conceptual model. *The Counseling Psychologist, 10,* 3–42.

McGoldrick, M., Pearce, J. K., & Giordano, J. (Eds.). (1982). *Ethnicity and family therapy.* New York: Guilford.

Neufeldt, S. A., Iversen, J. N., & Juntunen, C. L. (1995). *Supervision strategies for the first practicum.* Alexandria, VA: American Counseling Association Press.

Putney, M. W., Worthington, E. L., Jr., & McCullough, M. E. (1992). Effects of supervisor and supervisee theoretical orientation and supervisor-supervisee matching on interns' perception of supervision. *Journal of Counseling Psychology, 39,* 258–265.

Rabinowitz, F. E., Heppner, P. P., & Roehlke, H. J. (1986). Descriptive study of process and outcome variables of supervision over time. *Journal of Counseling Psychology, 33,* 292–300.

Reising, G. N., & Daniels, M. H. (1983). A study of Hogan's model of counselor development and supervision. *Journal of Counseling Psychology, 30,* 235–244.

Stenack, R. J., & Dye, H. A. (1982). Behavioral descriptions of counseling supervision roles. *Counselor Education and Supervision, 22,* 295–304.

Stenack, R. J., & Dye, H. A. (1983). Practicum supervision roles: Effects on supervisee statements. *Counselor Education and Supervision, 23*, 157–168.

Stoltenberg, C. D., & Delworth, U. (1987). *Supervising counselors and therapists: A developmental approach.* San Francisco: Jossey-Bass.

Stoltenberg, C. D., McNeill, B. W., & Crethar, H. C. (1994). Changes in supervision as counselors and therapists gain experience. *Professional Psychology: Research and Practice, 25,* 416–449.

Sue, D. W., & Sue, D. (1990). *Counseling the culturally different: Theory and practice* (2nd ed.). New York: Wiley.

Worthington, E. L., Jr. (1987). Changes in supervision as counselors and supervisors gain experience: A review. *Professional Psychology: Research and Practice, 18,* 189–208.

Worthington, E. L., Jr., & Roehlke, H. J. (1979). Effective supervision as perceived by beginning counselors-in-training. *Journal of Counseling Psychology, 26,* 64–73.

Yager, G. G., Wilson, F. R., Brewer, D., & Kinnetz, P. (1989, March). *The development and validation of an instrument to measure counseling supervisor focus and style.* Paper presented at the annual meeting of the American Educational Research Association, San Francisco.

CHAPTER 19

The Major Formats of Psychotherapy Supervision

RODNEY K. GOODYEAR
University of Southern California
MARY LEE NELSON
University of Washington

We begin this chapter by inviting you, the reader, to imagine a "typical" supervision session. As you create this mental picture, consider the following: Who is present? What are their respective roles? By what means is the supervisor in this session obtaining information about the trainee's work? By what means is the trainee receiving feedback?

We speculate that whatever image you may just have formed was of but a single supervision format.[1] For example, you might have imagined individual supervision in which the supervisor is reviewing one of the trainee's audiotapes; or you might have imagined a group session in which each trainee was making a verbal case presentation. But, in fact, supervisors have available to them a range of formats. Young (1986), for example, discussed seven, Pruitt, McColgan, Pugh, and Kister (1986), 10. And West, Bubenzer, Pinsoneault, and Holeman (1993) described three broad types of supervision formats: supervision through verbal reports, delayed review supervision (i.e., using audio- and videotape), and live supervision.

It is possible that the supervisor's employing institution will mandate how supervision is to be done. But usually a supervisor exercises some choice in the matter. In making that choice, the supervisor likely will be influenced by a chain of determinants (see, e.g., Schroll & Walton, 1991), including theoretical orientation and the trainee's developmental level.

There have been curiously few investigations to determine either the prevalence with which particular supervision formats are used or the efficacy supervisors perceive them to have. We did find several, however, all of which concerned supervision by AAMFT-approved supervisors. Table 19.1 summarizes some of the data from the surveys of McKenzie, Atkinson, Quinn, and Heath (1986) and Wetchler, Piercy, and Sprenkle (1989). McKenzie et al., updating an earlier study by Everett (1980), obtained information from 61% (i.e., 550) of all supervisors who were AAMFT approved at the time of the study. Wetchler et al., in turn, also obtained data from 318 AAMFT-approved supervisors, along with 299 of their supervisees.

Both studies examined the proportions of respondents who report employing particular supervision formats. There were some between-study differences in those proportions,

---

[1]Note that what we term *format* in this chapter, others have called *approaches, modalities, strategies,* or *techniques.*

Table 19.1 Supervisors' and Trainees' Most Used Supervisory Formats and Ratings of Effectiveness

Format	Wetchler et al. Study						McKenzie et al. Study	
	Supervisors' M Rating	Supervisors who use		Trainees' M Rating	Trainees who use		Supervisors who use the particular method	
		n	%		n	%	n	%
Supervisor and trainee review videotapes of therapy sessions	4.71(1)	217	68.2(5)	4.74(1)	145	48.5(5)	364	66.2(2)
Trainees participate on a treatment team behind the one-way mirror	4.59 (3)	134	42.1 (10)	4.58 (3)	87	29.1 (10)	—	—
Group supervision	4.35 (5)	260	81.8 (2)	4.44 (9)	203	67.9 (2)	—	—
Supervisor demonstrates specific therapy skills for supervisee	4.27 (12)	251	78.9 (3)	4.57 (15)	156	52.2 (4)	—	—
Individual case consultation	4.12 (14)	279	87.7 (1)	4.34 (10)	258	86.3 (1)	—	—
Live supervision with feedback after the session and no interruptions during the session	4.30 (11)	129	40.6 (12)	4.46 (8)	50	16.7 (13)	—	—
Trainee role-plays therapy situations and therapist skills	4.34 (7)	202	63.5 (6)	4.29 (13)	136	45.5 (6)	—	—
Live supervision using a mid-session break to consult with trainee	4.55 (4)	132	41.5 (11)	4.57 (5)	78	26.1 (12)	263	47.8 (6)
Live supervision using phone call-ins to direct trainee	4.70 (2)	120	37.7 (13)	4.63 (2)	79	26.4 (11)	153	27.8 (7)
Supervisor and trainee review audiotapes of therapy sessions	4.25 (13)	200	62.9 (7)	4.34 (10)	134	44.8 (7)	424	77.1 (1)
Supervisor helps trainee work on own family-of-origin	4.33 (8)	197	61.9 (8)	4.50 (7)	123	41.4 (8)	—	—
Use of assigned readings related to a specific case	4.03 (16)	249	78.3 (4)	4.05 (16)	179	59.9 (3)	—	—
Supervisor conducts co-therapy with trainee	4.37 (6)	166	52.2 (9)	4.58 (3)	90	30.1 (9)	357	64.9 (3)

(table continues)

Table 19.1 (Continued)

Format	Wetchler et al. Study						McKenzie et al. Study	
	Supervisors' M Rating	Supervisors who use n	%	Trainees' M Rating	Trainees who use n	%	Supervisors who use the particular method n	%
Employ family sculpting	4.08 (15)	85	26.7 (14)	4.19 (14)	48	16.1 (14)	—	—
Live supervision using an earphone to direct supervisee	4.33 (8)	24	7.5 (17)	4.14 (15)	15	5.0 (17)	—	—
Live supervision by entering the therapy room to intervene	4.31 (10)	83	26.1 (15)	3.95 (17)	39	13.0 (16)	128	23.3 (9)
Review written verbatim transcripts with supervisee	3.87 (17)	69	21.7 (16)	4.13 (16)	40	13.4 (15)	—	—
Written process notes	—	—	—	—	—	—	339	61.6 (4)
One-way mirror	—	—	—	—	—	—	299	54.4 (5)
Watching trainee live via video monitor	—	—	—	—	—	—	150	27.3 (8)
Hearing trainee live via audio monitor	—	—	—	—	—	—	44	8.0 (11)
Other	—	37	11.6	—	13	4.3	124	22.5 (10)

Note. Numbers in parentheses are ranks. Ratings are of perceived effectiveness of the format, using a five-point scale. The Wetchler et al. study is based on responses of 318 AAMFT-approved supervisors and 299 of their trainees. The McKenzie et al. study is based on responses from 550 AAMFT supervisors.

Summarized from Wetchler, Piercy, and Sprenkle (1989) and McKenzie, Atkinson, Quinn, and Heath (1986).

but it is difficult to know to what extent these were a function of nonparallel questionnaires. Yet, despite some discrepancies, the combined data do provide a general sense of the frequency with which family therapy supervisors use particular formats. For example, in both studies, more than 60% of the supervisors report using (a) videotape review of trainee sessions, (b) audiotape review of trainee sessions, and (c) individual case consultation (or, in the McKenzie et al. study, "written process notes").

To supplement these data from family therapy supervisors, we used e-mail to conduct an informal survey of directors of training of university counseling centers. Our results are summarized in Table 19.2. Respondents in both ours and the Wetchler et al. survey reported using group supervision frequently (McKenzie et al. did not address this matter); interestingly, too, both show using an earphone to direct the trainee (e.g., "bug-in-the-ear") to be used relatively infrequently, even though respondents in the Wetchler et al. study seemed to rate its effectiveness relatively highly.

The purpose of this chapter is to review the more commonly employed supervision formats. That is, we address actual practices as well as some of their particular advantages and disadvantages. In organizing the chapter, we follow the general scheme suggested by West et al. (1993). We begin with trainee reports, then progress to audio- and video-assisted reviews, followed by co-therapy, and then live supervision. Also, we briefly address group supervision.

THE USE OF TRAINEE REPORTS IN SUPERVISION

The most commonly used supervision format apparently involves the trainee providing verbal reports of the client and of treatment (e.g., McCarthy, Kulakowski, & Kenfield, 1994; McKenzie et al., 1986; Wetchler et al., 1989). This may take place with the trainee offering a verbal recounting of the counseling that is the focus of supervision; more often, it occurs with the trainee presenting during supervision the process notes he or she has writ-

Table 19.2   Frequencies With Which Selected Supervision Formats Are Used in a National Sample of University Counseling Centers

Format	M
Individual one-to-one supervision	4.86
Group supervision	4.27
Case review with audiotapes	3.90
in using audiotapes, how many reviewed the tapes *prior* to meeting with the trainee?	
18% did not	
45% sometimes did	
36% did	
Case review with videotapes	3.45
Case review from supervisee report only	3.27
Live observation (one-way mirror)	1.96
Live observation with reflection team	1.27
Live observation with telephone call-ins	1.23
Bug-in-the-ear	1.05

Note. n = 22. 1 = not at all; 2 = once in a while; 3 = sometimes; 4 = frequently; 5 = always

ten on the case. In either instance, the trainee's report of the treatment provides the basis for the supervision.

It is possible that the frequency with which this format is used may derive more from its convenience and ease of implementation than from supervisors' perceptions of its effectiveness. For example, whereas Wetchler et al. found their sample of supervisors used it most frequently, they actually rated its effectiveness below that of 13 other formats.

Certainly one important limitation of trainee reports is the veracity and completeness of the information to which the supervisor has access. The trainee provides his or her own account about the client and about the client-therapist dynamics, and this inevitably is subject to omissions and distortions that occur both outside the trainee's awareness and also with intention (e.g., to manage the impression the supervisee has of him or her). Also, the trainee simply may have failed to notice particular phenomena that the supervisor or external observers in general would consider important.

Yet despite these limitations, most of us can verify from our own experiences as trainees that supervision based on self-report can be quite valuable, in part because it often is not so much the story the trainee tells as *how* he or she tells it. This type of supervision format recapitulates the format of therapy itself, and psychodynamic supervisors in particular are interested in observing how the trainee "plays the role of the client"—and thereby reveals the client to the supervisor—through unconscious or automatic processes (Levenson, 1984). Therefore, the supervisor might note that in discussing this particular client, the trainee behaves in some uncharacteristic manner such as organizing and telling the story in a "scattered" way, or seems atypically "flat" in affect, or seems especially vulnerable. Observing this, the supervisor might entertain the hypothesis that this is the trainee's depiction of the client.

This isomorphism between supervision and therapy works in another way as well. That is, the supervisor and trainee develop a relationship that at times can closely approximate a therapist-client relationship. This can provide experiential learning for the trainee: The supervisor's responses to the trainee's interventions can serve as a model the trainee can extrapolate to his or her work with the client. Put another way, this format is especially useful in allowing the supervisor to focus on parallel processes (e.g., McNeil & Worthen, 1989).

Goldberg (1985) mentions another strength of this format, especially as it employs process notes. That is, it can be useful in helping the trainee learn to attend to patterns. These include the sequences of thoughts, images, and feelings the trainee is having toward the client. They also include the repetitive interpersonal processes that occur between therapist and client. Goldberg asserts that the use of process notes helps to identify and to link issues that occur from session to session. In this way, supervision based on process notes allows a broader, longer-term perspective than supervision that occurs in other formats.

It is reasonable to believe, too, that the usefulness of this format may vary according to the stage of the trainee's development. That is, the more novice the trainee, the more he or she may require the specific feedback that is allowed in audio- or videotape review or in live supervision; also, the supervisor's concern for client well-being make these formats more important. The more advanced trainee, however, is better able to self-monitor and to discriminate the most salient aspects of the therapy to relate in supervision.

We would assert that, in general, there is an optimal degree and type of structure in any supervision format. Process notes can provide that sort of structure. Presser and Pfost (1985) point out, though, that the format trainees use for process notes can affect his or her learning in supervision. In particular, they argue that traditional, medically oriented methods of writing cases notes (e.g., the Problem Oriented Medical Record; Weed, 1968) are focused on problems rather than process. They offer their own format that would encourage the trainee to think in terms of client, therapist, and client-therapist processes.

When we work with trainees who do not have process notes (e.g., in group supervision that occurs immediately after a therapy session observed behind one-way glass), we ask them to begin the supervision with a formal presentation that has the following elements. We do this in the belief that it not only aids the supervisor in understanding, but that it also helps the trainee in developing better conceptualizations of the treatment.

- What were the content, events, and processes of which you were most aware during this particular session? (In supervision based on audio and video review, playing selected tape segments at this point could be useful.)
- What do you believe is the most likely explanation for the content/events/processes? (Note that a good scientist will generate, then rule out alternative hypotheses: What alternative hypotheses do you have about the content/events/processes?)
- What *feelings* were you experiencing toward the client during the session (e.g., scared, confused, attracted, repulsed)? Also, were you aware of any *thoughts or fantasies* about the client during the session (e.g., "I wish I could take this person home and protect her." "Someone should lock this guy up!" etc.)?
- What feelings and thoughts do you believe the client was having about you during the session?
- What specific feedback would you like during supervision?

THE USE OF ELECTRONICALLY RECORDED INTERVIEWS
IN SUPERVISION

Rogers (1942) and Covner (1942a, 1942b) reported the first use of electronically recorded interviews for supervision purposes. Their articles described recording the therapy interviews directly onto phonograph records. Those interviews then were transcribed, and both the recordings and transcripts were used in supervision. Rogers (1942) identified three primary advantages to using recordings of therapy sessions for supervision. First, he observed that clinical trainees tended to be much more directive in their interviews than they had supposed. Rogers's early experiences with recording therapy interviews revealed that mere didactic training in nondirective methods was insufficient for training many students and that only when the students had direct access to the content of their interviews could they identify their natural tendencies to provide advice and otherwise control their sessions. He provided a quotation from margin notes that a student had made on one of his training transcripts:

> Not until the counselor read these interviews did he realize the deep dark depths to which his counseling had fallen. He could hardly believe that he actually had said such things. The assumption is made that he knew better. He thinks that he can recognize many of his errors, even though he evidently didn't, during the interview. (Rogers, 1942, p. 432)

Such an observation directly illustrates the type of advance in clinical training that was to develop as a result of the capacity to observe oneself in action in the therapy session.

Rogers suggested that a second advantage to session recordings was their capacity to reveal resistances, conflicts, and blocks that occur in session. He referred to the common experience of being aware of something happening in session but being unable to pinpoint what it was. Electronic recordings provided the means by which trainee and supervisor could return to a specific moment in the session and examine particular processes and the dynamics. They enabled the supervisory pair mutually to evaluate specific trainee interventions and to design fine modifications for use in future sessions.

Whereas observation of the actual therapy process enabled trainee and supervisor to identify problem areas in the trainee's style, it also allowed them to specify trainee interventions and in-session behaviors that led to insight and change on the part of the client (i.e., the third advantage). Thus, Rogers saw recordings as providing information about areas for trainee growth and development as well as about trainee abilities and strengths. The use of electronic recordings enabled Rogers to identify therapist behaviors that he deemed most helpful, such as recognition and clarification of feelings, allowing for spontaneous insight, and abstention from praise, criticism, and advice.

Audiotaping

Audiotaping is one of the most widely used forms of recording in psychotherapy training (Bernard & Goodyear, 1992; Wetchler et al., 1989). One of the reasons for its popularity is the degree of mobility provided by the size and portability of audio recorders (Bernard & Goodyear, 1992). Offices of therapists-in-training often are not equipped with special observation equipment such as one-way mirrors and video recorders. The audio recorder is easy to transport and may be placed unobtrusively on the therapist's desk or table.

Supervising clinicians assume various approaches to using audiotaped therapy sessions in supervision. Of the 21 training sites we surveyed for this chapter, 18 reported that supervisors listened to audiotapes of their trainees' sessions before meeting with the trainees. The frequency of this practice ranged from once in a while to always. One advantage of this approach is that the supervisor gets a picture of how the trainee manages a whole session, from orienting to concluding material. The supervisor can make feedback notes while going through the tape, and these notes can be shared with the trainee before or during the following supervision session. The supervisor also can cue the tape to a segment he or she wishes to review with the trainee for feedback and instruction.

Another common practice is for the trainee to review his or her tape and then to select a segment or two for examination in the supervision session. Bernard and Goodyear (1992) emphasize the importance of planning a focus for supervision sessions. To this end, they recommend that trainees come to session prepared to provide the reason for selecting a particular segment, describe what transpired in the session up to that point, explain their goals for the session and for that segment of the session, and state what specific kind of assistance they desire from the supervisor. Trainees should be encouraged to share their moments of excitement and success as well as their moments of confusion or discouragement. As Rogers (1942) pointed out, it is just as important for trainees to identify what they do that works as it is to focus on what they need to improve.

There are other means of using audiotapes in supervision. For example, Smith (1984) used a dual-channel audiotape device that permitted him to record feedback to a trainee as he observed a live counseling session. The trainee was then given a tape of his or her session that also provided the supervisor's running commentary on the session. By switching channels, the student could play back the session only or the session combined with the supervisor's comments. Hurt and Mattox (1990) reported a similar procedure.

And Miller and Crago (1989) documented their use of audiotaped family therapy sessions along with written letters to provide supervision to isolated family therapists in the Australian countryside. They emphasize that some trainees and professionals who provide services in remote areas and who cannot travel to a city for frequent supervision sessions can make good use of audio recordings as a source of data about the trainee's performance.

Videotaping

Videotaping currently is the technology most valued by supervisors and trainees in individual and family counseling and therapy (Bernard & Goodyear, 1992; Stoltenberg & Delworth, 1987; Wetchler et al., 1989). It has been in wide use in counseling and therapy training programs since Kagan (1976) recommended its use in his Interpersonal Process Recall (IPR) model. Videotaping has distinct advantages over audiotaping because it provides access to nonverbal cues and nonverbal interpersonal exchanges that would not be detectable on audiotape. It is also more difficult to undertake because of its cost, size, and complexity. Many modern training clinics have video cameras installed in their counseling rooms or behind one-way mirrors between observation and counseling rooms. The tapes themselves are installed by students or clinic technicians in or outside the counseling rooms. Video equipment has become so compact that cameras now can be installed in extremely small areas and still provide high-quality images of the activity in a room while remaining relatively unobtrusive. Thus, the videotaping of counseling and therapy sessions has become much more convenient.

Some practitioners, especially from the family therapy tradition, have made highly innovative use of videotape recordings in supervision. As with audiotape, videotape can be used to carry out long-distance supervision in the absence of resources to conduct supervision face-to-face. Wetchler, Trepper, McCollum, and Nelson (1993) describe a seven-step procedure for incorporating videotape and telephone calls in the supervision process. In their process, the trainee videotapes and reviews the therapy session and then mails the videotape with notes to the supervisor. The supervisor then views the session, making notes, and finally the supervisor and trainee discuss the session via telephone, using their individual notes.

Another interesting innovation is the meta-level use of videotaping in supervision of supervision. Wilcoxon (1992) described a process of videotaping the supervisor-in-training working with the therapist-in-training, then having both parties process their session, using the videotape, with the senior supervisor. The rationale for this procedure was that making the communications between the senior supervisor and the supervisor-in-training explicit for the therapist-in-training would eliminate misunderstandings that inevitably occur when ideas get passed from the senior supervisor through the supervisor-in-training, to the therapist-in-training, and eventually to the client.

The Interpersonal Process Recall method (Kagan, 1976) is the most widely taught set of guidelines for using videotape as a supervision tool (Bernard & Goodyear, 1992). Because that method is described in another chapter of this book, the present discussion focuses on the use of videotaped sessions to facilitate the process of reflective supervision (Neufeldt, Iversen, & Juntunen, 1995; Neufeldt, Karno, & Nelson, 1996; Schön, 1983) and on general guidelines for using videotape in supervision sessions.

The reflective process (Neufeldt et al., 1996; Schön, 1983) involves assuming an observant stance toward the work one is undertaking for the purpose of identifying what works and what doesn't work, in addition to gaining understanding about self and other. Schön distinguishes between reflection-*in*-action and reflection-*on*-action. Reflection-in-action involves observing one's process while it is taking place, or deliberately noticing one's feeling states, actions, and reactions to others while involved in an undertaking.

Reflection-on-action involves looking back on a process that is finished to reflect on feelings about and reactions to how one engaged in the process. Videotaping of therapy sessions provides an opportunity to examine past behaviors in light of present reflections. In supervision, videotape allows for the supervisor to facilitate the reflective process for the trainee as both examine the dynamics of the therapy session. The reflective process is multilayered in that it involves not only examining one's feelings, expectations, and speculations about one's observed behaviors or the client's behaviors in session (as in IPR), but it also involves examining the trainee's explicit and implicit theories about the meanings of those observations (Neufeldt et al., 1996).

Having interviewed several experts on the topic of reflectivity in supervision, Neufeldt et al. (1996) identified the willingness to be vulnerable as an essential quality of the reflective process. To truly get the most out of a reflective supervision process, a trainee must examine his or her work from a humble posture and be open to looking at feelings as well as areas for change and improvement. This requirement can present special problems for the video- (or audio-) taping of supervision sessions. Having one's work videotaped can automatically render the trainee vulnerable (Goldberg, 1983), not to mention having his or her work examined and evaluated by a person with greater expert power. Thus, for reflective supervision to be successful, a trusting relationship must exist between the supervisor and trainee. A lack of trust can result in trainee resistance and hinder or block the supervision process. The following section addresses the issue of resistance, specifically as it relates to the taping of supervision sessions.

Taping and Resistance.   Goldberg (1983) discussed two potential hazards inherent to videotaping of therapy sessions for the purpose of supervision: (a) the resistance of the client and (b) the resistance of the therapist-in-training. Indeed, Pharis (1986) described in detail a case example of how the audiotaping of therapy sessions produced profound resistance in a client. In her example, the therapist was able to uncover the meaning of the resistance and use it to help the client understand the dynamics of the therapy and how they related to other issues in the client's life. Such a skill level is not common in therapists in their early training. Nevertheless, if clients are properly informed prior to their therapy that they will be taped, they generally exhibit little resistance as they move beyond the first few sessions (Barnes & Pilowsky, 1969; Haggard, Hilsen, & Isaacs, 1965).

The psychiatric training literature has documented that both clients and therapists-in-training tend to be anxious about taping initially and to adapt over time (Barnes & Pilowsky, 1969; Benschoter, Eaton, & Smith, 1965; Geertsma & Reivich, 1965; Schiff & Reivich, 1964; Suess, 1970). Therapists-in-training are more anxious about videotaping, however, than are the clients, presumably because of the evaluative nature of supervision and the vulnerability involved with having their every move in session open for scrutiny.

Goldberg (1983) contends that the central reasons for trainee resistance to videotaping are the fears of exposure and criticism. These fears are heightened in therapists-in-training, as the therapists are learning to deal with intense emotions (their own and others'), and they realize that the work being scrutinized is an expression of their personhood. Goldberg also discusses the kind of competition that is inherent to professional training settings and that occurs not only between students, but also between students and their supervisors.

Absent from Goldberg's discussion is mention of how the power differential in supervision may interact with other power differences resulting from gender, race, culture, sexual identity, or socioeconomic status. For instance, a minority trainee from a low SES background might feel highly intimidated by a white supervisor from a background of privilege. Whatever confidence the trainee might have mustered to climb the educational and cultural ladder might feel highly vulnerable when his or her in-session behavior is completely visible to an evaluative other from a powerful sector of society. Thus, having one's therapy sessions taped can be threatening to the trainee for a number of reasons, some more obvious than others.

Goldberg (1983) proposes introducing videotaping early in the therapy process and using it over time so that it becomes familiar. He recommends educating therapists-in-training thoroughly about the use of the equipment and ensuring that the equipment setup is simple and stable. He emphasizes that working with resistance in supervision is essential to the training process. Whereas taping may initially increase defensiveness and resistance, it can also provide an opportunity for the supervisor and trainee to work on trust. It can provide stimuli for the supervisory pair to discuss obstacles to their open cooperation, and for the trainee to understand his or her issues around performance and criticism.

The responsibility for creating a safe environment in supervision lies with the supervisor. It is incumbent upon him or her to anticipate the degree and type of resistance the trainee might feel regarding the taping, to work on neutralizing whatever effects power differences other than the supervisory role would have on the resistance, and to utilize a sensitive situation to create a growth experience for the trainee.

THE USE OF DIRECT OBSERVATION IN SUPERVISION

All supervision formats discussed in this chapter are designed to promote trainees' professional development. But supervisors also are charged with protecting clients' well-being, and supervision formats that are based on direct observation of the trainee's work are especially effective for that purpose. This and other aspects of direct observation formats make it possible to allow beginning trainees to handle difficult cases sooner than they ordinarily would (Goodman, 1985).

The formats we discuss in this section are distinctive in another way. That is, in these formats the supervisor actively can participate in the treatment. Supervision and therapy are intertwined and co-occur (see, e.g., Berger & Dammann, 1982).

Braver, Graffin, and Holahan (1990) have discussed and Kaplan (1987) has confirmed in a survey of supervisors that trainee anxiety at the beginning of supervision is frequent in formats involving direct observation. But in our experience, most of that anxiety dissipates as trainees begin supervised work in these formats. Moreover, they come to value the support it offers during periods when they feel they are in "over their heads" (e.g., with a suicidal client who is experiencing command hallucinations; with a couple whose interactions are volatile and potentially violent).

Direct observation can take two major forms. In one form, the supervisor may participate directly in the session with the trainee as a co-therapist. In the other, the supervisor observes the trainee conducting therapy, either through one-way glass or through closed-circuit TV.

Co-Therapy as Supervision

In this format, supervisor and trainee participate as co-therapists. The supervisor is available not only as a role model, but also as a fellow therapist who can provide support at crucial times within and outside the session. During supervision, the supervisor and trainee have available to them a shared experience for discussion. This format has been used with group (Alpher & Kobos, 1988) and with family therapy (Connell & Russell, 1986). Sometimes also called multiple therapy, it also has been employed in the supervision of individual therapy (Braver et al., 1990).

Kell and Burow (1970) discussed multiple therapy as a means of treatment rather than as supervision. Nevertheless, many of their observations are useful for anyone considering multiple therapy as a supervision format. They suggest, for example, that a multiple therapy team include a man and a woman, which is especially useful with particular clients (e.g., those who express a strong preference for one gender over another, who are emotionally labile, or who are overtly hostile). They suggest ways in which this collaboration is beneficial to both the treating team and to the client.

A potential problem with this format is having a too-great discrepancy between supervisor and trainee skill and perceived expertise. This can lead clients to discount the trainee in favor of the "real" therapist, which not only affects the treatment, but also the integrity of the learning experience for the trainee. For this reason, co-therapy of this type may be best used with more experienced trainees. In that case, there is optimal chance of the supervisor-trainee relationship evolving into one that is a collegial one between near-equals.

A variant on this format is the in-session consultation, in which the supervisor enters the session no more than occasionally. Connell and Russell (1986), Connell, Whitaker, Garfield, and Connell (1990), and Richman, Aitken, and Prather (1990) all have described this as a procedure to use during impasses in family therapy. Magee and Pierce (1986) argued for this as an intervention that requires minimal time investment by the supervisor, even while offering immediately useful feedback to both client and therapist. They caution, though, that the supervisor must function within-session as a consultant whose interventions preserve the therapist's autonomy and responsibility for the session.

Live Supervision

Direct observation of a session is a necessary condition for live supervision. It is not sufficient, however, for live supervision implies that the supervisor actively intervenes in one way or another during the therapy session. We already have discussed how the verbal report supervision format generally is isomorphic with individual therapy; the same is true with respect to the relationship between live supervision and family treatment (e.g., Liddle & Schwartz, 1983). Therefore, family therapists have been the primary, though not the exclusive, proponents of live supervision (cf. Heppner et al., 1994; Kivlighan, Angelone, & Swafford, 1991).

Goodman (1985) has summarized strategies in conducting live supervision, including the supervisor communicating directly with the trainee via intercom or telephone and using a consultation break during which the trainee leaves the session (or the supervisor enters the session). To those, we would add the bug-in-the-ear technique. Each is considered briefly now.

Phone-Ins and Consultation Breaks.   In these versions of live supervision, the supervisor interrupts the therapy session to intervene in some manner with the trainee. This can be by making a telephone call into the session, by coming into the session to make a direct intervention, or by bringing the trainee out from the session to consult with him or her.

Liddle and Schwartz (1983) suggested questions supervisors should entertain as they consider making a live intervention. For example, what are the consequences if the intervention is not delivered? If the supervisor waits, what is the likelihood that the trainee will make the desired intervention on his or her own? Is the trainee capable of actually conducting the desired intervention if the supervisor suggests it? Will the intervention foster excessive dependency on the supervisor? Liddle and Schwartz also suggest factors to consider in evaluating an intervention. For example, if the supervisor's directive was not followed, to what extent did this reflect one or more the following: (a) a relationship problem between supervisor and trainee, (b) lack of clarity by the supervisor in making the intervention, (c) the trainee's inability to carry out the directive, or (d) the trainee's decision not to follow the directive?

Based on her review of more than 150 phone-ins, Wright (1986) suggested that the supervisor

- Should practice phone-ins with the trainee (e.g., via role plays) prior to actually using it to supervise a therapy session
- Should use phone-ins sparingly (e.g., she recommended there be no phone-in during the first 10 minutes of a session and that there be no more than five per session)
- Should limit the phone-in to 25 seconds or less and generally save process statements for after the session, for these can confuse and/or preoccupy the trainee during the session
- Should give no more than two instructions per phone-in
- Should provide positive comments to the trainee in at least the first one or two phone-ins of a session
- Should use more specific and concrete directives with beginning trainees; more global and abstract directives with the more advanced trainee
- Should—at least initially—be the *only* team member to conduct the phone-ins

As a reversal of the usual phone-in procedure, Keeney (1990) discussed calling into session to talk with clients to encourage them to help the therapist to help them. This is conceptually similar to Goodman's (1985) interventions of either sending in a note to the client for support or encouragement or to give suggestions, or of having the supervisor and trainee jointly compose an intervention letter in which the client disagrees with the supervisor. Each of these has more of a treatment than a supervisory intent. Nevertheless, they do offer additional possibilities for the supervisor.

As widely as live supervision seems to be used, it is interesting that so little research on it has been conducted. One exception is the investigation Heppner et al. (1994) conducted of supervisors' intentions while delivering interventions during live supervision. Using a multidimensional scaling procedure, they found six dimensions to characterize the intentions. For example, directing-instructing versus deepening; cognitive clarification versus emotional encouragement; and confronting versus encouraging the client. And in a study comparing live supervision with videotape review, Kivlighan et al. (1991) found that trainees receiving live supervision developed better working alliances with their clients and had more relationship and support intentions.

One reasonable concern about phone-ins is whether they disrupt the quality of the trainee's work. Fortunately, Bistline, Matthews, and Frieden (1985) found that call-ins did not disrupt the quality of trainees' verbal and nonverbal behavior (assessed in terms of such constructs as immediacy, genuineness, and anxiety). In fact, Frankel and Piercy (1990) found that the quality of supervisors' teach and support behaviors during call-ins was directly related to trainees' use of teach and support behaviors with their clients immediately subsequent to the call-in.

Bug-in-the-Ear (or Eye).   Another variant of the live supervision format is to have the trainee wear a wireless earphone during the therapy session. This often is referred to as the bug-in-the-ear (BITE). Gallant and Thyer (1989) concluded from their review of research that there still is insufficient evidence to support effectiveness claims for the technique. They did, on the other hand, find little evidence that the technique is inhibiting to the trainee. And in a subsequent study, Gallant, Thyer, and Bailey (1991) found that BITE produced "specific and immediate" improvements in trainees' clinical skills.

BITE does give the supervisor an immediate role as coach. The challenge to the supervisor, though, is not to give in to any impulse to conduct "remote control therapy." Most of the guidelines we have summarized for phone-ins and other live interventions pertain to BITE as well.

An alternative to BITE is what Klitzke and Lombardo (1991) playfully dub the "bug-in-the-eye" procedure. They note that by mounting a TV monitor behind the client but within view of the trainee, the supervisor can send more complex messages to the trainee than would be possible with BITE. Moreover, these messages are less potentially disruptive.

THE USE OF GROUPS IN SUPERVISION

The status of group supervision is succinctly summarized in the title of Holloway and Johnston's (1985) article: "widely practiced, but little understood." Group supervision in one form or another is ubiquitous in the training of not only mental health professionals but of other health professionals as well (e.g., Balint, 1985; Brock & Stock, 1990). Nevertheless, there has been only a small empirical literature devoted to it (cf. Holloway & Johnston, 1985; Prieto, 1996).

Group supervision is, in many ways, a format that is "discontinuous" with others discussed in this chapter. By this we mean that all of the previously discussed formats can be employed in group as well as individual supervision. For that reason, we limit our comments about group supervision. Nevertheless, there are aspects of working in groups that merit specific attention.

As compared to individual supervision, groups do offer several relatively specific advantages. The first of these, of course, concerns economies of time and energy. That is, because trainees in a group can learn vicariously from one another, to work with a group of trainees means that each can be learning even while one is the particular focus of the attention. As Rioch, Coulter, and Weinberger (1976) documented, groups can be a context in which trainees compete with one another to be the "best," but simultaneously can provide a strong basis for support to one another. And, Hillerbrand (1989) has pointed out that group members often are able to give one another feedback that is more understandable than what the supervisor offers.

CONCLUSIONS

One fact this chapter should have made clear is that the various supervision formats can be differentiated according to a number of factors. We have constructed Table 19.3 to illustrate this. It shows, for example, the types of feedback that each supervision format provides the supervisor and also makes clear which of the supervision formats can be used *both* as supervision and treatment. It also illustrates that the formats can be graded in the extent to which they permit (a) vicarious learning for other trainees, (b) supervisor monitoring and protection of the client, and (c) the supervisee to accelerate the difficulty level of the clients

he or she treats. Reivich and Geertsma (1969) captured much of this when they characterized verbal reports by the trainee as being trainee oriented and quasi-therapeutic, and audio
and video review as being, on the other hand, client oriented and didactic.

The salient question in evaluating the merits of the various formats really is, which is the
best in this particular situation, with this particular trainee, these particular training goals, and
this particular supervisor? In fact, the optimal situation likely is one in which the trainee is
exposed during training to a number of different formats and thereby is able to benefit from
the particular strengths of each. Unfortunately, there is scant research comparing different
supervision formats. One exception is the study by Kivlighan et al. (1991). Absent other
research of this type, the supervisor generally is left to his or her own best judgments.

In making those judgments, the supervisor almost certainly will be influenced heavily
by constraints of time, expense, and available resources. This is a reasonable explanation
for the frequency with which both verbal reporting and audiotape review are used.

Evolving technology also affects the possibilities of supervision. We already have noted
how the advent of audiotaping more than a half-century ago affected supervision (e.g.,
Rogers, 1942). But technology is evolving particularly quickly now, with concomitant
price decreases. For example, any supervisor wishing to listen to a counseling session as
it occurs can do so using baby monitors that readily are available in department stores for
about $30; using them is as easy as plugging them in. Similarly, equipment for bug-in-the-
ear live supervision is readily available at most local home electronics stores. And the
cost of video cameras and VCRs continues to drop, making them readily available for
almost any training situation (also, see Hargrave, 1991).

We predict, too, that computer technology soon will provide new supervision formats.
For example, it already is possible for therapists to use the Internet to solicit consultation
from colleagues around the world about particular clinical issues via specific newsgroups
or listservs. And Tracy et al. (1995) have described a supervision and training process in
which, using common software, a user screen has 14 icons, each representing a different
category on the Hill Counselor Verbal Response Category System (Hill, 1978). Coders can
either code each counselor response in real time as it occurs during live observation or
employ videotape review. The computer generates tables and graphs that the counselor can
use in supervision.

Table 19.3   Comparison of Selected Attributes of Supervision Formats

Supervisor Goals	Verbal Report	Audio Review	Video Review	Co-Therapy	Live Supervision
Immediate feedback (vs. delayed)				X	X
Access to actual trainee and client nonverbal behaviors			X	X	X
Access to actual trainee and client verbal behaviors		X	X	X	X
Can serve *both* as supervision and as a treatment intervention				X	X
Vicarious learning for other trainees	less	———————————————			more
Degree of client protection	less	———————————————			more
Permits trainee to take more difficult clients	less	———————————————			more

Videoconferencing, using current telephone technology, already is being used for supervision in rural areas (Troster, Paolo, Glatt, Hubble, & Koller, 1995). As we write this, newspaper articles describe soon-to-be-available software that will allow inexpensive videoconferencing to occur over the Internet. It is quite conceivable that this may allow more utilization of supervisors with special expertise who are many miles away from trainees—something already being done via audiotape and the mail (e.g., Dryden, 1983) and videotape and the telephone (Wetchler et al., 1993).

REFERENCES

Alpher, V. S., & Kobos, J. C. (1988). Cotherapy in psychodynamic group psychotherapy: An approach to training. *Group, 12,* 135–144.

Balint, E. (1985). The history of training and research in Balint groups. *Psychoanalytic Psychotherapy, 1,* 1–9.

Barnes, L. H., & Pilowsky, I. (1969). Psychiatric patients and closed-circuit television teaching: A study of their reactions. *British Journal of Medical Education, 3,* 58–61.

Benschoter, R. A., Eaton, M. T., & Smith, P. (1965). Use of videotape to provide individual instruction in techniques of psychotherapy. *Journal of Medical Education, 40,* 1159–1161.

Berger, M., & Dammann, C. (1982). Live supervision as context, treatment, and training. *Family Process, 21,* 337–344.

Bernard, J. M., & Goodyear, R. G. (1992). *Fundamentals of clinical supervision.* Boston: Allyn & Bacon.

Bistline, J. L., Matthews, C. O., & Frieden, F. P. (1985). The impact of live supervision on supervisees' verbal and nonverbal behavior: A preliminary investigation. *Journal of Marital and Family Therapy, 11,* 203–205.

Braver, M., Graffin, N., & Holahan, W. (1990). Supervising the advanced trainee: A multiple therapy training model. *Psychotherapy, 27,* 561–567.

Brock, C. D., & Stock, R. D. (1990). A survey of Balint group activities in U.S. family practice residency programs. *Family Medicine, 22,* 33–37.

Connell, G. M., & Russell, L. A. (1986). In-therapy consultation: A supervision and therapy technique of symbolic-experiential family therapy. *American Journal of Family Therapy, 14,* 313–323.

Connell, G. M., Whitaker, C., Garfield, R., & Connell, L. (1990). The process of in-therapy consultation: A symbolic-experiential perspective. *Journal of Strategic & Systemic Therapies, 9,* 32–38.

Covner, B. J. (1942a). Studies in phonographic recordings of verbal material: I. The use of phonographic recordings in counseling practise and research. *Journal of Consulting Psychology, 6,* 105–113.

Covner, B. J. (1942b). Studies in phonographic recordings of verbal material: II. A device for transcribing phonographic recordings of verbal material. *Journal of Consulting Psychology, 6,* 149–151.

Dryden, W. (1983). Audiotape supervision by mail: A rational-emotive perspective. *British Journal of Cognitive Psychotherapy, 1,* 57–64.

Everett, C. A. (1980). An analysis of AAMFT supervisors: Their identities, roles, and resources. *Journal of Marital and Family Therapy, 6,* 215–226.

Frankel, B. R., & Piercy, F. P. (1990). The relationship among selected supervisor, therapist, and client behaviors. *Journal of Marital and Family Therapy, 16,* 407–421.

Gallant, J. P., & Thyer, B. A. (1989). The "bug-in-the-ear" in clinical supervision: A review. *Clinical Supervisor, 7* (2–3), 43–58.

Gallant, J. P., Thyer, B. A., & Bailey, J. S. (1991). Using bug-in-the-ear feedback in clinical supervision. *Research on Social Work Practice, 1,* 175–187.

Geertsma, R. H., & Reivich, R. S. (1965). Repetitive self-observation by videotape playback. *Journal of Nervous and Mental Disease, 141,* 29–41.

Goldberg, D. A. (1983). Resistance to the use of video in individual psychotherapy training. *American Journal of Psychiatry, 140,* 1172–1176.

Goldberg, D. A. (1985). Process notes, audio, and videotape: Modes of presentation in psychotherapy training. *Clinical Supervisor, 3*(3), 3–13.

Goodman, R. W (1985). The live supervision model in clinical training. *Clinical Supervisor, 3*(2), 43–49.

Haggard, E. A., Hilsen, J. R., & Isaccs, K. S. (1965). Some effects of recording and filming on the psychotherapeutic process. *Psychiatry, 28,* 169–191.

Hargrave, T. D. (1991). Utilizing inexpensive communication systems: Building one-way mirrors for private practice consultation and supervision. *Journal of Marital and Family Therapy, 17,* 89–91.

Heppner, P. P., Kivlighan, D. M., Burnett, J. W., Berry, T. R., et al. (1994). Dimensions that characterize supervisor interventions delivered in the context of live supervision of practicum counselors. *Journal of Counseling Psychology, 41,* 227–235.

Hill, C. E. (1978). Development of a counselor verbal response category system. *Journal of Counseling Psychology, 25,* 461–468.

Hillerbrand, E. T. (1989). Cognitive differences between experts and novices: Implications for group supervision. *Journal of Counseling and Development, 67,* 293–296.

Holloway, E. L., & Johnston, R. (1985). Group supervision: Widely practiced but poorly understood. *Counselor Education and Supervision, 24,* 332–340.

Hurt, D. J., & Mattox, R. J. (1990). Supervisor feedback using a dual-cassette recorder. *Clinical Supervisor, 8*(2), 169–172.

Kagan, N. (1976). *Influencing human interaction.* Mason, MI: Mason Media; or Washington, DC: American Counseling Association.

Kaplan, R. (1987). The current use of live supervision within marriage and family therapy training programs. *Clinical Supervisor, 5*(3), 43–52.

Keeney, B. P. (1990). Supervising client conversation: A note on a contextual structure for evoking therapeutic creativity. *Journal of Family Psychotherapy, 1*(2), 51–56.

Kell, B. L., & Burow, J. M. (1970). *Developmental counseling and therapy.* Boston: Houghton Mifflin.

Kivlighan, D. M., Angelone, E. O., & Swafford, K. G. (1991). Live supervision in individual psychotherapy: Effects on therapist's intention use and client's evaluation of session effect and working alliance. *Journal of Counseling Psychology, 22,* 489–495.

Klitzke, M. J., & Lombardo, T. W. (1991). A "bug-in-the-eye" can be better than a "bug-in-the-ear": A teleprompter technique for on-line therapy skills training. *Behavior Modification, 15,* 113–117.

Levenson, E. A. (1984). Follow the fox. In L. Caligor, P. M. Bromberg, & J. D. Meltzer (Eds.), *Clinical perspectives on the supervision of psychoanalysis and psychotherapy* (pp. 153–167). New York: Plenum.

Liddle, H. A., & Schwartz, R. C. (1983). Live supervision/consultation: Conceptual and pragmatic guidelines for family therapy trainers. *Family Process, 22,* 477–490.

Magee, J. J., & Pierce, D. (1986). When the supervisor serves as participating consultant for both client and social worker. *Clinical Supervisor, 4*(4), 85–89.

McCarthy, P., Kulakowski, D., & Kenfield, J. A. (1994). Clinical supervision practices of licensed psychologists. *Professional Psychology: Research and Practice, 25,* 177–181.

McKenzie, P. N., Atkinson, B. J., Quinn, W. H., & Heath, A. W. (1986). Training and supervision in marriage and family therapy: A national survey. *American Journal of Family Therapy, 14,* 293–303.

McNeil, B., & Worthen, V. (1989). The parallel process in psychotherapy supervision. *Professional Psychology: Theory, Research, and Practice, 20,* 329–333.

Miller, N., & Crago, M. (1989). The supervision of two isolated practitioners: It's supervision, Jim, but not as you know it. *Australian & New Zealand Journal of Family Therapy, 10,* 21–25.

Neufeldt, S. A., Iverson, J. N., & Juntunen, C. L. (1995). *Supervision strategies for the first practicum.* Alexandria, VA: American Counseling Association.

Neufeldt, S. A., Karno, M. P., & Nelson, M. L. (1996). A qualitative analysis of experts' conceptualization of supervisee reflectivity. *Journal of Counseling Psychology, 43,* 3–9.

Pharis, M. E. (1986). The object relations implications of taping individual therapy sessions. *Clinical Social Work Journal, 14,* 361–374.

Presser, N. R., & Pfost, K. S. (1985). A format for Individual Psychotherapy Session Notes. *Professional Psychology: Research and Practice, 16,* 11–16.

Prieto, L. R. (1996). Group supervision: Still widely practiced but poorly understood. *Counselor Education and Supervision, 35,* 295–307.

Pruitt, D. B., McColgan, E. B., Pugh, R. L., & Kister, L. J. (1986). Approaches to psychotherapy supervision. *Journal of Psychiatric Education, 10,* 129–147.

Reivich, R. S., & Geertsma, R. H. (1969). Observational media and psychotherapy training. *Journal of Nervous and Mental Disease, 148,* 310–327.

Richman, J. M., Aitken, D., & Prather, D. L. (1990). In-therapy consultation: A supervisory and therapeutic experience from practice. *Clinical Supervisor, 8*(2), 81–89.

Rioch, M. J., Coulter, W. R., & Weinberger, D. M. (1976). *Dialogues for therapists: Dynamics of learning and supervision.* San Francisco: Jossey-Bass.

Rogers, C. R. (1942). The use of electrically recorded interviews in improving psychotherapeutic techniques. *American Journal of Orthopsychiatry, 12,* 429–434.

Schiff, S. B., & Reivich, R. (1964). Use of television as an aid to psychotherapy supervision. *Archives of General Psychiatry, 10,* 84–88.

Schön, D. (1983). *The reflective practitioner: How professionals think in action.* New York: Basic Books.

Schroll, J. T., & Walton, R. N. (1991). The interaction of supervision needs with technique and context in the practice of live supervision. *Clinical Supervisor, 9*(1), 1–14.

Smith, H. D. (1984). Moment-to-moment counseling process feedback using a dual-channel audiotape recording. *Counselor Education and Supervision, 23,* 346–349.

Stoltenberg, C. D., & Delworth, U. (1987). *Supervising counselors and therapists: A developmental approach.* San Francisco: Jossey-Bass.

Suess, J. (1970). Self-confrontation of videotaped psychotherapy as a teaching device for psychiatric students. *Journal of Medical Education, 45,* 271–282.

Tracy, M., Froehle, T., Kelbley, T., Chilton, T., Sandhofer, R., Woodward, D., Blanchard, D., & Benkert, R. (1995, April). *Data centric counseling: The development of a computer-assisted observation system for use in process studies in counseling, supervision, and counselor training.* Paper presented at the annual meeting of the American Educational Research Association, San Francisco.

Troster, A. I., Paolo, A. M., Glatt, S. L., Hubble, J. P., & Koller, W. C. (1995). Interactive video conferencing in the provision of neuropsychological services in rural areas. *Journal of Community Psychology, 23,* 85–88.

Weed, L. (1968). Medical records that guide and teach. *New England Journal of Medicine, 278,* 593–600, 652–657.

West, J. D., Bubenzer, D. L., Pinsoneault, T., & Holeman, V. (1993). Three supervision modalities for training marital and family counselors. *Counselor Education & Supervision, 33,* 127–138.

Wetchler, J. L., Piercy, F. P., & Sprenkle, D. H. (1989). Supervisors' and supervisees' perceptions of the effectiveness of family therapy supervisory techniques. *American Journal of Family Therapy, 17*(1), 35–47.

Wetchler, J. L., Trepper, T. S., McCollum, E. E., & Nelson, T. S. (1993). Videotape supervision via long-distance telephone. *American Journal of Family Therapy, 21,* 242–247.

Wilcoxon, S. A. (1992). Videotape review of supervision-of-supervision in concurrent training: Allowing trainees to peer through the door. *Family Therapy, 19,* 143–152.

Wright, L. M. (1986). An analysis of live supervision "phone-ins" in family therapy. *Journal of Marital and Family Therapy, 12,* 187–191.

Young, R. A. (1986). The functions of supervision and means of accessing interview data. *Clinical Supervisor, 4*(3), 25–37.

PART IV

Specialized Forms and Modes

CHAPTER 20

Child and Adolescent Psychotherapy Supervision

THOMAS R. KRATOCHWILL
KATHLEEN M. LEPAGE
JULIA McGIVERN
University of Wisconsin-Madison

Professional psychology is growing in sophistication in the areas of diagnosis, assessment, treatment, and related areas of practice. In fact, the knowledge base in psychology is growing extraordinarily diverse and continues to expand rapidly along with the other social and biological sciences. Educating professional psychologists in the expanding knowledge base in the field requires tremendous amounts of knowledge, insight into the teaching process, and skills in supervision of clinical practice. Some areas in which the field is expanding rapidly and in which major challenges are likely to occur in training can be seen in the American Psychological Association Division 12 Task Force on Promotion and Dissemination of Psychological Procedures (1995). As the list of treatments for child and adolescent disorders grows, individuals will increasingly be confronted with a sophisticated empirical knowledge base for implementation of psychological services. Teaching these treatments may be mandated in training programs and internship sites. Another example of challenges for trainers and supervisors of child treatment can be seen in the area of prescription privileges for psychologists. The possibility that psychologists will receive prescription privileges raises new and challenging issues in the design of curriculum and supervision of professional practice (Kratochwill, 1994).

As the knowledge base for the practice of child and adolescent psychotherapy develops, issues related to educating practitioners and supervising their practice have assumed an increasingly prominent place in professional literature. The publication of this handbook is testimony to the importance of this topic in the professional education of psychologists. Historically, the knowledge base in the area of teaching assessment and therapeutic skills has been considered important but has lagged behind other professional areas (Garfield, 1977; Hess, 1980, 1987; Matarazzo, 1971, 1978). Several major works have been published that provide an overview of research in the area of supervision (e.g., Bernard & Goodyear, 1992; Holloway, 1992; Stoltenberg, McNeill, & Crethar, 1994; Worthington, 1987), references on supervision (Robiner & Schofield, 1990), as well as works on conceptual issues (e.g., Knoff, 1986; Watkins, 1995). A special issue of *Professional Psychology: Research and Practice* has been devoted to the topic (Hess, 1987). In this literature, consideration first must be given to several terminological issues. To begin, we should offer a definition of *psychotherapy*. In this regard, we concur with the general definition offered by Kazdin (1988) in his discussion of child and adolescent psychotherapy:

The definition of psychotherapy is restricted to *psychosocial interventions*, in which the means rely primarily on various interpersonal sources of influence such as learning, persuasion, discussion, and similar processes. The focus is on some facet regarding how clients feel (affect), think (cognition), and act (behavior). The definition is necessarily general because of the range of approaches that need to be accommodated. Thus the definition includes a variety of treatments subsumed under many general rubrics such as individual, group, family, insight-oriented, behavioral, and cognitive therapies. (p. 2)

With regard to psychotherapy terminology, it also is important to take into account the manner in which much of child therapy is practiced. In a traditional approach, the therapist works directly with the child or adolescent client. Supervision of this direct relationship is a major part of the knowledge base of supervision research and writing in the field. Another type of psychotherapeutic relationship is very common, however, and typically involves a mediator-based model such as that characterized in mental health consultation approaches. The mediator-based models can provide, at least theoretically, a more difficult and challenging supervisory relationship. We discuss these issues in depth later in the chapter.

Second, the concept of teaching or training psychotherapy or therapeutic skills must be defined. By *professional training* we mean the education of professional child psychologists in a variety of diagnostic, assessment, and therapeutic techniques subsumed under the rubric of psychotherapy. Education of clinicians can be facilitated through a variety of procedures such as didactic instruction, modeling, role play, rehearsal, and media such as audio, video, and hypermedia technology. *Supervision*, a closely linked concept, refers to the monitoring and professional mentoring of individuals in the application of psychotherapy and its associated skills. Although most of the literature on supervision has focused on psychotherapy, we include related professional activities within the scope of supervision such as diagnosis, assessment, consultation, research, and teaching because they have been neglected in research (Robiner & Schofield, 1990). We do not consider supervision to be a homogeneous construct or unitary variable, but as Lambert and Arnold (1987, p. 217) do, we identify common activities: didactic instruction and training activities to facilitate "in therapy" behaviors. The distinction between the terms *training* and *supervision* can appear somewhat arbitrary, inasmuch as during teaching or training individuals often are supervised as part of the skill-acquisition process. Traditionally, supervision has been featured as a component of the process of applying skills learned in a training program under naturalistic conditions such as in a field practicum or internship setting. The concept can, however, be applied at any place during the educational experience of a graduate student learning psychotherapy skills or as a process to facilitate professional development. In the latter case, supervision can occur in professional practice, where it may be called peer supervision or review.

The purpose of this chapter is to provide an overview of major issues in the teaching and supervision of child and adolescent psychotherapy skills. We begin with a theoretical framework for our approach to supervision; thereafter, we describe some principles and practice of supervision including a framework for supervision, methodologies for training and supervision, and various components that can be used in the supervisory process. Examples of these various issues are presented in the context of casework from our practice and work in graduate education of psychologists at the University of Wisconsin-Madison.

THEORETICAL FRAMEWORK FOR SUPERVISION

Our presentation of issues and principles of psychotherapy supervision takes into account a theoretical framework for the methodology and process of supervision. We have embraced the theoretical focus that incorporates an ecological-behavioral model (Kratochwill, Bergan, & Mace, 1981). This model emphasizes the role that learning theory plays in the principles and practice of training and supervision. The theoretical framework has been available in the scientific literature for many years and as an approach has probably remained stable in terms of the relationship between the focus of therapy and the components of supervision. Technically, it is not part of the zeitgeist of developmental paradigms in the field (Watkins, 1995). It features an emphasis on the broad environmental or ecological influences in understanding the supervision process. The rationale for this particular focus of our work is based on the following considerations. First, behavioral theory has expanded considerably in recent years and now represents a sophisticated knowledge domain based on empirical research (O'Donohue & Krasner, 1995). Building on the technology of applied behavior analysis (Follette & Callaghan, 1995) and increasing diversity in theoretical work incorporating both cognitive features as well as an ecological or systems framework for understanding human behavior makes this theoretical approach a useful heuristic in supervision research and practice.

Second, there is a growing body of literature on training and supervision that has developed affiliated with this approach (e.g., Gambrill & Stein, 1983; Milne, 1986), and historically it has been an active area in the field (e.g., Matarazzo, 1978). Early reviews featuring behavioral training and supervision (Ford, 1979; Hung & Rosenthal, 1978; Kratochwill et al., 1981; Linehan, 1980; Loeber & Weisman, 1975) provide a good basis for conceptual work in this area. Specifically, within the training and supervision area writers have described variables that influence the generalization of skills acquired through training and supervision (e.g., Robinson & Swanton, 1980), and methodological and conceptual features of behavioral training and supervision (e.g., Follette & Callaghan, 1995; Linehan, 1980). The first author's research program on competency-based training and supervision in consultation serves as an account of how this methodology can facilitate the acquisition of skills, incorporate competency-based training, and facilitate the supervisory process (e.g., Kratochwill, Carrington-Rotto, Sheridan, & Salmon, 1992; Kratochwill, Elliott, & Busse, 1995).

Finally, the APA Division 12 Task Force on Promotion and Dissemination of Psychological Procedures (1995), hereafter called the Task Force, features behavior therapy as a major treatment technology for a wide range of child and adolescent disorders. Other approaches are considered important as well and should be featured in training and supervision. For example, although Crits-Christoph, Frank, Chambless, Brody, and Karp (1995) featured many behavior therapy programs in their survey, training in empirically validated psychodynamic and interpersonal theory was not well represented. In view of the content of emerging technologies for treatment of child and adolescent disorders, the ecobehavioral framework blends very well with the model of training and supervision in a variety of areas.

Implications for Supervision

The ecobehavioral model of supervision that guides our presentation in this chapter has several distinct features with implications for enacting the model in training and practice.

These features include the empirical focus, operational focus on skills, focus on adaptive functioning, and the emphasis and focus on specific measurable competencies.

Empirical Analysis.   A primary characteristic of the ecobehavioral approach that has important implications for supervision is the emphasis on evaluation of trainee performance and competencies throughout the process of supervision. Traditionally, a problem in the supervision area has been monitoring specific competencies and behaviors to establish a performance criterion for effective psychotherapeutic skills. It is essential that during the supervision process data are provided that document assessment and intervention skills and the role the supervisory process has on this outcome. In the former case the trainer/supervisor would establish a baseline on the trainee's skills and abilities for a particular therapeutic technique. Following training and supervision, the trainee's performance is measured to determine competency in the performance area. An assessment of the role that supervision plays in contributing to positive therapeutic outcomes also can be determined. For example, if skills acquired through supervision can be shown to positively affect client outcomes, then conceptually such a supervisor role might be linked empirically to the positive and desirable outcome on the client. In this regard, the concept of treatment utility of supervision might be invoked (Hayes, Nelson, & Jarrett, 1986, 1987).

Within the context of this approach, the supervisory process is an ongoing and multifaceted evaluation of the trainee's performance in multiple domains (discussed later in the chapter). Evaluation during the training and supervision process includes multiple measures used to assess the trainee's behavior under conditions that approximate performance in natural settings. Supervisory sessions are data based, and data are used to provide feedback regarding methods to improve performance in multiple areas of psychotherapeutic applications (and related areas). This empirical clinical practice approach to the training and supervisory process is closely linked with the ecobehavioral model inasmuch as individual case methodology can be used to frame the process of supervision (e.g., Barlow, Hayes, & Nelson, 1984). Empirically based theoretical frameworks also can be used to focus supervisory efforts and use the existing theoretical and scientific knowledge base to facilitate the supervisory role and ultimately the acquisition of skills in the professional psychologist.

Operational Focus on Skills and Specific Measurable Competencies.   Within the psychotherapy field, there is increasing emphasis on operational specification of the content of the psychotherapy process and technology (Kazdin, 1988). For example, the Task Force (APA, 1995) emphasizes establishing specific manual-based formats for the implementation of various therapies for children and adolescents. The use of manuals makes the therapy process operational and allows replication (Lambert & Arnold, 1987) and extension into practice (Kazdin, Kratochwill, & Vanden Bos, 1986). Lambert and Arnold (1987, pp. 220–221) specifically noted the following advantages of treatment manuals:

> (a) standardize (to a greater degree) the treatment being offered and thus allow for more concrete interventions by supervisors, (b) provide a method of training and supervising therapists to ensure that they offer a standard treatment, (c) allow for the development of rating scales to judge whether a therapy is being properly offered and thereby alert the supervisor and trainee to the need for further supervision with specific interventions and (d) allow researchers another method of sorting out the common factors from the unique factors associated with specific treatment approaches.

This manual tactic provides one of the important procedures for linking the supervisory process to the conceptual model presented in this chapter. One of the major hallmarks of the ecobehavioral approach presented here is the specification of interventions in operational terms to allow the intervention to be implemented with integrity in applied settings (Kratochwill et al., 1981). We also are aware of the limitations of a manual-based approach as outlined by Follette and Callaghan (1995). A manual-based approach may be a starting point in the process of therapeutic interactions; it may not be sufficient to change trainee behavior during the treatment process.

We also would add that only after the therapeutic procedures have been specified can effective supervision occur. Historically, specification of the content of therapy was considered critical, as this early quote by Garfield (1977) conveys:

> Only after we can first specify the operations which make for positive change in psychotherapy can we go on to develop and evaluate effective means of teaching such skills and procedures. The objectives must first be stated, then translated into meaningful operations, and later validated. Only then can worthwhile training procedures be developed, utilized, and appraised. (p. 80)

Nevertheless, effective psychotherapies extend beyond the treatment technique per se. The trainee must have knowledge of the scope of the dysfunction and threats to social adjustment (Kazdin & Johnson, 1994).

Increasingly, there has been an emphasis on identifying specific competencies that individuals need to develop in implementing psychotherapy in applied settings. Traditionally, developments such as competency-based models have embraced this theoretical framework and have provided frameworks for how therapy skills might be taught. Work featured from our own area of training and supervision of consultation skills provides some examples of how the operational focus on competency-based training can make the supervision process specific in teaching professional therapeutic skills.

Focus on Adaptive Functioning.   The ecobehavioral approach advanced in this chapter is based on learning theory broadly conceived. It is assumed that the supervisory process is one of facilitating the acquisition of adaptive and prosocial knowledge, skills, and affect in the professional therapist. This approach stands in contrast to some of the traditional methodologies used in supervision in which relationship dynamics between the client and therapist have been the primary focus of teaching/supervision efforts. We emphasize that the supervisory approach must be aimed at developing and facilitating specific technical skills in therapists to promote competencies in both mediators and clients. As mentioned earlier, training individuals in therapeutic skills cannot remain at a global or unspecified level. Specific adaptive and prosocial therapist skills need to be taught and facilitated across multiple settings in which therapies will be implemented (Follette & Callaghan, 1995). This proactive approach to education allows the application of a large body of educational and psychological research that can have a positive influence on the supervision process (e.g., applied behavior analysis, instructional psychology).

Emphasis on Observable Competencies.   The supervision process is aimed at developing competencies across multiple areas of functioning, including cognitive and affective domains. Nevertheless, the ultimate criterion within the theoretical framework presented here is that individuals be able to demonstrate through their professional behavior that they have mastered specific skills that allow them to function in a professional manner and facilitate change in clients. Therefore, one of the major criteria that is given priority within this model is observable change in professional therapists as they function during the training and supervisory process. Indeed, the ultimate criterion for change in professional practice would be that the professional psychologist demonstrates new skills that can be documented through independent and observable measures. Such an approach necessitates the development of sophisticated assessment tools that currently have lagged behind other developments in the field of supervision. Specifically, it has been suggested that using standardized rating scales would enable better assessment of trainee performance. For example, Robiner and Schofield (1990) have suggested developing standardized rating scales to assess skills. Furthermore, it has been proposed that developing psychotherapy treatment manuals could facilitate the development and use of rating scales to assess whether treatment is implemented correctly (Lambert & Arnold, 1987). McElfresh (1986) has suggested several measures, but they lack reliability and validity information. Although clinical ratings or global judgments can be used to supplement methods to document professional therapy skills, direct observational measures are given priority because they typically reduce the influence of bias and subjective impression in the process of evaluation.

PRINCIPLES AND PRACTICE OF SUPERVISION

Given that supervisors have a significant role in training professionals, one could expect they have been trained to offer supervision. This, however, is often not true. Because training in supervision rarely occurs, several areas of need have been identified. Tanenbaum and Berman (1990) discussed the need for supervisors to be fully aware of the legal and ethical responsibilities surrounding supervision. Also, they proposed that supervisors need to be able to vary the psychotherapy model they use, based on specific situations.

Because little research has been done to examine the supervisory process, areas in need of research also have been identified. For example, Watkins (1993) proposed a developmental model in which supervisors gain skills and competence as they pass through four stages of development. However, research has not been performed to test this model. One reason for this lack of research could be a lack of methods. Bear and Kivlighan (1994) proposed that the supervision field lacks the methods to evaluate the effect of supervisor behavior on the development of the supervisee.

It is important to emphasize that the framework presented here for promoting high-quality supervision of psychotherapeutic skills in child and adolescent therapists is guided by a model that is equally applied to training and to supervision. Thus, the model can be used with individuals who are participating in a competency-based approach to learning specific therapeutic skills as well as in supervision of practice in field or internship settings. Within the context of this approach, some conceptual frameworks for the supervision process can be advanced.

Supervision Framework

When considering the role of the professional supervisor and his or her role in facilitating professional functioning of the psychologist in training, it is important to conceptualize the domains or areas of functioning that need to be the focus of supervision efforts. In this regard, we embrace a model presented by Linehan (1980) that serves as a useful conceptual framework for structuring the role of the professional supervisor. Linehan's model is based on a tripartite approach to functioning that conceptualizes performance in three response systems: a cognitive system (thinking), an overt motor system (actions), and a physiological-affective system (feelings). The supervisor facilitates functioning of the supervisee within the domains of thinking, actions, and feelings when conducting therapy. Each of these frameworks is reviewed and expanded to provide a conceptual scheme for how it might be integrated into the supervisory process (see Linehan, 1980, pp. 163–165 for detail on the content of each of these areas of functioning).

Cognitive Focus.   Functioning in the cognitive domain, the supervisee should have knowledge in the following areas:

1. Knowledge of the theoretical and empirical literature relevant to the problem areas under treatment
2. Knowledge of fundamental principles of behavioral functioning and behavior influence
3. Competence in ethical and legal issues
4. An ability to organize and integrate information gained from experience
5. An ability to conceptualize a case and identify problems through assessment
6. Knowledge of classification systems and diagnostic criteria
7. An ability to plan and evaluate interventions
8. An awareness of the complementary roles of objective data and clinical judgment
9. An awareness of the influence of personal values, beliefs, and expectations in provision of psychological services

Overt Therapy Skills.   In keeping with the ecobehavioral focus on observable skills in functioning in a psychotherapeutic role, specific skills also should be a part of the professional areas of functioning. Linehan (1980) outlines the following five components as important in this domain: (a) procedural skills that pertain to actual implementation of assessment and intervention techniques; (b) interpersonal-clinical skills in assessment and intervention; (c) skills that involve the ability to explain assessment and treatment techniques to clients, identify and solve barriers to treatment implementation, and revise or modify treatments when they are not working; (d) professional skills that include such activities as report writing, communicating progress on treatments, negotiating contracts, and so forth; and (e) professional self-development skills that allow the supervisee to take part in learning activities other than those specified during actual supervision activities. These usually involve managing one's own learning activities. Implicit in Linehan's model, though not explicitly stated, is the need for professionals to develop skills in monitoring and evaluating treatments (e.g., Kazdin, 1988).

Affective Skills.   It is important that the supervisor facilitate appropriate affective functioning of the supervisee during the provision of child and adolescent psychotherapy services. Therapists in training often experience a wide range of affective responses to clients and their care providers (e.g., teachers, parents). The ability to manage affective responses to a wide range of stimuli is necessary for effective functioning as a psychologist. The supervisory process would be designed to identify, discuss, and deal with a wide range of affective issues and specific arousal that often accompanies these issues. Given that affective issues emerge, the first tactic is to discuss the concerns the trainee has over the issues that are considered problematic. For example, beginning therapists often are quite frustrated by the resistance that emerges during the course of therapy. A client who cancels appointments or who shows little commitment to the treatment protocol often invokes anger and frustration in the therapist. In such a case, the supervisor might provide specific tactics such as relationship enhancement techniques (e.g., Goldstein & Myers, 1986). In addition, the supervisor could help the supervisee consider other issues that might influence the client's behavior, such as the acceptability of the treatment to the client (e.g., Elliott, 1988).

More significant concerns might be handled by the actual application of therapeutic techniques that the supervisee can self-administer, such as relaxation or self-desensitization. In this case, it is important to make clear distinctions between dealing with these high-arousal situations in a supervisory role versus actually engaging in direct therapy with the supervisee. We are not advocating that the supervisor conduct therapy with the individual or establish the usual professional psychotherapeutic relationship. Supervision is not psychotherapy (Watkins, 1995). Nevertheless, methods of intervention and education used to address affective responses sometimes can blur the role between therapy and supervision. Should the supervisor decide that the supervisee could profit from actual therapy to deal with a wide range of problematic affective or behavioral responses, a referral would be appropriate at this stage. Similar to the therapeutic relationship, however, the development of appropriate affective functioning of the supervisee often is facilitated by a high-quality relationship between the supervisor and supervisee in which the usual therapeutic skills of the professional therapist can be used to encourage independent functioning.

It can be observed that the performance of supervisees within the supervision framework discussed here will require ongoing assessment of the three domains. The most challenging areas of assessment obviously will be in the cognitive and affective areas, which has prompted Linehan (1980) to recommend multimethod, multisetting assessment of performance. Table 20.1 provides an overview of Linehan's recommendations for assessment that can facilitate understanding the supervisee in the context of the three domains represented. We have added dimensions to this table based on our own experience and work in the supervisory process.

Framework for Training/Supervision

A variety of tactics traditionally have been used to facilitate the supervision of individuals engaged in professional psychology education (see Ford, 1979; Gray, 1974; Kratochwill & Bergan, 1978; Levine & Tilker, 1974; Linehan, 1980).

Table 20.1   Assessment of Supervisee Performance Across Multiple Domains

Assessment Tactics
1. Assess supervisee performance across multiple settings, including (a) classroom performance, (b) analogue performance, and (c) field performance.
2. Assess student performance across multiple modalities, including (a) direct observation, (b) self-report, (c) educational personnel report, (d) client report, (e) physiological measures when possible or feasible, (f) formal written examination/assessment, and (g) informal measures.
3. Obtain repeated samples of student performance across time, settings, and clients.
4. Assess broad range of specific skills (e.g., diagnostic-classification, direct therapy, consultation, administration, report writing, evaluation, etc.)

Adapted from Linehan (1980).

Didactic Instruction. One of the primary roles in the supervisory process is to ensure that the supervisee has well-grounded knowledge and information pertaining to academic and applied psychology. In the typical graduate program, students master coursework through a curriculum that incorporates both academic and applied experiences across areas of professional and legal issues, diagnosis, assessment, intervention, and program evaluation. The methodology for didactic instruction includes many different formats, such as program textbooks, journal articles, videotapes, hypermedia, case observations, and courses and seminars. In addition to traditional coursework, supervisors can schedule a variety of self-instructional activities into the supervisee's training. We emphasize the broad exposure to the academic scholarly literature needed to provide psychologists with the ever-growing body of information in the field.

With regard to specific areas of emphasis on acquiring psychotherapeutic skills, it is important to emphasize the knowledge base first in broad areas of theoretical approaches to psychotherapy. Thereafter, we emphasize that students be taught specific skills in empirically supported psychotherapeutic approaches. At this time, a database for this activity has been initiated by the Task Force (1995). Table 20.2 provides an illustration of some of the major child psychotherapeutic techniques that could be presented during didactic instruction across models. Didactic instruction would be facilitated through the application of specific therapy manuals in each of these areas. Other information is available from literature reviews of successful treatments across various childhood disorders in child therapy texts (e.g., Kratochwill & Morris, 1991). An especially useful resource is the review of meta-analysis studies presented by Lipsey and Wilson (1993).

Gradual Exposure-Based Training and Supervision. Most graduate training programs and internship-based training centers provide a gradual exposure of individuals to the demands for practice. This approach typically involves beginning with minimal requirements for direct work with clients and gradually increasing the exposure of individuals to the range and scope of problem areas as well as the severity of problems. Implicit in the exposure process is the role of continuing demands for demonstrating greater sophistication, independence, and expertise in assessing and treating child and adolescent disorders. The role of the supervisor in this process is to facilitate the training process through a variety of tactics (discussed later). The gradual exposure of individuals to increasing demands is useful in the context of the ecobehavioral model presented here. First, the individual gradually acquires skills and abilities to function in an independent fashion. The supervisor specifically facilitates the individual's skills across the three content areas in the context of this exposure model. Second, as the individual receives positive feedback and acquires skills, he or she increases in self-efficacy in being able to solve problems of both a routine and novel manner. The supervisor's role in this process can be to provide actual models of practice and ensure the individual is acquiring the skills as a natural progression occurs.

Self-Change Projects. An important option in professional supervision of students that can be implemented but often is overlooked is a project that involves a self-change intervention. This training involves having the supervisee design with the supervisor a program of intervention designed to change his or her own behavior. Such a program typically is implemented during the early phases of training when the individual can identify aspects of his or her performance to change. The focus of this program can be eliminating problematic behaviors in the context of provision of assessment or psychotherapeutic skills or

Table 20.2   Examples of Empirically Validated Treatments

Well-Established Treatments	Citation for Efficacy Evidence
Beck's cognitive therapy for depression	Dobson (1989)
Behavior modification for developmentally disabled individuals	Scotti et al. (1991)
Behavior modification for enuresis and encopresis	Kupfersmid (1989) Wright & Walker (1978)
Behavior therapy for headache and for irritable bowel syndrome	Blanchard et al. (1987) Blanchard et al. (1980)
Behavior therapy for female orgasmic dysfunction and male erectile dysfunction	LoPiccolo & Stock (1986) Auerbach & Kilmann (1977)
Behavioral marital therapy	Azrin, Bersalel et al. (1980) Jacobson & Follette (1985)
Cognitive behavior therapy for chronic pain	Keefe et al. (1992)
Cognitive behavior therapy for panic disorder with and without agoraphobia	Barlow et al. (1989) Clark et al. (in press)
Cognitive behavior therapy for generalized anxiety disorder	Butler et al. (1991) Borkovec et al. (1987) Chambless & Gillis (1993)
Exposure treatment for phobias (agoraphobia, social phobia, simple phobia) and PTSD	Mattick et al. (1990) Trull et al. (1988) Foa et al. (1991)
Exposure and response prevention for obsessive-compulsive disorder	Mark & O'Sullivan (1988) Steketee et al. (1982)
Family education programs for schizophrenia	Hogarty et al. (1986) Falloon et al. (1988)
Group cognitive behavioral therapy for social phobia	Heimberg et al. (1990) Mattick & Peters (1988)
Interpersonal therapy for bulimia	Fairburn et al. (1993) Wilfley et al. (1993)
Klerman & Weissman's interpersonal therapy for depression	DiMascio et al. (1979) Elkin et al. (1989)
Parent training programs for children with oppositional behavior	Wells & Egan (1988) Walter & Gilmore (1973)
Systematic desensitization for simple phobia	Kazdin & Wilcoxin (1976)
Token economy programs	Liberman (1972)

Probably Efficacious Treatments	Citation for Efficacy Evidence
Applied relaxation for panic disorder	Ost (1988); Ost & Westling (1991)
Brief psychodynamic therapies	Piper et al. (1990) Shefler & Dasberg (1989) Thompson et al. (1987) Winston et al. (1991) Woody et al. (1990)
Behavior modification for sex offenders	Marshall et al. (1991)
Dialectical behavior therapy for borderline personality disorder	Linehan et al. (1991)
Emotionally focused couples therapy	Johnson & Greenberg (1985)

Table 20.2   (Continued)

Probably Efficacious Treatments	Citation for Efficacy Evidence
Habit reversal and control techniques	Azrin, Nunn & Frantz (1980)
	Azrin, Nunn & Frantz-Renshaw (1980)
Lewinsohn's psychoeducational treatment for depression	Lewinsohn et al. (1989)

Note: From "Training in and Dissemination of Empirically-Validated Psychological Procedures: Report and Recommendations," by Task Force on Promotion and Dissemination of Psychological Procedures, 1995. *The Clinical Psychologist, 48*, pp. 22–23. Copyright 1995 by Division of Clinical Psychology, American Psychological Association. Reprinted with permission.

targeting the acquisition of some specific skills during the course of training. Such tactics as goal setting, feedback, self-reinforcement, and self-monitoring can be implemented in this type of self-change project (see Ford, 1979).

Competency-Based Training.   Competency-based training involves establishing preset criteria for mastery of particular content domains that are the focus of training/supervision (Kratochwill et al., 1992). Not all areas of psychotherapeutic skills can be equally organized into a competency-based model. Nevertheless, this approach is a useful technology in demonstrating mastery of specific skills that can be operationalized. A variety of competency-based models have been used and featured in the professional literature. We mention briefly two models that have application to supervision. The first involves microcounseling, which is based on the work of Ivey and his colleagues (e.g., Ivey, 1971, 1974; Ivey, Normington, Miller, Merrill, & Hasse, 1968; Moreland, Ivey, & Phillips, 1973). Reviews of the work on microcounseling have suggested it is effective in basic training of interview counseling skills; it typically involves several specific components (see Ford, 1979, for an overview of early research in this area):

Didactic Instruction. It is essential that the supervisee receive a well-grounded background in academic psychology, including course work and experiences relating to research and theory. The didactic instruction may include programmed texts, books, journal articles, and formal courses and seminars. Such exposure to the academic literature must be broad enough to provide psychologists with a good overview of the field.

Direct Observation. Gradual exposure to practice provides a good training/education approach to applied work (Levine & Tilker, 1974). Training and supervision in this area can take the form of modeling through such procedures as direct observation, audiotapes and videotapes, and simulated experiences (Ford, 1979). In such activities, the supervisor can provide cues as well as direct instructions. It must be emphasized that feedback through such procedures as video-feedback replay can be helpful when used in combination with other procedures (Follette & Callaghan, 1995). Yet, modeling research suggests that the mere presentation of information will not ensure that individuals viewing it will extract the meaning intended. Moreover, successful performance of various skills may not occur unless they exist in the viewer's repertoire (Hung & Rosenthal, 1978; Rosenthal & Bandura, 1978).

Self-Change Project. An important component in training involves having the supervisee design (with assistance), implement, and evaluate a self-change project of an intervention designed to change his or her own behavior (Ford, 1979). When specific assessment and intervention skills are involved, the student can self-monitor the implementation of these skills as well. Such monitoring may also facilitate generalization of the skills to other settings and in future practice (Loeber & Weisman, 1975).

Microcounseling. Based on the work of Ivey and his colleagues (Ivey, 1971, 1974; Ivey et al., 1968; Moreland et al., 1973), microcounseling has been found to be an effective training package and an analogue for basic training and interview skills (cf. Ford, 1979). A standardized format for microcounseling training has been developed:

1. Videotaping a 5-minute segment of therapy or counseling of a couple or a family, or 5 minutes of interaction around a selected topic.
2. Training. (a) A written manual describing the single skills being taught is presented to the trainees. (b) Video models of an "expert" therapist or "good" communication illustrating the skill are shown, thus giving the trainee(s) a gauge against which to examine the quality of their own behavior. (c) Trainees then view their own videotapes and compare their performance on the skill in question against the written manual and video model. Seeing yourself as others see you is a particularly high impact part of the training procedure. (d) A trainer-supervisor provides didactic instruction and emotional support for the trainees.
3. A second 5- to 10-minute session is videotaped.
4. Examination of the last session and/or recycling of the entire procedure as in Step 2, depending on the acquired skill levels of the trainees. (Ivey, 1974, p. 6)

Another approach to competency-based training involves a model presented by Kratochwill and his associates (Kratochwill & Bergan, 1978; Brown, Kratochwill, & Bergan, 1982; Kratochwill, Van Someren, & Sheridan, 1989; Kratochwill et al., 1992; Kratochwill et al., 1995). This model involves training individuals in assessment and therapy procedures that are linked to the behavioral consultation model. The model incorporates a four-stage problem-solving interview process (Bergan & Kratochwill, 1990; Kratochwill & Bergan, 1990). The tactics of training are designed to ensure mastery of objectives associated with each of three interview technologies that focus on identification of the problem, analysis of the problem, and implementation and evaluation of the intervention. Considerable support exists for the competency-based approach to training and the documentation of efficacy at the consultee and client outcome level (see Kratochwill et al., 1992, for a review of recent work in this area).

Components Used in Supervision

Over the years, a variety of specific components have been found to be effective to teach a broad range of psychotherapeutic skills. Most of these procedures are used in combination in a package format and can be applied to facilitate acquisition of psychotherapeutic skills in academic and applied settings (Lambert & Arnold, 1987). Each of these components is illustrated along with a brief example of how it can be used in practice. These components include the following areas: feedback, instructions, program instruction/computer programs, modeling, collaborative supervision, rehearsal/role play, and generalization and transfer of skills (Ford, 1979).

Feedback.   Feedback is a central component of the supervisory process and typically incorporates a focus on the message content, valence, source, and a medium. Feedback can be obtained from a variety of sources, including the supervisor, self-feedback from a self-monitoring process, videotape, instructions, and a variety of other mechanisms. For example, a supervisor could observe the supervisee's performance conducting an interview and then provide feedback about performance to the supervisee. Alternatively, the supervisee, with support from a supervisor, could develop an evaluation form to use to generate feedback about his or her own performance conducting an interview. Following the interview, the supervisee could review a videotape of the interview and complete the evaluation form. This tactic transfers some of the responsibility for developing performance criteria and generating feedback to the supervisee. In a third option, both the supervisor and the supervisee generate feedback about performance and compare information.

Instructions.   Similar to feedback, virtually all supervisory relationships involve the provision of instructions in either written or verbal formats. Some research has suggested that instructions alone may not facilitate acquisition of applied skills (e.g., Kazdin & Moyer, 1976; Sepler & Myers, 1978), and this outcome likely generalizes to the supervision process. Instructions are typically part of didactic formats and are usually available through conventional text. Individuals may need actual applied experience in addition to instructions to function effectively in the provision of psychotherapy skills. In fact, Follette and Callaghan (1995) have argued that providing instructions may actually promote rigid rule-governed behavior that causes problems during therapy.

Programmed Instruction.   Programmed instruction formats are typically used in the context of several other mechanisms of professional training and supervision featured in this chapter. Typically, programmed texts have been found to be more effective than prose texts, modeling, lectures, or no training when teaching specific discrimination skills (Ford, 1979). More recently, computer-based models of professional training have been found to be effective. For example, Kratochwill and his associates documented the efficacy of a hypermedia program in teaching applied consultation skills. The program was as effective as and took less time than a more conventional format that involves didactic instruction, mentoring, and workshop formats in training consultants (Kratochwill et al., 1995).

Modeling.   Observational learning or modeling approaches to training and supervision emanate from the social learning theory of Bandura and his associates (e.g., Bandura, 1977). Modeling typically involves a message, valence, model, and medium. Modeling has been shown to be an important source of acquiring both cognitive and applied psychotherapeutic skills. The role of the supervisor in this process is typically to model a variety of interaction patterns in the implementation of psychotherapy. Such an approach can be extremely effective in teaching individuals specific and complex psychotherapeutic skills.

Collaborative Supervision.   Collaborative supervision typically involves an approach in which the supervisor and the supervisee collaborate in developing interventions for psychotherapy. This context allows a format for the other dimensions outlined earlier to be incorporated into professional supervision. This approach can incorporate feedback, instructions, modeling, and opportunities to role-play or use rehearsal with feedback.

One particular investigation that incorporated the collaborative approach involved a tactic called mentoring (Salmon & Fenning, 1993). Mentoring involves the consultants (supervisor and supervisee) working with consultees (e.g., parent or teacher) to facilitate implementation of an intervention program for a child client.

Behavioral Rehearsal/Role Play.   Critical in the development of psychotherapeutic skills is the opportunity to actually rehearse particular aspects of implementation of the psychotherapeutic approach or tactic. Rehearsal can occur under analogue role-play conditions or can be rehearsed in the natural setting with real clients. When analogue tactics are used, there should be plenty of opportunity for the supervisee to apply what has been learned in an analogue context in the natural environment and in the same setting in the future. The supervisor should gradually structure training opportunities to provide the kind of gradual exposure that will facilitate transfer to the natural setting that involves actual cases and problems.

Skill Generalization and Transfer.   Generalization or transfer of psychotherapeutic skills in the course of training and supervision is a gradual process. Skills must transfer from one course to the next, ultimately to be integrated into practicum settings and eventually the internship experience, and later into professional practice on the job. In this process, it is well known that the generalization of skills must be specifically programmed and measured to document training effects (Drabman, Hammer, & Rosenbaum, 1979; Robinson & Swanton, 1980; Stokes & Baer, 1977). To generalize from the training setting to practice settings, we suggest that training must incorporate skill acquisition under a wide range of conditions in the natural setting and many opportunities for gradual feedback and opportunities to practice the skills that are being acquired.

CONCLUDING COMMENTS AND RESEARCH ISSUES

In this brief overview of issues pertaining to the training and supervision of child and adolescent psychotherapy, a variety of mechanisms, formats, and theoretical concepts have been introduced. In this final section, we provide some perspectives on measures of the supervision process that should be incorporated in future applied work and discuss some salient priorities in research as we see them in the field of child and adolescent psychotherapy supervision.

A number of striking issues can be raised regarding future research in the supervision area. Among the numerous possible issues we present five that seem especially important. One major issue that needs to be considered involves the selection of the therapeutic approach or tactic. Until recently, guidance for selection of various psychotherapeutic techniques revolved around theoretical or philosophical allegiance to particular models of therapy. With recent developments in empirical criteria as applied to effective psychotherapeutic techniques, however, a case can be made for the selection of the content of training and supervision based on empirically supportable techniques. The Task Force (1995) on effective treatments provides one conceptual framework for the selection of these therapeutic techniques. Table 20.3 provides an example of the criteria the Task Force used to select empirically based treatments. Research on teaching these particular techniques and the role a supervisor plays in these models would seem to be a high priority for the future. That is, we have information available in the field of applied psychology pertaining to effective techniques, but we do not have good information on how individuals should be trained and supervised in this process or even the role that supervision plays in developing effective therapy skills. Therefore, this issue stands as a major research priority in the future.

Second, despite the fact that the issue of assessing supervisory behaviors in terms of their impact on supervisee competence has been raised repeatedly in the professional lit-

Table 20.3   Criteria for Empirically Validated Treatments: Well-Established Treatments

   I. At least two good group design studies, conducted by different investigators, demonstrating efficacy in one or more of the following ways:
   A. Superior to pill or psychological placebo or to another treatment.
   B. Equivalent to an already established treatment in studies with adequate statistical power (about 30 per group).

OR

  II. A large series of single case design studies demonstrating efficacy. These studies must have:
   A. Used good experimental designs and
   B. Compared the intervention to another treatment as in I.A.

FURTHER CRITERIA FOR BOTH I and II:

 III. Studies must be conducted with treatment manuals.
 IV. Characteristics of the client samples must be clearly specified.

Note: From "Training in and Dissemination of Empirically Validated Psychological Procedures: Report and Recommendations," by Task Force on Promotion and Dissemination of Psychological Procedures, 1995. *The Clinical Psychologist, 48,* pp. 22–23. Copyright 1995 by Division of Clinical Psychology, American Psychological Association. Reprinted with permission.

erature (e.g., Holloway, 1987; Kratochwill et al., 1981), generally modest progress has been made in this area (Watkins, 1995). Much of the research on assessing supervisee behavior as related to supervision has depended on self-report data (Bear & Kivlighan, 1994). Research incorporating measures of supervisory activities in the professional practice of supervision will advance theoretical and practical knowledge pertaining to how supervision occurs and the mechanisms for the supervisory process. As an illustration of this approach, we provide one example of a model of supervision of consultation and therapy that has been used with some success in teaching school psychologists to work with various mediators (e.g., parents, teachers) in the provision of psychological services in schools and other applied settings. In this consultative approach to service delivery, the supervisor oversees the training of the consultant. This supervisory process then may be facilitated through the use of training logs and audiotapes of consultant interactions (Kratochwill et al., 1992). Using these methods may have several benefits for the consultant-in-training, including self-reflection.

Third, little research is available to suggest the most efficacious models of supervision as related to specific therapy techniques. An agenda of research in which supervision as a dimension of the therapeutic process is incorporated into the research needs to be implemented. Such an approach might initially begin with single-case research designs to show the role that supervision plays in the process of the treatment outcomes. Eventually, parametric variation of supervisor roles might be provided to eventually answer questions related to which techniques of supervision are appropriate to feature in the supervisory process as related to specific therapy techniques. For example, different types of supervisory relationships and tactics might be needed for different behavior disorders. Some childhood disorders that are treated through mediator or consultation-based approaches may require supervision roles different from those models based on direct therapeutic services. As a further example, consider that individuals supervising novice therapists who are implementing exposure-based tactics for treatment of a variety of childhood phobias could use supervision strategies that differ considerably from those used in supervision of treatment methods aimed at externalizing disorders such as conduct disorder, attention deficit hyperactivity disorder, and other related problems. The former cases may need greater focus on specific behavior therapy procedures; the latter cases may need considerably more focus on communication among the various therapeutic agents including family, physician, and others. Therefore, the supervisory role may vary depending on the childhood disorder involved. Research has not allowed us to answer questions about supervision methods unique to the childhood disorder area.

As argued in previous work (e.g., Ford, 1979), questions about the efficacy of various techniques in teaching psychotherapeutic skills to psychologists need to be investigated. There is still a paucity of research in this area considering the importance of applied and clinical significance of treating a variety of childhood and adolescent disorders.

Another area we regard as critically important in the process of professional training is the role that training of supervisors should take in graduate programs. Because there are few training programs that explicitly provide training in supervision, it would seem critical that graduate programs begin to incorporate opportunities for professional training in supervision in their programs and that these programs be empirically evaluated. Such an action research agenda could facilitate a whole new generation of individuals who contribute to the theoretical, empirical, and conceptual literature on effective supervision tactics in professional psychology.

A final area in need of research is the possible effects of cultural differences on the supervision process. Professional organizations such as the American Psychological Association have stressed the importance of considering cultural differences when providing psychological services (Myers, Wohford, Guzman, & Echemendia, 1991). Although the effects of cultural and ethnic differences have been researched in psychotherapy, research is needed to examine their effects on the supervisory process.

REFERENCES

American Psychological Association. (1995). *Template for developing guidelines: Interventions for mental disorders and psychosocial aspects of physical disorders.* Washington, DC: Author.

Bandura, A. (1977). *Social learning theory.* Englewood Cliffs, NJ: Prentice Hall.

Barlow, D. H., Hayes, S. C., & Nelson, R. O. (1984). *The scientist practitioner: Research and accountability in clinical and educational settings.* Elmsford, NY: Pergamon.

Bear, T. M., & Kivlighan, D. M., Jr. (1994). Single-subject examination of the process of supervision of beginning and advanced supervisees. *Professional Psychology: Research and Practice, 25,* 450–457.

Bergan, J. R., & Kratochwill, T. R. (1990). *Behavioral consultation and therapy.* New York: Plenum.

Bernard, J. M., & Goodyear, R. K. (1992). *Fundamentals of clinical supervision.* Needham Heights, MA: Allyn & Bacon.

Brown, D. K., Kratochwill, T. R., & Bergan, J. R. (1982). Teaching interview skills for problem identification: An analogue study. *Behavioral Assessment, 4,* 63–73.

Crits-Christoph, P., Frank, E., Chambless, D. L., Brody, C., & Karp, J. F. (1995). Training in empirically validated treatments: What are clinical psychology students learning? *Professional Psychology: Research and Practice, 26,* 514–522.

Drabman, R. S., Hammer, D., & Rosenbaum, M. S. (1979). Assessing generalization in behavior modification with children: The generalization map. *Behavioral Assessment, 1,* 203–219.

Elliott, S. N. (1988). Acceptability of behavioral treatments in educational settings. In J. C. Witt, S. N. Elliott, & F. M. Gresham (Eds.), *Handbook of behavior therapy in education* (pp. 121–150). New York: Plenum.

Follette, W. C., & Callaghan, G. M. (1995). Do as I do, not as I say: A behavior-analytic approach to supervision. *Professional Psychology: Research and Practice, 26,* 413–421.

Ford, J. D. (1979). Research on training counselors and clinicians. *Review of Educational Research, 49,* 87–130.

Gambrill, E., & Stein, T. J. (1983). *Supervision: A decision-making approach.* Beverly Hills, CA: Sage.

Garfield, S. L. (1977). Research on the training of professional psychotherapists. In A. S. Garman & A. M. Razin (Eds.), *Effective psychotherapy: A handbook of research.* Elmsford, NY: Pergamon.

Goldstein, A. P., & Myers, C. R. (1986). Relationship-enhancement methods. In F. H. Kanfer & A. P. Goldstein (Eds.), *Helping people change: A textbook of methods* (3rd ed., pp. 19–65). Elmsford, NY: Pergamon.

Gray, J. J. (1974). Methods of training psychiatric residents in individual behavior therapy. *Journal of Behavior Therapy and Experimental Psychology, 5,* 19–25.

Hayes, S. C., Nelson, R. O., & Jarrett, R. B. (1986). Evaluating the quality of behavioral assessment. In R. O. Nelson & S. C. Hayes (Eds.), *Conceptual foundations of behavioral assessment* (pp. 463–503). New York: Guilford.

Hayes, S. C., Nelson, R. O., & Jarrett, R. B. (1987). The treatment utility of assessment: A functional approach to evaluating assessment quality. *American Psychologist, 42,* 963–974.

Hess, A. K. (Ed.) (1980). *Psychotherapy supervision: Theory, research and practice.* New York: Wiley.

Hess, A. K. (1987). Advances in psychotherapy supervision: Introduction. *Professional Psychology: Research and Practice, 18,* 187–188.

Holloway, E. L. (1987). Developmental models of supervision: Is it development? *Professional Psychology: Research and Practice, 18,* 209–216.

Holloway, E. L. (1992). Supervision: A way of teaching and learning. In S. D. Brown & R. W. Lent (Eds.), *Handbook of counseling psychology* (2nd ed., pp. 177–214). New York: Wiley.

Hung, J. H. F., & Rosenthal, T. L. (1978). Therapeutic videotaped playback: A critical review. *Advances in Behavioral Research and Therapy, 1,* 103–135.

Ivey, A. E. (1971). *Microcounseling: Innovations in interviewing training.* Springfield, IL: Charles C Thomas.

Ivey, A. E. (1974). The clinician as teacher of interpersonal skills: Let's give away what we've got. *Clinical Psychologist, 27,* 6–9.

Ivey, A. E., Normington, C. J., Miller, D. C., Merrill, W. H., & Hasse, R. F. (1968). Microcounseling and attending behavior: An approach to prepracticum counselor training. *Journal of Counseling Psychology, Monograph Supplement, 15,* 1–12.

Kazdin, A. E. (1988). *Child psychotherapy: Developing and identifying effective treatments.* Elmsford, NY: Pergamon.

Kazdin, A. E., & Johnson, B. (1994). Advances in psychotherapy for children and adolescents: Interrelations of adjustment, development, and intervention. *Journal of School Psychology, 32,* 217–246.

Kazdin, A. E., Kratochwill, T. R., & Vanden Bos, G. (1986). Beyond clinical trials: Generalizing from research to practice. *Professional Psychology: Research and Practice, 3,* 391–398.

Kazdin, A. E., & Moyer, W. (1976). Training teachers to use behavior modification. In S. Yen & R. McIntire (Eds.), *Teaching behavior modification.* Kalamazoo, MI: Behaviordelia.

Knoff, H. M. (1986). Supervision in school psychology: The forgotten or future path to effective services? *School Psychology Review, 15,* 529–545.

Kratochwill, T. R. (1994). Psychopharmacology for children and adolescents: Commentary on current issues and future challenges. *School Psychology Quarterly, 9,* 53–59.

Kratochwill, T. R., & Bergan, J. R. (1978). Training school psychologists: Some perspectives on a competency based behavioral consultation model. *Professional Psychology, 9,* 71–82.

Kratochwill, T R., & Bergan, J. R. (1990). *Behavioral consultation: An individual guide.* New York: Plenum.

Kratochwill, T. R., Bergan, J. R., & Mace, F. C. (1981). Practitioner competencies needed for implementation of behavioral psychology in the schools: Issues in supervision. *School Psychology Review, 10,* 434–444.

Kratochwill, T. R., Carrington-Rotto, P., Sheridan, S. M., & Salmon, D. (1992). Preparation of school psychologists in behavioral consultation service delivery. In T. R. Kratochwill, S. N. Elliott, & M. Gettinger (Eds.), *Advances in school psychology* (Vol. III, pp. 115–152). Hillsdale, NJ: Lawrence Erlbaum.

Kratochwill, T. R., Elliott, S. N., & Busse, R. T. (1995). Behavioral consultation training: A five-year evaluation of consultant and client outcomes. *School Psychology Quarterly, 10,* 87–117.

Kratochwill, T. R., & Morris, R. J. (Eds.). (1991). *The practice of child therapy* (2nd ed.). Elmsford, NY: Pergamon.

Kratochwill, T. R., Van Someren, K. R., & Sheridan, S. M. (1989). Training behavioral consultants: A competency-based model to teach interview skills. *Professional School Psychology, 4,* 41–58.

Lambert, M. J., & Arnold, R. C. (1987). Research and the supervisory process. *Professional Psychology: Research and Practice, 18,* 217–224.

Levine, F. M., & Tilker, H. A. (1974). A behavior modification approach to supervision of psychotherapy. *Psychotherapy: Theory, Research and Practice, 11,* 182–188.

Linehan, M. M. (1980). Supervision of behavior therapy. In A. K. Hess (Ed.), *Psychotherapy supervision: Theory, research and practice.* New York: Wiley.

Lipsey, M. W., & Wilson, D. B. (1993). The efficacy of psychological, educational, and behavioral treatment: Confirmation from meta-analysis. *American Psychologist, 48,* 1181–1209.

Loeber, R., & Weisman, R. G. (1975). Contingencies of therapist and trainer performance: A review. *Psychological Bulletin, 82,* 660–688.

Matarazzo, R. G. (1971). Research on the teaching and learning of psychotherapeutic skills. In A. E. Bergin & S. L. Garfield (Eds.), *Handbook of psychotherapy and behavior change: An empirical analysis.* New York: Wiley.

Matarazzo, R. G. (1978). Research on the training and learning of psychotherapeutic skills. In S. L. Garfield & A. E. Bergin (Eds.), *Handbook of psychotherapy and behavioral change* (2nd ed.). New York: Wiley.

McElfresh, T. A. (1986). *Psychotherapy supervision: A model for professional training.* Paper presented at the annual meeting of the American Psychological Association.

Milne, D. (1986). *Training behavior therapists: Methods, evaluation and implementation with parents, nurses and teachers.* Cambridge, MA: Brookline Books.

Moreland, J. R., Ivey, A. E., & Phillips, J. S. (1973). An evaluation of microcounseling as an interviewer training tool. *Journal of Consulting and Clinical Psychology, 4,* 327–330.

Myers, H. F., Wohford, P., Guzman, L. P., & Echemendia, R. J. (1991). *Ethnic minority perspectives on clinical training and services in psychology.* Washington, DC: American Psychological Association.

O'Donohue, W., & Krasner, L. (Eds.). (1995). *Theories of behavior therapy: Exploring behavior changes.* Washington, DC: American Psychological Association.

Robiner, W. N., & Schofield, W. (1990). References on supervision in clinical and counseling psychology. *Professional Psychology: Research and Practice, 21,* 297–312.

Robinson, V., & Swanton, C. (1980). The generalization of behavioral teacher training. *Review of Educational Research, 50,* 487–498.

Rosenthal, T. L., & Bandura, A. (1978). Psychological modeling: Theory and practice. In S. L. Garfield & A. E. Bergin (Eds.), *Handbook of psychotherapy and behavior change* (2nd ed.). New York: Wiley.

Salmon, D., & Fenning, P. (1993). A process of mentorship in school consultation. *Journal of Educational and Psychological Consultation, 4,* 69–87.

Sepler, J. J., & Myers, S. L. (1978). The effectiveness of verbal instruction on teaching behavior modification skills to nonprofessionals. *Journal of Applied Behavior Analysis, 11,* 198.

Stokes, T. F., & Baer, D. M. (1977). An implicit technology generalization. *Journal of Applied Behavior Analysis, 10,* 349–367.

Stoltenberg, C. D., McNeill, B. V., & Crethar, H. C. (1994). Changes in supervision as counselors and therapists gain experience: A review. *Professional Psychology: Research and Practice, 25,* 416–449.

Tanenbaum, R. L., & Berman, M. A. (1990). Ethical and legal issues in psychotherapy supervision. *Psychotherapy in Private Practice, 8,* 65–77.

Task Force on Promotion and Dissemination of Psychological Procedures. (1995). Training in and dissemination of empirically-validated psychological procedures: Report and recommendations. *The Clinical Psychologist, 48*(1), 3–23.

Watkins, C. E., Jr. (1993). Development of the psychotherapy supervisor: Concepts, assumptions, and hypotheses of the supervisor complexity model. *American Journal of Psychotherapy, 47,* 58–74.

Watkins, C. E., Jr. (1995). Psychotherapy supervision in the 1990s: Some observations and reflections. *American Journal of Psychotherapy, 49,* 568–581.

Worthington, E. L., Jr. (1987). Changes in supervision as counselors and supervisors gain experience: A review. *Professional Psychology: Research and Practice, 18,* 189–208.

CHAPTER 21

Supervision of Psychotherapy
With Older Patients

MICHAEL DUFFY
PAMILLA MORALES
Texas A&M University

CLINICAL SUPERVISION IN GEROPSYCHOLOGY

All new specialties progress from the general to the specific as there is development in the knowledge base and an advance of associated technologies. So, for example, the field of aging as a whole has benefited from an explosion of gerontological knowledge. Upon entering the job market, graduates from general programs in gerontology (the study of aging), however, although well equipped with knowledge "about" aging have often been found lacking in *specific skills* in working with older adults. The same point can be made specifically about geropsychology (the psychology of aging). Psychology programs have done relatively well in instructing students about psychological processes of aging—especially in academic cognitive, memory, and developmental areas. They have done less well in developing specific *clinical* and *applied* training opportunities in graduate and postdoctoral programs. A strong clinical geropsychology is therefore the next stage of development within geropsychology; this applied emphasis represents the fruition of many years of scholarly preparation and research. (Indeed, this same point might be made of the current science versus practice tension in psychology as a whole: Practice can be viewed, not as antagonistic to science, but as its flowering and inevitable achievement.)

The central proposition of this chapter is that clinical supervision, as opposed to academic training alone, is the most powerful tool for advancing a strong clinical (applied) geropsychology. This is particularly the case in developing an effective subspecialty in the practice of psychotherapy with older adults. In the development of new specialty standards and certifications with the American Psychological Association and the National College of Professional Psychology, respectively, supervised practice is being given a primary role. Specifically, in proposed training standards' development in clinical geropsychology, in which this first author has participated, supervised experience in working with older adults is central. Proposed training guidelines would include practice, with at least some direct observation, in both predoctoral and postdoctoral specialty training in clinical geropsychology (Niederehe, Hinrichsen, Duffy, & Gatz, 1995).

In order to frame this discussion of psychotherapy supervision in geropsychology, it is helpful to characterize the geriatric psychotherapy process itself, including differences in setting, psychological development, and utilization of psychotherapy services, as well as similarities with general psychotherapy.

CONTEXTUAL ISSUES IN PSYCHOTHERAPY
WITH OLDER CLIENTS

Perhaps the first point to make is that there is much more the same than different when doing psychotherapy with older adults (Duffy, 1992b). The differences, as will be discussed, are of great importance. But the most serious mistake is to assume that geriatric psychotherapy requires totally new and different skills. This assumption leads to the avoidance of working with older patients by skilled and experienced therapists. Most of the body of knowledge and skills in behavioral therapies and psychotherapies is pertinent and effective in working with older persons. Selection of method, as always, is best based on the individual's needs and dynamics, rather than on the broad categorization of an age group. Put another way, older adults are much more similar than they are different from other age groups; an overspecialized approach runs the risk of ignoring basic human dynamics that transcend age or gender or ethnicity. Although therapists need to be increasingly sophisticated and trained in geropsychology, the most critical source of knowledge for the psychotherapist is listening, attending, and total absorption in the experienced world of the client.

There will always be a small number of psychologists who attend less to their limitations than to their entrepreneurial instincts and become "instant experts" in geropsychology (or any other "hot" specialty). Most colleagues, however, tend to underestimate the generalizability and level of their skills and consequently deprive older clients of much needed help (Duffy, 1992).

Working with older clients does require a greater versatility in the setting of psychotherapy. Many psychotherapy clients are living in nursing homes or retirement facilities, and therapists need to gain comfort and familiarity in such contexts. Upward of 25% of persons will spend some time in a nursing home (5%+ at any given point of time), and increased longevity will probably increase this number. Getting used to the medical settings (despite the nursing *home* designation) and the "booming, buzzing confusion" of such places will enormously facilitate the effectiveness of the therapist. Many older adults who are not in nursing homes are semi-immobilized at home, and willingness to do home-visit psychotherapy will also increase effectiveness (and business!) for the therapist. Many older adults, of course, are well and independent and can easily come for in-office psychotherapy. As will be discussed later, however, such "well elderly" are members of a current cohort who do not frequently seek out psychotherapy services (except on the advice of a physician). Geriatric psychotherapy frequently is just that: provided by referral of physicians and family members in geriatric settings where elderly are very old and very sick—the fastest growing segment of the older population.

Working with older adults is fast becoming an inevitability for psychotherapy. As is obvious in the upwardly shifting patient age in Veteran Affairs hospitals, for example, sheer demographics and increased longevity are affecting the practice of psychology. And psychology at large has been slow to recognize this. What, then, are some of the psychological dimensions relevant to understanding older clients in psychotherapy and supervision?

Psychological Features of Late Life

Aging has been defined as changes or differentiation in function that occur after the age of physical maturity (Birren & Renner, 1977; Kermis, 1986). Some of these changes are selective reductions in function; however, not all of the changes are or will become disabling (Edinberg, 1985; Kermis, 1986). Other changes involve the reorganization of functions and structures that allows individuals in late life to adapt to the altered realities of their lives in regard to social functioning and their environments (Kermis, 1986).

Aging occurs in various environmental contexts that affect individuals' coping, adaptation, and behavior in late life (Edinberg, 1985). These contexts include the family, the support network, and the environments in which they reside (Kermis, 1986). Aging is a process that all individuals will experience; it discriminates against no groups or individuals, unless there is premature death resulting from illness or accident, all individuals will encounter the phase of late life.

Many individuals in late life are able to successfully negotiate their later years, There are, however, a significant number of individuals for whom aging is a negative event, not only to themselves, but also to their families, supportive friends, and/or caretakers, because of a variety of factors (Kermis, 1986).

Positive psychosocial health is reflected by relatively sustained psychosocial efficacy or psychological and intellectual vigor, independence, and the continued capacity for success in varied environments (Vaillant, 1994). Negative psychosocial health has been defined as the opposite of positive psychosocial health with a decline in physical and mental vitality, dependence, and functional failure in varied environments. New technology has provided "cures" for many old-age diseases that have allowed people to live longer. This increase in health care has provided an extension in longevity, but not without its complications. For many individuals, technology has cured some, but not all of the diseases of the late-life adult. Illnesses such as pneumonia and influenza are easily treated by antibiotic therapy, but the increase in life span has created an increase in dementia and other progressive organic disorders that are not currently treatable. For many in today's society, recurring or chronically disabling illnesses or both have led many late-life adults to experience a medicated life revolving around clinics, hospitals, and pharmacies with a decrease in life satisfaction due to the dependence on these institutions and their social environment.

Another important psychological feature of late life is the predominant theme of loss in characterizing the emotional and psychological experiences of older people (Butler & Lewis, 1983; Butler, Lewis, & Sunderland, 1991). Individuals in late life experience loss in every aspect of living and are faced with expending enormous amounts of physical and emotional energy in grieving, resolving grief, and adaptation (Butler & Lewis, 1983; Butler et al., 1991). This experience of loss generally occurs on many fronts, both extrinsic and intrinsic. These losses for the late-life adult often occur multiply rather than singularly, with many of these losses occurring simultaneously (Duffy & Iscoe, 1990).

Extrinsic/environmental factors include the death of a marital partner, friends, colleagues, relatives; socioeconomic adversities; income drop; inflation; unwanted retirement or arbitrary retirement policies that force the late-life individual from his or her employment; and loss of status, prestige, and overall participation in society (Butler & Lewis, 1983).

Intrinsic factors include the decline of physical health; physical diseases; perceptual decrements; sexual losses; brain damage; arteriosclerosis; senile dementia; loss of speed in processing and response; regressive alterations of the body; changes in body size and appearance; changes in vision, hearing, taste, smell, touch, and mobility; and coming to terms with death (Butler & Lewis, 1983).

Common emotional reactions as expressed by late-life adults include grief, guilt, loneliness, depression, anxiety, rage, and a sense of impotence and helplessness (Butler & Lewis, 1983).

In spite of these varied reactions expressed by late-life adults, however, Maddox (1980) found that development, change, and growth can continue through the later years of the life span in spite of the decrement of social, psychological, and physiological functioning that typically accompanies the aging process.

Utilization of Psychotherapy

Government agencies and organizations have documented that the elderly have the lowest rate of mental illness of any age group, with the primary mental health problem being cognitive impairment; depression was transitory, and other forms of mental illness were rare in the upper age ranges (Kermis, 1986).

These low rates of mental disorders may be explained by the fact that late-life adults utilize mental health facilities at half the rate of the general population (Butler et al., 1991). Further, issues with epidemiological research have compounded the problem as a result of the tendency to overestimate the incidence of dementia while underestimating mental illness (Butler & Lewis, 1982; Eisdorfer & Cohen, 1982). These errors in reporting may result from the symptoms of dementia and mental illness being similar, as well as by the confounding of differential diagnosis by advancing age (Butler & Lewis, 1982; Eisdorfer & Cohen, 1982).

Another issue in the delivery of psychological services to the elderly has been the incidence of drug and alcohol abuse. Alcohol and drug abuse by late-life adults has typically been underestimated by researchers and has become a serious problem whose detection is also complicated by advancing age (Kermis, 1986; Wood, 1978). Researchers have documented that approximately 20% of all people in treatment for alcoholism are older than 55 years of age (Peterson, 1983).

Physician- and patient-induced medication abuse is also emerging as a serious problem among late-life adults (Kermis, 1986; Peterson, 1983). Four of the ten drugs most often prescribed for older patients by their physicians are psychoactive medications and 16.9 million prescriptions for tranquilizers are written for late-life adults, making them second to heart medications in usage (Kermis, 1986; Lofholm, 1978). With the prescribing of these drugs come negative side effects that often increase the risk of misdiagnosing dementia in late-life individuals along with the additional negative side affects of addiction, delirium, and toxicity (Kermis, 1986).

Burnside (1980) stated that in 1974 there were 3.3 million mentally ill late-life adults. Of the elderly chronically ill, 111,000 were in mental institutions, 1.5 million required home care, and 500,000 required nursing home care. Gurland and Toner (1982) stated that 10% to 15% of older people have clinically significant depression, with another 2% to 3% diagnosed as having a major affective disorder or bipolar depression. Roybal (1984) stated that 15% to 25% of the elderly have significant mental health problems. This percentage includes those in both long-term care facilities and community residences. These statistics, when combined with those regarding drug and alcohol abuse, suggest a potentially high demand for mental health services by the elderly. Even though these numbers reflect the need for psychological services to be provided, late-life adults continue to be the lowest group in the utilization of services.

The explanation for the underutilization of mental health services can be partially accounted for by the deinstitutionalization of elderly patients from mental hospitals and the reinstitutionalizing of the elderly in nursing homes and long-term care facilities (Bassuk & Gerson, 1978; Kermis, 1986; Moss & Halamandaris, 1977; Sherwood & Mor, 1980; Vladeck, 1980).

Another issue has been the underutilization of community mental health clinics. Late-life adults comprise a small percentage of clients in community mental health centers and private practice with approximately 85% of care provided by in-patient treatment (Gatz, Smyer, & Lawton, 1980). The lack of availability of community mental health centers can be partially explained by lack of funding. Currently only 5% of federal mental health care dollars are given to community mental health centers, which are expected to care for all individuals within their communities (Kermis, 1986). Another possibility for the under-utilization of mental health services may be the result of the stereotypic attitude of many mental health professionals that organic problems are commonplace in late-life adults and untreatable by psychotherapy (Gatz et al., 1980; Vladeck, 1980). These individuals are then referred to institutions to provide medical treatment as opposed to psychological care.

Increasingly, general hospital emergency rooms have become one-way transfers to nursing homes. Nursing homes, in turn, have become the "repositories" for the mentally ill aged (Moss & Halamandaris, 1977). What has become increasingly documented, however, is the lack of treatment provided by nursing homes as a result of lack of staff, expertise, and funding, as well as misdiagnosis of the mentally ill late-life adult. Nursing homes are generally unprepared to provide the type of treatment that is required for the mentally ill elderly.

Another important element of underutilization has been the accelerating cost of mental health services for the late-life adult and the lack of adequate reimbursement (Kermis, 1986). Even when the mentally ill late-life adult has been correctly diagnosed, within many institutionalized environments it has become easier to medicate such a patient into sedation or merely provide "warehousing" (Edinberg, 1985).

Other reasons for the underutilization may be the reactions of older persons against treatment (Butler et al., 1991). Late-life adults may resist mental health interventions for many reasons: desire for independence, fear of institutionalization, fear of change, cost, lack of insurance coverage, suspiciousness, realistic appraisal of the inadequacies of mental health programs for the elderly, and a generalized feeling that the problems associated with aging cannot be altered (Butler et al., 1991).

Possibility of Psychotherapeutic Change

Personality is a constantly changing record of individuals' adaptation to their environment. In late life, the normal personality adapts to the challenges that confront older people in a fluid manner rather than in the recapitulation of early patterns (Kermis, 1986). Therefore, abnormal personality can be distinguished by inflexibility and rigidity. Further, personality is defined as an individual's pattern of organizing his or her beliefs, perceptions, and behavior and is composed of a permanent core and temporary adaptations (Back, 1976).

The personality characteristics of any individual will affect psychotherapeutic change. There are two main components of personality: traits that remained stable over the life span and those traits that were capable of change and modification, even into extreme old age. Both adaptive and maladaptive features of an individual's personality are brought into old age (Butler & Lewis, 1983; Butler et al., 1991). Therefore, the more adaptable the individual in late life, the better the outcome for psychotherapeutic change.

A noticeable personality change for many late-life adults that can compound the therapeutic process is the tendency to turn inward (Edinberg, 1985). Individuals who turn inward show less energy and emotionality in relating to the world. This response appears to be a reflection of cautiousness by late-life adults to their environment as well as an overall life reflection (Botwinick, 1978). Turning inward for the late-life adult does not necessarily indicate increased mental health problems, nor does it mean that all older adults dramatically change with age, but it is an indication of the general slowing down of sensory and physical systems that many individuals in late life experience (Edinberg, 1985). In fact, this increased interiority can also be a positive indicator for psychotherapeutic change.

Late-life adults' personalities adapt to the challenges that confront them, and these challenges may occur at any point in the life cycle (Kermis, 1986). Personal losses, physical disabilities, and cultural prejudices against late-life adults are only three of the many stresses they are likely to encounter that will necessitate adaptation (Kermis, 1986).

Mental health can be impeded by varied experiences within the late-life adult. Older people often face simultaneous losses that lead to an attrition of their coping resources, and they may lack faith in their recovery powers and fear becoming a burden or becoming "senile" at the same time as they are encountering overwhelming transitions in their personal lives (Brink, 1979).

Late-life adults may also be less able to fulfill the goals of therapy because of their reduced sensory and physical vitality (Fries & Crapo, 1981; Verwoerdt, 1981). Counselors involved with late-life adults are likely to encounter special problems that require modification of their usual methods of counseling (Knight, 1986). Modifications such as becoming more active in the interchange, speaking slowly, and pacing sessions may benefit the client and increase the possibility of psychotherapeutic change (Knight, 1986). Many traditional methods of psychotherapy or counseling require the client to perform most of the action in a counseling session; however, with elderly or frail clients, the counselor may need to delineate and clarify problems as well as uncover their causes in order to facilitate change (Knight, 1986).

The perceived possibility of therapeutic change in late life is influenced strongly by the therapist's view of aging. There are several models of aging, each of which bears on various aspects of the change process.

Developmental theory evolved from Erikson's developmental stage perspective (Erikson, 1963). This perspective describes development as a sequence of eight steps or stages, with each stage encompassing specific tasks, problems, and outcomes. Individuals within each stage had the task of adaptation or nonadaptation. If stages were resolved with a high degree of adaptation, then the individual moved smoothly into the next developmental phase. Individuals could successfully negotiate through one stage and get stuck in another; therefore, the successful completion of one stage did not indicate success in another. If individuals had a poor adaptation in one developmental stage, they could not successfully negotiate through any further stages.

The developmental stage theory for psychological features of late life has important considerations in terms of psychotherapeutic change and process. Specifically, early experiences influence many aspects of current behavior for individuals in late life, and identifying and working through the various developmental stages that the client initially had difficulty negotiating could be therapeutic to the late-life adult and could facilitate psychotherapeutic change.

Continuity theory (Atchley, 1977) arises from the aspect of developmental theory that individuals in late life have a range of coping styles and approaches to life's problems that they have developed over the course of their lives (Edinberg, 1985). Many of their styles and approaches that were successfully utilized at other points in their lives have become ineffective in late life. An individual who is "resistant" in therapy may simply be holding on to those coping patterns that have proved effective sometime in the past. This implies for the therapist that psychotherapeutic change is not impossible, but rather that the integration of the client's social and personal history may prove important in helping the late-life adult implement new coping patterns that are more effective (Edinberg, 1985).

Disengagement theory (Cumming & Henry, 1960) is based on the basic tenet that there is a mutual and desirable separation between late-life adults and society as the elderly prepare for death (Edinberg, 1985). Disengagement has four basic characteristics: Disengagement happens slowly and continually; it is universal; it is mutual and satisfying for the individual and society; and it is sanctioned by society through mechanisms such as retirement (Crandall, 1980). The implications for psychotherapeutic change within this theory would be its emphasis on a passive acceptance of reduced functionality. Disengagement theory suggests working through an individual's decreasing interaction with society (Edinberg, 1985; Hussian, 1981). Note that disengagement, in this sense, does not imply a lowering of morale or happiness, but rather an increase in interiority that may derive from an enhanced and secure sense of self.

The last model of aging developed in opposition to the disengagement model and is based on the premise that successful aging occurs only when the previously active individual can find other activities to replace the ones lost in late life (Hussian, 1981). Activity theory (Maddox, 1964) relates to the successful adjustment to the maintenance of activities that characterize middle-life satisfaction and to the development of new activities in the late-life adult (Havighurst, 1968; Hussian, 1981; Neugarten, 1977). Various researchers have found that life satisfaction was correlated with various indices of involvement in social activities and integration with the environment (Havighurst, 1968; Hussian, 1981; Neugarten, 1977). The implications for psychotherapeutic change within this theory are the emphases on remaining active and engaging in meaningful activities for the late-life client. This may be an effective preventative measure and source of satisfaction to compensate for the losses in status and role that often accompany aging (Edinberg, 1985; Woods & Britton, 1985).

Each of these theories may be seen, not as opposing doctrines, but rather as contributory perspectives of change in late life. Indeed, they may pinpoint different personality styles in adapting to change. Change within introverted personalities, for example, may be reflected in disengagement theory, whereas activity theory may better describe extroverted personality styles.

Although the geriatric psychotherapist needs to have a realistic assessment of the constraints and limits of change in older adults, belief in exploring the possibility of therapeutic change would seem critical. If the therapist subscribes to ageist views of inherent late-life rigidity, he or she is unlikely to enhance or release the power of psychotherapy for older adults.

Age Versus Cohort Attitudes to Seeking Help

An important concept in gerontology for the therapist and supervisor to grasp is the difference between age and cohort effects. So often negative stereotypes about older adults are incorrect, not necessarily because they are untrue (often the case, however), but because they are wrongly interpreted as relating to *age itself* rather than, for example, being attributable to other factors such as the influence of a cohort.

A *cohort* is generally defined as a group of persons born at about the same time. Although cohorts are often defined differently in research studies, they are usually made up of people born within a 5- to 10-year period. They can also be defined by individuals who are born in distinct eras, who experience different historical events, or who experience the same events at varying stages of their lives. Individuals in cohort groups may have been exposed to different social structures that have had unique influences on their personal development (Knight, 1986).

Although age changes are often assumed to result from adult developmental processes, cohort effects describe other reasons why older people and younger people may differ from one another and why individuals may have different reactions to the same environmental stimuli. Schaie (1983) found that errors occurred when drawing conclusions about development from cross-sectional studies that compared groups of old and young people at a certain point in time and that these errors included confounding age changes with cohort effects and historical changes that can affect several cohorts at once, but with varying results.

Another source of differentiation among cohorts would be historical changes that affect attitudes and beliefs in a broad sense (Knight, 1986). World War II was a historical event that affected Americans' attitudes and beliefs about war and Japanese and German peoples and the changed labor force. Many of these cohort beliefs have continued for 30 years or more (i.e., the reluctance to purchase Japanese products). These effects may be moderated by cohort membership so that early-born cohorts had strong beliefs about patriotism after World War II, whereas later-born cohorts may have been more affected by the Korean War and still later-born cohorts experienced the Vietnam War and have patriotic feelings different from those individuals who served in World War II. Each one of these individuals has varying intensities of feelings, attitudes, and beliefs that continue with them through the aging process. Further, these beliefs and attitudes affect the psychotherapeutic process.

Another apparent cohort difference is the tendency of older generations to present many kinds of complaints in somatic form (Knight, 1986). Anxiety may be presented in terms of its physical manifestations, and depression may be described in terms of physical fatigue and vague aches and pains (Knight, 1986).

Psychotherapeutic change in therapy with older clients can also be the result of cohort effects. Cohorts who grew up with the notion of self-sufficiency and self-fulfillment are less likely to become willing candidates for therapy. There are a variety of cohort differences that can affect therapy and the client-therapist relationship, including differences in moral values, religious orientations, education, attitudes toward the family, and a tendency to somaticize complaints (Knight, 1986). It is not necessary for the therapist to adopt the values of older cohorts; however, it will be important to understand these values and be comfortable talking about them within the client's system.

CLINICAL SUPERVISION AS THE PRIMARY TRAINING METHOD IN GEROPSYCHOLOGY

Much of the training provided in graduate programs in professional psychology is didactic in nature. Although important knowledge about aging processes may be efficiently provided in academic courses, effective learning is often limited by lack of clinical experience. The instructional logic of traditional didactic training in psychotherapy, for example, is frequently in the following sequential order: first, theories of psychotherapy, then techniques of psychotherapy, and finally, practicum in psychotherapy. The appealingly simple logic of this didactic method, however, is ingenuous and often falls victim to reality; practicum supervisors often discover that much ill-digested theory and technique have to be unlearned in order to be relearned in an experiential and internalized manner. The experiential training method, on the other hand, uses the experiential context of a practicum, laboratory, or case analysis to convey theoretical or technical content in a more meaningful manner. As a concrete example of these contrasting instructional methods, we can compare professional psychology programs in which practicum is delayed until at least the second year to allow for "adequate preparation" and programs in which early supervised practicum training is seen as the major vehicle and context for learning. It is interesting to note that the current Accreditation Guidelines of the American Psychological Association also place practicum training in the first semester of the doctoral program—a recommendation that is frequently honored in the breach.

In either instructional model, practicum and internship are key vehicles to providing a professional expertise that reaches beyond academic content alone. Practicum placements, however, do not in themselves ensure professional competency; supervision is the ingredient that promotes clinical expertise. There are three propositions we would like to advance.

The first proposition is that there is a vast difference between supervised experience and experience alone. A well-supervised practicum experience differs greatly from a practicum that is just "being out there." In either case, students often enjoy the experience but are unaware of what is being missed when they have not been intensively supervised. When they lack intensive supervision, students often fail to become psychologically connected with older adults, especially in nursing homes. The physical disabilities that accompany age can block the trainee's internal contact with the person behind the sickness and leave him or her disconnected in a way that disallows a therapeutic relationship. Without this "vital" psychological contact, trainees are liable to feel less effective, to "drift" away, to lose interest, and to become bored with geropsychology. Is this not always the case—we drift away from relationships in which we have no intensive connections? Supervision can bring those relationships into an intense psychological sphere, and this is particularly critical in geropsychology, especially in nursing homes, where physical and cognitive disability can create a barrier to intimate therapeutic contact. Unless these experiences are well supervised and their meaning is understood and dealt with, therapeutic power will be lost.

The second proposition is that clinical supervision, even in accredited and respected professional programs, is of mixed quality. In the supervision that we have personally received, we probably saw considerable differences in quality and, of course, in type. Supervision in many accredited psychology programs becomes the responsibility of junior faculty or adjunct clinical faculty, its labor intensity avoided by more senior faculty. Thus, perhaps the most critical task in clinical training is conducted by the least experienced supervisors. When this pattern is present, it suggests how supervision is understood and valued and how it takes place (Qualls, Duffy, & Crose, 1995). There is a wide range of supervisory quality and activities. It can include arranging field practicum sites accompanied by superficial "corridor supervision," in which probes are a nonspecific "How are you doing? Any problems?" It sometimes implies a general case conference in which discussion is not based on direct access to data and easily degenerates into "the (therapeutic) fish that got away." Supervision, however, can also mean a more intensive and substantial process that focuses (by recording or direct observation) on the actual interactions between therapist and client. This allows detailed examination of the dynamics of the therapist, the client, and also of the therapist-client interaction in a way that enhances the therapist's skill over time and allows the therapist to learn richly from experience. To *have* experiences is valuable—to *learn* from them is exponentially more useful. This is equally relevant in a nursing home and in any geropsychological setting as it is in conventional training clinics. If such supervision is not there, students will not be enriched in skill and empathetic understanding of this age group.

A third proposition, therefore, is that the quality of clinical supervision is the single most important ingredient in the quality of geropsychology training. Training remains abstract and remote for students until they actually experience successes in ongoing therapeutic relationships with older adults. This, we think, can stop the drift away from clinical geropsychology.

Many trainers have experienced the reticence of graduate professional psychology students to approach geropsychology as a potential specialty. We have also experienced the challenge of maintaining the student's interest in an area in which they are frequently burdened by age prejudice and the temptation to either aggrandize or infantilize older clients in a transferential manner. Learning to "meet the person" without being preoccupied with age differences and disability allows an intense "personalized" psychological relationship that is necessary in being therapeutic with any client. In our experience, this process is best facilitated through close supervision. Without this, the "differentness" and related stress of the geriatric practicum experience can have the effect of alienating and discouraging trainees.

Detailed clinical supervision is also the most effective tool for developing specific, high-level skills in working with older clients. As mentioned, geropsychology as a whole has a history over the last 20 years of moving from the general to the specific. At one time, it was enough for us to be master of the demographics of aging. Geropsychologists were people who knew things about older adults. We have moved away from that to specific clinical skills in which geropsychologists know how to *do* something for older adults and are willing to work with students at the bedside in order to bring therapeutic change (Qualls et al., 1995). Even in our formal geropsychology programs, however, there has not been great progress in achieving a level of clinical specificity in our training. In a national survey in the mid-1980s of counseling psychology programs, there were few accredited programs that had detailed, organized practicum experience in geropsychology: About 2 out of 50 programs had an organized geropsychology practicum (Duffy, 1985). This situation has changed somewhat, and clinical psychology training programs have probably developed more practica. But, in general, our geropsychology programs emphasize "talking about" aging and often stop somewhat short of "doing" with older clients; practicum is too frequently limited to relatively unsupervised field experiences.

Clinical supervision raises special difficulties in the nursing home context. A major problem is that there have generally been few mental health professionals in nursing homes, and those that exist often are at the bachelor's level in social work (which frequently means a primary degree in some other discipline with specialty experience in social work). Another difficulty in working in nursing homes and providing psychological services is that there is little mental health ambiance. Nursing homes are focused on medical services, and although many day-to-day problems are behavioral and psychological, the mental health dimension is poorly recognized. Nursing home personnel (and older people themselves) do not recognize mental health needs as part of health care, and this is especially so in nursing homes. Consequently, therapists have to work in a much more naturalistic manner in geriatric clinical services and supervision, using naturalistic rather than technical language. Therapy groups, for example, become "conversation groups." Another limitation in long-term care settings is the lack of physical facilities and resources and the lack of privacy to conduct therapy and supervision. In a parallel situation, school psychologist colleagues have commented about how difficult it is to do supervision in schools. They recount stories of doing supervision in broom closets and corridors. These authors are able to recount similar geropsychology experiences; during one whole semester, supervision was conducted in a nursing home beauty salon sitting under the hairdryers!

SUPERVISORY TECHNIQUE IN GEROPSYCHOLOGY: A MULTIMETHOD MODEL

Doing psychotherapy with older adults can be complex in a number of ways. It involves working in nontraditional settings such as nursing homes, hospitals, and private homes. It involves working with clients who are non-self-referred in the traditional sense and who do not view themselves as mental health patients at all. It involves working in settings in which privacy is difficult, in which audio and video recording is a challenging process, and in which there is no formal role for the psychotherapist. In a similar way, supervision of geriatric psychotherapy has to face such complexity with a flexibility that maintains high-level quality.

Duffy (1992a) and Qualls et al. (1995) have developed a multimethod model of geriatric supervision that capitalizes on these situational complexities. Using three complementary supervisory techniques, the supervisor "triangulates" on the therapy process to maximize the comprehensiveness and accuracy of the supervisory work. Each method contributes individual benefits, and together they form a continuum of immediacy and access to the therapeutic interactions under review. These techniques are *grand rounds*, which provide a live experience of the patient; *intensive process supervision,* which can explore the detailed therapist-patient interactions via audio- or videotape; and *case conferences,* which, more distant from the experiential data, but based on it, can better frame a systemic view of the case. Because of the situational difficulties, it is usually impossible to use any one of the methods exclusively and continuously. Serendipitously, however, their juxtaposition adds significantly to the supervisory perspective gained. More detail of this approach can be found in Duffy (1992a). What follows is a brief overview of the approaches and their uses.

Grand rounds were developed in medical education and are the bedside equivalent of "live supervision." Supervisors and supervisees together visit the rooms of assigned patients, often meeting beforehand to select an appropriate therapeutic theme for the visit. This is essentially a "home visit" for the patient in which the therapeutic issue is developed and discussed in a conversational and naturalistic manner that is sensitive to the patient's non-clinical perception of the experience. The visit also allows the supervisor to demonstrate therapeutic techniques, such as affect deepening, use of humor for confrontation, and "tracking" therapeutic issues within the conversation. This opportunity to see the supervisor work is always reported by supervisees as the most useful part of supervision.

Intensive process supervision is based on recordings (usually using a hand-held audio recorder) made during therapy sessions by the supervisee. Although not as immediate as "live" sessions, it has the opposite benefit of psychological distance, allowing perspective on the therapeutic interactions and the facility to track therapeutic issues and patterns over time. It is probably through this detailed examination of client-therapist interactions and their meaning across the relationship that most therapeutic skill gains are achieved. It is also in process supervision that the therapist is helped to gain self-awareness and track transferential and countertransferential issues as they occur. In turn, this process both increases therapeutic effectiveness and personal growth in the therapist.

Building on the immediacy and therapeutic detail of the grand rounds and process supervision, respectively, the more traditional case conference approach gains greater effectiveness also; other supervisee colleagues can assist more effectively in conceptualizing and strategizing because they have had the opportunity to actually meet their colleague's client in live session and track progress through audio recording. Thus, the case conference presentation is protected from the dangers of "intellectual" discussion and remote "second guessing." The case conference can usefully be devoted to systemic case planning in which overall therapeutic strategies can be developed based on an accurate picture of the situation.

These methods are used in such a way that each supervisee is exposed to each method sequentially and has the benefit of each. Although developed in a nursing home setting and with groups of supervisees, this multimethod approach easily adapts to other settings and to individual supervisees.

ISSUES AND DYNAMICS OF GERIATRIC SUPERVISION

Supervisees in geropsychology come from a wide range of disciplines, roles, and levels of expertise, and clinical settings include private offices, health care institutions, family homes, group homes, and senior recreational centers. Personal feelings about aging, disability, death, competence, and professional roles are salient in the supervisory process as most of the supervisees are younger than their clients and have had few personal experiences to draw on in understanding the problems of their older clients. This makes the therapeutic alliance fertile ground for transference and countertransference dynamics (Brockett & Gleckman, 1991; Crose, 1991). This diversity and complexity within the practice of geropsychology make supervision challenging and interesting.

Because much of geropsychology is centered in multidisciplinary teamwork, the potential supervisees for a geropsychologist include fellow psychologists interested in developing expertise in geropsychology, physicians, nurses, nurses' aides, social workers, welfare workers, counselors, family members, and volunteer paraprofessionals, as well as psychology and counseling students. These supervisees are at many different levels of expertise in psychological understanding and abilities and thus require different considerations in supervision. Most of these professional and paraprofessional health care workers probably never think of themselves as supervisees of the geropsychologist, but the process of consultation with these professionals is in many ways similar to more traditional supervisory processes. As supervisor, the geropsychologist is responsible for ensuring that supervisees understand the diversity within their older clients and is also responsible for supervising different levels of expertise and disciplinary perspectives so that the individual mental health needs of older people are holistically and effectively addressed.

Although geropsychology supervisees are almost always younger than their clients, their different ages and stages of life may be important to the supervisory process. Midlife supervisees are often struggling with their own fears of aging and mortality and need help from the supervisor in sorting out some of these issues, whereas younger supervisees may be more concerned with issues of competency and intergenerational roles. Many older clients may respond favorably to helping young persons learn about aging and will cooperate more readily with psychological interventions if they believe they are making a contribution to the education of a "student." Other older clients want assurance that their clinician is mature, has experience, and is highly competent before they trust that they can be helpful. These factors make for interesting and challenging dynamics in the therapeutic relationship between clinician and client. Supervision of these dynamics becomes rich with opportunities for personal growth as well as for professional development (Genevay & Katz, 1990; Hubbard, 1984).

CONCLUSION

Clinical supervision is a complex and rewarding component in geropsychology. In the future development of clinical geropsychology as a specialty in psychology, we believe that high-quality supervision has a critical instrumental role. It will be challenging to get faculty in graduate programs to invest in this rewarding, but labor-intensive procedure. We are also being challenged to make supervision or consultation available through continuing education experiences for experienced professionals wishing to specialize in geropsychology. The proposed National College of Professional Psychology and, at a more advanced level, the American Board of Professional Psychology are promising potential sponsors and models for such applied specialty training. The experiential, applied emphasis of "supervised practice" will certainly add significantly to continuing education for professionals in the field of geropsychology. Without the benefit of such clinical guidance in geropsychology training, even well-disposed and highly competent professionals can tend to lose interest and drift away.

A final comment of "gerophobia" among professionals: Gerophobia tends to decrease the closer we approach a particular human being. And it is through intensive supervision that our supervisees begin to find that fascinating inner world of the person, of any person, of any age. It is that which takes us back time and again to work with our older clients and enlivens our curiosity, interest, and comfort.

REFERENCES

Atchley, R. C. (1977). *The social forces of later life: An introduction to social gerontology.* Belmont, CA: Wadsworth.

Back, K. W. (1976). Personal characteristics and social behavior: Theory and method. In R. Binstock & E. Shanas (Eds.), *Handbook of aging and the social sciences* (pp. 403–431). New York: Van Nostrand Reinhold.

Bassuk, E. L., & Gerson, S. (1978, February). Deinstitutionalization and mental health services. *Scientific American,* 46–53.

Birren, J. E., & Renner, V. J. (1977). Research on the psychology of aging: Principles and experimentation. In J. E. Birren & K. W. Schaie (Eds.), *Handbook of aging* (pp. 3–38). New York: Van Nostrand Reinhold.

Botwinick, J. (1978). *Aging and behavior* (2nd ed.). New York: Springer.

Brink, T. L. (1979). *Geriatric psychotherapy.* New York: Human Sciences Press.

Brockett, D. R., & Gleckman, A. D. (1991). Countertransference with the older adult: The importance of mental health counselor awareness and strategies for effective management. *Journal of Mental Health Counseling, 13,* 343–355.

Burnside, I. M. (1980). Symptomatic behaviors in the elderly. In J. E. Birren & R. B. Sloane (Eds.), *Handbook of mental health and aging* (pp. 719–744). Englewood Cliffs, NJ: Prentice Hall.

Butler, R. N., & Lewis, M. I. (1983). *Aging and mental health*. New York: Macmillan.

Butler, R. N., Lewis, M. I., & Sunderland, T. (1991). *Aging and mental health: Positive psychosocial and biomedical approaches* (4th ed.). New York: Macmillan.

Crandall, R. C. (1980). *Gerontology: A behavioral science approach*. Reading, MA: Addison-Wesley.

Crose, R. (1991). What's special about counseling older women? *Canadian Journal of Counseling, 25,* 617–623.

Cumming, E., & Henry, W. E. (1960). *Growing old: The process of disengagement*. New York: Basic Books.

Duffy, M. (1985). *A survey of practicum training in geropsychology in counseling psychology programs*. Unpublished manuscript.

Duffy, M. (1992a). A multimethod model for practicum and clinical supervision in nursing homes. *Counselor Education and Supervision, 32,* 61–69.

Duffy, M. (1992b). Challenges in geriatric psychotherapy. *Individual Psychology, 48*(4), 432–440.

Duffy, M., & Iscoe, I. (1990). Crisis theory and management: The case of the older person. *Journal of Mental Health Counseling, 12,* 303–313.

Edinberg, M. A. (1985). *Mental health practice with the elderly*. Englewood Cliffs, NJ: Prentice Hall.

Eisdorfer, C., & Cohen, D. (1982). *Mental health care of the aging: A multidisciplinary curriculum for professional training*. New York: Springer.

Erikson, E. H. (1963). *Childhood and society*. New York: Norton.

Fries, J. F., & Crapo, L. M. (1981). *Vitality and aging*. San Francisco: Freeman.

Gatz, M., Smyer, M. A., & Lawton, M. P. (1980). The mental health system and the older adult. In L. Poon (Ed.), *Aging in the 1980's*. Washington, DC: American Psychological Association.

Genevay, B., & Katz, R. S. (1990). *Countertransference and older clients*. Newbury Park, CA: Sage.

Gurland, B. J., & Toner, J. A. (1982). Depression in the elderly: A review of recently published studies. In C. Eisdorfer (Ed.), *Annual review of geriatrics and gerontology*. New York: Springer.

Havighurst, R. J. (1968). A social-psychological perspective on aging. *Gerontologist, 8,* 67–71.

Hubbard, R. W. (1984). Clinical issues in the supervision of geriatric mental health trainees. *Educational Gerontology, 10,* 317–323.

Hussian, R. A. (1981). *Geriatric psychology: A behavioral perspective*. New York: Van Nostrand.

Kazdin, A. E. (1978). *History of behavior modification: Experimental foundations of contemporary research*. Baltimore: University Park Press.

Kermis, M. D. (1986). *Mental health in late life: The adaptive process*. Boston: Jones and Bartlett.

Knight, B. (1986). *Psychotherapy with older adults*. Beverly Hills, CA: Sage.

Lofholm, P. (1978). Self-medication by the elderly. In R. C. Kayne (Ed.), *Drugs and the elderly* (pp. 8–28). Los Angeles: University of Southern California Press.

Maddox, G. L. (1964). Disengagement theory: A critical evaluation. *Gerontologist, 4,* 80–82.

Maddox, G. L. (1980). The continuum of care: Movement toward the community. In E. W. Busse & D. Blazer (Eds.), *Handbook of geriatric psychiatry* (pp. 501–520). New York: Van Nostrand Reinhold.

Moss, F. E., & Halamandaris, V. J. (1977). *Too old, too sick, too bad: Nursing homes in America*. Germantown, MD: Aspen Systems.

Neugarten, B. (1977). Personality and aging. In J. E. Birren & K. W. Schaie (Eds.), *Handbook of the psychology of aging* (pp. 626–649). New York: Van Nostrand.

Niederehe, G., Hinrichsen, G., Duffy M., & Gatz, M. (1995). *Knowledge and skills subcommittee draft report*. Washington, DC: NIMH.

Peterson, D. M. (1983). Epidemiology of drug use. In M. D. Glantz, D. M. Peterson & F. J. Whittington (Eds.), *Drugs and the elderly adult* (pp. 13–16). Washington, DC: U.S. Department of Health and Human Services.

Qualls, S. H., Duffy, M., & Crose, R. (1995). Supervision in community practicum settings. In B. G. Knight, L. Teri, J. Santos, & P. Wohlford (Eds.), *Applying geropsychology to services for older adults: Implications for training and practice.* Washington, DC: American Psychological Association.

Roybal, E. R. (1984). Federal involvement in mental health care for the aged. *American Psychologist, 39,* 163–166.

Schaie, K. W. (Ed.). (1983). *Longitudinal studies of adult psychological development.* New York: Guilford.

Sherwood, S., & Mor, V. (1980). Mental health institutions and the elderly. In J. E. Birren & R. B. Sloane (Eds.), *Handbook of mental health and aging* (pp. 854–884). Englewood Cliffs, NJ: Prentice Hall.

Vaillant, G. E. (1994). Successful aging and psychosocial well-being: Evidence from a 45-year study. In E. H. Thompson Jr. (Ed.), *Older men's lives* (pp. 22–40). London: Sage.

Verwoerdt, A. (1981). *Clinical geropsychiatry.* Baltimore: Williams & Wilkins.

Vladeck, B. C. (1980). *Unloving care: The nursing home tragedy.* New York: Basic Books.

Wood, W. G. (1978). The elderly alcoholic: Some diagnostic problems and considerations. In M. Storandt, I. C. Siegler, & M. F. Elias (Eds.), *The clinical psychology of aging* (pp. 97–113). New York: Plenum.

Woods, R. T., & Britton, P. G. (1985). *Clinical psychology with the elderly.* Rockville, MD: Aspen.

CHAPTER 22

An Experiential Group Model for Group Psychotherapy Supervision

DAVID A. ALTFELD
National Institute for the Psychotherapies
and New York University Medical Center
HAROLD S. BERNARD
New York University Medical Center

The practice of group psychotherapy is widely accepted today as a specialized discipline, distinct from that of individual psychotherapy. Different theoretical models, separate training programs and procedures, and often enough differing goals all signal group psychotherapy as having come of age. In the early course of this development, however, basic concepts from individually focused psychoanalytic theories were applied directly to patient behavior in groups. Concepts such as transference, resistance, regression, defense, symbiosis, oedipal conflict, sibling rivalry, and psychosexual development dominated much of the literature and teaching. As with individual work, technique focused on interpretation of resistance, analysis of (multiple) transferences, and genetic reconstruction as key curative factors in treatment, with the individual being the major focus of analysis, albeit in a group setting. Training in group therapy was often not available, and therapists who wanted to provide a group experience began running groups with patients from their own practices and "winging it." Today, all this has changed. The development of theory that elevated group process to center stage in the treatment of individuals has been accompanied by a proliferation of training programs, an ever-increasing body of literature and research, as well as national and local organizations providing conferences, journals, and forums for exchange.

Has supervision, the teaching and learning of group therapy through examination of a group leader's work, kept pace with these developments? Has the field of supervision developed its own methodologies for transmitting knowledge from senior to junior practitioners? Has the field of group psychotherapy evolved its own forms of supervision, whose success depends on understanding and utilizing group phenomena and behaviors? Our brief answer here to these questions is both yes and no. Some models of supervision continue in traditional dyadic and triadic form; some utilize groups but in that context focus on the individual practitioner; and some use the power, energy, and uniqueness of groups to shape the supervisory process. In an attempt to provide fuller answers to these questions, this chapter reviews various current forms of group supervision, following which we introduce a model of supervision that we believe is particularly illustrative of a supervisory process that depends on group theory and member interaction for its rationale and spirit.

SUPERVISION MODELS

Earlier literature on supervision was often included within the larger framework of discussions of general training procedures, programs, and issues (Dies, 1980; Tauber, 1978). This is not surprising, since a great deal of energy, thought, and resources have gone into developing methods that effectively transmit the growing body of knowledge to the next generation of practitioners. For example Dies (1980), in his comprehensive review included in a handbook on supervision, writes of both training and supervision. He divides training into four components, only one of which is supervisory. The others, which he labels "academic," "observation," and "experiential," get equal attention. In this chapter, however, we limit ourselves to supervision only and do not take up the broad questions of current overall group training procedures.

Dyadic Supervision

The dyadic, or one-on-one model, in which a group therapist presents his or her work to a supervisor is a time-honored form of supervision, taken directly from psychoanalytic institutes where it has been considered the bedrock of the teaching and learning experience for individual psychotherapy. This makes sense, because most if not all therapists originally begin their training doing individual psychotherapy. A large body of literature has accumulated over the years focusing on this form of psychoanalytic or psychodynamic supervision, and much of it is repetitive. Several basic texts summarize issues of dyadic individual supervision (Alonso, 1985; Dewald, 1987; Eckstein & Wallerstein, 1958; Fleming & Benedek, 1966; Hess, 1980; Wallerstein, 1981). Issues discussed focus on the relationship between the two parties, the place of transference and countertransference in the supervisory relationship, and the place and degree of didactic work that should be included in the supervisory mix. Reports of sessions from memory, process notes made during sessions or immediately afterward, and tape recordings are the methods of data transmission utilized, and their relative merits have been discussed and debated. Dyadic group supervision is widely used, having the advantages of simplicity of arrangement, ease of scheduling, and a regular weekly presentation time. It is not, however, considered the most effective form by many group supervisors, lacking as it does the utilization of any group process.

Dyadic Cotherapy Supervision

Another form of dyadic supervision involves a cotherapy arrangement between supervisor and therapist, in which both conduct the group therapy session, usually followed by a discussion of what occurred and why. This arrangement (Berman, 1975; Coché, 1977; McGee & Schuman, 1970; Sadock & Kaplan, 1971) allows the therapist-in-training to observe an experienced therapist at work in the setting in which he or she also functions as a therapist. In many ways, this is a priceless opportunity and not one that many training centers provide, for obvious reasons of time pressures and allocation of both finances and personnel. There are also disadvantages to this arrangement. One most frequently discussed is the junior therapist's tendency to defer or the senior therapist's tendency to take over or both, inhibiting the junior therapist's natural spontaneous flow and promoting feelings of inferiority concerning his or her ability to work effectively.

In a broad-ranging discussion of the merits and liabilities of traditional dyadic and cotherapy dyadic supervision, Abroms (1977) forcefully argues for the increased use of supervisor/supervisee cotherapy, on both theoretical and clinical grounds. Viewing the traditional dyadic model as restrictive observationally, he argues that it gives the supervisor more direct access to the trainee's modes of working, increases diagnostic accuracy in formulating a correct treatment plan, and provides the trainee with an experienced therapist to imitate and utilize as a model in his or her development as a therapist. Abroms does not focus specifically on group treatment, but his arguments are applicable to the supervision of that modality. Abroms, while not unmindful of the disadvantages mentioned earlier, believes these can be taken into account on balance and overcome.

Short of an ongoing cotherapy arrangement, Yalom (1985) recommends that the supervisor attend a couple of meetings early on in the supervisee's group, in order to fix names and faces to clinical material and to "savor the affective climate of the group" (p. 520). If that is not possible, videotapes can still accomplish the purpose and to a much lesser extent, so can audiotaping. Yalom also offers specific recommendations concerning the nature and structure of a therapist-in-training's group notes for supervision, including the identification of major themes and transitions, each member's contributions, the therapist's interventions, and the therapist's feelings about the meeting as a whole.

Triadic Supervision

An extension of the dyadic form, called "triadic" (Dies, 1980; McGee, 1974) pairs two trainees as cotherapists who then meet together with a supervisor. This model is popular in psychiatric medical centers for training residents and psychology interns. Some advantages of this method are that two therapists reporting the data will increase the accuracy of the report and the potential for transferential intensity between supervisor and supervisee is diminished, since it is distributed across all the relationships in the triad. The authors, in their own supervisory experience, have found this to be an effective form of group supervision.

Group Supervision

Utilizing a group setting in which to conduct supervision was but a short step away. Placing a number of trainees in a group in which to present their work provided a powerful new experience for both supervisors and supervisees in the teaching and learning of individual and group psychotherapy: "We claim that supervision in small leader-led groups can provide learning opportunities not found in individual supervision or in peer supervision groups (p. 25)" (Counselman & Gumpert, 1993). Aronson (1990, p. 93) describes some of the advantages of this form of supervision as well as the conditions for its success. He maintains that "superior creative insights" can be generated by a supervisor in interaction with a group as opposed to those generated by a supervisor alone. Aronson's conviction that a group is a valuable place to supervise rests also on his dislike of the authoritarian leader stance and his respect for others regardless of their professional standing. He asserts that less well-trained therapists sometimes possess talents that are lacking in others with more impressive credentials. The collaborative and democratic nature of these groups, in which trainees can share their anxieties and concerns about their work with one another in a safe atmosphere, has proven to be an extremely beneficial experience. Without doubt, it also requires considerable skill on the part of the nonauthoritarian leader.

Hearst and Brown (1995) assert that competitiveness is best managed in a group setting, and Sproul-Boulton, Nitsun, and Knowles (1995) claim that dependency issues between supervisor and supervisee are minimized when supervision is conducted in a group. Furthermore, there is the pleasure and advantage of collaborating in what can otherwise be a lonely and isolated profession: "A supervision group provides a place not only to continue to learn, but also to let off steam, share one's anxieties and insecurities, laugh, cry, and be with other professionals who care about each other and share concerns about the work" (Counselman & Gumpert, 1995, p. 27).

Those authors advocating the supervisory group have considered its disadvantages as well. The most obvious is that in most of these groups members do not present weekly, as in individual supervision, but more usually once every 5 to 6 weeks. Some group supervision leaders (Behr, 1995), however, structure their groups so that each member has the opportunity to bring up issues in every session, even if only for a few minutes. Also, personality conflicts occur and must be dealt with, as well as other group issues that arise, which also decrease the amount of presenting time. Finally, as there is potential for camaraderie, support, and sharing, so is there potential for discord, competition, shame, humiliation, isolation, and feelings of inferiority and incompetence before one's peers.

Experiential Group Supervision

One of the earliest attempts to use the group energy, resources, and experience for supervision is described by Mintz (1978). She begins with the premise that if clinicians have developed basic skills in diagnosis and technique, the difficulties they will encounter in treating their patients will be caused by unrecognized emotional conflicts in the therapist. She further believes the best way to uncover and work on such conflicts is in the context of an experiential group. Three of the methods she offers are the therapist role-playing the patient, the therapist speaking his or her mind to the patient (much like Gestalt empty-chair work), and group members engaging in fantasy about the patient.

A paper that closely approximates the kind of work we present in this chapter is by Ettin (1995). He describes the difference between group consultation and group supervision, a distinction we do not employ. He offers a model, however, that, like ours, makes use of both primary process and the parallel process to discern the meaning of the issue being presented to the supervisory group. Ettin presents a structured protocol by which the consultation or supervision is conducted; it begins with a statement of the problem and ends with the leader's formulation that it is hoped the therapist can utilize in his or her continuing work with the group in question.

THE NEW MODEL

Rationale

A serious problem that frequently arises when using a group setting to conduct supervision stems from the large amount of information that can flow from the group to the presenting member in a short period of time. In fact, the presenter can become overwhelmed with the amount of information offered. This is not an unusual state of affairs in group supervisory work, since it is often not difficult for group members to interpret psychodynamically given a modest amount of clinical information. The more experienced the clinician, the more facile he or she will be in this task. Further, in a field in which much is hypothesized and little proven and in which many opposing theoretical viewpoints hold sway, the possibilities for challenging, refuting, and criticizing the presenter are ever present, however well intentioned such critiques may be. Before such judgments of his or her peers, the presenter can experience feelings of inadequacy and shame (Alonso & Rutan, 1988).

It is hoped that experienced group supervisory leaders are mindful of these issues and of the formidable task a therapist has in presenting his or her work to colleagues and fellow students for evaluation and scrutiny. Yet even the most sensitive leader, attuned to both individual members and group process, can falter in the task of teaching while protecting group members from undue exposure and narcissistic injury. It is unfortunately not unusual for a presenting therapist to report months later that a high anxiety level prevented absorbing more than a modest amount of what was offered by the supervisory group.

Method

Partially in an effort to deal with this difficulty, the senior author began running workshops and supervisory group sessions in a different format. The guiding spirit of this new format is experiential rather than cognitive: The group is asked to respond to clinical material personally rather than intellectually. Typically, the group is told that a member will present a case, and other members are instructed to respond in the following way: Members are asked to take note of whatever images, fantasies, feelings, associations, and bodily sensations they experience while the case material is being presented and to report these "inner" data to the group. Members are asked to assume these reactions are related to the case material, no matter how personal, bizarre, embarrassing, or unrelated to the task they may seem. In fact, it is stressed that these reactions likely hold some key for the group supervisory process at hand. Members are also asked to report responses they are having to one another or to the leader and to trust that such responses also belong to the case and not merely to their own idiosyncratic private world.

This is all easier said than done. Members unpracticed in the procedure respond, not unexpectedly, in more customary ways and offer interpretive comments to the presenter. A typical statement might begin compliantly with the leader's request, such as "I feel . . ." but continue with "that this patient is angry with you and you're not seeing it." The leader interrupts this kind of communication, asking gently whether the member had any feelings while the therapist was presenting the case, or about the perception he or she had of the therapist's presumed blind spot. If the member persists in a more traditional formulation, the leader repeats the question until the person, and presumably others, understands the task. This section of the method can take some time because people characteristically tend to offer perceptions, opinions, and formulations rather than their own internal experience. The leader also models what he or she is after by giving his or her own reactions, and members typically find this helpful. No pressure is put on the presenter to respond to the group's many reactions, especially in this initial phase of the group task induction. Presenters, however, often begin responding and verifying that what is being said relates to the case, to their process with the patient, sometimes to the history of the patient, and often to their own internal psychological history.

Assumptions Underlying the Procedure

There are five assumptions that are made about the supervisory group model under discussion and they are as follows:

1. The leader assumes that the therapist is presenting because he or she wants help with the case, is stuck in some way, and is not seeing clearly what is going on in the therapy. Something is not moving in the treatment, as reflected in the therapist's feelings of anger, frustration, confusion, alienation, boredom, or rage.

2. A corollary assumption is made that the therapist's countertransference feelings will be brought into the room in some form or fashion, and that a parallel process will begin in the supervisory group. The group will unself-consciously, and probably unconsciously, begin functioning as a holding environment for the unaware feelings, thoughts, and experiences the therapist is experiencing with the patient, but with regard to which he has not yet achieved understanding. This process is congruent with how object relations theorists most frequently conceptualize individual psychoanalytic work today and is nicely summarized by Ogden (1982) in his work on projective identification. The analyst "holds" the feelings and anxieties of the patient until such time as the patient is able to take them back, bit by bit, assimilating the previously undigestible affective components aroused in the relationship with the therapist.

3. All reactions in the group are considered valuable countertransference responses to the case material. Although this assumption underlies the entire methodology in this kind of group, some participants question its validity. The most frequent objection encountered is that a member's response may simply be a product of his or her own subjective countertransference rather than a response induced by the case dynamic. This may, of course, be true from an intrapsychic perspective, but from the group or systems perspective, *it is not a great leap to view responses as also group determined* (Agazarian & Peters, 1981). In any case, the assumption has large heuristic value. In addition, so many issues in group emerge from a deep existential base that when the group regression begins, the feelings and associations stimulated and expressed often resonate with the struggle the presenting therapist is having with the case presented.

4. Group-as-a-whole phenomena exist and are a crucial part of the theoretical orientation of this work. This assumption follows directly from Assumption 3.

5. Another corollary to Assumption 3 is that Bion's (1961) work group and basic assumption groups coincide in this work, rather than being antagonistic forces in the group process, as Bion contended.

Theorists today accept Bion's notion that the work group's task will often be impeded by unconscious group forces, which he termed the basic assumptions. Although Bion (1961) acknowledges potentially positive aspects of basic assumption groups, he gives these short shrift in comparison to his descriptions of how they undermine work group functioning. In her description of Bion's theory, Rioch describes basic assumption life as follows:

> Basic assumption life is not oriented outward toward reality but inward toward fantasy, which is then impulsively and uncritically acted out. There is little pausing to consider or to test consequences, little patience with an inquiring attitude, and great insistence upon feeling. (Rioch, 1970, p. 61)

In the model presented here, Bion's characterization of basic assumption groups is in the service of work as we define it. As such, his distinction between work groups and basic assumption groups loses meaning. It is from the work with regressive phenomena that this kind of supervisory group derives its power, force, intensity, and feeling of immediacy. From a psychoanalytic perspective, our model is a pure distillation in a group environment of regression working in the service of the group ego. The ego directs the work task of the group, namely to solve the riddle of the case, while the unconscious provides the primitive and creative raw material—the group fantasies, spontaneous associations, and interactions—that makes it possible.

Theoretical Concepts

To summarize, the key theoretical concepts underlying this work are that of holding environment, group as container, the frame, parallel process, projective identification, and reassimilation, as well as the general concept of guided unconscious communication. The special character of this supervisory group work is defined by the interweaving of these phenomena into the unique process we are attempting to describe.

Considerable attention has been paid to the parallel process concept in the literature on individual supervision since the publication of Searles's (1955) seminal article on the subject, but less so in the supervisory literature on group work. Searles viewed the basic mechanism as caused by a transitory unconscious identification of the therapist with the patient, which causes a block in the treatment, and the parallel process as the therapist's subsequently responding to the supervisor in a manner parallel to the way the patient is responding to the therapist. The dyadic therapeutic interaction is stored unconsciously by the therapist, who then plays out with the supervisor the same dyadic interaction that the patient is experiencing with him. Of course, the successful resolution of this parallel response is contingent on the supervisor's understanding of this process, as well as his or her skill in opening it for discussion. Subsequent literature on parallel process elaborates the basic mechanism (Eckstein & Wallerstein, 1958), describes it as having various points of origin (Doehrman, 1976; Gediman & Wolkenfeld, 1980), and debates its importance and centrality (Bromberg, 1982). Still, the basic description contained in the Searles article has not been fundamentally altered. Searles himself never used the term *parallel process,* calling the phenomenon a *reflection process.* There is now widespread acceptance of the parallel process as a bona fide phenomenon that is ever present, although not always a desirable focus of supervision. Its successful handling makes a twofold demand on the supervisor, namely, (a) to distinguish between therapist subjective countertransference versus objective or induced countertransference (Ormont, 1970), and (b) to handle and resolve the process in a way that does not threaten or make the supervisee defensive and does not encroach on those aspects of his or her personality that are rightfully explored in personal treatment.

As has been noted, a few writers have recognized and applied the parallel-process notion in group supervisory work (Ettin, 1995; Kutter, 1993; Schuman & Fulop, 1989), though it does not seem that the concept has undergone any serious modification in its application to group work and functioning. Interestingly, it was Searles (1955) in the same article who described the phenomenon at work in a supervisory study group in which he was a participating member.

The Actual Group

The following are excerpts from a workshop employing this method that provide the reader with a sense of how such a group might proceed. Along with these excerpts is a running commentary on the possible meanings of the developing group text. This particular group met at a conference for one 2½-hour session. Following the group introductions and the leader's task instructions (described earlier), a group member volunteered to present case material. She was "feeling a need to get feedback" on a problem she was having in a group she was running.

PRESENTER: The issue I am struggling with now, and it's fresh, concerns one male member who is also doing a residency, who wants more from me in terms of teaching, and learning about group. It's his ongoing agenda. *(P. unconsciously introduces the first theme, namely someone of the opposite gender who wants more from her than he feels he is getting, and he couches it in intellectual terms.)*

PRESENTER: Two weeks ago he caught me in the hall before group and was interested in a recommendation for a family therapist. He had been talking in group about problems with his relationship and now was planning to get family therapy. *(The request for more from the therapist gets fleshed out further and contains the potential for competition from an alternative therapist. If the patient can't get more here, perhaps he will go elsewhere.)*

PRESENTER: I said "Please talk to the group about it." But he brought it up toward the end and we started to process it, and he never got a recommendation from me. I was handling it as competition between therapies. He was doing individual therapy with another therapist, and this has also been an issue, that he is doing well in his individual treatment and says to me, "I wish you'd get in there and be more confrontational and directive," and also at the end he said he didn't get the recommendation. I ended the group saying there are more issues than just getting a recommendation, and we need to talk more. Then I got a call canceling, with him indicating he is going into family therapy, and our group time was the only time he could get for the interview for that therapy. I am having all sorts of feelings about this. I'm feeling annoyance with him, set up by him, devalued by him, and I want to work on all this before I go in there again, and know what's going on. *(The presenter makes a clear call for help, which aids the work assumption, specifically asking for help with her anger at the patient who is setting her aside, abandoning her for another parent. She states these feelings are disruptive and therefore not conducive to working therapeutically.)*

LEADER: I was having an image of eating ice cream while you were talking. *(The first comment following the presenter's initial description is here made by the leader who begins modeling in a seemingly whimsical manner, in order to prompt group members to respond on a personal level. In so doing, the leader is communicating to the group that this is not going to be a cognitive group supervisory effort.)*

CONNIE: My association is that he is taking so much away from you. David (the workshop leader) is needing some nurturance, and this guy is depriving of any esteem to you. He's undercutting you. *(This group member seems to recognize that the issue of nurturance may be important in this supervision, but she has not yet been inducted into the more personal mode of responding.)*

LEADER: I mean to stop you, not because what you are saying is incorrect, but I am more interested in what your own personal reaction is. *(He thus begins to train not only Connie, but the entire group.)*

CONNIE: Deprivation. I felt deprived. Underfed.

(Following a few more group responses, the presenter asks the leader if she can react or should wait, in effect asking for further clarification of the contract and its boundaries. The leader responds with "You can react as you like." A few minutes later, several other

members help the group to further clarify the supervisory process in the following exchanges:)

JAN: I thought about rejection.

LEADER: Did you think about you being rejected?

JAN: Yeah (but she was unwilling at this moment to elaborate).

TRISH: I thought about machines, the messages, and avoidance.

LEADER: I'm not clear. Did this contain anything about you?

TRISH: Yes, about important messages, and communication, and connecting with people, and wondering when is the right time for me. *(This member is speaking for the group, of course, in wondering how much to communicate about herself at this early time in the group's life.)*

LEADER: (Testing the waters) Anybody in particular? A particular image?

TRISH: No

BETSY: This is a hard process. A struggle with not interpreting, with . . . I don't know where to put my hands. *(A wonderful image combining uncertainty and awkwardness in responding to a new and unusual situation.)* What you want and don't want. *(This response brings up the contract and the question of whether or not to work at complying with it.)*

BILL: I have an image of two people trying to go through a door, both moving in the same direction. You get mixed up, and finally you struggle but you get through, but it's not smooth. Then I thought of a student, a Jesuit, who has powerful training in philosophy. We were talking at cross-purposes; I am trying to explain to him and he to me about his struggles with his system, and what it told him about personal relationships. I was having trouble reaching him, and it felt like trying to get through the same doorway and bumping into each other. The outcome was that, through our efforts, a good deal of trust was developing and he told me a lot of personal stuff. *(Bill consciously believes he is describing the presenter's experience with her patient, but he is also describing covertly and unconsciously the group process at work and our initial bumpy efforts at developing some cohesion.)*

CLIFF: I'm thinking about the celibacy. That tension in me felt like some excitement. I felt frustration, and a sexual feeling, and not being able to get to it. Reminded me of a patient I had where I felt trapped with a wonderful patient I had, and I think he (Bill's priest) had some sexual feelings and he couldn't talk about it. *(This is a new level of statement, which represents a member getting into the work of the group. He is pointing to feeling trapped with feelings he does not feel he can express, and by implication, that others feel they also cannot express. It also begins to excite the group libido and the group defense against such feelings at this early stage. The parallel process is forming. There is the beginning suggestion of some unspoken sexual tension between the presenter and her patient, and more important, of unacceptable feelings in general. This is precisely what is implicit in the presenter's opening statement to the group.)*

PRESENTER: When Bill was talking, that was the trust piece. I want to say to Doug, "You are acting out around this. Get in the group. Do the work." That's my affect here. And a woman in the group started talking to another member about her sexual feelings toward him. It's been between these two people, and you are saying maybe another piece may be sexual feelings Doug is having toward the therapist. *(Here the presenter is working hard to join the group as she wants Doug to do in her therapy group and is relating in a parallel way to all that is being said. Her feelings, however, still need some focusing.)*

LEADER: (Continuing the training focus) You felt what when Cliff was talking?

PRESENTER: I felt he was right. (Leader questions further) I was with the anger, and wanted to let it out. I am really ticked off.

BEVERLY: I can't get beyond my anger at him, and it reminds me of my anger at a patient of mine. His mistreatment of you and his provocations enrage me.

LEADER: Can you get into it?

BEVERLY: A young man I have seen briefly sent me a patient who then became very demanding. What he lusts after he can never get. He's setting himself up for disappointment. He says to me, "I wish you did hypnosis." He formed a very positive relationship with me immediately, but then did a flip-flop.

LEADER: What are you feeling then?

BEVERLY: Fed up. After one session we had, he says, "This is really disappointing." In the next session, I work my ass off and he shakes my hand. "I'm seeing Barbra Streisand," he tells his friends. (Referring to a then current popular movie in which Streisand plays a psychiatrist.) *(This group member is giving a complicated report to the group. She is working at the basic assumption level, exploring the issue of ambivalence: love and hate toward the therapist, idealization, and disappointment. The grandiose reference to Streisand could be viewed at this stage as a group defense against the powerlessness of what may lie ahead.)*

CONNIE: She also had an affair with the patient (referring to the movie). Back to sex. Is it sex? Or seduction? What's Cliff talking about? I had a reaction to it: I thought it was seductive and exhibitionistic.

LEADER: What was your feeling? *(Leader continues to train, rather than going with the pull of the group to abandon his instructions and do the workshop the way they would like to do it, namely in a more traditional way.)*

CONNIE: Distrust. (And a few moments later) I had a reaction. I started feeling anxious, and the room was warming up, and we were moving into a more intimate process. This might get interesting.

BEVERLY: Cliff is trying to be a wiseguy.

LEADER: How do you mean?

BEVERLY: There it is, a man again, doing this, taking over the show. *(In this introduction of the gender issue, we hear some anger and perhaps a covert displaced anger at complying with the task set by the male leader.)*

BONNIE: I reacted by being reminded of a patient who left my office in a huff. And I thought, "Am I so rigid?" But I felt taken aback by your comment (addressed to Cliff) that I had already interrupted by coming. *(This is a reference to the fact that this person has announced that she has to leave the workshop early because of staff responsibilities in the setting where we are meeting. She states she didn't want to interrupt through leaving, and Cliff said she had already interrupted by coming. As things "begin warming up," this person makes the first clear introduction of frame and boundary issues, a fear of our losing our frame, that somebody besides her might walk out.)*

PRESENTER: I want to talk about certain issues now. I feel an enormous need to tell about the group. Confessing. A power struggle. I went out a year ago on leave, and this summer he wanted to take a short leave, and I said "No," indicating there were no leaves from this group. *(In this comment, the presenter introduces boundary and frame issues that were important in her relationship with Doug and her group, which she was able to pick up on because of the preceding remark by Bonnie. The issue of the shaky or unstable holding environment enters and will be developed further as a parallel process to the case material. The group material presented to this point allows the reader to see directly how amazingly tight the group's responses are in terms of the case material presented as the parallel process is developing. In fact, it continues in the next remark by a group member.)*

CONNIE: When you said sexual issues toward the therapist, like putting some distance between her and Doug, I slipped and started to say "Cliff" instead. *(She recognizes that unconscious forces are taking over here. A moment later, we hear the strongest statement of the developing frame issue.)*

BETSY: I want to leave and am struggling with the door. I didn't realize that my supervisee would be in this group. I needed to get this out. I'm in the wrong place.

LEADER: And what do you feel about it?

BETSY: I feel exposed, and I am wondering what her feelings might be (referring to the supervisee).

TRISH (the supervisee):   I share Betsy's feelings. The minute you (talking to the leader) said how to start, I said great, but I got upset when she said I want to talk about this, and it took this direction. Oh God, I need to get out of here. I need to be out of here. How could I leave? Slip out.

LEADER: I wonder if you are the only two who are uncomfortable and want to leave. (Others raise their hands.) *(Here the group leader recognizes that though their situation sounds unique, the feelings are being generated by the group experience. Otherwise, we believe the two would have dealt with the issue earlier.)*

LEADER: (repeating) I don't think this is only about your issue. I think this is about what we are doing.

BETSY: But I can't get to cohesion and trust without going through this stuff. *(She is right, and she reaffirms, despite her misgivings, the group task. Several other members now join this issue of leaving the group, which culminates in Penny's memory of a shattering group experience in which the frame was entirely destroyed.)*

LISA: I got anxious that Beverly wasn't handling it. I felt frightened. I thought my therapist, being a man, could handle the sexual feeling better. I felt I should leave the room, I wasn't in the right room. You're all more experienced. *(She voices for the group that she feels out of her depth, needs to leave, but perhaps this group leader will be able to handle it.)*

CINDY: You got to own up to it and deal with it. It's hard. This guy is having sexual feelings toward you and you have to deal with it. I want to pull back and keep things safe and therapeutic. *(Here Cindy talks about the demands of the work task and how attractive it would be to become cognitive again.)*

CONNIE: I'm feeling nervous between the sex and the mother thing. But I'm worrying about the people who want to leave. *(With this statement, one can see that the parallel process has taken hold. The group pressure to parallel the presented patient's behavior by leaving and breaking the frame becomes a strong pull in this group.)*

PENNY: Can I talk about a group I am in? I had brought in some cider to this group. I made it myself, we served it, saying how wonderful it was. Within 15 minutes everyone said, "We've all been poisoned." All claimed this. It scared me half to death. They had been saying how motherly it was for me to serve this, but I felt these people were going to die. I don't know how it fits in, but I was afraid I was going to throw up. I'm having the same feelings now.

KIM: I thought you were going to tell us about conflict and it scared me *(picking up on the terror theme expressed by Penny but talking to Cliff)*. I got scared. I felt anger here—direct conflict. The image I had was this fleeting one of a group I did years ago in which a client began decompensating in the group and raging at me. I didn't know how to handle it. I felt angry and scared. The terror is what scares me here: competition, control, issues of sex, anger at not being nice, it includes all that here. That's when I felt it's just going to go away, but will come back and get me. I want it to be expressed right now. *(This member's associations and feelings indicate that a level of terror is now in the room, and its source is the possibility of loss of control with group or individual decompensation. Also, there is fear of the unknown and the potential emergence of chaos.)*

LEADER: By whom?

KIM: By Jan. I was feeling you were being singled out to engage in battle. Like saying "What are you picking on me for?"

LEADER: Also, there is a feeling that the leader, taking in this delicious drink, had poisoned the group, brought in contaminated food for the group, and I'm wondering if people might not be feeling that I have done the same thing here, and the only way out would be to break the frame and go get a real doctor to take care of the damage. *(The leader obviously feels that interpretation of the process is indicated and that a greater level of awareness of the meaning of the material is desirable at this point.)*

BEVERLY: I don't feel this. I find the group interesting and exciting, and not dangerous. *(She comes out on the excitement side of the danger and terror, and also the approaching of the unknown. She is speaking also for the subgroup that feels able to support this search. On the other hand, it can also be seen as a resistance to further exploration of the terror.)*

LEADER: But are there people here to join Penny in this?

LISA: I had an image of one hostile woman in a bereavement group, who got provocative, and a man got up and grabbed this woman by the arm, and we asked him to leave. Had we set enough boundaries? And here, we didn't have a sense of what the boundaries would be. And here, what were we going to face here? No real framework or contract here. In our group, we didn't do it clearly enough.

LEADER: Faulty leading. *(Here the leader begins trying to accept the projective identification, that is, anger from group members for not taking better care of them. At this moment, the group process and the parallel process merge. That is, it is the leader's supposition that a basic dependency assumption is at work here, not only because it is a beginning group supervisory session, but more important because it is at the heart of the psychodynamics of the case being presented and is given full sway through the parallel process in the group.)*

CLIFF: I felt like you structured it for us, you said you don't want us to interpret and analyze, just share what we have about what's coming up. It released me from the concern about being appropriate: Am I supervising, etc.? The frame was set. *(This group member reiterates his feeling of safety and affirms the creative unconscious work the group has been doing. The dialectic between safety versus danger, risk versus retreat, and exploration versus flight is getting articulated.)*

PRESENTER: (Joining Cliff's subgroup) I must have felt safe too, because I have no idea now of what was so scary. What happened that people are talking about being poisoned?

KIM: I was scared about the anger being expressed and that I can't trust anyone will deal with this. Aren't we going to talk about it? I better do it myself. Then I get angry at not being taken care of by the leader. *(This member fully verbalizes the recent group dynamic.)*

PRESENTER: That is helpful.

JAN: I've been waiting it out here, and watching what was happening, not wanting to make it a therapy experience as much as whatever this is. David brought me into the fray, and where is he now? It's not my job to take care of all the spontaneous reactions. He's the leader, that's his job, he is supposed to take care of all this. I thought about how we say this to patients, pull them into it when we say, "Say whatever you want," and then we react, and what happens with it?

LEADER: I stimulated you to speak and then dropped you. *(A new but similar way of expressing the dynamic between the presenter and Doug is paralleled in Jan's reaction to the leader.)*

KIM: I was feeling angry with David. It had to do with the hostility. It felt like a potential fight. I feared that it could get out of control. Someone I worked with did get out of control.

LEADER: And what happened?

KIM: He raged at me and others and left. And was hospitalized. And your Doug is leaving. And people were leaving. And that's my issue.

LEADER: So could you talk to me directly?

KIM: I feel like you should make sure that nobody leaves, and nobody gets hurt, and nobody goes crazy. I want you to make sure that they get taken care of. *(Thus the frame, safety, boundaries containing the affect and unconscious rage are the paramount issues. As in all analytic work, these verbalizations work to secure the frame further and diminish the potential for acting out.)*

KIM: I'm struggling with these issues, not wanting to hurt and not wanting anyone to get hurt and yet wanting people to express feelings and get through them. I wasn't angry at you when you brought up sex. It was safe to say sex. But when it turned into anger, I wanted you (addressing the leader) to make it safe. Maybe that goes to the beginning, when you got up and locked the door. I thought that was wonderful. Thank you. Safety is the issue for me and how you should make it safe. And how it makes me angry if I get an intimation that you are not doing that.

BETSY: When Penny moved (she had changed her seat), I felt like moving over there, and I'll tell you why. It was okay for Cliff to have his opinion. He said it. And she worked it out. She needed to say that, and he needed to say that. I said what I needed to say so I reached a level of comfort. I have struggled with not interpreting for others . . . I have respect for the process. And I can just get up and go there *(change her seat, or change her internal situation in the group).* Maybe I will. It was also very hot until I said that (a lot of laughter). *(This group member affirms the proposition that whatever we feel and need to say in the group is okay. And this is in spite of the residue of anxiety that she and others still feel.)*

PENNY: She said she was hot, and I was sitting and watching her and realized that you (Susan) haven't gotten into the water yet. *(No one in this group is to be left out. No one is to contain anything without making it a part of the group experience and knowledge bank.)*

SUSAN: I was getting a headache. I was making too many judgments about what I was thinking to say anything. I felt unable to say any of them. I will. One thing: I kept having an image of a client of mine who has a sexualized transference to me, and I have thought a lot about whether I have provoked that in him. Was I responsible? This is a 17 year old, and I thought about one time he was in my office, and he pushed the table across the room toward me, and another time he pushed something off the table onto the floor and I kept thinking that the anger and the sexuality are all mixed up in it. Maybe your client is the same. There's something coercive about it: He's not just sexual, it's angry sexual. He's provocative. *(This is a complex communication to the group, expressing first a psychosomatic complaint—the headache—that she is sitting with, the source of which seems to be suppression of thoughts and feelings for fear of judgment about them. With the lifting of censorship comes an association to a young man who is full of libidinal and aggressive energy that is unable to find direct expression in the therapy. She now allows for the possibility that she has participated in some way in stimulating these feelings in the treatment while not providing some way to verbally deal with them, a likely connection and parallel to the presenter and Doug.)*

CONNIE: Feels hungry again, like with Doug.

LEADER: (To the presenter) I wonder now if you could bring the two of you a little more directly into the room. Just imagining the two of you here.

PRESENTER: It's a real sense of sadness (begins to cry). I feel how vulnerable and alone he feels. He can't use what's around him. The group cares for him genuinely, and he doesn't allow himself to use that. *(There is a shift in the presenter's feelings toward the patient. She is not, however, fully allowing herself to care for him, substituting the group response to Doug for her own feelings. The leader's directive suggestion to her represented a shift in his position indicating, probably, an awareness that the experiential part of the workshop will soon end, and a desire to bring meaningful closure to the experience.)*

BETSY: When you were talking, I kind of got in your shoes with you, and thinking he wants me to take care of him, and maybe I want to and maybe I don't. And the conflict was with me. Making that decision. *(She accurately and empathically picks up the presenter's softening in her feelings toward Doug as well as her continued ambivalence about actually taking care of him.)*

PENNY: I was getting sad. Loss, everything was about loss. I just lost a lot of people this year, including my mother. I was walking around mourning, and I was so shocked when you were sad, and crying, and I thought that it is not just me. It put me back in the room. I don't want him to leave your group. *(The group seems focused now on the loss theme and may reflect the loss the presenter felt underneath her anger at Doug's talk of leaving the group or moving away from her emotionally, as well as the loss he felt when she left the group and stopped attending to him. Penny in her comment exhibits the satisfaction that often occurs in group when a member who thought his or her feelings were privately painful finds them resonating with others in the group.)*

CINDY: I was very admiring of how clear and direct you were about coming here and wanting some help and asking for it. But I have been wondering . . . because I have to leave now. . . . (This member also announced early that she had to leave one half hour early, the second member to leave.)

PRESENTER: I wish you weren't leaving. *(Continuing the parallel process.)*

BEVERLY: I was wondering about Doug's losses.

PRESENTER: They have been tremendous. His dad left when he was young, and his mom was unable to cope emotionally, and Doug was taking care of things for her and never feeling he was taken care of. I was trying to make the connection between this and the issues of mine that are getting kicked off.

LEADER: Can you say what issues of yours?

PRESENTER: I haven't had any obvious losses. The closest thing I can associate to is one day when the sitter called up crying and said, "The baby . . ." and for a split second, I thought my baby had died, and for three days I was incredibly off base.

LEADER: I think that is very relevant. About what he needs from you.

PRESENTER: I did think about groups I do when I'm with my little girl, and I think of the parenting she gets, and I think of all those people who don't get it and will never get it. In my head, I know that therapy is helpful, but I think you can't do enough.

CLIFF: Did you get it as a child?

PRESENTER: Yes, I did. I got a lot of stuff.

LEADER: Well, you left and came back. Doug shared a great deal with you around that: His wife had a baby, and he's your baby.

PRESENTER: He lost both his mothers, his wife is taking care of this baby, and he has anger about it.

BILL: I get very close to the people in the groups I run and then there is the deprivation, and then there is nothing.

LEADER: (Watching the clock) I would like us to wind down now.

CONNIE: It was a help when you expressed that sadness.

PRESENTER: I was crying this morning. I don't do that when I am running groups.

CONNIE: I don't sob, but I get teary, and it helps me to get fed more there, giving myself permission to let this happen.

CLIFF: I was very moved by how much Doug is getting from you. How much concern you have for him, trying to treat him right, bringing him up here.

LEADER: I'd like to switch into a more didactic mode and process what we did today. What we learned and didn't learn. How people feel.

CONNIE: The group seemed to get animated quickly around sex and anger, and now I'm hearing so much about depression and sadness. Was the early sexuality a defense against the sadness and emptiness? Did we move into an as-if intimacy, running from the feeling of being underfed?

BEVERLY: The hunger we picked up early. Your ice cream image picked it up quickly, and my hunger at the time aligned with that.

KIM: I learned more about everybody, and a lot made sense. It's sort of amazing.

CLIFF: Your instructions helped a lot in keeping the frame, in terms of not being a therapist. And we participated in something in a parallel way with what is going on with Doug and you. Your issues got played out here, and I hope you can integrate some of that.

TRISH: I feel okay. I started out feeling anxious because of no set rules. I learned I don't have to do everything. I can let things take their course, and if things aren't okay you can deal with it. That's been hard for me over the years.

PENNY: This clarified many things that have not been clear to me in the last few weeks. I feel more clear about things. But where to go? . . . I need to be fed by you didactically now.

BILL: I liked the way you kept us with our emotional experience. We touched a basic human experience here.

SUSAN: What often stops me in my own work is wanting to stop ambiguity and make everything make sense, and here everything was ambiguous. I had no idea where anything was going, and in some way it made sense inside even when things were totally ambiguous, and I liked that feeling. It felt good to feel it.

(The leader briefly reviews the key concepts outlined earlier and applies them to this group process.)

LEADER: The presenter brought in the unconscious block that existed between her and Doug. The group started to work on that. If we had told her what it was about and what to do directly, she would have heard it in an undigestible form. The work of the group was to work out what she has not worked out yet. We the group worked unconsciously to identify with her, and that is what took place. My first image of ice cream told me there was a nutritional, feeding, mother-child dependency component here. I didn't know exactly what it meant; you then came forth with hunger, there's a hunger here, so that's one central dimension of the case.

Another important feature of this process is ambiguity, which Susan refers to as "things making sense even when nothing was clear, when things felt totally ambiguous." We know what we are doing even when we don't know that we know it. At the same time, the process is tenuous and feels as if it can be broken off at any point without resolution, and no one will ever come to feel that they know anything at all. One can liken this process to the creating of anything: a book, a poem, a painting, or what not, in which the product is not known in advance and is often described by its creator as discovered along the way. What keeps it going frequently is the abiding faith and energy of the creator; in our case, conviction or faith that the group's turmoil, anxiety, and suffering will produce clarity, growth, and understanding without hurting, defiling, or injuring the presenter or fellow group members.

Keeping the frame, having the frame tested, was a prominent aspect both in this particular group, through the parallel process, and more generally in this kind of group. Very early, we had two people saying they had to leave early without explaining to the group anything about why. They announced they were not happy about doing so at the time of their leaving. At another time, I locked the door to keep people from coming in, and one of you felt grateful for that, as it made you feel the frame was tight and we could hold it. Of course, the presenter began the presentation with information about her patient breaking the frame. Also, the presenter broke the frame of her group by taking leave. In a parallel way, in our process, it seemed very important that we remain a group by maintaining our frame.

But more generally, in this kind of group you can frequently reach a point at which it can become extremely uncomfortable, just as in therapy when projective identification occurs. In this group, the first important moment was when Betsy wanted to leave: You were speaking for the group. The second important moment concerned a leader failing to do something (referring to Cliff and Jan). The poison thing was important. That association was to breaking the frame by bad mothering, poisoned food leading to the break in the mother-child bond, which leads to panic, and a "let's get out of here" reaction. These are very important moments in groups, when the leader feels "I'm really losing it, it's really going down the drain, I can't hold onto it." So I focused my energies on the frame, interpreting it in terms of the group process, keeping it alive. Going through the bad moments and getting to the other side. The sexual part? I think that's a component of this case. I don't think we worked it through enough, which is why this meal feels only partially digested; it's still a stumbling block. I'm referring to unfinished pieces to our work that we would need to work out.

PRESENTER: When I came here, my sense was, if I don't talk about this, I am going to go back into group and become rigid because of my anger at him. Now I am not so angry with him. I'm feeling softer and more nurturing and wanting to work on it with him with that sense of myself.

(The patient's longings for love and nurturing and his powerful unfulfilled dependency needs gave rise transferentially to anger at the therapist, which led to devaluing comments and dis-

tancing as well as acting out behaviors. These behaviors stimulated a countertransferential anger in the therapist, who felt devalued and abandoned by the patient. In accord with Searles' (1955) analysis of the parallel process, it seems that the therapist unconsciously identified with the criticisms and the devalued feelings stimulated by the patient. Because of her own internal resentment of this state of being, she felt unable to explore analytically the meaning of Doug's behavior in relation to her. This was not openly analyzed and explained to her, in keeping with the rationale and methodology of this group supervisory model. What the group attempted was a working through of the unexplored longings between them, which when unexpressed led to the devaluing, critical, competitive behavior of the patient. In this group, the different perspectives offered through immediate emotional contact among the members allowed the presenter to move to a different emotional stance vis-à-vis the patient. In her last comment, she expresses this quite nicely. A full cognitive explanation of what took place in the group as just described would, at this stage of the process, probably have been a useful offering to her, and one we believe she would have grasped immediately.)

CONCLUSION

Those advocating a group setting in which to conduct supervision believe that two heads (or three, or four, etc.) are better, wiser, and more creative than one. Those advocating for experiential group supervision believe additionally that two heads are qualitatively different from one and that the potential for creative work finds its source in waters other than the more traditional form of case discussion.

The latter group believes that most therapist difficulties brought to supervision that are not a result of inexperience or lack of knowledge or both are due to not well-understood countertransference issues of the therapist. The more usual group supervision format involves a therapist presenting his or her difficulty to six or seven listeners who act as supervising colleagues in an attempt to unravel the case problem in order to help the therapist in difficulty. We have presented a model in which the blocked state will "come into the room" in a parallel way and can be most effectively handled through the unconscious of the group, whose members agree to undergo their own emotional process along with the presenter. We construe it as really working along with one's colleague instead of just empathizing and sharing ideas. From our perspective, it is this collaboration, as demonstrated in the excerpts we have presented, that released the creative energy that allowed the presenter to move from the place she began to an entirely different one emotionally by the end of the session.

This kind of supervisory experience is like taking a journey with destination unknown and, in that sense, resembles a therapy process without being one. It can be a powerful experience, often quite moving, and has been described by participants over time as valuable, different, freeing, and intense. The procedure assumes a certain level of therapeutic sophistication and training and is generally not advised for beginning group therapists. When one is trying to learn the rudiments of practicing individual and/or group psychotherapy, the notion of parallel process seems like just so much icing on a huge and undigested piece of cake. Beginning practitioners usually have not had enough personal therapy and are not used to delving inside and using themselves in the way this method requires. A more experienced group can absorb and integrate a less experienced person, but such a participant often defers to the more experienced, feels out of his or her depth, and gets less from the experience.

The leader must also be experienced in running groups, since he or she is often required to do considerable holding and containing for the group. Our example included a clear instance of this. Often these groups reach a point at which the group integrity becomes threatened. It feels as if a high anxiety wave has entered the room and gripped the leader and members. They become unsure whether to go on, and the entire supervisory effort feels as if it is about to fail. If at those moments the leader holds course, the result is a further freeing of the energy and resources of the group, which then continues its process and moves on toward solution. In this sense, the method can be thought of as radioactive, in that it is rich in energy and power, but potentially destructive if held in the wrong hands or used in the wrong way. The group does not succeed when the parallel process is not fully understood by the leader and the group, but rather is taken too literally, a parallel to what occurred in the therapy session that provided the raw material for the excerpts in this chapter. Schermer (1994) points out in his chapter on group therapy theory and history, "so-called 'regressive' group phenomena are not merely 'primitive' or 'distorted' but also possess the potential for self and group transformations. Further, that deep internal changes cannot occur without allowing regressive processes which may at times be quite disturbing and distressing to all concerned" (p. 31). This description fairly captures the process we have presented in our example of experiential group supervision. Another special advantage of the model is that it also has a training function. Not only is supervision taking place, but members have the opportunity to work with their own countertransferential responses to the clinical and personal material presented. This becomes a reproduction in milder form of what a therapist is asked to do in all therapy sessions, namely, to perceive, feel, process, and reflect the material in a form that is useful to the patient.

REFERENCES

Abroms, G. M. (1977). Supervision as metatherapy. In F. W. Kaslow & Associates (Eds.), *Supervision, consultation, and staff training in the helping professions* (pp. 81–99). San Francisco: Jossey-Bass.

Agazarian, Y., & Peters, R. (1981). *The visible and invisible group.* London and New York: Tavistock/Routledge.

Alonso, A. (1985). *The quiet profession.* New York: Macmillan.

Alonso, A., & Rutan, S. (1988). Shame and guilt in supervision. *Psychotherapy, 25,* 576–581.

Aronson, M. (1990). A group therapist's perspectives on the use of supervisory groups in the training of psychotherapists. *Psychoanalysis and Psychotherapy, 8,* 88–94.

Behr, H. L. (1995). The integration of theory and practice. In M. Sharpe (Ed.), *The third eye: Supervision of analytic groups* (pp. 4–17). London and New York: Routledge.

Berman, A. L. (1975). Group psychotherapy training. *Small Group Behavior, 6,* 325–344.

Bion, W. R. (1961). *Experiences in groups.* London: Tavistock.

Bromberg, P. (1982). The supervisory process and parallel process in psychoanalysis. *Contemporary Psychoanalysis, 18,* 92–111.

Coché, E. (1977). Supervision in the training of group therapists. In F. W. Kaslow & Associates (Eds.), *Supervision, consultation, and staff training in the helping professions.* San Francisco: Jossey-Bass.

Counselman, E., & Gompert, P. (1993). Psychotherapy supervision in small leader-led groups. *Group, 17,* 25–32.

Dewald, P. (1987). *Learning process in psychoanalytic supervision: complexities and challenges.* Madison, CT: International Universities Press.

Dies, R. R. (1980). Group psychotherapy: Training and supervision. In A. K. Hess (Ed.), *Psychotherapy supervision: Theory, research and practice* (pp. 337–366). New York: Wiley.

Doehrman, M. (1976). Parallel processes in supervision and psychotherapy. *Bulletin of the Menninger Clinic, 40,* 1–104.

Eckstein, R., & Wallerstein, R. S. (1958). *The teaching and learning of psychotherapy.* Madison, CT: International Universities Press.

Ettin, M. F. (1995). From one to another: Group consultation for group psychotherapy. *Group, 19,* 3–18.

Fleming, J., & Benedek, T. (1966). *Psychoanalytic supervision.* Madison, CT: International Universities Press.

Gediman, H. K., & Wolkenfeld, F. (1980). The parallelism phenomenon in psychoanalysis and supervision: Its reconsideration as a triadic system. *Psychoanalytic Quarterly, 49,* 234–254.

Hearst, L. E., & Brown, R. (1995). Simultaneous supervision and personal analysis. In M. Sharpe (Ed.). *The third eye: Supervision of analytic groups* (pp. 25–35). London and New York: Routledge.

Hess, A. K. (Ed.). (1980). *Psychotherapy supervision.* New York: Wiley.

Kutter, P. (1993). Direct and indirect ("reversed") mirror phenomena in group supervision. *Group Analysis, 26,* 177–181.

McGee, T. F. (1974). The triadic approach to supervision in group psychotherapy. *International Journal of Group Psychotherapy, 28,* 471–476.

McGee, T. F., & Schuman, B. N. (1970). The nature of the co-therapy relationship. *International Journal of Group Psychotherapy, 20,* 25–36.

Mintz, E. E. (1978). Group supervision: An experiential approach. *International Journal of Group Psychotherapy, 28,* 467–479.

Ogden, T. H. (1982). Projective identification and psychotherapeutic technique. Northvale, NJ: Jason Aronson.

Ormont, L. (1970). The use of objective countertransference to resolve group resistances. *Group Process, 3,* 95–110.

Rioch, M. (1970). The work of Wilfred Bion on groups. *Psychiatry, 33,* 56–66.

Sadock, B. J. & Kaplan, H. I. (1971). Training and standards in group psychotherapy. In H. I. Kaplan & B. J. Sadock (Eds.), *Comprehensive group psychotherapy.* Baltimore: Williams & Wilkins.

Schermer, V. L. (1994). Between theory and practice, light and heat: On the use of theory in the "Ring of Fire." In V. L. Schermer & M. Pines (Eds.), *Ring of fire: Primitive affects and object relations in group psychotherapy* (pp. 9–35). London and New York: Routledge.

Schuman, E. P., & Fulop, G. (1989). Experiential group supervision. *Group Analysis, 22,* 387–396.

Searles, H. F. (1955). The informational value of the supervisor's emotional experiences. *Psychiatry, 18,* 135–146.

Sproul-Boulton, R., Nitsun, M., & Knowles, J. (1995). Supervision in the national health service. In M. Sharpe (Ed.), *The third eye: Supervision of analytic groups* (pp. 71–87). London and New York: Routledge.

Tauber, L. E. (1978). Choice point analysis-formulation, strategy, intervention, and result in group process therapy and supervision. *International Journal of Group Psychotherapy, 28,* 163–184.

Wallerstein, R. S. (Ed.) (1981). *Becoming a psychoanalyst.* Madison, CT: International Universities Press.

Yalom, I. D. (1985). *The theory and practice of group psychotherapy* (3rd ed.). New York: Basic Books.

CHAPTER 23

Family Therapy Supervision

HOWARD A. LIDDLE
University of Miami School of Medicine
DANA BECKER
Temple University
GARY M. DIAMOND
Temple University

Clinical supervision is a robust and diverse specialty within contemporary psychotherapy (Alberts & Edelstein, 1990). New debates have begun with many implications for the practice of clinical supervision (Beutler & Kendall, 1995; Christensen & Jacobson, 1994), with a renewed emphasis on the important role of therapist issues in treatment outcome (Crits-Christoph, 1991; Crits-Christoph et al., 1991; Rounsaville, Chevron, Weissman, Prusoff, & Frank, 1986; Rounsaville, O'Malley, Foley, & Weissman, 1988). Essential to the field's survival and development, clinical supervision is a foundational activity within all of the psychotherapeutic professions. Unique literatures, revealing specialty-specific ideas and supervision techniques, exist within fields such as psychology, psychiatry, social work, mental health counseling, nursing, and family therapy. But there is a pronounced lack of relationship among these subspecialties. Whether a version of "disciplinary imperialism" (Wilden, 1985) is at play remains a matter for chroniclers of these specialties to take up, but it is safe to say that communication among the factions within psychotherapy supervision has been less than optimal. Of greater relevance to this chapter is the fact that family therapy supervision and psychotherapy supervision, paralleling the ideological divides that have existed between the parent fields of family therapy and psychotherapy, have not interacted much throughout their respective histories. Like proverbial ships passing in the night, these kindred areas of thinking, research, and practice do not interrelate. For that matter, each barely acknowledges the existence of the other, and they remain intellectual strangers. We address this circumstance—a reality that limits the development of each specialty and, more generally, the development of the specialty of clinical supervision. We present the highlights, core ideas, and innovative and unique methods characteristic of the family-therapy supervision and training specialty. The chapter concludes with recommendations for a multimodal approach to family therapy supervision. This supervision philosophy is presented within a discussion of our experience with *multidimensional family therapy* (Liddle, 1992, 1995), a specialized approach for adolescent drug and behavior problems, developed in clinical research contexts over the last 12 years.

FAMILY THERAPY TRAINING AND SUPERVISION:
GENESIS AND DEVELOPMENT OF A SPECIALTY

Family therapy training and supervision has been a specialty within the family therapy field for more than 25 years (Liddle, 1991). Some family therapy supervisors have an independent identity, sometimes apart from and sometimes in addition to their first professional affiliations (e.g., psychology, psychiatry, social work) (Saba & Liddle, 1986). The first papers in training and supervision were written beginning in the late 1960s and extending through the mid-1970s (Ferber & Mendelsohn, 1969; Ferber, Mendelsohn, & Napier, 1972; Kempster & Savitsky, 1967; Mendelsohn & Ferber, 1972; Sander & Beels, 1970). Early writings tended to focus on narrow content areas, such as the use of cotherapy as a training device (Stier & Goldenberg, 1975). Bodin (1969) was among the first to specify the varied content spheres of the disciplines or specialties, many of which would become core elements over the years. Bodin addressed trainee characteristics and context (i.e., how training differs according to professional settings and discipline) and training methods that would become characteristic of family therapy teaching methods (e.g., videotape, group supervision).

By the mid-1970s, a more complex literature was taking form in the family therapy training and supervision specialty. Papers appeared on new techniques (Bardill, 1976; Bodin, 1972; Hare-Mustin, 1976), models of supervision (Ard, 1973; Birchler, 1975; Cohen, Gross, & Turner, 1976), training program descriptions (Constantine, 1976; Hare & Frankena, 1972; Miyoshi & Lieberman, 1969; Tucker, Hart, & Liddle, 1976), trainee's own family as it relates to becoming a family therapist (Ferber, 1972; Framo, 1975; Guerin & Fogarty, 1972), training tailored to a specific context (Epstein & Levin, 1973; Malone, 1974; Talmadge, 1975), and implementation problems and politics idiosyncratic to training (Ehrlich, 1973; Framo, 1976; Haley, 1976; Liddle, 1978; Shapiro, 1975a, 1975b; Stanton, 1975a, 1975b). Throughout this phase, despite an increase in both volume and sophistication, this body of literature still lacked any coherent conceptual, technical, or evaluative focus.

Several seminal works were published during this era, however, and they remain historically and conceptually significant. The first of these, written by Cleghorn and Levin (1973), offered a systematic framework for organizing the individual's thinking about training. These authors identified and categorized three sets of skills for the family therapist: perceptual, conceptual, and executive. Their classification framework provided family therapy teachers with a valuable detailed and practical conceptual scaffolding. The Cleghorn and Levin framework was generative, eventually allowing particular family therapy schools to classify the methods of their approach according to similar categories, setting into stark relief, for the first time, the divergences and similarities among the models of the day (Tomm & Wright, 1979).

A second seminal work of this first era was Montalvo's (1973) article on live supervision. This paper defined the process of live supervision, a revolutionary supervision method that positioned the supervisor to observe and guide a session as it occurred by telephoning instructions into the therapist. This article is noteworthy for its lack of dramatic treatment of this specialty-transforming topic. In subsequent years, although live supervision was to become controversial (Nichols, Nichols, & Hardy, 1990), Montalvo's paper still stood as the definition of a unique and novel supervision method, containing as it did ideas that eventually would cohere into a new philosophy of supervision consistent with family therapy's theoretical and methodological framework.

The most comprehensive early exposition of the new epistemology of family therapy training was a chapter by Haley (1976) in his influential text *Problem Solving Therapy*. This single chapter constitutes a third major contribution: an organization and extension of the ideas outlined in Montalvo's classic live supervision paper. "Problems of Training Therapists" (Haley, 1976) proposed a multifaceted conceptual framework for devising a training orientation. Haley articulated therapy orientations on four dimensions: spontaneous versus planned change, personal growth of the trainee versus orientation, insight or understanding versus action as a cause for change, and self-report (of the therapist's work to a supervisor) versus live and videotape observation of the therapist's sessions. This framework defined and cast the molar-level ideas that were taking shape in family therapy at the time into an organizing schema for conceptualizing therapy and supervision. Haley (1988) extended this training framework by including three additional dimensions of possible training focus: the problem situation, the therapist's personality, and skill supervision. Taken together, these two publications of what would become fundamental parameters for conceptualizing family therapy training and supervision organized the increasingly diverse and numerous family therapy training models. They provided a template for supervisors to use in their clinical supervision. Today, Haley's ideas about supervision and training are best summarized in his text on the topic (Haley, 1996).

Using many of these early ideas to represent the existing organization of the specialty, Liddle, Breunlin, and Schwartz (1988) reflected the heterogeneity of the family therapy field during the 1980s. The central theme of isomorphism between an individual's training philosophy and therapy methods offered a core element to the summarization of the specialty (as did a focus on how to teach the interactional or family therapy viewpoint; Sluzki, 1974). Liddle, Davidson, and Barrett (1988) set out to represent the wide range of topics, ideas, subspecialties, contexts, and literature of the family therapy training and supervision specialty at the time.

A second era in the development of family therapy training and supervision began in the late 1970s and early 1980s as the field began to reevaluate its assumptions and methods and raise questions about its effectiveness. Several comprehensive reviews reached similar conclusions about the family therapy training specialty. Concrete suggestions were made about the lack of theory development, the failure to integrate knowledge from psychotherapy supervision, the need to investigate the role that context plays in the training of family therapists; and the urgent need to evaluate procedures for determining the effectiveness of supervision and training models and techniques (Everett & Koerpel, 1986; Ganahl, Ferguson, & L'Abate, 1985; Liddle & Halpin, 1978; Olson, Russell, & Sprenkle, 1980). Over the next decade, certain areas of the specialty were developed (e.g., increase in specificity about training procedures and articulation of training program structures and contents, tailored to contexts and disciplines). At the same time, other areas that were deemed in need of significant development (e.g., theory development and research) did not evolve at a rapid pace (Anderson, Rigazio-DiGilio, & Kunkler, 1995; Liddle, 1991).

Distinctions and Similarities Between Family Therapy Supervision and Individual Psychotherapy Supervision

There are theoretical and practical characteristics that distinguish family therapy supervision from supervision ideas and methods in individual psychotherapy. Perhaps the most clear distinctions can be illustrated in terms of the isomorphic nature of training and supervision (Haley, 1976; Liddle & Saba, 1983; Montalvo, 1973; Sluzki, 1974). This framework, an attempt to build theory in the family therapy training and supervision area, argued for the use of an individual's theory of therapy (e.g., principles about how change is brought about) as a guiding force in developing a theory of training/supervision (e.g., if a "learning by doing" philosophy is used in one's therapy, it can be used in one's supervision as well). Isomorphism can clarify the differences between family therapy and individual therapy supervision. It suggests we examine the theoretical and method/technique variances between family and individual therapy to understand the root differences between their corresponding models of training and supervision. In family therapy, much attention has been paid to patterns of interaction among family members, and in recent years, to patterns of interaction between family members and extrafamilial sources of influence (i.e., neighborhood, schools, health or welfare systems, juvenile justice systems). Individual dynamics, at least in classic versions of family therapy, are not attended to and are certainly not given the same theoretical weight or emphasis on mechanisms of change as are interactional processes (particularly interactions among family members). With these distinctions between therapies drawn, it is not surprising that in family therapy supervision, it is preferable to have direct access to the interaction among family members via live or videotape supervision. Furthermore, because particular models of family therapy emphasize an active, directive, non-insight-oriented approach to change, the live supervision method is syntonic with this therapy philosophy, because it presents the supervisor, the therapist, and the case with immediate opportunities for supervisory input. These within-session, midcourse corrections are not intended to provide a therapist with insight into interactional processes (either into himself or herself vis-à-vis family members or family members vis-à-vis one another). Their aim is to offer immediate, practical, concrete directives or suggestions about how to rechart the course and outcome of a session. Thus, it is important to the tradition of family that the development of particular training and supervision methods is thought of as reflecting the theoretical principles of the therapy approach that the supervision methods are designed to teach (Liddle, 1988).

Family therapy supervision faces challenges similar to those being addressed in the individual psychotherapy supervision field (Liddle, 1991; Watkins, 1995). For example, considerable energies have been expended in the service of creating new training and supervision models that account for gender, race, ethnicity, and cultural factors (Falicov, 1988; Hardy & Laszloffy, 1992; Lappin, 1983; Wheeler, Avis, Miller, & Chaney, 1985). Also, attempts have been made to use empirically based developmental knowledge in treatment and clinical training (Kaye, 1985; Liddle, 1988). As in the field of individual psychotherapy, contemporary family therapy models and supervision models have become more integrative and idiosyncratic to meet the demands of specific populations and specific clinical problems (Anderson et al., 1995; Liddle, 1996).

CHARACTERISTICS OF CONTEMPORARY FAMILY THERAPY SUPERVISION

Teaching the Observation and Analysis of Family and Multisystem Processes

The emphasis on teaching trainees to conceptualize a person's or family's behavior in systemic terms varies greatly according to the model of family therapy treatment/training, and it has not been until recently that attempts have been made to provide a unifying framework (Sluzki, 1983). Certain supervision models, such as the Milan systemic training program, place great emphasis on the trainees' theoretical development and on fostering an epistemological shift, whereas other therapy schools have focused on the therapist's family of origin (Bowen theory) or on technique acquisition (Liddle et al., 1988).

Methods used to teach therapists how to think in family therapy terms and how to conduct therapy consistent with a family systems philosophy vary considerably. Several important publications have provided versions of how to facilitate this conceptual shift (Haley, 1980; Minuchin, 1974; Sluzki, 1974; Watzlawick, Weakland, & Fisch, 1974). Some approaches are more didactic, others more experiential. For example, Coppersmith (1985) devised a series of exercises to teach trainees to think in terms of triads; Green and Sager (1982) created a series of writing assignments; and Street and Foot (1984) used videotape vignettes to help trainees practice formulation of presenting problems in interactional terms. Sometimes particular techniques of therapy are taught through methods devised just for that technique. Fleuridas, Nelson, and Rosenthal (1986) have devised a training protocol to teach the circular questioning technique; and Constantine, Stone-Fish, and Piercy (1984) have developed a procedure for teaching positive connotation. Other approaches to teach systems thinking include techniques used by therapists during the course of treatment. The use of case conceptualization outlines (Schwartz, 1981), concept cards that use case material to help ideas from the literature come alive in an immediate and personally meaningful way (Liddle, 1981), and structured interviews (Weber, McKeever, & McDaniel, 1985) are tools designed to help trainees perceive and conceptualize cases systemically.

Live and Videotape Supervision

Live supervision in family therapy was first introduced by Jay Haley, Braulio Montalvo, and Salvador Minuchin in the development of an innovative clinical model at the Philadelphia Child Guidance Clinic in the early 1970s, and it was first described by Montalvo (1973) in his now classic paper. This procedure refers to the supervisor's observation of a session and guidance of the events and interactions of that same session *as they happen* (Colapinto, 1988). Live supervision allowed supervisors and colleagues to witness the actual content and process of a session without relying on the therapist's memory or interpretation of therapy events. Through direct observation, supervisors identify patterns, redundancies, behaviors, or important content that the therapist did not observe or to which he or she did not attend. Then, critically, these observations are transformed into suggestions during the session, which help to reshape the course and outcome of a given session. Live supervision is not without its critics. Criticisms have included concerns about the encouragement of trainee dependence, intrusion into the privacy of the therapy, disruption of the natural rhythms and processes of sessions, family members' reactions to the call-ins, and the potential development of a mechanical approach to therapy, among others (see review by Liddle, 1991). One response to these criticisms has been the identification of common processes that lead to ineffective live supervision and suggestions for conducting live supervision competently (Schwartz, Liddle, & Breunlin, 1988; Westheafer, 1984). Research on the impact of live supervision on therapists and trainees has not supported fears about potentially harmful effects (e.g., Liddle et al., 1988).

Like live supervision, videotape supervision affords the supervisor a delayed but uncensored view of in-session client and therapist behaviors. Without the opportunity or requirement to respond to therapy events in real time, the supervisor functions more as an analyst of or commentator on the session's events. This permits the supervisor to challenge the supervisee to generate therapeutic alternatives in a context with fewer immediate performance demands. There have been remarkably few systematic descriptions or studies of videotape use in training and supervision. Breunlin, Karrer, McGuire, and Cimmarusti (1988) suggest that videotape supervision is most effective when there are focused goals, when tape segments are selected to offer views of diverse therapist behavior, and when the supervisor moderates the therapist's reactions and self-evaluation when watching the tapes. There are different benefits to be gained by using live supervision, videotape supervision, and case review/delayed supervision. One contribution of the new, comprehensive supervision models is their specification of the links, boundary conditions (i.e., limits), synergistic effects, and guidelines for the concurrent use of diverse supervision methods such as case management and live and videotape supervision (see Haber, 1996; Mead, 1990).

Isomorphism

The concept of isomorphism has been used in the family therapy literature to describe the reciprocal relationship between the therapist-client interaction and the supervisor-therapist relationship (Haley, 1980; Sluzki, 1974). This phenomenon, referred to as the isomorphic nature of training/supervision and therapy, has been described and proposed as a framework that can underlie one's theory of supervision and training. Similar to the psychodynamic concept of parallel processes, isomorphism refers to the tendency of interactions and relational processes between the therapist and client to replicate themselves in the supervisory relationship. Identifying and exploring these patterns can offer important assessment information. Unlike the concept of parallel process, which is meaningful primarily in a perceptual or diagnostic sense, the use of the term *isomorphism* in family therapy connotes that these interactions are subject to change. The family-therapy supervisor uses isomorphism as a cognitive organizer that directs the intention and choice of supervisory interventions. Additionally, the concept of isomorphism provides a template for supervisors to identify the replication of processes across system boundaries that can be facilitative or can be detrimental to both the therapeutic and supervisory systems. Using this perspective, for instance, the supervisor can transform this replication into an intervention, redirecting a therapist's behavior and thereby influencing interactions at various levels of the system. Finally, isomorphism refers to the parallels among the principles that organize therapy and training. One's guiding principles about the goals, methods, mechanisms of change, and means for assessment in therapy aid in guiding one's conceptualization of and behavior in training. In a study providing support for the importance of the isomorphic relationship between supervision and family therapy, when supervisors effectively used support and taught behaviors in phone-in interventions, there was a corresponding effectiveness in trainee's use of these behaviors (Frankel & Piercy, 1990). Furthermore, when both supervisors and therapists effectively used support and taught behaviors, family members responded in a more cooperative fashion (Frankel & Piercy, 1990). The psychotherapy literature has also been interested in the notion of parallelism of therapy and supervision (see Doehrman, 1976).

Developmental Theory

Family therapy has traditionally appreciated the conceptual importance of life-cycle and developmental theory in clinical practice. Life-cycle theory has been used as a lens for understanding both psychopathology in families (Singer & Wynne, 1965) and normal family functioning (Carter & McGoldrick, 1989; Falicov, 1988; Karpel, 1986; Liddle, 1984; Walsh, 1987). Although some in family therapy eschew normative conceptions of families and individuals (e.g., Fisch, 1988), a growing body of work has examined the specific implications of informing the training process with developmental findings. This meaning of the importance of developmental thinking is different from that usually afforded the term in the psychotherapy supervision literature. Developmental thinking in this context refers to the developmental stages of the therapist (Stoltenberg, McNeil, & Crethar, 1994) or the supervisor (Watkins, 1995).

Introducing developmental thinking and content into supervision provides a means of broadening and making more complex a therapist's systemic conceptualization. Whereas the systemic view helps a clinician appreciate the interconnectedness of various system levels and components, developmental thinking locates these levels and components in a life-span context, while also introducing the notion of normative developmental tasks as an informer of therapeutic aims and methods. Therapists can use concepts and findings from the risk and protective factor literature to organize case conceptualization, intervention design, and execution (Liddle, Diamond, Rowe, Schmidt, & Ettinger, in press). For example, two decades of research on adolescent development have reformed psychology's conception of the adolescent individuation process and health-promoting parent-adolescent relationships (Baumrind, 1991; Steinberg, 1990). Establishing a developmental frame around the presenting problem can organize therapy along nonpathological and nontrait-oriented lines (Liddle, 1988). Despite the utility of developmental knowledge in clinical work, there has been almost no literature regarding exactly how to integrate developmental knowledge into family therapy training. Rigazio-DiGilio (Chapter 14, this volume) designed a systemic cognitive-developmental family therapy training model in which therapists are taught to assess and then expand each family member's and family's cognitive worldview. Liddle et al. (in press) have offered a general overview for utilizing developmental knowledge in the clinical practice of family therapy. There remain many questions, however, about how supervisors can go about training therapists to be developmentally oriented (Liddle, 1988).

Developmental frameworks have utility not only for understanding the client but as a metaphor for conceptualizing the process of training therapists. Much as individuals and families pass through definable developmental stages, therapists are thought to follow a developmental path on their way to becoming effective clinicians. In a review examining changes in supervision as therapists gained experience, Stoltenberg et al. (1994) found considerable support for the notion of trainee developmental stage progression. In family therapy, several authors have delineated stages in the development of family therapy trainees (Kantor, 1983; Napier & Whitaker, 1973; Whitaker, 1976). Examples of development in a family therapy trainee might include the acquisition of systemic thinking, increased accommodation to video and live supervision, and the ability to grapple successfully with the complex issues of model integration (Liddle, 1988).

Person of the Therapist

This dimension of the family therapy supervision and training literature should be considered as a potential source of contribution to the psychotherapy literature (e.g., Aponte, 1992, 1994; Minuchin & Fishman, 1981). Although theory and technique are important to the practice of therapy, it is the personal interaction between the therapist and the client/family that provides the context for potential change. Structural family therapy recognizes the central role of the clinician in the therapeutic relationship and process (Colapinto, 1988; Minuchin, 1974; Minuchin & Fishman, 1981), noting that therapists both observe and direct enactments from the *outside* and become actors *within* the family system (Aponte, 1992). The style of the therapist and his or her ability to join with, be a part of, and direct the family effectively is in large part a function of who the clinician is as a person. This includes the therapist's values, experience within his or her family of origin, and relational patterns. Family therapy requires therapists to use themselves (Minuchin & Fishman, 1981). In order to be most effective, therapists must be flexible and have a sufficient repertoire of responses to meet the respective needs of families and family members.

Inevitably, family therapists find themselves in particular interactions or relationships with clients who are familiar to them from their own lives, and these interactions may elicit patterned responses. This phenomenon is similar to what psychodynamic authors term *countertransference*. In order for family therapists not to be driven or constrained in their responses to certain family members or situations, the clinician must have a reasonable sense of the relationship between his or her functioning as a therapist and his or her functioning as a person. When challenged by situations that he or she has found personally difficult, the family therapist must be able to extend him- or herself beyond reflexive responses and find a way to interact that creates an alternative experience for the family. Integrating structural and existential principles and techniques, Aponte (1992) suggests that through live and videotape observation of the therapist's functioning in enactments, supervisors and trainers can gain insight into the therapist's style, strengths, and limitations. Supervisors and trainers help trainees recognize the interrelationship among the relational patterns in client families, their own relational patterns, and how each of these sets of patterns influences the others: "Therapists are trained to observe their own reactions during client transactions and use themselves to create experiences that promote change in the client" (Aponte, 1992, p. 275).

In an attempt to help trainees become aware of their own relational patterns, supervision often focuses on the trainees' relationships with their families of origin and other significant people in their lives. The theory is that by helping supervisees gain insight into such relationships, they will better be able to understand their functioning as clinicians and recognize those areas they must challenge themselves to change. Understandably, such training can become personal, and the boundary between supervision and therapy may appear blurred. The field of family therapy is justly concerned about addressing the issue of dual relationships and the difference between supervision and therapy. In an effort to make a distinction between training and therapy for the therapist, Aponte (1994) emphasizes that personal work on the clinician's family of origin should be related to the trainees' professional work. By helping clinicians become aware of and alter their own functioning in relation to various client families, trainers and supervisors can promote trainees' widest possible use of self in the therapy room (Minuchin & Fishman, 1981).

Research on Family Therapy Training and Supervision

Despite a proliferation of family therapy training and supervision programs, it was not until the last 15 years that research was conducted to assess outcomes. Reviews of research on family therapy training by Kniskern and Gurman (1988) and Avis and Sprenkle (1990) present comprehensive summaries of the current state of the science and outline the conceptual and methodological challenges facing future researchers. Both reviews suggest that in order to evaluate the outcomes of family therapy training and supervision, researchers must identify the specific therapist behaviors and/or skills that the training is seeking to help the therapist acquire, describe in detail the training or supervisory method, adopt or develop valid and reliable instruments to measure change on the salient behaviors or skills, and demonstrate that the acquisition of these behaviors or skills is related to the therapist's heightened effectiveness in helping families to change. Avis and Sprenkle's (1990) literature review on this topic located nine studies that evaluated training outcome and six that pertained to instrument development. Several findings were noteworthy. First, it appears that various forms of family therapy training can increase trainees' cognitive and intervention skills (Churven & McKinnon, 1982; Pulleybank & Shapiro, 1986; Tomm & Leahey, 1980; Tucker & Pinsof, 1984), although the benefit of a particular training program may be mediated by the trainee's level of previous family therapy experience (Zaken-Greenberg & Neimeyer, 1986). Second, cognitive and intervention skills may develop independently of each other (Avis & Sprenkle, 1990). This information has implications for the designing and implementation of training and supervisory models, suggesting that programs should strive to address several areas of therapist functioning (e.g., perceptual, conceptual, and executive skills). These studies mark an important beginning in the attempt by the family therapy field to evaluate if, in what realms, when, and with whom training and supervision are effective. Future research should be designed not only to ensure more methodological control, but also to answer questions about the effectiveness of different training tools and techniques (live supervision, videotape review, readings) and the different contexts and times in which these techniques are employed (in groups, individually, early in training, etc.) (Kniskern & Gurman, 1988).

Multidimensional Therapy and Training Models

As family therapy evolves, treatment models have become less "pure" and more integrative. Integrative treatments frequently employ conceptualizations and techniques derived from multiple family therapy models (i.e., structural and strategic) and can be complex for therapists to learn. Some models require that therapists think and work in multiple domains (i.e., cognitive, affective, and behavioral) and work with clients involved with multiple systems (school, juvenile justice). Therapists working with multidimensional models must be trained to maintain multiple alliances (Liddle, 1995).

In this same tradition, a growing number of agencies and treatment models are incorporating home-based family therapy. Home-based family therapy raises new supervisory challenges. Therapists have less control of the environment when they meet with the family in the family's home. Therapists sometimes encounter ringing phones, uninvited family members, neighbors and friends of the family, some of whom may want to relax or watch television in the room designated for the session. Therapists need to be prepared in supervision to deal with these unexpected circumstances.

A second difficulty with home-based work is the logistics of live supervision. Unlike a clinic office, it is impossible for the supervisor to observe through a one-way mirror. One alternative is to have the supervisor join the therapist for one or more sessions in the family's home. Terming this the *invisible-mirror* technique, Zarski, Greenbank, Sand-Pringle, and Cibik (1991) suggested a framework for incorporating a live supervision session in the middle stage of home-based family therapy. The model addresses issues such as preparing the family for the live-supervised session, the procedure for the session, and processing the experience with the family.

FAMILY THERAPY SUPERVISION IN THE 1990S:
THE CASE OF MULTIDIMENSIONAL FAMILY THERAPY

To illustrate some defining features of the family therapy supervision specialty, the remainder of the chapter outlines the supervision guidelines and methods of multidimensional family therapy (MDFT). A treatment for substance-abusing adolescents and their families (Liddle, 1992, 1995), MDFT is representative of a genre of contemporary family therapy approaches that have been (a) manualized, (b) designed for specific populations and clinical problems, and (c) submitted to empirical scrutiny (Alexander, Holtzworth-Munroe, & Jameson, 1994; Lebow & Gurman, 1995) in outcome (Liddle & Dakof, 1994) and therapy process domains (Diamond & Liddle, 1996; Schmidt, Liddle, & Dakof, 1996).

Supervision in MDFT is illustrative of the changes in and challenges to family therapy training models in the 1980s and 1990s. Therapy models for youths have become more ambitious in recent years. Contemporary family therapy models are influenced by a number of fields and specialties, and these models often try to incorporate many of these influences into their theory and methods. Drawing theory from different sources creates the challenge of mastering more concepts. It also raises the possibility of confusion, because today's integrative models, although inclusive and comprehensive, may not have had sufficient time for the diverse content/methods to cohere into an integrative whole.

The advent of therapy manuals may be a mixed blessing for some of the new family therapy approaches (see Binder & Strupp, 1993; Moras, 1993, for excellent discussions of these issues in psychotherapy). On the one hand, the manualized family therapies create clarity about how the approach is structured and what behaviors are required. Manualized models also offer specifics about the proscribed behaviors, that is, those therapist behaviors that are not permitted or are not recommended within the approach (see Waltz, Addis, Koerner, & Jacobson, 1993). This degree of directiveness rubs some clinicians the wrong way. Just as some therapists were turned off to some of the school-specific precision and exclusion of certain techniques ("That method does not belong in this approach"), today's manualized therapies, in creating a new precision, may also turn away therapists who are disinclined to try models they believe will inhibit their creativity.

Conceptualization and implementation of research-based and population-specific models that have multiple streams of therapeutic and clinical influence make extraordinary and unique demands of therapists—demands that are outside the realm of their experience. These demands must be identified by supervisors in advance, communicated to the therapists, and, from the outset, should be carefully considered when recruiting and training therapists (i.e., in situations in which recruitment is relevant, such as a clinical setting vs. many academic settings). In the MDFT approach, the therapist may spend as much as 40% of his or her time alone with the adolescent and may spend considerable time alone with the teenager's parent(s), preparing each for discussions (enactments) to come and working with each individual as a subsystem of change as well. Consequently, the therapist is expected to have considerable skill in individual psychotherapy as well as an understanding of systems theory and the ability to use family therapy techniques (Liddle, 1995). In contemporary practice, however, it is helpful if clinicians do not make rigid distinctions between individual and family work or categorize some skills as individual therapy skills and others as family therapy skills. In specialized approaches such as MDFT, we look a priori for certain qualities, interests, and skills that are compatible with and seem to be reasonable predictors of a clinician's resonance to and facility with the approach. These predictors are deduced from experience with many clinicians in multiple projects. Thus, the model itself is a primary selector of the therapist.

Multimodal Approaches to Training and Supervision

Family therapy training and supervision, just as the therapy itself, should integrate a variety of modalities, including readings on theory and research, live supervision and videotape review, and written case formulations. Supervision methods are as organic as the therapy methods they seek to teach, and they require the same skills of judgment, context assessment, and clarity about immediate and longer-term supervisory goals (weighed in the context of clinical goals and needs—in Liddle & Schwartz, 1983, see the "urgency principle" of live supervision in which clinical and supervision goals are assessed simultaneously). Supervision methods are crafted to the circumstances and needs of the supervision system, the clinician, and sometimes the case. The supervision system is defined as the gestalt of therapist, case, and context, and this is the unit of assessment and intervention by the supervisor. The complexity inherent in supervision parallels the complexity of family therapy (Liddle, 1988). Inexperienced or unskilled supervisors, like their clinical counterparts who misapply or rigidly apply therapy techniques and watch them fail, often blame the supervision method or the trainee for failure. Some of the pioneers of the family therapy training and supervision specialty, particularly Haley (1976) and Montalvo (1973), were correct to remind us how to take responsibility as supervisors.

Supervisors must be skilled in applying training modalities differently at different stages of supervision and of a therapist's development. For example, live supervision in the early stages of training provides a way for supervisor and therapist to "walk through" cases together. Live supervision gives the supervisee an opportunity to be both supported and challenged, as some research on this method indicates (Liddle et al., 1988; Wright, 1986). Live supervision closely resembles an apprenticeship model of teaching and learning (Montalvo, 1973). Later in training, when the supervisee works on aspects of the approach that are inherently difficult, the therapist knows that, anxiety notwithstanding, he or she will be pushed in live supervision to attack these aspects. At the same time, however, the therapist can be secure in the knowledge that he or she will be assisted when the going gets rough. As we discuss later, many therapists find it difficult to challenge family members' statements or behavior. When used skillfully, live supervision provides emotional support and technical guidance to therapists of all skill and experience levels. Live supervision allows a more knowledgeable and experienced clinician to have access to the family, the therapist, and their interaction. It is frequently this interaction between the family and the therapist that is the assessment unit and target of intervention in live supervision.

For all its manifold uses, live supervision does not provide the opportunity for reflection and observation of greater detail that videotapes can yield. Using videotapes in family therapy supervision is popular and could be considered a hallmark of this approach. Detailed guidelines have been constructed about how to supervise clinicians with videotapes of their sessions (Breunlin et al., 1988). As with live supervision, videotapes are used differently at different stages of training. Initially, therapist and supervisor may watch entire sessions or large portions of sessions together. Later in a therapist's development, when therapist and supervisor are clear on which areas need attention, the therapist, who has become an excellent judge of what has gone well or badly in a session, will select portions of recent videotapes and use his or her supervisor increasingly as a consultant.

The Challenges of Conceptualization

A multisystemic approach reflects recent trends aimed at expanding the clinical focus and scope in the treatment of youth (Henggeler & Borduin, 1990; Liddle, 1996). In MDFT, the therapist must consider the choice of content themes for therapy (e.g., the need for parents of adolescents to understand the difference between parental influence and parental control). In addition, the therapist will have to consider not only who should attend sessions, but also with whom he or she needs to work alone within the space of a single session. The therapist will have to maintain multiple, simultaneous alliances; his or her supervisor will need to assist him or her with the appropriate selection of content, composition, and focus.

As is true in other models of family therapy, therapists who learn the multidimensional approach must develop equal facility in the different realms—the affective, the cognitive, and the behavioral—in which individuals and families operate. Because most clinicians are not equally comfortable in all domains, supervision assists them in developing greater skill in one or more specific areas of work. A supervisor assesses a clinician's strengths and areas needing change. Complex therapy approaches require clinicians to think with complexity and to plan with flexibility, all within a framework in which constituent elements must remain in a given relation to one another. For the MDFT therapist, the premium placed in supervision on "thinking in the room" can initially feel burdensome as he or she struggles to take account of family idiosyncrasies, situational variables, and individual personality styles, as well as the strength of his or her alliance with individual family members and the stage of the therapy.

Process or Content? Not an Either/Or Proposition

In MDFT, as a form of family therapy that seeks to address specific problems with certain populations (i.e., adolescent drug use and associated behavior problems), the content of the therapy matters a great deal. For the supervisee, the need to introduce content themes can pose several dilemmas. If the supervisee concentrates too exclusively on introducing thematic material, he or she will lose focus on other important content and on valuable process information. In order to have resonance, themes must be relevant to issues with which family members are struggling. Inattention to content may cost the therapist valuable opportunities to capitalize on (or, conversely, to challenge) statements by family members that directly relate to the problems they are having. The supervisor aims to direct the therapist's attention to such opportunities ("Do you remember when Mr. Jones said that he just can't follow Tom around everywhere? That would have been a great opportunity to talk about the difference between parental influence and parental control."), just as the therapist aims to direct the family toward issues that are vital to tackle if change is to occur.

Engineering Enactments

Engineering enactments (in-session conversations between family members) is a task for family therapists in many approaches and a critical endeavor in MDFT because of the key role played by enactments in helping to improve the relationship between adolescents and their families. Typically, trainees have a variety of problems helping families with these in-session conversations. Some trainees are reluctant to enter this domain of work entirely. Others appear to be preparing family members almost indefinitely, but actual enactments never ensue. Reluctance seems to stem from therapists' fears that the discussion will "blow up." Trainees do not trust that they have the tools to "fix" a faltering enactment. They may be frightened of the conflict that may emerge, or they may feel uncertain as to how to help people proceed if they have difficulty articulating their feelings or positions.

For trainees who are more willing to lead the family toward enactments, other difficulties can present themselves. Therapists may find themselves taking too much responsibility for moving the discussion along. In practice, they become too central and find themselves talking for individuals. Alternatively, trainees may allow themselves to become so peripheral to the action that they are not able to structure the discussion in productive ways. Some supervisees time enactments poorly, forcing difficult discussions when it is clear that the participants do not have the tools to engage in them or are not in agreement with the aims of the therapy; others wait until the end of a session to push for discussion of emotionally laden issues that need a good deal of time and care to develop. These common therapist difficulties again underscore the interdependence of supervision objectives and the objectives of a particular model of therapy. In these examples, a supervisor assesses a therapist's performance and development against the criteria and demands of a particular approach. Experienced supervisors are experts in knowing about and in communicating concrete suggestions for addressing particular, common challenges within their therapy model. The relationship between the ability to be an expert therapist and an expert supervisor is not established. Our speculation is that, although strong, the relationship is not without variation and complexity. Supervisors certainly must be good communicators about therapy and must know the terrain of therapy thoroughly, including the particular challenges and pitfalls inherent in learning and conducting a specific approach. Certainly the relationship skills used in therapy transfer to supervision. Just as the therapeutic alliance in therapy has been found to have predictive power vis-à-vis outcomes, the same will probably be so in the supervision arena. Many of the supervision methods that are mainstays of family therapy, particularly those that would likely be novel to and that might prove stressful for any clinician (e.g., live supervision), require a supervision relationship characterized by trust, respect, and support.

The supervisor must take care to assess the underlying difficulties so that he or she can plan a series of steps over the course of training to address them. The first stage of this plan necessarily involves ensuring that the trainee has adequate tools for the task; the midphase involves monitoring enactments closely in live supervision. In the final phase, the supervisor supports the therapist by reminding him or her that both the therapist's good alliances with family members and the tools he or she brings to bear are sufficient for the task.

Challenging and/or creating emotional intensity with families can pose particular problems for therapists-in-training. Discussion of these issues in supervision must include not only an assessment by therapist and supervisor of what is holding the therapist back, but also the strength of the alliances between the therapist and family members. If alliances are strong, but the therapist continually hesitates to elicit emotional content, or the stage of therapy is advanced and still important challenges have not been posed by the therapist, live supervision may be useful. The therapist will be pushed to confront what appear to him or her to be risky situations but will receive support in doing this. Overcoming anxiety is essential if the therapist is to cultivate the fearlessness necessary to help the family abandon the status quo for new ways of interacting. For any therapist, the expectation that families will necessarily enter such a brave new relational world without trepidation and without challenging the new order would be naive. For the family therapist, pushing for change implies the need not to overrespect the power of families by holding back, but at the same time understanding how the system may react and how to deal with this response. For the supervisor, both challenging and supporting the supervisee in this endeavor are critical.

CONCLUSION

Certainly there is skill involved in conducting supervision and in conducting therapy, but there is also skill involved in being a supervisee. Therapists vary a great deal in how they use supervision and the expertise of a supervisor. How well or how poorly supervision is used by the therapist-in-training not only has an impact upon the quality of training received by the therapist but also upon the quality of treatment received by the family.

Family therapy supervision is much like family therapy itself—active, directive, and collaborative. When the family therapy supervisor does not achieve a balance in these three domains, the therapist and the therapy are the poorer for it. Because of its multisystemic nature, family therapy supervision poses a tremendous challenge for the supervisor. He or she must attend to the family system and systems outside it, the system that is comprised of the family and the therapist, and the system that includes supervisor and supervisee. Each system is itself a complex set of relationships. Herein lies the challenge of family therapy supervision.

REFERENCES

Alberts, G., & Edelstein, B. (1990). Therapist training: A critical review of skill training studies. *Clinical Psychology Review, 10,* 497–311.

Alexander, J. F., Holtzworth-Munroe, A., & Jameson, P. B. (1994). Research on the process and outcome of marriage and family therapy. In A. E. Bergin & S. L. Garfield (Eds.), *Handbook of psychotherapy and behavior change* (4th ed.). New York: Wiley.

Anderson, S. A., Rigazio-Digilio, S. A., & Kunkler, K. P. (1995). Training of family professionals: Training and supervision in family therapy—Current issues and future directions. *Family Relations, 44,* 489–500.

Aponte, H. J. (1992). Training the person of the therapist in structural family therapy. *Journal of Marital and Family Therapy, 18*(3), 269–281.

Aponte, H. J. (1994). How personal can training get? *Journal of Marital and Family Therapy, 20*(1), 3–15.

Ard, D. (1973). Providing clinical supervision for marriage counselors: A model for supervisor and supervisee. *Family Coordinator, 22,* 91–98.

Avis, J. M., & Sprenkle, D. H. (1990). Outcome research on family therapy training: A substantive and methodological review. *Journal of Marital and Family Therapy, 16*(3), 241–264.

Bardill, D. (1976). The simulated family as an aid to learning family group treatment. *Child Welfare, 55,* 703–709.

Baumrind, D. (1991). Effective parenting during the early adolescent transition. In P. A. Cowan & M. Heatherington (Eds.), *Family transitions* (pp. 111–163). Hillsdale, NJ: Lawrence Erlbaum.

Beutler, L. E., & Kendall, P. C. (1995). Introduction to the special section: The case for training in the provision of psychological therapy. *Journal of Consulting and Clinical Psychology, 63*(2), 179–181.

Binder, J. L., & Strupp, H. H. (1993). Recommendations for improving psychotherapy training based on experiences with manual-guided training and research: An introduction. *Psychotherapy, 30*(4), 571–572.

Birchler, G. (1975). Live supervision and instant feed-back in marriage and family therapy. *Journal of Marriage and Family Counseling, 1,* 331–342.

Bodin, A. M. (1969). Family therapy training literature: A brief guide. *Family Process, 8,* 272–279.

Bodin, A. M. (1972). Video-tape applications in training family therapists. *Journal of Nervous and Mental Disease, 143,* 251–261.

Breunlin, D. C., Karrer, B., McGuire, D., & Cimmarusti, R. (1988). Cybernetics of videotape supervision. In H. A. Liddle, D. C. Breunlin, & R. C. Schwartz (Eds.), *Handbook of family therapy training and supervision* (pp. 194–206). New York: Guilford.

Carter, B., & McGoldrick, M. (Eds.). (1989). *The changing family life cycle* (2nd ed.). Boston: Allyn & Bacon.

Christensen, A., & Jacobson, N. S. (1994). Who (or what) can do psychotherapy: The status and challenge of nonprofessional therapies. *Psychological Science, 5*(1), 8–14.

Churven, P., & McKinnon, T. (1982). Family therapy training: An evaluation of a workshop. *Family Process, 21,* 345–352.

Cleghorn, J., & Levin, S. (1973). Training family therapists by setting learning objectives. *American Journal of Orthopsychiatry, 43,* 439–446.

Cohen, M., Gross, S., & Turner, M. (1976). A note on a developmental model for training family therapists through group supervision. *Journal of Marriage and Family Counseling, 2,* 48–76.

Colapinto, J. (1988). Teaching the structural way. In H. A. Liddle, D. C. Breunlin, & R. C. Schwartz (Eds.), *Handbook of family therapy training and supervision* (pp. 17–37). New York: Guilford.

Constantine, J., Stone-Fish, L., & Piercy, F. (1984). A systemic procedure for teaching positive connotation. *Journal of Marital and Family Therapy, 10*(3), 313–316.

Constantine, L. (1976). Designed experience: A multiple, goal directed training program in family therapy. *Family Process, 15,* 373–396.

Coppersmith, E. I. (1985). Teaching trainees to think in triads. *Journal of Marital and Family Therapy, 11,* 61–66.

Crits-Christoph, P. (1991). Implications of therapist effects for the design and analysis of comparative studies of psychotherapies. *Journal of Consulting and Clinical Psychology, 59,* 20–26.

Crits-Christoph, P., Baranackie, K., Kurcias, J., Beck, A. T., Carroll, C., Perry, K., Luborsky, L., McLellan, A. T., Woody, G., Thompson, L., Gallagher, D., & Zitrin, C. (1991). Meta-analysis of therapist effects in psychotherapy outcome studies. *Psychotherapy Research, 1,* 81–91.

Diamond, G., & Liddle, H. A. (1996). Resolving a therapeutic impasse between parents and adolescents in multidimensional family therapy. *Journal of Consulting and Clinical Psychology, 64*(3), 1–8.

Doehrman, M. J. G. (1976). Parallel processes in supervision and psychotherapy. *Bulletin of the Menninger Clinic, 40,* 3–10.

Ehrlich, F. (1973). Family therapy training in child psychiatry. *Journal of the American Academy of Child Psychiatry, 12,* 461–472.

Epstein, N., & Levin, S. (1973). Training for family therapy within a faculty of medicine. *Canadian Psychiatric Association Journal, 18,* 203–207.

Everett, C. A., & Koerpel, B. J. (1986). Family therapy supervision: A review and critique of the literature. *Contemporary Family Therapy, 8*(1), 62–74.

Falicov, C. (1988). Learning to think culturally. In H. A. Liddle, D. C. Breunlin, & R. C. Schwartz (Eds.), *Handbook of family therapy training and supervision* (pp. 335–357). New York: Guilford.

Ferber, A. (1972). Follow the path with heart. *International Journal of Psychiatry, 10,* 6–22.

Ferber, A., & Mendelsohn, M. (1969). Training for family therapy. *Family Process, 8,* 25–32.

Ferber, A., Mendelsohn, M., & Napier, A. (Eds.). (1972). *The book of family therapy.* New York: Science House.

Fisch, R. (1988). Training in the brief therapy model of the M. R. I. In H. A. Liddle, D. C. Breunlin, & R. C. Schwartz (Eds.), *Handbook of family therapy training and supervision* (pp. 78–92). New York: Guilford.

Fleuridas, C., Nelson, T., & Rosenthal, D. M. (1986). The evolution of circular questions: Training family therapists. *Journal of Marital and Family Therapy, 12*(2), 113–128.

Framo, J. I. (1975). Personal reflections of a family therapist. *Journal of Marriage and Family Counseling, 1,* 15–28.

Framo, J. I. (1976). Chronicle of a struggle to establish a family unit within a community mental health center. In P. Guerin (Ed.), *Family therapy: Theory and practice*. New York: Gardner.

Frankel, B. R., & Piercy, F. P. (1990). The relationship among selected supervisor, therapist, and client behaviors. *Journal of Marital and Family Therapy, 16,* 407–421.

Ganahl, G., Ferguson, L. R., & L'Abate, L. (1985). Training in family therapy. In L. L'Abate (Ed.), *The handbook of family psychology and therapy*. Homewood, IL: Dorsey.

Green, R., & Sager, K. (1982). Learning to think systems: Five writing assignments. *Journal of Marital and Family Therapy, 8,* 285–294.

Guerin, P., & Fogarty, T. (1972). The family therapist's own family. *International Journal of Psychiatry, 10*(1), 6–22.

Haber, R. (1996). *Family therapy supervision*. New York: Norton.

Haley, J. (1976). Problems of training therapists. In J. Haley (Ed.), *Problem-solving therapy* (pp. 164–194). San Francisco: Jossey-Bass.

Haley, J. (1980). *Leaving home: Therapy of disturbed young people*. New York: McGraw-Hill.

Haley, J. (1988). Reflections on supervision. In H. A. Liddle, D. Breunlin, & R. Schwartz (Eds.), *Handbook of family therapy training and supervision*. New York: Guilford.

Haley, J. (1996). *Teaching and learning therapy*. New York: Guilford.

Hardy, K. V., & Laszloffy, T. A. (1992). Training racially sensitive family therapists: Context, content, and contact. *Families in Society: The Journal of Contemporary Human Services, 73*(6), 364–370.

Hare, R., & Frankena, S. (1972). Peer group supervision. *American Journal of Orthopsychiatry, 42,* 527–529.

Hare-Mustin, R. (1976). Live supervision in psychotherapy. *Voices, 12,* 21–24.

Henggeler, S. W., & Borduin, C. M. (1990). *Family therapy and beyond: A multisystemic approach to treating the behavior problems of children and adolescents*. Pacific Grove, CA: Brooks/Cole.

Kantor, D. (1983). The structural-analytic approach to the treatment of family developmental crisis. *Family Therapy Collections, 7,* 12–34.

Karpel, M. (1986). *Family resources*. New York: Guilford.

Kaye, K. (1985). Toward a developmental psychology of the family. In L. L'Abate (Ed.), *The handbook of family psychology and therapy* (Vol. 2). Homewood, IL: Dorsey.

Kempster, S. W., & Savitsky, E. (1967). Training family therapists through live supervision. In N. Ackerman, F. Beatman, & S. Sherman (Eds.), *Expanding theory and practice in family therapy*. New York: Family Service Association of America.

Kniskern, D. P., & Gurman, A. S. (1988). Research on family therapy training and supervision. In H. A. Liddle, D. C. Breunlin, & R. C. Schwartz (Eds.), *Handbook of family therapy training and supervision* (pp. 368–378). New York: Guilford.

Lappin, J. (1983). On becoming a culturally conscious family therapist. In J. C. Hanson & C. J. Falicov (Eds.), *Cultural perspectives in family therapy*. London: Aspen Publications.

Lebow, J. L., & Gurman, A. S. (1995). Research assessing couple and family therapy. *Annual Review of Psychology, 46,* 27–57.

Liddle, H. A. (1978). The emotional and political hazards of teaching and learning family therapy. *Family Therapy, 5,* 1–12.

Liddle, H. A. (1984). Family therapy training: Current issues, future trends. *International Journal of Family Therapy, 4,* 81–97.

Liddle, H. A. (1988). Integrating developmental thinking and the family life cycle paradigm into training. In C. Falicov (Ed.), *Family transitions: Continuity and change over the life cycle* (pp. 449–465). New York: Guilford.

Liddle, H. A. (1991). Training and supervision in family therapy: A comprehensive and critical analysis. In A. S. Gurman & D. P. Kniskern (Eds.), *Handbook of family therapy* (Vol. 2, pp. 638–697). New York: Brunner/Mazel.

Liddle, H. A. (1992). A multidimensional model for the adolescent who is abusing drugs and alcohol. In W. Snyder & T. Ooms (Eds.), *Empowering families, helping adolescents: Family-centered treatment of adolescents with alcohol, drug abuse, and other mental health problems*. U.S. Department of Health and Human Services, Office for Treatment Improvement, ADAMHA, Washington, DC: United States Public Health Service, U.S. Government Printing Office.

Liddle, H. A. (1995). Conceptual and clinical dimensions of a multidimensional, multisystems engagement strategy in family-based adolescent treatment. *Psychotherapy, 32,* 39–58.

Liddle, H. A. (1996). Family-based treatments for adolescent problem behaviors: Overview of contemporary developments and introduction to the special section. *Journal of Family Psychology, 10*(1), 1–9.

Liddle, H. A., Breunlin, D. C., & Schwartz, R. C. (Eds.). (1988). *Handbook of family therapy training and supervision*. New York: Guilford.

Liddle, H. A., & Dakof, G. A. (1994, February). *Multidimensional family therapy and its impact on adolescent drug use and school performance*. Paper presented at Society for Psychotherapy Research Conference, Sante Fe, NM.

Liddle, H. A., Davidson, G., & Barrett, M. J. (1988). Outcomes of live supervision: Trainee perspectives. In H. A. Liddle, D. C. Breunlin, & R. C. Schwartz (Eds.), *Handbook of family therapy training and supervision* (pp. 386–398). New York: Guilford.

Liddle, H. A., Diamond, G. M., Rowe, C., Schmidt, S., & Ettinger, D. (in press). The clinical utility of adolescent development research: The case of multidimensional family therapy. *Journal of Marital and Family Therapy*.

Liddle, H. A., & Halpin, R. (1978). Family therapy training and supervision literature: A comparative review. *Journal of Marriage and Family Counseling, 4,* 77–98.

Liddle, H. A., & Saba, G. (1983). On context replication: The isomorphic nature of training and therapy. *Journal of Strategic Systemic Therapies, 2*(3), 3–11.

Liddle, H. A., & Schwartz, R. C. (1983). Live supervision/consultation: Conceptual and pragmatic guidelines for family therapy training. *Family Process, 22,* 477–490.

Malone, C. (1974). Observations on the role of family therapy in child psychiatry training. *Journal of the American Academy of Child Psychiatry, 13,* 437–458.

Mead, E. (1990). *Effective clinical supervision*. New York: Brunner/Mazel.

Mendelsohn, M., & Ferber, A. (1972). Training program. In A. Ferber, M. Mendelsohn, & A. Napier (Eds.), *The book of family therapy* (pp. 239–271). New York: Science House.

Minuchin, S. (1974). *Families and family therapy*. Cambridge, MA: Harvard University Press.

Minuchin, S., & Fishman, H. C. (1981). *Family therapy techniques*. Cambridge, MA: Harvard University Press.

Miyoshi, N., & Liebman, R. (1969). Training psychiatric residents in family therapy. *Family Process, 8,* 97–105.

Montalvo, B. (1973). Aspects of live supervision. *Family Process, 12,* 343–359.

Moras, K. (1993). The use of treatment manuals to train psychotherapists: Observations and recommendations. *Psychotherapy, 30*(4), 581–586.

Napier, A. Y., & Whitaker, C. (1973). Problems of the beginning family therapist. In D. Bloch (Ed.), *Techniques of family psychotherapy: A primer* (pp. 109–122). New York: Grune and Stratton.

Nichols, W. C., Nichols, D. P., & Hardy, K. V. (1990). Supervision in family therapy: A decade restudy. *Journal of Marital and Family Therapy, 16,* 275–285.

Olson, P. H., Russell, C. S., & Sprenkle, D. (1980). Marital and family therapy: A decade review. *Journal of Marriage and the Family, 42*(4), 973–993.

Pulleybank, E., & Shapiro, R. (1986). Evaluation of family therapy trainees: Acquisition of cognitive and therapeutic behavior skills. *Family Process, 25,* 591–598.

Rigazio-DiGilio, S. A. (1994). Systemic cognitive-developmental therapy: Training practitioners to access and assess cognitive-developmental orientations. *Simulation & Gaming, 25*(1), 61–74.

Rounsaville, B. J., Chevron, E. S., Weissman, M. M., Prusoff, B. A., & Frank, E. (1986). Training therapists to perform interpersonal psychotherapy in clinical trials. *Comprehensive Psychiatry 27*(4), 364–371.

Rounsaville, B. J., O'Malley, S., Foley, S., & Weissman, M. M. (1988). Role of manual-guided training in the conduct and efficacy of interpersonal psychotherapy for depression. *Journal of Consulting and Clinical Psychology, 56*(5), 681–688.

Saba, G. W., & Liddle, H. A. (1986). Perceptions of professional needs, practice patterns and critical issues facing family therapy trainers and supervisors. *American Journal of Family Therapy, 14*, 109–122.

Sander, F., & Beels, C. (1970). A didactic course for family therapy trainees. *Family Process, 9*, 411–424.

Schmidt, S. E., Liddle, H. A., & Dakof, G. A. (1996). Changes in parenting practices and adolescent drug abuse during multidimensional family therapy. *Journal of Family Psychology, 10*(1), 1–16.

Schwartz, R. (1981). The pre-session worksheet as an adjunct to training. *American Journal of Family Therapy, 9*(3), 89–90.

Schwartz, R., Liddle, H. A., & Breunlin, D. (1988). Muddles of live supervision. In H. A. Liddle, D. C. Breunlin, & R. C. Schwartz (Eds.), *Handbook of family therapy training and supervision* (pp. 183–193). New York: Guilford.

Shapiro, R. (1975a). Problems in teaching family therapy. *Professional Psychology, 6*, 41–44.

Shapiro, R. (1975b). Some implications of training psychiatric nurses in family therapy. *Journal of Marriage and Family Counseling, 1*, 323–330.

Singer, M. T., & Wynne, L. C. (1965). Thought disorder and family relations of schizophrenics: IV. Results and implications. *Archives of General Psychiatry, 12*, 201–212.

Sluzki, C. (1974). On training to think interactionally. *Social Science and Medicine, 8*, 483–485.

Sluzki, C. (1983). Process, structure, and world views: Toward an integrated view of systemic models and family therapy. *Family Process, 22*, 469–476.

Stanton, M. D. (1975a). Family therapy training: Academic and internship opportunities for psychologists. *Family Process, 14*, 433–439.

Stanton, M. D. (1975b). Psychology and family therapy. *Professional Psychology, 6*, 45–49.

Steinberg, L. (1990). Autonomy, conflict, and harmony in the family relationship. In S. S. Feldman & G. R. Elliot (Eds.), *At the threshold: The developing adolescent* (pp. 255–276). Cambridge, MA: Harvard University Press.

Stier, S., & Goldenberg, I. (1975). Training issues in family therapy. *Journal of Marriage and Family Counseling, 1*, 63–68.

Stoltenberg, C. D., McNeill, B. W., & Crethar, H. C. (1994). Changes in supervision as counselors and therapists gain experience: A review. *Professional Psychology: Research and Practice, 25*(4), 416–449.

Street, E., & Foot, H. (1984). Training family therapists in observational skills. *Journal of Family Therapy, 6*, 335–345.

Talmadge, J. (1975). Psychiatric residents, medical students and families: Teaching family therapy to the uninitiated. *Family Therapy, 2*, 11–16.

Tomm, K., & Leahey, M. (1980). Training in family assessment: A comparison of three methods. *Journal of Marital and Family Therapy, 6*, 453–458.

Tomm, K., & Wright, L. (1979). Training in family therapy: Perceptual, conceptual, and executive skills. *Family Process, 18*, 227–250.

Tucker, B., Hart, G., & Liddle, H. A. (1976). Supervision in family therapy: A developmental perspective. *Journal of Marriage and Family Counseling, 2*, 269–276.

Tucker, S., & Pinsof, W. (1984). The empirical evaluation of family therapy training. *Family Process, 23*, 437–456.

Walsh, F. W. (1987). The clinical utility of normal family research. *Psychotherapy, 24*, 496–503.

Waltz, J., Addis, M. E., Koerner, K., & Jacobson, N. S. (1993). Testing the integrity of a psychotherapy protocol: Assessment of adherence and competence. *Journal of Consulting and Clinical Psychology, 61*(4), 620–630.

Watkins, E. (1995). Psychotherapy supervision in the 1990s. *American Journal of Psychotherapy, 49*, 568–581.

Watzlawick, P., Weakland, J., & Fisch, R. (1974). *Change: Principles of problem formation and resolution.* New York: Norton.

Weber, T., McKeever, J. E., & McDaniel, S. H. (1985). A beginner's guide to the problem oriented first family interview. *Family Process, 24*(3), 357–364.

Westheafer, C. (1984). An aspect of live supervision: The pathological triangle. *Australian Journal of Family Therapy, 5,* 169–175.

Wheeler, D., Avis, J., Miller, L., & Chaney, S. (1985). Rethinking family therapy education and supervision: A feminist model. *Journal of Psychotherapy and the Family, 1*(4), 53–72.

Whitaker, C. (1976). Comment: Live supervision in psychotherapy. *Voices, 12,* 24–25.

Wilden, A. (1982). *System and structure.* London: Tavistock.

Wright, L. M. (1986). An analysis of live supervision "phone-ins" in family therapy. *Journal of Marital and Family Therapy, 12*(2), 187–190.

Zaken-Greenberg, F., & Neimeyer, G. J. (1986). The impact of structural family therapy training on conceptual and executive therapy skills. *Family Process, 25,* 599–608.

Zarski, J. J., Greenbank, M., Sand-Pringle, C., & Cibik, P. (1991). The invisible mirror: In-home family therapy and supervision. *Journal of Marital and Family Therapy, 17*(2), 133–143.

PART V

Researching Psychotherapy Supervision

CHAPTER 24

The Effectiveness of Psychotherapy Supervision

MICHAEL J. LAMBERT
Brigham Young University
BENJAMIN M. OGLES
Ohio University

Although there are many elements in graduate study that are necessary for training competent practitioners, supervision is the principal method of preparing students for psychotherapeutic practice. Despite the divergence in systems of psychotherapy, their goals and varied training practices, supervision remains the one component considered essential to all (e.g., Gerkin, 1969; Hess, 1983). The role and function of supervision are fairly broad. In the early training of analysts, an attempt was made to separate therapeutic and affective functions of supervision from the trainee's personal therapy, leaving the supervisor free to deal with more of the technical aspects of the trainee's interactions with his or her patient. For example, Newman, Kopta, McGovern, Howard, and McNeilly (1988) suggested two more technical functions of supervision: to help trainees conceptualize clinical material and to select and apply therapeutic interventions. Guest and Beutler (1988) claimed that supervision focuses not only on the technical proficiency of the trainee but, to a large extent, on the broad professional development of trainees, including their beliefs and values. Shanfield, Matthews, and Hetherly (1993) stressed the ability of supervisors to "track the concerns" of psychiatry students as a central ingredient of successful supervision. Vasquez (1992) emphasized the supervisor's role in following the ethical behavior of trainees. In addition to the aforementioned roles and functions of supervisors, several researchers have emphasized the importance of developmental issues in supervision (Stoltenberg & Delworth, 1987) and have shown how the focus and goals of supervision change over time, within a single session, as well as in the career of a therapist (Loganbill, Hardy, & Delworth, 1982; Rodenhauser, Rudisill, & Painter, 1989; Ronnestad & Skovholt, 1993).

Given the perceived importance of supervision and the obvious diversity in the conceptualization, roles, functions, and goals of supervision, there is considerable variability in the purposes and methods of research on supervision. A comprehensive list of this literature on supervision has been published by Robiner and Schofield (1990). There is also great variability in the value this research has for changing the process and practice of supervision and psychotherapy itself. Although there are many ways in which we might focus a review of research on supervision, we have tried to keep central our interest in patient outcome. That is, rather than becoming especially interested in the process of supervision, we emphasize research that has implications for the practice of effective supervision and subsequent psychotherapy. We also emphasize the effects of supervision on the trainee rather than focusing on the experience of the supervisor. We divide research on supervision into three sections: (a) research on therapist interviewing and interpersonal skills; (b) research on therapist technical skills, including the use of treatment manuals to enhance technical skills; and (c) measurement strategies for assessing supervision outcomes.

EFFECTS OF SUPERVISION AND TRAINING ON THERAPIST INTERVIEWING AND INTERPERSONAL SKILLS

General Interviewing Skills

Although there is little research support for the importance of certain "basic interviewing skills," there are certainly differences between novice and experienced clinicians in the way they conduct interviews (Matarazzo & Patterson, 1986). In spite of the fact that there is room for great diversity (Gustavson, Cundick, & Lambert, 1981) there is also agreement that certain behaviors are more helpful than are others in conducting an interview.

Research on general interviewing skills will be dealt with only superficially here since they are not central to the role of supervision. By general or basic interviewing skills, we mean those behaviors that therapists learn that facilitate the general purposes of an effective interview. They include behaviors such as asking open-ended questions, tolerating silence, limiting verbal activity, limiting interruptions, talking in shorter utterances, and the like. Matarazzo and her associates (Matarazzo, Phillips, Wiens, & Saslow, 1965) studied variables such as length of utterance, reaction time, and frequency of interruptions in an attempt to analyze interviewing "errors." A great deal of research has accumulated regarding the application of methods of teaching therapist interviewing skills and related concepts. Much of this research was summarized by Matarazzo (1978) and Matarazzo and Patterson (1986). Although in the past learning these skills was often accomplished through individual and group supervision, nowadays, clinical, counseling, social work, psychiatry, and marriage and family therapy training programs accomplish this goal through the use of class instruction, modeling, and feedback, turning more complex training tasks over to supervisory relationships. General interviewing skills are often combined with basic training in interpersonal skills, our next topic.

Therapist Interpersonal Skills

Regardless of the theoretical orientation of the training program or the therapeutic modality in use, there is considerable consensus that certain therapist attitudes and behaviors facilitate the general purposes of psychotherapy (Lambert, 1983). The client-centered school can be credited with the active research interest in therapist attitudes that eventually led to an expansion of research and the establishment of training programs that teach a variety of therapist facilitative attitudes or interpersonal skills. Carl Rogers (1959) was able to state the conditions he believed led to positive outcomes and to many research reports on the effects of these therapist-offered conditions. This research, in turn, resulted in the growing specification of these variables. Training raters to judge the level of empathy, warmth, congruence, and respect offered by therapists resulted in the application of these same training methods with student therapists.

Truax and Carkhuff (1967) published an influential volume of research related to these dimensions and outlined an experiential/didactic training program. They emphasized the importance of measuring changes in trainee skill subsequent to training. Ivey, Norming-ton, Miller, Merrill, and Haase (1968) also outlined the use of related methods, or "micro-counseling" procedures. During the late 1960s, numerous methods using similar training procedures were developed and applied in counselor education programs, graduate schools of social work and psychology, and medical schools.

Because interpersonal skills were once taught as part of early practicum experiences, research on training in interpersonal skills is dealt with here. These skills can no longer be considered a central function of supervision, however, because they can be learned more efficiently prior to the initial counseling experiences that are accompanied by super-vision. As a result, most interpersonal skills training is now conducted as a part of presu-pervisory experiences.

Table 24.1 focuses on studies of interpersonal skills training with an emphasis on stud-ies that involve supervision. The typical training program involves variants on a general procedure. This procedure includes (a) focus on a specific skill such as empathic respond-ing, (b) the presentation of a rationale for this skill, (c) audiotape or videotape examples of the presence and absence of the skill in actual therapy interaction, and (d) practice at the skill, with (e) feedback about performance from the supervisor. Changes in trainee performance are typically tested in a pretest-posttest experimental design that assesses the skills themselves rather than their effects on client outcome.

Table 24.1 lists numerous—but hardly exhaustive—groups of studies aimed at testing the effects of different forms of supervision and interviewing skills training. They are orga-nized in such a way as to suggest the primary intent of each study. Thus, under the "A" heading are studies that deal with the question, Does training (supervision) help? Later research (summarized under "B") is designed to compare the effects of a traditional method with an innovative method: Does training paradigm z work better than paradigms x and y?

More recently, investigators have been interested in studying the most essential com-ponents of an already effective training program. Studies with this goal in mind have been listed under heading "C." These dismantling studies usually ask: Given the effectiveness of training program z, what specific activities are necessary and sufficient to obtain which results?[1] In addition, some of the studies under "C" deal with the differential effects of training on different trainees or specific trainee "types," the interaction of supervisor per-sonality variables with trainee personality, and demographic variables.

Those studies listed under section "C" of Table 24.1 represent attempts at specifying *the most efficient* way to achieve the goals of training. All these studies compare two or more combinations of a training procedure. If such a design results in a clearer specifica-tion of the necessary and sufficient procedures to be used in training, then the training can be streamlined and supervision can have a specific focus. As an example, microcounsel-ing procedures usually include reading a manual that describes the skill to be learned and a plausible rationale for its importance, viewing experts model the skill, practicing the skill, receiving feedback about performance, and observing others who are receiving sim-ilar training. A natural question is: Can one or more of these steps be eliminated without reducing the effectiveness of training? A representative study is described in order to help the reader appreciate the nature of research in this area.

Peters, Cormier, and Cormier (1978) analyzed the effects of four training methods on

---

[1]For an excellent discussion of these research questions as applied to psychotherapy, see Gottman and Markman (1978).

Table 24.1 Studies Examining the Effects of Counseling and Psychotherapy Training and Supervision on Trainee Interpersonal Skills

A Studies comparing training with a no-treatment control group	B Studies comparing training vs. traditional supervision or a competing experimental group	C Studies dismantling the process of supervision/training
Austin and Altekruse (1972)	Berg and Stone (1980)	Authier and Gustafson (1975)
Barrington (1958)	Boyd (1973)	Baker, Johnson et al. (1986)
Biasco and Redfering (1976)	Cash and Vellema (1979)	Baker, Schofield et al. (1984)
Blocksma and Porter (1947)	Cormier, Hackney, and Segrist (1974)	Berenson, Carkhuff, and Myrus (1966)
Butler and Hansen (1973)	Dalton and Sunblad (1976)	Canada (1973)
Cunningham and Stewart (1983)	Deshaies (1974)	Dowling and Franz (1975)
Hart (1973)	DiMattia and Arndt (1974)	Forestandi (1973)
Ivey et al. (1968)	Dowal (1973)	Forge (1973)
	Gormally, Hill, Gulanick, and McGovern (1975)	Frankl (1971)
	Hodge, Payne, and Wheeler (1978)	Fry (1973)
	Kagan, Krathwhol, and Farquhar (1965)	Fyffe and Ori (1979)
	Kingdon (1975)	Kloba and Zimpfer (1976)
	Moreland, Ivey, and Phillips (1973)	Kuna (1975)
	Richardson (1974)	Olson (1973)
	Roffers, Cooper, and Sultanoff (1988)	O'Toole (1979)
		Perry (1975)

Table 24.1 (Continued)

| A
Studies comparing training with a no-treatment control group | B
Studies comparing training vs. traditional supervision or a competing experimental group | C
Studies dismantling the process of supervision/training |
|---|---|---|
| | Ross (1973) | Peters, Cormier, and Cormier (1978) |
| | Silverman (1972) | Richardson and Stone (1981) |
| | Spirack (1972) | Robinson and Cabianca (1985) |
| | Toukmanian and Rennie (1975) | Robinson, Froehel, and Kurpius (1979) |
| | Vander Kolk (1973) | Ronnestad (1973) |
| | | Rosenthal (1977) |
| | | Shear (1994) |
| | | Stone (1981) |
| | | Stone and Stein (1978) |
| | | Stone and Vance (1976) |
| | | Tosi and Eshbaugh (1978) |
| | | Uhlemann, Lea, and Stone (1976) |
| | | Uhlemann, Stone, Evans, and Hearn (1982) |
| | | Wallace, Horan, Baker, and Hudson (1975) |
| | | Young and Beck (1980) |

the acquisition of a counseling strategy (a goal-development procedure) in 40 beginning counseling students. The comparison methods were adopted from microcounseling procedures and involved four experimental groups: (a) written and videotaped model, (b) written and videotaped model plus practice, (c) written and videotaped model, practice, plus feedback, and (d) written and videotaped model, practice, and feedback, plus remediation practice following feedback.

The dependent measures included both a written test and a role-play interview with a standard client in which trainees were to demonstrate the counseling strategy they had learned. The results showed all students had improved significantly in their ability to formulate client goals, and these changes were maintained at the 2-week follow-up. Differences between the groups were not found to be significant. The authors concluded that there was little evidence to suggest that behavior rehearsal and feedback were necessary for skill acquisition. Thus, the most efficient training procedure would exclude these components and rely solely on reading and viewing examples of how the skill is to be practiced.

Much research on supervision of therapist interpersonal skills conducted during the late 1970s and early 1980s has focused on the effects of microtraining and variants of the microtraining model. In these studies, researchers have been concerned with comparing microtraining with other programmed learning packages or skill-training techniques (Crabb, Moracco, & Bender, 1983; Evans, Uhlemann, & Hearn, 1978; Uhlemann, Hearn, & Evans, 1980) or comparing microtraining strategies with other techniques, such as supervisor modeling (Thompson & Blocher, 1979).

Researchers have also tried to measure the relative contribution of different elements of the didactic-experiential program elaborated by Truax and Carkhuff (1967). Those authors suggested that effective training should include (a) highly specific didactic training in interpersonal skills, (b) an experientially based interaction among trainees about personal feelings, personal reactions to clients, and the role of the therapist, and (c) a "therapeutic context" wherein the supervisor provides high levels of the therapeutic conditions of empathy, warmth, respect, and congruence to the trainees while in supervision.

Researchers in several studies have tested the third assumption, that the trainee is affected by the level of facilitative conditions (such as empathy, warmth, and respect) offered by the supervisor. Pierce, Carkhuff, and Berenson (1967) and Pierce and Schuable (1970, 1971) found support for the idea that trainees move in the direction of empathy (either higher or lower) that their supervisors exhibit. A problem with this research is that the authors assumed that supervisors behave identically with regard to empathy and other skills with trainees as they do with clients. Lambert (1974) tested this assumption and found that a clear difference existed between the two situations. It appears that facilitative conditions are not as high in supervision as in counseling. There exists little empirical evidence supporting the absolute necessity of a therapeutic climate for the acquisition of interpersonal skills (Lane, 1974; Payne & Gralinsky, 1968; Ronnestad, 1974), and it appears that learning these skills can occur without especially high levels of empathy, genuineness, and unconditional positive regard, as long as the trainee perceives that the supervisor is indeed trying to be helpful.

Conclusions From Studies of Supervision Listed in Table 24.1

1. Generally, studies comparing training versus a no-training control group have found that training is superior to no training, both in producing greater personal adjustment and in increasing skill development.

2. Studies comparing "traditional supervision" (usually facilitated by listening to audio-tapes) with systematic training procedures that involved learning specific interpersonal or counseling skills indicate a superiority for the systematic training. Results of research on acquisition of skills by graduate-level trainees have been subjected to both narrative and meta-analytic review. For example, Baker, Daniels, and Greeley (1990) conducted a meta-analytic review of the three most frequently studied training approaches (interpersonal process recall, microcounseling, and human resource training) and found all to be effective; however, Kagan's (1984) interpersonal process recall approach had the smallest effect, while Carkhuff's (1971) human resource training model enjoyed the largest.

In a separate review of Ivey's microcounseling, Baker and Daniels (1989) located 81 relevant studies and related training effect sizes to variables such as length of training (2 to 25 hours) and type of trainee (professional, paraprofessional, etc.). Overall, the mean effect size for training was .83, suggesting that the average trainee moved from the 50th to the 80th percentile of the control group following training. Microcounseling appears to be an effective approach to learning basic skills; it surpassed "no-training" and "attention-placebo" control comparisons. Thus, one can expect trainees who receive no systematic training in areas such as empathic responding, confrontation, attending behaviors, and the like to make much slower progress in developing these skills than do the trainees who are involved in a systematic training program. Unfortunately, many of the research designs used to test this hypothesis have methodological weaknesses that favor the experimental group. In addition, the studies consist of an inordinately large number of unpublished doctoral dissertations. Still, the research is rather unequivocal. If a mental health training program values the development of basic interpersonal or interviewing skills, this can best be achieved with a program that clearly specifies the skills to be learned and then develops training (including modeling and practice) directed at this goal. Systematic teaching is superior to unsystematic teaching.

3. Several conclusions can be drawn from the research listed in column "C" using dismantling designs: (a) Simple behavioral skills can be quickly learned through instruction without modeling, feedback, and rehearsal; (b) more complex skills require more time and more components of the training package, primarily modeling and (to a lesser extent) feedback and rehearsal; and (c) it is indicated by some researchers that the teachability of microskills hits a ceiling in the acquisition of simple tasks, that microskills training is a good initial supervisory program for beginning counselors (Fyffe & Oei, 1979; Uhlemann, Stone, Evans, & Hearn, 1982) but is less effective and even unnecessary with more experienced therapists.

4. The specification of therapist attitudes and behavior that contribute to positive personality or behavior change has resulted in some exciting advances in training and supervision. The amount of research generated on questions related to the development of these attitudes and skills is impressive. The research itself has been a source of additional hypotheses about therapy and changes in the requirements and role of supervision in the overall training of therapists. In our opinion, the importance of therapist-offered attitudes or common factors cannot be underestimated, although research has, at this point, been able to demonstrate only a modestly positive relationship between empathy, regard, and genuineness and psychotherapy outcome (Lambert, DeJulio, & Stein, 1978; Mitchell, Bozarth, & Krauft, 1977).

5. How long-lasting are the effects of supervision? Does training on specific skills generalize to actual therapeutic practice? Few follow-up studies have been reported in the literature, and even when included as part of the research design, follow-up studies are marred by uncontrolled variables. Psychotherapy trainees almost invariably have additional training experiences beyond those included in the supervision research project. Furthermore, researchers in follow-up studies have not always applied the same criteria at treatment termination and follow-up. Those studies that have included a follow-up are therefore inconclusive. For example, Pierce and Schuable (1970, 1971) found in a 9-month follow-up on trainees who learned therapy skills (empathy, regard, genuineness, and concreteness) that the group trained by "high-functioning" supervisors (high on empathy, regard, etc.) remained superior over the "low" group at using the skills in a test situation. Unfortunately, the trainees did not appear to be randomly assigned to high- and low-functioning supervisors, which thus raised serious interpretive questions.

Gormally, Hill, Gulanick, and McGovern (1975) found that communication skills learned in a 40-hour training group were maintained at the 6-month follow-up for their graduate trainees but not for undergraduates. Collingwood (1971) also suggested that although interpersonal skills are learned by undergraduates, they gradually erode and require retraining, which thus raises the question as to the difference between internalization of skills and attitudes versus mere performance of targeted behaviors by trainees.

Research on microtraining indicates that although the procedure is effective in imparting the specifically targeted skill, some studies indicate modest generalization of skills, but others do not. For example, in attempting to increase the generalization effects derived from microtraining, Richardson and Stone (1981) added a cognitive element ("cognitive adjunct procedure") to a microtraining situation, in the belief that "a method that incorporates cognitive strategies and rules as well as discrete skills will foster generalization" (p. 168). A clear enhancement to skills performance was not demonstrated. The study, however, did indicate a clear superiority (retention) of cognitive-behavioral methods to that of a typical programmed learning module. In an examination of competence in cognitive behavior therapy that examined complex therapist behaviors, Beck (1986) found intensive (3-month) training in cognitive therapy, although initially successful, resulted in regression to pretreatment levels after 9 months. In contrast, he also reported that continual supervision over a year's time resulted in cumulative increases in competence.

The results of follow-up studies encourage the view that changes resulting from supervision and training can be maintained without retraining and often generalize to practical situations. There is a hint in the literature that supervision results in the ability of therapists to provide technically sound responses but that these abilities may not be widely practiced outside the research setting. Alberts and Edelstein (1990), after reviewing literature on training in interpersonal skills and more complex verbal skills, as well as Bootzin and Ruggill (1988) in their review of behavior therapy training raise doubt about the generalizability of training outcomes to actual therapy settings. Many more investigations dealing with the long-term retention and generalization of skills are needed before the limits of retention/generalization will be understood, but it appears that supervision could play a central role in assisting therapists to both generalize skills and maintain them over longer periods of time. Promising methods of supervision (i.e., anchored instruction) have been outlined by Binder (1993).

THERAPIST TECHNICAL SKILLS

Although research on the interpersonal skills has been plentiful, less attention has been directed toward research on therapy-specific skills. In the following section, we discuss the use of treatment manuals accompanied by supervision for learning or enhancing therapist technical skills along with three new areas of research regarding more complex therapist skills.

Treatment Manuals

Psychotherapy treatment manuals are an important development that will certainly come to affect the training of therapists using specific techniques with specific patient populations. A number of psychotherapy treatment manuals have been developed primarily for training beginning therapists who participate in psychotherapy outcome studies. Researchers were the first to use manuals as a way of standardizing the administration of treatments across therapists. This trend in psychotherapy outcome research is now beginning to have a substantial impact on the training of psychotherapists generally, particularly as extended to specialized techniques. These manuals have been successfully used in outcome studies and may be useful tools at training institutions with inexperienced therapists. To date, this proposition has not been well examined. But it is a relief to see a way to evaluate supervision with highly experienced therapists and to have more detailed and concrete suggestions for effective practice, training, and evaluation of less experienced trainees. A rationale for the development of manuals has been presented by Hurt and Clarkin (1990).

Although the proponents of behavioral therapies have been using treatment manuals in psychotherapy research and training since the 1960s, their use in the verbal therapies is more contemporary. Currently, there are a number of psychotherapy treatment manuals that have been used in psychotherapy outcome research. Some of these manuals have been reviewed elsewhere (Lambert & Arnold, 1987; Lambert & Ogles, 1988). The development of training manuals for verbal therapies has largely been the result of three factors: (a) the demonstrated efficacy of behavioral therapies having encouraged the further testing of verbal therapies; (b) the need for specificity of treatments in controlled comparisons of different treatments with homogeneous patient samples; and (c) the movement toward short-term treatment.

Treatment manuals have already impacted the training of psychotherapists in outcome studies. Investigators have taken great lengths to ensure the standardized administration of treatments in some studies (e.g., Bouchard et al., 1980; NIMH collaborative depression study, Waskow, 1984). Primarily experienced therapists are trained to administer a specific orientation and modality of therapy. They are typically trained by the developer of the treatment or one of their students, and rating scales have been developed and used to review tapes of actual therapy in progress. Criterion levels are then set for treatment conformity as well as competence, and supervision occurs both during training and during treatment. This supervision is considered essential when therapists perform below the cutoff level for adherence to the treatment protocol. Thus, a certain level of treatment conformity if not competence can be said to occur. Supervision becomes focused and its effects are easier to evaluate when the practice of therapy is clearly specified.

Manualized approaches to therapy are gaining in importance as guides to trainee performance in graduate training. In a recent survey of directors of clinical training and directors of APA-approved internships, most programs reported providing students with supervised clinical experience with manual-based therapies (Crits-Christoph, Frank, Chambliss, Brody, & Karp, 1995). Although the coverage was not extensive across the broadest range of therapies, there was significant coverage of some of the most well-researched interventions.

In a special issue on training of *The Journal of Consulting and Clinical Psychology*

(1988, *56,* Number 4), several articles address the success of using manuals for treatment conformity and/or competence. For example, Dobson and Shaw (1988) discuss the application of cognitive therapy treatment manuals in outcome research. They describe conformance in terms of *treatment integrity* (adherence to treatment) and *treatment differentiability* (extent to which the treatment can be differentiated from other treatments). Obviously, internal validity in research studies related to treatment adherence is of little utility if the treatment cannot be distinguished from other treatments. They also report the success of researchers in developing measures for both applications (DeRubeis, Hollon, Evans, & Bemis, 1982; Dobson, 1989). Others have also had success in measuring treatment adherence to manuals (e.g., Rounsaville, O'Malley, Foley, & Weissman, 1988; Strupp, Butler, & Rosser, 1988).

Although several research groups have had success in measuring treatment adherence or conformity, a number of issues still need to be addressed. First, measures used to address adherence typically neglect differentiability (Newman et al., 1988). That is, they neglect to include items from competing orientations, leaving little room for alternatives. Measures aimed at showing a therapist is using one technique or method of therapy should probably include items covering a broad range of the major schools of therapy. In this way, conformance with the treatment can also be interpreted as nonconformance with other methods. Second, the rating of conformity is often global rather than focusing on specific in-session behaviors and techniques. And finally, the utility of adherence has yet to be demonstrated. Whereas conformance with a treatment is useful for internal validity in an empirical investigation of a treatment, it may be useless as a predictor of outcome. In fact, competent therapists may deviate from treatment conformance when they deem it necessary (see Rounsaville et al., 1988). Since in the usual treatment setting and in graduate training, conformance is not as important as competence, the supervisor wishing to employ a manual will need to give careful consideration to instances in which competence is actually facilitated by what may appear to be a deviation from treatment conformity.

Competence takes adherence one step further by addressing important issues such as the timing of interventions, skill in technique implementation, therapist personal qualities, and appropriateness of the intervention in the first place. Rating scales have also been developed for some manualized therapies that measure competency in the given treatment rather than mere conformity. Typically, these scales are used prior to allowing the therapist to administer treatment or participate in the outcome study in order to assure that they meet minimum competency levels. They could just as easily be used to measure the effects of supervision in future research. A list of manuals including their focus and the extent to which they have developed rating scales that can be used in research on supervision is presented in Table 24.2.

The preliminary effectiveness of treatment manuals along with supervision to facilitate both conformance and competence demonstrated in recent outcome studies suggests the possible application of treatment manuals in training facilities. Recently, Barlow (1993) edited the second edition of his *Clinical Handbook of Psychological Disorders.* This text contains treatment manuals for 12 specific disorders (five anxiety-based disorders, two eating disorders, and one each on alcoholism, depression, sexual dysfunction, marital conflict, and borderline personality disorder). The chapters provide step-by-step manuals that are certain to enhance didactic training in graduate school, but also may enable supervisors to focus their attention on advanced technical issues in supervision of specific cases. In addition, Division 12 of the American Psychological Association recently established a task force that is producing a list of manuals for empirically validated treatments (Sander-

Table 24.2 Characteristics of Treatment Manuals

Author/Manual Subject	Patient Population	Orientation	Modality	Minimum Trainee Sophistication	Conformance Scales[1]	Competency Scales[2]	Research[3]
Luborsky et al. (1984) Supportive/expressive	Outpatient	Dynamic	Individual	Graduate students	Y	Y	Y
Klerman et al. (1984) Interpersonal	Depression	Interpersonal/ dynamic	Individual	Experienced clinicians	Y	Y	Y
Strupp and Binder (1984) Time-limited dynamics	Outpatient	Interpersonal/ dynamic systems	Individual	Graduate students	Y	N	N
Beck et al. (1979) Cognitive depression	Depression	Cognitive/ behavioral	Individual	Graduate students	Y	Y	Y
Beck and Emery (1977) Cognitive: anxiety	Anxiety and phobias	Cognitive/ behavioral	Individual	Graduate students	Y	Y	?
Yost et al. (1986) Cognitive: depression	Depressed older adults	Cognitive/ behavioral	Group	?	?	?	?
Lewinsohn et al. (1984) Coping with depression	Depression	Behavioral	Group	Paraprofessionals	N	N	Y
Rehm (1982) Self-control	Depression	Behavioral	Group	?	N	N	Y
Bellack et al. (1980) Social skills training and depression	Female depression	Behavioral	Individual	?	N	N	Y
Beidel et al. (1981) Social skills training: chronic psychiatric	Chronic psychiatric	Behavioral	Group	?	N	N	Y

(table continues)

Table 24.2 (Continued)

Author/Manual Subject	Patient Population	Orientation	Modality	Minimum Trainee Sophistication	Conformance Scales[1]	Competency Scales[2]	Research[3]
Ammerman et al. (in press) Social skills training: visually impaired children	Visually impaired children	Behavioral	Individual	?	N	N	Y
Daldrup et al. (1988) Experiential	Problems with constricted emotion	Focused expressive	Individual	?	Y	N	?
Greenberg and Goldman (1987) Gestalt experiential	Outpatient	Gestalt experiential	Individual	?	Y	N	Y
Elliot et al. (1987) Experiential	Outpatient	Gestalt experiential	Individual	?	Y	Y	Y
Rennie (1987) Person-centered	Outpatient	Rogerian	Individual	?	N	N	N
Toukmanian (1984) Experiential-cognitive	Outpatient	Rogerian cognitive	Individual	?	N	N	N

[1]Conformance scales available to rate the degree to which therapists are offering the therapy in a "pure" form.
[2]Competency scales available to rate the degree to which therapists are offering high (ideal) levels of the therapy.
[3]Manual has been tested in empirical research.

son & Woody, 1995). Clearly, the use of treatment manuals in outcome research is beginning to have an impact on the training and practice of psychotherapy.

Because treatment manuals have not been used in studies investigating their effectiveness in supervising and training graduate-level students, it is not known if training in the specific manualized techniques is a beneficial tool for graduate-training programs and internship agencies. Several issues will probably affect the efficacy of manuals in training novice therapists. Most manuals suggest that, as a minimum requirement, supervision be done by someone who is familiar with the techniques specified in the manual. Other manuals suggest participating in the treatment as an observer before attempting to administer the treatment (Lewinsohn, Antonuccio, Breckenridge, & Teri, 1984). To receive supervision in some techniques, the trainee may have to travel to the location where the manual was developed, a burden that is impractical. Even attendance at extended workshops at national conventions would be a hardship for many students. It is not known if training conducted by typical faculty members can occur at facilities other than those where the manual was first used (see for example, Linehan, Heard, & Armstrong's, 1993, manual for treating borderline personality disorders). Our own experience in applying Luborsky's (1984) supportive-expressive manual, without exposure to expert supervisors, suggests at least limited success with third-year clinical students, especially for those who had demonstrated a strong interest in psychoanalytic treatments in the past.

Another issue that must be covered when evaluating the effectiveness of treatment manuals for training is comparative effectiveness of supervision versus reading of the manuals. Perhaps supervision is the more important aspect of training with manuals, and manuals are really not superior to any other book on psychotherapy theory. This will undoubtedly depend on the particular treatment that is under consideration as some are much more explicit than others, and some are more easily implemented than others. Research on the contribution of supervision to manualized therapies awaits further evaluation.

Therapists-in-training might also misuse techniques that are so succinctly summarized in manuals. Both Luborsky (1984) and Strupp and Binder (1984) warn the reader/therapist in their treatment manuals not to confront the client with an overintellectualized interpretation of their problematic relationship styles. Inexperienced therapists may be inflexible with the specific formulations and interventions of manualized therapy. This may represent the single most important contribution of the supervisor, providing feedback and tempering the behavior of trainees who have already familiarized themselves with the content of the manual.

In some ways, the results of research on training via theory-based manuals parallels research on psychotherapy and the early research on training in interpersonal skills. There is evidence that training outcomes can be both positive and negative and that there are individual differences in effectiveness for trainees using the same material as a consequence of different trainers. For example, Henry, Schacht, Strupp, Butler, and Binder (1993) reported on the effects of manuals on training and outcome of time-limited dynamic psychotherapy. Among other conclusions, they caution that use of the manual successfully changed therapists' technical interventions but had unexpected negative effects on some therapeutic behaviors. Among the unhelpful changes was a tendency for therapists to become less approving and supportive, less optimistic, and more authoritative and defensive. It is important to note that these attitudes and behaviors have been strongly linked to psychotherapy outcome. Henry et al. (1993) suggest that one of the paradoxical results of training was that at the same time therapists were becoming more intellectually sensitized to the importance of in-session dyadic process, they were actually delivering a higher "toxic-dose" of disaffiliative communications. Negative effects of training manuals have also been discussed in a broader context.

In an auxiliary report of the same project, Henry, Strupp, Butler, Schacht, and Binder (1993) demonstrated clear differences in trainee outcome as a function of the trainer's teaching style. Effect sizes indicate that trainees of one trainer showed much higher levels of change than those of the other trainer. Evidence was presented to suggest specific differences in teaching style that may be related to more effective learning, and their report has numerous suggestions for future research. But the implications for training are clear. Training can be for better or for worse and, as in therapy, the supervisor may be even more important than the manual itself (Moras, 1989). Anecdotal evidence for negative effects has also been offered by Lazarus (1990) in an interesting and challenging personal statement about learning to be an effective psychotherapist.

Another aspect of treatment manuals that must be considered is the degree to which they require prerequisite skills. Some behavioral treatment manuals have been used by paraprofessionals (Lewinsohn et al., 1984), whereas the authors of psychodynamic manuals recommend use by experienced clinicians who have demonstrated a basic understanding of psychotherapy and the psychotherapeutic relationship (Luborsky, 1984; Strupp & Binder, 1984). Until the utility of manuals for training is more extensively investigated, little can be said about the importance of using them at a particular time in the trainee's development. Most would consider the basics of interpersonal skills to be primary; however, specific skills that could be learned from treatment manuals may give the trainees confidence early in their training experience. The utility of treatment manuals for trainees with different conceptual skills and different levels of psychotherapy sophistication remains to be seen.

Needless to say, numerous issues confront the investigator who is testing the efficacy of supervision via treatment manuals. Because no research has been published on this relatively new area, many questions must remain unanswered. At the very least, however, treatment manuals can be used as reading material in psychotherapy classes. More likely, they will provide the needed clarity of goals that will sharpen the efficiency of supervision and the ease with which it can be evaluated in research.

One final comment about treatment manuals and perhaps training should be made. Given that specific interventions or techniques account for approximately 15% of the variance associated with treatment effects whereas relationship variables common to all treatments and placebo effects account for more than 50% of the variance (Lambert, 1986), it may be more beneficial and cost effective to concentrate training efforts on relationship enhancement skills and therapist attitudes. Although most would agree that both technique and attitude or relationship are important, it seems as though manual-based supervision may further encourage reliance on technique rather than on relationship variables. This is especially true in psychotherapy and supervision research because technique training is easier to operationalize, conduct, and report. Nevertheless, common factors seem to be more important than technique to outcome and therefore should not be neglected in research on manual-based therapy supervision.

Other Technical Skills

The numerous treatment manuals for specifying technical aspects of psychotherapy are a welcome and potentially useful arrival for supervision practice and research. Although many studies have been conducted to examine the impact of training and supervision for learning basic interviewing and interpersonal skills, fewer studies have tackled the difficulties associated with understanding the best methods for helping supervisees to gain more complex skills such as conceptualization of cases, appropriate confrontation, or the timing of interpretations. Treatment manuals help to operationalize technical skills so that a newer generation of supervision studies can be conducted to examine the process of complex skill acquisition. To date, a limited amount of research has been conducted on technical skills. Three more recent areas of research that are related to therapist technical skills are briefly discussed in this section: family therapy training, theories of supervisee development, and training in conceptualization.

Family Therapy Training.   In general, empirical studies of supervision have been a series of isolated studies with little connection to previous research (Hansen, Robins, & Grimes, 1982). However, a few pockets of coordinated research exist. Research considering the supervision and training of family therapists is one such area. For example, Piercy, Laird, and Mohammed (1983) evaluated two methods of training family therapists: an observation feedback (OF) approach and a skills-based approach (SB). No differences were noted between the two methods, but relationship skills were learned more effectively when the OF training preceded the SB training. This and other studies are being conducted to better understand the process of skill acquisition for family therapists (e.g., Doty, 1986; Tucker & Pinsof, 1984). More detailed discussion of this body of literature is presented in Chapter 25.

Developmental Issues.   During the past two decades, there has been a growing interest in the development of the supervisee. These issues center on changes in supervisees' knowledge, skills, and experience over the course of their training. For example, Worthington (1987) reviewed and summarized no fewer than 16 different developmental models. Developmental issues serve to complicate supervision research since effective supervision will depend on the developmental stage of the supervisee. Several studies, mostly conducted in the 1980s, examine one or another developmental paradigm (e.g., Boyer, 1984; Weaver, 1987; Winter 1987; and numerous others), yet more and better research is needed to substantiate the developmental theories and rule out other interpretations of trainee skill acquisition (e.g., learning theory; Holloway, 1987).

Training in Conceptualization.   As part of the emphasis on developmental models of trainee growth, several researchers have conducted studies or produced theories of supervisee cognitive development. For example, Biggs (1988) presented a method for developing conceptualization skills through case presentations, and Patterson (1988) presented a model of training using the concept of automaticity. That is, movement from one stage of training to the next is based on the degree to which the skills have become automatic or habitual. Since trainees cannot focus on simultaneous processes, skills are broken down into stages with movement to the next skill or stage dependent on the automaticity of learning for the previous skill. Although a number of ideas exist concerning supervisee ability to conceptualize or process information, little research regarding the best methods for training or supervising exists. In addition, minimal evidence exists to support the notion that the ability to conceptualize cases is an important skill to begin with. In one study, Kurpius, Benjamin, and Morran (1985) found that counselors who were taught what and how to look for information generated superior hypotheses about clients. Other studies have noted that trainees with a higher conceptual level are more empathic, more self-aware, and more autonomous (Berg & Stone, 1980; Goldberg, 1974; McNeill, Stoltenberg, & Pierce, 1985). Yet overall, more research is needed to draw any meaningful conclusions.

SUPERVISORY AND TRAINING OUTCOME CRITERIA

In order to measure the effects of training and supervision, it is necessary to use procedures that reliably reflect the changes that are occurring in the trainee. Clearly, this aspect of research has a powerful effect on the supervisory process in that the measurement of training outcomes requires the clear specification of the goals and methods of supervision. Rosenbaum (1984) has reported that although APA has specifically recommended that training programs formulate and publish explicit criteria by which their psychotherapy practice can be evaluated, an amazing 77% of the students polled either did not know the criteria or thought evaluations of their therapy were based on the professors' personal biases. It is hoped that the use of meaningful and valid outcome measures will greatly facilitate the practice of supervision as well as the discovery of the most useful supervisory methods.

What Are the Goals of Supervision?

The goals of supervision so far discussed in this chapter can be categorized as focusing on trainee interviewing skills, interpersonal skills, and technical skills. In addition, supervision can be directed at changing supervisee values and attitudes and personal growth (Holloway & Neufeldt, 1995). Under the heading of personal growth are numerous changes in cognition and feeling. The student becomes more aware of self and of behavioral patterns and tendencies, resolves conflicts, becomes less anxious and more confident, and—one hopes—identifies with the supervisor in a significant and positive way. Criteria for measuring these kinds of changes will not be reviewed here because the measures typically employed have included a host of personality scales and measures of trainees' symptomatic states (e.g., anxiety) or self-actualization (see Lambert, Christensen, & DeJulio, 1983, for measures of this type).

The present review focuses on measures of training outcome as they impact the trainees' conceptual skills, intervention skills, and experience as a supervisee. Holloway (1984) suggested that a limited range of measures may unduly restrict the future study of supervision and suggested expanding the types of measures reviewed. Although not in complete agreement with this appraisal of the best direction for future research, we have included a review of measures of supervisor performance in supervision. Instruments in this area tap either trainees' perception of the supervisor or supervisors' self-perception of their role and behavior in supervision. These instruments have the advantage of helping supervisors improve their performance while they also allow trainees to express their satisfaction with the process. Instruments measuring attitudes, perceptions, and behavior of trainees and supervisors are listed in Table 24.3 along with an indication of the situation or context in which or about which evaluations are made. The person providing the evaluation of the trainee or supervisor is indicated. Finally, an attempt is made to describe the primary area of interest assessed by the questionnaire, or rating device.

As can be seen, the devices that have been typically employed are widely varied and have different purposes. Even when two devices have the same purpose (i.e., assess the same component of trainee change), they differ in (a) the focus of evaluation, such as the trainee or the client; (b) data-gathering techniques, such as structured personality tests or actual interaction with patients who have sought help; (c) the fact that the data provided sometimes come from the client, sometimes from the supervisor, and frequently from the trainee; and (d) the fact that data are collected at different times, both during and after

Table 24.3   Instruments Used to Measure the Effects and Process of Supervision

Measures of Trainee Performance			Primary Area of Assessment
Instrument Name and Primary Reference	Context[1]	Evaluator[2]	
Affective Sensitivity Scale (Kagan et al., 1967)	An	O	Interviewing skills
Barrett-Lennard Relationship Inventory (Barrett-Lennard, 1962)	Pt/Sup	C/T	Therapist-client relationship
Blumberg's Interactional Analysis (1970)	Sup	O	Positive interactions
Bowers Psychotherapy Skills Rating Scale (Bowers, Bauron, & Mines, 1984)	Pt	S/peer	Characteristics of
Carkhuff Communication Index (Carkhuff, 1969a)	An	O	Interpersonal skills
Carkhuff Discrimination Index (Carkhuff, 1969a)	An	O	Interpersonal skills
Carkhuff Scales of Empathy, Respect, Genuineness, Self Disclosure, Specificity, Confrontation, and Immediacy (Carkhuf, 1969b)	Pt/Sup	O	Interpersonal skills
Counseling Evaluation Inventory (Linden, Stone, & Shertzer, 1965)	Pt	C/T/S	Therapist-client relationship
Counseling Session Report (Silverman, 1972)	Pt	T	Supervisee perception of
Counseling Strategies Checklist (Hackney & Nye, 1973)	Pt	O	Interviewing skills
Counselor Development Questionnaire (Reising & Daniels, 1983)	Sup	T	Supervisee self-perception
Counselor Effectiveness Scale (Ivey et al., 1968)	Pt	C	Therapist-client relationship
Counselor Evaluation Rating Scale (Loesch & Rucker, 1977)	Sup/Pt	S	Counselor behavior
Counselor Interview Competence Scale (Jenkins, 1982)			
Counselor Perception Questionnaire (Blocher et al., 1985)	An	O	Cognitive/conceptual operations
Counselor Rating Form (Barack & LaCrosse, 1977)	Pt	S	Effective counseling
Counselor Training Questionnaire (Rosenthal, 1977)	An	O	Response preference-counselor
Counselor Verbal Response Scale (Kagan et al., 1967)	Pt	O	Interviewing skills
Family Concept Assessment (Tucker & Pinsof, 1984)	Pt	O	Observational/ conceptual ability
Family Therapy Assessment Exercise (Breunlin, Schwartz, Drauss, & Selby, 1983)	An	O	Observational/ conceptual
Family Therapist Rating Scale (Piercy, Laird, & Mohammed, 1983)	An	S/O	Goal-directed therapist activity
Field Practice Checklist (Dilley, 1964)	Pt	S	Self-ratings of counselor behavior

(table continues)

Table 24.3   (Continued)

Measures of Trainee Performance			Primary Area of Assessment
Instrument Name and Primary Reference	Context[1]	Evaluator[2]	
Flanders Interaction System (Amidon, 1965)	Sup	O	Verbal behavior
Hill Interaction Matrix (Hill, 1965)	Sup	O	Verbal behavior
Hogan Empathy Scale (Hogan, 1969)		T	Therapist personality trait
Ideal Therapeutic Relationship Scale (Authier & Gustafson, 1975)	Pt	O	Therapist-client relationship
Interaction Process Analysis (Bales, 1950)	Sup	O	Verbal behavior
Interview Checklist (Waltz & Johnson, 1963)	Pt	S	Effective counseling behavior
Interview Rating Scale (Anderson & Anderson, 1962)	Pt	C	Rapport, ideal relationship
Ivey's Rating Scale of Counselor Effectiveness (Ivey, 1971)	Pt	S	Effective counseling behavior
Level of Supervision Survey (Miars et al., 1983)	Sup	S	Supervisors' perception of selves
Microcounseling Skill Discrimination Scale (Lee, Zingle, Patterson, Ivey, & Haase, 1976)	An	O	Interviewing skills
No name (Allen, Szollos, & Williams, 1986)	Sup	T	Supervisee perception of supervision
Paragraph Completion Method (Hunt, Butler, Noy, & Rosser, 1976)	An	O	Cognitive/conceptual operations
Porter Test of Counselor Attitudes (Porter, 1950)		O	Response preference-psychotherapy
Professional History Form (Mead, 1990)	Sup	S	Readiness to assume professional practice
Judgment Rating Scale (Newman et al., 1988)		O	Conceptualization of therapy
Psychotherapy Session Report (Orlinsky & Howard, 1975)	Pt	O/S/T	Reactions to session
Role-Play Behavior (Gallacher & Hargie, 1989)			
Supervisor Behavior Checklist (Davis & Avery, 1978)	Sup	T	Effective supervisor behavior
Supervisor Role Analysis (Johnson & Gysbers, 1966)	Sup	S	Self-perception of supervisory preferences
Supervisor Questionnaire (Worthington & Roelke, 1979)	Sup	S	Self-perception of supervisory experience
Supervisory Styles Inventory (Friedlander & Ward, 1984)	Sup	S/T	Preferred focus of supervision
The Depth of Interpretation Scale (Harway, Dittmann, Raush, Bordin, & Rigler, 1955)	Pt	O	Verbal behavior
Therapeutic Procedures Inventory (Orlinsky et al., 1986)	Pt	T	Use of specific treatment procedures
Therapist Action Scale (Hoyt, Marmus, Harowitz, & Alvarez, 1981)	Pt	T	Therapeutic orientation

Table 24.3   (Continued)

Measures of Trainee Performance			Primary Area of Assessment
Instrument Name and Primary Reference	Context[1]	Evaluator[2]	
Therapist Activity Level Scales (Howe & Pope, 1961)	Pt	O	Verbal behavior
Therapist Orientations Questionnaire (Sundland, 1977)		S/T	Response preference
Trainee Personal Reaction Scale (Holloway & Wampald, 1983)	Sup	T	Perception of supervision
Trainee Value of Cues Scale (McClure & Vriend, 1976)		T	Intervention style
Training Reaction Questionnaire (Berg & Stone, 1980)	Sup	T	Supervisor ratings of trainee reactions to supervision
Truax Relationship Questionnaire (Truax & Carkhuff, 1967)	Pt/Sup	C/T	Therapist-client relationship
Usual Therapeutic Practices Scale (Walloch & Strupp, 1964)	Pt	T	Therapeutic orientation
Verbal Response Modes (Stiles, 1986)	Pt	O	Therapist in-session behaviors

[1]The context for ratings was classified as in supervision (Sup), in psychotherapy (Pt), from an analogue (An) situation, or not classified in the case of personality inventories.
[2]The person doing the evaluation was classified as trained observer (O), the client (C), the supervisor (S), or the trainee (T).

counseling. All these dissimilarities, plus usual errors of measurement, have the cumulative effect of making it difficult for agreement to be reached between measures.

One important dimension of criterion measures that should be stressed is the degree to which tests and ratings of trainee behavior are actually based on their behavior while in counseling sessions or whether they merely attempt to generalize to their performance in actual counseling interviews. The most ambitious designs have involved the measurement of trainee behaviors such as empathy and confrontation during therapy with actual clients. Less ambitious but still rigorous have been studies that measured trainee behavior with persons invited to act as patients. These "role-play" situations allow for considerable experimental control, but unfortunately they require the assumption that the results in this situation will generalize to situations in which role playing is not involved. A step further from actual counseling has been the use of a coached client who plays a designated role. This approach is currently most popular in training marital and family therapy interventions. Another method often employed in research involves videotaped sessions. Because no personal relationship exists in such situations, the use of a filmed or videotaped client to whom the therapist responds verbally (on tape), by writing out a response, or by picking a response from those provided by the experimenter, these techniques are far from actual counseling. Another simulation least like counseling has involved the use of a typescript of client expressions. Finally, some researchers have used a questionnaire to ask the therapist to indicate how he or she thinks he or she responds in the therapy situation.

Research on these analogue measurement procedures has been disappointing. Porter's (1950) test—the first actual simulation, and one that reflected obvious pre- and posttraining changes—never was found to correlate with actual counselor behavior. More recent simulations have followed this trend. Butler and Hansen (1973), for example, found no relationship between written and oral performance after training. Perry (1975) also found no carry-over from simulated counseling and a 15-minute live interview. Gormally, Hill, Gulanick, and McGovern (1975) found written responses and interviews with a volunteer client were not significantly correlated. Similar results were reported by Rosenthal (1977). As yet, those researchers studying marital and family therapy (e.g., Tucker & Pinsof, 1984) have not investigated the degree to which their measures generalize to actual therapy behavior. Research in the 1990s has been characterized by both analogue and live therapy demonstrations (Holloway & Neufeldt, 1995).

In general, it can be concluded that the more distant the criterion measure is from the actual criterion (performance in psychotherapy), the less representative it will be. Stated more strongly, simulated counseling criteria, especially paper-pencil devices, seemingly have little relationship to the phenomena they are supposed to represent. This appears to be even more true, however, for measures that make no attempt to simulate situational stimuli. The Hogan Empathy Scale, for example, relies on a traditional True-False personality test format (items come directly from the CPI). This scale has shown no relationship with other measures of empathy, nor any relationship to therapy outcome.

The following conclusions seem to be warranted by the current review of training outcome measures:

1. The most useful of these measures focus on specific observable behavior of trainees in therapy. They minimize inferences drawn by the raters and concentrate on observable behavior. Specific measures would include, for example, the Counselor Verbal Response Scale, Counseling Strategies Checklist, and Matarazzo Check List of Therapist Behavior. Frequency counts of carefully specified behaviors have proved quite useful and enjoy continued use.

2. The observer rating scales developed by Rogers's students (mainly, Truax & Carkhuff, 1967) have many problems associated with their use. They are time consuming and expensive to employ properly. They require considerable inference on the part of judges and quite possibly are not measuring the same dimensions when used by different experimenters. Finally, they do not have a strong relationship with psychotherapy outcome despite frequent use in the past. They have nearly disappeared from use in contemporary research. Despite the many problems associated with their use, their impact on training and practice has been substantial. They continue to be used in prepracticum training. The Barrett-Lennard Relationship Inventory has the advantage of having been used in numerous outcomes studies, and it has been shown to have at least a modest relationship to psychotherapy outcome. It has several shortcomings but, at this time, is perhaps the best measure of the therapeutic relationship as it is perceived by the client.

3. The most convincing procedure has been the evaluation of training through criteria from several sources. This is considered absolutely necessary in psychotherapy outcome research and seems desirable in the domain of supervisory research. Frequency counts of specified therapist behaviors proved a valuable source of information from the point of view of ideal therapist behavior. It seems desirable to collect data about the therapist from clients, the supervisor, and the trainees themselves. Related measures include a host of focal scales intended to rate the therapeutic alliance (see Orlinsky & Howard, 1986).

4. Devices that are based on simulations of psychotherapy, especially those that rely on a fixed client role and fixed therapist responses, are not yet acceptable and convincing training criteria. In part, their use depends on the extent to which researchers and supervisors wish to generalize their results. As long as no inference is made suggesting that changes on these measures reflect similar changes in other situations, such as actual therapy session, their use is acceptable but of limited value. At present, however, there is little information to allow generalization to actual performance and much information to the contrary.

5. The most persuasive studies of the effects of training and supervision will include an analysis of trainee behaviors with actual clients, as well as a measure of the effects of these behaviors on clients. If, for example, a trainee is being supervised specifically on variables that are supposed to affect the therapist-client relationship, then not only is a measure of those variables necessary, but some measure of the quality of the relationship is also called for. It would also be ideal to test the effects of supervision by examining patient outcome. Given the state of empirical findings in this area, however, this remains an ideal that will not be achieved in the near future. Perhaps the use of treatment manuals along with adherence and competency measures will help to fill in the gaps.

6. The field is still characterized by a plethora of homemade devices that are used only once and discarded. In addition, few researchers bother to publish reliability or validity data on their scales. This is a tolerable situation given the general chaos prevalent in psychotherapy outcome research and practice. Nevertheless, advances in knowledge can be expected to increase with advances in criterion measurement. Research in this area is highly recommended and promises to affect theory as well as practice.

CONCLUSION

It is tempting to justify graduate and postgraduate education in professional psychology by deferring to the firm foundation of empirical evidence supporting the positive effects of psychological interventions. Indeed, more than 50 years of outcome research have clearly shown that many psychotherapies have demonstrable effects on a wide variety of client problems. These effects are not only statistically significant, but also clinically meaningful and lasting. In addition to establishing the efficacy of psychotherapy, considerable research has helped identify the aspects or components of psychotherapy that promote improvement of symptoms. The interested reader is encouraged to peruse the numerous, carefully conducted reviews of the literature that elaborate on the aforementioned conclusions (e.g., Lambert & Bergin, 1994).

Although literature on the effectiveness of psychotherapy might tempt one to embrace the inference that graduate training in psychotherapy is crucial, it must be recognized that researchers have yet to conduct sufficient outcome studies that adequately explore the relationship between specific aspects of training programs (e.g., therapy courses, supervision) and therapy outcome. Despite the shortage of studies examining patient outcome and its link to supervision and other training experiences, some evidence can be found linking these two variables (cf. Burlingame, Fuhriman, Paul, & Ogles, 1989; Strupp et al., 1989; Henry, Schacht et al., 1993).

A recent review of graduate training in psychotherapy and patient outcome suggests a clear but modest treatment effect size is associated with training. These treatment effects are present on a variety of measures of patient improvement (Stein & Lambert, 1995). It also appears that lay therapists who work in community mental health centers and clinics appear to produce higher premature dropout rates than their more highly trained or experienced colleagues (Stein & Lambert, 1995).

There is no shortage of topics for future study—the interested researcher will probably find conducting such research a rich and interesting source of satisfaction as well as a worthy contribution to effective treatment.

REFERENCES

Alberts, G., & Edelstein, B. (1990). Therapist training: A critical review of skill training studies. *Clinical Psychology Review, 10,* 497–511.

Baker, S. B., & Daniels, T. (1989). Integrating research on the microcounseling program: A meta-analysis. *Journal of Counseling Psychology, 36,* 213–222.

Baker, S. B., Daniels, T. G., & Greeley, A. T. (1990). Systematic training of graduate-level counselors: Narrative and meta-analytic reviews of three major programs. *The Counseling Psychologist, 18,* 355–421.

Barlow, D. A. (1993). *Handbook of psychological disorders* (2nd ed.). New York: Guilford.

Beck, A. T. (1986). Cognitive therapy: A sign of retrogression or progress. *Behavior Therapist, 9,* 2–3.

Berg, K. S., & Stone, G. L. (1980). Effects on conceptual level and supervision structure on counselor skill development. *Journal of Counseling Psychology, 27,* 500–509.

Biggs, D. A. (1988). The case presentation approach in clinical supervision. *Counselor Education and Supervision, 27,* 240–248.

Binder, J. L. (1993). Is it time to improve psychotherapy training? *Clinical Psychology Review, 13,* 310–318.

Bootzin, R. R., & Ruggill, J. S. (1988). Training issues in behavior therapy. *Journal of Consulting and Clinical Psychology, 56,* 703–709.

Bouchard, M., Wright, J., Mathieu, M., Lalonde, F., Bergeson, G., & Toupin, J. (1980). Structured learning in teaching therapists social skills training: Acquisition, maintenance, and impact on client outcome. *Journal of Consulting and Clinical Psychology, 48,* 491–502.

Boyer, M. C. (1984). *Influence of conceptual system and training in supervision on supervision behavior. Dissertation Abstracts International, 45,* 412A.

Burlingame, G. M., Fuhriman, A., Paul, S., & Ogles, B. M. (1989). Implementing a time-limited therapy program: Differential effects of training and experience. *Psychotherapy, 26,* 303–313.

Butler, E. R., & Hansen, J. C. (1973). Facilitative training: Acquisition, retention and modes assessment. *Journal of Counseling Psychology, 20,* 60–65.

Carkuff, R. R. (1971). *The development of human resources.* New York: Holt, Rinehart and Winston.

Collingwood, T. (1971). Retention and retraining of interpersonal communications skills. *Journal of Clinical Psychology, 27,* 294–296.

Crabb, W. T., Moracco, J. C., & Bender, R. C. (1983). A comparative study of empathy training with programmed instruction for lay helpers. *Journal of Counseling Psychology, 30,* 221–226.

Crits-Christoph, P., Frank, E., Chambliss, D. L., Brody, C., & Karp, J. (1995). Training in empirically-validated treatments: What are clinical psychology students learning? *Psychotherapy, 26,* 210–216.

DeRubeis, R. J., Hollon, S. D., Evans, M. D., & Bemis, K. M. (1982). Can psychotherapies for depression be discriminated? A systematic investigation of cognitive therapy and interpersonal therapy. *Journal of Consulting and Clinical Psychology, 50,* 744–756.

Dobson, K. S. (1989). A meta-analysis of the efficacy of cognitive therapy for depression. *Journal of Consulting and Clinical Psychology, 57,* 414–419.

Dobson, K. S., & Shaw, B. F. (1988). The use of treatment manuals in cognitive therapy: Experience and issues. *Journal of Consulting and Clinical Psychology, 56,* 673–680.

Doty, D. R. (1986). Family therapy supervision: Assessment of skill attainment by trainee and supervisor. *Dissertation Abstracts International, 46,* 3589B.

Evans, D. R., Uhlemann, M. R., & Hearn, M. T. (1978). Microcounseling and sensitivity training with hotline workers. *Journal of Community Psychology, 6,* 139–146.

Fyffe, A. E., & Oei, T. P. S. (1979). Influence of modeling and feedback provided by the supervisors in a microskills training program for beginning counselors. *Journal of Clinical Psychology, 35,* 651–656.

Gerkin, C. (1969). An objective method for evaluating training programs in counseling psychology. *Journal of Counseling Psychology, 16,* 227–237.

Goldberg, A. D. (1974). Conceptual system as a predisposition toward therapeutic communication. *Journal of Counseling Psychology, 21,* 364–368.

Gormally, J., Hill, C. E., Gulanick, N., & McGovern, T. (1975). The persistence of communication skills for undergraduate and graduate students. *Journal of Clinical Psychology, 31,* 369–372.

Gottman, J. M., & Markman, H. J. (1978). Experimental designs in psychotherapy research. In A. E. Bergin & S. L. Garfield (Eds.), *Handbook of psychotherapy and behavior change* (2nd ed., pp. 23–62). New York: Wiley.

Guest, P. D., & Beutler, L. E. (1988). Impact of psychotherapy supervision on therapist orientation and values. *Journal of Consulting and Clinical Psychology, 56,* 653–658.

Gustavson, J. L., Cundick, B. P., & Lambert, M. J. (1981). Analysis of observed responses to the Rogers, Perls, and Ellis films. *Perceptual and Motor Skills, 53,* 759–764.

Hansen, J. C., Robins, T. H., & Grimes, J. (1982). Review of research on practicum supervision. *Counselor Education and Supervision, 22,* 15–24.

Henry, W. P., Schacht, T. E., Strupp, H. H., Butler, S. F., & Binder, J. L. (1993). Effects of training in time-limited dynamic psychotherapy: Mediators of therapists' responses to training. *Journal of Consulting and Clinical Psychology, 61,* 441–447.

Henry, W. P., Strupp, H. H., Butler, S. F., Schacht, T. E., & Binder, J. L. (1993). Effects of training in time-limited dynamic psychotherapy: Changes in therapist behavior. *Journal of Consulting and Clinical Psychology, 61,* 434–440.

Hess, A. K. (1983). Learning counseling and psychotherapy skills: A challenge in personal and professional identity. In G. Jumprer & S. Walfish (Eds.), *Clinical counseling and community psychology: A student guide to graduate training and professional practice.* New York: Irvington.

Holloway, E. L. (1984). Outcome evaluation in supervision research. *The Counseling Psychologist, 12,* 167–174.

Holloway, E. L. (1987). Developmental models of supervision: Is it development? *Professional Psychology: Research and Practice, 28,* 209–216.

Holloway, E. L., & Neufeldt, S. A. (1995). Supervision: Its contribution to treatment efficacy. *Journal of Consulting and Clinical Psychology, 63,* 207–213.

Hurt, S. W., & Clarkin, J. F. (1990). Borderline personality disorder: Prototypic typology and the development of treatment manuals. *Psychiatric Annals, 20,* 13–18.

Ivey, A. E., Normington, C. J., Miller, D. C., Merrill, W. H., & Haase, R. F. (1968). Microcounseling and attending behavior: An approach to prepracticum counselor training. *Journal of Counseling Psychology, Monograph Supplement, 15,* 1–12.

Kagan, N. (1984). Interpersonal process recall: Basic methods and recent research. In D. Larson (Ed.), *Teaching psychological skills: Models for giving psychology away* (pp. 229–244). Monterey, CA: Brooks/Cole.

Kurpius, D. J., Benjamin, D., & Morran, D. K. (1985). Effects of teaching a cognitive strategy on counselor trainee internal dialogue and clinical hypothesis formulation. *Journal of Counseling Psychology, 32,* 263–271.

Lambert, M. J. (1974). Supervisory and counseling process: A comparative study. *Counselor Education and Supervision, 14,* 54–60.

Lambert, M. J. (Ed.). (1983). *Psychotherapy and patient relationships.* Homewood, IL: Dorsey.

Lambert, M. J. (1986). Psychotherapy outcome: Implications for eclectic psychotherapy. In J. C. Norcross (Ed.), *Handbook of eclectic psychotherapy* (pp. 36–62). New York: Brunner/Mazel.

Lambert, M. J., & Arnold, R. C. (1987). Research and the supervisory process. *Professional Psychology: Research and Practice, 18,* 217–224.

Lambert, M. J., & Bergin, A. E. (1994). The effectiveness of psychotherapy. In A. E. Bergin & S. L. Garfield (Eds.), *Handbook of psychotherapy and behavior change* (4th ed., pp. 143–189). New York: Wiley.

Lambert, M. J., Christensen, E. R., & DeJulio, S. S. (1983). *The assessment of psychotherapy outcome.* New York: Wiley-Interscience.

Lambert, M. J., DeJulio, S. S., & Stein, D. M. (1978). Therapist interpersonal skills: Process, outcome, methodological considerations, and recommendations for future research. *Psychological Bulletin, 85,* 467–489.

Lambert, M. J., & Ogles, B. M. (1988). Treatment manuals: Problems and promise. *Journal of Integration & Eclectic Psychotherapy, 7,* 187–204.

Lane, R. G. (1974). *The influence of supervision on the trainee's development of facilitative skills in counseling.* Unpublished doctoral dissertation, Arizona State University.

Lazarus, A. (1990). The effects of training on providers. *Journal of Behavior Therapy, 21,* 190–192.

Lewinsohn, P. M., Antonuccio, D. O., Breckenridge, J. S., & Teri, L. (1984). *The coping with depression course.* Eugene, OR: Castalia.

Linehan, M. M., Heard, H. L., & Armstrong, H. E. (1993). Naturalistic follow-up of a behavioral treatment for chronically parasuicidal borderline patients. *Archives of General Psychiatry, 50,* 971–974.

Loganbill, C., Hardy, E., & Delworth, U. (1982). Supervision: A conceptual model. *Counseling Psychologist, 10,* 3–42.

Luborsky, L. (1984). *Principles of psycho-analytic psychotherapy: A manual for supportive-expressive treatment.* New York: Basic Books.

Matarazzo, R. G. (1978). Research on the teaching and learning of psychotherapeutic skills. In S. L. Garfield & A. E. Bergin (Eds.), *Handbook of psychotherapy and behavior change* (2nd ed., pp. 941–966). New York: Wiley.

Matarazzo, R. G., & Patterson, D. R. (1986). Methods of teaching therapeutic skills. In A. Bergin & S. Garfield (Eds.), *Handbook of psychotherapy and behavior change* (3rd ed., pp. 821–843). New York: Wiley.

Matarazzo, R. G., Phillips, J. S., Wiens, A. N., & Saslow, G. (1965). Learning the art of interviewing: A study of what beginning students do and their pattern of change. *Psychotherapy: Theory, Research and Practice, 2,* 49–60.

McNeill, B. W., Stoltenberg, C. D., & Pierce, R. A. (1985). Supervisees' perceptions of their development: A test of the counselor complexity model. *Journal of Counseling Psychology, 32,* 630–633.

Mitchell, K. M., Bozarth, J. D., & Krauft, C. C. (1977). A reappraisal of the therapeutic effectiveness of accurate empathy, nonpossessive warmth, and genuineness. In A. S. Gurman & A. M. Razin (Eds.), *Effective psychotherapy* (pp. 482–502). Elmsford, NY: Pergamon.

Moras, K. (1989). The U. Mass group and the psychotherapy integration movement. *Journal of Integration and Eclectic Psychotherapy, 8,* 157–160.

Newman, F. L., Kopta, S. M., McGovern, M. P., Howard, K. I., & McNeilly, C. L. (1988). Evaluating trainees relative to their supervisors during the psychology internship. *Journal of Consulting and Clinical Psychology, 56,* 659–665.

Orlinsky, D. E., & Howard, K. I. (1986). Process and outcome in psychotherapy. In S. L. Garfield & A. E. Bergin (Eds.), *Handbook of psychotherapy and behavior change* (3rd ed., pp. 311–381). New York: Wiley.

Patterson, L. E. (1988). The function of automaticity in counselor information processing. *Counselor Education and Supervision, 27,* 195–202.

Payne, P. A., & Gralinsky, D. M. (1968). Effects of supervision style and empathy upon counselor learning. *Journal of Counseling Psychology, 15,* 517–521.

Perry, M. A. (1975). Modeling and instructions in training for counselor empathy. *Journal of Counseling Psychology, 22,* 173–179.

Peters, G. A., Cormier, L. S., & Cormier, W. H. (1978). Effects of modeling, rehearsal, feedback, and remediation on acquisition of a counseling strategy. *Journal of Counseling Psychology, 25,* 231–237.

Pierce, R. M., Carkhuff, R. R., & Berenson, B. G. (1967). The effects of high- and low-functioning supervisors upon counselors in training. *Journal of Clinical Psychology, 23,* 212–215.

Pierce, R. M., & Schuable P. G. (1970). Graduate training of facilitative counselors: The effects of individual supervision. *Journal of Counseling Psychology, 17*, 210–215.

Pierce, R. M., & Schuable, P. G. (1971). Study on the effects of individual supervision in graduate school training. *Journal of Counseling Psychology, 18*, 186–187.

Piercy, F. P., Laird, R. A., & Mohammed, Z. (1983). A family therapist rating scale. *Journal of Marital and Family Therapy, 9*, 49–59.

Porter, E. H. (1950). A simple measure of counselor attitudes. In E. G. Williamson (Ed.), *Trends in student personnel work* (pp. 120–139). Minneapolis: University of Minnesota Press.

Richardson, B., & Stone, G. L. (1981). Effects of a cognitive adjunct procedure within a microtraining situation. *Journal of Counseling Psychology, 28*, 168–175.

Robiner, W. N., Fuhrman, M., Ristredts, S., & Bobbitt, B. (1994). The Minnesota Supervisory Inventory (MSI): Development, psychometric characteristics, and supervisory evaluation issues. *The Clinical Psychologist, 47*, 4–17.

Robiner, W. N., & Schofield, W. (1990). References on supervision in clinical and counseling psychology. *Professional Psychology: Research and Practice, 21*, 297–312.

Rodenhauser, P., Rudisill, J. R., & Painter, A. F. (1989). Attributes conducive to learning in psychotherapy supervision. *American Journal of Psychotherapy, 43*, 368–377.

Rogers, C. R. (1959). A theory of therapy, personality, and interpersonal relationships, as developed in the client-centered framework. In S. Koch (Ed.), *Psychology: A study of a science (Vol. 3: Formulations of the person and the social context)* (pp. 184–256). New York: McGraw-Hill.

Ronnestad, M. H. (1974). Effects of modeling, feedback, and experiential supervision on beginning counseling students' communication of empathic understanding. *Dissertation Abstracts International, 35*, 6985A (University Microfilms No. 74-9982).

Ronnestad, M. H., & Skovholt, T. M. (1993). Supervision of beginning and advanced graduate students of counseling and psychotherapy. *Journal of Counseling and Development, 71*, 396–405.

Rosenbaum, D. N. (1984). Evaluation of student performance in psychotherapy. *Journal of Clinical Psychology, 40*, 1106–1110.

Rosenthal, N. R. (1977). A prescriptive approach for counselor training. *Journal of Counseling Psychology, 24*, 231–237.

Rounsaville, B. J., O'Malley, S., Foley, S., & Weissman, M. M. (1988). Role of manual-guided training in the conduct and efficacy of interpersonal psychotherapy of depression. *Journal of Consulting and Clinical Psychology, 56*, 681–688.

Sanderson, W. C., & Woody, S. (1995). Manuals for empirically validated treatments: A project of the task force on psychological interventions. *The Clinical Psychologist: Division of Clinical Psychology*. Washington, DC: American Psychological Association.

Shanfield, S. B., Matthews, K. L., & Hetherly, V. (1993). What do excellent psychotherapy supervisors do? 144th Annual Meeting of the American Psychiatric Association (1991, New Orleans, Louisiana). *American Journal of Psychiatry, 150*, 1081–1084.

Stein, D. M., & Lambert, M. J. (1995). Graduate training in psychotherapy: Are therapy outcomes enhanced? *Journal of Consulting and Clinical Psychology, 63*, 182–196.

Stoltenberg, C. D., & Delworth, U. (1987). *Supervising counselors and therapists: A developmental approach.* San Francisco: Jossey-Bass.

Strupp, H. H., & Binder, J. L. (1984). *Psychotherapy in a new key: A guide to time-limited dynamic psychotherapy.* New York: Basic Books.

Strupp, H. H., Butler, S. F., & Rosser, C. L. (1988). Training in psychodynamic therapy. *Journal of Consulting and Clinical Psychology, 56*, 689–695.

Thompson, A. J. M., & Blocher, D. H. (1979). Co-counseling supervision in microcounseling. *Journal of Counseling Psychology, 26*, 413–418.

Truax, C. B., & Carkhuff, R. R. (1967). *Toward effective counseling and psychotherapy.* Chicago: Aldine.

Tucker, S., & Pinsof, W. M. (1984). The empirical evaluation of family therapy training. *Family Process, 23*, 437–456.

Uhlemann, M. R., Hearn, M. T., & Evans, D. R. (1980). Programmed learning in the microtraining paradigm with hotline workers. *American Journal of Community Psychology, 8,* 603–612.

Uhlemann, M. R., Stone, G. L., Evans, D. R., & Hearn, M. (1982). Evaluation of microtraining modifications: Implications for paraprofessional training within community counseling agencies. *Canadian Counselor, 16,* 115–121.

Vasquez, M. J. T. (1992). Psychologist as clinical supervisor: Promoting ethical practice. *Professional Psychology, Research and Practice, 23,* 197–202.

Waskow, I. E. (1984). Standardization of the technique variable in the NIMH treatment of depression collaborative research program. In J. B. W. Williams & R. L. Spitzer (Eds.), *Psychotherapy research: Where are we and where should we go?* (pp. 150–159). New York: Guilford.

Weaver, G. C. Z. (1987). An empirical investigation of Stoltenberg's counselor complexity model. *Dissertation Abstracts International, 47,* 2464A.

Winter, L. M., Jr. (1987). The effects of supervisor approach and trainee conceptual level on trainee selection of audiotape counseling passages in supervision. *Dissertation Abstracts International, 47,* 2464A.

Worthington, E. L., Jr. (1987). Changes in supervision as counselors and supervisors gain experience: A review. *Professional Psychology: Research and Practice, 18,* 189–208.

CHAPTER 25

Inferences Concerning Supervisees and Clients in Clinical Supervision: An Integrative Review

MICHAEL V. ELLIS
University at Albany, State University of New York
NICHOLAS LADANY
Lehigh University

The primary reasons for conducting reviews of the extant literature in a field of inquiry, such as clinical supervision, are to assess substantive and methodological advances, generalize from a set of studies, synthesize knowledge, and verify and develop theory (Jackson, 1980). As Feldman (1971, p. 100) and others (e.g., Bem, 1995; Cooper, 1982, 1989; Cooper & Hedges, 1994; Corcoran, 1985; Green & Hall, 1984; Light & Smith, 1971; Rosenthal & Rubin, 1979, 1982; Taveggia, 1974) have argued, a good review "shows how much is known in an area, [and] also shows how little is known." To be able to determine what is known, it is incumbent on the reviewer to ascertain if the variability among the studies reviewed is "due to sampling error, differences in the methodological adequacy of the studies, or differences in the phenomena that were studied" (Jackson, 1980, p. 447). To determine this, a review of the clinical supervision literature includes an in-depth evaluation of the methodological and statistical rigor of the studies. Thus, the reviewer takes into account the salient rival explanations for the results obtained in each study (e.g., methodological flaws) when making inferences from the studies (e.g., Cooper, 1989; Hogarty, 1989; Kazdin, 1983; Kline, 1983). This seems particularly important given that research reports sometimes contain misinterpretations of the data or do not disclose methodological and statistical flaws (e.g., Cooper, 1989; Dar, Serlin, & Omer, 1994; Ellis, Ladany, Krengel, & Schult, 1996; Fagley, 1985; Holloway, 1987; Huck & Sandler, 1979; Meehl, 1990; Sedlmeier & Gigerenzer, 1989). Reviews that fail to evaluate systematically the quality of the research may (a) incorrectly equate (or even outweigh) the results of excellent research with poor quality research (Hogarty, 1989; Kline, 1983), (b) draw erroneous inferences and conclusions (Cooper, 1989), and (c) intensify the theoretical ambiguity in the field (Meehl, 1990). Nevertheless, we discovered that many reviews of the clinical supervision literature did not systematically evaluate the scientific rigor (i.e., research quality) of the studies reviewed.

Note: An earlier version of this chapter was presented at the August 1995 meeting of the American Psychological Association, New York. We gratefully acknowledge Maxine Krengel and Deborah Schult for rating the studies and Kris Bronson, Marjorie Dennin, Erica Robbins Ellis, and Arpana Inman for their insightful comments on earlier drafts of this manuscript.

Over the past four decades, at least 34 reviews of research in therapist training and clinical supervision appeared in the literature. Many reviews took a noncritical stance in regard to the scientific rigor of the studies reviewed (e.g., Harkness & Poertner, 1989; Holloway, 1984, 1992; Holloway & Neufeldt, 1995; Lambert & Arnold, 1987; Leddick & Bernard, 1980; Liddle & Halpin, 1978; Matarazzo, 1971, 1978; Matarazzo & Garner, 1992; Matarazzo & Patterson, 1986; Russell & Petrie, 1994; Stoltenberg, McNeill, & Crethar, 1994; Yutrzenka, 1995). Other reviews (Baker & Daniels, 1989; Baker, Daniels, & Greeley, 1990; Ford, 1979; Hansen, Pound, & Petro, 1976; Hansen, Robins, & Grimes, 1982; Hansen & Warner, 1971; Holloway & Johnston, 1985; Holloway & Wampold, 1986; Kurtz, Marshall, & Banspach, 1985; Loganbill, Hardy, & Delworth, 1982; Stein & Lambert, 1995; Worthington, 1987) examined, usually informally, some aspects of research methodology (e.g., type of research designs, quality of the dependent measures). One review presented details of the conceptual and methodological flaws encountered in the studies reviewed (Holloway, 1987, 1988), and four reviews evaluated systematically the methodological rigor of each study (Alberts & Edelstein, 1990; Avis & Sprenkle, 1990; Ellis et al., 1996; Russell, Crimmings, & Lent, 1984). In combination, these 34 reviews provide a comprehensive assessment of the status of research and theory in clinical supervision. Thus, given these reviews, one might question the utility, if not necessity, of conducting yet another review.

The purpose of this review-study was to address the limitations of previous reviews by replicating and extending the work of Ellis et al. (1996). To this end, we conducted a more focused review of the clinical supervision research (i.e., inferences regarding supervisees and clients) that (a) incorporated a systematic evaluation of the scientific rigor of each study (i.e., a quantitative review), (b) reinterpreted the findings (if necessary) in light of the conceptual and methodological limitations, and (c) organized and reviewed the studies according to the inferences under investigation (rather than to the independent variables, dependent variables, or type of research design). We focused on inferences about supervisees and clients for two reasons. The focus on inferences underscores the importance of testing theories or theorizing (i.e., the relations among constructs or variables; Ellis, 1991b); whereas organizing a review on the basis of the variables researched (e.g., Russell et al., 1984; Stoltenberg et al., 1994) or research design (Hansen et al., 1982) contravenes the centrality of theory and theory testing (cf. Holloway, 1992). The second reason to focus on supervisees and clients was twofold: Supervisee variables are the most extensively researched aspect of supervision (Holloway, 1992; Worthington, 1987), and some consider client outcome the acid test for clinical supervision (Avis & Sprenkle, 1990; Holloway & Neufeldt, 1995). We anticipated that incorporating these three components into our review-study would provide a more rigorous assessment of research and theory pertaining to inferences about the supervisee and the client in supervision.

In order to evaluate the quality of the research assessing supervisee and client inferences in clinical supervision research, we replicated Ellis et al.'s (1996) methodology, the most recent comprehensive methodological evaluation of clinical supervision research. Specifically, each study was evaluated by means of a comprehensive set of criteria (Cooper, 1989; Heppner, Kivlighan, & Wampold, 1992; Wampold & Poulin, 1992). The criteria incorporated Wampold, Davis, and Good's (1990) four threats to hypothesis validity (defined as inferences about the fit of the research hypotheses with theory and with statistical analyses) as well as Cook and Campbell's (1979) 33 threats to validity. Cook and Campbell's threats included statistical conclusion validity (defined as inferences from statistical data about covariation of the variables), internal validity (inferences about causality and change), construct validity (inferences about the fit of operations and constructs), external validity (generalizability of results to and across time and populations of setting and people). In addition to the evaluative variables, we used statistical procedures to define operationally some evaluation criteria (e.g., sample size, effect size, statistical power, per comparison error, and experimentwise error rates).

We use the term *inference* two ways in this chapter. Primarily, we use inference to refer to rudimentary core premises (or assumptions) about supervision, supervisees, or clients. These are inferences, or basic assumptions, believed to be central to clinical supervision or supervisees. We define inference to include both broad generic inferences (e.g., inferences about the supervisory relationship) as well as more focused inferences, such as a specific theory of supervision (e.g., Bernard, 1979). Second, we use *inference* to refer to tentative conclusions formulated on the basis of data (i.e., consistent with Kerlinger, 1986; Pepinsky & Pepinsky, 1954, pp. 144–170); for example, drawing conclusions from the results of reviewed studies.

In order to identify the major inferences pertaining to supervisees and clients, we examined closely the theoretical and empirical supervision literature, prior literature reviews, and prominent books on clinical supervision (e.g., Bernard & Goodyear, 1992; Bradley, 1989; Ekstein & Wallerstein, 1972; Hawkins & Shohet, 1989; Holloway, 1995; Munson, 1983; Williams, 1994). We also drew upon the psychotherapy and counseling literature (e.g., Garfield & Bergin, 1994). We operated on four assumptions. The foremost assumption was the preeminence of theory and its testing and winnowing (see Ellis, 1991b; Serlin, 1987; Wampold et al., 1990). That is, we sought to identify those theories and models of supervision that were directly or implicitly tested by researchers since 1981. Second, we strove to identify rudimentary core inferences or assumptions that elucidate relations among constructs (i.e., theorizing) fundamental to clinical supervision and supervisees. Third, we assumed that the inferences would be pan-theoretical, applicable across theoretical orientations and supervision theories. Finally, we were not attempting to present a new model of supervision by which to organize the studies reviewed (e.g., Holloway, 1992); instead, we strove to offer a descriptive topology.

On the basis of our examination of the literature, we identified six cardinal inferences. Each of these cardinal inferences contained at least one more focused subinference (see Table 25.1). Supervisory theories were incorporated as more focused subinferences (i.e., subsumed by the broader cardinal inference). The most prominent inferences about supervisees encompassed the broad premise of supervisee development (Holloway, 1987, 1992, 1995; Stoltenberg et al., 1994; Worthington, 1987). More specific inferences about supervisee development included a variety of theories of supervisee development (e.g., Littrell, Lee-Borden, & Lorenz, 1979; Loganbill et al., 1982; Stoltenberg, 1981; Stoltenberg & Delworth, 1987), supervisee ego development (e.g., Borders, 1989b), and supervisee conceptual development (e.g., Blocher et al., 1985; Ellis, 1988; Holloway & Wampold, 1986).

The second most prevalent inference in the literature concerned the supervisory relationship (e.g., Bernard & Goodyear, 1992; Holloway, 1992). More specific inferences about the supervisory relationship were inferences about the working alliance (e.g., Bordin, 1983), about client-centered conditions (e.g., Schact, Howe, & Berman, 1988), about social influence theory (e.g., Strong, 1968), about role expectations (e.g., Olk & Friedlander, 1992), and about the structure of supervisory interactions (e.g., Holloway, 1982).

A third cardinal or core inference was the premise of matching supervisees and supervision (e.g., Bernard & Goodyear, 1992). This broad inference entailed more focused

Table 25.1   Six Sets of Inferences and Subinferences Pertaining to Supervisees and Clients in Clinical Supervision

Inferences About the Supervisory Relationship	*Inferences Regarding Supervisee Development*
Supervisory Working Alliance Model	Ego Development
Client-Centered Conditions	Conceptual Development
Strong's (1968) Social Influence Theory	Littrell et al.'s (1979) Model
Role Conflict and Ambiguity	Hogan's (1964) Model
Structure of the Supervisory Relationship	Loganbill et al.'s (1982) and Sansbury's (1982) Models
Inferences Entailing Matching in Supervision	Stoltenberg's (1981) Model
Bernard's (1979) Discrimination Model	Stoltenberg and Delworth's (1987) Model
Supervisee Needs	Generic Supervisee Development and Experience Level
Individual Differences	
Cognitive Style	*Inferences Relating to Supervisee Evaluation*
Reactance	
Sex/Gender	*Inferences About Client Outcome*
Race	Parallel Process
Theoretical Orientation	
Supervisory Environmental	*Inferences About Supervisees: New Measures*

Note. Inferences are presented in the order used in the qualitative review.

subinferences, including inferences about matching supervisee and supervisors in terms of individual differences (e.g., gender, theoretical orientation, race, cognitive style), inferences regarding the match of supervisee and supervisory environment (e.g., Stoltenberg, 1981), and inferences about matching supervisee needs (e.g., Bernard, 1979). Fourth, we observed a core inference regarding evaluation of supervisees (e.g., Dodenhoff, 1981). The fifth broad inference encompassed inferences about client outcome (e.g., Holloway & Neufeldt, 1995). Finally, given the dearth of psychometrically sound measures specifically developed to assess constructs and inferences about supervisees (e.g., Ellis et al., 1996; Russell et al., 1984), we assembled research developing and testing new measures into a generic inference about new measures.

Reiterating, our first purpose was to replicate and extend Ellis et al. (1996) by performing a more circumscribed methodological review. Thus, we assessed the status of research on inferences about supervisees and clients in clinical supervision by a thorough evaluation of the conceptual-methodological rigor (i.e., validity threats in conjunction with statistically based measures of effect size, power, and error rates). A second purpose was to conduct a comprehensive and rigorous integrative review of this literature that accentuated the theory-testing nature of scientific research (see Cooper, 1989; Cooper & Hedges, 1994; Ellis, 1991a, 1991b; Ellis & Blustein, 1991a, 1991b; Kerlinger, 1986; Serlin, 1987; Serlin & Lapsley, 1985; Wampold et al., 1990; Wampold & Poulin, 1992). We attempted to accomplish this by codifying the basic assumptions or inferences pertaining to supervisees and clients and subsequently organizing the integrative review in terms of these inferences (i.e., theorizing).

METHOD

For all practical purposes, the methods used in this review duplicate those of Ellis et al. (1996). Hence, there is considerable duplication of the method section presented here and in our prior methodological critique.

Sample

Search Procedures.   The research articles reviewed were identified through three retrieval sources and screened on the basis of explicit criteria (Cooper, 1989; Ellis, 1991a). More than two thousand potential supervision articles involving supervisee and client variables were identified by (a) the ancestry approach (i.e., reference list of previous articles; Cooper, 1989), (b) searching *Psychological Abstracts* and related databases (e.g., ERIC), and (c) examining journals that publish clinical supervision research (e.g., *The Clinical Supervisor, Counselor Education and Supervision, The Counseling Psychologist, Journal of Counseling and Development, Journal of Counseling Psychology, Professional Psychology: Research and Practice,* and *Psychotherapy*). Following Bernard and Goodyear (1992), supervision was defined as an intensive interpersonally focused relationship in which one or more persons are designated to facilitate the development of therapeutic competence in the other person(s).

Inclusion-Exclusion Criteria.   The inclusion criteria were that the study (a) addressed supervision of individual counseling or therapy as an integral part of the study (i.e., purpose, research question, hypotheses, methods, procedures), (b) was an empirically based article published in a professional journal since 1981, and (c) focused on inferences about supervisee and/or client variables. Inclusion criteria extended to empirical case studies, postdegree supervision, and peer supervision. Fields of therapy included school psychology, counseling psychology, clinical psychology, counseling (e.g., school, community mental health, rehabilitation), social work, psychiatry, and psychiatric nursing. The exclusion criteria were that the article did not meet the inclusion criteria stipulated earlier or that the research involved prepracticum training, teacher supervision, supervision of group therapy or speech pathology, or anecdotal case studies, or it was an unpublished manuscript. We did not review prepracticum training research (e.g., interpersonal skills training), given Alberts and Edelstein's (1990), Baker and Daniels's (1989), and Baker et al.'s (1990) excellent critiques and meta-analyses of this literature.

Sample Description.   To avoid confusion, we use the terms *article* to refer to a published journal article or book that reports one or more empirical studies and *study* to refer to a separate empirical investigation reported in an article (i.e., an article may report multiple studies). The final sample consisted of 95 research articles, one book (Skovholt & Rønnestad, 1992), and 104 studies. Four multistudy articles accounted for eight studies (i.e., Borders & Fong, 1989; Ellis, Dell, & Good, 1988; Heppner & Roehlke, 1984; Larson et al., 1992). Ellis et al.'s (1996) sample included 87.5% of these studies; however, these 91 studies comprised 63.2% of their sample. The breakdown of articles by journal was *Journal of Counseling Psychology* ($n = 30$; 31.6%), *The Clinical Supervisor* ($n = 18$; 19.0%), *Counselor Education and Supervision* ($n = 13$; 13.7%), *Professional Psychology: Research and Practice* ($n = 14$; 14.7%), *Psychotherapy* ($n = 4$; 4.2%), and 12 other journals in which three or fewer relevant supervision articles were published (e.g., *Journal of Con-*

sulting and Clinical Psychology, Journal of Counseling and Development, Psychological Reports, Social Work; $n = 16$, 16.8%). The distribution of articles by year of publication was 4.2% published in 1981 ($n = 4$), 3.2% in 1982 ($n = 3$), 9.5% in 1983 ($n = 9$), 9.5% in 1984 ($n = 9$), 5.3% in 1985 ($n = 5$), 11.6% in 1986 ($n = 11$), 6.3% in 1987 ($n = 6$), 9.5% in 1988 ($n = 9$), 6.3% in 1989 ($n = 6$), 6.3% in 1990 ($n = 6$), 10.5% in 1991 ($n = 10$), 6.3% in 1992 ($n = 6$), 8.4% in 1993 ($n = 8$), 2.1% in 1994 ($n = 2$), and 1.1% in 1995 ($n = 1$). The 104 studies utilized ex post facto research (72.1%; no random assignment and independent variable not manipulated), experimental (6.7%; random assignment and manipulated independent variable), quasi-experimental (9.6%; no random assignment and manipulated independent variable) designs, and case studies (4.8%). In addition, 6.7% ($n = 7$) of the studies were developing new measures and providing validity data.

Methodological Evaluation Variables

We evaluated the scientific rigor of each study according to 37 potential threats to the validity of the results. That is, we used Wampold et al.'s (1990) four threats to hypothesis validity in combination with Cook and Campbell's (1979) four classes of validity threats (statistical conclusion validity, internal validity, construct validity, and external validity). Each threat was rated "yes" (definitely a threat), "no" (not a threat), or "not enough information to evaluate" if the threat applied. Studies were further assessed on eight supplemental variables. In the ensuing paragraphs, we describe the 37 validity threats and supplemental variables.

Hypothesis Validity. "Hypothesis validity addresses the interrelations of theory, research hypotheses, and statistical hypotheses" (Wampold et al., 1990, p. 361). The threats to hypothesis validity are inconsequential hypotheses (the extent to which hypotheses neither corroborate one theory nor falsify others); ambiguous hypotheses (hypotheses are not specified, or if provided, the conditions under which hypotheses will fail or succeed are not delineated); noncongruence of research and statistical hypotheses (i.e., incorrect statistical procedures or the statistical tests do not test the research hypotheses); and diffuse statistical hypotheses and tests (at least one of the following: using multiple statistical tests per hypothesis, using omnibus tests and subsequent follow-up or post hoc tests, or the statistical analyses include extraneous independent variables not specified in the hypotheses).

Statistical Conclusion Validity. Statistical conclusion validity entails the validity of inferences about the covariation of independent and dependent variables (i.e., are the variables related?). Such inferences are made from statistical data. Cook and Campbell's (1979) seven threats to statistical conclusion validity are (a) low statistical power (e.g., the probability of detecting a true effect; determined by the population effect size, per comparison alpha, and N); (b) violating the assumptions of statistical tests (e.g., heterogeneity of variances); (c) Type I error (falsely rejecting a true null hypothesis; e.g., multiple statistical tests each with alpha = .05); (d) measures that are unreliable (reliability coefficients below .80; e.g., using a measure with unknown reliability in a supervision context); (e) unreliable treatment implementation (e.g., supervision interventions inconsistently delivered to trainees); (f) random irrelevancies in the experimental setting (e.g., setting idiosyncrasies induce error variance); and (g) random heterogeneity of respondents (e.g., not controlling for supervisee developmental level).

Internal Validity.   Internal validity refers to questions about the relations among variables and causality (i.e., why are the variables related, and why did change occur in the dependent variable?). The 13 internal validity threats are (a) history (events occurring between pretest and posttest produce the observed effect; e.g., academic training); maturation (e.g., the effect of supervisees or clients maturing or becoming more experienced between pretest and posttest); (c) testing (e.g., taking a test multiple times causes higher scores at posttest); (d) instrumentation (e.g., ceiling or floor effects); (e) statistical regression (e.g., regression to the mean accounts for pretest-posttest changes); (f) selection (no random assignment to treatment conditions, nonequivalent groups); (g) mortality (e.g., differential dropout among treatment conditions); (h) interactions with selection (e.g., selection bias interacts with maturation, history, or instrumentation); (i) ambiguity about the direction of causal influence (e.g., unclear whether the independent variable influences the dependent variable or vice versa); (j) diffusion of treatments (e.g., participants in control groups learn about experimental interventions); (k) compensatory equalization of treatments (e.g., supervisors attempt to equalize supervisees in less desirable treatments); (l) compensatory rivalry by respondents receiving less desirable treatments (e.g., control group participants change behavior positively to compensate for experimental group's advantage); and (m) resentful demoralization of respondents receiving less desirable treatment (e.g., control group respondents' change behavior negatively due to being demoralized when compared to the experimental group's advantage).

Construct Validity.   Construct validity concerns "generalizations about higher-order constructs from research operations" (i.e., to what extent can we generalize from the operations to the referent construct?; issues of confounding; Cook & Campbell, 1979, p. 38). The 10 construct validity threats are (a) inadequate preoperational explication of constructs (constructs central to the study are inadequately defined); (b) mono-operation bias (operationalizing a construct with only one measure); (c) mono-method bias (e.g., operationalizing a construct by one method; e.g., self-report); (d) hypothesis-guessing within experimental conditions (e.g., participants guessed what experimenters wanted them to do and reacted accordingly); (e) evaluation apprehension (e.g., supervisee's responses were affected by evaluation anxiety or social desirability); (f) experimenter expectancies (e.g., raters inadvertently favored the desired treatment conditions); (g) confounding constructs and levels of constructs (e.g., dichotomizing a continuous independent variable); (h) interaction of different treatments (e.g., exposure to two treatments produces a synergetic effect); (i) interaction of testing and treatment (e.g., participants reacting to pretreatment testing); and (j) restricted generalizability across constructs (e.g., operational definitions of constructs were so circumscribed to preclude generalizing to related constructs).

External Validity.   External validity pertains to "the generalizability of an observed causal relationship to and across populations of persons, settings, and times" (Cook & Campbell, 1979, p. 39). The three external validity threats are (a) interaction of selection and treatment (e.g., limited generalizability of effects to and across samples or populations of supervisees or clients); (b) interaction of setting and treatment (e.g., limited generalizability to and across supervisory settings); and (c) interaction of history and treatment (e.g., limited generalizability to and across time frames).

Supplemental Evaluation Criteria.   Seven methodological variables were culled from the literature and used to rate the studies (Chen, 1990; Ellis, 1991a; Kazdin, 1986; Kerlinger, 1986; Serlin, 1987; Wampold & Poulin, 1992). The supplemental variables included assessing whether the investigators (a) were explicitly testing theory or models; (b) explicated research hypotheses; (c) used measures with established reliability and validity data in a clinical supervision context; (d) tested developmental inferences using cross-sectional data; and (e) identified the limitations of their research. We evaluated the studies for inconsistencies (a mismatch) among the stated purpose, the research hypotheses, the methods, design, procedures, and the data analyses (Chen, 1990; Serlin, 1987). Finally, for each study two raters independently identified the two to six most plausible rival explanations for the observed data and results (i.e., we determined the study's most salient validity threats).

Raters and Rating Procedures

The four raters (includes the two authors) were all counseling psychologists (two white females and two white males) and were the same rating team from Ellis et al. (1996). They were between 1 and 12 years postdoctorate and between the ages of 31 and 41. Raters received training until achieving 90% agreement on all rating variables including the screening criteria (approximately 10 hours).

Potential articles were first screened for inclusion on the basis of the abstract. The full article was then subjected to the inclusion and exclusion criteria. Studies were subsequently rated in random order on the methodological variables such that two judges rated each study. Rater discrepancies were resolved by consensus. Interrater agreement among the four raters was checked randomly; the agreement rate was consistently above 90%. We computed two types of interrater agreement as well as kappas (Cone, 1988; Suen, 1988). The average interrater agreement per study (calculated across the 37 rating threats within each study, then averaged across studies) was 90.82% (Mdn = 91.11%, SD = 7.40, range: 64.4%–100%). The agreement between each rater and the final consensus ratings across the 37 threats within each study was computed, then averaged across studies yielding an average rater-final rating agreement rate. The average rater-final agreement rates ranged from 94.1% (Mdn = 95.6, SD = 5.94; range: 66.7–100%) to 96.53% (Mdn = 97.8, SD = 5.02, range: 80–100%). Thus, it appears that no bias existed for one rater within each rater pair nor was one rater unduly influencing the final consensus ratings. Lower interrater agreements for a particular study were typically due to the lack of detailed information reported in the article. It should be noted that the lack of variability among several of the threats necessarily limits the values of kappa at minimum and often prohibits computing kappa. Hence, the kappas reported herein represent lower bound estimates of interrater agreement.

Statistical Variables

For the quantitative analysis, we selected and computed several statistical variables that served as quantitative operational definitions of some methodological threats (e.g., N, effect size and statistical power, per comparison and experimentwise error rates). Statistical analyses that were reported in sufficient detail were treated as separate entities. That is, follow-up statistical procedures that did not control for Type I error (e.g., following MANOVAs with univariate ANOVAs) were regarded as separate tests (Dar et al., 1994; Huberty & Morris, 1989). The following quantitative variables were computed or tallied for each statistical test: sample size (N), sample effect size (η^2) and estimated population effect size ($\hat{\rho}^2$), post hoc statistical power ($1 - \beta_{PC(\eta^2)}$) and a priori power ($1 - \beta_{PC(\hat{\rho}^2)}$), and per comparison Type II error ($\beta_{PC(\eta^2)}$). These statistical data were aggregated by study and by statistical test (i.e., the unit of analysis was either each study or each test). For each study we computed or recorded the overall sample size, the number of statistical tests conducted per study, the number of nonsignificant and significant statistical results per study, the average sample effect size (η^2), the average population effect size estimate ($\hat{\rho}^2$), the corresponding average post hoc statistical power ($1 - \beta_{PC(\eta^2)}$) and a priori power ($1 - \beta_{PC(\hat{\rho}^2)}$), the average per comparison Type II error ($\beta_{PC(\eta^2)}$), and the experimentwise Type I (α_{EW}) and Type II (β_{EW}) error rates.

Effect Size.   Strength of association (i.e., effect size) was measured by eta squared (η^2), a descriptive sample statistic representing the proportion of dependent variable (DV) variance accounted for by the independent variable (IV). Because eta squared (η^2) was computed using a formula that employs the value of the test statistic (t, F) and relevant degrees of freedom (Haase, 1983, 1991; Haase, Ellis, & Ladany, 1989), some of the values of η^2 reported here are actually values of partial η^2 rather than classical η^2 (Kennedy, 1970). We expected that the overestimate of sample effect size due to partial η^2 values would not have serious consequences for the other measures computed using η^2 (see Haase et al., 1989). The estimated population effect size (estimated rho squared, $\hat{\rho}^2$) was computed using Ezekiel's (1930) shrinkage formula (also known as Wherry's formula), which is a negatively biased estimator. The bias of $\hat{\rho}^2$, however, should be less than $.1/N$ (Montgomery & Morrison, 1973). Cohen and Nee's (1984) formulas were used to compute multivariate effect sizes (both sample and population estimates). Jaspen's (1965) procedure was used to compute the exact probability (p) of the statistical test (e.g., F, t, χ^2).

Statistical Power.   Statistical power is the conditional probability of detecting an effect given that the effect exists in the population (i.e., the probability of rejecting a false null hypothesis). Post hoc power of the statistical test, $1 - \beta_{PC(\eta^2)}$, was derived using η^2 whereas a priori power, $1 - \beta_{PC(\hat{\rho}^2)}$, was estimated using $\hat{\rho}^2$ (Cohen, 1988). Both statistical power probabilities were computed using Abramowitz and Stegun's (1972) algorithm with Cohen's (1988) formulas.

Per Comparison and Experimentwise Error Rates.   The per comparison Type II error rate was estimated by $\beta_{PC(\eta^2)} = 1 - (1 - \beta_{PC(\eta^2)})$. Experimentwise Type I error rate (α_{EW}) was computed by $\alpha_{EW} = 1 - (1 - \alpha_{PC})^s$, where α_{PC} is the per comparison alpha (usually .05) and s is the number of separate statistical tests performed in a study (Haase & Ellis, 1987). Experimentwise Type II error rate (β_{EW}) was estimated by $\beta_{EW} = 1 - (1 - \beta_{PC})^s$ using $\beta_{PC(\eta^2)}$. This yields a smaller (more liberal) estimate of experimentwise Type II error than using the a priori estimate ($\beta_{PC(\hat{\rho}^2)}$) in the computations.

Procedures

Each study was evaluated using the 37 threats to validity plus the 8 additional variables, and statistical variables were computed. After critiquing the 104 studies, we classified the studies according to the explicit or implicit inferences under investigation (Ellis, 1991a, 1991b) and subsequently assigned the studies to the appropriate core inferences and more focused subinferences (interrater agreement = 99%). For each subinference, the targeted studies were examined individually and collectively considering the conceptual and methodological strengths and limitations identified from the quantitative evaluation. If necessary, the results of each study were reinterpreted given the conceptual and methodological strengths and limitations and then aggregated across the studies to arrive at the conclusions for each subinference.

QUANTITATIVE RESULTS

Statistical Variables

Of the 104 studies reviewed, 76 include sufficient information about at least one statistical test to permit computing the quantitative statistics (e.g., η^2, $\hat{\rho}^2$, and power). In Table 25.2 we present the quantitative data averaged across the 2,394 adequately reported statistical tests. Given that the distributions of the quantitative variables are highly skewed, we focus our presentation on median values. Nonetheless, means, standard deviations, standard errors, and 95% confidence intervals about the median values are presented.

Methodological Evaluations

The frequency percentages for the 37 evaluation variables aggregated across the 104 studies are presented in Table 25.3. The pattern of threats is fairly clear, especially regarding the threats to hypothesis validity. The most salient rival explanations are aggregated across the 104 studies and presented in Table 25.4. The average interrater agreement for Table 25.4

Table 25.2   **Means, Standard Deviations, Standard Errors, and 95% Confidence Intervals for Statistical Variables**

	M	SD	Mdn	Standard Error	95% CI (Mdn)
Across 2,394 statistical tests					
N per analysis	71.881	60.417	51.000	1.235	48.530–53.470
Sample effect size (η^2)	.166	.212	.073	.004	.065–.081
Estimated population effect size $\hat{\rho}^2$	.147	.211	.048	.004	.040–.056
Post hoc power ($1 - \beta_{PC(\eta^2)}$)	.497	.378	.432	.008	.416–.448
A priori power ($1 - \beta_{PC(\hat{\rho}^2)}$)	.425	.390	.257	.008	.241–.273
Type II error ($\beta_{PC(\eta^2)}$)	.503	.378	.568	.008	.552–.584
Across 76 studies (sufficient information presented)					
N per study[a]	87.853	99.221	63.500	9.729	41.042–79.958
Sample effect size (η^2)	.143	.152	.098	.017	.064–.132
Estimated population effect size $\hat{\rho}^2$	.113	.142	.057	.016	.025–.089
Post hoc power ($1 - \beta_{PC(\eta^2)}$)	.619	.296	.674	.034	.606–.742
A priori power ($1 - \beta_{PC(\hat{\rho}^2)}$)	.497	.341	.454	.039	.376–.532
Type II error ($\beta_{PC(\eta^2)}$)	.381	.296	.326	.034	.258–.394
Statistical tests per study[b]	62.744	96.528	33.000	9.701	13.598–52.402
Number of tests nonsignificant[b]	45.181	84.322	18.000	8.605	.790–35.210
Number of tests significant[b]	17.270	19.813	11.000	2.011	6.978–15.022
Experimentwise Type I error (α_{EW})[c]	.738	.278	.842	.028	.786–.898
Experimentwise Type II error (β_{EW})	.810	.363	1.000	.042	.916–1.000
Number of threats per study (of 37)[b]	15.482	5.200	15.000	.509	13.982–16.018

[a]$n = 76$.
[b]$n = 104$.
[c]$n = 99$ studies included sufficient information to compute α_{EW}.

Table 25.3 Percentages, Interrater Agreement, and Kappas for 37 Methodological Threats Across 104 Studies

Threat	Category (%)			Interrater Agreement[a]	Kappa[b]
	Not a Threat	Insufficient Information	Definitely a Threat		
Hypothesis validity					
Inconsequential hypotheses	10.60	0.0	89.4	91.21	.776
Ambiguous hypotheses	19.2	0.0	80.8	97.24	.871
Noncongruence of research and statistical hypotheses	55.8	16.3	27.9	84.54	
Diffuse statistical hypotheses and tests	1.0	0.00	99.0	96.64	.881
Statistical conclusion validity					
Low statistical power	20.2	4.8	75.0	91.21	.776
Violated assumptions of statistics	49.0	17.3	33.7	86.12	.786
Inflated error rate	10.6	0.0	89.4	96.28	.862
Unreliability of DV or IV measures	4.8	9.6	85.6	87.13	.620
Unreliability of treatment implementation	79.8	4.8	15.4	88.20	.639
Irrelevance in experimental setting	61.5	4.8	33.7	84.59	.691
Heterogeneity of participants	36.5	3.8	59.6	78.58	.582
Internal validity					
History	74.0	0.0	26.0	97.24	.891
Maturation	74.0	1.0	25.0	97.24	.871
Testing	73.1	1.0	26.0	93.47	.529
Instrumentation	93.1	1.9	4.8	94.83	.474
Statistical regression	82.7	0.0	17.3	96.64	.881
Selection	17.3	1.0	81.7	90.74	.768
Differential attrition	66.3	10.6	23.1	80.99	.618
Interactions with selection	62.5	0.0	37.5	88.58	.773
Ambiguity of causal direction	25.0	1. 0	74.0	95.67	.806
Diffusion of treatment	98.1	1.0	1.0	100.00	1.000
Compensatory equalization of treatments	100.0	0.0	0.0	100.00	
Rivalry by participants	100.0	0.0	0.0	100.00	1.000
Resentful demoralization	99.0	1.0	0.0	99.40	
Construct validity					
Inadequate preoperationalization explication	26.0	0.0	74.0	83.76	.683
Mono-operation bias	76.9	0.0	23.1	91.46	.794
Mono-method bias	22.1	1.0	76.9	84.15	.576
Hypothesis guessing within treatments	78.8	8.7	12.5	88.20	.690

(table continues)

Table 25.3 (Continued)

Threat	Category (%)				
	Not a Threat	Insufficient Information	Definitely a Threat	Interrater Agreement[a]	Kappa[b]
Construct validity (continued)					
Evaluation apprehension	79.8	3.8	16.3	91.21	.648
Experimenter expectancies	70.2	11.5	18.3	91.46	.778
Confounding construct with levels of construct	22.1	1.9	76.0	81.95	.432
Interaction of treatments	93.3	1.0	5.8	93.62	.652
Interaction of testing and treatments	74.0	1.0	25.0	91.21	.749
Restricted generalizability across constructs	39.4	1.0	59.6	77.13	
External validity					
Interaction of selection and treatment	2.9	0.0	97.1	98.44	.875
Interaction of setting and treatment	6.7	0.0	93.3	100.00	1.000
Interaction of history and treatment	10.6	0.0	89.4	98.44	.938

Note. Numbers are the percent of 104 studies rated per category for that methodological threat (criteria).
[a]Unanimous agreement in percentages.
[b]A blank field occurs where Kappa was not computable.

Table 25.4   Top 14 Most Salient Methodological Threats

Type of Threat	Percent[a]	Validity
Inflated Type I error rate	76.0	s
Unreliability or invalidity of independent or dependent measures	64.4	s
Inflated Type II error rate/low statistical power	51.0	s
Nonrandom/nonrepresentative sample	39.4	e
Nonrandom assignment	37.5	i
Mismatch of purpose, hypotheses, design-methods, and analyses	28.9	h
Violated assumptions of statistics	14.4	s
Cohort effects (e.g., developmental inferences from cross-sectional data)	10.6	c
Confounded IVs (e.g., participants in multiple roles [supervisor and supervisee], supervisors with an unequal number of supervisees)	9.6	s, c, h
Uncontrolled variables	8.7	s, c
Differential attrition across groups	7.7	i
Mono-method bias	6.7	c
Di- or multi-chotomized a continuously distributed IV or DV	6.7	s
Participant heterogeneity	6.7	s

Note. s = statistical conclusion validity, i = internal validity, c = construct validity, e = external validity, h = hypothesis validity.
[a]Percent of the 104 studies that the particular threat was judged a major flaw. The average interrater agreement was 70.3%.

ratings is 70.30%. The 6 most pervasive threats or plausible explanations for the pattern of results across the studies reviewed here are experimentwise Type I error (76%); measures not psychometrically sound (64%); experimentwise Type II error (51%); samples neither random nor representative of the target population (39%); nonrandom assignment to treatment conditions (38%); and clear inconsistencies among the purpose, hypotheses, design-methods, and analyses (29%). (Tables specifying the 37 threats plus the most salient threats for each of the 104 studies are available from the first author.)

Finally, data from the supplemental evaluation measures reveal that 22.1% of the studies explicitly tested theory (39.4% implicitly tested theory and 38.5% did not test theory). Authors explicated research hypotheses in 24.0% of the studies and left hypotheses implicit in 38.5%. In 84.6% of the studies, measures psychometrically inadequate for a clinical supervision context were used. For 76.9% of the studies, a mismatch existed among the purpose, hypotheses, design-methods-procedures, and statistical analyses. Only 10.0% of the studies attempted to control systematically Type I error rates. Finally, 55.8% of the studies did not explicate the pertinent limitations of the studies.

Quantitative Discussion

Although no statistical tests were performed (due to sample overlap), the results observed here were basically equivalent to Ellis et al. (1996). It is not surprising that the quantitative results closely parallel those of Ellis et al. because the two samples overlap substantially. For this reason and due to space restrictions, we refer interested readers to Ellis et al. for a more detailed presentation of the implications of the quantitative review, especially pages 43 to 48. Using the quantitative results, Ellis et al. describe an "aggregate study" to portray the status of research in clinical supervision (pp. 44–45) as well offer guidelines for conducting "a feasible and well-designed supervision study" (pp. 45–47). Nevertheless, we briefly discuss the most striking findings from this review.

An inspection of Table 25.2 highlights some of the most ominous threats to the reviewed research. For data averaged across statistical tests, the statistical power was meager (i.e., less than a 26% chance of detecting an effect existing in the population) even with medium effect sizes ($\hat{\rho}^2 = .048$), and the post hoc per comparison Type II error rate was 57%. The values for effect size were comparable to research in counseling psychology ($\hat{\rho}^2 = .050$; Haase et al., 1989), yet smaller than the medium effect size for generic psychology ($\hat{\rho}^2 = .0588$; Cohen, 1988). The values for a priori statistical power were noticeably smaller than those found previously for medium effect sizes in counselor education ($1 - \beta = .365$; Haase, 1974), in abnormal-social psychology ($1 - \beta = .460$; Cohen, 1962), and in psychological research ($1 - \beta = .53$; Rossi, 1990; Sedlmeier & Gigerenzer, 1989).

Examining the data averaged across the 104 studies, several findings were striking. The median experimentwise Type I and Type II error rates were distinctively larger ($\alpha_{EW} = .84$, $\beta_{EW} = 1.00$) than previous reports ($\alpha_{EW} = .37$, $\beta_{EW} = .87$; Haase & Ellis, 1987). On average, investigators conducted 33 statistical tests per study, of which more than 18 were nonsignificant. The large number of nonsignificant results per study is disquieting given that the experimentwise Type II error rate was 100% (i.e., one or more nonsignificant results per study were erroneous). Given this in combination with the high experimentwise Type I error rate (i.e., an 84% chance that one or more significant findings were spurious), and the lack of replication studies or a priori power analyses, how can we know which results were trustworthy and which were not? That is, on average, investigations were simultaneously both unlikely to detect true effects and very likely to find spurious significant results (Ellis et al., 1996). The implications from the statistical data are clear: Investigators are compelled to attend more carefully to issues of Type I and Type II error rates (Dar et al., 1994; Fagley, 1985; Rossi, 1990).

The data from Tables 25.3 and 25.4 accentuate some of the strengths as well as the abundance of problems that pertain to studies of supervisee and client outcome inferences. On the positive side, some threats to Cook and Campbell's (1979) internal validity (i.e., 9 of 13 threats) and construct validity (5 of 10 threats) occurred relatively infrequently (i.e., pertained to less than 26% of the studies). Unfortunately, the low frequency of most of these threats may be imputed to the preponderance of ex post facto studies (i.e., these threats are not applicable to designs in which the independent variable was not manipulated) or to the nearly exclusive use of cross-sectional designs (i.e., internal validity threats mostly relate to pretreatment-posttreatment designs).

Perhaps the most salient observation from the quantitative findings was that the majority of investigators conducted unrigorous, atheoretical (exploratory) research (Ellis et al., 1996; Omer & Dar, 1992). As is readily apparent in the tables, few studies were attempts to test and refine theories, explicate unambiguous hypotheses, or pair statistical tests with research hypotheses (Serlin, 1987; Wampold et al., 1990; Wampold & Poulin, 1992). Indeed, most studies had little control over rival explanations of the data or threats to the validity of the results and data (Ellis, 1991b; Kerlinger, 1986; Wampold et al., 1990). These threats and conceptual-methodological problems necessarily delimited the interpretability of the data and results from these studies. Thus, we expected the quantitative data to impact severely the integrative review of inferences pertaining to supervisees and clients.

Quantitative Limitations

Perhaps the most obvious limitations of our quantitative review concerns the criteria used to evaluate the studies. There was little or no variability on 6 of the 37 threats (see Table 25.3; e.g., instrumentation, statistical regression, diffusion of treatment, compensatory equalization, rivalry by participants, and resentful demoralization). One interpretation of this observation is that these evaluation criteria were not applicable to the research designs currently employed to investigate clinical supervision (we adhered closely to Cook & Campbell's, 1979, and Wampold et al.'s, 1990, definitions). Given that Ellis et al. (1996) were the only other investigators using these criteria to evaluate systematically a sample of research articles, it is unknown how the distributions observed here for the 37 threats compare to other research domains. We found the 37 threats effective in assessing the conceptual and methodological rigor of clinical supervision research studies. Nevertheless, it is important to point out that the criteria are not all-inclusive (e.g., cohort effects and specific confounds such as some supervisors providing multiple data sets). For this reason, we endeavored in the integrative review to prioritize the threats for each study in terms of the degree to which the threat offered a viable alternative explanation of the observed results within the context of the authors' theorizing and the research design (Cook & Campbell, 1979; Huck & Sandler, 1979; Wampold & Poulin, 1992).

Another limitation was the moderate interrater agreement (i.e., .77) for Cook and Campbell's (1979) "restricted generalizability across constructs" criteria (see Table 25.3). Hence, the results for these criteria or threats should be viewed somewhat cautiously. A related limitation of the study was that other ways of assessing interrater reliability and consistency could not be computed (e.g., Suen, 1988). Also, due to the overlap of data with Ellis et al. (1996), our review had no direct comparison group with which to contrast the methodological findings (i.e., Cook & Campbell's, 1979, and Wampold et al.'s, 1990, threats). That is, we could not test statistically the distributions of this review with Ellis et al. because 91 studies occurred in both samples.

Finally and perhaps most important of all, we surmise that the statistical data were biased in at least three fundamental ways (Cooper & Hedges, 1994). First, 26.9% of the authors provided incomplete or no statistical information for the tests performed, thus obviating our computation of quantitative data for these studies. The statistical results are thus biased by the attrition of these 28 studies (i.e., not representative of the full set of reviewed studies). Second, the tendency for most authors was to report complete statistical data for significant tests and either partial or no statistical data for nonsignificant tests. This fact is consequential inasmuch as nonsignificant tests are typically associated with trivial effects or near zero population effect sizes. Hence, the aggregate statistical values presented in Table 25.2 and those reported at the end of each inference section were the result of averaging *completely reported* statistical information (i.e., chiefly significant tests) and were therefore optimistically biased estimates of the statistical variables (e.g., sample and populations effect size, per comparison and experimentwise error rates).

The third source of bias encompassed the statistical data as well as the methodological evaluations (37 threats). Most reviewers concur that the published literature embodies the best research (e.g., Cooper, 1989) and that studies reporting mostly nonsignificant results are generally not published (e.g., Jackson, 1980; Rosenthal, 1995). Thus, in comparison with all clinical supervision research involving supervisee and client inferences completed from 1981 through 1995 (published and unpublished), the quantitative and evaluation data reported herein were favorably biased. We expect unpublished research to evidence more methodological and conceptual threats and less favorable statistical data (smaller effect sizes, higher error rates).

These three sources of bias examined collectively almost guarantee that the statistical and methodological data were biased and overly optimistic. We offer some additional data to substantiate our assertion. A total of 6,988 tests were performed across the 104 studies. Of these, fully 4,885 tests were not significant (69.9%) and 1,904 were significant. Sufficient statistical data, however, were presented for just 2,394 tests (34.3% of the total) of which 1,271 tests were nonsignificant (53.1% of fully reported tests). Hence, studies reported fully 59.0% (1,123) of the significant tests, and only 26.0% of the nonsignificant tests. The implications of these data are both obvious and profound. The results reported in Tables 25.2 and 25.3 should be viewed as representing the upper bounds or best-case scenario of the status of research on supervisee and client inferences since 1981. The results overestimated the actual effect sizes and statistical power and underestimated the per comparison and experimentwise error rates. Although the extent of the bias (overestimation and underestimation) is not known, we assert that it may be appreciable (see Cooper & Hedges, 1994).

INTEGRATIVE REVIEW

The integrative review was organized according to the six core inferences pertaining to supervisees or clients (Table 25.1). Several models of supervision were subsumed by these broader inferences as more focused subinferences (e.g., Bernard, 1979; Bordin, 1983; Loganbill et al., 1982; Stoltenberg, 1981). Due to space restrictions, we did not explicate these supervisory models or theories, or the specific constructs and inferences thereof. Instead, we encourage readers to acquaint themselves with the particulars of the supervisory model of interest. Whenever necessary, the results of the studies were reinterpreted in view of the conceptual and methodological limitations identified from the evaluation and statistical variables. In essence, we examined the interpretability of the data and results for each analysis, set of analyses, and collectively for each study (Huck & Sandler, 1979; Kerlinger, 1986). The results were judged uninterpretable if obvious and more plausible rival explanations of the results existed (i.e., other than the authors' theorizing or conclusions; see Cook & Campbell, 1979; Huck & Sandler, 1979; Wampold & Poulin, 1992). For example, results were considered uninterpretable if one or more of the following prevailed: The statistical procedures were grossly inappropriate (e.g., underlying assumptions severely violated, misapplication of statistical procedures, or striking inconsistencies among the hypotheses, data, and statistics); the data were blatantly confounded; the operational definitions were flagrantly inconsistent with the intended construct or theorizing; the measures evidenced inadequate psychometric properties; or the accumulation of Type I and Type II error rates plus conceptual-methodological threats overwhelmed the credibility of the data or pattern of results. If the study was replicated and a similar pattern of results was observed, the results might have been interpretable. We use the term *replication* to mean duplicating a prior study with minor changes, for example, to increase the rigor of the study. Thus, a replication study uses the same hypotheses, methods-procedures, variables, measures, treatments, and analyses as the original study, except allowing for some modifications to enhance the methodological rigor (e.g., controlling for Type I and Type II errors). A study may be replicated fully or in part, for example, when an investigator duplicates a previous study and also incorporates a new relation in the theorizing and includes the attendant set of hypotheses and measures.

The reinterpreted results were aggregated across the set of studies to arrive at the conclusions for each subinference and inference. At the end of each set of studies reviewed, we reported median statistical data aggregated across the set of studies. That is, we reported median values for sample size, the number of statistical tests performed and the number that the authors reported as statistically significant, the sample and shrunken (population estimate) effect sizes, sample and population statistical power, sample Type II per comparison error rate, the experimentwise Type I and Type II error rates, and the number of threats of the 37 judged to be salient.

Inferences Regarding the Supervisory Relationship

The primary inference regarding the supervisory relationship is that aspects or components of the supervisory relationship are related to supervisee outcome (e.g., supervisee skills and satisfaction). As in the counseling literature, the onus of the supervisory relationship has been attributed either to the supervisor (i.e., social influence), the supervisee (i.e., client-centered conditions), or a mutual collaboration of both partners (i.e., the supervisory working alliance). A series of studies examined the supervisory relationship from the perspective of roles of the supervisor and supervisee, the structural interactions between the supervisor and supervisee, and atheoretical components of the supervisory relationship.

Inferences About Social Influence Theory.   The most often examined counseling relationship construct applied to the supervision context was that of social influence theory

(Strong, 1968). In short, seven studies interpreted the theory to imply that a supervisor perceived as expert, attractive, and trustworthy will likely bring about various changes in the supervisee (Carey, Williams, & Wells, 1988; Dodenhoff, 1981; Friedlander & Snyder, 1983; Heppner & Handley, 1981, 1982; Heppner & Roehlke, 1984; Rickards, 1984). Most of the time, the supervisor's social influence was assessed via the Supervisor Rating Form (an abridged version of the Counselor Rating Form; Barak & LaCrosse, 1975).

The strengths of these studies were that social influence was examined across a variety of contexts, was possibly related to theoretically relevant supervision variables, and was studied using quasi-experimental and ex post facto designs. Overall, however, the results assessing the salience of the social influence factors were equivocal, due to the methodological flaws. A primary methodological threat to these studies was the potential misapplication of a counseling construct to the supervision process, without acknowledging inherent differences between the two domains (i.e., the evaluative supervisory relationship). Another primary methodological threat was the experimentwise Type I and Type II error rates. With a 92% probability that one or more significant results were spurious and a 100% probability that one or more nonsignificant results were erroneous, the data from these studies were generally not credible.

Tentative inferences based on the findings across the seven studies were that the social influence factors (a) may be related to supervisory impact on counseling skills (Heppner & Roehlke, 1984); (b) appear to be related to novice supervisee satisfaction (Heppner & Handley, 1981); (c) seem to be more often related to evaluative supervisor behaviors than to supportive behaviors (Heppner & Handley, 1982); and (d) may be potentially related to verbal interactions in supervision (Rickards, 1984). There was some evidence to suggest that the social influence factors were related to supervisor perceptions of supervisee performance (Carey et al., 1988; Dodenhoff, 1981). There was also some support for the conclusions that more self-efficacious trainees had expected supervisors to be more expert and that across experience levels, supervisees expected supervisors to be mostly trustworthy followed by expert followed by attractive (Friedlander & Snyder, 1983). In light of the methodological problems within which these tentative inferences are based, perhaps Heppner and Handley (1981) stated it best by noting that the supervision process may be more complex than previously postulated. The median statistical values for these seven studies were $N = 37$, 49 tests, of which 18 were significant, $\eta^2 = .068$, $\hat{\rho}^2 = .034$, $1 - \beta_{PC(\eta^2)} = .328$, $1 - \beta_{PC(\hat{\rho}^2)} = .189$, $\beta_{PC(\eta^2)} = .672$, $\alpha_{EW} = .919$, $\beta_{EW} = 1.00$, 15 threats.

Inferences About Client-Centered Conditions. Two studies examined client-centered counseling conditions as perceived by the supervisor (i.e., regard, unconditionality, empathic understanding, and congruence) (Schact, Howe, & Berman, 1988, 1989). Both studies, which appeared to use the same sample of 152 participants, used a modified version of the Barrett-Lennard Relationship Inventory (Barrett-Lennard, 1962) to assess the traditional facilitative client-centered counseling conditions to rate supervisors retrospectively. The primary methodological flaws involved the potential misapplication of a counseling condition to supervision, questionable operationalization of constructs, and statistical analyses that were mismatched with the purpose and presented in a confusing manner. Given the numerous methodological problems, no discernible inferences could be justified. Nonetheless, given the large effect sizes, this theory merits more rigorous investigation. The median statistical values for the two studies were $N = 140.5$, 57 tests, of which 47 were significant, $\eta^2 = .339$, $\hat{\rho}^2 = .334$, $1 - \beta_{PC(\eta^2)} = 1.00$, $1 - \beta_{PC(\hat{\rho}^2)} = 1.00$, $\beta_{PC(\eta^2)} = 0.00$, $\alpha_{EW} = .940$, $\beta_{EW} = 0.00$, 7 threats.

Inferences About the Supervisory Working Alliance.   The supervisory alliance, a third relationship construct derived from the counseling literature, in general refers to a mutuality between the supervisor and supervisee perceptions of the supervisory relationship (Bordin, 1983). As in the counseling literature, however, supervision researchers have begun to define and operationalize the supervisory working alliance differently. The supervisory alliance refers to either client focus, rapport, and identification from the supervisor's perspective, and client focus and rapport from the supervisee's perspective (Efstation, Patton, & Kardash, 1990), or a mutual agreement on the goals and tasks of supervision and an emotional bond between the supervisor and supervisee, from both supervisor and supervisee perspectives (Ladany & Friedlander, 1995). Large sample sizes were strengths of both studies ($Ns > 123$), as was the attempt to measure a construct that was modified from the therapy context to the supervision context. Ladany and Friedlander (1995) additionally attempted to test the impact of third variables interacting with the primary predictor and criterion variables (i.e., examining the relationships between the demographic variables and the predictor and criterion variables). The primary methodological problems involved the use of new measures with only preliminary psychometric data, and because these studies were both field based and did not randomize, there were many threats to internal validity. Thus, many potential third variables were not controlled. In terms of inferences based on the empirical findings, the two studies seem to indicate that, at best, the supervisory alliance, as defined by client focus, rapport, and identification, may be related to supervisor style and supervisee self-efficacy for advanced practicum and intern supervisees (Efstation et al., 1990) and the supervisory alliance, as defined by goals, tasks, and bond, may be related to supervisee role conflict and ambiguity for beginning practicum to intern-level supervisees (Ladany & Friedlander, 1995). The median statistical values for the two studies were $N = 150.5$, 64 tests, of which 24.5 were significant, $\eta^2 = .076$, $\hat{\rho}^2 = .056$, $1 - \beta_{PC(\eta^2)} = .760$, $1 - \beta_{PC(\hat{\rho}^2)} = .700$, $\beta_{PC(\eta^2)} = .241$, $\alpha_{EW} = .962$, $\beta_{EW} = .529$, 14 threats.

Inferences About Role Expectations.   Within inferences about the supervisory relationship, we included five studies that examined supervisors' and supervisees' role expectations and their effect on supervisee outcome. Three studies specifically defined role expectations as including role conflict or role ambiguity (Friedlander, Keller, Peca-Baker, & Olk, 1986; Ladany & Friedlander, 1995; Olk & Friedlander, 1992). Role conflict was defined as a supervisee's experiencing competing or opposing roles or expectations. Role ambiguity was defined as a supervisee's experience of unclear roles or expectations. In the context of creating the Role Conflict and Role Ambiguity Inventory (RCRAI), Olk and Friedlander (1992) attempted to compare supervisee experiences of role conflict and ambiguity with counseling experience, supervisee anxiety, and supervisee satisfaction with supervision and clinical work. Overall, this investigation was well conceptualized and theoretically driven. It also included a large sample and adequately addressed the limitations. The weaknesses were the attempt to make longitudinal inferences from cross-sectional data and threats to internal validity due to lack of randomization. Tentative inferences based on ex post facto field investigations for Ph.D. psychology students suggest that both role conflict and ambiguity may be positively related to work-related anxiety, general work dissatisfaction, and dissatisfaction with supervision (Olk & Friedlander, 1992). Furthermore, beginning supervisees appeared to report significantly more role ambiguity than did advanced supervisees (Olk & Friedlander, 1992).

In an experimental analog counterpart, Friedlander et al. (1986) attempted to determine the extent to which role conflict affected supervisees' self-statements, anxiety level, and performance. This investigation rigorously controlled internal validity threats and was well conceptualized. Due to a relatively small sample size ($N = 52$; low power) and a 100% chance of one or more Type II errors, however, no inferences were permitted from the non-significant results.

In the context of testing Bordin's (1983) model of the supervisory alliance (i.e., agreement on the goals and tasks of supervision and on the supervisee-supervisor emotional bond), Ladany and Friedlander (1995) set out to study the relationship between the supervisory alliance and role conflict and ambiguity. As noted previously, given weaknesses based on questionable validity of the measures and high intercorrelations among the predictor and criterion variables, the only tentative inference permissible was that the supervisory alliance may be inversely related to role conflict and ambiguity.

Bahrick, Russell, and Salmi (1991) set out to examine the effects of a role-induction procedure on supervisee perceptions, hypothesizing that conceptualizations pertaining to the supervision process would become clearer for those who receive role induction. Although the study's strength lay in the relatively tight control over the stimulus materials, the measures lacked adequate reliability and validity to permit interpretation of the results. At best, we tentatively inferred that the role-induction procedure may have altered beginning supervisee perceptions about the supervision process, but the nature and extent of this alteration in perceptions are unknown.

Finally, Moskowitz and Rupert (1983) attempted to examine conflicts in the supervisory relationship. Although a novel idea for supervision research at the time of the study, inflated Type I error and questionable reliability and validity of the measures obviate making specific inferences from the results. A tentative inference, based on the reports from 38% of the supervisees ($N = 158$ first-year through internship-year clinical psychology graduate students) is that frequent conflicts with supervisors may have something to do with theoretical approach, style of supervision, and personality issues.

In summary, the overall findings tentatively suggest that beginning supervisees may experience role conflict and ambiguity and that these role difficulties were related to supervision outcome. However, a number of methodological issues mitigate the findings. First, the studies offered little control for internal validity threats (e.g., randomization) and possible third variable confounds. Also, no causal links between the variables examined or temporal inferences can be inferred due to the limitations of the studies. The median statistical values for these studies were $N = 123$, 17 tests, of which 10 were significant, $\eta^2 = .119$, $\hat{\rho}^2 = .089$, $1 - \beta_{PC(\eta^2)} = .999$, $1 - \beta_{PC(\hat{\rho}^2)} = .960$, $\beta_{PC(\eta^2)} = .001$, $\alpha_{EW} = .785$, $\beta_{EW} = .058$, 14 threats.

Inferences About the Structure of the Supervisory Relationship. Two studies investigated the nature of supervisor-trainee verbal exchanges using an interactional observation system (i.e., Blumberg's Interactional Analysis System; Holloway, 1982; Holloway & Wampold, 1983). A primary strength of these studies was analyzing the reciprocal nature of supervision interactions and identifying potential supervisee-supervisor response patterns. The primary methodological threats included experimentwise Type I and Type II error and a circumscribed sample from which the data were derived. In addition, because these studies were descriptive in nature, strategies for effective supervision were not determined. For example, even though supervisors responded to supervisee's requests for information with information, this did not indicate whether doing so was the most effective method for supervisee growth (i.e., it may be better for supervisees to explore further their own questions). Given these methodological issues, interpretations based on the results must be tempered. We may tentatively infer that supervisors and supervisees may respond to each other in a predictable manner (e.g., supervisees responded positively to supervisor supportive comments and supervisors responded with information when trainees requested information, opinions, or suggestions; Holloway, 1982) and that verbal behavior patterns may predict supervisor and supervisee judgments of satisfaction (Holloway & Wampold, 1983). The median statistical values for these studies were $N = 80.25$, 22.5 tests, of which 12 were significant, $\eta^2 = .049$, $\hat{\rho}^2 = .023$, $1 - \beta_{PC(\eta^2)} = .386$, $1 - \beta_{PC(\hat{\rho}^2)} = .320$, $\beta_{PC(\eta^2)} = .615$, $\alpha_{EW} = .565$, $\beta_{EW} = 1.00$, 14 threats.

Generic Inferences About the Supervisory Relationship.   A final series of four studies examined aspects of the supervisory relationship in a largely atheoretical manner. That is, the studies assumed the supervisory relationship was associated with particular variables without explicating the relations among the constructs or the rationale for the relations. The implicit hypotheses included relations between the supervisory relationship and supervisee course grade (Lazar & Mosek, 1993), type of supervision (i.e., clinical vs. administrative; Greenspan, Hanfling, Parker, Primm, & Waldfogel, 1991), supervisee satisfaction (Fortune & Abramson, 1993), and changes in the relationship over time (Kauderer & Herron, 1990). Both individually and collectively, the results from these studies were uninterpretable or indeterminate. Inferences from the data and results were thus not warranted. The median statistical values for these studies were $N = 97.5$, 14 tests, of which 4.5 were significant, $\eta^2 = .250$, $\hat{\rho}^2 = .235$, $1 - \beta_{PC(\eta^2)} = .872$, $1 - \beta_{PC(\hat{\rho}^2)} = .825$, $\beta_{PC(\eta^2)} = .128$, $\alpha_{EW} = .633$, $\beta_{EW} = .746$, 7 threats.

Conclusions.   The consensus in the field of clinical supervision appears to be that the supervisory relationship is theorized as an important aspect of supervision process and outcome (e.g., Bernard & Goodyear, 1992). The studies reviewed here presented some evidence that the supervision relationship may be related to a few delimited and specific supervision processes and outcomes. The data did not, however, clarify of what the supervision relationship consists. We propose that the lack of clarity regarding the supervisory relationship may be attributed to the application to the supervision context of knowledge about counseling relationships without taking into account the dissimilarities inherent in the supervisory relationship (e.g., supervision is typically evaluative and involuntary; Bernard & Goodyear, 1992). We further assert that until the unique qualities of the supervisory relationship are both acknowledged and integrated into theorizing about the supervisory relationship, our understanding will continue to falter.

Inferences Entailing Matching in Supervision

A large number of studies investigated inferences that entailed matching supervisees and supervisors on numerous attributes (e.g., sex, race, cognitive style, theoretical orientation). That is, investigations attempted to examine the impact of supervisee and supervisor match (in terms of either individual differences or of matching supervisee needs with supervisor roles) on supervision process and outcome. The basic premise was that a supervisee-supervisor match enhances supervisory process and outcome in comparison to a mismatch. Overall, with the exception of the studies testing Bernard's (1979) Discrimination Model, little theoretical rationale for the study of the match phenomenon was delineated.

Inferences Regarding Bernard's (1979) Discrimination Model. Five studies examined Bernard's (1979) Discrimination Model for supervisee training. Bernard proposed a 3×3 grid of supervisor roles (teacher, counselor, consultant) and supervision functions (process, conceptualization, personalization) such that the supervisor (or supervisee) may choose one of the nine cells of the grid to match the supervisee's needs in supervision. Of the studies investigating Bernard's model, only those that explicitly focused on inferences about supervisees were reviewed. Stenack and Dye (1983) attempted to assess the supervisee's ability to differentiate supervisor behaviors on the basis of supervisor roles of teacher, counselor, and consultant. Although the analog design was rather rigorous, the Type I and Type II error rates were extreme, which encumbered interpretation of the results. Overall, we may tentatively infer that supervisees may be able to label supervisor behaviors as falling within the three supervisor roles; however, their ability to discriminate clearly between these roles has yet to be demonstrated.

Bahrick et al. (1991) examined the effects of a role-induction procedure wherein supervisees were presented Bernard's (1979) model. As noted previously, strengths included tight control over the stimulus materials; however, the measures lacked adequate reliability or validity to assist in the interpretation of the results. Overall, we may tentatively infer that exposure to the role-induction procedure may have altered supervisee perceptions about the supervision process, but the nature and extent of the alteration in perceptions are unknown. Davis, Savicki, Cooley, and Firth (1989) took a novel approach to examine the extent to which the supervisor roles of teacher, counselor, and consultant were related to supervisee burnout. Unfortunately, due to problems with hypothesis validity, inflated Type I error rates, and questionable reliability and validity of the measures, even tentative inferences from their results would be premature.

Ellis, Dell, and Good (1988), in two studies, explicitly tested Bernard's (1979) 3×3 model using supervisee judgments of dissimilarities among the nine role-function combinations (i.e., cells of the grid). Strengths of both studies include the explicit testing of a theoretical model of supervision and an extension of the model, replication of a previous study, meticulous attention to the procedures for the statistical analyses, and use of a unique design methodology for studying supervision (i.e., multidimensional scaling). Weaknesses include unknown reliability and validity of the attribute scales used to rate the dimensions, inflated Type I error rate, and questionable generalizability of the samples. Tentative inferences from the results include (a) supervisee perceptions of the nine role functions may be similar to supervisor perceptions, (b) Bernard's model may be somewhat consistent with supervisee perceptions of supervision, and (c) Bernard's model was simplistic—three, not two, dimensions were necessary to understand perceptions of supervisor roles and functions inasmuch as relationship issues (e.g., support) were not included. Continued examination into alternative configurations of the model via replications and extensions seems warranted.

In summary, the investigations into Bernard's (1979) model have not provided compelling evidence for either its adequacy or inadequacy. At best, the model appears to provide researchers and practitioners useful heuristics in which to conceptualize supervisor roles in relation to supervisee needs. It appears that Bernard's model oversimplifies perceptions of clinical supervision. The median statistical values for these studies were $N = 20$, 34 tests, of which 13 were significant, $\eta^2 = .138$, $\hat{\rho}^2 = .119$, $1 - \beta_{PC(\eta^2)} = .530$, $1 - \beta_{PC(\hat{\rho}^2)} = .441$, $\beta_{PC(\eta^2)} = .470$, $\alpha_{EW} = .825$, $\beta_{EW} = 1.00$, 13 threats.

Inferences Regarding Individual Differences: Gender.   A number of studies included inferences about the match of supervisee-supervisor gender. Petty and Odewahn (1983) tested the sex role congruency hypothesis that stereotypically female behaviors by female supervisors (e.g., considerate) and stereotypically male behaviors by male supervisors (e.g., initiating structure) were perceived as more satisfying by supervisees. A strength of the study was the delineation of directional hypotheses. There was a clear mismatch of the hypotheses with the design and analyses, however, that is, the study provided a cursory review of the correlations between supervisee satisfaction and supervisor consideration and structure across different gender matches, but never operationalized congruence. Moreover, virtually no demographic information about the samples of supervisees (other than $N = 144$) or the supervisors was provided. The tentative conclusions from the data were that regardless of supervisee and supervisor gender, supervisees were more satisfied with supervisors who displayed considerate and structured behaviors. However, nothing can be inferred regarding the congruency hypothesis given the problems with the data analysis.

As part of a test of Bernard's (1979) model, Stenack and Dye (1983) examined supervisee-supervisor gender match and adherence to supervisor roles of teacher, counselor, and consultant. A strength of this study was the use of actual supervisor-supervisee dyads and the manipulation of supervisor behavior. Given the high Type I and Type II error rates ($\alpha_{EW} = .94$ and $\beta_{EW} = 1.00$) and extremely low statistical power ($1 - \beta_{PC} = .08$), however, the pattern of findings (1 of 12 tests was significant) had a host of plausible rival explanations. As such, no inferences were tenable in terms of supervisor roles for various supervisee-supervisor gender combinations.

Worthington and Stern (1985) examined supervisee-supervisor dyads that varied on gender (matched vs. unmatched dyads), degree level (doctoral vs. masters), and time (three occasions during a semester). Although highly ambitious, the threats to validity were so profound (i.e., extreme Type I and Type II errors, no reliability or validity for the single-item measures, and incorrect statistical analyses), that no conclusions from the results are merited. This study does, however, bring to light a problem unique to gender-matching research. Specifically, Worthington and Stern oversimplified gender matching by creating two types of matches, matched and unmatched. On closer inspection, there are actually two types of unmatched pairs, those with a male supervisor and those with a female supervisor. The importance in this distinction arises when one considers that interpersonal power may be different depending on the gender of the supervisor (e.g., Nelson & Holloway, 1990).

Nelson and Holloway (1990), in fact, examined different combinations of supervisee-supervisor gender in a study of the dimensions of power and involvement within multiple supervisory discourses. Strengths of this inventive study included the use of multivariate analyses, the use of actual supervisory dyads, and a psychometrically sound coding system for supervision. The weaknesses included Type II error, which most probably accounted for some of the nonsignificant findings, and limited representativeness of the sample. Thus, we tentatively infer that gender of masters-level counselors may influence their reactions in supervision depending on supervisor gender. Specifically, female counselors may be less encouraged and supported to assume power in supervision by both female and male supervisors, and female supervisees may more often defer power to female and male supervisors than do male supervisees. Nelson and Holloway probably put it best when they stated that "the findings suggest that gender differences exist in supervision but . . . they are subtle and highly complex" (p. 478).

Schiavone and Jessell (1988) examined the effects of supervisor status (expert, nonexpert) and supervisor and supervisee gender on supervisees' perceptions of supervisor characteristics of expertness and competence. A strength of this study was the thorough description given to the procedures used for informed consent and confidentiality of participant identity. Problems with the study include little validity data for the 5-minute videotape stimulus, dependent measures with questionable psychometric properties, and excessive experimentwise Type I and Type II errors. The study attempted to interpret nonsignificant findings to mean that there were no gender differences; however, interpreting nonsignificant findings is rarely workable (Fagley, 1985). Therefore, the results were uninterpretable.

Goodyear (1990) investigated the extent to which supervisee-supervisor gender combinations affected supervisee interpersonal influence strategies and supervisor perceptions of supervisee skills. Although a MANOVA was used to help control Type I error, follow-up analyses were examined even though multivariate significance was not reached. Subsequent to examining the follow-up tests, the one significant result was interpreted and discussed. An even more salient threat was the lack of reliability or validity data for the measures used. Given the severe methodological problems, inferences derived from the results were not justifiable. Within the context of an atheoretical investigation of supervisor theoretical orientation, Putney, Worthington, and McCullough (1992) examined whether various supervisee-supervisor gender combinations were related to 11 supervision variables. Given the exorbitant experimentwise Type I and Type II error rates, as well as the lack of psychometric data for the measures, inferences from these findings were also not warranted.

In summary, with the abundance of nonsignificant findings compared to the infrequent significant findings, inferences pertaining to gender effects in supervision seem inappropriate. As stated previously, researchers are encouraged to avoid oversimplification of matched versus unmatched gender pairs. Also, the use of oversimplified demographic characteristics was given preference over potentially more salient psychological variables such as gender identity. The median statistical values for these studies were $N = 86$, 24 tests, of which 10 were significant, $\eta^2 = .079$, $\hat{\rho}^2 = .057$, $1 - \beta_{PC(\eta^2)} = .650$, $1 - \beta_{PC(\hat{\rho}^2)} = .318$, $\beta_{PC(\eta^2)} = .350$, $\alpha_{EW} = .708$, $\beta_{EW} = 1.00$, 13 threats.

Inferences Regarding Individual Differences: Race. The paucity of empirical investigations of inferences about racial issues in supervision points to a gap in the empirical supervision literature. Only three investigations specifically addressed inferences about race in supervision. Cook and Helms (1988) investigated Asian, African American, Hispanic, and Native American (visible racial-ethnic groups) supervisees' perceptions of supervision and the relation between racial groups and satisfaction. This ground-breaking study had many strengths, including the attempt to modify a scale (via exploratory factor analysis) for underrepresented populations, the use of a large sample size ($N = 225$), and an elaborate and extensive sampling procedure. The study's shortcomings were violations of the assumptions of factor analysis and questionable psychometric properties of the measures. In particular, although the measures were modified for specific racial groups, the items were not specifically originated to encompass ethnic-racial populations. As such, the scales themselves were etic (i.e., assumed to be universally applicable) versus emic (i.e., culturally specific) in nature. We tentatively infer that supervisor's liking may be an important component for ethnic-racial diverse supervisees, which in turn may be related to supervisee satisfaction.

Hilton, Russell, and Salmi (1995) investigated the effects of supervisee-supervisor racial matching on supervisee perceptions of the supervisory relationship and supervisor effectiveness. The analog study was unique in that confederate supervisors and clients were used and participants were randomly assigned to conditions. Although the effect sizes were large, few significant effects were observed. This plus the other conceptual and methodological problems suggests that the results offered few indications as to any effect of supervisor race on supervisee perceptions. Pope-Davis, Reynolds, Dings, and Ottavi (1994) investigated the relationship among demographic variables and multicultural education and self-reported multicultural competencies (e.g., awareness and knowledge-skills). Although acknowledging the importance and uniqueness of the area as strengths of the study, the methodology was fraught with methodological flaws, which make the interpretability of the results unfeasible. Specifically, the primary threats to the validity of the study included excessive Type I and Type II errors, violations of the assumptions of the statistical tests, and the misapplication of statistical procedures (use of stepwise regression analyses; Pedhazur, 1983). Instead, a simultaneous multiple regression analysis should have been employed (Wampold & Freund, 1987).

In summary, the authors investigating inferences about supervisee race should be commended for pursuing a potentially important area of supervision. Overall, the data indicated that race may play an important role in supervision process and outcome; however, the extent and nature of that role have yet to be adequately tested to make any tentative inferences. As with gender, researchers would do well to examine psychological variables such as racial identity versus the less complex variable of race (Helms, 1990). The median statistical values for the three studies were $N = 141$, 34 tests, of which 14 were significant, $\eta^2 = .022$, $\hat{\rho}^2 = .018$, $1 - \beta_{PC(\eta^2)} = .611$, $1 - \beta_{PC(\hat{\rho}^2)} = .512$, $\beta_{PC(\eta^2)} = .389$, $\alpha_{EW} = .825$, $\beta_{EW} = 1.00$, 16 threats.

Inferences Regarding Individual Differences: Theoretical Orientation. Several investigators examined the relation of supervisee-supervisor theoretical orientation and various supervision variables. Steinhelber, Patterson, Cliffe, and LeGoullon (1984) assessed the extent to which theoretical orientation congruence (defined as the match of supervisee and supervisor based on 17 different theoretical orientations) was related to aspects of client change. Little theoretical rationale and numerous statistical violations precluded making inferences from the data and results. In a unique longitudinal design, Guest and Beutler (1988) investigated the impact of supervisor theoretical orientation on supervisees; however, given the numerous methodological problems (e.g., extremely high Type I and II error rates and lack of reliability and validity data for the measures), no inferences are defensible.

In Schact et al.'s (1989) investigation of the relation of supervisees' Myers-Briggs type to most and least effective supervisor, the study also examined whether supervisees' theoretical orientation (behavioral, client centered, or analytic) was related to differences in their perceptions of most effective and least effective supervisors. Unfortunately, even with a large sample size ($N = 152$), the interpretations of the results become problematic due to extreme Type I error rates and very questionable validity and reliability of the measures. The only tentative inference that may be deduced from this investigation was that supervisees differentially perceived their most and least effective supervisors, regardless of the supervisee's or supervisor's theoretical orientation. A more detailed analysis of these differences is unclear as of yet. Putney et al. (1992) endeavored to determine the extent to which supervisee-supervisor theoretical orientation combinations were related to supervisee perceptions of his or her own autonomy (assessed by 13 dependent variables), supervisor approach (models, roles, and foci) and effectiveness (the same 13 dependent variables). Of the 84 participants, 64 were theoretically matched (theoretical orientation was generalized to two types, cognitive-behavioral or humanistic-psychodynamic) and 20 were unmatched. Unfortunately, due to the excessive Type I error rates, unknown validity and reliability of the measures, and questionable operationalization of theoretical match, no tentative inferences can be postulated with confidence.

In summary, beyond the numerous methodological difficulties mentioned, the most salient issue for studying supervisor theoretical orientation may be the question of relevance. Theoretically, as well as empirically, it is shaky reasoning to believe that supervisors who ascribe to a given theoretical orientation for counseling will directly translate that theoretical orientation into the process of supervision. For example, there is little reason to believe that a supervisor who conceptualizes and treats clients from a psychodynamic perspective will not, in supervision, be didactic about psychodynamic principles. Moreover, it is a dubious assumption to presume that supervisors can be categorized as working from a predominant theoretical orientation and not from an integrationist or eclectic orientation. Supervision researchers would probably do better to focus on supervisory orientations (e.g., developmental models of supervision) in attempting to understand supervision process and outcome. The median statistical values for these studies were: $N = 67.5$, 76.5 tests, of which 16 were significant, $\eta^2 = .287$, $\hat{\rho}^2 = .263$, $1 - \beta_{PC(\eta^2)} = .919$, $1 - \beta_{PC(\hat{\rho}^2)} = .863$, $\beta_{PC(\eta^2)} = .081$, $\alpha_{EW} = .977$ $\beta_{EW} = .774$, 22 threats.

Inferences Regarding Individual Differences: Environmental Setting.   Two investigations attempted to assess the extent to which perceptions of supervisee-environment match related to supervisee developmental level (Krause & Allen, 1988; Wiley & Ray, 1986). Although interesting and seemingly important to consider environmental conditions, as noted in the section on inferences regarding supervisee developmental level, the methodological problems associated with these investigations prohibit making inferences from the results. The median statistical values for these studies were $N = 85$, 37 tests, of which 13.5 were significant, $\eta^2 = .069$, $\hat{\rho}^2 = .029$, $1 - \beta_{PC(\eta^2)} = .570$, $1 - \beta_{PC(\hat{\rho}^2)} = .298$, $\beta_{PC(\eta^2)} = .431$, $\alpha_{EW} = .733$, $\beta_{EW} = 1.00$, 14.5 threats.

Inferences Regarding Individual Differences: Reactance.   In the context of examining inferences pertaining to supervisee developmental level, one study investigated the moderating effects of reactance potential (i.e., a personality variable defined as the extent to which a person resists structure when imposed) on trainee responses to crisis versus noncrisis materials (Tracey, Ellickson, & Sherry, 1989). As one of the more theoretically and methodologically sound studies, this study provided directional theoretically based hypotheses, extensive validity checks for the analog conditions, and generally rigorous methodology. As noted in the developmental inferences subsection that follows, however, a number of methodological threats tempered the potential inferences from the data. More specifically, we may tentatively infer that reactance potential may be an important personality variable to examine in supervisees. The median statistical values for these studies were $N = 78$, 68 tests, of which 11 were significant, $\eta^2 = .064$, $\hat{\rho}^2 = .041$, $1 - \beta_{PC(\eta^2)} = .560$, $1 - \beta_{PC(\hat{\rho}^2)} = .428$, $\beta_{PC(\eta^2)} = .572$, $\alpha_{EW} = .834$, $\beta_{EW} = 1.00$, 14 threats.

Inferences Regarding Individual Differences: Cognitive Style.   Four investigations considered the extent to which cognitive style, typically operationalized via Myers-Briggs personality types, plays a role in supervision process and outcome. Handley (1982) postulated that supervisee and supervisor Myers-Briggs type would predict differences in supervisee perceptions of the supervisory relationship and supervisor evaluation ratings.

Carey and Williams (1986) attempted to replicate and extend Handley's (1982) study, after identifying accurately the Type I error problems. Both studies had similar glaring weaknesses, however, which included inflated Type I and Type II error, confounding due to some supervisors rating up to four supervisees, and failure to articulate a rationale for the effect of supervisees and supervisors matching or differing in cognitive styles. As such, no tenable inferences can be postulated from these investigations. One study examined the relation of supervisee MBTI types to least and most effective supervisor (Schact et al., 1989). Numerous methodological problems, as well as poorly described and confusing presentation of the results, however, prohibited inferences from the data. Performing more than 235 statistical tests, the final study (Swanson & O'Saben, 1993) investigated whether cognitive style (i.e., MBTI type) was related to supervisory needs or experience. Beset with numerous methodological and statistical flaws, the results were uninterpretable.

Summarizing the four separate investigations, it is unfortunate that no clear inferences can be made regarding cognitive style and supervision. Perhaps the most glaring problem with using the MBTI is that whereas it may assess general cognitive style, it may not adequately assess cognitive style in the supervisory relationship or in counseling (i.e., is it more state or trait based for supervisory contexts?). Lacking from all studies was an adequate, logical rationale for why the MBTI may be useful to understand supervision process and outcome. Future researchers would do well to discuss these implications and their associated hypotheses. The median statistical values for these studies were $N = 60.5$, 104.5 tests, of which 29.5 were significant, $\eta^2 = .140$, $\hat{\rho}^2 = .123$, $1 - \beta_{PC(\eta^2)} = .282$, $1 - \beta_{PC(\hat{\rho}^2)} = .075$, $\beta_{PC(\eta^2)} = .718$, $\alpha_{EW} = .983$, $\beta_{EW} = 1.00$, 15 threats.

Inferences Regarding Supervisee Needs.   Sixteen studies seemed to take the perspective that supervisees were an important source of information for understanding the effectiveness of supervision. These studies appeared to approach this understanding from the common theme of matching supervisee needs with specific supervisor interventions, which were labeled in a variety of ways, such as good versus bad supervision, successful versus unsuccessful supervision, and critical issues in supervision. In general, these studies lacked the logical and theoretical arguments to explain the importance of matching supervisees' needs.

Lowe and McLeod (1985) examined the relation of supervisory needs of practicing clinicians with experience, training, certification, and client description. This study was unique in that it focused on postdoctoral and masters-degreed clinicians. A conspicuous weakness was the lack of validity or reliability data for the stimulus materials. As such, the tentative inference derived from the results was that practitioners may be less likely to have a supervisor as they became more experienced and more educated and were licensed.

In a well-designed case study, Martin, Goodyear, and Newton (1987) used a best-worst supervision session strategy to examine supervision process and outcome. The study was strong in many respects, including the use of pre- and posttest assessment and assessment from multiple sources. Interestingly, both supervisee and supervisor agreed on the session labeled "the best." The shortcomings of the study were (a) no description was given regarding the authors' biases, which may have impacted the qualitative assessment; (b) the participants were likely operating from demand characteristics; (c) the measures had questionable validity; and (d) the findings had clearly limited generalizability. We may tentatively infer from a 33-year-old female supervisee with a 41-year-old male supervisor that the supervisee and supervisor found sessions most productive when discussing personal issues related to work with clients; the least productive session, as perceived by the supervisee, involved conflict; supervisory styles and supervisee evaluations of supervision changed over time; and the case study design may be a fruitful approach to study supervision. Given the case study methodology, the tenuousness of the results can be lessened only via multiple replications.

Usher and Borders (1993) set out to examine supervisor style and emphasis preferences for postdegree school and nonschool counselors-supervisees. Strengths of this study were the use of multivariate statistical analyses and the inclusion of school counselors as a population. The rationale for comparing two "types" of counselors was weak, however, as there were high Type I and Type II error rates, the reliability of one of the dependent measures was discreditable, and longitudinal inferences were inappropriately made from cross-sectional data. Also, this study erroneously made inferences regarding the relative preference of the various supervisor styles and emphasis, without testing these hypotheses statistically. Overall, we tentatively infer from the results that postdegree school counselors may prefer supervisors to be more task oriented and to emphasize process skills more and personalization skills less than do counselors in other settings.

Thirteen studies were so seriously methodologically flawed, particularly in areas such as the validity of the measures, extreme Type I or Type II error rates, inadequate hypothesis validity, and inadequate description of the methodological procedures, that trustworthy inferences could not be made from the results (Allen, Szollos, & Williams, 1986; Curiel & Rosenthal, 1987; Eisikovits, Shurka, & Baizeman, 1983; Fortune & Abramson, 1993; Gandolfo & Brown, 1987; Hutt, Scott, & King, 1983; Kennard, Stewart, & Gluck, 1987; Perez, Krul, & Kapoor, 1984; Rodway & Rogers, 1993; Rotholz & Werk, 1984; Strozier, Kivlighan, & Thoreson, 1993; Talen & Schindler, 1993; Tracey & Sherry, 1993). At best, some of these studies raised several important issues concerning supervision theory, research, and practice. These include (a) the notion that supervisees seemed to be able to differentiate between their best and worst supervision experiences (Allen et al., 1986), (b) the potential importance of setting goals in supervision (Talen & Schindler, 1993), (c) supervision methods may differ depending on clinical population (e.g., individual, group, long-term; Perez et al., 1984), (d) supervision may be experienced differently by undergraduate- and graduate-level counselors (Curiel & Rosenthal, 1987), (e) supervisor behaviors may be valued differently by supervisees (Rotholz & Werk, 1984), (f) supervisees and supervisors may perceive supervision differently (Kennard et al., 1987), (g) there may be discrepancies between actual and ideal supervision (Gandolfo & Brown, 1987), (h) the case study format can provide much information about supervision (Hutt et al., 1983; Strozier et al., 1993), (i) the potential importance of faculty-field instructor coordination (Rodway & Rogers, 1993), and (j) successful versus unsuccessful supervision interactions may be contingent upon the complementary responses of supervisor (i.e., dominant-submissive, friendly-hostile; Tracey & Sherry, 1993).

In summary, very little can be inferred from the findings of studies investigating supervisee needs. The general lack of conceptual and methodological rigor seems pernicious. Supervision researchers interested in matching interventions with supervisee needs would do well to address hypothesis validity, creating a priori hypotheses and delineating the rationale regarding matching of supervisee needs. Another salient issue when attempting to determine intervention matches with supervisee needs is that investigators ought to establish clearly their purpose: to create descriptive inferences about what is done, or what supervisees would prefer to be done, rather than creating inferences about optimal methods for effective supervisee outcome (i.e., a descriptive versus prescriptive approach; Holloway & Hosford, 1983). The median statistical values for these studies were $N = 88$,

23 tests, of which 8.5 were significant, $\eta^2 = .064$, $\hat{\rho}^2 = .053$, $1 - \beta_{PC(\eta^2)} = .917$, $1 - \beta_{PC(\hat{\rho}^2)} = .880$, $\beta_{PC(\eta^2)} = .083$, $\alpha_{EW} = .743$, $\beta_{EW} = .777$, 14.5 threats.

Conclusions.   The second overarching inference that supervision researchers addressed was the matching inference. The matching inference is based on the premise that supervisee-supervisor dyads having the same characteristics (i.e., individual differences variables) and that matching supervisee needs (i.e., developmental level tasks) and supervisory interventions result in better supervision and enhanced supervisee learning. In general, these assumptions may be oversimplified and seem to lack empirical validation. One example of this oversimplification occurs when researchers examine the matching of basic demographic characteristics such as race or biological sex instead of examining the more relevant complex psychological constructs of racial identity or gender identity. Furthermore, more extensive research into specific models, Bernard's (1979) model in particular, is warranted.

Inferences Regarding Supervisee Development

The premise of supervisees progressing through a developmental sequence as they gain supervised clinical experience has a rich and long-standing tradition in the clinical supervision literature (e.g., Ekstein & Wallerstein, 1958; Holloway, 1987; Russell et al., 1984). Since 1981, researchers explicitly or implicitly investigated a variety of inferences regarding supervisee development and supervisee experience. More specifically, investigators tested inferences regarding ego development, conceptual development, several models of supervisee development (e.g., Loganbill et al., 1982; Stoltenberg, 1981), and generic supervisee development and experience level. Even though extensively studied, the data for these inferences were largely uninterpretable and offered few viable conclusions. In essence, the crucial inferences of supervisee development still have not been adequately tested (Holloway, 1987).

Inferences Regarding Ego Development.   Borders and her associates conducted a series of studies investigating the relationship of ego development (e.g., Loevinger, 1976) with the structural complexity and content of supervisees' perceptions of clients (Borders, Fong, & Neimeyer, 1986), with the frequency of counselors' in-session cognitions (Borders, 1989b), with the mastery of prepracticum counseling skills and counseling effectiveness (Borders & Fong, 1989, Study 1), and with counselor effectiveness and performance with "real" clients (Borders & Fong, 1989, Study 2). At best, these studies offer inconsistent and equivocal results. The logic explicating the potential relations of ego development to the efficacy of counselor training and supervision appeared well argued. It is our contention, however, that these propositions have yet to be tested adequately. That is, given the statistical and methodological problems with this set of studies (e.g., threats to hypothesis validity, inappropriate statistical procedures, low statistical power, conceptual-methodological mismatch) in combination with the lack of replication of the effects (both significant and nonsignificant), it is premature to draw any inferences from these data. The median statistical values across the four studies were $N = 53.5$, 9.5 tests, of which 3 were significant, $\eta^2 = .076$, $\hat{\rho}^2 = .054$, $1 - \beta_{PC(\eta^2)} = .439$, $1 - \beta_{PC(\hat{\rho}^2)} = .320$, $\beta_{PC(\eta^2)} = .561$, $\alpha_{EW} = .678$, $\beta_{EW} = .920$, 15.5 threats.

Inferences Regarding Conceptual Development.   Three studies were conducted to test inferences about the cognitive development (more specifically, cognitive complexity) of therapist trainees (Blocher et al., 1985; Malikiosi-Loizos, Gold, Mehnert, & Work, 1981; Winter & Holloway, 1991). As part of developing and providing preliminary validity data for the Counselor Perception Questionnaire rating system, Blocher et al. (1985) tested the hypothesis that Ph.D.-level psychologists were more conceptually differentiated than neophyte counselors (i.e., able to identify distinct issues and the cues from which these inferences were drawn). Given the methodological problems discussed in the "New Measures" section that follows, we may tentatively conclude that doctoral-level psychologists may be more cognitively differentiated than neophyte masters-student counselors, if the finding is treated as very preliminary, restricted to clients presenting vocational indecision issues, and is subject to cohort effects (e.g., age, maturity) and selection bias. Malikiosi-Loizos et al. (1981) tested the hypothesis that cognitive complexity mediates the efficacy of the type of supervision (didactic vs. experiential) received by inexperienced counselors. Given that no psychometric data were offered for the five new dependent measures, the low statistical power, and use of 15-minute sessions with coached clients, the only conclusion that seems warranted is that for inexperienced therapists, didactic supervision may be more effective for supervisees high in cognitive complexity than low cognitively complex supervisees; however, what constitutes high or low cognitive complexity is not known. Because the relevant findings were nonsignificant, no inferences can be made about the efficacy of experiential supervision in terms of cognitive complexity.

Winter and Holloway (1991) used an intriguing and innovative method to assess supervisee needs. The supervisee first rated all 90-second segments of an entire audiotaped therapy session in terms of four types of supervisory focus it would elicit. Then the supervisee selected a 3- to 6-minute segment of the audiotape to present in supervision. These segments were analyzed by tallying the ratings for each of the four supervisory foci. Other notable strengths of the study were that the authors incorporated explicit hypotheses and theorizing and assessed experience conceptual level as a continuous variable (e.g., months of clinical experience rather than trichotomizing practicum level). Regrettably, the study suffered from too many methodological and statistical problems to permit drawing inferences from the results. For example, the statistical procedures did not match the hypotheses (did not yield unique variances), the Type I and Type II error rates were excessive, the group sizes were small ($ns = 19$; i.e., low power), the four dependent variables lacked psychometric data, and having the supervisee rate the audiotape on the four supervisory foci before selecting the segment may have significantly biased the segment chosen.

In short, we know very little about the relations among supervision and the cognitive complexity and cognitive development of supervisees. Bestowed with large effect sizes (Holloway & Wampold, 1986), inferences about cognitive development remain an attractive and potentially fertile line of inquiry. We especially encourage researchers to replicate (after addressing the salient problems) Winter and Holloway's (1991) research. The median statistical values for these three studies were $N = 24$, 15 tests, of which 7 were significant, $\eta^2 = .176$, $\hat{\rho}^2 = .125$, $1 - \beta_{PC(\eta^2)} = .453$, $1 - \beta_{PC(\hat{\rho}^2)} = .319$, $\beta_{PC(\eta^2)} = .547$, $\alpha_{EW} = .560$, $\beta_{EW} = .996$, 16 threats.

Inferences Regarding Models of Supervisee Development

Littrell, Lee-Borden, and Lorenz's (1979) Developmental Model.   Ellis et al. (1988, Study 2) conducted the only empirical test of Littrell et al.'s unidimensional model to date. They did not, however, test the developmental components of the model per se. Although the study was subject to threats to hypothesis validity and inflated Type I error rate and was limited by the circumscribed set of stimuli, the data suggest that Littrell et al.'s model is simplistic. At least three dimensions are used by supervisees when making judgments about supervision (emotional vs. behavioral, directive vs. nondirective, and supervision focus: process-personal vs. conceptual). The median statistical values for this study were $N = 48$, 34 tests, of which 13 were significant, $\eta^2 = .138$, $\hat{\rho}^2 = .119$, $1 - \beta_{PC(\eta^2)} = .530$, $1 - \beta_{PC(\hat{\rho}^2)} = .441$, $\beta_{PC(\eta^2)} = .470$, $\alpha_{EW} = .785$, $\beta_{EW} = 1.00$, 13 threats.

Hogan's (1964) Developmental Model.   To date, only one set of authors (Reising & Daniels, 1983) explicitly tested Hogan's developmental model. Although the research was laudable on several criteria (e.g., theory testing, relatively large sample size, and use of planned comparisons), the credibility of their results rests largely on the 16 dependent variables (i.e., the 16 subscales of the Counselor Development Questionnaire), for which minimal psychometric data exist. Of the psychometric data presented by the authors, the use of exploratory (vs. confirmatory) factor-analysis procedures, the inadequate ratio of sample size to number of items (yielding unstable factor structures and factor loadings), and the lack of cross-validation data thoroughly compromise the validity of the results. Hence, conclusions about the application of Hogan's model to clinical supervision seem improper. The median statistical values were $N = 141$, 52 tests, of which 13 were significant, $\alpha_{EW} = .931$, 14 threats.

Loganbill et al.'s (1982) Conceptual Model and Sansbury's (1982) Skills-Based Developmental Model.   Heppner and Roehlke (1984, Study 3) and Rabinowitz, Heppner, and Roehlke (1986) indirectly tested Loganbill et al.'s model. In fact, Heppner and Roehlke's study employed an innovative procedure to test Loganbill et al.'s supervisory issues. The substantive methodological and statistical problems associated with Rabinowitz et al.'s study (e.g., unacceptably high Type I and Type II error rates, very low statistical power, inappropriate statistical procedures, confounded data, conceptual and methodological inconsistencies, and the lack of hypothesis validities), however, suggest that the data are largely uninterpretable. Although the results pertaining to trainee level and to the combined categories are highly problematic (e.g., violated statistical assumptions, small ns and low statistical power, and a mismatch among the data, underlying construct, and labels for the combined categories), we may cautiously infer from Heppner and Roehlke's study that supervisory issues of emotional awareness-confrontation and support occur frequently, whereas issue of theoretical identity, individual differences, personal motivation, ethics, and autonomy occur infrequently. The median statistical values for the two studies were $N = 42.5$, 20 tests, of which 10 were significant, $\eta^2 = .083$, $\hat{\rho}^2 = .039$, $1 - \beta_{PC(\eta^2)} = .528$, $1 - \beta_{PC(\hat{\rho}^2)} = .300$, $\beta_{PC(\eta^2)} = .472$, $\alpha_{EW} = .633$, $\beta_{EW} = 1.00$, 16 threats.

In a comparative test of Loganbill et al.'s (1982) model and Sansbury's (1982) model, Ellis (1991c) investigated whether 10 supervisory issues occur as predicted by the models both in therapy supervision and in supervisor supervision. In light of the methodological problems (e.g., lack of psychometric data for the rating system, threats to internal validity, diffuse statistical hypotheses, novice therapists, and novice supervisor samples), the results should be interpreted with caution. Therefore, considering the three studies collectively (Ellis, 1991c; Heppner & Roehlke, 1984, Study 3; Rabinowitz et al., 1986) and taking into account their methodological strengths and weaknesses, we tentatively conclude that for supervisees and novice supervisors (a) relationship issues and personal issues affecting treatment, which were not included by either Loganbill et al. or Sansbury, seem to be viable supervisory issues; (b) four of Loganbill et al.'s supervisory issues (i.e., individual differences, ethics, personal motivation, and theoretical identity) occur infrequently; (c) closely paralleling Sansbury's proposed hierarchy, there appears to exist a hierarchy among the supervisory issues that may be dependent on the developmental level of the supervisee; and (d) supervisory issues reported in therapy supervision and supervisor supervision are highly similar. These two models await further testing, in particular the extent to which Sansbury's hierarchy of supervisory issues is observed among a more diverse sample of therapists and supervisors (e.g., more advanced and experienced). The median statistical values for Ellis (1991c) were $N = 18$, 20 tests, of which 10 were significant, $\eta^2 = .695$, $\hat{\rho}^2 = .542$, $1 - \beta_{PC(\eta^2)} = 1.000$, $1 - \beta_{PC(\hat{\rho}^2)} = 1.000$, $\beta_{PC(\eta^2)} = 0.00$, $\alpha_{EW} = .642$, $\beta_{EW} = 0.00$, 19 threats.

Stoltenberg's (1981) Counselor Complexity Model.   Seven studies were published wherein the investigators explicitly tested Stoltenberg's model (Borders, 1990; Friedlander & Snyder, 1983; Krause & Allen, 1988; McNeill, Stoltenberg, & Pierce, 1985; Stoltenberg, Pierce, & McNeill, 1987; Stoltenberg, Soloman, & Ogden, 1986; Wiley & Ray, 1986). Unfortunately, the methodological and conceptual quality of the studies was so poor that the interpretability of the results was either severely compromised or precluded. We briefly review each study to elucidate the shortcomings and strengths.

Friedlander and Snyder (1983) set out to test Stoltenberg's (1981) model; however, the study is more accurately a test of social influence theory (see Heppner & Handley, 1981, 1982). The problem entails both a conceptual and a methodological mismatch: The methods and operational definitions were not compatible with the authors' implicit theorizing and implicit hypotheses (i.e., the logic linking the variables and data to Stoltenberg's model is weak and unsubstantiated). Second, the statistical tests that were performed did not test the authors' theorizing or implicit hypotheses. The lack of psychometric data for the criterion and predictor variables in combination with the conceptual and methodological mismatches suggests that the only highly tentative inferences from the data are that no significant relations were observed between supervisee level of experience and supervisor expertness, attractiveness, and trustworthiness.

In an impressive departure from the traditional assessment of supervisee developmental level, McNeill et al. (1985) used a composite trainee experience measure, which they regrettably trichotomized, rather than using just the supervisee's level of practicum. The authors also created the Supervisee Levels Questionnaire (SLQ) on the basis of Stoltenberg's (1981) model. The only psychometric data reported for either of these new measures were Cronbach alpha coefficients for the three SLQ scales. The alpha coefficients indicated that two of the three scales had inadequate internal consistency reliability (Self-Awareness $\alpha = .55$, Theory/Skills Acquisitions $\alpha = .67$; i.e., 45% and 33% measurement error, respectively). Hence, given the data and results, drawing inferences from these two SLQ scales is unfounded. In addition, McNeill et al. conducted "preplanned comparisons" (as did Stoltenberg et al., 1987). The term *preplanned comparisons* is deceiving. The authors appear to have performed ordinary *t*-tests for all possible paired comparisons. This procedure does not comply with established protocols for a priori planned (orthogonal) comparisons (e.g., Hays, 1988), thus constituting a mismatch (i.e., Wampold et al.'s, 1990, noncongruence of research and statistical hypotheses threat to hypothesis validity). The only tentative inference we can defend is that the advanced supervisees reported higher autonomy (Cronbach's $\alpha = .76$) than did the group of beginning supervisees.

Wiley and Ray (1986) tested the match between the supervisee's developmental level and the supervisory environment developmental level. Elaborating on Stoltenberg's (1981) model, they constructed the Supervision Level Scale (SLS), which consisted of four Person scales (i.e., four developmental levels) and four Environment scales (i.e., four developmental levels). Supervisors use the SLS to rate their supervisees and the supervision he or she provided to them. Although marginal to excellent 2-week test-retest reliabilities were reported (.71 to .95), the data were provided by a sample of *seven* supervisors. Thus, the reliabilities are highly dubious.

Two other salient problems exist. First, the data were doubly confounded: Approximately half the sample of supervisors provided multiple data sets (i.e., more than one supervisee), and 12 interns participated as both supervisee and supervisor. That is, some supervisors provided repeated measures or nested data, but the authors treated and analyzed the data as independent observations, thus violating a critically important assumption for the statistical procedures used (i.e., uncorrelated error terms). Hence, the results of the data analyses are erroneous and cannot be trusted. The second problem was the use of single-item measures as dependent variables. Single-item scales are notoriously unstable (test-retest reliability) and inaccurate (i.e., subject to many biases and vagaries), and it is virtually impossible to test their psychometric properties. Finally, the authors offer no sound data to suggest that the SLS classifies supervisees appropriately. Hence, we have no confidence in the data and results from this study and therefore believe that any inferences from the data are inappropriate.

Stoltenberg et al. (1986) also investigated the match of the supervisee's developmental level and the supervisory environment level. Similar to Wiley and Ray (1986), data from supervisors were confounded; 11 supervisors provided data for 30 supervisees. Thus, the results from any analyses using supervisor data were judged invalid. In addition to unacceptably high Type I and Type II error rates and multiple threats to hypothesis validity (ambiguous and diffuse hypotheses), the authors did not provide validity data for the stimulus materials (i.e., the items; descriptions of supervisees and supervisory environments) nor psychometric data for this new scale. We might cautiously infer that supervisees' self-classified developmental level may be related to their preferences for supervisory environment level such that they may prefer a supervisory environment at or below their perceived developmental level. Considering the magnitude of the problems, no other inferences are warranted.

Stoltenberg et al. (1987) tested the hypothesis that supervisees at different developmental levels express different supervisory needs as specified in Stoltenberg's (1981) model. To assess supervisory needs, the authors developed a new measure (Supervisory Needs Questionnaire, SNQ) but did not test or report any of the psychometric properties of the SNQ. In contrast to McNeill et al. (1985), the authors did not use a composite trainee experience measure, but rather treated the three experience variables (education, counseling experience, and supervised counseling experience) as separate, trichotomized independent variables, thus sacrificing a great deal of statistical power. As mentioned earlier, the authors inappropriately performed preplanned comparisons. Without validity data for the SNQ, not knowing the meaning of Experience Level 1, 2, or 3 (groupings may have differed across the three variables), and with the probability of observing at least one Type I error (.94) and one Type II error (1.0), drawing inferences from the data seems untenable.

Krause and Allen (1988) investigated the match between supervisees' developmental level and the supervisory environment level. Of the numerous problems besetting this study, perhaps the more compelling ones included the following. Supervisors were instructed to provide data for two supervisees, yet the number of supervisors providing multiple data sets was not reported. Supervisor data were analyzed as independent observations, thus supervisor data were confounded. Hence, any results involving supervisor data were deemed invalid.

Second, there were both conceptual and methodological mismatches (inconsistencies). Exploratory factor analyses were performed on two of the new measures created by the authors (see later discussion regarding scale construction and validity) even though the sample size to number of items ratio was well below the minimal 5:1 required for factor analysis (Tinsley & Tinsley, 1987). Although factor analyses were performed and Cronbach's alphas were computed for the resulting factors (mislabeled *clusters*), the analyses were performed at the item level, thus negating the factor analysis and internal consistency reliability analysis (see earlier discussion about single-item dependent variables). That is, there were 35 supervisor dependent variables (35 items), not the 8 factors or scales, and 33 supervisee dependent variables, not the 5 factor scales, yielding a total of 68 dependent variables for this set of analyses. Essentially, psychometric data were not provided for the authors' new measures, including the new single-item measure of supervisee developmental level. These problems coupled with the experimentwise Type I and Type II error rates (.95 and 1.0, respectively) and the circumscribed sample of predoctoral interns and their supervisors (plus several other methodological problems with the satisfaction and impact variables) suggest that the results are untrustworthy, permitting no inferences or conclusions.

Borders (1990) contributed the only longitudinal investigation of Stoltenberg's model (over one semester). The author prudently tested for differences among the three supervisors (i.e., groups) before conducting the major analysis. Given the low reliabilities associated with the Self-Awareness and Theory/Skills Acquisition scales of McNeill et al.'s (1985) SLQ, only data pertaining to the Autonomy scale seem viable. It should be noted that no psychometric data exist for the SLQ total scale (sum of all items), thus precluding interpreting total scale results. The various threats to validity notwithstanding, we might tentatively infer that Autonomy scores for novice supervisees significantly increased over the 14-week counseling practicum. Without a comparison group, however, we do not know if the significant increase in Autonomy was due to regression to the mean, maturation, testing effects, measurement error, hypothesis guessing, sample bias, or Type I error.

In summation, Stoltenberg's (1981) Counselor Complexity Model remains largely untested. In particular, the majority of the fundamental premises of the model have not been tested adequately (e.g., matching supervisory environment to supervisees' developmental level, the appropriateness of the four levels, hierarchical progression from Level 1 to Level 4, and so forth). The nearly exclusive reliance on cross-sectional data (vs. longitudinal data) is a major obstruction to testing the developmental and sequential components of Stoltenberg's model (Holloway, 1987). On the basis of our review, which takes into account the conceptual and methodological rigor of these studies, we tentatively conclude that per Stoltenberg's model, supervisees may significantly increase in autonomy as they gain experience, beginning supervisees may prefer more structured supervision, and self-perceived developmental level may not be equivalent to practicum level. No viable supervisor data or results were found because of confounded data (some supervisors contributed multiple data sets or participated as both supervisor and supervisee).

In their effort to test Stoltenberg's (1981) model, several of these authors constructed new measures and scales. Inasmuch as these scales are enticing, the lack of psychometric data, and in some instances the poor conceptual match to Stoltenberg's model, prohibits drawing inferences from the scale scores. One of the most important contributions from this set of investigators was to develop more suitable measures of supervisee developmental level rather than using practicum level (e.g., first practicum, advanced practicum, internship) as a proxy for level of experience. The most salient problems encountered among these seven studies were conceptual and methodological mismatches, ambiguous hypotheses and diffuse statistical tests, confounded data, excessive Type I and Type II error rates, and lack of psychometrically sound measures. The median statistical values for these studies were $N = 82$, 16 tests, of which 12 were significant, $\eta^2 = .067$, $\hat{\rho}^2 = .021$, $1 - \beta_{PC(\eta^2)} = .349$, $1 - \beta_{PC(\hat{\rho}^2)} = .226$, $\beta_{PC(\eta^2)} = .651$, $\alpha_{EW} = .560$, $\beta_{EW} = .996$, 16 threats.

Stoltenberg and Delworth's (1987) Integrated Developmental Model (IDM). The two published empirical tests of Stoltenberg and Delworth's IDM were done by McNeill, Stoltenberg, and Romans (1992) and Bear and Kivilighan (1994). McNeill et al. revised the Supervisory Levels Questionnaire (SLQ-R; McNeill et al., 1985) to be consistent with Stoltenberg and Delworth's IDM and tested several psychometric properties. Although laudable on many accounts, the study offers little in terms of testing Stoltenberg and Delworth's model. In addition to trichotomizing the composite supervisee experience variable (a continuous measure), the resulting three experience levels do not appear consistent with Levels 1 to 3 as specified in Stoltenberg and Delworth's model (i.e., producing a conceptual-methodological mismatch). Perhaps the most appropriate inference from these data is that the SLQ-R may become a potentially useful measure if it is more adequately developed and tested psychometrically.

Although several aspects of Bear and Kivilighan's (1994) multiple case study design were commendable (e.g., theory testing, observational data, sequential analyses, and attention to Type I error rates), the results are not interpretable in terms of Stoltenberg and Delworth's (1987) model. One of the most salient threats to the study pertains to the use of the unpublished Interpersonal Communications Rating Scale (ICRS) and the Deep-Elaborative versus Shallow-Reiterative scale (which was dichotomized, thus sacrificing 36% of the statistical power). Only limited psychometric data (i.e., interrater agreement) are available for these scales. Perhaps more important, the ICRS affiliation and control dimensions (i.e., yielding friendly dominant, hostile dominant, friendly submissive, hostile submissive subscales) do not seem defensible operational definitions of Stoltenberg and Delworth's theory and constructs (e.g., using the ICRS to measure directive-structured supervision and collegial-consultative supervision). Due to methodological and statistical problems, the study may offer somewhat dubious findings about the affiliation and control interpersonal behaviors of one beginning and one advanced supervisory dyad (e.g., are the results due to idiosyncrasies of the supervisees and supervisory dyads, or to developmental level?). It is not, however, a viable test of Stoltenberg and Delworth's developmental theory. Thus, Stoltenberg and Delworth's IDM has not been adequately tested and no tentative inferences seem justifiable given the poor rigor of the two studies. The median statistical values for the two studies were $N = 102.5$, 111.5 tests, of which 43 were significant, $\eta^2 = .022$, $\hat{\rho}^2 = .008$, $1 - \beta_{PC(\eta^2)} = .319$, $1 - \beta_{PC(\hat{\rho}^2)} = .195$, $\beta_{PC(\eta^2)} = .682$, $\alpha_{EW} = .805$, $\beta_{EW} = 1.00$, and 16 threats.

Inferences About Generic Supervisee Development and Experience Level. Fifteen studies were published since 1980 that tested vague inferences about supervisee experience level or generic supervisee development (Borders & Fong, 1991; Cross & Brown, 1983; Heppner & Roehlke, 1984, Study 1 & 2; Hill, Charles, & Reed, 1981; Larson et al., 1992, Study 3; Mallinckrodt & Nelson, 1991; Robyak, Goodyear, Prange, & Donham, 1986; Shiffman, 1987; Skovholt & Rønnestad, 1992; Tracey et al., 1989; Worthington, 1984; Worthington & Stern, 1985; Yogev & Pion, 1984; Zucker & Worthington, 1986). Of these, Hill et al. (1981) and Shiffman (1987) were the only investigators to test inferences about supervisee development via longitudinal data, a refreshing and welcomed departure from the prevailing cross-sectional designs. Both studies sought to assess the effect of doctoral training on therapists' interviewing skills (i.e., not specific to the effects of clinical supervision). It is noteworthy that Hill et al. utilized real clients whereas Shiffman used peer-role-played clients in "therapy sessions" of 10 minutes and 5 minutes duration, respectively. The generalizability of these "therapy sessions" to typical 50-minute therapy sessions is highly questionable (e.g., Friedlander et al., 1986). Hence, both of these studies suffer from a serious conceptual-methodological mismatch.

Shiffman (1987) used a combination of cross-sectional and longitudinal research designs. In fact, we see this as a major contribution (see Baltes, Reese, & Nesselroade, 1977). Unfortunately the severity of conceptual and methodological threats besetting Shiffman's study (e.g., violations of assumptions for statistics, inappropriate statistical procedures, severe conceptual-methodological mismatches, unacceptable experimentwise Type I and Type II error rates) make the data and results uninterpretable. Given the extremely low sample sizes ($N = 12$, $ns = 6$) and subsequent inadequate statistical power, the lack of an appropriate comparison group, and generally unknown psychometric properties of the dependent variables, our tentative inferences from Hill et al.'s (1981) data are limited to the following: Therapists' significantly increase their use of minimal encouragers while decreasing questions during 10-minute "therapy sessions" as the therapists progress in doctoral training. The median statistical values for the two studies were $N = 77$, 308 tests, of which 28.5 were significant, $\alpha_{EW} = .830$, and 22 threats.

In general, the remaining 13 studies were beleaguered by conceptual, methodological, and statistical problems. In fact, the problems were so severe as to obviate making inferences from the data for most of the studies. Because the majority of these authors attempted an exploratory and atheoretical approach (see Ellis, 1991b), the studies lacked hypothesis validities, contained conceptual-methodological inconsistencies, had excessive Type I and Type II error rates, violated the assumptions underlying the statistical procedures (e.g., heterogeneity of variances and disproportional group sizes, inadequate sample size relative to the number of items in a principal components or factor analysis, repeated measures data not analyzed as such), and used measures (both independent variables and dependent variables) with either unknown or poor psychometric properties in a supervisory context. More specific problems included conducting an excessive number of statistical tests (Cross & Brown, 1983; Heppner & Roehlke, 1984; Worthington, 1984; Worthington & Stern, 1985; Zucker & Worthington, 1986); analyzing scales or principal components (mislabeled *factor*; see "New Measures" section) at the item level rather than as a scale (Cross & Brown, 1983; Heppner & Roehlke, 1984; Worthington, 1984; Worthington & Stern, 1985; Yogev & Pion, 1984; Zucker & Worthington, 1986); and interpreting nonsignificant results (Worthington, 1984; Worthington & Stern, 1985; Yogev & Pion, 1984; Zucker & Worthington, 1986; see Fagley, 1985, for a discussion). Taking into account these problems, we tentatively infer that master's-level supervisees may get along better with their supervisor than do doctoral-level supervisees (Worthington & Stern, 1985); prepracticum supervisees have lower counselor self-estimate scores than do more experienced supervisees (Larson et al., 1992, Study 3), and a new model of professional development awaits empirical testing (Skovholt & Rønnestad, 1992).

Three studies stood out among the 15 in terms of their rigor and merits: Mallinckrodt and Nelson (1991), Robyak et al. (1986), and Tracey et al. (1989). Mallinckrodt and Nelson investigated supervisee experience level and the therapeutic working alliance among 50 counselor-client dyads. Obtaining such a sizable sample of counselor-client dyads is a major strength of the study. Taking into consideration the limitations of the study (e.g., analyses failed to control highly correlated dependent variables, disproportional group sizes), we may tentatively infer that experience level may be related to working alliance perceptions; however, we cannot ascertain the pattern of differences among experience levels.

In their investigation of supervisee preferences for power bases in supervision, Robyak et al. (1986) addressed numerous potential threats to their study by including a large overall sample size ($N = 102$), performing several manipulation checks, and randomly assigning participants to treatment conditions. Upon closer examination, we made a puzzling discovery: According to the authors' presentation in the article, they manipulated the *dependent* variable. In fact, the power base condition was a repeated measures independent variable and should have been analyzed accordingly. Thus, there exists a conceptual-methodological-statistical mismatch. We tentatively infer from the data that the amount of supervised clinical experience may be related to supervisees' preferences for a legitimate power base (i.e., a socially sanctioned role built on trust).

Tracey et al. (1989) was perhaps the most rigorous of the 15 investigations of supervisee experience level. They incorporated explicit hypotheses, delineated cogent theorizing, included numerous manipulation and procedural validity checks, randomly assigned participants to treatment conditions, and computed Cronbach alpha coefficients (internal consistency reliability) for each variable. Even with these strengths, there were a few, yet substantive problems. Because they were primarily interested in interactions among the variables, the sample sizes for each cell were small ($ns = 9$ to 11) and more important, evidenced unequal variances (violating the homogeneity of variances assumption). Their data were yoked or nested but were not analyzed as such; indeed, no statistical tests were made of the client content independent variable (a mismatch of the hypotheses and analyses). Given the salient problems, the results are equivocal at best relative to the hypotheses. We might tentatively infer the following from the study: The potential moderating effects of supervisee experience, reactance, and client variables in supervision merit further investigation.

Summarizing, the major conclusions from research on inferences of generic supervisee development and experience given the conceptual and methodological problems are limited: Therapists use more minimal encouragers and fewer questions during 10-minute "therapy sessions" as they progress in doctoral training (Hill et al., 1981); master's-level supervisees may get along better with their supervisor than do doctoral-level supervisees (Worthington & Stern, 1985); and the amount of supervised clinical experience may be inversely related to supervisees' preferences for a legitimate power base (Robyak et al., 1986). The median statistical values for these 13 studies were $N = 59$, 56 tests, of which 11 were significant, $\eta^2 = .098$, $\hat{\rho}^2 = .065$, $1 - \beta_{PC(\eta^2)} = .650$, $1 - \beta_{PC(\hat{\rho}^2)} = .428$, $\beta_{PC(\eta^2)} = .350$, $\alpha_{EW} = .841$, $\beta_{EW} = 1.00$, and 16 threats.

Conclusions.   Our review of the research on inferences about supervisee development and models of supervisee development is disheartening. Three findings from our review are noteworthy. Perhaps the foremost finding is the unpleasantly conspicuous conceptual and methodological problems that beleaguer this set of studies. The most grievous problems are the pervasive threats to the theoretical and hypothesis validities of the studies; the nearly exclusive use of cross-sectional research designs to test developmental inferences; the numerous conceptual, methodological, and statistical mismatches and confounds; the unacceptably high Type I and Type II error rates (and corresponding deficient statistical power); the paucity of psychometrically sound measures; improper statistical analyses; and violations of statistical assumptions. Most of these threats and problems, however, are readily remediable (Ellis et al., 1996).

A second finding is that the data from these studies are largely uninterpretable. In contrast to recent reviewers (e.g., Holloway, 1992; Holloway & Neufeldt, 1995; Stoltenberg et al., 1994; Worthington, 1987), we conclude that little viable information about supervisee development has been gained. It is only in those few instances in which the data had few plausible rival explanations or in which the specific results were replicated in at least one other study that tentative inferences from the data seemed justifiable. Hence, given the substantial problems with the conceptual and methodological rigor of the research, we argue that inferences about the ego development, cognitive complexity, and cognitive development of supervisees have yet to be tested adequately. In addition, the data suggest that existing models of supervisee development are simplistic (Littrell et al., 1979) and at least partially inaccurate (Loganbill et al., 1982; Sansbury, 1982). Indeed, most theories of supervisee development, for example, Hogan's (1964) model, Stoltenberg's (1981) Counselor Complexity Model, and Stoltenberg and Delworth's (1987) Integrative Developmental Model, have not been acceptably tested, and no tentative inferences from the data to the models seem justifiable given the inadequate rigor of the studies.

A third finding is in fact reasserting Holloway's (1987, 1988) incisive and enlightening commentary on the supervisee developmental hypothesis (inference). Eight years after Holloway published her penetrating review, the fact remains that the basic question "Is it development?" remains unaddressed. Researchers have not rigorously tested this hypothesis. We ardently endorse Holloway's (1987, 1988) position and call on investigators to test rigorously the developmental propositions underlying the developmental models of supervision. To this end, the use of practicum level as a proxy for experience level is ill advised. Furthermore, we assert that clinical experience level or supervised clinical experience are proxies for a more influential underlying construct. Like Holloway (1987) and Blocher (1983), we suggest that this more potent construct may prove to be cognitive development or cognitive complexity (Ellis, 1988).

Inferences Relating to Supervisee Evaluation

It can be argued that supervisee evaluation is the sine quo non of supervision outcome. It is through supervisee evaluation that supervisee and client progress can be made and the importance and relevance of supervision can be assessed. Interestingly and unfortunately, only 10 investigations attempted to assess aspects of supervisee evaluation. Investigations of inferences regarding supervisee evaluation typically attended to the manner in which, and the criteria by which, supervisees were evaluated.

Limited to a population of clinical psychology training programs (Norcross & Stevenson, 1984) and internships (Norcross, Stevenson, & Nash, 1986), these studies investigated how supervisees were evaluated. Although the studies were novel, the results of the studies need to be considered in light of the restrictive samples and quality of the measures utilized. We may tentatively infer that the supervisees were evaluated by informal, qualitative measures that were used more frequently than were quantitative measures. Similarly, Mathews (1986) attempted to determine the manner in which performance appraisals are conducted in human service agencies. Questionable validity and reliability of the measures and Type II error rates limited the interpretation of the results. The tentative inferences were that for a group of social workers, performance evaluations were typically conducted annually, allowed for supervisee feedback, and were not always clearly defined for supervisees.

Snepp and Peterson (1988), using measures lacking psychometric data, attempted to assess supervisors' perceptions of preinternship preparation as well as comparative competency of Psy.D. versus Ph.D. interns. Only 2 of 46 statistical tests were significant; however, statistical data were not reported. Hence, the substantive conceptual and methodological problems plus the pattern of results suggest that the data cannot support any inferences.

The Counselor Evaluation Rating Scale (CERS; Myrick & Kelly, 1971) was the most frequently used criterion to examine inferences about supervisee evaluation. The scale was designed for supervisors to rate supervisee behavior in counseling and supervision. Three studies assessed the extent to which supervisor evaluations were related to supervisees' perceptions of their supervisors (Carey et al., 1988; Dodenhoff, 1981) and to external judges' ratings (Borders & Fong, 1991). The most serious threats for these three studies were the inflated Type I and Type II error rates and ceiling effects. For instance, Borders and Fong (1991) noted that three participants received perfect scores of 189 and 11 reached scores of 180 or greater. Specifically pertaining to the CERS, none of the studies provided current reliability estimates (e.g., Cronbach's alpha; Meier & Davis, 1990), and only Borders and Fong reported means and standard deviations for their sample ($M = 162.28$, $SD = 24.99$). Finally, supervisors may have inflated their ratings of supervisees' competence because the supervisees liked them (i.e., a halo effect; Carey et al., 1988; Dodenhoff, 1981). These threats notwithstanding, we tentatively infer that CERS ratings by supervisors may be related to supervisee perceptions of their supervisors' attractiveness (based on a shortened version of the Counselor Rating Form; Dodenhoff, 1981) and supervisee perceptions of their supervisors' trustworthiness, attractiveness, and expertness (based on the Supervisor Rating Form; Carey et al., 1988), and supervisor's global CERS ratings of the supervisee may not compare to specific session evaluations (Borders & Fong, 1991).

In an investigation of a descriptive model of evaluating trainees (i.e., constant stimulus technique), Newman, Kopta, McGovern, Howard, and McNeilly (1988) compared supervisor and trainee ratings of conceptualizations and interventions. The model described appeared to have merit for the training of interns; however, the obtained results are equally explained by the lack of validity and reliability information, as well as the high Type I and II error rates. Thus, a tentative preliminary inference from this study was that interns and supervisors may be fairly consistent in their ratings about client conceptualizations and treatment interventions.

Two studies that had largely uninterpretable data investigated a loosely defined construct of the supervisory relationship and grade (Lazar & Mosek, 1993) and supervisor perceptions of good and bad nonacademic characteristics of supervisees (Fordham, May, Boyle, Bentall, & Slade, 1990). It should be noted that the ideas presented in these investigations seem interesting and warrant more rigorous testing; however, the conceptual and methodological problems resulted in uninterpretable data and results. Hence, no conclusions were justifiable. The median statistical values for the 10 studies were $N = 58$, 17.5 tests, of which 2.5 were significant, $\eta^2 = .249$, $\hat{\rho}^2 = .224$, $1 - \beta_{PC(\eta^2)} = .754$, $1 - \beta_{PC(\hat{\rho}^2)} = .715$, $\beta_{PC(\eta^2)} = .246$, $\alpha_{EW} = .602$, $\beta_{EW} = .996$, 11 threats.

Conclusions.   With regard to the inference or question of whether supervisees can be evaluated effectively by supervisors, the answer seems to be "yes and no." Yes, they can be evaluated, yet there is little evidence indicating how or what is being evaluated. Overall, it seems that supervisees may be evaluated primarily qualitatively, perceptions of the supervisee by the supervisor may influence evaluation, and the primary measure used to assess supervisee competence may consist of many flaws bringing into question its usefulness.

It seems clear that supervisee evaluation is one area of supervision research that needs much attention, in particular, an infusion of new and innovative measures. It is suggested that researchers attend to the following issues when attempting to evaluate supervisee competence. First, clearly define the context for evaluation; that is, one needs to specify the overall scope (e.g., general professional competence; competence particular to site, setting, client population, or disorder), the domain of supervisee behaviors (e.g., therapy or supervision), mode of therapy (e.g., individual, group, family, or couples), the specific supervisee behaviors or skills (e.g., therapy, assessment, conceptual, administrative, or written skills), and the time period (e.g., a semester, a specific session, or a segment of a session). In addition, clearly describe the method of the assessment, that is, the extent to which it is based on the quantitative-qualitative and structured-unstructured continuums. Specify the individuals who are engaging in the evaluation (e.g., supervisor, clients, objective third raters, and so forth). Finally, as reviewed in the "New Measures" section of this chapter, reliability and validity data for the evaluation measures need to be assessed and described in adequate detail.

Inferences About Client Outcomes in Supervision

The impact of clinical supervision on client outcome is considered by many to be the acid test of the efficacy of supervision (e.g., Avis & Sprenkle, 1990; Holloway & Hosford, 1983; Holloway & Neufeldt, 1995; Matarazzo, 1978; Stein & Lambert, 1995). Even with the continued call for supervision research that includes clients' data, there were only nine studies published since 1981 to do so (Alpher, 1991; Couchon & Bernard, 1984; Friedlander, Siegal, & Brenock, 1989; Harkness & Hensley, 1991; Iberg, 1991; Kivlighan, Angelone, & Swafford, 1991; Mallinckrodt & Nelson, 1991; Sandell, 1985; Steinhelber et al., 1984). It is not surprising that few researchers attempted to assess the supervisor-supervisee-client triad given the enormous difficulties inherent in such an endeavor (Friedlander et al., 1989).

Of these, three studies had such extensive conceptual and methodological problems as to obviate inferences from the data (Couchon & Bernard, 1984; Sandell, 1985; Steinhelber et al., 1984). More specifically, these studies had little hypothesis validity, confounded data (participants contributing multiple data sets but not analyzed as such), had numerous violations of the assumptions for the statistical procedures used, and relied on supervisees' perceptions of client change (Steinhelber et al., 1984). Couchon and Bernard's (1984) study was the most compelling of the three. With a couple of attainable changes, this could have been a rigorous and intriguing test of the timing of supervision. That is, the authors could have dropped client-counselor-supervisor triads with incomplete data (as disagreeable as this may be), continued to collect data according to the original design until an adequate sample was attained, and analyzed the data to control statistically both the repeated measures and nested independent variables.

Kivlighan et al. (1991) investigated the efficacy of live supervision versus videotape-based supervision. In addition to testing two types of supervision, a major strength of the study was testing the equivalence of the supervision groups through a series of preliminary analyses. Nevertheless, some of the salient threats were diffuse hypotheses and statistical tests, attempting to affirm a null hypothesis (see Fagley, 1985), excessive Type I and Type II error rates (low statistical power), the attrition in both groups for working alliance data, and violations of the assumptions underlying the statistics (i.e., heterogeneity of variances for therapist intentions and working alliance, even after the arc sine transformation of WAI data). We may tentatively infer that for inexperienced supervisors working with beginning supervisees, live supervision is rougher (less smooth) than is video-taped-based supervision.

In a fascinating application of statistical control theory (SCT) to clinical supervision, Iberg (1991) investigated the effect of supervisor instructions on first-session therapist performance. Although there are many strengths of the study (e.g., random assignment to treatment condition), the author's primary focus appears to have been demonstrating the application of a statistical technique rather than research rigor per se. Thus, the author did not provide the theorizing for the 13 hypotheses (i.e., deficient hypothesis validity); the study had low statistical power, especially for the tests of interactions ($ns = 6$) and excessive Type I error rates and used 7 dependent measures of unknown psychometric properties. Even if we assumed that these threats were negligible, our inferences would nonetheless be limited to beginning therapists' performance in one-shot counseling sessions of unspecified duration with friends and colleagues. The safer inferences from these data seem to be that (a) SCT may be a useful procedure to partition and control therapists' effects and therapist-by-treatment effects in investigations of therapists in-session behaviors, and (b) clients' input and ratings of therapist behaviors are important to assessing the effects of supervision. One needs to recognize that withholding some therapist behaviors (e.g., empathy) may raise ethical concerns for real clients.

Mallinckrodt and Nelson (1991) investigated the therapeutic working alliance among supervisees of various experience levels (see earlier review of this study). Remarkably, they obtained a sample of 50 therapist-client dyads. Given the methodological problems, we may tentatively infer that clients' perceptions of the working alliance exceeded counselor ratings. Although statistically significant, this difference in perceptions appears trivial (i.e., 3 points in a 72-point range).

Harkness and Hensley (1991) investigated the effects of adding client-focused supervision to traditional supervision. In general, they conducted a good field study using a multiple-baseline–multiple-participant design (see Kazdin, 1982; Kratochwill, 1978). It is noteworthy that their definition of traditional supervision appears to be more consistent with what many label administrative supervision. Likewise, their client-focused supervision is more accurately labeled as traditional clinical supervision (Bernard & Goodyear, 1992). Although not clear, it appears that the two treatments (mixed-focus supervision and client-focused supervision) were confounded by the type of supervision (i.e., client focused was individual supervision whereas mixed supervision occurred in groups). Moreover, client-focused supervision consisted of an hour of individual supervision that focused on the client at least 35% of the time plus one hour of mixed supervision. The mislabeling constitutes a conceptual mismatch. These problems in combination with the inordinate Type I and Type II error rates, lack of psychometric data for the dependent variables, and caseload confounds (data were averaged across a therapist's caseload of approximately 40 clients) suggest the following tentative inference from the data: The substitution of individual clinical supervision to replace in part administrative group supervision, in those situations in which traditional clinical supervision is minimal, may increase satisfaction with the therapeutic relationship, goal attainment, and therapist helpfulness across the therapist's caseload. The median statistical values for these seven studies were $N = 50$, 60 tests, of which 23 were significant, $\eta^2 = .134$, $\hat{\rho}^2 = .090$, $1 - \beta_{PC(\eta^2)} = .833$, $1 - \beta_{PC(\hat{\rho}^2)} = .691$, $\beta_{PC(\eta^2)} = .167$, $\alpha_{EW} = .954$, $\beta_{EW} = 1.00$, and 22 threats.

Inferences About Parallel Process.   The parallel process phenomenon typically refers to those instances in which supervisees present themselves in supervision as their clients presented to them in therapy (Bernard & Goodyear, 1992; Ekstein & Wallerstein, 1958; Friedlander et al., 1989). Thus, the interpersonal interactions between the supervisee and supervisor parallel the therapist-client interactions. The notion of parallel processes has intuitive and heuristic appeal. Hence, it is not surprising that this concept has been prominent in the supervision literature for more than 40 years (Bernard & Goodyear, 1992; Ekstein & Wallerstein, 1958, 1972; Searles, 1955). Yet, the parallel process hypothesis has essentially remained untested. Only two studies published since 1981 specifically tested it (Alpher, 1991; Friedlander et al., 1989).

Alpher (1991) and Friedlander et al. (1989) both employed an intensive case study methodology to investigate parallel process. The study by Friedlander et al. represents a fairly good example of case study research, especially by incorporating numerous auxiliary measures both to rule out alternative explanations of the results and to establish the context for interpreting the data (e.g., detailed information about the supervisor, supervisee, and client, the therapeutic and supervisory relationships). For example, the low frequency of supervisor feedback statements may have been due to the type or focus of supervision. That is, except for observing the third therapy session, the supervisor did not use or rely on audiotaped, videotaped, or observations of therapy sessions. If Friedlander et al. had not supplied such detailed information, the supervisory context for the data would be ambiguous, thus delimiting the interpretability of the data.

A few key problems were common to both studies. The authors did not formulate or test hypotheses. Second, the authors did not perform statistical tests, even though statistical procedures exist for data such as theirs (see Edgington, 1987; Hersen & Barlow, 1976; Kratochwill, 1978). Given the legion of implicit and explicit comparisons made by the authors, the Type I and Type II error rates are clearly excessive. Third, the theoretical orientation of the therapists and supervisees (psychodynamic and relationship focus) may have predisposed the occurrence of parallel processes. Or, perhaps the type of supervision (e.g., reliance on supervisee self-reports and perceptions) engenders parallel processes. Given these threats and in the absence of replication data, we do not know which of their findings are spurious, which findings are trivial (nonsignificant), and which findings are meaningful.

The only tentatively defensible inference from Alpher's (1991) data given the numerous threats and problems is that within the context of short-term psychodynamic therapy (25 sessions) in which therapy session audiotapes may be used in supervision (of unknown type or focus), there may be a possible link between interpersonal behaviors in therapy and supervision. Similarly for Friedlander et al. (1989), within the context of a positive supervisory relationship characterized by little conflict, compatible theoretical orientations, minimal supervisor's observation of therapy, and a somewhat positive therapy experience, we may infer the interconnectedness of therapy and supervision. In short, there is insufficient evidence from these two studies to make inferences from the observed links between therapy and supervision to the parallel process theorizing. Such theorizing awaits more rigorous testing. The median statistical values for these two studies were $N = 3$, α_{EW} = .954, and 20 threats.

Conclusions.   Although researchers investigated inferences about the relationship of supervision to client outcome, the quality and rigor of these studies were poor overall. More often than not, researchers incorporated innovative procedures or multiple procedures to augment substantially the rigor of the study, only to somehow undermine these strengths. For instance, Sandell (1985) was the only investigator to conduct an a priori power analysis; however, he did not adhere to the recommended sample size.

There are few justifiable conclusions from this set of studies. Perhaps foremost, the poor rigor of the studies notwithstanding, these studies underscore the importance of including clients as participants (i.e., extending inferences about supervisees and clinical supervision to include clients and client outcome, and collecting data from and about clients and client outcome). This puts an additional burden on clinical supervision researchers who operate in a domain with many inherent obstacles to conducting rigorous research (Russell et al., 1984). Nonetheless, the importance of formulating and testing inferences about the relations of clinical supervision to client and client outcome seems obvious (see Holloway & Neufeldt, 1995). Second, there appear to be interconnections between therapist-client interactions and supervisee-supervisor interactions. The link of these interconnections to parallel process theorizing has yet to be established, however, and in particular the causal relation between therapist-client interactions and subsequent supervisee-supervisor interactions. Finally, statistical control theory and methodology may be an alternative approach to deal effectively with therapist effects and therapist-by-treatment interaction effects, assuming the therapist or supervisory behaviors do not put the client at risk.

Inferences About Supervisees: New Measures

One of the most pernicious problems confronting supervision researchers is the dearth of psychometrically sound measures specific to a clinical supervision context (Ellis et al., 1996; Russell et al., 1984). It is thus heartening that over the past 15 years at least seven new measures were specifically developed to assess supervisee variables (Benshoff & Thomas, 1992; Blocher et al., 1985; Efstation et al., 1990; Larson et al., 1992; McNeill et al., 1985, 1992; Olk & Friedlander, 1992; Schact et al., 1988). Of these seven, two (Olk & Friedlander, 1992; Schact et al., 1988) had sufficient data to merit recommending their use for practice and as dependent measures in research endeavors. We did not review new measures developed for clients or client variables as it was beyond the scope of this chapter.

A Context for Measure Development and Validation.   Among measurement specialists, the predominate view is that test (or measure) construction and validation are nothing more or less than traditional hypothesis-testing research (Ellis & Blustein, 1991a, 1991b; Landy, 1986; Messick, 1989). This perspective of validation emphasizes that tests and measures are measuring theoretical constructs (e.g., latent variables) that should be explicated before constructing a measure. That is, psychological measures and tests are theoretically driven even if the authors have not made their implicit theorizing explicit. The measure constitutes an operational definition of a construct and the attendant theorizing. The central focus is that the authors are testing inferences from the scores (data) to the construct(s), the relations among the constructs, the population, the individual, the norms and norm sample, and the setting and context for which the measure was designed. All of these should be specified before the investigator begins collecting data. From this perspective, the study should adhere to traditional standards of scientific research that include explicating the theoretical basis and the research hypotheses for the study (see Chen, 1990; Ellis, 1991b; Serlin, 1987; Serlin & Lapsley, 1985; Wampold et al., 1990) in addition to established standards of scientific rigor (e.g., Cook & Campbell, 1979; Huck & Sandler, 1979; Kerlinger, 1986). A related issue from the hypothesis-testing perspective is the importance of explicating a priori the target population of interest for the theorizing and the measure, as well as the procedures to obtain a representative sample of persons. Thus, it is important to provide as complete demographic information of the sample as possible to facilitate the reader in assessing the extent to which the measure, norms (if any), and scores are generalizable to his or her research context, target population (supervisee), supervision setting, and so forth.

Recommended Measures

Self-Report Measures.   The Role Conflict and Role Ambiguity Inventory (RCRAI) was developed by Olk and Friedlander (1992) to assess two role difficulties (role conflict and role ambiguity) in supervisory relationships (past and present). As such, the RCRAI was not designed to measure role difficulties in a specific supervisory relationship. The authors did a laudable job of test construction and in testing a variety of inferences pertaining to the RCRAI. Users of the RCRAI should be aware that (a) the two scales are highly correlated with several role ambiguity items factorially loading on both scales; (b) both scales and in particular Role Conflict, appear to have marked floor effects (i.e., most respondents indicated that role conflict rarely occurred), thus the RCRAI will most likely yield highly skewed, nonnormal data; and (c) the RCRAI had not been cross-validated, for example, with a more heterogeneous sample of therapists (beyond clinical and counseling psychology supervisees). The median statistical values for the study were $N = 240$, 17 tests, of which 17 were significant, $\eta^2 = .190$, $\hat{\rho}^2 = .141$, $1 - \beta_{PC(\eta^2)} = 1.000$, $1 - \beta_{PC(\hat{\rho}^2)} = 1.000$, $\beta_{PC(\eta^2)} = 0.00$, $\alpha_{EW} = .923$, $\beta_{EW} = 0.00$, 14 threats.

Schact et al. (1988) substantially revised a short form of the Barrett-Lennard Relationship Inventory (BLRI; Dalton, 1983; Wiebe & Pearce, 1973) creating two forms specific to the clinical supervision relationship: Relationship Inventory Forms L and M (we designate these RI-M and RI-L). Each form was constructed to measure five constructs (Regard, Empathy, Congruence, Unconditionally, Willingness to Be Known, and Total Score [i.e., Quality of Relationship]). Supervisees rated a former supervisor who contributed the *most* (Form M) or *least* (Form L) to their therapeutic effectiveness. In general, the data are compelling; within the limits of the target population (supervisees holding a doctorate in clinical or counseling psychology) and instructions (rating previous best and worst supervision, *not* concurrent supervision as suggested by the authors), the Relationship Inventory total score may be a viable measure of most (or least) effective supervision. To this we add the following caveats: (a) The RI (both M and L forms) and its primary theoretical and psychometric inferences (e.g., convergent and divergent validity and stability) should be subjected to more rigorous testing (e.g., cross-validation) before widespread use; (b) the RI does not appear to measure the same constructs as the BLRI; and (c) due to the high interscale correlations and the results of the exploratory factor analysis, the RI total score is the preferred measure of the supervisory relationship (avoid using the five scales, except, for example, in a structural equation-modeling design in which multiple, highly related measures of a construct are required; see Hoyle, 1994). Adapting and using the RI with a more heterogeneous supervisee population (e.g., predegree trainees from divergent mental health disciplines) or to assess a current supervisory relationship are inappropriate because of the lack of supporting validity data. The median statistical values for this study were $N = 143$, 48 tests, of which 48 were significant, $\eta^2 = .202$, $\hat{\rho}^2 = .197$, $1 - \beta_{PC(\eta^2)} = 1.000$, $1 - \beta_{PC(\hat{\rho}^2)} = 1.000$, $\beta_{PC(\eta^2)} = 0.00$, $\alpha_{EW} = .915$, $\beta_{EW} = 0.00$, 12 threats.

Measures Not Recommended

Self-Report Measures.   Benshoff and Thomas (1992) set out to test the supposition that the Counselor Evaluation Rating Scale (CERS; Myrick & Kelly, 1971) was suitable for self-administration (i.e., self-rating). (The CERS was originally designed to measure the supervisor's evaluation of the supervisee.) They accomplished this by investigating the factor structure of the self-administered CERS on a sample of predominately school counselor supervisees (masters students). Although a six-factor CERS model was tested via confirmatory factor analysis (yet, no statistical data were reported), the authors relied instead on an exploratory factor analysis to develop a four-factor CERS model. Benshoff and Thomas appeared not to have tested Myrick and Kelly's original two-factor model or the general-factor (total score) model. Given the lack of a comparison group of supervisor CERS data, the homogeneous school counselor supervisee sample, possible ceiling effects (i.e., nonnormal data), exploratory analyses, and lack of cross-validation, their conclusion that self-ratings and supervisor ratings yield different factor structures seems precipitous. In essence, they are suggesting that the CERS measures different constructs when supervisees versus supervisors make the ratings. The data are too equivocal to substantiate either this inference or the use of the CERS for self-ratings.

The Counseling Self-Estimate Inventory (COSE) was developed by Larson et al. (1992), ostensibly to measure counselor self-efficacy. Although Larson et al. subjected the COSE to a series of five investigations testing a variety of inferences, there were sufficient methodological and conceptual problems to limit fundamentally its utility. Most notably, the COSE is *not* a measure of self-efficacy expectations because the authors did not adhere to Bandura's theory or test construction methods. Even though the authors acknowledge this, they erroneously interpret and discuss their results in the context of self-efficacy. Thus, it is not clear what constructs the COSE and its subscales are measuring. Second, the authors tested two versions of the COSE (COSE and a short form COSE-SF) and treated the two versions as if they were the same measure, which they are not. That is, two of the five studies pertain to the COSE-SF (Larson et al., 1992, p. 112). Hence, incomplete data are available for either the COSE or COSE-SF. We believe these two issues in combination with the use of exploratory factor analysis to develop the COSE and five self-estimate subscales (Microskills, Process, Difficult Client Behaviors, Cultural Competence, and Awareness of Values); the lack of cross-validation data; the extremely small sample sizes for Studies 2, 4, and 5; and the exclusive use of prepracticum students to develop and "validate" the COSE preclude recommending use of the COSE; data from the COSE and the COSE-SF are uninterpretable.

Efstation et al. (1990) constructed the Supervisory Working Alliance Inventory with *non*parallel supervisee and supervisor forms (SWAI-T and SWAI-S). The results of several exploratory factor analyses (mislabeled principal components analysis by the authors) suggested three SWAI-S factors (Client Focus, Rapport, and Identification) and two SWAI-T factors (Rapport and Client Focus). Internal consistency reliabilities were all below .77 except for SWAI-T Rapport (.90). Within each form, the scales were moderately to highly intercorrelated (i.e., scales are not orthogonal), and several items loaded substantively on more than one scale (i.e., the constructs being measured are not conceptually clean). Perhaps more troubling because the data were from supervisory dyads, the trainee and supervisor Rapport scales (SWAI-T & SWAI-S) were minimally correlated as were the trainee and supervisor Client Focus scales ($rs \leq .23$). Similarly, the within dyad correlations of the Supervisory Styles Inventory (Friedlander & Ward, 1984) and SWAI scales were small. Collectively, these data strongly suggest that the two SWAI forms are measuring different constructs. In short, until the psychometric properties of both forms of the SWAI are improved, the theoretical inferences explicitly tested, and they are cross-validated with a larger and more representative sample (beyond a predoctoral internship context), use of Efstation et al.'s SWAI would appear to be imprudent.

McNeill et al. (1992) expanded and revised the Supervisory Levels Questionnaire (SLQ-R; McNeill et al., 1985) to be consistent with Stoltenberg and Delworth's (1987) Integrated Developmental Model. Comprised of 30 items, the SLQ-R yields three highly related scales (rs = .43 to .58) and a total SLQ-R score. The four scales evidenced inadequate to good internal consistency reliabilities: Cronbach alphas of .64 (Dependency-Autonomy), .74 (Motivation), .83 (Self and Other Awareness), and .88 (total score). Unfortunately the more appropriate statistical procedures (i.e., multivariate trend analyses or multiple discriminate analysis) were not performed to test whether SLQ-R scores significantly increased with and discriminated among developmental levels. The "preplanned comparisons" resulted in highly inflated Type I and Type II error rates (see earlier discussion). These issues, along with the threats to hypothesis validity and the use of cross-sectional data, suggest that the Self and Other Awareness scale and the total SLQ-R scale may have the potential to become viable measures for some aspects of Stoltenberg and Delworth's model. Until the SLQ-R has viable data to substantiate the numerous inferences from its scores (e.g., performing confirmatory factor analysis studies, testing divergent and convergent validities, conducting cross-validation studies, and so forth), its use, except for additional validity work, seems ill advised. The median statistical values for these seven studies were N = 51, 85.5 tests, of which 25 were significant, η^2 = .068, $\hat{\rho}^2$ = .041, $1 - \beta_{PC(\eta^2)}$ = .520, $1 - \beta_{PC(\hat{\rho}^2)}$ = .440, $\beta_{PC(\eta^2)}$ = .480, α_{EW} = .982, β_{EW} = 1.00, 18 threats.

Rating Systems.   Blocher et al. (1985) developed the Counselor Perception Questionnaire (CPQ) and rating protocols to measure two constructs of supervisees' cognitive complexity: differentiation and integration. Blocher et al. attempted to test several key inferences regarding the theoretical (construct) validity of the CPQ; this was a clear strength of the study. However, the limitations of the study were conspicuous: extremely small samples (ns < 14), use of cross-sectional data to test developmental inferences, unknown generalizability of the CPQ beyond the specific stimulus materials and situation (a vocational indecision case), and generally weak tests of the key inferences. Although the CPQ has the potential to become a viable measure of supervisee cognitive complexity and veridicality, the preliminary data do not adequately test the key theoretical and psychometric properties of the CPQ. Hence, use of the PCQ is not recommended until it has undergone and held up well to more rigorous testing. The median statistical values for the two studies were N = 14, 7 tests, of which 4 were significant, η^2 = .176, $\hat{\rho}^2$ = .125, $1 - \beta_{PC(\eta^2)}$ = .453, $1 - \beta_{PC(\hat{\rho}^2)}$ = .319, $\beta_{PC(\eta^2)}$ = .547, α_{EW} = .302, β_{EW} = 1.00, 17 threats.

Untested Measures.   With the dearth of available measures suitable for the supervisory context (Ellis et al., 1996; Russell et al., 1984), many authors either constructed their own measures (e.g., Friedlander & Snyder, 1983; McNeil et al., 1985; Reising & Daniels, 1983; Stoltenberg et al., 1987; Wiley & Ray, 1986; Worthington & Roehlke, 1979) or imported measures developed for other contexts, adapting them to clinical supervision (e.g., Bahrick et al., 1991; Heppner & Roehlke, 1984; Miars et al., 1983). That is, several additional measures were developed and used by researchers; however, construction and validation of the new measures were incidental parts of the research. Thus, these measures have little if any psychometric data specific to a supervision context and have not undergone systematic attempts to test the underlying theoretical and psychometric inferences. It may be that these researchers did not realize that modifying an existing measure originates a new measure. It is obligatory that the authors establish the psychometric and theoretical (construct) properties of the new measure before its usage. In short, we conclude that although several of these new measures are inviting, their usage for research (other than testing their psychometric properties) or practice is premature and not recommended at this time.

Conclusions.   Confronted with the rather substantial obstacles, it appears that investigators attempting to construct new measures or adapt existing measures to the supervisory context have largely done an admirable job. Nonetheless, we can recommend only two of the numerous measures included in our review (the Relationship Inventory and the RCRAI). The primary reasons contributing to this state of affairs are often the lack of attention to the theoretical basis of the measure (i.e., testing inferences), the use of less sophisticated and sometimes inappropriate statistical procedures, not specifying a priori the target population or settings and attending to sampling issues, the lack of data bearing on the inferences of interest (e.g., cross-validity data, divergent and convergent construct data), and the poor to inadequate psychometric properties of the measures. Although not recommended for practice or use as research variables, we strongly encourage researchers to perform the requisite psychometric investigations for the tests and measures we reviewed but did not recommend.

One recurring error among these studies has been using exploratory principal components analysis and mislabeling principal components analysis as factor analysis (or vice versa) and calling the resulting principal components *factors*. Strictly speaking, principal components analysis is not factor analysis (e.g., Tinsley & Tinsley, 1987). Principal components analysis is a noniterative procedure that assumes that there are no errors in measurement (i.e., reliability of 1.0), an untenable assumption in clinical supervision research, whereas factor analysis procedures systematically partition and control error variance, including measurement error. The statistical procedure of choice, however, is confirmatory factor analysis (e.g., Byrne, 1994; Hoyle, 1994; Long, 1983). In confirmatory factor analysis, the investigator first specifies the hypothesized factor structure (number of factors, factor intercorrelations, and how individual items load on each factor), then statistically tests to determine how well the model fits the data. Hence, exploratory factor analysis and principal components analysis are largely inappropriate as the primary methodological and statistical procedures for scale development and validation (Ellis & Blustein, 1991a, 1991b).

IMPLICATIONS

To put in perspective the rather intimidating amount of information presented thus far, we posed two questions: What were the prominent findings? and What are the implications of these data? Several findings were prominent. (Our intent is not to duplicate the conclusion sections introduced previously, but to draw attention to the more prominent or heretofore undiscussed findings.) Perhaps foremost, the overall quality of research during the past 15 years was substandard. This cannot be taken lightly. As is evident in the previous sections, few conclusions were justifiable given the lack of replicated results and the conceptual and methodological problems besetting the studies. We agree with Meehl (1990) that poorly conceived and executed studies, like many of those reviewed here, obfuscate our knowledge and understanding and proliferate weak theories of clinical supervision and supervisees (Wampold et al., 1990).

A second prominent finding was the relative inattention to testing existing supervisory theory. Abundant theories pertaining to supervisees and clients in clinical supervision exist (see Bernard & Goodyear, 1992; Russell et al., 1984), however, just seven were explicitly tested (i.e., Bernard, 1979; Bordin, 1983; Littrell et al., 1979; Loganbill et al., 1982; Sansbury, 1982; Stoltenberg, 1981; Stoltenberg & Delworth, 1987). Only two of these seven theories were investigated on more than two occasions (Bernard, 1979; Stoltenberg, 1981). In our opinion, this is an obvious deficiency in the empirical and therefore theoretical literature.

The third prominent finding was the scarcity of replication studies. The crux of this issue is that replication is the heart of the self-correcting process of science (e.g., Serlin & Lapsley, 1985). Without replications, there is no way of establishing the veracity of theories or previous findings. That is, to help rule out rival explanations (i.e., to ascertain whether a particular pattern of results was due to Type I or Type II errors, or other rival explanations), the results over several replication or replication and extension studies need to be virtually identical to those of the original study. If the accepted practice was to conduct and publish replication studies, the current status of research reviewed here would not be encumbered. Indeed, merely four studies were replications or replication-extensions (Carey & Williams, 1986; Ellis et al., 1988; Ellis, 1991c). Even the studies replicating the use of Worthington and Roehlke's (1979) 42 supervisor behaviors items, but no other procedures or variables, did not find highly consistent results (Cross & Brown, 1983; Heppner & Roehlke, 1984, Study 2; Worthington, 1984; Yogev & Pion, 1984; Zucker & Worthington, 1986). Therefore, without replication, we are left in a quandary: Which findings are "real" and which are not?

A fourth prominent finding was the continued dearth of viable measures specific to clinical supervision. Of particular importance are measures to assess supervisee competence and to evaluate supervisee performance. Whereas several new measures may be promising, a good deal of psychometric testing needs to be completed before they merit recommendation.

Implications for Supervisory Theory.   Although some key theories of clinical supervision were investigated on multiple occasions (e.g., Stoltenberg, 1981; Stoltenberg & Delworth, 1987), we essentially concluded that these theories and the central premises thereof remain untested. Of the few defensible and tentative conclusions about theory, the data suggested that existing theories and models of supervision and supervisees (i.e., Bernard, 1979; Littrell et al., 1979; Loganbill et al., 1982; Sansbury, 1982) are simplistic and incomplete, partially accurate and partially inaccurate (i.e., weak theory). The implications for theorists and for theory are relatively straightforward. Clinical supervision appears to be a more complex phenomenon than represented in current theories about supervision and supervisees. Existing theories need to be revised on the basis of the interpretable empirical data pertaining to each theory. For instance, the majority of supervision models (theories) presume a good, quality supervisory relationship (i.e., relationship is held as a nonvarying construct in the theory). The data suggest that relationship quality may have mediating or moderating effects on other constructs in the theory (i.e., it is variable and not constant). Hence, one expedient step would be to integrate relationship quality as a mediating or moderating construct into existing theories.

Implications for Researchers.   The four most prominent messages to convey to researchers are to test the extant theories pertaining to supervisees and clients in clinical supervision, to attend more scrupulously to the conceptual and methodological rigor of their research (e.g., hypothesis validity, statistical power), to develop and use psychometrically sound measures, and to conduct programmatic research (Bausell, 1994; Frost & Stablein, 1992). At this point, we hope we have convincingly argued the exigency of testing theories (or theorizing) about supervisees and clients in clinical supervision.

Over the last two and a half decades, reviewers have encouraged investigators to pursue more rigorous research (e.g., Alberts & Edelstein, 1990; Hansen & Warner, 1971; Holloway, 1987; Russell et al., 1984). Ellis et al. (1996) provide a thorough discussion of conceptual and methodological rigor, including recommendations for investigators to enhance the quality of clinical supervision research. We refer readers to Ellis et al. for a more in-depth presentation than permitted here. In short, the issue is not the design (e.g., experimental, ex post facto, or case study) or type of research (e.g., pragmatic research, Borders, 1989a) per se, but rather the issue is rigor (Ellis, 1991b); to test more vigorously the fundamental core inferences and existing theories pertaining to supervisees and clinical supervision. The dominant conceptual and methodological issues to which researchers are encouraged to attend are listed in Table 25.5. We assume that the recommendations and rationale for them are reasonably self-evident, within the context of the material presented in this chapter.

One of the more potent and obvious remedies to enhance the rigor of research is to attend scrupulously to Type I and Type II error rates. Type I error can be controlled by adjusting the per comparison alpha level (e.g., Holland & Copenhaver, 1988), by performing only those statistical tests directly linked to a research hypothesis (e.g., Wampold et al., 1990), by avoiding omnibus testing strategies (e.g., Huberty & Morris, 1989), and by performing a priori rather than post hoc statistical procedures (e.g., simultaneous or hierarchical regression rather than stepwise regression, Wampold & Freund, 1987; confirmatory rather than exploratory factor analysis, Hoyle, 1994; and so forth).

We cannot proclaim strongly enough the importance, if not the necessity, of attending to Type II error and statistical power (e.g., Haase & Ellis, 1987). Type II error can be effectively controlled by performing a priori statistical power analyses to determine the appropriate sample size *before* beginning data collection (see Cohen, 1988; Fagley, 1985; Goldstein, 1989; Kraemer & Thiemann, 1987; Lipsey, 1990; Rossi, 1990). To this end, the effect sizes presented herein at the end of each set of studies may facilitate performing a priori power analyses. Researchers should bear in mind that our effect sizes are overestimates. An often neglected approach to control Type II error is to maximize the magnitude of effects, in particular by reducing sources of error variance (e.g., randomly assign participants to treatment condition; use psychometrically sound measures; use more sensitive research designs such as repeated measures, factorial, or covariate designs; eliminate or control confounding variables; use the appropriate statistical procedures) and by maximizing the differences among the treatment conditions or levels of the independent variables (see Kerlinger, 1986).

One of the auspicious observations from the review is the emergence of several new measures assessing attributes of supervisees. Included are measures that researchers imported or adapted from other settings and contexts. Even though most of these promising measures were not recommended, they are alluring. Indeed, we enthusiastically invite investigators to test vigorously the psychometric inferences of these measures and the associated constructs and theorizing. It is incumbent on researchers to establish empirically the viability in a supervisory context of any measures imported or adapted from another context. Numerous resources are available to assist researchers in addressing the conceptual, methodological, and statistical issues affiliated with constructing and validating measures (e.g., Dawis, 1987; Ellis & Blustein, 1991a, 1991b; Ellis et al., 1996; Landy, 1986;

**Table 25.5   Recommendations for Researchers Investigating Inferences
About Supervisees and Clients**

Section of Manuscript	Recommendation
Introduction	Explicate and test theory or theorizing (attend to hypothesis validity)
	Define central constructs and terms (attend to construct validity)
	Formulate unambiguous hypotheses
	Assure internal consistency of purpose, hypotheses, methods, and analyses
Methods	Perform a priori statistical power analyses (i.e., control Type II error)
	Sample representatively from the target population and setting (attend to external validity)
	Use longitudinal designs to test developmental inferences (e.g., cross-sequential or lag panel)
	Randomize wherever possible
	Control for confounds and incorporate manipulation-treatment checks (attend to internal validity and statistical conclusion validity)
	Use psychometrically sound measures specific to the supervision context
	Do not split continuous measures (e.g., dichotomized or extreme groups)
Results	Control Type I error
	Control diffuse statistical hypotheses and tests
	Test assumptions underlying statistical procedures
	Perform a priori statistical tests directly tied to research hypotheses
Discussion	Recognize the strengths of the study
	Thoroughly evaluate the limitations and threats (rival explanations for the results)
	Make inferences within the context of the threats, limitations, and strengths
	Offer defensible, data-based generalizability of the results

Messick, 1989). Once serviceable, these new measures and their constructs will offer new domains of inferences about supervisees and clients for empirical testing.

The importance of pursuing programmatic research that incorporates at least partial replications of prior work cannot be overstated (Bausell, 1994; Frost & Stablein, 1992). Rendering programmatic research that incorporates replications allows empirical evidence to build on itself in addition to winnowing theories and theorizing about supervisees. A scientific understanding of the supervisees and clinical supervision is attainable (i.e., empirically verifiable), if intrepid researchers pursue rigorous programmatic investigations.

Implications for Supervisors.   Conceivably, the most telling implication of this review is for practitioners to be extremely cautious and skeptical of the empirical literature we have reviewed. There are few practical implications of the research reviewed here. The research suggests that the quality of the supervisory relationship is paramount to successful supervision. What constitutes a high-quality relationship, however, is largely untested and equivocal. There is evidence that supervisors may want to clarify the supervisee's role to minimize role conflict and role ambiguity for beginning therapists. Given that evaluation is inherent to most supervisory relationships, supervisors may want to attend explicitly to evaluation issues such as specifying the context and domain of evaluation and recognizing the lack of psychometrically sound measures to promote evaluation (see Bernard

& Goodyear, 1992). Equally important, practitioners should be reticent to use the supervision theories that have not been adequately tested (e.g., Loganbill et al., 1982; Stoltenberg, 1981; Stoltenberg & Delworth, 1987).

Implications for Consumers of Research.   Given that at least 60% of the authors reviewed here either did not or only minimally acknowledged the salient threats to the validity of their research, readers should approach the empirical literature with skepticism. Avoid accepting the results and discussion sections of a study at face value. Read the article with a critical eye, especially toward the validity of the study (Cook & Campbell, 1979; Wampold et al., 1990; Wampold & Poulin, 1992). If the statistical procedures are ambiguous and confusing, assume that this is due to a poor description and presentation rather than to the reader's level of statistical expertise. Look for unrecognized flaws and confounds as well as strengths of the study. To this end, the recommendations delineated in Table 25.5 may prove helpful (see Ellis, 1991b). Finally, reinterpret the findings in light of these confounds, limitations, and alternative explanations (Huck & Sandler, 1979). Obviously, the more rigorous the study, the more credible and interpretable the findings.

Implications for Reviewers.   Frankly, we were somewhat puzzled that few reviewers appeared to be aware of the literature pertaining to conducting and reporting integrative reviews (e.g., Cook & Leviton, 1980; Cooper, 1982, 1989; Cooper & Hedges, 1994; Corcoran, 1985; Ellis, 1991a; Feldman, 1971; Green & Hall, 1984; Jackson, 1980; Light & Pillemar, 1984; Light & Smith, 1971; Meehl, 1990; Rosenthal & Rubin, 1979, 1982; Taveggia, 1974; Walberg & Haertel, 1980; Wolf, 1986). We suggest that the conclusions reached by uncritical reviewers, who weight equally the findings from high- and poor-quality studies, may contain more artifact than fact (Cooper, 1989; Hogarty, 1989; Jackson, 1980; Meehl, 1990). As a result of uncritical review articles, erroneous practices may be employed and additional resources may be allocated to unfruitful lines of inquiry.

Of the available resources, we recommend Cooper's (1989) concise and thorough compendium (see also Cooper & Hedges's, 1994, excellent compilation and the articles edited by Sternberg, 1995). As indicated in the previous section, it seems clear that reviewers put their review-based conclusions at great risk if the quality of each study is not evaluated and the results are reinterpreted on the basis of the plausible rival explanations and threats to validity. High-quality studies should not be weighted equally to or outweighed by poor-quality and faulty research studies (Cooper, 1989; Hogarty, 1989; Jackson, 1980; Kline, 1983). Second, we strongly encourage future reviewers to adopt a theory-grounded, scientific approach to integrative reviews (Cooper, 1989; Ellis, 1991a, 1991b). Rather than combine studies on the basis of independent or dependent variables, we advocate using inferences or a comparable schema, such as relations among constructs and theoretical models.

Conducting an integrative review of the literature is an ambitious and immense task. Yet, a review, like any other form of research, needs to be conceptually and methodologically rigorous (Cooper, 1989; Jackson, 1980). We exhort future reviewers to consider carefully and implement subsequently the recommendations set forth by Cooper (1982, 1989), Cooper and Hedges (1994), and Ellis (1991a).

Implications for Editorial Boards.   The profound Type I and Type II error rates occurring in the supervision literature reviewed here suggest that manuscripts were not scrutinized routinely on these issues. We entreat members of editorial boards to be more cognizant of and vigilant about Type I and Type II error rates and issues of statistical power when reviewing supervision research. We further encourage manuscript reviewers to be more discerning in evaluating the threats to the validity of studies involving supervision, especially hypothesis validity. Recognizing the conflicts inherent in allocating pages in journals, we nevertheless appeal to editors (a) to reconsider policies of not soliciting replication studies (e.g., perhaps as one-journal-page reports) and (b) to advocate for the full specification of statistical test results (both significant and nonsignificant) in order to expedite quantitative reviews of the literature.

Limitations.   A compelling limitation of the integrative review resides in the application of the quantitative review data to each study and to sets of studies. In general, we were highly consistent in evaluating the conceptual and methodological threats to the studies and in identifying the most salient threats. The reformation of conclusions from each study and set of studies, however, reflects a bias consistent with the definition of "uninterpretable data or results" (see criteria specified earlier). That is, we were unwilling to make inferences or draw conclusions from severely confounded data or seriously compromised statistical results (Alberts & Edelstein, 1990; Avis & Sprenkle, 1990; Huck & Sandler, 1979). There are no clear criteria by which to judge whether the data and results of a study are interpretable. Thus, other definitions of uninterpretable results may yield conclusions different from those reached here.

A second set of limitations regards the lack of hypothesis validity. Our purpose, however, was a descriptive one. Nevertheless, threats to hypothesis validity are a limitation of the review. Finally, our inferences and conclusions are only as good as the research from which the inferences were drawn. Thus, the major flaws besetting the reviewed studies apply to the conclusions reached here. Most notable of these are issues of Type I and Type II error rates. Because the experimentwise Type II error rate was 100% for more than two thirds of the studies, the review was also subject to Type II error (i.e., many genuine effects were not detected or interpreted). That is, our conclusions necessarily did not include many effects and relations that truly exist but were not detected empirically. It is also conceivable that our reinterpretations of the empirical findings, of which most were statistically significant, discounted genuine effects (i.e., contributing to review-wise Type II error). Similarly, we suspect that some of the review-based conclusions are spurious (i.e., Type I error). Hence, only through replication of the studies and this review will the veracity of the results and conclusions offered here be ascertained.

CONCLUSION

We initiated this review with the intention of highlighting the theories, theorizing, and inferences both directly and implicitly tested in investigations of supervisees and clients in clinical supervision. To this end, we organized and reviewed the studies according to the inferences under investigation. That is, we identified and organized the integrative review according to the six fundamental inferences extensively researched over the past 15 years (see Table 25.1). A second purpose was to assess and illuminate the scientific rigor of research on inferences about supervisees and clients. To accomplish this, the conceptual and methodological evaluation paradigm of Ellis et al. (1996) was replicated. In some ways, the data and findings are sobering (e.g., methodological threats and the number of studies with uninterpretable data and results). In other ways, the findings are encouraging (e.g., new measures, and some theories held up partially to empirical testing). In comparison to the status of the field 15 years ago, the specialty of clinical supervision continues to evolve and mature (cf. the findings presented here with Hansen & Warner, 1971; Hansen et al., 1976, 1982; Russell et al., 1984). The fact is that we do have a better scientific understanding of supervisees and clinical supervision. Given that one criterion of a good review is to elucidate how much and how little is known in an area (Feldman, 1971), we endeavored to articulate both. To the extent that we accomplished these goals, the quantitative data and integrative review findings may promote yet further advances in understanding supervision, supervisees, and the impact on clients.

REFERENCES

References marked with an asterisk indicate studies included in the review.

Abramowitz, B., & Stegun, A. (1972). *Handbook of mathematical functions.* New York: Dover.

Alberts, G., & Edelstein, B. (1990). Therapist training: A critical review of skill training studies. *Clinical Psychology Review, 10,* 487–511.

*Allen, G. J., Szollos, S. J., & Williams, B. E. (1986). Doctoral students' comparative evaluations of best and worst psychotherapy supervision. *Professional Psychology: Research and Practice, 17,* 91–99.

*Alpher, V. S. (1991). Interdependence and parallel processes: A case study of structural analysis of social behavior in supervision and short-term dynamic psychotherapy. *Psychotherapy, 28,* 218–231.

Avis, J. M., & Sprenkle, D. H. (1990). Outcome research on family therapy training: A substantive and methodological review. *Journal of Marital and Family Therapy, 16,* 241–264.

*Bahrick, A. S., Russell, R. K., & Salmi, S. W. (1991). The effects of role induction on trainees' perceptions of supervision. *Journal of Counseling and Development, 69,* 434–438.

Baker, S. B., & Daniels, T. G. (1989). Integrating research on the microtraining program: A meta-analysis. *Journal of Counseling Psychology, 36,* 213–222.

Baker, S. B., Daniels, T. C., & Greeley, A. T. (1990). Systematic training of graduate-level counselors: Narrative and meta-analytic reviews of three major programs. *The Counseling Psychologist, 18,* 355–421.

Baltes, P. B., Reese, H. W., & Nesselroade, J. R. (1977). *Life-span developmental psychology: Introduction to research methods.* Monterey, CA: Brooks/Cole.

Barak, A., & LaCrosse, M. B. (1975). Multidimensional perceptions of counselor behavior. *Journal of Counseling Psychology, 22,* 471–476.

Barrett-Lennard, G. T. (1962). Dimensions of therapist response as causal factors in therapeutic change. *Psychological Monographs, 76,* 1–33.

Bausell, R. B. (1994). *Conducting meaningful experiments: 40 steps to becoming a scientist.* Thousand Oaks, CA: Sage.

Bear, T. M., & Kivlighan, D. M., Jr. (1994). Single-subject examination of the process of supervision of beginning and advanced supervisees. *Professional Psychology: Research and Practice, 25,* 450–457.

Bem, D. J. (1995). Writing a review article for *Psychological Bulletin. Psychological Bulletin, 118,* 172–177.

*Benshoff, J. M., & Thomas, W. P. (1992). A new look at the Counselor Evaluation Rating Scale. *The Clinical Supervisor, 9*(2), 42–51.

Bernard, J. M. (1979). Supervisory training: A discrimination model. *Counselor Education and Supervision, 19,* 60–68.

Bernard, J. M., & Goodyear, R. K. (1992). *Fundamentals of clinical supervision.* Boston: Allyn & Bacon.

Blocher, D. H. (1983). Toward a cognitive developmental approach to counseling supervision. *The Counseling Psychologist, 11*(1), 27–34.

*Blocher, D., Christensen, E. W., Hale-Fiske, R., Neren, S. H., Spencer, T., & Fowlkes, S. (1985). Development and preliminary validation of an instrument to measure cognitive growth. *Counselor Education and Supervision, 25,* 21–30.

Borders, L. D. (1989a). A pragmatic agenda for developmental supervision research. *Counselor Education and Supervision, 29,* 16–24.

*Borders, L. D. (1989b). Developmental cognitions of first practicum supervisors. *Journal of Counseling Psychology, 36,* 163–169.

*Borders, L. D. (1990). Developmental changes during supervisees' first practicum. *The Clinical Supervisor, 8*(2), 157–167.

*Borders, L. D., & Fong, M. L. (1989). Ego development and counseling ability during training. *Counselor Education and Supervision, 29,* 71–83.

*Borders, L., & Fong, M. L. (1991). Evaluations of supervisees: Brief commentary and research report. *The Clinical Supervisor, 9*(2), 42–51.

*Borders, L. D., Fong, M. L., & Neimeyer, G. J. (1986). Counseling students' level of ego development and perceptions of clients. *Counselor Education and Supervision, 26,* 36–49.

Bordin, E. S. (1983). A working alliance based model of supervision. *The Counseling Psychologist, 11*(1), 35–41.

Bradley, L. J. (1989). *Counselor supervision: Principles, process, and practice* (2nd ed.). Muncie, IN: Accelerated Development.

Byrne, B. M. (1994). *Structural equation modeling with EQS and EQS/Windows: Basic concepts, applications, and programming.* Thousand Oaks, CA: Sage.

*Carey, J. C., & Williams, K. S. (1986). Cognitive style in counselor education: A comparison of practicum supervisors and counselors in training. *Counselor Education and Supervision, 26,* 128–136.

Carey, J. C., Williams, K. S., & Wells, M. (1988). Relationships between dimensions of supervisors' influence and counselor trainees' performance. *Counselor Education and Supervision, 28,* 130–139.

Chen, H. T. (1990). *Theory driven evaluations.* Newbury Park, CA: Sage.

Cohen, J. (1962). The statistical power of abnormal-social psychological research: A review. *Journal of Abnormal and Social Psychology, 65,* 145–163.

Cohen, J. (1988). *Statistical power analysis for the behavioral sciences* (3rd ed.). New York: Academic Press.

Cohen, J., & Nee, J. C. M. (1984). Estimators for two measures of association for set correlation. *Educational and Psychological Measurement, 44,* 907–917.

Cone, J. D. (1988). Psychometric considerations and the multiple models of behavioral assessment. In A. S. Bellack & M. Hersen (Eds.), *Behavioral assessment: A practical handbook* (3rd ed., pp. 42–66). Elmsford, NY: Pergamon.

*Cook, D. A., & Helms, J. E. (1988). Visible racial/ethnic group supervisees' satisfaction with cross-cultural supervision as predicted by relationship characteristics. *Journal of Counseling Psychology, 35,* 268–274.

Cook, T. D., & Campbell, D. T. (1979). *Quasi-experimentation: Design and analysis for field settings.* Boston: Houghton Mifflin.

Cook, T. D., & Leviton, L. C. (1980). Reviewing the literature: A comparison of traditional methods with meta-analysis. *Journal of Personality, 48,* 449–472.

Cooper, H. M. (1982). Scientific guidelines for conducting integrative research reviews. *Review of Educational Research, 52,* 291–302.

Cooper, H. M. (1989). *Integrating research: A guide for literature reviews* (2nd ed.). Newbury Park, CA: Sage.

Cooper, H. M., & Hedges, L. V. (Eds.). (1994). *Handbook of research synthesis.* New York: Russell Sage Foundation.

Corcoran, K. J. (1985). Aggregating the idiographic data of single-subject research. *Social Work Research and Abstracts, 21*(2), 9–12.

*Couchon, W. D., & Bernard, J. M. (1984). Effects of timing of supervision on supervisor and counselor performance. *The Clinical Supervisor, 2,* 3–20.

*Cross, D. G., & Brown, D. (1983). Counselor supervision as a function of trainee experience: Analysis of specific behaviors. *Counselor Education and Supervision, 22,* 333–341.

*Curiel, H., & Rosenthal, J. A. (1987). Comparing structure in student supervision by social work program level. *The Clinical Supervisor, 5*(2), 53–67.

Dalton, J. E. (1983). Sex differences in communications skills as measured by a modified Relationship Inventory. *Sex Roles, 9,* 195–204.

Dar, R., Serlin, R. C., & Omer, H. (1994). Misuse of statistical tests in three decades of psychotherapy research. *Journal of Consulting and Clinical Psychology, 62,* 75–82.

*Davis, A. H., Savicki, V., Cooley, E. J., & Firth, J. L. (1989). Burnout and counselor practitioner expectations of supervision. *Counselor Education and Supervision, 28,* 234–241.

Dawis, R. V. (1987). Scale construction. *Journal of Counseling Psychology, 34,* 481–489.

*Dodenhoff, J. T. (1981). Interpersonal attraction and direct-indirect supervisor influence as predictors of counselor trainee effectiveness. *Journal of Counseling Psychology, 28,* 47–52.

Edgington, E. S. (1987). Randomized single-subject experiments and statistical tests. *Journal of Counseling Psychology, 34,* 437–442.

*Efstation, J. F., Patton, M. J., & Kardash, C. M. (1990). Measuring the working alliance in counseling supervision. *Journal of Counseling Psychology, 37,* 322–329.

*Eisikovits, Z., Shurka, E., & Baizeman, M. (1983). Israeli social workers' supervision preferences and practices: An example of a professional ideology. *The Clinical Supervisor, 1,* 35–42.

Ekstein, R., & Wallerstein, R. S. (1958). *The teaching and learning of psychotherapy.* New York: Basic Books.

Ekstein, R., & Wallerstein, R. S. (1972). *The teaching and learning of psychotherapy* (2nd ed.). New York: Basic Books.

Ellis, M. V. (1988). The cognitive developmental approach to case presentation in clinical supervision: A reaction and extension. *Counselor Education and Supervision, 27,* 259–264.

Ellis, M. V. (1991a). Conducting and reporting integrative research reviews: Accumulating scientific knowledge. *Counselor Education and Supervision, 30,* 225–237.

Ellis, M. V. (1991b). Research in clinical supervision: Revitalizing a scientific agenda. *Counselor Education and Supervision, 30,* 238–251.

*Ellis, M. V. (1991c). Critical incidents in clinical supervision. *Journal of Counseling Psychology, 38,* 342–349.

Ellis, M. V., & Blustein, D. L. (1991a). Developing and using educational and psychological tests and measures: The unificationist perspective. *Journal of Counseling and Development, 69,* 550–555.

Ellis, M. V., & Blustein, D. L. (1991b). The unificationist view: A context for validity. *Journal of Counseling and Development, 69,* 561–563.

*Ellis, M. V., Dell, D. M., & Good, G. E. (1988). Counselor trainees' perceptions of supervisor roles: Two studies testing the dimensionality of supervision. *Journal of Counseling Psychology, 35,* 315–324.

Ellis, M. V., Ladany, N., Krengel, M., & Schult, D. (1996). Clinical supervision research from 1981 to 1993: A methodological critique. *Journal of Counseling Psychology, 43,* 35–50.

Ezekiel, M. (1930). *Methods of correlational analysis.* New York: Wiley.

Fagley, N. S. (1985). Applied statistical power analysis and the interpretation of nonsignificant results by research consumers. *Journal of Counseling Psychology, 32,* 391–396.

Feldman, K. A. (1971). Using the work of others: Some observations on reviewing and integrating. *Sociology of Education, 44,* 86–102.

Ford, J. D. (1979). Research in training counselors and clinicians. *Review of Educational Research, 49,* 87–130.

*Fordham, A. S., May, B., Boyle, M., Bentall, R. P., & Slade, P. D. (1990). Good and bad clinicians: Supervisors' judgments of trainees' competence. *British Journal of Clinical Psychology, 29,* 113–114.

*Fortune, A., & Abramson, J. (1993). Predictors of satisfaction with field practicum among social work students. *The Clinical Supervisor, 11*(1), 95–110.

*Friedlander, M. L., Keller, K. E., Peca-Baker, T. A., & Olk, M. E. (1986). Effects of role conflict on counselor trainees' self-statements, anxiety level, and performance. *Journal of Counseling Psychology, 33,* 73–77.

*Friedlander, M. L., Siegel, S. M., & Brenock, K. (1989). Parallel process in counseling and supervision: A case study. *Journal of Counseling Psychology, 36,* 149–157.

*Friedlander, M. L., & Snyder, J. (1983). Trainees' expectations for the supervisory process: Testing a developmental model. *Counselor Education and Supervision, 22,* 342–348.

Friedlander, M., L., & Ward, L. G. (1984). Development and validation of the Supervisory Styles Inventory. *Journal of Counseling Psychology, 31,* 541–557.

Frost, P., & Stablein, R. (Eds.). (1992). *Doing exemplary research.* Newbury Park, CA: Sage.

*Gandolfo, R. L., & Brown, R. (1987). Psychology intern ratings of actual and ideal supervision of psychotherapy. *The Journal of Training and Practice in Professional Psychology, 1*(1), 15–28.

Garfield, S., & Bergin, A. (Eds.). (1994). *Handbook of psychotherapy and behavior change* (4th ed.). New York: Wiley.

Goldstein, R. (1989). Power and sample size via MS/PC-DOS computers. *American Statistician, 43,* 253–260.

*Goodyear, R. K. (1990). Gender configurations in supervisory dyads: Their relation to supervisee influence strategies and to skill evaluations of the supervisee. *The Clinical Supervisor, 8*(2), 67–79.

Green, B. F., & Hall, J. A. (1984). Quantitative methods for literature reviews. *Annual Review of Psychology, 35,* 37–53.

*Greenspan, R., Hanfling, S., Parker, E., Primm, S., & Waldfogel, D. (1991). Supervision of experienced agency workers: A descriptive study. *The Clinical Supervisor, 9*(2), 31–42.

*Guest, P. D., & Beutler, L. E. (1988). Impact of psychotherapy supervision on therapist orientation and values. *Journal of Consulting and Clinical Psychology, 56*(5), 653–658.

Haase, R. F. (1974). Power analysis of research in counselor education. *Counselor Education and Supervision, 14,* 124–132.

Haase, R. F. (1983). Classical and partial eta square in multifactor ANOVA designs. *Educational and Psychological Measurement, 43,* 35–39.

Haase, R. F. (1991). Computational formulas for multivariate strength of association from approximate F and χ^2 tests. *Multivariate Behavioral Research, 26,* 227–245.

Haase, R. F., & Ellis, M. V. (1987). Multivariate analysis of variance. *Journal of Counseling Psychology, 34,* 404–413.

Haase, R. F., Ellis, M. V., & Ladany, N. (1989). Multiple criteria for evaluating the magnitude of effects. *Journal of Counseling Psychology, 36,* 511–516.

*Handley, P. (1982). Relationship between supervisors' and trainees' cognitive styles and the supervision process. *Journal of Counseling Psychology, 29,* 508–515.

Hansen, J. C., Pound, R., & Petro, C. (1976). Review of research on practicum supervision. *Counselor Education and Supervision, 16,* 107–116.

Hansen, J. C., Robins, T. H., & Grimes, J. (1982). Review of research on practicum supervision. *Counselor Education and Supervision, 22,* 15–24.

Hansen, J. C., & Warner, R. W., Jr. (1971). Review of research on practicum supervision. *Counselor Education and Supervision, 10,* 261–272.

*Harkness, D., & Hensley, H. (1991). Changing the focus of social work supervision: Effects on client satisfaction and generalized contentment. *Social Work, 36,* 506–512.

Harkness, D., & Poertner, J. (1989). Research and social work supervision: A conceptual review. *Social Work, 34,* 115–119.

Hawkins, P., & Shohet, R. (1989). *Supervision in the helping professions.* Cambridge: Open Univeristy Press.

Hays, W. L. (1988). *Statistics* (4th ed.). Fort Worth, TX: Harcourt Brace Jovanovich.

Helms, J. E. (1990). *Black and white racial identity: Theory, research, and practice.* Westport, CT: Greenwood Press.

*Heppner, P. P., & Handley, P. G. (1981). A study of the interpersonal influence process in supervision. *Journal of Counseling Psychology, 28,* 437–444.

*Heppner, P. P., & Handley, P. G. (1982). The relationship between supervisory behaviors and perceived supervisor expertness, attractiveness, or trustworthiness. *Counselor Education and Supervision, 22,* 37–46.

Heppner, P. P., Kivlighan, D. M., Jr., & Wampold, B. E. (1992). *Research design in counseling.* Pacific Grove, CA: Brooks/Cole.

*Heppner, P. P., & Roehlke, J. J. (1984). Differences among supervisees at different levels of training: Implications for a developmental model of supervision. *Journal of Counseling Psychology, 31,* 76–90.

Hersen, M., & Barlow, D. H. (Eds.). (1976). *Single-case experimental designs: Strategies for studying behavior change.* Oxford: Pergamon.

*Hill, C. E., Charles, D., & Reed, K. G. (1981). A longitudinal analysis of changes in counseling skills during doctoral training in counseling psychology. *Journal of Counseling Psychology, 28,* 428–436.

Hilton, D. B., Russell, R. K., & Salmi, S. W. (1995). The effects of supervisor's race and level of support on perceptions of supervision. *Journal of Counseling and Development, 73,* 557–563.

Hogan, R. A. (1964). Issues and approaches in supervision. *Psychotherapy: Theory, Research, and Practice, 1,* 139–141.

Hogarty, G. E. (1989). Metaanalysis of the effects of practice with the chronically mental ill: A critique and reappraisal of the literature. *Social Work, 34,* 363–373.

Holland, B. S., & Copenhaver, M. D. (1988). Improved Bonferroni-type multiple testing procedures. *Psychological Bulletin, 104,* 145–149.

*Holloway, E. L. (1982). Interactional structure of the supervision interview. *Journal of Counseling Psychology, 29,* 309–317.

Holloway, E. L. (1984). Outcome evaluation in supervision research. *The Counseling Psychologist, 12*(4), 167–174.

Holloway, E. L. (1987). Developmental models of supervision: Is it development? *Professional Psychology: Research and Practice, 18,* 209–216.

Holloway, E. L. (1988). Models of counselor development or training models for supervision? Rejoinder to Stoltenberg and Delworth. *Professional Psychology: Research and Practice, 19,* 138–140.

Holloway, E. L. (1992). Supervision: A way of teaching and learning. In S. D. Brown & R. D. Lent (Eds.), *Handbook of counseling psychology* (2nd ed., pp. 177–214). New York: Wiley.

Holloway, E. L. (1995). *Clinical supervision: A systems approach.* Thousand Oaks, CA: Sage.

Holloway, E. L., & Hosford, R. E. (1983). Towards a prescriptive technology of counselor supervision. *The Counseling Psychologist, 11*(1), 73–77.

Holloway, E. L., & Johnston, R. (1985). Group supervision: Widely practiced but poorly understood. *Counselor Education and Supervision, 24,* 332–340.

Holloway, E. L., & Neufeldt, S. A. (1995). Supervision: Its contribution to treatment efficacy. *Journal of Consulting and Clinical Psychology, 63,* 207–213.

*Holloway, E. L., & Wampold, B. E. (1983). Patterns of verbal behavior and judgments of satisfaction in the supervision interview. *Journal of Counseling Psychology, 30,* 227–234.

Holloway, E. L., & Wampold, B. E. (1986). Relation between conceptual level and counseling-related tasks: A meta-analysis. *Journal of Counseling Psychology, 33,* 310–319.

Hoyle, R. H. (Ed.). (1994). Structural equation modeling in clinical research (Special Section). *Journal of Consulting and Clinical Psychology, 62,* 429–521.

Huberty, C. J., & Morris, J. D. (1989). Multivariate analysis versus multiple univariate analyses. *Psychological Bulletin, 105,* 302–308.

Huck, S. W., & Sandler, H. M. (1979). *Rival hypotheses: Alternative interpretations of data based conclusions.* New York: Harper & Row.

*Hutt, C. H., Scott, J., & King, M. (1983). A phenomenological study of supervisees' positive and negative experiences in supervision. *Psychotherapy: Theory, Research, and Practice, 20,* 118–123.

*Iberg, J. R. (1991). Applying statistical control theory to bring together clinical supervision and psychotherapy research. *Journal of Consulting and Clinical Psychology, 59,* 573–588.

Jackson, G. B. (1980). Methods for integrative reviews. *Review of Educational Research, 50,* 438–460.

Jaspen, N. (1965). The calculation of probabilities corresponding to values of z, t, F, and chi-square. *Educational and Psychological Measurement, 25,* 877–880.

*Kauderer, S., & Herron, W. G. (1990). The supervisory relationship in psychotherapy over time. *Psychological Reports, 67,* 471–480.

Kazdin, A. E. (1982). *Single-case research designs: Methods for clinical and applied settings.* New York: Oxford University Press.

Kazdin, A. E. (1983). Meta-analysis of psychotherapy: Criteria for selecting investigations. *Behavioral and Brain Sciences, 6,* 296.

Kazdin, A. E. (1986). Research designs and methodology. In S. L. Garfield & A. E. Bergin (Eds.), *Handbook of psychotherapy and behavior change* (3rd ed., pp. 23–68). New York: Wiley.

*Kennard, B. D., Stewart, S. M., & Gluck, M. M. (1987). The supervision relationship: Variables contributing to positive versus negative experiences. *Professional Psychology: Research and Practice, 18,* 172–175.

Kennedy, J. J. (1970). The eta coefficient in complex ANOVA designs. *Educational and Psychological Measurement, 30,* 885–889.

Kerlinger, F. N. (1986). *Foundations of behavioral research* (3rd ed.). New York: Holt, Rinehart and Winston.

*Kivlighan, D. M., Jr., Angelone, E. O., & Swafford, K. G. (1991). Live supervision in individual psychotherapy: Effects on therapist's intention use and client's evaluation of session effect and working alliance. *Professional Psychology: Research and Practice, 22,* 489–495.

Kline, P. (1983). Meta-analysis, measurement, and methodological problems in the study of psychotherapy. *Behavioral and Brain Sciences, 6,* 296–297.

Kraemer, H. C., & Thiemann, S. (1987). *How many subjects? Statistical power analysis in research.* Newbury Park, CA: Sage.

Kratochwill, T. R. (1978). *Single subject research: Strategies for evaluating change.* New York: Academic Pess.

*Krause, A. A., & Allen, G. J. (1988). Perceptions of counselor supervision: An examination of Stoltenberg's model from the perspectives of supervisor and supervisee. *Journal of Counseling Psychology, 35,* 77–80.

Kurtz, P. D., Marshall, E. K., & Banspach, S. W. (1985). Interpersonal skill-training research: A 12-year review and analysis. *Counselor Education and Supervision, 24,* 249–263.

Ladany, N., & Friedlander, M. L. (1995). The relationship between the supervisory working alliance and supervisee role conflict and role ambiguity. *Counselor Education and Supervision, 34,* 220–231.

Lambert, M. J., & Arnold, R. C. (1987). Research and the supervisory process. *Professional Psychology: Research and Practice, 18,* 217–224.

Landy, F. J. (1986). Stamp collecting versus science: Validation as hypothesis testing. *American Psychologist, 41,* 1183–1192.

*Larson, L. M., Suzuki, L. A., Gillespie, K. N., Potenza, M. T., Bechtel, M. A., & Toulouse, A. L. (1992). Development and validation of the Counseling Self-Estimate Inventory. *Journal of Counseling Psychology, 39,* 105–120.

*Lazar, A., & Mosek, A. (1993). The influence of the field instructor-student relationship on evaluation of students' practice. *The Clinical Supervisor, 11*(1), 111–120.

Leddick, G. R., & Bernard, J. M. (1980). The history of supervision: A critical review. *Counselor Education and Supervision, 20,* 187–196.

Liddle, H. A., & Halpin, R. J. (1978). Family therapy and supervision literature: A comparative review. *Journal of Marriage and Family Counseling, 4,* 77–98.

Light, R. J., & Pillemar, D. (1984). *Summing up: The science of reviewing research.* Cambridge, MA: Harvard University Press.

Light, R. J., & Smith, P. V. (1971). Accumulating evidence: Procedures for resolving contradictions among different research studies. *Harvard Educational Review, 41,* 429–471.

Lipsey, M. W. (1990). *Design sensitivity: Statistical power for experimental research.* Newbury Park, CA: Sage.

Littrell, J. M., Lee-Borden, N., & Lorenz, J. (1979). A developmental framework for counseling supervision. *Counselor Education and Supervision, 19,* 129–136.

Loevinger, J. (1976). *Ego development.* San Francisco: Jossey-Bass.

Loganbill, C., Hardy, E., & Delworth, U. (1982). Supervision: A conceptual model. *The Counseling Psychologist, 10*(1), 3–42.

Long, J. (1983). *Confirmatory factor analysis.* Beverly Hills, CA: Sage.

*Lowe, C. F., & McLeod, M. (1985). Role of supervision in assuring quality mental health services in university counseling centers. *Professional Psychology: Research and Practice, 16,* 898–901.

*Malikiosi-Loizos, M., Gold, J., Mehnert, W. O., & Work, G. G. (1981). Differential supervision and cognitive structure effects on empathy and counseling effectiveness. *International Journal of Advanced Counseling, 4,* 119–129.

*Mallinckrodt, B., & Nelson, M. L. (1991). Counselor training level and the formation of the psychotherapeutic working alliance. *Journal of Counseling Psychology, 38,* 133–138.

*Martin, J. S., Goodyear, R. K., & Newton, F. B. (1987). Clinical supervision: An intensive case study. *Professional Psychology: Research and Practice, 18,* 225–235.

Matarazzo, R. G. (1971). Research in the teaching and learning of psychotherapeutic skills. In A. E. Bergin & S. L. Garfield (Eds.), *Handbook of psychotherapy and behavior change* (pp. 859–924). New York: Wiley.

Matarazzo, R. G. (1978). Research in the teaching and learning of psychotherapeutic skills. In S. L. Garfield & A. E. Bergin (Eds.), *Handbook of psychotherapy and behavior change* (2nd ed., pp. 859–924). New York: Wiley.

Matarazzo, R. G., & Garner, A. M. (1992). Research on training for psychotherapy. In D. K. Freedheim (Ed.), *History of psychotherapy: A century of change* (pp. 850–877). Washington, DC: American Psychological Association.

Matarazzo, R. G., & Patterson, D. (1986). Research on the teaching and learning of therapeutic skills. In S. L. Garfield & A. E. Bergin (Eds.), *Handbook of psychotherapy and behavior change* (3rd ed., pp. 821–843). New York: Wiley.

*Mathews, G. (1986). Performance appraisal in the human services: A survey. *The Clinical Supervisor, 3*(4), 47–61.

*McNeill, B. W., Stoltenberg, C. D., & Pierce, R. A. (1985). Supervisees' perceptions of their development: A test of the Counselor Complexity Model. *Journal of Counseling Psychology, 32,* 630–633.

*McNeill, B. W., Stoltenberg, C. D., & Romans, J. S. C. (1992). The integrated developmental model of supervision: Scale development and validation procedures. *Professional Psychology: Research and Practice, 23,* 504–508.

Meehl, P. E. (1990). Why summaries of research on psychological theories are often uninterpretable. *Psychological Reports, 66,* 195–244.

Meier, S. T., & Davis, S. R. (1990). Trends in reporting psychometric properties of scales used in counseling psychology research. *Journal of Counseling Psychology, 37,* 113–115.

Messick, S. (1989). Validity. In R. L. Linn (Ed.), *Educational measurement* (3rd ed., pp. 13–103). New York: Macmillan.

Miars, R. D., Tracey, T. J., Ray, P. B., Cornfeld, J. L., O'Farrell, M., & Gelso, C. J. (1983). Variation in supervision process across trainee experience levels. *Journal of Counseling Psychology, 30,* 403–412.

Montgomery, D. B., & Morrison, D. A. (1973). A note on adjusting R^2. *Journal of Finance, 28,* 1009–1013.

*Moskowitz, S. A., & Rupert, P. A. (1983). Conflict resolution within the supervisory relationship. *Professional Psychology: Research and Practice, 14,* 632–641.

Munson, C. E. (1983). *An introduction to clinical social work supervision.* New York: Haworth.

Myrick, R. D., & Kelly, F. D., Jr. (1971). A scale for evaluating practicum students in counseling and supervision. *Counselor Education and Supervision, 10,* 330–336.

*Nelson, M. L., & Holloway, E. L. (1990). Relation of gender to power and involvement in supervision. *Journal of Counseling Psychology, 37,* 473–481.

*Newman, F. L., Kopta, S. M., McGovern, M. P., Howard, K. I., & McNeilly, C. L. (1988). Evaluating trainees relative to their supervisors during the psychology internship. *Journal of Consulting and Clinical Psychology, 56*(5), 659–665.

*Norcross, J. C., & Stevenson, J. F. (1984). How shall we judge ourselves? Training evaluation in clinical psychology programs. *Professional Psychology: Research and Practice, 15*(4), 497–508.

*Norcross, J. C., Stevenson, J. F., & Nash, J. M. (1986). Evaluation of internship training: Practices, problems and prospects. *Professional Psychology: Research and Practice, 17,* 280–282.

*Olk, M. E., & Friedlander, M. L. (1992). Trainees' experience of role conflict and role ambiguity in supervisory relationships. *Journal of Counseling Psychology, 39,* 389–397.

Omer, H., & Dar, R. (1992). Changing trends in three decades of psychotherapy research: The flight from theory into pragmatics. *Journal of Consulting and Clinical Psychology, 60,* 88–93.

Pedhazur, E. J. (1983). *Multiple regression in behavioral research: Explanation and prediction* (2nd ed.). New York: Holt, Rinehart and Winston.

Pepinsky, H. B., & Pepinsky, P. N. (1954). *Counseling: Theory and practice.* New York: Ronald Press.

*Perez, E. L., Krul, L. E., & Kapoor, R. (1984). The teaching of psychotherapy in Canadian psychiatric residency programs: Residents' perceptions. *Canadian Journal of Psychiatry, 29,* 658–663.

*Petty, M. M., & Odewahn, C. A. (1983). Supervisory behavior and sex role stereotypes in human service organizations. *The Clinical Supervisor, 1,* 13–20.

Pope-Davis, D. B., Reynolds, A. L., Dings, J. G., & Ottavi, T. M. (1994). Multicultural competencies of doctoral interns at university counseling centers: An exploratory investigation. *Professional Psychology: Research and Practice, 25,* 466–470.

*Putney, M. W., Worthington, E. L., Jr., & McCullough, M. E. (1992). Effects of supervisor and supervisee theoretical orientation and supervisor-supervisee matching on interns' perceptions of supervision. *Journal of Counseling Psychology, 39,* 258–265.

*Rabinowitz, F. E., Heppner, P. P., & Roehlke, H. J. (1986). Descriptive study of process and outcome variables of supervision over time. *Journal of Counseling Psychology, 33,* 292–300.

*Reising, G. N., & Daniels, M. H. (1983). A study of Hogan's model of counselor development and supervision. *Journal of Counseling Psychology, 30,* 235–244.

*Rickards, L. D. (1984). Verbal interaction and supervisor perception in counselor supervision. *Journal of Counseling Psychology, 31,* 262–265.

*Robyak, J. E., Goodyear, R. K., Prange, M. E., & Donham, G. (1986). Effects of gender, supervision, and presenting problems on practicum students' preference for interpersonal power bases. *Journal of Counseling Psychology, 33,* 159–163.

*Rodway, M., & Rogers, G. (1993). A comparison of the academic and articulated approaches to graduate field education. *The Clinical Supervisor, 11*(2), 37–54.

Rosenthal, R. (1995). Writing meta-analytic reviews. *Psychological Bulletin, 118,* 183–192.

Rosenthal, R., & Rubin, D. B. (1979). Comparing significance levels of independent studies. *Psychological Bulletin, 86,* 1165–1168.

Rosenthal, R., & Rubin, D. B. (1982). Comparing effect sizes of independent studies. *Psychological Bulletin, 92,* 500–504.

Rossi, J. S. (1990). Statistical power of psychological research: What have we gained in 20 years? *Journal of Consulting and Clinical Psychology, 58,* 646–656.

*Rotholz, T., & Werk, A. (1984). Student supervision: An educational process. *The Clinical Supervisor, 2,* 15–27.

Russell, R. K., Crimmings, A. M., & Lent, R. W. (1984). Counselor training and supervision: Theory and research. In S. D. Brown & R. W. Lent (Eds.), *Handbook of counseling psychology* (pp. 625–681). New York: Wiley.

Russell, R. K., & Petrie, T. (1994). Issues in training effective supervisors. *Applied and Preventive Psychology, 3,* 27–42.

*Sandell, R. (1985). Influence of supervision, therapist's competence and patient's ego level on the effects of time-limited psychotherapy. *Psychotherapy and Psychosomatics, 44,* 103–109.

Sansbury, D. L. (1982). Developmental supervision from a skills perspective. *The Counseling Psychologist, 10*(1), 53–57.

*Schact, A. J., Howe, H. E., Jr., & Berman, J. J. (1988). A short form of the Barrett-Lennard Relationship Inventory for supervisor relationships. *Psychological Reports, 63,* 699–706.

*Schact, A. J., Howe, H. E., Jr., & Berman, J. J. (1989). Supervisor facilitative conditions and effectiveness as perceived by thinking- and feeling-type supervisees. *Psychotherapy, 26,* 475–483.

*Schiavone, C. D., & Jessell, J. C. (1988). Influence of attributed expertness and gender in counselor supervision. *Counselor Education and Supervision, 28,* 29–42.

Searles, H. F. (1955). The informational value of the supervisor's emotional experience. *Psychiatry, 18,* 135–146.

Sedlmeier, P., & Gigerenzer, G. (1989). Do studies of statistical power have an effect on the power of studies? *Psychological Bulletin, 105,* 309–316.

Serlin, R. C. (1987). Hypothesis testing, theory building, and the philosophy of science. *Journal of Counseling Psychology, 34,* 365–371.

Serlin, R. C., & Lapsley, D. K. (1985). Rationality in psychological research: The good-enough principle. *American Psychologist, 40,* 73–83.

*Shiffman, S. (1987). Clinical psychology training and psychotherapy interview performance. *Psychotherapy, 24,* 71–84.

*Skovholt, T. M., & Rønnestad, M. H. (1992). *The evolving professional self: Stages and themes in therapist and counselor development.* Chichester, West Sussex, England: Wiley.

*Snepp, F. P., & Peterson, D. R. (1988). Evaluative comparison of Psy.D. and Ph.D. students by clinical internship supervisors. *Professional Psychology: Research and Practice, 19,* 180–183.

Stein, D. M., & Lambert, M. J. (1995). Graduate training in psychotherapy: Are therapy outcomes enhanced? *Journal of Consulting and Clinical Psychology, 63,* 182–196.

*Steinhelber, J., Patterson, V., Cliffe, K., & LeGoullon, M. (1984). An investigation of some relationships between psychotherapy supervision and patient change. *Journal of Clinical Psychology, 40,* 1346–1353.

*Stenack, R. J., & Dye, H. A. (1983). Practicum supervision roles: Effects on supervisee statements. *Counselor Education and Supervision, 23,* 157–168.

Sternberg, R. J. (1995). Introduction to the special symposium on writing articles for *Psychological Bulletin. Psychological Bulletin, 118,* 171.

Stoltenberg, C. (1981). Approaching supervision from a developmental perspective: The counselor complexity model. *Journal of Counseling Psychology, 28,* 59–65.

Stoltenberg, C. D., & Delworth, U. (1987). *Supervising counselors and therapists: A developmental approach.* San Francisco: Jossey-Bass.

Stoltenberg, C. D., McNeill, B. W., & Crethar, H. C. (1994). Changes in supervision as counselors and therapists gain experience: A review. *Professional Psychology: Research and Practice, 25,* 416–449.

*Stoltenberg, C. D., Pierce, K. A., & McNeill, B. W. (1987). Effects of experience on counselor trainee needs. *The Clinical Supervisor, 5,* 23–32.

*Stoltenberg, C. D., Solomon, G. S., & Ogden, L. (1986). Comparing supervisee and supervisor initial perceptions of supervision: Do they agree? *The Clinical Supervisor, 4*(3), 53–61.

Strong, S. R. (1968). Counseling: An interpersonal influence process. *Journal of Counseling Psychology, 15,* 215–224.

*Strozier, A. L., Kivlighan, D. M., & Thoreson, R. W. (1993). Supervisor intentions, supervisee reactions and helpfulness: A case study of the process of supervision. *Professional Psychology: Research and Practice, 1,* 13–19.

Suen, H. K. (1988). Agreement, reliability, accuracy, and validity: Toward a clarification. *Behavioral Assessment, 10,* 343–366.

*Swanson, J. L., & O'Saben, C. L. (1993). Difference in supervisory needs and expectations by trainee experience, cognitive style, and program membership. *Journal of Counseling and Development, 71,* 457–464.

*Talen, M., & Schindler, N. (1993). Goal-directed supervision plans: A model for trainee supervision and evaluation. *The Clinical Supervisor, 11*(2), 77–88.

Taveggia, T. C. (1974). Resolving research controversy through empirical cumulation: Toward reliable sociological knowledge. *Sociological Methods and Research, 2,* 395–407.

Tinsley, H. E. A., & Tinsley, D. J. (1987). Uses of factor analysis in counseling psychology research. *Journal of Counseling Psychology, 34,* 414–424.

*Tracey, T. J., Ellickson, J. L., & Sherry, D. (1989). Reactance in relation to different supervisory environments and counselor development. *Journal of Counseling Psychology, 36,* 336–344.

*Tracey, T. J., & Sherry, P. (1993). Complementary interaction over time in successful and less successful supervision. *Professional Psychology: Research and Practice, 24,* 304–311.

*Usher, C. H., & Borders, L. D. (1993). Practicing counselors' preferences for supervisory style and supervisory emphasis. *Counselor Education and Supervision, 33,* 66–79.

Walberg, H. J., & Haertel, E. H. (Eds.). (1980). Research integration: The state of the art (Special Issue). *Evaluation of Education: An International Review Service, 4,* 1–135.

Wampold, B. E., Davis, B., & Good, R. H., III (1990). Hypothesis validity of clinical research. *Journal of Consulting and Clinical Psychology, 58,* 360–367.

Wampold, B. E., & Freund, R. D. (1987). Use of multiple regression in counseling psychology research: A flexible data-analytic strategy. *Journal of Counseling Psychology, 34*(4), 372–382.

Wampold, B. E., & Poulin, K. L. (1992). Counseling research methods: Art and artifact. In S. D. Brown & R. D. Lent (Eds.), *Handbook of counseling psychology* (2nd ed., pp. 71–109). New York: Wiley.

Wiebe, B., & Pearce, W. B. (1973). An item analysis and revision of the Barrett-Lennard Relationship Inventory. *Journal of Clinical Psychology, 29,* 495–497.

*Wiley, M. O., & Ray, P. B. (1986). Counseling supervision by developmental level. *Journal of Counseling Psychology, 33,* 439–445.

Williams, A. (1994). *Visual and active supervision: Roles, focus, technique.* New York: Norton.

*Winter, M., & Holloway, E. L. (1991). Relation of trainee experience, conceptual level, and supervisor approach to selection of audiotaped counseling passages. *The Clinical Supervisor, 9*(2), 87–103.

Wolf, F. M. (1986). *Meta-analysis: Quantitative methods for research synthesis.* Beverly Hills: Sage.

*Worthington, E. L., Jr. (1984). Empirical investigation of supervision of counselors as they gain experience. *Journal of Counseling Psychology, 31,* 63–75.

Worthington, E. L., Jr. (1987). Changes in supervision as counselors and supervisors gain experience: A review. *Professional Psychology: Research and Practice, 18,* 189–208.

Worthington, E. L., Jr., & Roehlke, H. J. (1979). Effective supervision as perceived by beginning counselors-in-training. *Journal of Counseling Psychology, 26,* 64–73.

*Worthington, E. L., Jr., & Stern, A. (1985). Effects of supervisor and supervisee degree level and gender on the supervisory relationship. *Journal of Counseling Psychology, 32,* 252–262.

*Yogev, S., & Pion, G. M. (1984). Do supervisors modify psychotherapy supervision according to supervisees' levels of experience? *Psychotherapy, 21,* 206–208.

Yutrzenka, B. A. (1995). Making a case for training in ethnic and cultural diversity in increasing treatment efficacy. *Journal of Consulting and Clinical Psychology, 63,* 197–206.

*Zucker, P. L., & Worthington, E. L., Jr. (1986). Supervision of interns and postdoctoral applicants for licensure in university counseling centers. *Journal of Counseling Psychology, 33,* 87–89.

CHAPTER 26

Research on Supervisor Variables
in Psychotherapy Supervision

SUSAN ALLSTETTER NEUFELDT
LARRY E. BEUTLER
ROBERT BANCHERO
University of California at Santa Barbara

Supervision is defined as a relationship between two or more people whose purpose is the development of the supervisee as a professional psychotherapist. The supervisor's tasks ordinarily include development of not only the supervisee's therapeutic skill in a given therapist-client relationship but also the supervisee's growth in clinical wisdom and identification with the therapist role across clients. In order to measure the supervisor's effectiveness, it is necessary to look at immediate outcomes, intermediate outcomes, and final outcomes. Immediate outcomes include the trainee's internal reactions and external behaviors within the supervision session. These, in turn, can be linked to the intermediate outcomes of the trainee's internal reactions and external behaviors while conducting psychotherapy. And finally, the supervisor's effects can be seen in clients' internal reactions and external behaviors within psychotherapy and within the client's life after psychotherapy. To date, more supervision research has been conducted on supervisees' responses within supervision than in either of the other two areas.

Research in supervision, while still limited relative to the body of research in psychotherapy, has grown in the past two decades. Holloway and Hosford (1983) identified goals for research in the nascent field. They suggested that development of this new scientific area should proceed in an orderly fashion. Phase 1 should include descriptive naturalistic research with hypotheses to be generated from its results. In Phase 2, researchers incorporate analyses involving inferential strategies and use experimentation to confirm the hypotheses of Phase 1. Theories are developed in Phase 3 as a basis for supervisory practice.

The literature on supervisor variables has included work in all three areas. In this chapter, we identify and present the extant research of the first two phases in a systematic way that adapts the taxonomy developed by Beutler, Machado, and Neufeldt (1994) to describe therapist variables. Supervisor characteristics are described along two dimensions. Figure 26.1 illustrates this. The first describes supervisor characteristics as those that can be objectively observed, on the one hand, and those characteristics that must be inferred from self-report or other means on the other. The second dimension ranges from those supervisor characteristics that are consistent across all situations to those that are specific to supervision. In each instance, we describe the variable as it relates to supervision processes, supervisee

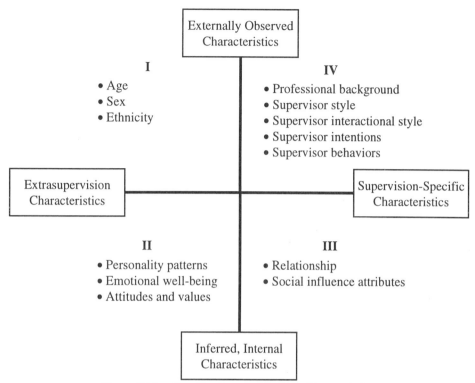

Figure 26.1 Classification of Supervisor Characteristics

satisfaction, and supervision outcome. When measures of independent variables specific to the supervisor have been developed, we discuss them in the appropriate category.

In the final portion of this chapter, we discuss the state of research in Phases 1 and 2 and suggest areas for further exploration. In particular, we identify promising independent variables and present possibilities for the development of appropriate dependent variables.

RESEARCH TO DATE

Objective Cross-Situational Traits

Objective, cross-situational traits are those supervisor characteristics that are observable and consistent across situations. We pay particular attention to the effects of age, sex, and ethnicity in this review; there is a paucity of research on the effect of these supervisor variables on either trainees or clients. No studies indicated significant effects of supervisor's age along any dimension.

Gender. Early research frequently involved surveys of supervisors and supervisees about their behaviors, preferences, and satisfaction with supervision. In a survey of graduate students from 50 APA-accredited programs in clinical and counseling psychology, Allen, Szollos, and Williams (1986) found that the rated quality of supervision was unrelated to the supervisor's gender. Likewise, Schiavone and Jessell (1988) found that supervisees' ratings of supervisor expertness and competence did not differ as a function of supervisor gender. Nonetheless, there is some evidence that male and female supervisors provide supervision differently. Robyak, Goodyear, and Prange (1987) surveyed female and male supervisors from seven counselor-center training programs. Supervisors rated the usefulness of responses reflecting interpersonal power bases. Men rated responses associated with referent power as more useful than did women. Referent power in supervision is that which is based on the attractiveness of the supervisor's attitudes, values, beliefs, and behaviors to the supervisee.

In a systematic effort to describe what actually happens in supervision, researchers in two recent studies examined interactions of supervisory dyads. Lichtenberg and Goodyear (1996) examined the extent to which the structure of patterning and of interaction is enhanced or moderated by a number of factors. Recordings of 54 actual supervisory dyads were analyzed for nonrandomness in relational patterning. The investigators reported that supervisor gender was a reliable predictor of whether the supervisor or the supervisee had the greater influence on the supervision structure. If the supervisor were male, he structured the session; if the supervisor were female, the supervisee was more likely to structure the supervision session.

In a multiple case study of four sessions each of four supervisory dyads, Nelson and her colleagues (1996) found that the female supervisor used more minimal encouragement, whereas the male used more self-enhancing and critical messages. Again, this suggests that male and female supervisors differ in their behavior toward supervisees.

In a survey of 84 interns from 32 training sites, Putney, Worthington, and McCullough (1992) found that women were perceived as more effective supervisors than men. More research is needed in this area to determine both how female and male supervisors differ in their behavior and whether those differences impact the performance of the supervisee. There is no research that shows how supervisor gender influences counseling behavior or client outcome.

Ethnicity.   Prior to 1995, there was no published empirical study of supervisor race or ethnicity (Brown & Landrum-Brown, 1995). Recently, Hilton, Russell, and Salmi (1995) explored the effects of supervisor race on trainee feelings and perceptions in the supervisory relationship. Sixty Caucasian women served as counselors in two counseling sessions with a confederate client and were supervised by one of six experienced supervisors—three African American and three Caucasian. Trainees reported that anxiety, perceived performance, satisfaction, and perceptions of the supervisory relationship did not differ on the basis of supervisor race. This finding, although descriptive of supervisee feelings, does not provide information about actual supervisor or supervisee behaviors in the supervision or counseling sessions.

Subjective, Cross-Situational Traits

Subjective, cross-situational traits are those that endure across a variety of settings, but are not available for objective measurement. We have included the supervisor's personality patterns, emotional well-being, and attitudes and values. There were no empirical studies found on supervisor emotional well-being.

Personality.   In the psychotherapy literature, research on correlates between general therapist personality factors and the outcome of psychotherapy has diminished in recent years (Beutler et al., 1994) because of the lack of significant findings. What little research exists in the supervision literature likewise suggests that general personality factors of supervisors or matching of these factors between supervisors and supervisees has little to do with supervision outcome. Nelson's (1978) survey of preferences of psychology, psychiatry, and social work trainees revealed that highly desired personality descriptors for supervisors included flexible, self-revealing, permissive, and outgoing. Powell (1991) examined highly rated and experienced clinical supervisors in a military substance-abuse program with a standardized test. He found that the supervisors, not surprisingly, demonstrated the "counselor" profile common among therapists in general.

Handley (1982) studied the relationship of similarity between supervisors and supervisees on the Myers-Briggs Type Indicator (MBTI; Myers-Briggs, 1962) to their perceptions of the supervisory relationship along dimensions of the Barrett-Lennard Relationship Inventory (Barrett-Lennard, 1962). Supervisees who were similar to their supervisors along the sensing-intuitive dimension were more likely to rate their supervisory relationships highly than those who were not. In an effort to link personality traits to supervision outcome, Davidson, Christiansen, and Dillon (1982) studied the relationship of similarity between supervisors and supervisees on the MBTI to fieldwork performance reports. The laudable effort to base their results on fieldwork performance did not produce significant results, however. Likewise, Deming (1980) attempted to base her study of supervisor personality on supervision outcome; she found, however, that counseling students tended to gain in self-actualization as they proceeded through training, whether or not they were enrolled in a practicum and regardless of the level of self-actualization of their supervisors.

Attitudes and Values.   No empirical studies were found on supervisor attitudes. In the only study available on supervisor values, Guest and Beutler (1988) found that supervisor values included a sense of accomplishment, imagination, self-respect, inner harmony, and wisdom. This pattern is distinct from the value patterns reported for other occupations but consistent with those of psychotherapists generally. Trainees had similar values. Over the course of the training year, trainees came to value ambition somewhat more and politeness somewhat less.

Subjective, Supervision-Specific States

Subjective, supervision-specific states are those that are inferred from data on supervisors. There is no way to observe the states directly. Rather, researchers decide on the basis of questions and observations whether the state exists in that supervision session.

Supervisory Relationship.   Given that supervision is an interactional process and given that the therapy alliance has been a good predictor of psychotherapy outcome, this is a likely arena for research. Not surprisingly, much of the supervision research is focused here.

As in psychotherapy (Beutler et al., 1994), early literature in supervision on the relationship between supervisor and supervisee focused on the provision of the facilitative conditions (Rogers, 1957). Because provision of the facilitative conditions was seen as necessary and in some cases, sufficient, for client change, therapists were expected to learn and demonstrate them in their sessions with clients; as such, their demonstration became a supervision outcome measure for effective supervision. Scales to measure the facilitative conditions were developed by Truax and modified by Carkhuff (Carkhuff & Berenson, 1967). Pierce and Schauble (1970, 1971) identified them as potential supervisor variables, that is, that the supervisor could provide facilitative conditions for the supervisee.

They found that those trainees whose supervisors provided high levels of empathy, regard, genuineness, and concreteness in their supervision sessions demonstrated growth in the use of the facilitative conditions in their therapy sessions over an academic year. Those therapists whose supervisors provided low levels of facilitative conditions, however, demonstrated a slight decline in provision of the facilitative conditions in therapy. These differences held constant 9 months later. Similarly, Karr and Geist (1977) found that supervisor dimensions of genuineness, respect, and concreteness were significantly related to trainee levels of functioning in counseling; there was no relationship on dimensions of empathy, however.

That this is subjectively important to supervisees is demonstrated in a recent survey of graduates of doctoral programs in clinical and counseling psychology by Schacht, Howe, and Berman (1989). Graduates rated the supervisors who contributed most to their therapeutic effectiveness as high on the facilitative conditions. Likewise, Wetchler (1989) found in a survey of family therapy supervisors and supervisees that both rated respect for the supervisee as a highly important characteristic of the supervisor.

As in psychotherapy (Beutler et al., 1994), the supervisory relationship has come to incorporate not only what the supervisor offers in the way of facilitative conditions but also the perceptions of the supervisee. The working alliance (Bordin, 1979) has come to embody the facilitative conditions as understood in the context of the psychodynamic therapeutic relationship. Bordin (1983) extended the concept of the working alliance to supervision, and he predicted that it would be equally important to measure. In a further development, Efstation, Patton, and Kardash (1990) published their reliable and validated measure, the Supervision Working Alliance Inventory (SWAI). They extracted three supervisor factors (Client Focus, Rapport, and Identification) and two trainee factors (Rapport and Client Focus) by factor analysis. The supervisor factors are of particular interest for future research on therapist contributions to the supervisory relationship. To date, we have found no published research using the SWAI in an empirical study of the supervisor.

In a laboratory analogue study that links supervision-specific relationship characteristics, Sundblad (1973) found, in a survey of rehabilitation counseling supervisors, that the supervisor's commitment to the supervisee was related to the levels of empathy and warmth they indicated they would provide to supervisees in 15 hypothetical vignettes on the Supervisor Response Questionnaire (SRQ), an investigator-designed measure. Although this is an interesting finding, it is not a measure of actual supervisor relationship behavior.

Social Influence Attributes.   Strong (1968) argued that the social influence attributes of expertness, trustworthiness, and attractiveness provided a therapist with a power base from which he or she could influence clients in a desired direction. Likewise, the supervisor's goal is to influence therapists, so that they perform in the professional role in an effective manner. Briefly, expertness refers to perception of the supervisor, in this case, as a source of valid assertions and trustworthiness to the perception that the supervisor is honest and sincere and has nothing to gain from the interaction; both enhance the supervisor's credibility and persuasiveness. The supervisor's attractiveness is the degree to which he or she is seen as likable by, compatible with, or similar to the supervisee.

Heppner and Handley (1981) modified the Counselor Rating Form (Barak & LaCrosse, 1975) into the Supervisor Rating Form (SRF) in order to examine trainee perceptions of supervisors along the dimensions of expertness, trustworthiness, and attractiveness. In a study in which they surveyed both trainees and supervisors at the end of a semester-long practicum in a counseling center, they found that there was a positive correlation between trainees' perceptions of supervisors' social influence characteristics and trainees' perceptions of the therapeutic relationship and satisfaction with supervision, but there was not a high correlation of these ratings with ratings of supervisor impact on their professional and personal behavior, perhaps a more salient variable. Interestingly, the ratings on perceived attractiveness and trustworthiness were related to the supervisors' ratings of trainee performance and their willingness to supervise the trainees again, which leads one to question the evaluations given by supervisors to trainees as legitimate outcome variable, especially in view of the fact that in one psychotherapy study (Najavits & Strupp, 1994), supervisors' evaluations of therapists were not correlated with those of outside observers or clients. At the same time, in a subsequent study, Heppner and Handley (1982) found that supervisors were rated as more credible and attractive when they were perceived as utilizing evaluative behavior.

Allen et al.'s (1986) survey revealed that trainees rated the quality of supervision high when the supervisor was perceived as trustworthy and expert. Dodenhoff (1981) found that trainees who were attracted to their supervisors were rated as more effective by supervisors on the Counselor Evaluation Rating Scale (CERS; Myrick & Kelly, 1971), although attraction was not related to clients' perceptions of outcome. In an extension of this study, Carey, Williams, and Wells (1988) found that the element of trustworthiness proved to be the strongest predictor of ratings of trainee performance as measured on the CERS. In an analogue study, Hester, Weitz, Anchor, and Roback (1976) found that when trainees were shown videotapes of high- and low-skilled supervisors whom they perceived to be similar or dissimilar to themselves, trainees overlooked attitude dissimilarity in finding the highly skilled supervisors more attractive. In a study in which trainees viewed videotapes of supervisors who had been previously described as varying in expertise, trainees rated those supervisors with the greatest ascribed expertness more highly. In all these studies, credibility, that is, expertise and trustworthiness, proved to be highly correlated with supervisee satisfaction, evaluations of supervisors, and/or counseling performance as rated by their supervisors.

Objective, Supervision-Specific States

Objective, supervision-specific states are those variables that occur in supervision and can be verified by an observer. Among these are descriptive variables such as experience and professional background in the areas of supervision and therapy, as well as those variables that objectively measure supervisor style, behavior, and intent. By far the largest number of studies in supervision fall into this area.

In an effort to describe what happens in supervision, a number of researchers have developed or adapted observation systems. These approaches to the measurement of the supervision process initially offer Phase 1 descriptions and then begin to examine the relationships between a number of variables in the manner of Phase 2. These are among the most promising studies in the area of supervision and offer possibilities to future researchers who want to link events that occur in supervision with those that occur in counseling.

In the following paragraphs, we present observational systems as we describe research results. As we do this, we recognize that it is difficult to separate the supervisor's relational behavior from the supervisee's. Many observational systems incorporate the interactions between the supervisor and the supervisee. We include these studies with particular attention to the behavior of the supervisor rather than the supervisee, except as the former influences the latter.

Professional Background and Experience.   Two analogue studies of supervisor planning behaviors were found in this area. In the initial study, Stone (1980) examined planning behaviors of 10 inexperienced undergraduates and 17 experienced supervisors from various settings and found the experienced supervisors generated more planning statements. In a follow-up study, Marikis, Russell, and Dell (1985) compared beginning graduate students in counseling with no supervision experience, advanced doctoral student supervisors who had up to 100 hours of supervision experience, and Ph.D.-level supervisors with from 2 to 18 years of supervision experience. They found no differences in planning statements, nor did they find a relationship between the planning statements and the follow-up supervisory conferences. Those supervisors who had some experience, however, made significantly more self-revealing statements and more instructional statements than did their no-experience counterparts during the actual supervisory session. Counselors rated the experienced supervisors more highly than the inexperienced ones. Surprisingly, there were no differences noted between those supervisors with limited experience and those with advanced experience, which would indicate that the practice of using graduate student supervisors with beginning counseling students can be as effective as using those whose training is complete. Caution is encouraged, however, because this is one study and because only beginning counselors were supervised.

In a survey of 237 counselors from 11 counseling centers, Worthington (1984) found that supervisors with more experience were reported to have used humor more frequently than did their less experienced colleagues. This is consistent with Skovholt and Rønnestad's (1992) finding that therapists lose their sense of humor during training and then regain it as they acquire postdoctoral experience. In a subsequent survey of 34 predoctoral interns and 25 postdoctoral licensure applicants employed at university counseling centers, Zucker and Worthington (1986) found that neither licensure status nor post-Ph.D. supervisory experience affected supervisees' ratings of their effectiveness. There are no studies that compare the behavior of more and less experienced supervisors' in-session behaviors nor their effects on supervisees' responses in supervision or in therapy.

Supervisor Style as Perceived by Supervisees.   Supervisor style describes patterns of supervisory behavior used by a given individual within a supervision session, and in some cases, across sessions with different supervisees. To date, all empirical descriptions of supervisory behavior fall within the style category. Supervision style has been described along a number of dimensions by researchers. In the initial studies, researchers asked supervisees what they valued in their supervisors' behavior. It is not clear that supervisee appreciation of supervision is predictive of supervisee performance in therapy, but as Russell and Petrie (1994) point out in their extensive review, it would be foolish to ignore such information in the absence of other data. Nelson (1978) surveyed 48 trainees across the disciplines of clinical psychology, counseling psychology, psychiatry, and social work and found them to agree that their goal was to gain competence as therapists. To that end, therapists preferred supervisors to observe them directly, either live or on videotape, and to provide feedback. Supervisors who were practicing therapists and modeled therapeutic skill and theoretical knowledge were highly valued, as were those who were flexible, self-disclosing, permissive, and congenial. Beginning therapists preferred more supervisor activity in sessions than did advanced trainees.

Similarly, Worthington and Roehlke (1979), in a survey of 237 counseling center trainees at the end of their first practicum semester, found that these beginners rated supervisors who provided structure, teaching, and support as highly competent. They wanted to be taught how to counsel, through literature and didactic instruction, and they wanted ways to think about and conceptualize their cases. Given this instruction, they wanted their supervisors to support them as they tried out their new skills. As Worthington (1987) noted, the need for support and encouragement appears to be high at transition points, such as in the first practicum and during internship.

In a study of group supervision, a common mode of supervision in training programs, Savickas, Marquart, and Supinski (1986) surveyed medical residents in psychiatry. They found that students preferred the same basic qualities in their supervisors described earlier, that is, didactic instruction, modeling, and cognitive schemes for case conceptualization.

Tackling the issue in a different way, Rosenblatt and Mayer (1975) examined the complaints of social work students. What did they find objectionable in their supervisors? Supervisors who limited supervisees' autonomy; failed to provide adequate direction and clarity; or were cold, aloof, and/or hostile, contributed to students' stress. Trainees also objected to supervisors who acted as therapists and explored trainees' personal issues.

In a more recent survey of 84 social work trainees and their supervisors, Rotholz and Werk (1984) found that supervisor styles could be described as consistent with two models, a goal-directed model and an apprenticeship model. The goal-directed model, in which students were encouraged to accept responsibility for their current practice and future development, was more attractive to students than was the apprenticeship model, based on learning by doing under close supervision.

Because each of these studies has been conducted with different trainees and used different terms to describe supervisor styles, it is difficult to compare them. One gathers, however, that supervisees want their supervisors to provide a positive relationship along with teaching and feedback that enables them to gain in competence. Beginners particularly express a desire for instruction. Stoltenberg and Delworth (1987) recommended that supervisors vary their behavior with supervisees of different levels of development, but in an extensive review, Worthington (1987) found only weak support for the idea that supervisors actually do so. In a more recent study, Krause and Allen (1988) assessed whether supervisors provided different supervision to beginners than they did to those at later points of development. They found that whereas supervisors thought they were providing supervision calibrated to the level of the trainee, trainees at different developmental levels were unable to detect the differences supervisors described in the supervisors' counseling, collegial, and consultative behaviors. As in prior studies, supervisors were valued when they provided a collegial atmosphere. In some contrast to studies cited earlier in which trainees preferred a focus on teaching, these trainees preferred supervision that was characterized by a focus on trainee personal development and self-understanding.

We suggest that little more is to be gained by asking students what their supervisors do and what they like about it, at least until we have evidence that supervisee perceptions of what happens in supervision translate into therapist in-session behavior and client outcomes. To describe what actually happens in supervision, direct observation must occur. To that end, researchers have developed observation systems that explicitly illuminate supervisor behavior and style.

Supervisor Style Based on Direct Observation.   In the first of these, Holloway and Wolleat (1981) posited that supervision is a teaching, rather than a counseling, activity. They adapted Blumberg's (1970) system for observation of teachers to the supervision arena and observed 12 supervisors who each conducted a supervision interview with 2 trainees. In support of the idea that supervisors develop a preferred pattern of behavior or style of supervision, they found that individual supervisors' interactional patterns were consistent across supervisees and different from those of other supervisors.

Friedlander and Ward (1984) developed a measure specific to supervision that identifies distinct supervision styles. In a series of studies of supervision, four separate analyses yielded three supervisory style dimensions: attractiveness, interpersonal sensitivity, and task orientation. Scales were constructed to measure these, with parallel versions for supervisors and trainees. Twenty-eight counseling trainees used the trainee version to observe prominent supervisors with different theoretical orientations (Ekstein, Ellis, Polster, and Rogers on videotape; Goodyear, 1982) and distinguish among their supervision styles. Results indicated that the cognitive-behavioral supervisor was task oriented and the psychodynamic and humanistic supervisors displayed highly interpersonal styles, which is consistent with reported supervision theory (cf. Bordin, 1983; Hosford & Barmann, 1983).

More recently, Shanfield, Mohl, Matthews, and Hetherly (1989) developed the Psychotherapy Supervision Inventory on the basis of observed sessions between psychiatry residents and their supervisors. Dimensions of supervisor behavior included focus on the therapist and the patient, intellectual and experiential orientation, number of clarifying and interpreting comments, intensity of confrontation, depth of exploration, verbal activity level of the supervisor, dominance of the supervisor and the therapist, and comfort and tension among supervisors. In a subsequent study (Shanfield, Mohl, Matthews, & Hetherly, 1992), trained raters reliably distinguished among styles of 34 supervisors in 53 videotaped supervision sessions. Supervisors who were observed with two residents behaved in the same style in both sessions. An analysis of the raters' judgments of excellent supervisors revealed that 72% of the variance in judgments could be accounted for by empathy, with the focus on the therapist accounting for an additional 5%. In a subsequent analysis of the data, Shanfield, Matthews, and Hetherly (1993) reported that those supervisors rated as excellent allowed the residents to develop their stories of their therapeutic encounter, paid close attention to the residents' affectively charged concerns, based their comments on the material presented in the session, and focused on helping the resident to understand the patient.

Heppner et al. (1994) used multidimensional scaling of supervisory statements during actual supervision interviews and found six dimensions to describe supervisory interventions: (a) Directing-Instructing Versus Deepening, (b) Cognitive Clarification Versus Emotional Encouragement, (c) Confronting Versus Encouraging the Client, (d) Didactic-Distant Versus Emotionally Involved, (e) Joining With Versus Challenging the Trainee, and (f) Providing Direction Versus Resignation. These dimensions bear some relation to those measured by the aforementioned Psychotherapy Supervision Inventory but may offer a basis for describing supervisory styles and behaviors more precisely in the future. Each of these efforts to describe supervision styles on the basis of observation provides a selection of process variables that can be related in the future to therapist behavior in session and to client outcome when clients have similar characteristics and present similar problems.

Supervisor Interactional Style.   Supervision is clearly an interactive process, and numerous researchers have begun to look at supervisors in terms of their interaction with trainees. Some of these studies are described in other sections of this volume, but they are notable for their microanalytic content analysis of supervision interactions. They fulfill the task of describing what goes on in supervision in a precise way. Those interactional studies that effectively describe supervisor interpersonal styles are described next.

Holloway and Wolleat's (1981) study provided a means for identifying not only supervisor behaviors but those of the trainee. In a subsequent study, Holloway (1982) analyzed the sequences of doctoral student supervisor and beginning trainee behaviors in 20-minute segments of 43 supervision interviews. Results indicated that patterns existed in which certain supervisor behaviors were likely to elicit particular supervisee responses. In particular, when supervisors reflected trainees' feelings, praised trainees, and developed their ideas, they elicited trainees' positive social-emotional behavior such as self-disclosure or praise for the supervisor. When supervisors directly questioned supervisees, however, trainees were silent in response. This finding suggests that the task of the supervisor with beginning trainees is more complex than might be imagined. The supervisor, for instance, who wishes to stimulate trainees' thoughtful and creative discussion about a case is not likely to do so by asking direct questions. In fact, cognitive formulations were not elicited from trainees by either direct questions or supportive communications.

Martin, Goodyear, and Newton (1987) used the Penman (1980) scheme of interaction to analyze supervisory transactions in an intensive case study of an experienced supervisor with an experienced counselor over one semester. The Penman system provides a lens through which observers can view the interactions of supervision participants with unequal power; it allows observers to analyze the interactional behaviors of each participant along dimensions of power and involvement. Holloway, Freund, Gardner, Nelson, and Walker (1989) utilized the Penman scheme to differentiate between the supervisory activity of Ekstein, Ellis, Polster, Rogers, and Kagan (Goodyear, 1982) and amplified Friedlander and Ward's (1984) finding that the supervisors had different styles. They found a primary pattern of teacher-learner interaction in all interviews, such that the supervisor delivered high-power messages followed by the trainees' low-power messages. The most egalitarian supervisor appeared to be Kagan, whereas Ellis appeared to be the most critical. A subsequent study by Nelson and Holloway (1990) extended the methodology beyond the case study approach to examine 15-minute segments of sessions of 40 supervisory dyads. Their findings supported the notion of the supervisor in relational control of the supervision sessions. This proved to be even more true when the supervisees were female; male and female supervisors delivered more high-power messages to female trainees and supported the female trainees' own high-power messages less often than they did those of male supervisees. This finding suggests that supervisors reflect the male-dominant culture, at least within the academic training environment.

Similar to the Penman scheme, the Strong, Hills, and Nelson (1988) rating scale measures interactional behavior along dimensions of status and affiliation, in a system based on Leary's (1957) circumplex model of behavior. Nelson et al. (1996) used this measure, along with qualitative analyses, to chart the interactions of four supervisory dyads in four supervision sessions during a semester. Consistent with prior studies, they found that all supervisors attempted to establish hierarchical relationships with their trainees and were successful in dominating the relationship to varying degrees. One supervisor, however, was unable to establish the complementary relationship of teacher-learner satisfactorily, and her female trainee contested her leadership, using a third more high-power, leading responses than the other trainees in the study. That this supervisee found the supervision somewhat unsatisfactory leads us to wonder whether it is important for both the supervisor and the supervisee that the supervisor be dominant, at least in relationships with beginning counselors.

Supervisor Intentions.   Subsequent studies of moment-by-moment interactions between supervisors and trainees focused on supervisor intentions and trainee reactions. The methodology of Hill and her colleagues (Hill, Helms, Spiegel, & Tichenor, 1988; Hill &

O'Grady, 1985) in the counseling process was adapted by Corbett and Hill (1991) for use in supervisory dyads. Strozier, Kivlighan, and Thoreson (1993) used supervisor intentions and trainee reactions to conduct an intensive case study of one supervision dyad throughout an academic semester. Sequential analyses and descriptive statistics were used to analyze the data. Results showed promise for the dilemma we posed in reaction to Holloway's (1982) study: How does a supervisor provoke intellectual and emotional work, defined as therapeutic work, on the part of the supervisee? The supervisor's intentions of explore, restructure, assess, and change led to supervisee reactions of therapeutic work. Whether this therapeutic work was demonstrated by supervisee verbalizations in session was not described. The issue of the impact of supervisor intentions on the internal emotional and cognitive responses of the trainee is not an inconsiderable one. If, as Rønnestad and Skovholt (1993) and Stoltenberg and Delworth (1987) have suggested, a primary task for supervisors is to provoke the professional development of the supervisee, then which supervisor activity leads to therapeutic work is important. A subsequent study might look beyond supervisor intentions to supervisor behavior in order to answer that question.

These moment-by-moment systems of coding interactions have yielded considerable information about which supervisor behaviors and intentions lead to which supervisee responses. The task of describing what goes on in supervision, as laid out by Holloway and Hosford (1983), has been handled effectively by these interactional studies. Whether there are relationships between such interactions and the therapist's behavior in counseling sessions or cogitation about cases remains to be seen.

Impact of Supervisor Behavior on Therapist Behavior.   In an effort to examine the effects of the supervisor's relationship with the therapist on the therapist's relationship with the client, several researchers have examined the existence of parallel process between the supervisory relationship and the psychotherapy relationship. Initially a psychoanalytic concept, parallel process was defined by McNeill and Worthen (1989, p. 330) as one in which "certain vestiges of the relationship between a supervisee and his or her client" appear in supervision and "certain vestiges of the supervisory relationship . . . manifest themselves in a reciprocal manner in the therapeutic setting."

Doehrman (1976) explored the links between the supervisor-therapist relationship and the therapist-patient relationship by interviewing two faculty supervisors, their four intern therapists, and in turn, their eight patients, in semi-structured interviews conducted after supervisory or therapy sessions. Qualitative and quantitative data indicated that therapists acted out their transference-countertransference from their supervisory relationships within their therapy relationship, either by mimicking the supervisory relationship or acting out its opposite.

Friedlander, Siegel, and Brenock (1989) extended the methodology from supervisor and trainee reports to direct observations of a single supervisory relationship and its attached psychotherapy relationship over eight sessions in 3 months. The supervisor's social role, interpersonal influence strategies, and strategies of self-presentation were largely repeated by the therapist in interaction with the client. It is difficult to determine from either of these studies whether the supervisor's behavior influenced the supervisee's counseling behavior more than the counselor's behavior influenced the supervisor's behavior in supervision, but one can speculate that the supervisor, who holds the relational control, is more likely to influence the course of events.

In order to prepare to conduct time-limited psychodynamic psychotherapy, experienced therapists in the Vanderbilt project (Henry, Butler, Strupp, Schacht, & Binder, 1993) participated in a year-long manual training program accompanied by supervision. Therapists increased their ability to perform the therapy but showed a slight decrement in relationship skills. Differences appeared between therapists trained by two different supervisors in their ability to perform the prescribed therapy with patients (Henry, Schacht, Strupp, Butler, & Binder, 1993). Therapists who adhered to the treatment protocols most thoroughly had a supervisor who presented therapists with specific learning tasks during each supervision session, stopped the tape regularly, and posed specific questions that often addressed the therapists' own thought processes, systematically reviewed core concepts, and spelled out precisely what the therapist had done and said that was desirable in the interaction. This is consistent with the finding that both supervisors and trainees prefer the supervisor to dominate supervision and, at least when providing supervision for new skills, structure it closely. Again, whether such moment-to-moment control leads to the long-term ability of the therapist to conceptualize about clients, accurately estimate the effects of their interventions on the client, and develop as a therapist is unknown. No empirical studies have shown a link between specific supervisor behaviors and client outcome (Holloway & Neufeldt, 1995). As Strupp (1986) suggested, so many client variables intervene between a systematic measurement of the supervisor's behavior and the outcome of psychotherapy for the client that such a link is difficult to make. Only with a circumscribed client population could this be adequately tested.

CONCLUSION

Within the framework proposed by Holloway and Hosford (1983), supervision research to date has done a credible job of describing what goes on in supervision, the task laid out for Phase 1. In the past 15 years, the research evolved from descriptions based on supervisor and supervisee report to microanalytic content analyses of supervision sessions. Quantitative and, to a much lesser extent, qualitative analyses have illuminated the nature of supervision. Reliable scales designed for supervision differentiate among supervisors on the basis of style and behavior. Observational measures adapted from other relational contexts clarify transactions between supervision participants. These measures of supervision process do provide potential variables for research on the relationships among them as well as between them and other variables of interest.

Research in Phase 2, however, is limited. Relationships between in-session variables, such as between supervisor high-power messages and supervisee low-power messages, have been established. Hypothesis-testing is limited however, to comparisons of transactions with behavior expected by chance. To this date, no researchers have systematically varied supervisor transactions in order to determine their effects on the supervisee's behavior or thinking as a therapist or on client outcome.

Several problems must be overcome in order to further the progress of research on supervisor variables. First, as Lambert and Arnold (1987) declared, supervision research is limited by the extent to which effective therapist behaviors have been identified. The progress in psychotherapy research and the advent of therapy manuals provide potential standards of therapist behavior.

Second, it is difficult to compare therapist behaviors across clients and even more difficult to compare therapy outcome across clients with differing presenting problems and diagnoses. The most promising possibility for outcome research on the effects of supervision on specific therapy transactions appears to be in the area of large-scale outcome studies of manualized treatments for specific diagnostic groups. In such a situation, supervision behaviors could be systematically varied and outcomes could be determined. The possibility that one approach, for instance, is effective in supervising therapists who provide cognitive-behavioral therapy and another more effective with psychodynamic therapists could be tested in a study that involved several supervisors with a large number of therapists who were trained by manual. Supervision of their ongoing therapy could be varied systematically. Because clients in such studies are chosen for their diagnostic similarity, client outcome could be examined as well. Current levels of research funding, however, may make such large-scale studies rare in the future.

How supervision affects the development of novice therapists into seasoned professionals has not been explored, despite the fact that a long-stated goal of supervisors has been to facilitate the development of their supervisees (Neufeldt, Iversen, & Juntunen, 1995; Neufeldt, Karno, & Nelson, 1996; Stoltenberg & Delworth, 1987). Two factors have made this a difficult area of research to pursue. First, such research is time consuming and expensive. Therapist development implies change in the ways therapists consistently behave with and think about clients. To get behavior samples and reported thoughts from therapists with several clients at several points in training is difficult. It is research probably best left to full professors who do not need to generate a number of discrete research studies for professional promotion.

Second, even if the data were collected, there are as yet no valid, reliable ways of relating therapist thoughts and behaviors to therapist development. If the effect of supervision on therapist development is to be explored, instruments must be advanced that relate these thoughts and behaviors to empirically defined models of therapist development, such as that presented by Skovholt and Rønnestad (1992). Until such measures are available, whether specific supervision strategies are more effective than others in provoking therapist development cannot be known.

REFERENCES

Allen, G. J., Szollos, S. J., & Williams, B. E. (1986). Doctoral students' comparative evaluations of best and worst psychotherapy supervision. *Professional Psychology: Research and Practice, 17*, 91–99.

Barak, A., & LaCrosse, M. B. (1975). Multidimensional perception of counselor behavior. *Journal of Counseling Psychology, 22*, 471–476.

Barrett-Lennard, G. T. (1962). Dimensions of therapist responses as a causal factor in therapeutic changes. *Psychological Monographs, 76* (43, Whole No. 562).

Beutler, L. E., Machado, P. P. P., & Neufeldt, S. A. (1994). Therapist variables. In A. E. Bergin & S. L. Garfield (Eds.), *Handbook of psychotherapy and behavior change* (3rd ed., pp. 229–269). New York: Wiley.

Blumberg, A. (1970). A system for analyzing supervisor-teacher interaction. In A. Simon & G. Boyer (Eds.), *Mirrors for behavior* (Vol. 3). Philadelphia: Research for Better Schools.

Bordin, E. S. (1979). The generalizability of the psychoanalytic concept of the working alliance. *Psychotherapy: Theory, Research, and Practice, 16*, 252–260.

Bordin, E. S. (1983). A working alliance model of supervision. *The Counseling Psychologist, 11*(1), 35–42.

Brown, M. T., & Landrum-Brown, J. (1995). Counselor supervision: Cross-cultural perspectives. In J. G. Ponterotto, J. M. Casas, L. A. Suzuki, & C. M. Alexander (Eds.), *Handbook of multicultural counseling* (pp. 263–286). Thousand Oaks, CA: Sage.

Carey, J. C., Williams, K. S., & Wells, M. (1988). Relationships between dimensions of supervisors' influence and counselor trainees' performance. *Counselor Education and Supervision, 28,* 130–139.

Carkhuff, R. R., & Berenson, B. G. (1967). *Beyond counseling and therapy.* New York: Holt, Rinehart and Winston.

Corbett, M. M., & Hill, C. E. (1991, August). *Participant perceptions of intentions, reactions, and outcome in supervision.* Paper presented at the annual meeting of the American Psychological Association, San Francisco.

Davidson, D. A., Christiansen, C. H., & Dillon, M. A. (1982). Personality process variables and their relationship to occupational therapy fieldwork performance. *The Occupational Therapy Journal of Research, 2,* 50–52.

Deming, A. L. (1980). Self-actualization level as a predictor of practicum supervisor effectiveness. *Journal of Counseling Psychology, 27,* 213–216.

Dodenhoff, J. T. (1981). Interpersonal attraction and direct-indirect supervisor influence as predictors of counselor trainee effectiveness. *Journal of Counseling Psychology, 28,* 47–52.

Doehrman, M. J. (1976). Parallel processes in supervision and psychotherapy. *Bulletin of the Menninger Clinic, 40,* 9–104.

Efstation, J. F., Patton, M. J., & Kardash, C. M. (1990). Measuring the working alliance in counselor supervision. *Journal of Counseling Psychology, 37,* 322–329.

Friedlander, M. L., Siegel, S. M., & Brenock, K. (1989). Parallel processes in counseling and supervision: A case study. *Journal of Counseling Psychology, 36,* 149–157.

Friedlander, M. L., & Ward, L. G. (1984). Development and validation of the Supervision Styles Inventory. *Journal of Counseling Psychology, 31,* 541–557.

Goodyear, R. K. (1982). *Psychotherapy supervision by major theorists* (Videotape series). Manhattan, KS: Instructional Media Center.

Guest, P. D., & Beutler, L. E. (1988). Impact of psychotherapy supervision on therapist orientation and values. *Journal of Consulting and Clinical Psychology, 56,* 653–658.

Handley, P. (1982). Relationship between supervisors' and trainees' cognitive styles and the supervision process. *Journal of Counseling Psychology, 29,* 508–515.

Henry, W. P., Butler, S. F., Strupp, H. H., Schacht, T. E., & Binder, J. L. (1993). Effects of training in time-limited dynamic psychotherapy: Changes in therapist behavior. *Journal of Consulting and Clinical Psychology, 61,* 434–440.

Henry, W. P., Schacht, T. E., Strupp, H. H., Butler, S. F., & Binder, J. L. (1993). Effects of training in time-limited dynamic psychotherapy: Mediators of therapists' responses to training. *Journal of Consulting and Clinical Psychology, 61,* 441–447.

Heppner, P. P., & Handley, P. G. (1981). A study of the interpersonal influence process in supervision. *Journal of Counseling Psychology, 28,* 437–444.

Heppner, P. P., & Handley, P. (1982). The relationship between supervisory behaviors and perceived supervisor expertness, attractiveness, or trustworthiness. *Counselor Education and Supervision, 22,* 37–46.

Heppner, P. P., Kivlighan, D. M., Jr., Burnett, J. W., Berry, T. R., Goedinghaus, M., Doxsee, D. J., Hendricks, F. M., Krull, L. A., Wright, G. E., Bellatin, A. M., Durham, R. J., Tharp, A., Kim, H., Brossart, D. F., Wang, L.-F., Witty, T. E., Kinder, M. H., Hertel, J. B., & Wallace, D. L. (1994). Dimensions that characterize supervisor interventions delivered in the context of live supervision of practicum counselors. *Journal of Counseling Psychology, 41,* 227–235.

Hester, L. R., Weitz, L. J., Anchor, K. N., & Roback, H. B. (1976). Supervisor attraction as a function of level of supervisor skillfulness and supervisees' perceived similarity. *Journal of Counseling Psychology, 23,* 254–258.

Hill, C. E., Helms, J. E., Spiegel, S. B., & Tichenor, V. (1988). Development of a system for categorizing client reactions to therapist interventions. *Journal of Counseling Psychology, 35,* 27–36.

Hill, C. E., & O'Grady, K. D. (1985). List of therapist intentions illustrated in a case study and with therapists of varying theoretical orientations. *Journal of Counseling Psychology, 32,* 3–22.

Hilton, D. B., Russell, R. K., & Salmi, S. W. (1995). The effects of supervisor's race and level of support on perceptions of supervision. *Journal of Counseling and Development, 73,* 559–563.

Holloway, E. L. (1982). Interactional structure of the supervision interview. *Journal of Counseling Psychology, 29,* 309–317.

Holloway, E. L., Freund, R. D., Gardner, S. L., Nelson, M. L., & Walker, B. R. (1989). Relation of power and involvement to theoretical orientation in supervision: An analysis of discourse. *Journal of Counseling Psychology, 36,* 88–102.

Holloway, E. L., & Hosford, R. E. (1983). Towards developing a prescriptive technology of counselor supervision. *The Counseling Psychologist, 11*(1), 73–77.

Holloway, E. L., & Neufeldt, S. A. (1995). Supervision: Its contributions to treatment efficacy. *Journal of Consulting and Clinical Psychology, 63,* 207–213.

Holloway, E. L., & Wolleat, P. L. (1981). Style differences of beginning supervisors: An interactional analysis. *Journal of Counseling Psychology, 28,* 373–376.

Hosford, R. E., & Barmann, B. (1983). A social-learning approach to supervision. *The Counseling Psychologist, 11*(1), 51–58.

Karr, J. T., & Geist, G. O. (1977). Facilitation in supervision as related to facilitation in therapy. *Counselor Education and Supervision, 16,* 263–268.

Krause, A. A., & Allen, G. J. (1988). Perceptions of counselor supervision: An examination of Stoltenberg's model from the perspectives of supervisor and supervisee. *Journal of Counseling Psychology, 35,* 77–80.

Lambert, M. J., & Arnold, R. C. (1987). Research and the supervisory process. *Professional Psychology: Research and Practice, 18,* 217–224.

Leary, T. (1957). *Interpersonal diagnosis of personality: A theory and a methodology for personality evaluation.* New York: Ronald Press.

Lichtenberg, J. W., & Goodyear, R. K. (1996). *The structure of supervisor-supervisee interactions.* ERIC: Resources in Education, ED. 387–759.

Marikis, D. A., Russell, R. K., & Dell, D. M. (1985). Effects of supervisor experience level on planning and in-session supervisor verbal behavior. *Journal of Counseling Psychology, 32,* 410–416.

Martin, J. S., Goodyear, R. K., & Newton, F. B. (1987). Clinical supervision: An intensive case study. *Professional Psychology: Research and Practice, 18,* 225–235.

McNeill, B. W., & Worthen, V. (1989). The parallel process in psychotherapy supervision. *Professional Psychology: Research and Practice, 20,* 329–333.

Myers-Briggs, I. (1962). *The Myers-Briggs Type Indicator.* Palo Alto, CA: Consulting Psychologists Press.

Myrick, R. D., & Kelly, F. J. (1971). A scale for evaluating practicum students in counseling and supervision. *Counselor Education and Supervision, 10,* 330–336.

Najavits, L. M., & Strupp, H. H. (1994). Differences in the effectiveness of psychodynamic therapists: A process-outcome study. *Psychotherapy, 31,* 114–123.

Nelson, G. L. (1978). Psychotherapy from a trainee's perspective: A survey of preferences. *Professional Psychology, 9,* 539–550.

Nelson, M. L., & Holloway, E. L. (1990). The relation of gender to power and involvement in supervision. *Journal of Counseling Psychology, 37,* 473–481.

Nelson, M. L., MacDonald, G., Blume, A., Coulon, A. E., Elliott, E., Rodriguez, J., & Milo M. (1996). *Development of four supervision relationships over time.* Submitted for publication.

Neufeldt, S. A., Iversen, J. N., & Juntunen, C. L. (1995). *Supervision strategies for the first practicum.* Alexandria, VA: American Counseling Association.

Neufeldt, S. A., Karno, M. P., & Nelson, M. L. (1996). A qualitative study of experts' conceptualization of supervisee reflectivity. *Journal of Counseling Psychology, 43,* 3–9.

Penman, S. R. (1980). *Communication processes and relationships.* London: Academic Press.

Pierce, R. M., & Schauble, P. G. (1970). Graduate training of facilitative counselors: The effects of individual supervision. *Journal of Counseling Psychology, 17,* 210–215.

Pierce, R. M., & Schauble, P. G. (1971). Follow-up study on the effects of individual supervision in graduate school training. *Journal of Counseling Psychology, 18*, 186–187.

Powell, D. J. (1991). Supervision: Profile of a clinical supervisor. *Alcoholism Treatment Quarterly, 8*, 69-86.

Putney, M. W., Worthington, E. L., & McCullough, M. E. (1992). Effects of supervisor and supervisee theoretical orientation and supervisor-supervisee matching on interns' perceptions of supervision. *Journal of Counseling Psychology, 39*, 258–265.

Robyak, J. T., Goodyear, R. K., & Prange, M. (1987). Effects of supervisors' sex, focus, and experience on preferences for interpersonal power bases. *Counselor Education and Supervision, 26*, 299–309.

Rogers, C. R. (1957). The necessary and sufficient conditions of therapeutic personality change. *Journal of Consulting Psychology, 21*, 95–103.

Rønnestad, M. H., & Skovholt, T. M. (1993). Supervision of beginning and advanced graduate students of counseling and psychotherapy. *Journal of Counseling and Development, 71*, 396–405.

Rosenblatt, A., & Mayer, J. (1975). Objectionable supervising styles: Student views. *Social Work, 20*, 184–189.

Rotholz, T., & Werk, A. (1984). Student supervision: An educational process. *The Clinical Supervisor, 2*, 15–27.

Russell, R. K., & Petrie, T. (1994). Issues in training effective supervisors. *Applied and Preventive Psychology, 3*, 27–42.

Savickas, M. L., Marquart, C. D., & Supinski, C. R. (1986). Effective supervision in groups. *Counselor Education and Supervision, 26*, 17–25.

Schacht, A. J., Howe, H. E., Jr., & Berman, J. J. (1989). Supervisor facilitative conditions and effectiveness as perceived by thinking- and feeling-type supervisees. *Psychotherapy, 26*, 475–483.

Schiavone, C. D., & Jessell, J. C. (1988). Influence of attributed expertness and gender in counselor supervision. *Counselor Education and Supervision, 28*, 29–42.

Shanfield, S. B., Matthews, K. L., & Hetherly, V. (1993). What do excellent psychotherapy supervisors do? *American Journal of Psychiatry, 150*, 1081–1084.

Shanfield, S. B., Mohl, P. C., Matthews, K. L., & Hetherly, V. (1989). A reliability assessment of the Psychotherapy Supervisory Inventory. *American Journal of Psychiatry, 146*, 1447–1450.

Shanfield, S. B., Mohl, P. C., Matthews, K. L., & Hetherly, V. (1992). Quantitative assessment of the behavior of psychotherapy supervisors. *American Journal of Psychiatry, 149*, 352–357.

Skovholt, T. M., & Rønnestad, M. H. (1992). *The evolving professional self: Stages and themes in therapist and counselor development.* Chichester, United Kingdom: Wiley.

Stoltenberg, C. D., & Delworth, U. (1987). *Supervising counselors and therapists: A developmental approach.* San Francisco: Jossey-Bass.

Stone, G. L. (1980). Effects of experience on supervisor planning. *Journal of Counseling Psychology, 27*, 84–88.

Strong, S. R. (1968). Counseling: An interpersonal influence process. *Journal of Counseling Psychology, 15*, 215–224.

Strong, S. R., Hills, H. I., & Nelson, B. N. (1988). *Interpersonal Communication Rating Scale.* Unpublished manuscript, Department of Psychology, Virginia Commonwealth University, Richmond, VA.

Strozier, A. L., Kivlighan, D. M., Jr., & Thoreson, R. W. (1993). Supervisor intentions, supervisee reactions, and helpfulness: A case study of the process of supervision. *Professional Psychology: Research and Practice, 24*, 13–19.

Strupp, H. H. (1986). Psychotherapy: Research, practice, and public policy: How to avoid dead ends. *American Psychologist, 41*, 120–130.

Sundblad, L. M. (1973). The relationship of commitment to supervisor level of functioning in rehabilitation counseling. *The Rehabilitation Counseling Bulletin, 16*, 131–136.

Wetchler, J. L. (1989). Supervisors' and supervisees' perceptions of the effectiveness of family therapy supervisor interpersonal skills. *The American Journal of Family Therapy, 17,* 244–256.

Worthington, E. L., Jr. (1984). Empirical investigation of supervision of counselors as they gain experience. *Journal of Counseling Psychology, 31,* 63–75.

Worthington, E. L., Jr. (1987). Changes in supervision as counselors and supervisors gain experience: A review. *Professional Psychology: Research and Practice, 18,* 189–208.

Worthington, E. L., Jr., & Roehlke, H. J. (1979). Effective supervision as perceived by beginning counselors-in-training. *Journal of Counseling Psychology, 26,* 64–73.

Zucker, P. J., & Worthington, E. L., Jr. (1986). Supervision of interns and postdoctoral applicants for licensure in university counseling centers. *Journal of Counseling Psychology, 33,* 87–89.

PART VI

Professional, Ethical, and Legal Issues

CHAPTER 27

Psychotherapy Supervision:
Prerequisites and Problems in the Process

PAUL RODENHAUSER
Tulane University School of Medicine

Effective psychotherapy supervision requires careful attention to innumerable factors. Perhaps the complexity of this instructional mode can be most readily appreciated from a comprehensive developmental perspective of the dynamics contributed by all participants in the supervisory triangle. At the least, this perspective must include simultaneous consideration of the supervisor's level of expertise both as a clinician and as an educator, the supervisee's knowledge base, prior experience, and openness to learning, as well as the patient's motivation, accessibility, and capacity for change.

Identifiable forms of psychotherapy numbered at least 250 in 1980, and in 1985 over 450 were reported (Herink, 1980; Karasu, 1986). In 1987, Beitman published *The Structure of Individual Psychotherapy,* which effectively collapsed the major schools of psychotherapy into three broad categories that he labeled psychodynamic, cognitive-behavioral, and existential-humanistic approaches to psychotherapy. Furthermore, Beitman postulated common stages through which patients progress in the process of individual psychotherapy regardless of the category into which the form of psychotherapy fits. Thus, a patient-centered developmental perspective emerged. Whereas most of the literature on psychotherapy has focused on the patient, most of the literature on instruction in psychotherapy has focused on the supervisee, particularly the supervisee's developmental stages. One of the earliest models and the one most applicable across mental health disciplines was described by Ralph (1980). Until recently, when several articles appeared almost simultaneously (Rodenhauser, 1994; Russell & Petrie, 1994; Watkins, 1993, 1995), supervisor development has received little attention. The earliest of the models of supervisor development reviewed by Russell and Petrie (1994) dates back to 1983 (Alonso, 1983).

Supervision is one of the four major modes of instruction employed in clinical educational settings; however, its use in psychiatric education, that is, for instruction in psychotherapy, is, unfortunately, neither well conceptualized nor reasonably systematic. Although it is advisable that educators be able to define supervision as a distinct instructional mode, knowing how psychotherapy supervision differs from lectures, tutorials, and small group instruction will provide supervisors and supervisees with a clearer sense of its purpose and characteristics. The distinguishing characteristics of these clinical instructional modes have been contrasted and compared by Rudisill, Painter, and Rodenhauser (1988). Bedside teaching, which is sometimes considered a distinct instructional mode in clinical settings, and problem-based learning, the newest method of instruction in medical education, utilize a combination of approaches. As such, they are not readily confused with psychotherapy supervision; however, arguments could be made for similarities between problem-based learning, which closely resembles the tutorial model, and psychotherapy supervision, particularly in groups. The characteristics of psychotherapy supervision that set it apart from the other instructional modes differ in terms of group size, information flow, task emphasis, resources, instructor posture, and learner attitude. Table 27.1 summarizes these characteristics for all four major modes of clinical instruction in psychiatric education and distinguishes one from the other. To further complicate matters, psychotherapy supervision involves a variety of models, methods, styles, and strategies that sometimes require clarification to ensure their conformity with the definition of this instructional mode (Rodenhauser, 1994). These models, methods, styles, and strategies are described subsequently.

Unless the emphasis is primarily on the supervisee's countertransference, as in one of the three major models of psychotherapy supervision described by Thorbeck (1992), the information flow in psychotherapy supervision depends much more on the patient's contributions than it does in other instructional modes. The flow of information and the relationships involved in the supervisory process can be readily visualized in the supervisory triangle displayed in Figure 27.1. This diagram also serves as a basis for dynamic considerations such as parallel process and transference-countertransference issues discussed later in this chapter. The model that focuses on the supervisee's countertransference is also the model that most closely resembles psychotherapy. With regard to all models of psychotherapy supervision, however, it is prudent for supervisors to maintain a clear distinction between supervision and psychotherapy. Although opinions about combining the two have always varied, as theoretical underpinnings of dynamic psychotherapy have moved away from adherence to strict psychoanalytic theory, the trend in supervision has been toward a clearer separation of psychotherapy supervision and psychotherapy. This is

Table 27.1   Characteristics of Major Modes of Clinical Instruction

	Lecture	Tutorial	Small Group	Clinical Supervision
Group Size	Greater than 12 (unlimited)	1-4 people	6-12 people	1-6 people
Information Flow	Instructor to participants	Interactive (emphasis on participant)	Interactive	Patient-participant-instructor
Task Emphasis	To impart *information*	To promote acquisition of *knowledge* through enhancement of content-seeking behavior	To reinforce *attitudes* and content learning by also focusing on process learning	To develop dynamic and therapeutic *skills* through mutual understanding of content and process
Resources	Instructor	Learner	Group	Patient
Instructor Attitude	Directive	Coaching	Facilitative	Reflective
Participant Attitude	Receptive	Searching	Sharing	Open

From Rodenhauser, P. (1994). Toward a multi-dimensional model for psychotherapy supervision based on developmental stages. *Journal of Psychotherapy Practice and Research, 3,* 1–15. Reproduced with permission.

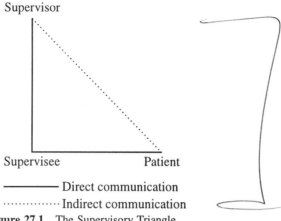

Supervisor

Supervisee   Patient

———— Direct communication

············ Indirect communication

Figure 27.1   The Supervisory Triangle

From Rodenhauser, P. (1994). Toward a multi-dimensional model for psychotherapy supervision based on developmental stages. *Journal of Psychotherapy Practice and Research, 3*, 1–15. Reproduced with permission.

not to say that counseling skills are not necessary in the process of supervision to facilitate the possibility of treatment for supervisees with obvious characterologic or other problems manifested in the process of adapting to the demands of providing effective psychotherapy (Trachtman, 1985). For some supervisees, as they recognize their level of function and limitations as psychotherapists and measure these against a newly formulated ego ideal, the process of involvement in psychotherapy supervision can be disturbing. It is generally believed, however, that psychotherapy supervision and psychotherapy should remain distinctly separate modalities and that recommendations for supervisees to pursue psychotherapy should be addressed administratively (Yager, 1982). Psychotherapy supervision, therefore, is distinguishable from a number of other interpersonal exchanges of an educational nature. It is neither a lecture, a small-group discussion, a tutorial, a problem-based learning session, nor psychotherapy.

The task of psychotherapy supervision is to develop psychotherapeutic skills through the supervisor's and the supervisee's understanding of both the content and process of psychotherapy. In the case of psychodynamic psychotherapy, this entails an understanding of elements such as defense mechanisms; resistances; transference and countertransference; and the instrumental role of the therapist's own thoughts, emotions, and behaviors. It also requires an understanding of stages such as engagement in the therapeutic process, the search for patterns, effecting change in perceptions and behaviors, and keeping the termination process therapeutic (Greben, 1979). Although the supervisor's posture might be best characterized as primarily reflective, and the primary task to be skill development, transmittal of knowledge about psychotherapy, consultation on clinical problems or questions, and assistance with development of attitudes essential for a psychotherapist (Greben, 1979) are additional tasks of the supervisory process.

Schein (1983) developed a list of topics important in teaching the application of psychoanalytic theory to psychotherapy:

(1) How to arrive at a dynamic formulation and what to do with it; (2) differences between manifest and latent content; (3) how to elicit and work with dreams and fantasies; (4) the meaning of fees and time; (5) the importance of interruptions such as therapist's vacations and holidays; (6) the use of different types of interventions—clarification, confrontation, and inter-

pretation; (7) seeing interpretations as informed guesses which may or may not be validated; (8) the importance of the beginnings and endings of sessions; and, (9) learning to listen to each session as a separate unit but also as part of an ongoing process. (p. 7)

Although directors of residency education in psychiatry have identified psychotherapy as one of the most difficult skills to teach (Rodenhauser, 1992), the dynamic formulation seems to be one of several particularly difficult concepts for supervisees to master. Models and examples of psychodynamic formulations have been aptly described by Perry, Cooper, and Michels (1987), although the literature offers many studies and examples (McDougall & Read, 1993; Melchiode, 1988; Weersaekera, 1993). More troublesome than the notion of difficulty with mastery of certain concepts in psychotherapy is the observation by Buckley, Conte, Plutchik, Karasu, and Wild (1982) that for many trainees, psychotherapy skills do not change over time. Significant changes were discovered in use of clarification and confrontation, the management of resistance, awareness of positive transference, and abilities to tolerate seductiveness (Buckley et al., 1982). Tolerance of regression, capacity for empathy, and awareness of countertransference issues did not change over time, however. Although Melchiode (1991) proposed that cultivating the use of empathy is a developmental stage in teaching psychodynamic psychotherapy, he also acknowledged that some trainees cannot make this step. These observations and the documented characteristics that distinguish more from less skilled psychotherapy trainees (Buckley et al., 1981) suggest the wisdom of applying criteria for entry into psychotherapy training programs based on trainee attributes that enable the process of psychotherapy supervision. These have been identified by psychotherapy supervisors and discussed by this author and colleagues (Rodenhauser, Rudisill, & Painter, 1989).

In addition to psychodynamic psychotherapy, other models such as cognitive, behavioral, family, and group therapies are commonly incorporated into the curricula of training programs. Irrespective of the form of psychotherapy to be learned, however, there are fundamental principles applicable to the instructional process for which supervisors are responsible. With regard to the beginnings of the supervisory relationship, an assessment of the supervisee's background and level of competency is essential. A discussion of the supervisor's and supervisee's mutual expectations of the process is equally important (Chessick, 1971). Insofar as ongoing performance in supervision is concerned, supervisee comfort and supervisee responsibility are paramount concerns. Support is necessary to facilitate an atmosphere of openness, as are guidance and assistance with the therapeutic process as it rests in the hands of the supervisee. Evaluation, which is one of the most difficult procedures for supervisors—particularly new supervisors—but also for supervisees, is critical to the learning involved in psychotherapy supervision. It must be continuous and involve the supervisee's opinion, ongoing supervisor feedback, and a plan for corrective learning.

The basic characteristics and principles of psychotherapy supervision described here provide the infrastructure for the discussions that follow. Although recognizing that readers of this book and this chapter will have a wide variety of backgrounds, interests, and degrees of expertise in one or more forms of psychotherapy, clarity of information necessitates that choices be made on which to base communication. Supervision of psychodynamic psychotherapy from the perspective of post-graduate education in psychiatry is, therefore, the orientation of this chapter. This chapter is geared to provide the reader with the conceptual tools necessary to provide effective psychodynamic psychotherapy supervision and an understanding of the issues, problems, and concerns surrounding the process of psychotherapy supervision at this point in the evolution of psychiatric treatment.

Because the current climate in which the treatment of psychiatric disorders is carried out affects instruction significantly, this element will be considered early in the chapter. If the characteristics and principles already described serve as a platform for what follows, then the climate might be likened to the sociocultural situation in which the supervisory process takes place. Within these contexts, this chapter considers and enlarges on various aspects of psychotherapy supervision, including (a) what basic conceptual tools and information psychotherapy supervisors need; (b) what communication and other elements are conducive to optimum learning in psychotherapy supervision; (c) what trouble spots exist for the supervisor, the supervisee, the patient, the supervisory triangle, and the instructional system as a whole; and (d) what constitutes desirable education for the supervisor.

THE CURRENT CLIMATE OF PSYCHOTHERAPY

Changes in the delivery of mental health services brought about by the burgeoning knowledge base in biological psychiatry have been endangering psychotherapy education and practice. Not only have recent scientific, social, political, and economic factors negatively influenced the role of psychotherapy in patient care, but this trend has also progressed to minimize—or in some cases even to disavow—the possibility of psychosocial etiologies in psychiatric disorders. The idea of "a chemical imbalance" has caught the attention of clinicians and the general public. Attempts to explain the existence of a neurochemical or neurophysiologic dysfunction on the basis of environmental influences are likewise available in the lay press (Wright, 1995), but these ideas have failed to attract attention away from the concept that supports interest in a quick fix. The newest medications are so effective and their effects are so well known that designing one's own personality is a currently popular notion (Begley, Rosenberg, & Ramo, 1994; Seiver, 1994).

In defense of its effectiveness and desirability (Elkin et al., 1989; Smith, Glass, & Miller, 1980), considerable attention has been devoted in the past decade not only to the preservation of psychotherapy as a distinct form of treatment, but also to the need for strengthening instruction in psychotherapy in training programs (Gabbard, 1992; Mohl et al., 1990). Many compelling arguments for enhanced, systematic education in psychodynamic psychotherapy have emerged in the context of universal demands for effectiveness and efficiency in health care (Krupnick & Pincus, 1992; Rodenhauser & Greenblatt, 1989), an increasing number of self-help groups (Lewis, 1991), constraints on health-care education and practice produced by managed care (Blackwell & Schmidt, 1992), an increasing array of effective psychotropic medications, and the increasing need to understand and utilize the complex psychology of psychopharmacology in mental health care delivery (Gutheil, 1982).

Despite these developments and the challenges they offer the various mental health care disciplines and their educational systems, the renewed interest in standards for education in psychotherapy for psychiatrists (Mohl et al., 1990; Tasman, 1993) has not had its counterpart in the development of standards for education in psychotherapy supervision (Rodenhauser, 1996). Apparently, the last set of American Psychiatric Association standards for supervisors was published in 1957 (Fleming & Benedek, 1983). In the field of counselor education and supervision, however, Borders et al. (1991) have developed a curriculum guide for training counseling supervisors as well as standards for their preparation and practice. The guide is organized on the basis of seven core curriculum areas and contains specific learning objectives clustered according to the three "threads" emphasized in each of the standards for effective supervisors: (a) self-awareness, (b) theoretical and conceptual knowledge, and (c) skills and techniques. Standards for counseling supervisors (Dye & Borders, 1990) contain 11 core areas of knowledge, competencies, and personal traits that serve as recommendations for training and professional activities.

In psychiatry, the basic qualification for serving as a psychotherapy supervisor continues to be one's own experience as a psychotherapy supervisee. At the same time, trainee experience in psychotherapy is changing qualitatively and quantitatively as exposures to short- and long-term psychotherapy cases—particularly long-term intensive psychotherapy cases (Altshuler, 1990)—is diminishing (MacDonald, 1992; Wallerstein, 1991). As scientific, social, political, and economic factors continue to influence the landscape of health care and as the numbers, characteristics, distribution, and proportions of various providers change, competition for psychiatric patients will increase. The national initiative to significantly increase the number of physician-generalists from 35% to 50% of the physician workforce will significantly augment the ranks of practitioners who currently treat a sizable proportion of the population seeking mental health care (Narrow, Regier, Rae, Manderscheid, & Locke, 1993). Patients with psychiatric problems are not now being referred by managed care organizations to psychiatrists or Ph.D. psychologists, but rather they are managed by primary-care physicians. The expansion of the primary care physician workforce will impact the education and practice of all mental health care providers.

Considering the known superior benefits of combined psychotherapy and psychopharmacotherapy for many psychiatric disorders (Elkin et al., 1989), psychiatrists and their patients might benefit from state-of-the-art paradigms for teaching the integration of psychotherapy and psychopharmacotherapy, whereas psychologists, psychiatric social workers, psychiatric nurse practitioners, and mental health counselors might benefit from educational emphasis on the communication and therapeutic skills required to optimize treatment in a therapeutic triangle involving a prescribing physician, particularly one with limited training in psychiatry.

CONCEPTUAL TOOLS FOR PSYCHOTHERAPY SUPERVISORS

In his view of the psychotherapy supervision literature, Albott (1984, p. 27) discovered "considerable agreement in terms of basic assumptions." These included the premise that supervision is essential for psychotherapy skill development, that it is a "teaching" procedure, and that the generally understood goal is the learning of psychotherapy. Other assumptions that have guided the nature and direction of supervision include the beliefs that (a) supervisory skills are derived from a combination of having been supervised and having some clinical practice experience, and (b) that models and theories of psychotherapy are sufficient bases for understanding how supervisees learn (Albott, 1984). The literature of psychotherapy supervision is now sufficient not only to challenge the latter two beliefs but also to provide theoretical structures on which to base research (Watkins, 1995).

Clinical knowledge and expertise, a consolidated professional identity, and enthusiasm for teaching are prerequisites for effective psychotherapy supervision. Foreknowledge of the problems usually encountered in the transition from supervisee to supervisor would be extremely beneficial for neophyte supervisors. Granet, Kalman, and Sacks (1980) characterize these as problems with inexperience, competition, identity, and administration matters. New supervisors are not only usually inexperienced clinically, they frequently have no exposure to instructional methodology regarding the supervisory process. Therefore, and also because of the usual closeness in age, there is a tendency for them to feel competitive with supervisees. This process might be enhanced by a supervisor's feelings of inadequacy and uncertainty about his or her identity, for example, perceiving himself/herself to be an advanced trainee rather than a junior faculty member. Administrative issues such as evaluations are particularly difficult for all of the reasons given. New supervisors might be particularly reluctant to submit negative evaluations. Insofar as supervisor inexperience is concerned, both clinically and pedagogically, the structure derived from systematic perspectives such as Beitman's (1987) reductionistic views of individual psychotherapy might be particularly helpful as a focus within the supervisory relationship. The structure of psychotherapy can be reduced to the aforementioned four elementary patient-centered stages: engagement, pattern search, change, and termination (Beitman, 1987).

Not only can the stages of a patient's progress through the process of psychotherapy be categorized, so also can the developmental stages of supervisees and supervisors (Rodenhauser, 1994). Ralph's (1980) theory of supervisee development has significant implications for both the therapeutic relationship between the patient and the supervisee as well as the educational relationship between the supervisee and the supervisor. Inspired in part, also, by the patient's expectations, most trainees in the beginning stages of their development as therapists are inclined to want to fix the problems presented by the patient. This is reinforced by the patient's tendency to want to be fixed. For psychiatric residents, there is a distinct carryover of the medical model into the psychotherapeutic relationship. As a result of additional learning and plenty of frustration, trainees soon adopt a theoretical basis for their work. While fitting the patients' problems into their chosen model of psychotherapy, they drop "pearls of wisdom" as the process unfolds. A supervisee of mine once shared considerable pride in his discovery that he could be himself in the psychotherapy hour. This revelation announced his readiness for the transition to the next stage in which neophyte psychotherapists become aware of the relationship aspects of psychotherapy, the complexities of transference and countertransference, and their effects. Movement into the final stage in the development of a psychotherapist results from increasing abilities to use awareness of personal thoughts and feelings as instruments in the process. This is accompanied by an awareness of one's limitations and sometimes one's need for personal work.

The stages of supervisor development can also be characterized as a four-step process, ranging from unconscious identification with and/or unconscious emulation of one's former supervisors through a personal search for concepts, then also learning, as the supervisee learns regarding psychotherapy, that psychotherapy supervision is a relationship, and, finally, consolidating knowledge and experience into a predictable and workable instructional model (Rodenhauser, 1994). Table 27.2 summarizes stages of development for all three participants in the supervisory triangle.

Psychotherapy supervisors are apparently limited, generally, in their skill diversity and flexibility across a variety of forms of psychotherapy from both theoretical and practical perspectives (Rodenhauser, 1992), and their tendency to polarize into psychotherapy versus psychopharmacotherapy camps also creates difficulties for supervisees, most of whom require assistance in integrating the combination dynamically (Gutheil, 1982). Figure 27.2 illustrates a simplistic view of some dynamic factors involved in the combination of psychotherapy and psychopharmacotherapy. Whereas the interactions between the psychiatrist/psychotherapist and the patient are based on the therapeutic and working alliances (Beitman, 1987; Gutheil, 1982), the introduction of psychopharmacotherapy significantly

Table 27.2   Stages of Development Among Participants in the Supervisory Triangle

	Supervisor Developmental Stages	Supervisee Developmental Stages	Patient Developmental Stages
Stage I	Emulation	Restoration	Engagement
Stage II	Conceptualization	Interpretation	Pattern Search
Stage III	Incorporation	Realization	Change
Stage IV	Consolidation	Instrumentation	Termination

Note: Patient development stages adapted from Beitman, B. D. (1987). *The structure of individual psychotherapy.* New York: Guilford Press.

influences those alliances by creating shifts in transference-countertransference, autonomy-control, and therapeutic emphases. Gutheil (1982) described the tendency among many psychiatrists to be subject to a "mind-brain barrier" and a "delusion of precision" when resorting to prescribing. In the practice of modern psychiatry, the ability to combine psychotherapy and psychopharmacotherapy effectively and to integrate their dynamic implications into a unified approach to treatment is a critical skill (Krull, 1990). It is equally important for nonprescribing psychotherapists to appreciate not only the psychology of psychopharmacology, but also the dynamics of the therapeutic triangle. This is particularly important when the prescribing physician might suffer from behavior similar to that of a "split-brain preparation" (Group for the Advancement of Psychiatry, 1975).

Other limiting factors include supervisor comfort, flexibility, and creativity in using var-

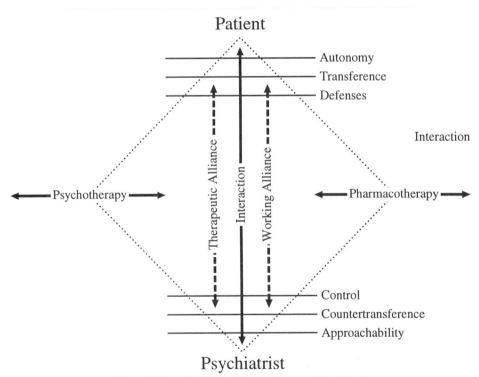

Figure 27.2   Psychology/Psychopharmacology Model

ious approaches within the framework of psychotherapy supervision as an instructional mode. Although on the one hand it is said that psychotherapy supervision embodies characteristics distinctly different from the other major modes of clinical instruction in psychiatric education, there are, on the other hand, strategies within psychotherapy supervision that augment its flexibility as a teaching mode. Administrative, instructional, consultative, and interactive strategies are available to supervisees depending on the supervisee's learning needs and the supervisory focus, which might be (a) patient evaluation and initial treatment planning, (b) treatment implementation and ongoing evaluation, (c) professional and/or organizational factors, or (d) personal factors. Table 27.3 demonstrates the relationships between strategies in supervision and supervisory foci while providing brief examples of the various strategies. Bernard's (1979) discriminational model for supervision lends itself to a 3 × 3 grid crossing functions of supervision (process skills, conceptualization skills, and personalization skills) with basic supervisor roles (teachers, counselors, consultants).

In addition to the requisite skills and flexibility necessary to meet the tasks of instruction, psychotherapy supervisors are required to abide by and instill knowledge of the legal and ethical issues applicable to the practice of psychotherapy and psychotherapy supervision (Cavenar, Rhoads, & Sullivan, 1980; Pope, 1990; Russell & Petrie, 1994; Tanenbaum & Berman, 1990). Illegal or unethical conduct could occur in either arena and could be encouraged by parallel process (Deering, 1994; Doeherman, 1976) or parallel process in reverse (Springmann, 1989).

Supervisors need to be able not only to understand the theoretical and appreciate the actual vicissitudes of transference and countertransference in the cases being discussed, they also need to continuously consider the possibilities of parallel process in their work with supervisees, that is, be sensitive to the likelihood that the supervisee's relationship with the supervisor will be qualitatively similar to the patient's relationship with the supervisee-therapist. Just as the patient, therefore, indirectly has an impact on the supervisor, the reverse can occur. The supervisee's experience in his or her relationship with the supervisor can be played out in the therapeutic relationship. Although there are reports of analysands' transferences (Luber, 1991) and fantasies (Myers, 1991) about a candidate's supervisor, a candidate's dreams of her patient (Robertson & Yack, 1993), and supervisees' dreams regarding the supervisory process (Olsson, 1991), there are no explicit reports of a similar nature relating to supervisors' participation in the process. Salvendy (1993), however, does address supervisors' countertransference reactions to their supervisees.

COMMUNICATION AND OTHER ENABLERS
OF OPTIMUM LEARNING

In addition to clinical expertise, a consolidated professional identity, enthusiasm for teaching, and knowledge of the tools available for psychotherapy supervision, effective supervisors need to have well-developed communication skills. A thorough assessment of the supervisee's knowledge base and prior experience as a psychotherapist, as outlined in the principles of psychotherapy supervision, should include the development of a learning contract between supervisor and supervisee. Disappointments between supervisor and supervisee stem particularly from unexplored assumptions about supervisee's background knowledge and experience (Chessick, 1971).

Although unexplored assumptions can explain dysfunctional regression in the supervisory process, some regression in psychotherapy supervision is considered to be functional.

Table 27.3 Strategies in Psychotherapy Supervision

	Administration	Instruction	Consultative	Interactive
Assessment and Treatment Planning	Describing institutional requirements for accreditation or payor agencies	Discussing indications and contraindications for treatment approaches	Suggesting a clinical intervention with supportive reasons	Exploring supervisee experience, skills, and comfort with them
Implementation, Intervention, Ongoing Evaluation	Requiring that treatment plans be checked by supervisor before implementation	Providing examples of transference/countertransference, defense mechanisms	Commenting on therapist/patient relationship	Comparing aspects of supervisor/supervisee therapeutic relationship
Professional/ Organizational Factors	Explaining documentation and record-keeping requirements	Sharing legal and ethical guidelines relevant to discipline in practice	Reflecting on supervisee concerns about professional development and identity	Exploring possible resistances in the process of supervision
Personal Factors	Making a decision about advisability of continuing a therapy relationship	Discussing the impact of personal differences on psychotherapy	Eliciting supervisee's perceptions of cultural differences and suggesting methods of exploration	Exploring transference/countertransference in supervisory relationship

The supervisory task of distinguishing between dysfunctional regression and regression in the service of the learning process is a difficult one. The primary source of functional regression is based on the stress of intensive long-term work with patients and the dynamics derived from alternately observing and identifying with the patient (Arlow, 1963). Ultimately, this process results in identification with the supervisor (Drucker, Klass, & Strizich, 1978) at least on a theoretical basis and facilitates in the supervisee a consolidation of skills developed as a result of the association. This phenomenon is dynamically interrelated to the concepts of parallel process (Doeherman, 1976) and transference and countertransference (Book, 1987) and the process involving the supervisee's separation-individuation from the supervisor (Watkins, 1990).

The supervisory triangle is multidimensional. It contains a plethora of conscious and unconscious components among the relationships; the latter components (transference and countertransference) are influential in both direct relationships, that is, between supervisor-supervisee and supervisee-patient, and in the usually indirect relationship between supervisor and patient (see Figure 27.1). As implied previously, it is important that supervisors appreciate another dimension, the developmental stages of *all* members of the supervisory triangle (see Table 27.2), including their own, and factor this information into a dynamic understanding of the supervisory process (Rodenhauser, 1994). Psychotherapy supervision would benefit from supervisor appreciation of the process in terms not unlike a dynamic formulation of a patient's presentation, but one in which the supervisor participates. A schematic multidimensional representation of possible combinations of developmental stages of the members of the supervisory triangle is depicted in Figure 27.3.

Studies indicate that the supervisor's intuition and facility regarding two-way communication is as important as the ability to actively teach (Shanfield, Matthews, & Hetherly, 1993). Excellent supervisors are also known to track supervisee's concerns and to remain specific to the material presented (Kline, Goin, & Zimmerman, 1977; Shanfield et al., 1993). Excellent psychotherapy supervisors are also able to give meaningful feedback in the context of the cases discussed. Feedback in medical education is an ongoing process involving an alliance between teacher and learner. It is qualitatively different from evaluation (Ende, 1983). In the context of control and power in supervision, Salvendy (1993) addresses many of the issues involved in the supervisory communication process, including supervisee vulnerability and sensitivity to supervisor feedback and the inherent need for support. Negative supervisor characteristics have also been reported and discussed (Allen, Szollos, & Williams, 1986; Rosenblatt & Mayer, 1975).

Differences in status, gender, race, ethnic background, religion, and lifestyle between supervisor and supervisee and/or supervisee and patient (Rubin, 1989; Salvendy, 1993) usually require explicit attention in the supervisory and therapeutic relationships as do resistances to the supervisory and therapeutic processes. Tension derived from these dynamics can possibly be the cause or effect of regression and can otherwise be played out in the arenas of parallel process and/or transference/countertransference. The ability to exchange information effectively within the supervisory relationship (Hassenfeld & Sarris, 1978) depends, in part, on the supervisee's capacity to avoid defensive warding off of information, a confining characteristic described by Szecsoky (1990) in his study of the psychotherapy supervision learning process.

Not having nearly as much control over their work in psychotherapy as do supervisors, for example, supervisees suffer from a variety of affronts to their narcissism. The unusual nature of psychotherapeutic relationships and supervisory relationships can be understandably discomforting to developing psychotherapists. Furthermore, there seems to be

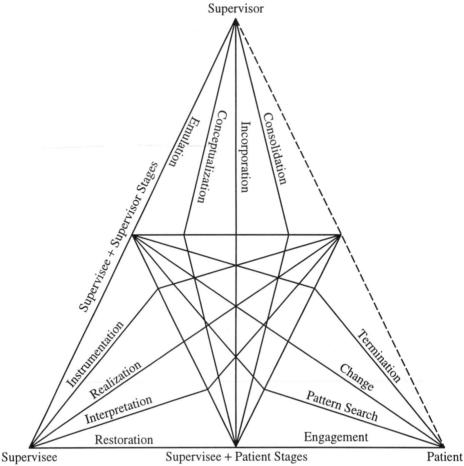

Figure 27.3   Possible Developmental Stage Combinations in the Supervisory Triangle

a tendency to first blame the supervisee if there are problems in the process. Compared to the assessments of psychotherapy supervisor qualities considered by supervisees to be most desirable (Kline et al., 1977; Shanfield et al., 1993), the literature regarding attributes of supervisees conducive to learning in psychotherapy supervision is more limited. Yager (1982) described desirable supervisee attitudes and characteristics, and a study conducted by Rodenhauser et al. (1989) revealed interesting impressions from groups of psychotherapy supervisors of desirable supervisee attributes. At the top of the lists into which responses naturally clustered were characteristics such as psychological mindedness, motivation, initiative, interpersonal curiosity, flexibility, intellectual openness, minimal defensiveness, and a capacity for introspection (Rodenhauser et al., 1989).

TROUBLE SPOTS IN PSYCHOTHERAPY SUPERVISION

In this chapter, several problems with the "institution" of psychotherapy supervision have been identified. While recognizing that the ramifications of these problems are far-reaching, only the core issues of some of the most obvious problems are addressed herein.

- *Uniform standards for training in psychotherapy have not been established* (Tasman, 1993). Advocates for uniform standards for psychotherapy training struggle with numerous controversies, including "whether the model curriculum should be designed so that every psychiatric resident would achieve a full level of competence as a psychodynamic psychotherapist" (Mohl et al., 1990, p. 13). Mohl et al. proposed a model curriculum for minimum training in psychodynamic psychotherapy that would allow graduates to become at least "psychodynamically informed psychiatrists."

- *Social, political, and economic pressures are rapidly changing the configuration and accessibility of psychotherapy—particularly the availability of long-term psychotherapy.* Therefore, the breadth and depth of education that can be derived from experience with various forms of psychotherapy while in psychotherapy supervision might suffer. The shifts toward biological psychiatry have inspired strong arguments for the preservation of a psychodynamic perspective (Gabbard, 1992), and educational programs have considered an integrationist approach in their curriculum designs (Verhulst, 1991).

- *Standards for competency to provide psychodynamic psychotherapy supervision have not been developed.* Anyone interested in teaching might be asked to be a supervisor. The most common qualification for serving as a psychotherapy supervisor is one's own experience as a supervisee (Rodenhauser, 1996; Watkins, 1992). Watkins (1992) noted that supervision skills are often not considered in selecting new psychologists whose roles will involve supervision as a primary responsibility. Some supervisors are possibly more interested in the benefits of a teaching appointment than in imparting knowledge and skills (Rodenhauser, 1992). It is not common practice for supervisors to consult with one another, review the literature on supervision independently, or attend courses on supervision.

- *There is no generally accepted theoretical model of supervision.* Within given models, such as the educational, "treatment," and parallel process models outlined by Thorbeck (1992), there is wide variability regarding implementation and application. Watkins (1995) has suggested a moratorium on theoretical formulations and research into a selected few.

- *Many supervisors lack skill diversity and flexibility with a variety of theories and practices of psychotherapy.* Advances in the practice and definition of a supervisor have not kept pace with recent quantitative changes in psychiatric skills (Langsley & Yager, 1988). Care must be taken in the selection of supervisors in order to satisfy the supervisee's learning goals. It has been demonstrated that patient progress benefits from congruence between supervisor's and supervisee's theoretical orientation (Steinhelber, Patterson, Cliffe, & LeGoullon, 1984). The capability among supervisors to help the supervisee to integrate psychopharmacology with psychotherapy is also a skill apparently in short supply. Availability of suitable supervisors is a problem in psychiatry (Rodenhauser, 1992).

- *Supervision of psychotherapy supervisors is uncommon.* Supervisor excellence seems to be assumed on the basis of supervisee evaluations exclusively. Supervisor groups for purposes of education and monitoring their performance is the method of supervising supervisors most frequently reported (Rodenhauser, 1992); however, others have been recommended, including written reports and supervisory session attendance by an objective observer (Wallerstein, 1981).

- *Personal and professional boundaries are often violated in the process of psychotherapy supervision.* The tendency to confuse psychotherapy supervision with psychotherapy creates a variety of possible problems for the supervisee (Glass, 1986; Spiegel & Gruenbaum, 1977). There are strong arguments for making recommendations for psychotherapy the responsibility of program administration (Yager, 1982). There are also strong arguments against personal long-term psychotherapy for psychotherapy trainees (Dubovsky & Scully, 1990). Other boundary violations in psychotherapy supervision have taken the form of sexual improprieties (Salvendy, 1993) or other abuses, including overinvolvement in case management and other forms of undermining a supervisee's confidence (Rosenblatt & Mayer, 1975).

• *Courses and seminars for psychotherapy supervisors are at a premium.* Although successful models for educational sessions at the program level have been described in some detail, meetings of psychotherapy supervisors for their own ongoing education are uncommon in academic settings. Courses and workshops on psychotherapy supervision are not readily available or accessible.

DESIRABLE EDUCATION FOR THE SUPERVISOR

Another assumption about psychotherapy supervision described by Albott (1984) involves the belief that one will automatically imitate the "best" of a variety of psychotherapy supervisors exposed to in the course of learning psychotherapy. Not only does this belief raise questions about the existence of a "best" supervisor, it suggests that the imitation is a conscious process (Albott, 1984). Indeed, scholars in psychiatric education (Arlow, 1963; Drucker et al., 1978) postulate that supervisee identification with the supervisor is the product of regression in the supervisory relationship enhanced by conducting long-term intensive psychotherapy. Although this theory pertains to the supervisee's identity as a psychotherapist, it is reasonable to assume that identification with other functions would occur as well. Given the present-day premium on training in intensive long-term psychotherapy, however, conscious but tentative imitation might be the likely recourse in the absence of additional instruction in how to provide psychotherapy supervision.

Participation in educational programs on instructional methodology is a sine qua non for psychotherapy supervisors. Approaches to supervision can take many forms, and the literature describes a variety of models, methods, styles, and strategies. Models of psychotherapy supervision fit into the three categories described previously: the educational model, the "treatment" model, and the parallel process model (Thorbeck, 1992). Methods of supervision refer to the mechanism or vehicle mainly responsible for conveyance of the material on which supervision is based. These methods include process notes, videotapes, audiotapes, or direct observation. Shanfield and Gil (1985) characterized styles of supervision as facilitative, confrontative-directive, expert, or task-oriented. Strategies for supervision have been described previously. Although models, methods, styles, or strategies vary from program to program, from supervisor to supervisor, and from session to session, only through supervisor education can the quality of the process be enhanced.

Studies of supervisee perceptions suggest that experience as a psychotherapy supervisor in itself, beyond that which is necessary for the establishment of a foundation from which to provide satisfactory supervision, does not translate into better quality or more effective supervision (Russell & Petrie, 1994). It is strongly recommended that all new supervisors participate in a series of sessions designed to orient and expose them to the basic knowledge previously outlined. Many aspects of the supervisor-supervisee relationship, that is, the supervisory process, need to be understood as well as do content elements. Recent recommendations for supervisor training by Russell and Petrie (1994) include formal didactic and experiential components. Critical elements of the recommended didactic component are: theoretical models of supervision, supervision research, and ethical and professional issues (Russell & Petrie, 1994). Responsibility for encouraging supervisor education, initial and ongoing, whether locally, regionally, or nationally based, resides within the educational program. Several models of instruction for psychotherapy supervisors have been described (Frayn, 1991; Morgan, Hamilton, & Harris, 1984; Rodenhauser, Painter, & Rudisill, 1985; Swiller & Davis, 1992).

Because the most available forum for supervisor education exists within the program responsible for instruction in psychotherapy, regularly scheduled ongoing seminars for psychotherapy supervisors within programs are highly recommended. Frayn (1991) considers the wisdom of separate agendas for inexperienced and seasoned supervisors. Seminars can be organized on the basis of discussions of cases or topics from the literature. The appendix to this chapter lists topics relevant to proficiencies for psychotherapy supervisors and relates references for use by supervisor groups or as individual readings. Although additional references are scattered throughout this chapter, neither source is exhaustive. The observation that literature searches will uncover almost as many perspectives on psychotherapy supervision as there are authors is perhaps beneficial to the ongoing educational process and professional development of supervisors. Although, on the one hand, this same pluralism of perspectives is symptomatic of the complexities involved in understanding and carrying out effective psychotherapy supervision, it is also emblematic of the many challenges involved in further defining and refining the process.

REFERENCES

Albott, W. L. (1984). Supervisory characteristics and other sources of supervision variance. In R. P. Archer & T. H. Peake (Eds.), *Clinical training in psychotherapy* (pp. 27–35). Binghamton, NY: Haworth.

Allen, G. J., Szollos, S. J., & Williams, B. E. (1986). Doctoral students' comparative evaluations of best and worst psychotherapy supervision. *Professional Psychology: Research and Practice, 17,* 91–99.

Alonso, A. (1983). A developmental theory of psycho-dynamic supervision. *The Clinical Supervisor, 1,* 23–26.

Altshuler, K. Z. (1990). Whatever happened to intensive psychotherapy? *American Journal of Psychiatry, 147,* 428–430.

Arlow, J. (1963). The supervisory situation. *Journal of the American Psychoanalytic Association, 11,* 576–596.

Begley, S., Rosenberg, D., & Ramo, J. C. (1994, February 7). One makes you feel larger, and one makes you small. *Newsweek,* pp. 37–40.

Beitman, B. D. (1987). *The structure of individual psychotherapy.* New York: Guilford.

Bernard, J. (1979). Supervision training: A discrimination model. *Counselor Education and Supervision, 19,* 60–68.

Blackwell, B., & Schmidt, G. L. (1992). The educational implications of managed mental health care. *Hospital & Community Psychiatry, 43*(10), 962–964.

Book, H. E. (1987). The resident's countertransference: Approaching an avoided topic. *American Journal of Psychotherapy, 41,* 555–562.

Borders, L. D., Bernard, J. M., Dye, H. A., Fong, M. L., Henderson, P., & Nance, D. W. (1991). Curriculum guide for training counseling supervisors "rational development and implementation." *Counselor Education and Supervision, 31,* 58–80.

Buckley, P., Conte, H., Plutchik R., & Karasu, T. B. (1981). Psychotherapy skill profiles of psychiatric residents. *Journal of Nervous and Mental Disease, 169,* 733–737.

Buckley, P., Conte, H., Plutchik, R., Karasu, T. B. & Wild, K. V. (1982). Learning dynamic psychotherapy: A longitudinal study. *American Journal of Psychiatry, 139,* 1607–1610.

Cavenar, J. O., Rhoads, E. J., & Sullivan, J. L. (1980). Ethical and legal aspects of supervision. *Bulletin of the Menninger Clinic, 44,* 15–22.

Chessick, R. D. (1971). How the resident and supervisor disappoint each other. *American Journal of Psychotherapy, 25,* 272–283.

Deering, C. G. (1994). Parallel process in the supervision of child psychotherapy. *American Journal of Psychotherapy, 48,* 102–110.

Doeherman, M. J. G. (1976). Parallel processes in supervision and psychotherapy. *Bulletin of the Menninger Clinic, 40,* 1–104.

Drucker, J. J., Klass, D. B., & Strizich, M. (1978). Supervision and the professional development of the psychiatric resident. *American Journal of Psychiatry, 135,* 1516–1519.

Dubovsky, S. L., & Scully, J. H. (1990). Hazards of long-term psychotherapy during psychiatric residency. *Psychiatry, 53,* 185–199.

Dye, H. A., & Borders, L. D. (1990). Counseling supervisors: Standards for preparation in practice. *Journal of Counseling & Development, 69,* 27–32.

Elkin, I., Shea, T., Watkins, J. T., Imber, S. D., Sotsky, S. M., Collins, J. F., Glass, D. R., Pilkonis, P. A., Leber, W. R., Docherty, J. P., Fiester, S. J., & Parloff, M. B. (1989). National Institute of Mental Health Treatment of Depression Collaborative Research Program: General effectiveness of treatments. *Archives of General Psychiatry, 46,* 971–982.

Ende, J. (1983). Feedback in clinical medical education. *Journal of the American Medical Association, 250,* 777–781.

Fleming, J., & Benedek, T. F. (1983). *Psychoanalytic supervision: A method of clinical teaching.* New York: International Universities Press.

Frayn, D. (1991). Supervision of the supervisors: The evolution of a psychotherapy supervisors' group. *American Journal of Psychotherapy, 45,* 31–42.

Gabbard, G. (1992). Psychodynamic psychiatry in the "decade of the brain." *American Journal of Psychiatry, 149,* 991–998.

Glass, J. (1986). Personal therapy and the student therapist. *Canadian Journal of Psychiatry, 31,* 304–312.

Granet, R. B., Kalman, T. P., & Sacks, M. H. (1980). From supervisee to supervisor: An unexplored aspect of the psychiatrist's education. *American Journal of Psychiatry, 137,* 1443–1446.

Greben, S. E. (1979). The influence of the supervision of psychotherapy upon being therapeutic: II. Modes of influence of the supervisory relationship. *Canadian Journal of Psychiatry, 24,* 507–513.

Group for the Advancement of Psychiatry Committee on Research. (1975). Pharmacotherapy and psychotherapy: Paradoxes, problems and progress. *GAP Report, 9.* New York: Brunner/Mazel.

Gutheil, T. G. (1982). The psychology of pharmacology. *Bulletin of the Menninger Clinic, 46,* 321–330.

Hassenfeld, I. N., & Sarris, J. G. (1978). Hazards and horizons of psychotherapy supervision. *American Journal of Psychotherapy, 32,* 393–401.

Herink, R. (1980). *The psychotherapy handbook: The A to Z guide to more than 250 different therapies in use today.* New York: New American Library (Meridian).

Karasu, T. B. (1986). Psychotherapies: Benefits and limitations. *American Journal of Psychotherapy, 40,* 324–342.

Kline, F., Goin, M. K., & Zimmerman, W. (1977). You can be a better supervisor. *The Journal of Psychiatric Education, 1,* 174–179.

Krull, F. (1990). The problem of integrating biological and psychodynamic views in psychotherapeutic training of physicians. *Psychotherapy and Psychosomatics, 53,* 115–118.

Krupnick, J. L., & Pincus, H. A. (1992). The cost-effectiveness of psychotherapy: A plan for research. *American Journal of Psychiatry, 149,* 1295–1305.

Langsley, D. G., & Yager, J. (1988). The definition of a psychiatrist: Eight years later. *American Journal of Psychiatry, 145,* 469–475.

Lewis, J. M. (1991). Thirty years of teaching psychotherapy skills. *International Journal of Group Psychotherapy, 41,* 419–432.

Luber, M. P. (1991). A patient's transference to the analyst's supervisor: Effect of the setting on the analytic process. *Journal of the American Psychoanalytic Association, 39,* 705–725.

MacDonald, D. (1992). Trends in the teaching of analytically oriented psychiatry and psychotherapy. *Academic Psychiatry, 16,* 83–89.

McDougall, G. M., & Read, B. (1993). Teaching biopsychosocial integration and formulation. *Canadian Journal of Psychiatry, 38,* 359–362.

Melchiode, G. A. (1988). The psychodynamic formulation: How and why. *General Hospital Psychiatry, 10,* 41–45.

Melchiode, G. (1991). On teaching today's residents psychoanalytic concepts. *Journal of the American Academy of Psychoanalysis, 19,* 648–659.

Mohl, P., Lomax, J., Tasman, A., Chan, C., Slege, W., Summergrad, P., & Notman, M. (1990). Psychotherapy training for the psychiatrist of the future. *American Journal of Psychiatry, 147,* 7–13.

Morgan, D., Hamilton, C., & Harris, L. (1984). Enhancing supervision of psychotherapy. *Southern Medical Journal, 77,* 1406–1409.

Myers, W. A. (1991). Survey concerning the frequency of fantasies about the supervisor in candidate analysis. *Journal of the American Psychoanalytic Association, 39,* 578–580.

Narrow, W. E., Regier, D. A., Rae, D. S., Manderscheid, R. W., & Locke, V. Z. (1993). Use of services by persons with mental and addictive disorders. *Archives of General Psychiatry, 50,* 95–107.

Olsson, G. (1991). The supervisory process reflected in dreams of supervisees. *American Journal of Psychotherapy, 45,* 511–526.

Perry, S., Cooper, A. M., & Michels, R. (1987). The psychodynamic formulation: Its purpose, structure, and clinical application. *American Journal of Psychiatry, 144,* 543–550.

Pope, G. G. (1990). Abuse of psychotherapy: Psychotherapist-patient intimacy. *Psychotherapy and Psychosomatics, 53,* 191–198.

Ralph, N. B. (1980). Learning psychotherapy: A developmental perspective. *Psychiatry, 43,* 243–250.

Robertson, B. M., & Yack, M. E. (1993). A candidate dreams of her patient: A report and some observations on the supervisory process. *International Journal of Psychoanalysis, 74,* 993–1003.

Rodenhauser, P. (1992). Psychiatry residency programs: Trends in psychotherapy supervision. *American Journal of Psychotherapy, 46,* 240–249.

Rodenhauser, P. (1994). Toward a multidimensional model for psychotherapy supervision based on developmental stages. *Journal of Psychotherapy Practice and Research, 3,* 1–15.

Rodenhauser, P. (1996). On the future of psychotherapy supervision and psychiatry. *Academic Psychiatry, 20,* 82–91.

Rodenhauser, P., & Greenblatt, M. G. (1989). Transformation in mental health system management: An overview. *Psychiatric Annals, 19,* 408–411.

Rodenhauser, P., Painter, A. F., & Rudisill, J. R. (1985). Supervising supervisors: A series of workshops. *The Journal of Psychiatric Education, 9,* 217–224.

Rodenhauser, P., Rudisill, J. R., & Painter, A. F. (1989). Attributes conducive to learning psychotherapy supervision. *American Journal of Psychotherapy, 43,* 368–377.

Rosenblatt, A., & Mayer J. (1975). Objectionable supervising styles: Students' views. *Social Work, 18,* 184–189.

Rubin, S. (1989). Choice points in psychotherapy supervision: On experiences of supervisors in supervision. *Clinical Supervisor, 7,* 24–41.

Rudisill, J. R., Painter, A. F., & Rodenhauser, P. (1988). Clinical teaching modes: A usage guide. *The Clinical Supervisor, 6,* 3–19.

Russell, R. K., & Petrie, T. (1994). Issues in training effective supervisors. *Applied & Preventive Psychology, 3,* 27–42.

Salvendy, J. T. (1993). Control and power in supervision. *International Journal of Group Psychotherapy, 43,* 363–376.

Schein, J. W. (1983). Supervision. *Psychiatric Residents Newsletter of the APA, 3*(1).

Seiver, L. J. (1994, January/February). The frontiers of pharmacology. *Psychology Today,* pp. 40–44, 70, 72, 85.

Shanfield, S. B., & Gil, D. (1985). Styles of psychotherapy supervision. *Journal of Psychiatric Education, 9,* 225–232.

Shanfield, S.B., Matthews, K. L., & Hetherly, V. (1993). What do excellent psychotherapy supervisors do? *American Journal of Psychiatry, 150,* 1081–1084.

Smith, M., Glass, G., & Miller, T. (1980). *The benefits of psychotherapy.* Baltimore: Johns Hopkins University Press.

Spiegel, D., & Gruenbaum, H. (1977). Training versus treating the psychiatric resident. *American Journal of Psychotherapy, 31,* 618–625.

Springmann, R. R. (1989). Reflection on the role of the supervisor. *British Journal of Medical Psychology, 62,* 217–228.

Steinhelber, J., Patterson, W., Cliffe, E. K., & LeGoullon, M. (1984). An investigation of some relationships between psychotherapy supervision and patient change. *Journal of Clinical Psychology, 40,* 1346–1353.

Swiller, H. I., & Davis, K. L. (1992). Continuing education in psychotherapy as a method to attract and involve voluntary faculty in an academic department of psychiatry. *Academic Psychiatry, 16,* 186–191.

Szecsoky, I. (1990). Supervision: A didactic or mutative situation. *Psychoanalytic Psychotherapy, 4,* 245–261.

Tanenbaum, R. L., & Berman, M. A. (1990). Ethical and legal issues in psychotherapy supervision. *Psychotherapy in Private Practice, 8,* 65–98.

Tasman, A. (1993). Setting standards for psychotherapy training: It's time to do our homework. *Journal of Psychotherapy Practice and Research, 2*(2), 93–96.

Thorbeck, J. (1992). The development of the psychodynamic psychotherapist in supervision. *Academic Psychiatry, 16,* 72–82.

Trachtman, R. (1985). Addressing the therapist's characterological problems in supervision. *Issues of Ego Psychology, 8,* 63–66.

Verhulst, J. (1991). The psychotherapy curriculum in the age of biological psychiatry. *Academic Psychiatry, 15,* 120–131.

Wallerstein, R. S. (1981). *Becoming a psychoanalyst: A study of psychoanalytic supervision.* New York: International Universities Press.

Wallerstein, R. S. (1991). The future of psychotherapy. *Bulletin of the Menninger Clinic, 55,* 421–443.

Watkins, C. E., Jr. (1990). The separation-individuation process in psychotherapy supervision. *Psychotherapy, 27,* 202–209.

Watkins, C. E., Jr. (1992). Reflections on the preparation of psychotherapy supervisors. *Journal of Clinical Psychology, 47,* 145–147.

Watkins, C. E., Jr. (1993). Development of the psychotherapy supervisor: Concepts, assumptions, and hypotheses of the supervisor complexity model. *American Journal of Psychotherapy, 47,* 58–74.

Watkins, C. E., Jr. (1995). Psychotherapy supervisor development: On musings, models, and metaphor. *The Journal of Psychotherapy Practice and Research, 4,* 150–158.

Weersaekera, R. (1993). Formulation: A multiperspective model. *Canadian Journal of Psychotherapy, 38,* 351–358.

Wright, R. (1995, March 13). The biology of violence. *New Yorker,* pp. 68–77.

Yager, J. (1982). Supervising psychiatric residents for eclectic practice. In J. Yager (Ed.), *Teaching behavioral sciences* (pp. 133–149). Orlando, FL: Grune and Stratton.

APPENDIX

Proficiencies for Psychodynamic Psychotherapy Supervisors

I. Prerequisites
  A. Clinical knowledge and experience
  B. A consolidated professional identity
  C. Enthusiasm for teaching
  D. Awareness of supervisee to supervisor transition issues

  Rodenhauser, P. (1995). Experiences and issues in the professional development of psychiatrists for supervising psychotherapy. *The Clinical Supervisor, 13,* 7–22.

  Granet, R. B., Kalman, T. P., & Sacks, M. H. (1980). From supervisee to supervisor: An unexpolored aspect of the psychiatrist's education. *American Journal of Psychiatry, 137,* 1443–1446.

II. Factors Primarily Related to Theoretical and Clinical Expertise
  A. Theoretical bases of psychotherapies

  Beitman B. D. (1987). *The structure of individual psychotherapy.* New York: Guilford.
  B. The psychology of psychopharmacology

  Chalfin, R. M., & Altieri, J. (1991). Supervised treatment of an obsessional patient by a psychiatric resident utilizing psychotherapy and pharmacotherapy. *American Journal of Psychotherapy, 45,* 43–52.

  Gutheil, T. G. (1982). The psychology of pharmacology. *Bulletin of the Menninger Clinic, 46,* 321–330.

  Karasu, T. B. (1982). Psychotherapy and pharmacotherapy: Toward an integrative model. *American Journal of Psychiatry, 139,* 1102-1103.

  Krull, F. (1990). The problem of integrating biological and psychodynamic views in psychotherapeutic training of physicians. *Psychotherapy and Psychosomatics, 53,* 115–118.
  C. Legal/ethical principles

  Cavenar, J. O., Rhoads, E. J., & Sullivan, J. L. (1980). Ethical and legal aspects of supervision. *Bulletin of the Menninger Clinic, 44,* 15–22.

  Pope, G. G. (1990). Abuse of psychotherapy: Psychotherapist-patient intimacy. *Psychotherapy and Psychosomatics, 53,* 191–198.
  D. Counseling skills for troubled supervisees

  Dubovksy, S. L., & Scully, J. H. (1990). Hazards of long-term psychotherapy during psychiatric residency. *Psychiatry, 53,* 185–199.

  Glass, J. (1986). Personal therapy and the student therapist. *Canadian Journal of Psychiatry, 31,* 304–312.

  Spiegel, D., & Grunebaum, H. (1977). Training versus treating the psychiatric resident. *American Journal of Psychotherapy, 31,* 618–625.

  Trachtman, R. (1985). Addressing the therapist's characterological problems in supervision. *Issues in Ego Psychology, 8,* 63–66.

III. Factors Primarily Related to Communication Skills
  A. Contracting for learning

  Chessick, R. D. (1971). How the resident and supervisor disappoint each other. *American Journal of Psychotherapy, 25,* 272–283.
  B. Exchanging information

  Hassenfeld, I. N., & Sarris, J. G. (1978). Hazards and horizons of psychotherapy supervision. *American Journal of Psychotherapy, 32,* 393–401.
  C. Commenting appropriately

  Kline, F., Goin, M. K., Zimmerman, W. (1977). You can be a better supervisor. *The Journal of Psychiatric Education, 1,* 174–179.

D. Tracking residents' concerns

Shanfield, S. B., Matthew, K. L., & Hetherly, V. (1993). What do excellent psychotherapy supervisors do? *American Journal of Psychiatry, 150,* 1081–1084.

E. Active teaching

Perez, E. L., Krul, L. E., & Kapoor, R. (1984). The teaching of psychotherapy in Canadian psychiatry residency programs: Residents' perceptions. *Canadian Journal of Psychiatry, 29,* 658–664.

F. Monitoring progress

Cobb, J. P., & Lieberman, S. (1987). The grammar of psychotherapy: A descriptive account. *British Journal of Psychiatry, 151,* 589–594.

G. Giving meaningful feedback

Ende, J. (1983). Feedback in clinical medical education. *Journal of the American Medical Association, 250,* 777–781.

IV. Factors Primarily Related to Supervisory Relationships/Dynamics

A. Avoiding disappointments

Chessick, R. D. (1971). How the resident and supervisor disappoint each other. *American Journal of Psychotherapy, 25,* 272–283.

B. Monitoring regressions

Arlow, J. (1963). The supervisory situation. *Journal of the American Psychoanalytic Association, 11,* 576–594.

Drucker, J. J., Klass, D. B., & Strizich, M. (1978). Supervision and the professional development of the psychiatric resident. *American Journal of Psychiatry, 135,* 1516–1519.

C. Utilizing parallel process

Baudry, F D. (1993). The personal dimension and management of the supervison situation with a special note on the parallel process. *Psychoanalytic Quarterly, 62,* 588–614.

Doeherman, M. J. G. (1976). Parallel processes in supervision and psychotherapy. *Bulletin of the Menninger Clinic, 40,* 1–104.

McNeill, B. W., & Worthen, V. (1989). The parallel process in psychotherapy supervision. *Professional Psychology: Research and Practice, 20,* 329–333.

Phillips, G. L., & Kanter, C. N. (1984). Mutuality in psychotherapy supervision. *Psychotherapy, 21,* 178–183.

Springman, R. R., (1989) Reflection on the role of the supervisor. *British Journal of Medical Psychology, 62,* 217–228.

D. Understanding transference/countertransference

Book, H. E. (1987). The resident's countertransference: Approaching an avoided topic. *American Journal of Psychotherapy, 41,* 555–562.

Haldipur, C. V., Dewan, M., & Beal, M. (1982). On fear in the countertransference. *American Journal of Psychotherapy, 26,* 240–247.

E. Addressing mental mechanisms of defense

F. Appreciating differences in culture, race, gender, lifestyle

Davidson, L. (1987). Supervision of psychotherapy East and West. *American Journal of Psychoanalysis, 47,* 230–236.

Mendel, D. (1986). Cross-gender supervision of cross-gender therapy: female supervisor, male candidate, female patient. *American Journal of Psychoanalysis, 46,* 270–275.

Oliver, N., & Fingas, W. (1986). The teaching of psychotherapy to foreign medical graduate residents in psychiatry. *Psychiatric Journal of the University of Ottawa, 11,* 223–227.

Peterson, F. K. (1991). Issues of race and ethnicity in supervision: Emphasizing who you are, not what you know. In T. H. Peake & J. Ball (Eds.), *Psychotherapy training: Contextual and developmental influences in settings, stages, and mind sets.* (pp. 15–31). Binghamton, NY: Haworth.

Remington, G., & DaCosta, G. (1989). Ethnocultural factors in resident supervision: Black supervisor and white supervisees. *American Journal of Psychotherapy, 63,* 398–404.

G. Reducing resistance/difficult supervisee (or patient)

Greben, S. E. (1985). Dear Brutus: Dealing with unresponsiveness through supervision. *Canadian Journal of Psychiatry, 30,* 48–53.

Rubin, S. S. (1989). At the border of supervision: Critical moments in psychotherapists' development. *American Journal of Psychotherapy, 63,* 387–397.

H. Conceptualizing developmental stages

1. Supervisor

Watkins, C. E., Jr. (1993). Development of the psychotherapy supervisor: Concepts, assumptions, and hypothesis of the supervisory complexity model. *American Journal of Psychotherapy, 47,* 58–74.

2. Supervisee

Altshuler, K. Z. (1989). Common mistakes made by beginning psychotherapists. *Academic Psychiatry 1989, 13,* 73–80.

Hess, A. K, (1987). Psychotherapy, supervision: Stages, Buber, and the theory of relationship. *Professional Psychology, 18,* 251–259.

Ralph, N. B. (1980). Learning psychotherapy: A developmental perspective. *Psychiatry, 43,* 243–250.

3. Supervisor, supervisee, and patient

Rodenhauser, P. (1994). Toward a multidimensional model for psychotherapy supervision based on developmental stages. *Journal of Psychotherapy Practice and Research, 3,* 1–15.

I. Appreciating interpersonal interactions

Greben, S. E. (1991). Interpersonal aspects of the supervision of individual psychotherapy. *American Journal of Psychotherapy, 45,* 306–316.

J. Facilitating the separation-individuation process

Watkins, C. E., Jr. (1990). The separation-individuation process in psychotherapy supervision. *Psychotherapy, 27,* 202–209.

V. Factors Primarily Related to Educational Technology

A. Major modes of clinical instruction

1. Characteristics of psychotherapy supervision

Albott, W. L. (1984). Supervisory characteristics and other sources of supervision variance. In R. P. Archer & T. H. Peak (Eds.), *Clinical training in psychotherapy* (pp. 27–36). Binghamton, NY: Haworth.

2. Characteristics of lectures, tutorials, small group instruction

Rudisill, J. R., Painter, A. F., & Rodenhauser, P. (1988). Clinical teaching modes: A usage guide. *Clinical Supervisor, 6,* 3–19.

3. Principles of psychotherapy supervision

Rudisill, J. R., Painter, A. F., & Rodenhauser, P. (1988). Clinical teaching modes: A usage guide. *Clinical Supervisor, 6,* 3–19.

B. Models of psychotherapy supervision

1. Educational model
2. "Treatment" model
3. Parallel process model

Thorbeck, J. (1992). The development of the psychodynamic psychotherapist in supervision. *Academic Psychiatry, 16,* 72–82.

Yager, J. (Ed.) (1982). Supervising psychiatric residents for eclectic practice. In J. Yager (Ed.), *Teaching psychiatry and behavioral sciences.* New York: Grune and Stratton.

C. Methods of psychotherapy supervision

1. Process notes

Silberman, E. K., & Mazza, D. (1985). Supervision of the psychotherapeutic process. *Archives of General Psychiatry, 42,* 739–740.

   2. Videotape

     Brown, E. (1990). Problems in the use of videorecordings in training for psychotherapy. *Psychotherapy and Psychosomatics, 53,* 139–141.

     Goldberg, D. (1983). Resistance to the use of video in individual psvchotherapy training. *American Journal of Psychiatry, 140,* 1172–1176.

   3. Audiotape

   4. Direct observation

     Betcher, R. W., & Zinber, N. E. (1988). Supervision and privacy in psychotherapy training. *American Journal of Psychiatry, 145,* 796–803.

     Boylston, W. H., & Tuma, J. M. (1972). Training of mental health professional, through the use of the "bug in the ear." *American Journal of Psychiatry, 129,* 124–127.

     Klitzke, M. J., & Lombardo, T. W. (1991). A "bug-in-the-eye" can be better than a "bug-in-the-ear." *Behavioral Modification, 15,* 113–117.

D. Styles of psychotherapy supervision

   1. Faciliatative

   2. Confrontative/directive

   3. Expert

   4. Task oriented

     Shanfield, S. B., & Gil, D. (1985). Styles of psychotherapy supervision. *Journal of Psychiatric Education, 9,* 225–232.

E. Documentation requirements

   1. Supervision

     Bridge, P., & Bascue, L. O. (1990). Documentation of psychotherapy supervision. *Psychotherapy in Private Practice, 8,* 79–85.

   2. Psychotherapy

     Albeck. J. H., & Goldman, C. (1991). Patient-therapist codocumentation: Implications of jointly authored progress notes for psychotherapy practice, research, training, supervision, and risk management. *American Journal of Psychotherapy, 45,* 317–334.

F. Organizational/departmental requirements

G. Evaluation methodology

     Chevron, E. S., & Rounsaville, B. J. (1983). Evaluating the clinical skills of psychotherapists: A comparison of techniques. *Archives of General Psychiatry, 40,* 1129–1132.

     Jones, S. H., Krasner, R. F., & Howard, K. I. (1992). Components of supervisors' ratings of therapists' skillfulness. *Academic Psychiatry, 16,* 29–36.

     Liston, E. H., Yager, J., & Strauss, G. D. (1981). Assessment of psychotherapy skills: The problem of interrater agreement. *American Journal of Psychiatry, 138,* 1069–1074.

     Silberman, E. K., & Mazza, D. (1985). Supervision of the psychotherapeutic process. *Archives of General Psychiatry, 42,* 739–740.

     Steinhelber, J., Patterson, V., Cliffe, K., & LeGoullon, M. (1984). An investigation of some relationships between psychotherapy supervision and patient change. *Journal of Clinical Psychology, 40,* 1346–1353.

From Rodenhausen, P. (1996). On the future of psychotherapy supervision in psychiatry. *Academic Psychiatry, 20.* Reproduced with permission.

CHAPTER 28

Gender and Psychotherapy Supervision: The Partnership Model

CARLTON E. MUNSON
University of Maryland at Baltimore

This chapter deals with the role of gender in psychotherapy supervision. Issues in supervision of practitioners using an integrated partnership perspective are explored, as well as how supervisors can assist the practitioner to apply this perspective in practice. The model is based on the structural units of societal, professional/agency, supervisory, and client system. The concept of a partnership model is used to craft a more effective perspective that reconceptualizes the traditional model of supervision through interrelating the structures.

Gender issues have not been the focus of research or theoretical writing in the historical evolution of psychotherapy supervision. Recent attention to gender differences in various aspects of functioning (Elson, 1986; Flax, 1990; Tannen, 1990) and psychotherapy practice (Howard, 1986; Lewis, 1989; Rosewater & Walker, 1985; Rothblum & Cole, 1991) have given rise to literature that focuses on gender and supervision, especially communication issues and patterns (Atkins, 1994; Conn, 1993; Hartman & Brieger, 1992; Leighton, 1991; Munson, 1986; Powell, 1993).

The psychotherapy professions are evolving to females being in the majority, but the literature has not been consistent with this evolution. For example, in the field of clinical social work, which is made up of the largest professional group delivering psychotherapy services in the United States, supervision books have been historically written by females; however, with the significant decline of males in the clinical social work profession over the last 40 years, the more recent supervision texts have been written by males. There are several reasons for this change, but most likely it reflects the modern tendency of women to remain in practice positions, while men gravitate to administrative and academic positions. Changes in enrollment patterns in graduate programs suggest that this pattern is reversing, and women are becoming the majority in practice, administrative, and academic positions.

The primary professions providing psychotherapy services in the United States are clinical social workers, psychologists, and psychiatrists. The three disciplines will be referred to in unison as the psychotherapy professions. Research has demonstrated no significant differences in the three professions with respect to clinical supervision (Smith-Harrison, 1981). The psychotherapy professions have become increasingly female since the 1970s. In 1975, 60% of professional social workers, 27% of psychologists, and 12% of psychiatrists were female. By 1994, 83% of professional social workers, 44% of psychologists, and 28% of psychiatrists were female. No reliable statistics exist regarding the percentage of female supervisors. These trends indicate that the pool of available professionally trained practitioners will increasingly be female (Philipson, 1994). This has implications for supervision, which is the focus of discussion in this chapter.

BACKGROUND

From the beginning of the psychotherapy professions in the 1800s to the mid-1970s, most of the major works on supervision were written by men except in social work, where the reverse was true. This male dominance has led to a male stereotype of the supervisory relationships. Psychiatry, psychology, and social work have historically engaged in little exploration of the roles of males and females in supervision. In one of the first studies of males in supervision, Kadushin (1976) found that only 21% viewed being supervised by a female as a problem, but 37% preferred to be supervised by a male. Kadushin considered the movement of males toward administration in part as an attempt to resolve the concerns associated with being supervised by a female. He concluded that his findings supported previous speculation that males resist subordination to women. Chafetz (1972) summarized this orientation in an extreme fashion by stating, "In short, no one seems to want a woman boss!" (p. 14). In contrast to Kadushin's finding, another early study (Munson, 1979) found that males supervising males produced the lowest level of positive outcomes and satisfaction with supervision. In a study of supervision that compared race and gender differences, males were found to be less supportive, more undermining, and more critical (Jayaratne et al., 1992).

If these attitudes and behaviors persist, then supervisors and supervisees need to alter their beliefs and practices to enhance the supervisory process. In supervision, it has been pointed out that helping supervisees gain knowledge involves processes different from those required to change attitudes (Pettes, 1979). Acquiring knowledge and changing attitudes are fundamental in dealing with gender issues in supervision. Changing attitudes in large measure is dependent on acquisition of knowledge. Through use of facts, concepts, theories, and guidelines, the conditions for developing positive attitudes toward supervision based on gender can be explored.

Although feminist literature in sociology, political science, and psychology has been evolving for centuries (Schneir, 1992) and has increased dramatically during the last three decades (Schneir, 1994), psychotherapists have produced limited literature on feminist practice and even less literature on feminist-oriented psychotherapy supervision. Practitioners have criticized educational programs for not preparing them for practice related to women and changing roles (Goodrich, Rampage, Ellman, & Halstead, 1988; Kaplan, 1985). A modern supervision model must take into account the significant changes that have occurred in gender relations and gender balance in the psychotherapy professions. A feminist model of psychotherapy supervision can contribute to a more effective and balanced model of modern supervision practice.

A feminist perspective of supervision requires a knowledge and attitude paradigm shift that takes into account client need, agency function, and practitioner preferences. Much of psychotherapy knowledge has been historically compatible with modern feminist theory, but it has not been framed in such a context that would permit comprehensive application in practice. What has been lacking is specific guidelines for practice application. Supervision/consultation practice based on a partnership model described in this chapter can be used to recast traditional orientations into a new partnership model of intervention.

GENDER AND SUPERVISION

The neglect of clinical supervision issues related to gender is ironic because supervision is the arena in which many of the issues that have been raised regarding gender are usually encountered and handled. For example, sanctioning practice decisions, communicating clinical wisdom, exercising authority, granting salary increases, evaluating performance, making employment decisions, and granting promotions are all components of supervision that have been identified as the major sources of discrimination against women in professions. Discrimination in these areas is related to hierarchical organizational arrangements in which supervisors get paid more than clinicians, and administrators get higher salaries than supervisors. Power is position in the psychotherapy organizational world. Although sex typing of positions has diminished, the salary and promotional inequities still exist, often leading to covert resentment and open conflict in some instances.

The psychotherapy field has not been as vigorous as other disciplines in investigating and documenting expectations and performance that are based on sex role stereotypes of men and women. In business and management, past research on perceptions of leadership styles has demonstrated that both men and women stereotype females as possessing characteristics that are considered inappropriate for management positions (Bass, Krusell, & Alexander, 1971; Schein, 1973, 1975). Research that has gone beyond attitudes to evaluate actual performance has not supported the stereotypes. No differences have been found in male and female leadership styles, particularly when leaders were evaluated by their subordinates. Most studies have found no significant difference between workers who had a male or a female for a superior in job satisfaction, satisfaction with salary, satisfaction with supervision, or promotional opportunity. Changes in clinical practice and the role of women and men over the past two decades require reexamination of supervision practice and male and female practitioner relationships in the psychotherapy professions. The literature has indicated that gender conflict continues to exist in the psychotherapy professions.

WOMEN AND EVOLUTION OF SUPERVISION

In the past, in the day-to-day life of agency practice, the average female practitioner and supervisee lived in a traditional society in which women showed deference to men and were rarely afforded the professional promotional opportunities men experienced. Women supervising women was a common occurrence in the past, but women supervising men was a unique, brief encounter in the man's rise to higher levels of administration (Reynolds, 1965).

Historically, the female supervisor's lot was a difficult and suppressed one. Many of the skilled, knowledgeable female supervisors and teachers had to live in the shadow of male psychiatrists even though much of what the psychiatrists had to offer was at best ineffective and at worst inappropriate in meeting practice demands (Reynolds, 1965). Many of the inroads and creative practice methods made by females relied on the influence of psychiatrists, as illustrated by the wife of Adolf Meyer, a psychiatrist, when she became the first psychiatric social worker in New York in 1907 (Munson, 1993). Although this model prevailed for more than a century, the women's movement during the past two decades has produced many changes and demands a new perspective of supervision based on a partnership model rather than on the historical hierarchical model.

FEMINIST PRACTICE

Current supervisory practice and gender issues can be portrayed as revolving around the emerging literature on a feminist approach to practice. Feminist therapy has emerged from the modern women's movement, which began in the early 1960s (Sturdivant, 1980). The initial rejection of psychotherapy by the general feminist movement was subsequently refocused by therapists into a specific model of feminist therapy. Sturdivant (1980) has conceptualized feminist therapy around the idea of a "philosophy of treatment." The core of feminist therapy is a set of values and attitudes that get translated into practice skill. Feminist therapists reject traditional sex roles and view societal and cultural values as necessarily making traditional therapy sexist.

Because approximately 20% of Americans (about 34 million people) hold to traditional values, the practitioner subscribing to the feminist therapeutic approach can be subjected to many conflicting pressures, just as the population as a whole is caught in conflicting expectations (Yankelovich, 1981). This conflict increases the importance of the role of the supervisor. The supervisor must give the practitioner the opportunity to explore the philosophy of practice and how it is manifested in what the practitioner does with the client. Without the opportunity to explore these attitudes, values, thoughts, and actions, the treatment can be misguided and confusing for the client. Symptoms, problems, roles, and responsibilities take on different meanings when a feminist perspective is introduced into the professional relationship.

The literature on feminist practice does not mention supervision as a way to help one build a feminist perspective, but implies this can be done through reading, introspection, and drawing on life experiences (Gibbs, 1984). The literature suggests the "going it alone" approach is necessary to emulate the male-dominated professions (Robbins & Siegel, 1983, p. 1), and others have pointed out the loneliness, doubt, and fear that can accompany the solitary approach (Milwid, 1983). This constitutes a paradox. Since feminist theory and therapy are relatively new, "going it alone" will only isolate the practitioner and prevent the spread of the approach. Historically, supervision has been the source of theory development and the spread of theory (application) in practice. Supervision is the place where the practitioner grappled with theory and case material to produce a rewarding, skilled, and confident practice style.

The evolution of theory is essential. For example, modern research on psychoanalytic theory is confirming some of its tenets, modifying others, and causing some to be discarded. Some feminist therapists have attempted to build feminist theory by devaluing psychoanalytic theory. This has neither helped feminist theory nor greatly altered psychoanalytic practices. Both approaches have much to offer, and the focus in supervision, research, and practice should be the advancement of each theory and their differential applications. There is not agreement on whether feminist approaches to therapy constitute a method, a modality, a theory, or a philosophy. Some have argued that feminist therapy is a philosophy that can be used to enhance other approaches (Porter, 1985). Much more research and application are needed before this process can be considered complete.

The practitioner cannot merge philosophy and practice of feminist treatment alone. Commitment to the theory and philosophy is not sufficient, and the supervisor plays a crucial role in a successful outcome of a course of treatment. Intervention based solely on academic abstractions can result in loss of confidence, disillusionment, and withdrawal from a feminist or any approach. Such shifts on the part of the practitioner can result in the client's becoming discouraged, lapsing into former ineffective coping strategies, or withdrawing from treatment. The feminist therapist must be comfortable and secure in that practice orientation to be effective (Sturdivant, 1980). The practitioner who adopts this perspective out of insecurity, rather than security, can do harm in therapy and expose the client to potential harm outside the treatment. The supervisor's role in monitoring such limitations is critical. There is evidence that supervision is essential to identifying feminist therapists' blind spots and anger they "did not hear" in treating female clients (Kaplan, Brooks, McComb, Shapiro, & Sodano, 1983) when therapists are struggling with their own role and status.

FEMINIST PRACTICE AND SUPERVISION

The emergence of feminist practice raises many issues for supervision and practice. There is debate whether males should treat female clients (Kaplan, 1985), there is disagreement whether the supervisor of a feminist practitioner should necessarily be a woman (Mendell, 1993), and whether men are capable of a feminist perspective. Another issue that needs exploration is the advisability of feminist therapists treating men. With so many underlying issues, the feminist therapist should undergo adequate supervision or consultation rather than being left to resolve the issues without support.

Female practitioners are less likely to have experienced supervision by a female during training (Seiden, 1982), and given the high percentage of men who have moved into administrative and supervisory positions, the chances of a female practitioner having a female supervisor in many settings are limited. Male supervisors of women often have limited preparation and lack awareness of many of the relevant practice issues because of their own lack of exposure to female supervisors or feminist issues. Some supervisees, both male and female, will not understand the necessity of a feminist approach with certain clients, and these supervisees offer a special challenge for the feminist supervisor.

In the situation in which the male is the supervisor of a feminist practitioner, there is a high risk of surprise, confusion, frustration, and defensiveness (Keefe & Maypole, 1983) on the part of the supervisor who lacks insight into traditional male behavior. The female supervisee can also experience the same reactions to an insensitive male supervisor. In such a situation, it is incumbent upon the supervisor to be open and aware and to develop understanding of the supervisee's position and examine his own possible biases about women. The same advice holds for the female supervisor who does not subscribe to the feminist philosophy. It is unrealistic to expect that because the supervisor is a woman, she will necessarily accept, understand, and advocate a feminist view. Although the women's movement has had an effect on psychotherapy education and practice, the theory of female sexuality and feminine development is based on a conventional variation of the male model, which could result in history repeating itself (Gould, 1984) in the supervisory arena.

Feminist therapists hold that more equality of power and authority between supervisor and supervisee is a basic notion just as it is in the relationship between therapist and client (Porter, 1985). The power relationship can be effectively altered in some situations, such as when a male supervisor can be given insight about female clients by a female supervisee (Brodsky, 1980; Nelson & Holloway, 1990). The question that remains to be addressed is, How much equality is necessary for effective feminist supervision? If there is to be total equality, it is no longer supervision. Porter (1985) offers helpful insights in this area related to authority, conflicts, autonomy, use of power, use of technology, and the process and stages of feminist supervision.

GENDER BIAS

Sex bias in the practitioner-client relationship can be a difficult problem to deal with in supervision, whether it be a male practitioner with a female client, or a female practitioner with a male client. Gender bias has been found to be inversely correlated with self-concept and positively correlated with homophobia. Homophobia is lowest among psychologists, moderate among psychiatrists, and highest among social workers (Anderson & Henderson, 1985). In supervision, dealing with such issues can be clarified by supervising the position, not the *person* (Munson, 1993). To avoid conflict and combativeness, the supervisor can focus on the case, tasks to be carried out, goals to be accomplished, and problems to be solved, rather than on the personality, attitudes, and values of the practitioner. Awareness techniques and exercises have been developed to explore stereotypes and biases in relation to clients of the opposite sex (Brodsky, 1980). In efforts to enhance feminist practice, some have held that feminist supervisors should use the supervisory relationship to foster a sensitivity to feminist issues in treatment in order to promote understanding that a cultural gender problem exists (Marecek & Kravetz, 1982). This approach can lead to conflict. In order to avoid supervisory conflict, any awareness development-oriented supervision must be client related and connected to specific case material. In some cases, avoidance of feminist issues in supervision is preferable. This is especially the case when authority is highly structured. These principles should also be followed when parallel process and sexuality are issues in the supervisory process (Hartman & Brieger, 1992).

In highly structured organizations in which authority is emphasized, the potential for supervisory conflict is increased. For example, in hospitals in which authority is structurally defined and divided along lines of professional disciplines, supervisees are more acutely aware of authority division, and this awareness carries over to the supervisory relationships.

For example, Tim, an advanced graduate student placed in a large government hospital, was required to do three rotations of 4 weeks each. He began his first rotation with a sense of superiority and spent much supervisory time ridiculing the bureaucracy and being sarcastic about his perceived insensitivity of the staff. He manifested a need to convince the supervisor he knew more than the regular staff; had insights into patients and the organization that others could not see; and that he had taken an existential view of the plight of the patients, the staff, and himself in the situation. The supervisor, a seasoned feminist practitioner, allowed Tim to express these views and did not challenge them or attempt to defend or explain the system. The supervisor used Tim's observations to help him learn about organizations, patients, and staff at a conceptual level. Also, the supervisor managed each supervision session in a way that guided Tim to focus on "Under these circumstances, what could be done to help the patient?" She led Tim to express his views in the context of specific cases and what could be done to aid the patient, the family, or both. By the middle of the second rotation, Tim talked less about organizational and staff issues and focused on patient dynamics and difficulties to be addressed. He began to identify skilled and committed staff who were important to his learning. By the end of the third rotation, all the "old bravado" was gone, replaced with professional exploration of strengths, weaknesses, limitations, and problems to be managed. The supervisor's patience and skill led to overcoming the student's defensiveness and anxiety produced by an underlying sense of inadequacy. The positive outcome in this case is best described in the words of the supervisor: "I know Tim was feeling overwhelmed and needed to defend against it. I gave him the flexibility to express his views. I knew he would come around when he realized that superiority stuff would not get him very far around here." The supervisor avoided conflict by not allowing this situation to become a sex-based power struggle and focused instead on the practice issues facing the supervisee.

Not all gender-linked supervisory authority relationships result in positive outcomes as in Tim's case. When supervisees have more deep authority problems and the supervisor is less skilled and not open to exploring feminist issues, the conflicts can escalate to a point that resolution is impossible and the struggles become upsetting to an entire staff. This is illustrated by the case of Pat, who was a graduate student receiving a fellowship in a large regional medical complex that had a psychotherapy unit. Pat was assigned several cases on different services in the hospital. The problem was complicated because her husband was the radiologist on the cancer service. Other staff complained to the supervisor about Pat's taking advantage of her husband's status in the unit and using her position as a basis for going around the rules. The supervisor attempted to discuss this with Pat by telling her to "cool it" on the ward. Pat viewed this as the supervisor "picking" on her and being "jealous" of her status. This low-grade conflict continued for several weeks and reached the crisis stage when the hospital implemented a regulation that each discipline wear a designated color lab coat in the hospital. Pat refused to wear the coat and said it "clashed with many of my clothes." Pat's husband, embarrassed by the situation, refused to get involved. The director of the psychotherapy unit entered the conflict, and when Pat became verbally combative with him, he terminated her from the fellowship. The hospital administrator withdrew the fellowship and assigned it to another department. The supervisor in this case was a traditional male who had little understanding of the worker and withdrew. He expressed little interest in the emotional content and felt "the rules are the rules." He saw the student as a "feminist" because she had raised some feminist issues in supervision. This was not the issue, but it became an excuse for the supervisor and further isolated the student. With more openness and looking beyond slogans, the supervisor could have avoided the extreme actions that resulted.

FEMINIST FAMILY THERAPY

One of the most significant developments in the helping professions during the past two decades has been the increase of family therapy. The theory of feminist family therapy has contributed significantly to our understanding of the feminist practice model (Ault-Riche, 1988; Goldner, 1985; Hare-Mustin, 1978; Libow, Raskin, & Caust, 1982; Luepnitz, 1988; Nelson, 1991; Wheeler, Avis, Miller, & Chaney, 1986). This development raises a number of questions that remain to be addressed and interpreted for the practitioner and supervisor. Some of the more salient questions are, How does the feminist therapist foster equality of the sexes in family practice? What is the effect of a feminist perspective in family treatment regarding the treatment process and outcome? How does a supervisor who is not schooled in a feminist perspective supervise a practitioner with a feminist perspective? Another related question is, Because more practitioners are entering private practice and often seek supervision from practitioners from other disciplines, mainly psychiatrists, how can a practitioner engage in a sustained career development process based on a feminist perspective? Because most psychiatrists are male, does the psychiatrist supervisor and psychotherapist supervisee constellation foster reinforcement of the old traditional, potentially sexist model of supervision and practice? These questions need attention in the family therapy field, as well as in supervision in general. In family therapy supervision, it has been pointed out that "The supervisory process will be most successful . . . if it constantly focuses on the skills that the therapist in training needs and must gradually begin to demonstrate" (Clarkin & Glick, 1982, p. 89). This is a good rule to follow to avoid conflict in all forms of supervision.

AGENCY FUNCTION

Supervision of a feminist-oriented practitioner must take into account the needs of the client and the function of the agency. Although there are feminist practitioners, there are few feminist agencies per se. When the client comes to a specific agency with a specific problem or a set of problems, a feminist approach to service must be compatible with client needs and agency function. Service should be based on client problems, not on practitioner interest. This does not mean agency function and intervention cannot be integrated with a feminist approach. It is critical that the feminist perspective, the agency function, and the client needs parallel. An example of the failure to reconcile practitioner perspective, agency function, and client need would be the battered wife whose therapist recommends marital or family therapy when the client requires shelter and protection. The supervisor should conceptualize treatment issues in the context of client-identified problems and agency function. This should be the background consideration of any treatment issues explored in supervision.

Supervision should focus on the interventions to be made by the practitioner. In analyzing these interventions, supervision can be oriented toward (a) the practitioner, (b) the client, or (c) the context of the treatment. In discussing feminist material in supervision, clearly the emphasis is on the practitioner or the client. The question remains whether this is the most efficient way to learn about or supervise treatment. Some theorists have placed more emphasis on the treatment context because it is a more comprehensive approach. In this approach, the focus is on exposure, interventions, and techniques (Lecker, 1976, p. 185). Any treatment supervision that fails to integrate all components of the treatment will be necessarily limited in utility (Gurman, 1981). Haley (1967) holds that self-expression of the client (and in the supervisory framework, the practitioner) cannot be separated from the context of the treatment. The main consideration is that any exploration of feminist material in supervision should be case related to avoid the supervision's going astray. This approach can help promote a feminist orientation rather than detract from it. For example, Gould (1984) holds that the use of Freudian theory in practice prohibited the development of feminist psychology. This inhibiting factor was reinforced through extension of Freudian theory use in the supervisory relationship to promote self-awareness. The more factual knowledge the practitioner has, the less likely that he or she will make practice errors. The supervisor has a responsibility to assist the supervisee in developing accurate client-based information. If both the therapist and the supervisor lack such knowledge, both can become anxious when client dynamics are presented in supervision for exploration (Bradshaw, 1982, pp. 202–203).

Feminist material in supervision is relevant in the context of other practice questions, such as, What are the problems that face the client? What techniques are most appropriate in relating to client problems? What are the goals of the treatment? How will outcomes be measured? How will practitioner "blind spots" be identified and overcome? Within the framework of these questions and other similar questions, feminist material can ultimately be useful to the practitioner and client.

ADMINISTRATION

The feminist practitioner must grapple with many issues to define and build a practice orientation, but this struggle will be intensified for the feminist practitioner who desires to move to administration. Given the rise in the number of female practitioners and the decline of males entering the psychotherapy professions, there is increased speculation about the nature of the opportunities for and role of women in administrative positions.

As opportunities in administration expand for women, new issues and choices are produced. New role models must be developed and supervisory opportunities and experiences provided that encourage and support women to pursue administrative positions, as well as the use of supervision as an arena to identify women who desire administrative careers. The role of the supervisor as a model for aspiring female administrators needs more focus of attention. The importance of this area is highlighted by one study (Munson, 1982) that found females in non-administrative positions who desire to be administrators undergo more conflict and negative perceptions than do other groups of women who have no desire to be administrators. This could be due to lack of encouragement, support, and adequate role models.

It is not valid to assume that because someone is a helping professional, he or she will be free of gender biases. Women holding administrative positions is a relatively new development; therefore, women can encounter more serious biases on the part of "old-time" colleagues that can be distressing. Distortion can result, leading to lack of understanding of the basis of older colleagues' views and actions by younger practitioners seeking role models. In the organizational world, the woman is easily made aware of the odds, resistances, and lack of role models she faces in a "man's world" (Kanter & Stein, 1979). The female professional in the clinical organizational world faces a more bewildering situation in that she is part of a profession that is moving toward a female majority but still offers few female role models because males have gravitated to the majority of administrative positions. Under these circumstances, the support group concept for women becomes just as important in clinical settings as in the business world (Faver, Fox, & Shannon, 1983). On the other hand, given the sex typing of occupations in our society (Pogrebin, 1980), the new majority status of women could enhance women's efforts to overcome the traditional sex typing of occupations in their preparation for and movement into middle-management and upper-level positions of leadership. Much could be learned from patterns of women's work groups and support groups in the corporate world (Kanter, 1977). The increase of women in administrative positions will most likely increase more rapidly as the number of men in the psychotherapy professions decreases. One study (Schwartz, 1990) shows that the old pattern of promoting clinicians to administrative positions continues to be the predominant practice in most agencies. Given the proportion of women to men in the practice ranks, the male domination of administrative positions should decrease. It is quite possible, however, that traditional biases could persist and impede gender equality in administrative positions.

SUPERVISION AND CAREER ADVANCEMENT

In clinical practice, it is appropriate for the supervisor of female practitioners to not only supervise job performance, but to also assist the female supervisee in preparation for career advancement. This has not always been recognized in the past. Women need to be encouraged to pursue and trained to perform supervisory and management roles, and their own supervisory experience can be an excellent arena for such preparation. The findings of one study (Munson, 1982) reveal that women who are practitioners with ambition to be administrators believe sexist practices exist at a high level, feel they need to be aggressive to get ahead, undergo more professional conflict, and desire more organization supports for their career goals when compared to female practitioners who have no desire for administrative positions. Although all of these problems may not be as severe for women in clinical settings as for women in business and industry, they do exist at a significantly higher level for women with administrative ambitions. The psychotherapy professions need to establish training programs to aid women in achieving their career aspirations. Zunz (1991), in a study of gender-related issues in career development of managers, found that although both women and men were helped in their promotions by people of their own sex, women mentored by women were promoted at a slower pace than were men mentored by men. This illustrates that traditional models do not promote equal treatment of people even in settings that may have an illusion of equality.

Supervisors of women with clinical management career aspirations should take these aspirations into account in their supervisory practices. For example, assertiveness by women in clinical managerial positions has been described as difficult for many women to engage in and hard for many other participants to accept (Drury, 1984). This is an example of one area in which supervisors can be helpful to supervisees with managerial ambitions. In order to do this, the supervisor must have experience and skill at being assertive.

SUPERVISION PARADIGM SHIFT

A feminist perspective of supervision has been slow to emerge because it requires a major paradigm shift that takes into account client need, agency function, and practitioner preferences. Feminist practice and supervision focus on change in structures in order to alter unjust practices. Fostering a feminist perspective in supervision through the use of what is referred to as a partnership model (Hipp & Munson, 1995) can assist in overcoming some of the outmoded aspects of the traditional hierarchical model. A feminist-based paradigm of partnership, although a departure from traditional models, is an attempt to modify and supplement existing models, rather than to replace them. At the same time, the partnership model is a way to enhance supervision.

Much of supervision knowledge has been historically compatible with modern feminist theory, but it has not been framed in such a context that would permit comprehensive application in practice. Specific guidelines for practice and supervision application have been lacking. The role of the supervisor using a partnership model is to foster comprehensive application. For example, a description of feminist family therapy practice by Papp in an interview with Simon (1992) illustrates how a feminist perspective can be used to apply dynamics and therapeutic outcome in supervision and practice:

> This family came in with an adolescent daughter who wouldn't go to school. The parents disagreed on the way the situation should be handled, but the mother went along with the father because she was afraid to say "no" to him. Meanwhile, she would subtly undermine their joint efforts because her heart wasn't really in it. The wife felt dominated and controlled by her husband and resented his authoritarian approach with the daughter, just as she resented it with herself.
>
> Now, in the past I would have seen the problem as the mother's being overly protective and undermining the father's efforts to establish rules. But because of my growing awareness

of women's issues I listened very carefully to the mother and found out where she was coming from. I then put her in charge of getting her daughter to school and asked the father to let mother handle the situation on her own. I put him in charge of his son, who was beginning to have problems.

The mother came in to the next session feeling wonderful. She said, "You don't know what it did for me when you gave me permission to take charge. I felt I had the power to follow through on my own ideals without interference—something I've never been able to do before." The daughter shaped up immediately and the father was actually relieved because he was in over his head. He had been so intent on winning the power struggle with his daughter that he frequently got out of control, and that was scary for him. The power struggle could now be fought where it belonged, between the husband and the wife, because I had empowered the wife so she could assert herself rather than undermine her husband. (pp. 52–53)

This case example illustrates the conceptual shift that is required to implement a feminist model of practice. Supervision/consultation models based on a feminist perspective can use this approach in recasting practitioners' past theoretical and practical orientations into new ways of intervening with families and individuals. Such strategic and cognitive shifts are basic to developing a partnership model of supervision.

THE PARTNERSHIP MODEL

Rainer Eisler's (1987) work in the study of civilization and creation of a "cultural transformation" theory is the focus for creating a new model in supervision. This model is unique because it can be used to integrate culture, society, professional practice, and supervision. In *The Chalice and the Blade,* Eisler describes two major patterns in history—the dominator and the partnership models. The dominator model is the one that has been operative historically. Eisler describes this model as based on cultural patterns that are

> male dominant, a hierarchy and authoritarian social structure and a high degree of institutionalized violence. They are also societies where so-called "masculine" values such as toughness, strength, conquest, and domination are given high social and economic priority (as in the emphasis in weaponry) and so called "feminine" values such as caring, compassion, empathy, and nonviolence are, along with women, generally held in contempt by men and relegated to a secondary, subservient sphere that is cut off from the "real world" of politics and economics. Finally, this is a model where difference (be it on the basis of sex, race, tribal or ethnic origin, religion, or belief system) is equated with inferiority or superiority, and where ingroup versus out-group thinking and behavior are the norm. (p. xvii)

We have accepted this paradigm and have not acknowledged other ways of relating until recent reinterpretations of relationships. Eisler (1987) describes alternatives to the hierarchical models in societies in which

> the characteristic social and ideological configuration or pattern appears to have been basically non hierarchic or equalitarian; although there were differences in status and wealth, they were not extreme. There are also specific indications that these were not male-dominator societies. (p. xix)

Eisler (1987) uses a reinterpretation of the past to develop a new paradigm through advocating a partnership model in which women, men, and nature are linked rather than

ranked, and it is more important to work together to create a better world than to dominate others. Eisler's partnership model views gender relations as basic to humanness.
Efforts to shift to relations between males and females deal with the core of human relations and with the most fundamental questions of values, ethics, and social structure. Eisler
uses the dominator and partnership models to demonstrate that those working for a more
human and ethical society need to give high priority to developing gender roles based on
partnership rather than on domination (Eisler, 1992). This formulation is basic to conceptualizing feminist supervision and practice.

The partnership model from a feminist perspective focuses on the sexes working
together for a different world. Feminists and psychotherapists have had a primary goal of
establishing a better world through raising the quality of life to its highest level. The partnership model concentrates on the need for change in both women and men practitioners
and supervisors as they work together. Although the partnership model is a major paradigm shift, it is not intended to create false dichotomies. Partnership is not the other side
of the coin of the dominator model and consequently is not one that would be equally limiting. It is a different view of the world. For example, competition and cooperation may
be found in both models, but it is used and viewed differently. Table 28.1 summarizes
some of the differences between the dominator model and the partnership model in super-

Table 28.1 Dominator and Partnership Models of Supervision

	Orientation	
Structure	Dominator	Partnership
Societal	Power	Relationship
	Patriarchal	Feminist
	Hierarchal	Egalitarian
	Individualist	Communal
	Violent	Nurturing
	Self-centered	Other-centered
	Feminine devalued	Feminine respected
Agency	Power	Relationship
	Authoritarian	Democratic
	Survival dependent	Survival dependent
	Task and function	Relationship
	Separation	Affiliation
	Competition	Cooperation
	Product	Process
Supervision	Power	Relationship
	Learning and support	Learning and support
	Dependence	Independence
	Compliance	Shared decisions
	Obedience	Initiative
	Authoritarian	Democratic
	Indoctrination	Education
Client	Powerless	Relationship
	Passive	Active
	Directive	Nurturing
	Concern	Caring
	Object/recipient	Subject
	Practitioner doing *for,* not *with,* client	Working through and with

vision and lists the operational terms used in the two models. These operational terms are explored further in the following sections.

Conceptualizing a feminist perspective of supervision using Eisler's (1987) model requires articulation of supervision structural systems issues at four levels: societal, agency, supervisory, and client system. These will be explored in relationship to the partnership model.

SOCIETAL STRUCTURE

The concept of power is the key to the dominator society and constitutes power over people rather than shared relationships. For example, a dominator model is enacted at the societal level in a social welfare system that asserts power over everyone involved in a way that lauds individualist values and a patriarchal system while it devalues femininity. Miller (1990) examines the "patriarchal necessity" that controls our welfare systems and calls for "new models" that "combine masculine and feminine world orientations," and "acknowledge the common experiences that women share in their relationship to the social welfare system throughout the life span" (pp. 160–161). Society dictates roles and expectations that get acted out through interaction. These expectations are brought to supervision and overtly and covertly characterize the interaction of the supervisor and the supervisee. Analysis of supervision conversations can reveal the underlying patterns that are the basis of a person's subjectivity and dominator worldview. Tannen (1990), a linguist, gives an excellent example of this in her book about men and women in conversation. She describes her experience of the difference in exchanges when she talks with men and women about her work:

> My experience is that if I mention the kind of work I do to women they usually ask me about it. When I tell them about conversational style or gender differences, they offer their own experiences to support the patterns I describe. . . . But when I announce my line of work to men, many give me a lecture on language. . . . Others challenge me, for example questioning me about my research methods. Many others change the subject to something they know more about. (p. 126)

This description of gender exchange in social situations can be applied to supervisory and practice situations. It can be characterized as the difference between "self-centered" and "other-centered" responses derived from cultural socialization patterns. In partnership-oriented supervision, there must be acknowledgment of these patterns and how they can foster or impede supervision work and practice. Men have difficulty moving from the "self-centered" mode, just as women have difficulty moving into this mode. With concerted effort, the change can be made. Recognition of the patterns and willingness to work to change them within oneself set the stage for a genuine partnership model of supervision/consultation to occur.

Supervisors need to understand the difference in communication patterns between women and men that Tannen (1990) describes. In supervision, there is a need to discuss these differences and how they influence client communication styles and patterns. It is empowering to share knowledge with clients to help them learn to understand their own behavior. Knowledge sharing is a large part of empowerment and fosters a genuine partnership model in supervision.

Supervisors can foster the understanding of larger societal issues by discussing them as essential material for case consultation. Societal and cultural influences are appropriate topics in supervision; as Mary Richmond (1917) observed, "Good supervision must include this consideration of wider aspects" (p. 351).

PROFESSIONAL AND AGENCY STRUCTURE

In authoritarian (dominator) models in agencies and group practices in which separateness is the rule, survival is dependent on task and function. The stress is on power over others rather than on fostering interdependent relationships. A partnership model in organizations is centered more on relationships and less on task and function. The supervisor must be alert to how an agency may engage in dominator acts that limit client options. The supervisor must work to overcome the bias in individual cases and to change organizational bias at the policy, personnel, and operational levels. A partnership perspective must be part of a larger learning experience for both the supervisor and the supervisee. Education for psychotherapy practice has not moved to such a model of supervision/consultation or practice. Most courses on feminism deal with women's issues from a societal context and offer little in the way of intervention strategies in professional relationships or supervisory or consultative practice. A number of strategies compatible with psychotherapy methods and a partnership model need to be developed in agency settings. One strategy is a greater use of groups in agencies. The rich tradition of group intervention is particularly suited to a partnership model of practice and supervision.

The group intervention model is as useful for practitioners working together on goals and issues as for working with clients. It also allows for a discussion of process as well as product. It fosters an opportunity to develop better relationships between women and men at various staff levels (Lewis, 1989). The use of codirectors and cochairs in various positions can also foster a sharing of power and a stronger sense of relationship. Group methods can lead to greater cooperation and less competition. Supervisors with a partnership perspective can encourage, support, and promote these different agency structures. It is important to note that it is advantageous to have female-male teams operating in co-facilitation positions. The dichotomy between females and males is a primary factor in the dominator model. This can be changed only as the sexes see that working together as partners is more effective. This form of partnership model reconceptualizes power. This does not imply that a democratic structuring of power means that all are alike or equally powerful at all times, but it does mean that structures can be created to give everyone equal access to resources and information (Hooyman & Cunningham, 1986).

The majority of psychotherapists in practice are women, and the majority of administrators and supervisors are men. For example, in clinical social work, men hold two thirds of the managerial jobs in a profession that is two thirds women (Austin, 1988; Fortune & Hanks, 1988). As long as the primary recipients of psychotherapy services are women, the majority of practitioners are women, and the administrators and supervisors are men, we will have a gap in the empowerment of women. That missing link is a partnership model. In order for fundamental change to occur, women and men will need to develop more effective models of communication. A shift is essential for social change because if the recent trend in graduate school enrollments continues, during the next decade the psychotherapy professions will be 85% to 95% female. As this occurs, women need to teach men about women and relationships. Men need to seek out women for this knowledge and develop a capacity to listen. Supervision is the arena to begin the dialogue. Women have much to offer men about treatment of women clients. For example, women practitioners with a feminist perspective can help men supervisors understand how difficult it is for battered women to leave abusive situations. Psychotherapists need feminist mentors regardless of whether the person is the supervisor or a supervisee. The essence of the partnership model is that both the supervisor and the supervisee can have shared input and influence.

SUPERVISORY STRUCTURE

Psychotherapy supervision has structurally followed a dominator model and continues to do so. Practitioners cannot rely on the supervisor to learn and apply a feminist perspective unless there is an explicit request for such an approach. Professional, licensure, and agency supervisory requirements usually follow the dominator model. This is normally referred to as the authority model used in supervision (Kadushin, 1992; Munson, 1993).

The theoretical orientation of the supervisor and the supervisee is a component of the supervisory structure. There has not been much empirical research on the congruence between the theoretical orientations of the supervisor and the supervisee, but there has been much speculation that congruence is important to positive supervision outcome. Steinhelber, Patterson, Cliffe, and Le Goullon (1984), in a study of 237 psychotherapy clients, found that clients reported significantly greater improvement when the supervisor's and the supervisee's theoretical orientations were congruent. This raises questions regarding how compatibility between supervisor and supervisee can be accomplished when either party to the supervisory relationship wishes to use a feminist orientation. The feminist-oriented supervisor of a nonfeminist supervisee must find a way to reconcile the differing perspectives, and the supervisee who desires to develop a feminist practice approach must accommodate to the methods of a nonfeminist supervisor. In the partnership model, there is an explanation and negotiation of the orientation that will be the focus of the supervision. Even if one party does not have a feminist orientation, when the strived-for model is made explicit, it is easier to overcome differences and to develop a new perspective.

Supervision and practice power can be misused, as it is in dominator societies, or it can be reframed as a shared resource in a partnership model. The feminist partnership model reconceptualizes "power as affiliation." Eisler (1987) sees this nondestructive view of power as a "win-win" rather than a "win-lose" view of power. A partnership model fosters supervisory relationships in which the relationship is based on joining and sharing to meet client and professional needs for a more humane world, rather than being viewed as a competitive activity (Bernstein, 1993; Ellis & Robbins, 1993; Twohey & Volker, 1993). This is done in supervision through a respect for the sharing of different viewpoints as normative, cooperative, and constructive interaction.

The traditional model in supervision has been the dominator model. Chernesky (1986) has argued that the dominator model of power is a hierarchy in which those higher up in the organization control and dominate subordinates. This can be addressed through the use of alternative models, such as the peer group model used at a counseling service that Chernesky describes as an experiment to demonstrate that highly experienced staff can carry out their professional roles and provide quality service to clients without constant supervision.

Group supervision can be conducted as a form of sharing and increasing awareness. This is a basic feminist tool. Women who experience such groups develop a much deeper understanding of themselves and their role in society. Wood and Middleman (1992) discuss such intervention with battered women. They draw on the concept of mutual aid and its significance for helping women understand their situations. They emphasize that as women draw closer together in the group experience, they develop more self-awareness. Similar findings have occurred in research on gender-based drug treatment programs (Nelson-Zlupko, Kauffman, & Dore, 1995).

CLIENT SYSTEM STRUCTURE

A partnership perspective in supervision can be viewed as an extension of a feminist practice perspective. Bricker-Jenkins, Hooyman, and Gottlieb (1991) state that feminist practice is a "work in progress" and resist rigid guidelines because it is "an open and dynamic system that has as its core an open and dynamic world view" (p. 4). There is no specific definition of practice used by feminists, and this is true of partnership-based supervision. Feminism is a way of thinking and being that is constantly emerging and changing. The control aspects of a dominator model filter down to the client level, and the authoritarian effect is cumulative. The power structure model results in those at the bottom being powerless, passive recipients who do not engage in the change process.

A central component of a partnership perspective is valuing the process as well as the outcome. A dominator model places emphasis and value only on the goal or product. The prevailing philosophy of the dominator model is product oriented, and the focus is on how goals are achieved rather than what happens to people in the process. The increased use of managed care models in mental health practice is resulting in more focus on the product aspect of the dominator model. A partnership model considers the people in the process and seeks to empower them by involving them through encouraging their input. In supervision, this allows for greater focus on what is actually happening during intervention.

This valuing of the other is related to a caring ethic. Caring has been associated with feminine culture and minimized by dominator culture. Gilligan's (1992) work has legitimized caring, but there remains a tendency to split caring and justice into two categories. A partnership model combines caring and justice. It allows for the valuing of feminine qualities that view feelings as a valid subject. Supervisors can facilitate the process of valuing by discussing the feeling ethic as it relates to work with clients. The feminine ethic of care is basic to supervisory inquiry and can be effectively related to supervision and practice activity (Freeberg, 1993).

A partnership model is based on an active, caring relationship that views the client as participant in working through problems. Wedenoja (1991) describes a feminist approach to working with the mothers of seriously mentally ill patients that is illustrative of a partnership with clients. Her interventions are guided by the premise that "valuing and acknowledging caregiving efforts that have been socially devalued [can be enhanced] by working with family caregivers . . . by facing with them the . . . challenge . . . of transforming an inadequate service system and reducing the stigma of mental illness . . . fostered and cultivated a sense of a working partnership" (p. 193).

Gorman (1993) discusses the partnership orientation in relationship to grounding our efforts to understanding in empathy. She explores the importance of the uses of narrative as a method of inquiry to document the efforts to promote individual and societal transformation. The role of narratives in psychotherapy practice is growing (Luborsky, Barber, Jacques, & Diguer, 1992; Russell & Lucariello, 1992; Russell, Van-den-Broek, Adams, & Rosenberger, 1993) and will need to become a focus in supervision. In the past, especially at the turn of the century, narratives were used in documenting the daily lives of immigrants. Other disciplines have long used narratives. A partnership model allows for deeper exploration of our work with others in their daily lives. Caring and life-enhancing activities are at the core of a partnership model. Practitioners should be gender specialists who work to change roles and not just role performance.

In conjunction with the partnership model, Eisler (1992) discusses the use of archetypes that reflect a revaluing of the feminine and an equality between the sexes. The archetype model reframes heroes and heroines in a more egalitarian way. The archetypes can have influence in practice and supervision. The archetypes for the partnership model are different from those for the dominator model. Eisler (1992) describes dominator heroines as passive and incompetent, such as the Helpless Heroine in "Sleeping Beauty." Dominator heros are Conquerors or Warriors. In the partnership model, it is possible to have the Wise Heroine or Hero as Mediator. Supervisors can model these behaviors. They can also encourage and discuss them and their significance for clients.

The practitioner faces many issues in the client relationship that can be better understood and more likely to be brought to supervisory discussion if a partnership perspective is openly shared. The female practitioner with a male client and a male practitioner with a female client will encounter conscious dynamics based on the societal socialization processes that impede client change that should be discussed in supervision/consultation. Lukton (1992) has pointed out that gender combinations in the treatment situation are permeated by gender role expectations and influence the essence of the therapeutic relationship. This has led to a debate regarding whether therapeutic relationships should ever involve mixed gender (Lukton, 1992). Sex role and power relationships need further exploration in terms of the limitations of the dominator model and the positive effects of the partnership model. This is especially true in the case of mixed gender practice and supervisee/consultation gender combinations.

CONCLUSION

The partnership model, based on a feminist perspective, is more compatible with the values and goals of the psychotherapy professions than is the dominator model. The supervisory/consultive role is an excellent place for practitioners to assess and model their professional strengths as they seek to enhance the quality of life. There is much work to be done to effect social change at the foundation of our relationships with one another. A partnership model provides the conceptual framework for doing this. Some critical questions need further exploration. Do supervisors view themselves as feminists? How do supervisors present a feminist perspective and a partnership model? Can education or training alter the male socialization process to the extent males could supervise from a partnership model? How do we foster a partnership model across the curriculum in psychotherapy education? Can a partnership model be implemented and sustained within institutions that remain hierarchical in orientation and structure? Further research is needed on supervision from a partnership model that addresses these questions.

REFERENCES

Anderson, S. C., & Henderson, D. C. (1985). Working with lesbian alcoholics. *Social Work, 30,* 518–524.

Atkins, C. P. (1994). Does genderlect exist? Implications for a predominately female profession. *The Clinical Supervisor, 12*(2), 129–141.

Ault-Riche, M. (1988). Teaching an integrated model of family therapy: Women as students, women as supervisors. *Journal of Psychotherapy and the Family, 3*(4), 175–192.

Austin, D. M. (1988). Women's career choices and human service organizations. *Social Work, 33,* 51–52.

Bass, B. M., Krusell, J., & Alexander, R. A. (1971). Male managers' attitudes toward working women. *American Behavioral Scientist, 15,* 221–236.

Bernstein, B. L. (1993). Promoting gender equality in counselor supervision: Challenges and opportunites. *Counselor Education and Supervision, 32*(3,, 198–202.

Bradshaw, W. H., Jr. (1982). Supervision in black and white: Race as a factor in supervision. In M. Blumenfield (Ed.), *Applied supervision in psychotherapy* (pp. 199–220). New York: Grune and Stratton.

Bricker-Jenkins, M., Hooyman, N. R., & Gottlieb, N. (Eds.). (1991). *Feminist social work practice in clinical settings.* Newbury Park, CA: Sage.

Brodsky, A. M. (1980). Sex role issues in the supervision of therapy. In A. K. Hess (Ed.), *Psychotherapy supervision: Theory, research and practice* (pp. 509–522). New York: Wiley.

Chafetz, J. S. (1972). Women in social work. *Social Work, 17,* 12–18.

Chernesky, R. H. (1986). *A new model for supervision: Feminist visions for social work.* Silver Spring, MD: National Association of Social Workers Press.

Clarkin, J. F., & Glick, I. D. (1982). Supervision of family therapy. In M. Blumenfield (Ed.), *Applied supervision in psychotherapy* (pp. 87–106). New York: Grune and Stratton.

Conn, J. D. (1993). Delicate liaisons: The impact of gender differences on the supervisory relationship within social services. *Journal of Social Work Practice, 7*(1), 41–53.

Drury, S. S. (1984). *Assertive supervision: Building involved teamwork.* Champaign, IL: Research Press.

Eisler, R. (1987). *The chalice and the blade.* New York: Harper & Row.

Eisler, R. (1992). Lecture. Association of Humanist Psychology, Chicago, IL.

Ellis, M. V., & Robbins, E. (1993). Voices of care and justice in clinical supervision: Issues and interventions. *Counselor Education and Supervision, 32*(2), 203–212.

Elson, M. (1986). Gender formation from the viewpoint of self psychology. In M. Elson (Ed.), *Self psychology in clinical social work* (pp. 23–34). New York: Norton.

Faver, C. A., Fox, M. F., & Shannon, C. (1983). The educational process and job equity for the sexes in social work. *Journal of Education for Social Work, 19*(3), 78–87.

Flax, J. (1990). *Thinking fragments: Psychoanalysis, feminism, and postmodernism in the contemporary west.* Los Angeles: University of California Press.

Fortune, A., & Hanks, L. (1988). Gender inequities in early social work careers. *Social Work, 33,* 221–225.

Freeberg, S. (1993). The feminine ethic of care and the professionalization of social work. *Social Work, 38*(5), 535–540.

Gibbs, M. S. (1984). The therapist as imposter. In C. M. Brody (Ed.), *Women therapists working with women: New theory and process of feminist therapy* (pp. 22–33). New York: Springer.

Gilligan, C. (1992). *In a different voice: Psychological theory and women's development.* Cambridge, MA: Harvard University Press.

Goldner, V. (1985). Feminism and family therapy. *Family Process, 24,* 31–47.

Goodrich, T. J., Rampage, C., Ellman, B., & Halstead, K. (1988). *Feminist family therapy: A casebook.* New York: Norton.

Gorman, J. (1993). Post modernism and the conduct of inquiry in social work. *Affilia, 8*(3), 247–264.

Gould, K. H. (1984). Original works of Freud on women: Social work references. *Social Casework, 65,* 94–101.

Gurman, A. S. (1981). Integrative marital therapy: Toward the development of an interpersonal approach. In S. H. Budman (Ed.), *Forms of brief therapy* (pp. 415–457). New York: Guilford.

Haley, J. (1967). Marriage therapy. In H. Greenwald (Ed.), *Active psychotherapy* (pp. 189–223). New York: Atherton.

Hare-Mustin, R. T. (1978). A feminist approach to family therapy. *Family Process, 17,* 181–194.

Hartman, C., & Brieger, K. (1992). Cross-gender supervision and sexuality. *The Clinical Supervisor, 10*(1), 71–81.

Hipp, J. L., & Munson, C. E. (1995). The partnership model: A feminist supervision/consultation perspective. *The Clinical Supervisor, 13*(1), 23-38.

Hooyman, N., & Cunningham, N. (1986). *An alternative administrative style. Feminist visions for social work.* Silver Spring, MD.: National Association of Social Workers Press.

Howard, D. (Ed.). (1986). *A guide to dynamics of feminist therapy.* Binghamton, NY: Haworth.

Jayaratne, S., Brabson, H. V., Gant, L. M., Nagda, B. A., Singh, A. K., & Chess, W. A. (1992). African-American practitioners' perceptions of their supervisors: Emotional support, social undermining, and criticism. *Administration in Social Work, 16*(2), 27–43.

Kadushin, A. (1976). Men in a women's profession. *Social Work, 21,* 440–447.

Kadushin, A. (1992). *Supervision in social work.* New York: Columbia University Press.

Kanter, R. M. (1977). *Men and women of the corporation.* New York: Basic Books.

Kanter, R. M., & Stein, B. A. (1979). The gender pioneers: Women in an industrial sales force. In R. M. Kanter & B. A. Stein (Eds.), *Life in organizations: Work places as people experience them* (pp. 134–160). New York: Basic Books.

Kaplan, A. G. (1985). Female or male therapists for women patients: New formations. *Psychiatry, 48,* 111–121.

Kaplan, A. G., Brooks, B., McComb, A. L., Shapiro, E. R., & Sodano, A. (1983). Women and anger in psychotherapy. In J. H. Robbins & R. J. Siegel (Eds.), *Women changing therapy* (pp. 29–40). Binghamton, NY: Haworth.

Keefe, T., & Maypole, D. E. (1983). *Relationships in social service practice.* Monterey, CA: Brooks/Cole.

Lecker, S. (1976). Family therapies. In B. B. Wolman (Ed.), *The therapist's handbook: Treatment methods of mental disorders* (pp. 184–198). New York: Van Nostrand Reinhold.

Leighton, J. (1991). Gender stereotyping in supervisory styles. *The Psychoanalytic Review, 78*(3), 347–363.

Lewis, K. G. (1989). Teaching gender issues to male/female group therapists. *Journal of Independent Social Work, 4*(3), 125–139.

Libow, J. A., Raskin, P. A., & Caust, B. L. (1982). Feminist and family systems therapy: Are they reconcilable? *The American Journal of Family Therapy, 10*(3), 3–12.

Luborsky, L., Barber, J. P., Jacques, P., & Diguer, L. (1992). The meaning of narratives told during psychotherapy: The fruits of a new observational unit. *Psychotherapy Research, 2*(4), 277–290.

Luepnitz, D. A. (1988). *The family interpreted: Feminist theory in clinical practice.* New York: Basic Books.

Lukton, R. C. (1992). Gender as an element in the intersubjective field: The female therapist and the male patient. *Clinical Social Work Journal, 20*(2), 153–167.

Marecek, J., & Kravetz, D. (1982). Women and mental health: A review of feminist change efforts. In H. Rubenstein & M. H. Bloch (Eds.), *Things that matter* (pp. 296–303). New York: Macmillan.

Mendell, D. (1993). Supervising female therapists: A comparison of dynamics while treating male and female patients. *Psychoanalytic Inquiry, 13*(2), 270–285.

Miller, D. (1990). *Women and social welfare: A feminist analysis.* New York: Praeger.

Milwid, B. (1983). Breaking in: Experience in male-dominated professions. In J. H. Robbins & R. J. Siegel (Eds.), *Women changing therapy: New assessments, values and strategies in feminist therapy* (pp. 67–79). Binghamton, NY: Haworth.

Munson, C. E. (1979). Evaluation of male and female supervisors. *Social Work, 24,* 104–110.

Munson, C. E. (1982). Perceptions of female social workers toward administrative positions. *Social Casework, 63,* 54–59.

Munson, C. E. (1986). Sex roles and power relationships in supervision. *Professional Psychology, 18*(3), 236–243.

Munson, C. (1993). *Clinical social work supervision.* Binghamton, NY: Haworth.

Nelson, M. L., & Holloway, E. L. (1990). Relation of gender to power and involvement in supervision. *Journal of Counseling Psychology, 37*(4), 473–481.

Nelson, T. S. (1991). Gender in family therapy supervision. *Contemporary Family Therapy: An International Journal, 13*(4), 357–369.

Nelson-Zlopko, L., Kauffman, E., & Dore, M. M. (1995). Gender differences in drug addiction and treatment: Implications for social work intervention with substance-abusing women. *Social Work, 40*(1), 45–54.

Pettes, D. E. (1979). *Student and staff supervision: A task centered approach.* London: George Allen & Unwin.

Philipson, I. (1994, March/April). Following the money: Why fewer and fewer men are becoming therapists. *The Family Therapy Networker,* pp. 40–44.

Pogrebin, L. C. (1980). *Growing up free.* New York: Bantam.

Porter, N. (1985). New perspectives on therapy supervision. In L. B. Rosewater & L. E. A. Walker (Eds.), *Handbook of feminist therapy: Women's issues in psychotherapy* (pp. 332–343). New York: Springer.

Powell, D. J. (1993). She said . . . he said gender differences in supervision. *Alcoholism Treatment Quarterly, 10*(1/2), 187–193.

Reynolds, B. C. (1965). *Learning and teaching in the practice of social work.* New York: Russell and Russell.

Richmond, M. (1917). *Social diagnosis.* New York: Russell Sage Foundation.

Robbins, J. H., & Siegel, R. J. (Eds.). (1983). *Women changing therapy: New assessments, values and strategies in feminist therapy* (p. 1). Binghamton, NY: Haworth.

Rosewater, L. B., & Walker, L. E. A. (Eds.). (1985). *Handbook of feminist therapy: Women's issues in psychotherapy.* New York: Springer.

Rothblum, E. D., & Cole E. (Eds.). (1991). *Professional training for feminist therapists: Personal memoirs.* Binghamton, NY: Haworth.

Russell, R. L., & Lucariello, J. (1992). Narrative, yes: Narrative ad infinitum, no. *American Psychologist, 47*(5), 671–672.

Russell, R. L., Van-den-Broek, P., Adams, S., & Rosenberger, K. (1993). Analyzing narratives in psychotherapy: A formal framework and empirical analyses. *Journal of Narrative and Life History, 3*(4), 337–360.

Schein, V. E. (1973). Relationship between sex role stereotypes and requisite management characteristics. *Journal of Applied Psychology, 57,* 95–100.

Schein, V. E. (1975). Relationship between sex role stereotypes and requisite management characteristics among female managers. *Journal of Applied Psychology, 60,* 340–344.

Schneir, M. (1992). *Feminism: The essential historical writings.* New York: Vintage.

Schneir, M. (1994). *Feminism in our time: The essential writings, World War II to the present.* New York: Vintage.

Schwartz, H. (1990). *Transition to administration: A comparative study of social workers and psychologists.* Unpublished Ph.D. dissertation, University of Tennessee.

Seiden, A. M. (1982). Overview: Research on the psychology of women. In H. Rubenstein & M. H. Bloch (Eds.), *Things that matter: Influences on helping relationships* (pp. 185–195). New York: Macmillan.

Simon, R. (1992). *One on one: Conversations with shapers of family therapy.* New York: Guilford.

Smith-Harrison, Y. (1981). *An interdisciplinary comparison of clinical supervision as a function of clinical quality assurance in community mental health centers.* Unpublished Ph.D. dissertation, University of Denver.

Steinhelber, J., Patterson, V., Cliffe, K., & Le Goullon, M. (1984). An investigation of some relationship between psychotherapy supervision and patient change. *Journal of Clinical Psychology, 40*(6), 1314–1353.

Sturdivant, S. (1980). *Therapy with women: A feminist philosophy of treatment.* New York: Springer.

Tannen, D. (1990). *You just don't understand me: Conversations between men and women.* New York: Ballantine Books.

Twohey, D., & Volker, J. (1993). Listening to the voices of care and justice in counselor supervision. *Counselor Education and Supervision, 32*(3), 189–197.

Wedenoja, M. (1991). Mothers are not to blame: Confronting cultural bias in the area of serious mental illness. In M. Bricker-Jenkins, N. Hooyman, & N. Gottlieb (Eds.), *Feminist social work practice in clinical settings* (pp. 179–196). Newbury Park, CA: Sage.

Wheeler, D., Avis, J. M., Miller, L. A., & Chaney, S. (1986). Rethinking family therapy education and supervision: A feminist model. *Journal of Psychotherapy and the Family, 1*(4), 53–71.

Wood, G., & Middleman, R. (1992). Groups to empower battered women. *Affilia, 7*(4), 82–95.

Yankelovich, D. (1981). *New rules: Searching for self-fulfillment in a world turned upside down.* New York: Random House.

Zunz, S. (1991). Gender-related issues in the career development of social work managers. *Affilia, 6*(4), 39–52.

CHAPTER 29

Cultural Competence in Psychotherapy: A Guide for Clinicians and Their Supervisors

STEVEN R. LÓPEZ
University of California, Los Angeles

The purpose of this chapter is to outline a model of culturally competent psychotherapy that can be used to guide both supervisors and trainees in their clinical work with culturally diverse clients.[1] Since López (1977), I have been interested in operationalizing what it means for clinicians to integrate a cultural perspective. Cultural competence, multicultural competence, and cultural sensitivity all concern therapists' ability to treat people of diverse cultural backgrounds in ways that respect, value, and integrate their sociocultural context (Comas-Díaz & Griffith, 1988; Cross, Bazron, Dennis, & Isaacs, 1989; Kleinman, 1988; Pedersen & Ivey, 1993; Ridley, Mendoza, Kanitz, Angermeier, & Zenk, 1994; D. W. Sue & D. Sue, 1990; S. Sue & Zane, 1987; Vargas & Koss-Chioino, 1992). In an effort to study the empirical basis of cultural competence, I first began by examining practitioners' clinical judgment, particularly their judgment of clients' presenting problems and symptomatology (López, 1983, 1989; López & Hernandez, 1986, 1987). Based on qualitative observations of clinical trainees, I then extended my work to psychotherapy (López et al., 1989). More recently, I have applied these ideas to formal psychological assessment (López, in press; López & Taussig, 1991).

In this chapter, I critically review this line of research and the model of cultural competence that it suggests. Next I address the model's limitations, in part by drawing on Kleinman's (1988) cultural perspective. I then present a revised model of cultural competence and illustrate the model with clinical cases of my own. I have chosen to present some of my mistakes and oversights as a means to discuss what culturally competent psychotherapy is. Addressing cultural issues in one's clinical practice can at times be difficult. It is important to establish and maintain an open dialogue about these matters with colleagues, supervisors, and trainees. By discussing my slips and errors, I want to demonstrate that part of maintaining such a dialogue requires that we reveal our vulnerabilities, which include our errors, oversights, questions, and uncertainties.

The model of cultural competence presented here is applicable to one's clinical work

---

[1] I refer to culturally diverse individuals as those from U.S. ethnic and racial groups other than the majority group of Euro-American backgrounds. These groups include the four largest ethnoracial groups in the United States, African American, American Indian, Asian American, and Latino American, as well as groups of mixed ethnoracial heritage and other recent immigrants (e.g., Persians).

Note: I would like to thank Rena Repetti for her most helpful comments on a previous version of this chapter.

570

with ethnic majority and minority clients alike. The principles of effective psychotherapy and culturally competent psychotherapy overlap. I believe, however, that the application of a cultural perspective is particularly important in working with clients from ethnocultural minority groups. In working with clients from culturally diverse backgrounds, the implicit and explicit models of human behavior are less likely shared by the client and clinician, particularly when the clinician is from a different ethnocultural background than that of the client. These differences may impede the provision of effective mental health care. Thus, although the model of culturally competent psychotherapy presented here is likely to be applicable to the treatment of clients from all ethnocultural groups, it may be most applicable to the treatment of people from ethnocultural minority groups.

DEVELOPMENT OF A CULTURAL COMPETENCE MODEL

In my prior clinical judgment research, I demonstrated that clinicians can both overpathologize and minimize actual pathology given their understanding of the cultural context of their clients' behavior (López, 1989; López & Hernandez, 1986). Let us consider the case of a highly religious and spiritual person who reports hearing God's voice directing him to take certain actions in his life. If a clinician assumes that hearing voices reflects psychosis, without assessing the possibility that this experience may reflect a culturally normative belief, then the clinician is at risk to judge culturally normative behavior as reflecting pathology. If hearing God's voice is indeed reflective of the patient's religious or spiritual belief system and not psychosis, then this would be an instance of *overpathologizing,* judging normative behavior within a specific cultural context to reflect more pathology than is actually the case. This is the type of mistake that most writers refer to when pointing out errors that clinicians can make when not familiar with the cultural context (e.g., Jones & Korchin, 1981).

Much less attention has been given to a second type of error, first recognized by Chess, Clark, and Thomas (1953). This error is referred to as a *minimizing* error or underpathologizing actual symptomatology. To continue with the example of hearing God's voice, if this experience is judged to be reflective of a client's religious or spiritual background, without careful assessment of the client's religious or spiritual values, or of the possibility that this may be psychosis, then the clinician is at risk to judge a symptom of psychosis as normal behavior. If hearing God's voice is indeed reflective of psychosis, then this would be an instance of a minimizing error, that is, judging abnormal behavior within a specific cultural context to reflect more normative behavior than is actually the case. The main difference between the overpathologizing and the minimizing errors is that in the former case, the clinician fails to consider the client's cultural context. In the latter case, the clinician indeed considers cultural factors but does so without taking into account the applicability of such factors for the specific client.

To assist clinicians in considering the role of culture in their evaluations, my colleagues and I argued that it was important for clinicians to keep in mind the cultural context in evaluating clients, but to do so carefully. Given the increasing push for clinicians to apply alternative cultural norms, clinicians may not be carefully applying these alternative cultural norms. For example, one therapist described in the following case summary how she considered the client's cultural background:

> In my work with a particular Hispanic female, my judgment of her ego-strength or self image was quite different than it would have been had I not taken into account cultural patterns which "condoned" the male being unfaithful and having other relationships. Accepting this

practice is not considered a deviant choice in a female of the Hispanic culture. (López & Hernandez, 1986, p. 603)

In this example, it is not clear how this practitioner knew that the client accepted extramarital affairs as part of her cultural norm. Given the great heterogeneity among Latinos, there are many women and men who do not hold this cultural norm. Thus, whereas it is important to consider culture-specific norms in clinical evaluations, it is equally important to assess the client's adherence to the presumed cultural behavior pattern.

In a qualitative study of how student-therapists take culture into account in their clinical work with culturally diverse clients (López et al., 1989), we expanded the notion of considering the cultural basis of specific presenting problems to identifying cultural competence in psychotherapy. We learned that cultural competence reflects moving between alternative cultural frameworks. We argued that the alternative cultural lenses were those that reflected *culture-specific* (emic) belief systems and *culture-general* (etic) belief systems. We drew from previous cross-cultural research (Draguns, 1981) that suggested working with culture requires balancing both culture-specific and culture-general norms. Culture-specific belief systems were thought to pertain to the cultural group to which the client belonged. For example, a parent who often interrupts his or her son during family therapy sessions may be judged as reflecting culture-specific processes, such as beliefs that adults' roles have greater value than those of children. Thus, in this context, the interruptions would not be viewed as family dysfunction. Culture-general belief systems, on the other hand, were thought to pertain to most if not all groups, those which could be considered universal. Therefore, the same behavior of a parent's interruptions in family therapy sessions could be construed from a culture-general position to reflect intrusiveness, an aspect of the family's behavior that reflects dysfunction. In López et al. (1989), we argued that a culturally competent therapist collects data to test hypotheses derived from both culture-specific and culture-general frameworks. The culturally competent therapist does not assume that any one perspective is applicable. Instead, he or she checks out their applicability with each individual. By doing so, the clinician considers the cultural context without stereotyping.

We later applied the notion of entertaining presumed culture-specific and culture-general norms to psychological testing, particularly in the assessment of Spanish-speaking adults (López & Romero, 1988; López & Taussig, 1991). We argued that the norms based on a U.S. standardization sample could be considered culture-general norms, as psychologists oftentimes apply such norms in assessing people from many different cultural backgrounds. (We later discuss the limitation of this assumption.) When using these presumed culture-general norms, Spanish-speaking elderly were found to be functioning at an impaired level when they were not impaired. In other words, normal elderly, without any history of impairment, were found to be functioning in the below-average range of cognitive-intellectual functioning because the test norm was not appropriate for them. The U.S. standardization sample was higher in educational level and socioeconomic status than the Spanish-speaking adults, thus leading to the impression that they were low functioning. This finding is similar to the overpathologizing error that was noted earlier, that is, failing to consider the cultural context and thus overestimating the degree of pathology. On the other hand, we also found evidence that when presumed culture-specific norms were used, that is, norms based on Spanish-speaking adults from a low-income and a low educational background, Spanish-speaking elderly with significant cognitive impairment were found to be functioning at a higher level than they actually were. Specifically, using such culture-specific measures underestimated the degree of cognitive impairment when compared to other measures of impairment, such as activities of daily living (e.g., ability to eat by oneself) and a global cognitive impairment measure. Based on a standardization sample characterized by low education and low socioeconomic status, the presumed culture-specific norms then may not have been sensitive enough to identify low functioning. This pattern of findings is similar to the previously mentioned minimizing error of underestimating the degree of pathology because an inappropriate cultural-specific norm is applied.

Given the potential error in using either the presumed culture-general and presumed culture-specific normed tests, we argued that a culturally sensitive psychologist carefully considers which norm might be most appropriate for the given individual being tested. This means, for example, not assuming that a primarily Spanish-speaking person requires Spanish language tests and their corresponding norms, particularly norms derived from a Spanish-speaking community with limited education and low socioeconomic status. Such norms might not be appropriate for a given individual, for instance, a highly educated Mexican professional. Thus, it is important to consider the fit between the individual's sociocultural background and the normative sample's sociocultural background. In addition, a culturally competent psychologist would include multiple sources of data, for example, a good history, other tests, and reports of significant others to assess properly the person from a cultural and linguistic background that is different from the majority of U.S. residents. Considering the applicability of different norms and integrating the findings from other measures reflect culturally competent psychological assessment.

EVALUATION OF PAST RESEARCH

The main contribution of this line of research is that it points out that two cultural perspectives are needed to identify the cultural meaning of given observations, whether the observations concern symptomatology, therapy-related behavior, or psychological test results. Prior research and writings that have advanced a cultural perspective have largely argued for using culture-specific norms with people of diverse cultural backgrounds (e.g., Dana, 1993; Malgady, Rogler, & Costantino, 1987). This is an important point as psychological research, in general, and models of psychopathology, therapy, and testing, in particular, too often ignore the sociocultural context (Betancourt & López, 1993; Graham, 1992; Guthrie, 1976). The disadvantage of the culture-specific perspective is that there is great heterogeneity among people from the same broad cultural group. Due to individual variability and subcultural variability within given cultural groups, what clinicians presume to be culture-specific norms may not be applicable for a given individual. Therefore, if clinicians assume that culture-specific norms are needed for specific Latino, African American, Asian American, or American Indian clients, they are at risk of misapplying norms. This is reflected in minimizing actual pathology, misunderstanding the clinical behavior of one's client in therapy, and judging someone to be less impaired based on presumed culture-specific test results. To guard against the potential errors in ignoring the sociocultural context or overattributing clients' behavior to their sociocultural background, it is important that the clinician consider two cultural frameworks simultaneously. In my view, this represents the essence of cultural competence, the ability of the therapist to move between two cultural perspectives in understanding the culturally based meaning of clients from diverse cultural backgrounds. Considering both cultural perspectives has been an important contribution of this work thus far.

A related strength of this work is that it focuses on process, not content. Process refers to *how* therapists ascribe meaning rather than *what* therapists know about specific groups. Much of the past literature advancing a cultural perspective emphasizes the ways in which cultural groups differ from the majority group with regard to illness categories, cultural values (e.g., individualism versus collectivism), reliance on families, use of alternative healers, and so forth. Oftentimes, books about cultural issues in clinical practice are organized around the different ethnocultural groups. In these books, authors highlight the specific issues relevant to providing clinical services to these groups. On the one hand, it is important for clinicians to learn about the different sociocultural issues pertinent to each group. However, the data to support much of what is believed to be culture-specific is limited (López, 1988). For example, the notion that Latinos somaticize psychological distress, a notion commonly held by clinicians (López, Nuñez, & Magaña, 1993), is based on very limited data. Yet, it is frequently noted as a culturally acceptable way in which Latinos express their distress. Given the limited database, content approaches to cultural competence can lead to either creating or reinforcing stereotypes of given groups. Ultimately, as educators and researchers, we want to broaden, not limit, clinicians' thinking about specific cultural groups. (See S. Sue & Zane, 1987, for another process model regarding culture and therapy.)

The advantage of focusing on the process of how to ascribe meaning in one's clinical work is twofold. First, it recognizes the importance of culture-specific norms. In other words, this process orientation acknowledges that there are alternative meanings of given behaviors depending on specific sociocultural contexts. Accordingly, this approach addresses past concerns of clinicians overlooking the clients' cultural context. Second, this process (meaning) approach recognizes the considerable heterogeneity within cultural groups. By focusing on how clinicians know which cultural meaning to apply in specific contexts, stereoptying can be significantly reduced. The focus on process in ascribing cultural meaning is an important strength of this past research.

In addition to considering the strengths of the ideas generated by the prior research, it is also important to recognize their limitations. The first weakness is that the two cultural perspectives used by clinicians cannot be considered culture-specific and culture-general. What we first labeled in López et al. (1989) as culture-general is really the therapist's culture-specific framework. It was rather presumptuous of us to consider the therapist's framework as reflecting what might be considered culture-general or universal belief systems. The therapist is immersed in his or her culture-specific context to the same degree as the client. Although an imposed-etic or a tentative culture-general view (Berry, Poortinga, Segall, & Dasen, 1992) perhaps best captures how we applied this notion in the past, it still implies a hierarchy. According to this view, the clinician's framework is thought to be closest to what might be considered universal, whereas the culturally diverse client's framework is simply reflective of a specific cultural perspective. Assuming such a hierarchy, whether implicit or explicit, is wrong. It is important to recognize that both the client's and the clinician's frameworks reflect specific cultural lenses. This does not mean that universals or shared human processes do not exist. Universals indeed exist. However, for the clinical context, ascribing meaning to specific cultural contexts is most important. For that reason, I emphasize the cultural particulars of clients' and clinicians' perspectives.

A second limitation of this line of research is that it has primarily focused on assessment, from clinical judgment of presenting problems and symptomatology to formal psychological testing. In López et al. (1989), we applied and extended the initial ideas identified in a clinical judgment context to the broader context of psychotherapy. The examples we used, however, still very much reflected a clinical judgment perspective. This may not be surprising, as clinical judgment underlies a great deal of clinical work throughout therapy. Nevertheless, our use of clinical judgment tended to reflect one aspect of therapy, assessment. Although assessment is an important component of psychotherapy, there are other aspects to consider, specifically those directly related to intervention. It is important that models of cultural competence in clinical practice apply to intervention as well as to assessment. I now address the noted limitations, and, in doing so, present for the first time this process model of cultural competence across several specific domains of psychotherapy.

A PROCESS MODEL OF CULTURAL COMPETENCE

The essence of cultural competence in working with clients from diverse cultural groups is moving between two cultural perspectives, that of the therapist and that of the client. It is important to recognize that each perspective reflects a specific sociocultural context. Both the therapist and the client maintain their own culture-specific frameworks. One advantage of this view is that no hierarchy in meanings or cultural frameworks is assumed. The client's cultural perspective is thought to be as valuable as the clinician's cultural perspective. For example, some clients express distress in somatic terms (e.g., headaches, physical weakness), whereas most clinicians frame distress in psychological terms (e.g., anxiety and depression). The differences in conceptualizing distress may reflect different cultural frameworks. Recognizing that both clients and clinicians operate from their own culture-specific perspectives, particularly when they are from different ethnocultural backgrounds, may contribute to reducing the risk of clinicians imposing their model of functioning as the ideal model. Instead, the clinician's culture-specific model may simply be an alternative model to that of the client's.

Moving between two culture-specific models is consistent with the work of Kleinman (1988). Drawing from anthropological theory and methods, he has advanced a cultural perspective for mental health research, practice, and training. In my view, Kleinman's single most important contribution has been to communicate for the mental health researcher and clinician the value of moving between the professional and lay systems of meaning to ascribe meaning to behavioral observations. This is captured in the following quote about the ethnographer's mission:

> The ethnographer's focus moves back and forth. The task is to interpret patterns of meaning within situations understood in experience-near categories; yet, ethnographers also bring with them a liberating distance that comes from their own experience-near categories and their existential appreciation of shared human conditions. . . . Getting at mediating psychological processes requires that eventually we shift to the view from afar—we cannot otherwise abstract universalizing processes from the particularizing content of ethnopsychological meaning—but to understand actual situations we must use both lenses. (Kleinman & Kleinman, 1991, p. 278)

Kleinman has demonstrated the utility of this ethnographic approach or anthropologically informed perspective to several clinical research domains, for example, the study of depression and neurasthenia in China (Kleinman, 1986), patients' and healers' explanatory models (Kleinman, 1980), and more recently pain (Kleinman, 1992). He has also outlined in general terms the application of this perspective to clinical training and practice (Kleinman, 1988).

It is important to translate the notion of moving between the lay and the professional systems of meanings for treating clients of culturally diverse backgrounds. Building on both my prior research and Kleinman's important conceptual contribution, I now extend this cultural perspective to four specific domains of clinical practice: engagement, assessment, theory, and method. These domains are not unlike what Kleinman (1988) has identified as three universal aspects of symbolic healing: identifying the casual agent (assessment and theory), applying therapeutic procedures (methods), and removing the casual agent within an interpretative system (theory). Nor are they unlike the areas of psychotherapy identified by S. Sue and Zane (1987) in their influential work on culture and psychotherapy. They argued that therapists' credibility, or client's perception of the therapist as an effective helper, can be achieved in three specific domains; conceptualization of the problem, means for problem resolution, and treatment goals. Also, the clinical observations of Bernal and Flores-Ortiz (1982) in treating Latino families overlaps with the areas of psychotherapy that I have identified, particularly their concern with engagement and evaluation.

There probably is no one correct way to organize the domains of psychotherapy, in part because there is considerable interrelatedness between domains. What the client presents as the problem during the engagement process is going to be related to the therapist's assessment, theoretical formulation, and treatment. Despite this overlap, it is useful to discuss the different domains to ensure that most aspects of psychotherapy are considered.

Given that the focus of this book is on clinical supervision, it is important to consider cultural issues in contexts other than those pertaining to the specific interaction between a therapist and a client. These include observations of other therapist-client interactions, case conferences, and interactions with one's supervisors. A cultural perspective that respects the sociocultural context of the specific interactions can be applied to these areas as well.

Engagement

Two of the most important issues that arise in the early phase of psychotherapy are defining the problem and setting the treatment goal(s). A culturally competent therapist is able to understand what the client views as the problem and what the client wishes to gain from therapy. At the same time he or she may need to maintain a formulation of the problem and treatment goals that differ in significant ways from those of the client. If this is the case, it is important that the clinician consider simultaneously both the lay and the professional perspectives in the early phases of therapy. From the point of view of the client, the therapist understands his or her specific circumstances well. From the point of view of the therapist, key theoretical issues, diagnostic formulations, and historical factors are entertained as hypotheses. A careful balancing of both perspectives is oftentimes necessary to successfully engage the client in psychotherapy. In the following case, such a balance was not achieved. I did not adequately assess the client's views with regard to her problem, nor did I properly consider her perception of appropriate treatment goals:

Maria[2] is a single Mexican American woman, 23 years of age. She has some college education and was working in a law firm as a high-level secretary. During the first session, she pointed out a number of factors that contributed to her seeking help. Her boyfriend had left her, and she felt her brothers and sister were taking advantage of her occasional financial assistance. Maria reported that a minor incident occurred at work, and she went to the bathroom crying for about 15 minutes. She indicated that she had overreacted and probably needed

[2]In presenting case material, the client's name and, in some cases, the client's background information have been changed to maintain his or her anonymity.

psychological help. She acknowledged some depressive symptoms, but not severe enough to warrant a diagnosis of major depression or dysthymia.

During the second session, Maria focused primarily on her relationship with her father. She stated that her father held rather traditional beliefs. He did not allow her to date till she was 18 years old, to receive phone calls at home, or to participate in after-school activities. In addition, Maria reported that he had a drinking problem and was at times "emotionally" abusive toward her through his yelling and his other reactions. For example, she recalled that when she decided to move out of the house at the age of 20, her father said that he would be unable to help her move. So she asked her uncle for assistance, which bothered her father quite a bit. When she and her uncle arrived at the house, the father took her keys, told her to take all her belongings, and insisted that she never come by without first calling. Maria acknowledged feeling a little angry and hurt over this and related incidents, but, in general, she appeared to minimize her emotional reactions. Toward the end of the initial session, I suggested some possible goals for therapy. One such goal was to improve her communication with her father. I indicated that eventually it would be a good idea for him to know how she feels about the way he treats her. Maria said that it would be very difficult for her to let him know this. I said that we could work on it. The possibility of opening the lines of communication with her father may have been threatening to Maria, as she responded to this possible treatment goal in an anxious manner.

At the end of the session, we set an appointment for the next visit to take place the following week. She never showed. I called and left a message on her answering machine. A week later I sent her a letter indicating that she could set an appointment at her convenience. I never heard from her again.

It is hard to know exactly why Maria did not return. Given her reaction to the possibility of speaking more directly to her father, she may not have been willing to work on improving communication with her father. In part, I had defined the problem as poor communication with her father (and others). She, on the other hand, defined the problem as her being "too emotional."

In working with culturally diverse patients, it is important that the therapist validate the client's definition of the problem and work toward the corresponding treatment goal. In many cases, the client and the therapist will agree on what the problem is and what the treatment goals are. In other cases, such as that of Maria, there may not be agreement. The therapist may have different ideas of what the problems and treatment goals are. In these cases, the therapist should be careful not to impose what he or she believes to be the problem and the treatment goal. Instead, within certain limits, it would be best for the therapist to demonstrate that he or she understands and accepts the client's definition of the problem. The clinician may then entertain parallel problem definitions and treatment goals, those defined by the client and those defined by the therapist. Over time, additional problems and solutions can be identified and addressed, including those defined by the therapist. But this will take place only after having established a positive working relationship. In the case of Maria, such a relationship had not been established.

Assessment

The collection of data regarding the client's functioning is an ongoing process that takes place throughout psychotherapy. It can be based on both formal assessment procedures (e.g., MMPI-2) and informal procedures (e.g., clinical interviews). Because of space limitations, only the use of formal assessment tools is discussed here.

As noted earlier, culturally competent assessment requires the application of two sets of cultural-specific norms, that of the mainstream culture and that of the client's culture. Using both sets of norms reduces the potential errors in using just one set of norms. There are two ways of using two sets of norms. First of all, one can administer two versions of the same test, one that is normed on an English-speaking U.S. standardization sample and one that is normed on a standardization sample reflective of the cultural and linguistic background of the individual client. For example, in assessing a bilingual Latino child, a psychologist might administer the English-language WISC-III as well as one of the two Spanish-language versions of the WISC-R that were normed on a Mexico City public school sample (WISC-RM; Gomez Palacios, Padilla, & Roll, 1984) and on a Puerto Rican Island standarization sample (EIWN; Herrans & Rodríguez, 1992). Although ideal, having available two sets of empirically derived norms for the same test is more the exception than the rule. There are few standardized tests that have been normed on an English-speaking U.S. standardization sample and on a linguistic, ethnic, or racial minority group standardization sample as well.

With no alternate group-specific normed tests, psychologists may then entertain subjectively determined norms. In other words, psychologists may adjust their interpretation of the test scores on the basis of the client's linguistic or cultural background. Take the example of a limited English-speaking woman from Southeast Asia who runs a successful business. On a given test, her scores fall within the borderline range of cognitive-intellectual functioning. One set of culture-specific norms that could be used then are the test's "mainstream norms." The psychologist, however, may judge that the person's limited English language skills contributed to the test scores as underestimating her psychological functioning. This interpretation rests on the assumption that there are no data to suggest other plausible explanations for the inconsistency between her test performance and her functioning in daily life. By interpreting the test data in this manner, the psychologist is adjusting the available set of norms and, in essence, applying a second set of culture-specific norms, specifically, norms for people with limited English-language skills. In this case, the culture-specific norms are subjectively derived.

Clinical judgment is required in deciding how to use the two culture-specific norms, whether they are empirically derived norms or a combination of empirically derived and subjectively derived norms. It is important that the psychologist carefully consider all available data to decide how best to use both sets of norms. It could be that the data from the two sets of norms converge. In that case, the psychologist can argue with some confidence that the person's level of functioning is the same across cultural contexts. It could also occur that the data from each set of norms suggest a different level of functioning. In that case, the psychologist has two options: to argue that either the data from one set of norms are more applicable or that the data from the both sets of norms are equally applicable, depending on the cultural context. In the former case, the client's clinical history, the report of significant others, and other test data may converge to support one set of norms more than the other. Accordingly, the psychologist would apply what appears to be the more appropriate test norm. When there is not a clear convergence of the available data, however, it could be that both sets of norms are applicable, depending on the sociocultural context. In other words, when compared to an English-speaking U.S. standardization sample the client is functioning at a particular level, and when compared to a standardization sample from the person's linguistic and cultural background the client is functioning at a different level. This interpretation reflects the possibility that an individual's psychological functioning may vary depending on the sociocultural context. A slightly different interpretation is that the person's actual performance may change under different linguistic circumstances because of anxiety or other factors.

Regardless of how psychologists interpret data from two sets of culture-specific norms, the important point is that culturally competent assessment requires that data be obtained from the vantage point of mainstream norms as well as culture-specific norms. The following case, which took place during my internship year, illustrates the value of using two cultural perspectives:

> Mrs. Encinas, a 42-year-old Mexican American, was being seen by a fellow intern. He was having some difficulty in teaching her parenting skills, so he decided to assess her cognitive-intellectual functioning to determine whether it was a factor in her slow progress. Mrs. Encinas spoke English with a heavy accent. As part of the clinical training, I and the other interns, as well as our supervisor, watched the assessment through a one-way mirror. Mrs. Encinas performed poorly on the Wechsler Adult Intelligence Scale—Revised, which I attributed to her apparent limited English-language skills. After the testing, I approached both my peer and supervisor and asked if I could test her in Spanish. They agreed, as did Mrs. Encinas. We arranged an appointment for the following week.
>
> For the second testing, I conducted the evaluation solely in Spanish; at least, that was my intention. After the first three or four questions from the information subtest, most of which she failed, Mrs. Encinas asked me, in her thick accented English, "Could we please do this in English?" I was dumbfounded—in part by her low performance in what I thought was her dominant language, but more importantly by my failure to assess her language skills. On the basis of her heavy accent, I had *assumed* that Spanish was her dominant language. I did not even ask her what language she preferred. It was clear that Mrs. Encinas was low functioning in both English and Spanish.

This case points out the value of using two culture norms. Had we relied strictly on the results from the English-language version, we would have had some doubt about her "true" level of functioning. We might have concluded that she was low functioning, as this was consistent with our clinical observations as well. But then, given her accented speech, the degree to which her presumed limited English-language skills were responsible for the test scores would not have been known. On the other hand, we might have simply assumed that her low performance was due to what we thought were poor English-language skills. Taking this position would have been similar to applying a second set of culture-specific norms, ones that are subjectively derived based on adjusting the English-language set of norms. In applying these norms, however, it would have been unclear how much adjustment would actually be needed. Interpretations based on only one set of norms, whether empirically derived or subjectively derived, are limited. By administering two empirically derived sets of linguistic and cultural norms, we were able to avoid having to adhere solely to the English-language norms or to the adjusted set of norms. With both sets of norms, we learned that language was not a significant factor in Mrs. Encinas's cognitive-intellectual functioning.

Cultural competence requires the consideration of two culture-specific norms. Questioning the validity of the interpretations generated by Mrs. Encinas's responses on the WAIS-R was necessary for two reasons: People of Mrs. Encinas's background were either not included or were not well represented in the normative sample of these tests, and the tests are administered in English, frequently their second language. Applying a second set of cultural norms has the potential, such as in Mrs. Encinas's case, to rule out the possibility that the observed level of functioning is related to linguistic or to cultural factors.

Theory

Theory refers to the explanatory models used to explain a person's psychological functioning and correspondingly how therapy works to affect behavior change. For example, cognitive models of depression suggest that dysfunctional thoughts lead to depressed mood.

Therefore, to alleviate depression, therapists must help clients alter their dysfunctional thinking. A cultural perspective to psychotherapy recognizes that clients may hold theoretical models different from those held by practitioners. Accordingly, it is important that clinicians identify, recognize, and discuss the client's model that is embedded in his or her culturally specific framework. After having defined the problem and treatment goals, the clinician would do best to understand what the client believes to be the causes of the problem and the means by which the problem is maintained. In some cases, clients may not know. In most cases, clients entertain certain notions. Some of these beliefs include that they are being punished by God; as children, they had poor relations with their parents; they are bewitched; they have an unspecified physical disorder that leads to the psychological problems; their spouse treats them poorly; they do not like their job; they can't get a certain thought out of their minds; and so forth. The important point is that clients' beliefs and explanations for their problems are embedded in their cultural context. Clinicians would do well to recognize these beliefs as part of their client's cultural context and work within that context. How one integrates the client's explanatory model is central to culturally competent psychotherapy. The following case illustrates the importance of integrating the client's explanatory model:

> Janet and her husband Jorge sought psychotherapy to help them address their long-standing marital difficulties. At the time, Janet was 37 years old and Jorge was 42 years old. They were married in Argentina 17 years earlier and had come to this country to flee the political conflict at that time. Both are college educated, but because of their limited English-speaking skills they were employed in jobs well below their level of preparation. They have two adolescent children, a boy and a girl. Therapy was conducted in Spanish.
>
> Initially, I saw them both in conjoint therapy to improve their communication and problem-solving skills, with occasional individual sessions for each partner. In the third session, Janet reported having experienced some panic symptoms. Based on her responses to selected questions from the Anxiety Diagnostic Interview Schedule—Revised, taken from Barlow and Cerny (1988), it was clear that she met criteria for panic disorder. Nevertheless, she preferred focusing on improving the marriage. I gave her some reading about panic disorder and regularly inquired about her anxiety symptoms and panic attacks, which she reported had decreased during the course of marital treatment.
>
> After four months of couple's therapy, Janet experienced an increase in her anxiety symptoms and some depressive symptoms as well. We continued marital therapy, but I also initiated regular individual sessions with Janet. I adhered to the cognitive-behavioral treatment model of panic disorder (Barlow & Cerny, 1988).[3] Janet learned the progressive muscle relaxation technique. She learned the role of automatic thinking and poor hypothesis testing in maintaining anxiety. During the first few sessions, it was clear that she was not consistently practicing her relaxation exercises, nor was she regularly completing her cognitive homework assignments. At the beginning of the fifth session, Janet stated that she did not agree with the cognitive model of anxiety. "I don't think first and then feel. I feel first and then think." She went on to say that she thought learning ways to combat anxiety would not help her. She wanted to understand why she was anxious. I then asked her what she wanted to do. She said she wanted to talk about her childhood. I agreed to shift the direction of therapy. Janet then went on to talk about the impact her father's death had had on her and her family's life. She was 12 at the time. Her mother became very depressed after his death and for years did not fulfill her parental role. I saw Janet for four more sessions, and then Janet and Jorge terminated, primarily because of their

---

[3]At the time of treating this case, the important component of focusing on interoceptive bodily cues in cognitive-behavioral treatment of panic disorder had not been introduced.

limited finances. Janet reported that she benefited a great deal from therapy; this was supported by some reduction in her anxiety symptoms since she was first evaluated. Jorge, on the other hand, reported that there was little change in their marriage.

The important point of this case is that there was not a good match between the theoretical basis of treatment and the set of issues (theory) that Janet expected the therapy to address. I presented the assumptions of the model through written material and through didactic presentations. One could think of this as the therapist's culture-specific explanatory model. Janet learned the main points of the model, and, although not consistently, she did make some efforts to implement the therapeutic strategies. After five sessions, she informed me that she did not agree with the basic assumptions of the model. She expressed a set of beliefs with a psychodynamic bent, that is, learning skills is not important; understanding her childhood is what matters.

As a therapist, I had the choice of following Janet's lead in helping her to understand her childhood or of redirecting her back to cognitive-behavioral therapy. At the time, I remember thinking that I might not have presented the treatment effectively and that was why she was doubtful of the treatment approach. I considered reviewing the basic premises of cognitive therapy with her. Instead, I opted for following her lead and shifting the focus of therapy. To clarify, I did not see myself as shifting to a psychodynamic approach to meet her expectations. My goal was to allow her to talk about her childhood and related experiences, and through reflection and "supportive" therapy I hoped to help her better understand that experience. Furthermore, I was open to the possibility of reintroducing cognitive-behavioral principles and methods as needed. I was not going to push that perspective; however, I was going to be ready should the opportunity present itself. For instance, if Janet's recollection of her childhood experiences contained cognitive distortions, which I had no doubt they did, I would have used or at least recommended cognitive-behavioral means of addressing them.

The mistake I made with Janet is that I did not provide her adequate opportunity to express her views as to why she suffered from panic disorder. In part this was due to the original focus of treatment being on their marital relationship. When we began working in individual therapy, however, I moved immediately into the cognitive-behavioral approach, teaching her about the model. There was little opportunity for her to propose other explanatory models. Given that she was motivated to attain symptom relief as soon as possible, she may not have given as much thought to her own beliefs about what underlay her problem.

It is difficult to know if I made the right decision to shift the direction of therapy. We are not able to compare the achieved outcome with the outcome that would have been associated with having stayed the course. I believe, however, that being open to following the client's direction reflects cultural competence. It demonstrates a willingness to respect and validate the client's theoretical model, which I believe was related to her sociocultural beliefs.[4] The theoretical notion that changing thoughts can alter one's mood may run counter to some people's belief systems, which place more significance on emotions than on thoughts. This is not to say that I completely disregarded the culturally embedded theoretical framework from which I worked. I was open to incorporate it at an appropriate

---

[4]It is important to note that the therapist should have some background in the treatment approach suggested by the client's framework. If not, it would be best to refer the client to a therapist whose treatment approach would provide a better match.

time in the future, after Janet could see that I had accepted and worked within her framework. Furthermore, the use of my perspective at a future time would probably work only if I grounded it in the framework of helping her understand her childhood, at least initially.

It is worth noting that there are risks in agreeing to work within the client's theoretical model. It could be that the client's framework may reflect more than just an alternative way of understanding the presenting problem; it could also reflect dysfunction, an effort to undermine the treatment, or both. In this case, Janet's efforts to shift the therapy focus, whether they were intentional or not, could have led to less effective treatment. A therapist should not follow the client in whichever direction he or she wishes to go at any given time. A careful consideration of the pros and cons of such treatment modifications is necessary at all times, particularly if changes are being requested often. Nevertheless, an openness to consider working within the client's proposed theoretical model, however presented, is likely to be useful in working with culturally diverse clients.

Methods

The treatment methods refer to the procedures clinicians use to facilitate behavioral change in their clients. These methods are frequently tied to the practitioner's theoretical orientation, which now can include an integration of different therapeutic methods and theoretical approaches. For example, Wachtel (1977) discusses the integration of behavioral and psychodynamic principles and methods. Cultural competence reflects an openness on the part of the therapist to adapt one's intervention to the client's cultural belief system. This could range from referring clients to other healers to receive treatment that the mental health professional is not capable of providing (e.g., folk healing) to maintaining one's treatment methods intact but describing the method as being similar to a known culturally syntonic method. An example of the latter is encouraging patients to use injectable long-lasting depot medication rather than oral medication by alluding to cultural beliefs in which injections are viewed as a most effective form of medical practice, a belief adhered to by some Mexican and Latino families. In order for the clinician to adapt his or her intervention to the client's cultural perspective, it is important that the clinician learn about culturally syntonic treatment methods for his or her clients. This can come about during the initial evaluation after the problem has been defined. The practitioner can inquire as to how such problems have been addressed in the past by the client and his or her family. Or the practitioner can be open to the clients' reactions to the treatment methods that are implemented and consider adapting the procedures to better fit the client's cultural background.

I now present a couple's case in which I attempted to improve their communication and problem-solving skills. It was not until therapy had ended unsuccessfully that I realized the lack of congruence between their cultural belief system and my efforts to increase "appropriate" communication of both positive and negative affect. This case, and others like it, taught me the importance of making sure that the treatment methods one uses are compatible with the clients' cultural system of meanings.

> The eldest of four adult daughters initiated the first contact between me and the Siqueiros family. Mr. and Mrs. Siqueiros were born in northern Mexico and came to the United States as young adults. They were both 54 years old, and their four daughters were in their twenties. The parents had been married for about 30 years. The family ran a business from their house; the father was the owner, two daughters ran the office, and the mother helped out occasionally. The main presenting problem was the couple's considerable and long-standing

marital strain. According to the daughters, they were either not talking to each other or were verbally abusive. The couple agreed to begin therapy, but Mr. Siqueiros would do so only on an individual basis. Although couples therapy was my preference, I agreed to see them individually for three or four sessions and then to reevaluate the treatment plan. My goals were to establish a working relationship with each of them, help them define goals for their marriage, and then bring them together for conjoint therapy. After seeing each one for three consecutive sessions, Mr. Siqueiros ended therapy, stating, "My feet are on the ground—she's the one who needs help." He further added that he fulfilled his obligations as a husband; he worked hard and provided well for the family. However, he indicated that his wife intentionally refused to fulfill her responsibilities, particularly cooking meals for him, washing his clothes, and being available for sexual relations. Because of this, Mr. Siqueiros believed his wife was to blame for their marital problems. Mrs. Siqueiros was disappointed that her husband had decided not to continue psychotherapy; nevertheless, she continued for six more sessions. Before ending therapy, she stated that Mr. Siqueiros was depending on her more and she found him to be more communicative.

Fourteen months later, Mr. and Mrs. Siqueiros returned and requested to be seen for family therapy with their daughters. They agreed to have short-term therapy, five weeks only. As was the case a year earlier, there was considerable marital strain, and the daughters took turns in trying to mediate their difficulties. Furthermore, the mother was seen by all as intrusive. In an effort to decrease the tension, as one treatment goal I attempted to teach them how to communicate both positive and negative feelings following Gottman, Notarius, Gonso, and Markman (1976). In the last session, in an effort to assist Mr. Siqueiros further with communicating negative feelings in a specific situation, I suggested that he might have felt hurt that his needs were not considered by his wife. He responded vehemently that no one had ever hurt him, but if they ever did he would make sure that they would know it. I interpreted his comments as meaning that he does not let others know when he is hurt by their actions. Expressing hurt would mean that he was not strong. He stated that his wife and daughters have tried to make him a *mandilon* [wimp], but he was never going to succumb to their wishes. At the end of the session, I referred the couple for marital therapy. They did not follow through.

Therapy helped the family in some ways. For example, the daughters learned that their mother's intrusiveness was in part due to her feeling excluded from their lives, both in terms of the family business and their personal lives. As a result of family therapy, the daughters began taking steps to spend time with their mother in ways not related to the business or to their father (e.g., going shopping or going out to eat). Little progress was made, however, in improving the central problem, Mr. and Mrs. Siqueiros's chronic marital distress. There were many factors that contributed to my unsuccessful efforts in working with the couple. One factor that was particularly significant from a cultural perspective was the mismatch between the treatment methods and the clients' cultural values. I attempted to teach the couple and daughters ways to communicate their considerable negative feelings in a manner that would enhance their relationships. Mr. Siqueiros's clear rejection of my interpretation that his wife may have hurt him is an example that his cultural views ran counter to this approach. Directly expressing to his wife that she did something to hurt him violated some sociocultural standard. From his view, he was not supposed to show vulnerability; as the head of the household, he had to be strong. As a result, he was not at all receptive to learning how to communicate negative feelings, let alone acknowledge that his family did things to offend or hurt him.

In retrospect, I had assumed that the direct communication of negative (and positive) feelings was the cultural standard in effective communication in marriages and families. It made sense to me, it was written up in treatment manuals, but it may not be the cultural standard for all families. This direct form of communication may run counter to the standard in some cultural groups. In the case of the Siqueiros family, particularly from the father's perspective, normative communication between spouses may not be directly stating negative or even positive feelings. Words may be valued less. Action or behaviors may be emphasized. This is consistent with what Mr. Siqueiros had said; he had fulfilled his obligations, yet his wife had not.

The important point is that as clinicians we need to recognize that the treatment methods we use are embedded in culture-specific models of human behavior. Rather than proceed along usual treatment paths, particularly with clients from diverse cultural backgrounds, the effectiveness of one's treatment might be enhanced by first assessing whether the assumptions underlying chosen treatments are consistent with clients' models of human behavior. By collecting this type of information, not only will clinicians learn how their clients' cultural ways of life are important for their treatment, but also clinicians will inform their clients that they are interested in learning from them what treatment models might work best. As a result, the clinician will be in a position to adjust his or her tools to meet the specific needs of the client. For instance, had I assessed the Siqueiros's ideal form of communication, I might have learned that they prefer expressing negative sentiment in indirect or subtle ways. If that was the case, then we could have structured the communication skill building around those forms of communication.

It is important to note here, as is the case in other therapy domains, that there are risks in trying to adapt one's treatment methods to the clients' cultural belief system. For the cultural outsider, it can be difficult to distinguish culturally different forms of adaptive functioning from simply maladaptive forms of functioning. For example, indirect forms of communication may be the norm for the Siqueiros family, but had I worked with them in improving the effectiveness of their supposed indirect forms of expressions, we might have learned that they were actually unable to communicate effectively in that mode as well. So it is important that clinicians carefully consider the cultural context of their intervention methods, but not completely abandon their methods or radically modify them on the basis of limited information about the cultural congruence between their method and the client's belief system. It is possible that little modification is necessary. Or, it may be that initially a major change is thought to be needed but after pursuing that path for some time both the therapist and client(s) may agree that still further modification is needed. That modification could even be a return to the standard treatment method used by the therapist. Culturally competent psychotherapy requires an openness to consider the lack of fit between one's treatment methods and the client's cultural background. Deciding whether or not changes are necessary and then knowing when and how to implement such changes reflect culturally competent practice.

Extraclinical Aspects of Therapy and Training

Issues of culture can be difficult to address with one's clients or with the clients of one's trainees. Addressing such issues can be even more challenging when they come about outside the therapist-client relationship, in case conferences, and in observing colleagues' clinical work. I now present a case in which culture was a salient theme during a case conference I attended during my internship. What made this incident especially challenging for me is that the case concerned a Mexican woman, and part of the discussion focused on the Mexican culture. Being Mexican American, I could not help but think that the discussion of the Mexican culture was at least in part a discussion of my culture as well.

At a case conference of the adult outpatient clinic within the Department of Psychiatry, a psychiatry resident presented the case of Mrs. Sambrano, an 18-year-old Mexican woman. She had been living with her common-law husband for more than 2 years. They were the parents of a 5-month-old baby. At the age of 12, Mrs. Sambrano immigrated to the United States from Mexico with her family. She was referred by the psychiatric emergency unit for having significant depressive symptomatology that began after the birth of her child. The depression had been exacerbated recently by a series of life events: becoming pregnant again, her spouse threatening to leave her, and obtaining an abortion one week prior to her ER visit. In addition to her depressive symptoms, Mrs. Sambrano also presented "seizurelike" behaviors described in the ER records as an "arching back, flinging arms, rolling eyes up in her head" and "alternating periods of unresponsiveness."

After presenting the case, the resident brought the patient into the conference room from the hallway where she had been waiting. Mrs. Sambrano was then interviewed by a psychiatrist with approximately 30 clinical staff members observing. The client spoke English with a marked accent but was easily understood. After a 15-minute interview, her husband, who had also been waiting, was called in. The psychiatrist interviewed the couple together. Interestingly, Mr. Sambrano took it upon himself to serve as his wife's translator. When the psychiatrist asked Mrs. Sambrano a question, he translated the question into Spanish, she responded to her husband in Spanish, and then he translated into English what she had said. This was rather curious given that we knew that she communicated well in English.

After the interview ended and the patient and her husband left, an interesting discussion about diagnostic and treatment issues took place primarily among the psychiatrists and residents. Near the end of the discussion one of the experienced and well-regarded psychiatrists commented that his wife's aunt, who was also Mexican, had a similar hysterical style as that of the patient. He then went on to argue that the patient's reactions reflected a "cultural pattern," in part due to the controlling nature of the spouse. No one questioned or challenged his comments; as a whole, the clinical staff appeared to have been persuaded by his argument.

This case conference raises many issues. One issue is the limited evidence that the psychiatrist had regarding the cultural basis of the client's symptoms and his tendency to explain away her considerable distress as a "cultural thing." His explanation reminds me of one of Meehl's (1973) comments as to why he does not attend clinical case conferences. He says that in case conferences, clinicians tolerate "feeble inferences." Had the psychiatrist commented on the literature with regard to *ataque de nervois,* or had he expressed even the slightest tentativeness in his assessment, then perhaps an interesting discussion could have evolved about the cultural basis of Mrs. Sambrano's presenting problems. But that did not happen. Instead, this well-regarded psychiatrist convinced the clinical staff that the symptoms were cultural in nature, his argument largely based on the fact that his aunt-in-law, who was also Mexican, had similar symptoms.

During this discussion, I recall feeling considerable tension. I am not one to speak out in public settings, particularly when I have little status. A psychology intern in a department of psychiatry has little status. But I had hoped that my supervisors would speak up, especially the two who were Mexican American. They did not. It is awkward when a member of your ethnic group is being discussed by a group of people who are largely not from your same ethnicity. You want to contribute and shed some light on the issue, but you want to do it in a way in which your ethnicity is irrelevant. You simply want to be judged on the quality of your ideas. However, one cannot divorce one's ethnicity from the discussion, let alone one's thinking. Perhaps my supervisors felt this awkwardness as well. As a result of not questioning the psychiatrist, many people left the staff meeting with a presumed better understanding of the Mexican culture. Later on, the psychiatry resident who was treating Mrs. Sambrano told me that he agreed with the cultural interpretation. I should have spoken up at the case conference.

This incident occurred 15 years ago, when the awareness of cultural issues was more limited and the ethnic composition of mental health professionals reflected little cultural diversity. Although I have not encountered this situation now as a clinical supervisor, I am sure that similar issues arise in case conferences today. Supervisors should model appropriate professional behavior by critically evaluating claims about the role of culture in the lives of clients with the goal of enhancing an understanding of the case. Modeling such behavior would likely help all trainees feel more comfortable in contributing to such professional discussions. It would be especially helpful for trainees of ethnocultural minority groups to help them learn how to integrate their own local cultural experience in professional activities, perhaps without feeling the awkwardness that some of us have experienced.

CONCLUSION

Culture matters in psychotherapy and in clinical supervision. I have presented a model of cultural competence derived from both research and clinical practice to serve as a guide in providing culturally appropriate mental health services for culturally diverse clientele. Cultural competence is not a simple formula that can be easily followed from session to session. Nor is it a set of cultural facts that one can apply. Instead it is a perspective that respects the complexity of each individual and his or her cultural context. Moving between the cultural frames of the client and the clinician is essential to cultural competence. To develop this skill, supervisors and trainees alike must think critically about the role of culture in clinical practice.

REFERENCES

Barlow, D. H., & Cerny, J. A. (1988). *Psychological treatment of panic.* New York: Guilford.

Bernal, G., & Flores-Ortiz, Y. (1982). Latino families in therapy: Engagement and evaluation. *Journal of Marital and Family Therapy, 357–365.*

Berry, J. W. Poortinga. Y. H., Segall, M. H., & Dasen, P. R. (1992). *Cross-cultural psychology: Research and applications.* Cambridge, United Kingdom: Cambridge University Press.

Betancourt, H., & López, S. R. (1993). The study of culture, ethnicity, and race in American psychology. *American Psychologist, 48,* 629–637.

Chess, S., Clark, K. B., & Thomas, A. (1953). The importance of cultural evaluation in psychiatric diagnosis and treatment. *Psychiatric Quarterly, 27,* 102–114.

Comas-Díaz, L., & Griffith, E. H. E. (Eds.) (1988). *Clinical guidelines in cross-cultural mental health.* New York: Wiley.

Cross, T. L., Bazron, B. J., Dennis, K. W., & Isaacs, M. R. (1989). *Towards a culturally competent system of care.* Washington, DC: CAASP Technical Assistance Center.

Dana, R. H. (1993). *Multicultural assessment perspectives for professional psychology.* Boston: Allyn & Bacon.

Draguns, J. G. (1981). Counseling across cultures: Common themes and distinct approaches. In P. B. Pedersen, J. G. Draguns, W. J. Lonner, & S. E. Trimble (Eds.), *Counseling across cultures* (2nd ed., pp. 3–21). Honolulu: University of Hawaii Press.

Gomez Palacios, M., Padilla, E. R., & Roll, S. (1984). *Escala de inteligencia para nivel escolar Wechsler: WISC-RM.* Mexico, D.F.: El Manual Moderno.

Gottman, J., Notarius, C., Gonso, J., & Markman, H. (1976). *A couple's guide to communication.* Champaign, IL: Research Press.

Graham, S. (1992). Most of the subjects were white and middle class: Trends in published research on African Americans in selected APA journals, 1970–1989. *American Psychologist, 47,* 629–639.

Guthrie, R. V. (1976). *Even the rat was white.* New York: Harper & Row.

Herrans, L. L., & Rodríguez, J. M. (1992). *Escala de inteligencia Wechsler para niños—Revisada.* San Antonio: The Psychological Corporation, Harcourt Brace Jovanovich.

Jones, E. E., & Korchin, S. (1981). Minority mental health: Perspectives. In E. E. Jones & S. J. Korchin (Eds.), *Minority mental health* (pp. 3–36). New York: Praeger.

Kleinman, A. (1980). *Patients and healers in the context of culture.* Berkeley: University of California Press.

Kleinman, A. (1986). *Social origins of distress and disease: Depression, neurasthenia and pain in modern China.* New Haven: Yale University Press.

Kleinman, A. (1988). *Rethinking psychiatry: From cultural category to personal experience.* New York: Free Press.

Kleinman, A. (1992). Pain and resistance: The delegitimation and relegitimation of local worlds. In M. G. Good, P. Brodwin, A. Kleinman, & B. J. Goods (Eds.), *Pain as human experience* (pp. 169–196). Berkeley: University of California Press.

Kleinman, A., & Kleinman, J. (1991). Suffering and its professional transformation: Toward an ethnography of interpersonal experience. *Culture, Psychiatry, and Medicine, 15,* 275–301.

López, S. (1977). Clinical stereotypes of the Mexican-American. In J. L. Martinez (Ed.), *Chicano psychology* (pp. 263–275). New York: Academic Press.

López, S. (1983). Ethnic bias in clinical judgment: An attributional analysis (doctoral dissertation, University of California, Los Angeles). *Dissertation Abstracts, 44,* 2561B.

López, S. (1988). The empirical basis to ethnocultural and linguistic bias in mental health evaluation of Hispanics. *American Psychologist, 43,* 1095–1097.

López, S. R. (1989). Patient variable biases in clinical judgment: Conceptual overview and methodological considerations. *Psychological Bulletin, 6,* 184–203.

López, S. R. (in press). Testing ethnic minority children. In B. B. Wolman (Ed.), *The encyclopedia of psychology, psychiatry, and psychoanalysis.* New York: Holt.

López, S. R., Grover, K. P., Holland, D., Johnson, M. J., Kain, C. D., Kanel, K., Mellins, C. A., & Rhyne, M. C. (1989). Development of culturally sensitive psychotherapy. *Professional Psychology: Research Practice,* 369–376.

López, S., & Hernandez, P. (1986). How culture is considered in evaluations of psychopathology. *Journal of Nervous and Mental Disease, 174,* 598–606.

López, S., & Hernandez, P. (1987). When culture is considered in the evaluation and treatment of Hispanic patients. *Psychotherapy, 24,* 120–126.

López, S. R., Nuñez, J. A., & Magaña, B. (1993). *Cultural attributions, ethnic base rates and clinical judgment of a depressed Mexican American woman.* Unpublished research.

López, S., & Romero, A. (1988). Assessing the intellectual functioning of Spanish-speaking adults: A comparison of the EIWA and WAIS. *Professional Psychology: Research and Practice, 19,* 263–270.

López, S. R., & Taussig, I. M. (1991). Cognitive-intellectual functioning of impaired and nonimpaired Spanish-speaking elderly: Implications for culturally sensitive assessment. *Psychological Assessment: Journal of Consulting and Clinical Psychology, 3,* 448–454.

Malgady, R. G., Rogler, L. H., & Costantino, G. (1987). Ethnocultural and linguistic bias in mental health evaluations of Hispanics. *American Psychologist, 42,* 227–234.

Meehl, P. (1973). Why I do not attend clinical case conferences. In P. E. Meehl, *Psychodiagnosis: Selected papers* (pp. 225–302). Minneapolis: University of Minnesota Press.

Pedersen, P. B., & Ivey, A. (1993). *Culture-centered counseling and interviewing skills: A practical guide.* New York: Praeger.

Ridley, C. R., Mendoza, D. W., Kanitz, B. E., Angermeier, L., & Zenk, R. (1994). Cultural sensitivity in multicultural counseling: A perceptual schema model. *Journal of Counseling Psychology, 41,* 125–136.

Sue, D. W., & Sue, D. (1990). *Counseling the culturally different: Theory and practice.* New York: Wiley.

Sue, S., & Zane, N. (1987). The role of culture and cultural techniques in psychotherapy: A critique and reformulation. *American Psychologist, 47,* 37–45.

Vargas, L. A., & Koss-Chioino, J. D. (1992). *Working with culture: Psychotherapeutic interventions with ethnic minority children and adolescents.* San Francisco: Jossey-Bass.

Wachtel, P. (1977). *Psychoanalysis and behavior therapy: Toward an integration.* New York: Basic Books.

CHAPTER 30

Ethical and Legal Aspects
of Clinical Supervision

SAMUEL KNAPP
Pennsylvania Psychological Association
LEON VANDECREEK
Wright State University

The supervision of trainees or employees is an expected responsibility for many professional psychologists. In a job analysis of licensed psychologists in the United States and Canada, Rosenfeld, Shimberg, and Thornton (1983) found that 64% of the 1,585 licensed psychologists surveyed reported spending part of their time in teaching, including supervision of students and interns. More than half (57%) of the respondents spent less than a quarter of their working time in this pursuit, but 25% reported spending 25% to 50% of their time on such activities.

Bowers and Knapp (1993) found that one third of the members of the Pennsylvania Psychological Association who were in independent practice were supervising other psychotherapists. Each respondent supervised an average of two persons. Sixty percent were supervising persons who were gaining the experience necessary to become licensed as a psychologist.

The educational backgrounds of supervised persons varies greatly. Psychologists may supervise interns or students from psychology, social work, counseling, medical, nursing, or other fields. Also, psychologists may hire licensed or engage unlicensed professionals, paraprofessionals, or volunteers to provide services under their direction.

The legal and ethical requirements of supervision vary according to the type of supervision provided. In general, licensing boards require that the supervising psychologists assume a greater degree of control and provide more intensive supervision to psychologists-in-training (those who are accruing supervised hours to qualify for the licensing examination) than to employees. In both of these situations, however, the psychologist has the authority to direct the treatment and has the ultimate responsibility for patient welfare.

Consultation is distinct from supervision. Although many persons use the terms *consultation* and *supervision* interchangeably, the consultative arrangement is not real supervision and is not discussed in detail in this chapter. The consultant provides advice to an independent professional and has no authority over the services provided.

Supervisors need to be familiar with legal and ethical aspects of supervision that tran-

Note: The views expressed do not necessarily represent those of the Pennsylvania Psychological Association.

scend their theoretical orientations and teaching skills. Ethical principles apply to supervision, as they do to all professional activities. Supervision, like all professional services, contains a unique liability component because when patients claim they were harmed by a supervisee, the supervisor may be held liable as well.

Licensed psychologists who are supervisors can find guidance on ethical and legal issues from sources within and outside the profession, including the Ethical Principles of Psychologists and the Code of Conduct of the American Psychological Association (APA, 1992). Acceptance of membership in the American Psychological Association commits psychologists to adhere to these principles. In addition, these principles may take on the force of law because they or similar ethical codes are often incorporated into the regulations pursuant to the licensing laws for psychologists. Licensing laws also frequently adopt the supervisory guidelines recommended by the Association of State and Provincial Psychology Boards (ASPPB). Finally, precedents from malpractice cases impact on psychological supervisors.

This chapter reviews the ethical and legal guidelines for psychologists who provide supervision. The issues covered include ensuring the proper qualifications of supervisors, handling impaired supervisees, handling sexual attraction to patients, dealing with multiple relationships, treating life-endangering patients, ensuring that the consent of patients to receive treatment is informed, and learning of the unique malpractice issues of direct and vicarious liability. Recommendations for supervisors are made at the end of the chapter.

Having been trained in psychology and having worked as psychologists, we have written this chapter from that vantage point. Consequently, our primary attention will be given to the ethical code and the issues confronted by psychologists in their practice of psychotherapy supervision. It is important, however, to emphasize that the issues and concerns of psychologists discussed here readily apply to supervisors from other mental health professions.

QUALIFICATIONS OF SUPERVISORS

According to the APA Code of Ethics, "psychologists provide services, teach, and conduct research only within the boundaries of their competence, based on their education, training, supervised experience, or appropriate professional experience" (Principle 1.04). The ASPPB guidelines (no date) provide more specific statements of qualifications:

> Supervising psychologists shall be licensed or certified for the practice of psychology and have adequate training, knowledge, and skill to render competently any psychological service which their supervisee undertakes. They shall not supervise or permit their supervisee to engage in any psychological practice which they cannot perform competently themselves. (Guideline A. Qualifications)

Therefore, these guidelines require supervisors of health care services to have competencies as practitioners. Supervision requires not only a thorough knowledge of patient care, but also an understanding of the unique cultural issues in the population receiving services (Vasquez, 1992).

The guidelines also imply that psychologists/supervisors should have specific knowledge and skills as supervisors. Yet acquiring these skills is currently a haphazard endeavor. Training as a supervisor occurs mostly through informal experiences, such as reading about how to do supervision or relying on past experience as a supervisee. And although newly graduated psychologists are familiar with the role of supervisee, they may not be prepared to assume the role of supervisor. Furthermore, APA accreditation of doctoral programs does not require training in how to supervise (APA, 1986), and licensing boards and other credentialing bodies rarely inspect the qualifications of supervisors.

DUTIES AND RESPONSIBILITIES OF THE SUPERVISOR

Ethical Principle 1.22 reads as follows:

> Psychologists delegate to their employees, supervisees, and research assistants only those responsibilities that such persons can reasonably be expected to perform competently, on the basis of their education, training, or experience, either independently or with the level of supervision being provided. (APA, 1992)

This ethical guideline makes it clear that supervisors should delegate responsibilities carefully and deliberately to their supervisees. Because training centers typically accept trainees from many different university programs, the skill level of the trainees may vary greatly. It is important for the supervising psychologist to determine the adequacy of preparation and level of skill of the trainee even though previous supervisors and sponsoring academic departments may claim that the student has superior skills. The supervisors' knowledge of patient progress must also be thorough enough to ensure that they fulfill their legal and professional responsibilities. This may include using face-to-face contact when necessary to develop and monitor effective treatment plans. Supervisors must also be available for emergency consultation and direct intervention.

Psychologists should not supervise more trainees than they can responsibly manage at one time, remembering that the ultimate responsibility for all patients rests with the supervisor. The ASPPB Guidelines (which are incorporated in the licensing regulations of many states) say that "no more than three full-time persons may be registered for any one supervisor" (p. 3). Theoretically, a court could view overextended supervisors as negligent if they did not adequately monitor the progress of patients or trainees.

The duties of supervisors include more than just providing a basic "safety net" to ensure that minimal standards of treatment are being provided. Ethical Principle 1.22 (APA, 1992) states that "Psychologists provide proper training and supervision to their employees or supervisees and take reasonable steps to see that such persons perform services responsibly, competently, and ethically." Special problems identified by supervisors are helping supervisees who have psychological impairments, who have difficulties dealing with their sexual feelings toward patients, and who are treating patients who threaten to harm themselves or others.

The Impaired Supervisee

Impairment can be distinguished from distress. Impairment refers to the inability of professionals to fulfill the minimal responsibilities of their profession because of a mental or physical disability. When an individual is distressed, he or she may feel subjective discomfort but may still be able to perform his or her job responsibly.

The frequency of impairment among psychologists is not known, but Guy, Poelstra, and

Stark (1989) reported that 4.6% of psychologists reported that they had been impaired some time in their careers. At least 6% of psychologists use alcohol to excess (Thoreson, Nathan, Skorina, & Kilburg, 1983). Other psychologists may have depressive or other disorders that significantly impair them.

Skorina, Bissell, and DeSoto (1990) found that older psychologists in recovery from alcoholism reported that they first noticed the harmful effects of their drinking at the median age of 24. Thus, most psychologists with alcoholism would have had significant drinking problems by the time they entered their practicums or internships.

Regrettably, psychologists are reluctant to confront colleagues with drinking problems, although they are better at confronting colleagues with other mental health problems (Thoreson, Budd, & Krauskopf, 1986). Skorina et al. (1990) found that only 41% of the psychologists in recovery were ever confronted by their colleagues about their drinking.

Supervisors may be liable if they fail to take appropriate action against supervisees whom they know or reasonably should know to have an impairment. Some public indications of impairment may include smelling alcohol on their breath, arriving at work intoxicated, or being arrested for driving under the influence. A more subtle indication may be a serious deterioration in work performance.

Sexual Attraction to Patients

Pope, Keith-Spiegel, and Tabachnick (1986) reported that 87% of psychologists (95% men and 76% women) reported feeling sexual attraction to patients at least once in their careers. Yet only 9% believed their training or supervision had been adequate to help them deal with this issue.

Supervisors are responsible for investigating all suggestions of harm to patients. In *Andrews v. United States* (1982), a physician's assistant and the physician who supervised him were found liable. The physician's assistant was having sex with a patient, and one of the staff physicians did not adequately investigate the complaint when he heard about it from another patient. The supervising physician probably would not have been liable if he had made a thorough response to the allegation, such as speaking with the patient directly.

The issue of sexual relationship goes far beyond warnings to avoid patient-therapist sex or investigating complaints when they occur. Intensive sexual feelings (even if not acted on) can impair a positive transference and the success of psychotherapy. It is more important, however, for supervisors to deal with sexual attraction to patients as part of their overall supervisory functions.

Many people are uncomfortable talking about sexual feelings or perceive that discussions of sexual feelings are indicative of insensitivity, excessive machismo, or "bad taste." Regardless of whether the psychologists welcome or fear it, however, patients may have sexual attractions toward them or their supervisees. Supervisors can help their supervisees provide better health care services by discussing sexual feelings in a safe environment with respect, sensitivity, and openness (Pope, Sonne, & Holroyd, 1993).

Special Issues With Life-Endangering Patients

Supervisors also need to be especially careful with life-endangering patients. Kleespies (1993) reported that 1 out of 9 psychology interns had a patient successfully commit suicide and more than 1 in 4 had a patient who made a suicide attempt during his or her training years. That means 40% of the psychology trainees had a patient who either succeeded in or attempted suicide.

Although no mental health professional can claim to have the ability to predict or prevent all potential suicides, Kleespies (1993) reported that the psychology trainees did not believe they were well trained to deal with suicidal patients. Few therapists had the course work or experience to treat such patients, let alone deal with the emotional aftershock of the patient's death.

Although the potential of the supervisees' patients to harm identifiable third parties is less rare than patient suicides, supervisors also need to be aware of this potential problem. The need to make an exception to confidentiality to warn or protect others from harm is especially troublesome for supervisors. Because supervisees are normally expected to provide the same standard of care as does a licensed professional, supervisees have the same duty to warn or protect others from harm (VandeCreek & Knapp, 1994).

The most widely known case pertinent to this issue is *Tarasoff* v. *Regents of the University of California* (1976). The California court ruled that the psychologist should have done more to prevent the murder committed by his patient, and it established the duty of a psychotherapist to protect when a patient presents an imminent degree of danger to an identifiable victim. The psychologist's supervisor, a psychiatrist, was held responsible as well, along with the University of California. If the supervisor had examined the patient and decided that he was not dangerous, the grounds for liability based on foreseeability might have been less clear.

A related case underscores the need for written policies to guide the agency in the management of dangerous patients. In *Peck* v. *The Counseling Service of Addison County, Inc.* (1985), Peck told his counselor that he was considering burning down his father's barn. After talking with Peck, the counselor was satisfied that the threat was not serious, and she did not discuss the matter with her supervisor or take any preventive action. She did send for Peck's medical records but did not contact any of the physicians who had previously treated him. The next day, Peck burned the barn down. The court found that the counselor was negligent in failing to protect the barn, based on her failure to obtain the past medical records more quickly, failure to take an adequate history, and failure to consult her supervisors.

The Counseling Service was negligent because it did not have any written policy regarding supervision when a patient presented a serious danger. The lack of policy may be seen as the agency's failure to exercise proper control over its supervisees. Had the center had such a policy, there might have been no grounds for action against it if the counselor had been acting outside the scope of the agency's policy.

The Peck case illustrates the importance of specifying the lines of authority within an agency and defining the limits of independent action and decision making by each employee. The descriptions of responsibility must specify the means and critical patient situations in which supervisees will contact the supervisor.

TIMELINESS AND DOCUMENTATION OF SUPERVISION

Supervision must be provided on a scheduled basis with additional supervision available as needed. The lack of timely feedback is the root of many ethical complaints brought against supervisors (Keith-Spiegel & Koocher, 1985).

Just as practitioners maintain case records on their clients to document services, they should also document their supervisory work. The goals of supervision should be clarified in writing, and written evaluations of trainees should be completed on a regular basis. Bridge and Bascue (1988) have developed a one-page supervisory record form that includes most of the information needed for documentation: the date and session number of supervision, identification of the cases discussed along with client progress and problems, suggestions for further treatment, and remedial plans for the supervisee. The supervisors should prepare this record with concern for the quality of care given the patient, the quality of training given the supervisee, and the ethical and legal issues involved if there should be a complaint from the supervisee or the patient.

Ratings of poor performance should never come as a surprise to a supervisee. The trainee who practices at an unsatisfactory level, is not given a remedial plan, and is later given a poor performance rating that affects future employment could have grounds for an ethical complaint for failure to provide constructive and timely feedback.

Similarly, supervisors should provide accurate information in response to requests for references. These may include factual information such as hours worked and the nature of the job responsibilities as well as quality of performance, strengths, and weaknesses. Supervisees should be aware of the general nature of the reference and could therefore be in the position of declining to use the supervisor as a reference (Bennett, Bryant, VandenBos, & Greenwood, 1990).

MULTIPLE RELATIONSHIPS

Ethical Principle 1.19 states the following:

> (a) Psychologists do not exploit persons over whom they have supervisory, evaluative, or other authority such as students, supervisees, employees, research participants, and clients or patients. (b) Psychologists do not engage in sexual relationships with students or supervisees in training over whom the psychologist has evaluative or direct authority, because such relationships are so likely to impair judgment or be exploitative. (APA, 1992)

Supervisors, by definition, occupy a position of power and trust and are expected to advocate for the welfare of the supervisee. Although this principle appears straightforward, a sizable percentage of supervisors fail to adhere to these standards. In a survey of female members of APA Division 12 (Clinical Psychology), 17% of the respondents reported that they had sexual relationships with psychology educators while graduate students (Glaser & Thorpe, 1986). Pope, Levenson, and Schover (1979) found that 1 out of 4 women who received her doctoral degree within the prior 6 years had had sexual contact with a supervisor.

One possible explanation for these findings is the lack of formal education for supervisors and supervisees concerning competent ethical standards of supervision. Only 3% of the respondents in the Glaser and Thorpe (1986) survey reported a thorough coverage of ethical considerations concerning sexual involvement with educators, and only 9% reported receiving some coverage of the issue. The remaining 88% reported that no coverage at all was given to educator-student sexual intimacies. If students are expected to master the intricacies of supervision through informal observation of their own supervisors, the data from the Glaser and Thorpe study suggest that a poor role model is often provided.

Other forms of dual relationships may arise between supervisee and supervisor. Although it is difficult to establish absolute guidelines to cover all possible conflict-of-interest situations, the general rule is that psychologists must hold the fiduciary role of supervisor as paramount. This means that psychologists should not supervise trainees who are relatives, spouses, friends, prior clients, employers, or others with whom they would find a potential conflict of interest or with whom they cannot be candid about performance.

Even the most cautious supervisor cannot avoid all dual relationships. It is inevitable that supervisors will encounter trainees in social settings, in community activities, and in other professional settings. This issue is considered in Ethical Principle 1.17, which reads, in part,

> In many communities and situations, it may not be feasible or reasonable for psychologists to avoid social or other nonprofessional contacts with persons such as patients, clients, students, supervisees, or research participants. Psychologists must always be sensitive to the potential harmful effects of other contacts on their work and on those persons with whom they deal. A psychologist refrains from entering into or promising another personal, scientific, professional, financial, or other relationship with such persons if it appears likely that such a relationship reasonably might impair the psychologist's objectivity or otherwise interfere with the psychologist's effectively performing his or her functions as a psychologist, or might harm or exploit the other party. (APA, 1992)

This can be interpreted to mean that supervisors do not need to shun the trainee on all nonprofessional occasions, unless the supervisor believes that the supervisee-supervisor relationship will be compromised.

INFORMED CONSENT AND THE USE OF SUPERVISION

Being introduced as "doctor," even though a person is a resident or a psychological trainee who is completing a year of postdoctoral supervision, may mislead the patient into believing that the practitioner is licensed to provide independent service. Patients have a right to know if they are receiving services from a trainee (ASPPB Guidelines, C.9). The patient's informed consent is especially important when the trainee is in the early stages of training because the patient may elect not to receive the service under these conditions. Furthermore, patients should be told who the supervisor is, that they may contact the supervisor if they are dissatisfied with the treatment, and how they can reach the supervisor.

It is easy for patients to misunderstand or misconstrue their therapists as acting in independent practice. Consequently, all aspects of the practice, from billing statements, business cards, signs on the office door, and so forth, should be prepared carefully so as not to mislead patients into thinking their therapist is an independent professional. The supervising psychologist should countersign all written reports (ASPPB, no date). Failure to inform a patient of a student's or trainee's status may expose the student and the supervisor to possible lawsuits alleging fraud, deceit, misrepresentation, invasion of privacy, breach of confidentiality, and lack of informed consent. Informed consent is not required for consultations in which the therapist is a licensed professional, possesses primary responsibility for the patient, and does not disclose identifying information.

MARKETPLACE ISSUES FOR SUPERVISORS

Supervisees may not advertise or market services, collect fees, or make public announcements as an independent provider. Payments for services provided by a psychology trainee or employees must be made to the supervisor or agency and never to the trainee. Titles of trainees must indicate their supervised status, and business cards and letterheads must not mislead the public into believing that the unlicensed supervisee delivers services independently. Titles such as "psychological intern," "psychological assistant," "psychologist resident," or "psychologist-in-training" may be appropriate.

One of the most distressing marketplace issues is the matter of the supervisor signing insurance forms for reimbursement for a trainee when the form requires the signature of the professional who actually provided the service. Although it may be unfair for insurance companies to refuse reimbursement for services not personally provided by the licensed psychologist, it is nonetheless fraudulent for supervisors to sign the form as if they had provided services (Knapp & VandeCreek, 1993). At the very least, the supervisor should cosign the form as "supervisor." Challenging this restrictive practice of insurance companies should be done through the courts or the legislature, not by fraudulently signing the form.

PENALTIES FOR ETHICAL VIOLATIONS

Psychologists who violate any of the APA's ethical principles face a variety of internal sanctions, ranging from a reprimand to being dropped from membership in APA. In addition, state licensing boards may restrict or revoke a psychologist's privilege to practice. The APA Ethics Committee has taken sanctions against psychologists who have exploited employees or supervisees. Malpractice cases may also be brought against supervisors for inadequate supervision.

Psychologists may find themselves liable for their actions (direct liability) or for the actions of their supervisees (vicarious liability) that harm patients. The legal liability of supervisors and employers arises primarily out of the common law, or the legal precedents established by the courts. Even when patients consent to treatment by a trainee, the patient does not thereby consent to receive substandard care or to be injured. In general, a trainee or an employee is held to the same standard of care as is a licensed professional. For example, in *Emory* v. *Porubiansky* (1981), the Georgia Supreme Court concluded that the status of a university as a training institution did not lower its duty to exercise reasonable care and skill in treating dental patients. Supervisors, however, are not liable for the acts of supervisees that occur outside their scope of employment.

Direct Liability

Charges of direct liability may be based on the supervisor's erroneous actions or omissions even though the injury to the patient occurred at the hands of the supervisee. This could occur for negligent procedures in the selection or hiring of the supervisee or dereliction of basic duties in providing supervision.

When it comes to employee selection, a court might ask if the supervisee or trainee was chosen in accordance with acceptable evaluation procedures. Does the supervisee have the minimal standards for a person of trainee status? Has he or she completed the course work necessary to perform the duties required of the traineeship or supervised status? Did the trainee have the recommendation of faculty members, former employers, or others familiar with his or her work? Does the person have personal skills as well as the technical skills necessary to function adequately within the work setting?

In selecting supervisees, the supervisor must have a clear understanding of the types of questions that can and cannot be asked according to current federal or state law. Generally speaking, questions about religion, sexual orientation, race, age, or marital status are not appropriate. Conversely, dismissals must be made only with clearly documented reasons and after previous warnings (Calfee, 1992).

Another area in which liability could occur is if the supervisor failed in his or her minimal responsibilities of providing supervision. The supervisor is expected to know the level of skill of the supervisee. Liability could occur if the supervisor directed the supervisee to perform a procedure that the supervisee was not qualified to perform or that was not appropriate for the patient. Inadequate treatment may also occur if the supervisor failed to consider the opinions or warnings of the supervisee when making decisions about a case and therefore failed to comprehend the needs of the patient. The supervisee is the conduit between the patient and the supervisor.

Most state boards of psychology establish standards concerning the minimum number of hours of face-to-face supervision and the proper procedures to follow with supervisees when the supervisor is on vacation or otherwise unavailable for prolonged periods of time. Failure to follow these standards could raise a presumption of negligence on the part of the supervisor.

It is crucial to investigate any allegations of misconduct thoroughly. As noted earlier, in *Andrews* v. *United States* (1982), a physician was held liable for the actions of a physician's assistant in the treatment of a woman with depression. The court ruled that the physician had failed to investigate the allegations adequately, "thereby failing to properly supervise the medical treatment that was being given a patient for whom he was responsible" (p. 611).

Vicarious Liability

The doctrine that has established the vicarious liability of supervisors is respondeat superior ("let the master respond"). According to this legal theory, the supervisors are the "masters" and the supervisees are the "borrowed servants." Courts assume that the supervisor is responsible for the conduct of the supervisee the same as the captain of the ship is responsible for the behavior of the crew or a surgeon is responsible for the performance of the operating room staff during surgery. The supervisee must be working under the direction and control of the supervisor and must have acted within the defined scope of tasks permitted by the supervisor.

The legal and ethical responsibility is the same whether the supervisee is an independent contractor or a salaried employee of the training agency. The issue is primarily a question of who has control over the patient. From an ethical and training standpoint, supervisees should not assume final responsibility for the patient. The supervisor carries the decision-making responsibility.

Vicarious liability would not likely accrue against supervisors of fully licensed professionals who carry full responsibility for their patients (although direct liability might be charged). Professionals who contract with licensed professionals are not vicariously liable for any harm resulting from their negligence. The professional must, however, have used reasonable care in hiring the practitioner and contract him or her only to perform duties within the scope of the practitioner's training, competence, and licenses.

DISCUSSION AND RECOMMENDATIONS

Some aspects of the preceding discussion may lead licensed psychologists to be reluctant to provide supervision, but this need not be so for the responsible professional. If supervisors are aware of the issues discussed within this chapter and act with the expected circumspection and responsibility, their welfare as well as that of the supervisees and the clients should be protected.

The internal and external guidelines for supervision are convergent, rather than divergent in nature. Both are intended to protect the public, the supervisee, and the supervisor. Neither contradicts the other. Both establish a safety net for the public by establishing minimum standards to follow in training future practitioners to deliver services to the public.

We make the following recommendations to training facilities, direct service agencies, and psychologists in independent practices. First, we encourage more thorough teaching of ethics within academic and nonacademic training programs. Learning ethics by osmosis or by example alone is seldom effective.

Second, we encourage training facilities, licensure and credentialing boards, and the APA to reconsider the view that supervision skills can be obtained informally. Course work on the practical skills and ethical standards of behavior for supervisors should be provided during predoctoral training. Training centers should require that every trainee acquire some guided experience as a supervisor.

Third, we encourage academic and nonacademic training programs to attend to the psychological needs of trainees, including identifying and helping those who have signs of impairment and who have problems dealing with sexual attraction to patients. Training programs should also help trainees anticipate and cope with negative professional events such as patient suicides or assaults on others. The concern for psychological health should go beyond helping those with noticeable problems and should include guiding all trainees to career and personal decisions that will improve their likelihood of personal and professional fulfillment.

Finally, both supervisors and supervisees should purchase professional liability insurance that covers their scope of practice.

REFERENCES

American Psychological Association. (1986). *Accreditation handbook.* Washington, DC: Author.

American Psychological Association. (1992). *Ethical principles of psychologists and code of conduct.* Washington, DC: Author.

Andrews v. United States, 548, F. Supp. 603 (1982).

Association of State and Provincial Psychology Boards. (no date). *Guidelines for the employment and supervision of uncredentialed persons providing psychological services.* Montgomery, AL: Author.

Bennett, B., Bryant, B., VandenBos, G., & Greenwood, A. (1990). *Professional liability and risk management.* Washington, DC: American Psychological Association.

Bowers, T., & Knapp, S. (1993). Reimbursement issues for psychologists in independent practice. *Psychotherapy in Private Practice, 12,* 73–86.

Bridge, P., & Bascue, L. (1988). A record form for psychotherapy supervision. In P. Keller & S. Heyman (Eds.), *Innovations in clinical practice* (Vol. 7, pp. 331–336). Sarasota, FL: Professional Resource Press.

Calfee, B. (1992). *Lawsuit prevention techniques for mental health professionals, chemical dependency specialists and clergy.* Cleveland, OH: ARC Associates.

Emroy University v. Porubiansky, 282 S.E.2nd 903 (GA 1981).

Glaser, R. D., & Thorpe, J. S. (1986). Unethical intimacy: A survey of sexual contact and advances between psychology educators and female graduate students. *American Psychologist, 41,* 43–51.

Guy, J., Poelstra, P., & Stark M. (1989). Personal distress and therapeutic effectiveness: National survey of psychologists practicing psychotherapy. *Professional Psychology: Theory and Research, 20,* 48–50.

Keith-Spiegel, P., & Koocher, G. P. (1985). *Ethics in psychology*. New York: Random House.

Kleespies, P. (1993). The stress of patient suicidal behavior: Implications for interns and training programs in psychology. *Professional Psychology: Research and Practice, 24,* 477–482.

Knapp, S., & VandeCreek, L. (1993). Legal and ethical issues in billing patients and collecting fees. *Psychotherapy: Theory, Research, and Practice, 30,* 25–31.

Peck v. The Counseling Service of Addison County, Inc., 499 A.2d 422 (1985).

Pope, K., Keith-Spiegel, P., & Tabachnick, B. (1986). Sexual attraction to clients: The human therapist and the (sometimes) inhuman training system. *American Psychologist, 41,* 147–158.

Pope, K., Levenson, H., & Schover, L. (1979). Sexual intimacy in psychology training: Results and implications of a national survey. *American Psychologist, 34,* 682–689.

Pope, K., Sonne, J., & Holroyd, J. (1993). *Sexual feelings in psychotherapy*. Washington, DC: American Psychological Association.

Rosenfeld, M., Shimberg, B., & Thornton, R. (1983). *Job analysis of licensed psychologists in the United States and Canada: A study of responsibilities and requirements*. Princeton, NJ: Educational Testing Services.

Skorina, J., Bissell, L., & DeSoto, C. (1990). Alcoholic psychologists: Route to recovery. *Professional Psychology: Research and Practice, 21,* 248–251.

Tarasoff v. Regents of the University of California, 551 P.2d 334 (1976).

Thoreson, R., Budd, F., & Krauskopf, C. (1986). Perceptions of alcohol misuse and work behavior among professionals: Identification and intervention. *Professional Psychology: Research and Practice, 17,* 210–216.

Thoreson, R., Nathan, P., Skorina, J., & Kilburg, R. (1983). The alcoholic psychologist: Issues, problems, and implications for the professional. *Professional Psychology: Research and Practice, 14,* 670–684.

VandeCreek, L., & Knapp, S. (1994). *Tarasoff and beyond: Legal and clinical considerations with life-endangering patients* (2nd ed.). Sarasota, FL: Professional Resource Press.

Vasquez, M. (1992). Psychologist as clinical supervisor: Promoting ethical practice. *Professional Psychology: Research and Practice, 23,* 196–202.

PART VII

Endnotes

CHAPTER 31

Some Concluding Thoughts
About Psychotherapy Supervision

C. EDWARD WATKINS JR.
University of North Texas, Denton

In this chapter, I would like to offer some final thoughts about psychotherapy supervision—its theory, research, practice, and training. It has been an interesting journey to read the foregoing chapters and to be informed about the status of many supervision areas. In reading those chapters, I found that they touched off a number of thoughts in me, some of which were directly related to the topic at hand and others of which were in some way more distal or only tangentially related. Nevertheless, in what follows I would like to share with you some of those thoughts. And I will do this in a more free-flowing fashion than otherwise, thinking out loud I guess you could say, about what struck me in all of this.

I am sure that for every point or issue that I mention I will leave many others unsaid. Without question, these chapters are rich, informative, and full of valuable material. I think they are worth reading and rereading. So with that recognized, I offer a few of my own observations or reflections—limited though they may be—about psychotherapy supervision as it is portrayed in this book.

RANDOM AND NONRANDOM MUSINGS
AND MEANDERING THOUGHTS

On Matters of Practice and Training

1. When I began to put together this volume, it was with the firm conviction that psychotherapy supervision is extremely important for and highly critical to the teaching and learning of psychotherapy. Although perhaps that goes without saying, I come away from this project with an even firmer conviction and deeper appreciation for the criticality of psychotherapy supervision. Such supervision, as these chapters have shown, is a key means if not *the* key means by which (a) we learn about and improve our skills at psychotherapy, (b) quality control gets exercised, and (c) quality service gets assured. In addition, clinical supervision also transmits, protects, and enhances a valuable culture, the culture of psychotherapy. The importance of that culture has been attested to time and again (e.g., *Consumer Reports,* 1995). Based on much of what we have read here, the case could be made that supervision contributes significantly to therapy's ultimate vitality and viability (e.g., Rodenhauser, 1996). Without the enterprise of psychotherapy supervision, the practice of psychotherapy, in my opinion, would become highly suspect and would or should cease to exist.

2. If psychotherapy supervision is really all that important, then why is training in how to supervise and become a supervisor so limited? That is a difficult question that eludes easy answers. Still, some, perhaps many, perhaps all, in this volume see a clear and definite need for would-be supervisors to be trained in how to supervise. Again, perhaps that too goes without saying, but the facts here are staggering: (a) Psychotherapists-in-training typically are closely scrutinized and supervised because becoming a therapist is considered to be a labor-intensive endeavor for which much training and supervision are needed; (b) supervisors have the charge of facilitating the growth and development of their supervisees and, in turn, helping those supervisees facilitate the growth and development of their patients; and (c) though being the ultimately responsible party in the supervisor-supervisee-patient triad, supervisors typically receive little to no training in how to supervise and do supervision (Rodenhauser, 1995; Watkins, 1992). Something does not compute. We would never dream of turning untrained therapists loose on needy patients, so why would we turn untrained supervisors loose on those untrained therapists who help those needy patients? Just as becoming a therapist is a labor-intensive endeavor for which training and supervision are needed, so too can the same be said about becoming a supervisor. Psychotherapy supervision training, I think, should be accorded the same importance as psychotherapy training. Until that happens, it seems reasonable to assume that supervisors' supervision efforts will generally be compromised, as will the therapy efforts of their supervisees.

3. If training in psychotherapy supervision is needed, and I am asserting here that it is, then do we also need standards to help the training and practice of supervision? That seems like a legitimate question to entertain. Standards for some groups can be found (e.g., American Association for Marriage and Family Therapy, 1987), but they have been criticized for being either too brief and general or too specific (Dye & Borders, 1990). In my opinion, the standards and accompanying curriculum guide developed to help the preparation and practice of counselor supervisors (Borders et al., 1991; Supervision Interest Network, Association for Counselor Education and Supervision, 1990) stand as a noteworthy exception; they may be equally usable by other professional groups, for example, psychiatrists, psychologists, and social workers, but it remains for them to be evaluated as such. If nothing else, those standards and that guide provide a useful model for other groups to consider and scrutinize when taking up the issue of standards. Standards are by no means a panacea, but I believe it is time that their potential value and merit be more seriously considered across all disciplines that train and supervise psychotherapists (Rodenhauser, 1996; Watkins, in press-a).

4. If you want trainees to learn a set of specific, systematic, basic therapeutic skills, then it seems best to teach them those skills in a highly specific, systematic manner. Systematic training is more apt to beget systematic learning than otherwise. In that regard, systematic training approaches such as microskills (Chapter 16, this volume), interpersonal process recall (Chapter 17, this volume), and human resource training (Truax & Carkhuff, 1967) have proven to be of value in helping beginning therapists learn those basic therapeutic, facilitative skills that we consider so essential. That seems to be attested to by means of both narrative and meta-analytic reviews (Baker & Daniels, 1989; Baker, Daniels, & Greeley, 1990; Chapter 24, this volume), and some of the chapters (also 16 and 17) presented in this volume. Some important questions about one or more of the systematic training approaches have been raised, however: Are they cost effective? If they are, how can they be made more cost efficient? How can behavioral maintenance of those skills learned be enhanced? Can these approaches be effective in the teaching and learning of higher order therapeutic skills? Those questions remain as challenges yet to be substantively addressed in the systematic training literature (Baker & Daniels, 1989; Baker et al., 1990) and provide rich, viable directions for future research in this area.

5. Just as specificity and structure are important for the learning of basic therapeutic skills, some degree of specificity and structure also seems important if learning is to occur in psychotherapy supervision. For example, Binder et al. (1993), in summarizing the main points of several contributors to a special *Psychotherapy* section on manualized training, noted that "[a] common observation, whether expressed explicitly or implicitly, is that psychotherapy supervision tends to be too unstructured" (p. 600). Beutler (1995), in proposing his "germ theory" of psychotherapy education, asserted the following: "The assumption that . . . supervision . . . in the absence of specifically targeted skills and systematic feedback methods result[s] in the acquisition of [therapeutic] skills . . . is unjustified" (p. 491).

To assume that any amorphous, unstructured supervision could be helpful does indeed seem wrongheaded. Supervision is about learning, about helping supervisees learn to become better therapists. Supervision appears to work best when (a) it is guided by a set of goals and tasks shared between supervisor and supervisee; (b) the roles and responsibilities of both supervisor and supervisee are clearly defined at the outset of the supervisory relationship; (c) supervisory feedback is provided in a constructive, specific, clear manner; (d) guided practice is a part of the supervision experience; (e) supervision sessions are defined by purpose, direction, and goal orientedness; and (f) the criteria for and process of evaluation are made as concrete as possible at the outset of supervision (cf. Bernard & Goodyear, in press; Beutler, 1995; Bordin, 1983; Freeman, 1993).

On Matters of Theory

6. The major difference that exists across most of the approaches to supervision covered in Part II comes down to one simple point for me: The supervision is oriented around and driven by the theory of therapy that one is trying to teach. For example, those supervising cognitive therapists would often focus on session contents different from those supervising Gestalt therapists. The theory of therapy that one is attempting to teach brings a particular lens to the work of supervision, which colors and guides it. The one exception here would seem to be the developmental approach, which is more of a metamodel perspective on the supervisory process and not wedded to any particular theory of therapy.

Some similarities do exist across most of the approaches to supervision covered in Part II. For instance, many emphasize the importance of (a) a supportive, noncritical supervisor-supervisee relationship or learning alliance; (b) teaching and instructing supervisees as needed; (c) modeling desired therapeutic behaviors or attitudes for supervisees; and (d) stimulating supervisee curiosity. Most use audiotape or videotape recordings so that what supervisees actually do in session can be heard and seen; most use individual and group modes of providing supervision. All have as their ultimate goal the development of competent, informed, autonomous professionals who can provide quality therapeutic services.

7. Do psychotherapy-based approaches to supervision really exist? As Bernard and Goodyear (1992) have stated, "the psychotherapy-based supervisor is one whose supervision is based totally and consistently on the supervisor's theory of psychotherapy and counseling" (p. 11). In considering the chapters in Part II, I think we could question if such psychotherapy-based approaches to supervision actually exist. Instead, it seems that one's theory of therapy may inform one's supervision work, for example, when the client-centered supervisor provides a facilitative supervisory relationship to his or her supervisees or when the rational-emotive-behavioral supervisor is called on to identify a supervisee's irrational ideas that are impeding the supervision or therapeutic process. But I think we find little evidence here of a supervision approach "based totally and consistently on the supervisor's theory of psychotherapy or counseling" (Bernard & Goodyear, 1992, p. 11). Perhaps no such approaches exist in reality. After all, analytic supervisees are not analysands, cognitive therapy supervisees are not cognitive therapy clients, and so forth. Supervision may have its therapeutic elements, but it is not therapy; it is primarily education, and I believe the chapters in Part II clearly reflect that fact.

On Matters of Research

8. In researching psychotherapy supervision, we need to work toward developing reliable, valid measures that are supervision specific—that assess variables specific to the supervision process and that are developed with the supervision endeavor in mind and are not takeoffs on a psychotherapy measure. Too often, as Lambert and Ogles (Chapter 24, this volume) pointed out, supervision research has involved the one-time use of homemade assessment devices with little to nothing being said about their reliability or validity; that needs to change. In recent years, some useful supervision measures, for example, the Psychotherapy Supervisory Inventory (Shanfield, Mohl, Matthews, & Hetherly, 1989), the Supervisory Working Alliance Inventory (Efstation, Patton, & Kardash, 1990), and the Role Conflict and Role Ambiguity Inventory (Olk & Friedlander, 1992), have been produced, and their promise has been noted in several reviews (Ellis, Ladany, Krengel, & Schult, 1996; Stoltenberg, McNeill, & Crethar, 1994; Watkins, 1995b). Those efforts provide a good beginning toward the needed development of more reliable, valid supervision-specific measures.

9. Over the last couple of decades, we see that increasingly sophisticated research questions, designs, and statistical analyses have been brought to bear on the supervision research process and that an increasing openness to and use of alternative experimental approaches—single-case studies and qualitative investigations—has been in evidence as well (Watkins, 1995c). The need for methodological pluralism and diversity in our researching of the supervision enterprise has increasingly been emphasized (e.g., Worthen & McNeill, 1996; see Chapter 2, this volume); however, the need to maintain acceptable methodological rigor can never be forgotten and continues to receive emphasis, as well (Ellis et al., 1996; Chapter 25, this volume). Relevance without adequate rigor means nothing and vice versa. If supervision research is to most fruitfully advance, we must continue to make as rigorous, yet broad-based and pluralistic an attack on the supervision process as we possibly can. Rigor plus diversity will beget an increasingly informed, informative, expanded knowledge base about supervision; either without the other will not.

10. What has psychotherapy training and supervision research told us or led us to conclude thus far? Lambert and Ogles (Chapter 24, this volume) and Stein and Lambert (1995) have stated that psychotherapy training programs should give primary emphasis to helping their student trainees learn core facilitative relationship skills (e.g., empathy), because those skills or "common factors" are still the best predictors of therapeutic outcome; supervision efforts, as a key part of that training endeavor, seemingly would do well to consider that advice. Furthermore, some of those same common factors may be just as critical to effective supervision as they are to effective psychotherapy (Carifio & Hess, 1987; Russell & Petrie, 1994; Chapter 26, this volume). Effective supervision, however, seemingly involves good instructional and didactic elements as well: "Supervisees want their supervisors to provide a positive relationship along with teaching and feedback that enables them to gain competence" (Chapter 26, this volume). Good supervision appears to involve, among other qualities, a healthy blending of relationship and instructional factors, which seemingly potentiate each other in the making of any supervision. How to best blend those relationship factors and instructional factors, along with other key supervision factors (e.g., patient problem, supervisee reactance), across supervisees remains a potent area for future investigation and study.

We have some evidence that supervisors vary in their styles of and behaviors in supervision, that some of the characteristics of those styles and behaviors can be identified, and that those styles and behaviors remain stable over time (Friedlander & Ward, 1984; Shanfield & Gil, 1985; Shanfield, Mohl, Matthews, & Hetherly, 1989, 1992). We also have evidence that identifies some of the underlying dimensions of the supervisor role itself (e.g., joining with versus challenging the trainee; Ellis & Dell, 1986; Ellis, Dell, & Good, 1988; Heppner et al., 1994). Those lines of research, though carried out independently, seem to complement one another and could be conceptually integrated for further heuristic purposes.

Neufeldt, Beutler, and Banchero (Chapter 26, this volume) speak favorably about "moment-by-moment systems of coding [supervision] interactions." Holloway and Neufeldt (1995) earlier echoed the same sentiment, indicating that

> Content analysis has substantiated that (a) supervision is interactionally different from counseling, (b) there are different predominant styles of supervision, (c) the quality and actual discourse of supervision are related to trainees' satisfaction in supervision, (d) style of supervision may be related to a supervisor's theoretical orientation in therapy, and (e) trainees and objective observers can recognize different types of supervisory styles. (pp. 209–210)

As can be seen, some of the findings from these microanalytic studies are also consistent with some of the findings mentioned in the preceding paragraph.

Those selected findings are interesting to consider. Equally if not more interesting to consider, however, is what we need to know with regard to supervision. To highlight those needs, let me pull out a few quotes that stood out for me:

> Very few follow-up studies have been reported in the literature, and, even when included as part of the research design, follow-up studies are marred by uncontrolled variables. (Chapter 24)

> Researchers have yet to conduct sufficient outcome studies that adequately explore the relationship between specific aspects of training programs . . . and therapy outcome. (Chapter 24)

> [There was a] scarcity of replication studies. . . . Without replication, we are left in a quandry: Which findings are "real" and which are not? (Chapter 25)

> [Supervision] theories and the central premises thereof remain untested. (Chapter 25)

> There is a paucity of research on the effect of . . . supervisor . . . [age, sex, and ethnicity] on either trainees or clients. (Chapter 26)

> No empirical studies were found on supervisor attitudes. . . . only [one] study [was] available on supervisor values . . . (Chapter 26)

> There are no studies that compare the behavior of more- and less-experienced supervisors' in-session behaviors nor their effects on supervisee's responses in supervision or in therapy. (Chapter 26)

> No empirical studies have shown a link between specific supervisor behaviors and client outcome. (Chapter 26)

If we push this even further and consider a few quotes from other recent reviews and papers, we hear still others echoing what we most need:

No studies have as yet examined change over time for trainees. (Stoltenberg et al., 1994, p. 421)

There is no research on standardized and empirically validated training program[s] for supervisors. (Holloway & Neufeldt, 1995, p. 211)

Limited research has been done relating supervision variables to supervisee functioning . . . and even less research has directly linked supervision variables to client outcome. (Holloway & Neufeldt, 1995, p. 207)

Given the enormous national investment of physical and human resources in graduate programs, it is quite remarkable that more compelling evidence is not available that demonstrates that graduate training directly relates to enhanced therapy outcome. (Stein & Lambert, 1995, p. 194)

Put bluntly, we have little evidence that our teaching methods (courses and supervision) change students' behavior in the direction of training objectives or foster effective therapeutic performance. (Binder & Strupp, 1993b, p. 571, emphasis in original)

These selected quotes point us in the direction of significant research gaps that we must start to fill. Although some modest, indirect evidence appears to support a training/supervision-therapy outcome link (Beutler & Kendall, 1995), we need to work more vigorously to establish a direct link between them. Furthermore, there seems to be agreement among some supervision researchers about the importance of (a) developing more reliable, valid supervision-specific research measures so that we may better study the supervision process itself (Ellis et al., 1996; Stoltenberg et al., 1994; Chapters 24 to 26, this volume); (b) doing more observational investigations of the supervision enterprise, studying what supervisors and supervisees actually do in therapy (Chapters 24 to 26, this volume); (c) better incorporating blocking variables (e.g., supervisee reactance), which moderate the supervision process in some way or other, into supervision theory, research, and practice (Bernard & Goodyear, in press; Watkins, 1995b); and (d) where possible, using multiple indices (e.g., client outcome data; Stoltenberg et al., 1994) and multiple raters (e.g., therapist, supervisor, and patient; Chapters 24 and 25, this volume) in an effort to provide a more complete, comprehensive picture about the supervision variables under examination. Last, there were also some opinions that training manuals may be quite useful to us in our struggles to better understand and more solidly research psychotherapy training and supervision and their effects (Chapters 24 and 26, this volume; cf. Holloway & Neufeldt, 1995; Moras, 1993; Stein & Lambert, 1995).

Research is critical to the advancement of psychotherapy supervision. And as some of the preceding shows, and as Lambert and Ogles (Chapter 24, this volume) made clear, "[t]here is no shortage of topics for future study." If the scientific base of clinical supervision is to move forward, then those topics must be actively, vigorously, and tenaciously pursued.

11. Let me belabor one aspect of the preceding point: that training manuals potentially hold promise for enhancing our knowledge base about supervision. I think that is truly the case, and I foresee much more manualized attention being given to the teaching, learning, and researching of psychotherapy supervision in the near future. As yet, we have only one manual that has been designed specifically with the intent of training supervisors (Neufeldt, 1994; Neufeldt, Iversen, & Juntenen, 1995). We had 10 times that many therapy training manuals 10 years ago (Lambert & Ogles, 1988); because of that, however, some of what has been learned about manualized therapy training seemingly would have implications for and could serve as a useful guide to our further development of manualized supervision training. In that regard, the special sections on manualized training appearing in the *Journal of Consulting and Clinical Psychology* (Beutler, 1988) and *Psychotherapy* (Binder & Strupp, 1993a) are instructive.

In the study of manuals, one simple, straightforward, yet interesting point that in my view bears emphasis here is the following: Just as the person and procedures of the therapist can be critical for outcome in psychotherapy, so too the person and procedures of the supervisor or trainer can be critical for outcome in psychotherapy supervision and training. For example, in their study of training time-limited psychodynamically oriented psychotherapists, Henry, Schacht, Strupp, Butler, and Binder (1993b) concluded that teaching style appeared to affect trainee learning. The most favorable results were obtained when the supervisor structured the use of recorded therapy material in supervision, explicitly encouraged supervisees to track a focal therapy theme and provided them with methods for doing that, and supported desirable therapist behaviors by means of clear, specific feedback. I think their study, its companion piece (Henry, Schacht, Strupp, Butler, & Binder, 1993a), and other recent discussions (Binder, 1993a, 1993b, in press) point to the following: A good supervision manual is but one piece of the puzzle, a tool that is used to stimulate and structure learning; the person and procedures of the supervisor or trainer may be equally if not more important (Stein & Lambert, 1995); if we are to develop effective manualized supervision efforts, then we must not lose sight of the contributions that relationship factors, instructional style, and teaching methods exert in making the teaching-learning process happen. In doing that, the work of cognitive-instructional psychologists may prove of much value for us to consider if we are to ultimately improve psychotherapy training, supervision, and manualization (Binder, 1993a, 1993b, in press).

12. In 1975, Waskow and Parloff recommended that a core battery, or standardized set of assessment measures, be used to assess psychotherapy outcome; that was the first time such a recommendation had been made:

> A hope behind the proposal for such a battery was that, if researchers working in different settings with different treatment orientations were to use the same standard set of instruments, it would become possible to compare and integrate the results of different studies. (Waskow & Parloff, 1975, p. 3)

Since that proposal, the concept of the core battery has not died; it has continued to receive its share of attention in the psychotherapy literature (e.g., McCullough, 1993; Ogles, Lambert, Weight, & Payne, 1990). With that in mind, I could not help but wonder, should we begin to think about a "core battery" that could be used in our supervision research efforts? Is such a battery even possible? If such a battery were to happen, I am sure it would be a good way off. Still, I think there is merit to that concept. If advances in the development of supervision assessment tools continue to occur and if more supervision-specific measures come to be, then we may be in a better position to at least entertain the idea of putting together a core battery designed to assess the outcomes of supervision. That would be an intriguing addition to the field and would no doubt reflect much evolution in our efforts to study the supervision process.

On the Developmental Perspective

13. I have long thought and continue to think that developmental theorizing about supervision has much to offer us. Since most of my supervision efforts over the last 8 years have been along developmental lines, I cannot lay claim to lack of bias here. Still, with my bias readily acknowledged, I think I am safe in saying that the developmental metaphor has proven quite useful for our thinking about supervision (Stoltenberg & Delworth, 1988), having led to the generation of some valuable supervisee and supervisor models (see Chapters 12 and 14, this volume), having been heuristic with regard to research (Stoltenberg et al., 1994), and having emerged as the zeitgeist of supervision lore for the 1980s (Holloway, 1987), 1990s (Watkins, 1994a), and beyond. But just why is this so-called developmental perspective on supervision so robust?

Developmental models (a) provide a meaningful structure for conceptualizing how supervisor, supervisee, and even patients change and grow into their respective roles over time (e.g., Rodenhauser, 1994); (b) provide a conceptual map for what supervisors should expect of and how they should intervene with their supervisor and therapy trainees over time (Watkins, 1994b; Chapter 12, this volume); (c) are easy to understand and have an intuitive appeal (Bernard & Goodyear, in press); and (d) because of their metatheoretical nature, can be readily applied to the supervision of trainees learning diverse therapeutic approaches (Watkins, 1995c). Developmental model research, although not without its critics (e.g., Holloway, 1987; Chapter 25, this volume), has tended to support a developmental structure for supervision and supervisee growth, to show that supervisors modify their behaviors as supervisees change, and to show that beginning supervisees generally need more structure, direction, and guidance, whereas advanced supervisees generally need less of those and are more willing to consider their own personal issues and how those affect the therapy process (Stoltenberg et al., 1994; Watkins, 1995b, 1995d; Worthington, 1987). So the theory-research-practice base of the developmental view has become more refined and grown stronger over time; that no doubt further contributes to its appeal.

But some legitimate, constructive criticisms have been put forth with regard to developmental models. Based on some of the material presented in this book and other recent reviews and commentaries (e.g., Stoltenberg et al., 1994; Watkins, 1995b), supervisor and supervisee models are in need of the following: (a) more specific, precise "descriptions of the thoughts, feelings, and behaviors of supervisees [and supervisors] at various developmental stages" (Borders, 1989, p. 17); (b) a transition theory, explaining how transitions take place between stages (Worthington, 1987); (c) better accommodation of divergent developmental paths and addressing of matters of relapse and no progress (Bernard & Goodyear, in press); (d) fuller and more precise incorporation of moderator variables (e.g., self-efficacy, psychological reactance, session content) into the fabric of the models themselves (e.g., Tracey et al., 1989); and (e) "more precise depictions of the supervision environments (i.e., interventions, supervisor traits) that 'match' each stage or foster movement toward higher stages" (Borders, 1989, p. 17), that is, a fuller, more specific developmental supervision theory that is completely translated into actual developmental supervision practice (Watkins, 1996).

In addition to those needs, I think, too, the integration of a developmental perspective with the supervision of trainees learning particular approaches to psychotherapy could be useful conceptually. For example, if certain supervisees are learning and being supervised in cognitive therapy, what sort of progression might be expected of them developmentally with regard to skills, identity, affect, and intentions? The same question could be asked for supervisees learning psychodynamic, Gestalt, and other forms of therapy. That type of blend—the developmental with theory-specific supervision—could provide a useful, more specific road map for supervisors who are attempting to help their supervisees learn a particular form of therapy.

14. As for research, developmental models of supervisor and supervisee are in need of the following: (a) a more substantive focus on the actual behaviors of supervisors and supervisees, determining what they really do (Borders, 1989); (b) longitudinal studies that track supervisor and supervisee over time (Stoltenberg et al., 1994); (c) the incorporation of key moderator variables (e.g., self-criticality) into experimental efforts (Watkins, 1995b, 1995d); (d) the use of more developmentally sensitive methods and methodologies (Holloway, 1987); and (e) more cross-disciplinary and cross-setting research involving, for example, psychiatry and social work supervisees and being conducted in settings such as hospitals, outpatient clinics, and inpatient units (Watkins, 1994a).

The research and theoretical needs mentioned here pose a number of real challenges for a developmental view of supervision. Though possessing robustness and enjoying much popularity, if the developmental perspective is to advance most viably and become increasingly informed and informative to supervisors, those challenges must be addressed in the years ahead.

Miscellaneous and Other Comments

15. Evaluation has been, is, and will no doubt remain one of the key definitional features of clinical supervision. Yet certain aspects of the evaluative component of supervision have been little addressed in the literature and seemingly merit more attention. For example, Samec (1995) examined the process by which supervisors terminate supervisees from supervision—the causes for the termination, how it was done, what made the process difficult, and the outcomes for both supervisor and supervisee. I think this paper struck me because, although we find various materials related to evaluation in supervision, the issue of supervisee failure and termination and its effects on both supervisee and supervisor has received all too limited attention. Considering that those effects can prove quite traumatic for both parties and require some working through (see Samec, 1995; cf. Watkins, 1995a), perhaps more thorough examination of that issue is in order.

16. Mahrer (1995b), one of the contributors to this volume, recently edited a special section of the journal *Psychotherapy* that dealt with myths in psychotherapy. Specifically, he asked Beutler (1995), Ellis (1995), and Norcross (1995) to identify some *disposable* myths in psychotherapy, that is, "relatively widely held belief[s] . . . uncritically accepted as . . . truth . . . [that] psychotherapy practice, theory, research, or training could probably develop better without . . ." (Mahrer, 1995a, p. 484). Whereas most of the identified myths focused on therapy practice and research, Beutler (1995) put forth one—his "germ theory of education"—that focused on therapy training and supervision; in that, he asserted that the following idea or myth was disposable: "Exposure to psychotherapy, through supervision and class instruction, over a finite period of time, will result in competence and expertise" (p. 490). Beutler went on to argue that targeted goals, specific feedback, and the assessment of therapist skill level all are important if effective training and supervision are to occur.

Point well taken. But at the same time, that paper and Mahrer's (1995a) special section raised two questions for me. First, what other disposable myths underlie our psychotherapy training and supervision efforts? And second, what might be some of the *nondisposable* myths that underlie those same efforts? After all, myths can be for good, providing us with meaning and direction, as Rollo May (1991) pointed out so well in his book *The Cry for Myth*. With that in mind, I could not help but wonder what those disposable and nondisposable training-supervision myths that we adhere to might be. I have no ready answers for my wondering; still it seems an interesting supervision issue we might wish to consider in the times ahead.

17. More than 3 decades ago, Kiesler (1966) put forth his idea of the "client uniformity myth," that all patients with the same disorder make for a homogeneous group and that they all will benefit equally from the same treatment. Just as the uniformity myth has relevance for psychotherapy practice and research, it can have relevance for psychotherapy supervision practice and research as well. Several of the contributors to this volume, either here or in other publications, have cautioned us about applying a "supervisee uniformity myth"—assuming that all supervisees have the same needs and should all be dealt with accordingly (Bernard & Goodyear, in press; Beutler, Clarkin, & Norcross, 1990; Stoltenberg & Delworth, 1987). That caution seems to merit much consideration. To the extent that we subscribe to such a myth, overlooking or failing to take into account supervisee differences and needs, we compromise the practice of and research about supervision (Stoltenberg et al., 1994); some suggestions for avoiding such compromises have been made (e.g., conducting a needs assessment at the outset of supervision; see Beutler, Clarkin, & Norcross, 1990; Norcross & Beutler, in press; Chapter 13, this volume; conducting more aptitude-treatment interaction studies; Bernard & Goodyear, 1992) and seem worth heeding if our supervision efforts are to be most solidly informed.

18. How does managed care affect our thinking about and implementation of psychotherapy supervision? We are all well aware of the effects of managed care on psychotherapy. Issues of insurance reimbursement, cost containment, and short-term treatment loom large in today's world of psychotherapy. Brief therapy has emerged as the major player in securing the psychotherapy dollar. In turn, therapists generally have become more informed about and practitioners of more abbreviated treatments; furthermore, the need to train students in how to do brief therapy seems more a priority now in many therapy-training programs. But what does all that mean for psychotherapy supervision? Just as some models of therapy have been adapted to better accommodate a briefer time frame, models of therapy supervision may need to be adapted accordingly as well (Watkins, 1995e). Supervisors must think about how they can help their supervisees do as much or more with less. Brief therapy seemingly calls for brief-therapy–minded supervision. But what exactly is that? It seems to me that more explicit, concrete efforts to answer that question are needed, but as yet none have been made.

19. Much attention, as should be the case, has been given to identifying and studying the characteristics of the effective psychotherapy supervisor (e.g., Carifio & Hess, 1987; Russell & Petrie, 1994). By contrast, attention to the "ineffective supervisor" and "ineffective supervision" has been quite limited. More than a decade ago, Worthington (1987) emphasized the need for a theory of ineffective supervisor behaviors. With but one exception (Watkins, in press-b), his call has gone unheeded. Research providing data about ineffective or poor supervision (e.g., Allen, Szollos, & Williams, 1986; Shanfield, Matthews, & Hetherly, 1993), while informative, has been sparse. What is ineffective or poor may not always be the exact opposite of what is effective (see Hutt, Scott, & King, 1983). If we are to have the most comprehensive, fully informed, and complete picture about supervision—good and bad—then we need substantive theoretical and research efforts to be advanced toward the topics of both effective *and* ineffective supervision.

20. It is clear from reading these chapters that this book's contributors strongly believe in the importance of psychotherapy supervision. But when does supervision of the therapist cease to be important? Once we graduate and obtain our respective licenses or certifications, do we then no longer need supervision of our therapeutic work? LeShan (1996) has some interesting words to offer on that matter:

A therapist who is not in supervision should be regarded either with suspicion or awe. He or she is making a statement that they have learned all that is needed for one of the most complex problems in existence—helping others to be as fully human as possible and to survive and exult in being in the human condition. If they have arrived at this august state (I, personally, have never met anyone who has), they deserve our awe; otherwise, our suspicion. (p. 91)

LeShan's opinion is worth some reflection. Supervision is not just a graduate school necessity; it is a means by which we can continue to grow and enhance ourselves as therapists even after formal training is done. Furthermore, I think supervision for supervisors can be equally valuable and is a means by which they, too, can continue to enhance their skills as supervisors. Whereas such supervision for either supervisors or therapists need not be continuous, as LeShan seems to prefer, periodic supervision can be a real asset in pushing us forward, challenging us, helping us remain as current as possible, a growth option we may wish to exercise time and again.

CONCLUSION

Perhaps that is enough. I could muse on, but I will stop here. Let us end our journey—or are we just beginning it? We have seen much about psychotherapy supervision in these pages. The authors have all done an excellent job in informing us about this most important of enterprises. This volume reflects some of the breadth, richness, and maturity that characterize psychotherapy supervision now. But as Bernard and Goodyear (1992) have stated, "[b]ecause supervision is a young field, practitioners and researchers alike have much yet to learn" (p. 242). We have a way to go yet, but we are getting there. And I think this book is a good testament to that fact.

REFERENCES

Allen, G. J., Szollos, S. J., & Williams, B. E. (1986). Doctoral students' comparative evaluation of best and worst psychotherapy supervision. *Professional Psychology: Research and Practice, 17,* 91–99.

American Association for Marriage and Family Therapy. (1987). *The approved supervisor designation.* Washington, DC: Author.

Baker, S. B., & Daniels, T. (1989). Integrating research on the microcounseling program: A meta-analysis. *Journal of Counseling Psychology, 36,* 213–222.

Baker, S. B., Daniels, T. G., & Greeley, A. T. (1990). Systematic training of graduate-level counselors: Narrative and meta-analytic reviews of three major programs. *The Counseling Psychologist, 18,* 355–421.

Bernard, J. M., & Goodyear, R. K. (1992). *Fundamentals of clinical supervision.* Boston: Allyn & Bacon.

Bernard, J. M., & Goodyear, R. K. (in press). *Fundamentals of clinical supervision* (2nd ed.). Boston: Allyn & Bacon.

Beutler, L. E. (Ed.). (1988). Special series: Training to competency in psychotherapy. *Journal of Consulting and Clinical Psychology, 56,* 651–709.

Beutler, L. E. (1995). The germ theory myth and the myth of outcome homogeneity. *Psychotherapy, 32,* 489–494.

Beutler, L. E., Clarkin, J. F., & Norcross, J. C. (1990). Training in differential treatment selection. In L. E. Beutler & J. F. Clarkin, *Systematic treatment selection: Toward targeted therapeutic interventions* (pp. 289–307). New York: Brunner/Mazel.

Beutler, L. E., & Kendall, P. C. (1995). Introduction to the special section: The case for training in the provision of psychological therapy. *Journal of Consulting and Clinical Psychology, 63,* 179–181.

Binder, J. L. (1993a). Is it time to improve psychotherapy training? *Clinical Psychology Review, 13,* 301–318.

Binder, J. L. (1993b). Observations on the training of therapists in time-limited dynamic psychotherapy. *Psychotherapy, 30,* 592–598.

Binder, J. L. (in press). A proposal for improving the conceptual foundations and methods for teaching psychodynamic therapies. *The Clinical Supervisor.*

Binder, J. L., & Strupp, H. H. (Eds.). (1993a). Special section: Recommendations for improving psychotherapy training based on experiences with manual-guided training and research. *Psychotherapy, 30,* 571–600.

Binder, J. L., & Strupp, H. H. (1993b). Recommendations for improving psychotherapy training based on experiences with manual-guided training and research: An introduction. *Psychotherapy, 30,* 571–572.

Binder, J. L., Strupp, H. H., Bongar, B., Lee, S. S., Messer, S., & Peake, J. H. (1993). Recommendations for improving psychotherapy training based on experiences with manual-guided training and research: Epilogue. *Psychotherapy, 30,* 599–600.

Borders, L. D. (1989). A pragmatic agenda for developmental supervision research. *Counselor Education and Supervision, 29,* 16–24.

Borders, L. D., Bernard, J. M., Dye, H. A., Fong, M. L., Henderson, P., & Nance, D. W. (1991). Curriculum guide for training counseling supervisors: Rationale, development, and implementation. *Counselor Education and Supervision, 31,* 58–80.

Bordin, E. S. (1983). A working alliance based model of supervision. *The Counseling Psychologist, 11*(1), 35–42.

Carifio, M. S., & Hess, A. K. (1987). Who is the ideal supervisor? *Professional Psychology: Research and Practice, 18,* 244–250.

Consumer Reports (1995, November). Mental health: Does therapy help?, pp. 734–739.

Dye, H. L., & Borders, L. D. (1990). Counseling supervisors: Standards for preparation and practice. *Journal of Counseling and Development, 69,* 27–29.

Efstation, J. F., Patton, M. J., & Kardash, C. M. (1990). Measuring the working alliance in counselor supervision. *Journal of Counseling Psychology, 37,* 322–329.

Ellis, A. (1995). Psychotherapy is alarmingly encumbered with disposable myths. *Psychotherapy, 32,* 495–499.

Ellis, M. V., & Dell, D. M. (1986). Dimensionality of supervisor roles: Supervisors' perceptions of supervision. *Journal of Counseling Psychology, 33,* 282–291.

Ellis, M. V., Dell, D. M., & Good, G. E. (1988). Counselor trainees' perceptions of supervisor roles: Two studies testing the dimensionality of supervision. *Journal of Counseling Psychology, 35,* 315–324.

Ellis, M. V., Ladany, N., Krengel, M., & Schult, D. (1996). Clinical supervision research from 1981 to 1993: A methodological critique. *Journal of Counseling Psychology, 43,* 35–50.

Freeman, S. C. (1993). Structure in counseling supervision. *The Clinical Supervisor, 11,* 245–252.

Friedlander, M. L., & Ward, L. G. (1984). Development and validation of the Supervisory Styles Inventory. *Journal of Counseling Psychology, 31,* 541–557.

Henry, W. P., Schacht, T. E., Strupp, H. H., Butler, S. F., & Binder, J. L. (1993a). Effects of training in time-limited dynamic psychotherapy: Changes in therapist behavior. *Journal of Consulting and Clinical Psychology, 61,* 434–440.

Henry, W. P., Schacht, T. E., Strupp, H. H., Butler, S. F., & Binder, J. L. (1993b). Effects of training in time-limited dynamic psychotherapy: Mediators of therapists' response to training. *Journal of Consulting and Clinical Psychology, 61,* 441–447.

Heppner, P. P., Kivlighan, D. M., Jr., Burnett, J. W., Berry, T. R., Goedinghaus, M., Doxsee, D. J., Hendricks, F. M., Krull, L. A., Wright, G. E., Bellatin, A. M., Durham, R. J., Tharp, A.,

Kim, H., Brossart, D. F., Wang, L., Witty, T. E., Kinder, M. H., Hertel, J. B., & Wallace, D. L. (1994). Dimensions that characterize supervisor interventions delivered in the context of live supervisors of practicum counselors. *Journal of Counseling Psychology, 41,* 227–235.

Holloway, E. L. (1987). Developmental models of supervision: Is it development? *Professional Psychology: Research and Practice, 18,* 209–216.

Holloway, E. L., & Neufeldt, S. A. (1995). Supervision: Its contributions to treatment efficacy. *Journal of Consulting and Clinical Psychology, 63,* 207–213.

Hutt, C. H., Scott, J., & King, M. (1983). A phenomenological study of supervisees' positive and negative experiences in supervision. *Psychotherapy: Theory, Research, and Practice, 20,* 118–123.

Kiesler, D. J. (1966). Some myths of psychotherapy research and the search for a paradigm. *Psychological Bulletin, 65,* 110–136.

Lambert, M. J., & Ogles, B. M. (1988). Treatment manuals: Problems and promise. *Journal of Integrative and Eclectic Psychotherapy, 7,* 187–204.

LeShan, L. (1996). *Beyond technique: Psychotherapy for the 21st century.* Northvale, NJ: Jason Aronson.

Mahrer, A. R. (Ed.). (1995a). Special section: Are there any disposable myths in the field of psychotherapy? *Psychotherapy, 32,* 484–504.

Mahrer, A. R. (1995b). An introduction to some disposable myths, how to detect them, and a short list. *Psychotherapy, 32,* 484-488.

May, R. (1991). *The cry for myth.* New York: Dell.

McCullough, L. (1993). Standard and individualized psychotherapy outcome measures: A core battery. In N. E. Miller, L. Luborsky, J. P. Barber, & J. P. Docherty (Eds.), *Psychodynamic treatment research: A handbook for clinical practice* (pp. 469–496). New York: Basic Books.

Moras, K. (1993). The use of treatment manuals to train psychotherapists: Observations and recommendations. *Psychotherapy, 30,* 581–586.

Neufeldt, S. A. (1994). Use of a manual to train supervisors. *Counselor Education and Supervision, 33,* 327–336.

Neufeldt, S. A., Iversen, J. N., & Juntenen, C. L. (1995). *Supervision strategies for the first practicum.* Alexandria, VA: American Counseling Association.

Norcross, J. C. (1995). Dispelling the dodo bird verdict and the exclusivity myth in psychotherapy. *Psychotherapy, 32,* 500–504.

Norcross, J. C., & Beutler, L. E. (in press). Advances and possibilities in supervising eclectic psychotherapy. *The Clinical Supervisor.*

Ogles, B. M., Lambert, M. J., Weight, D. G., & Payne, I. R. (1990). Agoraphobia outcome measurement: A review and meta-analysis. *Psychological Assessment: A Journal of Consulting and Clinical Psychology, 2,* 317–325.

Olk, M. E., & Friedlander, M. L. (1992). Trainees' experiences of role conflict and role ambiguity in supervisory relationships. *Journal of Counseling Psychology, 39,* 389–397.

Rodenhauser, P. (1994). Toward a multidimensional model for psychotherapy supervision based on developmental stages. *The Journal of Psychotherapy Practice and Research, 3,* 1–15.

Rodenhauser, P. (1995). Experiences and issues in the professional development of psychiatrists supervising psychotherapy. *The Clinical Supervisor, 13,* 7–22.

Rodenhauser, P. (1996). On the future of psychotherapy supervision in psychiatry. *Academic Psychiatry, 20,* 82–91.

Russell, R. K., & Petrie, T. (1994). Issues in training effective supervisors. *Applied and Preventive Psychology, 3,* 27–42.

Samec, J. R. (1995). Shame, guilt, and trauma: Failing the psychotherapy candidate's clinical work. *The Clinical Supervisor, 13,* 1–18.

Shanfield, S. B., & Gil, D. (1985). Styles of psychotherapy supervision. *Journal of Psychiatric Education, 9,* 225–232.

Shanfield, S. B., Matthews, K. L., & Hetherly, V. (1993). What do excellent psychotherapy supervisors do? *American Journal of Psychiatry, 150,* 1081–1084.

Shanfield, S. B., Mohl, P. C., Matthews, K., & Hetherly, V. (1989). A reliability assessment of the Psychotherapy Supervisory Inventory. *American Journal of Psychiatry, 146,* 1447–1450.

Shanfield, S. B., Mohl, P. C., Matthews, K. L., & Hetherly, V. (1992). Quantitative assessment of the behavior of psychotherapy supervisors. *American Journal of Psychiatry, 149,* 352–357.

Stein, D. M., & Lambert, M. J. (1995). Graduate training in psychotherapy: Are therapy outcomes enhanced? *Journal of Consulting and Clinical Psychology, 63,* 182–196.

Stoltenberg, C. D., & Delworth, U. (1987). *Supervising counselors and therapists: A developmental approach.* San Francisco: Jossey-Bass.

Stoltenberg, C. D., & Delworth, U. (1988). Developmental models of supervision: It is development—response to Holloway. *Professional Psychology: Research and Practice, 19,* 134–137.

Stoltenberg, C. D., McNeill, B. W., & Crethar, H. C. (1994). Changes in supervision as counselors and therapists gain experience: A review. *Professional Psychology: Research and Practice, 25,* 416–449.

Supervision Interest Network, Association for Counselor Education and Supervision. (1990). Standards for counselor supervisors. *Journal of Counseling and Development, 69,* 30–32.

Tracey, T. J., Ellickson, J. L., & Sherry, P. (1989). Reactance in relation to different supervisory environments and counselor development. *Journal of Counseling Psychology, 36,* 336–344.

Truax, C. B., & Carkhuff, R. R. (1967). *Toward effective counseling and psychotherapy.* Chicago: Aldine.

Waskow, I. E., & Parloff, M. B. (1975). *Psychotherapy change measures.* Rockville, MD: National Institutes of Mental Health.

Watkins, C. E., Jr. (1992). Reflections on the preparation of psychotherapy supervisors. *Journal of Clinical Psychology, 48,* 145–147.

Watkins, C. E., Jr. (1994a). Developmental models, psychotherapy supervisors, and clinical supervision research [Letter to the editor]. *The Journal of Psychotherapy Practice and Research, 3,* 274–275.

Watkins, C. E., Jr. (1994b). The supervision of psychotherapy supervisor trainees. *American Journal of Psychotherapy, 48,* 417–431.

Watkins, C. E., Jr. (1995a). Pathological attachment styles in psychotherapy supervision. *Psychotherapy, 32,* 333–340.

Watkins, C. E., Jr. (1995b). Psychotherapy supervisor development: On musings, models, and metaphor. *The Journal of Psychotherapy Practice and Research, 4,* 150–158.

Watkins, C. E., Jr. (1995c). Psychotherapy supervision in the 1990s: Some observations and reflections. *American Journal of Psychotherapy, 49,* 568–581.

Watkins, C. E., Jr. (1995d). Psychotherapy supervisor and supervisee: Developmental models and research nine years later. *Clinical Psychology Review, 15,* 647–680.

Watkins, C. E., Jr. (1995e). And then there is psychotherapy supervision too [Letter to the editor]. *American Journal of Psychotherapy, 49,* 313.

Watkins, C. E., Jr. (Chair). (1996, August). *Developmental approaches to psychotherapy supervision: Translating theory into practice.* Symposium conducted at the annual meeting of the American Psychological Association, Toronto, Canada.

Watkins, C. E., Jr. (in press-a). Reflections on contemporary psychotherapy practice, research, and training. *Journal of Contemporary Psychotherapy.*

Watkins, C. E., Jr. (in press-b). The ineffective psychotherapy supervisor: Reflections on bad behaviors, poor process, and offensive outcomes. *The Clinical Supervisor.*

Worthen, V., & McNeill, B. W. (1996). A phenomenological investigation of "good" supervision events. *Journal of Counseling Psychology, 43,* 25–34.

Worthington, E. L., Jr. (1987). Changes in supervision as counselors and supervisors gain experience: A review. *Professional Psychology: Research and Practice, 18,* 189–208.

Author Index

Italic page numbers refer to reference citations.

617

Subject Index

ABC theory of emotional and behavioral
    disturbance, 102–6
Abstinence, learning therapist, 77
Activating event in ABC theory, 102–6
Activity theory of aging, 372
Adaptive functioning, ecological-behavioral model
    focus on, 351
Administration, women in, 557
Administrative component of Gestalt therapy
    supervision, 150–51
Administrative responsibility for client, 169–70
Adolescent psychotherapy supervision. *See* Child
    and adolescent psychotherapy supervision
Advanced supervision strategies, 317–18
Advantages-disadvantages analysis, 119
Affective skills, 353–54
Affiliation, 254, 563
Agency function, supervision of feminist-oriented
    practitioner and, 556
Agency structure in partnership vs. dominator
    models, 560, 562–63
Agenda
    in cognitive therapy supervision, 121, 122
    of dialectical behavior therapy consultation
        group, 92–93
Age vs. cohort attitudes to seeking help, 372–73
Aggressive therapists, 130
Aging. *See also* Older patients, psychotherapy with
    defined, 368
    environmental contexts of, 368
    psychology of. *See* Geropsychology
    therapist's view of, 371–72
Alcohol and drug abuse
    impairment of psychologists due to, 592
    by late-life adults, underestimation of, 369
Aligning with patient in experiential
    psychotherapy, 171
Alliance
    learning, 33, 40, 52
    supervisory working, 490, 512, 606
    therapeutic, 54–55
Ambiguity in integrative supervision, 217
American Board of Professional Psychology, 378
American Psychiatric Association, standards for
    supervisors, 531–32
American Psychoanalytic Association
    Committee on Institutes, 42
    COPE Study Group on Supervision of the, 42
American Psychological Association
    Accreditation Guidelines of, 374
    Code of Conduct of the, 590

Ethics Committee, 596
Analogic mode of communication, 65
Andrews v. *United States*, 592, 597
Anthropologically informed perspective, 575
Anxiety
    cognitive therapy applied to, 115–16
    learning by, 76
Appreciation of diversity, 90
Apprenticeship model, 56, 515
Approach-avoidance behavior, 298–300
Archetypes, for partnership vs. dominator model,
    565
Ascending patterns, 16
Asocial, psychotherapist as, 68, 77
Assertive behavior in inquirer role, 302, 307
Assessment, 8
    in cultural competence process model, 577–79
    across developmental levels, 191
    via linguistic channels in SCDS, 233–40
    across multiple domains, 354
    of therapeutic skills, 212
Assimilation, 149, 155
Association of State and Provincial Psychology
    Boards (ASPPB), 590, 591
Assumptive world of supervisor, 6
Attack response style, 300
Attending behavior and skills, 280, 281, 282, 284
Attila the supervisor, 129
Attitudes, supervisor, 511
Attractiveness, trainee perceptions of, 512–13
Audiotape supervision, 334–35, 341
    approaches to, 334–35
    in cognitive therapy, 123
    COPE study of, 42
    in experiential on-the-job teaching, 175–79
        for improved competency and skill, 176–78
        studying teacher's own sessions, 178–79
        trainee's preparation of audiotapes, 175–76
    in psychodynamic supervision, 51
Authentic communication, 68–69
Authority relationships, gender-linked supervisory,
    554–55. *See also* Power
Automaticity, training using concept of, 435
Autonomy, developmental level and, 187–88, 190,
    193, 194, 197
Avoidant therapist, 130
Awareness
    emotional, task of, 257
    Gestalt therapy focus on, 149
    of mental life, 65–66
    self and other, 187–88, 190, 194, 195, 197

633

Process of supervision *(cont.)*
  in systems approach, 258–59
  therapist training affecting, 23
Process skills, 310–11
Product orientation of dominator model, 564
Professional background and experience, 260, 514
Professional behavior, 311
  evaluation criteria, 322
Professional functioning, enhancement of, 5
Professional/organizational factors, 8
Professional role, task of, 257
Professional self-development skills, 353
Professional self-esteem of novice therapist, 47,
    154–55
Professional skills, 353
Professional structure in partnership vs. dominator
    models, 560, 562–63
Professional training, definition of, 348
Programmed instruction, in child and adolescent
    psychotherapy supervision, 359
Psychoanalytic supervision, 31–43
  author's example of, 39–41
  differences in pedagogic theory and, 36–38
  frequency of, 39
  goals of, 32
  psychoanalytic theory of supervision
    and, 33–36
  research on, 41–43
  styles of, 32–33, 36–38, 39
  tripartite model of psychoanalytic training,
    31–32, 35, 40, 44
Psychoanalytic theory, topics important in teaching
    application of, 529–30
Psychodynamic psychotherapies, supervision of,
    44–62
  brief history of, 44–46
  data sources and formats for, 51–52
  difficulty with mastery of certain skills and, 530
  goals and outcomes of, 53–55
  models of supervisory process, 48–51
  proposal for, 56–59
  reflections on, 56
  research on, 46
  strategies and techniques for, 51–53
  supervisor characteristics and, 47–48
  task of, 529, 530
  trainee characteristics and, 46–47
Psychologically "safe" distances, 298–99
Psychological reality, 64–65
Psychopathology, trainee, 47
Psychopharmacotherapy, integration of
    psychotherapy with, 532, 533–34, 539
Psychosocial health, negative vs. positive, 368
Psychotherapy
  current climate of, 531–32, 539
  definition of, 347–48
  interpersonal interaction as theater for, 67
  supervision vs., 71–72
Psychotherapy professions, women in, 549–50,
    562
Psychotherapy supervision
  basic characteristics and principles of, 530
  communication and other enablers of optimum
    learning, 535–38

conceptual tools for supervisors, 532–35
consultation as distinct from, 589
desirable education for supervisor, 540–41
difference between supervised experience and
    experience alone, 374
discrimination model operating parallel to,
    323–24
distinction from other major modes of clinical
    instruction, 527–28
importance of, 3, 603
information flows in, 528–29
literature, shifts in, 223–24
prerequisites for effective, 532, 545
psychotherapy as distinct from, 71–72
purpose of, 11
quality-control function of, 3, 5
specificity and structure in, need for, 605
topics relevant to proficiencies for, 545–48
training in, need for, 604
trouble spots in, 538–40
working definition of, 4–6
Psychotherapy Supervision Inventory, 516, 606
Purposive eclecticism, 69

Qualifications of supervisors, legal and ethical,
    590–91
Qualitative learning environment in
    microcounseling, 287–88
Quality
  of professional service, monitoring, 3, 5
  of research on inferences, 492
  supervisory, range of, 374–75
Questioning
  in basic listening sequence, 280
  in systemic cognitive-developmental supervision,
    233–36, 341

Race and ethnicity, 14. *See also* Cultural
    competence model; Cultural
    issues/differences
  as contextual factor in SAS supervision, 261,
    264
  inferences about match of supervisee-supervisor,
    469–70
  issues involving, 199
  as objective cross-situational supervisor trait,
    510
Rating perspective, 19–20
Rating scales, 430
  criteria-based, 212
  DBT Expert Rating Scale, 86, 97
  observer, 440
  standardized, 352
Rating systems, not recommended, 491
Rational emotive behavior therapy (REBT),
    supervision in, 101–13
  complexity of ABC model of emotional and
    behavioral disturbance, 102–6
  educational aspects of, 101–2
  evaluation of supervisees' performance, 111
  fundamentals of, 102–6
  preferable characteristics and traits for REBT
    practitioners, 111–12
  training aspects of, 106–9

subjective, cross-situational traits, 510–11
subjective, supervision-specific states, 511–13
trainees' views on, 48
Supervisor factor in systems approach, 252,
260–62
Supervisor functioning, 6–9
Supervisor intentions, 517–18
Supervisor interactional style, 516–17
Supervisor Rating Form (SRF), 512
Supervisor Response Questionnaire (SRQ), 512
Supervisor style. *See under* Style, supervisory
Supervisory Levels Questionnaire (SLQ-R), 491
Supervisory relationship. *See* Relationship,
supervisory
Supervisory structure in partnership vs. dominator
models, 560, 563–64
Supervisory triangle, 528–29
stages of development among participants in,
533, 534, 537
possible combinations in, 537, 538
Supervisory Working Alliance Inventory, 490, 512,
606
Supporting/sharing function, 258
Surveys of student satisfaction, 54
Systematic eclecticism. *See* Technical eclecticism
Systematic referral, 206
Systematic training. *See also* Interpersonal process
recall (IPR); Microcounseling
approaches, 604–5
research findings on effectiveness of, 427
Systemic cognitive-developmental supervision
(SCDS), 223–45
cognitive-developmental orientations, 226–27,
230, 231–32
psychotherapy environments associated with,
228–29
research on identification and use in clinical
practice of, 240–41
style-matching/reinforcing psychotherapist's
foundations and, 237
style-shifting/expanding supervisee
development and, 237–40
supervisory environments associated with,
236–39
framework of, 229
psychotherapy theory underlying, 224–29
questioning strategies in, 233–36, 341
research on, 240–42
status of developmental supervisory perspectives
and, 223–24
status of integrative supervisory perspectives
and, 224
theoretical underpinnings of, 229–40
assessing and stimulating supervisee growth
via linguistic channels, 233–40, 241
cultural experience of supervision, 233
supervisee development as holistic, 230
supervision as co-constructive process,
230–33
Systemic cognitive-developmental therapy (SCDT),
225–29
co-constructing therapeutic environments to
enhance client development, 228–29
cognitive-developmental orientations, 226–27

framework of, 225
theoretical underpinnings of, 225–26
Systemic therapy
dialectical behavior therapy as, 86
family systems therapy, 85–86
Systems approach to supervision (SAS), 249–76
applying model to teaching supervision, 267–72
supervision consultation case analysis, 268–72
contextual factors of supervision in, 12, 252,
259–67
client factors, 252, 264–65
institutional factors, 252, 265–67
supervisor factor, 252, 260–62
trainee factor, 252, 262–64
dimensions of, 250–51, 252–53
functions of supervision in, 253, 257–58
goals of model, 250
process of supervision in, 258–59
relationship of supervision in, 250, 251–56
interpersonal structure of, 251–54
phases of, 254–55, 256
supervision contracts, 255–56
tasks of supervision in, 252, 253, 256–57

Tarasoff v. *Regent of the University of California*,
593
Tasks of supervision, 529–30
in systems approach, 252, 253, 256–57
Teacher-learner interaction in supervision, 517
Teacher role of supervisor, 312
activities for, 316
choosing, 313–15
research on, 325
Team building in dialectical behavior therapy, 98
Technical eclecticism, 204–5, 209
distinctions among theoretical integration and,
205
Technical skills, therapist, 428–35
developmental issues in, 435
in family therapy training, 435
pedagogic emphasis in psychoanalytic
supervision on, 36
training in conceptualization, 435
treatment manuals and, 429–34
Techniques, 8
differences in, as alternative ways of observing
primary data, 40–41
teaching of, as learning task, 70
Technology. *See also* Audiotape supervision;
Videotape supervision
computer, 58–59, 341
importance of, in discrimination model, 315–16
Telephone, supervision by, 41, 96
Termination from supervision, 611
Termination phase
frequency of supervision during, 39
in interpersonal approach, 80
Theoretical integration, 205–6
Theoretical orientation
conflict between supervisor and supervisee, 15
across developmental levels, 192
interpersonal approach and, 75
matching of supervisor and supervisee, 135,
470–71, 563